DEXA 90

A M. Tjoa and R. Wagner (eds.)

Database and Expert Systems Applications

Proceedings of the International Conference
in Vienna, Austria, 1990

Springer-Verlag Wien New York

Prof. Dipl.-Ing. Dr. A Min Tjoa
Institut für Statistik und Informatik
Universität Wien, Vienna, Austria

Prof. Dipl.-Ing. Dr. Roland Wagner
Institut für Informatik
Johannes Kepler Universität Linz, Linz, Austria

With 336 Figures

ISBN -13:978-3-211-82234-0   e-ISBN-13:978-3-7091-7553-8
DOI: 10.1007/978-3-7091-7553-8

International Conference on Database and Expert Systems Applications

DEXA 90

August 29 - 31, 1990

Technical University of Vienna

Gußhausstraße 25-27, Vienna, Austria

TABLE OF CONTENTS

SESSION 7C   Engineering Applications in Science and Engineering

SESSION 8A   Implementation Aspects

SESSION 8B   User-Interfaces and Hypertext

SESSION 8C   Office Applications

X

Information Retrieval Tools for Literary Analysis

Abraham Bookstein   and   Shmuel T. Klein

Center for Information and Language Studies
University of Chicago, 1100 East 57-th Street
Chicago, IL 60637

ABSTRACT

The advent of the CD-ROM as a means of distributing massive bodies of textual data increases the importance of developing automatic techniques for textual analysis. To accomplish this task, we should be alert to existing techniques, perhaps developed for other purposes, that can be of value. We here report on observations we made while carrying out research on information storage and retrieval that promise to be helpful. Specifically, auxiliary information and data structures created incidental to our IR investigations are rich in semantic content, and can be useful in suggesting or confirming relations among concepts in text. Two examples are given: one based on a term weighting scheme for IR, the other on a tree structure for compressing bitmaps.

1. Introduction

Over the past ten years, we have gained considerable experience on how to store and retrieve textual information by machine [12]. Elaborating on pioneering research carried out in the 50's and 60's, rather sophisticated models now exist that describe the retrieval process, that allow us to take advantage of feedback information in a systematic manner, and that permit the retrieval of documents on the basis of information only indirectly related to the request initially presented by a user of the Information Retrieval (IR) system [1]. These models are probability based and, within the confines of the model's assumptions, make optimal use of available information. Similarly, algorithms have have been developed, also based on a detailed understanding of the structure of text, that allow us to store text in an efficient manner [13].

The type of processing that takes place when these techniques are used are parallel to processes that take place as a human expert intermediary surveys his corpus to understand its character; interacts with a user to learn the peculiarities of the information need to be satisfied; and formulates an effective search strategy that takes advantage of available information. In current approaches to IR, preliminary statistical analysis results in a knowledge representation of the text, and a Bayesian learning procedure, based on user feedback, mirrors the role of human learning.

Given the parallels between modern automatic IR and IR based on human interactions with a text library, it should not be surprising that intermediate information generated in the course of storing and retrieving information should be rich in semantic content, and that this derivative information should have value for understanding the relationships between concepts in the database beyond that needed for retrieval itself. As information retrieval is increasingly carried out on full text databases, such possibilities will become more prominent. In this paper we describe our experience in using data structures and information generated in the course of retrieving information as a tool for literary analysis. Indeed, we have come to believe that the type of methods that have become standard in IR has considerable potential for serving as a component of an intelligent assistant for literary scholars — suggesting relations that may not be obvious from a preliminary examination of the texts; integrating a broad range of quantitative and often subtle information and relating these to a corpus of interest; and providing objective confirmation of subjectively arrived at conclusions about a text.

Below we shall give two examples of spin-offs of IR for literary understanding. The first [5] indicates how the weights that are automatically assigned to terms in a feedback IR process can be used to identify concepts associated with a topic of interest: in our case, concepts associated with the emperor, Charlemagne, in a large French text database. The second example indicates some data structures that resulted as we tried to find efficient ways to compress a set of bitmaps associated with a large body of text [3]. The tree structures resulting from that effort are interesting in their own right and convey information about the relationship between individuals and ideas in the database at hand. We have applied the algorithm to the Hebrew Bible; by comparision with a similar analysis of the English language Bible, we found interesting insights into differences between the languages.

2. Identification of key concepts in text

The first task of literary scholarship involves defining a corpus of materials suited for further examination. The need to provide assistance at this stage of the research has long been recognized and has resulted in such tools as concordances. The existence of machine readable text, such as the joint CNRS/University of Chicago project for American and French Research on the Treasury of the French Language (ARTFL) [11] makes it tempting to search for new techniques that assist the literary scholar in locating interesting passages of text. Our research began with the intention of adapting techniques developed in the area of computerized IR to aid the literary scholar in locating a corpus. The problems in the two areas are very much the same: how to use textual clues to determine whether an entity (a document/passage) should be retrieved, given an imperfectly formulated request. We used techniques in which words are assigned weights automatically on the basis of how likely they are to distingush useful passages from not useful passages, and in which passages containing the words with the largest weights are retrieved. An advantage of this approach is that it provides the ability to assign weights to terms, ideally in a manner that can be theoretically justified, so as to be able to incorporate weak information, including that in terms not obviously semantically related to the research objectives, into our requests: the motivation here is that large amounts of weak information may collectively be strongly informative.

2.1 Methodology

There remains the question of how weights are to be assigned. The details of the retrieval mechanism we were testing have been explained elsewhere [2]. However, it is possible to give an overview. Since the main purpose of the search is to retrieve interesting segments, the weight assigned to a given word is based on how much its presence or absence is statistically indicative of the relevance or non-relevance of a given passage. Thus in a first step we divide the corpus into two components, the first containing the segments desired (the *relevant* segments), the other the contrast set of segments (those *not relevant*). Since we do not initially know all the relevant segments (that is the objective of the search), the process begins with a known *sample* of these, and uses the rest of the corpus as the contrast component. We must try to find terms that occur significantly more in the first set than in the second and assign weights accordingly. There are many possibilities for assigning weights. We made use of a weighting scheme derived from Bayesian arguments that are currently being used heavily in the theory of information retrieval [6]. Bayesian theory assumes that terms occurring in text have known, similar distributional properties in both relevant and nonrelevant segments of text, differing in the two classes of text in the values taken by the parameters defining the distribution within a known family of distributions. The actual parameter values in the two classes are estimated by means of feedback information, such as noted above; these values are then used to assign weights to terms. This procedure is purely automatic and based on the relative rate of occurrences of each word in the relevant and non-relevant corpora.

For computational convenience, in this preliminary study, we used weights defined on the basis of the simple assumption that in each class of text, terms are Poisson distributed and are distributed independently of one another. (That is, the probability of n occurrences of a term is given by $(\lambda^n e^{-n})/n!$, where λ is the parameter defining the specific Poisson distribution [10].) If we make this assumption, the weight, w, assigned to a term is given by $w = \log(\lambda_0/\lambda_1)$. Here λ_0 is the expected number of times the term will occur in a segment of relevant text and λ_1 is the corresponding quantity for non-relevant text. If the word occurs n times in a segment, that word contributes a weight of nw to that segment. The intuitive content of this formula is evident: λ_0 and λ_1 measure the likelihoods of the word occurring in relevant and non-relevant segments respectively, and their ratio measures the ability of the word to distinguish between the two sets. Note that terms that do distinguish classes of text, but do so only weakly, can have an impact; they collectively influence the outcome of a search. Such words are those least likely to occur to a researcher trying to formulate a request without machine assistance. Further, in principle at least, some terms will have negative weights — in effect simulating a NOT operator. Thus, this mechanism can be used very flexibly.

Although the intuitive justification for the form of the weighting formula is understandable, the detailed form, and particularly the appearance of the logarithm function, depends on the assumption of Poisson distributivity. Other distributional assumptions yield other functional forms, though generally with a similar interpretation.

We looked at the statistical properties of terms in passages where Charlemagne is mentioned, using the Poisson distribution as a means for assigning weights. The database consisted of all the works in the ARTFL corpus from 1715 to 1900. Each occurrence was examined in a context of 6 sentences in either direction of the word. The output was a list of terms with weights assigned on a purely statistical basis, with large weights distinguishing terms that discriminate between passages about Charlemagne and the rest of the corpus. The Charlemagne corpus was made up of 240,000 words; the contrast corpus, of which the Charlemagne corpus was a subset, was made up of 112,000,000 terms.

2.2 Results

When the statistical techniques described above were applied to the ARTFL database, the weights ranged from 0 (no association) to $+2.72$ on the positive side and to -1.17 on the negative side. We thus immediately see that this method is much more effective in determining clues pointing to passages about Charlemagne than in locating words that indicate a passage is *not* about Charlemagne. Our discussion will accordingly be only of positive terms.

The first question we shall ask is whether significant terms exist that are given low weights. We found that among the low weight terms (absolute value near zero) are such functional grammatical words, as `la`, `cet`, `et`, `son`, and `du`. Such words do not carry content and would be expected to have low weight; nonetheless, it is satisfying to find that a purely statistic method does classify such words as useless for discriminating interesting passages. (It is also the case that no such clearly contentless words are found among words with the highest weights.) This is also consistent with the results in [9], where each term is assigned a *selectivity index*, again on a purely statistical basis.

Other words exist with low weights, for example, `élégant`, `gauche`, `accourut`, `huile`, and `indigne`. Although such words have content, they do not distinguish passages about Charlemagne. For the most part, words given low weight are similar to these, in that one would not expect them to be particularly associated with passages about Charlemagne. However, a few exceptions were found: `chrétien`, and `majestueuse`. To some extent, this is an artifact of the format of the database — that is, the absence of lemmatization or stemming. For example, `christianisme` has a higher, though not very high, weight.

But even the surprises are informative, and indicate important features and strengths of this technique. Recall that the approach we are taking is purely statistical — no explicitly semantic information is provided, nor was the technique designed to retrieve semantically significant terms. Rather, the intention was to generate words (and weights) that separate desired from undesired passages. The strength of our approach is its single-mindedness. It focuses on the task given it and is not diverted by other, more human attractions. People, on the other hand, given the task of generating terms separating out passages about Charlemagne, will rather often provide words descriptive of Charlemagne, without considering whether such terms are effective discriminators. `Majestueuse` appears to be an example of a term that might be mistakingly produced in this way. The word does very well characterize our image of Charlemagne, but apparently is used in enough other contexts as well to make it ineffective for the task of interest. It is the ability of this technique to take into account *other* passages that gives it its power.

The words with higher weights are more interesting. We first note the peculiarities of words with the highest weights. These tend disproportionately to be proper names (e.g., `Ebre`, the name of a river in Germany, weight (wt) = 2.67; 9 occurrences in the whole subset examined, of which 8 occur in the Charlemagne corpus; `Roncevaux`, site of battle in *Chanson de Roland*, (wt = 2.3; 62 vs 24 occurrences)). Also included are words referring to events in Charlemagne's life: `capitulaires` (wt = 2.3; 109 vs 42 occurrences). But by far, proper names dominated the words with weights greater than 2.0. These tended to be names closely associated with Charlemagne, and for the most part occur very infrequently. They do very well discriminate passages about

Charlemagne, but are not very useful because of their few occurrences.

Some of the most significant words are found with weights near 1.0. Examples include: `monument` (wt = 0.58), `membre` (wt = 0.60), forms of the word `établir` (wt = 0.61), `fondateur` (wt = 1.12), `couronne` (wt = 1.13), `fondation` (wt = 1.13), `sceptre` (wt = 1.19). Going to higher weights: `vassaux` (wt = 1.47), `conquérant` (wt = 1.53), `heaume` (wt = 1.54) and `fief` (wt = 1.74). These terms are important in that they reflect key concepts associated with Charlemagne. `Electif` (wt = 1.81), for example, is representative of a class of terms (`élection`, `établir`, `souveraineté` and `républiques`) referring to government and having moderate weight. They confirm the categories found by hand in earlier studies. Although the density of interesting words increases with weight, except at the highest weights, there is a large number of non-indicative terms that got through for various reasons. Also, many highly weighted terms occur rather infrequently. Although these results are very preliminary, they do show that a purely statistical technique that has proven successful in the context of bibliographic retrieval has promise in the domain of full-text retrieval as well.

Examining the results of our preliminary study left us hopeful. We have in effect designed a statistically driven filter that, in addition to producing, as intended, terms discriminating passages about one topic from others, has also yielded a set of terms that is rich in words that are informative about Charlemagne. Thus, while intended as a text retrieval mechanism, our approach can be used also as a word retrieval mechanism. As such it can serve two complementary functions: an exploratory function, which can yield unexpected terms, and thereby motifs or themes, associated with a topic of interest, or distinguishing two such topics; and a confirmatory function, providing additional, objective evidence to support an argument initiated through more traditional analysis.

In the course of our work, other intriguing potential applications arose. For example, considering this technique as a theme retrieval mechanism, it would be of interest to create corpora of text about two comparable individuals and use the technique to isolate terms that most effectively separate what is said about the two individuals. Other pairs of corpora could be analyzed in the same way. Continuing with examples based on persons, we could identify automatically themes associated with different writers or different schools when writing about a single person, or we can search for terms that capture the differences in discussions about a particular historical figure over two different periods.

3. Concept association

The second example deals with the spin-offs of a compression algorithm we considered recently [3] for a large file of sparse bitmaps. Bitmaps occur often in information retrieval. They can represent the occurrences of a word in the

4

sentences or paragraphs making up a text; they can indicate the documents associated with an index term; they appear as bit slices of a matrix of signatures; they might represent pixels in rows of a raster graphics display.

3.1 Methodology

In our application, each bit-position corresponds to a specified sub-unit of the database, referred to as a *segment*. For each different word (or index term) W in the database, there is a map $B(W)$, such that the i-th bit of $B(W)$ is 1 if and only if W appears in (or is assigned to) segment i. How such bitmaps can be used to enhance an IR system is discussed in [4] and [8]. These bitmaps are generally very large and sparse, and many methods have been suggested for their compression (see, for example, [14] or [7]). The present method is based on the observation that the occurrences of certain words are sometimes strongly correlated accross segments in the sense that if one word appears in a certain segment, the other is also very likely to do so. Such pairs of bitmaps are likely to be quite similar. This similarity is exploited in a two-stage compression process: the first stage is to partition the bitmaps of our IR system into clusters of correlated bitmaps; the resulting clusters are then used to transform the original bitmaps into another set of bitmaps that are sparser and therefore more effectively compressed in stage 2 of the process, by means of some standard bitmap compression technique. If two bitmaps X_1 and X_2 are strongly associated in the sense that the presence of a 1-bit in one map increases the likelihood of a 1-bit occurring in the same position in the other, then the bitmap $X_3 = X_1$ XOR X_2 will very possibly have fewer 1-bits than, say, X_2. If we store X_1 and X_3, we can reconstruct X_2. Since our intention when XORing two vectors is to reduce the number of 1-bits, it is useful to take as a measure of association between two vectors, the number of 1-bits in the XORed vector. This quantity is the familiar *Hamming distance* between the two vectors.

The algorithm now proceeds by adding a vector of zeros to the set of bitmaps and constructing a minimum spanning tree on a labelled complete graph G. The vertices of G are our bitmaps and the label on edge (x, y) is the Hamming distance between the maps x and y. This non-directed minimum spanning tree is then transformed into a directed spanning tree, by choosing the 0-vector as the root and orienting all the edges to point in the direction of the root. The root of each sub-tree of the 0-vector is compressed directly. All the other bitmaps are first XORed with their successor in the oriented tree and then the XORed map is compressed. It is easy to see that this procedure minimizes the number of 1-bits in the set of vectors to be compressed, thereby improving their compressibility in the second stage of the algorithm. For some sets of bitmaps, this two stage method almost doubles the compression savings.

3.2 Results

We would here like to discuss mainly a side-effect of this method: the generation of clusters of related words. The database we chose is the Hebrew Bible, consisting of 305514 words which are partitioned into 929 chapters. The number of different words is 39647. We restricted ourselves to the 1478 words which appeared in at least 20 chapters. A segment was defined to be one chapter, so the length of each bitmap was 929 bits. The overall probability of a 1-bit was very low (6.9%). About two thirds of the bitmaps formed singleton clusters, i.e., could not be profitably associated with any others. While most of the remaining clusters were still small (two to four elements), some formed deep trees with tens of bitmaps. A closer look at some of the larger clusters revealed interesting associations. Figure 1 shows a typical example. For each node in the tree, the Hebrew word is given in English translitteration, using {**ABGDHVZXtYKLMNsaPCQRST**} respectively for {*aleph, beth, . . . , tav*}, as well as the translation of the word into English.

Almost all the words in this cluster are typical of the historical descriptions of the reigns of the various kings cited in the Bible. Note that 6 of the 31 words in the cluster belong to the Hebrew root **MLK** (king). Many words in Hebrew must be translated into several English words, because Hebrew morphology provides the possibility of prefixing a root by articles and prepositions (the, and, to, . . .) and suffixing it by possessive pronouns (mine, his, . . .). Sometimes, the root (consisting generally of 3 letters) may undergo slight changes such as loosing a letter, but in this example, the root **MLK** can be found in all the six words as a substring.

The tree draws attention to formulæ occurring in the Bible when a new king is presented. Generally, reference is given to his age and the name of his mother. The father is not mentioned, as he is generally the previous king. A typical phrase form is: ... **was** ... **years (SNH) old when he became king (BMLKV), and he reigned ... years in Jerusalem (BYRVSLM), and the name (VSM) of his mother (AMV) was** .... Then comes a global description of his actions: **and he did (VYaS)** [good or evil] **in the eyes of God** .... Toward the end of the description, the following phrase can often be found: **and the rest of (VYTR) the actions of (DBRY) ... and the ... he did (aSH), are not (HLVA or HLA) they (HM) written (KTVBYM) in the book (sPR) of chronicles** [literally: **the acts of (DBRY) the days (HYMYM)**] **of the kings of (LMLKY)** .... There are actually 26 occurrences of such a sentence in the Bible; all except one (in the book of Esther) are in the two books of Kings.

Finally, the phrases reporting the death of the king can be found in two subtrees of the cluster. A biblical idiom for *dying* is to *lay with his fathers*: **and ... lay (VYSKB) with his fathers (ABTYV), and he was buried in**

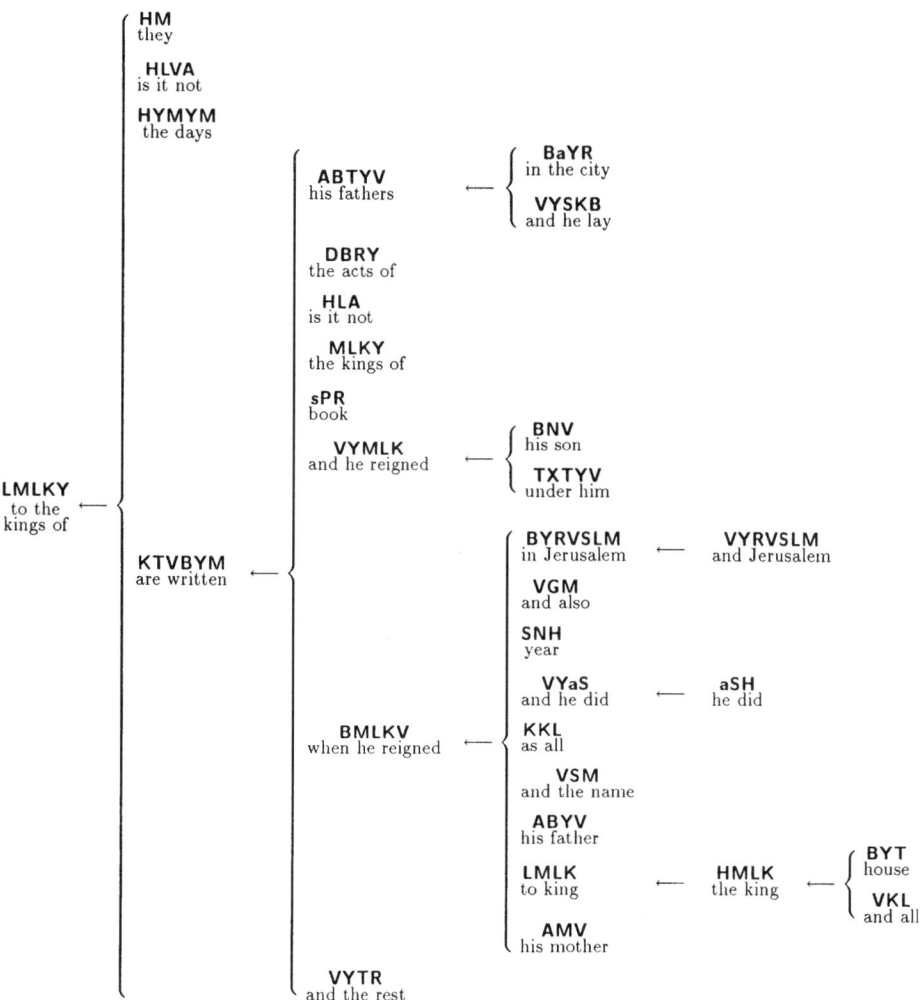

Figure 1: *The Kings cluster (Hebrew)*

the city (**BaYR**) of ..., and reigned (**VYMLK**) ...
his son (**BNV**) in his place [literally: under him
(**TXTYV**)]. An example of the above sentence forms can
be found in Kings I, 22:41–51, which describe the reign of
King Jehoshaphat. The word **HLA** (**are they not** or **is it
not**) appears in this sentence in two possible forms, with (10
times) or without (16 times) the letter **V**, and it is notewor-
thy that both forms can be found in the cluster. The word
SNH (**year**) appears here in singular, though the referred
ages and periods would require a plural; this is because Hebrew allows the use of a singular form of a noun if the number
of items exceeds ten.

Not all the words in the cluster are mutually related. For
example the word **VYRVSLM** (**and Jerusalem**) has no connection with the descriptions of the reigns, but it is clearly
related to **BYRVSLM** (**in Jerusalem**). Words like **VGM** (**and**

also) or **VKL** (**and all**) do not obviously relate to this context; we have no special explanation for their appearence in
this tree.

In a subsequent analysis, we redefined a text segment
to consist of four consecutive chapters, which leads to the
generation of more and larger clusters. The new bitmaps
were thus of length $\lceil 929/4 \rceil$ = 233 bits, of which 19.1%
on the average were 1-bits. With these denser maps, only
about a third formed singleton clusters, and 948 bitmaps
were partitioned into 186 clusters, each containing at least
two elements. Most of the clusters were still small, but some
were large — the largest consisted of a tree of depth 15 with
112 vertices. An interesting example of the trees produced
is depicted in Figure 2.

In this cluster, 18 out of 28 words are numerals; these are

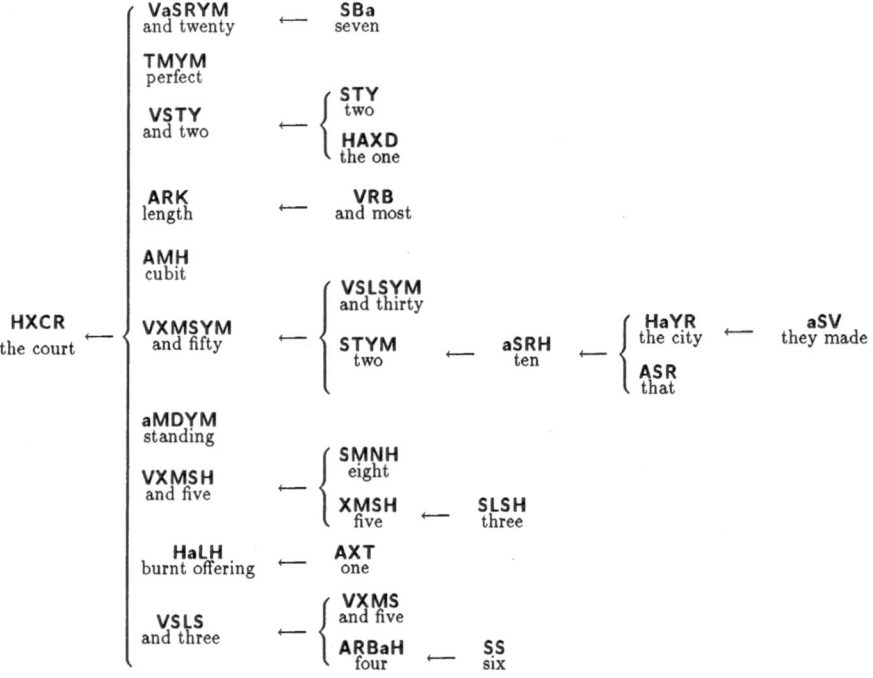

Figure 2: *The Court cluster*

clearly connected, as the Bible tends to give exact dimensions (note the words `length` and `cubit`) in certain detailed descriptions. See, for instance, Exodus 27:9–19, where a description of the `court` of the tabernacle, the root of this cluster, is given. The multiple occurrence of certain numerals is due to the fact that they may take various forms in Hebrew (masculine, feminine and others).

In order to check the influence of the language of the database on the algorithm, we repeated the experiments with the *King James Bible*, again with a segment equal to one chapter. Figure 3 shows one of the trees we got. This cluster can probably be considered as the couterpart of the one in Figure 1, if we note the large number of words they have in common: `chronicles`, `book`, `written`, `years`, `rest`, `acts`, `kings`, `stead`, `died`, `reigned`, `reign`, `Jerusalem`. The word `slept` is the translation of the He-

brew paraphrase for *died*. The word `began` does not appear in the Hebrew cluster, but is implicit in the phrases: `... was ... years old when he reigned (BMLKV)`, which in fact means when he began to reign.

Another interesting cluster can be found in Figure 4. This cluster contains the names of all the tribes, except `Judah`, and does not contain anything else. `Judah` appeared in the cluster in Figure 3, together with words like `Jerusalem`, `kings`, etc. Clearly, `Judah` differs from the other tribes as his name often refers to the kingdom or land of `Judah`. Some of the internal connections in the cluster can also be explained. `Levi` and `Simeon` are connected because they appear several times as a couple (e.g., Genesis 34:25 or Genesis 49:5). `Reuben` and `Gad` are the two tribes which settled east of the Jordan river and are therefore often mentioned together (e.g., Numeri 32, Joshua 13:23–24). `Zebulun` and `Naph-`

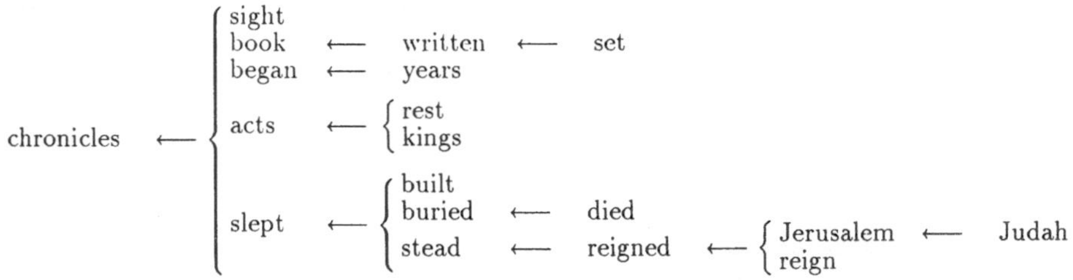

Figure 3: *The Kings cluster (English)*

tali appear together at the time of the prophetess Deborah (e.g., Judges 4 : 6).

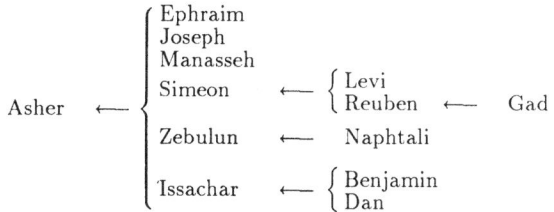

Figure 4: *The Tribes cluster*

It may be surprising that the algorithm, when applied on the Hebrew text, did not generate such a cluster of the names of the tribes. There might be two causes for this. First, since Hebrew is written without vowels, almost every Hebrew word has more than one possible meaning. This is also true for certain names. For instance, `Asher`, the root of the tree, is written in Hebrew **ASR**. But this is also the spelling of the preposition *that*, and therefore appears in many different contexts (see the cluster in Figure 2). `Dan`, in Hebrew **DN**, is also the verb *to judge* in present singular; `Joseph`, in Hebrew **YVSP** means also *[he] should add*. The second reason is again that the names may be prefixed by prepositions. Thus the set corresponding to the references to the name x in the English text is partitioned for the Hebrew text into several smaller subsets corresponding to the words *and x, from x, to x*, etc. Thus our automatically generated trees carry a great deal of semantic content, but also strongly reflect linguistic considerations.

References

[1]   **Bookstein A.,** Probability and Fuzzy-Set Applications to Information Retrieval, *Annual Review of Information Science and Technology* **20** (1985) 117–151.

[2]   **Bookstein A.,** Explanation and Generalization of Vector Models in Information Retrieval, *Proc. 5-th ACM-SIGIR Conf.,* Berlin (1982) 118–132.

[3]   **Bookstein A., Klein S.T.,** Construction of Optimal Graphs for Bit-Vector Compression, to appear in *Proc. 13-th ACM-SIGIR Conf.,* Brussels (1990).

[4]   **Bookstein A., Klein S.T.,** Using Bitmaps for Medium Sized Information Retrieval Systems, to appear in *Information Processing & Management* (1990).

[5]   **Bookstein A., Morrissey R., Deerwester S., Waclena K., Ziff D.,** Statistical Guides for Literary Analysis, to appear in *Festschrift for Quemada,* edited by Antonio Zampolli.

[6]   **Bookstein A., Swanson D.,** A Decision Theoretic Foundation for Indexing, *J. Amer. Soc. for Inf. Sc.* **26** (1975) 45–50.

[7]   **Choueka Y., Fraenkel A.S., Klein S.T., Segal E.,** Improved hierarchical bit-vector compression in document retrieval systems, *Proc. 9-th ACM-SIGIR Conf.,* Pisa, Italy (1986) 88–97.

[8]   **Choueka Y., Fraenkel A.S., Klein S.T., Segal E.,** Improved Techniques for Processing Queries in Full-Text Systems, *Proc. 10-th ACM-SIGIR Conf.,* New Orleans (1987) 306–315.

[9]   **Choueka Y., Klein S.T., Neuvitz E.,** Automatic Retrieval of Frequent Idiomatic and Collocational Expressions in a Large Corpus, *J. Assoc. Literary and Linguistic Computing,* Vol. **4** (1983) 34–38.

[10] **Feller W.,** *An Introduction to Probability Theory and Its Applications,* Wiley, New York (1968).

[11] **Morrissey R., Del Vigna C.,** A Natural Language Data Base, *Educom* **18** (1983).

[12] **Salton G.,** *Automatic Text Processing: The Transformation, Analysis, and Retrieval of Information by Computer,* Addison-Wesley, Reading, Mass. (1989).

[13] **Storer J.A.,** *Data Compression, Methods and Theory,* Computer Science Press, Rockville, Maryland (1988).

[14] **Teuhola J.,** A Compression method for Clustered Bit-Vectors, *Inf. Processing Letters* **7** (1978) 308–311.

Automatic Indexing of Document Databases by Cooperating Expert Systems

Ernst J. Schuegraf, Martin F. van Bommel

Department of Mathematics and Computing Sciences
St. Francis Xavier University
Antigonish, Nova Scotia. Canada. B2G 1C0

ABSTRACT

Early and current approaches to automatic indexing of document databases are reviewed, together with some attempts at incorporating artificial intelligence techniques into the indexing process. A fully automatic indexing system currently under development is described. It combines pre-indexing by statistical techniques with knowledge based indexing carried out by two cooperating expert systems. The architecture of the system, databases and functions of each module are outlined. Reasons that justify the approach are given.

Introduction

It has been known for some time that adding index terms to the description of a document in a database results in increased precision during retrieval [1]. These extra keywords or index terms are normally assigned by a human indexer familiar with the topic discussed and the indexing vocabulary. Automatic indexing, the generation of index terms by a computer without human assistance has been studied intensively since the late fifties beginning with H.P. Luhn [2]. Successive work, especially by Salton [3] has mainly applied statistical techniques to the input text to identify terms that could serve as meaningful index terms. The general idea on which this approach is based, is that word frequency within a document is related to the content. A detailed summary of results in automatic indexing up to 1973 can be found in a paper by Sparck-Jones [4]. Most of the research in automatic indexing carried out after the publication of this paper applied statistical techniques. Many experimental systems based on different statistical methodologies have been built, but only one is currently used commercially [5]. The statistical approaches to automatic indexing and retrieval offer significant advantages in terms of efficiency and performance, but absolute performance measured in terms of precision and recall show their limitations [6].

In an attempt to overcome these restrictions many researchers in information retrieval have been trying improve performance with techniques borrowed from artificial intelligence, especially from the areas of knowledge representation and natural language processing.

Artificial Intelligence Methods and Automatic Indexing

Researchers in automatic indexing have basically adopted two approaches from AI, with the first one coming from natural language processing. Even though statistical schemes for the identification of descriptors are computationally easy and efficient, they fail to provide "good" index terms when the descriptor is very general. This problem can be remedied by the introduction of index phrases; for example, the phrases "information retrieval", "information science" are more specific than the descriptors "retrieval", "science", "information". However, statistical techniques have great difficulty in identifying such phrases since they may occur in the text separated by other words, or in a different order, for example "retrieval of information", "science of information processing". A number of methods have been suggested for the automatic identification of phrases to index documents [7,8,9] and a detailed comparison of various schemes was reported by Fagan [10]. The methods proposed vary in complexity and range from incorporation of word co-occurrence frequencies, use of a thesaurus to automatic syntactic analysis. The main conclusion is that all schemes are only marginally better than systems using single words or stems [6] and that they offer little promise for improvement [8] at great computational effort.

The other approach based on artificial intelligence is to employ the computer as an expert assistant. This avenue has been pursued by using a computerized intermediary for formulation of search requests [11], user modelling [12], selection of search keys [13] and lastly for indexing. An expert assistant to a human indexer has, normally, access to a thesaurus, semantic net or the indexing vocabulary, which represents a form of knowledge base. The assistant's function is to assure indexing consistency - the use of terms is restricted to those found in the knowledge base; indexing precision - the most precise terms should be used; and indexing exhaustivity -

all terms that are relevant should be attached to the document. The National Library of Medicine in the U.S. has reported great success with its interactive knowledge-based indexing [14,15]. A description of the Med-IndEx system [16] shows that the system is an assistant to a human indexer. The assistants knowledge base is organized around frames which form a thesaurus containing the MeSH terms. The assistant assures that the human indexer follows the rules with regard to conformity, consistency, specificity and multiplicity.

A similar system using a rule based expert system to aid the indexing of patents and technical literature of interest to the petroleum industry has been developed by the American Petroleum Institute [17]. The API thesaurus is the knowledge base and the expert system produces index terms which are reviewed by a human indexer. This system has been in operation since 1985. An automatic indexing and retrieval system for the law literature called ALLOY is under development and described in [18]. It needs human experts to set up a concept hierarchy and an expert dictionary before indexing can begin. The use of knowledge bases in the automatic indexing process has been thought of by several researchers, but was deemed to be too difficult due to the large amount of data required [19]. Despite this apparent obstacle and the fact that it is difficult in artificial intelligence to

represent commonsense knowledge [20], it has been suggested that the "rule-based activities of cataloguing, classification (and indexing) seem particularly worthwhile for developing expert systems" [21]. A fully automatic system for automatic indexing of general document databases has not yet been described in the literature. The major obstacles to such a development seem to be the large size of the knowledge base needed and the difficulty of representing commonsense knowledge. Such a fully automatic system currently being developed [22] tries to circumvent both of these difficulties by a unique combination of conventional and expert system techniques.

System Architecture

The major premise in the development of the system is that *"divide et impera"* can reduce the problem of fully automatic indexing to manageable dimensions. The structure of the system is shown in Figure 1. To describe the structure and operation of the system, one document is followed as it proceeds through the system. Initially the document to be indexed is to be input to a statistic extraction module (SEM). Its function is to identify the relevant content words in the document based on some form of term weight. From previous work in automatic indexing it is known [3] that terms identified in this

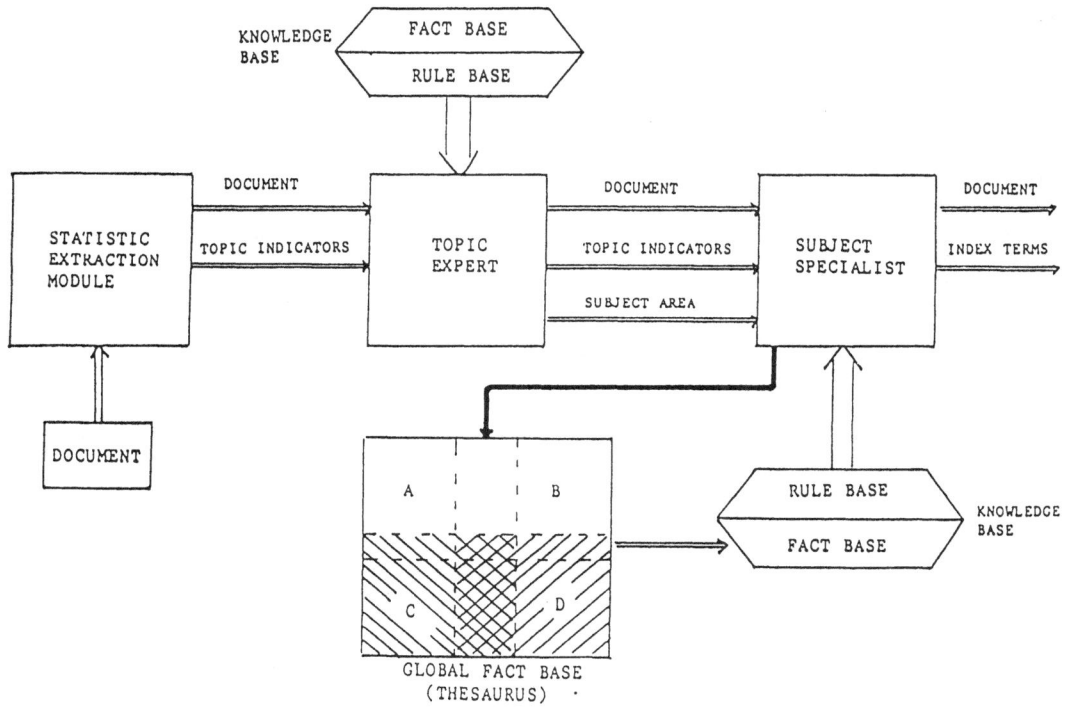

FIGURE 1.   SYSTEM STRUCTURE

fashion provide a reasonably good description of the documents content. This list of terms may not be very complete or specific, but certainly gives an indication of the topic the document is dealing with. The terms, called "topic indicators" and the document are passed to another module, the "topic expert." The module is a small expert system, rule based, that analyses the topic indicators produced by SEM, and decides which subject area is dealt with in the document. The fact knowledge base of the topic expert contains a coarse thesaurus and subject area designators. The function of the topic expert is to select an appropriate subject area and then to pass topic indicators, original document and subject area to another module. The rules of the topic expert facilitate navigation through the coarse thesaurus with the topic indicators as guides until the subject area has been determined.

The next module, called a "subject specialist," is another small expert system that will complete the indexing process by assigning very specific index terms to the document. The fact knowledge base of the subject specialist contains an enhanced thesaurus built with frames, representing and linking the entries. However, the subject expert does not need access to the global fact database, but only to a small one covering the subject area as chosen by the topic expert. Before the subject expert can assign index terms or phrases he must load the fact database associated with the subject area. The subject fact databases form a set which cover the entire domain knowledge. (See Figure 1). It is obvious that some degree of overlap must exist between different fact databases belonging to different subject areas. When a subject expert discovers during the indexing process that strong links exist to other subject areas, he can load the relevant subject areas fact database and continue with indexing. When the indexing process is finished the subject expert produces an ordered list of index terms and phrases together with an indication which subject area they were derived from. In the final stage the subject expert analyses the list and adjusts it to fit constraints; for instance, the maximum number of index terms may be limited. The document and the index terms are then stored in the database, and indexing is complete.

Justification and Conclusion

The architecture chosen for the system can be justified, since it circumvents most of the difficulties previously described. Using a statistical extraction module and a topic expert to narrow the field avoids the problems of having to represent a lot of general and common sense knowledge as well as a large knowledge base. It is relatively easy to give a general indication of a subject area a document is dealing with based on a few characteristic terms. Once the area has been restricted, interpretation of homonyms becomes much easier. For example, the word "series" is hard to interpret without knowing the area we are dealing with, but once we know whether it is mathematics, electrical engineering or geology, it is easy.

The system is very flexible since the number of subject areas is a parameter that can be chosen to fit external constraints such as disk space, response time, etc. The standard time-space tradeoff applies here, too, as subject areas which are too small will cause the subject expert to load too many fact databases for one document and thus slow the operation. The separation of the rule and fact data base offers all the advantages that are described in [23]. Rule and fact data bases can be updated easily and the rule base stays small. It is, however, imperative that the fact data bases, implemented as semantic nets built with frames, are checked for consistency, to avoid problems of looping, and methods described in [24] will be applied before the data is entered in the fact data base. The design of the subject expert and its rule base offers great flexibility since the operations carried out by this subsystem can be arbitrarily complex. It can include special methods for the generation of index phrases based on semantic and syntactic information or even a complete parsing of the document. Field specific rules must be included. They are needed for example to index documents in chemistry which contain structure formulas, documents in mathematics and physics which contain equations. The indexing rules will be derived, initially, by consultation with a human expert and later on by analysing "badly indexed" documents. As the quality of the index terms is very dependent on a good and comprehensive set of rules, considerable effort will be needed to build the rule base.

One well known problem in indexing is the introduction of new descriptions into the vocabulary, the shift in emphasis and frequency of term usage and the emergence of new fields. It is envisaged that some kind of learning mechanism which tracks usage of terms will have to be added. The aim is that the fact data base is either augmented automatically or the knowledge engineer is alerted to a shift in usage.

One major task remains once the project is concluded and the system is operational, namely, the evaluation. Does an improvement in recall and precision in comparison to other indexing methods exist and is it significant? Should the user who prepares a query have access to the subject expert to help her/him to formulate a good query?

Acknowledgements

This research was supported by the Natural Science and Engineering Council of Canada. Provision of facilities by the University of Essex for carrying out this research during a sabbatical leave are gratefully acknowledged.

References

[1] Lesk, M.E. "Word-Word Associations in Document Retrieval Systems," *American Documentation,* 20 (1969) pp. 27-38.

[2] Luhn, H.P. "The automatic creation of literature abstracts," *IBM Jrl. of Rs. and Develop.* Vol 2 (1958) pp. 159-165.

[3] Salton, G., McGill, M. *Introduction to Modern Information Retrieval,* McGraw Hill (1983).

[4] Sparck-Jones, K. "Automatic Indexing", *Jrl. of Documentation,* Vol. 30 (4) (1974) pp. 393-432.

[5] Biebricher, P. et al. "The automatic indexing system AIR/PHYS - from Research to Application". *Proceed. 11th SIGIR Conference,* (1988) pp. 333-342.

[6] Croft, B.W. "Approaches to Intelligent Retrieval", *Infor. Proc. & Mgmt.,* Vol. 23 (1987) pp. 247-254.

[7] Salton, G., Yang, S., Yu, C. "A Theory of Term Importance in Automatic Text Analysis". *Jrl. ASIS,* Vol. 26 (1975) pp. 33-44.

[8] Dillon, M., Gray, A.S. "FASIT: A fully automatic Syntactically based Indexing System". *Jrl. ASIS,* Vol. 34 (1983) pp. 99-108.

[9] Schuegraf, E.J., van Bommel, M.F. "The use of syntactic and semantic data for Document Retrieval". *Proceed. APICS Comp. Sc. Seminar,* (1987) pp. 1-10

[10] Fagan, J.L. "Automatic Phrase Indexing for Document Retrieval: An Examination of Syntactic and Non-syntactic Methods". *Proceed. 10th SIGIR Conf,* (1987) pp. 91-101.

[11] Pollitt, A.S. "An Expert System as an on-line search intermediary", *Proceed. Intern. Online Meeting,* (1981) Learned Info., Oxford, pp. 25-32.

[12] Brajnik, G., Guida, G. & Tasso, C. "User Modelling in Intelligent Information Retrieval". *Inform. Proc. & Mgmt.* Vol. 23 (1987) pp. 305-320.

[13] Fidel, R. "Towards Expert Systems for the selection of search keys". *Jrl. ASIS,* Vol. 37 (1986) pp. 37-44.

[14] Humphrey, S. & Miller, N.E. "Knowledge based indexing of the medical literature". *Jrl. ASIS,* Vol. 38 (1989) pp. 184-196.

[15] Humphrey, S. "Illustrated Description of an interactive knowledge-based Indexing System". *Proceed. 10th SIGIR Conf.,* (1987) pp. 91-101.

[16] Humphrey, S. "MedIndEx System: Medical Indexing Expert System". *Infor. Proc. & Mgmt.,* Vol. 25(1) (1989) pp. 73-88.

[17] Martinez, C., Lucey, J., Linder, E. "An Expert System for Machine Aided Indexing". *Jrl. Chem. Info. & Computer Science,* Vol. 27(4) (1987) pp. 158-162.

[18] Jones, L.P., Bessonet, C., Kundu, S. "ALLOY: An amalgamation of expert, linguistic and statistical Indexing Methods". *Proceed. 11th Intl. Conf. on Research & Development in Information Retrieval* (1988) pp. 191-199.

[19] Sparck-Jones, K. "A look back and a look forward." *Proceed. 11th SIGIR Conf.* (1988) pp. 13-30.

[20] Er, M.C. "Decision Support Systems: A Summary, Problems and Future Trends". *Decision Support Systems,* Vol. 4 (1988) pp. 355-363.

[21] Yaghmai, N.S., Maxin,I. "Expert Systems: A Tutorial". *Jrl. ASIS,* Vol. 35 (1984) pp. 297-305.

[22] Schuegraf, E.J. "Automatic Indexing of Documents Using Cooperating Expert Systems". *Proceed. 4th Intl. Sympos. on Computer and Information Science,* Cesme, Turkey, 1989, pp. 173-177.

[23] Defude, B. "Knowledge based system versus thesaurus: An architecture problem about expert systems design". *Proceed. 7th SIGIR Conference* (1984) pp. 267-280.

[24] Schäuble, P. "Thesaurus based concept spaces". *Proceed. 10th SIGIR Conference* (1987) pp. 254-262.

InfoGuide: A Full-Text Document Retrieval System

IJsbrand Jan Aalbersberg and Frans Sijstermans

Philips Research Laboratories – P.O. Box 80.000
5600 JA Eindhoven – THE NETHERLANDS

Abstract

This paper describes a full-text document retrieval system developed at the Philips Research Laboratories. The system is implemented on the POOMA machine, a parallel computer with a large main memory, and offers fast as well as high-quality retrieval on very large document bases.

1 Introduction

The increase in performance of computer systems means that the theory and practice of full-text document retrieval are receiving more and more attention. Another reason for this increase in interest can be found in the vast and growing amount of information currently stored in electronic form. To keep a clear overview of all the documents managed by an organization, a high-performance as well as high-quality full-text document retrieval system seems indispensable.

At the Philips Research Laboratories we have developed the parallel document retrieval system *InfoGuide*, which combines high-quality full-text retrieval with a high performance. The retrieval quality of *InfoGuide* is based on *term weighting* techniques (see, e.g., [18]), and supports ranking of documents in the order of relevance to a search request. Thus, using *InfoGuide*, one is able to initiate a full-text search the result of which is an ordered list of documents, in which the first document is the most relevant, the second one is less relevant, and so on.

The *InfoGuide* system is currently implemented on the parallel object-oriented POOMA machine (see, e.g., [5]). In a first prototype, the POOMA machine consists of 100 processing nodes, with in total 1.6 gigabytes of internal memory. This memory size makes it possible to store fast access structures – such as the *inverted files* (see, e.g., [9]) – in main memory. Using these structures as well as the parallelism, *InfoGuide* provides very fast computation of retrieval results on large document bases.

In this paper we present an overview of the *InfoGuide* system. Since we try to give a broad insight into all of the functionality, the design, and the current implementation, in this paper we are not able to elaborate on any single issue in depth. For detailed information, the reader is referred to [2], or to a forthcoming paper.

The paper is organized as follows. In Section 2 we provide some background knowledge on full-text retrieval techniques. Next, in Section 3, we concentrate on the *InfoGuide* system: here we mainly detail the functionality of the operation of searching for a document. Section 4 describes the user interface of *InfoGuide*: what does the user see, and what does he or she have to do to search for and retrieve documents? For the interested reader, in Section 5 we explain the term-weighting techniques as they are used by *InfoGuide* to rank the result of a search request. The hardware and the software platform on top of which the *InfoGuide* system is implemented are the key issues in Section 6. Section 7 indicates some design decisions and some current implementation aspects of *InfoGuide*. The paper culminates in Section 8: in this section we provide the performance analysis and results as they are measured on the first prototype implementation of *InfoGuide*. At the end of this paper, Section 9 concludes with some discussion and expectations for the future.

2 Full-Text Document Retrieval

Basically there are two different views on full-text document retrieval systems. First, there is the technique-oriented view on how to decide which document is in the result of a search request and which document is not. Second, there is the view on the implementation of the search process and of the search structures involved.

From the various techniques used for deciding which document is in the result of a search request, one of them completely outnumbers the others in frequency in commercially available full-text retrieval systems (see, e.g., [16]). This retrieval technique is the *boolean query* method, which is based on an exact boolean specification of the words that are wanted as well as of the words that are forbidden in the documents to be retrieved. A seldomly used retrieval technique is the *term weighting* approach,

---

*The work in this paper was conducted both as part of the PRISMA project, supported by the Dutch "Stimulerings-projectteam Informatica-onderzoek" (SPIN), and as part of the ES-PRIT 2427 TROPICS project, supported by the EC.

although it is shown that it gives a much higher retrieval quality than the boolean query approach (see, e.g., [18]). Here the high-quality retrieval originates from the fact that the term weighting method computes the importance of each word in each document. The most important reason for the low frequency usage of the term weighting method is the computational effort it takes to use it when searching in large document bases.

As far as the implementation of full-text document retrieval is concerned, there are three different approaches to implement full-text search on document bases (see, e.g., [16]). First, there is the simple *scan* through all the texts of the documents involved. Second, there is the *inverted file* approach, which makes use of an index, the inverted file, containing all the words that occur in the documents. Third, there is the *document signature* method, which translates the contents of each document into a bit string, the document signature.

Because of its efficiency in sequential computer environments, almost every commercially available full-text retrieval system is based on the inverted file method. However, the introduction of parallelism initially seemed to change this exclusiveness. In fact, on the one hand it was shown that multiple-instruction, multiple-data (MIMD) computers could be used efficiently to scan many documents in parallel (see, e.g., [10]). On the other hand, the introduction of single-instruction, multiple-data (SIMD) computers demonstrated that, especially on these computer systems, the document signature method is well suited to search in large document bases (see, e.g., [14, 19]). Here it has to be said that also the transputer networks have their influence in signature-based, full-text document retrieval (see, e.g., [8]).

Notwithstanding these two alternative implementation methods, the inverted file approach still remains a popular and efficient mechanism for searching in the full text of many documents. Actually, it even seems that also on parallel platforms the inverted file method can outperform both the scan approach and the document signature method (see, e.g., [2, 6, 17, 20, 21]).

The *InfoGuide* system as described in this paper follows the high-quality term weighting mechanism as the retrieval technique, and the inverted file method as the implementation approach. These choices originate from the choice for the underlying computer platform, a distributed network or a parallel machine, in which each node has a large local memory. For a more detailed treatment of the motivation behind these choices, the reader is referred to [2].

3 Functionality of InfoGuide

The basis of *InfoGuide* is the assumption that a user wants to search in the full text of a huge number of documents. These documents are managed by the *InfoGuide* system, which also guides the user through the document opera-

tions of insertion, search, and retrieval. Here, *InfoGuide* assumes that a document consists of a one-line *document description* and a *document text* of arbitrary length. Usually, the document text will contain an occurrence of the document description (e.g., the title, the header, or the subject of the document).

Insertion of a Document: Insertion of a document into the *InfoGuide* system can easily be done as follows. To insert a document with the name *name*, it is assumed that this document already exists somewhere in the computer working environment. Upon supplying the name *name* to *InfoGuide*, and upon taking the appropriate action, the document will be read and inserted.

Searching for a Document: Searching for a document managed by the *InfoGuide* system is based on the use of two types of queries: the boolean query and the weighted query. In the *boolean query* case, an *InfoGuide* user formally specifies the requirements to be matched by the documents searched for. Such a specification is a boolean expression over the words that have to be present or may not be present in the required documents. For instance, the boolean query

(NOT (sequential) AND (full OR free))

AND (text AND retrieval)

will result in the list of all documents managed by *Info-Guide* which contain the words text and retrieval, which do not contain the word sequential, and which contain either the word full or the word free or both.

For an *InfoGuide* user, a *weighted query* is a piece of text, informally describing the documents searched for. *InfoGuide* associates with each word in the query text a *term weight*, which indicates the relevance of the word in this text. These term weights are used to compute the result of a weighted query, which is an ordered list of *matching* documents. For instance, the weighted query

parallel full free text retrieval

will result in an ordered list of all documents managed by *InfoGuide* which contain at least one of the words parallel, full, free, text, and retrieval. Moreover, the documents in this *result list* are ranked in decreasing order of matching with the weighted query raised.

Searching for a document using a combination of a boolean and a weighted query is also possible. Whenever such a combination is requested, the result is the intersection of the results of the corresponding boolean and weighted query. One could say that this result is the result of a weighted query on those documents that are selected by the boolean query.

Retrieval of a Document: Depending on the point from which the retrieval starts, a document can be retrieved from the *InfoGuide* system along two different paths. First, a document which has been presented as a result of a query can be retrieved directly by selecting this document in the result list. Second, each document can also be retrieved by supplying its unique document identifier to the *InfoGuide* system.

Word Browsing: In the above we only described actions that can be performed on documents. There is also a function that allows the user to look inside the *InfoGuide* system without addressing any document at all. In fact, the *word browser* supplies the user with a view of all the words that occur in the documents stored. Here, also the number of documents in which a word occurs is presented.

4 User Interface of InfoGuide

The *InfoGuide* user interface plays the role of an access mechanism to the documents managed by *InfoGuide*. It is implemented on a workstation and uses a windowing system. All the operations described in Section 3 are accessible through 6 small subwindows (see Figure 1): five text windows, containing the various sorts of texts to be dealt with, and one panel window, containing the buttons that invoke the full *InfoGuide* functionality.

4.1 Text Windows

Each text window has the ordinary text editing functionality such as scrolling, cutting, and searching. Furthermore, since the text windows are all based on a standard text editor, interchanging text between the text windows within the user interface as well as to and from text windows outside it is easy.

The *scratch window* serves as a clipboard for the temporary storage of parts of text, for instance, a part of a query to be stored for later processing or a part of a text to be searched for in another text window.

The *boolean query window* and the *weighted query window* are reserved for the boolean query and the weighted query. In these windows the user can specify these queries according to the format, as explained in Section 3.

In the *result list window* the *InfoGuide* system presents the result of a query. Such a result is a list of triples, each of which corresponds to a document that matches the query. In fact, a triple (m, i, d) means that the document with description d and document identifier i matches the boolean query, and has a degree m of matching with the weighted query. The *match factor* (i.e., the first element) in such a triple informs the user of the difference in matching between resulting documents.

The *word browser window* provides the user with a word-oriented view to the *InfoGuide* documents: it contains all words that occur in some document that has been stored. More precisely, each element in this window is a tuple (x, n), where x is a word in a document stored, and n is the number of documents stored in which x occurs.

4.2 Panel Window

For the manipulation of the buttons on the panel window the *InfoGuide* user has to use a mouse. With this mouse he or she can invoke an operation, create a pop-up menu to detail an operation to be invoked, or select a text field.

By clicking the *document base button*, one determines the document base to operate on. In fact, *InfoGuide* can be used to address different document bases. The name of the document base has to be inserted in the *base* field. By using the document base button and choosing the appropriate option from the pop-up menu, a new document base can be created, an existing document base can be loaded, and a previously created or loaded document base can be exited, quited, or saved.

The *insert document button* can be used to insert a document from the computer working environment into the current *InfoGuide* document base. The file in which the document is stored has to be specified explicitly in the *file* field. If the name specified is *name* and if the user clicks the insert document button, *InfoGuide* searches for the files *name.desc* and *name.text*, assuming that they contain the document description and document text.

The search engine of the *InfoGuide* system is invoked when clicking the *query search button*. A search can be parametrized using the text fields that are associated with the subbuttons of the query search button.

- The origin of the boolean query has to be specified in the text field associated with the *boolean query button*. For this field the options are: *window* (the boolean query is in the boolean query window), *file : name* (the boolean query is in the file *name*), or *none* (there is no boolean query).

- The origin of the weighted query has to be specified in the text field associated with the *weighted query button*. Here the options are: *window* (the weighted query is in the weighted query window), *file : name* (the weighted query is in the file *name*), *identifier : ident* (the weighted query is in the *InfoGuide* document with document identifier *ident*), or *none* (there is no weighted query).

- The number of most matching documents (the result list) has to be specified in the text field associated with the *length result list button*. Here the value *all* as well as any positive integer value is allowed.

Upon clicking the query search button, the list of documents matching the query (the result list) is calculated, and presented to the user in the result list window.

To retrieve a document managed by the *InfoGuide* system, one has to click the *get document button*. The document has to be specified in the text field associated with the get document button. In this field one can have *identifier : ident*, indicating that the document with document identifier *ident* is selected for retrieval. On the other hand,

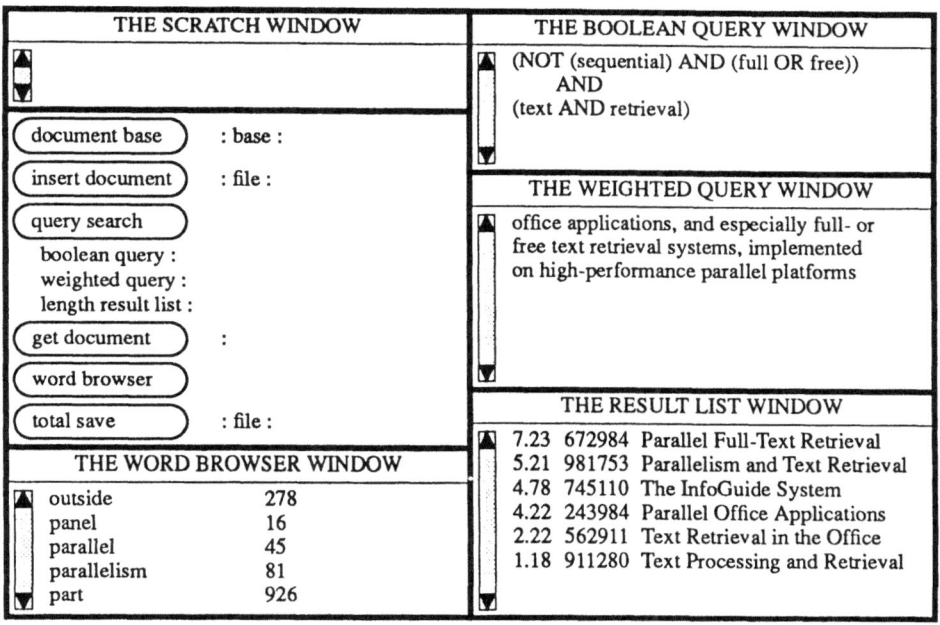

Figure 1: The user interface window of InfoGuide

selected result can also be typed in: now the document will be retrieved as selected in the result list window.

The word browser is invoked using the *word browser button*. By clicking it all words that occur in any document managed by *InfoGuide* are retrieved. The words as well the number of documents in which they occur are presented to the user in the word browser window. Each second and subsequent clicking the word browser button gives an update of the list of words.

To store a query and the corresponding result list in the computer working environment, the *InfoGuide* system contains the *total save button*. Whenever a user clicks this button, the current contents of the boolean query window, the weighted query window, and the result list window are stored in the file, the name of which is specified in the *file* field associated with the total save button.

5 Term Weighting

As mentioned, if an *InfoGuide* user raises a weighted query to search for documents, term weights become associated with the words that occur in the weighted query. Term weights also become associated with the words occurring in the documents managed by *InfoGuide*. This is done to separate the more relevant and selective words from the lesser relevant and selective ones. Out of the various term-weighting schemes that are known, *InfoGuide* uses one of the schemes with the highest retrieval quality (see, e.g., [18]). This term-weighting scheme is explained as follows.

For a text t, *InfoGuide* first determines the absolute relevance of each word x in t. This is done by calculating the word frequency $\#_x(t)$ of x in t. For each word x in t, *InfoGuide* then computes the relative relevance or the term weight $w_x(t)$ of x in t, by normalizing the word frequency $\#_x(t)$ to the total length of t:

$$w_x(t) = \frac{\#_x(t)}{\sqrt{\sum_{y \in t}(\#_y(t))^2}}.$$

Now, using the term weights of the words in a query text and the term weights of the same words in a document text, the *InfoGuide* system associates a match factor with every document managed. Such a match factor $m(q,d)$ indicates the degree of matching between a query q and a document d, and it is calculated as

$$m(q,d) = \sum_{x \in q} w_x(q) \cdot w_x(d) \cdot \log \frac{N}{n_x},$$

where N is the number of documents managed by *Info-Guide*, and n_x is the number of these documents that contain the word x. Here the logarithmic value ensures a low contribution from those words that occur in almost all documents.

6 Implementation Support

In this section we sketch the hardware and the software on top of which the current *InfoGuide* implementation is built. We present both the parallel main-memory machine POOMA and the parallel object-oriented programming language POOL.

The POOMA Machine: The POOMA (Parallel Object-Oriented MAchine) project is a large-scale research effort in the design and the implementation of a highly parallel machine (see, e.g., [5, 7]). The development of this machine is directed towards the efficient storage and manipulation of data and knowledge.

Conceptually, the POOMA machine will consist of at most some hundreds of *nodes*, connected via a high-bandwidth network. Each node will contain a data processor, a communication processor, and local storage. Each of these parts will be balanced in such a way that ultimately the nodes can be integrated in VLSI. In a first prototype set-up the POOMA machine consists of 100 nodes, each of which is composed of (i) a processing board containing a Motorola 68020 data processor, (ii) a bread-board communication unit, and (iii) 16 megabytes of local storage. The communication unit provides four communication links to other nodes, each link running at 20 megabits per second. Apart from the local storage, half of the nodes are connected to private disks, each providing 300 megabytes secondary storage.

The POOMA machine is connected to a SUN network using ethernet: one out of every five nodes has a connection to this ethernet.

The POOL Language: The POOMA machine implements the programming language POOL (Parallel Object-Oriented Language). This language is a member of the POOL family of parallel object-oriented programming languages, which are developed at the Philips Research Laboratories (see, e.g., [3, 4, 7]). It allows easy programming of complex parallel programs.

The basic concept in POOL is the *object*: an executing POOL program is thought of as a collection of executing objects. Each object is a run-time entity that contains data and methods. The data of an object is stored in variables, consisting of references to other objects. The methods of an object are the procedures acting on the data. One of the important points of POOL is that objects are protected against each other: the data of one object is not directly accessible from another object.

Objects can be created dynamically. Each object has a body, which is a local process that is started when the object is created. In principle, this body can execute in parallel with the bodies of other running objects. Hence, within the execution of a POOL program a large amount of parallelism can arise. Objects are grouped in classes: all objects in one class have the same variables, methods, and body.

Synchronization and communication between objects take place by sending messages, which are requests to execute a method. The sender of a message waits for the corresponding method execution without doing anything in the meantime. When the receiver accepts the message, a rendezvous takes place, during which the method is executed. After that, the result of the method is sent back to the sender and both objects proceed in parallel again.

7 Design and Implementation

7.1 Global Design

The design of *InfoGuide* is based on the following assumptions. Firstly, for each user there is a workstation, taking care of the presentation of the *InfoGuide* system. Secondly, there is the parallel POOMA machine, containing the heart of *InfoGuide*, i.e., the documents managed and the internal search structure (see Figure 2).

An *InfoGuide* user has access to the *InfoGuide* system through a workstation, at which a *user interface* program is running. For each *InfoGuide* user there is a separate workstation, and thus also a separate user interface program. The POOMA system communicates with the user interface programs through several *POOMA interface* programs. In fact, at each node of the POOMA machine that is connected to the ethernet, a copy of the POOMA interface program is available, and each of these copies is able to communicate with a number of user interface programs.

Connected to each POOMA interface program there is a private local lexicon, located at the same node of the POOMA machine. Such a local lexicon keeps track of all words the POOMA interface has encountered. Since the *InfoGuide* system internally works with stems of words, each local lexicon is also equipped with an operation that maps a word to a stem identifier. To keep this mapping consistent over the various local lexica, for new words each local lexicon communicates with a shared central lexicon. This central lexicon is located on a node of the POOMA system on its own, and it stores the complete sets of words and of stems of words.

The *word browser*, the *inverted files*, and the *document bases* are also *InfoGuide* components running on the POOMA machine. The latter two components control the documents and the associated search structures, and are distributed over the various nodes of the POOMA machine. The word browser, the inverted files, and the document bases are shared, in the sense that they can be addressed by each POOMA interface. Guided by the operations of insertion of and searching for a document, we now describe the design of these components.

Insertion of a Document: At insertion of a document into the *InfoGuide* system, the POOMA interface involved sends one copy to the *word browser*, and another copy to the local lexicon connected to it. As explained in Section 3, the word browser keeps track of all words that occur in the documents being managed by *InfoGuide*, together with the number of documents in which each word occurs.

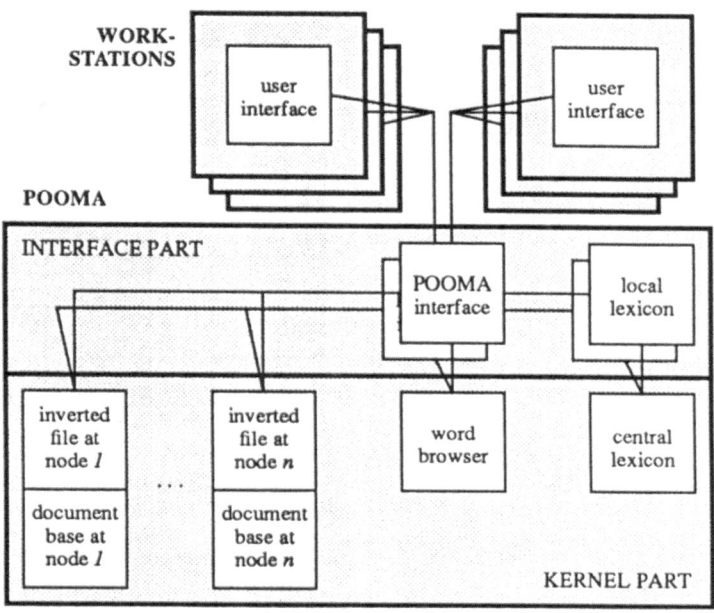

Figure 2: The internal architecture of InfoGuide

Upon receipt of a document, a local lexicon first transforms each word to its stem, and next translates each such stem to a unique stem identifier. The word-to-stem transformation is based on the suffix stripping algorithm as presented in [15], and aims to enhance the retrieval quality. The translation to stem identifiers is done to speed up the retrieval of documents: working with identifiers is much faster than working with strings. For a document received, a local lexicon also counts the occurrences of words with the same stem. It summarizes all the computations in a *frequency vector* of pairs of stem identifiers and stem frequencies, which is sent back to the POOMA interface from which the document was received.

A POOMA interface replaces in a frequency vector the stem frequencies by term weights, using the term-weighting scheme described in Section 5, and thus obtaining a *weight vector*. Note here that *InfoGuide* works with term weights of stems of words instead of with term weights of words themselves. After this replacement, the POOMA interface sends the resulting weight vector to an *inverted file* at some node of the POOMA machine, and the corresponding document to the *document base* at the same node. In fact, the documents managed by the *InfoGuide* system are distributed over the nodes of the POOMA machine. Each node that is connected to a disk manages a part of the documents: the document vectors are kept in the main memory and the documents themselves are stored on disk.

Searching for a Document: When searching for a doc-ument managed by *InfoGuide*, the appropriate POOMA interface receives both the boolean and the weighted query involved. The POOMA interface parses the boolean query, and uses its local lexicon to convert the words in the boolean query to the corresponding stem identifiers. For the weighted query, a similar action is taken as in the document insertion case: the local lexicon converts the weighted query to a frequency vector, and the POOMA interface replaces it by the corresponding weight vector.

After the parsing of the boolean query and the calculation of the weight vector, the POOMA interface sends the results to all inverted files. Next, each inverted file searches for those documents that are managed by the corresponding node, that match the boolean query, and that have a positive match factor with the weighted query. Finally, each inverted file sorts the resulting documents in order of decreasing match factor, and sends the best matching documents in this partial result list back to the POOMA interface at which the query was received.

Upon receipt of the various partial result lists, this POOMA interface merges them in the order of decreasing match factor. Next, it sends the best matching documents in the merged result list to the user interface program at which the query was raised. Finally, the result of the query can be shown to the user.

7.2 Implementation Aspects

In this paper we detail only two implementation aspects of *InfoGuide*. We first describe how the local and the

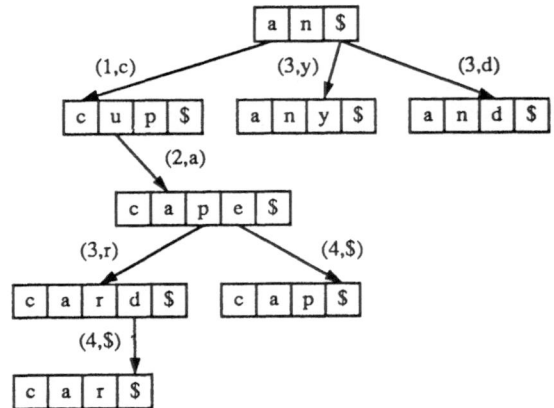

Figure 3: A compact trie

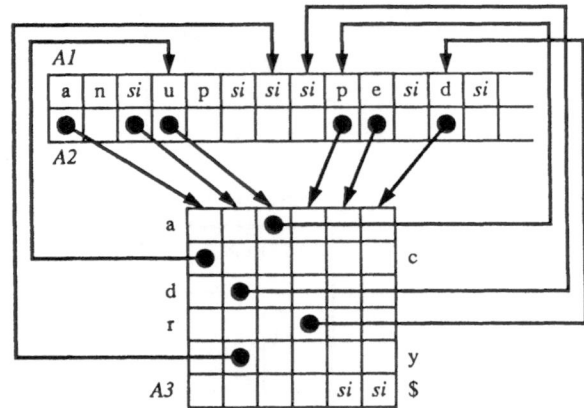

Figure 4: An implementation of a compact trie

central lexica are implemented. Next, we deal with the computation of the final result lists.

Using the Lexica: Each local lexicon returns, for an input word x, the stem identifier of the stem of x. Since each word in a document inserted or in a query raised has to undergo this mapping, we need an efficient implementation of a POOL class **Local-Lexicon**. The huge amount of main memory per node leads us to implement each object of the class **Local-Lexicon** by a *compact trie* (see [1]), a space-efficient version of the ordinary *trie* (see, e.g., [13]).

In Figure 3 we have depicted the compact trie of { *an$*, *cup$*, *cape$*, *any$*, *card$*, *car$*, *and$*, *cap$*}. Note that every word is extended with the end-of-word symbol *$*, to distinguish words from prefixes of other words. Searching in a compact trie for the stem identifier associated with a word x is easy. First, the first symbol in x is compared with the first symbol in the root node. If these symbols are equal, then the second symbols are compared, and so on. As soon as two symbols differ at position i, the search continues at position $i + 1$ in the node pointed at by the outgoing edge that is labeled by (i, σ), where σ is the i-th symbol in x. Whenever the node does not have this outgoing edge, then x is not present in the compact trie. On the other hand, if all symbols in x can be scanned successfully, then the final node in the search contains x.

In the implementation of the class **Local-Lexicon**, we replace the end-of-word symbol *$* by the appropriate stem identifier. Other implementation details can be described as follows (see Figure 4). Firstly, there is a one-dimensional "success" array *A1* that contains both characters and stem identifiers. Secondly, there is an equally long one-dimensional "failure" array *A2* that contains pointers to columns in a third array. This third array *A3* is a two-dimensional "pointer" array, which contains pointers to entries in the arrays *A1* and *A2*, and of which the number of rows equals the number of possible symbols. The rela-

tions between these arrays is best explained by following a search for a stem identifier associated with a word.

Consider the compact trie in Figure 3, and its implementation in Figure 4. To find the stem identifier associated with *cape$*, one compares the first symbol of *cape$* with the first entry in *A1*. Since $c \neq a$, one follows the corresponding failure pointer in *A2* to a column of *A3*, in which the *c*-entry is followed back to *A1* (the *c*-entry is taken because *c* is the first symbol of *cape$*). Now the second symbol of *cape$* is compared with the entry pointed at in *A1*, resulting in a similar following of pointers. Next one compares the third symbol of *cape$* with the current entry in *A1*: equality on *p*. Hence, one moves simultaneously to the fourth symbol in *cape$* and to the next entry in *A1*. Again there is equality, now on *e*, and one again moves. Since the fifth symbol in *cape$* is *$*, and since the current entry in *A1* contains a stem identifier (originally a *$*-symbol), one concludes that this stem identifier is associated with *cape$*.

Computing the Result List: On the input of a stem identifier s, the inverted file at node p returns a list of *postings* of document identifiers and term weights. A posting (i, w) in this list means that the document with identifier i is managed at p, and that w is the (positive) term weight of the stem with identifier s in the document with identifier i. *InfoGuide* keeps the postings sorted on the value of the insertion time of the corresponding documents.

To process a boolean query that is sent to the inverted file at node p, the inverted file locally retrieves all posting lists associated with the stem identifiers in this boolean query. Next, it applies the set operations intersection, union, and difference to the document identifiers in these lists, where the operations correspond to the AND, OR, and NOT operators in the boolean query.

To process the weight vector computed out of a weighted query, a similar procedure is followed: the inverted file

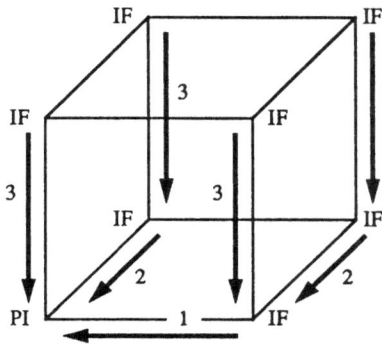

Figure 5: A sorting and merging hypercube

first retrieves all lists of postings associated with the stem identifiers in the weight vector. Then, each term weight in the list associated with the stem x is multiplied with the term weight of x in the weight vector and with the factor $log(N/n_x)$ (see Section 5). Next, all these lists are merged in such a way that the weights associated with the same document identifier are added to each other, and thus resulting in a list of pairs of document identifiers and match factors.

If both the boolean query and the weighted query originally existed, then this is the moment where the intersection of the results of their processing takes place: both partial result lists are sorted using the same sorting criterion. After this intersection, the last step performed locally by the inverted file at node p is to sort the resulting list on the value of the match factors: here an ordinary heap sort is used.

At the global level, there is still left the merging of the various local result lists. To do this, the inverted files and the POOMA interface involved can be considered to be mapped to virtual nodes in a k-dimensional hypercube (see, e.g., [11]). This hypercube is such that each node knows its own highest dimension, and also such that each node has a direct dimension pointer to the unique node that only differs in this highest dimension (in Figure 5 we have depicted the dimension pointers in the 3-dimensional hypercube). Furthermore, the POOMA interface corresponds to the unique hypercube node that has 0 as its highest dimension.

Assume now that from the union of all the local result lists as they are distributed over the inverted files at the various nodes of the POOMA machine, the n best matching document identifiers have to be transferred to the POOMA interface (which in turn has to send them to the user interface program from which the query was originally received). Then the merging of the local result lists is achieved by iterating the following steps for the values of $j = k$ down to $j = 1$:

- Each inverted file with j as its highest dimension sends the n uppermost pairs in its local result list to the inverted file pointed at by its dimension pointer.

- The receiving inverted file, which has at most $j - 1$ as its highest dimension, locally merges the result list received with the one it has available from its own, to obtain a new and updated local result list.

Since the POOMA interface corresponds to the node with 0 as its highest dimension, in k steps the POOMA interface will end up with a result list, of which the upper most n are the identifiers of the n documents that are managed by *InfoGuide* and that have the best match with the query originally raised.

8 Performance Analysis

Unfortunately, due to recent changes in the POOL language implementation, at the moment we are not yet able to measure the ultimate performance of *InfoGuide*. Therefore, in this paper we only present performance results of a first implementation, and estimate results which we expect to have within a couple of months.

For measuring the performance full-text retrieval systems, the search operation is usually considered to be the most time consuming. Moreover, since the evaluation of a weighted query is more expensive than the evaluation of a boolean query, in the *InfoGuide* performance analysis below we have only investigated the former. Thus, in our analysis the search operation consists of the following five phases:

- derivation of the weight vector out of the weighted query,

- distribution of the weight vector among all inverted files (nodes),

- computation of the match factors between the query and all documents,

- sorting the match factors into partial result lists, and

- merging the partial result lists into a final result list.

The time complexity of these phases is analyzed as follows.

Clearly, the number of steps needed to derive a weight vector out of a weighted query is linear to w, the number of words in the weighted query.

The number of operations needed to send a weight vector from one inverted file to another linearly depends on q, the number of terms in this vector. Using the hypercube described in Section 7, the distribution of a weight vector among n inverted files (distributed over n nodes) takes $log\, n$ iterations of possibly parallel sends. This amounts to a total distribution time that is linear to $q \cdot log\, n$.

The complexity of computing match factors is linearly related to the number of matching terms. This number equals the product of the number d of documents in the system, the number q of terms in the weight vector, and the percentage p of documents containing a term from the weight vector. Thus, in our analysis where we assume that the matching terms are perfectly distributed over the n inverted files (nodes), the match factors can be computed in time linear to $d \cdot q \cdot p/n$.

To estimate the number of operations required for locally sorting the match factors, we assume that all documents have some resemblance to the query. Furthermore, we again assume a perfect distribution of documents over the nodes. Then picking out the r highest match factors takes time linear to d/n, and locally sorting these match factors takes time proportional to $r \cdot \log r$.

Finally, merging the partial results is similar to distributing the query. Therefore, it is easily checked that the time required to do this is linear to $r \cdot \log n$.

The analysis results above are summarized in Table 1. In this table also the constant factors are added to the time complexity formulas, resulting in values in microseconds. However, since these constant factors are derived from experiments with only a small number of documents, they are probably somewhat overrated due to the unfavorable influence of once-only contributions. Note that in the "total" row in this table, only the calculated time related to the dominating number d of documents stored is taken into account.

In Table 1 we also provide the expected search time for a typical weighted query and a typical document base. Here we fill 80 nodes of the POOMA machine with in total 600,000 documents, each of them containing some 200 terms. Furthermore, we take a 200-term weighted query such that on average each query term occurs in 2 percent of the documents. Finally, we search for the 50 best matching documents.

As already mentioned, the POOL language implementation is being changed. Therefore, we expect to gain in the several phases of the query search at least a factor between 2 and 4. For our example document base of 600,000 documents, we already estimated the expected query time after the POOL changes, and depicted them in Table 1 between brackets. Consequently, it can be concluded that evaluation of large 200-term queries on 600,000 documents is expected to take about 2.5 seconds, and that small 5-term queries are expected to take less than 0.1 second.

9 Discussion

In this paper we have sketched the first prototype implementation of the parallel full-text document retrieval system *InfoGuide*. This implementation has been written in the parallel object-oriented language POOL, and has been executed on the parallel object-oriented machine POOMA. Based on term-weighting techniques, *InfoGuide* offers a high-quality retrieval in the sense that it ranks the output of a search request in the order of relevance to that search request. Furthermore, because of its implementation on the parallel POOMA machine, *InfoGuide* offers this extended functionality without any loss in retrieval performance.

In the world of full-text retrieval systems, we can state that *InfoGuide* nicely keeps pace with the retrieval performance of other parallel retrieval systems. More precisely, with respect to the Distributed Array Processor (DAP) as described in [14], our results on the document base with 600,000 documents show a scan rate (i.e., number of thousands of match factor computations per second) which is twice as high. Furthermore, in comparison with the first Connection Machine (CM-1) approach as evaluated in [19], our results demonstrate a similar performance: the CM-1 searches through 640,000 small documents in a little bit more than $2\frac{1}{2}$ second, while *InfoGuide* searches through 600,000 larger documents in a little bit less time.

In a more detailed comparison of the *InfoGuide* system with the systems mentioned in [14], [19], and [20], the following points have to be noted. First, the current main-memory implementation of the *InfoGuide* system cannot cope with extremely large document bases of several million documents or even a magnitude more. Therefore, especially a comparison with the second Connection Machine (CM-2) approach as sketched in [20] is very difficult at the moment. However, it will be clear that extensibility to extremely large document bases is a topic of future research (see, e.g., [12] for a possible direction), the outcome of which should be incorporated in a next implementation of *InfoGuide*. Second, a major advantage of the *InfoGuide* system is that the retrieval technique it uses is superior to the ones used by the other systems. In fact, comparison with the other retrieval techniques shows that the term-weighting scheme used by *InfoGuide* gives much higher recall and precision rates (see, e.g., [17, 21]).

However, the greatest difference between the *InfoGuide* system and the three systems presented in [14], [19], and [20], is that *InfoGuide* is not nailed down to any specific (SIMD) hardware platform. In fact, although currently implemented on the MIMD parallel object-oriented POOMA machine and written in the parallel object-oriented POOL language, *InfoGuide* can easily run on standard sequential systems or on networks of those systems. In particular this feature of scalability makes the *InfoGuide* approach extremely useful as well as cheap in various environments, from small office systems to large high-end retrieval servers.

References

[1] IJ.J. Aalbersberg, The Compact Trie of a Set of Words, PRISMA Doc. No. 0360, Philips Res. Labs., Eindhoven, The Netherlands (1989), submitted for publication

phase	calculated time (μs)	measured time (ms)
derivation	$3840 \cdot w$	1920 (480)
distribution	$325 \cdot q \cdot \log n$	455 (228)
computation	$281 \cdot d \cdot q \cdot p/n$	8430 (2100)
sorting	$160 \cdot d/n + 100 \cdot r \cdot \log r$	1230 (308)
merging	$740 \cdot r \cdot \log n$	259 (86)
"total"	$(281 \cdot q \cdot p + 160) \cdot d/n$	9660 (2408)

Table 1: The search performance of a 200-term query on 600,000 documents

[2] IJ.J. Aalbersberg, A Parallel Full-Text Document Retrieval System, Proc. Workshop on Object-Oriented Document Manipulation, Rennes, France (May 1989), 268 - 279

[3] P. America, POOL-T: A Parallel Object-Oriented Language, in *Object-Oriented Concurrent Programming*, eds. A. Yonezawa and M. Tokoro, MIT Press, Cambridge, Mass. (1987), 199 - 220

[4] P. America, Issues in the Design of a Parallel Object-Oriented Language, DOOM Doc. No. 0452, Philips Res. Labs., Eindhoven, The Netherlands (1989), to appear in *Formal Aspects of Computing*

[5] J.K. Annot and P.A.M. den Haan, POOL and DOOM: the Object-Oriented Approach, in: *Parallel Computers: Object-Oriented, Functional, Logic*, ed. P.C. Treleaven, Wiley, Chichester - New York (1990), 47 - 79

[6] N. Asokan, S. Ranka, and O. Frieder, A Parallel Free-Text Search System with Indexing, Proc. Intern. Conf. on Distributed, Parallel Architectures, and their Applications, Miami Beach, Flor. (March 1990), 519 - 521

[7] W.J.H.J. Bronnenberg, L. Nijman, E.A.M. Odijk, and R.A.H. van Twist, DOOM: A Decentralized Object-Oriented Machine, *IEEE Micro* 7 (October 1987), 52 - 69

[8] J.K. Cringean, M.F. Lynch, G.A. Manson, P. Willett, and G.A. Wilson, Parallel processing techniques for information retrieval, Proc. 13th Intern. Online Information Meeting, London, United Kingdom (December 1989), 447 - 462

[9] C. Faloutsos, Access Methods for Text, *Computing Surveys* 17 (1985), 50 - 74

[10] L.A. Hollaar, The Utah Text Search Engine: Implementation experiences and Future Plans, Proc. 4th Intern. Workshop on Database Machines, Grand Bahama Island (March 1985), 367 - 376

[11] J.M. Jansen and F.W. Sijstermans, Parallel Branch-and-Bound Algorithms, *Future Generation Computer Systems* 4 (1989), 271 - 279

[12] D. Lucarella, A Search Strategy for Large Document Bases, *Electronic Publishing* 1 (1988), 105 - 116

[13] K. Mehlhorn, *Data Structures and Algorithms; Vol. 1: Sorting and Searching*, Springer Verlag, Berlin (1984)

[14] C.A. Pogue and P. Willett, Use of Text Signatures for Document Retrieval in a Highly Parallel Environment, *Parallel Computing* 4 (1987), 259 - 268

[15] M.F. Porter, An Algorithm for Suffix Stripping, *Program* 14 (July 1980), 130 - 137

[16] G. Salton, *Automatic Text Processing: The Transformation, Analysis, and Retrieval of Information by Computer*, Addison Wesley, Reading, Mass. (1989)

[17] G. Salton and C. Buckley, Parallel Text Search Methods, *Comm. of the ACM* 31 (1988), 202 - 215

[18] G. Salton and C. Buckley, On the Use of Spreading Activation Methods in Automatic Information Retrieval, Proc. 11th Intern. Conf. on Research and Development in Information Retrieval, Grenoble, France (June 1988), 147 - 160

[19] C. Stanfill and B. Kahle, Parallel Free-Text Search on the Connection Machine System, *Comm. of the ACM* 29 (1986), 1229 - 1239

[20] C. Stanfill, R. Thau, and D. Waltz, A Parallel Indexed Algorithm for Information Retrieval, Proc. 12th Intern. Conf. on Research and Development in Information Retrieval, Cambridge, Mass. (June 1989), 88 - 97

[21] H.S. Stone, Parallel Querying of Large Databases: A Case Study, *Computer* 20 (October 1987) 11 - 21

Acknowledgements. The authors are indebted to Jan Martin Jansen, Hans Oerlemans, and Jan Turk, who also made a contribution to the definition of *InfoGuide*. We furthermore acknowledge the system support of Rogier Wester, who was always present when needed.

An Architecture for Full Text Retrieval Systems

Scott C. Deerwester, Donald A. Ziff, Keith Waclena

University of Chicago

Abstract

A novel architecture for full-text information retrieval systems is described. The architecture's most distinctive feature is a server that is implemented as an interpreter for a lazily evaluated functional programming language. The consequences of this approach for time and space performance are discussed, concentrating especially on the functionality provided for searching for occurrences of words in textual databases.

Introduction

We present here an architecture for full-text information retrieval systems. This architecture has several distinctive features:

- The retrieval system is implemented as a server to which client user interfaces may connect.

- The server is presented to both end users and client user interfaces as an interpreter for an assignment-free, referentially transparent functional programming language.

- The architecture allows a single client to obtain results from many servers simultaneously; in effect, the machine on which programs written in the server's language run is the network.

- Different user interfaces, with very different styles of interaction, use the same server for all retrieval and textual object management functionality.

We concentrate in particular on the means by which a retrieval system finds word occurrences. The reasons for this focus are:

- The demands of a modern distributed computing environment require an unusual degree of flexibility. A system may be used to search collections of text ranging from very large, relatively static text archives to small, dynamic collections. As a result, it is often not possible to know what the most effective method for searching is until search time. Further, search methods may become available as new classes of textual databases are added, and a retrieval system should be able to accomodate them.

- Much of the time and space complexity of operations performed by an information retrieval system are determined by its search methods. The strength of a retrieval system is largely determined by how well it searches.

The approach presented here may be compared with several other classes of systems. Special purpose information retrieval systems are those designed to be used with a particular database. Sometimes such systems can be used with other databases that are sufficiently similar. The Responsa Project is a good example of such a system [4]. The Responsa is a large body of literature composed of letters to Jewish authorities, with their responses. The database is large, static, and has a community of highly educated users. The system runs on a large IBM mainframe. Response time is extremely fast, almost never more than a few seconds. To reconstruct the indices is extremely costly, and a great deal of work has gone into the design of the indexing process to optimize for the Responsa database. The system is currently being extended to be used with a larger body of Jewish literature.

Although the Responsa Project is by any standards a very good text retrieval system, it is in no sense general purpose, and is running in essentially the same environment in which it was designed fifteen years ago.

Another example of a special purpose retrieval system is *refer*, written by Michael Lesk as part of the tools available with the UNIX operating system [9]. Refer is a preprocessor for the *troff* text formatter. It examines troff source files, which have embedded typesetting commands, for known-item queries, which it then searches for in one or more databases of bibliographic references in a particular format. These references are then formatted by troff. Refer is a good example of a well-designed tool for a special application. It uses very little space overhead, and takes very little time to find a citation for which it is given a non-ambiguous query. Refer would work much less well for unknown item searches, and quite legimately so, since it was not designed for this.

Laboratory systems are largely used only for information retrieval experiments, and not primarily, if at all, by end users. Two well-known examples of laboratory systems are IRx [6, 7], developed at the National Library of Medicine, and the SMART system, the most recent generation of which was written by Chris Buckley and Gerard Salton at Cornell University. From a programming methodology point of view IRx is similar to our approach. Although IRx uses a single indexing method, and was not intended to be a tool of the flexibility proposed here, it is highly modular, and allows different retrieval methods to be used with little modification to most of the retrieval system.

There are few systems that were designed for a modern computing environment. Since programming methodologies have consistently lagged behind hardware developments, this is certainly not surprising. One system that was designed for a distributed environment is MicroARRAS, written by John

B. Smith at the University of North Carolina [13].

The work that we describe here is the product of the Textual Information Retrieval and Analysis research group (TIRA). The TIRA system (whose architecture we describe below) is a full-function full text information retrieval system that runs on a network of UNIX workstations at the University of Chicago. It is used as the primary research environment for a group of information retrieval researchers, and is the primary research tool of a large group of literary scholars in many North American universities. The work described here is part of an ongoing project whose eventual outcome will be a comprehensive set of tools for performing textual information retrieval and analysis, providing access to textual resources anywhere on the Internet.

1 Architecture

The design of the TIRA system is based on an overall architecture that consists of a set of abstractions. Before discussing the individual levels (see section 3.2), we give here an overview of the whole system architecture in terms of these levels.

1.1 Abstraction

The TIRA system consists of code that implements progressively higher levels of abstraction, where each level accesses functionality provided by the next lower level through some well-defined interface (see figure 1).

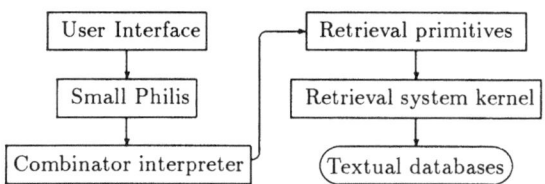

Figure 1: Levels of abstraction in the TIRA system

At the highest level the TIRA system is accessed by casual users with an interface that uses windows, menus and help screens. Two interfaces exist. The first, called PhiloLogic is one of the primary research tools for a large population of literary scholars through the project for American and French Research on the Treasury of the French Language (ARTFL). [12] An independent Macintosh interface (called MacPhilo) also exists. Interfaces work by communicating with a Philis interpreter. PhiloLogic constructs Philis expressions, which are passed to the Philis interpreter using some interprocess communication mechanism, reads the result and presents it in a nice way to the user. In response to a user query requesting all occurrences of the word "amour" in the works of Flaubert, PhiloLogic might pass the expression `"search (gimme "author=flaubert") "amour""` to Philis, where "`(gimme "author=flaubert")`" returns a single textual object of type *author*. This which would result in a list of *textual objects*, passed from Philis to PhiloLogic (see section 2). Users can also write Philis programs directly,

without using PhiloLogic. Philis has been used in this way in several (literary) research projects.

Philis has evolved over the past four years from a very simple UNIX shell-based command language to a sophisticated language in its own right. Its current implementation, presented in this paper, is based on an interpreter for the Small language, written in C by Lennart Augustsson. [1] This interpreter is a fully lazy language based on a combinator graph reduction machine that interprets Turner combinators [14]. We have extended this interpreter (the "combinator interpreter" in figure 1) to include special functions that, combined with auxiliary definitions in Small, implement all of Philis' functionality.

Each of Small Philis' retrieval-related functions is implemented by one or more C functions, compiled into the combinator interpreter, and called by the interpreter's driver function *eval()*. This set of retrieval primitives rely in turn on a larger and more complicated set of lower level functions that are the actual implementation of the system. It is only at the level of this retrieval system kernel that the system reads information from files and actually accesses stored data.

There are several advantages to adopting a rigorously modular and hierarchical approach to systems design. First, it is extraordinarily easy to add functionality to the system, since a function is implemented at the highest possible level. To take an example, a feature to store results and queries between PhiloLogic sessions required only modifications to the source code comprising PhiloLogic. No level below that of the interface required any modification. Similarly, the effects of changes at low levels of abstraction can be well contained; changes as fundamental as the definition of a textual object have been effected in a few weeks.

This last point illustrates, as well, the most important advantage of this strategy for TIRA researchers. While the TIRA system is a "production" tool for scholars, it is also the primary vehicle of research for several projects. The strict adherence to well defined levels of abstraction means that research at a given level—the programming language aspects of the retrieval server, for example—is both largely unconstrained by the dictates of other levels, and can bear direct fruit in the system as a whole.

1.2 Characteristics of Text Retrieval Systems

Text retrieval systems—considered as systems—bear a superficial resemblance to several other classes of large systems. It is tempting to view a text retrieval system as a sort of special purpose database management system or statistical analysis package. Since the latter are likely to be more familiar to many readers, and particularly since the approach to systems architecture taken in this paper would be much harder to justify in these other systems, we describe in this section those characteristics of text retrieval systems that have led to the choices presented here.

First, it is important to realize that text retrieval systems must routinely handle enormous lists; it is not at all unusual for a system to have to perform computations involving combinations of tens of lists, each of which may contain tens or hundreds of thousands of items. Second, text retrieval systems are used interactively. Users typically try a query—which might retrieve many items—examine the results, and then refine the query. A user might iterate many times before being satisfied with a search. There is almost never a single correct answer to a query. The user views the system as an aid in limiting the number of textual items that he has to examine to find ones that he is interested in. The system's function is to identify subsets of items and present them to the user for perusal.

The principal means by which we accomodate the demands imposed by these characteristics is *lazy evaluation*. Briefly, lazy evaluation may be defined as the delaying of the evaluation of the actual parameters of a function until it has been determined that they are required for the evaluation of the function. This allows the user to define non-strict functions. Non-strict constructor functions allow the manipulation of so-called "infinite" data structures; the original proponents of lazy evaluation [5, 8] considered this one of its most important advantages. The most visible advantages of lazy evaluation in the context of textual information retrieval are space and time savings:

- Space usage. Without lazy evaluation, it would be necessary to compute fully all the occurrence lists of all the words, requiring space to hold all of these intermediate results. For problems that require merging large lists, with lazy evaluation, we start to compute the merge before evaluating any of the intermediate lists. With careful implementation techniques, it may be possible to require only that the head of each list be in memory, with the information required to produce the next element when necessary. The space complexity of this method is much less than the space complexity of the intermediate lists, perhaps even linear in the number of lists to be merged, regardless of the size of the lists themselves.

- Prompt delivery of preliminary results. When a system such as this is used in conjunction with a user interface which permits interactive browsing of results, early results can be delivered to the user before the entire result is computed. This may give the user the impression that the system is functioning faster than an equivalent system based on applicative order evaluation.

- Avoiding unnecessary computation. In such situations, users may find, from examining the first few preliminary results, that it is not necessary to look at the remainder. Under a lazy evaluation regime, further computation is simply avoided, since it is not needed.

2 Textual Databases

There are many ways of modeling textual data. The most common is simply as a character string. We model document structure in a textual database, and we have thus chosen a hierarchical model. That is, we visualize a textual database as a tree. We call the internal nodes of the tree *textual objects*; in general, these correspond to natural textual divisions. For example, at the bottom of our tree are words; next above that are sentences. Above the sentence level are levels corresponding to document structure, such as chapter, act, scene, etc. Above these are document objects, then perhaps natural groupings of documents, such as all works by a single author, or works of the same genre, or century, etc. Finally, at the top level, the root of the tree is a single object which represents the entire database. The generic names or tags for each level of the tree (*word, sentence,* etc.) are called *object-types*. A list of the textual object types at each level of a tree is called a *marking*.

In general, the relation of parent to child in our text tree expresses containment, that is, a given paragraph contains several sentences, so each sentence object is a child of the common paragraph object. Similarly, sentences contain words, etc. Also, at each level, child nodes are ordered and numbered. Thus, a sequence of integers that corresponds to a path through the database tree may be identified with the corresponding textual object. The type of the object is implied by the length of the sequence.

A distance measure can be defined naturally between two children of a common parent, but generally this is only meaningful below the document level. Thus we can measure the distance in words between two words in the same sentence, or the distance in sentences between two sentences in the same paragraph. This distance measure can be extended to any two objects of the same type, even if they are not children of the same parent, but such a measure is not so easily calculated from the two sequences of integers identifying the paths to the two objects.

The set of all word objects in a database is mapped to a smaller set of objects called *word types*. These word types may correspond to dictionary head-words, or to distinct word forms. The word objects that map to a given word type are called the *occurrences* of the type; word objects are sometimes called *tokens*. Thus, in some databases, occurrences which are spelled "go" and "went" may be considered as separate occurrences of the same type, in another database, they may be considered as corresponding to different types. Word searching in a textual database is evaluating the inverse of this word-object to word-type mapping; that is, given a type, one must quickly find all the tokens that are occurrences of that type. Algorithms for solving the word-search problem are *word searching mechanisms* or, more loosely, *index methods*.

A database always has at least one marking that applies to all documents. More than one marking may be defined, however, on a per-database basis. In the ARTFL database, for example, a second marking that includes *pages* (and that could, but currently does not, include *lines*) is defined. The *contextualize* primitive works transparently across markings, so that a user could, for example, ask for all instances of "nation" that occur on the same page as a sentence that contains both "liberté" and "fraternité". This second marking is also used by the user interface to be able to tell users which page occurrences are on.

3 Textual Information Retrieval and Analysis

3.1 Access Methods

One of our primary goals in the design of a textual retrieval system is to have a retrieval language implemented as a programming environment in which high-level problems can be programmed without regard to specific word-search mechanisms. In this section we first consider some representative methods, to understand their differences and to further motivate our emphasis on flexibility of method selection. We then consider our implementation of a selection of these methods.

3.1.1 Overview

There are several word-search mechanisms in common use; these may be placed on a continuum of space-time trade-off. At one end of the spectrum is the most commonly used method for large databases, full indexing, or the "inverted file" method. Here an intermediate file is first created containing the set of pairs in the mapping from word tokens to types. This intermediate file is then sorted by type, and the list of tokens for each type is represented as a list in secondary storage. These token lists are called the *concordance*. An associative mechanism is devised for linking the types to their concordances; this can be either a hashed access list, or a trie, or any other representation of a sparse table. When well-designed and implemented, this method can provide very fast access to the occurrences of words, at the cost of enormous space usage. Space overhead of from 50% to 200% is common. Such methods may not allow for additions to a database, much less dynamic modification.

On the other end of the spectrum is the preferred method for small text databases, sequential searching. Here the word type to be searched is expressed as a character pattern, and the entire database is searched with some fast pattern matching algorithm. This method uses no space overhead and is compatible with dynamic databases, but can be impractically slow for large databases, particularly if the words involved are extremely infrequent.

As an example of a method which trades off between these two, let us consider Michael Lesk's "Grab" method [10]. First an intermediate file is created, as in the inverted-file method. Next, the set of types is hashed down to a smaller integer range. The intermediate file is then processed so that the types are replaced by their hash values, and the file is sorted by hash value, so that all of the occurrences of any word in a given hash bucket are grouped together. Now the database is divided into blocks, either arbitrarily or at natural divisions, and the intermediate file is then processed into a collection of bitmaps, indicating, for each hash-bucket, the set of blocks in which there is at least one occurrence of at least one of the words in the bucket. Word searching is then a two-step process: first the appropriate bitmaps are retrieved, then the corresponding blocks are searched sequentially. This method can be tuned by adjusting the number of hash buckets and the blocksize.

There are several other techniques which use bitmaps, and it should be noted that these have an advantage when used in a compound search, namely that bitwise logical operations can be efficiently performed to further limit the number of blocks which must be searched sequentially.

Because we are interested in experimenting with word-search mechanisms, one of our design goals is a platform that allows us to write query programs that are oblivious to the particular search methods used. This is even more important when one considers hybrid techniques, in which

different methods are available for the same database. For example, sequential searching makes good sense, even for a very large database, for words which are extremely frequent, say the 100 or so most frequent words (these words typically account for more than 50% of the tokens; in many database systems, they are called *stop words*, since they are not indexed and thus not searchable). On the other hand, full concordances are good for extremely infrequent words. So a Grab-like method would be best for medium-frequency words.

Another consideration that motivates a word-search abstraction is distributed databases. We wish to consider searches spanning different databases (either on one machine or across a network). We model this as a single database tree in which one must search for a given word by a particular set of methods in one subtree, and by another set in a different subtree. Again, we want our high-level search algorithms to be oblivious to this complication.

3.1.2 Implementation

Our system contains implementations of three word-search mechanisms: a fully-indexed method, a bitmap method, and a sequential searching method. All three were implemented in C; this was motivated by two main considerations:

- The low-level operating system interface available from C allows efficient use of secondary storage devices, which is essential for implementation of large-scale database software.

- We already had a fully-indexed method and other software written in C from our last implementation of a textual retrieval system. We wished to reuse this software, both to minimize recoding and to maintain compatability with the index files.

In our current implementation, the fully-indexed method is used for all the words except the 100 most frequent. In the previous system, it was impossible to search for these stop words; now, sequential searching fills this gap. Our sequential searching method is based on widely available, public domain regular-expression matching subroutines. Our bitmap oriented method is based on Lesk's, and uses a bitmap compression technique based on the work of Tomi Klein and his colleagues [3]. Once the blocks for search have been selected, they are searched sequentially using the same code as in the sequential search method (see section 3.1).

The performance of all of these methods could be improved; most particularly, our sequential searching method would benefit from the choice of an algorithm better suited to the range of patterns we expect. But our purpose for the moment is to demonstrate that several word-search mechanisms can be combined in a single system. Thus, it is most important to have representative methods to begin with, especially since our architecture permits us easily to fine-tune or replace our methods at any time later, as we have in fact done.

The C implementations of these methods share important support procedures and data structures. Some of these are used in the C interface to the combinator reduction machine; they are discussed below. Others perform important basic access functions, such as converting from the representation of a textual object to an indication of the files, offsets and lengths of the corresponding text. These structures are called *spans*; the operation, *spanify*, is made available as a C function to the access methods and, at the language level, to programs written in Philis.

3.2 Interpreter

We now discuss the interface of the access method software and the combinator reduction machine from the combinator graph point of view. In Philis, search results are returned from access methods as a *lazy list*. This is an important concept in functional languages and deserves special attention. In most imperative list oriented languages, lists are implemented by linking together CONS cells, each of which contains a pointer to a cell containing the value of a list item, and a pointer to the next CONS cell in the list (see figure 2d).

A lazy list is implemented by storing a pointer to a special function called a *generator* that returns a list composed of two elements: a value, and another pointer to itself (see figure 2). The generator indicates the end of the list by returning NIL (indicated by "∧" in figure 2). The interpreter, when asked for the next element of a lazy list, replaces the cell that points to the generator with the return value of the generator, effectively extending the list by one cell.

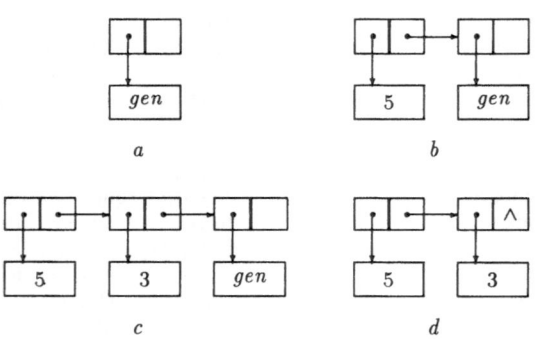

Figure 2: Steps in evaluating a lazy list [5, 3]

Philis' search-related primitive functions (or primitives) are implemented as extensions to the combinator interpreter. Implementing a primitive that returns a lazy list requires two components:

- A generator that returns successive elements of the list.

- Code that transforms a reference to the search primitive and its arguments into an invocation of the generator, with the appropriate arguments.

In general, this means that such a primitive depends on a second primitive, which is used to access the generator, and which is only callable from inside the combinator interpreter. The *read* primitive, for example, takes a string that

represents a file name, and returns all of the characters in the file as a lazy list of characters. The combinator interpreter evaluates *read* by calling the UNIX *open* system call, and replacing the call to *read* with a call to its internal *getc* primitive, with the file descriptor returned by *open* as its argument. Figure 3 shows the first few steps in evaluating "read "file";", where the first character in the file whose name is "file" is "a".

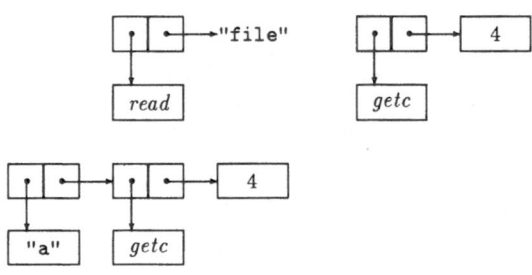

Figure 3: Evaluating the *read* primitive

In Philis, the interface to the externally compiled word-search mechanisms is through a special function—*M*—which is implemented similarly. *M* takes three arguments; an integer that determines the method to be called, a key for which to search, and an object within which to search. The combinator interpreter replaces such a call, for example, "M 0 "amour" obj;" with a list containing two elements. The first element is a *Boolean* that indicates whether the string is searchable using the method; it does this by calling the *open* for that method. The second element is either *nil*, if the string is not searchable, or a call to a generator (called *gethit*, and implemented by *getnext*) whose argument is the search descriptor returned by the *open* call. When the next occurrence of a word in an object is requested (the next "hit") the interpreter evaluates *gethit* to obtain it, until all of the hits have been found. In essence, *M* functions like *read* in figure 3, and *gethit* like *getc*, except that *gethit* takes a search descriptor and generates textual objects, and *getc* takes a file descriptor and generates characters.

3.3 Method/Interpreter Interface

The interface of our external word-search mechanisms with our combinator reduction machine brings up a general problem in the use of functional languages for real-world applications: the need for an interface to programs written in other languages and styles. This is a particular problem in functional languages, because it is difficult to enforce the semantic restriction that programs should have no side-effects. For this reason, we did not devise a general mechanism for linking arbitrary C into our interpreter; we restricted our attention to index methods written in C (or any other language linkable to C). In this way, we could make sure that the code linked in is free of side-effects, by making sure that the index method abstraction itself demands this.

In this section we discuss the C side of this interface; we then turn to the combinator reduction machine. Index methods written in C must provide three interface procedures, called generically *open, getnext,* and *close.* A special dispatch table keeps track of all the currently known external (C-callable) index methods, associating an integer with each one. The *open* routine takes a string and an object as arguments and returns an integer. If this integer is non-negative, it is interpreted as a unique search ID. The other return values and their meanings are:

Error	The search method failed
NotSearchable	The method cannot be used with the given combination of object and string
NotFound	The string/object pair *is* searchable, but no occurrences were found.

If a word is searchable by a particular method, *open* initializes an entry in a global state table giving all the information necessary to resume the search at any time. This is necessary since it is difficult to characterize exactly when the rest of a search will be needed after it has been initiated. It may be needed immediately, or many other searches may intervene before the rest of this search is needed, or it may never be needed. Thus this search state table must be managed centrally; support procedures must be provided to the methods to allocate and release space in the table, and to manage system file descriptors.

A search state table entry consists partly of information that applies to all search methods, such as:

- The target object in which to search

- An indication of the object's file, offset and length (the object's *span*)

- The string to search for

- An indication of the search method

Space is reserved in the state structure for method-specific information as well. Normally this information is used to indicate how far the search has proceeded. This is typically the last occurrence found, a file offset or any other information that the method-specific *getnext* requires to figure out where to begin looking for the "next" occurrence. The amount of information per search in the state table is on the order of several machine words; more information is, for some methods, accessed by pointers that are stored in the state structure.

All information pertinent to a search is kept in the search's state structure, and not in local or global variables in method-specific code. This is because, as mentioned above, the evaluation mechanism may end up calling the same method code for a different search before resuming any particular search.

The overhead of creating a state structure explains the necessity of the *NotFound* return value. If a given *open* routine knows that there are no occurrences of the given string in the specified object, there is little point in incurring the expense of allocating and initializing a search state structure, since the only thing that would ever be done with it is to *de*-allocate it.

The *getnext* routine takes a search descriptor and returns the next token which is an occurrence of the word in the object. To do so, it must consult the corresponding entry in the state structure table, and perhaps modify the corresponding private information pointed to there.

Exactly what a given method-specific *getnext* does is completely hidden from anything at or above the search abstraction level. The sequential *getnext* function, for example, uses (and hides) a relatively sophisticated least-recently-used buffer management scheme to minimize disk operations. Within a given call, it might access and advance a pointer to a buffer, modify the usage statistics, or allocate a new buffer. In any case, it uses only information in a particular search state structure, and modifies (side effects) only the information in this structure before returning the next occurrence, as a textual object, to its caller.

The *close* routine takes a search descriptor and frees up any local space allocated for it. It also calls the search-state table management software to let it know that this state entry is no longer needed.

3.4   The Philis Language

We now turn to a consideration of how word searching is viewed at the language level. To begin, we consider how our model of a textual database may be realized in a programming language. We then turn to the word-search abstraction.

3.4.1   The Database Model

First, we need data types to model the special objects we work with, and the primitive operations defined for them. The most important of these data types is the `TextObj`, which corresponds to our notion of *textual object.* That is, data of type `TextObj` represent nodes in our textual database tree. `TextObj` data are divided into subtypes, indicating the level in the tree: *word, sentence,* etc. The names of these levels are values of a special enumerated type called `OType`. The root of the database tree is a `TextObj` of type *library;* it is the only textual object of that type. This root object has the conventional global name `Library`. In our implementation, a `TextObj` is represented as the list of integers which corresponds to its path in the database tree.

A `contextualize` function is provided for moving up or down the database tree. Given the name of an object type and a textual object (presumably of a different type), it returns the list of all textual objects of the desired type that either contain or are contained by the object. That is, `contextualize` takes an `OType` and a `TextObj` and returns the list of all the descendants (or the ancestor) of its argument `TextObj` which are of the desired `OType`. It can be used to find the paragraph which contains a word, or all the sentences in a chapter, etc. As currently implemented, any `OType` below the level of *document* belongs to exactly one marking. A textual object is thus implicitly associated with some marking by the object types in terms of which it is expressed. We find this unsatisfying and intend to make the association between textual objects and markings explicit in a later version of our database model.

We use just one operator to move either up or down the database tree so that we may reserve the possibility of non-hierarchical object type structures or alternate markings (e.g., footnotes, or stanza-line-word vs. sentence-word in poetry). In general, `contextualize` is easy if one is going up the database tree; one merely truncates the list. Going down is more difficult, since one cannot predict how many children a given textual object has. Each object type is defined with respect to a *recognizer function*, currently written in C, that takes a span as an argument, and returns occurrences of some type (returned as spans) that are contained in it. Since contextualizing is an extremely frequent operation, most of the recognizer functions are memo functions[1] that are usually, but not necessarily, precomputed. We use large arrays for this purpose, implemented as external files. These arrays are also used to implement the translation from textual objects to the actual characters which they represent; this operation (called `get`) was not mentioned in our model, but is clearly necessary for viewing results. The same operation is used by most recognizer functions. Downward `contextualize` and `get` were implemented in C and linked into our interpreter.

The integration of recognizer functions and multiple word search methods into our software means that the system can operate on essentially any textual database, even with no primary or secondary indices, albeit more slowly.

The usual comparators ($<, >, \leq, \geq, =$) are defined for textual objects; they reflect the natural database order. Only textual objects of the same `OType` can be compared; that is, two words may be compared, or two sentences, but not a word and a sentence. Again, implementation of the comparators is straightforward; for example, one object precedes another if the sequence of integers in its representation is lexicographically smaller.

Word types, that is, search keywords, are modeled as character strings.

4 Performance

In section 1.2 we noted some of the characteristics of text retrieval systems that have led to our approach to system architecture. This approach is not without costs, both potential and actual. For the most part, we believe these costs to be more than regained by performance gains, but we have not yet undertaken a systematic evaluation of the performance of this approach. This is at least in part because the Small combinator interpreter was not designed to be efficient. Performance is thus dominated by factors that are not particularly relevant to the subject of this paper, and on which we expect to make substantial progress in the next generation of the language. We thus focus the present discussion on costs that result from using lazy evaluation.

Let us first consider the cost of evaluating a single list. As noted in section 3.1.2, all information pertinent to a search is stored in a per-search state structure. One (marginal) source of overhead is thus the access and maintainance of this structure. A more important source is that a given invocation of *getnext*, which might be one of many active invocations, and thus not benefit from block I/O. A sequential search method, for example, works by reading in sections of a document and

---

[1] Memo functions are functions that keep a table of argument–result pairs to avoid recomputing them in subsequent calls with the same argument. [11]

searching for the desired character string. This is normally quite efficient, since a program that is to find all occurrences of some pattern can read in large amounts of text in a single, efficient read operation, minimizing the number of disk accesses. If we are forced to return one occurrence at a time, with no guarantee that the next occurrence will ever be requested, the most straightforward implementation will have many times the I/O overhead, incurring one disk access per item rather than per storage block.

This cost is mitigated by several things:

1. Even though a method is not guaranteed that the next item will ever be requested, there is no particular reason *not* to evaluate (i.e. to precompute) several consecutive occurrences, and to return them only when they are requested. In other words even though at the level of the combinator interpreter we have no buffering of responses, there is nothing to prevent buffering at a lower level. In many ways this is exactly the same as a normal buffered I/O function that actually reads from disk a block at a time, but provides a *getchar()* function that simply returns characters from the buffer. All four of the search methods that have been implemented to date incorporate buffering of some kind.

2. More important, the evaluation regime implemented here means that most list items will probably never be evaluated at all, but can be used as if they were. What actually is evaluated depends almost entirely on what users actually ask to see. For this reason we are currently logging ARTFL users' sessions. We intend to look at the degree to which lazy evaluation helps in one of the next stages of this project.

A cost might also be incurred if the evaluation of a list is forced in order to perform some other computation. In particular, it is often desirable to know the length of a list. Several solutions are suggested:

1. Avoid computing the length if it is not really necessary.

2. Compute a rough estimate of the length. If the user merely wants to know about how many items were found, this may be sufficient.

3. Sometimes we know in advance how long it is, e.g. for the fully-indexed method.

Aside from the evaluation of lazy lists, there are several other factors that influence performance. Among those that we expect to have the largest impact are parallel evaluation and combining search methods.

In more traditional languages, exploiting parallelism is computationally difficult, and may be accomplished only with expensive dataflow analysis. Writing programs that take advantage of parallel evaluation requires the use of special parallel programming constructs, adding complexity, development time and often bugs. Assignment-free, referentially transparent functional languages can be parallelized automatically by the compiler because all data dependencies are manifest in the graph structure of the program.

A second potentially fruitful possibility that we intend to explore is combining search methods to optimize search performance. Several things are suggested:

- It should be possible to take advantage of bitmaps, for those methods that use them, to effect more efficient list joins for disjunctive or conjunctive searches.

- More standard search optimization techniques also apply: for example, in conjunctive searches where the terms have very different frequencies it clearly makes more sense to find the least frequent terms first, and then only look at passages containing these terms for the more frequent terms.

The appeal of these and other similar techniques will certainly influence the further design of searching functionality at most of the levels of our system. Our intention is to gain experience with the present abstraction over the next year, and to redesign the indexing abstraction concurrent with our redesign and reimplementation of other major system components.

5 Conclusions

Several problems associated with traditional text retrieval systems make them unattractive as primary tools in a modern computing environment. We have presented an approach to systems architecture that overcomes many of these problems. This approach is based on a clear model of textual databases, a set of well-defined levels of abstraction that ultimately lead to an efficient set of computer programs that implement this model, and a server that is implemented as an interpreter of a lazy functional programming language.

Our goal here has been to show the value of this approach. Future work will include at least:

1. Elaboration and testing of our concept of *markings*. We believe this concept to be of importance, and have already seen the benefits even in a limited implementation.

2. Elaboration of the search abstraction. The ability to write search functions at the language level that are oblivious to the underlying mechanisms used is very appealing. In future work we intend to explore how language level functions can take advantage of efficiencies and capabilities of individual methods, e.g. the use of bitmap operations.

3. Exploring the interaction between user interfaces and lazy evaluation. We expect that most lists will never be fully evaluated and that very efficient code will result from this, but we don't really know.

Finally, the work presented here is one of very few large projects that uses a functional programming approach, and the lack of such applications is acutely felt in the functional programming community. [2] There are many unanswered questions surrounding such applications, some of the answers to which we hope will come of further work with the TIRA system. We expect that both the questions and answers will be of interest to both the information retrieval and functional programming communities.

References

[1] Augustsson L. "Small", Chalmers University Computer Science Technical Report; (detailed reference unavailable).

[2] Augustsson L. Private communication, 1989.

[3] Choueka Y., A.S. Fraenkel and S.T. Klein. "Improved Hierarchical Bit-Vector Compression in Document Retrieval Systems," *Proceedings 9th ACM-SIGIR Conference*, 1986, pp. 88–97.

[4] Choueka Y. "Responsa: An operational full-text retrieval system with linguistic components for large corpora," 1989.

[5] Friedman D. P. and D. S. Wise. "CONS Should Not Evaluate its Arguments", *Proceedings 3rd International Colloquium on Automata Languages and Programming*, 1976.

[6] Goldstein C. "Full Text Retrieval from Structured Text," *Bulletin of the American Society for Information Science*, August/September 1989, p. 11.

[7] Harman D., D. Benson, L. Fitzpatrick, R. Huntzinger, and C. Goldstein. "IRX: An Information Retrieval System for Experimentation and User Applications," in *RIAO 88 Conference Proceedings*, vol. 2, Cambridge, MA, 1988.

[8] Henderson P., and J. M. Morris, "A Lazy Evaluator", *Proceedings 3rd Symposium on Principles of Programming Languages*, 1976.

[9] Lesk M.E. "Some Applications of Inverted Indexes on the UNIX System," in UNIX *User's Manual: Supplementary Documents*, 1984.

[10] Lesk M.E. "GRAB — Inverted Indices with Low Storage Overhead", *Computing Systems*, v. 1, pp. 207–220, 1988.

[11] Mitchie D. ""Memo" Functions and Machine Learning," Nature, v. 218, pp 19–22.

[12] Morrissey R. and C. del Vigna. "A Large Natural Language Data Base", *Educom*, 1983.

[13] Smith J. "MicroARRAS," Proceedings of *RIAO '88*, v. I, Cambridge, 1988.

[14] Turner D.A. "Another Algorithm for Bracket Abstraction," The Journal of Symbolic Logic, June 1979, v. 44, n. 2, pp. 267–270.

An Object-Oriented Approach to Modelling Relationships and Constraints based on Abstraction Concept

Soochan Hwang and *Sukho Lee*

Department of Computer Engineering
Seoul National University
Seoul, 151-742, Korea

ABSTRACT

In the new applications such as OIS, CAD/CAM, and AI, it is required to support not only fixed Is-A and Part-Of relationships but also various dynamic relationships including complicate constraints. However, existing object-oriented models have many weakness in representing and manipulating those complex relationships.

This paper presents a data model OORM whose main contribution is to provide facilities to represent and manipulate dynamically all of relationships modelled from the real-world. In OORM, the relationship is expressed as *relationship object* which provides an abstraction mechanism for the association as a conceptual construct and makes it possible to capture the semantics of the relationship more clearly such as constraints, generalization abstraction, and dynamic aspects.

1. INTRODUCTION

The object-oriented programming paradigm has been actively studied and has made much progress in various database application systems such as office information systems (OIS)[13], CAD/CAM[3,9], and AI[11,16]. These systems have enhanced the modelling capabilities of the database and have tried to complement the semantic scantiness in the traditional record-based database systems. However, these systems are lacking in representing and manipulating various complex relationships in the real-world. So far, there have been many attempts to support Is-A and Part-Of relationships and much work has been done[1,2,9]. However, new applications such as OIS, CAD/CAM, and AI require to support not only such static and fixed Is-A and Part-Of relationships but also various associations defined dynamically. And they also require to represent and maintain various integrity and consistency constraints related to the associations.

Even though existing OO systems can represent and maintain all sorts of relationships by the reference between two objects, they have many weakness in modelling the relationships, because they do not provide syntax and semantics to express relationships directly. We will discuss their problems and limitations with references to a sample ER diagram for a manufacturing company presented in figure 1.

This work was supported by *Korea Science and Engineering Foundation*.

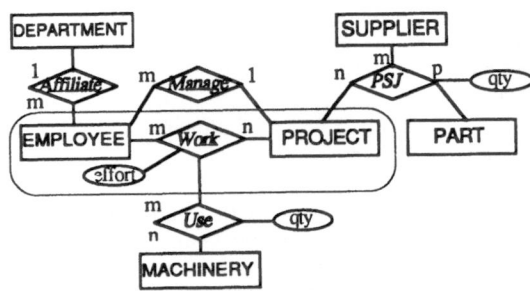

Figure 1. An ER Diagram for a Manufacturing Company

For example, representing a binary relationship as a pair of mutually interlocked attributes loses semantic information, because the standard OO model cannot represent the constraint that the two objects must point at each other[15,19]. Moreover, the n-ary relationships associating objects of n classes are merely represented by n*(n-1) decomposed binary relationships. For example, the ternary relationship `PSJ` in figure 1 can be replaced by three binary relationships: `Part-Supplier`, `Supplier -Project`, and `Project-Part`. However, if we want to get some information from these three binary relationships, we will get some nonfacts which do not exist in the original relationship[4].

Let's consider another relationship describing information about employees who work for a particular project and use many different machines for that project. In order to represent such relationships, an abstraction mechanism that can treat the relationship `Work` as higher-level entity is needed. However the existing OO systems do not support such an abstraction.

But the recent models developed by [11,12] provide the facilities to specify *inverse-of* constraint in the attribute specification. However, in those models, when a relationship itself includes some properties or constraints, it may be specified redundantly and distributed to many participating objects rather than gathering it into a single object[15,19].

There is an approach to represent the relationship as a seperate aggregate object such as [2,5,14,15]. In [2,5,14], a relationship can be represented as a first class object using the aggregation concept. But in these models, a class representing a relationship cannot properly express the semantics of the relationship such as cardinality, referential transparency between aggregate object and participating objects, and various constraints. Users have to maintain all the semantics. In [15], a relationship and its cardinality are represented as a set object called *relation* whose elements are composed of the oids of participating objects. But an object cannot reference related objects or relations directly, because the elements of relations are not first class objects. And in the above models, since the aggregate object contains only oids of participating objects as attributes, operations are only applied to each participating object as the target of a method.

Therefore, in order to manage properly all kinds of relationships in OODB, the following requirements need to be satisfied:

1) Relationships should be treated as higher-level objects through the abstraction, thus the information to be related to the relationship can be treated as a unit.
2) Since a relationship represents an inherent constraint between objects of two or more classes, it can be specified abstractly without imposing an implementation.
3) Operations to a relationship should be uniformly applied to all related objects as a whole.
4) Referential integrity and other consistency constraints can be represented and should be maintained in accordance with changing related information.

The purpose of this paper is: 1) to present how various relationships in the real-world can be represented in an object-oriented database system, 2) to provide the mechanism for representing integrity and consistency constraints related to the relationship, 3) and to show how relationships can be dynamically managed and a generalization hierarchy of relationships can be constructed. In the *Object-Oriented Relationship Data Model (OORM)* proposed in this paper, a *relationship object* is introduced to represent a relationship and its constraints. The relationship object can provide an abstraction mechanism for the relationship as a conceptual construct and can capture the semantics of the relationship more clearly.

The remainder of this paper is organized as follows. In section 2, we present the basic features of OORM. Section 3 introduces the concept of the relationship object and the method to express various relationships and its constraints. In section 4, we describe the way to support dynamic aspects of relationships and generalization abstractions between relationships. Finally, a brief conclusion is presented in section 5.

2. OVERVIEW OF OORM

This section describes the basic components of OORM: *objects, types, classes, attributes,* and *methods*. In OORM, all entities and concepts are represented as objects that are uniquely identified with their own *object identifiers(oids)*. Every object belongs to a class, and the objects belonging to the same class share common properties. The OORM distinguishes the *type class* used as a domain of an attribute from the *class* representing an entity.

2.1 Type Class

Type class provides the facility to define an abstract data type that enables a user to offer flexible domains of attributes. These type classes are divided into two categories: *atomic type classes* and *user-defined type classes*. Atomic type classes are defined by the system such as Integer, Char, String, and Boolean and user-defined type classes allow users to define their own data types. The type classes can be defined by using the atomic types and other user types as its components. In this paper, we will simply call the type class *type*.

2.2 Class

The class of OORM represents an entity or relationship. All classes of OORM participate in the class hierarchy according to their Is-A relationships. The root of the hierarchy is a system-defined class called *Object*. In order to support associative queries, OORM implicitly defines a set class for each class. One special instance of the set class is a set of all instances of a class, called an *instance set*.

Let's take an example of class definition. Figure 2 shows the definition of the class Employee. The syntax of a class definition is described in section 3.2.

```
Class Employee super Person
  ( birthdate : date,
    salary : integer with [x| x between:10000 and:100000],
    tax : integer with taxLimit,
    works : { Project }, affiliate : Department )
method taxLimit
  (salary > 50000)
    ifTrue: [(tax <= (salary * 0.07))]
    ifFalse:[(tax <= (salary * 0.05))].
```

Figure 2. Definition of the class Employee

The properties of a class consist of *attributes* and *methods*. The attributes hold the state of an object. An attribute specification syntax is as follows.

i) <Attribute name> : <Domain> **with** <constraint-spec>
ii) <Attribute name> : {<Domain>} **with** <constraint-spec>

In the above definition, the attribute of type (i) is a single-valued attribute and the attribute of type (ii) is a set-valued attribute. The domain of an attribute can be either a type or a class. The attribute value can be either a real value when it is defined on a type, or an oid of related object when it is defined on a class. The former *owns* the object and the latter *references* the object. The attribute defined on a class represents the relationship between the class itself and the class referenced through the attribute.This attribute is referred to *reference attribute*.

The optional *with*-clause specifies the constraint that the attribute must satisfy. This *attribute constraint* can be represented as either a block of code whose result is a Boolean value or a name of Boolean method which is defined in the method definition part. For example, the Boolean method taxLimit of figure 2 specifies the limit of an employee's tax. The constraint on the attribute salary is expressed in the attribute specification with the block of code. In the block, the variable x which is similar to a block argument of Smalltalk[6] represents the attribute `salary`. The constraint is enforced when the attribute value is changed.

The method specifies a behavior of an object. It consists of a method name, parameters, and a method body. For each attribute, the system defines a method, called an *attribute method*, with the same name as the attribute. If a message specifying the name of an attribute is sent to the class having that attribute, the message returns a set of the attribute values of all instances of that class. In OORM, a set of formal operations is defined to manipulate OO database, and those operations are implemented as an extension of the Smalltalk[6] which is used for specifying the method. A complete description of our language can be found in [10].

2.3 Concatenated Object

One of new features of OORM is that several kinds of objects can be grouped into a single object and share their properties without losing the advantages of data encapsulation. This operation is called *object concatenation*. If objects s and r are instances of class S and class R respectively, the object concatenation of these two objects, expressed as $s//r$, includes all properties of both objects. The concatenated object $s//r$ is not a physically combined object but an ordered collection of oids of those two objects. Actually, the sharing of properties can be implemented by a *message protocol* between these two objects. If a message m is sent to the concatenated object $s//r$, the message m is processed as follows:

$$(s//r \ m) = (s \ m) \quad \text{if } m \in Ps$$
$$(r \ m) \quad \text{if } m \in Pr \text{ and } m \notin Ps$$

where Ps and Pr are sets of properties of objects s and r, respectively

In order to explicitly specify the receiver class to process the message, a qualified name like $S@m$ is used.

On the basis of the object concatenation, OORM provides the *cartesian product* which combines information from several classes. It also supports the means that operations can be applied to all objects of several classes at a time. The definition of cartesian product of two classes S and R is as follows:

$$S \ X \ R = \{ \ s//r \mid s \in S \text{ and } r \in R \ \}$$

3. REPRESENTATION OF RELATIONSHIPS

3.1 Relationship Object

A relationship represents an association among several objects. Formally, it is a mathematical relation on $n \geq 2$ (possibly nondistinct) classes. If E_1, E_2, .., E_n are classes, then a relationship R is a subset of cartesian product of participating classes, $E_1 \ X \ E_2 \ X \ ...X \ E_n$ [9].

In OORM, a relationship is represented by a *relationship object*. The relationship object is a logical entity which contains the information and constraints of a relationship belonging to a relationship class. The relationship class of OORM includes the information about participating classes E_i, constraints on the relationship C, and the properties of the relationship itself P. Following is the definition of relationship class R which represents an association among classes E_1, E_2, .., E_n.

$$R = (E_1 \ X \ E_2 \ X \ ...X \ E_n \mid C, \ P)$$

In OORM, all classes representing either an entiy or a relationship are handled with a uniform manner. Thus, a class E representing an entity is also treated as a special kind of the relationship class which has an empty set of participant classes. That is, $E = (C, P)$, where C and P are the properties and the constraints of the class E, respectively.

The properties of R include both attributes and methods of the relationship itself. In addition, the properties of the participating classes can be also used like the properties of R. Thus, all the information related to a relationship is represented in the relationship class, and the operations to the relationship are uniformly applied to all participant classes. More details about the sharing of properties are described in the section.

The relationship object has similar characteristics to *complex object* in the sense that a set of related objects is treated as a single logical entity. A complex object consists of exclusive component objects and represents the *Part-Of* relationship between objects. The component object is one whose existence depends on the existence of the complex object and is owned by exactly one complex object[1]. On the other hand, a relationship object consists of nonexclusive participant objects and represents an *association* relationship between them. However, its existence depends on the existence of each participant object. Therefore, if either any one of participant objects within the association or the association itself is deleted, the relationship object representing the association is also deleted.

3.2 Representation of Relationships

A class specification syntax and the definition of sample relationships in figure 1 are shown in figure 3.

> **Class** <class-name> *for* <participant-list>
>   *super* <superclasses>
>   *constraint* <constraints>
>   (<attribute-list>)
>   <method-list>

Class Project **super** Object
(pid : integer, pName : string, city : string, manager : Employee)

Class Work **for** Employee(*), Project(*) **super** Object
(effort : integer **with** effortConst, tools : { Use })
  method effortConst
   (Work select: [wl w Employee = (self Employee)])
   effort sum < 100.

Class PSJ **for** Project(*), Supplier(*), Part(*) **super** Object
constraint Colocation:
  [(self Part city = (self Supplier city)) and:
  (self Supplier city = (self Project city))].
(qty : integer)

Class Use **for** Work(*), Machinery(*) **super** Object
(qty : integer)

Figure 3. Syntax of a class and sample definition of classes

In the syntax of a class, the *for*-clause specifies participating classes with their cardinalities, where the defined class represents a relationship. The cardinality of a participating class may be specified with one(1) or many(*). The *constraint*-clause specifies the *class constraint* that all objects of the class must satisfy.

In figure 3, the class `Work` represents the many-to-many relationship between `Employee` and `Project` including the relationship attribute `effort` and its attribute constraint. The constraint means that the total effort of an employee cannot exceed 100%. In the specification of the relationship class `Use`, the relationship `Work` is treated as an aggregate object which is an abstraction of `Employee`, `Project`, and its relationship `Work`. The ternary relationship among `Project`, `Supplier`, and `Part` and its constraint that all participants must be all colocated, are also represented as the relationship class `PSJ`. The constraint `Colocation` is enforced when the relationship is created and modified.

In the implementation of OORM, the information about participants is stored as a concatenation of all participant objects. For example, if the relationship object w of `Work` represent the relationship that an employee e works for the project p, w includes the information of participants as a form of $e//p$. For processing the message to the relationship object, the relationship object itself is concatenated to that concatenated object and the message is forwarded to this concatenated object. When the attribute message *pName* is sent to w, it is forwarded to the concatenated object $w//(e//p)$ and the name of the project p is returned.

4. DYNAMICITY AND GENERALIZATION OF RELATIONSHIPS

4.1 Dynamicity of Relationships

In the new applications such as OIS, CAD/CAM, and AI, it is necessary to manage not only static relationships supporting in the traditional DB systems but also dynamic relationships including complicate constraints. So far, much work has been done for schema changes in the OO databases such as [1,7], yet the dynamic management of relationships has been scarcely considered in the database systems and most existing OO systems cannot manage dynamic aspects of relationships very successfully.

In OORM, since relationships are represented by the relationship class through abstraction mechanisms, the management of relationships requires the facilities to create and delete relationship classes and to update the definitions of the participant classes dynamically. This should not affect the information of the participant objects which has no bearing on the relationship. Since the relationship class of OORM does not physically combine participant classes, the existence of the participants is not dependent on the existence of the relationship class. Therefore, relationship classes of OORM can be created and deleted dynamically without affecting other classes. When a relationship class is created, the reference attributes defined on that class are simply added to the participants of the relationship.

Deleting a relationship class may cause the deletion of the reference attributes of participants, if any, which are defined on that class. The schema changes which create and delete other classes follow the rules of the schema evolution of [1].

4.2 Virtual Class and Generalization of Relationships

OORM allows one to build new classes on the basis of existing ones, and alternative interfaces to the instances of existing classes can be provided. This scheme is called *virtual class*. The notion of virtual class and schema virtualization is proposed by [18]. However, the virtual class of [18] cannot exist as a super/subclass of the real class in the class hierarchy. The virtual schema can only be defined as an alternative to the real schema. This restriction reduces the utilization of the virtual class.

In OORM, the virtual class is defined by specifying derivation constraints on existing classes called the *base classes* and its instances can be derived from the instances of the base classes. In the class hierarchy, the virtual class can be located as a subclass of real classes or another virtual classes. It can also have real classes as its subclasses and inherits the derivation constraint to them as a class constraint. The syntax of a virtual class specification is similar to that of the base class except for the message receiver. The syntax is as follows.

> *Vclass* <class-name> *for* <participant-list>
> *super* <superclasses>
> *where* <derivation constraints>
> (<attribute-list>)
> <method-list>

The *where*-clause specifies the method to derive instances from the base class and also represents class constraint. The derivation constraints are expressed in the same way of the constraint of the base class.

The main advantage of the virtual class is to provide users with multiple views of data[11,18]. In addition, the virtual class of OORM provides the means to define and manage complex relationships dynamically. That is, virtual relationships can be represented in the database. The virtual relationship class can be defined in two ways: Firstly, it can be defined by participating classes. Secondly, it can be derived from the real relationship classes as a subclass of them.

In OORM, a generalization hierarchy of relationships can be also constructed according to their Is-A relationships like the general classes. A specialized relationship of a relationship can be defined in the following ways.

1) Modifying the cardinality of a relationship, but the only change is one of reduction.
2) Adding constraints to a relationship. Only the added constraints are specified and they are connected to the inherited constraints by *and*-condition.
3) Adding attributes and methods like the general classes.

Let's take an example of figure 4 that constructs a generalization hierarchy using the virtual class and Is-A relationships between relationships. For example, the relationship

34

Work of figure 1 can be specialized into two subclasses such as MajorWork, where the effort of an employee is greater than 50 % on a project, and MinorWork, where it is less than 50%. Then the cardinality of MajorWork has to be modified into many-to-one, because the total effort of an employee cannot exceed 100%. These two subclasses can be defined as virtual relationship classes with the above constraints on effort. If the manager of a project must be a major worker in the project, the relationship Manager can be defined as a subclass of the relationship MajorWork.

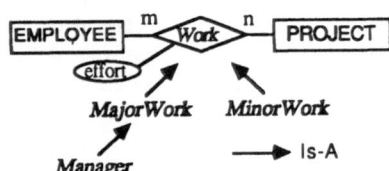

Class Work **for** Employee(*), Project(*) **super** Object
    (effort : integer with effortConst)

Vclass MajorWork **for** Employee(*), Project(1) **super** Work
    where [self effort > 50]

Vclass MinorWork **super** Work
    where [self effort <= 50]

Class Manager **super** MajorWork

Figure 4. Generalization of relationships

Using the facilities such as virtual relationships and generalization of relationships, various complex relationships, which have complicate constraints and are related to each other, can be systematically represented as super/subclasses according to their Is-A relationships. And the virtual relationships can be created and deleted at any time without affecting other classes.

5. CONCLUSIONS

We have presented in this paper a data model OORM for an object-oriented database system. The main contribution of OORM is to provide facilities for the representation and manipulation of all sorts of relationships including complicate constraints. The relationship object provides an abstraction mechanism for the association as a conceptual construct and captures the semantics of the relationship more clearly. The constraints are explicitly represented in the class specification and maintained as a property. And a generalization hierarchy of relationships can be constructed according to their Is-A relationships, in order that the complex relationships in the real-world can be systematically modelled into the database. The dynamic aspects of relationships have been considered, too. The relationship class can be created and deleted dynamically without affecting other classes. The virtual class and generalization of relationships can also support the dynamicity of relationships more easily.

The investigation of the efficient storage techniques for OORM such as indexing and clustering remains in the future research.

6. REFERENCES

[1] Banerjee, J., Chou, H., Garza, J.F., and et al., "Data Model Issues for Object-Oriented Applications", ACM Trans. on Office Information Syst., Vol.15, No.1, 1987.

[2] Brodie, M.L. and Ridjanovic, D., "On the Design and Specification of Database Transactions," in On Conceptual Modelling, Brodie,M.L. and et al(ed), Springer-Verlag, 1982

[3] Cammarata, S.J. and Melkanoff, M.A., "An Interactive Data Dictionary Facilities for CAD/CAM Data Bases," Expert Database Systems, Proc. of 1st Int. Workshop, Kerschberg, L.(ed), 1986

[4] Chen, P.P., "Database Design Based on Entity and Relationship," in Principles of Database Design, Vol.1, S. Bing Yao(ed), Prentice-Hall, 1985.

[5] Copeland, G. and Maier, D., "Making Smalltalk a Database System," Proc. of ACM SIGMOD Conf., 1984.

[6] Goldberg, A. and Robson, D., "Smalltalk-80: The language and its implementation", Addison-Wesley, Reading, 1983.

[7] Jason, D.P. and Stein, J., "Class Modification in the GemStone Object-Oriented DBMS," Proc. of ACM OOPSLA Conf., 1987.

[8] Korth, H.F. and Silberschatz, A., Database System Concepts, McGraw Hill, 1986.

[9] Lee, S. and Hong, B., "CAD Data Management Using Object -Oriented Paradigms," Proc. of 1st Int. Conf. on Industrial and Engineering Applications of Artificial Intelligence and Expert Systems, ACM Press, Tennessee, 1988.

[10] Lee, S., Hwang, S., and Nah, Y., "The Design of Object-Oriented Relationship Data Model," Seoul Nat. Univ., Dept. of Computer Eng., DBTR-9-1, 1989.

[11] Lee, K. and Lee, S., "An Object-Oriented Approach to Data/Knowledge Modeling Based on Logic, " Proc. of 6th Int. Conf. on Data Eng., 1990

[12] Mannino, M.V., Choi, I.J., and Batory, D.S., "An Overview of the Object-Oriented Functional Data Language," Proc. of 5th Int. Conf. on Data Eng., 1989

[13] Nierstrasz, O.M., "An Object-Oriented Environment for OIS Applications", Proc. of 11th Int. Conf. on VLDB, 1985.

[14] Rolland,C., Cauvet,C., and Proix,C., "A Design Methodology and Its Associated Tools for Object-Oriented Databases," Proc. of Advanced Database Syst. Symp., 1989

[15] Rumbaugh,J., "Relations as Semantic Constructs in an Object -Oriented Language", Proc. of ACM OOPSLA Conf., 1987.

[16] Shephard, A. and Kerschberg, L., "PRISM : A Knowledge Based System for Semantic Integrity Specification And Enforcementin Database Systems", Proc. of ACM SIGMOD Conf., 1984.

[17] Smith, J. and Smith, D., "Database Abstractions: Aggregation and Generalization", ACM Trans. on Database Syst., Vol.2, No.2, 1977.

[18] Tanaka,K.,Yoshikawa,M., and Ishihara,K., "Schema Virtualization in Object-Oriented Databases," Proc. of 4th Int. Conf. on Data Eng., 1988.

[19] Tsichritzis, D.C. and Nierstrasz, O.M., "Fitting Round Object Into Square Database," European Conf. on Object-Oriented Proc.'88, in Lecture Notes in Computer Science No 322, Springer-Verlag, 1988.

VALUE-ORIENTED AND OBJECT-ORIENTED DATABASE DESIGN WITH REFERENCE TO TIME

PRINCE Violaine

HABRIAS Henri

Ecole Normale Supérieure de Cachan
and LIMSI (Orsay) FRANCE

University of Nantes
FRANCE

ABSTRACT :

This paper discusses the problem of time representation in database modelling. Although temporal aspects have been the subject of many works and techniques within the Entity-Relationship and Relational conceptual frames (some of them are described in this communication), the "lively" features of entities and relationships have not been emphasized, whereas the technical aspects of time interference with data behaviour have been largely examined.
These "lively" features address the trajectory in time (life cycle), availability to query and various changes that occur to items in the database throughout the Information System's life. Our assumption relies on the observation that many "formal" changes that occur concerning a given amount of data, do no affect the very existence, thus the "semantics" of this data Therefore, we propose a conceptual model, related to object oriented approaches, that takes into account these features without involving heavy operations (such as "database versioning" or "history collections").

Database design in term of entities and relationships (E-R- approach, [11]), or as a relational setup [8] often involves an instantaneous conception of the modeled universe. The evolution of the database is thus captured as a collection of snapshots, in the literal sense[1], at different times. This collection is considered as a historical view of the system but is not recorded in the current model. The history of the database in an information system is deduced from different instanciations of timeless entities and/or relationships rather than expressed by the means of "temporal" entities and relationships.
Therefore, this paper proposes to evaluate both value-oriented and object-oriented modeling of time in database design. The first section describes the way value-oriented entities and/or relationships attempt to capture time, and the properties as well as the limitation of the operative side of their modeling. The second section refers to object-oriented methodology and the momentary/historical/permanent distinction between object-oriented entities and relationships. The third section shows how distinguishing time as a dimension might be useful in an "evolution-oriented" database design.

In conclusion we would like to point out the fact that an accurate reference to time can be a valuable aid in taking into account the complex evolutional aspects in information systems.

I- CLASSICAL VALUE-ORIENTED DESIGN AND ITS MODELING OF TEMPORAL FEATURES

Time has been captured in information systems as the chronological aspect of databases. This might be explained rather easily. Temporal aspects were presented in research about E-R and relational approaches ([12]) [14] [21] [24] as *tied to the concept of sets*. Being confronted to the problem of representing the real world, databases models have very early recognized **set structures** (entity-class or type, the same for relationships) [11], with the appropriate status (of set structures). The basic concepts in E-R or in the relational model are already "near-objects", - in the sense of object-oriented methodology, which is more general than object-oriented programming languages -, being intrinsically set-typed. The inheritance properties of classes (or types) of objects hold between the type and its population (this describes the effect of the $\in$ relationship). Further extensions of the models have given birth to an IS-A primitive such as in semantic network-based knowledge representation languages [6] and object-programming [28], making inheritance possible between entity-classes by defining a superclass and a subclass (this describes the $\supset$ relationship).

The two major techniques known in representing temporal features are time-stamping and time integration as an entity and/or an attribute.

I-1 Time-stamping

One of the best-known techniques of handling time in value-oriented database design consists in providing the model with the **time-stamping capability.**

Time-stamping was first applied to tuples [5] ,[10] and later at the attribute level [9] [21]. In the Time Relational Model, TRM, proposed by Ben-Zvi [5], Navathe and Rafi [21] represent time by two stamps : "time-start" and "time-end", one of which necessarily belongs to the temporal key of a relationship.

a-Main properties of the time-stamping capability :
Although represented by a <u>punctual form</u> (a stamp), time is considered as an <u>interval</u>, providing the constraint that <u>intervals do not overlap</u>. Therefore, the interval is logically equivalent to its extremities.
The concept of <u>duration</u>, which is the second major asèct of time, is implicitly the <u>sum of all consecutive intervals</u> contained in the interval determined by the two time stamps.

We can find then a "Time-slice" function in a system based on this principle such as TSQL [21]. According to its general use, the time-stamping function seems to be oriented

---

[1]to be distinguished from the concept of "snapshot" in historical databases introduced by [3] and [2] with which will be discussed later

toward attributes values of which are more or less regularly modified.

Example : Let us consider a relation schema representing a product as a set with the attributes Prno (product-number, serving as a key) and price. The relation schema is : PRODUCT (Prno, price). Price is an attribute subject to time changes. If every occurrence of PRODUCT is time-stamped with a couple of week-numbers such as :
(345, 115, 02, 15)
(345, 116, 16, 29), etc.
standing for PRODUCT (Prno, price, price(ts), price(te)).
the temporal key for PRODUCT will be for instance :
(Prno, price(ts)) and the E-R schema will contain a couple of stamps for the price attribute[2].

Notice that time-stamping the key (product-number) is difficult to represent : how are we going to write down the information that a product-number might be modified because of an error (for instance, a typing error which has been discovered much later), or that it is no more relevant because the corresponding product is obsolete ? In an information system lifetime, such a case might happen especially as a result of wrong or misled operations.

Example : if the same client has been recorded twice in the database because his change of address has not been recognized as such, he gets two client-numbers. If at a given time, somebody becomes aware of this, that person will either delete one of the occurrences for this client, or delete both wrong occurrences and issue a third one with a new client-number and correct information. The history record of this client will not be complete if it does not contain the key change, particularly if transactions have been made during the period of double-keying.

b- Some limitations of time-stamping :
1- the original key is timeless.
2- the temporal key might be very long : its length is directly proportional to the number of volatile attributes values.
3- the temporal variations's create new entities instead of representing the same entity's trajectory through time. It is the same old dilemma : is Mr John Smith at age 30 the same entity as Mr John Smith at age 60? It would be more economical for an information system to answer "yes".

I-2 Time as an entity

In order to avoid some peculiarities of time-stamping such as entity multiplication, time can be viewed as an entity (or a relation) with which other entities and/or relationships of the system might interact. This view is popular in French works on the subject [29], [31], [30].

a- Main properties :
Time-stamping is the differenciating principle between occurrences of the time entity which is in fact a date entity.
Occurrences are recognizable by values (dates), representing both a punctual aspect and a regular period of time.[29],[23]
The granularity of this period depends on the level of description necessary for the model.(ABP83)

The duration concept seems here to be a property of the period size. The possible interval of time is equivalent to one of its extremities.

Compared with the time-stamping technique, the time entity representation provides the following effects :
1- at the tuple-level stamping, time-end and time-start stamps merge ;
2- at the attribute-level stamping, it is necessary to introduce other entities and relationships to take into account the possible modification of some attributes values.

Example :
Refering to the time-stamping of orders, which is at the tuple level, one might give the following E-R schema :

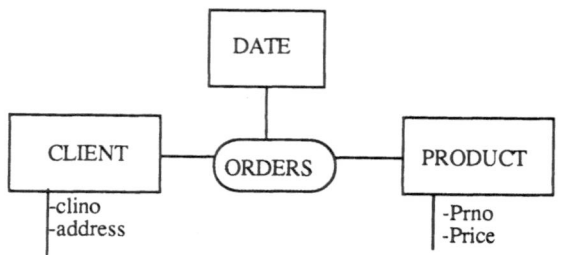

Here, the date gives information as much about the order date as about the product price at this moment.
This schema intents to provide the following functional dependencies :
clino,prno,date ---> order-attributes

The date entity might be replaced by other time-period synonyms such as DAY, WEEK, MONTH, YEAR, or whatever is relevant to the system.

In the preceding example, one should have to look for a "BUYER" entity which might interact with PRODUCT and DATE in order to take the pricing changes into account. Price would then be the attribute of the relationship between these three entities rather than a property of PRODUCT. We would have the following functional dependency :
Prno,buyer-no,date ---> price

b- Some limitations of time as an entity (or relation) :
1- At the attribute level, one would have to "create" an entity responsible for the attribute changes. This creation is artificial : it assumes that time is discrete and that entities might or might not interact with time. This proposition proves to be wrong : *every entity interacts with time.*
2- The representation of time as an independent object within the system gives rise to a confusion between two aspects of time's use in an information system : the date of occurence of an event ; the period of validity of an attribute value [16].

I-3 Time as an attribute

The first of the above mentioned limitations of time as an independant entity (or entity-class) might mislead the designer into considering time as a property of an entity (entity-class). However, time placed as an attribute is the most controversial representation in a "classical" E-R or relational schema.

The worst position for it seems to be as the attribute of a relationship. The semantics of time thus placed are often contradictory with the following proposition :
if K1 is the key of Entity E1
and K2 is the key of Entity E2
and RA1, RA2,...,RAn are the attributes of the relationship R existing between E1 and E2 then : K1,K2 --> RA1,RA2,...,RAn
Example :
if date-of-order was placed as the attribute of the relationship ORDERS in the preceding figure, this means that :
clino,prno --> date-of-order

Placed as an attribute of an entity, time leads us to consider entities as dated. But here confusion reigns about the semantics of the date (or the interval, if time is represented as such).

Just as in the representation of time in section I-2, two possible roles for time might be meant :

1- *Issuing time* : of an event ; typed as <u>punctual</u>.
Example : Date-of-order. Date-of-buying. Date-of-loan, etc.
2- Beginning of a *validity period* : for the occurrence as a whole. The key value must then change if the date is modified. In other words, it describes the validity of the set of values composing the occurrence.
<u>Example</u> : (<u>proposal-number</u>, date, object-designation).
This proposal is valid until another is received.
But it cannot describe the validity of one attribute value within the same recognizable object.
<u>Example</u> : if one writes (prno,price,pricing-date), the product-number is meant to be changed at every new pricing if one wants to preserve the normal form of the relation.

I-4 Major conclusions about value-oriented time representation

In considering the three preceding possibilities, we may conclude that :
1- Time as an attribute of a relationship leads to an incorrect relational model ;
2- Time as an attribute of an entity is a dangerous representation unless this entity is an event[3] ; time is then considered as punctual and describes the origin of the occurrence.
3- Time as an entity maintain the confusion between the two aspects of time : *time-stamping*, punctual and giving rise to the creation (updating, deletion) of other entity occurrences, and *duration*, which describes the activity or relevance of both occurrences and attributes values. Philosophically, this is bothersome, it means that objects are intrinsically timeless, that time is itself an object, and that some of those timeless objects might occasionnally interact with time, as with any other object.
4- Time as a stamp on the attribute level describes accurately some of the evolutional possibilities of the recognizable object (occurrence) providing both aspects of time. But stamping attributes relates to "permanent" object evolution, and does not describe time-typed objects such as events.

The question then is : what is the best model to design :
1- entities with some attributes, the values of which may be updated without modifying the entity as an individual ;
2- entities or relationships that are events and therefore totally dependent on punctual starts and/or ends ;
3- information items which are neither individuals (entities or relationships) nor events but a collection of images of the same individual, of a set of individuals or of a set of events.

II- OBJECT-ORIENTED METHODOLOGY AND TEMPORAL PROPERTIES

II-1 Where the problem lies

The two (among others) concepts of time, time-stamping and duration, have been either merged or one of them have been ignored in the value-oriented databases or data models. According to Maclennan [20], there are many uses for time in a data processing system. We personally see three major fields for time expression : one of them relates to the "state" of an object as mentioned by Maclennan and earlier by Backus [4] the second addresses the "temporal features" of a set structure (entities and relationships as classes of objects), and the third differenciates events as time-objects from other objects.

---

[3]Some authors [29] recommend representing events as entities.

II-2 Concepts of state, temporal features and time-objects

II-2-1 The Concept of state

The concept of state relates to two elements of our model : the entity (as a class of individuals) or relationship, and the occurrence (as the precise individual).
We shall define the **state of an entity** (or a **relationship**) as the configuration of its population at a given time. The collection of all the states of an entity (or a relationship) represent its *trajectory* through the database during its lifetime. The operations related to the population of an entity (or a relationship) are :
creation, deletion, activity, availability,validity of an occurrence.
Creation and deletion are stamped with a punctual time.
Activity , availability and validity are stamped with a duration. They might depend upon management rules, decisions or constraints.

These operations allow us to define the **state of an occurrence** as being the valuation for this precise occurrence of **boolean state-flags** such as :
- *suppressed* : yes (when),no
- *created* : yes(when),no;
- *active*: yes (period), no(period) ;
- *valid* : yes (containing no false indication)(period), no (since when) ; it expresses how long the occurrence data has been considered as true ;
- *available* : yes (to query), no (since when).

Time description at the tuple level described by Clifford, Warren and Ben-Zvi (op.cit.) for the relational model relates to the state concept.
<u>Examples</u> :
1) *creation* :
- At a time t, an occurrence of an entity or a relationship is created.
An occurrence of ORDER is created when a client issues an order.
When a new client is recorded there is a new occurrence for the entity CLIENT.
2) *validity of an occurrence* :
- At a time t, an occurrence of an entity or a relationship becomes no longer valid to the system.
A client of whom we have lost track for more than ten years (address no longer available) must no longer be a member of the CLIENT entity.
3) *Activity of an occurrence dependent upon management rules* :
At a time t, an entity or a relationship is no longer"active" because nothing in the information system refers to it. For instance, an occurrence of ORDER is no longer active when its contents has been wholly delivered and an occurrence of INVOICE referring to it has been issued.
4) *Availability of an occurrence* :
At a time t an entity is not available for updating or deletion because it is shared.

II-2-2 Temporal features

The **temporal features** of an entity (or a relationship) as a set, refer to its creation, updating (its set structure), activation, availability and destruction. In other words,these features account for its *species life* within the database, its *evolutional capabilities*.
We distinguish two major kinds of operations :
1- The **set operations** are creation, deletion and updating of the set structure (by changing the number, either by append or deletion operations, or the naming of the attributes) ;
2- the **attribute time-relations** which concern attribute updating (value updating or deletion), availability and activity according to management rules or caused by an exterior event.

The availability of an attribute might be defined as the availability of a value that can be associated to this attribute at the time of a query.

The set operations are punctually timed.The attribute time-relations refer to the concepts of interval (attributes updating, to relate to the [9] [21] approach) and duration (availability, activity). Some of them might be periodical.

Examples :

1)*Updating the set structure* :

-at a time t, a new attribute must be appended to the list of attributes of an entity.

A university campus, having had security troubles, might ask its students to apply for an insurance and will add an insurance-number to its STUDENT entity.

2)*Updating at the attribute level:*

exterior event modification :

- At a time t, some value modifications to attributes have to be recorded.

A client might have his address and phone number modified.

periodical modification :

At a time t, all the occurrences of an entity must be updated because one (or many) of their attributes must be reviewed. For example, the prices of all products are reviewed every six months.

3) *Attribute activity :*

- At a time t, an attribute of an entity E, necessary at t0 (first modelling) is no longer active because no longer valued in all new occurrences of the entity.

At t0, all clients were companies and there was a Contact-name attribute to the entity CLIENT. But for more than two years all new clients have been persons and the Contact-name is no longer used.

II-2-3 Time-objects

In a database, the representation of time is completed by the intrinsically time-related elements of an information system, sometime designed as entities and sometime designed as relationships[4] : **events.** Events have been the object of many studies. J-L Peaucelle has suggested distinct representations for "true" (permanent) objects and "dated" (events) objects [22]. C. Rolland has proposed an event-based representation of the database dynamics [25] [26]. Y. Tabourier [29] integrates events in the E-R model as entities but admits that this representation is partial.

An event is a time-object : all its occurrences must be dated. *In other words, time is also recognizable as a direct attribute of an event.*

II-3 Momentary/Historical/Permanent Objects
II-3-1 Permanent Objects

The preceding concepts allow us to define different types of object in the system depending on the characteristics of their state, temporal features and event-like properties.

We might call **permanent objects** those which are not event-born. They have a state (and therefore a trajectory) which is not subject to periodicity and time features as much punctual as periodical or durable.

Examples : CLIENT,PRODUCT,etc.

Note : The objects here are sets of occurrences, according to the vocabulary we have adopted. Of course, permanent objects may see their population grow or decline **eventually.**

In other words, *if permanent objects are not event-born, the creation (or deletion or appending) of their occurrences is event or decision-caused.*

---

[4]Some examples given by [31] show event-like elements represented as relationships.

Example : a new client, a client's change of address , the suppression of a product, etc.

In a classical E-R or relational representation, there is a confusion between the permanence of the object and the permanence of its associated values.

The state is only the current state and the time features are ignored.

In a history database some of the state and time features operations are recognized : but they concern punctual and interval defined operations. Concepts such as relevance, activity and availability, related to duration are not expressed.

II-3-2 Momentary Objects

At the other side events are the typical **momentary objects.**Their state is subject to precise management rules, periodicity and actions.

Their only time features are set operations : one does not modify the attributes values of an event. A modification is in itself the expression of a new event .

The state operations relating to duration, except availability in shared databases, can be the direct cause of other punctual operations. For instance, inactive or invalid event-like objects are subject to suppression from the set population.

Momentary objects include a temporal aspect at the attribute level. This attribute is of a punctual form.

Examples : INVOICE, ORDER, BUY, etc.

III-3-3 Historical Objects

There is also another type of object in a database with temporal properties : objects which are issued from "versioning" or statistical manipulations. These "**historical**" **objects** are created by query or programming, whenever they are needed. They have no state concept. They can be of many types.

1- The whole or partial trajectory (collection of state values) of a given permanent object :

ex: all clients belonging, or having belonged to the CLIENT entity from the beginning until now including mistaken-records, deletions and their dates (whole trajectory).

all clients recorded as active in the database since 1987.

2- The whole or partial trajectory of a given occurrence of a permanent object :

ex: Client number 45389 activity.

3-The trajectory of a given event -object :

ex: all the orders issued on march 22nd 1988.

all orders issued by client number 45389.

Note : the trajectory of an event-object is necessarily related to the trajectories of those permanent objects involved. Many integrity and referential constraints in database management have to be expressed in terms of state and temporal feature constraints.

4- The trajectory of a given occurrence of an event- object :

ex : the state of order number 8897 between april 1st and april 7th.

5- The image of a set of punctual states or punctual values of time features at a given time (a snapshot, according to the Adiba denomination in (ADL80),(ADB87)) :

ex : all clients whose orders are still on the waiting list (inactive).

III- A DATABASE DESIGN INVOLVING PERMANENT, HISTORICAL AND EVENT OBJECTS

The object-event distinction is not new as a concept. It has been at the core of many systems [25] [26] [27] and models [13] ,[15]. The object-oriented approach suggests the existence of a relationship between permanent objects and the events in which these objects play roles [17].

Let us call permanent objects P-Objects, events E-objects, historical objects H-objects. We may define relational primitives between :
1- One or many P-object(s) and an E-object .
2- Interdependent E-Objects.
3- A P-Object or an E-Object or a schema and an H-Object.
The first relationship describes the existence of the E-Object as a "play" in which the P-Object might take part.
The second expresses a "causal" and "chronological" chain between E-Objects.
We propose a representation for these in the following sections.

III-1 P-Objects, E-Object relationship

The relationship (drawn on the following schema as a curved line) between P-Object1(or P-Object2) and E-Obj1 means that the state of E-Obj1 is dependent upon the states of P-Object1 and P-Object2. A constraint might be asserted as : " occurrences of P-Object1 and P-Object2 involved in a given occurrence of an E-Object must both be created prior to this occurrence creation."
A representation of this constraint in terms of a *production rule* would be the following :

> *if occurrence(E-Obj$_i$) created and occurrence(P-Object1) not-created and occurrence(P-Object2) not-created and related(occurrence(P-Object1), occurrence (E-Obj$_i$)) and related (occurrence (P-Object2), occurrence (E-Obj$_i$)) then setup :*
>
> *occurrence(P-Object1) created and occurrence (P-Object2) created.*

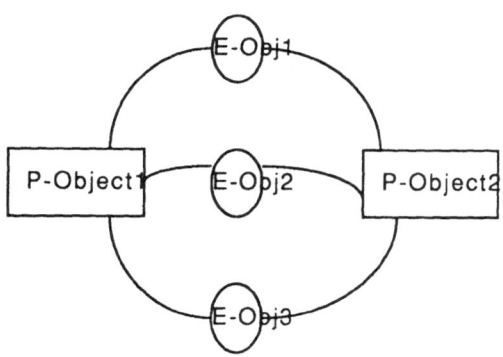

In an object-oriented database, this rule would be attached to the class of P-Objects as a whole.
Example :

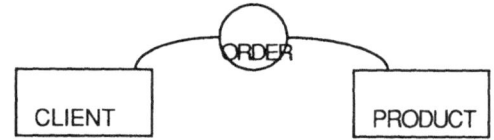

This means that a client and a product are related by an order event. This object is dated, it cannot be created unless both occurrences of client and product already exist.

If one of them is unavailable this causes the event also to be unavailable (a management rule might set the state-flags so to express the "waiting list" concept).
Note : an E-Object not being a relationship in the sense of the Entity-Relationship approach, there is no possible functional dependency between the P-Object keys and the E-object attributes. Being an object in itself, every occurrence of the E-object is identified by a unique key-value.

If one wants to express semantic functional dependencies resulting from management rules and constraints such as :
- every order is issued by only one client ;
- a client does not issue more than one order at a certain date (or during a certain interval) ;
these must be expressed by cardinalities on the line representing the relationship between the E-object and the P-object.
Example :

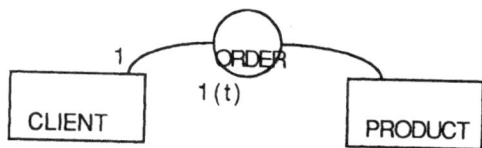

This constraint would be expressed by the production rule :

> *if occurrence(P-CLIENT) valid and related (occurrence (P-CLIENT), occurrence (E-ORDER) then = (count (related(occurrence (P-CLIENT), occurrence (E-ORDER)), 1) and = (time(E-ORDER, P-CLIENT), 1)*

This rule introduces primitive functions *count* and *time*. The arguments of function count are predicates and its result is an integer that represents the number of occurences of the E-Object that are issued by the P-Object. The function time accepts an E-Object as first argument (and only an E-Object) and another object as a second argument and returns the number of occurrences of the E-Object related to the P-Object that have the same time-stamping. This rule can be associated to the subclass P-CLIENT of the P-OBJECT class in an object-oriented database.

III-2 E-Objects relationship

The arrow gives the direction of the causal dependency and the chronology.
This schema means :
- the creation of an occurrence of E-Object1 causes the creation of an occurrence of E-Object2 ;
- an occurrence of E-Object2 cannot be created unless a corresponding occurrence of E-Object1 already exists.

It might also express a semantic functional dependency included in a causal predicate[18]. For every candidate key : E-Object1-Key ---> E-Object2-key
As in the preceding paragraph, these constraints are very easily expressed as a production rule associated to the E-Obj$_i$ subclasses of the E-Object class.
The returning line states the fact that set operations on the E-Objects are dependent on each other : the creation, deletion or appending of any of the E-objects (as a set) imposes a similar operation on the other E-objects.
Example :

Every new order must cause the later creation of a delivery which in turn creates an invoicing action. The creation or deletion or appending of the orders as a set must cause a similar operation on the set of deliveries and invoices.

40

If we want to express the fact that every order must cause the creation of only one delivery and thus only one invoice, in other words to express the functional dependencies :
order-number ---> delivery-number
delivery-number--->invoice-number
one can add a "cardinality" to the chaining as :

III-3 Historical objects

We might try to include some H-objects in an E-R schema . Most of them can be considered as unpredictable because they depend upon the user's will and queries at a given time. But some of them are classical : all the versions of an E or a P-Object for instance.
We may represent them as such :

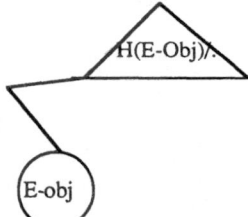

In this representation the historical object expresses the <u>length of the object trajectory</u> with a symbol following the slash.
The H-object of an E-object must respect the constraint of time consistency :
This means that the dating attribute's values must belong to the considered period of time.
<u>Example</u> :
Let us represent all the orders for the week number 43.

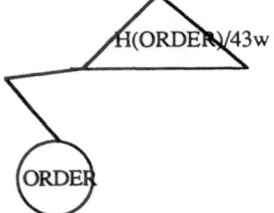

The formal representation of this H-Object is :
Setup : Subset (H-ORDER) created ;
   Type : E-ORDER ;
   Time representation : WEEK ;
   Trajectory : 43
   Constraints : ALL occurrence(E-ORDER) created and occurrence (E-ORDER) valid and date (occurrence(E-ORDER) in WEEK 43.
The representation of an H-object of a P-Object, for instance all the occurrences of products for the year 1988, might be the following :

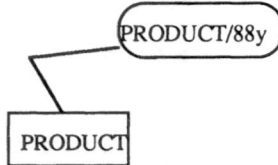

These are not of course the only possible representations for historical objects of which there are many types.

CONCLUDING REMARKS

Classical temporal relational databases may be complete with regards to time encapsulation but do not take into account the "lively" aspect of entities and relationships. Therefore, the dimensional aspect of time is removed and replaced by its image in "motion" (we consider this metaphor to apply to the technique of database versioning too).
It seems that object-orientation, being centered more upon objects as a whole than upon tuples as mathematical entities, provides the capability of distinguishing many object types according to temporal properties, and equally of creating objects with the main property of being time-driven.
Time is a component both of every live entity and of the processes in which it takes part to sustain the information system evolution.
The database relations thus express as much the knowledge as its dynamic capability. Being essentially both declarative (descriptive) and procedural (methods), the objects of object-oriented programming and design are able to support this duality.

REFERENCES

[1]   M. ADIBA, BUI QUANG, N., PALAZZO DE OLIVEIRA, J. "Notions de temps dans les Bases de Données Généralisées", in "Actes des Journées Bases de Données Avancées, INRIA ed. France.1986
[2]   M. ADIBA, and BUI QUANG, N. "Dynamic Database snapshots, Albums and Movies" in TAIS Conference "Temporal Aspects in Information Systems", IFIP, AFCET, INRIA eds., Sophia Antipolis, France.Pp 207-221.1987
[3]   M. ADIBA and LINDSAY, B. "Database snapshots", Proceedings of the Sith VLDB , Montreal, Canada.1980
[4]   J. BACKUS "Can programming be free from the Von Neumann Style?", Communications of the ACM. 1978.
[5]   J. BEN-ZVI "The Time Relational Model", PhD Dissertation, University of California, Los Angeles.1982
[6]   R. BRACHMAN and LEVESQUE,H."Readings in knowledge representation", Morgan Kaufman, Los Altos. 1985
[7]   J.A. BUBENKO. "The temporal dimension in information modeling", in Nijssen "Archtitecture and Models in Databases Management Systems" North-Holland. Pp 93-118.1977
[8]   E.F. CODD " Further normalization of the database relational model" Data base Systems (R.Rustin ed.), Prentice-Hall, Englewood Cliffs, New Jersey. Pp 33-64.1972
[9]   J.S. CLIFFORD and TANSEL, A.U. "On an algebra for Historical Databases : Two Views", Proceedings of the ACM, SIGMOD Conference, Austin, Texas.1985
[10] J.S. CLIFFORD and WARREN, D.S. "Formal Semantics of Time in Databases", ACM Transactions on Database Systems, vol. 6, n° 2, pp 73.1983
[11] P. CHEN " The Entity-Relationship Model : Toward a Unified Data", ACM Transactions on Database Systems, vol.1, n°9. Pp 41.1976
[12] DE ANTONELLIS, DEGLI ANTONI, MAURI, ZONTA, "Extending the ERA to take into account the historical aspects of systems", in "ERA to systems analysis and design", PP Chen ed, North-Holland.1980
[13] M. JACKSON "System Development", Prentice Hall , Hoare Series.1983
[14] H. HABRIAS "La prise en compte du temps dans la définition des besoins en information", in Travail et Méthodes, n°445-446.1986
[15] H. HABRIAS "Le Modèle Relationnel Binaire", Eyrolles. Paris.1988

[16]   H. HABRIAS "A proposal of concepts to avoid the natural ambiguity of expressions of time" , Proceedings of "Colloque Informatique et langue naturelle", PRC "Linguistique informatique"-SILFEC eds, Nantes, France.1988

[17]   H. HABRIAS "Le schema conceptuel ? Non! Les schémas conceptuels ou vers l'approche orientée objet", workpaper, LIANA, Nantes, France.1989

[18]   H. HABRIAS and PRINCE, V. "About the Semantics of Functional Dependencies", Fourth ISCIS Conference, Cesme, Turquey, vol. 1.Pp 561-567.1989

[19]   C.A.R HOARE "Communications sequential processes", Prentice-Hall.1985

[20]   B.J. MACLENNAN " Values and objects in programming languages" in Sigplan Notices, volume 17, N° 12, Pp.70-79.1982

[21]   S.B. NAVATHE and RAFI, A. "TSQL- A language interface for history database", in TAIS Conference "Temporal Aspects in Information Systems", IFIP, AFCET, INRIA eds, Sophi Antipolis, France. Pp 113-128.1987

[22]   J.L. PEAUCELLE "Les systèmes d'information. La représentation". Presses Universitaires de France. Paris.1981

[23]   R.PLANCHE "Maîtriser la modélisation conceptuelle", Editions Masson, collection MIPS, Paris.1988

[24]   C.ROLLAND, BODART, F., LEONARD, M. (eds) "Temporal aspects in information systems",North-Holland.1987

[25]   C. ROLLAND, FOUCAUT, O., BENCI, G. "Conception des systèmes d'information. La méthode REMORA", Eyrolles. Paris.1988

[26]   C. ROLLAND "Database Dynamics" in Database. Pp 32-42.1983 26.

[27]   C.ROLLAND and RICHARD, C. "Transactions Modelling", SIGMOD Conference, Orlando.1982

[28]   J.SCHOCH "An overview of the language Smalltalk-72" in Sigplan Notices, volume 14, N° 9, Pp.64-73. 1979

[29]   Y.TABOURIER " De l'autre côté de Merise", Les Editions d'Organisation. Paris.1986

[30]   H. TARDIEU "Contribution of the E.R.A to object management in an Information System Design Workbench", Tutorial 3, part 2. 5th International Conference on E.R.A, Dijon.1986

[31]   H.TARDIEU, ROCHFELD, A., COLLETTI, R. "La méthode Merise, tome 1 : Principes et outils", 2e édition. Les Editions d'Organisation. Paris.1984

An Object Behavior Modeling Method

Hirotaka Sakai

Faculty of Science and Engineering, Chuo University
1-13-27, Kasuga, Bunkyo-Ku, Tokyo 112, Japan

Abstract

The behavior modeling of objects is a critical task in the object oriented approach to database design. The behavior that describes dynamic characteristics of objects is analyzed based on the aggregation concept.

The behavior of objects is formally defined as a set of states and events representing the script of object life cycles. The simplified formalization of the behavior makes it easy to analyze and model the behavior in complex environments where many objects interact with each other. This helps a great deal to establish the integrity constraints concerning control structures of object activities.

1. Introduction

Methodologies for conceptual design of databases has become the central concern in data engineering stimulated by the data oriented approach to information systems developments. Semantic data models are now widely used as the fundamental tool for it[7,16]. Among other things, the Entity-Relationship model with the extended capabilities to support a variety of abstraction concepts are proposed and accepted in both research and practical areas[12,13,23].

The requirements that conceptual schemas should reflect the static and dynamic aspects of entities stimulated the object oriented approach to database design, and semantic data models are now being refined from the object oriented view of the real world[3,15]. Terminologies used in various semantic data models such as 'entities', 'relationships', and 'values' are uniformly viewed as 'objects' with the structural as well as dynamic characteristics encapsulated in them.

With the advance of the object oriented approach to database design, the behavior modeling of objects has grown into one of the major problem areas in data engineering. In order to complete the conceptual schema of objects, it is essential to analyze the behavior of objects and encapsulate it in objects. Some design methodologies are using the behavior analysis techniques of objects in a practical basis[8,19], and behavior modeling capabilities are becoming the important factor of semantic data models [1,9,10,11,14,18,20,21].

Though the word 'behavior' is used to stress the dynamic characteristics of objects, it refers essentially to both of structural and dynamic aspects as they are indivisible. This suggests that the behavior of objects should be induced from the structural characteristics. All the behavior models proposed so far follow this way. Among other things, Kappel-Schrefl established a behavior modeling method based on the aggregation concept[9]. According to this model, the behavior of an aggregate object is deaggregated into the behaviors of the component objects.

The behavior modeling method discussed in this paper is also based on the object abstraction concepts. The behavior of an object is formally defined as the totality of life cycles of the object. We further propose that the control structure of the behavior should be implemented based on the aggregation concept in the sense that the aggregate object acts as the scheduler of behaviors of component objects.In a complex environment where many behaviors interact with each other, the synchronization of behaviors has to be solved. The formalization of behavior descriptions makes it easy to uniformly model complex behavior interactions.

"We can understand complex systems only if they are composed of simple parts, so a method for specifying complex systems must have a simple conceptual basis [10]." The aim of this paper is to provide such a basis.

2. The Extended Entity-Relationship Model

2.1 Constructs of the Model

As the basic framework of the behavior modeling, we use an extended version of the ER model(abbreviated EER model). The model is defined by the elementary constructs of the ER model plus abstraction concepts.

We use the elementary constructs of the ER model without definitions[2]. These elements are 'entity', 'relationship', 'value', 'entity set', 'relationship set', 'value set', 'attribute', and 'role'. For the sake of brevity, we uniformly refer to 'entity', 'relationship', and 'value' as 'object', though 'value' is 'printable(or lexical) object' and distinguished from 'entity' and 'relationship' which are 'nonprintable(or nonlexical) object'. We also refer to 'attribute' and 'role' as 'property'. As each property of an object maps that object to a certain object or a set of objects of the same or different object sets, we say a property takes an object or a set of objects as its values. These terminologies come from the object oriented view of the real world.

The EER model has additional abstraction concepts such as aggregation, generalization, and association[1,22]. In this paper, we concentrate on the aggregation concept. The aggregation is an abstraction where a collection of certain component object sets makes up a higher level object set. We call the higher level object set an aggregate set and its component object sets simply component sets. Objects of each component set are considered as values to be assigned to an appropriate property of objects of the aggregate set. In the EER model, we can see the following aggregation.

(a) The aggregation of a collection of value sets into an entity set.

(b) The aggregation of a collection of entity sets and value sets into a relationship set.

(c) The aggregation of a collection of entity sets, relationship sets, and value sets into a relationship set.

An object of an aggregate set can exist only when a certain collection of objects of the component sets exists. Furthermore, in many cases, an aggregate set is defined to realize a function or a task in which the component sets play some roles as its resources. In this sense, an aggregate set is considered to be a functional or dependent object set, while its participant component sets exist as independent object sets relative to the functional object set. We alternatively call them a task object set and resource object sets respectively. Notice that the relation 'functional' vs 'independent', or 'task' vs 'resource' has a relative meaning in the aggregation hierarchy.

As a variation of the aggregation, we define the notion of partial aggregation. Let E and F be two object sets. When the object or the set of objects which a certain property of an object of E takes are turned over from the object or the set of objects which a property of an object of F takes, we say E is a partial aggregate set with a partial component set F. This meas that an object set E has the component set of F indirectly via F. An object set may have more than one partial component set.

2.2 The Graphical Representation of the EER Model - EERD

The EER model is diagrammatically represented in a directed graph (V, A) called EERD. In this graph, V is a set of vertices representing object sets and A is a set of directed edges representing properties. In the EERD, vertices are uniformly depicted in rectangular boxes and vertices standing for printable object sets are often omitted. Edges are labeled with the names of properties. The directionality of edges obeys the rule : 'from aggregate sets to component sets'. In the case of the partial aggregation, the edges are depicted in dotted lines.

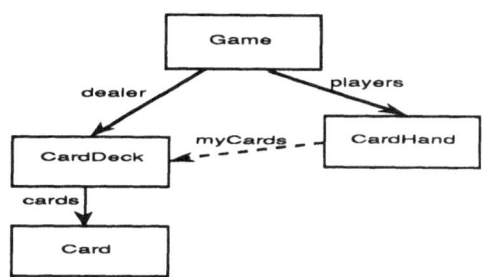

Figure 1 : The EERD of Playing Cards

As a simple example, we consider the 'playing cards' game the source of which appears in [6]. In this game, we have object sets shown in the EERD of Figure 1. Each set has the following roles in the game.

(a) An object of Card represents one card and has the properties *suit* which takes heart, club, spade, or diamond, and *rank* which takes 1 through 13 as their values respectively.

(b) The dealer is represented by an object of CardDeck and has the property *cards*. When an object of CardDeck is

created, a deck of cards as a shuffled collection of 52 objects of Card is assigned to *cards*. This implies that CardDeck is the aggregate set with the component set Card.

(c) Game players are represented by objects of CardHand. An object of CardHand has the property *myCards* to which a collection of cards selected from the value of *cards* of CardDeck is assigned. The value of *myCards* of each object of CardHand is handed from the value of *cards* of the object of CardDeck. This implies that CardHand is the partial aggregate set with the partial component set CardDeck.

(d) An object of Game has the properties *dealer* taking an object of CardDeck and *players* taking a set of objects of CardHand as their values respectively, and acts as the scheduler of the playing cards by activating the dealer and the players appropriately. By definition, Game is the aggregate set with the component sets CardDeck and CardHand.

3. Clustering of Objects

As suggested by the abstraction concepts, objects are clustered depending on the levels of representation details. The clustered ER model is introduced as a hierarchy of successively more detailed ER diagrams[5,24]. As suggested by the entity clustering methods, the aggregation hierarchy of the EER model represents the clustering of object sets[5]. Three levels of areas are recognized to be useful : 'a high level area', decomposition of this called 'subject area', further decomposition of this called 'information area', though the number of levels depends on the complexity and diversity of the real world.

Each area consists of an aggregate set (a functional or a task object set) and its component sets (independent or resource object sets). Some of the component sets may be shared by more than one aggregate set. In the behavior modeling, we start to analyze the behavior of object sets in information areas, and further follow the clustering hierarchy upwards and successively establish the behavior of higher level objects.

Figure 2 is the EERD of the aggregation hierarchy of a company consisting of three levels : a high level area (Company), subject areas (Product_Management, Employee_Management), and information areas (Order, Inventory, Personnel, Market). In this diagram, the independent object sets Product, Customer, and Staff are shared by more than one functional object set.

4. The Behavior Model

4.1 The Behavior with a Simple Life Cycle

Every object has its life cycle. Any object comes into existence in a certain mini world(e.g. an information area, a subject area, etc.), changes its states with time, and finally goes out from the environment in which it lived. We call this dynamic aspects the behavior of objects.

The behavior of an object expresses a script of functionality such as playing the game or performing the order business in an order entry application. Thus it is considered that each of Game and Order has its own life cycle in a given information area. The behavior is described by a set of states which represent the stages or milestones of functional processes, together with a set of events which cause state changes. The behavior model of

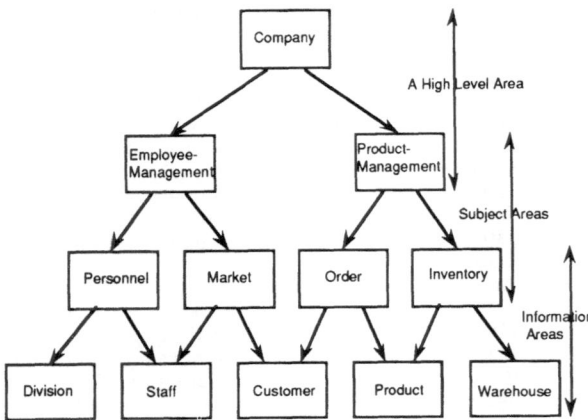

Figure 2 : The EERD Representing an Aggregation

object sets is built up using these notions. We first consider a single information area and define the behavior with a simple life cycle.

Let E be an object set. The behavior with a simple life cycle of E is a two-tuple (S,T), where $S = \{s_0, s_1, s_2, ..., s_n\}$ is an ordered set of symbols representing states such that $s_{i-1} \le s_i$ ($i = 1, 2, ..., n$), and $T = \{t_1, t_2, ..., t_n\}$ is a set of symbols representing events. Each event t_i of T is associated with s_{i-1} and s_i with the meaning that the execution of t_i causes the state change from s_{i-1} to s_i. To express this fact explicitly, we write t_i $(s_{i-1} \mid s_i)$ and say t_i has the prestate s_{i-1} and poststate s_i. Among the states of S, we call $s_0 = s_{INIT}$ standing for "an object created" the initial state and $s_n = s_{FIN}$ standing for "an object disappeared" the final state.

In the behavior of E, each state s_i stands for a general statement of a processing stage in the life cycle of objects of E. The behavior of an object set is not directly related to procedures that describe control structures of operations on objects, rather it should be taken as a script or integrity constraints which every object of that object set should obey. Thus the behavior of an object set is naturally encapsulated in the object set as a part of the schema representing the dynamic integrity constraints.

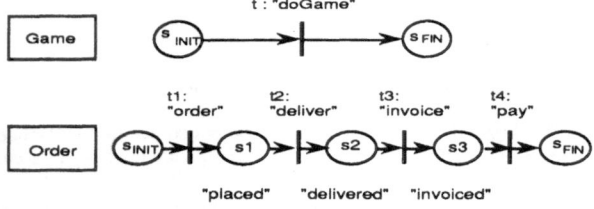

Figure 3 : The Behavior Diagram of Two Object Sets

The behavior of an object set is expressible in a graphic form using the Petri net graph[17] with places and transitions representing states and events respectively. The behavior diagram of an object set is a combined diagram of the rectangular box representing the object set and the Petri net representing its behavior. Figure 3 illustrates two examples of the behavior diagrams of Game and Order. Each diagram should be interpreted as representing states and events of an object of the object set that appears on the left, not of the object set itself.

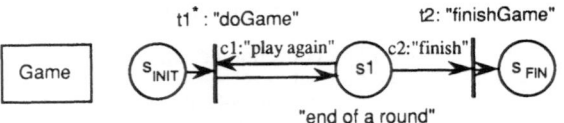

Figure 4 : The Behavior Diagram Having Iterated Events

In order to group a sequence of events, we define the group event as a consecutive sequence of events t_i, t_{i+1}, ..., t_k, and denote it $t = [t_i, t_{i+1}, ..., t_k]$. The group event t is also written $t(s_{i-1} \mid s_k)$ where s_{i-1} is the prestate of t_i and s_k is the poststate of t_k.

If execution of an event or a group event t is to occur repeatedly, it is denoted t^* and called an iterated event. The iterated event $t^*(u \mid v)$ is equivalently expressed as a group event $t^*(u \mid v) = [t(u \mid v), t(v \mid v)..., t(v \mid v)]$ which is interpreted as follows.

(1)   At the first execution of t, the prestate u is changed to the poststate v.
(2)   At the n-th (n > 1) execution of t, the poststate v of the (n-1)-th execution becomes the prestate of the n-th execution of t.

When it is required to specify the condition to execute the event $t(u \mid v)$ explicitly, that condition is attached in the form of a label to the input edge from u to t.

For example, if the game is played repeatedly, the iteration of the event t_1 : "doGame" is denoted t_1^* ($s_{INIT} \mid s_1$), where s_1 stands for the state "end of a round". The refined version of the behavior diagram of Game is shown in Figure 4, where c_1: "play again" and c_2: "finish" specify the branching conditions to t_1 and t_2 respectively.

4.2   The Behavior with Multiple Life Cycles

There are circumstances where an object participates in more than one information or subject area and plays different roles in different areas. In this case, we consider that the object has multiple life cycles as an integration of the life cycles in various areas in which it participates. For example, the object set Customer may have two different life cycles, one in the order entry and another in the marketing management. The former may include such states as $\{s_{INIT}, s$:"new debt", $s_{FIN}\}$, while the latter may have $\{s_{INIT}, s'$:"new address", $s_{FIN}\}$, though the states s_{INIT} and s_{FIN} are common to both life cycles.

We define the behavior with multiple life cycles of an object set E as a two-tuple (S,T) satisfying the following conditions.

(1) S is a set of states and the union of subsets $S_1, S_2, ...,$ and S_m such that $S_i \cap S_j \supseteq \{s_{INIT}, s_{FIN}\}$.
(2) T is a set of events and the union of subsets $T_1, T_2, ...,$ and T_m.
(3)   For each i ($1 \le i \le m$), the two-tuple (S_i, T_i) is a behavior with a simple life cycle of E.

The general behavior diagram of Customer with two life cycles is expressed in the form $(S_1 \cup S_2, T_1 \cup T_2)$ such that $S_1 = \{s_{INIT},$ s:"new debt", $s_{FIN}\}$, $S_2 = \{s_{INIT}, s'$:"new address", $s_{FIN}\}$, $T_1 = \{t^*(s_{INIT} \mid s)$:"changeDebt", $t_{FIN}\}$, and $T_2 = \{t'^*(s_{INIT} \mid s')$:"move", $t'_{FIN}\}$, and is illustrated in Figure 5.

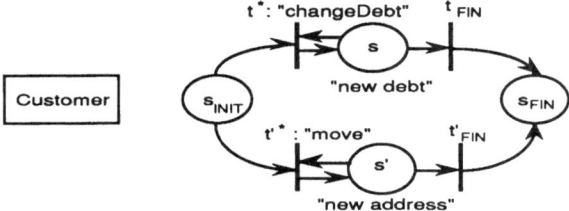

Figure 5 : The Behavior Diagram Having with Two Life Cycles

There is a case that Customer may have multiple life cycles even in a single information area, say in the order entry. This suggests the multiplicity of life cycles does not necessarily depend on the environments.

5. Decomposition of Behaviors

In the aggregation hierarchy of object sets, behaviors of the component sets participate in the behavior of the aggregate set. In other words, as also discussed in [9], the behavior of an object set is decomposed into behaviors of the component sets. Suppose for example that the event "changeDebt" of Customer causes updating values of two properties of Customer, say *currentDebt* and *amountOfMoneyPayed*. This event is then decomposed into two events, "changeCurrentDebt" and "change AmountOfMoneyPayed" which belong to the respective behaviors of the object sets taken by these properties as values. Namely, events of Customer are considered as an aggregate of events of the component sets (printable object sets in this case).

Furthermore, since the functional object set is an aggregate set of some independent object sets, these component sets participate in the behavior of their aggregate set playing certain roles like CardDeck and CardHand in Game, or Customer and Product in Order. In order to handle the granularity of events, we define the notion of the decomposition of behaviors.

Let E be an aggregate set with component sets E_1, E_2, ..., and E_n, and $t(u \mid v)$ be an event of E having the prestate u and the poststate v. Then t is decomposed into events $t_1(u_1 \mid v_1)$, $t_2(u_2 \mid v_2)$, ..., and $t_n(u_n \mid v_n)$ where each t_i is an event or a group event of E_i, and $u_i \mid v_i$ denotes its prestate and poststate respectively. Here the states u and v are considered to be decomposed into the respective sets of states $\{u_i\}$ and $\{v_i\}$. We call u and v the aggregate states with the respective sets of component states $\{u_i\}$ and $\{v_i\}$, and t the aggregate event with the set of component events $\{t_i\}$. The aggregate event t is denoted $t = aggregate(t_1, t_2, ..., t_n)$.

The decomposition means that each event of an aggregate set together with its prestate and poststate is broken down into the equivalent sets of events and states of the component sets. In other words, the execution of the aggregate event t is equivalent to the execution of the set of component events $\{t_1, t_2, ..., t_n\}$ that causes the change of the set of the component states from $\{u_1, u_2, ..., u_n\}$ to $\{v_1, v_2, ..., v_n\}$. In the implementation design of objects, the aggregate event should be transformed into a scheduler which determines the control structure of the component events. In this sense, we say the aggregate event t schedules the set of component events $\{t_i\}$, and the aggregate set E is the event scheduler of the component sets E_1, E_2, ..., and E_n.

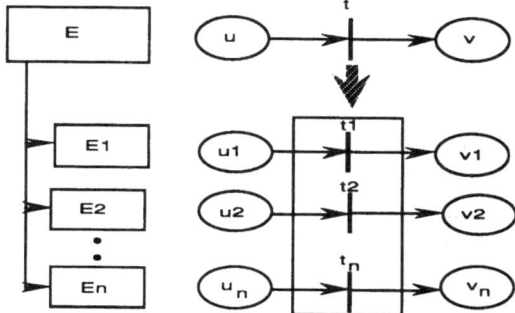

Figure 6 : Decomposition of the Behavior

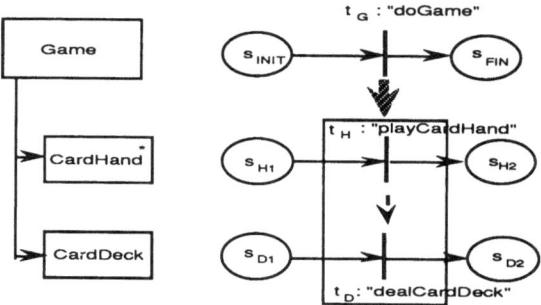

Figure 7 : Decomposition of the Behavior of Game

In the aggregation hierarchy of object sets, the decomposition of behaviors proceeds from the lower level to the higher level until it reaches the highest level area. The decomposition of behaviors is illustrated in Figure 6. Rectangular boxes on the left represent an aggregation hierarchy of object sets, and the Petri nets on the right are the associated behaviors. The decomposition is expressed by the arrow from the aggregate event to the component events. For the sake of brevity, behaviors in the lowest level representing updates of printable object sets do not appear in the diagram.

Figure 7 illustrates a part of the behavior of Game having the component sets CardDeck and CardHand. Suppose that the game is played by one dealer and more than one player. In Figure 7, the box CardHand* stands for a set of objects of CardHand.

The event t_G:"doGame" is decomposed into events of CardHand and CardDeck such that $t_G = aggregate(\{t_H\}, t_D)$, where $\{t_H\}$ stands for a set of events t_H for multiple players. Each event t_H:"playCardHand" is a group event of CardHand which performs a sequence of playing operations such as "takeCards" and "returnAllCards", and is denoted $t_H = [takeCards*, returnAllCards]$. The event t_D:"dealCardDeck" is a group event of CardDeck which performs a sequence of dealing operations such as "shuffleCards", "selectNextCards", and "collectCards", and is denoted $t_D = [shuffleCards, selectNextCards*, collectCards*]$. The aggregate event t_G schedules the component events $\{t_H\}$ and t_D.

Since CardHand is a partial aggregate set having the partial component set CardDeck, some events of CardHand may partially have some events of CardDeck as the component

46

events. Therefore the former may schedule the latter. Notice that the events to be scheduled is restricted only to those which handle the objects taken by the property *cards* of CardDeck as values. The dotted line in Figure 7 represents this partial scheduling.

The group events in this example are horizontally ungrouped into the sequence of events as shown in Figure 8. In effect, each event of Game sends messages to invoke appropriate events of the component sets. In this sense, we have relative relationships "message sender and receiver" between an aggregate and its component objects. The message flow is illustrated in Figure 9, where events at the arrow tails invoke events at the arrow heads.

The grouping notion of objects CardHand* indicates n objects of CardHand are playing the game. The events "distribute" and "return" cause n times repeating of [selectNextCard, takeCards]

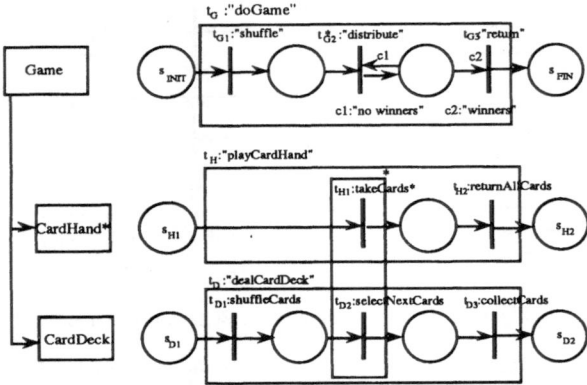

Figure 8 : Ungrouping of the Event "doGame"

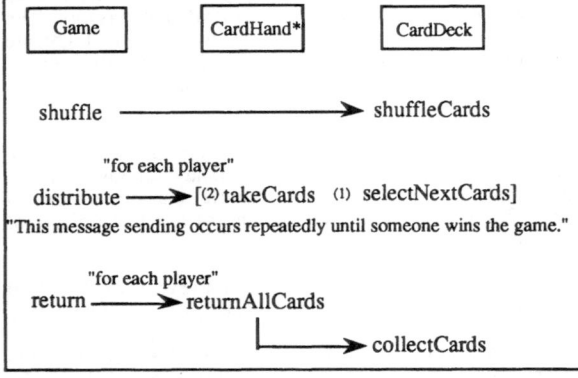

Figure 9 : The Message Flow in Game

and "returnAllCards" respectively. An execution of "returnAll Cards" in turn invokes the event "collectCards". We note here the events of component objects (message receivers) are "simple" having no control structures concerning iterations (while or for statements) and selections(if-then-else statements). Rather only the aggregate object is responsible for realizing the control structures of component sets.

6. Interactions of Behaviors

6.1 Sharing of Behaviors

In general, as seen in the example of the aggregation hierarchy in Figure 2, independent object sets participate in more than one information or subject area, and their behaviors are shared by behaviors of more than one functional object set. This could occur even if an independent object set has a behavior with a simple life cycle. In this case, the behavior may be scheduled by more than one aggregate set which requires a careful integrity control.

Figure 10 illustrates a part of behaviors of Order and Inventory sharing a common object set Product. Assume that Product has a behavior with a simple life cycle (S, T) such that $S = \{s_{INIT}, s:$"new qtyOnHand", $s_{FIN}\}$ and $T = \{t*:$"changeQtyOnHand", $t_{FIN}\}$. The event t is scheduled by the two aggregate events $t_O:$"deliver" of Order and $t_I*:$ "receiveStock" of Inventory. Since the granularity of each event is defined based on the associated object and its state, the event scheduling mechanism is safely implemented.

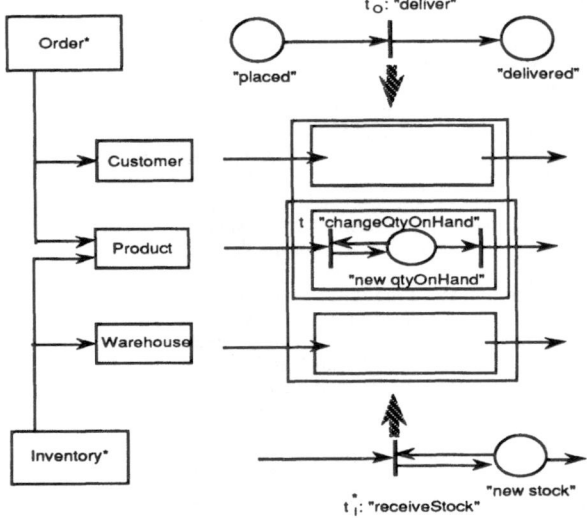

Figure 10 : Shared Behaviors

6.2 Synchronization of Events

Under the circumstances where many interrelated information or subject areas exist interacting with each other, modeling synchronization of behaviors becomes necessary. The typical problem occurs when an execution of an event of an object is forced to wait for certain states which should be caused by other events of the same or different objects as in the case that the event "deliver" of Order is forced to wait for the state "new stock" of Inventory which should be caused by the event "receiveStock". To handle this problem, we use the notion of primitiveness of events. An event is called primitive if its execution is instantaneous taking zero time. In the behavior with a simple life cycle, almost all the events are treated as primitive.

A nonprimitive event of an object is an event which does not take zero time. A nonprimitive event t(u | v) is converted into a group event that is a sequence of two primitive events such that $t = [t_{START}(u | s), t_{FINISH}(s | v)]$ where s is the state:"(the object) is waiting for some states" as illustrated in Figure 11.

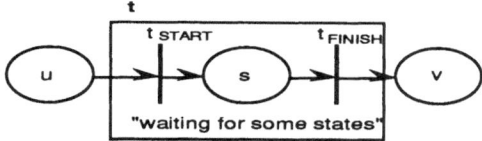

Figure 11 : Decomposition of a Nonprimitive Event

Suppose we have two functionally independent object sets E and E'. Let $t(u \mid v)$ be a nonprimitive event of E and $t'(u' \mid v')$ be a primitive event of E'. Consider a circumstance where the event t has to be delayed waiting for the poststate v' of the event t'. To solve this synchronization problem, we use the following modeling technique.

(1) Convert t into a group event that is a sequence of two primitive events $t_{START}(u \mid s)$ and $t_{FINISH}(s \mid v)$ with the intermediate state s:"waiting for some states".

(2) Consider an aggregate set EE'_Scheduler having the component sets E and E'. EE'_Scheduler should naturally coincide with the already existing aggregate set in a given area in the clustering hierarchy of object sets. EE'_Scheduler ought to have an event "doEE'" or the equivalent to it which schedules events of E and E'. Among other things, when the event t' of E' is executed bringing about the poststate v', "doEE'" invokes the event t_{FINISH} of E. Figure 12 is the behavior diagram representing this synchronization.

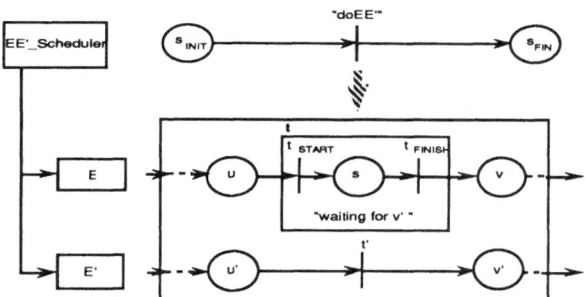

Figure 12 : Synchronization of Events

In the order entry application for example, as shown in a portion of Figure 13, the synchronization of the nonprimitive event "deliver" of Order and the primitive event "receiveStock" of Inventory is directly modeled under the interpretation : E = Order, E' = Inventory, the nonprimitive event of Order t_2 = deliver(s_1:"placed" | s_2:"delivered"), the iterated event of Inventory $t'*$ = receiveStock(s_{INIT} | s':"new stock"), EE'_Scheduler = Product_Management, and doEE' = doOrderInventory. This modeling technique is easily applied to more general cases where an event waits for the poststates of more than one event.

There is also the case that a nonprimitive event $t(u \mid v)$ of an object set E is forced to wait until a certain time arrives. This synchronization problem is directly solved if we define the object set Time having a single object representing time. Each event of Time brings about changes of time points. Since every object commonly uses time concepts, we assume that the object set Time is always defined implicitly.

Figure 13 represents that the behavior of an object of Product_Management, which appeared in Figure 2 and is

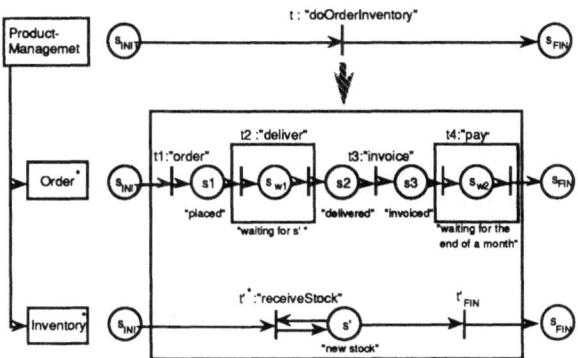

Figure 13 : Scheduling Behaviors of Order and Inventory

equivalent to OrderInventory_Scheduler, schedules the behaviors of all objects of the component sets Order and Inventory, including especially the synchronization of "deliver" waiting for the poststate of "receiveStock" as well as "pay" waiting for "the end of a month".

Notice that the event t:"doOrderInventory" schedules the behaviors of all objects of Order and Inventory as indicated by the asterisks in Figure 13. The event t is decomposed into events of Order* and Inventory* such that t = aggregate($\{t_{ORDER}\}, \{t_{INVENTORY}\}$), where t_{ORDER} and $t_{INVENTORY}$ are group events of Order and Inventory such that t_{ORDER}= [t_1, t_2, t_3, t_4] and $t_{INVENTORY}$ = [$t'*$, t'_{FIN}] respectively.

7. Conclusion

A method for behavior modeling of objects based on the aggregation concept is discussed. The summary is listed below.

(1) Analyze the aggregation hierarchy of object sets and establish the functional / independent relations among them.

(2) Analyze the life cycle of each object set in each of given areas and define its behavior consisting of states and events. If an object set is an aggregate set, refine the behavior by decomposing it into behaviors of the component sets.

(3) To each area of clustering hierarchy of objects, apply the above technique from the lower level to the higher level, and establish the hierarchical structure of behaviors. In this process, synchronize the behavior interactions by decomposing the nonprimitive events, and regulate the scheduling mechanism of the aggregate sets.

By encapsulating the identified behaviors in the associated object sets, we can refine the clustering hierarchy of objects representing the totality of the enterprise behavior. This contributes a great deal to achieving a high quality of integrity of the information resource. Problems that need further investigation are as follows.

(1) Analyze the behavior from the viewpoint of more sophisticated abstraction concepts where the notions such as aggregation, generalization, and association coexist.

(2) Enhance the behavior modeling method by investigating the time concept in detail. Reflect it to upgrading capabilities of semantic data models.

(3) Develop the method to describe the detailed control

structure of events in the conceptual design level as a basis for object oriented CASE tools.

References

[1] Brodie,M.L., Ridjanovic,D., On the Design and Specification of Database Transactions, in : On Conceptual Modeling, Springer-Verlag(1986).

[2] Chen,P.P., The Entity-Relationship Model - Toward a Unified View of Data, ACM Trans. on Database Systems, Vol.1, No.1(1976).

[3] Dittrich.K.R., Object-Oriented Database Systems : A Workshop Report, Proc. 5th Int. Conf. on Entity-Relationship Approach(1986).

[4] Eder,J., Kappel,G., Tjoa,A.M., Wagner,A.A., BIER - The Behavior Integrated Entity Relationship Approach, Proc. 5th Int. Conf. on Entity-Relationship Approach(1986).

[5] Feldman,P., Miller,D., Entity Model Clustering : Structuring a Data Model by Abstraction, The Computer Journal, Vol.29, No.4(1986).

[6] Goldberg,A., Robson,D., Smalltalk-80 : The Language and Its Implementation, Addison-Wesley(1983).

[7] Hull,R., King,R., Semantic Database Modeling : Surveys, Applications, and Research Issues, ACM Computing Surveys, Vol.19, No.3(1987).

[8] Jackson,M.A., System Development, Prentice-Hall(1983).

[9] Kappel,G., Schrefl,M., A Behavior Integrated Entity-Relationship Approach for the Design of Object-Oriented Databases, Proc. 7th Int. Conf. on Entity-Relationship Approach(1988).

[10] Lamport,L., A Simple Approach to Specifying Concurrent Systems, CACM Vol.32, No.1(1989).

[11] Kung,G.H., Solvberg,A., Activity Modeling and Behavior Modeling in : Information Systems Design Methodologies : Improving Practice, North-Holland(1986).

12] Markowitz,V.M., Shoshani,A., On the Correctness of Representing Extended Entity-Relationship Structures in the Relational Model, Proc. 1989 ACM SIGMOD Int. Conf. (1989).

[13] Mattos,N.M., Abstraction Concepts : The Basis for Data and Knowledge Modeling, Proc. 7th Int. Conf. on Entity-Relationship Approach(1988).

[14] Mees,M., Put,F., Extending a Dynamic Modeling Method Using Data Modeling Capabilities : The Case of JSD, Proc. 5th Int. Conf. on Entity-Relationship Approach(1986).

[15] Navathe,S.B., Pillamarri,M.K., Toward Making The E-R Approach Object-Oriented, Proc. 7th Int. Conf. on Entity-Relationship Approach(1988).

[16] Peckman,J. Maryanski,F., Semantic Data Models, ACM Computing Surveys, Vol.20, No.3(1988).

[17] Peterson,J.L., Petri Net Theory and the Modeling of Systems, North-Holland(1981).

[18] Put,F., The ER Approach Extended with the Action Concept as a Conceptual Modeling Tool, Proc. 7th Int. Conf. on Entity-Relationship Approach(1988).

[19] Robinson,R.A., An Entity/Event Data Modeling Method, The Computer Journal, Vol.22, No.3(1979).

[20] Sakai,H., A Method for Entity-Relationship Behavior Modeling, Proc. 3rd Int. Conf. on Entity-Relationship Approach(1983).

[21] Sakai,H., Horiuchi,H., A Method for Behavior Modeling in Data Oriented Approach to Systems Design, Proc. 1st Int. Conf. on Data Engineering(1984).

[22] Smith,J., Smith,D., Database Abstractions : Aggregation and Generalization, ACM Trans. on Database Systems, Vol.2, No.2(1977).

[23] Teorey,T.J., Yang,O., Fry,J.P., A Logical Design Methodology for Relational Databases Using the Extended Entity-Relationship Model, ACM Computing Surveys, Vol.18, No.2(1986).

[24] Teorey,T.J., Wei,G., Bolton,D.L., Koenig,J.A., ER Model Clustering as an Aid for User Communication and Documentation in Database Design, CACM, Vol.32, No.8(1989).

Correcting Anomalies of Standard Inheritance
—A Constraint-Based Approach—

Alfons Kemper   *Guido Moerkotte*

Universität Karlsruhe, Fakultät für Informatik, D-7500 Karlsruhe, West Germany, *kemper/moer*@ira.uka.de

Abstract

When using standard inheritance of attributes from superclasses one problem often arises: the subtype relation is conflicting with the subset relation. Inspired by geometrical modelling we will propose a solution to this problem on the basis of *constraint* inheritance which is—internally—modeled as a term rewriting system. We treat multiple inheritance and preserve strong typing. Further we discuss homogeneous and heterogeneous inheritance. In the case of homogeneous inheritance we treat both, fixed and overwritable defaults. Class constants can be seen as a special case of fixed defaults. For a set of type definitions, i.e., the user defined schema with type associated constraints, we derive sets of rewrite rules which are then used to model the different kinds of inheritance just mentioned. These rules serve two purposes: first, they are used to rewrite the user defined schema to derive an internal schema and, second, to rewrite the operators. The last step enhances efficiency because the type associated constraints can be utilized for operator optimization.

1 Introduction

Object-oriented database systems are emerging as the "next-generation" DBMSs for non-standard database application, e.g., VLSI design, CAD/CAM, software engineering, etc. One of the key concepts of object-orientation (see. [1]) is inheritance which supports the structured design of a database schema for these new applications which contain very complex structured object types.

When using standard inheritance the following problem often arises: the *subtype* relation of two types is conflicting with the *subset* relation of the types' extents (classes). A typical example—taken from the computer geometry application domain—illustrates this problem.

Consider modeling geometric objects like *RECTANGLE*s and *SQUARE*s. Obviously every *SQUARE* is a *RECTANGLE* (subset relation). On the other hand, there are two attributes, namely *Length* and *Height*, which are necessary to model a *RECTANGLE*, and there is only one attribute, say *Length*, necessary to model a *SQUARE*.

Thus the following type definitions would be typical in the context of subtype-based inheritance:

type SQUARE **is**   **type** *RECTANGLE* **is**
[Length : INT]   **supertypes** SQUARE
                              [Height : INT]

This makes *RECTANGLE* a subtype of *SQUARE*, which conflicts with the subset relation.

The main reason for this problem is the intermingling of three different concepts, namely the *is-a* (subset) relationship, the *subtype* relationship, and *inheritance*. The *subtype* relationship is directly tied to the *inheritance* relationship in a way such that all attributes of the supertype are inherited by the subtype. The problems associated with this approach were already observed by some other researchers ([3, 12], see also [2]). But, so far, no commonly agreed upon solution has been found to overcome this deficiency. Note that in the context of strong typing the approach of replacing the "inherits all" meaning of subtyping by "inherits all but" does not work because a subtype must provide all features of the supertype—unless one is willing to give up on type safety.

In order to alleviate (some of) the deficiencies induced by subtype-based inheritance we are going to introduce the notion of *constraint inheritance*. For example, a *SQUARE* is a special case of a *RECTANGLE*. This can be expressed as a relation between the attributes of a *RECTANGLE*, i.e., *Height = Length*, must hold for a *RECTANGLE* in order to be a *SQUARE*. This knowledge can now be used in two different ways. First, constraints can be introduced to check this relation. But there are two problems with this approach. One problem is the amount of checking that must be done every time a *SQUARE* is created or modified. The other problem is that there are still two attributes for the *SQUARE*. Thus the original problem is not solved. The same argument is true if *SQUARE*s are modeled via views.

The second approach—the one we follow here—is to use the constraints as rewrite rules. In order to allow the definition of these constraints we enhance the type definition syntactically by a **where** clause in which equalities of this kind can be specified.

We call the collection of types defined by the user the *external* or user defined schema. This schema is then rewritten to the *internal* schema using the equalities specified by the user as rewrite rules. This way the internal schema is freed from the **where** clause. The second step of rewriting concerns the defined operators. As we will see the rewrite rules serve to refine the operators given such that much efficiency is gained. This way we can avoid a performance decrease and solve the original problem.

The remainder of the paper is organized as follows. The next section outlines the very idea of our approach. The preliminaries needed are then presented in section 3. Section 3 and 4 formalize the schema and operator rewriting, respectively. An extended example is given in section 5. The discussion with a comparison to related work concludes this paper in section 6.

2 The Very Idea

We first give the solution of the problem for the example of the introduction. Then we define the syntax of a general type declaration.

Example 1: The solution to our problem for the example given in the introduction defines a *SQUARE* as a subtype of *RECTANGLE* (according to the subset relation). The consistency constraints, i.e., the fact that a *SQUARE* has equally long edges, is modeled as constraints which are associated with the *SQUARE* type.

type RECTANGLE is	type SQUARE is
[Length : INT,	**supertypes** RECTANGLE
Height : INT]	**where** Height ::= Length

We use "::=" for fixed defaults. This is opposed to overwritable defaults expressed by ":=".

For a rectangle the *area* operator is declared and defined as follows:

- **declare** *area* : RECTANGLE$\|$ → INT **code** *areaCode*

The **declare** statement introduces the signature of a newly defined operation. The "$\|$" denotes that the operation is type-associated, i.e., it can be refined within a subtype of the receiver type (i.e., the first argument). In our case *RECTANGLE* is the receiver type and *area* may be refined in subtypes thereof, e.g., *SQUARE*.

The implementation of an operation is supplied under different name (in the **code** clause), in our case *areaCode*. The implementation may simply look as follows:

- **define** *areaCode*$(X\|)$ X.Height $*$ X.Length

(Infix notation is used for the built-in arithmetic operators like $*$.)

To evaluate the function for a *SQUARE* the attribute access *X.Height* would be rewritten by the access to *X.Length*. A subsequent simplifier of algebraic expressions is then able to detect that the *SQUARE* function is needed and limits the number of accesses to the *Length* attribute to one instead of two. Of course, in the presence of more complicated **where** clauses and operators the simplifier can increase performance to a greater extent.

2.1 Syntactical Constructs

We now state the general syntax for a type definition under constrained inheritance:

> **type** t **is**
> > **supertypes** $s_1, \ldots, s_m$
> > $[a_1 : t_1, \ldots, a_n : t_n]$
> > **where** $b_1 = e_1$
> > > **renamed** c_1
> > > $\cdots$
> >
> > $b_k = e_k$
> > > **renamed** c_k

for $= \in \{:=, ::=\}$. In the simplest case all attribute accesses to an attribute constrained by "::=" are rewritten at compile time. For ":=" the create operation initializes the attribute with the given value (values for the **not null** specified attributes are supplied as the parameters of the create operation).

We call each s_i a *direct* supertype of t, and t a *direct* subtype of s_i. The a_i, b_h, $b^i_{j_h}$, and c_h are pairwise different attribute names, t, t_h and s_h types. The e_i are valid expressions of the type of b_i using only constants, operators and the attribute names $b^i_1, \ldots, b^i_{l_i}$. The $=$ clause or the **renamed** clause may be missing, but not both.

3 Preliminaries

3.1 Terminology

For formulating the conditions to be satisfied for a type definition a couple of sets and an ordering on attributes are needed:

- $STypes(t) := \{s_1, \ldots, s_m\}$
  $STypes(t)$ is the set of direct supertypes of t.

- $STypes^0(t) := \{t\}$

- $STypes^{i+1}(t) := \bigcup_{s \in STypes^i(t)} STypes(s)$
  $STypes^i(t)$ are the "i-th level" supertypes of t. Note that $STypes^1(t) = STypes(t)$.

- $Attr(t) := \{a_1, \ldots, a_n\}$
  These are the attributes defined in t.

- $CAttr(t) := \{c_1, \ldots, c_k\}$
  These are the attributes that have been renamed in t.

- $SAttr^*(t) := Attr(t) \cup SAttr^*(s_1) \cup \cdots \cup SAttr^*(s_m)$
  These are all the attributes "available" in t, i.e., the directly defined ones and the inherited ones.

- $SAttr^+(t) := SAttr^*(s_1) \cup \cdots \cup SAttr^*(s_m)$
  This set denotes the inherited attributes.

- $SCAttr^*(t) := SAttr(t) \cup CAttr(t) \cup SCAttr^*(s_1) \cup \cdots \cup SCAttr^*(s_m)$

- $SCAttr^+(t) := SCAttr(s_1) \cup \cdots \cup SCAttr(s_m)$

- $AType(a, t) := \begin{cases} t_i & \text{if } a = a_i \in Attr(t) \\ AType(a, s_{i_1}) & \text{if } AType(a, s_{i_1}) = \ldots \\ & = AType(a, s_{i_l}) \\ & \text{for all } s_{i_j} \text{ s.t.} \\ & a \in Attr(s_{i_j}) \\ \uparrow & \text{else} \end{cases}$

  The type of an attribute a in type t is either the defined type t_i or, if a is inherited, it corresponds to the unique type of all attributes a that are inherited from different supertypes. If no such unique type can be determined it is $\uparrow$ (denoting undefined).

- $depth(t)$
  $:= \begin{cases} 0 & \text{if } STypes(t) = \emptyset \\ 1 + max_{s \in STypes(t)} depth(s) & \text{else} \end{cases}$
  This variable denotes the maximum length of the paths from t to the root of the supertype DAG.

- the following partial order $\leq_A (t)$ on attributes is defined as the transitive closure of $\leq_A (t) := \{c_i \leq_A b_i | 1 \leq i \leq k\} \cup \{b_i \leq_A b_h^i | 1 \leq i \leq k, 1 \leq h \leq l_i\} \cup \leq_A (s_1) \cup \ldots \cup \leq_A (s_m)$
  If the type context is obvious we will write $\leq_A$ instead of $\leq_A (t)$

3.2 Validity Conditions

The following conditions on the attribute names must hold:

1. $a_h \notin SCAttr^+(t)$
   Inherited attributes cannot be redefined/retyped which is a necessary condition to preserve strong typing.

2. $b_h \in SCAttr^*(t)$
   The constrained attributes must have been declared.

3. $c_h \notin Attr(t) \cup SCAttr^+(t)$
   The attributes can only be renamed such that no new name conflict arises.

4. $b_j^i \in Attr(t) \cup SCAttr^+(t)$
   Every attribute used to constrain another one must have been declared in t or one of its supertypes.

The conditions on the type lattice are listed below:

(CF_TC) $\leq_T$ must be cycle free

(MI_TC) For every type t and every attribute a in $SAttr^*(t)$ the type $AType(a, t)$ exists.

While the last condition may seem to be very drastic it is needed to ensure type safety. Note that the attempt to resolve type conflicts in the case of multiple inheritance by taking the greatest lower bound within the user defined type lattice does not work because this would result in a retyping of attributes which is known to be illegal in the context of strong typing.

Example 2: Let us illustrate the impossibility of removing type conflicts of multiply inherited attributes of identical name but different type. Consider the following (cursory) type definitions:

type STUDENT **is**	**type** EMP **is**
[Rating: INT]	[Rating: STRING]

type RES_ASST **is**
supertypes STUDENT, EMP
$\ldots$

This type schema contains a type conflict in the form that *Rating* is multiply inherited with two different type constraints. A database variable, say *TopStudent*, of type *STUDENT* must provide an attribute *Rating* of type *INT* while a database variable of type *EMP*, say *TopEmp*, must have the same attribute of type *STRING*. Since both variables, *TopStudent* and *TopEmp*, may be associated with the same instance of type *RES_ASST* a type conflict is unavoidable. There is **no** way to consolidate the schema without redefining at least one of the supertypes, either *STUDENT* or *EMP*. Even encapsulation cannot solve this problem since the analogous problem would recur in the form of incompatible operator signatures.

In the case of attribute redefinition the following conditions must hold:

(CF_AC) $\leq_A$ is cycle free

(MI_AC) In the case of multiple inheritance, all the attribute names occurring on a left hand side in the **where** clauses of two different paths from the node under consideration to the root of the type hierarchy must be different.

The last condition is rather strict. For example, it does not allow for further refinement of the same attribute in subsequent subtypes. We will elaborate on the relaxation of the condition in the next section.

Summarizing, three new concepts have been introduced by using the above syntax for a type definition:

1. constraint (multiple) inheritance

2. renaming of attributes

3. computable attributes in the form of fixed and overwritable defaults with the special case of class constants.

If there is a class constant a defined for a type t then the attribute a of every instance of this type t assumes the value specified for a in the schema.

Note that the renaming of attributes is not a construct for resolving conflicts in the case of multiple inheritance as often used in the literature. This is of no use because the renaming of two inherited incompatible features (attributes or operators) does not really resolve a conflict in the light of strong typing—as demonstrated in Example 2.

Example 3: Let us now apply the concepts to a typical AI example. Here, we highlight the third concept introduced. Consider the definition of a type *ANIMAL* with subtype *BIRD* which in turn has the subtype *PENGUIN*. As everybody should know by now *BIRD*s *fly* whereas *ANIMAL*s, in general, and *PENGUIN*s, in particular, don't. Using constraint inheritance we can model these facts in two different ways. One is using fixed defaults, the other approach uses overwritable defaults. This corresponds to strict *is-a* and default *is-a* (see [4]).

(1) Fixed Defaults:	(2) Overwritable Defaults:
type ANIMAL **is**	**type** ANIMAL **is**
[fly : BOOL]	[fly : BOOL]
where fly ::= $false$	**where** fly := $false$
type BIRD **is**	**type** BIRD **is**
supertypes ANIMAL	**supertypes** ANIMAL
where fly ::= $true$	**where** fly := $true$
type PENGUIN **is**	**type** PENGUIN **is**
supertypes BIRD	**supertypes** BIRD
where fly ::= $false$	**where** fly := $false$

Using all three **where** clauses of each modelling in one term rewriting system results in a nonconfluent term rewriting system. Thus we will not put all rewrite rules gained from the **where** clause into a single rewrite system as, e.g., introduced in [7] but instead use ordered rewriting (cf. section 4). Note that both of the above modeling possibilities are not very satisfactory. In the first case all instances of

direct type *ANIMAL* must not fly despite the fact that there even exists a subclass of it, namely *BIRD*s, which do fly. In the second case the user is able to overwrite the *fly* attribute of *PENGUIN*s to true even though there does not exist any flying *PENGUIN*. These circumstances give rise to the introduction of what is called heterogeneous (as opposed to homogeneous inheritance as seen above) inheritance where the mixture of fixed and overwritable attributes is allowed ([13]). Consider again our *ANIMAL* example. This time we model:

(3) Heterogeneous Inheritance
    type ANIMAL **is**
    [fly : BOOL]
      where fly := $false$
    type BIRD **is**
      supertypes ANIMAL
      where fly := $true$
    type PENGUIN **is**
      supertypes BIRD
      where fly ::= $false$

The mixture of "::=" and ":=" in the same branch of the type lattice has the consequence that the *fly* attribute is fixed for the *PENGUIN* type but overwritable for the *ANIMAL* and *BIRD* type.

Example 4: Another example for heterogeneous inheritance is given in [5] (see also [4]):

1. Molluscs are normally shell-bearers.

2. Cephalopods must be Molluscs but normally are not shell-bearers

3. Nautili must be Cephalopods and must be shell-bearers which is modeled as:

    type MOLLUSC **is**
    [shell_bearer : BOOL]
      where shell_bearer := $true$
    type CEPHALOPOD **is**
      supertypes MOLLUSC
      where shell_bearer := $false$
    type NAUTILI **is**
      supertypes CEPHALOPOD
      where shell_bearer ::= $true$

4 Schema Rewriting

In this section we define the rewriting systems for the schema rewriting. Since the rewrite set is different for homogeneous and heterogeneous inheritance there is a subsection devoted to each.

4.1 Homogeneous Inheritance

We first define the base set B of rewrite rules independent of the defined types. B contains the following rules:

$$\begin{aligned} ,, &\to , \\ [, &\to [\\ ,] &\to] \end{aligned}$$

For each type definition

$$\begin{aligned} \textbf{type } t \textbf{ is } &[a_1 : t_1, \ldots, a_n : t_n] \\ &\textbf{supertypes } s_1, \ldots, s_m \\ &\textbf{where } b_1 = e_1 \\ &\qquad\qquad \textbf{renamed } c_1 \\ &\qquad\qquad \cdots \\ &\qquad b_k = e_k \\ &\qquad\qquad \textbf{renamed } c_k \end{aligned}$$

we define the following set $B(t)$:

$$B(t) := \{ b_i : u \to \epsilon \mid b_i ::= e_i \text{ occurs in the type definition}$$
$$\text{and } u = AType(b_i, t) \}$$

This removes all those attributes which are non-overwritable. A reference to such an attribute is handled by evaluating the expression e_i.

4.2 Heterogeneous Inheritance

To model heterogeneous inheritance we require the base set B to contain for all attribute names a and all type names t:

$$\begin{aligned} a : t \quad &\to a \circ : t \\ a - : t &\to \epsilon \\ ,, \qquad &\to , \\ [, \qquad &\to [\\ ,] \qquad &\to] \end{aligned}$$

We define the following set $B(t)$:

1. For each $b_i := e_i$ with $u = AType(b_i, t)$ the set $B(t)$ contains $b_i \circ : u \to b_i + : u$.

2. For each $b_i ::= e_i$ with $u = AType(b_i, t)$ the set $B(t)$ contains $b_i \circ : u \to b_i - : u$.

4.3 The Rewrite System

We now define the ordered rewrite system for a given type t. Using the sets B and $B(t)$ given above we define:

1. $R_0(t) := B(t) \cup B$

2. $R_i(t) := \bigcup_{s \in SType^{i+1}(t)} B(s) \cup B$ for $(1 \leq i \leq depth(t))$

4.4 The Rewriting Process

For each user defined type t the term rewriting system $R(t)$ is applied to the following internal type definition:

$$\textbf{internal type } t \textbf{ is } [a_1 : t_1, \ldots, a_m : t_m]$$

where the a_i are all the inherited attributes and the t_i the corresponding types, i.e., $\{a_1, \ldots, a_n\} = SAttr^*(t)$ and $t_i = AType(a_i, t)$. Let r_0 denote this term.

Rewriting proceeds as follows: $r_0 \to^*_{R_0} r_1 \cdots \to^*_{R_{depth(t)}} r_{depth(t)+1}$ where $\to^*_R$ means reduction until no further rule in R can be applied, i.e., the normal form is reached. There is only one normal form since any reduction system R_i for a given schema which obeys the given conditions is confluent. The rewriting process stops since any R_i is obviously Noetherian, i.e., the rewriting process is finite (see [7]). The resulting type definitions give the internal schema used for storage allocation.

4.5 Object Creation and Manipulation

In our approach objects can only be created by using create operations which are derived from the rewritten schema, i.e., the internal schema. For a given internal type definition

$$\textbf{internal type } t \textbf{ is } [a_1 : t_1, \ldots, a_m : t_m]$$

the following create operator is automatically derived:

$$\textbf{declare } t\$create : (a_1 : t_1, \ldots, a_m : t_m) \to t$$

Constrained attributes are not always updatable because their value may be derived from other attributes in such a way that the propagation of the update to the other attributes is not unique. An example should illustrate the intricacies of derived values:

$$\begin{aligned} \textbf{type } &DoubleLengthRectangle \textbf{ is} \\ &\textbf{supertypes } RECTANGLE \\ &\textbf{where } Length ::= 2 * Height \\ \textbf{type } &SpecialCuboid \textbf{ is} \\ &\textbf{supertypes } CUBOID \\ &\textbf{where } Length ::= Height + Width \end{aligned}$$

In the first type, *DoubleLengthRectangle*, an update to *Length* could still be propagated to the *Height* attribute, because it can be deduced that $Height = 1/2 * Length$. But in the second type definition, *SpecialCuboid*, an update to *Length* cannot unambiguously be mapped to an update of *Height* and *Width*. Therefore, we allow attribute update only through special operators which are refined for each type. If there is no potential unique update for a rewritten attribute the invocation of the update operator does not have any effects but does not result in any error, either.

5 Operator Rewriting

The term rewriting system for operator rewriting is defined as follows and the same for homogeneous and heterogeneous inheritance.

We define the following set O_t:

1. For each $b_i := e_i$, or $b_i ::= e_i$ the set O_t contains $X.b_i.Y \rightarrow e_i'.Y$

2. For each b_i **renamed** c_i the set O_t contains $c_i \rightarrow b_i$

where e_i' is derived by replacing each access of an attribute $a \in CAttr^*(t)$ in e_i by $X.a$.

5.1 The Rewrite System

We now define the ordered rewrite system for a given type t.

1. $O_0(t) := O_t$

2. $O_i(t) := \bigcup_{s \in SType^i(t)} O_s$ for $(1 \le i \le depth(t))$

We now shortly discuss the relaxation of condition MI_AC. The first step is to require the term rewriting system $O(t)$ to be confluent which in some cases is general enough but not always convenient. Consider the following type definitions:

> **type** s_1 **is** $[a : t_1, b : t_2, c : t_3]$
> **type** s_2 **supertypes** s_1 **where** $a ::= b * c$
> **type** s_3 **supertypes** s_1 **where** $a ::= c * b$
> **type** s_4 **supertypes** s_2, s_3

The resulting rewrite system is not confluent but the two possibilities for rewriting a which are $b * c$ and $c * b$ are equivalent due to the commutativity of $*$. For operators with a known theory, i.e, the set of laws (like commutativity, associativity, distributivity, etc.) we introduce an equivalence relation $\sim$ and restate condition MI_AC as follows:

MI_AC: For each defined type t the term rewriting system $O(t)$ must be confluent modulo $\sim$.

The term rewriting process with $O(t)$ is defined the same way as for $R(t)$ even though it is applied to the operator definitions instead of type definitions. Here we discuss two cases of operators separately, namely, attribute retrieval and general type associated operators (e.g., weight).

6 A More Sophisticated Example

Let us develop a more sophisticated example. This example is taken from the mechanical CAD/CAM application area. Different kinds of conical pipes are modeled. The most general definition of a conical pipe is as follows (the pipe may be conical in its inner (I) as well as its outer (O) circumference):

Example 5:

> **type** IO_CON_PIPE **is**
> [Length : FLOAT,
> OuterRadius_1 : FLOAT,
> OuterRadius_2 : FLOAT,
> InnerRadius_1 : FLOAT,
> InnerRadius_2 : FLOAT,
> Density : FLOAT]

Special cases arise if the inner radius or the outer radius stays constant.

> **type** I_CON_PIPE **is**
>   **supertypes** IO_CON_PIPE
>   **where** OuterRadius_1 ::= OuterRadius_2
>   **renamed as** OuterRadius.

> **type** O_CON_PIPE **is**
>   **supertypes** IO_CON_PIPE
>   **where** InnerRadius_1 ::= InnerRadius_2
>   **renamed as** InnerRadius.

If both radii stay constant we get a normal pipe:

> **type** PIPE **is**
>   **supertypes** O_CON_PIPE, I_CON_PIPE

A cylinder is a special case of a pipe. This is expressed as follows:

> **type** CYLINDER **is**
>   **supertypes** PIPE
>   **where** InnerRadius_2 ::= 0.

To give an example, the rewritten internal schema for a $CYLINDER$ is:

> **internal type** CYLINDER **is**
> [Length : FLOAT,
> OuterRadius_2 : FLOAT,
> Density : FLOAT]

We can now introduce a type associated function declaration $weight$ as follows.

- **declare** $weight : IO\_CON\_PIPE \| \rightarrow FLOAT$ **code** $WeightCode$

Using infix notation for built-in arithmetic operators the function $weight$ is defined as

define $WeightCode\ (X\|)$
$X.Density * X.Length * \pi$
$* ((0.5 * (X.OuterRadius\_1 + X.OuterRadius\_2))^2$
$- (0.5 * (X.InnerRadius\_1 + X.InnerRadius\_2))^2)$

This definition then is rewritten for the cylinder to:

define *cylinder$WeightCode* ($X$‖)
  $X.Density * X.Length * \pi$
  $* ((0.5 * (X.OuterRadius\_1 + X.OuterRadius\_2))^2$
  $- (0.5 * (0 + 0))^2)$

Here, *cylinder$WeightCode* denotes the version of *Weight-Code* that will be applied when invoked on a *CYLINDER* instance. Further simplification by an algebraic simplifier yields the final rewritten version:

define *cylinder$WeightCode*($X$)
  $X.Density * X.Length * \pi * (X.OuterRadius\_2)^2$

7 Discussion

The work described here is fundamentally different from several AI proposals on inheritance exceptions, e.g., [4, 5, 13]. Their work concerns the elimination of certain *is-a* links between classes within an inheritance hierarchy (or graph). For example, a typical problem they try to solve is the type hierarchy

Penguin **is-a** *Bird* **is-a** *FlyingThing*

The implicit membership of *Penguins* to *FlyingThings* has to be explicitly cancelled in order to have a precise model of the real world. However, this approach introduces type conflicts which cannot be resolved at compile time and, therfore, may lead to run-time errors.

Our approach—on the other hand—is not at the taxonomy level (*is-a* links) but, rather, at the structure level. The constraints determine the valid values that particular attributes which may have been inherited from subtypes assume. But these constraints always conform to the schema definition and thus preserve the type consistency. Admittedly, not all exceptional cases that arise due to the "irregularities" of the real world can be handled. But, as shown in this paper, many interesting and important examples where pure inheritance fails may be tackled this way.

Our approach has some resemblance to the class assertions in Eiffel [10]. However, class assertions can only be extended, i.e., an inherited assertion can only be "strengthened" by adding conjuncts. Our framework allows to override the constraints in order to being able to model exceptions that arise within specialized types (Eiffel does not address the exception problem).

We have introduced a term rewriting approach to inheritance serving the schema and operator level. We did not touch the instance level, e.g., there are no exceptions to defaults inherited by the instance from the type/class. Nevertheless we think it will be worthwhile to generalize the term rewriting approach to the instance level and thus building

up an alternative to non-monotonic logic [11, 9, 6] and logic for inheritance [8].

A major advantage of our approach to inheritance is that it can be implemented on top of existing object-oriented systems in order to enhance their inheritance mechanisms.

References

[1] M. Atkinson, F. Bancilhon, D. J. DeWitt, K. R. Dittrich, D. Maier, and S. Zdonik. The object-oriented database system manifesto. In *Proc. of the DOOD Conference*, Kyoto, Japan, Dec 1989.

[2] J. R. Brachmann. I lied about the trees. *AI Magazine*, 6(3):80–93, 1985.

[3] R. J. Brachmann. What IS-A is and isn't: An analysis of taxonomic links in semantic networks. *IEEE Computer*, 10:30–36, 1983.

[4] D. W. Etherington and R. Reiter. On inheritance hierarchies with exceptions. In *AAAI*, 1983.

[5] S. E. Fahlman, D. S. Touretzky, and W. van Roggen. Cancellation in a parallel semantic network. In *IJCAI*, pages 257–263, 1981.

[6] M.L. Ginsberg, editor. *Readings in Nonmonotonic Logic*. Morgan Kaufmann, 1988.

[7] G. Huet. Confluent reductions: Abstract properties and applications to term rewriting systems. *JACM*, 27(4):797-821, 1980.

[8] E. Laenens, D. Vermeir, B. Verdonk, and A. Cuyt. A logic for objects and inheritance. In *Proc. of Advanced Database System Symposium*, pages 55–135, 1989.

[9] J. McCarthy. Applications of circumscriptions to formalizing common sense knowledge. *Artificial Intelligence*, 28:89–116, 1986.

[10] B. Meyer. *Object-Oriented Software Construction*. International Series in Computer Science. Prentice Hall, 1988.

[11] R. Reiter. A logic for default reasoning. *Artificial Intelligence*, 13, 1980. 81-132.

[12] A. Snyder. Inheritance and the developement of encapsulated software components. In *Research Directions In Object-Oriented Programming (B. Shriver, P. Wegner (Eds.))*, 1987. 165-188.

[13] D.S. Touretzky, J.F. Horty, and R.H. Thomason. A clash of intuitions: The current state of inheritance. In *IJCAI*, pages 476–482, 1987.

AN INTELLIGENT INTERFACE TO LEGAL DATA BASES
COMBINING LOGIC PROGRAMMING AND HYPERTEXT

Andreas Hamfelt and Jonas Barklund
Uppsala University

UPMAIL, Computing Science Dept., Box 520, S-751 20 Uppsala, Sweden
ANDREAS@EMIL.CSD.UU.SE or JONAS@EMIL.CSD.UU.SE

Abstract

We propose an architecture for building expert systems in which the main subsystems are distinct but communicating programs: a Prolog inference engine, a multimedia interface tool and a data base management system. We have used this architecture for constructing a legal expert system for labour law.

We propose a novel approach for capturing vague concepts. The vagueness is not represented in the sense that its extent is quantified but instead rules are given for evaluating the concept in a given situation. The method is analogous to legal practice; lawyers develop methods for judging whether vague concepts apply to fact situations. These methods are used for identifying the relevant sub-questions and legal text documents for analyzing the case in issue. Our system reflects this and other aspects of a lawyer's practical work.

1. INTRODUCTION

We shall present an expert system for the legal domain of labour law, developed jointly by Uppsala Programming Methodology and Artficial Intelligence Laboratory, the Swedish Law & Informatics Research Institute, and a major Swedish employer organization (Verkstadsföreningen).

The system was developed to serve several purposes:

- a consultation aid for corporations,
- a tool for acquiring further expert knowledge on labour law, and
- an educational system for lawyers specializing in labour law.

The architecture of the system has three major components: a Prolog inference machine, a hypertext system, and a legal data base. These subsystems are connected in a network and interact with each other and the user [14]. The system is truly distributed in the sense that all subsystem can reside on distinct computers without any visible difference for the user.

The system features two innovative techniques: a method for capturing vague concepts, such as those central for legal reasoning, and an architecture which takes advantage of cutting edge technology for inference machinery, text management, and data base management.

An important feature of our approach is that when the expert system requests information from the user, it also provides access to documents in the legal data base which help the user give accurate answers. Our solution for handling vague concepts is based on the insight that although knowledge about a vague concept cannot always produce a definite answer, it will at least guide the user to relevant documents which enable her to draw a well-founded conclusion. In a sense, the expert system then turns into a decision support system.

The system was first presented to the Council of Europe: 9th Symposium on Legal Data Processing in Europe, (Bonn 1989) [2]. An earlier version of the system was presented by the same delegation to the Council of Europe: 7th Colloquy on the Use of Computers in the Administration of Justice (Lisboa 1988).

2. MOTIVATION

Failure to observe proper proceedings when dismissing an employee is expensive. The legislation on dismissal of employees is in Swedish labour law centered around the vague concept of *fair ground for dismissal*. Few lawyers are experts on this matter. These issues arise frequently and consequently the consultation costs for enterprises are significant. Moreover, an improperly conducted dismissal can have serious economical consequences for the employer, apart from the negative publicity.

There are two primary objectives for the system at hand:

- to reduce the amount of consultations with experts on labour law, and
- to minimize the number of incorrectly pursued dismissals of employees

and thereby decrease the associated costs.

The expert system is chiefly intended for two categories of organizations:

- small to medium corporations without in-house lawyers, and

- larger corporations with corporate lawyers who may not, however, be experts in labour law.

The system is expected to function as a "filter" between corporations and, e.g., a central employer organization providing legal expertise on labour law. Many problems should be possible to solve locally and only the hard questions need to be submitted for expert examination.

For an employer organization, a system such as this can serve as a knowledge acquisition tool. Lawyers can add their comments on legal material as well as on the behavior of the system, such as the questions posed. If the system is centralized so recently added information is immediately available to all users then it may also serve as a medium for distribution of knowledge in the field. The fast spreading of knowledge will reduce the incoherence in lawyers' interpretations of the law. The information can also be processed to attain a deeper understanding of the problem, enabling organizations to influence the content of future legislation in the field.

A widely deployed system is expected to bring about an increased uniformity in the handling of dismissal matters. This will add to the predictability of the outcome of disputes and have a positive psychological effect due to the perceived fairness of the procedure.

For the lawyer, whether being an expert on labour law or not, the system gives fast, easy and reliable access to relevant legal sources. Lawyers recognize the behaviour of the system since it reflects their usual procedure of work while increasing their efficiency.

3. PROBLEMS

Vague legal concepts

We say that a concept is vague when it lacks a complete definition, i.e., the extension of the concept is not fully known. In this section we shall present a practical methodology for representing vague concepts in knowledge systems.

In the legal domain vagueness does not only come from lack of understanding of the domain but is often intentional, to allow an exact interpretation to be given in each particular case. A central legal matter of labour law is dismissal of an employee. The 7th section of the Act of Employment in Swedish labour law simply states that:

7 sect. The employer's dismissal must have fair ground.

No indication is given to what is fair ground and the concept has been left open for interpretation by courts. Since the act was made law there have been a number of court decisions in particular cases and lawyers have now a conception as to the circumstances under which fair ground may exist.

The question is thus "how can we handle vague concepts?" We do not consider other approaches such fuzzy logic, probability etc appropriate where they for example give the extent of vagueness by numbers; where do these numbers come from [12]? The point of departure we have chosen is how the expert actually reasons about a vague concept. How does he solve, in his practical work, the often arising problem of assessing whether or not a vague concept applies to some fact situation?

Even though a concept is vague, it does not mean that the result of applying the concept to a particular situation always is inexact. Since in the legal domain cases are adjudicated by courts, the extension of a concept is often partially determined. The application of the concept may be fairly precise when there exist earlier cases being more or less similar to the situation in issue. What is more important, however, is that in legal usage there have often evolved a number of necessary or disqualifying conditions that are used for assessing new cases. Moreover, these conditions exhibit a structure enabling lawyers to methodically examine new cases. We can reproduce this structure in a form amenable to machine inferencing. The expert system examines a case in accordance with this structure and may conclude that the case belongs to the established extension of a concept. Otherwise the system may nevertheless be able to point out the most relevant conditions that should be further examined and come up with references to documentation sources.

Managing Legal Documents

Today's AI technology must be complemented with other techniques in order to capture vague legal concepts. The expert system suffices for identifying which text documents are relevant for the case at hand. At the text document level other techniques are employed for giving smooth and easy access to written material.

Legal databases contain text documents that can be accessed, for example, through keywords or by case titles. Legal documents have explicit or implicit links to other documentation. Therefore it does not suffice to examine them separately. For example, a precedent may explicitly refer to sources such as other precedents, legal writings, legislative material, etc. A doctrine for how to understand the precedent may have evolved. Ignorance of this may lead to erroneous decisions. Accessing a legal data base through a hypertext system can solve these problems, since:

- The texts can be presented in a "user-friendly" fashion with multiple windows, etc., allowing many documents to be examined simultaneously.

- Information in a document can be explicitly or implicitly *linked* to information in the same or other documents. Hypertext allows the user to navigate smoothly between documents and background material, such as statutes and legal writings, but also thesauri and dictionaries.

Together, the legal data base and the hypertext system constitute a sophisticated document management system. An aspect that ought not to be underestimated is that the full system reflects quite well the lawyer's traditional method of work. This is often determinative for user acceptance.

4. TOOLS

Prolog

An inference machine for an expert system must be able to express rule-based knowledge at a high level but efficiently. At the same time it must be flexible enough to express concepts that do not naturally fit into the standard framework. For the latter purpose a high-level programming language would be convenient.

The logic programming language Prolog [5] fulfills both these requirements in a single level formalism. Pattern matching is available directly in the form of unification. Unlike most other proposed AI languages, Prolog can be compiled to achieve high performance. Among the other advantages, Prolog has a potential for metaprogramming which seems essential for high-level knowledge representation [8].

Data Bases

Our system is primarily intended to access remote public text data bases, containing case descriptions, etc. Since these data bases are often accessed via modems the interfaces are usually text-based. Accessing them from inside a hypertext system such as HyperCard is technically not difficult. We also think that it would be useful to have access to a "local" data base system where, for example, information about the current case could be stored. We imagine that such a facility would make the system interesting for crime investigation.

Hypertext

Multimedia is a technique for communicating information that is attracting much attention today. Multimedia is a common name for communicating various kinds of information such as text or hypertext, speech, sound, graphics, etc. As an idea hypertext has been around since the 1940's, cf. Bush [4]. Actual implementations of the hypertext idea appeared in the 1960's, cf. Engelbart [6]. Today powerful commercial systems are available, e.g., Hypercard [1].

MultiProlog

While multimedia is a cutting-edge technology for man-machine communication, logic programming is powerful for developing computer reasoning systems. Our system has been developed in a logic programming language that has links to a multimedia system and data bases (see figure 1) [14].

UPMAIL MultiProlog is a portable implementation of Prolog with extraordinary capabilities to coexist and

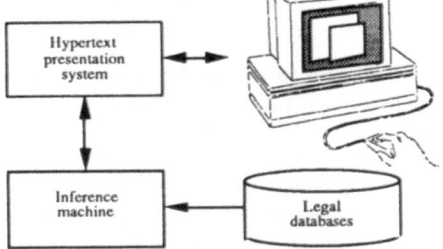

Figure 1. Architecture of knowledge system tool.

interact with other applications. For this particular system we have linked it with SuperCard, a state-of-the-art hypertext system, and with Oracle, a SQL relational data base management system.

Another advantage with this arrangement is that the modules can run on different computers. Communication between MultiProlog modules is done in exactly the same way regardless of whether the modules reside in the same computer or not. For example, it would be possible to run only the Hypertext system on a user's local machine while the expert system and legal data bases are remote. Such a configuration would have the advantage that changes to the system are immediately available to all users. In addition the system may serve as a communication channel for information, such as comments to cases, in the area.

The Development Environment

The most important advantages of our architecture are that it allows

- a high flexibility for exploiting new software developments, and
- the nature of the problem to be determinative for the choice of module (logic programming, data base or multimedia) in which the solution be programmed.

With our design of the system we can easily make use of further software developments. The subsystems are connected using a general serial communications protocol. Any subsystem can be replaced as long as the new component can use the communications protocol which means that we can use software from different developers. For example, the document management system was originally programmed in Hypercard. We are now employing further developments beyond Hypercard, i.e., Supercard. Due to the open architecture the switching from Hypercard to Supercard was carried out in a few hours. In the future multimedia will be increasingly flexible and powerful. The ability of our system to exchange modules is a necessary requirement for an adaptable system.

One might think that combining a reasoning system with multimedia could be carried out by using e.g., the imperative script language in Hypercard for programming an inference engine. This is awkward since that language is not adapted for developing such applications. Our approach enables us to develop the reasoning system in logic programming but the user interface and text handling system in Supercard. For these two different ends logic programming and Supercard are, respectively, among the most powerful programming environments available.

5. LEGAL KNOWLEDGE AND KNOWLEDGE REPRESENTATION

In order to create practical legal knowledge systems there is a basic problem that must be handled. The problem is the presence of vague legal concepts. Concepts that are more or less vague, or as it is also termed "open-textured," appear frequently in legal reasoning, see e.g., Hart [11]. Legal reasoning is not a mechanical application of rules in statutes and the like. Legal reasoning is more a process of interpreting legal rules and the concepts that form part of these rules. The primary problem is to see whether the rule applies or not to a certain fact situation. First when this is established a mechanical application of the rule is possible.

The background to the research described herein is a cooperation project with a major Swedish employer organization [10]. Activities carried out at the employer organization are primarily negotiation with the union on matters such as the interpretation of collective contracts, dismissal of employees etc. We chose to investigate the prospects of building a knowledge system for dismissal of employees. The primary reason for our interest in this legal issue was that the Swedish legislation concerning dismissal is centered around the vague legal concept "fair ground for dismissal."

The Norwegian legal theorist Sundby argues that lawyers often do not make a "free" evaluation of whether a vague legal concept—"fair price" in his example—applies to the case in issue ([13], p. 214). Our study of lawyers in practical legal work at the employer organization confirms Sundby's observation. Vague concepts were evaluated by decomposing them into several subquestions. The subquestions that could prove relevant to the case in issue were identified by applying a rather uniform procedure. As the subquestions were identified it was examined whether they applied to the case in issue. To this end the main method was comparing the case in issue with relevant text documents such as precedents, legal writings etc.

The work of the lawyer as it has been described here has been reflected in the system. The system helps the user to identify the subquestions that are relevant to the case in issue and retrieves the text documents needed to answer these. The level at which the document retrieval starts is the same as the level at which the lawyer began to look in books, law reports etc.

The reasoning part of the system is used to reflect logical relations between various subquestions. We give an example below. The document management part is used to give access to text documents needed to judge e.g., whether a particular measure is adequate or not.

Text documents may be presented in several levels. At the "top level" the legal matter at issue can be presented in the form of an abstract that includes general guidelines for its examination. In the abstract relevant legal sources are pointed out, e.g., precedents. Names for precedents can be connected to a full text accounts, to the relevant legal writings, etc. The user gets access to these levels just by clicking at the tokens of a precedent's name, e.g., "Jones vs Smith," wherever these appear in the text.

In figure 2 we see a schematic description of the system. At the top of the picture we have the reasoning part, at the bottom the document management part.

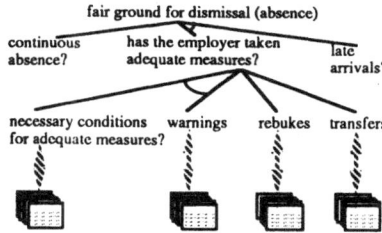

Figure 2. Schematic description of the expert system.

The vague concept "fair ground for dismissal" is, if the misdemeanour is absence, first decomposed by the legal experts into the three subquestions

- "is it a case of continuous absence?"
- "has the employer taken adequate measures to solve the problem?", and
- "is it a case of several shorter delays?"

These subquestions are logically related so that the employer's measures become relevant only if it is not a case of continuous absence. And in this case the question whether some other kind of absence exists is relevant only if the employer's actions are adequate. In the figure the arch between two branches stands for "and" and the lack of an arch stands for "or." By using these logical relations between subquestions we can sort out the relevant from the irrelevant subquestions leading the user to those relevant for his case.

These subquestions can be further decomposed. For example "adequate measures" can be split up into the four subquestions specified in the figure. At this level the lawyers at the employer organization began to look in text documents. And at the same level in the system we give the user access to these documents and guidelines for how to interpret them.

That is, we do not "define away" vagueness, instead we guide the user to the subquestions being relevant for his case. These subquestions are still vague but they are demarcated enough so that a human being, although ignorant of labour law, can handle their vagueness simply by browsing through the relevant text documents which, at this level, are made available automatically. It is thus the user's responsibility to make the final decision as to whether a vague concept applies or not, but this task is considerably simplified by the supplied information.

This is not to say that representation of vagueness as such is insurmountable. Perhaps, such a representation could be carried out along lines analogous to those developed by Hamfelt and Barklund for capturing legal interpretation principles for notions such as *analogia legis* and *e contrario* [7, 8, 9]. Such a project is however much more ambitious and still there exist several questions—both of technical and philosophical nature—that ought to be investigated before commercial systems based on that approach are launched. The approach described in the present paper is, on the contrary, at a stage of development where practical applications are feasible.

6. HYPERTEXT AND COMPUTER REASONING—AN INTELLIGENT LIBRARY

Hypertext, data bases, and computer reasoning can be used to create an "intelligent library." This is a library where the user in addition to the access to writings also gets a firm guidance for retrieving the texts relevant to his problem. Of course there exist a vast range of possible applications also outside the legal domain. Examples are libraries at large companies for various internal information on anything from research results to market analyses, education systems, etc.

To illustrate the prospects of combining a document management system with computer reasoning, let us show a few parts of a session with the system.

If the questions are vague the document management part helps the user to answer them. The reasoning system can only give little help to judge whether the measures taken are adequate. But at this level the document management system instead becomes dominant. It helps the user to examine vague questions by giving access to text documents in which similar questions have been examined or adjudicated (see figure 3). Pressing the "Cases" button gives a pop-up menu with all relevant precedents for the question in issue. Choosing "ALL" in the menu gives the abstracts of these precedents put side by side for convenient comparison. The abstracts are retrieved from the data base.

The user can also get access to the relevant legal writings about the legal matter in issue by pressing the button "Writings." If he wishes to browse the part of the library that contains the relevant doctrine and law reports this is also feasible. Clicking at a book in the shelf gives the list of content and clicking at an item in the list gives the actual text, etc.

Figure 3. A question supplemented with comments. By pressing "Cases" all relevant precedents can be viewed.

When the system finally reaches a conclusion the user gets help to fulfill the formal requirements for dismissal. Pressing the "dismissal form" button gives the form and notes concerning how to correctly fill it in (see figure 4).

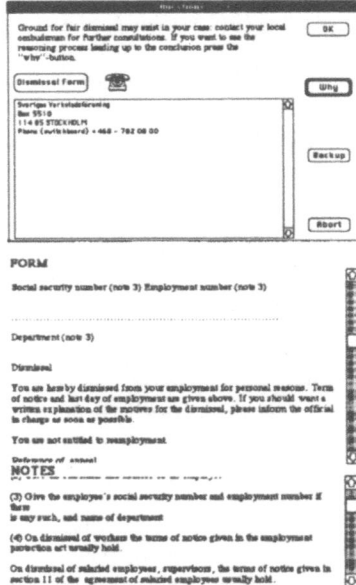

Figure 4. The system has reached a conclusion. By pressing "Dismissal Form" the proper form appears.

Features such as these are included because the system is intended to be self-contained, helping the user with all aspects of dismissal. Most necessary desk accessories—

forms, mail, fax, telephones etc.—can be made accessible directly from the computer screen.

7. RELATED WORK

There exist a variety of proposals for how to represent vague legal concepts, e.g., fuzzy logic, probability, approximation, and examples. Some of the most commonly suggested have been compared and evaluated by Bench-Capon and Sergot [3]. Their analysis resulted in a proposal quite akin to the approach developed in this paper. They propose a representation based on general rules supplemented with examples of actual or stereotypical legal cases relevant to the vague legal concept in question. The general rules are induced from the cases and, in a sense, a case may be conceived as an example of how some general rule might be applied. In the system the rules may be used for retrieving the examples from a data base. Ideally, general rules should be automatically induced from legal cases but, as a "practical solution which we can adopt for the present," the authors suggest that the constructor of the system be responsible for abstracting and formalizing general rules. We agree in all essential with this proposal but there exists also another important class of rules. These are the rules based on the lawyer's practical knowledge of applying a concept and are used to identify relevant precedents. Our project has shown that rules belonging to this category suffice for creating a practical and quite powerful information-retrieval system for the legal domain. The awkward problem of inducing general rules from legal cases does not arise at the level of document-retrieval but only if we require the system to analyse, without user-consultation, the legal matter at issue by comparing it for similarity to previously adjudicated legal cases.

8. CONCLUSIONS AND FUTURE WORK

- Logic programming combined with data base technology and multimedia provides an appropriate environment for developing applications of this kind.
- Document management and computer reasoning can be used to create an "intelligent library," i.e., a library where the user gets active support for retrieving the texts relevant to his problem. This is strictly more powerful than hypertext which is a passive medium.

Some aspects of legal knowledge representation have been clarified:

- Legal vagueness is genuine and it is therefore fruitless to try to give the extent of vagueness as numbers.
- An adequate way, or at least a way that can acquire acceptance among lawyers, is to handle vagueness by decomposing a problem into manageable subquestions and automatically provide the text documents needed to answer these.

An additional conclusion is that the multimedia system opens the possibility to create a genuine legal work station. Necessary materials and tools can be made accessible directly in the computer: forms, letters, fax, telephones and even bookshelves in a library including law reports, legal writings etc.

REFERENCES

1. B. Atkinson, *Hypercard* (Cupertino, CA.: Apple Comp. Inc., 1987).

2. J. Barklund, A. Hamfelt, S.-Å. Tärnlund, "A Legal Reasoning Assistant," *Council of Europe, report by Swedish delegation: 9th Symp. on Legal Data Processing in Europe*, (Bonn 1989).

3. T. Bench-Capon, M. Sergot, "Toward a Rule-Based Representation of Open Texture in Law," *Computer Power and Legal Language* (ed. C. Walter) (Westport, Conn.: Greenwood Press, 1988), 39–60.

4. V. Bush "As we may think," *Atlantic Monthly* (July 1945): 101–8.

5. A. Colmerauer, H. Kanoui, M. van Caneghem, R. Pasero, P. Roussel, *Un Système de Communication Homme-Machine en Francais* (Marseille: Univ. Aix-Marseille II, 1973).

6. D.C. Engelbart, W.K. English, "A research center for augmenting human intellect," *AFIPS Conf. Proc. 33* (Montvale, N.J.: AFIPS Press, 1968).

7. A. Hamfelt, *The Multilevel Structure of Legal Knowledge and its Representation*, Uppsala Theses in Computing Science 8/90 (Uppsala: Uppsala University, 1990).

8. A. Hamfelt, J. Barklund, "Meta Levels in Legal Knowledge and their Runnable Representation in Logic," *Proc. 3rd Intl. Congress—Logica, Informatica, Diritto —Expert Systems in Law*, (1989), 557–76.

9. A. Hamfelt, J. Barklund, "Metaprogramming for Representation of Legal Principles," *Proc. Meta90 Workshop*, (1990), 105–22.

10. A. Hamfelt, P. Wahlgren, "Datorstödda beslut—Artificiell Intelligens och juridik," *IRI-rapport 1988:4*, (Stockholm, Univ. of Stockholm, 1988).

11. H. L. A. Hart, *The Concept of Law* (Oxford: Clarendon Press, 1961).

12. P. J. Hayes, "Some Problems and Non-Problems in Representation Theory," *Proc. AISB Summer Conf.*, (1974), 63–79.

13. N. K. Sundby, *Om normer*, (Oslo-Bergen-Tromsø: Universitetsforlaget, 1974).

14. J. Wünsche, *Integrating Prolog and a Multimedia Environment*, MSc thesis (Uppsala: Uppsala university, 1990).

HyperTeX - A System for the Automatic Generation of Hypertext Textbooks from Linear Texts

F. Sarre [*]   M. Seidt [*]   U. Güntzer [†]

June 15, 1990

Abstract

This paper reports on the HyperTeX system from which electronic textbooks have been produced. In order to reconstruct the implicit, network-like structure of a textbook, basic ideas of the hypertext concept were used to develop the system. HyperTeX consists of two parts: One component (HyperTeX/G) generates a hypertext structure from a textbooks's linear, machine-readable version and stores this strucutre in a relational database system, whereas the other component (HyperTex/B) provides for access to the hypertext textbook by means of a window- and mouse-oriented user interface.

HyperTeX/G's task is on the one hand to recognize which units from the input text form hypertext nodes, on the other hand to discover explicit and implicit interrelations automatically and to establish them as hypertext links. Although the resulting hypertext has a static character at first, its links can be altered dynamically by drawing conclusions from instances of use of the system. HyperTeX/B has the special feature that teaching material can be displayed on a high resolution graphic screen in full photo type setting quality. Still, each word and parts of formulae are mouse-sensitive in the raster graphic.

1 Introduction

If the definition of a certain concept has to be looked up in a textbook, it goes without saying that the whole book will not be read from the beginning to the end for this purpose alone. Rather, the table of contents or the index serve as a means of finding the desired text passage. However, concepts might occur in the definition, which are unknown and have to be looked up in their turn. Reading the appropriate text passages, the necessity of following references to examples etc. might then arise. At the latest, the fingers of one hand are not enough to be able to mark all the passages in the book that have to be read in a certain sequence ...

In reality, a textbook is not a simple sequence of words but a complex structure. In addition, it does not only contain references explicitly specified by the author (e.g. "see page 45", "see section 2.3.4" or "see definition of the concept *resolution*"), but also interrelations between text passages that the reader may have difficulty determining, because the author has not given any explicit hints. For example, the Peano axioms are set up in lecture notes about mathematical logic on page 54. However, supplementary explanations for these axioms are given on page 95. This (implicit) interrelation is not recognizable (explicitly) in the text.

When an author *writes* a textbook, it generally involves an effort to put down his knowledge about a complex field in a linear fashion. During this process, much information about the interrelations between concepts or pieces of knowledge gets lost. When a reader *reads* the document, many of these interrelations can only be reconstructed with difficulty. The conclusion is that the one-dimensional, sequential representation obviously is not the best method for storing or making knowledge available. Especially for a textbook, which can be considered as a knowledge base consisting of pieces of knowledge, there must be more preferable means of representing material than a single huge character string (figures, tables and formulas not re-

---

[*]Department of Computer Science, Technical University of Munich, P.O. Box 20 24 20, D – 8000 Munich 2, FRG.

[†]Wilhelm-Schickard-Institut, University of Tübingen, Auf der Morgenstelle 10, D – 7400 Tübingen, FRG.

garded). In addition, the "usual" reading of a textbook should be supported by a computer.

These deliberations led to the development of an electronic textbook. As an example, we chose a set of lecture notes [Gue89]. How the system designated "HyperTeX" works and what concepts it is based on will be explained in the following.

2   The Hypertext Concept

The basic ideas of the hypertext concept were integrated into the HyperTeX system. For this reason, a summary of the main characteristic qualities of hypertext systems follows:

- The information to be managed is broken up into units. These units ("chunks of information") are called nodes, notecards, frames or pages in the various systems.

- The information units are connected by links and the system aids the user in following these links by the system, often by means of a window- and mouse-oriented user interface.

- The system provides for retrieval possibilities.

- The user often has the possibility of annotating the text under consideration or of creating new links by himself.

These characteristics of hypertext systems lead to several advantages for both readers and authors, to name a few:

- Pieces of information can be structured in any way.

- Several passages can be looked at simultaneously.

- Interrelations between text passages can be made recognizable by links.

- An author is not forced to linearize the knowledge he wants to make available. He is able to set up cross references without chapter or section numbers.

For a further discussion we recomend [Con87].

3   The HyperTeX System

3.1   Requirements of an Electronic Textbook

In the introduction we already explained the deliberations that led to the development of a new system. The following requirements were laid down for the HyperTeX system:

- Text has to be displayed in small, logically coherent units.

- The hierarchical structure of the original text has to be reflected by special links. This decreases the disorientation.

- For all explicit references of the author links should be generated.

- In addition to the possibility of following links a full text search should be provided because it makes no sense to have links between almost every pair of text passages.

- The cognitive overhead should be as small as possible. This means that the user should not do things that the system can handle (e.g. closing windows that are not needed anymore).

- A certain analogy to the printed text should exist. Layout and position of the text units should correspond to the original text. This feature eases the "acclimatization" to the hypertext system.

- Reactions to the user's actions should occur as quickly as possible. Only this way can the user be encouraged to use the functionality of the system.

- Lecture notes in mathematics or chemistry make exacting demands on layout and formula type setting. The hypertext system has to meet these requirements on the text representation.

3.2   Consequences of the Requirement Catalogue

Many lecture notes are available in a machine-readable version. This makes it possible to convert these lecture notes to hypertext documents automatically. Creating a lecture notes' hypertext version from the beginning would be an enormous amount of work and therefore, would not take place in most cases. Because the document preparation system LaTeX [Lam86] is based on macros that allow the recognition of the logical structure of a document automatically, and because LaTeX has achieved a wide spreading within the university area, the problem of the automatic generation of hypertext documents from already existing LaTeX documents arises. At the same time, the multidimensional structure that exists implicitly in a given document has to be "dissected".

A comparison of the requirement catalogue above with the qualities of already existing hypertext systems shows that none of the systems approximates the features required. Especially the automatic generation of hypertext documents have not been found in systems known to the authors. This plainly indicates that such systems should be developed.

3.3 System Architecture

The HyperTeX system consists of two components, the hypertext structure generation module HyperTeX/G and the browser component HyperTeX/B. Both components have an interface to the relational database system TRANSBASE [Tra88] (see fig. 1). HyperTeX/G generates a hypertext structure from a textbook's linear, machine readable version and stores this structure in a relational database (see section 3.5). HyperTeX/B is a window- and mouse-oriented browser that presents the text on high resolution screens in full photo type setting quality (see section 3.6). Both components were implemented in the C programming language. The browser uses the SunView window system. HyperTeX runs on Sun3 and Sparc workstations.

3.4 Use of a Relational Database System for Managing the Hypertext Structure

In hypertext systems nodes and links have to be stored on a disk. Basically, three methods are commonly used:

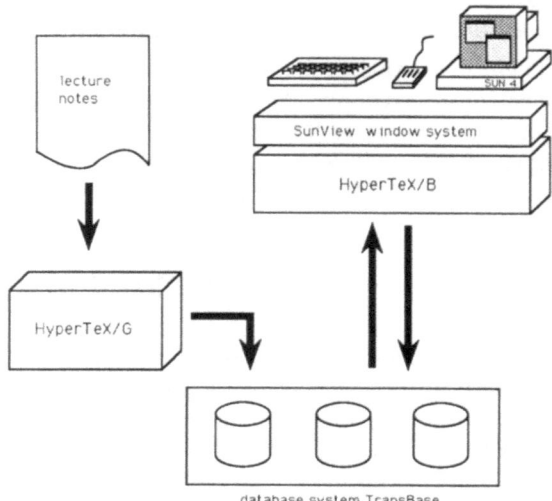

Figure 1: HyperTeX's system architecture

1. **Storage in the Standard File System**
   If the nodes are stored in the standard file system, every node can be stored in its own file as it is done, for example, in PlaneText, or all nodes are stored together in a single, huge file, as for example in NoteCards. Links are implemented as pointers that are in their turn stored in a separate file.

2. **Storage in a Database**
   Hypertext systems are often built upon a database, for example a relational database. The use of a relational database offers many advantages:

   - Fast access methods;
   - Transactions;
   - Well-tried mechanisms for locking and recovery;
   - Simultaneous use by several users.

   The systems "Intermedia" and "gIBIS" use relational database servers.

3. **Storage in a Special Network**
   The optimum solution with regard to access time is a specially developed network server that already "knows" about nodes and links. The first system based on this idea was "Neptune" [DeSc86].

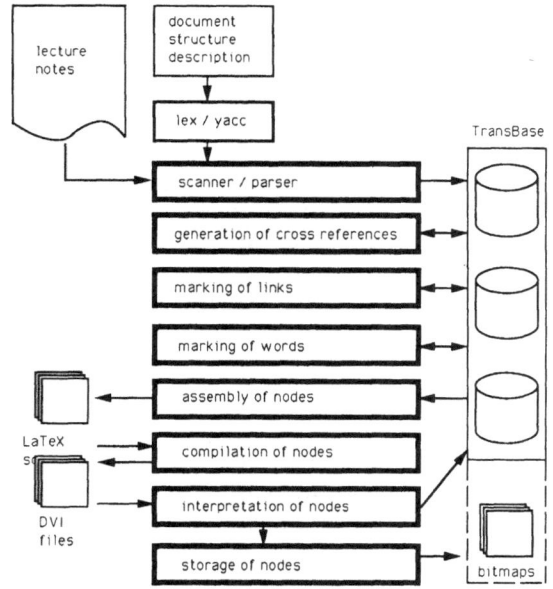

Figure 2: Process of a document's transformation into a hypertext structure

The HyperTeX system is based on the second approach, because a prototype could be implemented rather quickly with comparatively low expenditure. By doing this, we found that the combination of hypertext and database techniques is a promising approach for managing huge sets of interconnected pieces of information. As we use the database system TRANSBASE, a flexible query language is available, a superset of SQL. The demand on comprehensive full text retrieval possibilities could thus be easily met.

3.5 Transformation of a Set of Lecture Notes' Linear Version into a Hypertext Structure

The process of the document's transformation is shown in figure 2. It can be divided into the following steps executed one after the other:

1. **Breaking up the Original Text and Generating the Structure-Describing Links**
   First, the original document is analyzed by a parser generated by means of the UNIX tools LEX and YACC. The generation of the parser

```
document : cformseq BEG_DOCUMENT cformseq
    docbody END_DOCUMENT
    ;
docbody  : chapter
         | docbody chapter
         ;
    .
    .
    .
environ  : BEG_DFN subbody END_DFN
         | BEG_SATZ subbody END_SATZ ...
         ;
```

Figure 3: Example of a document structure description

is based on a document structure description in the form of a context-free grammar, which can be adapted to every document type. Figure 3 shows a cutting of such a grammar that refers to the lecture notes "Mathematische Logik" [Gue89].

The original document's text is broken up by the parser into single, hierarchically or sequentially connected nodes stored in their turn in several database relations.

2. **Generation of Cross References**
   Now links are created proceeding from explicit cross references. Methods for ascertaining implicit interrelations are being taken over from the HyperMan system [Sar90] at the present time.

3. **Marking Links and Words**
   Text passages have to be marked in order to be able to determine link and word positions later on. This kind of information is essential, if the user's mouse clicks for following a link or selecting a word are to be interpreted correctly.

4. **Assembly of Nodes**
   The node's source texts are extracted from the database and are compiled by means of LaTeX. The result of this compilation is a device-independent layout description.

5. **Interpretation of Nodes**

In the last step, the dvi files created by LaTeX are interpreted, in the course of which the exact word and link positions are determined by means of the markings inserted during step 3.) and raster graphics are created as well. The storage of the raster graphics in the database is projected [Elf90], but not implemented yet. Formating and interpreting the nodes just before they are displayed is still not possible with the hardware currently available because of insufficient performance.

3.6 HyperTeX's Window- and Mouse-oriented User Interface

The component HyperTeX/B forms the system's graphical user interface and combines the qualities of a simple hypertext browser with an extended window managment and a full text retrieval component. In order to facilitate fast responses to a user action (especially when following a link) a node cache that carries out and minimizes the database accesses by prefetching during waiting periods has been created. Following a link takes less than 0.5 seconds on a Sparc workstation due to the cache.

Windows for new nodes appear at certain positions on the screen depending on their type, for example, footnotes always appear below the corresponding window, whereby the window is shifted towards the top or made smaller, if necessary. The closing of windows not used anymore is done by the system in most cases. Windows not refered to and not activated for a longer time are closed automatically. However, the user has the possibility of influencing this mechanism by fixing or explicitly closing windows.

By means of a table of contents direct access to a desired node is possible. HyperTeX offers a standard and a detailed version of the table of contents. The standard table of contents exactly corresponds to the one that can be found in printed textbooks. In addition, the table of contents' detailled version lists all numbered theorems, definitions, examples and the like.

HyperTeX/B also offers a full text search. Within nodes any word can be selected and the search can be initiated. When search options are used, the search can be restricted to the first occurence, to definitions or, alternatively, a node with the most occurences of a given word can be found. Up to three search terms can be combined by AND, whereby the system assembles the appropriate SQL query from pre-made query units depending on the search options chosen and the terms selected. In order to get to a node of a certain type (for example to the next lemma) HyperTeX/B offers a special structure search.

4 Outlook

At the present time, HyperTeX is still a prototype system. However, we want to develop the system further, as will be explained in the following.

4.1 Annotations, User Links and Multi-User Operation

Many existing hypertext systems enable the user to annotate the text. Annotations are of great use especially for electronic textbooks, if the text has to be read a second time. An annotation can refer to a text passage by means of a link. In this context, the problem of how user links are managed has to be solved. Martin Hofmann suggests in [LaHo89] distinguishing between local and global hypertexts. If this were done, a user would have "private" links and annotations, and could also make them available to the public.

Another problem closely related to the ones just discussed is the multi-user operation; its introduction does not seem to pose many difficulties because the database system TransBase supports multi-user operation by locking mechanisms.

4.2 User Observation

The original lecture notes are not the only information source that can be used to gain knowledge about desirable properties of the hypertext system. The actions of every user of the system indirectly indicate its advantages and deficiencies. For this reason, the user should be observed while operating the system (it goes without saying anonymously) and his action should be recorded. An evaluation of the action can provide information

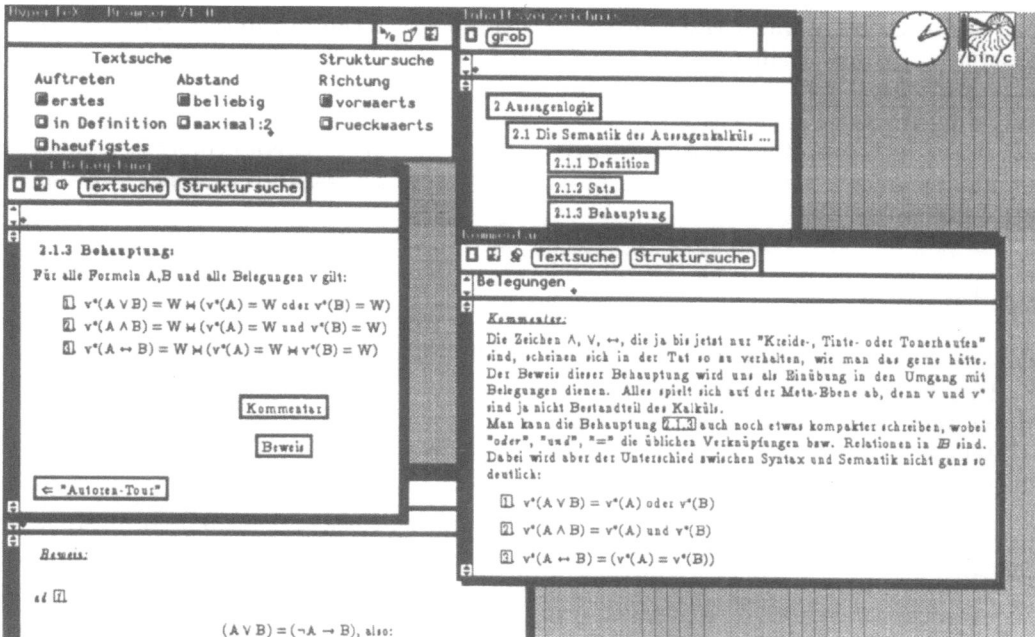

Figure 4: Snapshot during the work with HyperTeX

on how the system should be developed in the future.

In addition, the user observation can be utilized in several respects:

1. **Observation during the Following of a Link**

   If a certain sequence of links is traced many times, this suggests new interrelations within the document that can be utilized for the generation of new links implicitly defined by the users.

   The selection of a cross reference together with the dwelling time in the most recently activated node (which is not easy to measure) provides information about the quality of the cross reference.

2. **Activation Frequency of Nodes**

   The absolute frequency of a node being activated can give a hint on how much its content is relevant to the comprehension of the whole document.

   The relative frequency of usage of links from a fixed node to different destination nodes can give hints which nodes should be presented first to the user, if there are more than (say) three of them.

3. **Evaluation of Search Queries**

   Search queries give hints about interrelations for which links have not existed up to now in most cases. If the same search query is submitted sufficiently often, it can be materialized, that is, one or several links can be created.

   The frequent selection of search results in a certain sequence could cause the reordering of the materialized links, too.

4.3 Final Remarks

Finally, we would like to emphasize once again, that the HyperTeX system is not in the least intended to be a competitor for other research systems in the field of computer aided instruction (CAI). On the contrary, we wanted to show by means of our work that hypertext systems based on a relational database are, because of their performance, well-suited for applications in areas like electronic textbooks. In addition, we were interested in testing the usefulness of the concept of automatic transformation of linear texts into hypertext structures. A very challenging task was the integration of a text processing system like LaTeX into the hypertext node generation process in order to achieve full photo type setting quality for the original document, when the text is presented on the screen.

Acknowledgement

This work has been supported by the DFG (Deutsche Forschungsgesellschaft) within the project "Intelligent and Cooperative User Interfaces" (Intelligente und kooperative Benutzerschnittstellen).

References

[BoWe85] Borning, Alan H.; Weyer, Stephan A.: *A Prototype Electronic Encyclopedia.* ACM Transactions on Office Information Systems, Volume 3, No 1, January 1985, p. 63–88.

[Bus45] Bush, Vannevar: *As we may think.* Atlantic Monthly 176, 1, July 1945, p. 101–108.

[Con87] Conklin, Jeff: *Hypertext: An Introduction and Survey.* Revision 2, December 1987.

[DeSc86] Delisle, Norman; Schwartz, Mayer: *Neptune: A Hypertext System for CAD Applications.* Proceedings of ACM SIGMOD, International Conference of Management of Data, Washington D.C. p. 132–143, May 28–30, 1986.

[Elf90] Elfinger, Ralf: *Effiziente Verwaltung von Pixel-Graphiken in relationalen Datenbanken.* Diplomarbeit, Technische Universität München, to appear Nov. 1990.

[Gue89] Güntzer, U.; Schmidt, G.; Kempf M.; Möller B.: *Mathematische Logik.* TUM-Info Juli 1989, Technische Universität München, München 1989.

[Hah89] Hahn Andreas: *Entwurf und Implementierung einer hypertext-ähnlichen Oberfläche für die UNIX-Manuale als Beispiel einer kooperativen Benutzerschnittstelle.* Diplomarbeit, Technische Universität München, November 1989.

[Lam86] Lamport,Leslie: LaTeX : *A Document Preparation System.* Addison-Wesley, Sept. 1986.

[LaHo89] *Das Hypertextsystem CONCORDE.* Ed.: Langendörfer, H.; Hofmann, M., Informatik-Bericht 89-06 der Technischen Universität Braunschweig, December 1989.

[Nel88] Nelson, Theodor H.: *Managing Immense Storage.* BYTE, January 1988, p. 225–238.

[SaGu89] Sarre, Frank; Güntzer, Ulrich: *Einsatz von Hypertextsystemen für Dokumentationen technischer Systeme am Beispiel der UNIX-Manuale.* Proceedings of the GI-Fachtagung "Interaktive Schnittstellen für Informationssysteme", Clausthal-Zellerfeld, Nov. 1989, p. 133–148.

[Sar90] Sarre, F.: *Automatic Transformation of Linear Texts into Hypertext.* (to be published)

[Sei90] Seidt, Markus: *Einsatz von Hypertext-Techniken für die Realisierung eines intelligenten Zugangssystems zu einem Skriptum über mathematische Logik.* Diplomarbeit, Technische Universität München, January 1990.

[Tra88] TransAction Software GmbH.: *Transbase Relational Database System, Version 3.3*; TransAction Software GmbH, München, 1988.

A Hypertext Database Model for Information Management in Software Engineering

Sahar Jarwa   Marie-France Bruandet

Laboratoire Génie Informatique LGI - IMAG
BP 53X 38041 Grenoble Cedex   France

ABSTRACT

This paper presents a basic data model for a hypertext database that manages software information produced throughout the software life-cycle. This information is software documentation and programs (e.g. requirement documents, specification documents, test specification documents, source and object codes, etc). Our objective is to constitute an efficient aid in the development and the maintenance activities using an integrated engineering information system.

We propose an Object-Oriented data model supporting hypertext features. Documents and programs are modeled as composite objects, and links are supported between documentation fragments, between program fragments and between documentation and programs. The model aims to provide a definition of the semantics of hypertext links including a support for composite objects with shared components, and to distinguish hypertext composition links from simple ones. In addition to these static aspects, the model expresses the dynamic behaviour of objects and their evolution over time, e.g. version management and side effect propagation after updating code or documentation. In order to locate fragments of documents relevant to user's requests, information retrieval by content in addition to database-like queries and hypertext information navigation is supported.

INTRODUCTION

The main problem facing software maintenance is poor documentation. Documentation when present usually consists of a set of unstructured information which is difficult to be accessed, impossible to be maintained and out-of-date comparing with source code.

Viewing software development as an integrated information management problem, our purpose is to define a data model which should de able to represent and manage software documentation and code in a unified manner. Information management referred to here is the combination of hypertext, database and information retrieval aspects in a unique model taking the dynamic behaviour of documents and their evolution over time into account.

Life-cycle of a software is often considered as a sequence of phases[6, 17], each one depending on others : requirement definition, specification definition, software design, software implementation, software integration and test, and software maintenance. Information produced at each level of a software life-cycle is represented by documents validated at the end of this level and consulted in subsequent phases. The final product of a software development process is then a set of documents containing the information (documentation and code) produced and used during the software development. This information will be referred to as software database.

The hypertext systems seem to provide an appropriate environment for information management in software engineering applications [5, 15]. However, most hypertext databases implicitly use a directed graph data model, not powerful enough to meet related software database management requirements.

In this paper we propose a basic object-oriented data model for hypertext databases, in which documents are represented as structured objects. Semantics are provided to hypertext structural links in order to distinguish them from simple references between objects. Event-action rules are supported to maintain hypertext database consistency after modifying some hypertext objects. The model presented here is the basic layer of the project ELEN [8] whose objective is to give a suitable environment for software maintenance activities.

The paper is organized as follows : the following section identifies features needed for managing documents in a software engineering environment and gives a brief discussion on existing information management systems. Section 3 gives a short overview of hypertext systems; attention is focussed on their need for an explicit data model able to support software database features. Section 4 describes the basic data model that supports a number of issues and abstraction mechanisms, and uses it to model the software environment. In Section 5 and 6 special attention is given to dynamic aspects in software database management such as versions control and database consistency maintenance. Implementation issues are presented briefly in section 7.

DESIRABLE FEATURES FOR SOFTWARE DOCUMENT MANAGEMENT

Software environment is a type of an application that is not well supported by traditional information management systems. Below, we will identify some specific requirements to be met to manage software databases.

First, software components are highly structured entities. Documentation like programs should be organised as structured objects; documentation is recursively made up of a number of text fragments (chapters, sections, etc) and programs are constructed as a number of source code fragments (modules, procedures, variable declarations, etc). A collection of components has to be structured in a single hierarchy to constitute a logical unit, and documentation as well as programs should appear at their various abstraction levels.

Moreover, fragments of documents may be referenced as components in more than one document. For example, a fragment of text may be found in both requirement and specification documents, a procedure may be found in several programs. The ability of structured documents to share components is one of the software database objectives.

Further, software components are highly interrelated, so relationships should be provided between documentation fragments, between program fragments, and between documentation and programs. For example, a specification document is related to the design document of the same software component, a portion of specification is related to the code implementing it, etc. These relationships may be used extensively in data navigation to locate users' requests. Another interesting aspect of these relationships concerns the propagation of changes made in a program to all documents referencing this program in order to maintain documentation and programs consistency and actuality.

In addition, software components and their structure may change over time, so that, several versions of a software and its documents may exist simultaneously. Each version may be either created from scratch or derived from some existing version. Version control is an important aspect in a software database. However, this raises an important problem, that of ensuring consistency between versions of linked entities. In fact a software database should be active in the sense that it should automatically execute specified actions when specified events occur, providing thus a mechanism for maintaining consistency within interrelated data.

Finally, managing documents in software engineering involves retrieval of documents relevant to user's request. Because of the great amount of information and its textual nature, it must be possible to retrieve documents by their content. One of the system's objectives is to introduce information retrieval mechanisms and to combine them with hypertext information navigation and with database-like queries based on software components description.

Originally, software engineering environments supported an incomplete collection of software tools that managed traditional file systems. These often did not provide wide range of data management facilities and did not support operations on the hierarchical structure of programs and documents. Moreover, they neither supported the automation of software maintenance activities, nor the integration of software components and tools.

Database management systems support such features [10, 19]. They can efficiently store a large amount of structured data, and provide desirable characteristics including data sharing, data integrity, and consistency of data with its type definition. They constitute a support for high-level data access and retrieval operations. While supporting most information management features, current database systems do not support some important ones. For example, database systems do not support arbitrary connections between pieces of data, therefore, data navigation is impossible. Hypertext systems have recieved much attention in software engineering environment in recent years [5, 15]; its power lies in combining database methods that provide a way for directly accessing data, and interface modality that allows the user to browse the documents and traverse the links. In the next chapter, a brief overview of hypertext systems is presented but attention is focussed on their need for an explicit and more powerful data model to support software database features.

HYPERTEXT INSUFFICIENCY FOR SOFTWARE ENVIRONMENT

Hypertext is a structuring mechanism for information [4], which is particularly well suited for an interactive computer. Hypertext is not a new idea, a first proposal, the "memex" system, has been designed by Bush in 1945. Actually, some commercial systems are available such as Schneiderman's hyperties, and the Xerox's NoteCards. Commercial interest has led to an explosion in the development of hypertext systems. Hypertext permits the user to track down information by taking non-linear paths through text and to link a variety of documents in novel ways. Traditionally, hypertext or hypermedia systems are composed of nodes containing information fragments (such as textual information, graphics, bitmapped images, etc) and links representing relationships among them.

The implicit model in many hypertext systems is based on the labelled directed graph. A user browsing a hypertext, traverses the graph and views information fragments as he visits nodes. However, the simplicity of the model does not represent the structure of data adequately. Particularly, it does not allow many structures to be superimposed over a set of fragments or a fragment to be shared among nodes within a single structure. Generally, the basic hypertext or hypermedia model lacks a composition mechanism, e.g. a means of representing and dealing with groups of nodes and links as a unique abstract entity instead of just being an arbitrary collection of nodes. This leads to accounting the difference between *reference* links and *composition* links. Contrary to a reference link which is a looser one, a composition link implies that operations on the whole entity (e.g creation, deletion) will affect the components entities as well.

Another area which was not adequately been investigated by hypertext researchers is the consideration of typed information. For example, one may desire to ensure that all projects have the same structure (type) of documents which allows standardization of documents across projects. This captures the notion that information is created according to predefined structures and the system provide integrity checkers to ensure that information structure is consistent with its type definition. In addition to standardization purposes, explicit modeling of such structures helps in comprehending the layout of large networks, especially for the user not to be lost when navigating and browsing such networks.

Moreover, most (if not all) hypertext systems do not consider the problems related to maintaining their database consistency, wich is crucial to a software environment. In fact, changing an object in a hypertext database may have some side effects on the objects that refer to it. Hypertext databases must be active, that is, it must be possible to propagate modification side effects.

Finally, the user often needs to find all text fragments on a given topic, for example, text fragments talking about a certain module functionality. This concept lacks although it is basic to many retrieval requests. Information navigational access is adequate for a large number of applications, but becomes problematic when the application is characterized by a large, heterogeneously structured network. One solution to this problem as proposed in [7] is to augment navigation by a more efficient query-based access mechanism. The query mechanism would be composed of two kinds of searches : *structure search* and *content search*. The development of a structure search mechanism involves the definition of a more formal model for hypertext database. Content search involves the introduction of information retrieval system functionalities in order to locate documents relevant to users requests [3]. Actually, some researchers are beginning to realize the need for a more formal structure (e.g. [20, 21]).

The work described in this paper attempts to model data. This model which constitutes the kernel for the ELEN project is based on an object-oriented approach. It cannot be viewed as a complete model for a hypertext system, but an attempt to introduce mechanisms by which some important abstractions could be supported in a hypertext [4]. Special attention is given to the dynamic features in a software environment, therefore, a versioning model is studied and an event-action mechanism is provided to maintain consistency of software project components.

DATA MODEL FOR HYPERTEXT DATABASE

A Basic Data Model

In order to integrate software structured objects, their relationships and software tools and activities, our attention is focussed on semantic and object-oriented database models[2, 12, 13, 16]. This model [9] provides a mix of value-oriented and object-oriented semantics of data. In addition to its static aspects the model supports the objects' behaviour which constitute the dynamic aspects of objects.

The real world entities used and produced during software life-cycle are modeled as identified **objects**, to each object is assigned a value that describes it, it stands for its properties, its children in the hierachical structure and the other objects it refers to. Briefly, we can say an object is a concept which stands for hypertext nodes, it has an **identifier** by which it is accessed or referenced.

Objects are created according to a predefined type schemas, the object **type** concept is used to specify a common structure and a common behaviour to a collection of objects.

In addition to conventional types : integer, real, boolean, string, etc, we consider several other **basic types** in order to construct and to manage complex objects (documents, programs). These basic types include :

• *Text* and *Graphic* types which represent document content,

• *SourceCode* which represents program fragments,

• *ObjectCode* and *ExecCode* which represent object and executable codes related to source code,

• *IndexTerm* which represents indexing termes related to a text fragment in order to include the semantics of document content. This constitutes a minimal support to introduce information retrieval functionalities in database systems. Indexing terms can be generated automatically or be defined manually, but that is not the issue here(see [3, 18] for more details).

Applying a set of **type constructors** (*tuple, set, list*) to basic types we can obtain **constructed types**. A type constructor is defined as a data structuring operator to which is associated a set of data access operations.

The types are structured as an **inheritance hierarchy** that defines each type as a subtype of another one by means of the IsA relationship, we consider a predefined global supertype *Object* as a root of this hierarchy, it represents characteristics and behaviour shared by all objects.

A type definition includes the **name** of the type, the name of its **supertype**, a set of **attributes** that describe objects of this type and a set of **methods** which can be applied to these objects. Attributes reflect the static state of objects while methods may support dynamic behaviour and actions performed on objects such as software activities (compiling, editing, etc).

To each attribute is associated a **cardinality** indicating the minimal number of elements associated to the object as attribute values, e.g. an objects' attribute with 0 as cardinality means that the object may have no such attribute. By default, attributes are considered to have a cardinality of one.

Attribute values may be given by the user, they may also be obtained from the operating system (e.g. creation date, user name) or by some method activation (e.g. indexing terms associated to text, object code associated to source code). This last aspect provides a support for derived data which is particularly important in a software environment because a significant amount of information in a software system is derived.

Attribute values may be **atomic values** representing properties of the object, they may also be **identified objects** related to the considered object by links.

For example, a specification document has some properties such as Author, CreationDate, etc, it is composed of several chapters that constitute its components and it is related to the program that it specifies. Properties of a specification document are values of basic or constructed types associated to the document, its components need to be considered as identified objects to be referenced and shared by other objects, but the document should still be treated as a whole. The program is an independent object but related to its specification document in order to evolve with it.

To support these different cases we provide three kinds of attributes : **prop** attributes, **comp** attributes, **ref** attributes.

• **Prop** attributes are values of basic or constructed types, they are not identified objects. They stand for object properties of database models in their conventional form, and provide the value-oriented semantics for data. By default, all attributes are taken to be **prop** attributes unless otherwise specified. For example, the field "editDate : *Date*" in *SpecDoc* type definition (see figure 1) represents a value of type *Date* associated to a specification document object, this value is not an identified object, and therefore it cannot be referenced from elsewhere in the database. If a specification document is deleted its associated date value is also deleted.

• **Comp** attributes are used to declare an object as a part of another object. This captures the composition links between a parent object and its components and allows to link a collection of objects to constitute a **composite object**. A comp attribute value is an identified object with the additional constraint that it is owned by the objects that refer to it as a component. Being an identified object, a component can be referenced from elsewhere in the database. Contrary to exclusive semantics of component objects first proposed in ORION [11] which we do not find acceptable for a logical structure, we allow an object to be a component of more than one parent object (the later paper [12] eliminate this shortcoming in ORION). The possibility of refering to an object by more than one composition link provides a support for composite objects with shared components which constitutes an important aspect in software databases (see section 2).

The existence of a component is dependent on the existence of objects that refer to it as a component, this means that, if a composite object is deleted, all its components must also be deleted except those referenced as components of other existing objects. One example of composite objects is specification documents of type *SpecDoc* given in figure 1; chapters of a document are parts of it, they belong to it, but they should still be treated as identified objects and may be referenced by other objects in the database. It is also possible to consider them as components of another document.

• **Ref** attributes are used to represent simple references between objects. When an attribute is defined as a **ref** attribute, it represents simply a reference to another independent and identified object. No deletion semantics is associated to it, that is, the deletion of an object does not cause the automatic deletion of its referenced objects. These attributes are used to model simple references between software objects. For example, the field "specify : **ref** *Module*" in the definition of *ModuleDesc* type (see figure 1) represents a simple reference between a module specification and the object of type *Module* implementing it.

In fact, **ref** and **comp** attributes stand for hypertext links, and provide them with different semantics while **prop** attributes stand for node's attributes in hypertext.

To summarize, the proposed model is a semantic model, it supports a mix of value-oriented semantics of data provided by **prop** attributes and object-oriented semantics of data provided by **comp** and **ref** attributes. In addition to simple references provided between objects, it includes a support for representing composite objects with shared components. This allows us to take into account the difference between *reference* links and *composition* links in a hypertext database.

The complexity of our proposal resides in the project manager's task of data type specification, but he does not need to be aware of that if he only wants to use predefined data types which will be described in the next section. In fact, predefined types help in defining some project standards (see figure 1) which is possible to be modified when needed.

```
Type SpecDoc                    Type ModuleDesc
  IsA Document                    IsA Document
  (                               (
  title : Text                    title : Text
  introduction : comp Text        introduction : comp Text
  ch1 : comp GenDesc              parag1 : (0)comp InputDesc
  ch2 : comp InfoDesc             parag2 : (0)comp OutputDesc
  ch3 : comp FunDesc              parag3 : comp FunctionDesc
  ch4 : comp NonFunDesc           parag4 :(0)comp LimitsDesc
  annex : (0)[ comp Annex ]       specify: ref Module
  biblio : comp Bibliographic     )
  editDate : Date
  )

Type FunDesc                    Type InputDesc
  IsA Document                    IsA Document
  (                               (
  title : Text                    content : Text
  sections:[ comp ModuleDesc ]    title : Text
  specify : ref Program           definedBy : (0)ref Interface
  )                               )
```

figure-1

Application to Software Engineering

During its life-cycle, a software project generates a set of objects of different nature : programs, documentation, object and executable codes, etc. Using the above outlined data model we are studying concepts describing software objects and its relationships.

A software **project** is a composite object having specific characteristics, its components are a set of programs and documents (see figure 2).

```
Type Project
  IsA Object
  (
  projectName : String
  Date : Date
  director : String
  partners : [ String ]
  period : Integer
  programs : [ comp Program ]
  documentation : [ comp Document ]
  executables : [ comp ExecCode ]
  )
```

figure-2

Programs are objects of a big size so it is convenient to consider them as composite objects. The problem resides in components granularity choosing. For example, one may consider instructions to be the lowest level of program decomposition. But this causes an important problem of efficiency because of the large number of resulting objects.

```
Type Program
  IsA Source
  (
  modules : [ comp Module ]
  implements : ref DesignDoc
  manual : ref Manual
  commentedBy : (0)ref ImplNote
  executable : ref ExecCode
  )
```

figure-3

Some software engineering environments [1] offer a reasonable solution in taking the **module** as the lowest degree of granularity, the module concept is used here in the sense of modular programming languages such as ADA and Modula2. In this manner a **program** is defined as a set of modules (see figure 3) and is related to its documentation by reference attributes.

```
Type Module
  IsA Source
  (
  hasInterface : (0)comp Interface
  hasRealisation : comp Realisation
  implements : ref ModuleDesign
  commentedBy : ref CommModule
  dependsOn : (0) [ ref Module ]
  )
Type Interface
  IsA Source
  (
  uses : (0) [ ref Interface ]
  content : SourceCode
  )
Type Realisation
  IsA Source
  (
  uses : (0)[ ref Interface ]
  content : SourceCode
  )
```

figure-4

Each **module** is composed of an interface and a realisation. The **interface** is the visible part of the module. It generally includes declaration of its external procedures, variables, types, constants, etc, which are possibly used by other modules. The **realisation** of a module is its private portion; generally it is the body of the exported procedures, e.g. procedures defined by the interface (see figure 4).

Notice that modules are related using *dependsOn* relationship which is a reference attribute; a module is dependent on another module if it uses resources defined by that module. A dependency relationship defines an acyclic graph with modules as nodes and dependence links as arcs. This relationship may be calculated automatically by analysing the source code of modules.

The previous description shows that programs are composite objects, their basic components are objects of type *SourceCode* which represent their content. These features are represented in our data model, as shown above, using the predefined types *Program, Module, Interface, Realisation*. These are subtypes of type *Source*, a type defining all common characteristics of program components, e.g. programming language, operating system, programmers, etc.

Notice that the given definitions in previous figures represent only static aspects of the type definition, and there must be some defined methods associated to each type.

Documentation is also represented by composite objects, they have a hierarchical composition structure with objects of type *Text* as leaves to represent their content. All documentation types are subtypes of *Document*; a type defining characteristics and operations common to all documents, e.g. editing, formatting, printing. To each **document** is associated a set of indexing terms that represent the semantics of its content. Indexing terms are associated to leaves and deduced automatically for higher levels of document hierarchy [3]. To represent documentation associated to programs we define several types of documents, e.g. *SpecDoc, DesignDoc, Manual, ImplNotes*. Figure 1 shows an example of these documents.

Relationships exist between documentation and programs at different levels of their composition hierarchy, for example, a program is associated to its design document as a whole, but each module is associated also to its design which is a part of the program's design. Links between documentation and programs are of great interest; they allow the user to navigate between them and are used to maintain documentation and programs consistent and up-to-date.

VERSIONS

Basic Version Model

Software components (documents, programs) may evolve during their life-cycle for different reasons such as software development, error correction, software portability, software maintenance, etc. Keeping different versions is crucial to a sofware database. The ability of keeping several versions in a manner semantically suitable for the application is an important problem. This leads us to consider a set of versions for each object in order to capture its history or to support parallel developments of an object. We define an object version to be *an identifiable state of this object.* In this model we are in a position to define the semantics of versions at a level closer to the application domain.

In software engineering all objects are versionable. Versions are either totally ordered as a function of time, or partially ordered in terms of another development consideration. In practice, software objects evolve as follows :

A given object (document, program) may have a sequence of versions which stands for its evolution over time (e.g. error corrections, successive refinements, etc). Each version is **derived** from the previous one in the sequence by copying it and then performing desired modifications in its content. The derived version may replace its predecessor because it has a more "complete" or a more "correct" content. Derived versions of an object are often called **revisions**. A revision is an object which has basically the same semantics of content as in the original one, with few changes.

However, linear derivations are insufficient because in practice several versions may be derived from an existing version, this stands for parallel evolution of the same original object using different design strategies, or different ways to correct design errors. To support this kind of evolution we consider a **derivation tree** for each object .

Precedent concepts are not capable of expressing all forms of evolution, they do not represent parallel and independent developments of an object (e.g. programs written in different programming languages; those using different algorithms; documents written in English and in French; etc). In practice, each object may evolve in **several derivation trees**, the root of each tree is created from scratch and then has a different content comparing with roots of other trees. However, they have some invariants. In the example of a program implemented using different algorithms, resulting programs are functionnaly equivalent so they have the same specification document, but each program has evolved separately then it has its own derivation tree.

To gather up versions of an object, and to model their shared properties and invariants, we introduce the concept of **generic object**. A generic object (represented by the ellipse in figure 5) can be considered as an additional level of abstraction by which a collection of objects is referenced. This captures the essential similarity between the revisions of an object. The generic object describes the version structure (children, default version, last created version), and the invariants of the object. When a generic object is deleted, all its instances are deleted too. In addition, referencing a generic object means referencing its

default version. The default version is considered to be the last version created in the absence of user specified default version. Since all objects are versionable, each object (**revision**) must specify its original version, its descendants, e.g. derived versions, the creation date, the user who created it, etc. When no original is specified for an object it is considered to be the root of a derivation tree.

The previous concepts are illustrated in figure 5; objects *id1*, *id2* and id3 represent three derivation trees for the same object. They are grouped by the generic object identified by *id* which is represented by the ellipse. Nodes represent the revisions of the object, and arcs between nodes represent the derivation relationship. Note that *id11* and *id111* are the result of successive derivations of *id1*, while *id11* and *id12* are the result of parallel derivations of *id1*.

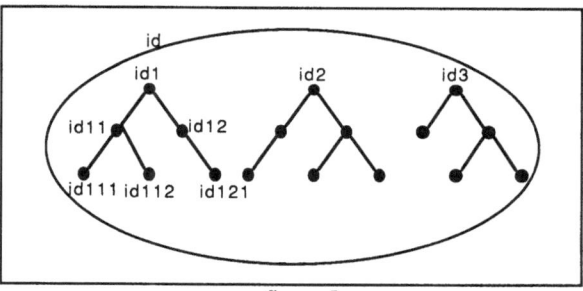

figure-5

Versions of Composite Objects

Since a generic object gathers all its versions, several composition links may exist between a parent and a child generic object. In order to extend the semantics of composite objects to generic objects, we can view all these composition links as a single one between the two generic objects. This defines composition links between generic objects and captures the semantics of composite objects to the more general **generic composite object**.

A particular version of a generic composite object, called a **configuration**, is defined by *the choice of a list of versions, one for each of its component generic objects.* The list of component versions may be specified *explicitly* by the user, or generated *automatically* by choosing the default version of each component or its current version. This list may also be specified using a logical expression based on version attribute values.

CHANGE SIDE EFFECT PROPAGATION

In a hypertext database an object may refer to any number of other objects. Because of the complexity of interconnection defined between objects, it is important that the consistency of the database be maintained automatically. Changes in referenced objects (e.g. updating, deletion, version creation) may have some side effects on objects that refer to it. In fact, a hypertxt database manager, especially in a software environment, must be active, that is, it must be able to control side effects of object modifications.

For example, updating a design document may imply modifications to be done in the code implementing it. Side effects of object modifications should be analysed, and the user must be notified of the possibly effected objects. There are cases where some actions are to be executed when specified events arise in order to maintain the reference consistency of objects. For example, a module modification may cause the recompilation of its dependent modules, and significant modifications in a document may imply a new indexing process.

The mechanism used here is similar to the so called Event-Action [3]. It is based on **Event-Condition-Action** (ECA) rules that define how to react to changes occurring on referenced objects. Rules, as methods, are associated to objects and described in their type definition. They are activated using links between objects. Links are used here by referenced objects as channels to propagate side effects of changes. *If there is no link between two objects the modification of one object can have no consequences on the other.*

A rule is defined as follows : **when** event **do if** condition **then** action **done**;

Rules may have no condition : **when** event **do** action **done**;

The semantics of a rule is defined as follows : when the event occurs and the rule condition is verified, rule action is executed in order to maintain the reference consistency between the object causing the event and the object containing the rule.

The **event** notion is associated to a change in an object status. A change in an object status means a change in one or more of its attribute values, which is the result of the activation of some associated method. If there is no relationship between the modified object and other objects in the database, no event is produced. An event is caracterized then by the name of the method which changed the object status, and the relationship used to propagate the change. The produced event and the context in which the event is produced is represented by an *event signal.* This holds, in addition to the event, information about it such that : the changed object, the activation date of the method which causes the change and the user who activated the method. This information is used to bind the parameters of the triggerred rule.

To control side effect propagation, we define the primitive **Propagate** which is responsible for event signal production. This primitive will be added to the method body by the project manager, who decides if the method activation should cause side effects. Since we consider that relationships are responsible of side effect propagation, the Propagate primitive must have as parameters the list of relationships (for which the modified object is a destination) used to produce events. If all relationships are concerned *All* is used as parameter of the primitive Propagate.

The rule **condition** is a logical expression, it may have variables to be bound to the actual values of the event signal. The condition is evaluated when the rule is triggered by its event.

Action is one or a combination of the following :

• a message sent to the user to notify him about the possibly affected objects or to ask him what to do in the actual situation.

• a message sent to the object to activate some associated method in order to maintain the database consistency. In this case, the method arguments are bound to the actual arguments of the event signal.

Action activation may maintain the object reference consistency by activating environment tools, it may undo the action causing the event using the predefined primitive *undo.*

For example, the rule illustrated in figure 6, which is associated to objects of type *Realisation,* express the fact that : if an interface is modified, all realisations (modules) that use this interface (e.g. realisations related to the interface by "uses" relationship) should be compiled. If the compilation of a module fails, the corresponding event is recorded in the module and the user is notified. This rule is triggerred by events of the form *(modify, uses)* .

```
Rules
When (modify, uses) do
            If not (compile $Self) then (recordEvent $Self);
                                        (assignAtt $Self 'state
                                        'ModifiedInterface);
                                        (tellUser "The module" $Self
                                        "must be modified because
                                        of the modification of" $D );
            fi
done
```

figure-6

Suppose that the method *modify* is activited at time *Date* by the user *User* on the interface I, and that the module M uses the interface I. If the method *modify* includes the primitive *propagate(uses)* in its body, an event signal *(modify, uses, I, Date, User)* is produced. This signal matches the event part of the rule of figure 6, associated to objects of type *Realisation.* The variable $Self, of the Condition and the Action parts of the rule, is bound to the actual value, that is, the module M recieving the event signal. The variable $D in the Action side of the rule is bound to the actual value I of the event signal. We assume for the moment that, for a certain object and an event signal, there is at most one matched rule. In the general case where several rules are matched, the database manager should provide some strategy to automatically order and activate them.

In fact using ECA rules many features may be expressed, e.g. version consistency, integrity constraints, access permissions, derived data control.

IMPLEMENTATION

We are currently implementing an object manager based on the defined data model using Loops. Loops is an Object-Oriented programmig language. It is used to build an additional level that implements our data model features. This level provides the hypertext system with the abstraction mechanisms defined by the data model. Object manager provides integrity checkers to ensure that object structures are consistent with their type definitions. In addition to static aspects of objects, the object manager control object consistency using ECA rules. Objects of the database correspond directly to nodes in a hypetext. Composite and reference attributes of objects are represented using hypertext links with predefined semantics on them. The hypertext used here is NoteCards. NoteCards is a hypertext system fully integrated in Xerox Lisp programming environment [29]. It allows users to formulate and structure ideas by providing them with a semantic network of electronic notecards interconnected by typed links. Navigation is the primary means for accessing information in NoteCards, but it also provides a limited search facility that can locate all notecards matching some user specification. In order to have a complete hypertext system, our user hypertext interface must provide the defined database operations to directly manipulate objects of the database.

CONCLUSION

In this paper we have presented the main concepts of our model. Work in hypertext systems has influenced our ideas in this article [4, 5, 7]. We also have taken into account related work on Object-Oriented databases [2, 12, 13] and on software engineering [1]. The aim of this model is to understand the different abstractions we can define to overcome the semantics of composite objects and the dynamic aspects of documents and programs. Using Event-Condition-Action rules, the model ensures the consistency between objects in the software hypertext database.

To increase the search capability of NoteCards limited to navigation, more investigations are necessary using database and information retrieval search facilities.

In order to constitute a support for information retrieval in a dynamic context, we count on using the Event-Action mechanism to maintain the consistency between documents and its indexing terms. More research is to be done in order to automatically deduce new indexing terms by indexing the difference between document versions.

In this paper we did not investigate other standard database features which must also be covered, e.g., object persistence, transaction management, recovery, etc. Moreover, a query language that combines database, content search, and hypertext aspects should be proposed as a subsequent step to this work.

REFERENCES

[1] BELKHATIR N. & ESTUBLIER J., Nomade : Noyau de Maintenance et de Developpement, Proc. Int. Workshop in Software Engineering and its Application, Toulouse, France, Decembre5-9, 1988, pp. 151-167.

[2] CAREY M. J., DEWITT D. J., VANDENBERG S. L., A Data Model and Query Language for EXODUS, Proc. ACM SIGMOD, Chicago, June 1-3, 1988.

[3] CHIARAMELLA Y., BRUANDET M. F., DEFUDE B., KERKOUBA D., IOTA: a Full-Text Information Retrieval System, in Proc. of SIGIR Conference on Research and Development in Information Retrieval, Pisa, Italy, 1986.

[4] GARG P.K., Abstraction Mechanisms in Hypertext; Communications of the ACM, Vol. 31, No. 7, July 1988.

[5] GARG P. G. & SCACCHI W., A Software Hypertext Environment, Int. Workshop on Software Version and Configuration Control, ACM, Jan. 1988, Grassau FRG.

[6] Software Engineering Handbook, Staff of General Electric Company, McGraw-Hill, 1986.

[7] HALASZ F.G., Reflections on NoteCards : Seven Isues for the Next Generation of Hypermedia System; Communications of the ACM, Vol. 31, No. 7, July 1988.

[8] JARWA S. & CHEVALLET J.P., Spécification d'ELEN un système pour la gestion et l'interrogation de document et de logiciel, Second Internqtional workshop, Software Engineering and its Applications, Toulouse, 4-8 december, 1989.

[9] JARWA S. & BRUANDET M.F., An Object-Oriented Model for Hypertext Databases : Application to Document Management in Software Engineering, Aristote Report, RAP004, January 1990.

[10] KATZ R. H., A Database Approch for Managing VLSI Design Data, Proc. 19th ACM/IEEE Designe Automation Conference, LAs Vegas, NV., June 1982.

[11] KIM W., BERTINO E. & Garza J.F., Composite Object Revisited, Proc. ACM-SIGMOD'89.

[12] KIM W. et al., Composite Object Support in an Object-Oriented Database System, Proc. 2nd OOPSLA Conf., Orlando, FL, 1987.

[13] LECLUSE C., RICHARD P., O2 an Object Oriented Data Model, Rapport Altaïr 10-87, Novembre, 1987.

[14] McCARTHY D.R. & DAYAL U., The Architecture of an Database management System, ACM SIGMOD'89.

[15] NORMAN M. D. & MAYER D. S., Context- A Partitionning Cocept for Hypertext, ACM trans. of Office Information Systems, Vol. 5, N°2, Apr. 1987, pp. 168-186.

[16] PILLAMARRI M. K., Toward a Semantic Data Model Based on Object-Oriented and Entity-Relationship Concepts, M. S., Departement of Electrical Engineering, University of Florida, December 1987.

[17] ROGER S. PRESSMANN, Software Engineering A Partitionner's Approch, 2eme Edition, Roger S. Pressmann, McGraw-Hill, 1987.

[18] SALTON G., McGILL M. J., Introduction to Modern Information Retrieval, Mcgraw Hill Book Company, New York, 1983.

[19] SCOTT E. H., KING R., The Cactis Project: Database Support for Software Environments, IEEE Transaction on Software Engineering, Vol. 14, No. 6, June 1988.

[20] STOTTS P. D., FURUTA R. Petri-Net-Based Hypertext: Document Structure with Browsing Semantics; ACM Transactions on Information Systems, Vol. 7, No. 1, January 1989, pp 3-29.

[21] TOMPA F. WN. , A Data Model for Flexible Hypetrtext Database Systems; ACM Transactions on Information Systems, Vol. 7, No. 1, January 1989, pp 85-100.

[22] Interlisp-D Reference Manual, Volume II Environment, 1985.

Two Level Hypermedia
An Improved Architecture for Hypertext

P.D. Bruza   Th.P. van der Weide*

Dept. of Information Systems
University of Nijmegen

Abstract

In this article we present the Two Level Hypermedia architecture. Both levels of this architecture are detailed in the framework of a conceptual model of hypermedia. A central aspect of this model is the notion of a view. The concept of a hyperindex is introduced, which is a novel approach to organizing indexing information relevant for hypermedia. In conjunction with the hyperindex, the notion of Query by Navigation (QBN) is introduced.

0   Introduction

Hypermedia is becoming more and more popular as a structure that enables user-friendly access to large amounts of information. The term *hypermedia* is used in order to stress the fact that data types other than text may be involved. *Hypertext* refers to text-only hypermedia.

There are however some problems. One of the most important problems is what is usually referred to as being *lost in hyperspace* [12]. This problem can be introduced by the analogy of the child who, walking home through the forest, sees a butterfly and starts chasing it, which leads him further and further from the original path, until he stops and realizes he is lost. The notable aspects of the above analogy are as follows: a *path to a goal*, followed by *distraction*, leading to *disorientation*.

In the context of hypermedia, the *goal* is the fulfillment of the user's information need which (s)he commonly tries to achieve by following a path through the linked node structure of hypermedia. The *distraction* may be caused by the

---
[1]This work has been partially supported by the **ESPRIT** project **APPED (2499)**.

fact that from any given node the user may become fascinated by some new information that was not relevant to the initial goal. This distraction, coupled with the possibility in hypermedia to be able to quickly and easily follow up on it, can lead to disorientation, sometimes referred to as lost in hyperspace. The above scenario demonstrates one facet of disorientation. Another possibility is when the user has a vague goal in mind, which (s)he tries to fulfill by trial-and-error.

This paper focuses on the question as to what can be done to help the user to re-orient when they become lost. In current hypermedia systems orientation is facilitated by mechanisms such as a *browser* or a *book-mark* [5] [12]. A browser is essentially a map of the hypermedia in which the current position of the user is marked. A book-mark is a place marker in the hypermedia to which the user can return after following a side-track.

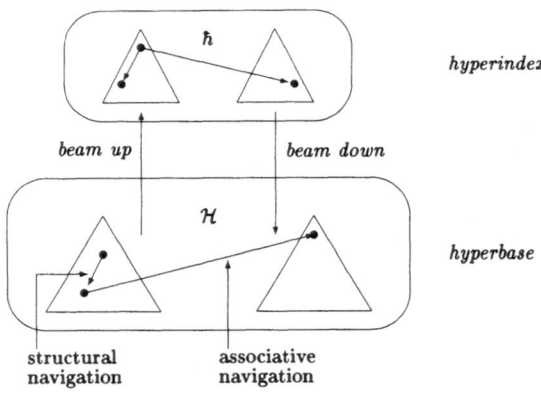

Figure 1: The architecture of $\frac{\hbar}{\mathcal{H}}$

In this paper a new mechanism is presented to structure the hypermedia in two levels as a means of facilitating user orientation. The bottom level of this mechanism is called the *hyperbase* and the upper level the *hyperindex*. We denote the hyperbase by $\mathcal{H}$ and the hyperindex by $\hbar$. The resulting structure is denoted as $\frac{\hbar}{\mathcal{H}}$ (see figure 1).

The hyperbase corresponds to hypermedia as is typical in current systems. The user has two forms of navigation to browse through the information:

Structural navigation is navigation whereby the user can move through the information on the basis of an underlying (hierarchical) structure. For example, moving from a chapter to a section, or from a chapter to the next chapter. Structural navigation is characterized by the fact that it extends (enlarges) or contracts (refines) the current context (see figure 2).

Associative navigation is navigation whereby the user moves through the information by following cross references that uni-directionally thread related information together. Associative navigation is characterized by the fact that it brings about a change of the context.

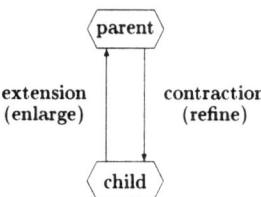

Figure 2: Contraction and Extension of Context

The top level (the hyperindex) consists of information, used to index the information in the hyperbase. It is only natural to structure the hyperindex in the same style as the hyperbase. Now the user can navigate through the hyperindex to better clarify their information needs. The structure of the hyperindex provides the opportunity to guide a (possibly distracted or lost) user, by taking advantage of the hyperindex structure. When the user arrives at some potentially interesting index information item, the nodes in the hyperbase, relevant to this particular index item, can be retrieved. In this way the user can move from the hyperindex level to the hyperbase level. This type of browsing, by navigating through the hyperindex, is termed *query by navigation* (QBN). Querying is thus reduced to a form of browsing which is an easily understood form of searching behaviour.

The movement between levels is also a form of navigation:

Inter-layer navigation is navigation whereby the user moves between the hyperbase and the hyperindex. If the user moves from the hyperbase to the hyperindex then this is termed a *beam up* operation. The inverse of this is termed the *beam down*.

The advantage of the hyperindex is that the user can view the underlying hypermedia at a higher abstraction level in the sense that, at this level, descriptions of objects are used rather than the objects themselves thus relieving the user from having to cope with a lot of detail. It is also advantageous that both levels are expressed in terms of the same underlying model, namely hypermedia. The user can thus deal with the system in a uniform way.

The two level structure is a natural extension of the lattice-based model of information retrieval presented in [9]. This model consists of a lattice of index entries built on a document set. The user interacts with the system essentially by walking over the lattice. A node in the lattice represents a query. The query can be refined or enlarged by moving to descendant or ancestor nodes respectively.

The organization of the paper is as follows. First we describe a sample session with a system based on the two level architecture. After that the two level architecture is formally introduced and applied in the context of hypermedia systems. Next there is particular emphasis on the use of the hyperindex as a useful abstraction layer of the underlying information. This layer can be used both for the purposes of querying and as an aid in helping user orientation.

1   The User Interface

In this section we describe the interaction with a two-level hypermedia so the reader can get some feel for how this works. This will provide the intuition to understand the formal definitions of the underlying concepts which are given in the following section.

Starting a session, the user may enter the two-level hypermedia via the hyperindex or directly via the hyperbase. If the user has entered via the hyperbase then (s)he can browse using structural and associative navigation, or move to the hyperindex by using the *beam up* navigation operation.

When the user enters the hyperindex (s)he is presented with a node like that depicted in figure 3.

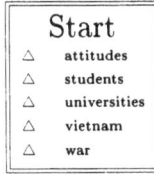

Figure 3: Example start node of the hyperindex

The node is a gateway into the hyperindex which is a

hypertext of indexing information. This information is organized in such a way that from any node in the hyperindex the user can navigate to more specific indexing information. This corresponds to *refining* the search criterium. The inverse of this is navigation to less specific information, termed *enlarging*.

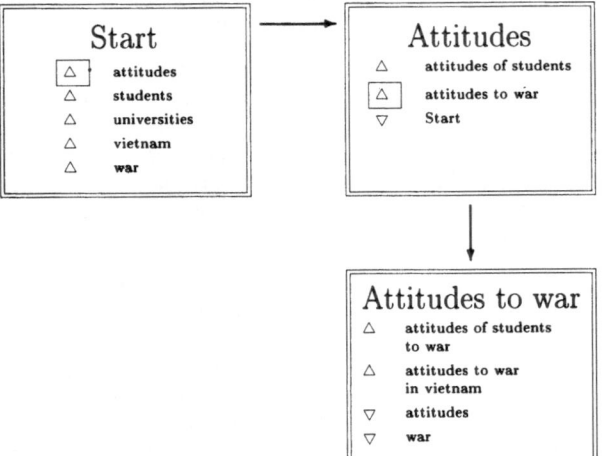

Figure 4: Example of Refining in the Hyperindex

Figure 4 shows two examples of refining, using the start node of figure 3 as begin point. In this figure we see that a node consists of a number of entries where all entries represent indexing information. The first entry represents the current focus of the user in the hyperindex, and the other entries are *buttons* which can be activated to refine ($\triangle$) or enlarge ($\triangledown$) the current focus. By enlargement or refinement, the button activated becomes the new focus.

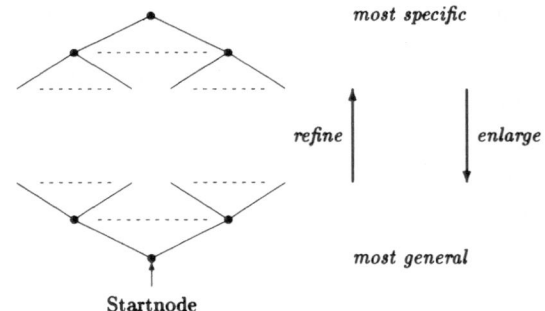

Figure 5: Conceptual view of the Hyperindex

Enlargement and refinement are inverse to each other (see figure 5). They form a partial order on the set of nodes.

This partial order will have a minimal element (least specific, indexing everything), and a maximal element (probably indexing nothing). The partial order is naturally represented as a graph. This graph demarcates a space within which the user can navigate. Vertices of this graph correspond to nodes consisting of index entries as we have shown in the examples above. For example the node associated with the minimal element is depicted in figure 3.

Rather than enlarging or refining the current focus in the hyperindex, the user can decide to inspect the set of objects, associated with the current focus. This set of objects will be ordered on relevancy. In order to reflect this structure, a query result is treated as a special view. This view has a trivial (empty) structural definition which implies that it contains a single molecule. The presentation of this molecule offers the query result to the user, giving the opportunity to select (by associative navigation) an object for further inspection. More details will be given about this special view in the section dealing with the hyperindex.

2 Two-Level Hypermedia

In the literature there have been a number of papers which focus on formally defining hypermedia at a *conceptual level*. Several approaches can be recognized; in [7] for example, a model of hypermedia is presented using first-order logic. In [14] hypermedia is modelled in terms of hypergraphs. We take a different approach, and consider hypermedia as more than just a way of *presenting* the underlying information (this is also recognized in [10]). In our approach of hypermedia, we have a clean separation between the *structure* of the information, the *presentation* of the information, and the information elements themselves (the *fragments*). At this point we introduce some terminology. The term *title* refers to a particular hypermedia application. A title has a *structure*, a *presentation*, and consists of a base of fragments.

Currently there are a number of description languages for documents, such as SGML [8], TEX and ODA [4]. The underlying conceptual model is implicit is the definition of these description languages, although it is recognized that the underlying conceptual model is relevant (see for example [11] for a conceptual description of SGML). We take the opposite approach, and define the conceptual model, without the introduction of a description language. For practical reasons however, SGML-based documents are easily mapped into the format of our conceptual model. A simple transducer will suffice for this.

Figure 6 depicts the syntactical structure of the conceptual model as a schema in the NIAM notation (see [6]). On the basis of this schema we will discuss the various components of the model.

Definition 2.1 *A* Title *is a structure* $\mathcal{T} = (\mathcal{R}, \mathcal{V}, \mathcal{F})$ *where*

- $\mathcal{R}$ *is a set of (context free) rules, called the* Title Structure.

- $\mathcal{V}$ *is a set of views, called the* Title Mask.

- $\mathcal{F}$ *is a set of information fragments, called the* Fragment Base.

2.1 Fragments

We start from a set $\mathcal{F}$ of so-called fragments. Fragments are the elementary parts of a document, which are not decomposed structurally into smaller components. Each fragment has associated data of a particular medium (such as text, video and audio). The criterium for judging whether a fragment is atomic or not is not necessarily a property of the fragment itself, but rather is dependent on the lowest level of granularity at which the information is to be considered. For example, animation can be considered as a single fragment, or as a sequence of frames.

2.1.1 Characterizations

A major difference with relational databases is the identification of objects. In relational databases each object can be uniquely denoted by an expression or description of some fixed type: the key of the object (tuple). This is not the case in hypermedia applications. When we want to retrieve an object we provide, as good as possible, a description of it. This description is then matched against descriptors associated with objects. If the matching algorithm deems that the description and the descriptors are sufficiently similar then the object is retrieved.

The object descriptors are termed *characterizations* because they only describe the associated object to some extent. Note that the quality of the retrieval is heavily dependent on how good the characterization describes the associated object.

A typical example of a characterization is a set of keywords or terms. There are other possibilities such as trigrams [13] or index expressions. For a detailed exposition of index expressions see [2].

In the model of figure 6 the characterizations, denoted as $\mathcal{C}$, are presented as a special sort of fragment. The characterizations form the basis of the hyperindex. Each fragment can

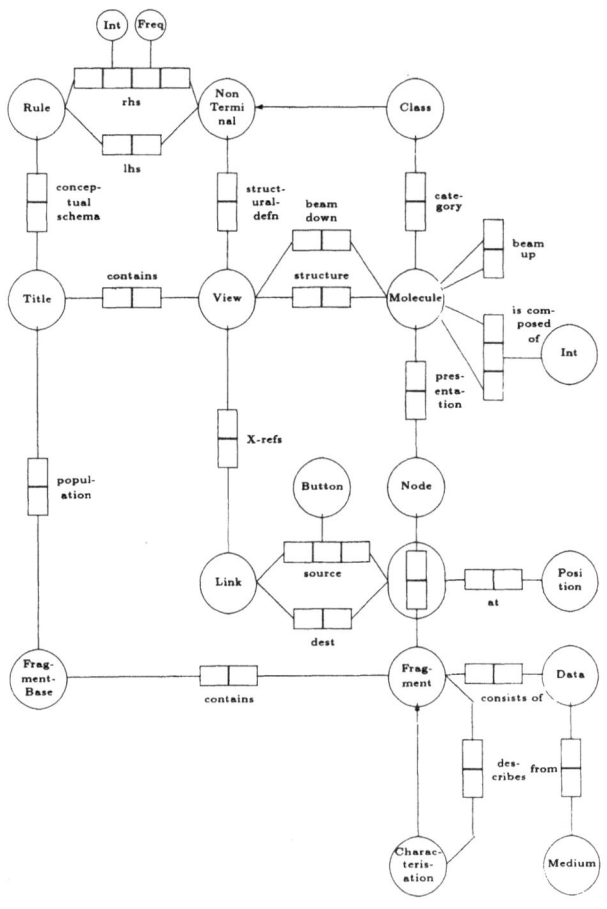

Figure 6: Conceptual Schema of the information model

have associated zero or more characterizations. This is modelled by the relation *describes* in figure 6. If f is a fragment, then the characterization of f is denoted $\chi(f)$.

2.1.2 Nodes

Nodes are units of presentation, and are used to present the structural components to the user. As a consequence, nodes are constructed from fragments. Formally, a node is a partially ordered set of fragments. In figure 6 the partial order is represented by the position of the fragment within the node. We denote a node by the letter N, and the set of nodes over $\mathcal{F}$ by $\mathcal{N}$.

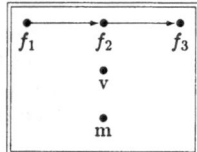

Figure 7: A multimedia presentation

As an example, in the node in figure 7 the fragments f_1, f_2 and f_3 are displayed on the screen, while at the same time the video v is played, accompanied with the audio fragment m. This node can be represented as the following expression:

$$(f_1; f_2; f_3)\|v\|m$$

A calculus for expressions of this sort has been described in [1].

fragment	position
f_1	$\langle s,1 \rangle$
f_2	$\langle s,2 \rangle$
f_3	$\langle s,3 \rangle$
v	$\langle v,1 \rangle$
m	$\langle a,1 \rangle$

Table 1: Ordering of fragments in node

In terms of the conceptual schema, the partial order of above example would be represented as in table 1.

2.2 Rules

Usually information is structured according to some rules. For example, if the information has the form of a book, a book consists of chapters, a chapter consists of sections, etc. In SGML terminology, these rules form the structural specification of the document (the DTD, or Document Type Definition). We adopt the convention of SGML, and (basically) allow context free rules only. As a consequence, a rule has a left hand side (LHS), which consists of a single symbol and a RHS, which is a series of one or more symbols, where each symbol may have one of the following occurrence indicators:

- *, the so-called Kleene star, denoting an optional repetition.
- +, the so-called Kleene plus, denoting a repetition.
- ?, denoting an optional occurrence.

This format for rules is not as rich as in SGML, where the following rule would be permitted:

$$A \rightarrow B(C|D)^*$$

In our case, we would introduce an extra non-terminal (say X) and rewrite the rule as:

$$A \rightarrow BX^*$$
$$X \rightarrow C|D$$

2.3 Views

One of the most powerful aspects of hypermedia is the ability to define several different views on the same underlying base of information fragments. In our model a view is defined to have the following components: A structural definition, a structure and a set of associative links.

Definition 2.2 *A* View *is a system* $V = (G, \omega, \mathcal{L})$ *where*

- G *is a set of rules, called the* structure definition *($G \subset \mathcal{R}$), and a start symbol S.*
- ω *is a parse tree conform G, called the* actual structure.
- $\mathcal{L}$ *is a set of* associative links.

The actual structure has the form of a parse tree where each node corresponds to an instance of a particular structural element, such as a *chapter* or *section*. We term these structural elements *molecules*. In the parse tree the terminal symbols are not the fragments as a fragment in itself is not a structural element. The connection of the structural elements with the fragments is via nodes.

The *context* of a molecule is defined as the path from the root molecule in the parse tree to the molecule in question.

By following this path the user becomes aware of the contextual framework in which the molecule exists. This awareness arises because the user constantly refines the context to arrive at the molecule in question.

The rules have a context free format. We allow however a more liberal application of those rules than is usual in the theory of context free grammars. In particular, it is possible that a molecule occurs in more than one parse tree.

Definition 2.3 *Let V be a view, then the set of molecules of V, denoted by $\mathcal{M}_V$ is the set nodes within ω.*

Finally, a view contains a set of *associative links*. These model cross references within the view structure. A link has a source and a destination. The source is a triple (f, b, n), where f is a fragment, b a button, and n a node. The destination of a link is a pair (f, n). The associative links support the concept of associative navigation.

When following an associative link the current context will be shifted. (This, by the way, is the main cause of user disorientation. After following the link the user arrives at a molecule which is part of an unfamiliar contextual framework.)

Context ambiguity can also occur. By traversing an associative link a molecule may be reached which is part of more than one parse tree. There is therefore more than one conceptual framework with which to continue. There are two possibilities to overcome this. The first is that the author constructs the hypermedia in such a way so that each molecule has a unique context. The alternative is that the system provides information about the possible contexts of molecule and lets the user decide with which context to continue.

2.4 Structural Presentation

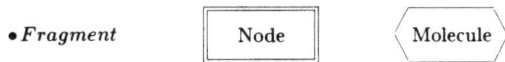

Figure 8: Drawing conventions for hypermedia

Molecules as such are abstract objects, and need a mechanism to be presented. For this we use the concept of presentation, or node, as introduced earlier.

Figure 9 shows an example in the context of document maintenance. (When drawing hypermedia structures, we use the conventions displayed in figure 8). The document readers view has no structure. It presents the document as a whole, so that the document can basically be read sequentially. The reader can deviate from this line by following an associative link.

The document maintenance view takes the full structure of the document into account. This is useful when the component parts of the document are to be manipulated.

The view structure (the molecules) must be mapped to a set of nodes. This is the job of a so-called author. In figure 6 this is represented as the function *presentation*, that maps molecules into nodes. This function, which is termed the *authoring function*, is not formalizable in the sense that there is an arbitrary number of ways in which this can be done. The author decides subjectively which is a "good" mapping of a view structure to a presentation.

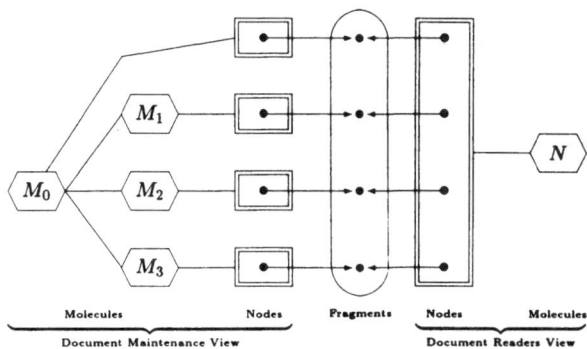

Figure 9: Document Maintenance Views

3 The Guiding Hyperindex

The hyperindex was introduced as a hypertext which indexes the hyperbase. In general, index items can be represented in the form of index expressions. Index expressions were introduced earlier in this paper (see figure 4). Unlike keywords or n-grams, index expressions have a structure. This structure is defined by the following grammar in extended BNF format:

```
IdxExpr  →  Term {Connector IdxExpr}*
Term  →  string
Connector  →  string
```

This grammar produces index expressions like the following:

attitudes of students of universities to war in vietnam

Index expressions can be ambiguous. For this reason they are often represented as trees. Figure 10 depicts the representation of the above expression.

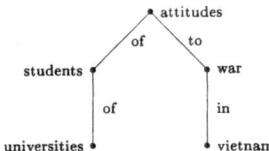

Figure 10: Example representation of an index expression

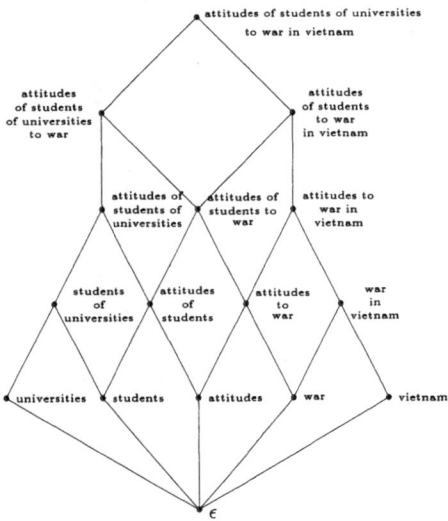

Figure 11: Example power index expression

From an index expression the so-called power index expression can be formed. This is the set of all index subexpressions of the original expression, including the empty index expression, which is denoted by ϵ. The power index expression forms a lattice-like structure in which every point corresponds to an index expression. Figure 11 is the power index expression derived from the above example.

From index expressions an elegant underlying structure of the hyperindex can be derived. It is this structure that supports Query By Navigation. We summarize the construction of the hyperindex is as follows. (Refer to [2] for a detailed exposition.)

Every object in the hyperbase is described by an index expression. The characterization of the object is the power index expression. The union of all such power index expressions forms a lattice-like structure. From any point in the lattice, the corresponding index expression can be enlarged or refined. For example, in the context of figure 11 the expression

attitudes to war can be refined to attitudes of students to war or attitudes to war in vietnam. Conversely, the same expression van be enlarged to attitudes or students. Note that these refinement and enlargement possibilities are also depicted in figure 4.

Figure 6 depicts the conceptual model of the two level architecture shown in figure 1. The hyperindex fits into this model as a special view. As such, it has an associated structural description (grammar), an actual structure and a set of associative links. Each molecule of this view corresponds to an index expression. Figure 4 shows presentations of such molecules. Associative links in the hyperindex are used to model cross references between index expressions which are deemed similar. This helps the user find related index information. For example, there may be an associative link between war in vietnam and rise of communism in south-east-asia.

Enlargement (context extension in the hyperindex) and refinement (context contraction in the hyperindex) are operations *within* the top level of the two level architecture. Beam-up and beam-down, on the other hand, are operations which act *between* the two levels. The beam down operation originates from an index expression in the hyperindex and results in a view with the following characteristics. The structural definition of the view is empty. As a result the view consists of a single molecule, M, with class S, where S is the start symbol. The presentation of this molecule M offers the possibility to access the molecules that are characterized by the original index expression. These molecules form the result set. Each fragment in the presentation of M identifies a molecule in the result set. These fragments are ordered with respect to decreasing relevance of the associated object to the original index expression. Associated with each fragment is a button which acts as the source of an associative link into the corresponding result node. As a consequence, the user can easily navigate through the result set. Note that traversing such an associative link brings about a change of the current contex, as it lands the user into the view which the molecule is a part of. The beam down operation is depicted in figure 12. In this figure the *focus* refers to the molecule in the hyperindex that was the source of the beam down operation.

The beam up operation originates from a molecule in the hyperbase and results in a molecule in the hyperindex. Each molecule in the hyperbase is characterized by a power index expression. Each index expression in this power expression more or less characterizes the molecule. The beam up operation results in the top element of this lattice, as it is the "best" characterization of the associated molecule.

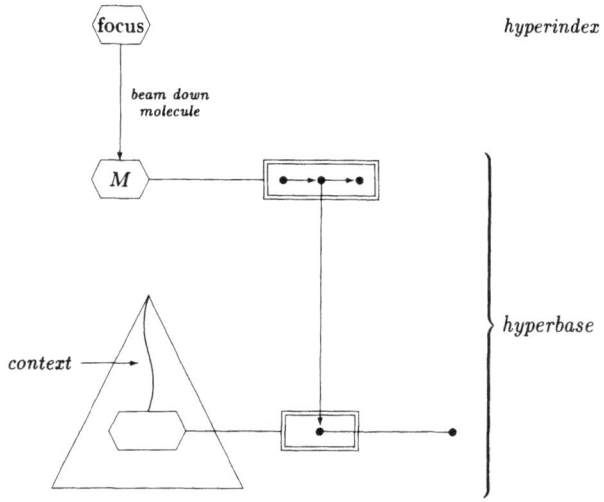

Figure 12: The Beam Down operation

4 Summary and Further Research

In this paper a two level architecture for hypermedia has been introduced as a means of countering the lost in hyperspace problem. If lost, the user can always move to the upper level of this architecture. Although the two-level hypermedia architecture has not yet been tested in practice, we feel that it is a promising and elegant new approach. Currently we are constructing a prototype implementation.

An important concept is Query By Navigation. This refers to navigation through the upper level to find the best characterization of the user's information need. When such a characterization is found, the user can retrieve the associated objects and inspect them. Further search can occur via navigation within the hyperbase or by beaming up to the hyperindex in order to adjust the result set by enlargement or refinement, or by possibly navigating to a completely new index expression.

The two-level architecture is a closed system in the sense that all navigational queries are *a priori* known. This offers possibilities for optimization. Further research is currently being performed to investigate this in relation to CD-ROM based hypermedia.

References

[1] P.D. Bruza. Hyperindices: A Novel Aid for Searching in Hypermedia. Technical Report 90-03. Afdeling Informatiesystemen, University of Nijmegen, The Netherlands, 1990. Research report.

[2] P.D. Bruza and Th. P. van der Weide. The semantics of data flow diagrams. In *Proceedings of Conference on Management of Data*, 1989. Hyderabad, India.

[3] I.R Campbell-Grant and P.J. Robinson. An Introduction to ISO DIS 8613 - Office Document Architecture - and its Application to Computer Graphics. *Comput and Graphics*, 11(4):325–341, 1987.

[4] J. Conklin. Hypertext: An Introduction and Survey. *IEEE Computer*, 20(9):17–41, September 1987.

[5] J.J.van Griethuysen (ed.). *Concepts and Terminology for the Conceptuel Schema and the Information Base.* 1982. ISO Report, Publ. nr. ISO/TC97/SC5-N695.

[6] P. Garg. Abstraction mechanisms in hypertext. *Communications ACM*, 31(7):863–870, July 1988.

[7] ISO8879. Information Processing - Text and Office Systems - Standard General Markup Language (SGML), 1986-10-15.

[8] J. Gecsei R. Godin and C. Pichet. Design of a Browsing Interface for Information Retrieval. In N.J. Belkin and C.J. van Rijsbergen, editors, *Proceedings of the Twelfth ACMSIGIR Conference*, pages 32–37, 1989.

[9] G. Salton. *Automatic Text Processing: the Translation, Analysis and Retrieval of Information by Computer.* Addison-Wesley Publishing Company, 1989.

[10] H. Schouten. SGML*CASE: The Storage of Documents in Databases. Technical Report 03-11, TFDL/ECIT, PO 356, 6700 Wageningen, The Netherlands, 1989. Internal Report.

[11] B. Shneiderman and G. Kearsley. *Hypertext Hands-On!* Addison-Wesley Publishing Company, 1989.

[12] B. Teufel and S. Schmidt. Full text retrieval based on syntactic similarities. *Information Systems*, 13(1):65–70, 1988.

[13] F. Tompa. A Data Model for Flexible Hypertext Database Systems. *ACM Transactions on Information Systems*, 7(1):85–100, January 1989.

A Tool Kit for Knowledge Based Production Planning Systems

Stefan Böttcher
IBM Deutschland GmbH
Scientific Center
Institute for Knowledge Based Systems
P.O.Box 80 08 80
D – 7000 Stuttgart 80
West Germany *

Abstract

This paper describes the logic programming language PROTOS-L and how to use it as a tool kit for the programming of knowledge based production planning system prototypes. PROTOS-L embeds transparent access to relational databases, supports the programming of deductive databases, provides a module concept similar to Modula-2 and contains a type concept with subtypes and polymorphism. The programming language PROTOS-L and the PROTOS-L system have been developed and implemented at IBM Stuttgart. PROTOS-L is currently used to reimplement parts of production planning systems which have been developed at Sandoz AG in Basel and at Hoechst AG in Frankfurt. The investigated production planning applications need an integration of both concepts: read access to relational databases (which contain the relevant planning data) and a logic programming language for the implementation of heuristic rules (which control the planning strategy). In order to support both facilities, PROTOS-L fully embeds database access into a logic programming language.

1 Introduction

The Eureka project PROTOS investigates logic programming tools for expert system applications, and focusses on tools for production planning systems. Production planning system prototypes have been developed at Sandoz AG in Basel and at Hoechst AG in Frankfurt. Currently, it is investigated how parts of a planning algorithm for the Sandoz production planning problem, namely finding a production schedule for several products under given production constraints, can be reimplemented in the logic programming language PROTOS-L.

The paper is organized as follows. The second section describes some requirements of the PROTOS production planning applications, which are relevant to the use of databases and knowledge based systems. Next, we describe which facilities PROTOS-L provides in order to meet these requirements, i.e. we describe the module concept of PROTOS-L and how PROTOS-L supports database access and the development of deductive databases.

---

*The research reported here has been carried out within the international EUREKA project PROTOS (EU56): Prolog Tools for Building Expert Systems. Project partners of the succeeding project PROTOS II are BIM, IBM Stuttgart, Sandoz AG Basel, Hoechst AG Frankfurt, IBM Montpellier, University of Dortmund and University of Oldenburg.

2 Requirements of the PROTOS production planning applications

The requirements of the PROTOS production planning applications result from many discussions with our industrial project partners.

2.1 A sketch of the production planning problems

Within the PROTOS project, there is already a production planning system prototype implemented at Sandoz in Basel [Sauer et al., 1989], [Sauer, 1990], [Slabor et al., 1990]. Another production planning system prototype has been implemented at Hoechst in Frankfurt. We summarize both applications and outline their requirements to databases and knowledge based systems.

A production planning system has to plan orders for several kinds of products and has to fulfill the production constraints. The most important production constraints for the production planning problem at Sandoz are the following:

- Each machine can only be used for one production step at a given time. If there are two production steps which are planned to use the same machine in overlapping time intervals, we call this a *planning conflict*.

- Each production step can be performed only on some of the machines, i.e. there are *different types* of machines.

- The production of a product must not be interrupted, i.e. intermediate products have to be processed immediately (*continuity constraint*).

Each order contains information about: which product is required, the order priority, the earliest time to begin the production and the time at which the order shall be carried out.

For each product there are several production alternatives. A production alternative consists of a sequence of production steps. Each step can be performed on several machines. Therefore, the order for a certain product can be carried out, if there exists a production time interval and a production alternative such that for all of steps of this production alternative there exists an available machine.

An important criterion for the quality of a plan is to carry out the production orders in time (or at least with a short delay). However, the search space is too large to find an optimal solution, e.g. to find the production plan with the minimal sum of delay days. Therefore, the planning algorithm combines heuristic rules and interaction with a human planner[1] in order to construct the

---

[1] The time needed for human interaction is acceptable, because

production plan. Human interaction is also required, because in the case of planning conflicts it is the decision of humans which product will be delayed.

The production planning system prototype developed at Hoechst AG in Frankfurt differs from that of Sandoz in several aspects. For example, the constraints and the criterion for the quality of a plan are different from the Sandoz production planning problem. In the case of Hoechst, the production planning system prototype is used for a couple of production lines, each of which is capable to fulfill any order for the given plant. It is desirable to produce many orders of the same kind sequentially on a single production line in order to reduce cleaning costs. The number of product changes on a production line shall be minimized. Moreover, if it is not possible to use a production line for a single kind of orders, then it is preferable to put similar production orders on a production line, which at least need less cleaning of machines than other production orders.

Both production planning scenarios have the following problems:

- The storage of data relevant to production in relational databases: for example, an order database contains the orders of customers and different production database contains information about used machines, product descriptions and information about which machines can can produce which products or can carry out which production steps.

- The search space is too large to find an optimal solution. Heuristic rules have to be used in order to find a good solution.

- Human planners must have the possibility to modify the planning strategy i.e. the decisions for conflict resolution.

In the next section, we summarize the requirements to a tool kit for the implementation of such production planning systems.

2.2 Requirements to a tool kit for knowledge based production planning systems

The need for database access

Embedding database access into a programming language for production planning systems is enforced by the following reasons:

- Most of the characteristics of products, production alternatives, production steps and machines are (or can be) stored in relational databases and have to be accessed efficiently.

- The production orders are stored in a relational database.

- Databases are used for information sharing, e.g. if the actual accessible set of machines changes because of repair or maintenance activities, then this information will be provided in a database relation.

The need for a logic programming language

A programming language for production planning systems should support the programming of rules for the following reason. As mentioned before, the search space for production planning problems is too large for an exhaustive search of an optimal solution. "Good" solutions found by heuristic rules and human

---

the time needed for interactive planning is only a small fraction of the time during which the production plan is carried out.

interaction are sufficient for the applications. Finally, in our applications the heuristic knowledge for finding a good solution is typically given in the form of rules as in logic programs. Alltogether, a logic programming language seems to be the most adequate approach for the implementation of heuristic planning knowledge.

Further useful language features

A knowledge structuring concept, a type concept and the support of rapid prototyping are further useful properties of a tool kit for the development of production planning systems for the following reasons.

- In our applications, production planning systems will only be accepted, if the production planner can control the planning algorithm, i.e. he must be supported by a simple facility to exchange parts of the planning algorithm. Therefore, some kind of knowledge structuring concept or module concept would be very useful.

- A type concept would be useful for data structuring and for avoiding type errors.

- Since production plans and the underlying algorithms are often developed interactively, the support of rapid prototyping is also necessary.

3 PROTOS-L

This section outlines the design goals and summarizes the main language features of the programming language PROTOS-L, which are described e.g. in [Beierle, 1989] and [Böttcher, 1990b]. It further describes how the PROTOS-L module concept supports the development of knowledge based production planning systems.

3.1 Design goals

The design goals of PROTOS-L are to meet the production planning system requirements, i.e.

- to embed database access in a logic programming language,

- to support both backtracking and set-oriented query evaluation,

- to support data structuring and a powerful type concept and

- to support knowledge structuring, separate compilation and rapid prototyping.

In order to meet these goals, the logic programming language PROTOS-L incorporates the following basic language features, c.f. [Beierle, 1989] and [Böttcher, 1990b].

- The module concept supports knowledge structuring, separate compilation and rapid prototyping. Similar to Modula-2 [Wirth, 1983], PROTOS-L distinguishes between interface and body of a module and hides the implementation of the exported predicates in the module body. The body of a PROTOS-L module is either a *program body* or a *database body*. Program bodies implement the predicates of a module by a set of facts and rules in the embedding logic programming language. However, database bodies implement the predicates by a set of views on database relations. At the interface of a module it is transparent how the predicates are implemented, i.e. whether the module body is a program body or a database body.

- The logic programming language PROTOS-L integrates access to external relational databases. Furthermore, PROTOS-L supports the programming of deductive databases. A database body is used to access an external relational database or a deductive database.

- Set-oriented evaluation is used for rules in database bodies (i.e. for deductive databases) whereas backtracking is used for program bodies.

- Program bodies for small amounts of data used by prototypes can be substituted by database bodies for the access to external databases, when the first prototyping phase is completed.

- As in TEL [Smolka, 1988], the PROTOS-L type system [Beierle and Böttcher, 1989] supports data structuring and writing more readable programs, and it helps to avoid typing errors. The type system requires to assign types to all arguments of a predicate, but it provides subtypes and polymorphism, i.e. type variables. However, PROTOS-L types are not only used by the PROTOS-L compiler for type checking purposes, but also by the PROTOS Abstract Machine (PAM) [Beierle, 1989], [Böttcher and Beierle, 1989] for type inferencing in order to reduce the search space. If a predicate is implemented in a database body, then the types of its arguments are restricted to integer and string.

The basic design goals are met by the language features of PROTOS-L as follows.

- The module concept supports knowledge structuring, separate compilation and rapid prototyping.

- Database bodies support both access to relational databases and the programming of deductive databases.

- The type concept supports data structuring and more readable programs, it leads to a reduction of the search space during query evaluation, and it helps to avoid typing errors. A description of the PROTOS-L type concept can be found e.g. in [Beierle and Böttcher, 1989] and [Beierle, 1989].

3.2 The module concept of PROTOS-L

The PROTOS-L module concept integrates ideas from the module concepts of Modula-2, DBPL [Eckhardt et al., 1985], [Böttcher, 1989] and TEL [Smolka, 1988]. As in TEL, the *interface* specifies only the predicate names and the types of their arguments. Different from DBPL, PROTOS-L supports database access by a special kind of module bodies and not by a special kind of interfaces. The advantage of this approach over the DBPL approach is that PROTOS-L allows to keep the database access transparent to the user of a module.

The example of figure 1 shows a part of an interface of that module in our production planning system which contains and computes the production data. The module computes

- which machines are used in which time intervals for which order and

- which production steps can be done by which machines.

It is hidden how the predicates are implemented, i.e. the concept of an interface supports knowledge encapsulation. Similarly, the distribution of rules into several separate modules supports knowledge structuring.

Separate compilation and thereby the maintenance of large program systems is supported as in Modula-2: interface and body

of a module are compiled separately. Since compilation units import only from interfaces, but never from bodies, the body of any module can be modified and recompiled independently of the rest of a module system.

The PROTOS-L module concept also supports two kinds of rapid prototyping: namely top-down and bottom-up system development. Top-down system implementation is facilitated as follows. The programmer can use dummy submodules which list only a few facts for rapid prototyping purposes in order to check whether an upper module works well. Later, the dummy submodules can be exchanged by modules which implement the desired predicates, without changing the interfaces of the module. Bottom-up system evaluation is even better supported than in many conventional programming languages, because in PROTOS-L the programmer can interactively query every predicate defined in any module, provided that the module and all its submodules are implemented.

Let us continue our example: During a rapid prototyping phase the predicates used_machines and step_machines could be implemeted in a program body, e.g. by listing some example facts. When the prototyping phase is completed successfully, this program body can be substituted by a database body selecting the facts from a relational or deductive database.

4 Access to relational and deductive databases

This section summarizes how access to relational and deductive databases is embedded in the programming language PROTOS-L, i.e. how database access is expressed within database bodies [Böttcher, 1990a]. The basic idea is to give the PROTOS-L programmer a uniform high-level database programming language. The impedance mismatch of other language integrations, e.g. the integration of SQL into C, should be avoided.

4.1 Transparent database access

The most important new aspect of the PROTOS-L module concept is that PROTOS-L offers two kinds of bodies of a module: *program bodies* and *database bodies*. Program bodies support logic programming with backtracking, whereas database bodies support set-oriented retrieval from external relational databases and user defined deductive databases.

Because access to an external database shall be transparent for the user of a module, at the interface of a module it is not visible, whether or not the corresponding implementation of the body accesses an external database and which kind of data retrieval is used.

For example, the predicates used_machines and step_machines could be implemented either as in Prolog by a set of facts and rules written down in a program body or by external databases as described in the third section. At the interface it is not visible how the predicates are implemented.

The database module can be used as an interface to a relational database as follows. The implementation of a module is a database body and the facts solving a predicate are taken from a relational database. Furthermore, for every database relation declared in the database body there has to exist a corresponding database relation in the database schema.

For example, the interface given in section 3.2 can be implemented by the database body given in figure 2.

```
interface production_data.

  rel  used_machines :   ?string x      ?int x      ?int x      ?int .
  %                      machine name   used from   used until  for order
  % Which machine is used in which time interval for which order ?
  % If the machine is available in the time interval, then the 4th argument has the value 0.


  rel  step_machines :   ?int x            ?string .
  %                      production step   machine name
  % Which production step can be done by which machine ?
  ...

endinterface.
```

Figure 1: Abstraction from details of the production data

```
database_body production_data using schedule_DB .

  rel     used_machines :   ?string x      ?int x      ?int x      ?int .
  %                         machine name   used from   used until  for order
  % Which machine is used in which time interval for which order ?
  % If the machine is available in the time interval, then the 4th argument has the value 0.

  dbrel   used_machines      is Machine_Rel( Machinename , From , Until , Order ).


  rel     step_machines :   ?int x            ?string .
  %                         production step   machine name
  % Which production step can be done by which machine ?

  dbrel   step_machines      is Machines_for_Productionstep( Step , Machinename ).
  ...
endmodule.
```

Figure 2: Implementation of relations containing the relevant production data

This database body requires that there are at least two relations in the database schedule_DB: Machine_Rel and Machines_for_Productionstep. Furthermore, Machine_Rel must have at least the four attributes: Machinename of type string, and From, Until and Order of the type integer. Similarly, Machines_for_Productionstep must have at least the attributes Step of the type integer and Machinename of type string.

However, the database module can also be used in order to program a deductive database. Therefore, a PROTOS-L database body may contain function free database rules in order to implement predicates specified in the module's interface. A function free database rule consists of a head and a number of goals, each of which does not contain a function symbol. Note that the PROTOS-L programmer may program recursive and nonrecursive rules in database bodies.

For example, the database body given above may additionally contain two non-recursive rules which are shown in figure 3. The first rule computes, which machines are available in which time interval, and the second rule computes which available machines can be used for a production step in a given time interval.

Since rules in program bodies and view definitions in database bodies are expressed in the same way, the PROTOS-L programmer has to learn only one single language for deductive databases and application programs. This avoids the impedance mismatch of other integrations of database query languages into host programming languages, e.g. of the integration of SQL into C.

Different from the rules in program bodies which are evaluated by backtracking, the rules in database bodies are evaluated by set-oriented query evaluation strategies. The implementation of these strategies is described e.g. in [Meyer, 1989]. Set-oriented query evaluation strategies are especially advantageous, if the accessed data sets are large.

4.2 Evaluation strategies for rules

PROTOS-L integrates two evaluation strategies for rules: set-oriented evaluation and backtracking. Whenever a rule uses facts that are stored in a database the programmer has the choice to select an adequate evaluation strategy for this rule.

Set-oriented evaluation is preferable for the goals of a rule, if many calls of the goals are needed in order to solve the rule or if many solutions of the rule are needed in order to solve a higher goal. However, backtracking is preferable for the goals of a rule, if few solutions of its goals are sufficient in order to solve this rule and if few solutions of this rule are sufficient in order to solve a higher goal. A typical case where backtracking may be preferable is a program execution which computes only few solutions to a subgoal before running over a cut.

In PROTOS-L, the choice of an appropriate evaluation strategy is left to the programmer, assuming that he knows best how much search is needed before a rule can be solved. Whenever the programmer assumes that there are many results of goals needed in order to solve a rule R, he may prefer set-oriented evaluation of the rule R. In this case, he codes the rule R in a database body, and the PROTOS-L system evaluates the rule set-oriented. On the other hand, if he assumes that there are only few results of goals needed to solve a rule R, he may prefer

```
database_body production_data using schedule_DB .

...

rel   available_machines :  ?string x      ?int x      ?int .
%                           machine name   used from   used until
% Which machines are available in which time interval ?

      available_machines( Machine , From , Until )
                     <--  used_machines( Machine , From , Until , 0 ) .


rel   step_can_use_machine :  ?int x  ?string x     ?int  ?int .
%                             step    machine name   from   until
% Which machines can be used for a production step and
% are available in a given time interval ?

      step_can_use_machine( Step , Machine , From , Until )
                     <--  step_machines( Step , Machine ) &
                          available_machines( Machine , F , U ) &
                          F ≤ From &
                          U ≥ Until .

endmodule .
```

Figure 3: Computation of available machines from the production data

```
database_body production_data using schedule_DB .

...

rel   single_step_product :  ?string x      ?int x          ?int .
%                            product name   production step   time needed
% Which products are produced by a single production step,
% and how many days are needed for this production step ?

dbrel  single_step_product    is
       Single_Step_Products( Product_name , Production_step , Time_needed ).
endmodule .
```

Figure 4: Products which require a single production step

```
database_body order_data using order_DB .

rel   order :  ?int x   ?string x      ?int x .
%              ordernr   product name   due date
% Which order for which product shall be performed until which due date ?

dbrel  order    is Order_Rel( Order_Id , Product_name , Due_date ).

endmodule .
```

Figure 5: Accessing the order database

```
module planning algorithms.
imports production_data , order_data .

...

rel   servable_order :  ?int x   ?string x      ?int x .
%                       ordernr   product name   due date
% Which order for which product can be performed on some available machine ?

      servable_order( Ordernr , Product , Duedate )
      <-- order( Ordernr , Product , Duedate )
      & single_step_product( Product , Step , Duration )
      & step_can_use_machine( Step , Machine , Duedate--Duration , Duedate ) .
endmodule .
```

Figure 6: Computating servable orders from the order data and the deductive database containing production data

an evaluation by backtracking and use a cut at that place of a program, where no more answers to a goal are needed. In this case, he codes the same rule R in a program body, and the PROTOS-L system evaluates the rule by backtracking.

Let us continue our example. If it is assumed that many calls of step_machines are needed in order to solve the rule step_can_use_machine, then the rule step_can_use_machine is preferably implemented in a database body as shown in figure 3, because the database body performs a set-oriented evaluation of the rule. However, if it is assumed that only few solutions of step_machines are needed in order to solve the planning problem, and therefore backtracking is preferred, then the rule should be implemented in another program body instead of the database body. Hence, whether a rule which accesses database relations should be implemented in a database body or in a program body depends on the desired evaluation strategy for this rule.

4.3 Accessing multiple databases

PROTOS-L can integrate the knowledge of many databases within a single application program. According to the claim that knowledge structuring is supported by the module concept, every database (like every other knowledge package) is enclosed in its own module. Hence, every database needs its own database body. The information of several databases can be integrated within program bodies that import all the predicates they need from the database modules.

In our example, the production data and the order data are stored in different databases. Nevertheless, the knowledge of both databases has to be integrated for the production planning process.

Assume that the database body production_data implements a further relation single_step_product, which contains information about each product that can be produced by a single production step and about the time required for that production step (c.f. figure 4).

Assume furthermore, a relation Order_Rel is stored in a different database and therefore is implemented in a different database body (c.f. figure 5).

Then the PROTOS-L programmer can integrate the knowledge of both databases in the program body outlined in figure 6. The rule for servable_order computes which orders for single_step_products can be performed by some available machine.

5 Summary and conclusion

The PROTOS production planning applications need a tool kit which supports data and knowledge structuring, which integrates logic programming and database access and which supports rapid prototyping.

PROTOS-L provides the facilities which are needed for our production planning system applications. The module concept supports rapid prototyping, knowledge structuring and transparent database access by hiding the implementation of predicates from the user of a module. Additionally, database bodies facilitate the programming of deductive databases. Furthermore, PROTOS-L supports the integration of knowledge from multiple databases.

Efficient set-oriented evaluation strategies are used for rules contained in database bodies and backtracking is used for rules contained in program bodies. The PROTOS-L programmer selects the appropriate evaluation strategy for a rule, simply by coding it in a program body or in a database body. Because program body rules and database views are expressed in the same way, the PROTOS-L programmer has to learn only one single language. This avoids the impedance mismatch.

Finally, the example showed how to implement small fragments of a production planning and scheduling system within PROTOS-L.

References

[Beierle, 1989] C. Beierle. Types, modules and databases in the logic programming language PROTOS-L. In K. H. Bläsius, U. Hedtstück, and C.-R. Rollinger, editors, *Sorts and Types for Artificial Intelligence*, Springer-Verlag, Berlin, Heidelberg, New York, 1989. (to appear).

[Beierle and Böttcher, 1989] C. Beierle and S. Böttcher. PROTOS-L: Towards a knowledge base programming language. In *Proceedings 3. GI-Kongreß Wissensbasierte Systeme, Informatik Fachberichte*, Springer-Verlag, 1989.

[Böttcher, 1989] S. Böttcher. *Prädikative Selektion als Grundlage für Transaktionssynchronisation und Datenintegrität*. PhD thesis, FB Informatik, Univ. Frankfurt, 1989.

[Böttcher, 1990a] S. Böttcher. Development and programming of deductive databases with PROTOS-L. In L. Belady, editor, *Proc. 2nd International Conference on Software Engineering and Knowledge Engineering*, Skokie, Illinois, USA, 1990. (to appear).

[Böttcher, 1990b] S. Böttcher. How to use PROTOS-L as a logic-based database programming language. In H.-J. Appelrath, A.B. Cremers, and O. Herzog, editors, *The EUREKA Project PROTOS*, Springer-Verlag, 1990. (to appear).

[Böttcher and Beierle, 1989] S. Böttcher and C. Beierle. Data base support for the PROTOS-L system. *Microprocessing and Microcomputing*, 27(1–5):25–30, August 1989.

[Eckhardt et al., 1985] H. Eckhardt, J. Edelmann, J. Koch, M. Mall, and J. W. Schmidt. *Draft Report on the Database Programming Language DBPL*. DBPL-Memo 091-85, Univ. Frankfurt, 1985.

[Meyer, 1989] G. Meyer. *Regelauswertung auf Datenbanken im Rahmen des PROTOS-L-Systems*. Diplomarbeit Nr. 630, Universität Stuttgart, December 1989.

[Sauer, 1990] J. Sauer. Design and implementation of a heuristic planning algorithm. In H.-J. Appelrath, A.B. Cremers, and O. Herzog, editors, *The EUREKA Project PROTOS*, Springer-Verlag, 1990. (to appear).

[Sauer et al., 1989] J. Sauer, G. Micheaux, and L. Slahor. Wissensbasierte feinplanung in PROTOS. In *Proceedings 3. GI-Kongreß Wissensbasierte Systeme, Informatik Fachberichte*, Springer-Verlag, 1989.

[Slahor et al., 1990] L. Slahor, F. Reuter, and H. Schildknecht. Scheduling problems: a user's perspective. In H.-J. Appelrath, A.B. Cremers, and O. Herzog, editors, *The EUREKA Project PROTOS*, Springer-Verlag, 1990. (to appear).

[Smolka, 1988] G. Smolka. *TEL (Version 0.9), Report and User Manual*. SEKI-Report SR 87-17, FB Informatik, Univ. Kaiserslautern, 1988.

[Wirth, 1983] N. Wirth. *Programming in Modula-2*. Springer, Berlin, Heidelberg, New York, 1983.

Application of hybrid expert systems in Computer Integrated Manufacturing

Henk de Swaan Arons   Eric-Paul Jansen

Faculty of Applied Mathematics and Informatics
Delft University of Technology
The Netherlands
E-mail: henk@dutisa.tudelft.nl and ericpaul@dutisa.tudelft.nl

Abstract

Delfi3 is a knowledge engineering environment which integrates a number of advanced knowledge representation and inference techniques such as a semantic net of objects and relations, a knowledge representation language and a backward/forward chaining interpreter for production rules. Delfi3 is a uniform and transparent system.

Delfi3's capabilities are very well suited to applications in CIM. Its knowledge bases are stored in modules which are separately compiled, can be stored in libraries and can be loaded very fast by various applications. Furthermore, it can be integrated with external databases and application software.

Delfi3 has partly been developed in the Esprit project 809 *Advanced Control Systems and Concepts in Small Batch Manufacturing* and is being used in Esprit project 2415 *Distributed Manufacturing, Planning and Control*.

In this paper some applications in CIM are outlined and it is explained how these will benefit of Delfi3's capabilities.

1 Introduction

The Faculty of Applied Mathematics and Informatics of Delft University of Technology is active in the field of knowledge-based systems since 1982, especially in building knowledge engineering tools.

In 1984 the first rule-based expert system shell (Delfi2) became operational and in 1987, its successor Delfi2+ emerged. This system was partly developed in Esprit project 809 in which it would be incorporated in a control system for Flexible Manufacturing System [Swa 89]. It has some important extensions with respect to knowledge representation, inference procedures (an intelligent combination of forward and backward reasoning), and it has considerably improved interfacing facilities to RDBMS. Furthermore, Delfi2+ has been made suited to on-line applications.

Nevertheless, because of its rather restricted knowledge representation capability (production rules) Delfi2+ has only a limited applicability. For this reason Delfi3 has been developed. This system has been built around Lore [Jon 90], a knowledge representation language based on objects and relations, both on definition and individual level. Another important part of Delfi3 is its rule base. Though objects and relations are an important and sufficient means to represent knowledge, experience with rule-based applications reflects that production rules can sometimes more suitably applied.

Many expert system shells are rather powerful in only a small class of applications, for instance in selection problems. Outside such an application area they have only little or no problem solving capability. However, in this respect Delfi3 is a general tool which can be applied in a wide range of applications. Furthermore, for a knowledge engineer there is no longer the need to implicitly specify the purpose within a given knowledge base as is the case in most rule-based systems; knowledge bases (e.g. stored in libraries) may contain more general knowledge which can be used for particular purposes.

Building an expert system requires adequate tools which can facilitate this task. The Delfi3 compiler is such a tool, helping to define the objects and relations in the domain and converting a given knowledge representation into an internal representation. In doing so, it also executes lexical, syntactical and semantical analysis [Ber 87].

With Delfi3 modular knowledge base can be built up, which is indispensable in the case of large knowledge bases.

Delfi3 is being used in Esprit project 2415 *Distributed Manufacturing, Planning and Control* in which Delft University of Technology participates.

In the following section Delfi3 is discussed in more detail. In section 3 two important applications in CIM are discussed; one application deals with knowledge-based scheduling, a second one concerns distributed knowledge-based systems in a manufacturing system. An example of how Delfi3 is used in this kind of applications is discussed in section 4. Section 5 presents some conclusions and prospects based on experience thus far.

2 Delfi3

Delfi3 is based on the data model DAMOR, it uses the knowledge representation language LORE and the rule base for inferences. Following each of these items will be looked at more closely.

2.1 The data model

DAMOR consists of objects and relations. The objects have attributes, which in turn have facets. Relations are used to express relationships between objects. The objects in DAMOR can be placed in a hierarchy that allows multiple inheritance. Also exceptions can be modelled using the so called CHANGES-construct.

DAMOR is a strongly typed data model; meaning that to each entity in DAMOR a type is assigned. These types are based on the object hierarchy, and called a hierarchical type system. Type rules are used to determine whether entities are correctly typed. Types have shown to be of great help with respect to the construction of correct programs.

In DAMOR there is a fundamental distinction between definitions and individuals. Definitions model prototype entities in the problem area, where individuals represent concrete entities in the problem area. Each individual has exactly one corresponding definition. The distinction between definitions and individuals holds for both objects and relations.

Objects model entities of the problem area. Objects can be placed in hierarchies allowing all kinds of inheritance rules. An object consists of a collection of attributes that describe relevant features of the object. There are two kinds of attributes: shared and private. Shared attributes describe features of a definition object that are common to all instances of that object (being individual objects). If such an attribute is bound to a value, this value is shared among all instances. Private attributes describe features that might differ for various instances. A value for a private attribute is determined by the instance itself.

Where attributes describe the features about objects, facets describe the various features of attributes. However, there is a limited set of facets. Beside the type facet (giving the type of the attribute) there are, for example, value facets to hold the value and if-needed facets that hold a method for obtaining a value when there is no value facet.

Definition objects can be placed in hierarchies. Most important about hierarchies are the structuring of the knowledge and the inheritance of information. In DAMOR the hierarchy of definition objects is constructed by so called SUPER-connections. If an object has a SUPER-connection to another object it inherits all attributes (and corresponding facets) from that object. Hierarchies may give rise to multiple inheritance. DAMOR can elegantly cope with this.

Relations are used to model all kind of relationships between objects that go beyond the simple SUPER-connections or object-attribute relationships. Just like objects, there are definition relations and individual relations. Relations can have any number of arguments, the type of these arguments determines the set of objects a relation may be applied to. A relation can be applied to any object that has a type compatible with the type of the corresponding argument.

There are two kinds of argument: DOMAIN and RANGE arguments. The DOMAIN arguments can be be considered as input arguments to the relations, where the RANGE parameters are input/output arguments.

2.2 The knowledge representation language

In LORE a view extension has been made to DAMOR to allow all kinds of inference. These inferences are based on first order predicate logic. The items added to DAMOR are expressions and variables. Expressions are found in facets (if-needed and if-added), views and queries. Variables can be introduced anywhere in combination with an expression.

A view is an expression in terms of the arguments (and variables) of the relation. The view of a definition relation is used to infer individual relations. The evaluation of views is very similar

to that of Prolog. Queries (both from within the knowledge base and from keyboard) can be used to extract information from LORE programs.

2.3 The rule base

From literature as well as from our own experiences with rule-based applications we find that rules are of great importance to the construction of expert systems; therefore, production rules are included in Delfi3. Because of the importance of a uniform system the rules have been completely integrated with DAMOR and LORE, allowing free interchange of reasoning between production rules and expressions in LORE.

A production rule in Delfi3 defines a prototype situation in terms of objects and relations. A rule has three parts: a declaration part, a condition part and a conclusion part. The declaration part determines the objects for which the rule can be used. The condition is simply an expression from LORE and the conclusion part consists of conclusions and actions. In example 1 a self-explaining Delfi3 rule is given.

```
Example 1: A Delfi3 production rule

RULE  Schedule_Acceptance_001
  GIVEN schedule, workplan: <Schedule>
  IF schedule.total_number_too_late >
        workplan.total_number_too_late
    AND schedule.number_too_late_of_class_1 >=
          workplan.number_too_late_of_class_1
    AND schedule.number_too_late_of_class_2 >=
          workplan.number_too_late_of_class_2
  THEN
    ABOUT schedule CONCLUDE acceptable := FALSE
ERULE
```

The structure of a rule base is closely related to the definition object hierarchy. The declaration part of a rule determines the object a rule can be applied to. Since more specific objects are placed lower in the hierarchy, rules concerning these objects should be defined lower in the hierarchy and cannot be applied to more general objects. The consequence of this approach is that the conflict set of rules becomes smaller for general objects. The rule selection from the conflict set is such that rules defined on more specific objects are chosen first, in this way more specific rules come before more general rules.

Both forward and backward chaining is used for inferences with the rules in Delfi3. These inferences can be started from any expression in Delfi3 (from views, facets, queries, conditions). On the other hand inferences in LORE can be started also in rule conditions. So the inferences can be completely interchanged.

To start backward inferences one must first set a goal (often tracing the value of an attribute); to start forward inferences one must give a set of data from which these inferences will start.

2.4 Embedding Delfi3

In many applications, Delfi3 will not work as an independent system, but has to be integrated with other programs. To allow this it must be possible to define interfaces to programs outside Delfi3. This is done by so-called external relations; external relations (XRELs) are normal definition relations except for the fact that they have no view. Instead of evaluating the view a corresponding external procedure is evaluated.

3 Modular knowledge base

It has been discussed that a rule base can be structured by the object hierarchy. Modules are another way of structuring a Delfi3 knowledge base. The advantages of using modules to improve maintainability is well known from the software engineering field. A Delfi3 program consists of a collection of modules; the interfaces between these modules are defined by using the import/export facilities of Delfi3.

Modules can be compiled separately with the only restriction that imported modules must already have been compiled. The compiles of all modules are finally linked to form the executable expert system. This program can be run by the Delfi3 interpreter.

Delfi3 programs are compiled before they can be executed. The compilation does more than only code generation. Of course, during the compilation process syntax checking is done, but also a number of so called semantic checks is performed. Among these checks are trivial checks on declaration of identifiers, but also more complex type-checks and checks on the correctness of the definition object hierarchy. The semantic checks performed distinguishes Delfi3 from many other systems. More details can be found in [Ber 87].

4 Application areas

Because of its integration of various knowledge representation techniques, the Delfi3 system can and is successfully applied applications in different application domains. In order to demonstrate this a few of these applications is briefly discussed. Two applications of Esprit projects are treated in more detail in next section.

A recent example concerns the re-implementation of the medical Plexus expert system. It was originally built in Delfi2+ and its knowledge base contained approximately 2000 production rules. Because of Delfi3's better knowledge representation facilities (particularly a better representation of the structural domain knowledge, allowing deep reasoning), Plexus is now being re-implemented in Delfi3 [Jas 90].

Another application is an expert system which configures a digital telephone switching system. The relations involved in this application have shown to be too complicated to be represented in a rule-based system [Waa 89].

Another promising application under development concerns mortgage selection, taking into account the mortgage conditions of all Dutch banks and insurance companies, related to a buyer's personal circumstances. This knowledge-based mortgage adviser enables any potential buyer to select the mortgage best suited to his personal circumstances without the help of a human expert.

In the following sections two applications of Delfi3 will be looked at in more detail. The first application concerns on-line decision-making with respect to dynamic re-scheduling, which has been one of the research topics in Esprit project 809 *Advanced Control Systems and Concepts in Small Batch Manufacturing*, in which Delft University of Technology is participating [Swa 89].

The second application concerns another Esprit project in which Delft University of Technology is involved: project 2415 *Distributed Manufacturing, Planning and Control*. The expert system will be an integrated component of both the OMS (Operator Management System) and the PMS (Production Management System). One of the interesting research topics is the distribution of knowledge over PMS and the various OMS.

5 CIM applications

In this sections two examples of Delfi3's involvement in CIM are briefly discussed. First, it is described how Delfi3 can help in re-scheduling in manufacturing. The second applications concerns distributed knowledge bases.

5.1 Knowledge-based job shop scheduling

In job shop scheduling it is attempted to solve the problem of scheduling a sequence of n jobs over a number m machines, in an optimal manner with respect to some criterion. he following methods and algorithms are known:

- Constructive algorithms
- Enumeration methods
- Priority and dispatching rules
- Interactive scheduling
- Knowledge-based scheduling

By a constructive scheduling an algorithm is meant which builds up an optimal solution from the data of the problem by following a simple set of rules which exactly determine the processing order. Unfortunately, due to the complexity of the problem, only for a few simple cases this method leads to useful rules.

Enumeration methods generate schedules one by one, searching for an optimal solution. The schedules are listed or enumerated, and the non-optimal schedules are removed from the list, leaving those which are optimal. Often they use clever elimination procedures to see if the non-optimality of one schedule implies the non-optimality of many others not yet generated. Thus the methods may not search all the set of feasible solutions. Nonetheless, they are methods that proceed by exhaustive enumeration, have serious computational consequences which may soon be quite prohibitive in many practical problems.

Experiments have demonstrated that schedule generation based on priority rules is a practicable method of obtaining sub-optimal solutions to job shop problems. A priority rule assigns a scalar to each waiting job that can be the object of the next scheduling decision. These priority rules could be directly used to dispatch a job when a machine becomes idle: take the job with the smallest priority. It must be noticed that mostly a priority will not be optimal.

The above-mentioned methods have some disadvantages. First, constructive algorithms can only successfully be applied in a very limited number of job shops. Second, in many applications the computational efforts of enumeration methods are quite soon prohibitive. Finally, the priority (dispatching) methods do guarantee a schedule, however, the solution could and will often be far from optimal. In [Nak 88] it is explained that there is no dispatching rule which is effective for all scheduling problems. The results obtained for a given rule differ according to the operating conditions. It is therefore important to know the type of assumptions and operating conditions used before dispatching rules can be selected for proper applications. These methods lack human experience, which is generally considered as a major drawback. In the same paper several experiments have been described demonstrating that humans with even little experience in manufacturing do have the ability to make good scheduling decisions.

In the foregoing paragraph it has been concluded that a combination of using priority rules and human experience is an attractive approach. Indeed, most priority rules are intended for use with all job files. When several rules are tested with a job shop simulator the "best" rule is sought, the one which will be most effective most of the time, regardless of the particular job files. However, experiments of Nakamura have shown that the priority rules should be chosen based on the actual job file.

The knowledge base must contain a description of both the job shop and how scheduling could be done. By the following objects a simple job shop is represented in which all relevant items such as *Order, Workstation, Tool,* and *Toolset* are modelled. These definition objects are grouped in one module. Explanations and other comments are printed in italic between bracelets, keywords are bold-faced.

```
DOBJ *Order
{The asterisk denotes that the object Order may
be imported from this module to other modules of
the knowledge base}
PRIVATE
   product: <INT>  {product-code}
| number_of_products: <INT>
| due_date: <Date>
{Date is also defined as an object, see follow-
ing DOBJ}
EOBJ


DOBJ *Date
PRIVATE
   year: <INT # 1990 TO 1999>
| month: <INT # 1 TO 12>
| day: <INT # 1 TO 31>
EOBJ


DOBJ *Workstation
PRIVATE
   occupied: <BOOL>
     DEF FALSE
{By default a workstation is not occupied}
| tools: <LIST <Tool>>
| present_job: <Job>
| present_tool: <Tool>
| expected_release_time: <INT>
EOBJ


DOBJ *Tool
PRIVATE
   setup_time: <INT>
| can_last_for: <INT>
| number_of_places_in_buffer: <INT>
EOBJ
```

Another module defines all relevant relations between the various objects. It is the task of the job shop to machine a list of jobs given by a startlist of jobs. The definition relation (DREL) *Simulate* starts the simulation of the job shop by first checking the availability of some necessary components (tool transport system, pallet transport system), next by showing the jobs to be machined and at last by starting the process.

```
DREL Go
{Go is a recursive relation calling itself as
long as there are jobs left to be machined, the
BOOL TRUE indicates whether a  job is ready}
VAR ws,helpws: <Workstation>
  | helplst: <LIST <Workstation>>
[Job_ready() AND ! AND
 Show_joblist("Ready jobs:",ready_jobs.contents)
    AND WRITE("Job done: end of simulation")
      OR
LISTER(helpws,helplst,available_ws.list)
{LISTER is a built-in relation.In this case it
splits a list into a head and a tail}
AND Look_for_ws(ws,helpws,available_ws.list)
AND Look_for_and_do_task(ws)
AND Go()]
EREL


DREL Simulate
VAR  head: <Workstation>
   | tail: <LIST <Workstation>>
[Initiate() AND
 Show_joblist("Startset:",startset.contents)
AND
 Go()]
EREL
```

It can be noticed that several other relations are called. For instance, in case that there are still jobs left to be machined the relation *look_for_ws* determines the first workstation that will be ready. The relation *look_for_and_do_task* tries to find a suited job for the machine just determined.

It is in this relation that knowledge-based scheduling can be performed. It may contain heuristic rules which determine the choice of the next job. For instance, if a job's next machining type could be done on the same machine, then it could be time-saving to take that job first for that machine. Another approach is to consider such a job together with all other jobs that can be machined on that machine, and to take the one with he highest priority, given some priority rules.

In the model described above, the complete simulation is carried out by Delfi3, but it could be better to have some special-purpose programs to be carried out outside the knowledge-based system. For instance, decisions on whether or not to re-schedule are preferably taken based on the results of the suggested priority rules. Then, the simulation itself (in fact a forecast which is calculated based on a process-plan, a cell configuration and a set of priority rules) is carried out outside the expert system. However, the decisions which priority rules to be taken for which machines, and whether re-scheduling will be carried out remain in the knowledge base.

5.2 Distributed knowledge-based decision-making

This part of the paper describes an area that is currently under

94

research and which is funded by the CEC as part of the Esprit project 2415 [TAE 88]. It shows an example of the usage of knowledge-based systems within the project and some preliminary results that are important to the further development of the project.

In manufacturing the allocation of resources such as machines, tools and human effort, plays an important role. To plan for a long period, especially in large manufacturing companies, MRPII systems can be used. However, in general an MRPII system can not adequately support manufacturing environments that produce products in small to medium size batches and it is not quite able to react on frequently changing situations such as rush orders and machine breakdowns. So, most of the adjustments to the original plans as offered by the MRPII systems, is being done by hand by production planners and cell operators (cell: collection of manufacturing machines to produce certain types or families of products). The production planner is responsible for assigning a shop order (order for a part) to a cell, either according to the plan (by MRPII or by hand) or based on events as rush orders. During this assignment process, there might be some negotiation between the production planner and the cell operator who is responsible for the allocation of the machines to be used for each shop order.

To support the production planner and the cell operator with these tasks two systems, the Production Management Support System (PMS) and the Operator Management System (OMS), are being developed. These systems support tasks such as scheduling, capacity loading and balancing and schedule progress evaluation, but they differ in the level of appliance (see Figure 1). Linked together, these systems form a multi-level distributed manufacturing support system for planning and control.

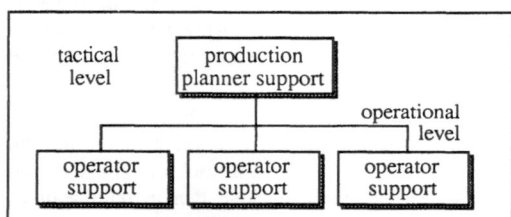

Figure 1. Multi-level manufacturing support system

Although each system can support its user, either the production planner or the operator, some of the system's functions can be enhanced in their functioning by allowing knowledge-based systems to support the decision making process. How the knowledge-based systems can be used for this support activity is one of the topics that are currently being researched at the Delft University.

Typical problem situation

One of the production planner's tasks is to schedule each shop order to be processed by a certain manufacturing cell. A constraint to the assignment of a shop order to a cell, is the ability of the cell to manufacture the part in time, i.e. the due date of the shop order has to be met. If this is not possible, the production planner tries to assign the shop order to another cell. If there is

no possibility that the due date can be met, an alternative solution has to be found.

In case of the PMS, this system assists the production planner with, among others, the scheduling task. The process of finding an alternative solution can also be supported by PMS, if PMS is able to use the knowledge and experience of an expert production planner. It is not necessary for PMS to actually contain this knowledge and experience. It suffices when PMS can interact with a knowledge-based system which does contain it. For this purpose the Delfi3 knowledge-based system will be used.

In this particular example, PMS will ask the knowledge-based system for advice on this due date violation. A due date violation can have several causes such as capacity or throughput-time problems. Based on the cause of the violation and some additional information from stored data, the knowledge-based system tries to find some alternative solutions to the due date violation problem, and offers them ordered to the PMS. During the process of determining solutions, communication between the PMS and the knowledge-based system can be necessary.

Distributed knowledge-based support

At operational level, the OMS systems are also supported by knowledge-based systems that may perform similar tasks as the knowledge-based system that supports the PMS. Supporting an OMS, the knowledge-based system starts to know facts that may be valuable to the knowledge-based system that is supporting the PMS.

Suppose the quality monitoring function of an OMS detects the wearing out of some of the tools. A knowledge-based system which is advising some function of the OMS gets hold of this information and concludes this to be of importance to the knowledge-based system which supports PMS with the problem solving concerning due date violation problems. In this way the various knowledge-based systems constitute a larger system, a distributed knowledge-based system, that supports the problem solving of the entire distributed manufacturing system and which deals with problems that occur on different levels within the manufacturing environment.

Implementation of a distributed knowledge-based system

The objective of the research is to develop knowledge-based systems that support the various functions of PMS and OMS. The knowledge-based systems will be implemented using Delfi3. As such, we have to find a way of using the Delfi3 system to build a distributed knowledge-based system, preferably with as little changes as possible to the Delfi3 system itself.

To investigate in how far the Delfi3 system can be used to implement a distributed knowledge-based system, a small testing system has been implemented. This testing system consists of several knowledge-based systems that communicate with each other through message exchange. If something that is known by a knowledge-based system A might be important or is described to be important to another knowledge-based system B, A will send a message to B stating the fact f known to A. The interpretation of f depends on the knowledge that is available to B. The following example shows a possible way of implementing message exchange.

```
DOBJ Message
PRIVATE
   Sender, Receiver: <TEXT>
| Mess: <LIST <TEXT>>
EOBJ

DOBJ MessageList
PRIVATE
  messages: <LIST <Message>>
EOBJ

IOBJ mList: MessageList([])
{mList is an instance of the MessageList object
and contains all received messages that are not
yet processed. Initially mList contains an empty
message list: mList.messages = []}
EOBJ

XREL ReceiveMessage
{The relation ReceiveMessage calls an external
program to obtain facts known to other knowl-
edge-based systems }
DOMAIN Sender, Receiver: <TEXT>
RANGE Mess: <LIST <TEXT>>
   CALL ReceiveMessage
EREL

XREL SendMessage
{The relation SendMessage calls an external pro-
gram to offer known facts to other knowledge-
based systems }
DOMAIN Sender, Receiver: <TEXT>
RANGE Mess: <LIST <TEXT>>
   CALL SendMessage
EREL

DREL CheckForMessageFrom
DOMAIN Sender: <TEXT>
VAR Receiver: <TEXT> | Mess: <LIST <TEXT>>
[Receiver = "A" AND
{The receiver is the knowledge-based system A }
  ReceiveMessage(Sender,Receiver,Mess) AND !
AND
     LISTER(Message(Sender,Receiver,Mess),
           mList.messages,mList.`messages)
   OR  TRUE]
EREL
```

Suppose knowledge-based system A supports the function of capacity planning of PMS and the knowledge-based systems B_1 and B_2 support the quality monitoring function of two OMS systems for cells C_1 and C_2. If B_1 or B_2 decides that certain facts may be important to A, messages containing information on these facts are sent to A. To retrieve the messages, A either constantly checks for incoming messages, or A only checks for messages at the time it needs additional information on a specific subject. E.g. A is searching for possible alternative cells to assign a shop order to. If the manufacturing of this shop order requires a high level of precision, A will not assign a shop order to a cell B_2 for which some of the machines cannot meet this level of precision because of tools wearing out. At the moment it needs information on this, A retrieves all messages to check for this information. This second option can be enhanced by checking only the messages from a specified knowledge-based system, e.g. all messages from B_2 .

```
DREL   PossibleAlternative
DOMAIN Sender: <TEXT>
VAR    message: <Message>
[mList.messages = [] AND ! AND TRUE OR
  LISTER(message,mList.`messages,
          mList.messages) AND
  [message.Sender=Sender AND
         "Tools wearing out" IN message.Mess
    AND ! AND FALSE
  OR PossibleAlternative(Sender)]]
EREL
```

The relation `PossibleAlternative` checks all messages for information on the wearing out of the tools for a specific cell. Knowledge-based system A uses the outcome of the relation `PossibleAlternative` in the process of generating possible solutions for the capacity planning function of PMS.

6 Conclusions

Delfi3 is still under development, some parts will have to be added or improved. Nevertheless, the present system has already been successfully applied. A reason for this is that Delfi3's knowledge representation and inference techniques can represent quite different applications. Moreover, it has a uniform structure meaning that the various parts are based on the same design principles. Nevertheless, only qualified users will be able to successfully use all offered features.

The use of a hybrid knowledge-based systems in CIM has shown several important advantages. The objects defined can easily identify all relevant items (machines, jobs etc) in a Flexible Manufacturing System or job shop environment, the built-in and user-defined relations can describe how the various items are related.

References

[Ber 87] Berg T van den. *Lore-compiler*. Graduate thesis of the Faculty of Technical Mathematics and Informatics of Delft University of Technology. Delft. August 1987.

[Jas 90] Jaspers R. *Medical decision support: an approach in the domain of brachial plexus injuries*. Dissertation. Faculty of Mechanical Engineering. Delft University of Technology. Delft. 1990.

[Jon 90] Jonker W. *The design and implementation of a knowledge representation and processing language*. Dissertation. Faculty of Applied Mathematics and Informatics. Delft University of Technology. Delft. 1990.

[Nak 88] Nakamura N., Salvendy G., *An experimental study of human decision-making in computer-based scheduling of flexible manufacturing system*, Int. J. Prod. Res., Vol. 26, no. 4, pp. 567 - 583, 1988.

[Swa 89] Swaan Arons H., Riewe D. *Integration of Dynamic Expert Scheduling in Production Control*. In: Proceedings of the 6th Annual Esprit Conference 1989. 27 November - 1 December 1989. pp 674 - 687. Kluwer Academic Publishers. Brussels.

[TAE 88] Technical Annex for Esprit Project 2415: Distributed Manufacturing, Planning and Control.

[Waa 89] Waal de JC. *The design of a knowledge-based system for the configuration of digital telephone switching systems*. Graduate thesis of the Faculty of Electrotechnics of Delft University of Technology. Delft. 1989.

Relational Database Applications in Manufacturing System Design

Elizabeth C. Scheyder

Member, Association for Computing Machinery

ABSTRACT

Relational databases can be implemented as an effective design tool during the Preliminary and Final Engineering phases of manufacturing system design projects. The use of a hierarchical relational database structure will be shown to enhance system development, handling detailed information about electrical, mechanical, chemical, or other parameters of system components and their applications. Holding such information in a central database structure as it becomes available maximizes its accessibility and coordinates communication between disciplines involved in the project. This enables calculations to be automated, ensures data integrity, and minimizes redundant compilation and typing of data. The ability to interface with a computer aided design (CAD) package can increase the labor savings of such a database even further. Techniques will be shown for assessing a particular project's needs and developing an overall structure which can be customized to suit the details of an application, providing an effective design tool for quality and efficiency in the project.

I. Introduction

While relational databases are widely recognized as a powerful tool for handling production data in a manufacturing environment, their application as a resource for designing manufacturing systems is not often recognized. When one considers the ability of relational databases to organize and manipulate large quantities of information about the equipment, instrumentation, and other components that are selected for such a system during the Preliminary and Final Engineering phases of a project, the value of relational databases in this implementation becomes apparent.

It is the intent of this paper to detail the application of a hierarchical relational database structure to the design of a manufacturing system of virtually any size. Although the author and her colleagues have implemented relational databases in manufacturing system design at a large professional consulting firm working on multimillion dollar projects, techniques presented here can be applied equally well by firms doing their own system design for projects large or small.

II. Problem Definition

During the design of any manufacturing system, large quantities of information are gathered pertaining to the various components of the system. Such information can include motor voltages and types, pipe sizes and materials of construction, instrument cabinet numbers and other highly detailed data. While it has been standard practice to maintain such information on paper, keeping such data up to date when it is held this way is nearly impossible as designs are modified and new information is acquired which has an impact on existing data. Problems inevitably arise when conflicting information is found in a paper file, and much time can be wasted considering which information is really "current". Information held in various forms on paper is difficult to share between disciplines, and when interim reports are required, information must be compiled by hand and the resulting report typed, requiring a great effort and leaving many chances for error. Even simple counts of particular types of components are a hand effort requiring a professional's time and concentration.

Despite these drawbacks, the adherence to the traditional "paper file" method of information storage and retrieval continues to be surprisingly prevalent in the design of manufacturing systems. This is most likely a consequence of the limited experience with databases of many engineers who work on such systems, as well as the somewhat formidable interfaces of many database packages. As database packages improve and more engineers become not only computer-literate, but also proficient, manufacturing system design is certain to become more computerized. Relational databases are an excellent tool in this case, organizing the great quantity of information that exists, and expanding the usefulness of component data.

The move to the use of a hierarchical relational database structure has been gradual. In the author's experience, individual engineers who are more computer literate have begun to implement databases for use during design, but have implemented only information directly useful to their work, and have used whatever database software package was easily available, Widely varied computer literacy and the incompatibility of information in different database languages has discouraged any larger computerization project. Now, as more and more engineers use personal computers on a daily basis, and with database software packages for personal computers becoming less expensive and more friendly, it becomes a much less formidable task to implement a relational database for manufacturing system design. The applications described here are intended to be accessible enough to be implemented by the engineers who will use them, possibly with the assistance of one person familiar with programming in the database package selected. If time and resources permit, a more formal Management Information Systems staff may become involved, but this is not a necessity. As will be described in more detail later, the database structure described here is hierarchical, with one parent and a flexible number of children, which makes it possible to pursue a phased implementation over the course of several projects, again depending upon the resources available.

III. Benefits of Relational Databases

The implementation of a relational database during manufacturing system design coordinates information from many disciplines contributing to the project, such as Civil Engineering, Electrical Engineering, Instrumentation Engineering, Process Engineering, Project Management, Purchasing, and Scheduling, by encouraging each discipline to codify its information and provide it for entry into a relational database where it can be accessed by everyone for reference and consideration. While the dissimilar parameters of different types of components would make a single database prohibitively large and difficult to manipulate, using several smaller related databases keeps particular types of components with similar attributes or uses grouped together. Furthermore, this centralization efficiently ensures data integrity, since all information is entered once and checked, and all further references to it are drawn directly from the database, eliminating typographical errors in reports and errors in interpreting handwritten information. This not only saves time, but also allows clerical time to be substituted for professional time in filling out reports, such as instrument indexes and equipment specifications.

Holding all information in a central relational database structure allows a clerk to access it with report generator, producing a uniform, computer generated report without filling out forms by hand or re-typing information that is already held in the database. This centralized structure can be held on a file server or networked personal computer with access to making modifications restricted by password, again maximizing the availability of information. A simple algorithm can be implemented to track the date a data record was last updated so that modifications can be monitored and information can be restored from a backup copy if a problem should arise. The ability to interface to computer-aided design (CAD) packages can further reduce drains on professional time in listing all equipment appearing on Piping and Instrumentation Diagrams and other drawings, since many CAD packages now include a utility for automatically transferring information from drawings into database files readable by several commercial database packages. Further, most database software packages provide a utility for transferring information in database fields to text files, which can be imported into the CAD package and used for annotation, again saving typing time and eliminating typographical errors.

With relational database programming languages available, algorithms can be developed easily to handle repetitive, non-creative tasks such as assigning input/output points, calculating electrical loads, and determining equipment sizes required. These languages can also provide user-friendly interfaces for clerks unfamiliar with database use, allowing them to enter and modify data, initiate automatic calculations, and prepare reports with minimal assistance or supervision. Programs can include protection of data entered, checking input for validity, and even password protection. Again, the sophistication required depends upon the application.

IV. Developing a Relational Database Structure for Manufacturing System Design

After realizing the ability of a relational database to contribute to a project, the next question is when and how to begin. When to begin is "early" - as soon as there is some concrete idea about what the project will encompass, and the types of equipment that will be used, even if these may change as the project progresses. In a large consulting firm, with industry-specific expertise, this information can be similar from project to project, and becomes somewhat intuitive. For a smaller company, or one unfamiliar with the use of databases or a particular application being approached, this may require more thought. Note, however, that the conceptual development of a relational database application should be done by a group rather than just one person, to avoid the biases and other pitfalls inherent in forcing the opinions of one designer on a varied group of users.

Beginning early encourages ongoing intermittent thought about the database, and ultimately leads to a series of revisions that will produce a maximally useful structure. Further, the earlier a relational database is structured and implemented, the earlier its rewards can be appreciated, and the more uses it will have, which provides more impetus to continue than would a last-minute attempt to create and input everything at once to produce only a final report.

IVa. Defining Goals

Contributors to developing the relational database structure should be those who provide the information necessary to build the database as well as those who will be determining the form of its output. White this is not a tremendously laborious endeavor, it is absolutely necessary that those who agree to contribute to the project be committed to it. If they should lose interest and fail to contribute what they have promised, there will be gaps in the results and goals will not be fully achieved.

Once the project team has been assembled and has some idea of what the intended manufacturing system will require and how it will be identified, the general goals of the relational database can be assessed. As mentioned previously, there can be a phased implementation of goals. If this is to be the case, the growth path of the database structure should be identified at the planning stage so that the overall structure can be implemented most efficiently and everyone understands and agrees with the proposed partial results and milestones. Overall intended goals are best divided into categories such as the following:

I. Input
    A. Engineering (all disciplines)
    B. Management
    C. Purchasing
    D. Scheduling

II. Data Handling
    A. User interface
    B. Automatic data generation
    C. Automatic data checking

III. Output
    A. Internal
        1. Interim reports for checking drawings

2. Equipment lists and engineering reports
3. Management/Purchasing/Scheduling reports
B. Customer (if applicable)
C. Vendors and Contractors
   1. Specifications
   2. Installation information

Again, these goals will be dependent upon the project and its participators, but they must be stated explicitly and agreed upon during the development of the relational database if the project is to be a success.

IV b. Defining a Structure

Once the relational database's goals have been defined, actual structuring can begin. Since the premise is to hold and manipulate information about the components of a system, the identifying part number or tag number of each component must be the backbone of the structure of the relational database. Each component must have an identifier that is completely unique, as this will provide the link between the databases holding the particular discipline information for each component. For the purposes of keeping information in databases of manageable size and avoiding allocating fields (and memory) which will not be necessary for each item, the child databases are best used to group particular discipline information. For example, every component in the manufacturing system is required to be a member of the parent database, that is, it will appear in the parent database with information that pertains to all components (such as its description, component type, and specification number). Every component is also required to be a member of the Reference drawings (child) database, since this indexes the particular drawings where each component appears. However, each component is not required to be a member of every child database (other than the Reference Drawings), since only electrical equipment will appear in the electrical database, and only instruments will appear in the instrumentation database. An example of a general structure, using the notation proposed by Howe, is given in Figure 1.[1]

Relational Database Sample Structure

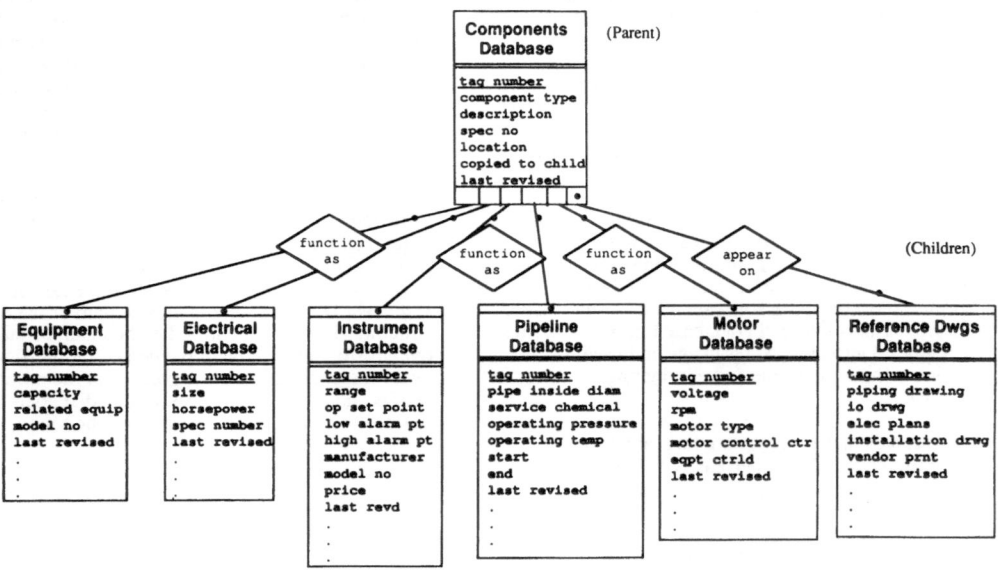

Example: every member of Equipment database must be a member of Parent database, but, not every member of Parent database is a member of Equipment database.

Figure 1

Typical Database Entries

Component Database (Parent)

Tag No.	Component Type	Description	Spec. No.	Location	Copied to Child	Last Rev'd
T-01	Equipment	Holding Tank	S-300	Process Area	Yes	2/1/90
XV-01	Instrument	Tank Inlet Valve	S-301	Tank T-01	Yes	2/1/90
LE-01	Instrument	Level Element	S-302	Tank T-01	Yes	2/2/90
LIT-01	Instrument	Level Transmitter	S-303	Tank T-01	Yes	2/2/90
TE-01	Instrument	Temp. Element	S-304	Tank T-01	Yes	2/1/90
P-001	Pipeline	Tank Feed Pipe	P-100	Process Area	Yes	2/8/90
P-002	Pipeline	Tank Drain Pipe	P-100	Process Area	Yes	2/8/90

Instrument Database (Child)

Tag Number	Range	Operating Set Point	Low Alarm	High Alarm	Manuf.	Model	Price	Last Rev'd
XV-01		Open			Brand A	V-1	$100	2/8/90
LE-01	0-100%		10%	90%	Brand B	E-1-a	$150	2/7/90
LIT-01	4-20 mA		5mA	18mA	Brand B	T-1-a	$250	2/7/90
TE-01	40-100°C		50°C	80°C	Brand C	TE-2	$150	2/8/90

Figure 2

Note that the tag number field appears in every database and provides the relation between databases. Each tag number is unique, providing a basis for sorting and indexing the records, so the tag number field is called the primary key of each database. Again, this provides the facility to access all information about a given component without allocating memory for inapplicable information or creating an extremely large database that becomes very difficult to manipulate or even backup.

Note also that it is required that every record in a child database also appear in the parent database. This is required if the structure is to be a hierarchical relational database, and it is fundamental to our original premise that the parent database will provide basic information about every component in the manufacturing system. It is also significant to note that this structure is Boyce Codd Normal Form (BCNF), since the tag number field is the basis of all of the relations, and is the primary key for them.[2,3] While it is not the intent of this paper to delve into the theory involved here, suffice it to say that a BCNF structure avoids complicated interdependencies which can lead to loss of information and compromised data integrity.

The percentage of all records which appear in each of the child databases depends directly on the manufacturing system being designed. Some applications, such as packaging systems, are electrically intensive, with many conveyors, motors and switches, while others, such as chemical processes, would have more control valves, measurement devices, transmitters, and related instrumentation, but proportionately fewer motors.

As a specific example, consider Figure 2, "typical" entries for a component (parent) database and instrument (child) database. Once a structure has been developed, database functions which will directly serve the goals of the system can be addressed.

V. Data Handling

The next consideration is the data handling that will be done, including automatic data generation and the user interface. As with the rest of the design, the sophistication here depends upon the requirements of the project and the resources of time and talent available to meet them. The simplest structure can be manipulated without sophisticated data handling, but a certain amount of user interface will make the system more friendly for clerks or other users unfamiliar with databases. In this phase of the system, it is particularly easy to modularize development, with features added as the system progresses, needs develop, and the time is available.

Depending upon the database package being used and requirements of the project, the interface can be a series of small programs to be run directly to perform tasks, or they can be incorporated into a menu-driven interface. Interface functions to be considered are:

1. Adding records to the database
2. Placing tag numbers in child databases appropriate to each component
3. Adding information to records in the child databases
4. Changing information held in databases
5. Changing a tag number (as the primary key field, it is crucial to the structure of the relational database, and it must include changes in all child databases)
6. Deleting records from parent database and all child databases where they appear
7. Calculating derived information
8. Preparing reports

Figure 3 shows a sample input screen for the parent database with the structure described in Figure 1. As a further example, the steps required in an algorithm to place tag numbers from the parent database into the child databases appropriate to a particular component would be the following:

1. Select a record and check if tag number is to be copied into the first child database

    a. If it is to be copied:
      (1) Open the first child database for use
      (2) Place an empty record in the database
      (3) Put the tag number in the child database record

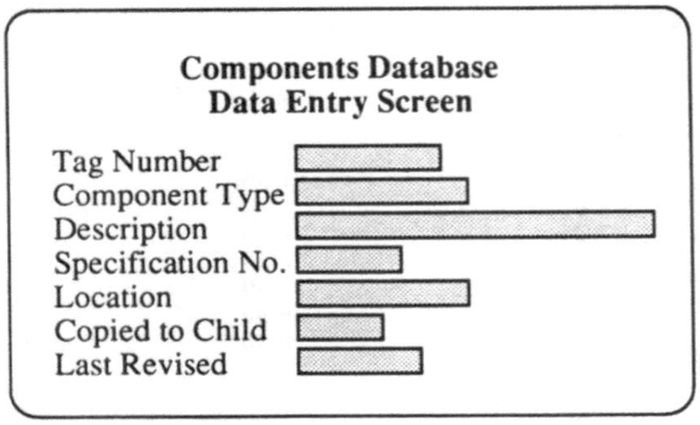

**Components Database
Data Entry Screen**

Tag Number
Component Type
Description
Specification No.
Location
Copied to Child
Last Revised

Figure 3

(4)   Put any other automatically generated information in the child database record

(5)   Change parent database record to show that record has been copied to first child database

(6)   Close first child database

b.   If it is not to be copied, do nothing to the first child database

2.   Step one is repeated for each successive child database, until the record has been checked for copying into each child database

3.   Steps one and two are repeated for all records being transferred

VI. Implementing the Relational Database

Once the structure and data handling have been developed, the implementation of the database in entering and manipulating information should be smooth and efficient. Experience is always the best way to polish a structure though, and one should not hesitate to make modifications as the project progresses. With a structure that has been considered carefully and follows the guidelines presented here, changes should be minor and should decrease rapidly over time. It is best to implement changes as they are discovered, so that a minimum number of records will need to be modified or re-entered because of the change. Once the data has been entered, it can be used for checking the completeness of drawings and producing partial reports, showing which data has yet to be determined. The ability to globally change certain information in the database can also be very helpful if, for example, all Brand A widgets are changed to Brand B, Model Number 1.

The preparation of reports becomes simple, with very professional results and easy modifications based on project needs. A sample Instrument Index is given in Figure 4. Note that all instruments can be listed, or only certain types, or only those located in a certain part of the manufacturing system. The power and advantage of the relational database is most apparent in this use.

VII. Conclusion

While paper output such as an equipment list is the most concrete example of the application of relational databases to manufacturing system design, it has been shown how labor can be reduced in several ways by investing a reasonably small amount of time in developing and implementing a relational database. The structures shown should be straightforward enough to be implemented by someone with only moderate experience in the database software selected for use. The modular structure also allows the implementation of a relational database to be selective, based on the needs of a given project, and even phased over several projects, with increasing capabilities installed on each successive project. Any time spent in such development will be recouped quickly in the savings of information sharing, CAD interfacing, automatic data generation, and report preparation. Reductions in design time and improvements in efficiency by using a relational database will provide tangible cost savings, while improvements in quality on a project can be even more valuable.

REFERENCES

[1] D. R. Howe, Data Analysis for Database Design. Baltimore, MD: Edward Arnold/University Park Press, 1983.

[2] G. A. Jackson, Relational Database Design with Microcomputer Applications. Englewood Cliffs, N.J.: Prentice Hall, 1988.

[3] E. F. Codd, "Recent Investigations in Relational Database Systems," Proceedings of the International Federation for Information Processing, 1974. Amsterdam: North-Holland, 1974.

INSTRUMENT INDEX
Engineering Database

Tag Number	Service description	Spec. No.	Oper. Range	Manufacturer	Model No.	Price
XV-01	Tank Inlet Valve	S-301		Brand A	V-1	100.00
LE-01	Level Element	S-302	0-100%	Brand B	E-1-a	150.00
LIT-01	Level Transmitter	S-303	4-20mA	Brand B	T-1-a	250.00
TE-01	Temperature	S-304	40-100 C	Brand C	TE-2	150.00

Figure 4

Integration of Knowledge-Based Modules into a Distributed Production Planning and Control System

C. Bolte   K. Kurbel   C. Rautenstrauch

Westfälische Wilhelms-Universität
Institut für Wirtschaftsinformatik
Grevener Str. 91, D-4400 Münster
Fed. Rep. of Germany

Abstract

In this paper we will describe the architecture of a distributed production planning, scheduling, and control system (PPC system), the functionality of integrated expert system components, and the way in which they are integrated into the system. This is followed by a discussion of our experience using the database and expert system tools. Most functions of the PPC system are based on a distributed relational database system. One main topic of this paper is the role of the database system as "integration instrument" in this context.

Concept

Our developmental activities focussed on building a low cost production planning, scheduling, and control system (PPC system) for small to medium sized manufacturers in the discrete part industry. In the past, traditional PPC systems have been based on mainframe or minicomputer technology. Therefore, from a business point of view, such systems have demanded high investments, before they could be used efficiently. Our idea was to build a distributed PPC system based on workstation, PC, distributed database, and LAN (local area network) technology. Small and medium sized companies require more and more

distributed systems of this kind. Such systems can only be implemented in an environment where both hardware and software offer considerable flexibility. A major advantage of the distributed system architecture is that the requisite capital investment in equipment grows relative to the stage of development of the total system.

In a distributed environment the complex PPC system is divided into "workplaces". Each workplace is a complete computer system representing a node in a LAN. On each node, a set of PPC system functions and data may be installed. From the database point of view, this is a multi-server architecture, because a workplace may function as both client and server. A typical configuration is shown in Figure 1.

Two expert system components have been developed and integrated into the distributed PPC system: a bill of materials (bom) generator and a production schedule generator.

Standard algorithms for presales order calculation and for shop order generation are based on the assumption that a bill of materials and production schedule already exist. But neither a bill of materials nor a production schedule is available when a customer specifies new or modified parts. Therefore the bom expert system constructs a bill of materials based on customer specifications. The bom can subsequently

Fig. 1: Workplace configuration in a distributed PPC system

be forwarded to and used by the production schedule generator. Both the bill of materials and the schedule may then be used as input for standard presales calculation and shop order generation algorithms.

The two expert system components are installed at the workplaces. They communicate with other system modules by means of a common database. The following sections describe the architecture of the distributed PPC system, the functionality of the expert system components, and the way in which they are integrated into the system. This is followed by a discussion of our experience using the database and expert system tools.

System Architecture

Workplaces and Functions

Our present prototype of the distributed PPC system goes under the name of VAIS (this is a German acronym for "Verteiltes Auftrags-InformationsSystem"): customer support, materials resource planning, master production scheduling, and short term production planning and control [2]. Four workplaces have been realized with major functions at the workplaces as follows:

- customer support (CS): customer orders management, retrieval functions for shop orders and parts, presales calculation,

- materials resource planning (MRP): management of parts, bills of materials (generation and maintenance), inventory control,

- master production scheduling (MPS): management of long term production schedules, shop orders, scheduling,

- short term production planning and control (STPPC): scheduling and sequencing based on graphics ("Leitstand"), interactive capacity planning and smoothing, and Gantt charts [1].

Hardware and Software Basis

Our implementation of VAIS is based on an Ethernet LAN (TCP/IP protocol) with four Unix workstations (SUN 3/60, SUN 4/110, HP 9000/350, Personal Computer with Xenix386) and a Personal Computer running under MS-DOS. The distributed database system is ORACLE RDBMS. An ORACLE 4GL tool (SQL*Forms) was used for implementation of most of the "non-expert-system" functions. Complex algorithms, such as shop order generation and scheduling, are, however, written in C and embedded SQL and are integrated with SQL*Forms modules.

A Mapping of workplaces to hardware systems is shown in Figure 2.

Data Distribution

The data allocation mode is dispersal which means that each relation is completely assigned to exactly one node of the network. This is a less than optimal data allocation scheme. Our data base management system (ORACLE) did not, however, offer a two phase commit protocol. Therefore, we had to design a distribution scheme, and work out a methodology for maintaining consistency in distributed update transactions. A description in more detail is given in [3].

The Unix-based-workplaces perform as both clients and servers (data suppliers) within the distributed database. The MS-DOS based work-place functions as a client using the database of the master production scheduling workplace as a "logical local database". When a workplace is directly connected to a remote database, then the database referred to is a "logical local database", since it behaves as if it were a database local to the workplace. This mode of coupling had to be chosen because an MS-DOS workplace cannot be a database server in a distributed environment. We were, however, working under the constraint that "Leitstand" data had to be available to other workplaces, too.

Expert Systems Integration

The two expert system components are quite different from each other with regard to their design and their integration into the VAIS system.

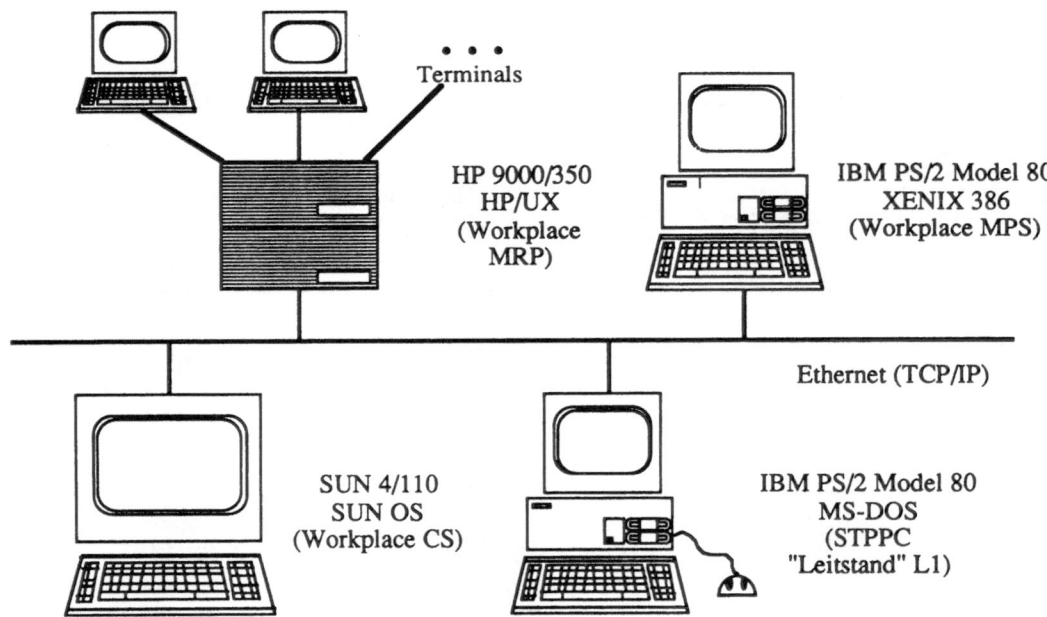

Fig. 2: Configuration of the prototype system

The bill of materials generator Stuelip was planned and designed as a part of VAIS from the very beginning, while PIA, the expert system for generating production schedules, was built as a stand-alone system by a different research group at the University of Dortmund [4].

The decision to integrate PIA into our distributed PPC system was made long after work on VAIS had already begun.

Because of these different starting points, communication between the knowledge based components and those VAIS components which are based on Oracle and its tools, was difficult for several reasons. When we started to design the Stuelip system a direct connection to the VAIS database and to ORACLE was planned. Stuelip was designed as a part of the "customer support" workplace, but it was supposed to use the "materials resource planning" database as its logical local database. Figure 3 shows the integration of Stuelip into VAIS and the access paths between the databases and the workplaces functions.

Stuelip runs on a SUN 4/110 workstation. A connection from Nexpert Object to ORACLE can be realized using the tool Nexpert Object ORACLE Bridge. Because of technical problems which appeared during the implementation process (see also last section), there is no direct connection between the expert system and the database currently. But it could be shown that it is possible to access to the database, not by using the ORACLE Bridge, but by simulating access as the following procedures:

- after the expert system session, an output including all knowledge base objects and their attributes is produced;

- the interface between SUN 4-Nexpert Object and HP 9000-ORACLE is implemented in Pro*C, one of those ORACLE tools which allow embedded SQL-statements for database access;

- these programs retrieve data from the master parts file and store the

generated bill of materials.

Integration of the stand-alone system PIA meant that an already existing expert system had to be connected to our PPC system workplaces. PIA is implemented in Prolog. As a first step, the connection had to be realized via textfile transfer, because there was no interface available between the Prolog based PIA system and ORACLE RDBMS. Integration via the database is planned for future activities.

Knowledge Based Components of VAIS

Bill of materials generator Stuelip

When a customer request for a new product has to be worked out, the bill of materials often does not exist. This makes it difficult or even impossible to calculate product cost in advance. In order to apply one of the standard calculation algorithms at least a preliminary bill of materials must first be generated. New products will often require

- that new parts have to be constructed,

- that existing parts have to be modified,

- that parts similar to existing ones have to be manufactured, or

- that a new configuration has to be assembled from a large number of parts under many restrictions as to which parts may or may not go together with other ones.

In each of these cases, the knowledge of an experienced engineer is required.

The expert system Stuelip handles the last two of these four cases. First of all, Stuelip helps to configure complex products from a large number of possibilities. Informations about parts that have been previously manufactured can be taken from the master parts file and the bom file.

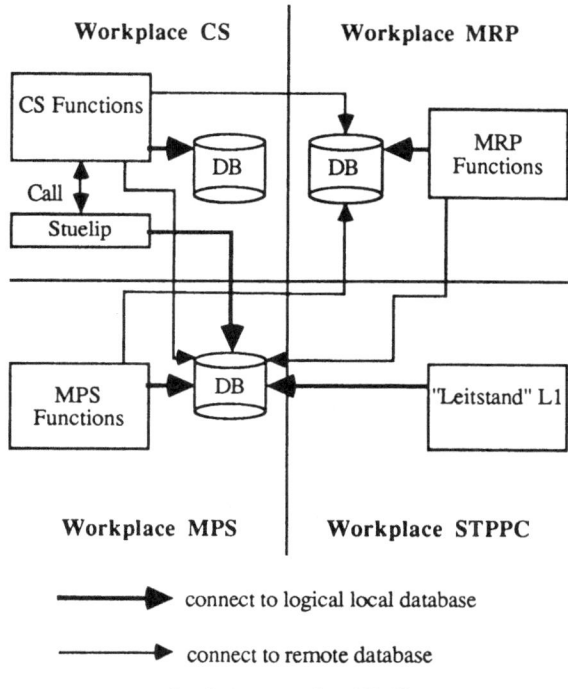

Fig. 3: Access paths of VAIS

Information about new parts or other similar parts has to be derived from a complex rule base which is divided into two parts. The first part contains rules which describe which parts may be combined. These rules will be evaluated after knowledge acquisition. The second part contains rules as to which parts must be combined, based on the requirements defined during knowledge acquisition. These rules will be evaluated after knowledge acquisition. Stuelip then generates a bill of materials and stores it in the ORACLE database. Subsequently, it can be used to calculate the cost of product at the "customer support" workplace.

During a consultation session, users are asked for the design features and production possibilities of those parts which are not stored in the database. Such a process requires detailed knowledge about product components as well as production steps. Our prototype bom generator currently incorporates a small portion of this knowledge.

Our goal, however, was not to construct an expert system for real world application, but to explore methods and flexible approaches for integrating knowledge-based components with a distributed PPC system, based on heterogenous hardware and software configurations. From this point of view, our interest in the expert system side was primarily driven by the additional heterogeniety introduced by knowledge-based technology. In order to apply Stuelip for daily use, the knowledge base would have to be extended. Our experience last led us to believe that considerable effort would have to be expended in order to acquire the knowledge necessary for this. An essential component in this effort would be the help of experts who solve problems like this - generate bills of materials and calculate costs of products specified by customers - in their daily work.

PIA - An Expert System for generating Production Schedules

The expert system PIA generates a production schedule using its knowledge base and a bill of materials as input. As a result, documentation and work orders will be produced.

Data on prerequisite physical units and resources, and rules for partitioning operation steps are stored in the knowledge base. The generation of production schedules starts with the description of a task and results in the production schedule data (all operational steps, their order, and the resources required).

The knowledge of a production scheduler and the boundary conditions are stored in the knowledge base for generating those plans.

Some redundancy occurs between the data stored in the knowledge base and the database. Physical units and resources will be stored as objects in both file systems. The knowledge about operational steps limits the generic application of the system. PIA has two nearly completely different knowledge bases for producing switch boxes and farm machines.

The integration of PIA and VAIS is planned by explorative prototyping. Our first step was to test possibilities for integrating these components. The first solution for transferring data was a "quick and dirty" usage of text files; but real integration is possible. VAIS can send text-files containing data about resources and bom and VAIS can receive text-files containing data on production schedules, which will later be used for generating shop orders.

The first step, "integration by textfile", was easy to implement successfully, but further steps are necessary. Direct access from PIA to VAIS using ORACLE may not be the last step. Integration will be complete when there is no redundancy between the data in the knowledge base and database.

PIA is implemented in PROLOG and can be started on IBM-compatible PC's with MS DOS. Access to those data from UNIX-machines is possible via linking C-routines with embedded SQL to PIA, so that the PC can work as a database client. Then the bill of materials can be taken from the database by the PC and a generated operation schedule can be stored on it.

Experiences

Our experiences during the implementation of VAIS and knowledge based components can be seen from two different points of view. One has to do with system distribution; the other one with integration of PIA and Stuelip into VAIS.

Two main problems had to be solved while developing the distributed PPC workplaces:

- how to maintain consistency in a distributed database without two-phase-commit, and

- how to keep the distributed application running when updates or upgrades of operating systems or database components have to be or have been installed.

The first problem was solved by developing special workarounds for consistency management. The second problem is really difficult to solve, because some software products might need upgrades which will not harmonize with the distributed application.

For the implementation of Stuelip, the operating system UNIX (SunOS) was necessary; XWindows, Nexpert Object, and ORACLE were also required. During our initial installation it seemed that it might be possible to install all components with no problems at all. Later it became clear that ORACLE and Nexpert Object would need different UNIX-libraries, and that there was no chance to get the system working with this configuration. The solution was to use HP 9000-ORACLE, programming C-routines with embedded SQL to get access to the database. A new version of SUN 4-ORACLE will help to solve these problems and direct access to the data needed will be possible.

There have been no problems integrating PIA into the distributed PPC-system up to now. We hope we will still be able to say the same thing when direct access has been implemented. Here the problems are more on a conceptual level, i.e. reducing redundancy between knowledge base and database.

Our actitvities have shown that a distributed and heterogenous application is a very fragile system. The more components involved in keeping the system alive, the greater is the probability that distributed application functions might fail.

References

[1]   Kurbel, K., Meynert, J.: "Flexibilität in der Fertigungssteuerung durch Einsatz eines elektronischen Leitstands", ZwF 83 (1988) 12, S. 581-585.

[2]   Kurbel, K., Rautenstrauch, C.: "Ein verteiltes PPS-System auf Arbeitsplatzbasis", in: Paul, M. (Ed.): GI-19. Jahrestagung: Der computergestützte Arbeitsplatz, Reihe Informatik Fachberichte, Band 223, Berlin, Heidelberg u. a. 1989, S. 476-490.

[3]   Rautenstrauch, C.: "Saving Consistency in Distributed ORACLE Databases", in: EOUG (Eds.): Proceedings of the 8th European Oracle Users Conference, Madrid 1990.

[4]   Heinz, K., Köhler, F.: "Expertensysteme helfen bei der Erstellung von Montagearbeitsplänen", VDI-Z 131 (1989), S. 21-26.

An Approach to the Integration of Legal Support Systems

T.J.M. Bench-Capon   P.E.S. Dunne

Department of Computer Science
University of Liverpool
Liverpool L69 3BX
Great Britain

Abstract

A single framework for the development of the range of systems available to support workers in the field of law is described. Correspondences between the components of the various classes of system are noted, and some current difficulties with integrating the systems described. The potential for and benefits accruing from the use of a uniform graph-theoretic model as a basis for the systems are outlined. A detailed description of the application of this approach to the construction and maintenance of knowledge bases, particularly in the legal domain is given.

Keywords: Legal Information Systems, Hypertext, Information Retrieval, Document Models.

1. Introduction

Computer systems have been developed to assist legal work in a variety of ways: in the retrieval of information, ranging from the keyword-in-context searching of LEXIS and WESTLAW, to more advanced methods of conceptual retrieval as in [9] and [17], and, more recently still, hypertext based systems such as JUSTUS [29]; in document preparation ranging from basic use of word processors, to semi-automated methods such as those of [24] for will preparation and [22]; and in assistance in the application of the law in systems such as the Retirement Pensions Forecast and Advice System of the UK Department of Social Security [25] and the Latent Damage Advisor of Capper and Susskind [13]. Additionally, of course, any organisation concerned in legal work will have the usual office systems and database requirements. Work on such systems has tended to progress independently, but we argue that these systems should not be conceived of as separate technologies, as there are sufficient grounds of commonality between them to give great potential synergy through integration. Such an integration requires, however, that the various technologies be put on a some uniform foundation, so that coherence and harmonisation can be achieved. The main purpose of this paper is to outline how a single coherent *document model* together with appropriate formal transformation rules could be used to provide such a foundation. We will therefore indicate some of the areas of commonality between the various types of system, indicate the need for harmonisation, propose a suitable document model, and show how it applies to some of the system types.

We note that although some work has been done on providing formal models of documents, e.g. [20], this has received less attention than it deserves with the result that, in some cases, implementation has outstripped understanding. The increasing popularity of hypertext systems [15], which seem to provide an excellent solution to the problem of catering to different reader needs, has meant that systems have been built upon a purely intuitive understanding of these models without much thought to their formal characterisation and how such might be exploited to yield better systems. While there have been attempts to put hypertext on a formal basis, such as [12] and [27], these have not been followed through to any significant extent. The situation that currently exists resembles that found in the field of semantic nets in the 1970s when excitement about what could be done with the new technique led to unsoundly characterised systems, which has retarded their exploitation despite attempts to rectify the defects by Brachman [10] and others e.g. [18] and [30].

2. Commonalities

The relationship between hypertext and knowledge based systems has previously been observed in [1] and [3]. Broadly these turn on the fact that the links in the hypertext system are typically construed as arcs of a semantic net: and these arcs correspond to the predicates that are found in a expert system. The relations represented in the two systems are common: the use made of them within the two classes of system are different: they are employed to facilitate document traversal in the hypertext system, whereas in the expert system they will provide a vocabulary for the construction of rules to licence inference, but there is considerable scope for the information latent within each of the systems to inform the other system. Turning to conceptual retrieval systems we see that the proposals of [17] combine the use both of semantic nets, which relate to hypertext like systems, with issue discrimination trees which have much in common with the rules of an expert system. Similarly alternative approaches are either founded ultimately on a semantic net or, as in the case of Bing's normative thesaurus [9], on expert system-like rules. Automated document creation systems also turn on the identification of rules to exploit relations between the individual facts of a case and the appropriate pieces of text which must form the final document. Relational databases, too, will contain extensional descriptions of sets of relations, which could of course be re-expressed as the binary relations of a semantic net. Therefore whether we are dealing with hypertext, expert systems, conceptual retrieval systems, conventional relational databases or automated document creation systems we are likely to find similar collections of predicates and executable rules composed of these predicates. Commonality with the remaining classes of systems, which deal with no more than documents, is found through our use of the notion of a *document* as the basic notion in which to model the sets of relations and rules found in the other systems. The most contentious use of this model is the construal of a rule base as a document: this is consequently discussed in detail in a later section of this paper.

3. Problems of Harmonisation

Given the similarities noted above, it might be thought that harmonisation through common predicates would be a straightforward task. But this is not so. Suppose, for example, we wished to integrate an expert system with an hyper document relating to its domain. Whilst it is true that hypertext systems are based on some form of semantic net, very often the relations represented by the arcs in this net are not defined with any great precision, rather relying on the connotations of the labels of the arcs to convey the meaning. Thus, for example, a typical net may use a relation "is-a" to link nodes without making it clear whether this class-superclass relation is intended to be exhaustive, so that any instance of the superclass must be an instance of at least one of the sub-classes, or whether it is intended to be exclusive, so that any instance of a super-class must be an instance of at most one of the sub-classes. Other decisions about the relation need to be made, and these are not necessarily taken consistently across the whole net. In a hypertext system, and probably a conceptual retrieval system also, this may not to matter too much, since the user of the system can impart intelligence allowing him to recognise and reconcile any inconsistencies that may occur. In contrast the relations of an expert system are precisely defined, because their extension can be computed from the system. Often too little attention is paid to thinking precisely about the relations, in which case the computation may conflict with the expectations of the systems builder, but none the less the executability of the expert system does mean that the relation has an objective definition. In an expert system the knowledge base will be debugged until the actual, computed interpretation, is not significantly different from that of the systems builder.

If the predicates of the various systems are to be merged into a single system, however, any lack of precision in relations becomes unacceptable. The expert system will apply its computation based understanding of relations to the more loosely used relations of the semantic net within the hypertext system, which may or may not coincide with the similar relations of the conceptual retrieval system, with the inevitable result that some uses of these relations will be inappropriate. Therefore it is essential that at least some of the relations employed in the different systems, namely those on which the systems will interact, should be harmonised through some common model. This means that the use of the relations in the hypertext and conceptual retrieval systems must be disciplined and based on some precise definition of those relations, and this definition must correspond to the computational behaviour of the expert system. The question thus becomes one of how we are to express the precise definitions of these relations and how such expressions are to be made operational when constructing the systems. It is clear that we must make the major change in our approach to the retrieval systems rather than expert systems, because an ambiguous relation cannot be used as if it were unambiguous without unwanted conclusions being drawn (or desired conclusions not being drawn), whereas an unambiguous relation can be catered for in a system which uses that relation in other senses also. The sentence "every student uses a computer" is ambiguous in that every student may use a different computer if they all have micros, or they may all use the same computer where they use a mainframe. This distinction must be made if we formalise the sentence into predicate logic, and different conclusions will follow, according to the choice made. In natural language, however, the ambiguity can be allowed to pass, relying on the reader to understand the intended meaning according to the context and his judgement. It is therefore the natural language that needs to be disciplined if correspondence to the formal logic is to be enforced. The first concern, therefore, must be to provide a means for making the relationships used within the hypertext system precise, and in such a way that this conformity with the chosen interpretation can be imposed on the system builder.

4. Document Models as a Foundation for Harmonisation

Any meaningful document has a structure, an understanding of which is essential if a reader is to interpret the text correctly. Over the years conventions for different classes of documents have developed; thus a textbook will typically comprise a preface, followed by a table of contents, followed by a series of chapters, followed by an index. Chapters themselves have structure, being broken down into sections, paragraphs and sentences. A law report will comprise a header note summarising the point of law, a statement of the facts of the case, and the decision. Statutes, of course, also follow strict structural conventions. Normally the reader will be expected to read these documents in a particular order: thus later chapters of a book may presuppose material in earlier chapters. Understanding of any document is enhanced if the reader is aware of the structural conventions, but this means in turn that the author must be aware of, and observe, these conventions.

Today many documents are prepared on computer systems, although intended for publication in hard copy. The electronic document on which the author is working thus may have a different set of structural conventions from the intended finished product. It is important therefore that there be correspondence between the two; which requires that the electronic document have a formal structure which can be used to map onto the output paper document. Only if these correspondences exist can the author ensure that he is observing the required conventions in a natural and effortless manner.

One structure which has attracted much attention as an underlying document model is directed acyclic graphs. Examples of such models may be found in [16], [19], [20], [21] all of which employ arbitrary directed acyclic graph structures; and [8], [14], [26], [28], which are restricted to tree structures. This model is appealing since it permits logical connections between sections to be represented simply and directly. [20] extends the earlier models of [16], [19] and [21] by introducing (amongst other ideas) the concept of *graph modification rules*. These are employed to control modifications to a graph in order that it should reflect changes (either in structure or interpretation) made to the underlying document: thus rules may encapsulate how to modify the graph in the event of sections being added or deleted and rules may indicate how new logical links in the document structure are to be reflected in the graph form. More formally a graph modification rule is a production rule in a graph grammar. A rule consists of 3 parts and acts on a given graph as follows: the rule consists of a predicate, P; a left-hand graph G_l; and a right-hand graph G_r. For a given input graph G if the predicate P holds for G and G contains G_l as a sub-graph then G_l is replaced by the graph G_r in G. [20] illustrates how a simple set of rules may be applied to create and modify tables of information and it is observed that the correctness of the given rules may be formally verified by a simple inductive proof.

The properties of directed acyclic graphs offer several advantages over more general representation methods particularly when their semantic capabilities are enhanced by the provision of a formal modification regime. These are discussed in [7].

The above formal model for electronic documents can, we contend, be applied to conventional documents, hyperdocuments, the semantics nets underpinning hyperdocuments and conceptual retrieval systems, and the rule bases of expert and other automated document creation systems. Essentially the formal model consists of a set of constraints on the allowed form of graphs, together with a set of traversal and modification rules. The formal representation of documents in this way has a number of advantages independent of integration: for example legal texts provide one example of documents which are sometimes the work of several individuals and which possess a highly structured form. A formal model would allow exploration of issues such as the automated production of a hyperdocument from legal documents, formal specification of classes of legal document (e.g. contracts, legislation, wills etc.) and the automated translation of such specifications into rewriting and production systems, managerial strategies for cooperative production of legal hyperdocuments, and the serialisation of such hyperdocuments, which will subsume current navigation problems. In addition, as has been argued in [2] a graph-theoretic approach allows the importation of formal models of concurrent behaviour as a vehicle with which to describe cooperative authorship activities.

When we move to intergrating the various systems, the need for a formal underpinning model ceases to be desirable and becomes essential. Although the traversal and modification rules will differ for different classes of document, they will ensure that the relations represented by the arcs in all the various documents will be precisely defined. This being so, where a relation is represented in the different documents identification can be made with confidence, and only the correct consequences will be drawn from this identification. The advantages of this are clear: a single representation may be used as the core of the various systems and communication between them in operation will be facilitated. This would enable, for example, the output of a conceptual retrieval system to be used in the explanation of the output from an expert system, or the product of document creation system to be offered to an expert system for validation.

5. Knowledge Bases as Documents

The above is critically dependent on our ability to represent all the various components of the system to be integrated within the single formalism of our document model. This is least obviously the case when we consider the rule based components. In this section therefore we will show the sense in which rules bases can, and arguably should, be seen in terms of the document model.

Knowledge bases, like documents, have structure: depending on the domain of application the knowledge represented may be classified into a number of categories and be of several different types e.g. conceptual, qualitative etc. In addition to the actual facts stored in the knowledge base various rules must be encoded which will attempt to mimic the reasoning processes employed by an expert practitioner in the relevant domain. Again such rules may be divided into several different classes depending on the style of reasoning they embody and by the degree of confidence which can be placed on the veracity of those conclusions which are inferred by their application to particular sets of data. This underlying core of factual knowledge and this battery of inferential techniques are obviously related: tight logical links connect facts in the former with rules in the latter. However there will, in general, also exist logical connections among divers collections of information in the factual database and similar links among subsets of the various reasoning techniques. An awareness of all such logical interdependencies is crucial at each stage from knowledge elicitation to verification of the final system if the knowledge engineer is to succeed in the aim of constructing a usable (let alone useful) knowledge based system for the specific target application.

Just as the writing of a document involves the organisation of ideas by an author into a form that can be communicated to readers, this being often accomplished using some computer representation as an intermediary so too the design and implementation of a knowledge base involves the systematic distillation of a core of expert knowledge into a form which an adept but non-specialist user can apply; and here again a computer system is used as a vehicle for building and storing the elicited knowledge. Thus, given these parallels between the preparation of complex documents and the codification of specialist knowledge, one can contend that those management approaches which endeavour to aid authors in communicating ideas by providing a computer representation supporting the underlying form of a particular class of document will also provide a valuable foundation for the synthesis of knowledge bases.

The analogy between document and knowledge base management extends beyond the creation and design phase. An electronic document is ultimately produced in a serial form corresponding to a sensible order in which some reader may traverse it. The process of reading and understanding a document is an interpretive one. Similarly, in application, a knowledge base is traversed by the inference engine applied to it during specific execution instantiations. The traversal is controlled by some execution strategy and just as different readership imposed orderings of a document may result in different interpretations of the text so different traversals of the knowledge base during execution will yield different results on each occasion e.g. if varying conflict resolution strategies are chosen. Underpinning the interpretation of a document there are implicit constraints on how the text should be read in order that a sensible understanding of its content be garnered; similar constraints guide the reasoning processes carried out on a knowledge base again to ensure both termination and the validity of conclusions arrived at.

The purpose of expressing a knowledge base in terms of the formal document model (as with any document) is to be aware of these differing execution strategies (readings of a document) in order to impose appropriate constraints on which strategies are permissible and which are not. That a formal management system is necessary arises from the fact that even a single designer will find it difficult to organise a complex database; this holds even more true for teams of designers who need to conform to a single homogeneous view and thereby require organisational support tools in order to ensure systemic correctness.

6. Use of the Model to Support the Construction and Maintenance of Knowledge Bases

The advantages of describing knowledge bases in terms of such a document model will be explored in this section by seeing how it supports their construction and maintenance. Before looking at the creation of knowledge bases, however, it is worth emphasising the contrast between differing structural views of a document through the following example.

Consider a programming language in which the order of execution of sequential statements is determined by associated line numbers. If we consider a program in such a language as a document and examine the creation and development of this then we have (at least) two different possible perspectives with which to analyse the structure present: that seen viewing the document (program) created, as a block of text by the author, solely in terms of its *physical* representation as an ASCII character file within the computer system - this is the low-level description; or we may consider the viewpoint, implicitly adopted by the interpreter or compiler of the program, that the document is a sequence of labelled instructions with this sequence proceeding from the lowest numbered statement to the highest numbered statement - this is the high-level description. Note that the writer(s) of such a program must be aware that the high-level description exists and must construct their program accordingly in order to ensure its correctness: the individual statements comprising the code must be assigned numbers in accordance with their intended order of execution. On the other hand the programmer does not have to worry about physically reproducing this order in the program text: statements can be typed in any order provided the numbering convention is correct, thus to insert a new statement between two existing ones it would be sufficient to add this to the *physical* end of the file containing the program provided that the label of the new statement fell between the numerical values of the two statements it was to be inserted among. Indeed if the program is listed in an environment, such as that of an interpreter which also uses this model, the lines will be automatically listed in the appropriate physical order. The key point here is that the editor has an underlying model of a program which can be used harmonise the source file with the ultimate execution strategy of the interpreter. In passing it should be noted that the whole thrust of structured programming methodologies, for conventional programming languages, is essentially to make explicit and uniform across contributors such a harmonising model.

It is one of the main contentions of this paper that an appreciation of the high-level structural semantics underlying any expert domain *is essential* in the realm of cooperative design ventures and the example just given provides some support for this claim. The rationale of a shared model is the same, although the model is likely to be more complex in the case of the knowledge base of an expert system. In this case the advantages of using a model of the document appropriate to the document type and built-in to the system over the superficially less constrained model of the finite text string are evident. In a similar fashion, a properly developed and enforced model of the knowledge base will support the integration of the contributions of multiple developers. To summarise, we contend that directed acyclic graphs provide the strongest basis for a high-level management tool.

One important feature of such graphs is that there are only a fixed number of finite paths from source nodes to terminal points permitted by the graph structure. This allows the sensible execution conventions on the final knowledge base, when processed by some inference system, to be reflected in the computer representation used for creating and maintaining the knowledge base. Here there is an underlying assumption that the sensible paths through in the reasoning process are acyclic. As a simple example consider the procedural definition of the factorial function in a language such as PROLOG. In a correct definition one rule must deal with the base case (i.e. $n = 0$); another rule must deal with definition for the remaining case. Conceptually, within the logic programming paradigm the *textual* order of the defining rules is irrelevant to the correctness of the definition. In practice logic programming systems (such as PROLOG) must adopt certain conventions in order to fix on the procedural expansion ordering to be used in evaluation: clearly if a naive strategy is used to process a recursive definition the execution may never terminate. By modelling the computational instantiations of procedures as a directed acyclic graph which is amended under the control of modifications rules it will be possible in this case to impose the terminating execution strategy (while hiding this from the user) and possible in simple cases to detect erroneous procedural definitions (e.g. when a recursive definition has omitted to specify a base case). Thus the graph could model sequences of *rule* followed by *action* followed by *rule* by labelling nodes with attributes such as *recursive call* or *base case* as appropriate (the attribute labelling scheme is another innovation of [20]). Note that this graph is acyclic; a recursive call affects the binding of ground terms and so since the procedural nodes in the computation graph model the system environment a new recursive call requires a new node to be introduced to the graph.

The constraints on ordering (both in representation and execution) are important in avoiding the confusion that can result in more liberal representation methodologies such as hypertext techniques and in particular the semantic shifts and inversions possible in the latter approach can be prevented. A fuller discussion of such issues is the subject of [4]. Of course it might be contended that by restricting oneself to a fragment of hypertext capabilities one can achieve the same ends and still have in reserve a battery of techniques for use with more general representations. However to argue as such indicates a failure to appreciate the expressive clarity of minimalism: it is easier to prove properties of systems whose behaviour is rigidly controlled by a concise set of construction principles than it is to reason about the outcome of methods which permit great laxity in specification, even if the latter can be artificially restricted to emulate the former. Other dangers in allowing over liberality in a system and relying on the discipline of the user to ensure that they are used in a sensible way are highlighted by the kind of confusions that can arise in ill-specified is-a hierarchies, well discussed in [11]. An additional advantage of the graph modification rule paradigm is that it provides a rigorous structure with which to regulate cooperative design ventures. The modification rules guarantee that, regardless of how many writers are working on the construction of the knowledge base and the specific changes they make to it, the global organisation of the data and rules will always conform to a predefined model so that the conventions of the target system are observed: while co-authors work on particular sections if changes are made in accordance with the modification rules then these will ensure that a homogeneous structure results. Note that this substantially reduces the requirement for multiple designers to expend considerable efforts in collating individual contributions. In total these two benefits suggest that graph modification rules offer a secure foundation on which to build a formal theory of Computer Supported Cooperative Working (CSCW), whether that work is to produce a document or a knowledge base: a complete exposition of such is beyond the scope of the present paper however bases for formal qualitative and metric theories have been proposed in [5] and [7].

The way to progress the development of a knowledge base is, therefore, to provide a consistent set of modification rules which will reflect the structure of the knowledge base and its target execution strategy. Creating the knowledge base within the constraints that this model will impose will ensure that it will execute in a sensible fashion, predictable from the model. Additionally, of course, appreciation of the model and obedience to its constraints will harmonise contributions from several members of a development team.

All the above applies to building and maintaining knowledge bases for expert systems in any domain whatsoever. If, however, the domain is law, then the use of the document model becomes still more pertinent. It has been cogently argued in [6] and [23], that a knowledge base grounded in a written legal source needs to have some clear correspondence to that source, if it is to be satisfactory in operation and capable of maintenance. Knowledge base and source text must be is some sense *isomorphic*. Whilst there is a intuitive understanding of what such isomorphism entails, the notion is insufficiently precise to be practical. If, however, we have both the source text and the knowledge base modelled in the formal terms sketched above such isomorphism can both be stated with precision, and, more importantly, enforced by the constraints that those models impose. In particular validation of the knowledge base which is a crucial issue for an expert system which is to make legally acceptable decisions, is greatly facilitated.

7. Conclusions

We have noted the existence of a range of currently separate systems for the support of legal work, and noted that many of them are grounded in common ideas, most notably, the existence of structured texts, sets of predicates describing the relationships between entities in the domain, and rules composed using these predicates which describe their logical relations, and manipulation in the performance of tasks. We have argued that these commonalities could form the basis for the integration of such systems, so that their development can be harmonised, components could be shared across systems, and benefits be derived from communication between the systems in operation. Such integration is possible only given a suitable formal basis which can underpin all such systems and serve as the common foundation for the integrated system. We have argued that modelling such systems in terms of electronic documents, described as directed acyclic graphs with associated traversal and transformation rules can provide the required common formal basis. Finally we have indicated the benefits of such an approach: the harmonisation achievable in the design of information retrieval and expert systems through the common representation of a single coherent model; the support that such a model provides for regulating the activity of several authors engaged in cooperatively producing texts; as has been discussed in detail, such an approach would facilitate the construction and maintenance of expert system knowledge bases. Finally the use of a common foundation for knowledge base and document synthesis would permit the development of information retrieval approaches which could operate in tandem with an expert reasoning system: the former being used to provide a natural language explanation of reasoning processes and the latter used to validate the correctness of generated documents.

This paper, of course, does not go into the specific aspects of models for particular classes of document: we believe, however, that it makes a strong case for their development, and the construction of such models is the subject of ongoing work. Some preliminary characterisations of document classes is described in [7].

8. References:

[1] Barlow, J; Beer, M.D; Bench-Capon, T.J.M; Diaper, D; Dunne, P.E.S; Rada, R: Expertext: Hypertext-Expert System theory, synergy and potential applications; In: Research and Development in Expert Systems VI (Ed: N. Shadbolt), Proc. of Expert Systems 89, Cambridge Univ. Press, 1989, 116-127

[2] Barlow, J; Dunne, P.E.S: Cooperative writing

schemes based on formal models of concurrency; Report CS/CSCW/7/1989, Dept. of Computer Science, Univ. of Liverpool, 1989

[3] Barlow, J; Dunne, P.E.S; Rada, R: EXPERTEXT: from Semantic Nets to Logic Petri Nets; To appear in: Expert systems with applications, Vol 1, (1), (ca. March 1990)

[4] Bench-Capon, T.J.M.; Dunne P.E.S.; McEnery, A.M.: A document model to support cohesive ties in text, Internal Report CS/CSCW/4/1989, Univ. of Liverpool, 1989

[5] Bench-Capon, T.J.M; Dunne, P.E.S: Some metrics for document complexity; Internal Report CS/CSCW/5/89, Univ. of Liverpool, 1989

[6] Bench-Capon, T.J.M., Deep Models, Normative Reasoning and legal Expert Systems, Proceedings of the 2nd International Conference on AI and Law, Vancouver 1989, ACM Press, 37-45.

[7] Bench-Capon, T.J.M; Dunne, P.E.S: Some computational properties of a model for electronic documents; (To appear: Electronic Publishing - Origination, Dissemination and Design)

[8] Bertino, E; Rabitti, F; Gibbs, S: Query processing in a multimedia document system; ACM Trans. on Office Information Systems, 6 (1), 1988, 1-41

[9] Bing, Jon, Designing Text Retrieval Systems for Conceptual Searching, Proceedings of 1st International Conference on AI and Law, Boston, 1987, ACM Press, 43-51.

[10] Brachman, R.J: On the epistemological status of semantic networks; In: Associative Networks: Representation and use of knowledge by computers (Ed: N.V. Findler); Academic Press, 1975, 3-50

[11] Brachman, R.J: "I Lied About the Trees" Or, Defaults and Definitions in Knowledge Representation, AI Magazine, Fall, 1985.

[12] Campbell, B; Goodman, J.M: HAM: A general purpose Hypertext Abstract Machine; Comm. ACM, 31 (7), 1988, 856-861

[13] Capper P., and Susskind, R., Latent Damage Law - The Expert System, Butterworths, 1988.

[14] Christodoulakis, S; Theodoridou, M; Ho, F; Papa, M; Pathria, A: Multimedia document presentation, information extraction, and document formation in minos: a model and a system; ACM Trans. on Office Information Systems; 4 (4), 1986, 345-383

[15] Conklin, J: Hypertext: an introduction and survey; Computer, 20 (9), 1987, 17-41

[16] Delisle, N; Schwartz, M: Neptune: a hypertext system for CAD applications; Proc. ACM Intnl. Conf. on Management of Data, 1986, 132-143

[17] Hafner, Carole D., Conceptual Organisation of Case Law Knowledge Bases, Proceedings of 1st International Conference on AI and Law, Boston, 1987, ACM Press, 35-41.

[18] Hobbs, J: Ontological promiscuity; Proc. 23rd Ann. Mtng. of the Association for Computational Linguistics, 1984

[19] Kimura, G.D; Shaw, A.C: The structure of abstract document objects; Proc. ACM Conf. on Office Information Systems, 1984, 161-169

[20] Koo, R: A model for electronic documents; ACM SIGOIS Bulletin, 10 (1), 1989, 23-33

[21] Meyrowitz, N: Intermedia: the architecture and construction of an object-oriented hypermedia system and applications framework; Proc. Object-Oriented Prog. Syst., Languages and Applications, 1986, 186-201

[22] Morris, G., Taylor, K, and Harwood, M., Handling Significant Deviations from Boilerplate Text, Proceedings of 1st International Conference on AI and Law, Boston, 1987, ACM Press, 145-154.

[23] Routen, T., Hierarchically Organised Formalisations, Proceedings of the 2nd International Conference on AI and Law, Vancouver 1989, ACM Press, 242-50.

[24] Sprowl, J.A., Automating the Legal Reasoning Process: A Computer that Uses Regulation and Statutes to Draft Legal Documents, American Bar Association Journal 1979, 1-81.

[25] Springel-Sinclair, S., The DHSS Retirement Pension Forecase and Advice System: an update, in Duffin, P., (ed) KBS in Government 1988, Blenheim Online, 1988, 89-106.

[26] Standard ECMA-101, Office Document Architecture; Euro. Compu. Manu. Assoc., 1985

[27] Stotts, P.D; Furuta, R: Adding browsing semantics to the hypertext model; Proc. ACM Conf. on Document Processing Systems, 1988, 43-50

[28] Thomas, R.H; Forsdick, H.C; Crowley, T.R; Robertson, G.G; Schaaf, R.W; Tomlinson, R.S; Travers, V.M: Diamond: a multimedia message system built upon a distributed architecture; Computer, 18 (12), 1985, 65-78

[29] Wilson, E: Converting legal texts into expert systems; Proc. National Conf. on Law, Computers and Artificial Intelligence, Univ. of Exeter, 1988

[30] Woods, W.A: "What's in a link?" Foundations for semantic networks; In: Representation and Understanding: Studies in Cognitive Science (Ed: D. Bobrow and A. Collins); Academic Press, 1975, 35-82

KNOWLEDGE SYSTEMS AND LAW - THE JURICAS PROJECT

Prof. R.V. De Mulder, C. van Noortwijk , H.O. Kerkmeester and J.G.L. van der Wees

Workshop for Computer Science and Law,
Erasmus University Rotterdam
Burg. Oudlaan 50
3062 PA ROTTERDAM (The Netherlands)

ABSTRACT

Due to the lack of empirical knowledge in the law, it is not possible to produce either legal expert systems or legal knowledge systems. Jurimetrics, the scientific studying of the law, may in the long term change this situation. Until then, the best alternative is the production of computerized legal advice systems. Such a system would advise its users about a specific legal subject on the basis of legal practice.

These systems have been developed by the Workshop for Computer Science and Law at Erasmus University as part of the JURICAS project. While responsibility remains with the user, it is ensured that all relevant criteria are examined. Each advice system is targeted at a particular sort of user, e.g. a judge or public prosecutor. It is also an ideal means for a legal author of a JURICAS system to convey his opinions. The JURICAS "Advice System Shell" has been made generally available and therefore it is now possible for Dutch lawyers to design their own advice systems.

Not only lawyers are using JURICAS, however. Policy-makers and managers also showed interest in the JURICAS shell. So what was designed as a legal advice system is now an advice system for the implementation of rules in general.

1.0. Systems based on knowledge about law

In recent years, within the field of specialization called artificial intelligence, particularly research into the possible applications of so-called knowledge systems has taken flight. From within the group of knowledge-based systems, it has been the expert systems which have received the most attention up till now. The term expert system indicates that these computer programmes intend to simulate the reasoning of a human expert.

For the present we will only deal with the knowledge aspect and therefore our subject is referred to as knowledge systems; computer programmes that are capable of containing the knowledge of one or more people and transferring it to others, the users of the programme.

When examples are given in literature of the kind of "knowledge" which is suitable for use in a knowledge system, "legal knowledge" is almost never omitted. Common examples given are:
- dismissal law: what chance does an employee have of successfully fighting his dismissal?
- private law: when will the judge consider a certain transaction to be illegal?

There are then dozens, if not hundreds, of other conceivable applications for a legal knowledge system.[1]

The core of a knowledge system is the so-called knowledge-base. In order to make a workable knowledge system, there must be enough knowledge available on the area of expertise in question. What sort of knowledge is concerned here? We will examine this by taking the above mentioned examples as a starting point.

A knowledge system for dismissal law that can make a good estimate of the chances of fighting a dismissal must have at its disposal an extensive knowledge of the way in which a lawsuit concerning labour law will progress in practice. For example, what information in the dossier will the judge consult, which matters will be of importance for the final verdict even though they are not in the case dossier? In this case, therefore, it is necessary to have knowledge of reality, in particular to have knowledge of how a decision in a lawsuit comes into existence.

The same goes for the second example: only when we have at our disposal certain knowledge of reality, in this case of the way in which a civil lawsuit will progress in practice, can we build a knowledge system with which the judge's decision can be "predicted".[2]

Again and again it would therefore appear that a certain knowledge of reality, often referred to by the term empirical knowledge, is essential in the making of a knowledge system. This is the core of the problem: empirical knowledge of the law falls short. For a long time

ledge can be used as a starting point. Extensive research would first be necessary before the empirical knowledge required could be obtained.

However, in the twentieth century some lawyers have become aware of this lack of a scientific basis to their area of specialization. Interest in an "empirical legal science" has steadily grown. The "legal realists" contributed to this development[3] and especially in Scandinavia there has always been a strong empirical influence.[4]

1.1. Jurimetrics

"Empirical legal science" is now often referred to by the term jurimetrics. The American advocate Lee Loevinger[5] has the honour of being the first to have used the term jurimetrics. In the article "Jurimetrics: The next step forward", he sketched out the development of legal science. He stated that the law had become a mystery that was barely understandable to its practitioners, let alone for the public at large. Jurimetrics had to change this. It had to take the achievements of science and use these in the service of the law. Loevinger thus derived his definition of jurimetrics as being "the scientific studying of legal problems".

De Mulder equates jurimetrics with "empirical legal science" by analogy with econometrics.[6] He calls jurimetrics "the empirical science which concerns itself with the study of syntax, semantics and pragmatics of demands and authorizations issuing from state organizations".

We must emphasize that jurimetrics and econometrics cannot simply be put side by side. Whereas the birth of econometrics was preceded by decades in which economists had concerned themselves with a model-building or quantitative approach to economic problems[7], the birth of jurimetrics was quite different. For a long time a model-building analysis of legal phenomena has been most unusual even though this is an important condition for a sufficient level of empirical research. Nowadays, however, the "Economic Analysis of Law" movement successfully applies (economic) models to legal issues.[8]

1.2. Examples of jurimetrical research

An important part of jurimetrics is the study of the effect of state legislation. If the severity of a sentence or the chance of being caught is increased, would this influence the number of offences being committed and, if so, which offences?[9] What is the relationship between legal demands and authorizations and other prevailing norms in society? These and similar questions cannot be answered without the help of empirical and model-building research.

As stated above, it is of great importance to the construction of a legal knowledge system that an appeal can be made to "real knowledge". An expert system which is not based on this cannot possibly satisfy its claim that it provides knowledge concerning reality. What has not been put in can never be got out.

Another example of the importance the use of jurimetrics could have in the construction of a legal knowledge system is the following. In an advice system which offers help in making decisions concerning whether or not to remand in custody, problems arise regarding the specification of terms like "danger of abscondence" or "danger of repetition". A knowledge system cannot, at present, do much more than ask the user whether he considers this danger of abscondence or repetition to be there and to give some explanation concerning the current notions of what these terms mean on the basis of case law. This situation could be improved if jurimetrical research on these subjects was carried out.[10]

1.3. Computer advice systems

As empirical knowledge of judicial matters is so limited it can be concluded that the construction of a legal knowledge system is, at this moment, impossible. With this limitation in mind, research was undertaken by the Workshop for Computer Science and Law as to alternative means for supporting lawyers' work with the aid of a computer. From that research, it has appeared that there is a substantial role for the computer to play if sufficient attention is paid to the interaction between system and user. What we are referring to here is not a knowledge system or an expert system but a computer advice system; a computer programme that is able to advise users about a specific legal subject. An important starting point for this sort of system is that it is a means for legal authors to convey their own opinions to the users. The term "opinion" is used deliberately. This is to emphasize the difference between empirical knowledge (that can be tested and falsified) and the kind of practical knowledge lawyers have, that cannot be tested and falsified.

2.0. The JURICAS project

In 1978 a start was made, at Erasmus University Rotterdam, on the designing of a programme which could support the user in the making of juridical decisions. In 1982, a prototype of such a programme came into existence. It was christened SENPRO, an abbreviation of Sentencing Programme.[11]

In the years after 1982, the prototype SENPRO was subject to further testing. New specifications were developed which were aimed at producing a SENPRO which would be satisfactory to a larger public. By adjusting the control programme for use on a PC, it became available to a wide group of users.

The control programme got the new name of JURICAS, Juridical Computer Advice Systems. By 1987, the following four computer advice systems had been published:
- Remand in custody: the question of its permissibility according to statute and case law
- Dismissal law
- Inheritance law, the division of the estate
- Sentencing according to Hulsman.

In 1990 two new commercial systems will be brought on the market. A system for military conscription rules and a travel documents system. The first one will advise young Dutch men with regards to their rights to obtain deferment or dispensation, the second will tell travellers which tavel documents they need for which country.

2.1. The basics of the JURICAS system

As the JURICAS project is based on the principle that interaction with the user is necessary in generating legal advice with the help of a computer, one of the first and most important basics of the system is that responsibility is left as far as possible to the user. The user should remain responsible for the juridical treatment and the supervision of his/her case.

A second basic point is that the programme can exert a certain compulsion to ensure that all the criteria considered to be relevant by the author will come up for examination so that a decision must be made on all separate criteria.

These two basic points may seem to be somewhat contradictory, but that is not the case. It appears to be perfectly possible to let the user retain responsibility and still - on the basis of the user's own choices - be able to present all the criteria considered relevant by the author to the decision.

A third basic point is that a particular position is adopted. In an advice system it has to be clear to whom the advice is directed i.e. whether the recipient of the advice is a judge, public prosecutor or other interested party.

2.2. Some characteristics of JURICAS programmes

One of the characteristics of the advice programme is the so-called "checklist function": all criteria are at hand and are also listed in a predetermined order. It is, therefore, difficult for the user to forget a criterium.

The computer programme can carry out a number of tasks more quickly and accurately than a person can, such as drawing conclusions on the basis of a series of choices.

One of the hallmarks of the JURICAS system is its ability to deal with different levels of information. The user may find that answering the most important questions is enough to be able to check that all the criteria have been satisfied. He may, however, ask for further information.

The programme also offers the possibility of trying out what the consequence would be of altering a particular answer. In this way, the user can try out all the alternatives when he is not sure of an answer. It is, therefore, possible to see what the conclusions would have been if a certain answer to a question had been given. For this reason this facility is referred to as the "What if?" facility.

2.3. Writing JURICAS programmes

Until recently, the JURICAS project always aimed at complete computer advice programmes. Apart from the JURICAS control programme a decision file was always provided with every system. It was not possible for the end-user to make changes in this file.

Many people have come into contact with computer advice technology via JURICAS. Sometimes they wanted to know whether an advice system could be "tailor made" for their specific situation. In order to satisfy this requirement, a special author's version of JURICAS has now been made and is, in fact, an "advice system shell".

With the help of a simple text processing programme, an author can make his own decision file, which can then be consulted with the JURICAS control programme.

In order to make it possible for experts themselves to work with this author's programme, and hence make their own advice systems, an author's course was set up by the Workshop for Computer Science and Law in co-operation with the publisher Royal Vermande.

It is expected that by using the expert's own skill together with the JURICAS shell, the drawing up of computer advice systems will become a viable option for an increasingly large group of lawyers. This way lawyers will have a new way of communicating their opinions to others and the law could be made more understandable to more people.

2.4. JURICAS. A legal advice system?

As stated above JURICAS was created to support the lawyer. So JURICAS had to be a system, which could cope with legal rules.

While they were using the system lawyers discovered errors and restrictions. Their remarks were passed on to the JURICAS developers, who improved the system to what it is now; a user-friendly system, which can cope with legal rules, has various calculating facilities and which can produce text (letters, pleadings, etc.).

Reactions from others than lawyers showed a broader interest in the JURICAS shell. When the shell was made commercially available in 1988, the system was adjusted to be able to cope with rules in general, rather than just legal rules.

3. Conclusion

In this paper, we have referred to some of the problems which arise in the construction of a legal knowledge system. It appears that in the field of law there is insufficient empirical knowledge available and this makes the drawing up of the required knowledge base an impossibility. The carrying out of jurimetrical research may, in the long term, provide a solution to this short-coming. Until that is the case, computerized legal advice systems form a "next best" alternative to legal knowledge systems.

Computer advice systems provide authors with the opportunity to convey their opinions to the users in an interactive way. The systems are casuistic and the advice is directed towards a specific group of users. Considering that the JURICAS shell was particularly aimed at lawyers and that special author's courses are now available, Dutch lawyers will be able to design such systems virtually independently.

Recently the JURICAS shell has been adjusted to deal with rules in general, rather than just with legal rules.

Notes

1. R. Susskind, Expert systems in law: a jurisprudential inquiry, Oxford, 1987.

2. There is some literature, however, in which methods have been developed for the prediction of verdicts from the facts of the case. See F. Kort, A special and a general multivariate theory of judicial decisions, Beverly Hills, 1976 and S.S. Nagel, "Case prediction by staircase tables and percentaging", Jurimetrics Journal, 1985, p.168.

3. C.f. O.W. Holmes, The path of law, [] 1920.

4. See H. Hyden, "Sociology of law in Scandinavia", Journal of Law and Society, 1986, p.131.

5. See L. Loevinger, "Jurimetrics: the next step forward", Minnesota Law Review, April 1949, p.455.

6. See R.V. De Mulder, Een model voor juridische informatica, Lelystad (Holland), 1984 (with a summary in English), R.V. De Mulder, "A model for legal decision making by computer" in A.A. Martino, F. Socci Natali (eds), Automated analysis of legal texts, Logic, Informatics, Law, North-Holland, 1986. p. 581 and R.V. De Mulder, "Juridische informatica: in de eerste plaats hulpmiddel bij de jurimetrie", in P. van den Berg c.a. (eds), RI-paradigmata, Lelystad (Holland) 1988, p. 7 (with a summary in English).

7. H. Landreth, History of economic theory: scope, method, and context, Boston, 1976, p. 369.

8. See several publications in The Journal of Legal Studies and The Journal of Law and Economics.

9. I. Ehrlich, "Participation in illegitimate activities: a theoretical and an empirical investigation", Journal of Political Economy, 1973, p.521.

10. See H.O. Kerkmeester and C.J. van de Velde, "De ontwikkeling van juridische computeradviessystemen", Computerrecht 1988/3, p.141.

11. See for a description of SENPRO the report: R.V. De Mulder, A. Oskamp, W. van der Heyden and H.M. Gubby, Sentencing by computer: an experiment, Oslo, 1982. For a summary, see R.V. De Mulder and H.M. Gubby, "Legal Decision-making by Computer: an Experiment in Sentencing", in: Computer Law Journal, Summer 1983, and R.V. De Mulder and H.M. Gubby, "Sentencing by computer: A Step forward?", in: Law/Technology, Vol. 17, 1984, No.1, p. 13.

AN EXPERT SYSTEM FOR LEGAL CASE RESEARCH SUPPORT

Amit Basu and L. Ramkumar
College of Business and Management
University of Maryland
College Park, MD 20742, USA.

Fredric D. Abramson
Hardlaw Software, Inc.
21155, Burnham Road
Gaithersberg, MD 20879, USA.

ABSTRACT

This paper discusses issues relating to the design of an expert system to aid lawyers in using statutory legal knowledge for case research. A brief survey of approaches to development of expert systems for law is provided. We identify some features that are important in the design of such expert systems. We then describe an expert system dealing with the U.S. Federal Rules of Civil Procedure, which is being developed jointly by Hardlaw Software, Inc. and the University of Maryland. In particular, we demonstrate the utility of some of the design features, by describing their use in this system.

1. Introduction

Most lawyers tend to be experts or specialists in specific areas of law (eg. Contract law, Patents, Copyrights etc). The large volume of legal knowledge that needs to be mastered forces even experts to frequently refer to statutes, case law or other material relevant to their area of specialization. In addition, many problems require experts to reference legal knowledge outside their area of specialization .

Lawyers seeking to prepare a good legal argument for a case are confronted with three major issues. First, the volume of legal knowledge that has to be referenced is very large. Accessing relevant legal knowledge for a problem may be a complex and time consuming task. Second, selecting appropriate references quickly, and using them to build a powerful legal argument may demand legal intuition or expertise in an area that the lawyer is not intimately familiar with. Third, the body of legal knowledge is constantly evolving and it is necessary to keep pace with these changes.

Automated Legal Information Systems that aid lawyers in addressing the above issues are of obvious value. These systems can be approached from several perspectives. They include legal document drafting systems (eg. [20]), text retrieval systems (eg. LEXIS and WESTLAW), and expert systems offering advice in specific legal domains (eg. [9]).

Document preparation systems serve a limited purpose. They aid drafting of standard legal documents, but do not aid lawyers in preparing legal arguments for problems (case preparation). Text retrieval as well as expert systems can assist lawyers in case preparation.

Text retrieval systems enable lawyers to retrieve relevant information rapidly. These systems incorporate sophisticated search techniques (including knowledge based techniques) for rapid information retrieval. While such systems are useful, they also have some drawbacks. They often require the user to compare and select search strategies and stop at pointing out relevant text to the user. Such systems may not help in analyzing the content of a document or piece of text, in order to offer advice specific to a problem or case.

Expert systems on the other hand, do not stop at pointing out relevant text. They can advise lawyers regarding specific courses of action in a case or examine the feasibility of pursuing alternative courses of action under different circumstances. Such systems may be of greater value to lawyers than text retrieval systems. However they are based on the premise that legal knowledge can be represented and retrieved as necessary, using knowledge representation and heuristic search techniques that are typical of Artificial Intelligence [13].

Major issues in developing expert systems for legal applications include knowledge engineering, knowledge representation, support of different types of reasoning and issues of system architecture. The scope of this paper is to identify and discuss the major features that need to be supported in legal expert systems and to describe an expert system being developed jointly by Hardlaw Software, Inc. and the University of Maryland, that implements these features. This paper is organized in sections. A brief survey of related work is presented in Section 2. Different views of jurisprudence and their relation to legal expert system development are discussed. In Section 3, we present some major characteristics of legal knowledge and propose an approach to legal knowledge representation. Some major features of legal expert systems are identified and discussed in Section 4. In Section 5, we describe a system being developed jointly by Hardlaw Software, Inc. and the University of Maryland and focus on the implementation of the features discussed in Sections 3 and 4. Finally, Section 6 discusses current status and directions for future work.

2. Related work

There have been several discussions regarding the nature of jurisprudence and use of Artificial Intelligence techniques in law [1, 6]. Conflicting theories have been proposed regarding the nature of jurisprudence. These have different implications for expert system development.

Mechanical Jurisprudence[15] is a view of law, as a set of axioms and legal reasoning as a process of deductive reasoning. However this is considered a naive view since there are several cases which are decided by use of discretion and not by strict application of legal rules. A number of researchers have built legal expert systems based primarily on the theory of Mechanical Jurisprudence, using production rule based systems [14, 9, 21] or logic programming [8, 19]. While these have been successful in limited domains, problems associated with the Mechanical Jurisprudential view, as discussed above have been reported.

A contradictory theory is Legal Realism or Nominalism [3], which views jurisprudence as evolving from individual decisions or cases. The validity of legal axioms is disputed. Reasoning based on case law is essentially reasoning by example. Artificial Intelligence work in this area is limited. One approach uses a frame based system for depicting and reasoning with case knowledge [16, 17].

A more popular view seems to be that of Legal Positivism [7, 3], which recognizes the fact that legal rules are valid provided they are properly pedigreed. However testing the pedigree or validity of rules is a complex problem. Positivism also recognizes the fact that all cases cannot be decided by applying these rules and several cases require application of discretion. The relevance of each of these views varies, depending on the specific legal domain. There may be some areas where legal knowledge is largely based on statutes or legal rules (eg. Rules of Procedure) and others where law is primarily case or individual decision based (eg. Offer and Acceptance in Contract Law). [6] discusses this in some detail and presents an approach for dealing with offer and acceptance problems in Contract Law using production rules and frames.

While there are a number of special issues that are relevant to legal expert system development, their relative importance depends on the specific domain being modelled.

3. Major Characteristics of Legal Knowledge

We take the view that law does not consist of structural truisms. Even statutory law cannot be viewed as axiomatic [18]. The semantic interpretation of legal knowledge is context dependent and subjective. This section highlights some major characteristics of legal knowledge that are relevant to the design of legal expert systems.

a) Ambiguous predicates (elements of rules): In some legal rules, the meaning of predicates may be ambiguous due to the language used. Consider a rule which details action to be taken when **reasonable** grounds exist for deducing that a person is driving under the influence of alcohol. A canonical definition of what is **reasonable** may not exist, though case law may provide a basis for argument.

b) Context dependent interpretation: Legal rules may require interpretation even in cases where the semantics of predicates is apparently clear. Consider the following excerpt from [6]:

Let us suppose that in leafing through the statutes, we come upon the following enactment: "It shall be a misdemeanor, punishable by a fine of five dollars to sleep in any railway station."......Suppose I am a judge, and two men are brought before me for violating this statute. The first is a passenger who was waiting at 3 A.M. for a delayed train. When he was arrested he was sitting upright in an orderly fashion, but was heard by the arresting officer to be gently snoring. The second is a man who had brought a blanket and pillow to the station and had obviously settled himself down for the night. He was arrested, however before he had a chance to go to sleep. [5]

It would be reasonable to expect that the second man is guilty but the first is not. However this is not the interpretation that would be obtained by a mechanical application of the enactment. The relevant issue here is the interpretation of "sleep". This interpretation could be provided by rulings (the judge mentioned above could hold that the second man was guilty while the first was not, and this could be cited in other legal arguments) or opinions provided by experts.

It is important to recognize that different levels of context sensitive interpretation are possible. At one level, context sensitivity can be viewed as the interpretation of specific words in the light of surrounding verbiage. At a higher level context sensitivity depends on other knowledge that the user of a system has (eg. an expert lawyers interpretation of law may differ from that of a novice). Interpretation may also differ depending on the goals and biases of the person using the system (eg. a prosecuting lawyer's interpretation may differ from that of a defending lawyer).

c) Example based reasoning: There are several areas where legal knowledge is available as a set of cases. Universally accepted rules or statutes may not be available. In some cases it might be possible for a group of experts to cull rules from cases. However this is a complex task and validation of such rules is both difficult and crucial. Hence, alternative methods of depicting and reasoning with such knowledge (which is essentially a set of examples) are required.

d) Inferential vs descriptive knowledge: Descriptive knowledge refers to knowledge that describes or amplifies the meaning of individual predicates in a rule or the entire rule itself. This knowledge is not used by the system for reasoning (eg. references to appropriate sections of the statute, opinions describing the meaning of predicates). However, an user may draw inferences based on this knowledge. Inferential knowledge on the other hand, is used by the system for inference. Different knowledge representation paradigms may be appropriate for these two types of knowledge. This is discussed in greater detail in the following section.

3.2 A Taxonomy for Knowledge Representation

A discussion of different knowledge representation techniques and their suitability for law can be found in [6]. A detailed discussion is outside the scope of this paper. We present an approach to represent different types of knowledge that we believe is well suited to represent statutory legal knowledge (fig.1).

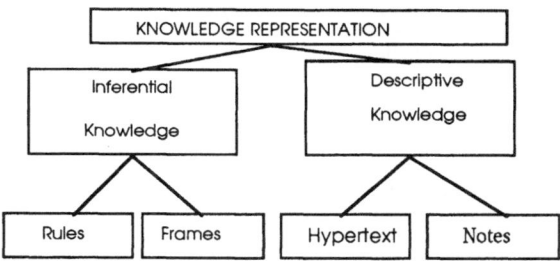

FIG.1. TAXONOMY FOR KNOWLEDGE REPRESENTATION

Hypertext or notes can be used to represent descriptive knowledge. Knowledge that refers to predicates can be depicted as hypertext. This may be based on text of the statute, case law or expert opinion. Knowledge that amplifies the meaning of production rules without relating to individual predicates is represented as notes or annotation. Individual words in the notes may in turn be defined as hypertext keywords.

Inferential knowledge can be represented as production rules or frames. Frames can be used to represent the taxonomy of the statute and to classify and organize production rules [5].

It is important to realize that the distinction between treating a particular piece of knowledge as inferential or descriptive is not always clear. The distinction between these types of knowledge is amplified in the following discussion. Consider the following example:

A user may be asked the following question:

How has service of summons and complaint been made ?
1. By mail
2. By delivering a copy to the party
3. By delivering a copy to the attorney

A rule associated with this predicate is:

If service has been made by delivering a copy to the attorney **then** ------------

NOTE: This rule deals with ------------
REFERENCE: Please refer to Rule 5 of Federal Rules of Civil Procedure.
Delivering is a hypertext keyword which is associated with the following text:
Delivering within the context of this rule means handing it over to the attorney or party, or leaving it at the attorney's office with a clerk or other person in charge thereof.
Rule 5 is a hypertext keyword which if selected displays the actual text of Federal Rule number 5.

In this example, amplification of "delivering" has been treated as descriptive knowledge. An alternate approach would be to treat this as inferential knowledge. In this case, amplification of delivering could be captured in the form of production rules. The user could be asked the following question:

How has service of summons and complaint been made?
  1. By mail
  2. By handing over a copy to the party
  3. By handing over a copy to the attorney
  4. By leaving a copy with a clerk or other person in charge of the attorney's office

Associated production rules are:

1) **If** service has been made by delivering a copy to the attorney **then** ---------
2) **If** service has been made by handing over a copy to the attorney **Or** by leaving a copy with the clerk or other person in charge of the attorney's office **then** service has been made by delivering a copy to the attorney.

In this case, the amplification of delivering has been treated as inferential knowledge. This relieves the user of drawing inferences from descriptive knowledge. However amplification of delivering may be based on opinions or case laws and may not be normative. In such situations treating this as descriptive knowledge may help to draw attention to this fact. Contradictory opinions can also be represented and the user can draw inferences based on his objectives.

In some cases this amplification may be considered trivial by most lawyers. If such knowledge is represented as inferential knowledge, this may result in a number of relatively trivial questions being asked of the user. Such knowledge could possibly be represented as descriptive knowledge. (eg. Consider a portion of the statute which specifies that "There shall be one form of action to be known as Civil Action.")

We can summarize this discussion by making the following points:

1) Knowledge that is normative and used for inference can be represented as production rules. This is particularly true of situations which involve long or complex chains of reasoning. Knowledge regarding structure of the domain is a candidate for frame based representation.
2) Knowledge that is descriptive in nature and deals with predicates can be represented as hypertext if it is based on opinion, case law (ie. not axiomatic), or if it is relatively simple in content. Information that is contained in a statute, but judged to be relatively unimportant or rarely used, can be represented as hypertext. This helps to reduce the size of the rule base and enhance quality of interaction with the user by ensuring that questions asked of the user are more "intelligent". Completeness of knowledge representation is not affected.
3) Descriptive knowledge which deals with amplification of the meaning of rules can be represented as a combination of notes and hypertext.

4. Desirable Characteristics of Legal Expert System

This section identifies some major characteristics of legal expert systems. These are issues which place the problem of legal expert system design in perspective. The relative importance of each of these issues would however vary, depending on the actual domain of law being studied.
(a) Multiple Knowledge Bases: Quite often, different areas of law reference each other (eg. Federal Rules refer to State Rules). It might therefore be prudent for expert system developers in a legal domain to plan for interaction with other legal domains. Blackboard architectures [11, 12] are well suited for this. This is discussed in greater detail in the following section.
(b) Database Access: Lawyers often maintain client databases which contain some information that may be relevant to legal expert systems. Legal expert system designers could consider using this information, instead of having the system ask the user for this. The database may be fairly large and interfacing may be a non trivial issue.
(c) Interface with Text Retrieval Systems: Lawyers frequently use text retrieval systems like LEXIS and WESTLAW. Expert systems which interface with these text retrieval systems would be valuable and serve as "intelligent" front ends.
(d) Reasoning in multiple worlds: Lawyers would often like to examine the outcomes of multiple scenarios, before deciding on a course of action. Legal expert systems could accommodate this by providing features for "what-if" analysis.
(e) Explanation: Explanation which allows lawyers to access relevant sections of legal documents, is likely to complement conventional methods like displaying rules. This would enhance the quality of explanation.
(f) Non-monotonic reasoning: It is also important to recognize that over time legal knowledge bases may evolve non-monotonically. It is possible for conflicting rules to coexist. Conclusions that can be drawn from existing legal knowledge may have to be withdrawn or modified when new legal knowledge (eg. new court decisions) is added.

5. An Expert System for Legal Case Research Support

5.1 Overview

An expert system for legal case research support is currently being developed at the University of Maryland in collaboration with Hardlaw Software, Inc. It is designed to be used by lawyers who seek information on aspects of the Federal Rules of Civil Procedure that might be relevant to a particular client or problem. Federal Rules of Civil Procedure is a body of statutory legal knowledge that lays down procedure to be complied with under several situations relating to civil action. Failure to take cognizance of these rules could jeopardize the case at a later date. This is a domain where lawyers have felt the need for assistance in keeping track of relevant rules for a problem. These rules also represent a stable body of statutory legal knowledge, on which different issues relating to legal expert system development can be tested.

A user who logs on to the system is allowed to enter relevant case data, if this is a new problem. A lawyer may use multiple sessions with the system in order to get relevant information for a particular case or problem. In this situation data that has already been entered can be retrieved and used. Information collected up front, represents answers to questions that a lawyer might typically ask a client during initial consultation.The user then chooses one of three modes of access:

(a) Hypertext access mode: This allows the user to access text of the statute, as well as other information like opinions which are stored as hypertext. Hypertext keywords were identified in consultation with the legal expert. The emphasis is on ease and naturalness of retrieval.
(b) A "guided search" mode: This enables the user to access knowledge related to a particular topic (eg. Service of Summons and Complaint) and is implemented by using "integrated forward and backward chaining". This mode is expected to be used by people who would like to obtain information relating to a topic. They would like to obtain information relevant to the case at hand but are not sure what specific questions should be asked in order to obtain an answer. The system guides the user towards possible specific questions through suggestions at various levels of specificity. During this process, the user can in effect get answers to a variety of questions pertaining to the current case.
(c) A "goal directed search" mode: This enables the user to obtain answers to a specific question (eg. who should serve the summons and complaint). The user can select from a set of predefined questions. This is essentially a backward chaining

mode. Such users are aware that one might expect the answer to this specific question would be provided in the Federal Rules. For such a user, use of the "guided search " mode described above may result in unnecessary questions being asked.

At first glance it might appear that hypertext alone could be used to retrieve relevant information instead of the methods described in (b) and (c) above. Consider the following example : A set of rules may define who should serve summons and complaint. One rule might be as follows:

If service is upon the United States **and** the action attacks the validity of the order of an officer of the United States **then** service shall be made by delivering a copy of the summons and complaint to the US Attorney of the court in which the action is brought.

There may be several rules which determine if service is upon the United States and several which determine if action attacks the validity of the order of an officer of the United states. In addition there may be several rules which deal with who should serve summons and complaint (eg. service upon corporations, persons of unsound mind etc). By asking appropriate questions relating to the if conditions, the expert system is able to prune the search space considerably, by firing appropriate rules only. The user gets answers that are specific to the particular case or problem at hand (eg. the expert system may determine that service is upon the United States and the action attacks validity of the order of an officer of the United States, by firing appropriate rules) and is not merely presented with the relevant text of the statute. This is due to inference performed by the expert system.

This scenario would be difficult to model using hypertext. While it may be possible to depict the text of the statute using hypertext, a user would merely be presented with relevant text of the statute. It is the user who will have to reason about what part of the text is relevant to the problem at hand. The expert system offers additional benefits by allowing the user to go back and look at multiple levels of previous questions (in case the user is confused) and is also able to provide explanations for questions as well as conclusions. A user may use multiple modes during a session and can analyze multiple scenarios. Facilities are available for display or printing of intermediate or final results. Hypertext information can also be accessed from screens in the specific question or browsing mode as well as from rules which are displayed during explanation. This enhances explanation as discussed in section 5.3.

5.2. System Architecture

A schematic diagram of the Expert System Architecture is provided is fig 2. The system consists of multiple interacting

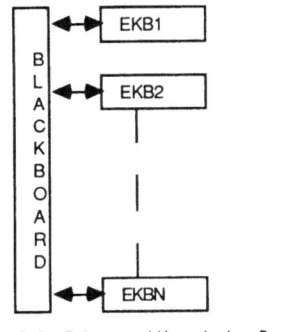

EKB - Enhanced Knowledge Base

FIG. 2.A BLACKBOARD ARCHITECTURE

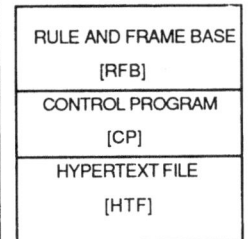

FIG 2.B. COMPONENTS OF AN ENHANCED KNOWLEDGE BASE.

knowledge bases. We refer to each of these knowledge bases as an enhanced knowledge base [EKB]. Interaction occurs through a blackboard mechanism that directs control to one of the EKBs at any time. The user's initial dialogue is with EKB1 which manages the initial interfacing and directs reference to the other EKBs as needed. Each EKB consists of the following:

(a) A rule and frame base [RFB]: This consists of knowledge that has been represented in the form of Production rules [2] and Frames [10]. The knowledge that is contained in a RFB is primarily declarative, though some production rules contain knowledge that is procedural.

(b) A hypertext file [HTF]: This contains hypertext associated with hypertext keywords in the RFB. Top level keywords are defined in the knowledge base and may be predicates (elements of rule text) or annotations associated with rules. Multiple levels of keyword definition are possible, so text associated with keywords may in turn contain hypertext keywords. Thus, the system can support arbitrarily complex hierarchies of descriptive knowledge. A hypertext file is associated with a RFB during the initial interaction with KB1. Hence, it is possible for a different hypertext file (representing different interpretations) to be associated with the same RFB during different sessions. Using hypertext in conjunction with production rules has resulted in a relatively small number of production rules, aiding interpretation of ambiguous words and enhancing the quality of explanation.

(c) A Control Program [CP]: The Control program associated with each knowledge base contains control knowledge or procedural knowledge that is used in guiding search and focusing system behavior during a session. The control program allows focus to be restricted to specific subsets of rules in different inferential modes (both forward and backward chaining are supported) through appropriate commands to the inference engine. Some of this procedural knowledge can be represented as control rules in the knowledge base. However, use of the control program helps to make the rule base more readable, by separating most of the control knowledge from the declarative domain knowledge. Control programs also facilitate interaction between multiple knowledge bases.

The use of multiple knowledge bases interacting through a blackboard is motivated by factors such as efficiency, context sensitive hypertext attachment, maintainability and expansibility. These are briefly discussed below:

a) Efficiency: The knowledge base can be partitioned into a few smaller knowledge bases, each of which contains portions of statutory law on civil procedures. Each knowledge base has limited interaction with others through a blackboard facility. Given that a typical user would access only a limited portion of the knowledge base, we have been able to increase efficiency of retrieval significantly, by partitioning the domain knowledge smartly. This is particularly significant due to the fact that the efficiency of the system is significantly dependant on the size of the RFB active at any time.

b) Attaching context specific information: Case information or opinions may be context specific as discussed in Section 3. This can be represented by choosing among different hypertext files (using the controlling knowledge base) and attaching relevant hypertext information each EKB. In other words, the same keyword can have different interpretations in different files (with cross referencing where necessary).

c) Maintainability: Organizing knowledge in the form of relatively small, structured knowledge bases aids maintenance. This is particularly relevant in a domain like law where a large amount of work in terms of knowledge representation is exploratory. It is expected that the knowledge base would be updated based on feedback from lawyers who use the system.

d) Expansibility: One legal statute may refer to another (eg. Federal Rules refer to State Rules). In such a situation, the knowledge bases representing State Rules can be developed independently and the controlling knowledge base can be modified to include this. This knowledge base (State Rules) can also be accessed independently, by users who might be interested in issues that do not involve Federal Rules. Care should be taken to ensure that information that is required for interaction between knowledge bases is written out to the blackboard.

5.3. Explanation

Explanation of questions is provided by one or more of the following:

(a) Display of hypertext associated with words on the question screen: These words may be associated with predicates or other text on the screen. The user is presented with hypertext based aids in order to answer questions that the system asks him. These include opinions or interpretations of words which require interpretation or amplification of meaning. Hypertext based access is also available to the actual text of the statute, as well as associated portions of other statutes, or relevant cases where necessary. This access can be made context sensitive where required.

(b) Display of relevant rules for a question or conclusion: Hypertext can be accessed from the rule display screen. This is similar to (a) and helps to enhance the quality of explanation.

(c) Display of notes and reference: Each rule is associated with a note and a reference. Notes contain text that would help to amplify the meaning of a rule. This may in turn contain hypertext keywords. Reference contains appropriate Federal Rule reference (eg. Rule 81). This is defined as a hypertext keyword and allows the user to see the actual text of the statute if required.

(d) Display of rules associated with conclusions: Rules associated with conclusions can be displayed if required. Reference to hypertext is possible from the rules or associated notes or references as discussed above.

6. Discussion and future work

Use of hypertext in conjunction with traditional knowledge representation techniques like rules and frames has proved extremely valuable. It has helped to make the expert system size more manageable by reducing the number of rules without affecting completeness of knowledge representation. In addition, it provides a convenient and effective framework for representing case knowledge and interpretations which may be context sensitive. Linking this context sensitive information to predicates in the rule base helps to enhance the quality of explanation and also provides a method for dealing with imprecision inherent in legal knowledge.

The system is currently being implemented on an IBM PS2, model 50 Z, using a C based expert system shell. The current prototype uses a knowledge base of about 200 rules and associated hypertext. This represents approximately one-tenth of the knowledge that has to be encoded. The different modes of access described above have been implemented and hypertext relevant to this rule base has been developed as well. The blackboard facility has been tested for multiple small knowledge bases. We hope to implement and test the system with larger EKBs within the next few months. Our experience in transfering the conceptual features into characteristics of the computer based system has been very positive. Currently, the system accesses case knowledge through hypertext associated with rules. However, this is not as powerful as a full blown case based reasoning. Such reasoning would involve reasoning by example, which is a relatively complex task.

Of the features that we have discussed earlier, those that have not yet been used in the system till date are frames, non monotonic reasoning and database access. However, the shell that we are using has built in support for incorporating these features. We hope to utilize some or all these features in later versions as we enhance the knowledge base.

Acknowledgements

This work was supported by the Maryland Industrial Partnerships Scheme (MIPS) and Hardlaw Software, Inc.

References

[1] C. Ciampi, (Ed), **Edited Version of Selected Papers from International Conference on Logic, Information and Law**, vol 1, North Holland, 1981.

[2] R. Davis, B. Buchanan and E.H.Shortlife, "Production Rules as a Representation for a Knowledge-Based Consultation System", *Artificial Intelligence,* vol-8, 1977, pp. 15-45.

[3] R. Dworkin, **Taking Rights Seriously,** Cambridge: Harvard University Press, 1977, pp.16.

[4] R.Fikes, and T. Kehler, "The role of Frame-Based Representation in Reasoning", *Communications of the ACM,* vol-28, 1985, pp. 904-920.

[5] L.L. Fuller, "Positivism and Fidelity to Law: A reply to Professor Hart", *Harvard Law Review,* vol-71, 1958, pp. 630-672.

[6] A.V.L. Gardner, **An Artificial Intelligence Approach to Legal Reasoning,** Cambridge-MIT Press, 1987.

[7] H.L.A. Hart, **The Concept of Law,** Oxford: Clarendon Press, 1961.

[8] A. Hustler, "Programming Law in Logic", Research Report, CS-82-13, Department of Computer Science, University of Waterloo, 1982.

[9] L.T. McCarthy, "Reflections on Taxman: An Experiment in Artificial Intelligence and Legal Reasoning, *Harvard Law Review,* vol-90, 1977, pp. 837-893.

[10] M. Minsky, "A Framework for Representing knowledge", in **The Psychology of Computer Vision,** P.H. Winston (ed), McGraw Hill, 1975.

[11] H.P. Nii, "Blackboard Systems: The Blackboard Model of Problem Solving and the Evolution of Blackboard Architectures", *AI Magazine,* vol-7, No.2, 1986a.

[12] H.P. Nii, "Blackboard Systems: Blackboard Application Systems from a Knowledge Based Perspective", *A I Magazine,* Vol-7, No.3, 1986b

[13] N.J. Nilson, "Principles of Artificial Intelligence", Palo Alto, Tioga Publishing, 1980.

[14] W.G. Popp, and B. Schlink, "JUDITH, a Computer Program to Advise Lawyers in Reasoning a Case", *Jurimetrics Journal,* vol-15, 1975, pp. 303-314.

[15] R. Pound, "Mechanical Jurisprudence", *Columbia Law Review,* vol-8, 1908, pp. 605-623.

[16] E.L. Rissland, "Examples in legal Reasoning: Legal Hypotheticals", in *Proceedings, Eighth International Joint Conference on Artificial Intelligence,* Karlsruhe, 1983, pp. 90-93.

[17] E.L. Rissland, E.M. Valcarce and K.D. Ashley, "Explaining and Arguing with Examples", in *AAAI-84, Proceedings, National Conference on Artificial Intelligence,* Austin, Texas, 1984, pp. 288-294.

[18] A.J. Ruggero, **Logic for Lawyers,** Clark Boardman, 1989.

[19] M.J. Sergot, et al "The British Nationality Act as a Logic Program", *Communications of the ACM,* vol-29, 198, pp. 370-386.

[20] J.A. Sprowl, "Automating Legal Reasoning Process: A Computer that uses Regulations and Statutes to draft Legal Documents", *American Bar Foundation Researc h Journal,* 1979, pp. 1-81.

[21] D.A. Waterman, and M.A. Peterson, "Models of Legal Decision Making", Report R-22727-ICJ, Rand Corporation, Institute for Civil Justice, 1981.

[22] D.A. Waterman, and M.A. Peterson, "Evaluating Civil Claims: An Expert Systems Approach", *Expert Systems,* vol-1, 1984, pp. 65-76.

TOWARD A COMPREHENSIVE LEGAL INFORMATION RETRIEVAL SYSTEM

DAPHNE GELBART   J.C. SMITH

University of British Columbia
Faculty of Law Artificial Intelligence Research Project
Vancouver, Canada V6T 1Y1

Abstract

The construction of comprehensive legal information systems require at least three different kinds of mechanisms of information retrieval and knowledge representation, ranging from domain-specific and knowledge-based to fully automatic and general purpose. This paper describes how different information needs are satisfied by different architectures, and in particular how the **FLEXICON** System[1] being developed by the FLAIR team can replace Boolean word searches with a system of information retrieval using weighted conceptual profiles to search automatically indexed databases.

Introduction

The essence of legal research is the retrieval of relevant decided cases and related legal information. While a number of computerized legal information retrieval systems are available, including QuickLaw and CAN/LAW in Canada, and LEXIS and WESTLAW in the US, it appears that no existing system fully addresses the special needs of judges, lawyers and legal researchers. Existing systems allow the user to conduct keyword search of mostly unstructured case databases, largely via boolean queries. Boolean searches can be confusing to legal or para-legal users and often result in the retrieval of a large number of cases not ranked by relevance to the user's query and including many irrelevant cases. In addition to a deficient search mechanism, existing systems usually provide little or no assistance to the user in formulating a query and lack any domain expertise that could improve the search outcome.

The cases retrieved by existing systems are generally recovered in full text, which the user must laboriously page through to ascertain whether or not the case is relevant. Legal research requires a set of tools which can summarize the numerous cases that are either published in the law reports or are unreported. Legal information in printed form generally provides summaries such as headnotes of cases, abstracts, indexes, and digests. These tools require extensive human time and expertise to prepare. When legal information is stored electronically, similar kinds of summaries are needed in order to facilitate retrieval and perusal of the primary documents. Depending upon the purpose of the legal research, a user may require either the full text of a case, some specific information which the case contains, a summary of the case, or some combination of the above.

The University of British Columbia **FLAIR** (Faculty of Law Artificial Intelligence Research) Project was established to develop techniques for the retrieval of legal information by adapting general retrieval tools for use in recovering legal information, and to explore new ways of representing legal knowledge to facilitate the use of such tools. The Project is investigating various information retrieval techniques ranging from domain-specific knowledge-based advisory systems to fully automatic general purpose information retrieval systems. We have found that at least three kinds of retrieval mechanisms and related databases are required to serve the needs of the legal community. The three types of systems described below satisfy diverse requirements and, we believe, provide the foundation for a complete legal information retrieval system.

Knowledge-Based Information Retrieval Systems

A knowledge-based legal information retrieval system is composed of a database of cases and a knowledge base of rules. The database design requires the selection of key attributes by a domain expert. Each case is then scanned manually and the values of the corresponding attributes are filled in. The knowledge base is built by extracting the domain expertise from an expert and representing it in the form of rules.

The retrieval mechanism of a knowledge-based information retrieval system is the reasoning over domain rules resulting in the automatic formulation of a query to the database. The user of a knowledge-based information retrieval system is not required to construct a query to search for relevant information. Rather, the system asks the user questions about the matter at hand, assists him or her in answering those questions and instructs the user to acquire additional information, if necessary. Based on the information supplied by the user, on domain expertise, on factual information, and on reasoning methods applied by the system, a forecast of the outcome of the case if presented in court is presented to the user. Then the system automatically formulates a query to retrieve relevant cases.

The Nervous Shock Advisor

The Nervous Shock Advisor (NSA)[2], FLAIR's first effort and one of the pioneering case-based expert systems, demonstrates the successful operation of a domain-specific knowledge-based legal information system built using a commercial shell. The Hearsay Advisor[3] demonstrated the applicability of that methodology to a different area of law. NSA is a rule-based expert system in the domain of remoteness that includes a knowledge base of domain rules linked to a database of legal judgments. It gives expert advice on the circumstances under which a plaintiff could recover damages in negligence for a case of post-traumatic stress disorder, commonly known as nervous shock. The system then retrieves relevant cases from the case database and displays them to the user. NSA uses its domain knowledge to separate the cases into those that are on point, relevant by analogy, or contra. As well, the system gives advice as to the most effective defences to nervous shock law suits.

Case-Based Reasoning

While NSA has proven a very useful tool, its construction has demonstrated the high degree of effort required to construct a knowledge base adequate for even a narrow domain of law. In order to move toward a more generally applicable architecture, FLAIR is redesigning NSA as a frame-based system using a case-based reasoning approach influenced by the pioneering work in legal case-based reasoners done by Rissland and Ashley[4,5]. While in a rule-based expert system the conclusion is reached on the basis of rules summarizing the domain expertise, the redesigned NSA system will reach conclusions based on characteristics of the retrieved cases. The system will retrieve cases related to a given case profile, based on user input, and will extract the decisions in those cases to produce a conclusion. The decisions are weighted to reflect the relative value as legal precedents of the cases retrieved, the number of cases found, the relative number of cases supporting the plaintiff versus those supporting the defendant, the degree to which each case matches the facts of the current case, and the consistency of the conclusions in comparing searches using more or less constrained search criteria.

The most effective form of legal case based reasoner is one which asks the user only factual questions, but presents a legal conclusion as dictated by the cases in the database. This requires the fields of the cases in the database to correspond with the questions to be directed to the user. The essential knowledge representation task is to select the right categories of facts to serve as fields, and as the basis of the inquiries from the user. This relationship cannot be established in terms of the legal doctrines argued and cited in the cases, as the adversarial system of legal argument leads to the development of legal doctrines in terms of opposing pairs of conceptual alternatives, those which favour plaintiffs, and those which favour defendants. It has been our experience that one must search for and use a deeper structure than is to be found at the doctrinal level. This structure can only be discovered through the development of a theory which explains the outcomes of the cases in a particular area of law.

The knowledge based system has many advantages to the user. It allows a user with minimal understanding of the domain to retrieve relevant cases by providing assistance in entering and acquiring necessary information, by predicting the outcome of the case at hand, and by offering explanations of its reasoning. However, the construction of a knowledge-based system and its accompanying database for each domain is a major undertaking requiring the employment of a domain expert, lengthy knowledge acquisition sessions, implementation and maintenance of the knowledge base, as well as the manual abstracting and summarizing of the cases required to construct the database.

The case-based approach, while requiring the same effort in manually constructing the database, reduces the effort required to construct and maintain the knowledge base and employs primarily meta-rules, i.e. rules that describe the search and pattern matching mechanism, which are more portable to other domains.

It is clear from our experience in building expert systems for case-based reasoning that one must have a jurisprudential foundation rich enough to provide a theory of relevancy which can furnish criteria for measuring when a certain factor is relevantly similar to another. Legal theory is essential for the representation of legal knowledge for expert systems[6], and the use of deep structure will be necessary if we are to create case-based reasoners which are capable of going beyond the heuristic instincts of their creators

Menu-Driven Case Retrieval Systems

The menu-driven case retrieval system is another domain-specific information retrieval model that provides some of the capabilities of the knowledge-based system, while requiring less effort in system construction. A menu-driven system is composed of a database of cases and related information and a user interface that extracts information from the user and displays results of the consultation to the user. Usually, a commercial database management system is used for the database component and a front end tool is used to build the user interface. Similarly to the knowledge-based system, the menu-driven or intelligent database asks the user intelligent questions, assists him or her in answering the questions and instructs the user to acquire additional information, when necessary. The entered information is used to automatically construct a query to search the database of cases, display relevant cases and provide additional information on the retrieval.

The Whiplash Knowledge System, constructed in 1988 by the FLAIR team, is an intelligently structured database of current British Columbia judgments awarding damages for soft-tissue injury to the neck and back. The objective of the Whiplash Knowledge System is to provide users with quick, up-to-date and easy to understand information about the quantum of pain and suffering awards for whiplash injury in the province, and to provide summaries of closely matched cases in support of a specific whiplash claim. The Whiplash Knowledge System allows the user to select cases from among those available by specifying search parameters such as sex, age and occupation of the plaintiff; recovery period and severity of injury; judge, date and quantum; medical conditions common to soft-tissue injury; legal issues relevant to the calculation of whiplash damages; and various types of pre-trial and future income loss indicators. Once cases are retrieved, a report is generated which produces summaries of those cases and summarizes the search results by displaying the number of cases retrieved, their average pain & suffering award, the inflation-adjusted average, and the range of awards involved. A multi-window menu-driven user-interface has been constructed for the Whiplash Knowledge System, incorporating hypertext links to meaningful help screens.

Like the case-based reasoning expert system, the menu-driven system extracts information, such as the range of damages, from the database. Unlike the knowledge-based system, it involves no reasoning and does not provide information on the likelihood of success of a cause of action for the case at hand. As well, constructing the database of cases demands less expertise than constructing the database for a knowledge-based system. Consequently, the effort required to construct a menu-based system consists primarily of building an intelligent and appropriate user interface, as well as the manual indexing and summarizing of cases required to construct the database. The most crucial and time-consuming step in building an expert system, the knowledge acquisition from an expert, is eliminated.

A General Purpose Legal Information Retrieval System

The two domain-specific systems discussed above require a manually structured and indexed database of case summaries. However, the large volume of legal information and the enormous effort required to manually abstract and index cases for every domain of law necessitates a general purpose system which automatically generates a database of document profiles. This process is facilitated by the recent trend of courts to produce decisions in a standard format using word processors which allows the cases to be simply transferred to a database upon release. In order to be effective, the system should provide assistance in entering and refining queries, match the queries against the automatically constructed document profiles and retrieve those documents that best match the query, ranked in order of their similarity to the query.

FLEXICON (Fast Legal EXpert Information CONsultant) is an automatic general purpose legal information retrieval system that will handle judgments in any domain of law, as well as other legal documents. Every case contains a factual story, a description of the set of legal issues which the story gives rise to, a statement of the applicable law, and a resolution to the issues when the law has been applied to the facts. The statements of law within the case, whether they relate to the issues raised, the law to be applied to them, or to the resolution, will contain legal concepts and references to cases and statutes. Legal concepts will be found to exist in clusters. Certain concepts generally appear in some form of relationship to other concepts. The citations of cases, as well, appear in clusters; that is, certain cases are generally found cited together. Furthermore, certain concept clusters will often be found in conjunction with certain case clusters. The same holds equally true for statutes and codes. We can build up a profile of a case in terms of the relationships between four parameters: concepts, cases, legislation, and facts. By measuring the frequency and proximity of these parameters in relationship to each other, we can produce a database of profiles of cases which can serve as summaries of their counterparts in the document database. We can then retrieve cases from the database by comparing a query composed of the four types of keyword terms and selecting those cases whose profiles are most similar to the query.

The potential of the connectionist approach for legal information retrieval has been persuasively argued by Below and Rose.[7,8] The approach taken in constructing FLEXICON differs from theirs, in that while we also make use of connections between keywords as part of our related terms network (as indicated below), we base the search for cases on a match between a user's query and case profiles.

Text Analysis and Automatic Indexing

Document analysis involves scanning the raw text of the document and automatically extracting key information that can serve as a document representative or profile. These keywords are listed in decreasing order of a weight factor, which is proportional to the document term frequency and inversely proportional to the number of documents in which the term occurs. The function of the document profile is twofold: the profile can serve as a summary of the document, allowing the user to rapidly familiarize him- or herself with the document's content and to establish its relevance to his or her needs. Its second and more important function is to serve as the document representative, containing information necessary and sufficient to match the document with a user's query and to determine the relevance of the document to the user's needs.

The document profiles produced by the automatic text analysis component of FLEXICON serve as a basis for the automatic construction of an electronic headnote that, in analogy to the manually constructed headnotes of printed law reports, provides an easily scanned summary of the judgment. In addition to the list of concepts, facts, case citations and statute citations ordered by relative significance, the electronic headnote includes a list of the fact words of the judgment in order of occurrence, and a number of automatically extracted key paragraphs that appear to express the essence of the judgment. For reports of legal judgments, in addition to extraction of keywords, the text analysis process involves automatic extraction of additional parameters from judgment headers, such as date, jurisdiction, etcetera. These can serve as additional search parameters that will allow a user to, optionally, narrow the domain of the search.

Search Mechanism

The search mechanism to be employed in FLEXICON will be an optimized version of the inverted index model based on a dictionary of terms where each term points to a list of all document profiles in which it occurs. While most information retrieval systems use boolean queries in conjunction with an inverted index structure, we feel that the boolean operators are too restrictive, as well as being a source of confusion to the user. Instead we will use the vector space model suggested by Salton [9], and represent both document profiles and queries as ordered lists of weighted keywords [9,10,11]. In order to reduce the number of cases retrieved and to return the best cases ranked by relevance, the inverted index will be used merely to produce an *initial* list of cases which *could* be relevant. The profile of each document in that list will be compared with the query using the cosine similarity measure suggested by Salton [9] to compute the degree of similarity between query and profile. The documents whose profiles score highest are returned to the user in decreasing order of matching score. In order to further increase the efficiency of the search, we may use the algorithm presented by Buckley and Lewit [12] which performs the match only on a subset of the documents pointed to by the index, relying on stopping rules to indicate the point in the search where the loss of effectiveness resulting from incomplete matching will be minimal.

User Interface

The FLEXICON user interface is simple and elegant. The user is instructed to enter legal concepts, facts, case and statute citations, which, together, characterize every legal document into four quadrants on the query screen. The user can, optionally, indicate the significance of each term entered by selecting a qualification (i.e. High, Medium, Low). The system allows the user to enter minimal information and presents a list of related keywords that can be used for query refinement. In addition to keyword search, the user can enter additional search parameters, such as date, court, etcetera, that will refine the search request. The result of the FLEXICON search will be a list of cases ranked in descending order of similarity to the query. The user will be able to indicate prior to the search the maximum number of cases he/she wishes to retrieve. The user will be able to view the headnote and full text of each retrieved case, and to print selected information.

Picture 1 describes the FLEXICON data entry screen.

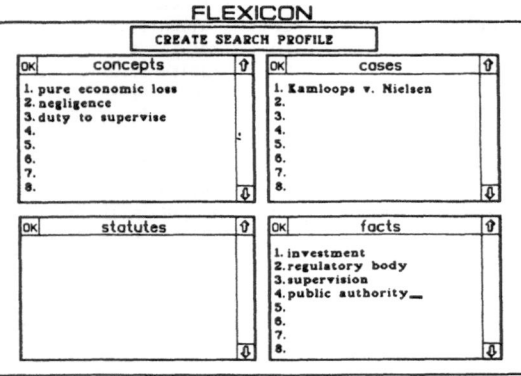

Picture 2 portrays the initial summary of the case profile which introduces the user to the full automatically created headnote or document summary.

Related Terms Network

For each query term the user enters, FLEXICON will present a list of related concepts, facts, case and/or statute citations which can, at the user's discretion, be added to the original query. Also, in order to determine the relevance of related terms that are case or statute citations, the user can view the profile and full text of

those cases and a summary or full text of statutes. The related terms network is automatically constructed for the four types of FLEXICON keywords by connecting terms that tend to co-occur in many legal documents. A measure of association is computed between each pair of terms that is inversely proportional to their distance in the document text and is incrementally computed over all documents in the database. Two terms are linked if their measure of association is above a certain threshold.

Since experimental results by Salton [11] and others indicate that only about 20% of the automatically generated related terms are globally relevant, we propose to assist the user in two ways:

(1) Use a thesaurus of synonyms whereby the similarity matching routine will recognize a match between any two terms belonging to the same thesaurus class. This thesaurus function will be performed automatically, without user intervention.

(2) Use an automatically generated related terms association network. These terms need not be synonyms, but are related to each other in the sense that they tend to co-occur in many document profiles. Control over the utilization of related terms should remain with the user. The user can be presented with lists of terms related to query terms and select those which will enhance the query in the given context. This process gives the user maximal control over the query refinement process.

A specialized association mechanism will be applied to case and statute citation terms to reflect the citation mechanism in legal text such that a document is linked with other documents which either cite it or are cited by it. As well, two cases cited by a third case are linked. A statute is linked with all cases that cite it and with related or equivalent statutes, such as statutes covering the same subject matter but originating in different jurisdictions.

Yet another association mechanism will be applied during system operation where the cases verified as relevant by the user will be associated with leading query terms that were used to retrieve those cases. This self-learning mode allows other users who are entering common terms in a different query (that may not retrieve the same cases) to benefit from previous users' knowledge. Cases retrieved by earlier users will be presented as related to the same terms entered by later users.

Relevance Feedback

Relevance feedback describes a process whereby terms found in profiles of documents retrieved by an initial query can be used to refine that query to allow the search to be repeated until the user is satisfied. While other authors, such as Salton [10], present this as an automated process, we prefer, as with related term substitution, to leave the FLEXICON user in control of which terms are added to the profile. The user will inspect the profiles of relevant retrieved documents and *selectively* add terms to his/her original profile.

Conclusion

The various models of legal information retrieval systems investigated by the FLAIR project represent a spectrum of information retrieval approaches, ranging from effort-intensive and domain-specific to automatic general purpose systems. The knowledge-based system seems especially suitable to documenting the expertise of a narrow and relatively specialized form of legal knowledge. The case-based reasoning technique could present a more general purpose approach to an expert system, whereby the rules, rather than documenting the domain expertise, serve primarily as meta-rules recording knowledge about the mechanism used by the expert to reach a conclusion. In addition to constructing working advisory systems, a case-based reasoner could conceivably be used to automatically generate domain rules and thus automatically document the domain expertise.

The menu-driven model seems to lend itself especially to domains that require the retrieval of specific information which will be found in a large set of cases. The specific information in a particular case is not generally important. The information which is required necessitates a comparison of the same kind of information across a set of cases, such as the range of damages awards for specific kinds of injuries or the penalties for specific kinds of crimes[13]. The user addressing a widely used domain usually has the expertise to arrive at an expected judgment and will probably be satisfied with assistance in formulating an intelligent query to retrieve relevant cases. A manually indexed database for a narrow domain like whiplash can be generated and maintained with reasonable effort and has the added advantage of being tailored to the needs of a user specializing in that domain.

For the requirements of general purpose legal information retrieval, a generalized retrieval system like FLEXICON seems most suitable. The same technology and implementation effort can be used not only for cases in all domains of law but for any type of legal document. Due to the quantity of legal decisions, a daunting effort would be required to manually index and maintain a legal database. The construction of knowledge bases for each domain of law would require an even larger effort. We believe that only a general purpose system can satisfy a significant share of the tremendous information retrieval requirements of legal practitioners. FLEXICON will assist the user in entering a well-formulated query and allow him or her to benefit from the expertise of earlier users. It has the capacity to provide the user with a complete legal library and to alleviate the need for manual handling of text. Combining generality of use with an emphasis on effectiveness and efficiency of retrieval will make FLEXICON a significant tool for legal information retrieval.

Upon the completion of FLEXICON we plan to modify it into a general tool which can be adapted to a variety of specific domains which lend themselves to the construction of profiles in terms of several kinds of conceptual parameters. Such a system would be fully menu driven, and would provide automatic document processing including the production of document summaries. A search would be based on a comparison of a weighted query (search profile) as a whole to automatically-generated document profiles. The system would provide relevance feedback and would be self-learning, making associations between documents retrieved by users and the conceptual patterns that retrieved them. A user would be able to view the summaries of retrieved documents to determine relevance and then jump to the location of user-indicated keywords in the test.

Given the existence of a suitable general purpose tool for a specific domain, it should only be necessary to build special purpose tools for tasks that have special additional information requirements or that are so heavily used as to justify a system tailored to that

application. Together the various system models can provide the foundation for a complete information retrieval system which could be adapted to a variety of knowledge domains.

REFERENCES

[1] Copyright 1989, Daphne Gelbart and J.C. Smith.

[2] Smith, J.C. and C. Deedman. The Application of Expert Systems Technology to Case-Based Reasoning. Proc. 1st International Conference on Artificial Intelligence and Law, (Boston) A.C.M. Press, New York, 1987, p. 84.

[3] MacCrimmon, Marilyn T. Expert Systems in Case-Based Law: The Hearsay Rule Advisor. Proc. 2nd International Conference on Artificial Intelligence and Law, (Vancouver) A.C.M. Press, New York, 1989, p. 68.

[4] Rissland, Edwina L. and Kevin D. Ashley. A Case-Based System for Trade Secrets Law. Proc. 1st International Conference on Artificial Intelligence and Law, (Boston) A.C.M. Press, New York, 1987, p. 60.

[5] Ashley, Kevin D. Modelling Legal Arguments: Reasoning with Cases and Hypotheticals. MIT Press, Cambridge, Mass., 1990 (in press).

[6] Susskind, Richard E. Expert Systems in Law. Oxford University Press, Oxford, 1987.

[7] Belew, Richard K. A Connectionist Approach to Conceptual Information Retrieval. Proc. 1st International Conference on Artificial Intelligence and Law, (Boston) A.C.M. Press, New York, 1987, p. 116.

[8] Rose, Daniel E. and Richard K. Belew. Legal Information Retrieval: A Hybrid Approach. Proc. 2nd International Conference on Artificial Intelligence and Law, (Vancouver) A.C.M. Press, New York, 1989, p. 138.

[9] Salton, G. and M.J. McGill. Introduction to Modern Information Retrieval, McGraw-Hill, 1983.

[10] Salton, G. Automatic Text Processing. Addison-Wesley, 1989.

[11] Salton, G. and C. Buckley. Term Weighting Approaches in Automatic Text Retrieval. Information Processing and Management, Vol 24 (1988), p 513.

[12] Buckley C. Optimization of Inverted Vector Searches. Eighth Annual International ACM SIGIR Conference on Research and Development in Information Retrieval, Montreal, 1985.

[13] A prime example of a menu-driven legal information system is the Sentencing Database developed by John Hogarth as part of the UBC Faculty of Law-IBM Canada Cooperative Project, now marketed by the LIST Foundation.

"TERESA: An Integrated System for Network Diagnoses"

Alan McMichael   Jennifer Thien   Jason Tsay

AT&T Bell Laboratories
Middletown, New Jersey 07748

ABSTRACT

The TERESA system (Trouble Evaluation and Resolution via Expert System Application) is a distributed expert system that provides automated diagnoses of transmission problems in AT&T's digital communication network. Its domain of operation is challenging, requiring collection and analysis of large amounts of information from equipment and systems in disparate locations and cooperation among the processors in the distributed system. Through its distributed design, TERESA secures reliable local communications with operations support systems throughout the network and can serve users in a variety of locations. TERESA employs its wide area networking capability to obtain global alarm correlation information and to perform cooperative trouble diagnosis from both ends of a circuit. The trouble shooting application program is an expert system knowledge base consisting of rules garnered from human experts.

This paper examines how database, communications, and expert system technology are integrated in TERESA to provide reliable, fault-tolerant automation of network maintenance tasks.

1. Introduction

The TERESA system (Trouble Evaluation and Resolution via Expert System Application) diagnoses transmission problems in AT&T's digital communication network. The TERESA system is a successful application of both expert system and database technology. Expert system technology allows TERESA to diagnose the source of network problems, while database technology extends the number of objects whose status may be considered in any one diagnoses without adversely affecting the performance.

The TERESA system seems to embody Brodie's concept of *intelligent interoperability* [1] [2] , that is, an environment in which communicating systems act as intelligent agents that cooperate to solve problems. It consists of several intelligent subsystems, each of which understands a subset of the diagnostic task. There is no controlling subsystem. Any subsystem may communicate with another subsystem to gather additional information needed in its task. Notice that this communication is not limited by physical machine boundaries. TERESAs can also communicate with each other to diagnose network problems.

2. Application Domain

A brief explanation of the long distance network is necessary to understand TERESA's functionality. Figure 1 shows a simplified view of a telecommunication network. Each node represents a network element, which can be either a switching system such as a 5ESS® electronic switch, or a transmission system. Network elements are connected by facilities. Specialized computer applications are required to manage, control, monitor and maintain the network elements. These computer systems, often called Operations Support Systems or simply Operations Systems (OS), are an integral part of the telecommunication network. Some complex network elements--such as 4ESS® switching systems--have several OSs to support the operation, while the smaller ones--such as intelligent transmission systems--have the control and monitoring programs embedded in the network elements.

One major function of an OS is to log the huge amount of diagnostic data generated by the network element it supports. A switching machine, for example, generates diagnostic messages whenever an attempted call cannot be completed. Sometimes these messages represent normal conditions in the network, but other times they are causes by real problems that need human assistance. The problem may occur at any point in the network--facilities, terminal equipment, trunks, or a component of the switch itself. Although redundancy will allow most network elements to continue to function

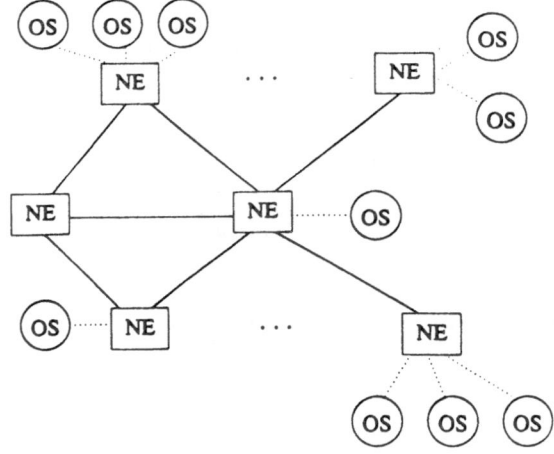

FIGURE 1: A simplified view of a telecommunication network NE is a network element such as a switching machine or a transmission system; OS is an Operations Support System.

when some components are failing, delay in fixing faulty components may degrade the performance of the network, as well as decrease its capacity. The redundancy of components and the availability of alternate routes hide most network problems from the end user. Therefore, network problems must be detected and reported by supporting technicians in work centers. Thus, network maintenance is heavily dependent on the internal diagnostics produced while the system is processing.

Since all network elements are tightly connected as shown in Figure 1, an alarm indicating a problem in one network element or link may propagate to other network elements. The facilities that connect network elements may be conceptualized as a hierarchy. A failure at one level will generally propagate to the lower levels in the hierarchy. However, the hierarchy is not strict, a lower level element may be associated with several higher level elements. Furthermore, the independent operations of network elements in each work center make it more difficult to determine the cause of a problem that affects several work centers. Each work center may be responsible for different levels in the facility hierarchy and may be unaware of problems at other levels. Determining the root cause of a set of alarms, called correlating the alarms, requires the interaction of both database and expert system technologies. It is also one of the important tasks of managing a telecommunication network effectively and efficiently. Before the dynamic alarm correlation expert system was deployed, technicians in one work center needed to contact technicians in other work centers, working together to resolve the problem. Using this approach, it often took hours to identify the root cause of the problem. By coupling an expert system with a database hundreds of alarm messages can be analyzed and correlated in close to real time.

Even after an alarm is traced down to the network element or link that caused the alarm, experienced technicians need to differentiate the alarm between normal conditions, transient problems, and serious problems. If the trouble is nontransient, the technician runs tests using OSs command to isolate the source of the problem. Often problem isolation requires communication with a person working at another work center, so that test commands can be issued to the far-end OS.

Telecommunications trouble-shooting--alarm correlation, trouble analyses, and trouble isolation--is a time-consuming task that demands highly specialized skills. Clearly, there are benefits to be realized by automating even a part of the process. TERESA uses a combination of database and expert system technology to automate the entire process.

3. Alarm Correlation

To determine the cause of a facility alarm, TERESA needs the status of the associated facilities. Since each TERESA can support more than twenty thousand facilities, this is a large amount of information to maintain. Also, there are thousands of changes in the status of facilities every day. To maintain the routing and status information for the facilities it supports, TERESA must be able to quickly select individual records from a large set. Ideally this information would be available to several diagnostic processes at one time. The application of a conventional database supports all the desired features.

TERESA correlates alarms in T1 facilities with alarms in the T3 facilities. A T1 facility is created by multiplexing together 24 voice paths. T3 facilities, in turn, consist of 28 T1 facilities multiplexed together. A T1 facility may be routed over several shorter distance T3 facilities between the two switching systems that are its termination points. Each TERESA processor monitors the alarm traffic for the T1 facilities that terminate on the switching systems it supports. The database in each processor contains the routing and status information for these facilities. However, the information in the database of a single TERESA processor is not adequate to determine the correlation between the alarms on the transmission systems that it is monitoring. Therefore, each TERESA forwards alarms that are likely to be related to alarms on other machines to a centralized database processor, FAMAS2. FAMAS2 contains the transmission system database for the entire network. When FAMAS2 receives a T1 alarm from a TERESA, it updates the global database and applies its correlation rules to decide whether there is enough evidence to generate a T3 alarm. If a T3 alarm is generated FAMAS2 reports it to any TERESA that would be effected by this alarm. Several TERESAs may be notified of a T3 alarm, even TERESAs whose associated T1's are not alarmed.

When TERESA receives an alarm on a T3 facility, it uses the routing and status information in the database to determine which T1 alarms were caused by the T3 alarm. When the system attempts to diagnose a problem with the T1 facility, it will consult the database to determine if the T1 alarm has been correlated to a T3 alarm. TERESA will not attempt to isolate T1 problems that have been correlated to T3 alarms.

3.1 Database Design

TERESA uses a relational database with three tables to encode the facility status and routing information. One table contains the status of each T1 facility. Similarly, the second table contains the status of each T3 facility. The third table contains the routing information for the facilities. This schema does not contain any duplicate data entries and allows the status to be accessed quickly.

Each TERESA contains a distinct subset of the FAMAS2 database. When the TERESA is initially deployed, its facility routing information is provisioned by FAMAS2 on a per-switch basis. The routing information is resynchronized at scheduled intervals by re-provisioning the entire TERESA. To prevent incomplete or inconsistent data from being used to downward correlate T3 alarms, TERESA may lock the facility database for any one switch. This is done whenever the database for one switch is being built or resynchronized.

Mechanisms exist to synchronize the status information when communication between FAMAS2 and TERESA is temporarily lost. Status information is more dynamic that routing information, therefore to preserve consistency between the FAMAS2 and TERESA, TERESA keeps track of any status changes that it is unable to report to FAMAS2. When communication is re-established, delayed status reports are sent to resynchronize the FAMAS2 database.

4. Trouble-Shooting

Within a single TERESA processor, up to twelve *inference processes*, each serving a particular switching machine, run simultaneously, making decisions necessary to diagnose the circuit problems. They send requests to other TERESA processes in order to access operations systems and network elements, at both the near and far ends of a troubled circuit, and to obtain alarm correlation information.

Because of the variety of network elements, problem symptoms, and underlying causes, circuit trouble-shooting involves sequences of decisions that, although not difficult for experienced humans, resist simple algorithmic programming techniques. In TERESA, this obstacle is overcome by using expert system technology. The inference processes utilize a trouble-shooting knowledge base, consisting of rules garnered from human experts, that is written in the OPS83 [1] language. The OPS rule format is a convenient vehicle for the representation of human trouble-shooting expertise, one that is suitable for handling the complexity of the domain and, at the same time, serves as a modular platform for modification and enhancement.

4.1 Knowledge Base Design

The "inference engine" that invokes the knowledge base rules employs a version of the MEA conflict resolution strategy (see [3]). More specifically, each rule has the form, "If <condition 1>, <condition 2>, ..., <condition n>, [<rank-option>], then do <actions>." When the left-hand side conditions (the "if" conditions) of a single rule are matched by elements in "working memory", the right-hand side actions are performed. If the left-hand conditions of several rules are matched simultaneously (or if a single rule's conditions are matched by more than one collection of working memory elements), the conflict resolution strategy picks a rule whose first condition (the "goal" or "context" condition) is most recently matched. If there are several such rules, the strategy defaults to a rule with a maximum ranking (if any). If there is still a tie, the strategy selects a rule with the largest number of left-hand side conditions. Any remaining tie is resolved arbitrarily.

Conflict resolution is a low-level aspect of TERESA's knowledge base design. Viewed from a higher perspective, the TERESA knowledge base can be seen to involve a division into three separate inference problems:

1. Task Selection — Selection of a trouble report to work on.

2. Trouble Analysis — Verifying the existence of a real, nontransient problem.

3. Trouble Isolation — Isolate the problem to a section of the circuit.

For each of these inference problems, specific decision making methods, of varying complexity, are used.

Task Selection is handled by a scanning search of work lists according to simple priority rules, namely, (1) that outage reports for circuit groups are more important than those for single "trunks", and (2) that handling new trouble reports is more important than the retesting and reverification of reports previously considered.

Trouble Analysis incorporates a more sophisticated decision scheme. In Trouble Analysis, TERESA must determine whether a trouble report indicates a real problem or a routine transient error. Also, if a problem does exist, TERESA must decide whether it is serious enough to warrant placing the circuit out of service or whether instead the circuit should be left in service but marked for maintenance. Because problems may be of an intermittent nature, because they may involve accumulation of error counts over varying periods of time, because the condition of a circuit may change, and because test results themselves are inevitably subject to errors, TERESA must base its decisions on uncertain information. The method chosen to implement this is Bayesian probabilistic reasoning.[4]

When an inference process selects a trouble report to work on, it forms a list of hypotheses about the condition of the circuit in question. These hypotheses divide into families. The members of a family represent different problem severities. In TERESA, each family has five members. (No use could be made of a significantly larger number, since TERESA would have to perform an unreasonable number of tests to make any distinction between adjacent hypotheses.) For example, the family of hypotheses for circuit noise consists of one hypothesis ("good") for acceptable circuit noise, two hypotheses ("low" and "medium" failure) for noise within service limits but requiring maintenance, and two hypotheses ("high" and "extreme" failure) for noise that requires taking the circuit out of service.

According to information provided by a domain expert, TERESA provides an initial estimate of the hypothesis probabilities. It then calculates, for each of the various tests it may perform, the expected total change in probability that the test provides (the expected "knowledge gain" of the test). TERESA performs the test with the highest expected gain. It uses Bayes' Theorem to adjust hypothesis probabilities in accordance with the test result, or "evidence", e:

$$p\ (h\ given\ e)\ =\ p(h\mid e)\ =\ p(e\mid h)\ \frac{p(h)}{\sum_i p(e\mid h_i)\,p(h_i)}$$

Here, $p(h)$ is the initial probability of the hypothesis in question. The inverse conditional probability, $p(e\mid h)$, is well-defined because the hypotheses TERESA considers have a direct impact on the

---

1. (OPS83 is a trademark of Production Systems Technologies.)

probabilities of test results. The summation on the bottom of the formula is the total probability of the evidence, calculated by summing over all the hypotheses in *h*'s family.

TERESA exits the trouble analysis process when none of the tests available to it would provide appreciable knowledge gain. If it has determined that a real problem exists on the circuit, it proceeds to the problem isolation phase.

Trouble isolation is a process of elimination. Intermediate circuit elements are tested to narrow the list of candidate faults. Trouble isolation ends when no further narrowing is possible. TERESA assumes a single fault, but it does check to make sure that a fault it finds is adequate to explain the result of its trouble analysis. (For example, TERESA would not regard a one Db noise discrepancy to be an adequate explanation of a total ten Db deviation from the acceptable level, and TERESA would find the principal source of the problem elsewhere.)

A major component of isolation is the filtering of problems correlated to higher-level alarms. Higher-level alarms are caused by faults outside the switching offices served by TERESA. To prevent technicians from wasting time on the lower-level effects, TERESA annotates the lower-level trouble reports and places them on a special work lists. To do this, the inference processes query the alarm correlation database, which has been assembled, as explained in previous sections, through TERESA's links to a centralized database system that contains the correlation rules.

4.2 Distributed Trouble-Shooting

To secure reliable and inexpensive communications with operations systems and personnel in widely separated locations, TERESA processors are installed in several sites. The TERESA processors do not function in a totally independent way, however, because trouble isolation requires communication and cooperation among them. If, for example, a TERESA system verifies the presence of an alarm being received on a circuit, then isolation typically requires that it determine whether the alarm is also being received by equipment at the far end of the circuit. (If it is, then the trouble is at the far end; otherwise, it is on the circuit section between the two locations.) Sometimes, the far end of the circuit is being served by the same TERESA processor, so that only interprocess communication is needed. But usually access to the far end involves a call, over a packet switching network, to another TERESA processor. TERESA is therefore a distributed trouble-shooting system; interprocessor communication is an essential part of its diagnostic capabilities.

Cooperation is needed from the far end TERESA for two reasons:

1. Trouble isolation requires communication with the far end OSs. For a given OS, TERESA is provided with only one, or few communication links, and they are under the control of the local (far end) TERESA. Remember that more than one distant TERESA may be in need of this resource at any given time!

2. Trouble isolation requires communication with far end circuit elements. The database for routing to these elements is stored

on the local (far end) TERESA. The TERESA calling in must access this routing information.

Later sections will describe the design of the software supporting TERESA's distributed operations.

5. A Wide-Area Distributed Expert System

TERESA's two-ended circuit trouble shooting feature necessitates some form of wide-area network. This could be achieved either through a centralized processor networked to all the OSs or, as in the design actually selected, through a network of less powerful processors co-located with the OSs. However, the centralized alternative has serious drawbacks and the distributed design offers many relative advantages.

In the centralized design, the central processor, undoubtably a mainframe, has communication links to 50+ OSs in ~10 widely separated locations. Since these links are in continuous operation, they would have to be dedicated to TERESA. Moreover, maintaining reliable communications over such long distances is a difficult task. The difficulty would be ameliorated if the OSs were designed to support such communications. However, TERESA does not have this luxury; it must interface with existing, difficult to modify OSs. In summary, the cost of provisioning and maintaining the connectivity required by the centralized design is prohibitive.

In the distributed design, there are one or more minicomputers in the ~10 locations. Communications with the OSs are dealt with locally and reliably. When two-end trouble shooting is performed (and when both ends are not served by a single processor), one processor calls up another over a packet switching network. It issues appropriate commands which the far-end processor passes on to *its* OSs. Naturally, two-end trouble shooting in this cooperative form somewhat more difficult to implement than in the centralized design and there is some loss of reliability. But the distributed design remains the only workable option.

Although the distributed design complicates two-end trouble shooting, characteristics of the application domain limit the importance of this disadvantage. The majority of trouble shooting tasks, perhaps 75%, can be performed satisfactorily using commands to only local OSs. Even when cooperation takes place, local commands predominate. So it seems acceptable to leave two-end trouble shooting process exposed to whatever risks are involved in wide-area networking.

Figure 2 displays the communications links involved in the TERESA system. It can be seen that, unlike most expert systems (see), which run in a stand-alone, advisory mode, the TERESA expert system knowledge base is integrated with a larger computing environment.

6. Overall System Architecture

6.1 Client-Server Model

One TERESA consists of a set of client and server processes. These UNIX® processes, based on the client-server model, are concurrent and communicating (each runs continuously as a daemon). This

130

architecture differs from the ordinary UNIX execution environment, which forks and executes a new process for every service.

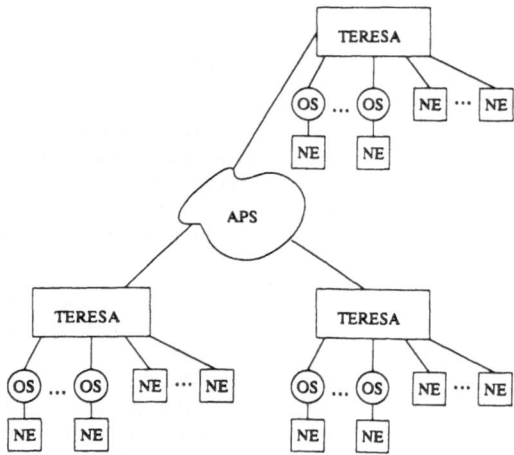

FIGURE 2: TERESA -- a distributed expert system: NE is a network element, OS an operations support system, APS AT&T Accunet Packet Service.

Message passing is the mechanism for inter-process communication (IPC). TERESA extends the IPC mechanism to the expert system network.

6.2 Layered Software Structure

TERESA runs on an AT&T 3B2/600 super microcomputer, hosts the inference and communications subsystems and the database manager. The major software components of TERESA are organized in a layered structure, as shown in Figure 3. The lower-layered software subsystems serve the higher-layered ones.

- Operating System Layer: UNIX is the kernel of the architecture. It provides a versatile environment for expert system development and an efficient environment for expert system execution.

- Execution Environment Layer: This layer is built on UNIX's inter-process communications utilities: messages, semaphores and shared memory. It defines the structure and skeleton of all TERESA processes, which share the same main procedure and the same subroutines for receiving and sending messages and handling signals. The layer also provides a library of subroutines for manipulating fields in the inter-process communication messages. The homogeneity of all concurrent processes facilitates a good environment for software development, integration, testing, execution, and growth.

- Communication and Networking Layer: Provides interface with external OSs, other TERESAs in the network, and FAMAS2.

- Database Management Layer: This layer, built on INFORMIX[2], provides the query processing and concurrency control necessary for transparent, efficient access to the facility database.

- Inference Layer: This layer consists of inference engines and knowledge bases.

- Presentation Layer: This layer provides all user interface capabilities.

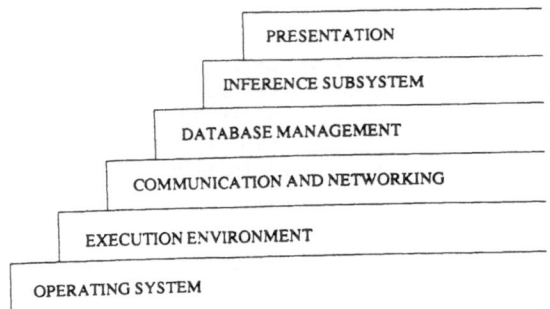

FIGURE 3: The layered structure of TERESA's software components

6.3 Communication Backbone

TERESA's network and the FAMAS2 interface are based on AT&T's Accunet® Packet Service (APS), which supports X.25 host-to-network interfaces and X.75 network-to-network interfaces. APS supports both switched virtual circuits (SVCs) and permanent virtual circuits (PVCs), over which data packets are delivered to the user in the same sequence as they were transmitted and without duplication. Reliability and performance (see [5] for the specifications) are the key criteria for choosing APS as the backbone of the TERESA network.

One physical APS link per TERESA system serves both types of circuits: PVC for the interface with FAMAS2 and SVCs for the TERESA network. Since all TERESAs cannot be simultaneously deployed using the PVC service for the TERESA networking may cause difficulties in the circuit subscription and provisioning. If the SVC service is chosen for the networking, TERESA can deployed gradually without retrofitting the configuration of the APS circuits of previously deployed TERESAs. When the network map files (maintained by TERESA) are modified, any newly added TERESAs will be recognized by all others in the network, without restarting the expert system.

6.4 Distributed Server Processes

To implement the distributed architecture, two service handling processes have been developed, a service dispatcher (SVC_DISP)

---

2. INFORMIX is a registered trademark of Informix Software, Inc.

and a remote handler (REM_HDL). The action of these processes can be illustrated by a simple example.

Suppose that an expert system inference process requests the activation of a circuit terminated at the XYZ switching machine. It does so by composing the following message:

    msg_chg (msg_ptr, SERVICE, ACTIVATE);
    msg_chg (msg_ptr, ID, "1234CITYSTATE");
    msg_chg (msg_ptr, SERVER, "XYZ");

Then the following statement sends the request message to SVC_DISP for forwarding to a server process:

    msg_send (msg_ptr, "XYZ");

SVC_DISP will fetch the SERVER field and decide to send the request to a server process according to the network map file. If the server process is on the same machine, SVC_DISP sends the message directly to it. Otherwise, via REM_HDL, it forwards the message to the server on a remote TERESA.

6.5 Homogeneity, Transparency and Runtime Binding

A client process in one host can access any server process in the network using the same IPC mechanism used in the intra-processor communications. No client process, such as the inference subsystem, needs information about the location of the server processes. They may reside on the same machine or on a remote TERESA. When an IPC message is sent to a server, the client process merely specifies the server's name and the type of service, as in the circuit-activation example above.

The binding of remote expert systems is done at runtime by the remote handler process. It then fetches the server name and consults the network map files to determine a remote host TERESA. If a virtual channel to the remote host already exists, the remote handler process sends the message directly to APS. Otherwise, the handler makes a call setup request and then forwards the message after receiving the connection confirmation.

Since all the binding is performed during runtime, changes to the network map files will allow the expert system to recognize immediately any new configuration of the distributed services.

7. Conclusions

By combining database and expert system technology in a distributed system, TERESA is able to fully automate the network maintenance task and achieve the goal of distributed artificial intelligence (DAI): To find mechanisms that can be employed by individual expert systems (or expert system builders) to coordinate the activities of a group into an effective organization for solving problems that the system share. Initially, TERESA was demonstrated by installations at only a few locations. However, its acceptance was quick and the excellence of the software design led easily to full deployment. That deployment (about 17 systems supporting all AT&T switches) is a significant indicator of TERESA's many benefits.

Three important benefits are as follows, though most of the benefits listed in [6] and [5] are also applicable:

- To capture and preserve expertise.

- To utilize automated expertise as a basis for automating other related tasks, thus allowing the complete automation of telecommunication maintenance.

- To ensure that expertise is applied uniformly, objectively, and consistently at all times — 24 hours a day and seven days a week.

REFERENCES

1. Mylopoulos, J. and Brodie, M. L., "Readings in Artificial Intelligence and Databases", Morgan Kaufman, 1988

2. Brodie, Michael J., "Future Intelligent Information Systems: AI and Database Technologies Working Together", from [1]

3. Brownston, L., Farrell, R., Kant, E., and Martin, N., *Programming Expert Systems in OPS5: An Introduction to Rule-Based Programming* (Reading, Massachusetts: Addison-Wesley, 1982).

4. Pearl, J., *Probabilistic Reasoning and Intelligent Systems: Networks of Plausible Inference* (Morgan Kaufman, 1989).

5. AT&T Communications Technical Reference: *X.25 Interface Specification and Packet Transport Network Capabilities*, PUB 54010, May 1986.

5. Liebowitz, J. (Ed.), *Expert Systems Applications to Telecommunications*, John Willey & Sons, 1988.

6. Prerau, D., *Developing and Managing Expert Systems*, Addison-Wesley, 1990.

DScheme, An Imbedable Interpreter

Alfred Kayser   Jan van Oorschot

Delft University of Technology
Faculty of Electrical Engineering
Laboratory of Computer Architecture and Digital Technique
P.O.Box 5031, 2600 GA DELFT
The Netherlands

ABSTRACT

This article describes the design and development of a data description language (DDL). The main purpose of this language is to provide an uniform syntax for data files spread on decentralized systems. The Data Network Performance Analyzing Project (DNPAP) group is currently building such a decentralized system. Its main purpose to collect, store and analyze network measurement and configuration files. The DDL described in this article is developed to ensure that all data files are self-documenting, system independent and readable by man and computer. DDL will also be used as the query language for the DNPAP data base system.

DDL is build on a subset of Scheme, to avoid the design of a complete new language. An imbedable Scheme interpreter called DScheme (Delft Scheme) is written to parse and evaluate data stored in DDL. DScheme meets the following requirements: small, system-independent, extensible in C and linkable to applications. The DScheme language can serve as an universal language for data, control and definition files in a distributed environment.

INTRODUCTION

This section explains why we selected Scheme as base to develop DDL. It describes the situation and the requirements to be met by the Data Description Language. Subsequent sections explain why Scheme was chosen and describe the language Scheme.

Situation

One of the main tasks of the Data Network Performance Analyzing Project (DNPAP)* is to build a measurement and network configuration data base. This data base maintains all the output of the measurement programs of DNPAP programs. Other DNPAP programs such as analyzers, modelling tools and configuration programs access this data base to extract information about tested networks.

Figure 1 shows the position of DDL in the DNPA system. The measurement programs store the results of the measurements in the

---

*DNPAP is a research project at the Laboratory of Computer Architecture and Digital Technique at the University of Technology at Delft, the Netherlands. The DNPAP group is building an environment in which data network performance analysis can be performed. This comprises measurements of existing networks, network modelling and configuration of new networks.

DBM in DDL format. Output of existing measurement programs is first converted to DDL and then stored in the DBM. Remote workstations consult the data base and receive the data in DDL format.

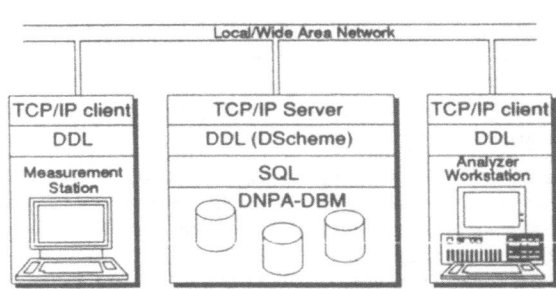

Figure 1. The data flow of the DNPA system.

This means that our DDL not only defines the syntax of the data files, but serves also as a query language to the data base. We have formulated some requirements for this language:

o **Readable by humans.** It should be possible for a human being to read the data file and to understand the contents of it. This means that the data should be stored in a readable form. It means also that it should be written in a natural or a simple well known computer language. (It should be easy to deduct the language when reading the file without knowing the context.) It is also convenient to test and analyze data generated by measurement programs by hand and thus avoiding writing special programs to just read and analyze it.

o **Readable by computers.** Computers are responsible to write, read and manipulate the data files, so they must be able to read the contents and to evaluate it. For this reason (and for performance reasons) the syntax must be simple.

o **System independent.** This follows partly from the previous two requirements. The other reason for this requirement is that most of the data files are spread over wide area networks consisting of computers with different hardware architectures and different word sizes.

o **Documentation included.** There must be enough documentation in a data file (understandable by both humans and computers) to determine the meaning and structure of the data. In this way the data file is reasonable independent to other files, such as programs and documents. This documentation should at least comprise the definition of the records, the data types and bounds of the fields.

The first requirement came from *The EJJO Standard*[1]. This document states that all the program source files, data files and documentation generated by members of the DNPAP group should be readable by humans. This requirement is caused by the problems met when deciphering the binairy files generated by existing tracing and measurement software. But readability of data files has also some penalties. Readable files are mostly bigger* in size, while binairy data files can be stored and read efficient in and time and space.

Why Scheme?

The first requirement gave us the choice between a natural and a computer language. The preferred natural language would be British, as most of the scientific world understands this language. But the natural langauge is not a clear and exact language to define data types. Also is the natural language to complicated to decode by a computer, because the syntax and semantics of a natural language is complicated. It takes years for a human being to learn a new natural langauge, while a new computer language can be learned in a few weeks. The conclusion is that the natural language isn't the preferred choice for a data description language.

So our choice is narrowed down to a computer language. One of the requirements is that the language is easy to understand, so we have to select our language from the existing and well-known computer languages. This language should have the following features: dynamic creation of procedures (easily extendable and new procedures can be defined in the data files), simple evaluation of procedures and expressions and system independent data types.

Languages such Pascal, Ada, C and Fortran aren't suitable for our purpose as they don't support definition of new procedures during run-time. Most of these languages need complicated interpreters. The class of languages such as Prolog, Snobol and Lisp are more flexible and allow dynamic generation of procedures. The attraction of Lisp is that both the syntax and the semantics are simple, so the evaluator for Lisp is relatively simple. One of the many 'dialects' of Lisp is called Scheme, a well defined language by itself. (See *Revised[3] Report on the Algorithmic Language Scheme.*[2])

Scheme has a small and clean set of functions and is easily extensible by defining new functions. The simple syntax and the small set of functions means that Scheme is a language easy to grasp. Scheme is also very flexible with its data types. Strings can be of any length, numbers of any size and any type. Each data type can easily translated to every other type.

---

*The problem of the size of readable files can be made less severe by compressing the data on a low level (between the application program and the operating system). This compressing can be transparant to the application program or even to the operating system itself. This means that the files aren't readable on disk or tape niveau, but who can read a tape just by looking at it. The software (or the hardware) which reads the tape can uncompress the data to the readable form.

About Scheme

The *Revised[3] Report on the Algorithmic Language Scheme*[2] gives the following description:

"Scheme is a statically scoped and properly tail-recursive dialect of the Lisp programming language invented by Guy Lewis Steel Jr. and Gerald Jay Sussman. It was designed to have an exceptionally clear and simple semantics and few different ways to form expressions. A wide variety of programming paradigms, including imperative, functional, and message passing styles, find convenient expression in Scheme."

The first version of Lisp was developed in 1960 by John McCarthy. And since then many dialects of Lisp were created. The mean purpose of developing Lisp was to create a language which is easy to understand by human readers. Lisp was also very convenient to experiment with, because it can change itself. In 1975 a graduate student (Guy Lewis Steele Jr.) of Gerald Jay Sussman[5] of M.I.T. implemented a Lisp with lexical scoping instead of dynamic scoping* of variables. This resulted in some interesting properties as efficient recursion, first class procedures and simple semantics. They decided to call this new language Scheme and in 1986 a standard Scheme was defined in the *Revised[3] Report on the Algorithmic Language Scheme*[2].

This report describes the essential functions (the functions which should always be present in a Scheme implementation), some extra preferred functions and the syntax and semantics of Scheme. The main features of Scheme are:

o simple and clear syntax,

o same format for data and programs,

o lexical scoping of variables (same as in PASCAL, and C, but different from most Lisp dialects),

o easy definition of procedures, data structures and new data types,

o untyped variables. In Scheme the variables aren't typed, but the data is. So it is perfectly legal to bind a variable *sum* to a number and then to a string or even to a procedure.

Excellent Scheme guides are: *The SCHEME Programming Language.* by R. Kent Dybvig[3] and *PC Scheme tutorial* of Texas Instruments Inc.[4].

IMPLEMENTATION

The Scheme interpreter which reads the data file formatted in DDL has the following requirements:

o Highly portable and thus system independent.
o Extendable. Extra functions should be easily linked to Scheme.
o Fast input and output.

---

*Lexical scoping means that the extend of the definitions is restricted to the block in which it is defined. Languages as Algol and Pascal have also lexical scoping. Dynamic scoping means that the extend of the definition is unlimited. In other words after a local variable is defined in the body of a procedure, it can be referenced outside the body.

134

o New data type: timestamp.
o Includable in C-programs.

Existing Scheme interpreters don't fulfill these requirements. Most commercial Scheme interpreters aren't portable, while others are written in another Lisp interpreter for experimental reasons. So a new Scheme interpreter had to be written to meet all the requirements. The following sections describe the various parts and extensions of the DScheme interpreter developed.

Extensions to Scheme

The standard Scheme had to be extended to make it usable as an Data Description Language (DDL). A data file, in particular a measurement data file consists of records, each consisting of multiple fields. We defined a new function *record* which takes an description of a record, and which returns a procedure which reads its arguments, checks their type and value and stores them in a list. An example:

```
(define (datrec
  (RECORD '((time timestamp)
            (name symbol)
            (count integer))
          '(> count 0)))

(datrec #@1989/03/28-12:34:00 dutrun 91234)
(datrec #@1989/03/28-12:34:10 dutesta 45877)
```

In this example an record type *datrec* is defined which contains a timestamp, a name and a count. The definition of the record consists of two parts: a field type definition and a validation function. The first part is a list of pairs whose car is the name of the field and the second is the type of the field. The second part is an expression which yields true when the values of the fields are correct.

The function *record* could easily be defined in Scheme, as the syntax of the definition and the use of the procedure is in Scheme notation. This means that a standard Scheme interpreter could read the data file without any problems.

The example shows also a new data type called *timestamp*. Most of the measurement programs include the time and date of the measurements in the data files. To represent the time and date efficient and unique, a new data type had to be developed. Scheme doesn't have such a type and the normal data types are inadequate. A string is awkward to handle and a number isn't readable.

The timestamp is handled as a first class data type, and it consists of 6 fields. The first three contain the date in 'year/month/day' format. The following two define the time and the last one the seconds and the fraction of seconds. The seconds are stored as a floating point number, with 9 digits signification. If a field is omitted, it means that it is unknown or irrelevant. The most significant field (the year) is on the left hand side, to allow easy sorting. Here are some examples:

```
#@1989/03/28-12:34:43.06   current date and time
#@-12:34                   without date and seconds
#@1989/03/28               only the date
#@::0.000001               one second
```

Figure 2 shows how the DScheme interpreter is called to read a data file in DDL format. The DScheme system will call an user defined handle function to handle (i.e. store or display) the fields of each record. To make it easy to combine DScheme with applications, the system is extendable with procedures written in other languages such as C.

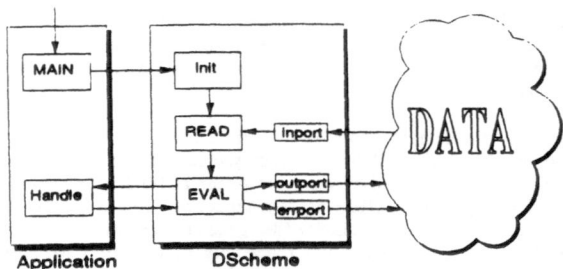

Figure 2. The program flow of the DScheme system.

Another extension of DScheme isn't really an extension as it is implemented in most of the Scheme versions. This is a macro system. There is no standard given in the *Revised³ Report* [2]. The most simple form of macros is to substitute at call time the formal parameters in the body of the macro with the actual parameters.

Memory Management

On a high end Lisp workstation about 100Mbytes virtual memory space is needed for compiler, editor, interpreter and symbol space (see page 61 of *Lisp Evolution and Standardization*[7]). The DScheme interpreter isn't allowed to require such a large memory space, so an efficient use of available memory is needed. The Scheme data objects should be stored in compact cells with a minimum of overhead. DScheme uses about 40k data space for constants and the system environment.

One of the most important features of Scheme is its automatic memory management. This is to create the illusion of infinite memory [6]. A program can continuously define new elements, lists and procedures. But memory is always limited, so a garbage collector is needed to release memory previously used by data. The garbage collector releases each cell of memory when it isn't needed anymore (in the sense that their contents can no longer influence the results of the program).

This type of memory management has two consequences. The first is that the memory must be allocated and freed by a fixed count of bytes. Normally whould the different data types consume different count of bytes. A floating point number needs 8 bytes while a character need only 1 byte. The second consequence is that some bookkeeping is needed about the cells. This means that a list of free cells is maintained and each cell contains a tag to indicate the type of data stored in it.

This memory is allocated at initialization time as an array of structures. A cell is defined as a structure consisting of a *tag* part and a *data* part. During initialization of DScheme a chunk of memory is allocated as string space. A linked list of string descriptors maintain the free parts of this space. When a used string part is released, during garbage collection, neighbouring free parts are joined to form a new bigger free part.

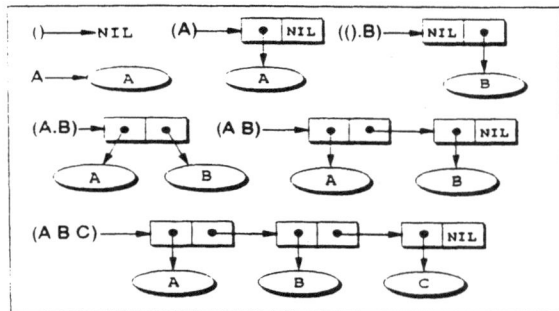

Figure 3. Examples of structures of DScheme cells.

A special type of cell is the pair cell. This cell contains not a first class data type, but two pointers (the CAR and the CDR) to other cells. A pair cell is used to construct lists of data. The most common form of list is the *simple* list. In such a list the car of a pair cell points to a data object (a simple data type of another list) and the cdr to the rest of the list. Figure 3. shows how cells are combined to lists.

Input & Output Ports

A port represent an input or output device. To Scheme, an input port is a Scheme object that can deliver characters upon command, while an output port is an Scheme object that can accept characters. Figure 2 shows where the ports reside in a DScheme system.

The Scheme standard[2] defines ports to read and write from files. DScheme had to be more flexible. It should be possible to read for example from a port connected to a network device and to write to an internal buffer. DScheme provides an easy way to define new ports.

A DScheme port is build on an input, an output and a control function. These are called by the DScheme system, when I/O is to be performed on that port.

An example is an user-friendly interface. The application program presents to the user an window system where the user types and edits the expressions. DScheme reads characters via the input function of the port and sends its output via the output function to the window manager.

The Parser

One of the main tasks of DScheme interpreter is to parse the input stream. In the development stage of DScheme the parser was written with assistance of YACC (Yet Another Compiler Compiler[8]) and LEX (LEXical analyzer[9]). These generate a piece of C code which parses the input and calls an user-supplied routine to handle the parsed data. This code isn't very flexible, as it is not reentrant. And it is called once for a complete file and each time an object is found a handle function is called. But we wanted to call the parser to get one object at the time.

So the parser was completely rewritten in C. This turned out to be not a complicate task as Scheme has a very simple syntax and most of the complicate functions as parsing timestamps and floating point numbers were already written in C, because YACC and LEX couldn't handle them. A conclusion may be these tools aren't adequate to speedup the development of the parser. But they force the user to describe the input in a structured way.

The Evaluator

The part of Scheme which handles the expressions and calculates the result is called traditionally the *evaluator*. This part is actually very simple. It evaluates the elements of each expression and applies then the first (which is mostly a kernel function or a lambda expression) to the other elements. An example:

```
(define apple 12)    ''    apple
(define add +)       ''    add
(add 3 apple)        ''    15
```

The evaluator looks very simple and can be defined easily in a few recursive C functions. But then some problems arise:

o The stack expands very quick.

o Scheme is defined to be properly tail-recursive. This allows the evaluation of a iterative computation in constant space, even if the iterative computation is described by a syntactically recursive procedure.

o Evaluating special forms. A special form is an expression of which one or more arguments must be passed unevaluated.

o Call-with-current-continuation or for short call/cc. This is a procedure which calls the argument (a procedure which accepts one argument) with the current continuation wrapped up in a Scheme object. The called procedure can store this object. When this object is evaluated (it is handled as a procedure) the continuation is set to the continuation stored in the object. This makes it possible to 'jump' out of an evaluation to another evaluation.

This implicates that the continuation shouldn't be stored in the standard stack but in a special stack maintained by the evaluator. This stack can be stored in a continuation object for the *call/cc* function.

A way to speed up evaluation and to make Scheme a smaller module without any supplementary files is to implement all the essential functions and some extra functions (such for the timestamp extension) in C. This increases the code size, but removes the need to implement a way of syntax extension (see *The SCHEME Programming Language*[3]) which is very slow and very complicated.

In an article about *Performance and Standardization* of *Lisp Evolution and Standardization*[7] are a few ways shown to speed up the interpreting of Lisp/Scheme expressions.

o Disable redefinition.
o Disable typechecking (partial/complete)
o Compacting space used by symbols.

Disabling redefinition decreases the number of lookups in the environment, but decreases also the flexibility of the language. A compromise is to store the top level bindings with the symbols. This makes the environment and the lookup time smaller. About 80% of processing time is used by the lookup function when evaluating *(fac 160)*, when *fac* is defined as:

```
(define (fac n)
    (if (= n 0)
        1.0
        (* n (fac (- n 1)))))
```

Disabling typechecking doesn't increase the performance very much, but could give serious problems when something goes wrong. The last suggested way is to compact the symbol space. A typical Lisp implementation has about 8000 symbols which needs about 300kbytes of memory. In systems with virtual memory and page swapping this result this in extra page swapping from and to disk. DScheme isn't mend to be used for such large implementations, therefore the symbol space is not compacted.

Error Handling

A large part of the code written for a production-quality lisp is for error handling and debugging tools. Debugging tools are very basic in DScheme as Scheme code can be debugged and tested in such a production-quality program as PC-Scheme which offers a good debugging tool. But errors which can occur in data files (when transmitted over serial lines or generated by programs) should be signalled as soon as possible and a very descriptive message should be generated.

When an error is signalled the DScheme interpreter returns an error code and other information can be retrieved from the DScheme interpreter. This information includes the context of the error, the object in error and a number describing the exact nature of the error and the function which signalled the error.

Linking to Applications

The first time the DScheme interpreter is called it allocates a piece of memory where all the global variables needed by DScheme are stored. This makes it possible to create multiple environments or to execute multiple DScheme interpreters in parallel.

The default configuration of the DScheme system is such that a simple application as a interactive Scheme interpreter is easy to make. Via the *DSinit* function this configuration can be altered.

The size of the cell space, port space, string space and hash table are configurated via this *DsInit* function. The hash table is called traditionally the obtable (page 494 of [6]) and contains all the pointers to the symbols. This table ensures that all symbols are interned. The *eq* function which tests if two objects are the same, compares only the pointers to the objects. By interning the symbols it is ensured that comparing *apples* with *apples* yields always a true value.

The standard ports of DScheme can also be defined via the *DsInit* function. DScheme has three standard ports: current input, current output and current error port. These are initialized to respectively *stdin*, *stdout* and *stderr*, if no ports are specified.

In a client-server system where a host is running the interpreter it sets the ports to the network connection and starts the interpreter. A local workstation sends queries in DScheme format to the host via the network connection. The network software at the host delivers the message to the DScheme interpreter, which evaluates this message (for example a query for a measurement file from the data base) and sends the result via the network port to the network, which passes this to the local workstation.

APPLICATIONS AND EXTENSIONS

This section describes some actual uses and some possible applications of the DScheme interpreter. The Data Network Performance Analyzing Project started the development of DScheme, so this is the first application where DScheme is used.

Data Network Performance Analyzing Project

The DNPAP group is developing tools and programs to measure computer networks. One of the goals is to assemble all the output (formatted in DDL) into a data base (called DNPA-DBM) so that analyzing tools can access all the information it needs.

DScheme is extended (with timestamps and records) to serve as the Data Description Language (DDL), so the DScheme interpreter can be used to read, analyze and write DDL files. The DNPAP group has defined a network data base. This data base stores four kinds of information:

o *Measurements files*. These contain the output of the measurement program written by the DNPAP group.

o *Network configuration files*. These describes the exact configuration of the network and its stations and server(s) on which the measurements are performed.

o *Note files*. These contain the results of the analyzing programs and calculations made by the users.

o *Program source files*. Here are all the sources of all the versions of the measurement programs stored. This enables checking measurement methods used by the programs.

This data base is a free format data base. This means that there is no restriction on the format of record of the files (except that there are in DDL). The DDL makes it possible to define the records in the data files themselves. Free format means also that the data base can be searched on any item, not only on predefined keys, but even on names, comments or parts of timestamps.

Interactive Interpreter

The DScheme interpreter could be used to build a Scheme development tool. If some debugging and trace tools are build and an editor is linked to DScheme, an environment is created which is highly portable and which is easely adjusted to the needs of the Scheme developer. It could also be used for experiments with Scheme such as implementing other ways of scoping variables, or building a compiler for Scheme or other languages.

Batch, Query and Definition Language

System files such as batch, job controls, definition and configuration files have always a new syntax and semantics. Piles of documentation are needed to describe the format of this kind of information. Examples of such files are: Batch files, config.sys and environment (not a file, but it has a syntax and functions to address it) on MSDOS system. Another example is the UNIX operating system, which has hundreds of configuration files with all different syntax.

If the DScheme interpreter is made part of the operating system, all that kind of files can be written in the same language. Expressions be included in configuration files, the interpreter evaluates them without having to extend the operating system programs with a expression evaluator. Some operating systems have more or less such an evaluator. On CMS is this called REXX and UNIX has SH and CSH but these can only evaluate batch files and not the configuration files such as terminal definition files.

Distributed Processing

One of the requirements to be fulfilled by the DScheme interpreter is the high portability. DScheme can easely be transferred to all kinds of systems. When DScheme is transferred to a group of systems on a network, they all speak the same language. Portions of programs written in Scheme can be distributed over the network to hosts with some free processing time. Evaluation of Scheme expressions yield always the same values independent of the system on which there are calculated.

Windows and Mouse

It is very easy to define new input/output ports in DScheme so it should be easy to link DScheme to a windows system. This could be the Presentation Manager on a OS/2 system or X-Windows on UNIX systems. The possibility to the call the interpreter to evaluate one expression at the time, makes it possible to link Scheme expressions to window and mouse events.

The article *AIDA: Machine Independent Window/Mouse Interface Development Tools for Le-Lisp*[7] describes a system build into Le-Lisp (another Lisp dialect) which handles windows and mouse and is build on top of the Virtual Display Interface of Le-Lisp.

CONCLUSION

DScheme is a very portable and flexible interpreter for the essential subset of Scheme. DScheme can be used for many applications. It replaces existing or new parse routines, which are most of the time complicated to write. DScheme is developed to be used as a Data Description Language (DDL) to read and format data files. These data files are readable by humans and computers. They are very independent of the programs which reads these files. Fields of records can be swapped or extra fields can be added, the description in the same file takes care of interfacing the data to the programs.

DScheme can also be used as a simple user interface. This gives the user to enter complicated expressions or construct a layer above the functions presented by the application. This is comparable to a macro system implemented by programs as *brief* and *emacs*. If DScheme is consequently used in an operating system, then all the interfacing to the users and applications can be handled via Scheme.

REFERENCES

[1] Bos, Erik-Jan and Jan P.M. van Oorschot. *The EJJO Standard*. Standard involving project management, documentation, software and hardware development. Delft, 1988

[2] Jonathan Rees and William Clinger (Editors). *Revised³ Report on the Algorithmic Language Scheme*. MIT, 1986

[3] R. Kent Dybvig. *The SCHEME Programming Language*. Englewood Cliffs, New Jersey 1986

[4] Texas Instruments Incorporated. *PC Scheme Tutorial*. Austin, Texas, July 1987

[5] Gerald Jay Sussman and Guy Lewis Jr. Steele. *Scheme: An Interpreter for Extended Lambda Calculus*. MIT, AI MEMO No 347, December 1975

[6] Harold Abelson and Gerald Jay Sussman with Julie Sussman. *Structure and Interpretation of Computer Programs*. Cambridge, Massachusetts 1985

[7] C. Queinnec and J. Chailloux (Editors). *Lisp Evolution and Standardization*. Amsterdam & Springfield, 1986

[8] S. C. Johnson. *Yacc: Yet Another Compiler Compiler*. Comp. Sci. Tech. Rep. No. 32, 1975, Bell Laboratories, Murray Hill

[9] M. E. Lesk. *LEX - A Lexical Analyzer Generator*. Comp. Sci. Techn. Rep. No. 39, 1975, Bell Laboratories, Murray Hill

[10] Texas Instruments Incorporated. *PC Scheme User's Guide*. Austin, Texas, July 1987

Suggestions for Further Reading.

[11] Guy Lewis Jr. Steele. *Rabbit: A Compiler for Scheme (A Study in Compiler Optimization)*. MIT AI LAB Technical Report 474, May 1978,

[12] Guy Lewis Jr. Steele. *Common Lisp, the Language*. Digital Press, 1984

[13] John Allen. *Anatomy of Lisp*. New York, McGraw-Hill, 1978

[14] Steven S. Muchnick and Uwe F. Pleban. *A Semantic Comparison of Lisp and Scheme*. The Lisp Conference 1980, ACM 1985, pages 56-60.

[15] David H. Bartley and John C. Jensen. *The Implementation of PC Scheme*. Proceedings of the 1986 ACM Conference on Lisp and Functional Programming, ACM 1986, pages 86-93

[16] H. Ganzinger (Editor). *Lecture Notes in Computer Science*. ESOP '88, 2nd European Symposium in Programming, Nancy, France, March 1988

Data-Intensive Applications in Open Networks:
Extending the Modelling, Programming and Communication Support

Winfried Lamersdorf

IBM European Networking Center

Tiergartenstraße 15, D-6900 HEIDELBERG, West-Germany

Abstract

New **requirements** for extended computer support arise from various areas of *advanced data-intensive applications*. For example, the increased integration of *data and knowledge* initiated a number of database system extensions. Other requirements of new data-intensive applications lead to extended support for *complex data objects*. Similarly, an increasing number of data-intensive applications today is based on *distributed application scenarios* with locally distributed cooperation. Such applications require extended communication facilities in 'Open Systems' computer networking environments. In all cases, services of advanced data management functions should be offered to programmers via appropriate high-level *programming language interfaces*. Consequently, integrated systems **realizing** computer support for advanced data intensive applications include the following DBMS extensions: support for data and knowledge modelling, communication facilities for accessing remote system components in distributed systems, programming language interfaces, etc..

This paper concentrates on concepts and implementation proposals for extending data-intensive applications into a **distributed open network** environment. After a brief classification of database management systems generalizations into distributed environments, the paper focuses in detail on three areas of supporting advanced data-intensive applications: the presented *data modelling* extensions introduce complex data objects into a distributed database environment following an object-oriented approach; at the *programming language* interface it is demonstrated how an appropriate database and programming language can be used to specify distributed applications; and, finally, the addressed *communication* facilities show how access to remote databases in a heterogeneous environment can be realized based on dedicated open systems communication protocols.

1. Introduction

For advanced data-intensive applications, improved computer network infrastructures are becoming increasingly important in order to support distributed and cooperative work patterns. In such environments, multiple computer nodes with different characteristics and capabilities can be interconnected in order to communicate with and support each other. Based on dedicated communication facilities, a 'client/ server' approach [22] frequently provides an appropriate conceptual framework to describe the cooperation patterns of such distributed communication partners. Following this approach, cheap and locally interconnected personal workstations can, for example, access - via wide-area and other local area networks - specialized and powerful server nodes in order to jointly realize an integrated distributed application.

An important area of applications for distributed cooperative work and the related communication services is that of remote access to **databases in computer networks**. In many cases, databases represent a costly to collect and to maintain set of data on which they offer information retrieval and management services to a great number of user. Based on an appropriate communication infrastructure, such centralized database application scenario can be generalized into distributed application environments where database users and providers can be located at different sites.

This allows for providing database services not only for a local but also for a remote set of potential user. So, all benefits as well as all (high !) costs of data management can be shared among a much greater number of users in an, in principle, unlimited open computer network. In such an environment, the heterogeneous nature of computer hard- and software involved requires 'Open Systems' communication facilities for transferring, e.g., request/ response messages between peer communication partners over the network.

This paper first gives a brief overview on architectural alternatives for supporting distributed and data-intensive applications in an open systems network. It then concentrates on extending the data modelling functions of traditional database models to describe the behaviour of complex objects in a distributed network environment. After outlining how an integrated and modular database and programming language interface can be used for programming distributed database applications, the paper finally focuses on the necessary communication support for accessing remote databases in open computer networks. In this section, the paper presents some of the most recent developments of an emerging International Standard on 'Remote Database Access' [8] as currently produced by the 'International Standards Organization' (ISO) SC21 WG3 ('Databases') in the framework of 'Open Systems Interconnection' (OSI) [7].

2. Databases in Computer Networks

2.1 Client - Server Cooperation

In a distributed database application environment, a frequent form of communication between two cooperating communication partners can, in many cases, be described by the concepts of a **'Client/ Server'** or 'Requestor/ Server' [22] model. In such a cooperation, a database client (or: requestor) asks for services from a database server which is able and willing to provide such services. According to such a model, clients can also request services from a number of different servers. In addition, sites which play the role of servers in one environment, can also become clients in a different context. In other cases, for example, complete (e.g. local area) subnetworks could play the role of compound servers providing, collectively, services to other nodes in a distributed client/ server network environment. It may also be possible that client systems (workstations and mainframes) maintain their own databases locally. So, in many cases, the client/server approach provides an appropriate model for describing the communication behaviour of peer system components at different levels of abstraction.

As an example for a client/ server interaction, the basic model underlying 'Remote Database Access' [8] supports - in the first phase - a simple one client to one or many server(s) cooperation. It assumes that there is no direct cooperation between any servers involved in a distributed remote database application. According to the client/ server model as currently supported by a standardized ISO/OSI RDA communication link, the RDA client acts as a coordinator which is responsible for managing and coordinating access to one or more remote database servers.

2.2 Architectural Choices for Database Applications in Computer Networks

Based on applying the requestor/ server approach to distributed database applications, alternate database architectures in open computer networks can be classified as a *generalization* from centralized to completely distributed systems (see, e.g., [3], or [20]). Such a generalization departs from traditional **centralized** database systems, includes simple **client/ server** or more complex **federative** database environments, and, finally, leads to environments of completely **distributed**, database applications in a cooperative networking environment. It can be briefly outlined as follows:

2.2.1 Centralized Database Systems : In a centralized database environment, all DBMS functions to support data query and manipulation requests, as well as all data reside on only one computer node. The DBMS allows access to the data to be shared among a number of 'parallel' users. Sometimes, so called centralized multi-processor database systems allow for distributing the location of the data (including the immediate access to it) among a (in general small) number of locally interconnected processors. In a centralized database system, however, all management of parallel user requests for the combined sets of data as well as data management functions are executed centrally. So, users may access data on all processors only through one centralized DBMS.

As a first step towards remote access to data, remote terminals have been introduced which may also access centralized databases via dedicated long-distance communications networks in so called 'TP-monitor' systems. Here, all data management functions as well as all data are still under the control of one, centralized database system. Only the end user interface of some specific application is distributed to, in general, very simple remote sites (application terminals). In such an architecture, a TP-monitor component supervises and handles requests from the re-

mote stations locally at the database system site where they are executed by the respective centralized DBMS functions.

2.2.2 Remote Database Access : The next step in generalizing a centralized database system into a networking environment allows for complete database applications to reside on remote computer nodes. All DBMS functions, however, still reside on one dedicated database 'server' node. In this model, the interaction between a remote application, called the database 'client', and the centralized and dedicated DBMS, called the database 'server', follows the client/ server cooperation model.

For data-intensive open systems applications, the communication links between clients and database servers have to provide dedicated support for database applications. External interfaces to the communication services have to be generally agreed, i.e. *standardized*. Such agreements form the basis for the so called *Remote Database Access* service and protocol standard [8] in the framework of communication support for 'Open Systems Interconnection' (OSI) [7].

2.2.3 Federated Databases : The basic idea underlying a federated database architecture [6] is that of a fairly loose cooperation of independent databases which, however, still provide some support for global (distributed) database integration. This also leads to a loose cooperation of the involved database management systems and not much system support in executing distributed requests. In such an architecture, definition and execution of distributed database operations is completely up to the application programmer. It also means that, in general, for federated databases there exists no global conceptual schema for the integrated distributed database, although some, partial, database integration is supported at the user interface for some classes of applications.

In federated database systems, some global coordination (e.g. naming conventions, im- and export mechanisms etc.) is provided by global rules which have to be obeyed by all local DBMS implementations. For instance, distributed user requests are first translated into a generally understood 'internal' representation, and may then be routed independently from each other to the respective local database components. This leads to still a fairly high degree of autonomy of the involved databases systems, but also supports a distributed application by some system-wide coordination functions.

Federative distributed databases provide an architectural compromise between system-wide integration on the one hand side and local site autonomy on the other based on a distributed and only partially integrated data management system. Members of such a federation may join or leave the integrated environment at any time - based only on their own and local decision. A distributed database management systems to support such kinds of federative database applications has been designed and implemented in a uniform database and programming language context as described in [4].

An even looser, partial integration of pre-existing and independently managed database systems of any kind for specific and relatively rare tasks is also called a *super- or multi-database* system (e.g. [21]).

2.2.4 Distributed Databases : Tightly coupled distributed database systems (e.g. [5]) integrate different databases distributed among different sites in a network closely by providing the application program with a logical view of only one, logically centralized database. So, at the user interface of a distributed database, there is only one global conceptual schema; all integrity and consistency constraints are expressed and enforced at the global database level. As a consequence, distributed databases require close cooperation, i.e. only little independence of all participating local database management systems. This reduces local control and autonomy considerably. On the other hand, much more support is given by a distributed database management system to relief the application programmer from problems of data distribution in a networking environment. Specifically, this means that a user may access data on a remote site without knowing it's exact location ("distribution" or "location" transparency).

In a distributed database environment, database operations are executable both at the local and at the remote (i.e. global) level. An integrated distributed *transaction management* involves - potentially - different and independent local (sub-) transaction management components at different sites. An integrated 'global' transaction management aims at guaranteeing the ('ACID'-) transaction properties also at the global level. This can, in general, only be achieved at the expense of an additional management overhead and of restrictions to the respective autonomy of the involved local database components.

Distributed databases may be either *homogeneous* or *heterogeneous* systems. The former type integrates local database system which are based on the same conceptual database model (e.g. relational or hierarchical), the latter those which are based on different databases models or, at least, designed differently based on the same database model.

3. Data Modelling for Distributed Data-Intensive Applications

Data Modelling for advanced data-intensive applications requires concepts that extend beyond what is known from traditional database management systems. One example for extending the 'flat' record structure of traditional DBMSs into a 'non first normal form' is given in [1] and has been realized successfully for locally centralized databases based on a completely new DBMS implementation.

The approach as presented in the following section follows the stepwise generalization from a simple, centralized to a more complex distributed environment: first, a high-level complex object model is defined which can be realized through a mapping to an existing programming language interface of a conventional database system [17]. Then, this model is extended into a distributed environment as presented in section 3.2.

For realizing the distributed object model - as in the centralized case - via a mapping to an existing underlying programming language interface, an appropriate distributed database language is required. Following such an approach, the second part of this chapter introduces the notion of a database programming language for distributed environ-

ments. Such a language can then be used as a target for mapping the high-level complex object model to an underlying distributed database system implementation.

3.1 A Recursive Complex Objects Model

Recursive object modelling aims at more adequately representing hierarchical complex objects structures for data-intensive applications and the related operations on such objects [18]. Instead of representing objects - as in traditional, e.g. relational, data models - by (sets of) fixed-format records, the recursive object model is based on powerful, orthogonal type mechanisms as can be derived from modern programming languages.

In the recursive data model, object types are not just defined as set of object occurrences, but rather specified as a number of - recursive - object instance and type **generators**. Using such type generators, single object instances can be generated dynamically and in extensions and numbers not necessarily fixed at type definition time. Each such instance generator takes a number of (maybe structured) named object components as input values and generates a new compound object instance at a higher level.

Along with the generalized object generation mechanisms, the recursive data model provides for a, similarly generalized, object **component selection** mechanism. Additionally, as complex object instances of the same type can now be generated based on different alternate instance generators, there is a need for an object **component identification** function which, for a given object instance, returns the name of the generator used to create the respective instance.

The following example demonstrates an application of the recursive high-level complex object data model. It defines the type of a 'document' which could either be a 'letter', or a 'compound document' or a 'memo'. Note that the 'content' component of the compound document 'compond_doc' is, recursively, defined as a 'document'.

```
Document  = ( Letter (sender, receiver: Name;
                      from, to: Address;
                      date_mailed, date_received: Date;
                      content: Text)

            | Compound_doc  (..; content: Document; ..)

            | Memo  ( ... )  |  ... )
```

Further notational extensions of the recursive data model allow for specifying complex objects ordered *list*, *sets* and *maps* based on corresponding **type generators**. So, for example, a 'file' type can be specified as a list of 'documents':

```
File  =  LIST OF Document,
```

a 'file cabinet' can be specified as a set of 'drawers':

```
FileCabinet  =  SET OF Drawer,
```

and, finally, a single drawer can be modelled as a mapping from 'FileIDs' to 'Files':

```
Drawer  =  ( FileID ---> File )
FileId  =     TOKEN.
```

Together with these type generators (i.e. 'list', 'set' and 'map') all well-known operations are implicitly defined for all corresponding instances of such types. Notationaly, square brackets represent component 'selections', and curly brackets denote expression 'generators' (with the type of the expression in front of them). For each recursively defined type, variables can be declared, and, in addition, the values of variables of recursively defined types can be changed based on alternate assignment operators (: = , : + for 'insert', :- for 'subtract', etc.). For example:

file [j]   or   file [last]

File { doc_1, doc_2, ..., doc_n }   or

file_cabinet_1 ∪ file_cabinet_2

FileCabinet {drawer IN file_cab SUCH THAT <predicate>}

drawer :+ Drawer { file_i --> file }.

Finally, it is important to note that all these operators can be freely and orthogonally applied to any complex objects expressions which have been generated in any possible way. Thus, the recursive approach to data object modelling provides a very flexible and powerful mechanism to describe complex hierarchical object structures which only share a common set of generation rules. Any such object can be of any size and may vary considerably over time. In addition, complex objects (and their components) can only be accessed and manipulated based on an well-defined set of - either implicit or explicit - operations. Such an **object-oriented** approach seems to be well suited for generalization into a distributed environment.

3.2 Distributed Objects Cooperation

The previous section gave a brief overview of recursive data object modelling without regard to specific characteristics of distributed systems. Basically, it introduced an abstract way to describe complex object structures recursively together with a set of corresponding operations on them, based on generalized type abstraction concepts.

For **generalizing** this approach to complex object modelling into a distributed systems environment, the underlying idea is the following: in principle, each recursively defined object is, in the distributed environment, allowed to reside on a separate node of the network. In a centralized environment, application programs access complex objects by 'using' any of the operations defined for them. This way of accessing objects can also be generalized to apply to distributed complex objects in a networking environment: any application program on any node in a is then allowed to 'use' any of the operations on any other object, regardless of whether this object is available locally or on any remote network site [19].

Thus, in the distributed environment, inter-object communication can be conceived as (potentially remote) 'calls' to other objects which 'offer' their operations (i.e. services) to programs on other nodes in the network. This still follows the basic paradigm of an *object-oriented* approach.

The set of operations offered by complex objects to other complex objects or application programs in a distributed environment includes **implicitly**: their respective operations to generate new object (component) instances, operations

to select object components, and the object instance type identifiers. In addition, **application dependent** operations can be user defined *explicitly* for all recursive object types. Such operations include *functions* which retrieve values, *procedures* which may have effects on objects or object components, and object (component) *selectors* which select object (component)s as variables to be used, e.g., on the left-hand side of assignment operations.

Using a 'class' notation, the following example shows a function to retrieve the (value of) the last 'letter' a given 'sender' has sent from a 'file' which is defined as a list of 'documents'. Similarly, the given procedure deletes a 'document' in such a 'file', and, finally, the given selector selects a 'form' with a given 'number' from that 'file'. Not surprisingly, all operations defined for this recursive types are themselves specified recursively:

```
CLASS FileClass

IS     LIST OF DocumentClass

WITH

FUNCTION last_letter_from (s: NameClass): DocumentClass;
  IF SELF = <>
    THEN <*EXCEPTION: "There is no letter from s !"*>
    ELSE IF SELF [LAST].is_Letter AND
            SELF [LAST] [sender]
            THEN RETURN SELF [LAST]
            ELSE RETURN SELF [REST].last_letter_from (s)
END last_letter_from;

PROCEDURE delete_doc (d: DocumentClass);
  IF SELF = <>
    THEN <*EXCEPTION: "Nothing to delete !"*>

    ELSE IF SELF [LAST] = d
            THEN SELF := SELF [REST]
            ELSE SELF := SELF [REST].delete_doc (d).
                       APPEND (SELF [LAST])
END delete_doc;

SELECTOR sel_form (n: INTEGER) : DocumentClass;
  IF SELF = <>
    THEN <* EXCEPTION: "No form with that number !" *>
    ELSE IF SELF [LAST].is_Form AND
            SELF [LAST] [serial_no]
            THEN SELECT SELF [LAST]
            ELSE SELECT SELF [REST] [sel_form (n)]
END sel_form;
  . . .
END FileClass.
```

3.3 Programming Language Support for Distributed Data-Intensive Applications

As already mentioned for the complex objects model in a centralized environment, its implementation shall not be realized *directly* but rather by a *mapping* to an appropriate underlying high-level programming language interface. (I.e. all data objects as well as all corresponding operations have to be 'implemented' by respective (sets of) basic objects or procedures at the underlying programming language inter-

142

face.) In order to be suited for such a mapping, the programming language interface has to fulfill a number of requirements: first, the language has to provide functions to describe the storage and management of persistent data objects; in addition, it has to provide functions for realizing all respective operations on them (including the application specific ones).

So, in addition to the abstract data object representation, an appropriate *algorithmic programming language environment* has to be supported. In order to provide for sophisticated type-checking mechanisms at application program *compile time*, both (database and algorithmic) language components should be closely integrated. These requirements lead to an integrated **database and programming language** approach.

In this paper as well as in the prototype realization as presented in [4], the database programming language DBPL [2] is used as the target language onto which the concepts of the abstract objects representations are to be mapped. The programming paradigm of DBPL is centered around a high-level im- and export mechanism for data and other programming language objects to be provided for independent program units (modules) in a centralized as well as in distributed environments. Thus, the basic idea of integrated database programming languages is extended into distributed systems: an abstract language interface for the definition, manipulation, and administration of **all** data objects of an application regardless on which node in a network they reside.

In the (relational) database programming languages, relations - as all other data objects - are regarded as typed variables; relation types are constructed orthogonally from types of the database programming language. *Database* variables are defined in a 'permanently' existing scope and can be 'imported' for manipulation by other program units. Database relations are updated by assignment statements, values are retrieved as expression, and iterators allow for programming loops on (sub-) sets of relation elements.

DBPL consists of Modula-2 as algorithmic language and of a relational extension with first-order predicate expressions for data retrieval and manipulation. DBPL programs are viewed as systems of independent program 'modules' which are related exclusively via well-defined interfaces. A specific type of ('database') module defines the permanent (relational) database which can be imported by other modules. A 'selector' mechanism allows for restricting the database access to a predicatively defined (sub-) relation, a 'transaction' mechanism allows for partitioning database programs for parallel database access as well as for ensuring data consistency.

In the DURESS project [4], the DBPL implementation was extended in such a way that independent program modules could be distributed over **different network nodes** while keeping the basic programming paradigm of im- and exporting modules as the communication interface. In the extended DBPL language, the separation of modules over different nodes of a computer network basically allows for im- and export of three different classes of program objects: data types, procedures/ transactions, and (database) variables. **Type declarations** can, for instance, be exported in order to generate objects of the same type in different modules (like a central office 'forms' administration). Im- and

export of **procedures/transactions** can be viewed as a 'remote procedure call' where the importing module sends a set of parameters to the exporting module where the operation is executed, and possible results are returned to the 'calling' module. Finally, export of a **variable** allows other modules to gain access to the exported variable.

4. Communication Support for Database Client-Server Cooperation in Open Systems

Open and heterogeneous networks integrate, in general, various subnetworks (i.e. local, wide-area networks, etc.) of different kinds which, in turn, interconnect a wide variety of machines which many different hard- and software characteristics. In order to provide for network integration in such an environment, an overall agreement about communication interfaces and protocols used has to be reached. This is achieved by *standardized communication services and protocols* as internationally specified in the 'Open Systems Interconnection' (OSI) framework [7] of the 'International Organization of Standardization' (ISO).

In addition to the *general* communication mechanisms which each system has to provide in order to be able to communicate at all in an open systems environment, adequate *application specific* interfaces also have be added within each local environment for supporting dedicated application functions. Such an application interface is - since it is defined specifically for a local computer environment - also generally subject to international standardization. As opposed to the generic communication support, this application specific communication interface is tailored to a specific class of applications only (e.g. message handling, remote file access, remote database access etc.).

4.1 Remote Database Access

The basic communication model underlying the ISO/OSI standard on 'Remote Database Access' (RDA) ([8]) is that of a 'Database Client' (e.g. on a personal workstation) using the ISO/OSI RDA communication services to access a remote 'Database Server' which provides database services from its local database management system to a set of (local or) remote clients in an open systems network environment (see Figure 1).

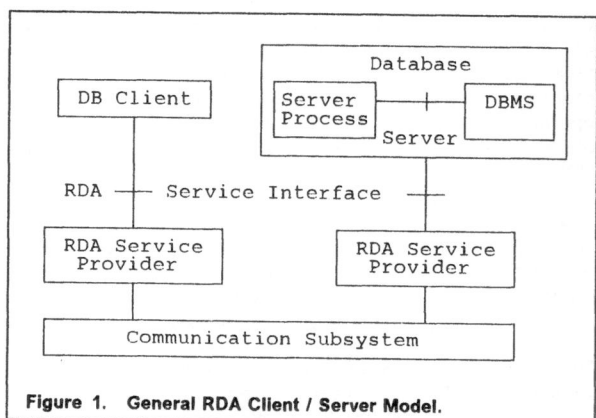

Figure 1. General RDA Client / Server Model.

According to this model, the 'RDA Service' is provided to both database client and database server based on the underlying services of the ISO/OSI communication layers 1 to 6 ('Communication Subsystem'). A dedicated 'Server Process' routes incoming requests on the RDA server to the 'Database Management Systems' (DBMS) on the server node and sends results - via the RDA communication services - back to the RDA client.

The 'RDA Services Interface' defines all RDA communication **services** which are provided to both RDA client and server in order to support their communication requirements. In the RDA communication standard, the RDA communication **protocol** then specifies in detail all message formats and communication rules which have to be followed by any RDA implementation which conforms to the RDA standard in order to allow for full interconnectivity with all other conforming RDA implementations in an open systems network environment.

4.2 RDA Communication Services

At the RDA service interface, a set of RDA services is provided to both the RDA client and the RDA server. According to the different classes of functions which RDA supports, these services can be subdivided into five different groups:

4.2.1 Dialogue Management Services : In line with most ISO/OSI communication standards, RDA provides a 'connection-oriented' communication service. So, any two RDA peer communication partners have to establish (resp. transmitting their communication requests. In order to support that, the RDA service interface includes two respective services, 'R-BeginDialogue' and R-EndDialogue'.

4.2.2 Resource Handling Services : After having established an RDA dialogue to a peer communication partner, an RDA client is supported by RDA services in accessing a remote database management system. First, 'resources' of such a DBMS may have to be opened. In order to do so, the RDA service interface includes two corresponding services, 'R-Open' and 'R-Close' which are used to transmit requests for opening or closing a database resource from the RDA client to the RDA server.

As the transmission and execution of RDA services usually produces a result, the RCA client/ server communication pattern as described in the RDA service tables always is the following: the RDA client requests a remote operation invocation, this request is indicated at the RDA server side, and, after execution of the respective operation, the server requests the transmission of the result (resp. error) which is then indicated at the client node.

4.2.3 Database Language Services : After having established a dialogue and opened the necessary database resources, a RDA database client may want to transmit database language (DBL) commands to the RDA database server in order to initiate execution of such commands at the server DBMS. This is supported in RDA by the 'R-ExecuteDBL' service. In addition to that, RDA provides for a way of transmitting DBL command to the server prior to their execution by pre-'defining' them (R-DefineDBL). At the RDA server side, such commands can then be validated and

stored for later execution which is initiated using the RDA service 'R-InvokeDBL'. Also, pre-defined DBL commands can be dropped at the RDA server side, initiated from the RDA client using a respective RDA 'R-DropDBL' service.

4.2.4 Control Services : In cases where the execution of a DBL command at the RDA server side takes a great amount of time, RDA provides for some means of controlling the execution of DBL commands from the client side. First, an RDA client can acquire information about the status of a DBL operation sent to the RDA server using the 'R-Status' service. (The status of such an operation could, e.g., be 'awaiting execution', 'executing', etc..) Second, the RDA client can initiate the prevention of an already sent DBL operation from execution at the RDA server side by using an 'R-Cancel' service.

4.2.5 Transaction Management Services : In many cases, RDA service users want to group their DBMS service requests into sets of services which have to be executed either altogether or not at all. In database management systems, such kinds of requirement are usually supported by realizing a database *transaction* concept. In order to initialize use of the respective DBMS services, but also to be able to synchronize transmission of sequences of communication requests between two communication partners, RDA also provides for basic communication services for supporting a transaction concept. The elementary RDA transaction management services consist of a service to start a transaction ('R-BeginTransaction'), and two alternate ways of ending it, either successfully ('R-Commit') or by withdrawing all changes since the start of the transaction ('R-Rollback').

More elaborate transaction management services for RDA - including communication support for managing more that one sub-transaction - are provided based on the ISO/OSI services for 'Transaction Processing' (TP) [14] and 'Commitment, Concurrency and Recovery' (CCR) [13] (see section 4.5).

4.3 The RDA Communication Protocol

The RDA communication protocol defines in detail the message formats for all RDA messages that can 'legally' flow between an RDA client and an RDA server. For uniquely defining the structure of such RDA '**Application Protocol Data Units**' (APDUs) is makes use of the ISO/OSI standardized 'Abstract Syntax Notation 1' [15]. Then, another ISO/OSI standard [16], for example, specifies how these structures can be translated ('encoded') uniquely into system independent Bit representations which then are to be sent over the communication link to the peer communication partner.

In addition to specifying the APDU structures, the RDA protocol defines *rules and restrictions* which any RDA implementation has to obey. The most important set of such rules are the so called '**sequencing rules**'. They define the set of legal sequences in which RDA services may be used. (For example, an 'R-BeginDialogue' has to precede any other RDA operation.).

4.4 RDA in the ISO/OSI Upper Layer Architecture

The ISO/OSI Upper Layer Architecture (ULA) [10] defines a common framework within which all ISO/OSI application layer standards shall be specified. As a basic building principle, it emphasizes 're-use' of partial or 'generic' OSI application layer standards whenever possible for defining specific application layer standards which support a dedicated class of applications only. For example, as association management has to be provided by all application layer standards, a corresponding generic standard 'Association Control Service Elements' (ACSE) [11], is included in all specific application layer standards.

In case of RDA, there is an 'generic' part of the RDA standard which describes those aspects of the RDA client/ server communication which are independent of the details of a particular database language used to access the remote database, called the 'Generic RDA' [8]. For using RDA in order to access a specific database, the generic RDA standard has to be augmented by the details of a specific database language, for example SQL when accessing a standardized relational database interface. This part of RDA is then specified in a corresponding RDA 'specialization', e.g. for the database language SQL [9].

In addition, RDA operations can be viewed as a specific way of using more general 'remote operation' calls in an open systems environment. Such calls are supported by the corresponding OSI standard 'Remote Operations Service Elements' (ROSE) [12]. Based on such an OSI ULA 'specialization hierarchy' the complete structure of the RDA standard is defined as a stepwise specification of OSI service parameters as follows:

ROSE: for generic calls of any remote operations,

Generic RDA: for DBL independent calls of remote RDA operations, and

Specific RDA: for remote calls of specific RDA DBL operations.

4.5 OSI ULA RDA Application Context Definition

According to the OSI Upper Layer Architecture (ULA) standard [10], a specific 'Application Process Invocation' is composed of the non-communication capabilities of an application and an 'Application Entity Invocation' (AEI) which supports the communication requirements of that application. Within such an AEI, single communication associations are controlled within the framework of a 'Single Association Object' (SAO) by a 'Single Association Control Function' (SACF). Besides the SACF, an SAO consists of the set of basic building blocks, or 'Application Service Elements' (ASEs). Whenever there is a need to coordinate more than one association, this is defined in the so called 'Multiple Association Control Function' (MACF).

In its AEI, the RDA SAO combines different ASEs in two alternate RDA application: I.e., depending on the level of transaction management supported, it specifies two alternate application context definitions:

4.5.1 RDA Basic Application Context :
In the 'Basic Application Context' for single-client/ single-server applications, only limited transaction management functions (as described in the RDA services section) are provided within the RDA-ASE. Therefore, in this context, the corresponding SAO contains an RDA-ASE and ACSE only.

4.5.2 RDA TP Application Context :
In RDA, full transaction management support - including a service for executing a two-phase commitment protocol over a tree of sub-transactions - is provided in the 'TP application context'. It uses the 'Transaction Processing' (TP) [14] standard for managing distributed transactions, including the necessary MACF-rules for coordinating more than one transaction branch. For supporting the transaction control protocol exchange of any two adjacent nodes, the RDA TP application context makes use of the ISO/OSI 'Commitment, Concurrency and Recovery Service Element' (CCR) [13]. So, the corresponding SAO for the RDA TP application context includes ACSE, the RDA-ASE, and TP (supported on a single branch by the CCR protocol) for transaction management.

5. Conclusions

The paper first aimed at motivating the need for extended database management system functions as motivated by requirements of new data-intensive applications. Explicitly, the paper focussed on requirements of *distributed database applications in open computer networks*. Using an approach which generalizes traditional, centralized database systems stepwise into various forms of data distribution in such networks, the paper then concentrated on extension to database systems in three related areas: first, traditional **data modelling** concepts were extended to accommodate the needs of both more adequate complex objects representations and the communication requirements of a distributed systems environment; second, in order to ease realizing abstract object models for distributed data-intensive applications, an appropriate **programming language** interface was identified; finally, this required - beyond what is already provided by existing, centralized database and programming languages - dedicated support for **communication with remote databases** which was defined for an open systems network environment.

In a basic form, the communication requirements of advanced databases in open computer networks are met by the current version of the ISO/OSI RDA standard. However, instead of 'specializing' RDA with SQL (as specified in [9]) exclusively, the modular structure of RDA also allows for alternate RDA specializations. So, for example, an RDA open systems communication mechanism could also be specialized according to the needs of an integrated database and programming languages as, e.g., DBPL as introduced in section 3.2. Such an approach has been taken in a research prototype as described in [4]. A distributed database programming language implementation based on communication mechanisms for open systems provides an ideal target interface for realizing the distributed complex object specifications. In principle, such an approach has already been taken earlier in a prototype for a recursive complex objects implementation for a *centralized* environment as described in [17]. A similar - but more complex realization - for the *distributed* open systems scenario has still been a promising but open research issue. This paper outlined a way of a extending the centralized prototype implementation into an open systems network environment. A prototype implementation for realizing the distributed high-level programming language interface as described in section 3.3 of this paper in an open systems network environment with communication support based on RDA as described in the previous chapter has been realized in the 'DURESS' project (see, e.g., [4]).

Acknowledgement

Parts of the practical results as described in this paper have been achieved in joint work, both in a research cooperation with the University of Frankfurt and together with colleagues at the IBM European Networking Center in Heidelberg.

6. References

[1] **P. Dadam, K. Küspert, F. Andersen, H. Blanken, R. Erbe, J. Günauer, V. Lum, P. Pistor, G. Walch** *A DBMS Prototype to Support Extended NF2 Relations: An Integrated View on Flat Tables and Hierarchies* Proc. ACM SIGMOD, Washington, DC, May 1986, pp. 356-367

[2] **H. Eckhardt, J. Edelmann, J. Koch, M. Mall, J.W. Schmidt** *Report on the Database Programming Language DBPL* DBPL Memo 091-85, Johann Wolfgang Goethe-Universität, Frankfurt, 1985

[3] **W. Effelsberg** *Datenbankzugriff in Rechnernetzen (Database Access in Computer Networks)* Technical Report TR 43.8707, IBM Deutschland, European Networking Center, July 1987

[4] **L. Ge, W. Johannsen, W. Lamersdorf, K. Reinhardt, J.W. Schmidt** *Database Application Support in Open Systems: Language Concepts and Implementation Architectures.* Proc. 4th Conference on Data Engineering, pp. 556-563, Los Angeles, CA, USA, February 1988

[5] **L. Haas et al.** *R*: A Research Project on Distributed Relational DBMS* Database Engineering, vol. 5, no. 4, 1982

[6] **D. Heimbigner, D. McLeod,** *Federated Architecture for Information Management* ACM Transaction on Office Information Systems, vol. 3, no. 3, pp. 253-278, July 1985

[7] **International Organization for Standardization** *Basic Reference Model* Information Processing Systems - Open Systems Interconnection, International Standard 7498, 1984

[8] **International Organization for Standardization** *Remote Database Access - Part 1: Generic* Information Processing Systems - Open Systems Interconnection, Draft Proposal 9579-2 (ISO/IEC JTC1/C21 WG3 N996), 1990

[9] **International Organization for Standardization** *Remote Database Access - Part 2: SQL Specialization* Information Processing Systems - Open Systems Interconnection, Draft Proposal 9579-2 (ISO/IEC JTC1/C21 WG3 N996), 1990

[10] **International Organization for Standardization** *Application Layer Structure* Information Processing Systems - Open Systems Interconnection, Draft Proposal 9545, 1989

[11] **International Organization for Standardization** *Service/Protocol Definition for Common Application Service Elements: Part 2: Association Control* Information Processing Systems - Open Systems Interconnection, International Standard 8649/50-2, 1988

[12] **International Organization for Standardization** *Remote Operations* Information Processing Systems - Open Systems Interconnection, Draft International Standard 9072-1 and -2, 1989

[13] **International Organization for Standardization** *Commitment, Concurrency and Recovery Service Element* Information Processing Systems - Open Systems Interconnection, Draft International Standard 9804, 1989

[14] **International Organization for Standardization** *Distributed Transaction Processing* Information Processing Systems - Open Systems Interconnection, Draft International Standard 10026-1, 10026-2, 10026-3, November 1989

[15] **International Organization for Standardization** *Abstract Syntax Notation One (ASN. 1)* Information Processing Systems - Open Systems Interconnection, International Standard 8824, 1989

[16] **International Organization for Standardization** *Basic Encoding Rules for Abstract Syntax Notation One* Information Processing Systems - Open Systems Interconnection, International Standard 8825, 1989

[17] **W. Lamersdorf, J.W. Schmidt** *Specification and Prototyping of Data Model Semantics* in: Procs. 'Approaches to Prototyping', R. Budde, K. Kuhlenkamp, L. Mathiassen, H. Züllighoven (Eds.), Springer-Verlag, Berlin Heidelberg New York Tokyo, 1984, pp. 214-231

[18] **W. Lamersdorf** *Recursive Data Models for Non-Conventional Database Applications* Proc. 1st International Conference on Data Engineering (COMPDEC), Los Angeles, CA, IEEE Computer Society Press, Order No. 530, Silver Spring, MD, April 1984, pp. 143-150

[19] **W. Lamersdorf** *Communicating Complex Objects* Technical Report TR 43.8606, IBM Deutschland, European Networking Center, Heidelberg, July 1986

[20] **J.A. Larson** *Four Reference Architectures for Distributed Database Management Systems,* Computer Standards and Interfaces, North-Holland Pub. Co., vol. 8, 1988/89, pp. 209-221

[21] **C. Pu** *Superdatabases for Composition of Heterogeneous Databases* Proc. 4th International Conference on Data Engineering (COMPDEC), Los Angeles, CA, IEEE Computer Society Press, Order No. 827, Silver Spring, MD, April 1988, pp. 548-555

[22] **L. Swobodova** *Client/Server Model of Distributed Processing* Proc. GI/NTG-Fachtagung 'Distributed Database Systems', Karlsruhe, W.-Germany, Informatik-Fachberichte, vol. 95, Springer Verlag, Heidelberg, 1985, pp. 485-498

Distributed Knowledge Based Systems supporting CIM Components on B-ISDN[1]

Hermann Krallmann

Technical University Berlin

ABSTRACT

The project "Distributed knowledge based systems supporting CIM components on B-ISDN" - called INTERBIT - is a strategic project that combines newest methodology from communications, distributed knowledge based systems and 2nd generation problem solving architectures to pave the way for innovative industrial applications of computer-integrated manufacturing (CIM). This document briefly reviews the relevant components of a real-world problem-solving-situation (PSS) in CIM, their functionality, and requirements derivable from functionality and application context. Next, a strategy for the implementation of distributed problem solving architectures is presented and described. This strategy is then applied to those components of the PSS which are to be tackled in the INTERBIT project.

1 INTERBIT CIM Model and Systems

This section gives an overview on the problem-solving situation under consideration and identifies the component systems that ultimately comprise the INTERBIT application.

1.1 Motivation

CIM has been one of the most misused and misunderstood terms in more recent computer terminology. Nevertheless, every project set up more or less in a CIM context has to define the meaning of the word and its own position within the field. Thus, we decided to include our definition of CIM in our documents to make ourselves better understood.

In our definition, CIM is an undertaking that aims at the complete and true integration of all activities regarding the design, production and marketing of products and any activities necessary or supportive to these tasks.

This definition takes a broad view of CIM and includes tasks such as the adequate presentation of an extraordinary wide variety of products, high-quality consultancy of customers, and the achievement of outstanding correctness and consistency in orders, prices and delivery dates. All of them have hardly been tackled up to now due to inadequate technology and methodology. This project is addressed to companies which are characterized by distributed components, e.g. with distributed sales structures, remote product development and manufacturing [see Fig. 1]. Companies meeting these criteria require new communication services like B-ISDN. INTERBIT specifically tries to work on these problems, because possible payoffs and the degree of innovation are very promising, as pointed out in [8].

---

[1] This paper is based on the INTERBIT working paper [1] and on the INTERBIT project report [5].

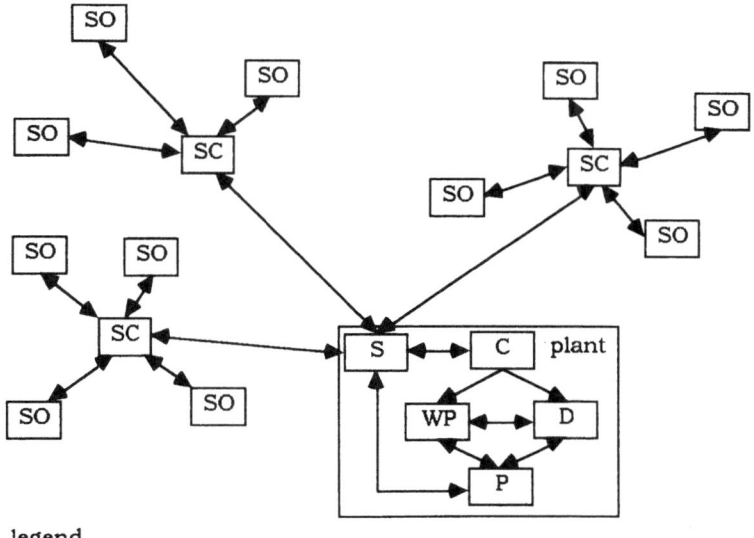

legend
S := sales
SC := sales center
SO := sales office
C := construction
WP := work planning
D := disposition
P := production

Fig. 1: Distributed Business Structure

1.2 Overview

The fundamental characteristics of the problem solving context considered by the INTERBIT group are as follows:

- Future generations of software systems will typically have knowledge-based components [10].

- Availability of communication services spurs integration of systems.

- New communication services (IBC[2]) allow for transmission of immense quantities of data across long-range distances.

- Combination of the above will result in new software architecture.

- New software architectures enable new and innovative applications.

One of the most pressing, yet unresolved problems of many manufacturers is handling a huge variety of products in sales offices and order processing departments. Oddly enough, this problem has been created by CIM - and the very idea of CIM - in the first place: It was the dissatisfaction of customers and sales departments that initiated the wish to produce truely customized products, to have lot size one and, thus, the CIM idea. While the mainstream of CIM has worked on the integration of such activities as design, process planning, manufacturing and quality assurance, the problems of handling variety and complexity in the sales offices order processing departments have been denied. Some of these problems are:

- Printed material is an expensive yet inadequate means of presenting hundreds or thousands of variants of a single product (1)[3].

- An upper limit on the variety and complexity sales people can manage (2).

---

2   IBC = Interconnected Broadband Communication

148

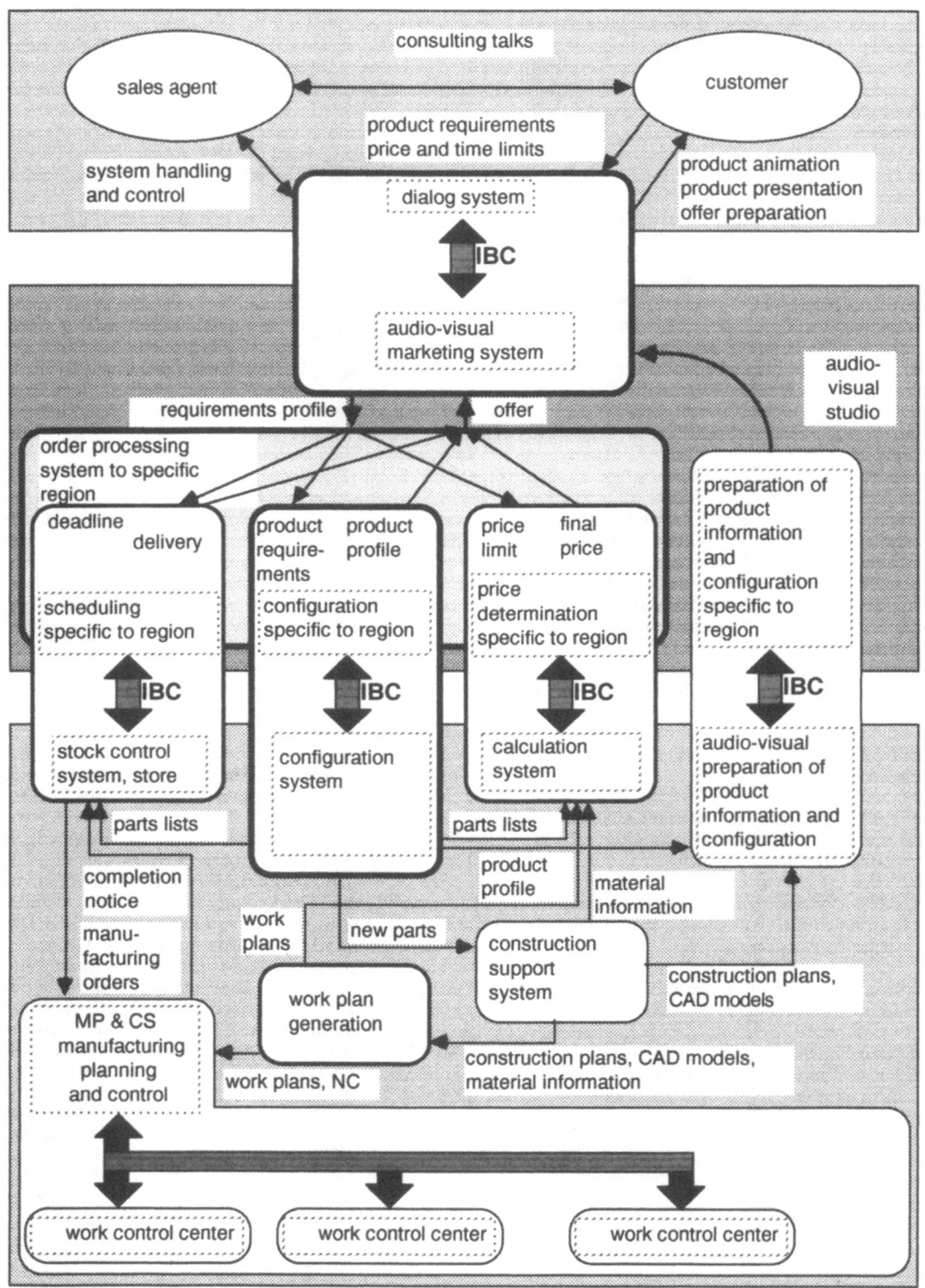

Fig. 2: The Comprehensive CIM Structure

- Increased variety makes orders much more complex; order acquisition is an error-prone process (3).

- Incomplete and inconsistent orders cause unnecessary delay, dissatisfaction of the customer, frustration of sales people, and extra cost (4).

- Calculation of prices becomes a complex task (5).

- Determination of tentative and definite delivery dates, especially for urgent orders, involves complex planning, simulation and calculation (6).

The problem solving situation selected as research topic in INTERBIT (see [9]) investigates these problems and develops approaches to solve them. One main component is the development of the konowledge represantation language called

AMOR for the classification of orders. The basic modules of a general CIM structure are shown in Fig. 2. The next chapter briefly overviews the particular component systems part of INTERBIT.

1.3 Briefings of the Functional Description of Components

1.3.1 Audio-Visual Marketing System (AVMS)

The AVMS tackles problems (1) and (2). The idea is to provide a system that takes the complexity load from sales people, makes printed product informations almost obsolete and yet provides very high quality of product presentation. Using IBC, small computer systems in sales offices or portable computers carried by travelling sales people are connected to bigger computers in sales centers. The smaller systems serve as front end to complex systems in the sales centers that provide animated, audio-visual product information, which may or may not be tailored to local requirements (language used, set of variants and options presented, etc.). A distributed implementation of the AVMS idea is necessary and reasonable for several reasons:

- Front ends must be small, with limited computing power, and very limited permanent storage space; thus they cannot store large quantities of audio-visual material and animated product presentations.

- Sales center systems may be much bigger and provide sufficient storage (> 1GB).

- Maintaining the AVMS is easier, if the dynamic parts are centered.

The AVMS is a very good example for an innovative application of IBC, because it requires the transmission of huge quantities of data over long distances. It allows to bring new and creative approaches to product presentation and sales from a few special situations (exhibitions, sales shows) to every sales office and make them work in a much more complex context.

The AVMS also serves as front end to systems that solve other problems. All the customer and the sales person sees is AVMS, although the actual work is done by other components that talk to the AVMS via IBC (see Fig. 2).

Main audio-visual components help in the preparation and creation of animated product presentations. It takes input from various sources, e.g. CAD design models for anatomic components, scanned images of prototype parts, partial or full configuration from CONS, etc. (see Fig. 3). Designers and other creative people in the central marketing department use this material, edit it, and prepare audio-visual units being used by the AVMS system. Marketing people in the regional sales office may tailor these units to local needs, e.g. translate texts, speech, filter out certain parts (on components/variants unavailable in that region) and so on.

1.3.2 Order Management and Acqusition (OMA)

The OMA system, located in regional sales centers, tackles problem areas (3) to (6). It gets its input from the AVMS systems in the sales centers and interacts with systems CONS (problem area 4, partially 3), PS (problem area 5) and DS (problem area 6). One of the main functions of OMA is the coordination of the communication with and interaction of configuration system CONS, the pricing system PS, and the disposition system DS. All these components provide unique services that different departments of a company are responsible for. In order to ease maintenance and stability of these subsystems each of them is put into the responsible department in the main

---

3   We assign numbers to the problems described here, which will later be used as reference to a specific problem.

150

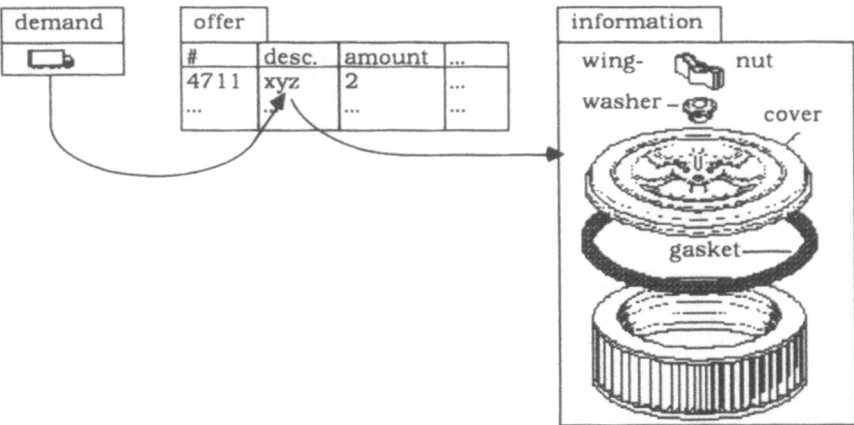

Fig. 3: CAD Design Model

offices. However, country-specific and regional considerations are best maintained in the regional sales centers, where all the country-specific know-how is located. OMA interacts with and controls the local parts of the CONS, PS and DS systems in order to achieve the overall task (see Fig. 2).

1.3.3 Configuration System (CONS)

The configuration system CONS is one of the central components of INTERBIT. CONS is responsible for the configuration of products, which includes the following tasks:

- checking the validity of constraints imposed by customers (can a variant exist at all)

- completing the partial specification of a product (add missing specifications; select options)

- completing an order (add necessary components non-interactively)

- consulting during order acquisition (useful components to add in order to get a good product)

CONS has to work on multiple configuration tasks simultaneously (many customers sit in front of the AVMS at the same time). Various other papers describe our approach to configuration ([2][6][7]).

1.3.4 Disposition System (Purchasing, Materials, Stock and Inventory Control) (DS)

The DS system takes partially or fully configured orders together with requested delivery dates. It checks whether the requested delivery dates can be met or generates earliest and/or most convenient delivery dates by communicating with the production management system, that does a tentative scheduling of production on those parts that are not available on stock. It also takes into account country-specific or regional circumstances that influence delivery (such as the duration of customs processes, local transportation, etc.). For reasons of maintenance and responsibilities (local responsibility for pricing, currency rates, etc.) the DS consists of a central component for providing basic pricing information and components located in sales centers for customizing products to country-specific or regional needs.

1.3.5 Pricing System (PS)

The PS is similar to the DS system. It works on partially or fully configured orders together with specified price limits and checks the consistency of the result of the current configuration against price limits. As for disposition, the pricing system is split up into a central component providing pricing information on specific components, standard models and configuration, etc. and a regional component that accounts for local adaptation of pricing (currency rates, extra transportation and delivery surcharges, customs fees, local taxes, etc.).

1.3.6 Production Management System (PMS)

The production management system PMS manages all the manufacturing facilities. It is responsible for timely production of orders and thus must take care of all necessary activities to achieve that. More recent insights into how CIM might be put to work suggest that a PMS must employ a rather dynamic planning facility working in the following context: Given a set of production facilities (manufacturing machines, robots, transportation devices, etc. and programs to control them), their current states (provided by a sensory network), a set of goals that reflect certain management decisions about planning and scheduling of manufacturing orders, and a dynamic set of orders (possibly categorized by different priorities; new orders coming in; processed orders falling out) a production schedule (and its distributed version for each (job or flow) shop) must be generated. The important factor is the inherent dynamics of a production environment which is responsible for the necessity to do incremental planning.

2 A Layered Implementation Model for Distributed Problem Solving Architectures (LIMODIPSA)

2.1 Motivation

Faced with the quite ambitious task of tying together knowledge-based systems technology and broadband communications networking of up-to-here unknown bandwiths, the chances to fail are substantial unless specific provisions are taken. The provisions taken by the INTERBIT group are based on a model for structuring the design and implementation of knowledge-based systems in a distributed environment. The main advantages are:

- The huge gap between application level and communication level is divided into several layers, which makes design and implementation more managable and allows working in parallel.

- Effort for redesigns necessary during implementation is decreasing as the scope is narrowed down with each redesign.

- The many problems arising in the application contexts are distributed across several levels and can be tackled in a more local and focussed manner; the set of problems to be solved is smaller in any specific layer.

- The closer a layer is towards communications, the more general it is. This allows other projects to share results developed by the INTERBIT core group; while still developing completely different things at the application level.

The basic ideas of the model are not new par se. They are applied in a more or less rigid manner in every serious software project; however we want to concisely present the complete model and its application in a distributed context.

2.2 Overview

LIMODIPSA (Layered Implementation Model for Distributed Problem Solving Architectures) models ([3][4]) consists of five layers. Similar approaches can be found in [11][12][13]. They structure design and implementation of problem solving components for distributed applications (see Fig. 4). These layers are (from bottom to top):

- Fundamental and Communications Layer

  This layer is the first level of abstraction of the hardware layer including partly the net topology. It represents the layers two to six of the ISO-reference model and provides communications services (broadband, local area net, inter-process communication) for the language processor layer.

- Language Processor Layer

  The language processor layer provides independence of a specific hardware environment, software distribution, process allocation, and network topology. We intend to achieve this by implementing DOOS, which stands for Distributed Object-Oriented System. The object-oriented programming paradigm seems to be best suited for this task at the moment. This layer will use the services of the fundamental and communications layer and will include systems like window systems and data base systems, etc.

- Technique Layer

The technique layer is made up by an extensible, generic set of tools (both AI and non-AI) which help programmers implement task specific shells at the task layer. The technique layer stresses flexibility, generality, efficiency and orthogonality of its components. In detail the technique layer will include a rule interpreter, a frame interpreter, a constraint interpreter and an assumption truth based maintenance system (ATMS).

- Task Layer

The task layer provides task-specific problem solving shells suitable to implement applications for a specific kind of task, such as configuration. Domain-specific shells may sit on top of task-specific shells and contain standard knowledge needed in applications taken from a specific domain (such as the configuration and layout of computer systems).

- Application layer

On the application layer specific application systems will be implemented based on cooperative agents which solve specific tasks of the application.

3 Some Aspects of Implementation

The central aspect we focus on is the configuration part (see Fig. 2). Thus, the CONS system will be fully implemented; i.e. a full-fledged, knowledge-based, distributed application for configuration is built, including all the underlying utilities at the task layer, the technique layer, the language processor layer, and the fundamental and communications layer. The CONS system itself is a distributed system. Aside from having the regional parts of CONS run at another site, the main configuration process itself may be distributed. The more complex the configuration object becomes, the more reasonable it is to distribute rather complex subtasks to available computing resources.

The DS and PS systems will be implemented as black boxes. We need at least two regional black box versions for both PS and DS. By a black box implementation we mean, that for our specific application a module is built that provides the correct output for a specific input without actually implementing the underlying problem solving processes. These systems are, among others prime candidates for satellite projects or for extra work to be done in the rather unlikely case that we will have time left to do it.

In the early spring 1990 the first two prototype versions are modulled in AMOR.

Naturally, as we need to demonstrate our configuration system in a working context, we also have to implement a prototype AVMS system. By prototype system we mean, that all the functionality of the AVMS, that is necessary to conduct the configuration dialog and perform the order acquisition process will be implemented. We will also implement the animated presentations and audio-visual parts to some extent. One of the constraints in this area is availability of equipment needed to fully implement the AVMS. For example, at the moment it is reasonable to expect the AVMS exhibiting the basic features of the HyperCard program on Macintosh computers, which includes the display and animation of graphic images, a reasonably nice user interface (sexy windows), and a dialog mechanism, that allows initiating sales presentations and walking through them based on mouse-controlled menus and mouse-sensitive items on the screen. It would be expecting too much, if video units and audio units would be included in this list.

All the other systems are not scheduled for implementation in the current setting of the INTERBIT project. However, it is both recommended and likely that INTERBIT satellite projects or other cooperatve research efforts add components like the PMS or the process plan generations system.

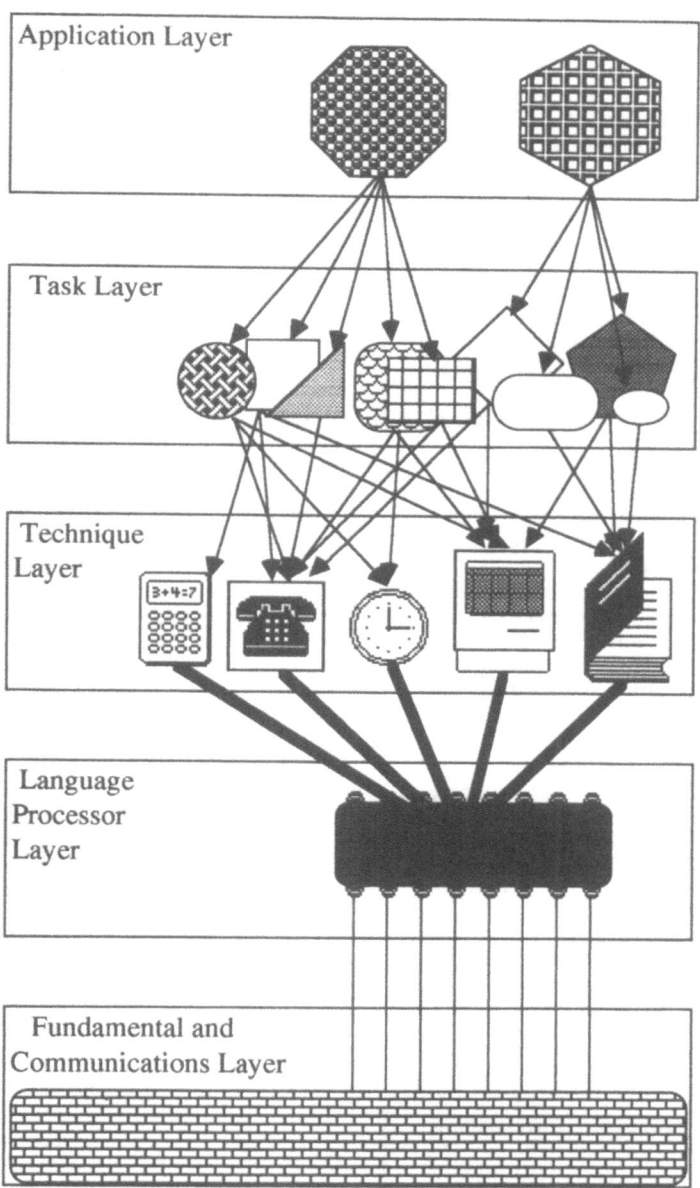

Fig. 4: Layered Implementation Model for Distributed Problem Solving
Architectures

REFERENCES

[1] S. Albayrak, M. Hein, G. K. Kraetzschmar, B. Messer, W. Tank: On Implementing INTERBIT, Working Paper TU Berlin, draft version 0.2, 14 March 1989

[2] M. Hein, W. Tank: Diskussion des Abhängigkeitsbegriffs in Konfigurationsproblemen. In: Arbeitspapiere der GMD, Nr. 310, April 1988

[3] M. Hein, J. Mertens, C. Unbehend: Architekturentwurf für eine Konfigurationsshell mit flexibler Kontrolle. Arbeitspapiere der GMD 388, 1989

[4] G. K. Kraetzschmar: Extending Object-Oriented Systems for Distributed Technical Applications. Diplomarbeit, Friedrich-Alexander Universität, Erlangen, 1988

[5] H. Krallmann, S. Albayrak, M. Hein, G. K. Kraetzschmar, B. Messer, W. Tank: Innerbetriebliche Integration wissensbasierter Systeme auf der Basis von Breitband-ISDN Diensten, Abschlußbericht zur Phase I des Projektes, TU Berlin, Mai 1989

[6] J. Mertens: Entwicklung eines Stellgerätekonfigurators auf der Basis eines objektzentrierten Gegenstandsmodells. Diplomarbeit, TU Berlin, 1988

[7] W. Tank: Entwurfsziele bei der Entwicklung von Expertensystemen. In: KI, Oldenbourg Verlag, 3/88

[8] W. Tank: What a Configuration Task is (and what it is not). Arbeitspapier, TU Berlin, 1989

[9] W. Tank: Pragmatik der Repräsentationssprache AMOR. To appear: Arbeitspapiere der GMD 388, 1989

[10] D. Partridge: Software Engineering und KI, McGraw Hill Verlag, 1989

[11] D., C. Brown, Chandrasekaran, B.: Knowledge and Control for System. IEEE EXPERT, Itelligent Systems and their Applications, IEEE, 1986

[12] Coyne: Logic Models of Design, Pitman Verlag 1989

[13] D., C. Brown, Chandrasekaran, B.: Design Problem Solving, Pitman Verlag, 1989

ALGRES Prototype of Reusable Software Modules based on Algebraic Specifications.

Hanna Oktaba (*)
Concepción Pérez de Célis (*)
Roberto Zicari (**)

(*) IIMAS, Universidad Nacional Autonoma de México, Mexico.
(**) Dipartimento di Elettronica, Politecnico di Milano,
Piazza Leonardo da Vinci, 32 , 20123 Milano, Italy.

Abstract

A catalog of software components designed using an advanced relational system is described.

1. Introduction

Every hardware design shop mantains a store of information, called *catalog*, about the components that are available for potential use in the electronic products. The catalog is a powerful system-building tool. The concept of catalog can be used to store software components as well. To achieve this goal we need some abstract and precise description of software components which permits to consider the software code as a sort of "black box" ready to be re-use. Formal specification languages can play this role.

In this paper we present the design of a catalog of reusable software modules based on algebraic specifications. The system has been implemented using the ALGRES advanced relational system [Cac*89], [Ceri*88], [Ceri*88a].

In the definition of the software catalog we made the following assumptions:

- A software component is associated to an algebraic specification which form its abstract description. (Through the paper we will use the LESPAL language [Okt89] as a representative algebraic specification language).

- Each specification stored in the catalog has at least one implementation in a conventional programming language. We suppose that the implementations meet the specifications and are correct.

- The specifications depend on each other by inheritance and/or import relationships.

The catalog we have designed has four components:

1. The general topic dictionary.
2. A part which stores all algebraic specifications.
3. A part which stores for each specification its implementation(s).
4. A part which stores the dependencies between specifications.

The goal of this work was twofold: First, we wanted to design a catalog in such a way that software designer could easily retrieve and analyze both software specifications and implementations in order to build new complex software components from the basic ones stored in the catalog. Second, we wanted to test the ALGRES system as a tool for rapid prototyping. This paper reports such an experience.

The rest of the paper is structured as follows: Section 2 briefly presents the LESPAL specification language. Section 3 introduces the functionalities offered by the ALGRES system. Section 4 presents the requirements for the design of the software catalog. Section 5 defines the static part and the dynamic part of the catalog. Finally section 6 presents some conclusions and future work.

2. LESPAL

LESPAL is an algebraic specification language developed at IIMAS [Okt89]. The language is similar to the ASF-formalism [BHK 87] and to CLEAR [BG 81]. LESPAL allows the definition of modularized, hierarchical and parameterazied abstract specifications of software components. An important factor for the practical utilization of abstract specification languages is to build a library of specifications which can be used in constructing other larger specifications. A specification module defines a set of sorts and operations. The meaning of the operations is described by a set of axioms. A specification module can be parameterized to achieve generality. One specification can import other specifications or can enrich (specialize) another specification.

The general schema of a LESPAL specification module is as follows:

```
SPEC    <spec-id>
        <enriched-by>
        <parameters>
        <exports>
        <imports>
        <sorts>
        <operations>
        <variables>
        <axioms>
END OF <spec-id>
```

The *enriched-by* part defines the inheritance relationships between specifications. We consider only single inheritance. The *import* part describes the "client of" relationships between specifications.

3. ALGRES

ALGRES is an advanced relational programming environment and database for the rapid-prototyping of data-intensive and non-standard applications which perform complex operations over hierarchical data structures.

The motivations for the design of ALGRES originates from the need to overcome the limits of (pure) relational algebra as a prototyping tool. In this respect, the (pure) relational algebra has two main drawbacks:

- the relational data model cannot directly model nested structures, as it requires to flatten structures and to introduce artificial entities, such as pointers or surrogates;

- the relational algebra is not computationally complete, hence it requires to be embedded into a traditional programming language. This creates a so called "impedance mismatch".

ALGRES overcomes these limitations, yet remaining as close as possible to the relational approach.

ALGRES is a vehicle for the integration of two research areas: The extension of the relational model to deal with complex objects, and the integration of databases with logic programming.

The ALGRES system consists of:

i) A data model which incorporates standard elementary types (characters, string, integer, real, boolean), and the type constructors tuple, set, multiset and list. An ALGRES object has a schema which consists of a hierarchical structure of arbitrary depth built with the above type constructors.

ii) An algebraic language, called *ALGRES-PREFIX* , which provides:

- Classical relational operators, such as selection, projection, Cartesian product, union, difference (and derived operators) suitable extended to deal with hierarchical relations;
- The restructuring operators of nested relations: Nest, Unnest which modify the structure of a nested relation;
- Aggregate functions;
- Operations for type transformation, which enable the coercion of any type into a different one;
- A fixpoint operator which applies to an algebraic expression and iterates the evaluation of the expression until a certain predicate is satisfied. This operator is very flexible and allows to emulate all different *closure* operators proposed to evaluate recursive queries.

The fixpoint operator has the following structure:

```
FIXPOINT [Temp:= TRANSF (Op);
          PRED (Temp, Op);
          COMB(Temp, Op) ] Op
```

where Op is the operand and Temp is a temporary object, the scope of which is limited to the FIXPOINT operation. TRANSF, PRED, COMB are three ALGRES expressions: TRANSFER computes a new instance of Temp from Op; PRED is the exit condition from the loop; COMB creates a new instance of Temp from Temp and Op. The three inner statements of the FIXPOINT operator are iteratively executed until Pred is not satisfied. Note

that, like every ALGRES statement, the FIXPOINT operator does not actually modify the original Op object; a copy of Op is used in the evaluation of the FIXPOINT, and it eventually becomes the final result.

The FIXPOINT operator corresponds to the following Pascal-like program:

```
end:= false;
Result := Op;
repeat
  Temp:= TRANSF (Result);
  if PRED(Temp, Result)
     then end:= true;
     else Result := COMB(Temp, Result);
until end
```

In particular the fixpoint operator can be used to simulate the *transitive closure* to evaluate recursive relational expressions: $R=f(R)$. The least fixpoint of this expression is a relation R^* such that $R^*=f(R^*)$ and $S \supseteq R^*$ for any S satisfying $S=f(S)$. The least fixpoint can be obtained using the FIXPOINT operator as follows:

```
FIXPOINT  [Temp := f(R0);
           NOT (R0 ⊇ Temp );
           UNION Temp R0] R0
```

where R0 is an empty collection with the required schema.

The ALGRES system constitutes a relational programming environment; in fact ALGRES is integrated with a commercial relational database system (Informix), but it is not implemented on top of it. ALGRES programs operate on main memory data structures, which are initially loaded from the external database, and returned to mass memory after manipulation. The abstract machine supporting the extended relational data model and its operations, named RA (Relational Algebra), reflects the following assumption: only a fraction of the database is supposed to be present in main memory at any time, and speed (rather than memory) is the limiting factor.

The core of the ALGRES environment (fig. 1) consists of the ALGRES to RA translator and RA interpreter. The translator maps ALGRES data structures and operators into conventional (flat) relations and RA instructions. The RA instruction set provides traditional algebraic operations on (flat) relations. The implementation of the RA interpreter ensures a good performance of execution in main memory of ALGRES expressions.

The ALGRES system compares favorably with other existing productivity tools or high-level languages used for rapid prototyping, such as SETL and Prolog.

Applications in ALGRES can be programmed using directly the rather low-level ALGRES-PREFIX language. However, to provide the programmer with a multi-paradigm, easy-to-use programming environment, the system supports an extension of SQL for nested relations and recursive queries, named ESQL. Programs in ESQL are translated into ALGRES-PREFIX before their execution. Both ALGRES-PREFIX and ESQL are interfaced with the C programming language in order to exploit existing C libraries.

The user , through a special interface can make ALGRES data structures persistent by loading (unloading) them in (from) the Informix database system.

ALGRES runs on SUN/360 and HP-9000 workstations with the Unix operating systems, and on IBM PCs with the OS/2 operating system.

fig.1: The ALGRES environment

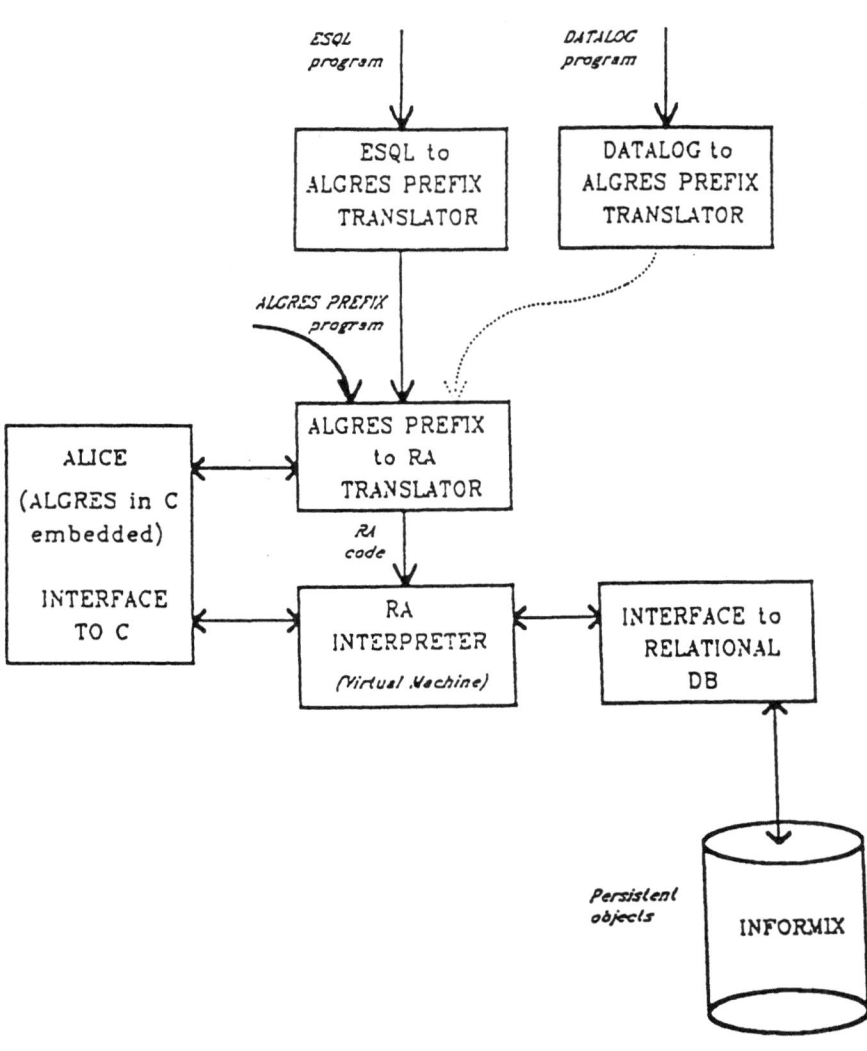

The ALGRES project is broad-spectrum, and to give a specialization of each of its part is outside the scope of this paper; the interested reader is referred to [Ceri*88], [Ceri*88a], and [Cac*89].

For the sake of readability we list in Table 1 the ALGRES full names of ALGRES-PREFIX operators used in the next sections.

TABLE 1.

PJ	PROJECT
SL	SELECT
UN	UNION
JN	JOIN
TE	TUPLE EXTENSION
FP	FIXPOINT

4. Catalog Requirements

ALGRES is suited for an evolutionary rapid prototyping approach to software construction, which replaces a complete requirement analysis phase by a continuous adjustment of the prototype functions and interfaces. When we started our development we had just scattered but representative indications of the kind of queries to be performed on the software components:

(1) To retrieve all modules meeting a condition which does not involve interrelations among other modules;

(2) To perform recursive queries involving the graph of the inheritance and clientship relation among modules.

In this paper, we do not consider updates. Starting with such loose requirements we designed the schema of the catalog described in the next section, and checked its suitability with respect to the sample of intended queries.

5. ALGRES representation of the catalog.

The static representation of the catalog in ALGRES is composed of the following complex relations:

1) Topic dictionary,
2) Specification set,
3) Implementation set,
4) Dependency set.

The topic dictionary contains the basic information of the catalog components; for example: Data structures, graphics, etc. The specification set contains the abstract description of the components in some specification language, in our case LESPAL. The implementation set contains the implementation code in various programming languages and relative descriptions.

The dependency relations are expressed by three auxiliary ALGRES relations generated by execution of recursive queries. These relations represents the inheritance and import relationships among specifications.

5.1 Topic dictionary

The topic dictionary contains the general information about the software components of the catalog. It is organized as a set of subjects (*Subject*). Each subject contains a set of modules which provide the information about the component's names (*comp-name*), the specification languages to choose (*spec-languages*) and the implementation languages (*impl-languages*).

The ALGRES schema of the topic dictionary is the following:

```
DEF Topic-Dictionary:
    { Subject: string,
      Modules: { comp-name: string,
                 spec-languages: <name:string>,
                 impl-languages:<name:string>
               }
    }
```

In ALGRES " < >" define a sequence of attributes and "{ }" define a set of attributes. The above schema can be graphically represented by a tree, where each node is a type constructor (i.e. list, multiset, set, tuple), and the leaves are the attributes.

An example of an instance object of the topic dictionary is as follows:

```
Topic-Dictionary <- { ("Primitive-Types",
                       { ("Boolean", <"LESPAL">, <"Modula-2>),

                         ("Natural", <"LESPAL">, <"Modula-2">)
                       }),
                     ( "Linear-Structures",
                       {"Stacks", <"LESPAL">, <"Modula-2", "Ada">),
                     ( "Bounded-Stacks", <"LESPAL">, <"Modula-2", "Ada">)
                       })
                   }
```

As it can be seen, the Topic-Dictionary is a complex relation which contains besides single-valued attributes, such as "Subject", also set (list,multiset in general)-valued attributes, such as "Modules". This is the characteristic of the nested relational model, where attributes of a nested relation can be relations themselves.

We consider this rather flat version of the topic dictionary as a first step in the prototyping process. We will consider more sophisticated solutions in the evolution of the prototype.

Note that we consider the possibility to have more than one specification language to define software components.

5.2 ALGRES schema for LESPAL specifications

To represent the LESPAL specifications (defined in section 2) as ALGRES objects we define the *Specifications* schema. First we need two auxiliary ALGRES relations for representing the sorts and the operations:

DEF Sorts: <Sort: string>

```
DEF Operations: < Operation:
                    (Op-name:string,
                     Domains: <Domain:string>,
                     Codomain: string
                    )
                >
```

The *Specifications* relation is a set of specification descriptions defined as follows:

DEF Specifications:
```
{
    Spec-name: string,
    Enriches:string,
    Parameters:
        <Parameter:
            (Param-name:string, Sorts: VS[ ], Operations: VS [ ] )
        >,
    Exports: (Sorts: VS[ ], Operations: VS[ ] ),
    Imports: {Spec-name: string},
    Sorts: VS[ ],
    Operations: VS[ ],
    Variables: <Var: (Name:string, Type:string) >,
    Axioms: <Text:string >
}.
```

"VS[ ]" means that the type of the attribute has been previously defined.

The information about the specification implementations is represented in the *Implementations* relation. For each specification we have a set of alternative implementations in various programming languages and possibly different versions. Each version has its code reference (e.g. the name of the executable file) and some other useful information such as: The author (*Auth*), complexity description and reuse information. The *Implementations* relation is defined as follows:

DEF Implementations
```
{
    Spec-name: string,
    Impl-set: { Language: string,
                Versions: {Code: string,
                           Auth: string,
                           Complexity: string,
                           Reuse-info: string
                          }
                }
}
```

5.3 Examples of ALGRES objects

We present an example of an ALGRES object modeling the specification of a Stack. The schema of the object is defined in section 5.2.

```
Specifications <--
    { ( "Stacks",
        "Null",
        <("Element:, <"Elem">, < >)>,
        (<"Stack">, <("empty", < >,"Stack"),
                         ("push", <"Elem", "Stack">, "Stack"),
                         ("pop", <"Stack">, "Stack"),
                         ("top", <"Stack">, "Elem"),
                         ("is-empty", <"Stack">, "Bool")>),
        {"Boolean"},
        < >,
        < >,
        <("e", "Elem"), ("s", "Stack")>,
        <"[P1] pop(empty) =error",.... >
        ) }
```

For this specification, suppose we have only one implementation , in the Ada programming language. Here is an example of the value of an object which gives this information:

```
Implementations <--
    { ("Stacks",
        { (ADA, {("Stacks.ADA",
                  "Brooch, 1988",
                  "Brooch book, page 80",
                  "Brooch book, page 56")
                 }
        ) }
    ) }
```

5.4 Generation of dependency

Specification modules do depend on each other. The dependency relationships are defined by the **IMPORT** (i.e. client of) and **ENRICHED BY** (i.e. inheritance) LESPAL clauses. The dependency information can be obtained from the instance values of the *Specifications* relation defined in section 5.2 by executing three queries Q1, Q2, and Q3 (fig.2) which will be described later in this section.

The dependency information between specifications will be structured according to three auxiliary relations: *Ancestor-struct, Descendent-struct,* and *Importation-struct. Ancestor-struct* will store for each specification the set of all its inherited specifications (by enriched clause). *Descendent-struct* will store for each specification the set of all specifications which enrich it. *Importation-struct* will store for each specification the set of all specifications which import it.

The generation of instance values for such relations is obtained by executing the three queries Q1, Q2, and Q3 defined as follows:

Query Q1: *Generation of ancestors*

The ancestors structure contains the information relative to the specifications with non empty value for the *Enriches* attribute and its correspondent ancestors set. The ALGRES schema of this structure is as follows:

DEF Ancestors-Struct: { Spec-name: string,
                        Ancestor-set: {Ancestor:string}
                       }

To generate this structure we need some temporal objects:

DEF Ancestors-temp: {Spec-name-temp:string,
                     Ancestors-set-temp: {Ancestor-temp:string}
                    }

DEF T: {Spec-name-T: string,
        Ancestor-set-T: {Ancestor-T: string }
       }

DEF Result: { Spec-name-Result: string,

              Ancestor-set-Result: {Ancestor-Result:string}
            }

The generation of *Ancestor-struct* starts with the creation of the following object:

Ancestor-temp <-- NEST[Ancestor-set-temp: {Enriches}]
                  PJ [Spec-name, Enriches]
                  SL[NOT(Enriches="Null")] Specifications

Ancestor-temp contains the information about each specification with non empty value for the *Enriches* attribute (obtained with a selection). Only the attribute "Spec-name" and "Enriches" are considered by removing the others with a projection. A Nest operator groups for same Spec-name the set of specification that "Enriches" it.

160

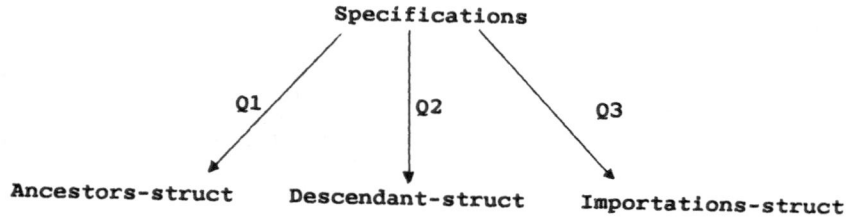

fig. 2   Dependency generation queries.

The algorithm start with a copy T of this object and for each specification generates a set of its ancestors using the fix point operator (FP):

T <-- Ancestor-temp

Result <--
   FP [Family:= PJ[Spec-name-T, Ancestor-set-temp]
            TU [Ancestors-set-temp:=
                   UN Ancestors-set-T Ancestors-set-temp]
            JN [MEMBER(Spec-name-temp; Ancestors-set-T)]
              T Ancestors-temp;

     CONTEQ (Family; Ancestors-temp);
     UN Ancestors-temp Family
   ] Ancestors-temp

The obtained relations contain some redundancy which is eliminated by first Unnesting on *Ancestor-set-Result* an then by Nesting on *Ancestor-set*::

Ancestors-set <-- NEST [Ancestor-set: {Ancestor-Result}]
                 UNNEST [Ancestor-set-Result] Result

Example: Consider the following value for the relation *Specifications:*

Specifications <--{ (a b < > ( ) { } < > < > < > < >)
               (b "Null" < > ( ) { } < > < > < > < >)
               (c e < > ( ) { } < > < > < > < >)
               (d f < > ( ) { } < > < > < > < >)
               (f "Null" < > ( ) { } < > < > < > < >)

the initial *Ancestor-temp* value is:

Ancestor-temp <-- { (a {b})
              (c {e})
              (d {f})
              (e {d}) }

The final result of the auxiliary structure *Ancestors-struct* after the fixpoint evaluation and the Nest-Unnest operations is:

Ancestor-struct <-- { (a {b})
               (c {e d f})
               (d {f})
               (e {d f }) }

Query Q2: *Generation of descendents*

The query computes the set of specifications that are "father" of at least one specification. To each "father" we associate the set of "sons". This query uses the copy of *Ancestors-struct* as an auxiliary object.

DEF Descendent-struct : { Father: string,
                     Descendant-set: {Son: string})

DEF Ancestor-aux: {Spec-name-aux:string,
                  Ancestors-set-aux: {Ancestor:string}
                  }

Ancestors-aux <-- Ancestors-struct

As the next step we build an auxiliary structure *Temp*. This structure is necessary because the *Ancestor-struct* lacks the information about the specifications that have no "father", that is the root specifications in the inheritance trees.

DEF Temp: {Spec-name-temp:string,
          Ancestors-set-temp: {Ancestor: string}
          }

Temp <-- UN Ancestors-aux
          TE [Ancestors-set-temp:={ }]
          PJ [Spec-name]
          SL [Enriches="Null"] Specifications

The expression begins with the selection of the root specifications (selection). The result is a set of root specifications. We obtain the set of specification names by projecting on the attribute *Spec-name*. Then we perform a Tuple Extension on the result by adding an empty set for each specification name. This is necessary in order to make the union with *Ancestor-aux*. (Note, the Union operator is defined for compatible schemas, i.e. schemas with the same structure). The result of the union is then assigned to a temporary structure *Temp* and this one is used to obtain the *Descendant-Struct*:

Descendant-struct <--
          NEST [Descendant-set: {Spec-name-aux}]
          PJ [Spec-name-temp, Spec-name-aux]
          JN [MEMBER(Spec-name-temp; Ancestor-set-aux)]
          Temp Ancestors-aux

We perform the join between *Temp* and *Ancestors-aux* with the condition that the name of the specification is a member of the set *Ancestor-set-aux* (i.e. it is a "father" of some specifications).

Then we project on *Spec-name-temp* and *Spec-name-aux* and in order to obtain the desired schema we nest by *Spec-name-aux*, that is we group together all values which have the same "father".

Query Q3: *Generation of importation dependencies*

This query returns for each specification a set of specifications which import the given specification. The structure of the result is:

DEF Importations-struct
       {Spec-name-imp: string,
        Imported-by-set: {Spec-name: string} }

To obtain the desired result we define two temporal structures *Test* and *Temp* :

DEF Test : {Spec-name-test: string }

DEF Temp: {Spec-name-temp: string,
        Imported-by-set-temp: {Spec-name: string}}

Test contains all specification names:

Test <-- PJ [Spec-name] Specifications

Temp retrieves from the initial specifications set the specification names and import sets:

Temp <-- PJ [Spec-name, Imports] Specifications

We have:

Importations-struct <--
      NEST [Imported-by-set: {Spec-name-temp}]
      PJ [Spec-name-test, Spec-name-temp]
      JN [MEMBER (Spec-name-test; Imported-by-set-temp)]
      Test Temp

The join operator selects all the specification names which appear in the importation set of another specification. Than we project by the specification names and finally we nest to group all specifications which import a give one.

6. Conclusions

We have outlined the design of a catalog of software components based on algebraic specifications using the ALGRES system. The implementation of the queries took a few sessions and confirmed the utility of ALGRES as a rapid prototyping tool. The next step is the development of a user-friendly implementation of the catalog using ALICE- the C language interface to ALGRES.

A more detailed description of the kind of queries which are possible to ask for the data stored in the catalog is reported in [OPZ90] .

Acknowledgments

This work has been sponsored by CNR (Italy) and CONACyT (Mexico) under a joint national research contract. The authors wish to thank all members of the ALGRES project, and in particular Filippo Cacace, Luigi Lavazza, and Gianfranco Lamperti. We also thank Armando Hernandénz Solis for the implementation of the catalog.

References

[BG 81] Burstall R. M., and J. A. Goguen, "An Informal Introduction to Specifications Using CLEAR", in "The Correctness Problem in Computer Science", (R.S. Boyer and J. Stothers Moore eds.), Academic Press, pp. 185-213, 1981.

[BHK 87] Bergstra J.A., J. Heering, and P. Klint, "ASF - An Algebraic Specification Formalism", Center for Mathematics and Computer Science, Amsterdam, Report CS-R8705, 1987.

[Cac* 89] Cacace F. et al., "ALGRES: and Extended Relational Database System for the Specification and Prototyping of Complex Applications", in Proc. CASE 89, Kista, Sweden, May 1989.

[Ceri* 88] Ceri S., Crespi-Reghizzi, G. Gottlob, G. Lamperti, L.Lavazza, L.Tanca, R. Zicari,"The ALGRES Project", in Proc. EDBT 88, Lectures Notes in Computer Science No. 303, Springer-Verlag, Venice, 1988.

[Ceri* 88a] Ceri S., Crespi-Reghizzi, G. Lamperti, L. Lavazza, R. Zicari, "ALGRES: An Advanced Database System for Complex Applications", IEEE Software, July 1990 (to appear).

[Okt 89] Oktaba H., "Tipos de datos abstractos y estruturas de datos", Lecture Notes in Spanish, IIMAS-UNAM, 1989.

[OPZ 90] Oktaba H. , C. Perez de Celis, R. Zicari, "ALGRES prototype of reusable software modules based on algebraic specifications", IIMAS report, 1990.

A DATABASE OF SOFTWARE COMPONENTS:
An Algebraic Structure and Its Implementation

Noureddine Boudriga and Ali Mili

Department of Informatics, Faculty of Sciences
1002 Belvedere Tunisia

Abstract

Software development will remain something
of a handcraft as long as each new program
is developed from scratch, without using
existing software components. On the
other hand, software components present
such a diversity of functional properties
that the problem of storing them and
retrieving them is very difficult. In
this paper we propose a structure for a
data base of software components, and
discuss how this structure addresses some
of the issues pertaining to the storage
and retrieval of software components.

1. INTRODUCTION: A SOFTWARE DATABASE

Introduction. Despite several decades of
research, the production of software under
acceptable conditions of predictability
and speed, and with acceptable degrees of
reliability and quality, remains an
unsurmountable problem [Wegner, 1984]. A
brief analysis of the issues, and a
comparison with other industries, leads to
a single most important factor: our
inability to reuse existing software
components in the design of software
products; most generally, each software
product is built from the ground up
[Mittermeir, 1983; Mittermeir and Oppitz,
1987; Mittermeir and Rossak, 1987;
Mittermeir, 1988].

The key to solving this problem is to
design a database of software components
from which the designer can tap components
which he combines together to derive his
solution.

Requirements for a Software Database. In
traditional databases, two features define
the storage structure: the *key*, which
serves to identify individual components;
the *ordering relation* among keys, which
facilitates retrieval of components in the
database. We discuss the requirements
that a software database must meet, so as
to derive from them, in the next section,
a proposal for the structure of a software
database. For the sake of separation of
concerns, we will present requirements
pertaining to the external behaviour of
the database, and will not, until the next
section, discuss internal details of the
database.

The first requirement that comes to
mind is that when one wishes to retrieve
an element, one produces a *program
specification* as parameter, and seeks to
find all the programs in the database that
are correct with respect to this
specification. Indeed it is rather
unnatural to be seeking a program that
computes precisely a given function; it is
more natural (not to mention more
effective) to seek a program that is
correct with respect to a particular
specification.

The second requirement is that
storage into the database is performed
with a program specification as a
parameter, in addition to the mere program
text. This allows in particular that
different versions of the same program
(e.g. a selection sort, insertion sort,
quicksort) are all stored together, and
are retrieved together (either all of them
are returned for a *retrieve* operation, or
none of them is).

Other requirements include the traditional properties one expects from any repository of data, such as: the ability to retrieve previously stored components; the commutativity of store operations (the state of the database does not depend on the order in which components are inserted); the idempotence of store operations (two stores of a given element are as good as one).

2. STRUCTURE FOR A SOFTWARE DATABASE

With the above requirements in mind, we now discuss our proposed structure for a database of software components; then we discuss the operations that are defined on this structure.

We have pointed out earlier that the two key decisions in the design of any database are: the choice of the key, and the choice of ordering relation among keys. Extending these premises to *software* databases, we discuss these two questions in turn, below.

The Key. In the previous section, we have found that store operations on a software database are best defined in terms of the aggregate made up of a specification and a program (as parameters), and that retrieve operations on such a database are best defined in terms of program specifications (as parameters). In order to cater for these two requirements, we have found it useful to define a component of the database in terms of a compound key:

<specification, program>,

where the program which is given in the second argument is correct with respect to the specification given in the first argument.

Also, following our previous work on program specification and program analysis [Mili et al, 1986; Boudriga et al, 1987; Mili et al, 1989], we have chosen to represent program specifications by means of binary relations. Hence if we let S be the space defined by the following Pascal-like declarations

    a: array [1..n] of real;
    i: 1..n+1;

then an example of component of this database is defined by the following entry:

<SORT, selectionsort>,

where *SORT* is the binary relation defined on S by

$$SORT = \{(s,s')| \quad perm(a(s),a(s')) \wedge sorted(a(s'))\},$$

and *selectionsort* is a Pascal program performing a selection sort on real arrays of size n.

The Ordering Relation Among Keys. The ordering relation is required, to organize the database in such a way that individual entries of the database can be indexed and retrieved efficiently when they are needed. The first decision we have taken in this regard is that the ordering relation involves the *specification* component of the key, and does not involve the *program* component. The idea behind this decision is that the database is structured in two layers, which correspond to two levels of abstraction. The *specification* layer is a device for classifying software components by a criterion of functional proximity: We wish that the programs that are correct with respect to a single specification of the database (and are presumably functionally similar) be clustered together around the specification. On the other hand, the requirements for *search* and *retrieve* operations on the database impose on us to define an ordering relation among these specifications.

Second, we have decided to use the following ordering relation, which we have found to be quite meaningful for our purposes [Mili et al, 1986; Boudriga et al, 1989]. Relation R is said to be *more-defined* than R' if and only if:

dom(R')⊆dom(R),

∀s∈dom(R'), s.R⊆s.R',

where s.R is the set of images of element s by relation R. Intuitively, R is more-defined than R' if and only if R carries more input output information than R'. As an illustrative example, we consider relations R and R' defined below:

    R = {(a,b),(b,c),(c,d),(d,e)}
    R'= {(a,b),(a,c),(a,d),
        (b,c),(b,d),(b,e)}

on space S = {a,b,c,d,e}. The reader can check that R is more-defined than R';

164

there are two intuitive reasons why one should consider that R carries more input output information than R'. The first is that R has a larger domain, hence knows about more inputs; the second is that for those inputs about which both relations know (i.e. {a,b}), relation R is more precise in its assignment of outputs than relation R'.

We have studied the structure that this ordering confers the set of specifications, and have found it to be a lattice (we assume the reader familiar with this notion [Liu, 1977]). Further, this lattice has a universal upper bound, namely the *miracle specification* (name due to [Morgan et al, 1988]) which no program can satisfy, and a universal lower bound, namely the *trivial specification* which any program can satisfy [Boudriga et al, 1990].

For the sake of illustration, we present below an example of a software database, and highlight the structuring defined on this database by the *more-defined* relation.

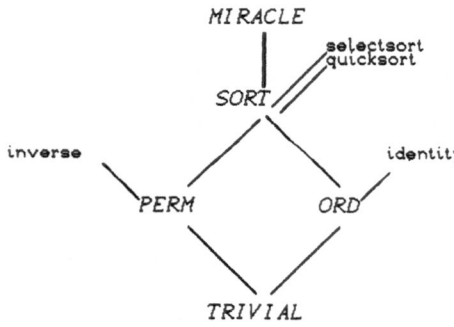

In this graph, specifications are represented in capital letters, while programs are represented in lower case letters, in small print. The links between specifications are oriented downwards; R is linked to R' if and only if R is more-defined than R'. A program is attached to a specification if it is correct with respect to that specification. It is a property of the relation *more-defined* that if p is correct with respect to R and R is more-defined than R' then p is correct with respect to R'. In our representation, each program

is attached to the *most-defined* specification with respect to which it is correct.

This graph represents the following set of entries:

<TRIVIAL,identity>,<TRIVIAL,inverse>, <TRIVIAL,selectsort>,<TRIVIAL,quicksort>,

<ORD,identity>,<ORD,selectsort>, <ORD,quicksort>,

<PERM,iverse>,<PERM,selectsort>, <PERM,quicksort>,

<SORT,selectsort>,   <SORT,quicksort>,

where *inverse* describes a program that returns the inverse of the given array, and *identity* describes a program that, in cell [i] of the array places i.

3. OPERATIONS ON THE DATABASE

Given the above structure, we show how *store* and *retrieve* operations can be carried out on this database.

Retrieve Operation. The problem that we address in this section is the following: *Given a specification R, find all the programs of the database that are correct with respect to R.*

In order to achieve this goal, we proceed in two steps: First, we find all the entries of the database whose *specification* field is more-defined than R. Second, we retrieve all the programs attached to these specifications.

Had our database been organized as a linear table of entries, the above description would have been sufficient as an indication of the algorithm that we must follow: we scan the whole database looking at the *specification* field and identifying those specifications that are more-defined than our retrieve key. We return all the programs that are in the *program* fields of the selected entries. Because our database is not arranged as a linear table but rather as a partial ordering graph, the retrieve algorithm is slightly more complex in that it handles a partial ordering.

As an illustrative example, we consider the database D given in the previous section, and show the result of submitting the query

$$retrieve(PM,D),$$

where specification PM is defined as

$$\{(s,s')|\ perm(a(s),a(s'))\ \wedge$$
$$\forall k:\ 1\le k\le n-1:\ a(s')[k]\le a(s')[n]\}.$$

The set of specifications of D that are more-defined than PM is: {SORT, MIRACLE}. Programs *selectsort* and *quicksort* are attached to specification *SORT* and no programs are attached to *MIRACLE*. The procedure retrieve returns the set {selectsort, quicksort}; both selectsort and quicksort correct with respect to *PM*, and they are the only two correct (with respect to PM) programs in the whole database.

Store Operation. The problem that we address in this section is the following: *we wish to store in the database an entry of the form <specification, program>.*

In order to store a database entry, say <R,p>, we proceed as follows:
- We identify the set, say $\mathcal{M}$, of all the specifications of D that are immediately more-defined than R; and the set, say m, of those that are immediately less-defined than R.
- We delete all the links between $\mathcal{M}$ and m, and link R below all the elements of $\mathcal{M}$, and above all the elements of m.
- If some element of m has attached to it a program that is correct with respect to R, then this program is attached to R and deleted from its original position.
- We identify the set, say μ, of all the specifications in D that are more-defined than R, and for which p is correct. Program p must be attached to all the maximal elements of set μ.

As an illustrative example, we show what becomes of the database given in the previous section when we submit the update

$$store(D,<MP,mp>),$$

where mp is a program that swaps the maximal element of array a with a[10]. We leave it to the reader to check that pm is correct with respect to *PM*.

We leave it to the reader to double check that execution of the update yields the following steps:

$$\mathcal{M} = \{SORT\}$$
$$m = \{PERM\}$$
link (PERM,SORT) is deleted
links (PERM,PM) and (PM,SORT) are
                          created
program *inverse* is attached to
                  specification *PM*
$$\mu = \{\},\ \text{and } pm \text{ remains attached to } PM$$

This yields the following database

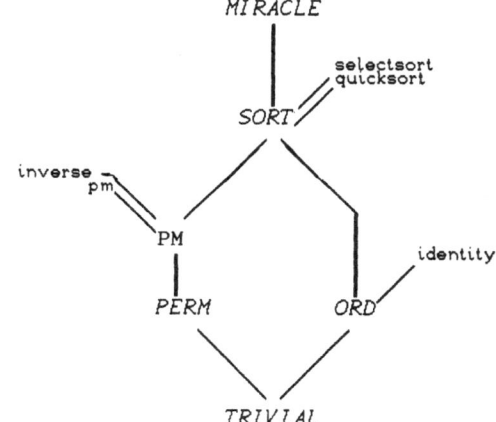

The set of entries that have been added by this store operations the following.

    <TRIVIAL,pm>
    <PERM,pm>
    <PM,pm>,<PM,inverse>
    <PM,quicksort>,<PM,selectsort>.

It is left to the reader to check that all these represent pairs whose second component (program) is correct with respect to their first component (specification).

4. CONCLUSION

In this paper, we have presented a formalism for the structure and the operation of a database of software components. The purpose of this database is to serve as a repository of software components, from which designers can tap to construct a software product from existing components.

This database is characterized by the following features: its *key*, which is the aggregate of a program specification and a program text; its *ordering relation*, which ranks relations by how much input/output information they carry; its *store* and *retrieve* operations, which are based on the lattice structure that this ordering gives our set of software component descriptions.

This database is currently being built at the University of Tunis, in cooperation with the University of Klagenfurt, with a sample of small programs and specifications, along the proposal outlined in [Ben Cherfia et al, 1989]. Experimentation with simple queries is currently under way.

Acknowledgement

The work presented here is a byproduct of a joint research project that is currently in progress between the University of Tunis, Tunisia, and the University of Klagenfurt, Austria. The authors whish to acknowledge the participation of Professor R.T. Mittermeir in the progress of this work.

5. BIBLIOGRAPHY

[Ben Cherfia et al, 89]: Ben Cherifa, A., N. Boudriga, A. Mili, R.T. Mittermeir, and W. Rossak. *A Formal Specification Structure for Software Reuse.* Submitted, 1989.

[Boudriga et al, 89]: Boudriga, N., A. Mili, F. Mili. *Towards Structured Specifying.* Chichester, UK: Ellis Horwood Ltd, 1989.

[Boudriga et al, 90]: Boudriga, N., F. Elloumi and A. Mili. *On the Lattice of Specifications.* Submitted, 1990.

[Liu, 77]: Liu, C.L. *Elements of Discrete Mathematics.* New York, NY: McGraw Hill, 1977.

[Mili et al, 86]: Mili, A., X-Y Wang, and Q Yu. Specification Methodology: An Integrated Relational Approach. *Software-Practice and Experience.* 16(11), november 1986, pp 1003-1030.

[Mili et al, 87]: Mili, A., J. Desharnais, F. Mili. Relational Heuristics for the Construction of Deterministic Programs. *Acta Informatica.* July 1987.

[Mittermeir, 83]: Mittermeir, R.T. Software Base for Adaptive Maintenance of Complex Software Systems. *Proceedings, 7th International ADV Congress.* Vienna, 1983.

[Mittermeir and Oppitz, 87]: Mittermeir, R.T. and M. Oppitz. Software Base for the Flexible Composition of Application Systems. *IEEE Transactions on Software Engineering.* Vol SE-13(4), April 1987, pp440-460.

[Mittermeir and Rossak, 87]: Mittermeir R.T. and W. Rossak. Software Bases and Software Archives- Alternatives to support Software Reuse. *Proceedings of the Fall Joint Computer Conference.* Dallas, USA, October 1987.

[Mittermeir, 88]: Mittermeir, R.T. "Specification Aspects for Software Reuse". First Algerian Conference on Software Engineering. Oran, Algeria, October 1988.

[Mittermeir and Rossak, 89]: Mittermeir, R.T and W. Rossak. *Reusability.* In: *Handbook of Computer Aided Software Engineering.* Ng, P.A. and R.T. Yeh, editors. Van Nostrand, 1989.

[Morgan, 88]: Morgan, C., K. Robinson, P. Gardiner. *On The Refinement Calculus.* Oxford University Computing Laboratory. Technical report PRG-70. October 1988.

[Wegner, 84]: Wegner, P. Capital Intensive Software Technology. *IEEE- Software.* Vol 1(3), July 1984, pp 7-45.

Legal knowledge elicitation: from textual databases to expert systems

Claude Thomasset,
François Blanchard

et Louis-Claude Paquin

Groupe de Rercherche en Informatique et Droit (GRID)
Université du Québec à Montréal

Centre d'Analyse de Textes par Ordinateur (ATO)
Université du Québec à Montréal

Summary

In this paper we intend to present the problems we encounter due to the textual nature of the knowledge in building an expert system for legal advice on Québec Housing Law. During the knowledge engineering process, we propose to take into consideration both the very textual aspects (morphology, syntax, discursive specificity e.g. legal) of the material and the reader's expertise, for instance, the jurist. Some simple methodological steps of textual data analyses by computer could help us solve the problem of satisfactory knowledge elicitation.

INTRODUCTION

The aims of the LOGE-EXPERT[1] project are twofold: first, to build a prototype of an Expert System on Québec Housing Law oriented towards non-expert users and second, to produce an ongoing evaluation of the effects of legal knowledge computerization on the legal system and on the users of legal services. This paper presents the latest state of the project's first aspect. After two versions of a micro-prototype to familiarize ourselves with both expert system technology and legal knowledge engineering[1] , we are working on an extensive prototype. We have recently settled upon the general design of the man-machine communications[2]. We now address the problems related to the legal text analyses and its knowledge elicitation.

In LOGE-EXPERT, we intend to feed the legal knowledge base with a data base of tribunal decisions. That data base should intervene at different stages in building the knowledge base. At the input stage, the data base will help its authors to validate rules according to decisions given by tribunals specialized in Housing Law. At the output stage, it will illustrate situations corresponding to the user's requests, by selecting pertinent decisions from those included in the tribunal decisions data base. Meanwhile, it will fulfill two other functions. It should keep the LOGE-EXPERT knowledge base constantly updated with information taken from the data base, in two ways: by adding new information to provide most recent decisions on matters included in the knowledge base; by inducing structural changes in the knowledge base, justified by substantial changes occurring in the way in which new tribunal decisions consider our specific legal field.

The process of knowledge elicitation in building an expert system is well documented for expertise which is technical in nature. This is far less the case for managerial expertise because the main source of knowledge lies in texts. This is not so at the technical level because during an interview, the technician gives information and direction which are of greater assistance than the general descriptions of the related texts. Generally speaking, management is to be carried out from a written policy. If this policy is complex, it comes with explanatory documents. When it is governmental management of law, the scope of the textual corpus is broad: law, regulations, decrees, tribunal decisions, etc. In our case, Québec Housing Law is to be read in light of the decisions, specially to figure out the proper acceptation of the law's terms.

Our contribution aims at knowledge eliciation from textual material. The initial form of the knowledge consists of words, the last being reconstructed out of context in the form of concepts and inference rules. Unfortunately, data does not arrive in neat little pre-delimited zones and fields ; in our case it comes as a huge mass of texts. In this paper we examine the following aspects related to the very textual nature of the pertinent material available for knowledge elicitation.
— What is specific to a text? to a legal text ?
— How to efficiently access the texts?
— Reading as an act of knowledge elicitation.
— How can computer-assisted textual analyses help knowledge elicitation?
The scope of the answers we propose to each of these points is related to our pragmatic task: to efficiently build a legal expert system.

What is specific to a text?

A text is both inflexible and unsettled: the text is an entanglement of systems that could take several forms. We only find in it what has been written: words and punctuation. A minimal definition of a text could be the following: an ordered set of segments written in a natural language recorded on a material (paper or magnetic). A more substantial definition of a text should include and present as such the set of linguistic systems, namely: the voicing system (phonological); the outside world referential system (lexical); the internal structure and forms system (morphological) and the system of the organization and relationship of words within groups, phrases, clauses and sentence. The higher levels of the linguistic model are less defined. For instance, the semantic level is conceived as a kind of calculus on the lexical properties of the words and/or their morpho-syntactic position in the segment. It is important to note that the gradual complexity is merely for didactic presentation. Under real life conditions, we have to deal with the inevitable entanglement of all the systems. For example, it is virtually impossible to automatically select between two or more potentially contradictory surface categorizations without a thorough description of the text's deep structure.

1 This project, which has been running since January 1987, received a grant from the Canadian Donner Foundation. See [1]

After more than 30 years of research in the field of automatic natural language processors, J. Sowa, a IBM System Research team member, stated that:

> "... the successes of language processors on small domains and their failure on unrestricted domains result from the fundamental nature of language. In particular, a large grammar and dictionary are not sufficient to scale up a small system to an unrestricted natural language processor"[3].

Problems arise when those systemic descriptions intersect at higher or at other levels of description which we called textual. Among the descriptions of proper textual systems, there are the figure of speech, the network of argumentation, the communicational environment, etc. Furthermore, not only must the reader possess a minimal knowledge of the particular universe of the text, but he must also be familiar with the social conventions from which the text emerged. This dimension of the text requires a decoding beyond its linguistic structures.

A text is both inflexible and unsettled. Its life is unpredictable: it may be destroyed; it may be duplicated; it may be quoted in another text with or without indication. This evanescent trajectory is called interdiscursivity and should be taken into account. There are several forms of text depending on its aim: report, study, directive, free-text answers to opinion pool, interview retranscription, etc. In the legal domain, texts have characteristics of their own.

What is specific to a legal text?

We should be aware of some characteristics of the legal texts, characteristics that have already been pointed out by different authors. For instance, both theorist (computer scientists or logicians who tackled the field of law as a means of testing their research program) and practicing lawyers who have tried to develop a "machine-like" understanding of legal texts came across several difficulties.

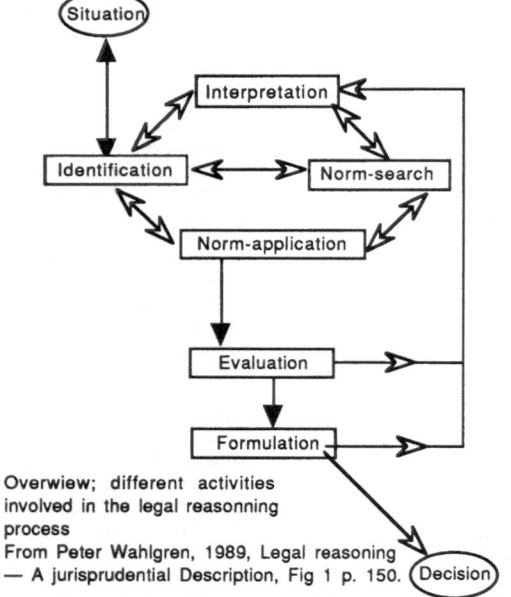

Overwiew; different activities involved in the legal reasonning process
From Peter Wahlgren, 1989, Legal reasoning — A jurisprudential Description, Fig 1 p. 150.

For those dealing with statutes, it became apparent that: "the structure of the text of the statute is no longer irrelevant but dictates the nature of the formalization"[4] and that the "definition of a concept" may have been distributed "across a number of fragments". Still others[5], have tried to describe the interactive play involved in the legal reasoning process.

This scheme (see the illustration in the previous column), which could perhaps be translated into a set of rules (with some of them expressly recursive), well illustrate the complexity of the process in which a legal text is interpreted and/or produced. But most authors, in trying to describe legal texts as a by-product of reason, subscribing to Toulmin[6] interpretation for example, seem to forget that texts are "artifacts" which exist independently of the individual reason which gave rise to them. On the other hand, there is an existing categorization of legal texts: a legal hierarchy.

Legal texts may be classified according to a hierarchy of norms in a written legal system such as the Québec's legal system. After the **Constitution**, which is the founding legal document, **Laws**, as documents issued by legislative bodies, are considered as the supreme norms. Then come **regulations** adopted by executive agencies, to give effect to laws. **Courts and Tribunals decisions** apply laws and regulations to specific situations, when litigation occurs. Some of these decisions are published and could become cases to be used as **precedents** for other decisions. To illustrate that hierarchy in legal texts, we have chosen excerpts from article 1659 of the Québec Civil code relating to repossession of premises for the benefit of landlords[1]. As we have selected an article of the Québec Civil code that usually does not require regulations for its implementation, we cannot find a corresponding regulation in the field of repossession. For example, no regulation exists which gives a definition to the legal concept "landlord". We must then examine tribunal decisions and legal doctrine to assess all the meanings this concept could carry in the field of landlord and tenant relationships; nevertheless, we have selected section 3 of a regulation related to obligatory dispositions of a residential lease, adopted to implement the *Law creating the Québec Rental Board* (la Régie du logement) *and amending the Civil code*,[2] to illustrate the way in which that kind of legal text intervenes in the hierarchy of legal norms. We have completed these legal texts with two types of Tribunal decisions: one from the Québec rental board[3] which has been published and its confirmation [4] by the appellate Tribunal.

How to access the texts efficiently ?

The information is always abundant; to access specific information, one must go through a huge mass of non-pertinent information. We only can assimilate a small proportion of the available relevant information. Management of the information requires a computerized information system and a hierarchy of administrative structures. The first computerized information systems were bibliographical: access to the document was not by way of its content but of its localization in a library shelf. The textual information systems are more recent. Skimming to obtain information is a time-consuming essential operation. Information retrieval researches are oriented towards the improvement of two measurements: recall rate and precision rate. The recall rate is the percentage of the relevant documents found as against the total number of relevant documents. The precision rate is the percentage of the relevant documents found as against the total number of documents found.

Every textual information system has its own (specialized) data structure and associate query language that one has to learn before getting access to the information. A format (rows, columns, fields or zones) or an index made in advance cannot foresee all the users'requests. This is especially so in the interactive, free-association and browsing process of reading with the help of the computer. Apart from the two rates, a textual information system should take input data in loosely structured formats (ad hoc protocol); it should allow easy, interactive free-association and browsing (hypertext, RDBMS). Lastly, it should not demand too much work to get data into the system.

There are however databases which are specialized in text handling; indeed, lawyers already know them. They exist as "on-line" services accessed by phone via a modem. They are Lexis or Westlaw in the USA and Quicklaw or Soquij in Québec. As such, they do require the users to learn of new skills. Each possesses its own query language and they are thereby almost incompatible. For example compare " *s locateur /5 usufruitier & possession*" from QUICKSEARCH (from Quicklaw) to "*..repere locateur avec usufruitier*" from SOQUIJ. But there are more limitations: they are only available through a communication process that cannot be easily built in an expert system without taxing the skills or the patience of the users.

One should dispose of a modem, a phone line, a communication program with a user-friendly interface. One should expect delays from datapac and the server for a sign-on procedure. Finally one should be ready to pay, because these on-line databases charge on a connect-time basis for their consultation. Their existence does point out that it is possible to transform legal text into factual data by the process of indexing [for instance Soquij in Montréal utilizes the software STAIRS (©IBM) for that purpose; Sonar for the Mac can almost do the same for a micro]. The result of this process permits the end user to ask for the occurrence(s) or the co-occurrence(s) of word(s) that are linked (more or less obviously) to the topic of his inquiry. This type of interaction with the data takes at least a couple of hours for a law student to master. At the beginning, the questions which spring to mind must be translated into a query language, which is simple but unforgiving in the amount of debris it can accumulate, and the search has to focus on the occurrences of words, not notions or concepts. In a sense, then, they are simply "too good a tool" to be built in: they are far too general and cumbersome not to intimidate the end user.

In order to accomplish all the tasks the tribunal decisions data base should fulfill in relation to the LOGE-EXPERT knowledge base, we could not limit the dimensions of the decisions to summaries and key-words. We need the full texts of the tribunal decisions. The necessary selective content access is not only with regard to patterns of words but also conceptual patterns. The main problem with conceptual patterns is that an indexation is needed. Indexing is intended as the transformation of prominent terms from a text into factual data. This tagging process was, until recently, performed by human readers. It is now done by computer in a rough way but at a relatively low (software and a personal computer) cost and at high speed when the texts are already machine-readable. This indexation, called "key word in context" (KWIC) could be selective when the KWIC is the result of an elaborate pattern matching of word chains. The criterion for the match should also be structural. This could be seen in two ways: the first is linguistic in that "we need a full structural description as deep as possible (at any cost?)"; the second is more pragmatic, in the sense that the text is not by itself an object of study.

Our textual database was primarily aimed at collecting all the decisions of an administrative body, " La Régie du Logement", and all decisions of superiors court pertaining to those decisions. "La Régie du Logement" does publish some of those decisions, about 150 per year (which represent less then 1/100 of the decisions that, for the most part, [rent determination] are fairly short and "automatic"). Since we are as yet unable to pick up decisions at the source as text file from a word processor, we opted for a mechanical transcription instead, by means of optical character recognition of only a small part of the decisions: those relative to "retaking of possession" as the index of the published decisions defines them, about 17 for 1988 for instance. After their transformation into a text file, we subject them to an orthographical revision (for , and ') and save them in two distinct formats: -one that we can manipulate [like inserting TAB to imported them into a database] and -one that preserves the formal appearance of the decision so that a consultation could produce an on-screen facsimile of the retrieved decision(s). The corpus is, at first, quite small but will certainly increase as we expand our coverage in time and in the domain of the law.

Reading as an act of knowledge elicitation

We have seen that knowledge does not lay at the text's surface. The only way to overcome the lack of certainty concerning the meaning of a text and still use the computer is to include the reader into the model of the meaning construction process. This intuition is confirmed by the most recent psychological and sociological theories stating that a univocal meaning is not set down in the text but is constructed by the reader through his cognitive structures and his socialization. But reading alone proves to be an inconsistent knowledge elicitation device at the low level of recognition; we need the regularity of the computer in complex pattern-matching situations to assist the reader to make a better judgmental choice. Gathering informations is what humans do worst, although making inferences and making decisions on uncertain facts are what humans do best. In this perspective the computer accumulates every context needed by the expert-reader to construct a meaning by correlating information gathered from throughout the corpus. This model is attractive because it includes the implicit possibility of a partial integration of the reading "expertise" (with the knowledge engineering inquiry techniques?).

According to J. Wroblewski, legal language comes from natural language[7] and adds to it specialized words and specific meanings corresponding to the legal nature of that discourse. Even if some researchers have attempted to establish that a legal grammar specific to legal language could be elaborated, for the purpose of this paper, we adopt the proposition of J. Wroblewski. The difference between natural language and legal language is not syntactic but semantic, and depends on the words as well as their specific meanings[7]. He distinguishes legal language, the language of legislative bodies, from meta-legal discourse, among which he classifies the discourse of Courts and tribunals, the discourse of legal authors (doctrine and jurisprudence), and the common legal discourse used by lawyers in their oral arguments in Courts or by the general population when they talk about law. The legal documents we use in the LOGE-EXPERT knowledge base, belong to all these kinds of legal language and discourse. The tribunal decisions data base, on the other hand, is devoted only to tribunal decisions which are expressed in a meta-legal discourse, the language in which the law is applied to specific situations by judges.

If we analyze the way a legal expert usually reads each kind of these legal documents, we may establish patterns of reading operating in order to catch all their possible meanings. These patterns of reading could be illustrated by successive readings of a legal document, each reading adding a new level of understanding and deciphering the specific meaning of legal concepts it includes. Depending on the legal expert's skill, these levels of reading could be accomplished in one or several reading experiments. The **first level** of reading is a common sense reading, or syntagmatic reading, that is, we read it as if it were expressed in natural language. A **second level** of reading or paradigmatic reading, implies that we focus on words as legal concepts. The **third level** of reading will be done to compare the legal document to a specific situation. The **fourth level** of reading will try to give meanings to the legal document, in order to apply it to a specific situation by interpreting it according to ad hoc methodology in use in the legal universe. A fifth level of reading could be reached when we want to analyze the symbolic dimensions of the legal document. We have tested this pattern with our samples of previously selected legal documents.

Article 1659 of Québec Code civil:

Le locateur d'un logement peut en reprendre possession pour s'y loger ou pour y loger ses ascendants ou descendants, son gendre, sa bru, son beau-père, sa belle-mère, son beau-fils, sa belle-fille, ou tout autre parent dont il est le principal soutien.

Le locateur d'un logement   peut
    en reprendre possession   pour s'y loger
                ou   y loger
         ses ascendants
            ou
         descendants
         son gendre, sa bru, son beau-père, sa belle-mère, son beau-fils,sa belle-fille
            ou
         tout autre parent
         dont il est le principal soutien.

At the **first reading level** (syntagmatic), we scrutinize the meanings of the words in the context: At the **second reading level** (paradigmatic) we focus on legal concepts, such as: *locateur, ascendant, descendant, parent, principal soutien, logement*. To better understand the meanings of these legal concepts, we have to get outside the document in order to perceive other possible meanings in co-texts. At that stage, the legal expert reader looks for indications in other parts of the legal document (law or regulation), or in other decisions or cases (the legal cases discourse according to J. Wroblewsky classification) as well as in legal doctrinal works (designated by J. Wroblewsky as scientific legal discourse). We carried out that search to obtain all the meanings of the legal concept *locateur*, and we could duplicate it for all the other legal concepts identified in that segment of section 1659 of Québec Civil code. The next step is the **third reading level** or the "analyse de correspondances", which usually involves applying the legal document as it is understood after the second reading and enriched with the search of meanings, to a specific situation. At that stage, the legal expert usually qualifies facts and makes hypotheses about the applicability of that legal document. When necessary, a **fourth reading level** could be done, in order to give effect to legal concepts in the specific situation under consideration. At that stage, a legal expert reader will focus then on general legal principals such as "the legislator 's will" or "the general meaning of the law", in order to enlarge the legal concept meanings obtained from the precedent searches. Usually, for the implementation of that segment of article 1659 of Québec Civil code, the legal expert will invoke the property rights of the landlord and its components like "usus", "abusus", and "fructus", or the tenant's right to stay in the dwelling according to article 1657 of the same Code. At that stage we are very near to the next level of reading. A **fifth reading level** is still possible, in order to identify the symbolic dimensions of a legal documents. This step is occasionally done when the legal expert wants to give effect to general assertions included in segments of that text. But for the purposes of the analyses of article 1659, it is not necessary to expand the level of reading to that stage.

Article 3 (Règlement sur les mentions obligatoires du bail, de l'écrit et de certains avis prévus au Code civil, **R.R.Q. R-8.1, r.2)**

Le bail, s'il est écrit, doit contenir la désignation du logement, le montant du loyer, et la date du début et de la fin du bail, s'il est à durée fixe.

le bail   s'il est écrit
    doit
       contenir
           la désignation du logement
           le montant du loyer
               et
        la date   du début
               et   de la fin
du bail
           s'il est à durée fixe

This is the segmentation done at the **syntagmatic level** and there are the selected legal concepts at the **paradigmatic level**: *bail, loyer, durée fixe, logement*. At this stage, it is necessary to find the meanings of these legal concepts in the enabling law. For example, we know that in the Québec Civil code, «un bail à durée fixe» implies the opposite concept, «bail à durée indéterminée», and «bail écrit» implies the opposite concept, «bail verbal». If the enabling law cannot help to understand these meanings, we look to new legal sources for further definition. The **third reading** is the same kind of reading as for laws, but instead of applying law, we want to give effect to a regulation in specific situation. Facts are systemized to fit with the regulation and its enabling law. At that stage of the **fourth reading**, it is important to evaluate the suppletive or imperative nature of the regulation and to expose the intention of the executive body which has enacted it or the legislative body which has delegated these powers. Even in regulations, we may find symbolic wordings which could have effect without any means of implementation; this is considered as a **fifth reading**.

Germaine Lalonde-Sarault et al. c. Huguette Masse, Gustave Hébert, régisseur, Régie du logement, Verdun, 34-870115-017-G, le 3 juin 1987. J.L. 88-12
Considérant que le frère de la locatrice, n'est ni locateur, ni propriétaire du logement;

Considérant que « la nue-propriété contient le droit de jouir pour l'époque où s'éteindra l'usufruit actuellement existant», le droit pour les nus-propriétaires indivis de reprendre possession du logement n'est que différé;

Considérant la preuve;

Rejette la demande de la locatrice.

Reprise de possession

This is an excerpt from a published decision. We have selected the final part of the decision because it sums up the legal reasoning of the administrative judge in that specific case. We have introduced the excerpt with key words enumerated for the purpose of editing the decision for publication it in Jurisprudence-Logement, a case reporter under the responsibility of the Québec Rental Board. A legal expert will read a law or a regulation quite differently from a Court or tribunal decision. We may relate this practice to the classification set up by J. Wroblewsky. The former constitute legal language according to that classification while the latter are kins of legal discourse. Nevertheless, we may establish a pattern which has some common elements. The first stage, when a decision is edited for publication, is to read key-words, and abstracts if they exists. They do not in our example. Then a legal expert will go the conclusive part of the decision to look at its ratio. The second stage will depend on the reader's purpose. He could be satisfied with the **first reading** if he only wants to update his knowledge about that legal field. But if he intends to use this decision in an argument for or against that decision, then his next reading will try to analyze the decision in order to give it the meanings he needs to complete his demonstration.

The **second reading** will focus on analyzing the facts of the case, in order to compare them with the specific situation he is confronted with. We may include all the procedural steps to get to the tribunal in the facts. The **third reading** will pay attention to the arguments of each party and to the way the administrative judge receives them. At this stage, the legal reasoning followed by the judge will be thouroughly analyzed. The **fourth reading** will help to evaluate the applicability of the decision to other situations. The legal expert at this stage will depart from the decision and compare the situation under consideration with the situation sanctioned in the decision. The **fifth reading** will be of greatest interest to legal academics who try to analyze the effectiveness of laws and regulations through Courts and Tribunal decisions. At that stage, it is important to analyze the work of the judge in further defining the meanings of legal concepts and giving them consequences. Legal concepts become objects of debate. In our case, we may confront key-words with the conclusions of the administrative judge: we understand that the issue is to know if the lessor (locateur) who is «usufruitière»of the rented premises, is entitled to repossession for the benefit of her brother, who is «nu-propriétaire». The conclusion is "no", because the «nu-propriétaire» does not have the right to use the premises during the lifetime of the «usufruitier». Article 1659 of Québec Civil code could not apply to the situation submitted to the judge.

There has been an appeal from the party against whom the decision was rendered to the appellate tribunal. The latter has confirmed the first level decision. The judgment has also been published.

Germaine Lalonde Sarault et al. c. Huguette Masse, monsieur le juge Jean-Louis Lamoureux, Cour provinciale, Montréal, 500-02-022192-871, le 29 janvier 1988 , J.L. 88-42.

Pour les motifs exprimés dans la décision du régisseur, le Tribunal en vient aux mêmes conclusions que le régisseur.

Le principe énoncé à l'article 1657 du Code civil que le locataire a droit au maintien dans les lieux exige que les articles 136.1 de la Loi sur la Régie du logement et l'article 1659 du Code civil soient interprétés restrictivement.

L'appelant Gaston Lalonde n'est que le nu-propriétaire de l'immeuble. Il n'en a ni «l'usus» ni le «fructus». De plus, il n'est pas le locateur au sens de l'article 1659C.c. C'est Germaine Lalonde Sarault qui est le locateur non seulement apparent mais réel du logement dont on veut reprendre possession. C'est elle qui signe les baux, retire les loyers et voit à l'administration de l'immeuble dont elle a l'usufruit. Ce n'est qu'occasionnellement qu'elle se fait aider par son frère, le co-appelant.

Par ces motifs, le tribunal:
Rejette l'appel sans frais.

The same pattern of reading could be followed to analyze this appellate decision. This decision is worthy of special interest because the appellate judge has set up the right of lessor to the repossession of rented dwellings against the tenant's right to stay in the rented premises. He gives effect to that right in restrictively interpreting the lessor's right, and the legal concept "lessor".

In contrast to a published decision which is edited and is processed with key-words and abstracts, an unpublished decision is a legal document which requires its readers to go through the editing process themselves to get key-words and a summary of the essential features. That means that the reading pattern has to take this processing step into account if we want to simulate the reader's work. The other stages of a legal expert reading pattern are similar in both cases.

How texual analyses assisted by a computer could help knowledge elicitation?

What could a computer do to simulate legal expert reading patterns? We have established two reading patterns, according to the types of legal documents a legal expert faces. If the legal document is a law or regulation, the reading pattern includes the analyses of contexts and co-texts of the written document in order to establish the specific meanings of words expressed in a legal language. If the legal document is a court or tribunal decision, we are confronted with a multi-dimensional analyses of that kind of legal discourse. The reading pattern has to cope with the argumentative nature of a decision, which implies that the judge has expressly stated the reasons which justify his decision. The legal expert usually finds all the references of the judgment reasoning in the decision. He does not have to search for them because the adversarial procedure facilitates the expression of the pro and contra arguments during the proceedings. The judge has to consider them and form his own opinion in order to write his decision. The contexts and co-texts are included in the decision which give it its multi-dimensional size.

For our purpose, which consists of building a data base with tribunal decisions in Housing Law, the computer does not have to proceed through all these stages. We only need the first and second levels of reading in order to identify legal concepts in use in the Housing law domain and common sense words which characterize specific situations. This means that the automated text analyses should be able to identify common sense words and legal concepts. It is not necessary to require a computer to accomplish the other levels of reading of legal texts and discourses. The human legal expert will do it at the input stage and the human legal expert users will intervene at the output stage.

The knowledge we are looking for is to be represented in a well-defined data model such as networks, frames, valuated objects, inference rules, etc. On the other hand, a term always comes included in the near context of a nominal group where it gets specification and determination from other terms or from various qualities. Between these two poles is the human expert reading. The relative slowness of the human process and the potential lack of attention make the computer's assistance desirable. Textual analyses with both its linguistic and discursive sides offers a suitable theoretical framework. Our aim is not the exhaustive description of all the textual systems, but the dissociation of the information from it's enunciation conditions. Because the highly structured approach are generally static, we favour the gathering of analyses procedures from various, sometimes opposite, point of views. But the scope of these procedures should be cautiously tuned to methodological principles.

The control of these analyses should not be left to the automatic processes. By taking the exclusive point of view of the author's (legislator for instance) intentions, the analyses will be normative. To avoid this bias, the reader must have control over the sequence and the modulation of textual manipulations and mesurements. Prior to any analyses, the reader must have formalize a hypothetical model of its corpus. The model should cover both formal and content aspects. A description in terms of break and consistency in front of the natural language should be made. Every significant difference at any systems should be taken down and investigated. From this model, the parsing focus and needed adaptations together with the "grain" of the pattern matching will show up. The reader should have the proper cognitive structure in order to match statements to events happening to "real word" objects. The model will help 1) formalize the problem's space; 2) evaluate the better computational approach to produce the needed description at the suited depth; 3) fix boundaries to the corpus, witch texts fit in and why those and not others? 4) determine the best description needed by both the model and the aims of the project, knowledge elicitation for instance.

The textual description is made in terms of groups, properties and relations. The more static element is the lexicon; its categorization out of context could be made automatically. If one want to search for surface structures, a morphological description is a minimum. The resulting informations should be tied to the lexical form; the valuated object seem to be the more adequate representation: beside the morphological one, a slot must be devoted to every aspects the analyses project is monitoring. This slot is to be filled when someting significant is observed or inherited from observation at other levels. Looking for reference of concepts, the nominal group interests us. Its variations are many but most of them are localized in a small word set. A surface pattern with masks and informed by a projected morphological description would seem sufficiant to give interesting results. In a computational framework, the conceptual indexation could be replace by nets of associated concepts; one node of the net being tagged with the concept name. The numerical co-occurrence of two words in the same limited context represent a statistical validation of their expressed relationships within the text. The KWIC search with annotation facilities represent an alternative way to interact with textual data: to sort and search in a multi-dimensions (proprieties) space.

On a text whose words have been morphologically categorized, vocabulary control could be peformed: 1) tie the words forming idiomatic expressions to track terminological phrases from the co-occurrence of categories, e.g. *traitement de textes* {[noun] preposition [noun]}; 2) reduce the different surface forms of the words to their dictionary entry (beside the verbs, in french each adjectives takes four different forms and the noun two), this task is called lemmatization; 3) cross-reference the synonymy, one term has to be preferred and the others non-preferred the links have to be validated by experts; 4) reconstitute the incomplete wordings with correct interpolations, substitution of the anaphora (pronom used as substitute); this last operation is up to now out of reach of the algorithmic modelisation, because it rests on jugment.

On a controlled vocabulary, a concept dictionary has to be built. A restriction of the lexicon to the words categorized «noun» is then to be reduced manually by experts in order to keep only those concepts related to the field of expertise. Then a transformation of the terms into concepts is performed. It is an operation of abstraction; a word or a locution is taken out of the context and the contextually relevant information is annotated. It is also an operation of condensation; for each concept, a general model of all the contexts found in the corpus is developed by classification of the dependant terms and adjectives. This model could then be implemented into an index for information retreival; into frames of an expert system, or into nodes of a hypertext. Every nouns validated by domain experts has to be analyzed in terms of configurations (called ingredients) that are associated with these concepts. These configurations are sought out. The search for hierarcherical relations explicitly stated is then made in term of word patterns such as « x has a y», «x is made of y», «x is part of», etc. Adjectival forms found in located contexts reveal quantifiers and argument scales that virtually position other possible qualitative or quantitative value. On the other hand, analyzing verbal groups helps in the inference rule writing process. Indeed, the study of action verbs allows the tracking of object-defined operations. Their inflection and context provide thus modulation (active, passive, necessary, optional, etc.), localization and temporality.

CONCLUSION

Textual analyses seems to be the available best approach to knowledge transfer from texts to expert systems assisted by computer. We advocate the use of computer packages for processing the search of knowledge. Resting on morpho-syntactical structural selective pattern matching, we use the metalanguage inherent to the text itself to single out organized and hierarchized invariants by their recurrence. It meets the criteria of consistency, objectivity, reproductiveness and independence as to the problematics defined in the texts. Furthermore, a methodological approach with general purpose analytical tools, seems to us both more trustworthy and more helpfull than a "black box" application. We believe the main obstacle to a full use of texts in expertise transfer lies in a lack of understanding of the nature of text. The words that compose it do not necessarily refer to realty through concepts, but may serve to recategorize them. Gaps and modification in the referential structure of the text bring the reader to produce several inferences. Finally we believe that expert-readers, jurists, should be included at all the steps of software or methodological developpements.

[1]THOMASSET, C., BLANCHARD, F., HEBERT, R. "L'informatisation du savoir juridique: conception d'un prototype de système expert en droit du logement." in : *Recueil des activités du CIEST*, 1986-1988, publié sous la direction de A. Caron et A.Michaud, Montréal, UQAM, 1988, pp301-314.
THOMASSET, C. "Expert System and Legal Formalization: Evaluation of a prototype in Québec Housing Law". Paper presented at the *International Conference on "Intelligence and Society"*, International Social Science Council, European Coordination Centre for Research and Documentation in Social Sciences, Vienna, March 1988, to be published by Reidel (Netherlands).
THOMASSET, C., " Expert System in Québec Housing Law: from HOME-Expert I to HOME-Expert II", paper presented at the International *Conference on Law and Artificial Intelligence: Expert Systems in Law*. CIRFID, Bologna, May 3-5, 1989, 29p.
[2]THOMASSET, C. PAQUIN L. C. "Expert Systems in Law and the Representation of Legal Knowledge: Can We Isolate It from the Why and the Who?", *Proceedings of the Third International Congress on: Logica, Informatica, Diritto: Legal Experts Systems*, Florence, 1989, Istituto per la documentazione giuridica, vol. 1, pp. 751-771.
[3]SOWA, J. F. "Multi-Domain Semantic Theory" draft given by the author at a Montreal conference dated November 28, 1988. See also: SOWA, J. F."There's More to Logic than the Predicate Calculus" draft given by the author at a Montreal conference dated November 28, 1988.
[4]Routen, Tom. " Hierachically Organised Formalisation." *The Second ICAIL*. Vancouver, BC: ACM, 1989. p. 242-250.
[5]Wahlgren, Peter. " Legal Reasoning A Jurisprudential Description." *The Second ICAIL*. Vancouver, BC: ACM, 1989. p. 147-156.
[6]Toulmin, Stephen. *The Uses of Argument*, C.U.P. 1958.
[7]Wroblewski, Jerzy. "Les langages juridiques: une typologie" *Droit et société Revue internationale de théorie du droit et de sociologie juridique*, No 8, 1988, p.14

Authors' affiliations:
Université du Québec à Montréal
Case postale 8888, succursale "A"
Montréal (Québec) H3C 3P8

Computer-aided Research and Teaching of Roman Law:
A Database of Justinianean Sources

Giancarlo Taddei Elmi

Istituto per la documentazione giuridica of the Italian National Research Council - Florence and the Catholic University (Italy)

Summary:

1. The Research Project 2. The Database 3. The Documentary Unit 4. Searching the Database 5. Retrieval by Sources 6. Bibliographical-Linguistic Retrieval.

1. THE RESEARCH PROJECT

Romanists in this century, up until World War II, have engaged in the research of a classical Roman law.

Since the 1930's, the more concentrated utilization made of the historical and comparative methods has illustrated better the various periods in the Roman legal system.

The research tools used by Romanists reflect the phases in the development of the discipline in this century.

The Interpolationum Index represents the first phase up until 1935. The bibliographical indices such as the Collectio Bibliographica of L. Caes and R. Henrion illustrate the interdisciplinary nature of the second phase. We can see how the initial tool (the index of the interpolations) commenced with the ancient text whilst the latter (bibliographical) tools are divided into "mots clés", selected in consideration of modern interpretation.

The experience gained in collecting the material for the continuation of the Interpolationum Index, between 1935 and 1965, marks the passage between the two phases and can be used to indicate a way to improve them.

The first step towards this improvement was suggested by Broggini, who suggested that the Interpolationum Index relating to the Codex Iustinianus presents "the study of the interpolationistic critique ..... set out in a source index".

Similarly, the research begun in 1965 by the editors of IURA, directed at "indexing the principal Roman legal texts which have been the subject of special critical or exegetic examination in monographs", tends to continue the tradition of the Index Interpolationum with an Index Interpretationum (see IURA 17, 1966, p. 805).

2. THE DATABASE

The "electronic file" proposed to the Italian National Research Council and in the course of construction under the direction of Professor Pierangelo Catalano of the La Sapienza University of Rome, permits an exhaustive work to be carried out on a predetermined "documentary base", avoiding subjective selection þy the researcher whose job it is to scan the documents. (see P. Catalano, Archivio elettronico per l'interpretazione delle fonti giuridiche romane, SDHI, 1985, pp. 453-457).

Furthermore, the database will give the user all the advantages of an information retrieval system and will permit him to overcome the limitations inherent in printed bibliographies and indices, including those drafted with the aid of the computer.

It must, however, be pointed out that the reordering of the enormous bibliography relating to the interpretation of Roman legal sources must have regard to order of these same sources.

The general objective of the research may be defined as the automated access to an ordered knowledge of the interpretation of Roman legal sources (from the ancient sacerdotal files up to modern classifications). For several reasons, this objective can only be reached in part. The first partial objective which can be practically reached is constituted by the "codified" sources of law or those enacted by Emperor Justinian I.

The works of Justinian, seen as the meeting point between the East and West, are also the starting point of the so-called "Bizantine" and "European" traditions, which are both encompassed within the perspective of this research.

It would also be advisable, during the course of the research, to accumulate the bibliographical data relative to both the Eastern and Western pre-and post-Justinanean sources, with a view to widening this partial objective in the future.

The delimitation of the documentary base potentially made up of all the written interpretations of the sources is also difficult, because of the implications of scientific policy inherent in all the formal criteria used in setting these limits.

The documentary base must be limited according to formal temporal, spatial (geocultural) regulatory and documentary criteria.

a) For the temporal limit, the starting date was fixed as the year in which the Interpolationum Index ended, that is, 1965.

b) As far as the spatial limit is concerned, research began on the works edited in the European countries which belong today to the Romanist legal order (Romano-Germanic): Belgium, France, the Federal Republic of Germany, Italy, Holland, Spain, etc.

c) With regard to the regulatory limit, research began on strictly Romanistic texts, or on the more generally legal- historical texts.

d) Regarding the documentary limit, both articles published in journals and those appearing in volumes which are not journals but which are reviewed in journals must be taken into consideration.

In practice, the research began with articles published in 1983 and then went back as far as 1965.

A group of researchers from the Faculty of Jurisprudence at the University of Cagliari, under the direction of Professor Francesco Sitzia, scans the following journals: "Anuario de historia del derecho Español"; "Bullettino dell'Istituto di diritto romano 'Vittorio Scialoja'"; "Iura. Rivista internazionale di diritto romano e antico"; "Index. Quaderni camerti di studi romanistici"; "Labeo. Rassegna di diritto romano"; "Revue historique de droit français et étranger"; "Revue internationale des droits de l'antiquité"; "Studia et documenta historiae et iuris"; "Tijdschrift voor Rechtsgeschiendenis"; "Zeitschrift der Savigny-Stiftung für Rechtsgeschichte. Rom. Abt."

Currently, 3,500 articles have been analysed and the same number of documents produced, of which 1,500 have already been recorded on magnetic tape.

The form outlining the structure of the documentary unit for retrieval, the software for generating the database with the Find retrieval system and the actual building of the experimental and provisional database storing 603 documents which can be searched by using all the Find functions were created in collaboration with the technicians of the Computer Centre of the Italian Corte Suprema di Cassazione. This database is called FIURIS.

3. THE DOCUMENTARY UNIT

The documentary unit must be defined at the level of in-put, retrieval and out-put if an on-line database is to be created.

Three kinds of relevant information are involved: relating to the sources, bibliographical and linguistic details.

Researchers analysing the articles extract the information and write it out on forms divided into lines and columns. All the lines containing the same kind of information are called cards. The lines and, therefore, the cards can be of unlimited number whilst there are 80 columns.

The information is subdivided by 'card' as follows:

card 01   data identifying the document and bibliographical details;

card 02   data relating to the author or editor;

card 03   title and/or equivalent information;

card 04   translated title (this has not as yet been used);

card 05   sources cited in full in the text and in full in the notes;

card 06   sources cited in the text;

card 07   sources cited in the notes.

Example of the structure of the document on in-put:

```
0101850047500089      000046000080      023602470000      04 005
010185004750restano+Riccardo.                               01
02018500475La 'cognitio extra ordinem': una chimera         01
0501850047513.12.PR./I4.15.8.(P.238) D43.1./D50.13./D47.11.(P.239) D50.13  01
05018500475.(P.240)                                         01
06018500475D19.1.52.2./D50.16.178.2./D3.5.46./D4.6.2.(P.239)  01
```

(document on in-put)

The documents on in-put are consecutively processed by programs which organize and transform them into a new 'defined' structure for 'retrieval'.

The form of the document during 'retrieval' takes into account the fact that articulated retrieval through the parts of the document (channels) is provided for in the Italgiure/Find System.

The subdivision into channels constitutes the logical structure of the document whilst the subdivision into 'cards' constitutes its physical structure.

Logical Structure		Physical Structure
Channel Name	Content	Card Type
CPER	journal code	01
AN	year of publication	01
TD	type of document	01
CL	language code	01
AUT	author's surname and Christian name	02
AUT1	surname and Christian name (sole datum)	02
PT	words in the title	03, 04
PNT	Latin or foreign words	03, 04
PK	key or conceptual words	03, 04
ED	editor (only for books)	04
F	quoted and cited sources	05, 06, 07
FCT	sources cited in the text	06
FCN	sources cited in the notes	07
FRCT	sources quoted and cited in the text	05, 06

The structure of the document shows that the information is mainly concerned with the sources. They are assigned the 'F' type retrieval channels (F, FR, FRCT, FCT, FCN). The other channels store linguistic-bibliographical information: the title of the document is assigned the PT, PK, PNT channels; the author, the AUT and AUT1 channels; the language, the CL channel; and the editor, the ED channel.

Example of the structure of the document on out-put:

```
REVUE HISTORIQUE DE DROIT FRANCAIS ET ETRANGER
00/03/1980
TD: articoli
BRISSET JACQUELINE
LE STOICISME ET LA VENGEANCE
D1.1.3. (P.59)

REVUE HISTORIQUE DE DROIT FRANCAIS ET ETRANGER
00/12/1981
TD: articoli
PIERI GEORGE
STATUT DES PERSONNES ET ORGANISATION POLITIQUE
AUX ORIGINES DE ROME
D50.16.105. (P.586) D49.15.7.1. (P.589)
D1.6.9. (P.592)
```

(document on out-put)

4. SEARCHING THE DATABASE

The data base can be searched through the Italgiure/Find information retrieval system. Like all large retrieval systems, the fundamental principles of this system are based on the complete indexing of the document, the capacity to logically combine several data during the search and the morphological flexibility of the access keys.

The first principle means that the database can be accessed through any linguistic signs used in the text: the document is indexed under all the signs of which it is composed and, therefore, the indexing language correponds exactly to the storage language.

Under the second principle, search strategies can be formulated by combining two or more signs through boolean-type logical operators (et=and, vel=or, non=not): these functions will be discussed in greater detail later in this paper in relation to retrieval at a logical level.

Flexibility of the access keys means the capacity to enter the system with linguistic forms of a fixed or variable length: this is so-called retrieval by truncated form or by roots which allows all the keys of a minimum lenght n and an unlimited maximum to be given as a response when starting off from a key made up of n characters.

The data in the FIURIS database can be placed in three homogeneous groups: the 'sources' to which the F, FR, FCT, FCN, FRCT channels are dedicated; language signs to which the PT, PK, PNT channels are dedicated and the bibliographical details to which CPER, AN, TD, CL, AUT, AUT1 are dedicated.

The logical combination between data belonging to different channels is possible.

The search language is a symbolic language and as such has a formalized lexicon and syntax: the language signs are divided into symbols, functional commands, logical operators and ordinary language signs (retrieval data).

The main symbols are the ($) which must be used at the beginning of every search and the semi colon (;) at the end of every search; a search here does not mean the complete search but each step in the search which is usually called a 'string': a 'string', in this sense, means a set of signs (data, symbols, commands, operators) required or sufficient from a formal point of view for obtaining a response.

A search can consist of one or more strings, but each string must begin with the dollar sign ($) and end with the symbol of the colon (;).

The commands can be divided into search, display, print or spectral analysis commands. The conventional names of the channels and the AND (asterisk *), OR (+), NOT (non monadic (-)) and AND NOT (non dyadic *(-)) boolean-logical operators are the most important of the search commands.

The syntactical structure of a string made up of two data is as follows:

$ sign/ name of channel/ : sign/ datum/ logical operator/ datum/ ; sign.

Example: $pt:datum*datum;.

5. RETRIEVAL BY SOURCES

All the sources found in the original article are recorded in their complete form in the document and, for each source, the page of the text in which it is cited or printed.

In order to make retrieval of the 'sources' more flexible and efficacious, the important passages of the Corpus Juris have been subdivided according to their 'weight' into passages printed in full in the text or in a note passages cited in the text and passages cited in a note: each type of passage is recored in a different section of the document as described above. This subdivision constitutes the physical structure of the document.

The computer allows a logical definition which is articulated in a diiferent way and which increases retrieval capacity to be added to the physical definition of the document.

Let us compare, in detail, the definition or logical structure relating to the 'sources' with their corresponding physical definition.

Logical Structure · Physical Structure

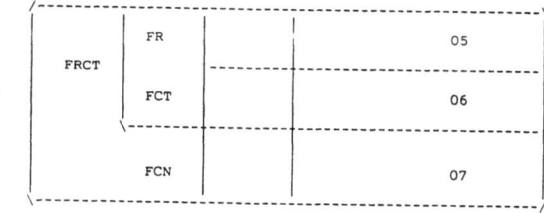

Starting with three physical fields, five logical fields representing combinations of physical fields have been defined. Each logical field constitutes a retrieval channel which can be searched independently.

The division into logical fields facilitates the extremely flexible and articulated retrieval of the 'sources' and, in this respect, makes the FIURIS database original and unique among tools of this kind. Not only is it possible to find all the places (page number of the article) where a particular passage is discussed but it is also possible to calculate the weight of the passage (printed in the text or in a note, cited in the text, cited in a note) and, to some degree, the weight of the relative discussion.

All the 'sources', no matter how they are indicated in the articles (printed in the text or in a note, cited in the text, cited in a note), can be retrieved through the 'F' channel.

Only the 'sources printed in the text or in a note' and the 'sources cited in the text' can be jointly selected in the 'FRCT' channel; all and only the 'sources printed in the text and/or in a note' in the 'FR' channel; all and only the 'sources cited in the text' in the 'FCT' channel; and in the 'FCN' channel, all and only the 'sources cited in a note'.

Examples:
$F:D50.13.;
$FR:D43.1.;
$FCT:D50.16.178.2.;
$FCN:D4.6.2.;
$FRCT:D19.1.52.2.;
$F:D50.13.*D43.1.;
$FCT:D50.16.178.2.+FCN=D4.6.2.;

The system, as mentioned earlier, permits the access keys to be exploited in both a rigid and flexible way by using the implicit or explicit truncation technique.

This provides greater articulation in retrieval by 'sources'in the sense that the 'source' 'd1.1', for example, can be considered in its entirety during a search and will give in out- put only the documents containing 'd1.1', or it can be considered as a minimum key resulting in the search being extended to all the 'sources' beginning with 'd1.1' and, therefore, to the whole 'title'.

Once the documents containing one or more 'sources' have been selected, the system is able to indicate the places (bibliographical details and page of the article) where the 'source' or 'sources' can be found.

A special procedure is at present being developed which will provide a print out of a document containing only the 'source' or 'sources' retrieved complete with the details about the journal or journals and the page or pages where the retrieved 'source' or 'sources' are to be located.

6. BIBLIOGRAPHICAL-LINGUISTIC RETRIEVAL

Retrieval by 'sources', which is the main objective of the FIURIS data base, is enriched by the capacity to search the documents through bibliographical and linguistic keys.

The search can be made on a textual, morphological, semantic and logical level.

6.1. Textual Level

The type of basic retrieval here is that which utilizes a fixed key and obtains in out-put all the documents where the exact linguistic sign used in the query appears. The language used in the query by the user is, in this case, exactly the same as the retrieval language and the language used in out-put; if the user uses the sign 'senatus', the system does not transform the sign, textual retrieval is carried out and only documents containing the sign 'senatus' without any conceptual expansion will given in out-put.

This type of retrieval is only possible in channels where the keys are not defined as 'truncated'; the PNT and AUT1 channels are of this kind. The PNT channel is used for retrieving Latin or foreign words as well as all the terms which cannot be found with the PT channel.

Examples:

$PNT:senatus;

$AUT1:Brisset;

$AUT1:Brisset Jacqueline;

The characteristic of working with complete or fixed forms (like those in so-called type 1 channels) is the impossibility of formulating truncated queries such as:

$PNT:senat;

$AUT1:Briss;

In these cases, it is necessary, as we shall see, to use a truncation symbol if the key of the type 1 channel is to be made flexible.

The PT command (channel) activates by definition an initial level of conceptual research, the expansion to declined or inflected forms; with the '$PT:senato' search, all the documents which have not only the lemma but also the feminine, plural and conjugated form can be retrieved.

6.2. Morphological Level

Morphological retrieval is of a higher level. An attempt is made through it to go beyond the mere text in order to reach a conceptual expansion starting off from a common root: this is called retrieval by morphological expansion given that a common formal base is always required.

This type of retrieval is also called retrieval by truncated forms because an incomplete form is fed into the computer: the truncation function, in type 1 channels, is expressed with the dollar sign ($) placed at the end of the linguistic sign.

Example: $pt:senat$;

The query is automatically transformed from a monodatum to a multidatum as follows:

$pt:senato+senati+senatore+senatori+all the signs of any length whatsoever but with the root or common minimum key 'senat'.

Some retrieval channels can be structured so that the signs contained in them are processed by definition as truncated forms or minimum keys (called type 2 channels).

In this case, the retrieval as a rule is always by morphological expansion without it being necessary to use the truncation symbol at the end of the sign.

All the channels relating to the 'sources' (F, FR, FCT, FCN, FRCT) have been defined in the FIURIS database as trucated type or type 2 channels; therefore, if the user formulates the search string '$F:d1.1' he receives in out-put all the documents containing the minimum key 'd1.1' as well as the documents containing longer keys, without limitation, such as 'd1.1.1.', 'd1.1.2.' but not 'd1.2.'

The AUT channel processes the signs as truncated signs and considers 'Christian name and surname' to be separate keys.

Example: $AUT:Briss;

$AUT:Briss*Jacqueline;

The AUT1 channnnel, as mentioned earlier, is a type 1 channel which processes complete or fixed keys, but which, unlike AUT, considers 'Christian name and surname' to be only one key. This means that if truncation is required the $ sign must be used ('AUT1:Briss$,') and that the 'asterisk' operator should not be used if the 'Christian name and surname' is sought ($AUT1:Brisset Jacqueline;).

Anyone who wishes to 'block' the effect of the implicit expansion and formulate queries without truncated keys by definition must utilize the '/' command (stroke or slash) and repeat the key: for example, '$F:d1.1./d1.1.'. In this way, all and only the documents containing 'd1.1' are given in out-put.

6.3. Semantic Level

Retrieval by semantic expansion, which allows the limitations arising out of synonymy and similarity in meaning to be overcome, is important but not essential in information retrieval systems which index texts in full text in natural language (statutes, abstracts of court decisions, summaries or abstracts in natural language of articles from legal journals, etc.).

The accent of the 'document' in the FIURIS database is not placed as much on the language, which limited to that of the title of the article, nor on the bibliographical details which are considered in relation to the 'sources', as mainly on the 'sources' which, as has already been emphasised several times, are referred to in their entirety in the analysis of the articles.

The need for tools which contend with the ambiguity, variety and vagueness of natural language is barely felt in relation to this database. It is, nevertheless, important to keep in mind that a search based on a given sign can be extended to signs within the semantic area centred on the initial sign with the PK command (channel).

There are two other help functions for conceptual retrieval: LINK and TEST. These permit chains of analogous terms (TEST) or chains of specific terms linked in the AND logical-semantic relation (LINK) to be activated with regard to a particular initial term.

The user, in practice, by using these functions, is provided with lists which aim at suggesting a range of possible terms for carrying out a specific search.

6.4. Logical Level

The FIURIS database, as described earlier, provides the possibility of using boolean-logical retrieval. The logical operations which can be used are co-presence or conjunction (AND), inclusive (OR) and exclusive disjunction (OR) and general (NOT) and specific exclusion (AND NOT).

The symbols for the operations are '*' for the AND-conjunction, '+' for the addition-inclusive disjunction, '(-)' for the general exclusion, '*(-)' for the specific exclusion; there is no direct operator for the exclusive disjunction operation in Find and if it is necessary to carry out a complex operation, more than one simple operators need to be utilized. The hierarchy of the operations establishes that the AND and the exclusion operations are developed firstly and then the addition operations, if the user wishes to change the logical order of the operations he must utilize the brackets as in algebra. The first operation developed among the AND and the subtraction-exclusion operations is that found in the string from left to right.

Searches can also be formulated with n operators and n operands belonging to different retrieval channels: for example, words contained in the 'title' (PT) combined with data stored in type 'F' channels devoted to the 'sources' can be retrieved and the data in the various 'F' type channels can, in turn, be combined.

Examples:
$FR:D50.13.*D50.16.178.2.;
$FR:D50.13.*PT=cognitio*extra*ordinem;
$PT:senato+tribunato;
$PT:cognitio*extra*ordinem*AUT1=Orestano Riccardo;
$PT:(senato+tribunato)*AUT1=Arangio Ruiz Vincenzo;

Distributed Evaluation of the DATALOG Query Language

Lars Stefan Jensen, Erik Johannes Kaae*

Department of Computer Science, Building 344,
Technical University of Denmark, DK-2800 Lyngby, Denmark

Abstract

We present a technique for distributed evaluation of the deductive database language DATALOG, that is, PROLOG without function symbols. DATALOG is both a powerful extension of relational database query languages like SQL and a suitable language for constructing expert systems. Both of these types of applications tend to be computationally complex and to exhibit parallelism of the kinds known as Or parallelism and All-solutions And parallelism. We therefore expect large speedup by exploiting this parallelism.

The lack of function symbols ensures a finite model, in spite of presence of recursive clauses. We therefore discuss how to ensure termination while retaining completeness. Our distributed implementation uses a top/down interpretation strategy and is based on the problem-heap paradigm and dynamic load balancing. Tests show up to 14.2 times speedup, obtained on a Transputer network containing 16 Transputers.

1   Introduction

The problem of how to implement a distributed interpreter for PROLOG has been described extensively in the literature, see e.g. [4], [6]. The obtained results have, however, not been impressive, as far from linear speedup has been obtained when many processors have been used. Some of the problems are due to the global nature of PROLOG, which manifests itself in the possibility of having chains of logical variables bound to one another. Binding of one of these will at the same time bind the others in the chain. That is, binding of a variable may have global effect. Our approach is therefore to identify a logical language which, while retaining many of PROLOG's facilities, circumvent this problem.

The chosen language, which supports database query languages like SQL etc., is a slightly limited version of DATALOG (see e.g. [3] and [14]). DATALOG is a subset of PROLOG which includes negation as failure but not function symbols. This ensures a finite model, hence DATALOG programs can

be interpreted in a purely declarative way since *all* programs can be made bound to stop. DATALOG is therefore interesting – in spite of its limited means of expression – in a number of applications including deductive databases and expert systems. In such systems the computation involved in retrieving information or decision-making is often large, as large amounts of data are present and/or many different paths must be searched to find all solutions. This suggests that parallel evaluation may be beneficial since different paths can be pursued concurrently using Or parallelism. Different solutions for the same subproblem can be computed in parallel using All-solutions And parallelism.

Distributed evaluation of DATALOG has not been described until recently in the literature. However, in both [7] and [16] parallel, bottom-up evaluation of a class of DATALOG programs is described. Moreover, the system described in [10] seems to be a distributed version of a language corresponding to DATALOG.

The advantages of our approach as opposed to several of those described in the above mentioned papers are that it

1. by using a top/down interpretation strategy is faster than bottom/up based interpreters** because it uses top/down propagation of constants to limit the search space.

2. uses dynamic load balancing thereby ensuring good exploitation of many processors at the cost of a slight run-time administration.

The rest of the paper is organised as follows: In section 2, we describe two archetypical applications of DATALOG and discuss the inherent parallelism at the example level. Then we define the syntax of DATALOG and discuss static and operational semantics for a sequential implementation (section 3). In section 4 we describe the different kinds of parallelism. In section 5 an example is presented which illustrates the behaviour of a sequential implementation. We then discuss how to use the problem-heap paradigm in section 6 and 7. Finally in section 8 the termination problem induced by certain recursive formulations is discussed.

---

*Present address: NCR Systems Engineering Copenhagen, Svanevej 14, DK-2400 Copenhagen NV, Denmark.

** Unless a preprocessing phase is introduced which compiles the program into an efficiently bottom/up evaluable form, see e.g. [14].

2 Applications of DATALOG

2.1 A Bibliography Database

We design a small bibliography database to illustrate how DATALOG can be seen as an extension of query languages like SQL.

We define two relations: **bibliography** and **references**, the former containing information about articles, that is, *title, author, journal* and *date,* and the latter containing references from articles to articles.

bibliography			
title	*author*	*journal*	*date*
an amateurs introduction ...	Bancilhon, Ramakrishnan	ACM	1986
parallel execution of logic programs.	Conery	Kluwer Ac. Publ.	1987
distributed evaluation of the datalog ...	Jensen, Kaae	proc. of DEXA 90	1990
recursive axioms in deductive databases ...	Vieille	proc. of First ...	1986
⋮	⋮	⋮	⋮

references	
title	*ref*
an amateurs introduction ...	recursive axioms in deductive databases ...
distributed evaluation of the datalog ...	an amateurs introduction ...
⋮	⋮

In DATALOG the relations are formed as fact clauses as follows:

    bibliography('an amateurs introduction ...', 'Bancilhon,
    Ramakrishnan', ACM, 1986).

    bibliography('distributed evaluation of the datalog ...',
    'Jensen, Kaae', 'proceedings of ...',1990).

    ⋮

    references('an amateurs introduction ...', 'recursive ax-
    ioms in deductive ...').

    references('distributed evaluation of the datalog ...', 'an
    amateurs introduction ...').

    ⋮

Below we compare queries of this base expressed in SQL and DATALOG. In DATALOG answers are obtained as bindings of variables (a sequence of letters the first of which is capital is considered to be a variable).

Finding the authors of articles referred to in this article can be expressed as follows in SQL

    SELECT   author
    FROM   bibliography, references
    WHERE   references.title = 'distributed evaluation of ...'
             AND references.ref = bibliography.title

and in DATALOG:

    query(Author) ← references('distributed evaluation ...',Ref),
                    bibliography(Ref,Author,Journal,Date).

Titles of all articles referred to in this article and in the articles that this article refers to can be extracted by the SQL query:

    (SELECT   ref
    FROM   references
    WHERE   title = 'distributed evaluation of ...')
    UNION
    (SELECT   R2.ref
    FROM   references R1, references R2
    WHERE   R1.title = 'distributed evaluation of ...'
              AND R1.ref = R2.title)

and in datalog

    titles(Ref)   ←   references('distributed evaluation of ...',Ref).
    titles(Ref)   ←   references('distributed evaluation ...',Ref1),
                      references(Ref1,Ref).
    query(Ref)   ←   titles(Ref).

But suppose we are interested in the names of all articles referred to in this article and in those articles *they* refer to and so on at all levels? This requires the possibility of expressing recursive queries which SQL does not provide for. In DATALOG, however, we would write:

    recursive_references(Title,Ref) ← references(Title,Ref).
    recursive_references(Title,Ref) ← references(Title,Ref1),
                                      recursive_references(Ref1,Ref).
    query(Ref) ← recursive_references('distributed eval ...',Ref).

Among others the paper 'recursive axioms in deductive databases...' is a solution.

2.2 The MYCIN Expert System

MYCIN is a production-rule based expert system for consultative advice on diagnosis of infectious diseases, see [5]. MYCIN handles uncertain knowledge through use of certainty factors (CF).

Below we reproduce two MYCIN rules both of which define a way of establishing the fact (with certainty respectively 0.7 and 0.6) that the infecting organism is *bacteroides.*

> *if   (1) the infection is primary-bacterimia, and*
> *(2) the site of the culture is one of the sterilesites, and*
> *(3) the suspected portal of entry of the organism is*
> *the gastro-intestinal tract,*
> *then there is suggestive evidence (.7) that*
> *the identity of the organism is bacteroides.*

> *if   (1) the gram stain of the organism is negative, and*
> *(2) the morphology of the organism is rod, and*
> *(3) the metabolism is anaerobic,*
> *then there is suggestive evidence (.6) that*
> *the identity of the organism is bacteroides.*

In DATALOG these rules become (postponing treatment of the certainty factors)

identity(Organism,Culture,Infection,bacteroides) ←

    infection(Infection,primary-bacteremia),

    site(Culture,Site),sterilesite(Site),

    portal-of-entry(Organism,gastro-intestinal-tract).

identity(Organism,Culture,Infection,bacteroides) ←

    gramstain(Organism,negative),

    morphology(Organism,rod),

    metabolism(Organism,anaerobic).

Here we have introduced an argument for each of the elements in what MYCIN calls the *context* of the organism, namely the culture and the infection.

The certainty factors can be incorporated as an extra argument for the conclusion of the rules and for each of the literals in the premise. Of course, the interpreter must then take care of manipulating them. In this case the interpreter must evaluate both rules (in fact all rules with this conclusion) and if they both succeed conclude that the identity of the organism is *bacteroides* with a certainty which is a function of the two CFs and the CFs of the conditions, see e.g. [1] for the details.

2.3 Parallelism in the Examples

In both examples there is a potential for parallelism. Consider e.g. the first query for the bibliography base. There are likely to be several references in the article 'distributed evaluation of the datalog ...'. For each of these we need to search the **bibligraphy** relation for the proper tuple in order to determine its author. As the search for the right tuple for a given article is independent of the search for the others it can be performed concurrently with these. Furthermore, there is no reason why the whole temporary relation containing the references of the given article should be computed before the search begins in the **bibliography** relation. Both the search for different solutions in the same relation and the search in different relations can thus be performed in parallel. (All-solutions And parallelism.)

In the MYCIN example the parallelism is due to the fact that there are two rules which can be evaluated in order to establish the identity of the organism. In fact, they *must* both be evaluated in order to compute the correct CF for the conclusion. As the rules are totally independent they can be evaluated in parallel. We can consider this as the parallel search for evidence for the same fact. If there are other rules expressing the conditions for establishing the identity of the organism, these can be evaluated in parallel with the rules above. (Or parallelism.)

These examples suggest that parallelism is present in ordinary applications of DATALOG. In large systems both sorts of parallelism can be expected to be present in large scale.

3 Language Definition

3.1 Syntax

DATALOG programs are constructed from sets of variables, constants and predicates. *Constants* are either symbols or numbers. *Variables*, *symbols* and *predicate names* consist of sequences of letters. The first letter in variable names is capital while only small letters are used in predicate names and symbols.

We define a predicate's *arity* to be the number of arguments it takes. An *atom* has the form $p(t_1, t_2, \ldots, t_n)$ where p is a predicate name with arity n and each t_i is a *term*, which is either a constant or a variable. A *literal* is either an atom or a negated atom, that is, an atom with prefix '¬'.

Schematically a *clause* has the form:

$$p \leftarrow l_1, l_2, l_3, \ldots, l_n.$$

where p is an atom and each l_i is a literal. The symbol '←' represents logical implication (from right to left) and ',' logical conjunction. p is called the *head* of the clause and the conjunction of the literals is called the *body*. A clause is said to *define* the predicate in its head atom.

Recursion is allowed, meaning that p may occur in one or more of the literals $l_1, l_2, l_3, \ldots, l_n$ or in the clauses defining the predicates these literals contain (mutual recursion).

Finally we define a *unit clause* to be a clause with empty body, corresponding to the case where $n=0$ above. A *fact* is a unit clause without variables.

A DATALOG *program* is a query and a set of clauses which can be divided into two parts: an *extensional* base which contains the facts and an *intensional* base containing the rest of the clauses. A *query* is a distinguished clause with the head predicate **query**.

Given the mentioned division of the base a corresponding division of the predicates into respectively base and derived predicates is natural. *Base* predicates are the predicates which occur in the extensional base only, while *derived* predicates are those which occur only in the intensional base. Such a division is not always possible, but a simple rewriting can be devised (cf. [3]) to ensure this.

3.2 Static Semantics

It is statically checked that recursion through negation does not occur. (Cf. [2] for a formal treatment.)

3.3 Dynamic Semantics

We will use a traditional top/down interpretation strategy. Informally described a clause is evaluated by (assuming that all solutions are sought):

    evaluating the first literal in the body of the clause by evaluating all clauses, whose head atom unifies with that literal, recursively.

For each solution returned for the literal, the corresponding instance of the clause, obtained through the substitution of variables by constants as determined by the solution, is formed. The newly evaluated literal is then removed from this instance which is then evaluated by a recursive call of the algorithm. When the last literal in the body has been evaluated the clause has been fully evaluated and its head terms form the solution.

A fact clause is evaluated by immediately extracting its head terms.

We postpone treatment of our solution to the (at least in a distributed setting) quite complex termination problem to section 8.

Negation is implemented as *negation as failure*, meaning that a negated atom is evaluated as if it was unsigned, and if solutions are returned, the negated version will be forced to fail. If, on the other hand, no solutions are returned, the negative literal will succeed.

A slight restriction is imposed on the language by the introduction of a demand on the form of the result of evaluating a clause. The *result* is considered to be the head terms of the clause after successful evaluation of its body. We now demand that all variables in the head *must* be bound after evaluation of the clause body. This implies

- The notorious problems with logical variables disappear since all communication takes place by transferring of constant tuples. Instead of binding variables we can simply substitute the constants for them. This ensures a higher degree of locality since the binding of a variable cannot indirectly bind another variable. This fact is essential for an algorithm to be efficiently implementable on a distributed system.

- Since we no longer have to bind variables we can dispense with binding environments, hereby reducing the amount of communication between the processors.

We enforce this restriction by a dynamic check.

4   Types of Parallelism in DATALOG

In DATALOG we find four types of independent, and thus concurrently evaluable, computations which will be described in the following.

All-solutions And parallelism: Parallel evaluation of the literals in the body of a clause, working on different solutions.

Restricted And parallelism: Parallel evaluation of literals in the body of a clause, which do not have variables in common (cf. [6]).

Stream And parallelism: Parallel evaluation of literals in the body of a clause, which have variables in common. When one of the literals finds a binding for a common variable this binding is to be sent to the processor which is evaluating the other literal.

Or parallelism: Parallel evaluation of candidate clauses for evaluating a given literal, that is, clauses with the same predicate in the head atom as the literal. This is possible since the evaluation of one clause cannot influence the evaluation of another clause since side-effects are not part of pure DATALOG.

Since the applications for which DATALOG is suitable are deductive databases and expert systems, where all solutions to a query are normally sought, exploitation of Or parallelism and All-solutions And parallelism seems most appropriate for our purpose.

The Or parallelism was explained in the MYCIN example above. All-solutions And parallelism corresponds to the parallelism described in the bibliography base example. It can be performed in two ways. Take as an example of a clause to be evaluated

$$query(X) \leftarrow q_1(X), q_2(X).$$

First the evaluation of $q_1(X)$ is commenced. If this results in a solution x_1, evaluation of $q_2(x_1)$ is performed simultaneously with a search for other solutions for $q_1(X)$. If $q_1(X)$ returns more solutions before the evaluation of $q_2(x_1)$ is finished, one can either

1. buffer the solutions until the evaluation of $q_2(x_1)$ is finished and then start evaluation of $q_2(X)$ with a new solution ("pipelining"), or

2. construct a new instance of $query(X) \leftarrow q_2(X)$ for each new solution. All these instances can be evaluated in parallel. This is the approach we have chosen to use.

5   Query Evaluation: An Example

When a query is evaluated according to the described algorithm a natural way to illustrate the process is to construct a tree containing the clauses participating in the evaluation. This means that each time a clause is invoked it is added to the tree and a connection between this clause and the clause whose first body literal called it, is established. In an implementation the nodes of the tree will be represented by frames on a stack.

When a clause is invoked, the frame created for it is referred to as an OR frame, whereas a frame created for a partly evaluated clause is referred to as an AND frame.

Below we demonstrate evaluation of a sample program. Consider the base and the query:

1. a(X, X).
2. a(X, Y) ← p(X, Y).
3. a(X, Y) ← t(X, Z), u(Z, Y).
4. u(...) ← ...
5. t(...) ← ...
   query(Y) ← a(1, Y).

The interpreter starts searching for candidate clauses for evaluating the main goal, that is, clauses with predicate name a, and finds 1, 2 and 3. This results in the addition of two new frames to the stack each with a reference to their parent, and a reference to the frame to which they shall later send their results (if any). In this situation the two references are identical. This will always be the case for frames of type OR.

The situation is now as shown in Figure 1. Thin arrows point at the parent of the clause, and thick arrows show the destination for solutions from the clause. We have not shown a thick arrow for the second OR frame. This is due to the fact that solutions will never be produced by this frame since the clause has more than one literal in the body.

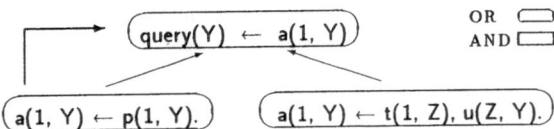

Figure 1: Search tree after the first expansion.

There is no frame corresponding to clause 1, since this clause is immediately solvable and therefore evaluated by successful unification with a(1, Y) producing the result tuple (1, 1), which is inserted into query(Y) ← a(1, Y). Because the returned result was a result for the last literal in the body, this clause is now fully evaluated and its head terms extracted as result. That is, the result is the tuple (1) which is presented to the user.

The two newly generated frames are now to be handled. a(1, Y) ← p(1, Y) has non-empty body. Therefore the corresponding frame is stacked and candidate clauses for solving p are added to the stack (there are none).

If results are returned to a literal, which is not the last in the clause, an AND frame is created for each solution and added to the stack. The first literal is removed and the unbound variables, which have been affected by the returned result, are instantiated in the rest of the clause. This is the case with evaluation of the clause a(1, Y) ← t(1, Z), u(Z, Y) since the created OR frame for t ← ... returns two solutions and thus gives occasion to the creation of two AND frames (see Figure 2).

Notice that the results produced by these AND frames are to be sent directly to the toplevel OR frame for insertion and not to their parent frame.

If we consider the figures again we note that in both cases the leaves in the tree can be evaluated in parallel as they are independent. A natural thing to do is therefore to distribute this data structure over a number of processors. A paradigm for this purpose has been developed, *the problem heap paradigm*.

6   The Problem-Heap Paradigm

The parallelism inherent in divide-and-conquer algorithms can be exploited by using a technique known as the *problem-*

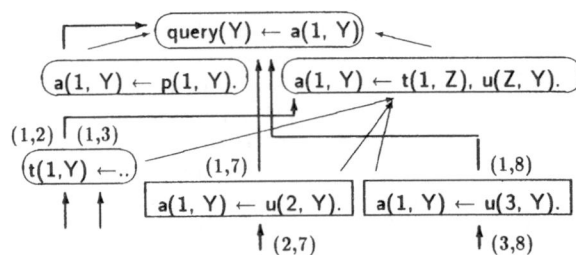

Figure 2: Further expanded search tree.

heap paradigm, see e.g. [11].

The idea behind such algorithms is that the problem which is to be solved can be divided into a number of *independent* smaller or simpler subproblems. Each of these can themselves be divided into new subproblems and so on until the subproblems can be solved immediately. Such immediately solvable problems are called *primitive problems*.

A problem-heap is now a set of such yet unsolved subproblems. This heap can be accessed by a number of processes. Whenever a process is ready to treat a problem, it obtains one from the heap. If the problem is primitive it is solved, if not, it is divided into subproblems, which are added to the heap. When the heap is empty, the initial problem has been solved. Problems which have been divided into subproblems are temporarily stored in a stack until they can be solved by using the solutions for the subproblems. A problem is referred to as *parent* of the subproblems it has been divided into. A snapshot of a problem-heap is shown in Figure 3.

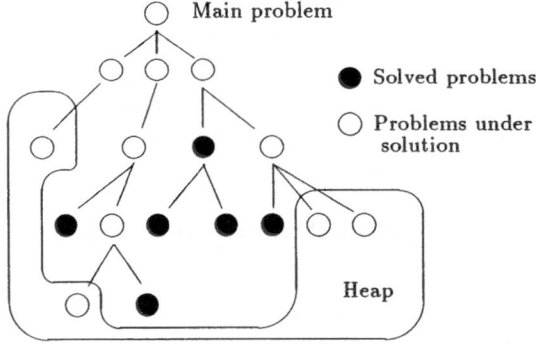

Figure 3: Problem tree

To implement this algorithm efficiently on a distributed system (that is, a multiprocessor without shared memory) the heap must be distributed over the processors in the system, such that each processor contains in its local memory a part of the heap. In order to obtain good load balancing, the processors must distribute problems between them, attempting to keep them evenly distributed. In addition to the problem solving/dividing process we therefore need a distribution process on each processor. This process exchanges information with its neighbours in order to decide if problems should be sent or received in order to keep them evenly distributed.

Let us briefly describe the tasks performed by each of the processes running on each processor:

- A heap process takes care of administrating the local part of the problem-heap.

- A stack administration process takes care of storing problems which await solutions from their descendants. It must be able to receive solutions, combine them with the destination problem, decide if this has been fully evaluated and act accordingly. That is, extract the solution from the destination problem and send it to the proper ancestor problem. Furthermore, the process must be able to decide when stack frames can be deallocated.

- The problem solving/dividing process receives problems from the heap process. A problem is treated in the following way:

  A copy of the problem is sent to the stack process for insertion and a reference to the position of the problem in the stack is received.

  Then the process checks whether the problem is primitive or not and takes the corresponding actions. That is, it respectively sends the result or generates new subproblems.

For a detailed description of the distribution algorithm used and a proof of its correctness we refer the reader to [8].

7 Using the Problem-Heap Paradigm

Having decided to use the problem-heap paradigm some definitions are required:

A *problem* is a frame containing information about an instantiation of a clause and a reference to the position of the parent problem.

A *reference* is a pair of identifiers, which uniquely identifies a problem in one of the stacks in the system. The first element of the pair is a number which identifies the processor in whose stack the problem is placed, while the second identifies the problem's position in this stack. A reference can therefore be considered as a generalized pointer. These stacks constitute a distributed version of a traditional PROLOG stack (assuming breadth first search) the frames being connected by the generalized pointers.

A *result* is a frame consisting of a tuple, containing ground terms, and a reference to the problem to which this result is to be sent.

A problem is *primitive* if the first literal in the body of the clause in the problem contains a base predicate. A problem is partly primitive if the first literal unifies with at least one intensional unit clause, as e.g. the clause id(X,X). Results from such clauses can be extracted immediately.

We now associate a problem with each of the stack frames in the sequential implementation outlined above and note that we cannot use the problem-heap paradigm in the version described above for two reasons:

- A problem can now have 0,1 or more solutions.

- A problem which awaits solutions from its descendants can, when solutions are returned, generate more subproblems. That is, for each solution returned for the first literal in the body of a clause a new problem is created which contains the corresponding instance of the remaining part of the clause, provided that there are still unevaluated literals left in the body.

The arrows shown in Figure 2 will now represent communication paths through which solutions (thick arrows) and what we have called *deallocation messages* (thin arrows) are sent. This means that a problem must have a reference to both the parent problem and to the problem to which solutions must be sent. The fact that solutions are sent directly to the final destination means that the problem of deciding when to deallocate stack frames becomes quite complicated as the number of solutions for a given problem is not known. Not even the number of descendants from which solutions can be expected is known. Details of how we have solved this problem are to be found in [9]. The basic idea in the solution is that deallocation messages are sent through the paths connecting parents to their children. A problem will then know how many of these messages to expect. Along with these messages the number of solutions generated by the problem and its subtree is sent. This ensures that a problem will know exactly how many solutions it must receive when it has received deallocation messages from all its children. This allows it to decide when it can be deallocated itself.

We can illustrate the interaction between the processes on each processor schematically (see Figure 4). The arrows represent flow of information in the direction indicated by the arrow. The sort of the information transferred from one process to another is attached the corresponding arrow. The communication and distribution processes take care of the interprocessor communication.

We assume that a copy of the base, that is, the DATALOG program, is available in the local memory of each processor in the system. This ensures efficient retrieval of clauses.

8 Dealing with Recursion

In this section we present a slightly modified version of a so-called *repetition cut-off algorithm* described in [13] which when combined with the described interpretation algorithm will ensure termination and completeness.

This algorithm is based on the fact that the set of solutions for a literal which is subsumed by a literal among

184

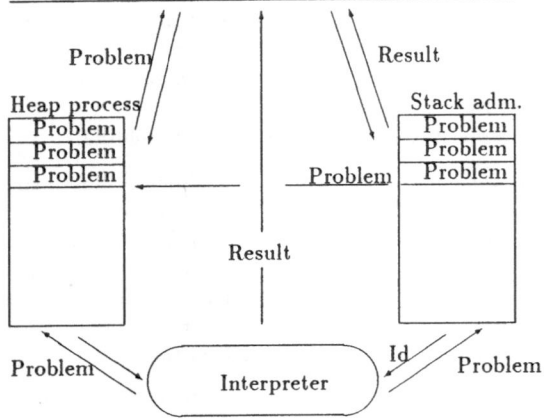

Communication and distribution processes

Figure 4: Communication between the processes on one processing node.

its ancestors is a subset of the solutions for the ancestor. We define such a literal to be a *repeating descendant* of the ancestor, which is called a *subsuming supergoal*. The algorithm is as follows:

- Whenever a solution is found to a goal, which contains a recursive predicate, the solution is cached.

- Before a goal, which contains a recursive predicate, is allowed expansion a search for a subsuming supergoal among its ancestors is performed. If such a goal is found, the current goal is a repeating descendant and is not allowed expansion. Instead cached solutions for the supergoal are tried as solutions for the current goal.

- When a new† solution is found for a supergoal it must be tried as a solution for all repeating instances of this goal. This may in turn lead to new solutions for the supergoal which are then to be inserted into the repeating descendants and so on.

  Only when no new solutions are generated for the supergoal have all solutions for this as well as for its repeating descendants been found and the evaluation can terminate.

The described extensions allow both All-solutions And parallelism and Or parallelism as usual since a supergoal sends *all* cached solutions and all incoming solutions to *all* repeating descendants. Furthermore, the search for a subsuming supergoal can be performed concurrently with the evaluation of other goals.

The algorithm can be implemented as described for a version of the language allowing only strongly linear recursion. This means that only one clause containing a recursive call

---

†That is, not just another solution, but a solution which is not a copy of one already found.

is allowed in the definition of a recursive predicate. This version requires an extended deallocation algorithm.

For general recursion, however, the deallocation problem is extremely complicated. We therefore propose to implement general recursion in a way corresponding to that described in [15] for sequential implementation.

We have not implemented either of these versions of the repetition cut-off algorithm. This means that the user is responsible for termination of recursive programs. The implementation guarantees completeness *if* the evaluation terminates.

9 Test Examples

We present test runs (see Table 1) from a prototype implementation of our parallel inference engine on a single transputer and on a network of 16 transputers. Three examples have been chosen, exhibiting different kinds of parallelism. The code is in the appendix.

Fibonacci: This example contains neither Or- nor All-solutions And parallelism. Therefore the runtime on one transputer compared with the runtime on the network gives an idea of the overhead for sequential problems.

Ancestor: This example contains mainly All-solutions And parallelism. It illustrates the obtainable speedup over the sequential implementation in tests with 50 - 70 generations in a linear parent base. The number of generations in each test appears from the query's suffix.

Construct: This test has been made to observe the speedup in an example containing large scale Or parallelism. This is obtained by adding a dummy clause, which always fails when recursion stops, to the above fibonacci example.

Table 1: Test results

Query	sequential	parallel	speedup
fibonacci(15,X)	67.4	67.5	1.0
ancestor50(1,X)	2.7	2.3	1.2
ancestor50(X,50)	31.7	6.5	4.9
ancestor50(X,50)	31.7	5.6	5.7
ancestor50(1,50)	1.3	1.3	1.0
ancestor70(1,X)	4.8	4.1	1.3
ancestor70(X,70)	79.3	9.5	8.4
ancestor70(X,70)	79.3	9.2	8.6
ancestor70(1,70)	2.3	2.3	1.0
construct(7,X)	27.4	2.7	10.0
construct(8,X)	74.9	6.5	11.6
construct(9,X)	204.6	15.2	13.5
construct(10,X)	559.7	39.4	14.2
	sec	sec	

The two tests for each of the queries *ancestor50* and *ancestor70*, show that the distribution of the problems over the local parts of the heap may vary from one execution to the next. This is due to the dynamic load balancing. Furthermore, it should be noted that since the parent base is linear, evaluation of the ancestor(1,X) query only exhibits a very limited amount of Or parallelism and no All-solutions And parallelism.

From the fibonacci test we can conclude that overhead is practically no problem. The ancestor tests show that we get the best utilization of the net with larger problems, since the speedup is increased from approx. 5 to 8.5 when increasing the number of generations from 50 to 70. This indicates that the parallel engine is suitable for working on large databases. The constructed test shows that even for minor problems we get a large speedup, which increases when the problem gets larger and more subproblems are generated. A speedup of 14.2 is very satisfactory when compared to the maximum 16.

10   Conclusion

On basis of our test results we conclude that the implementation is capable of exploiting both Or and All-solutions And parallelism efficiently and runs with almost no overhead for programs exhibiting none of these kinds of parallelism.

Further research might address the problems of how to use compilation techniques to further speed up the evaluation, see e.g. [12] for a suggestion of how to do this in the PROLOG context. Some of the ideas presented there might be of interest in the present context as well.

Acknowledgments

For their comments on a previous version of this paper we wish to thank A.P. Ravn, H.H. Løvengreen, M.R. Hansen and J.F. Nilsson. Part of this work has been supported by a grant from the Danish Technical Research Council (STVF).

References

[1] L. L. Alty and M. J. Coombs: Expert Systems, Concepts and Examples. NCC Publications, 1984.

[2] K. R. Apt, H. A. Blair and A. Walker: Towards a Theory of Declarative Knowledge. In J. Minker (ed.): Foundations of Deductive Databases and Logic Programming, edt. J. Minker. Morgan Kaufmann Publ. 1988.

[3] F. Bancilhon, R. Ramakrishnan: An Amateur's Introduction to Recursive Query Processing Strategies. *Proceedings of the ACM SIGMOD '86, Washington D.C., 1986*.

[4] J. S. Conery: Parallel Execution of Logic Programs. Kluwer Academic Publishers, 1987.

[5] R. Davis, B. Buchanan and E. Shortliffe: Production Rules as a Representation for a Knowledge-Based Consultation Program. *Artificial Intelligence 8(1), 1977, 15-45*.

[6] D. DeGroot: Restricted AND-Parallelism. *International conference on Fifth Generation Computer Systems 1984*.

[7] S. Ganguly, A. Silberschatz and S. Tsur: A Framework for the Parallel Processing of Datalog Queries. Department of Computer Science, The University of Texas at Austin, March 1989.

[8] P. Grønning, T.Q. Nielsen and H.H. Løvengreen: Development of an algorithm for Dynamic Load Balancing. Technical Report. Dept. of Computer Science, Technical University of Denmark.

[9] L.S. Jensen, H.H. Løvengreen: Distributed Interpretation of DATALOG. Technical Report. Dept of Computer Science, Technical University of Denmark.

[10] Y. Kiyoki et al: A Stream-Oriented Approach to Parallel Processing for Deductive Databases. *5th International Worpshop on Database Machines, 87'*.

[11] P. Møller Nielsen, Jørgen Staunstrup: Problem-heap: A Paradigm for Multiprocessor Algorithms. *Parallel Computing, Vol. 4, pp.63-74, 1987*.

[12] J.F. Nilsson: On The Compilation of a Domain-Based Prolog. *Proceedings of IFIP'83, Paris, 1983*.

[13] D. E. Smith, M. R. Genesereth and M. L. Ginsberg: Controlling Recursive Inference. *Artificial Intelligence* **30** *(1986), 343 - 389*.

[14] J. D. Ullman: Principles of Knowledge-Base Systems. Computer Science Press, 1988.

[15] L. Vieille: Recursive axioms in Deductive Databases: The Query/Subquery approach. *Proc. First Intl. Conference Expert Database Systems, Charleston, 1986*.

[16] O. Wolfson: Parallel Bottom-up Evaluation of Datalog Programs by Load Sharing. Technical report no. 564, TECHNION - Israel Institute of Technology, Computer Science Department, June 1989.

A   Test Programs

Fibonacci :

        id(X,X).
        fibonacci(N,M) ← id(N,0),id(M,1).
        fibonacci(N,M) ← id(N,1),id(M,1).
        fibonacci(N,M) ← ¬ id(N,0),¬ id(N,1),
                plus(1,N1,N),fibonacci(N1,M1),
                plus(1,N2,N1),fibonacci(N2,M2),
                plus(M1,M2,M).

Ancestor :

        ancestor(X,Y) ← parent(X,Y).
        ancestor(X,Y) ← parent(X,Z),ancestor(Z,Y).
        parent(1,2).
        parent(2,3).
        ⋮
        parent(69,70).

Construct :

        id(X,X).
        construct(N,M) ← id(N,0),id(M,1).
        construct(N,M) ← id(N,1),id(M,1).
        construct(N,M) ← ¬id(N,0),¬id(N,1),
                plus(1,N1,N),construct(N1,M1),
                plus(1,N2,N1),construct(N2,M2),
                plus(M1,M2,M).
        construct(N,M) ← ¬id(N,0),¬id(N,1),
                plus(1,N1,N),construct(N1,M1),
                plus(1,N2,N1),construct(N2,M2),
                plus(M1,M2,M),fail.

THE FEDERATED DATABASES AND SYSTEM:
A NEW GENERATION OF ADVANCED DATABASE SYSTEMS

David K. Hsiao   Magdi N. Kamel   C. Thomas Wu

Departments of Computer and Administrative Sciences
Naval Postgraduate School
Monterey, CA 93943

ABSTRACT

The presence of large numbers of heterogeneous databases in a given organization is prompted by the replacement of traditional data processing with modern database management systems (DBMS) for traditional applications, such as record keeping, product assemblies and inventory control, as well as for new applications, such as expert-system support, design automation and manufacturing engineering. These heterogeneous databases form a federation in the organization due to the desire to facilitate data sharing and resource consolidation while maintaining the local autonomy of individual databases, which are dictated by their particular security requirements, integrity constraints and application specificities. This paper outlines an architecture for the federated databases, based on the *multimodel, multilingual, and multibackend* approach, that facilitates data sharing and resource consolidation in a heterogeneous database environment without compromising the autonomy of individual databases.

1. INTRODUCTION

The proliferation of various Database Management Systems (DBMS) in recent years is prompted by the replacement of traditional data processing with modern DBMS and by the need to support new data-intensive applications [6]. Since traditional data processing covers a wide area of applications, such as record keeping, product assembly and inventory control, they are replaced by different kinds of DBMS. For instance, a relational DBMS is used for record keeping applications, a hierarchical DBMS for product assembly applications and a network DBMS for inventory control applications. Consequently, traditional data processing practice of using tapes and manual handling of transactions are being replaced by modern DBMS using disks and automatic handling of transactions. Since new data-intensive applications are also diverse, there are different kinds of DBMS for their support. For example, functional DBMS are used for supporting expert system applications and object oriented DBMS for supporting manufacturing processes.

The proliferation of these heterogeneous databases and their DBMS is gratifying, indicating the viability of heteroge-

This work is supported by by NADC, NOSC, NPMTC, NSGC and NRL.

neous DBMS in modernizing the traditional data processing practices and in supporting new data-intensive applications. However, in a modern organization, particularly large and complex, a number of data processing practices and new applications are on going. For example, a large company in the retail trade not only needs a network DBMS to recount details of its inventories, but also needs a relational DBMS to keep its payroll of employees. Thus, in this example, the company utilizes two separate and different DBMS. In a large and complex organization the number of separate and different DBMS, known as *heterogeneous DBMS*, is large, since the organization must maintain several traditional data processing as well as several new data-intensive applications. A modern organization of some size and complexity is therefore by nature a "hot house" for heterogeneous DBMS.

2. PROBLEMS OF HETEROGENEOUS DBMS

There are two major issues being faced by organizations with heterogeneous DBMS. The first issue is *data sharing*. Since all the corporate information have been computerized into heterogeneous databases, effective utilization of these information collections for business strategies, corporate planning, regulatory compliances and resource controls requires data sharing among the heterogeneous databases. In other words, the corporate user should be able to access the various heterogeneous databases with ease. Contemporary heterogeneous DBMS are stand-alone; i.e., they do not make their databases accessible to others who do not write transactions in the languages of their DBMS. For example, to access a network database, one must write a transaction in a network data language such as CODASYL-DML. If the corporate user is only familiar with a relational data language, e.g., SQL, he cannot access the network database. The user must learn the network model, write a transaction in its language, and submit the transaction to the network DBMS for execution. Such a demand forestalls data sharing among heterogeneous databases and among various database users.

The second issue is *resource consolidation*. As the proliferation of heterogeneous DBMS and their databases accelerates, the number of separate supporting hardware, software and personnel multiplies proportionally. Consequently, the cost and complexity of maintaining and supporting the ever increasing heterogeneous DBMS grows significantly. Ideally, we would like to minimize the cost and complexity by consolidating all the supporting resources into a single DBMS.

Most research has concentrated on addressing the problems associated with the first issue. These efforts include Computer Corporation of America MULTIBASE [8], IN-RIA's heterogeneous SIRIUS-DELTA [5], SDC mermaid [9], MRDSM [7], and LINDA [10]. The question is, therefore, whether or not it is possible to design a DBMS that facilitate *both* data sharing and resource consolidation while maintaining the individual autonomy of each database, which are dictated by their particular security requirements, integrity constraints and application specificities.

3. A NEW DBMS FOR DATA SHARING AND RE-SOURCE CONSOLIDATION

To overcome the problems associated with the current proposals and address the issues of resource consolidation, we present in this paper a new kind of DBMS called the *Federated Databases and System* that provides two kinds of capabilities. The first, the *multimodel and multilingual capability*, supports data sharing by allowing users to access different databases created under different models using their preferred data model and language. The second capability, the *multibackend capability*, supports resource consolidation by consolidating all hardware while providing for an expandable and configurable system with high level of performance throughput. In the following sections, we describe these two capabilities in more detail.

3.1. The Multimodel and Multilingual Capabilities

Unlike conventional DBMS each of which is *monomodel* and *monolingual* (i.e., each DBMS is based on a single data model and language), the federated databases and system is *multimodel* [1] and *multilingual* [2,3]. In other words, in the federated databases and system several heterogeneous databases may be created each of which is based on a different data model. Consequently, in the federated databases and system several databases of different data models co-exist in the same database system. Further, as a multilingual DBMS, the federated database system supports the corresponding data language of each data model it supports. For example, for relational databases, the federated database system provides a relational data language, e.g., SQL; for hierarchical databases, a hierarchical data language, DL/I; for the network databases, a network data language, CODASYL-DML; and so on. In Figure 1, we depict the architecture of our multimodel and multilingual DBMS capability.

The multimodel and multilingual capability allows also for *cross-model accessing*. More specifically, cross-model accessing allows the user to write transactions in a familiar data language to access other databases created under a different data model. For example, a relational user may write

transactions in SQL to access either hierarchical databases or network databases. The user is, therefore, not compelled to learn a hierarchical or a network data language to access his or her respective databases. Cross-model accessing in the multimodel and multilingual DBMS is accomplished by the DBMS' capability to provide schema transformation and language translation. Schema transformation allows databases unfamiliar to the user to look familiar, while language translation allows transactions written in a familiar language to be executed against databases created under an unfamiliar data model. The process of schema transformation and language translation is depicted in Figure 2.

3.2. The Multibackend Capability

In a multibackend DBMS, a number of dedicated computers and their respective disk units, known as *backends*, are connected in parallel via a *broadcast bus* [4]. One backend acts as a controller which is responsible for supervising the execution of database transactions and for interfacing with the users, as shown in Figure 3.

The characteristics of a multibackend DBMS are as follows:

(1) All the backends and their respective disk systems have identical hardware and software. They perform all primary database management functions.

(2) The controller functions are limited to the pre-processing of the user transactions, the post-processing of the transaction results, the sending and receiving of data from the backends and hosts. The controller is also responsible for overseeing the record-insertion process to ensure an even distribution of data among the backends.

(3) The communication bus functionality is limited to two capabilities. The first is broadcasting, i.e., the-controller-to-all-the-backends and one-backend-to-all-the-other-backends communications. The other is one-to-one communication, e.g., the-controller-to-a-specific-backend and a-specific-backend-to-the-controller communications. All other modes of communications, other than the ones mentioned above, are not needed nor used in the multibackend DBMS.

(4) The databases are partitioned into mutually exclusive sets of records, known as *clusters*. Clusters are collections of records which typically satisfy the predicates of the user's queries. A round-robin algorithm distributes these clusters evenly on the different backends' disks on a one-block-per-backend's-disk basis.

The characteristics of the multibackend approach results in a parallel and expandable DBMS architecture. Parallel data placement can facilitate either single-transaction-and-multiple-database-streams (STMD) or multiple-transactions-and-multiple-database-streams (MTMD) operations. Expandability is achieved by replicating the DBMS software on new and identical backends.

188

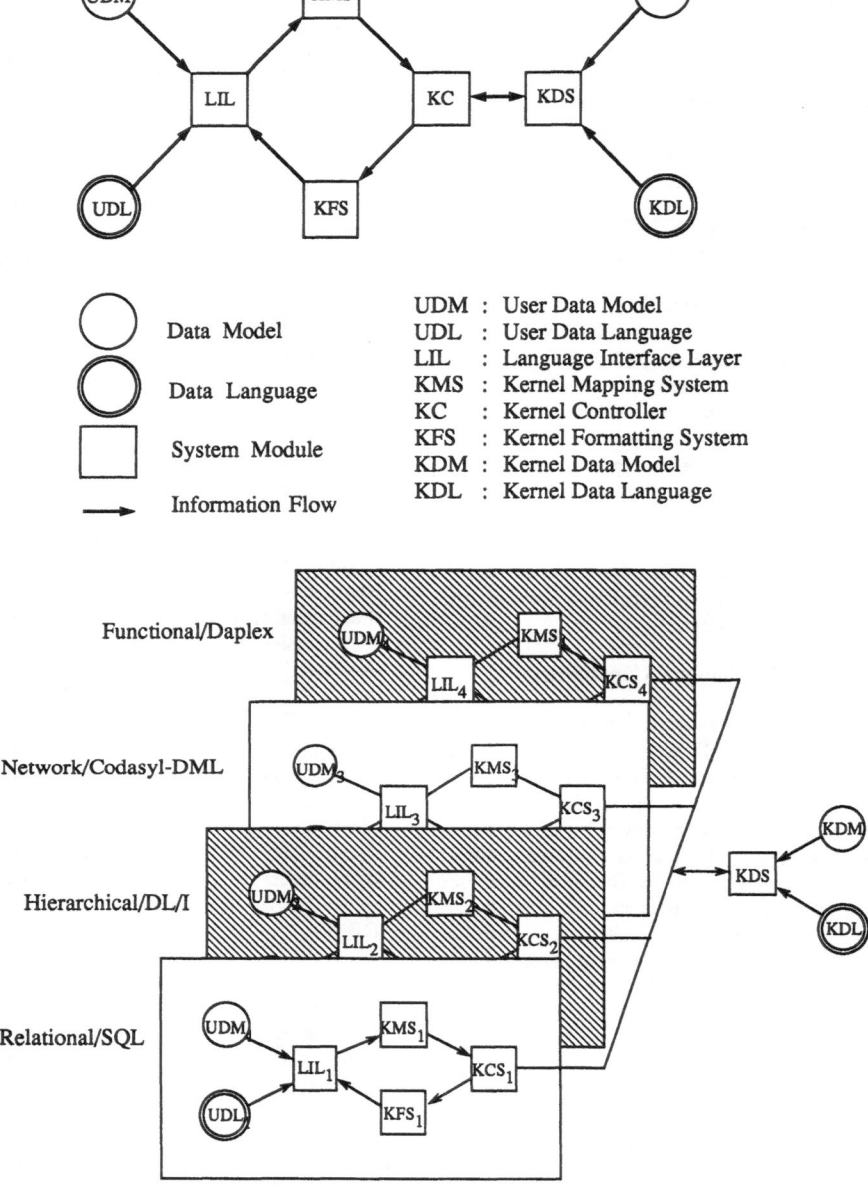

Figure 1. The Multimodel and Multilingual Capabilities.

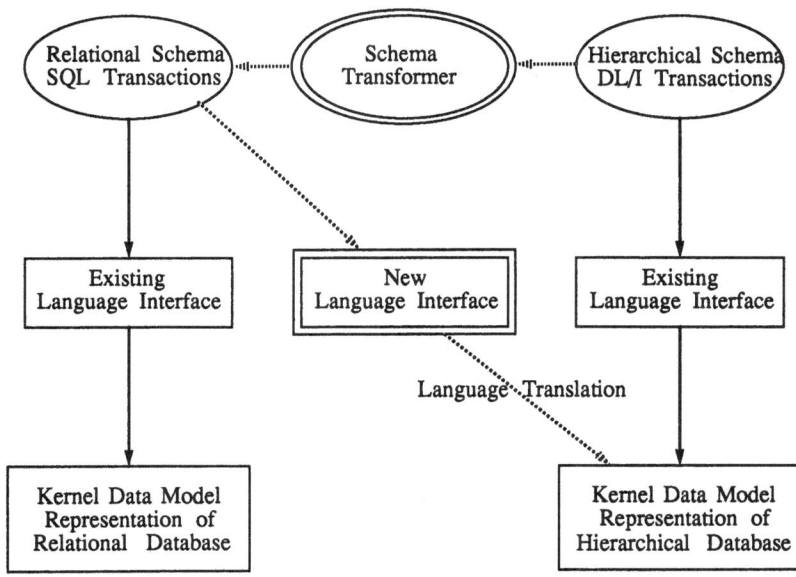

Figure 2. Cross-Model Accessing Capabilities via Schema Transformation and Language Translation.

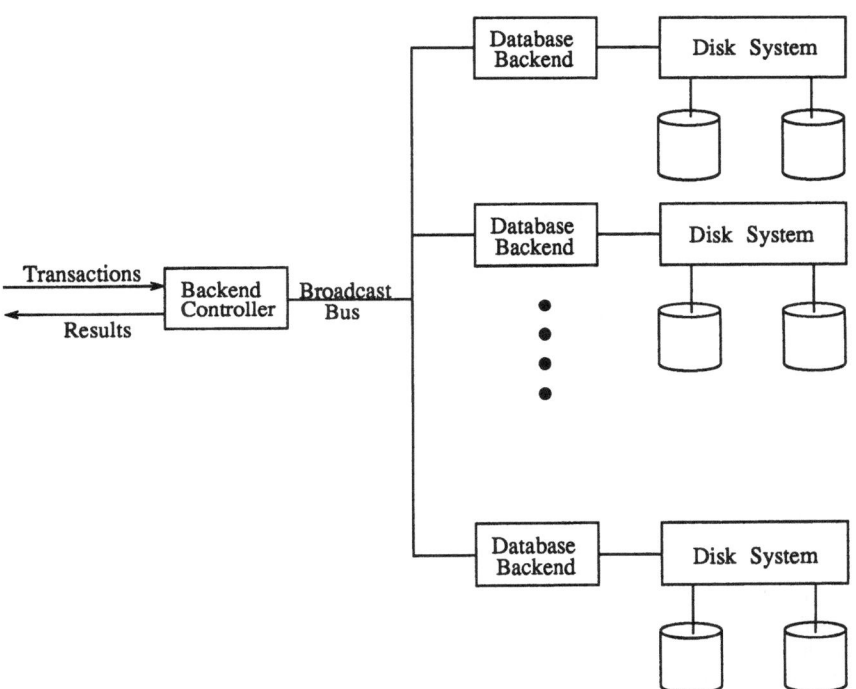

Figure 3. The Multibackend Capabilities

4. THE FEDERATED DATABASES AND SYSTEM

The multimodel, multilingual and multibackend approach may be an ideal answer for the federated databases and system. By providing multiple models and their corresponding languages on a kernel DBMS, the heterogeneity of databases and transactions is consolidated into one (kernel) DBMS. Further, this consolidation is at no cost of the functionality and diversity of the DBMS, since it effectively supports all the monomodel and monolingual DBMS and databases that it replaces.

The multibackend capability also consolidates all the hardware, making the replication of the software, placement of the databases and expanding the hardware an orderly and routine task. This case of resource consolidation can improve the response time and enhance the capacity growth of the system.

Finally, the cross-model accessing capability encourage data sharing. The user can access unfamiliar databases using a familiar data model and language without being compelled to learn either a new global data model and language or other unfamiliar data models and languages. The local autonomies are upheld, since individual database are created in their own data models and accessed via their own data languages, although they can be viewed as databases in other data models and accessed by other data languages. Access controls are facilitated centrally by the kernel DBMS.

5. CONCLUDING REMARKS

In this paper we outlined the DBMS architecture for the heterogeneous databases and system of the 90's and beyond. We believe that the federated databases and system requires the DBMS to have multimodel, multilingual, cross-model accessing, and multibackend capabilities. To this end, these capabilities are motivated and articulated. The experimental work on the federated databases and system is being pursued in earnest, indicating that the advent of multimodel, multilingual, and multibackend DBMS with cross-model accessing will soon be a viable solution towards data sharing and resource consolidation in heterogeneous database environments.

REFERENCES

[1] S. A. Demurjian and D. K. Hsiao, "The multimodel database system," in *Proc Int. Phoenix Conf. Computers and Communications*, Phoenix, AZ, March 1989.

[2] S. A. Demurjian and D. K. Hsiao, "Towards a better understanding of data models through the multilingual database system," *IEEE Transactions on Software Engineering*, vol. 14, no. 7, pp. 946-958, July 1988.

[3] S. A. Demurjian and D. K. Hsiao, "The multilingual database system," in *Proc. 3rd Int. conf. Data Engineering*, Los Angeles, CA, Feb. 1987.

[4] S. A. Demurjian, D. K. Hsiao, and J. Menon, "A multibackend database system for performance gains, capacity growth, and hardware upgrade," in *Proc. 2nd Int. Conf. Data Engineering*, Los Angeles, CA, Feb. 1986.

[5] A. Ferrier and C. Stangret, "Heterogeneity in the distributed database management system SIRIUS-DELTA," in *Proc. 8th Int. Conf. Very Large Data Bases*, Mexico City, Mexico, 1983.

[6] D. K. Hsiao and M. N. Kamel, "Heterogeneous databases: Proliferations, issues and solutions," *IEEE Transactions on Knowledge and Data Engineering*, vol. 1, no. 1, pp. 45-62, March 1989.

[7] W. Litwin and A. Abdellatif, "Multidatabase interoperability," *IEEE Computer*, vol. 19, no. 12, pp. 10-18, Dec. 1986.

[8] J. M. Smith *et al.*, "MULTIBASE: Integrating heterogeneous distributed database systems," in *Proc. National Comp. Conf.*, 1982.

[9] M. Templeton *et al.*, "Mermaid - Experiences with network operation," in *Proc. 2nd Int. Conf. Data Engineering*, Los Angeles, CA, Feb. 1986.

[10] A. Wolski, "LINDA: A system for loosely integrated databases," in *Proc. 5th Int.. Conf. on Data Engineering*, Los Angeles, CA, February 1989.

A High Speed Database Machine HDM and its Performance Evaluation

Harumi Minemura Takuya Asano Makoto Satoh Rika Kashima
Hisashi Hanabata[†] Shunichiro Nakamura Tatsuya Mutoh

Information Systems & Electronics Development Lab.,
Mitsubishi Electric Corporation
[†]Mitsubishi Electric Computer Systems (Tokyo) Corporation

ABSTRACT

To meet the increasing demand for speeding up relational database processing, we developed a database machine HDM and presented it at the 5th IWDM in 1987. Here, we present the results of a performance evaluation of HDM by 'Wisconsin Benchmark' and 'Expanded Wisconsin Benchmark.' The results of the evaluation show that HDM can execute various relational database operations fairly faster than some other database systems or database machines.

1. Introduction

Recently the research for database machines seems to become very active, such as GAMMA[2] and RINDA[3]. HDM is a parallel relational database machine which has a simple structure with one master processor and several slave processors. We showed the architecture of HDM in detail in [4]. Figure 1 shows the structure of 4 slave processor HDM, which was used for the evaluation in this paper. Each processor module has a Motorola MC 68020 microprocessor, several disk storage units and 4 mega bytes memory for work area and disk caches. Each processor is made of one 30cm square card, and same cards are used for both master and slave processors. The memory of the master processor is used as a common memory, to which all the slave processors are connected via a simple bus line. The common memory is used for communications between the master processor and the slave processors. The master processor communicates to a front-end computer, via which users access HDM, distributes database queries to the slave processors, and merges the results from them. The master processor has indices and various information about data allocation. Relations are partitioned horizontally and stored into the disks of the slave processors. The number of tuples of each relation stored in each slave processor is adjusted evenly.

In this paper, we show the results of a performance evaluation by 'Wisconsin Benchmark' and 'Expanded Wisconsin Benchmark' in section 2 and 3 respectively. We evaluated all the queries in the both benchmarks except modification of attributes with clustered indices. Comparison with other database systems or database machines is included in the same sections. In section 4, we present conclusions.

2. Performance Evaluation by 'Wisconsin Benchmark'

In this section, we present the performance evaluation results by 'Wisconsin Benchmark' [1], which is one of the most popular benchmarks for relational database systems. The database used for the evaluation is the same as used in [1]. It contains several 1,000 and 10,000 tuple relations. Each tuple is 182 bytes long and consists of thirteen 2-byte integer attributes and three 52-byte string attributes. All our tests were run with a front-end computer, an engineering workstation, ME 1100[1], connected to HDM with a SCSI cable.

We measured the response time at the terminal. It means the total elapsed time at the front-end computer — the time from when an evaluation query is entered from the keyboard through when the front-end computer receives whole the reply to the query from HDM and displays the first character of the result. We measured whole the benchmark twice and present the average time of them in this paper.

To examine the effect of the disk cache, we executed two same queries successively after invalidating the cache for each experiment. When the first query is executed, all the data to be retrieved must be read from the disks, but when the second query is executed, the amount of the data to be read from the disks becomes zero or less than the first for the effect of the cache. In all the tables reported below, HDM(1st) and HDM(2nd) mean the first and the second trial respectively.

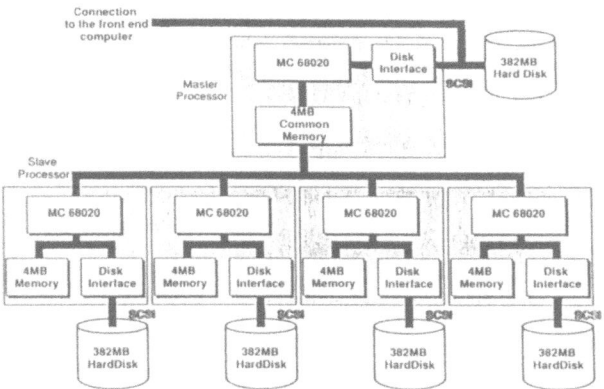

Figure 1: HDM — High Speed Database Machine

---

[1]ME 1100 is an engineering UNIX workstation made by Mitsubishi Electric Corp.

Table 1: Selection Queries without Indices
(Result Tuples Inserted into Relation)

[Total Elapsed Time in Seconds]

System	Number of Tuples Selected from 10,000 Tuple Relation	
	100	1000
INGRES	38.40	53.90
ORACLE	53.20	72.50
IDM(nodac)	20.30	27.20
IDM(dac)	19.90	23.40
HDM(1st)	1.89	2.03
HDM(2nd)	1.25	1.41

Table 2: Selection Queries with Indices
(Result Tuples Inserted into Relation)

[Total Elapsed Time in Seconds]

System	Number of Tuples Selected from 10,000 Tuple Relation			
	Clustered Index		Non-Clustered Index	
	100	1000	100	1000
INGRES	3.90	18.90	11.40	54.30
ORACLE	4.50	31.60	7.30	53.50
IDM(nodac)	1.80	8.90	4.10	29.80
IDM(dac)	1.10	7.40	3.30	24.80
HDM(1st)	1.75	2.46	2.17	2.81
HDM(2nd)	1.11	1.43	1.15	1.86

Table 3: Selection Queries with Clustered Indices
(Result Tuples Displayed on Screen)

[Total Elapsed Time in Seconds]

System	Number of Tuples Selected from 10,000 Tuple Relation	
	1	100
INGRES	0.90	5.00
ORACLE	0.70	6.90
IDM(nodac)	0.80	2.90
IDM(dac)	0.70	2.70
HDM(1st)	0.88	1.02
HDM(2nd)	0.58	0.62

Table 4: Join Queries

[Total Elapsed Time in Seconds]

System	Query		
	joinAselB	joinABprime	joinCselAselB
	Without Indices		
INGRES	108.00	156.00	126.00
ORACLE	>18000	>18000	>18000
IDM(nodac)	570.00	552.00	126.00
IDM(dac)	80.00	114.00	36.00
HDM(1st)	6.12	5.84	7.36
HDM(2nd)	5.39	5.25	6.59
	With Clustered Indices		
INGRES	54.00	102.60	64.20
ORACLE	77.50	73.50	111.40
IDM(nodac)	28.20	25.80	40.80
IDM(dac)	22.20	14.40	28.20
HDM(1st)	5.95	5.77	7.18
HDM(2nd)	4.92	4.99	6.03
	With Non-Clustered Indices		
INGRES	118.20	108.00	114.60
ORACLE	139.90	87.30	172.10
IDM(nodac)	52.80	40.20	75.00
IDM(dac)	39.00	37.80	48.60
HDM(1st)	6.02	5.72	7.25
HDM(2nd)	5.30	5.14	6.50

We have compared the performance evaluation results of HDM with the results of several database systems. The systems compared with HDM are as follows:

INGRES   software DBMS on VAX11/750
ORACLE   software DBMS on VAX11/750
IDMnodac   database machine IDM500 (without DAC)
IDMdac   database machine IDM500 (with DAC)
                (DAC : database accelerator)

The results of INGRES, ORACLE, and IDM are cited from [1], [5], and [6] respectively.

2.1 Selection Queries

The results of the performance evaluation for selection queries are presented in Tables 1, 2 and 3. Table 1 shows the total elapsed time of 1% or 10% selection queries for a 10,000 tuple relation without indices, and Table 2 shows the time of the same operations for a 10,000 tuple relation with clustered or non-clustered indices. Table 3 shows the time of 1 tuple or 100 tuple selection queries for 10,000 tuple relation with a clustered index. The result tuples are inserted into other relations in the experiments presented in Table 1 and 2, but on the contrary the result tuples are displayed on the screen of the front-end computer in the experiments showed in Table 3.

The results demonstrate that HDM can execute selection operations fairy faster than other database systems. Especially, in the case without indices, HDM executes these operations about 10 times as fast as IDM500.

2.2 Join Queries

Table 4 shows the results of join queries without indices, with clustered indices and non-clustered indices. In this table,

'joinAselB', 'joinABprime', and 'joinCselAselB' indicate following queries:

- joinAselB: Join query of 10,000 tuple relations A and B. Relation B has 10% selectivity factor.

- joinABprime: Join query of 10,000 tuple relation A and 1,000 tuple relation Bprime.

- joinCselAselB: Join query of 1,000 tuple relation C and 10,000 tuple relations A and B. Relation A and B have 10% selectivity factor.

These results reveal that HDM can execute join queries without indices very fast as well as with indices. The performance for join without indices of the other database systems, especially of ORACLE, are fairy lower than with indices.

2.3 Projection Queries

The results for projection queries are presented in Table 5. The experiments for projection queries are intended to evaluate the performance of sorting and eliminating duplicate tuples. The first query reduces a 10,000 tuple relation to 100 tuples while the second query is a projection of a 1,000 tuple

Table 5: Projection Queries
(Duplicate Tuples are Removed)

[Total Elapsed Time in Seconds]

System	100/10,000	1000/1000
INGRES	26.40	132.00
ORACLE	117.30	29.50
IDMnodac	58.90	31.50
IDMdac	33.00	22.00
HDM(1st)	2.56	2.07
HDM(2nd)	1.85	1.84

Table 6: Aggregate Queries

[Total Elapsed Time in Seconds]

System	Query Type		
	MIN Scalar Aggregate	MIN Aggregate (100 Partitions)	SUM Aggregate (100 Partitions)
	Without Indices		
INGRES	34.00	495.00	484.80
ORACLE	62.90	1198.10	1219.80
IDMnodac	22.00	61.50	62.30
IDMdac	19.00	36.00	36.00
HDM(1st)	1.68	2.49	2.55
HDM(2nd)	0.84	1.89	1.87
	With Indices		
INGRES	37.20	242.20	254.00
ORACLE	1.40	1200.10	1211.80
IDMnodac	22.00	61.50	62.30
IDMdac	19.00	36.00	36.00
HDM(1st)	1.82	2.63	2.69
HDM(2nd)	0.90	1.93	1.92

Table 7: Update Queries

[Total Elapsed Time in Seconds]

System	Query Type			
	Append	Delete	Modify	
			Without Indices	
INGRES	1.40	32.30	32.80	
ORACLE	1.00	46.70	32.00	
IDMnodac	0.90	22.80	29.50	
IDMdac	0.70	20.80	20.90	
HDM(1st)	1.31	1.45	1.25	
HDM(2nd)	0.60	0.78	0.74	
			With Indices	
			Cluster	Non-Cluster
INGRES	2.10	0.50	1.60	1.60
ORACLE	1.20	0.90	0.90	0.90
IDMnodac	0.90	0.40	0.60	0.50
IDMdac	0.80	0.40	0.50	0.50
HDM(1st)	1.07	1.04	—	1.02
HDM(2nd)	0.56	0.69	—	0.66

relation. As shown in Table 5, the performance of sorting and eliminating duplicate tuples of HDM is very high.

2.4 Aggregate Queries

We evaluated the performance of aggregate operations with following three queries:

- MIN Scalar Aggregate
  select the minimum on an integer attribute from a 10,000 tuple relation

- MIN Aggregate (100 Partitions)
  partition a 10,000 tuple relation into 100 subsets and select the minimum on an integer attribute for each subset

- SUM Aggregate (100 Partitions)
  partition a 10,000 tuple relation into 100 subsets and select the sum on an integer attribute for each subset

Table 6 shows the results of the performance evaluation for the aggregate queries without indices and with indices. As shown in this table, although indices have no effect for aggregate queries in HDM, the performance of HDM is fairy better than the other database systems.

2.5 Update Queries

The results of the performance evaluation for update (append, delete, and modify) queries are presented in Table 7. The current version of HDM cannot modify attributes with clustered indices, but HDM reveals that it is fairy faster than

other database systems for other update queries, especially for delete or modify queries without indices.

3. Performance Evaluation by 'Expanded Wisconsin Benchmark'

In this section, we show the results of the performance evaluation by 'Expanded Wisconsin Benchmark' [2], which is a new version of 'Wisconsin Benchmark', expanded to evaluate performance for large relations. The database used for the evaluation is the same as used in [2]. It contains several 1,000 through 1,000,000 tuple relations. Each tuple is 208 bytes long and consists of thirteen 4-byte integer attributes and three 52-byte string attributes. We measured the response time at the terminal as in section 2.

In the tables below, database machines compared with HDM are as follows:

- Teradata
  Teradata Corporation's database machine DBC/1012 with 24 Intel 80286 processors (4 Interface Processors and 20 Access Module Processors)

- GAMMA
  The GAMMA database machine developed by University of Wisconsin with 17 VAX11/750 processors

The results of these machines are cited from [2]. These database machines are larger and more expensive than HDM, and one of the objectives of this section is to compare the performance of these 'big' machines with the performance of HDM.

3.1 Selection Queries

Table 8 shows the results of the performance evaluation for various selection queries: 1% or 10% selection from 10,000, 100,000, and 1,000,000 tuple relations without indices (the experiments (a) and (b)), with non-clustered indices (the experiments (c) and (d)), and with clustered indices (the experiments (e), (f), and (g)). The result tuples are inserted into

Table 8: Selection Queries

(a)	1% nonindexed selection	(e)	1% selection using clustered index
(b)	10% nonindexed selection	(f)	10% selection using clustered index
(c)	1% selection using non-clustered index	(g)	1 tuple selection using clustered index
(d)	10% selection using non-clustered index		

[Total Elapsed Time in Seconds]

Source Relation	Database Machine	(a)	(b)	(c)	(d)	(e)	(f)	(g)
10,000 tuples	Teradata	6.86	15.97	7.81	16.82	—	—	—
	Gamma	1.63	2.11	1.03	2.61	0.59	1.26	0.15
	HDM(1st)	2.02	2.09	2.27	2.99	2.00	2.49	0.96
	HDM(2nd)	1.18	1.40	1.21	1.89	1.13	1.41	0.61
100,000 tuples	Teradata	28.22	110.96	29.94	111.40	—	—	1.08
	Gamma	13.83	17.44	5.32	17.65	1.25	7.27	0.15
	HDM(1st)	6.77	8.08	8.89	16.05	4.66	11.25	0.97
	HDM(2nd)	6.55	8.41	8.53	16.27	2.45	11.53	0.58
1,000,000 tuples	Teradata	213.13	1106.86	222.65	1107.59	—	—	—
	Gamma	134.86	181.72	53.86	182.00	7.50	69.60	0.20
	HDM(1st)	81.94	126.38	71.66	184.98	30.47	137.33	0.91
	HDM(2nd)	82.83	131.68	71.85	187.53	30.70	139.44	0.54

Table 9: Join Queries

(a)	joinAselB (without indices)	(d)	joinAselB (with indices)
(b)	joinABprime (without indices)	(e)	joinABprime (with indices)
(c)	joinCselAselB (without indices)	(f)	joinCselAselB (with indices)

[Total Elapsed Time in Seconds]

Source Relation	Database Machine	(a)	(b)	(c)	(d)	(e)	(f)
10,000 tuples	Teradata	35.60	34.90	27.80	25.00	22.20	23.80
	Gamma	5.10	6.50	7.00	5.00	5.70	7.20
	HDM(1st)	6.36	6.03	7.71	6.21	5.91	7.43
	HDM(2nd)	5.55	5.43	6.72	5.16	5.15	6.17
100,000 tuples	Teradata	331.70	321.80	191.80	170.30	131.30	156.70
	Gamma	36.30	46.50	38.40	36.90	45.60	37.90
	HDM(1st)	69.03	62.36	79.45	70.44	63.32	80.91
	HDM(2nd)	70.08	63.21	79.88	71.10	64.14	81.30
1,000,000 tuples	Teradata	3534.50	3419.40	2032.70	1584.30	1265.10	1509.60
	Gamma	703.10	2938.20	731.20	737.70	2926.70	712.80
	HDM(1st)	1123.79	1028.71	1233.16	1019.26	968.58	1118.39
	HDM(2nd)	1128.69	1031.94	1237.59	1022.00	970.17	1120.27

other relations in the experiments (a) ~ (f) while the result tuple is displayed on the screen of the front-end computer in the experiment (g).

As shown in Table 8, HDM is faster than Teradata in all the cases, and faster than GAMMA for queries without indices. HDM is not so slower than GAMMA in the experiments (c) and (d), but it is 2 or 4 times as slow as GAMMA in the experiments (e), (f), and (g).

3.2 Join Queries

The queries used for the performance evaluation of join are the same as in section 2, i.e., 'joinAselB' (the experiments (a) and (d)), 'joinABprime' (the experiments (b) and (e)), and 'joinCselAselB' (the experiments (c) and (f)), except for the size of relations; the relations A and B contain 10,000, 100,000 or 1,000,000 tuples and the relations Bprime and C contain 1,000, 10,000, or 100,000 tuples. In the experiments (a), (b), and (c), there are no indices on the join attributes, but the queries in the experiments (d), (e), and (f) used the attributes

with clustered indices as the join attributes. Table 9 shows the results: as shown in this table, HDM is faster than Teradata in all the cases, and almost as fast as GAMMA.

3.3 Aggregate Queries

The queries used for the evaluation are the same as in section 2 except for the size of source relations. These three queries involved no indices. The results are presented in Table 10. As shown in the table, HDM is almost as fast as or a little faster than Teradata and GAMMA.

3.4 Update Queries

Table 11 shows the results of the performance evaluation for update queries — append (the experiments (a) and (b)), delete (the experiment (c)), and modify (the experiments (d), (e) and (f)). As explained in section 2, because the current version of HDM cannot modify attributes with clustered indices, we didn't do the experiment (d). Except the experiment (d), HDM is almost as fast as Teradata and GAMMA.

Table 10: Aggregate Queries

[Total Elapsed Time in Seconds]

Source Relation	Database Machine	MIN scalar aggregate	MIN aggregate (100 partitions)	SUM aggregate (100 partitions)
10,000 tuples	Teradata	4.41	8.66	8.94
	Gamma	1.89	2.86	2.89
	HDM(1st)	1.80	2.61	2.61
	HDM(2nd)	0.88	1.91	1.91
100,000 tuples	Teradata	18.29	27.06	24.79
	Gamma	15.53	19.43	19.54
	HDM(1st)	6.18	14.86	14.97
	HDM(2nd)	5.96	14.65	14.77
1,000,000 tuples	Teradata	127.86	175.95	175.78
	Gamma	151.10	184.92	185.05
	HDM(1st)	80.81	176.35	177.33
	HDM(2nd)	80.59	176.21	177.16

Table 11: Update Queries

(a) Append 1 tuple (no indices exist)
(b) Append 1 tuple (one index exists)
(c) Delete 1 tuple using the key attribute
(d) Modify 1 tuple using the key attribute (the key attribute is modified)
(e) Modify 1 tuple using the key attribute (a non-indexed attribute is modified)
(f) Modify 1 tuple using a non-key attribute with non-clustered index (the non-key attribute is modified)

[Total Elapsed Time in Seconds]

Source Relation	Database Machine	(a)	(b)	(c)	(d)	(e)	(f)
10,000 tuples	Teradata	0.87	0.94	0.71	2.62	0.49	0.84
	Gamma	0.18	0.60	0.44	1.01	0.36	0.50
	HDM(1st)	0.77	0.89	0.99	—	0.94	0.91
	HDM(2nd)	0.63	0.50	0.61	—	0.61	0.60
100,000 tuples	Teradata	1.29	1.62	0.42	2.99	0.90	1.16
	Gamma	0.18	0.63	0.56	0.86	0.36	0.46
	HDM(1st)	0.70	0.93	1.03	—	0.92	0.96
	HDM(2nd)	0.61	0.50	0.60	—	0.65	0.53
1,000,000 tuples	Teradata	1.47	1.73	0.71	4.82	1.12	3.72
	Gamma	0.20	0.66	0.61	1.13	0.36	0.52
	HDM(1st)	0.71	0.86	0.90	—	0.75	0.80
	HDM(2nd)	0.63	0.49	0.59	—	0.58	0.53

4. Conclusion

In this paper we presented the results of a performance evaluation by 'Wisconsin Benchmark' and 'Expanded Wisconsin Benchmark.' The results of the performance evaluation demonstrate that HDM can execute various relational operations very fast.

HDM with its front end workstation is used as a database server on the TCP/IP network. In our laboratory, HDM is used in practice as a part of EOA (Engineering Office Automation) system for various technical information retrieval systems. HDM is going to be put on the market in the near future.

5. Acknowledgement

We wish to thank Mr. Masakazu Soga and Mr. Takaya Ishida for their continuing support and encouragement. We are also grateful to Messrs. Kuniji Itakura, Masaki Terai, Jun-ichi Shimodaira, Masao Imai, and Masahiro Osamura for their contribution to our work.

References

[1] Bitton, D., DeWitt, D.J., and Turbyfill, C., "Benchmarking Database Systems — A Systematic Approach," Proceedings of the 18th VLDB Conference, 1983.

[2] DeWitt, D.J., et. al., "A Single User Evaluation of the GAMMA Database Machine," Proceedings of the 5th IWDM, 1987, pp.43–59.

[3] Inoue, U., Hayami, H., Fukuoka, H., Suzuki, K., "RINDA — A Relational Database Processor for Non-Indexed Queries," Proceedings of the International Symposium on Database Systems for Advanced Applications, 1989, pp.382–386.

[4] Nakamura, S., et. al., "A High Speed Database Machine — HDM," Proceedings of the 5th IWDM, 1987, pp.340–353.

[5] "Oracle Corporation Response to the DeWitt Benchmark," Oracle Corp.

[6] Simon, E., "Update to December 1983 'DeWitt' Benchmark," Britton Lee, Inc., 1985.

Dynamic Scheduling of Transactions in Design Databases based on Version Consistency

(Extended Abstract)

Gottfried Vossen[*]
Institut für Informatik
Universität Koblenz (EWH)
Rheinau 3–4
D-5400 Koblenz, FRG

Roger Schwarz
Institut für Informatik
Universität Kiel
Olshausenstr. 40
D-2300 Kiel, FRG

Abstract

The concurrency control problem for design databases is considered. In such a database, used in engineering design applications, transactions operate concurrently on multiple versions of various design objects. Recently, a notion of *version consistency* has been proposed for schedules of such transactions, and it has been shown that a notion of serializability appropriate for schedules of design transactions can statically be tested in polynomial time in the presence of version consistency. However, no dynamic concurrency control mechanism based on these results has been reported yet. Such a mechanism is the subject of this paper. In particular, a dynamic scheduling algorithm for design transactions is presented which generates version consistent and τ_*-serializable schedules; various problems newly arising in a dynamic situation are identified, and solutions for them proposed where possible.

1 Introduction

In recent years there has been an increasing interest in making "database technology" feasible for nonstandard applications [14]. One of these is computer-integrated design and manufacturing, an area which requires the efficient management of design and manufacturing information [6]. While it is well-recognized nowadays that database technology can contribute positively to the solution of these problems, a variety of issues (including data modeling, database design, or storage structures) need to be reconsidered for making the "merger" work. One of these issues, *concurrency control in design databases*, is discussed in this paper (see also [2, 5]). Here, the situation to be investigated is that several transactions operate concurrently on multiple versions of various *design objects* (like VLSI circuits). Each transaction may access some version of one or more objects already produced (reflecting a certain stage of the design), and derive from these new versions to be made available to other transactions. What is crucial in this context is that "consistent" versions are used in each such derivation. Recently, a notion of *version consistency* has been formalized by Vidyasankar and Dampney [13], and it has been shown that a specific notion of correctness of schedules for design transactions (called τ_*-serializability) can be tested in polynomial time in the presence of version consistency. In this

[*]Permanent affiliation: Lehrstuhl für Angewandte Mathematik, insbes. Informatik, RWTH Aachen, Ahornstr. 55, D-5100 Aachen, FRG

paper, we add a dynamic scheduling protocol to the work of [13], which has not been reported before.

The model of transactions used in this paper is the standard one from [4] or [9], but it is assumed that updates of data objects are not made "in place", and each write step of a transaction writes a new *version* of the object in question. A *schedule* for a given set of transactions represents the order in which the transactions are executed, s.t. only versions are read which have previously been written (and hence "exist"). Clearly, not every schedule for a given set of transactions is "correct". For example, in the special case that at most one version of every object is around at any point in time, a schedule should be considered correct if it is *conflict-* or even *view-serializable*. In the presence of multiple versions, however, generalized notions of serializability are needed, which has previously been discussed for "ordinary" databases in [8, 3, 10, 7, 9, 4].

In the context of an engineering design database, there exists the additional complication that, due to the evolutionary nature of a design process, not only a version assignment needs to be taken into account, but also the derivation of versions from previously generated ones. This leads to the notion of version consistency introduced in [13], which, informally, calls a schedule *version consistent* if no transaction in the schedule directly or indirectly reads two distinct versions of the same object, where "indirect reading" refers to the fact that object versions are used to produce "revisions" of other versions. For example, if t_j reads version x_i of object x from t_i to produce x_j, and if t_k (directly) reads x_j from t_j and y_i from t_i, then t_k indirectly reads x_i as well, which should be forbidden since x_i and x_j must be assumed to be distinct (so that t_k gets an inconsistent "view" of x).

As has been discussed in [13], version consistency is a reasonable condition to be imposed on schedules of design transactions. Furthermore, it "interacts" nicely with the correctness criterion of τ_*-*serializability* [12], which is based on the intuition that the "final" version of some design object may depend on some previously "tried" ones, but not necessarily all of them. Consequently, a schedule s is "correct" if, for each transaction t occurring in it, s is (view-) "equivalent" to some serial schedule for those transactions contributing to the final versions produced by t.

It has been shown in [13] that τ_*-serializability can be characterized in terms of "history graphs" in the presence of version consistency. As a result, the criterion is efficiently testable for version consistent schedules. The goal of this paper is to present a corresponding dynamic scheduler which produces τ_*-serializable schedules in an online fashion, by maintaining a data structure suitable for testing version consistency, and by deciding serializability on the basis of the graph-theoretic characterization. To this end, we first consider a static environment (in which a finite set of transactions as well as a schedule for these is given) and then extend the results obtained to the dynamic case. Here, the two major issues to be considered are version control and concurrency control, which we discuss in turn. For the former, we introduce a new way in which a transaction manager can make version assignments such that the user gets what he wants and there is also an option of reassigning versions in case the scheduler discovers an inconsistency; for the latter, we describe a dynamic scheduling algorithm. Several problems, including transaction aborts and deleting completed ones from the history graph maintained by the scheduler, are discussed, and solutions proposed where possible.

The organization of this paper is as follows: In Section 2 we present the formal framework and notions crucial for our concurrency control mechanism, including the notion of a version consistent schedule. Some new properties of schedules and their correctness (serializability) are identified and investigated in Section 3. The dynamic scheduling protocol is then described in Section 4. Section 5 summarizes our work and poses several questions that deserve further study. The paper originally evolved from [11] and is an extended abstract of [15], in which proofs and further details can be found.

2 Preliminaries. Version Consistency

In this section we introduce our notation and review previous work from [13] on version consistency in design databases. We assume the reader to be familiar with the basics of concurrency control theory in standard databases [9, 4].

A *database* is a finite collection $d = \{x, y, z, \ldots\}$ of (design) objects. At each point in time, there exist one or more *versions* (instances) of each object comprising a database *state*; for simplicity, instances are not formally distinguished from objects, and versions will be distinguished by subscripts. A *transaction* is a (finite) sequence of steps of the form $r(x)$ ("read object x") or $w(x)$ ("write x"); each transaction reads and writes an object at most once. As is common in concurrency control theory, a transaction is viewed as a consistency-preserving unit whose execution is atomic. We assume that transactions do not make in-place updates. Instead, each write step of a transaction produces a new version of the object in question (unless a *revision* takes places through which an older version may get replaced); in the presence of several transactions, where unique identifiers are assigned to them (written as subscripts), the version of object x written by transaction t_i is denoted x_i.

In reality, transactions do not run in isolation, but concurrently with other transactions. To this end, a database system comprises a *transaction manager* whose central component is a *scheduler*; the task of the latter is to produce "execution sequences" that are consistency-preserving as a whole. To model this situation, we first consider a *static* environment, in which a set $T = \{t_1, \ldots, t_n\}$ of transaction is given. We now define the notion of "schedule" used in this paper and what it means for a schedule to be "correct": For given T, let shuffle(T) denote the *shuffle product* of T, i.e., the set of all sequences that have the elements of T as subsequences and contain no other elements. In addition, let $t_0 \notin T$ be a transaction consisting exclusively of write steps, at least one for each object read by any $t \in T$ (t_0 materializes an "initial" state). A *schedule* s for T is an element

of shuffle(t_0T), where the notation "t_0T" indicates that the steps of t_0 precede all steps of transactions from T in a schedule.

Since we assume that write steps produce new versions of objects, read steps occurring in a schedule need to be assigned some (previously written) version to read: For some given schedule $s \in$ shuffle(t_0T), a *version function* [9] V_s maps each read step of s to a previous write step on the same object, and maps each write step of s either to a previous write step (meaning that an old version is overwritten) or to one of the symbols "new" (meaning that a new version is created) or "empty" (meaning that this write step is ignored). For the purposes of this paper, it is sufficient to restrict the attention to version functions which assign read steps to previous write steps (which in particular implies that every version read by some transaction indeed exists) and write steps to "new" without exception; we term version functions of this kind *read-version functions* (rvf's) and consider those from now on.

Example 1 Let the following transactions be given: $t_1 = w_1(x) w_1(y) w_1(z)$, $t_2 = r_2(x) w_2(y)$, $t_3 = r_3(z) w_3(y) w_3(z)$. The following is a schedule for $T = \{t_1, t_2, t_3\}$: $s = w_0(x) w_0(y) w_0(z) w_1(x) r_2(x) w_1(y) w_1(z) r_3(z) w_2(y) w_3(y) w_3(z)$ The following is an rvf for s: $V_s(r_2(x)) = x_0$, $V_s(r_3(z)) = z_1$ □

Notice that, due to the special form of version functions used here, a version function need not be supplied separately; instead, we will "encode" it directly into the schedule in the sequel and hence write, for example, the schedule s from the previous example as $w_0(x_0) w_0(y_0) w_0(z_0) w_1(x_1) r_2(x_0) w_1(y_1) w_1(z_1) r_3(z_1) w_2(y_2) w_3(y_3) w_3(z_3)$.

With a given schedule $s \in$ shuffle(t_0T) we next associate a labelled graph $G(s)$ (called *history graph* in [13]) as follows: $G(s) := (T \cup \{t_0\}, E, l)$, where

$$E := \{(t_i, t_j) \mid r_j(x_i) \text{ occurs in } s\}$$
$$\cup \{(t_0, t_k) \mid t_k \text{ is a write-only transaction}, k \neq 0\}$$

and l assigns x_i to edges of the first type. For the example above, $G(s)$ is a shown in Figure 1.

The distinction between labelled and unlabelled edges in a graph $G(s)$ stems from the intuition that versions produced by write-only transactions are "consistent" because they are generated "from scratch", while versions produced by other transactions are "derived" from previous versions; since such a derivation may involve sequences of transaction steps, care must be taken that no mutually inconsistent versions are encountered in the process. This intuition is justified by the "Herbrand semantics" associated with read steps occurring in a schedule [9]: If some t_j reads x_i in s, then x_i potentially influences the versions written by t_j. However, if t_i was not write-only and has hence read, say, y_k (from t_k), then also y_k (indirectly) influences the versions produced by t_j. The important point is to make sure that y_k and x_i are "consistent", which is formally captured as follows:

Let $s \in$ shuffle(t_0T) and $t_i \in T$. The *extended read set* of t_i (w.r.t. s), abbreviated ers(t_i), is defined as follows: Let rs$(t_i) := \{x_j \mid r_i(x_j) \in s\}$ denote the *read set* of t_i, and let ws$(t_i) := \{x_i \mid w_i(x_i) \in s\}$ denote the *write set* of t_i. Next, rf$(s) := \{(t_i, x, t_j) \mid r_i(x_j) \in s, j \neq i\}$ denotes the *reads-from relation* of s. Then

$$\text{ers}(t_i) := \bigcup_{t_j, (t_i, ., t_j) \in \text{rf}(s)} (\text{ws}(t_j) \cup (\text{ers}(t_j) - \{x_k \mid x_j \in \text{ws}(t_j), k \neq j\}))$$

198

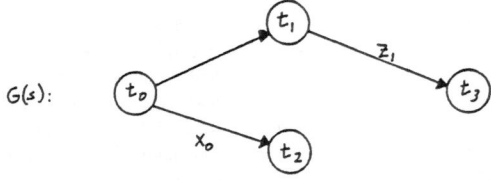

Figure 1: $G(s)$ for the schedule from Example 1.

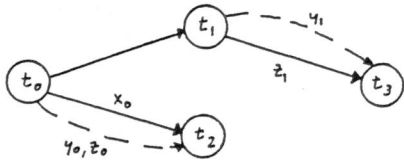

Figure 2: $EG(s)$ for the schedule from Example 1.

Once again a graph can be used to capture the "extended-read relationships" between transactions: With a given schedule s we associate a labelled graph $EG(s)$ (called *extended history graph* in [13]) as follows: $EG(s) := (T \cup \{t_0\}, E, l)$ where

$$E := \{(t_i, t_j) \mid x_i \in \mathrm{ers}(t_j)\}$$
$$\cup \{(t_0, t_k) \mid t_k \text{ is a write-only transaction, } k \neq 0\}$$

and l assigns x_i to edges of the first type. The graph $EG(s)$ for the schedule from Example 1 above is depicted in Figure 2.

Example 2 For a more complex example, consider the following transactions: $t_0 = w_0(x)w_0(y)$, $t_1 = r_1(y)w_1(y)r_1(x)w_1(x)$, $t_2 = w_2(v)w_2(z)$, $t_3 = r_3(y)w_3(u)$, $t_4 = r_4(x)w_4(x)r_4(y)r_4(v)w_4(v)$, $t_5 = r_5(x)r_5(v)$. Next let the following schedule be given:

$$s = w_0(x_0)w_0(y_0)r_1(y_0)w_2(v_2)w_1(y_1)r_1(x_0)r_3(y_1)w_3(u_3)$$
$$w_1(x_1)r_5(x_0)w_2(z_2)r_4(x_1)w_4(x_4)r_5(v_2)r_4(u_3)$$
$$r_4(v_2)w_4(v_4)$$

The graph $EG(s)$ is shown in Figure 3. □

Note that versions a transaction "inherits" via an ers-relationship appear as labels on (dashed) edges originating from the transaction which first produced that version. Also note that $EG(s)$ is in general not simply the transitive closure of $G(s)$, due to the fact that revisions "interrupt" previous "inheritance-chains" w.r.t. the object in question.

We are now ready to define version consistency: A schedule $s \in \mathrm{shuffle}(t_0 T)$ is *version consistent* if

$$|\{x_j \in \mathrm{ers}(t) \mid x \in d\}| \leq 1$$

for each $t \in T$.

Theorem 1 [13] A schedule s is version consistent iff there does not exist a node v in $EG(s) = (V, E, l)$ s.t. $(w, v), (w', v) \in E$, $l(w, v) = x_j$, $l(w', v) = x_i$ and $i \neq j$.

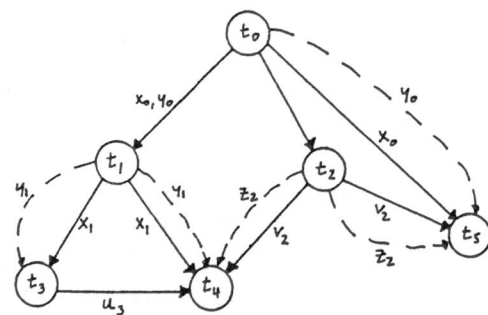

Figure 3: $EG(s)$ for the schedule from Example 2.

In the sequel, let $\mathrm{VC}(T)$ (or simply VC if T is understood or immaterial) denote the set of all version consistent schedules for a given set T of transactions.

3 Serializability of Schedules for Design Transactions

We discuss the issue of serializability next. As was pointed out in [13], the traditional notion of view-serializability [9] has serious shortcomings in the context of design databases, even when adapted to multiple versions. As a result, another correctness criterion for schedules was introduced, the basics of which are reviewed next. We start by looking at the case of single versions, in order to clarify several issues previously left open, and to clearly draw the line to the generalization we pursue.

Let s be a schedule for a given set T of transactions. We introduce the following binary relation on the steps of s (originally due to [17] and also called "immediately-useful" in [12]): A step u of s *immediately affects* another step v of s, written $u \leadsto_s v$, if either v reads some object from u, or u is a read step of $t \in T$ preceding the write step v of t. Stated differently, two types of step-pairs can be related via "$\leadsto_s$":

1. $r_i(x) \leadsto_s w_i(y)$ if $r_i(x)$ occurs in s before $w_i(y)$;

2. $w_j(x) \leadsto_s r_k(x)$ if $k \neq j$ and $(t_k, x, t_j) \in \mathrm{rf}(s)$

Let $\overset{*}{\leadsto}_s$ denote the transitive closure of $\leadsto_s$ (called "affects" in [17]). Notice that $w_j(x) \overset{*}{\leadsto}_s r_k(x)$ hence implies $k \neq j$ and $(t_k, x, t_j) \in \mathrm{rf}^*(s)$, the transitive closure of the reads-from relation of s (see above).

Next, let $T' \subseteq T$ be an arbitrary subset of T. Following [12], we say that a step u of t_i occurring in a given schedule s is T'-*useful*, denoted $u \overset{*}{\leadsto}_s T'$, if there exists a read step v of some transaction in T' s. t. $u \overset{*}{\leadsto}_s v$. The reads-from relation of s *restricted* to some $T' \subseteq T$ is the set

$$\mathrm{rf}(s, T') := \{(t_i, x, t_j) \in \mathrm{rf}(s) \mid r_i(x) \overset{*}{\leadsto}_s T'\}.$$

Two schedules s and s' for T are called T'-*equivalent* for $T' \subseteq T$ if $\mathrm{rf}(s, T') = \mathrm{rf}(s', T')$. Next, a schedule s for T is called T'-*serializable* if there exists some serial schedule s' which is T'-equivalent to s, *view-serializable* if it is T-serializable, and τ_*-*serializable* if it is $\{t\}$-serializable for every $t \in T$.

Let VSR(T) [TSR(T)] (or VSR [TSR] if T is understood) denote the set of all view-serializable [τ_*-serializable] schedules from shuffle(t_0T), resp. Intuitively, in a schedule $s \in$ TSR each transaction "thinks" an equivalent serial schedule exists, but each one may have a different such schedule in mind. In a schedule $s \in$ VSR, every transaction thinks of the same serial execution. Hence, it should intuitively be clear that every view-serializable schedule is τ_*-serializable, but not necessarily vice versa. Formally, we have:

Theorem 2 For each set T of transactions, VSR(T) $\subseteq$ TSR(T).

The following example shows that the inclusion stated in Theorem 2 is even strict:

Example 3 Consider $s = w_0(x)w_0(y)r_2(x)w_1(x)r_1(y)w_2(y)$. Then rf($s,T$) $= \{(t_2,x,t_0)\}$ (note that $(t_1,y,t_0) \notin$ rf(s,T), although $(t_1,y,t_0) \in$ rf(s), since $r_1(y)$ occurs "too late" to affect t_1). However, rf(t_1t_2,T) $= \{(t_1,y,t_0),(t_2,x,t_1)\}$ and rf(t_2t_1,T) $= \{(t_2,x,t_0),(t_1,y,t_2)\}$. Hence, $s \notin$ VSR. We next show that $s \in$ TSR: rf($s,\{t_2\}$) $= \{(t_2,x,t_0)\} =$ rf($t_2t_1,\{t_2\}$) and rf($s,\{t_1\}$) $= \emptyset =$ rf($t_1t_2,\{t_1\}$). $\square$

It follows from the above that τ_*-serializability is strictly more general than view-serializability, and clearly this remains valid if we return to the case of multiple versions. For this case, [13] has argued that view-serializability is no longer appropriate, in particular in the context of design transactions, in which, intuitively, it suffices for a schedule to be correct that each transaction in it can "recognize" some serial production sequence of the versions which affect it, and this sequence need not be the same for each transaction. We also adopt this view in this paper. The following was proven in [13]:

Theorem 3 Let $s \in$ shuffle(t_0T).

(i) If $s \in$ VC(T), then $s \in$ TSR(T) iff $G(s)$ is acyclic.

(ii) $G(s)$ is acyclic iff $EG(s)$ is acyclic.

This result will be used in the next section to develop a scheduling algorithm for design transactions. We conjecture that a similar result can be obtained for the more restricted class of view-serializable schedules, i.e., that membership in the class VSR can be decided in polynomial time in the presence of version consistency.

4 Dynamic Generation of Correct Schedules

According to Theorem 3, testing τ_*-serializability of a given schedule s reduces to testing whether $G(s)$ (or, equivalently, $EG(s)$) is acyclic if s is version consistent; clearly, acyclicity of $G(s)$ can be tested in time polynomial in the "size" of this graph. As a result, a scheduler needs to maintain this graph, test it for cycles from time to time, and make sure that the schedule generated is version consistent at any time.

In the dynamic case, the transactions to be scheduled are not known in advance; instead, they arrive in a step-by-step manner at a *transaction manager*, which performs some preprocessing (such as the assignment of a version to be read to read steps, see below) and then passes them to the *scheduler*. The scheduler maintains as data structures a copy of the *schedule* output so far

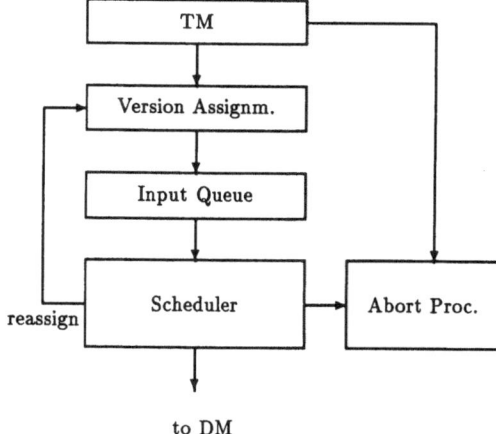

Figure 4: Dynamic scheduling environment.

(called "s" below), and a *graph* which represents the extended history graph of the "current" schedule (called "$EG(s)$" below). For a newly arriving step, the goal is to determine whether it can be placed at the end of the current output schedule without violating its version consistency or serializability.

The dynamic environment we assume to be underlying the situation considered is shown in Figure 4: The transaction manager (TM) is in charge of controlling the processing of each transaction. For reasons discussed below, this is here considered to include the assignment of versions to transaction steps (so that steps reaching the scheduler have been assigned versions already). Steps to be scheduled are then placed in an *input queue* from which the scheduler takes its input. For the scheduler, we adopt the implications of Theorem 3 outlined above appropriately; hence the basic idea is to consider each step newly placed in the input queue in turn, check whether its version assignment was made such that the overall situation obtained so far is kept version consistent, and, if so, check the extended history graph of the augmented schedule for cycles. In the positive case, the step will be output by the scheduler (appended to an execution queue to be processed by the data manager [DM]). If a version inconsistency is discovered for some current read step, the step is returned to the TM for reassignment of (another) version (satisfying the corresponding selection criteria). If such a version cannot be found, or if the graph maintained by the scheduler becomes cyclic, the step is rejected and the transaction aborted. We now consider the major aspects of this outline in more detail.

We consider the task of assigning a version to be read to a newly received read step first. As has been argued in [1], it is reasonable to decouple version control from concurrency control. We also adopt this view here and assume that assigning versions to read steps is accomplished by the TM. Clearly, if a step of the form $r_j(x)$ is currently under consideration, and if n versions of x have already been produced, the TM may choose any of them for $r_j(x)$. However, this choice cannot be arbitrary. In particular, the user of a design database may have a specific version or "type" of version in mind that he wants to elaborate upon, and this intuition must be taken into consideration by the TM.

To describe this formally, we assume that the user, when

writing down his transaction, specifies which version(s) to operate on by delivering a set Σ of *selection conditions* each such version must satisfy. We use the following notation: If x is a database object, x_i is a version of x already produced, and Σ_x is a set of conditions on x, we write $x_i \models \Sigma_x$ if x_i satisfies every condition in Σ_x; let $\text{Sat}(\Sigma_x)$ denote the set of all existing versions of x satisfying Σ_x. Note that we leave open at this point which language is used for specifying conditions; this is immaterial for what follows as long as satisfaction of conditions by versions is polynomially decidable.

If a transaction reaching the transaction manager has a set Σ_x of selection conditions associated with each $r(x)$ step, the TM can check the set of currently existing versions of x and assign to $r(x)$ any member of $\text{Sat}(\Sigma_x)$. Note that this choice is nondeterministic in case $|\text{Sat}(\Sigma_x)| > 1$; however, the more conditions Σ_x contains, the fewer versions will qualify (and the user may be assumed to be happy with any version that falls into the realm of his selection criteria). In addition, this approach leaves the transaction manager with some flexibility regarding retries of version assignments in case a current assignment leads to an inconsistency (discovered by the scheduler).

We finally notice that it can furthermore be assumed that each write step wishing to produce a new version of an object has an associated "procedure" which provides (a set of) conditions the new version will satisfy.

The basic dynamic scheduling algorithm can now be described as follows:

Algorithm (Dynamic) Scheduler:

```
begin
    initialize s and EG(s) to empty;
    while input queue ≠ ∅ do
        begin
            read(newstep); (* from input queue *)
            test(newstep)
        end
end.
```

Here, the while-loop is an infinite loop, which is executed as long as there are transaction steps available. The central test procedure is as follows (where VC and AC are Boolean variables which are assigned the result of corresponding procedures that perform the version consistency test and the acyclicity test on a given extended history graph, resp.):

Procedure test (p : step);

```
begin
    save current EG(s);
    augment EG(s) by p;
    VC := version_consistency(EG(s) "+" p);
    if not VC
        then
            begin
                restore former EG(s);
                if type(p) = 'read'
                    then return p to TM for reassignment of version
                    else reject p
            end
```

```
        else
            begin
                AC := acyclicity(EG(s) "+" p);
                if not AC
                    then reject p
                    else
                        begin
                            output p;
                            s := sp;
                            EG(s) := EG(s) "+" p;
                        end
            end
end;
```

Notice that several details are neglected in this description; for example, we do not elaborate here on such things like adding a node to the graph when a new transaction become active.

While the basic ideas underlying the scheduling algorithm are fairly easy to understand, various issues need additional attention; the most important of these are how to abort transactions, in particular how to assure that rejecting a step and hence aborting the corresponding transaction does not "compromise" what has been scheduled already, and when to remove a node representing a committed transaction from the graph $EG(s)$; these will be discussed in the remainder of this section.

To understand the problem arising in the context of rejecting a step currently being processed by the scheduler, consider the following example:

Example 4 Let the following prefix of an execution queue be given: $s = r_1(x_0)w_1(x_1)r_2(x_1)w_2(y_2)$. Notice that $s \in \text{TSR}$. Now suppose $p = r_1(y_2)$ is encountered next by the scheduler. Although $EG(s \circ p)$ remains version consistent, it is now cyclic, so that p is rejected according to the above algorithm. As a result, t_1 is aborted, and t_2, having read as "invalid" version of x, must be aborted too, a situation commonly termed *cascading aborts*. □

In order to cope with situations like the above, the obvious approach is to require that the output of the scheduler not only be serializable, but also *recoverable* (RC) or even *avoiding cascading aborts* (ACA). Following [4], a schedule is ACA if every transaction may only read values written by committed transactions; a schedule is RC if each transaction commits after the commitment of all transactions from which it read; finally, ACA implies RC, but not vice versa.

In our framework, it is easily seen that in order to make output schedules ACA, it is sufficient that the TM assigns to a read step coming with conditions Σ_x a version from $\text{Sat}(\Sigma_x)$ which has been written by an already committed transaction; if no such version is available, the step might be delayed and retried later. This can easily be implemented by having the TM distinguish *active* transactions from *committed* ones; details are omitted. With this addition, it is now easy to verify the following:

Theorem 4 The dynamic scheduling algorithm described above is safe, i.e., it outputs version consistent and τ_*-serializable schedules which are ACA, and runs in time polynomial in the number of currently active transactions.

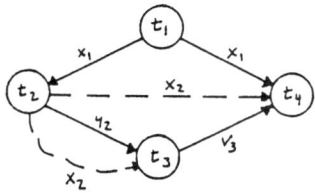

Figure 5: $EG(s)$ for the schedule from Example 5.

We finally look at the space requirements of our scheduler. To this end, there are two sources that might give rise to high space comsumption: One is the fact that the graph needed to test for version consistency and serializability continuously grows as new transactions arrive at the scheduler; the other is simply the fact that basically all versions are kept around. Since the latter is an aspect we want to make use of, there is nothing to do about it. So we consider the former in what follows.

First notice that a transaction will not be aborted any more as soon as it has committed. However, committed transactions cannot be removed from $EG(s)$.

Example 5 Consider the following schedule, whose graph $EG(s)$ is shown in Figure 5:

$$s = w_1(x_1)r_2(x_1)w_2(y_2)r_3(y_2)w_2(x_2)w_3(v_3)r_4(v_3)r_4(x_1)w_4(x_4)$$

Since t_4 reads x_1 as well as x_4, s is not version consistent. For being able to recognize this, the scheduler must keep t_1 represented, although it committed before t_4 started. □

As the example indicates, the problem of deleting completed transactions is difficult to solve for the above scheduling algorithm since, intuitively, the inheritance relationship between transactions regarding versions may grow arbitrarily long. This shows a fundamental difference to ordinary serialization graph testers for 1-version databases, which can remove completed transactions from their conflict graph as soon as the corresponding node has indegree zero [4]. Hence, the space needed by our scheduling algorithm is roughly proportional to $n \cdot m$, where n is the *overall* number of transactions (not just the currently active ones), and m is the size of the database (each transaction may in the worst case produce a new version of each database object), and $EG(s)$ needs space in $O(n^2)$. The only obvious improvement is achievable for read-only transactions, which can be deleted from $EG(s)$ after commitment, since they have not written anything to be kept around.

The fact that in general the space requirements of the scheduler can grow indefinitely seems to be the price to be paid for being able to base the scheduling algorithm on a correctness criterion that is difficult to test in the absence of version consistency. It remains open to improve the scheduler's space efficiency.

5 Conclusions

In this paper, we have added a scheduling algorithm to the work of [13] which dynamically generates version consistent and τ_*-serializable schedules; we have identified a number of problems arising in a dynamic environment where such a scheduler is to be applied, and proposed solutions where possible. One problem that remains is the inefficiency of the proposed scheduler

w.r.t. space complexity. It seems, however, that this can be overcome as soon as semantic information on the transaction becomes available. Suppose, for example, that the state of the underlying database is "refreshed" from time to time by eliminating versions no longer needed. As a result, their "generation history" becomes irrelevant and can also be deleted (e.g., from the graph $EG(s)$). In real-world applications, such information on what a "current" database state (or set of configurations) is can be expected to be available, although the time interval between two consecutive such updates may still be large.

A number of technical questions regarding the theoretical framework underlying our scheduler also remain open. For example, it is currently not clear whether the condition that a transaction "inheriting" some version from another inherits all that were associated with that transaction can be relaxed without invalidating the results obtained.

In general, it seems that the scheduling algorithm proposed in this paper can also be adopted to become a central synchronization mechanism for distributed fileserver-workstation environments, in which designers *check out* designs they want to operate upon from the fileserver to their workstation, and *check* it back *in* when they are done. Here, the centralized graph structure used by our scheduler may need to be broken down into components that can "accompagny" objects which are checked out, so that version consistency of newly created derivates can be controlled locally. In addition, a record must then be kept of the replicas of a version currently checked out, and locally updated graph-components need to be merged appropriately in order to let the system eventually return to something globally consistent. While this is sketchy only, it seems that a deviation from locking protocols usually employed in such architectures is possible.

Another question that seems worth looking into is the extension of the approach described here to (open) nested transactions in the sense of [16], in which each transaction in question is broken down into subtransactions that are allowed to commit before the transaction as a whole commits. In environments employing nested transactions, which seem particularly suited for coping with long transactions that even require user interaction, a more liberal version assignment strategy as well as a greater flexibility for derivations of new designs could become possible, at the expense of a more complicated scheduler. These questions deserve further study.

References

[1] D. Agrawal and S. Sengupta, "Modular Synchronization in Multiversion Databases: Version Control and Concurrency Control," *Proc. ACM SIGMOD Int. Conf. on Management of Data* 1989, 408–417.

[2] F. Bancilhon, W. Kim and H.F. Korth, "A Model of CAD Transactions," *Proc. 11th Int. Conf. on Very Large Data Bases* 1985, 25–33.

[3] P.A. Bernstein and N. Goodman, "Multiversion Concurrency Control: Theory and Algorithms," *ACM Trans. Database Systems* Vol. 8, 1983, 465–483.

[4] P.A. Bernstein, V. Hadzilacos and N. Goodman, "Concurrency Control and Recovery in Database Systems," Addison-Wesley Publ. Co., Reading, MA, 1987.

[5] H.T. Chou and W. Kim, "A Unifying Framework for Version Control in a CAD Environment," *Proc. 12th Int. Conf. on Very Large Data Bases* 1986, 336–344.

[6] R. Elmasri and S.B. Navathe, "Fundamentals of Database Systems," The Benjamin-Cummings Publ. Co., Redwood City, CA, 1989.

[7] T. Hadzilacos and C.H. Papadimitriou, "Algorithmic Aspects of Multiversion Concurrency Control," *J. Computers and System Sciences* Vol. 33, 1986, 297–310.

[8] G. Lausen, "Formal Aspects of Optimistic Concurrency Control in a Multiple Version Database System," *Information Systems* Vol. 8, 1983, 291–301.

[9] C.H. Papadimitriou, "The Theory of Database Concurrency Control," Computer Science Press, Rockville, MD, 1986.

[10] C.H. Papadimitriou and P.C. Kanellakis, "On Concurrency Control by Multiple Versions," *ACM Trans. Database Systems* Vol. 9, 1984, 89–99.

[11] R. Schwarz, "Dynamic Scheduling of Design Transactions based on Version Consistency," Master's Thesis (in German), University of Kiel, April 1990.

[12] K. Vidyasankar, "Generalized Theory of Serializability," *Acta Informatica* Vol. 24, 1987, 105–119.

[13] K. Vidyasankar and C.N.G. Dampney, "Version Consistency and Serializability in Design Databases," *Proc. 2nd Int. Conference on Database Theory (ICDT)* 1988, Springer LNCS 326, 368–382.

[14] G. Vossen, "Data Models, Database Languages and Database Management Systems", Addison-Wesley Publ. Co., Wokingham, England 1990, forthcoming.

[15] G. Vossen and R. Schwarz, "Dynamic Scheduling of Transactions in Design Databases based on Version Consistency," Informatik-Bericht 89-22, RWTH Aachen 1989.

[16] G. Weikum, "Enhancing Concurrency in Layered Systems," *Proc. 2nd Workshop on High Performance Transaction Systems* 1987, Springer LNCS 359, 200–218.

[17] M. Yannakakis, "Serializability by Locking," *J. ACM* Vol. 31, 1984, 227–244.

Design, Implementation and Performance Comparison of the Buddy-Tree[1,2]

Bernhard Seeger[3] and Hans-Peter Kriegel

Praktische Informatik, University of Bremen,
D-2800 Bremen 33, West-Germany

Abstract

In this paper, we introduce a new multidimensional access method, called the buddy-tree, to support point as well as spatial data in a dynamic environment. The buddy-tree can be seen as a compromise of the R-tree and the grid file, but it is fundamentally different from each of them. Because grid files loose performance for highly correlated data, the buddy-tree is designed to organize such data very efficiently, partitioning only such parts of the data space which contain data and not partitioning empty data space. The directory consists of a very flexible partitioning and reorganization scheme based on a generalization of the buddy-system. As for B-trees, the buddy-tree fulfills the property that insertions and deletions are restricted to exactly one path of the directory. Additional important properties which are in this combination not fulfilled by any other multidimensional tree-based access method are: (i) the directory grows linear in the number of records, (ii) no overflow pages are allowed, (iii) the data space is partitioned into minimum bounding rectangles of the actual data and (iv) the performance is mostly independent of the sequence of insertions. Using our standardized testbed, we present a performance comparison of the buddy-tree with other access methods demonstrating the superiority and robustness of the buddy-tree.

1. Introduction

In non-standard database applications, such as geographic information processing or CAD/CAM, access methods are required that support efficient manipulation of multidimensional geometric objects on secondary storage. Moreover, efficient access methods are an essential part in rule-based systems. We can basically distinguish between point access methods (PAMs) and spatial access methods (SAMs) which are designed to handle multidimensional point data, e.g. records ordered by a multidimensional key, and spatial data, e.g. polygons or rectangles, respectively.

First of all, these access methods must be dynamic, i.e. they should support arbitrary insertions and deletions of objects without any global reorganizations and without any loss of performance. Moreover they should efficiently support a large set of queries, such as range, partial match, join and nearest neighbors queries.

The basic principle of all multidimensional PAMs is to partition the data space into page regions, shortly regions, such that all records of a data page are taken from one region. We classify according to the following three properties of regions: the regions are pairwise disjoint or not, the regions are rectangular or not and the partition into regions is complete or not, i.e. the union of all regions spans the complete data space or not. Obviously, this classification yields six classes, four of which are filled with known PAMs, see table 1.

class	property		
	rectangular	complete	disjoint
(C1)	X	X	X
(C2)	X	X	
(C3)	X		X
(C4)		X	X

Table 1: Classification of multidimensional PAMs

All of the PAMs in class (C 1) such as the grid file [9], PLOP-hashing [6] or the K-D-B-tree [13] perform rather efficient for uniform and uncorrelated data. However, for highly correlated data their performance degenerates. Therefore other PAMs belonging to class (C4) like the BANG-file [2] or hB-tree [8] have been proposed allowing more general shapes of regions which are constructed by difference and union of rectangles.

Quite a different approach for the efficient organization of highly correlated data is the buddy-tree. The most important characteristic is that the union of all regions does not span the complete data space. Thus the buddy-tree avoids partitioning empty data space. Instead the buddy-tree uses a similar concept as the R-tree [3] for spatial data, but differs from the R-tree by avoiding overlap in the tree directory. In comparison to previously proposed tree structures such as the K-D-B-tree [13], the buddy-tree guarantees a more efficient dynamic behavior. Moreover, indirect splits which cause low storage utilization and high insertion costs in the K-D-B-tree, are completely avoided. Therefore, the same properties are fulfilled as for B-trees: deletions, insertions and exact match queries are restricted to one path of the directory.

Furthermore, we propose a special implementation technique for the buddy-tree which can be generalized to other access method, like the R*-tree [1]. From this the buddy-tree gains a high fan out of the directory nodes. Thus the height of the tree and the retrieval cost are reduced.

Most SAMs assume that geometric objects are approximated by a minimal bounding rectangle whose sides are parallel to the axis of the data space. One technique to generate such a SAM from a PAM is the transformation of d-dimen-

[1] This work was supported by grant no. Kr 670/4-3 from the Deutsche Forschungsgemeinschaft (German Research Society) and by the Ministry of Environmental and Urban Planing of Bremen.

[2] A long version of this paper is presented at the 16th VLDB Conference, Brisbane, Australia, August 13-16, 1990.

[3] Bernhard Seeger has a one year leave of absence from the University of Bremen which he presently is spending at the University of Waterloo, Canada, financially supported by a Post Doctoral Fellowship from the DFG.

sional rectangles into 2d-dimensional points where for example the first d components represent the center, the remaining d components represent the extension of the rectangle ([4], [14]). These 2d-dimensional points are highly correlated and occupy only a small part of the data space. In particular for such distributions the buddy-tree performs very efficiently.

In the paper we will use the following notations: The parameter d, $d \geq 1$, specifies the dimension of the data space D. The data space D is composed of the domains D_i, $1 \leq i \leq d$, of the i-th axis. On these domains an order relation should be well defined. Without loss of generality we assume that D is given by the d-dimensional unit square $[0,1)^d$. The parameters b, $b > 1$, and c, $c > 1$, denote the capacity of a data page and directory node, respectively. Furthermore we assume in this paper that rectangles are always parallel to the axes of the data space.

The paper is organized as follows. In section 2 we introduce the principles and the properties of the buddy-tree. In the third section we propose a generally applicable implementation technique for increasing the fan out of directory nodes. Eventually, in section 4 we present an experimental performance comparison which demonstrates the superiority of the buddy-tree to other PAMs, such as the hB-tree, the BANG-file and the grid file.

2. The Principles of the Buddy-Tree

The buddy-tree organizes data using a tree-based directory where each axis is treated equally. In contrast to the K-D-B-tree [13] (one of the first multidimensional trees), the buddy-tree performs well in a highly dynamic environment, i. e. insertions, deletions and a change of the data distribution do not affect performance. This property is achieved by applying a modified version of the so-called buddy-system which is well-known from the grid file [9] to the buddy-tree. Additionally, the performance of the buddy-tree is almost independent of the sequence of insertions which is an essential drawback of previous tree-structures, like the K-D-B-tree or hB-tree [8].

Another important feature of the buddy-tree is that it does not partition empty data space. Therefore queries, such as partial match queries, where the query region intersects with empty data space, can be performed much faster than by conventional structures partitioning the complete data space. This property is very similar to the R-tree [3], originally designed for spatial data. Contrary to the R-tree, the buddy-tree does not allow overlap in the directory nodes and can therefore guarantee that insertions, deletions and exact match queries are restricted to one path of the directory. Additionally we incorporate an implementation technique in the buddy-tree which increases the fan out of the directory nodes (see section 3).

The following catalogue summarizes the design properties of the buddy-tree:
- empty data space is not partitioned
- insertion and deletion of a record is restricted to exactly one path
- no overflow pages
- rectangles in directory pages are disjoint
- pointers are disjoint
- directory grows linear in the number of records
- performance is basically independent of the sequence of insertions
- efficient behavior for insertions and deletions
- very high fan out of the directory nodes

Before we present an example of the buddy-tree, we introduce two notations:

Given two d-dimensional rectangles R, S with $R \subseteq S$, R is called a **B-rectangle** of S, iff it can be generated by successive halfing of S (see figure 2.1).
For an arbitrary rectangle $R \subseteq D$, there exists a smallest B-rectangle B of D such that $R \subseteq B$. We call such a B-rectangle the **B-region** of R, short **B(R)**.

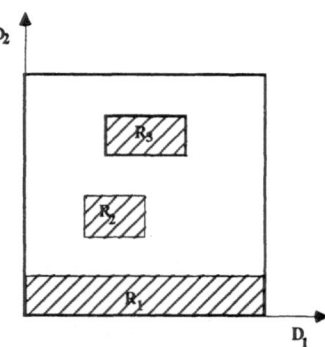

Fig. 2.1: The rectangles R_1 and R_2 are B-rectangles of D and R_3 is not a B-rectangle of D.

With the following example we intend to visualize the basic properties of the buddy-tree. Let the dimension be d = 2, the capacity of a directory page be c = 5 and the capacity of a data page be b = 4. Then the following snapshots illustrated in figure 2.2 depict the growth of the buddy-tree starting with an empty file. In the data pages the actual points are stored. Minimum bounding rectangles of at most four points are represented in the directory pages indicated by a light fill pattern. The white area corresponds to empty data space which is not managed by the buddy-tree. The first line in our example shows states of the buddy-tree with an overflowing data page depicted by a dark fill pattern. In the second line the corresponding subsequent state after the page split is depicted. The rightmost overflow of a data page implies an overflow of the one and only directory page resulting in a buddy-tree of height two.

To briefly summarize the way how a split of a page is performed let us consider the left most overflow. For the points in the overflow page we compute the B-region of the smallest rectangle which covers the points. In our example the B-region corresponds to the entire data space. Then we select a hyperplane perpendicular to the split axis, of the data space which halfens this B-region. In our situation the first axis is selected as the split axis. This hyperplane separates the records into two groups where the one group containing three points remains in the page and the other group is stored in a new page. After further insertions an overflow occurs in the left page. Again we compute the B-region of the points which is the left half of the data space. We determine the second axis as the split axis and separate the points according to a hyperplane perpendicular to the second axis.

To demonstrate that there is no basic difference whether a directory or a data page is split, let us consider the rightmost situation of our example. After performing a split of a data page is performed, an overflow occurs in the directory page. Then we compute the B-region for the minimum bounding rectangle of our directory rectangles. This B-region is again the entire data space. After determination the first axis as the split axis, the hyperplane perpendicular to the first axis divides the directory rectangles into two groups, each containing three entries.

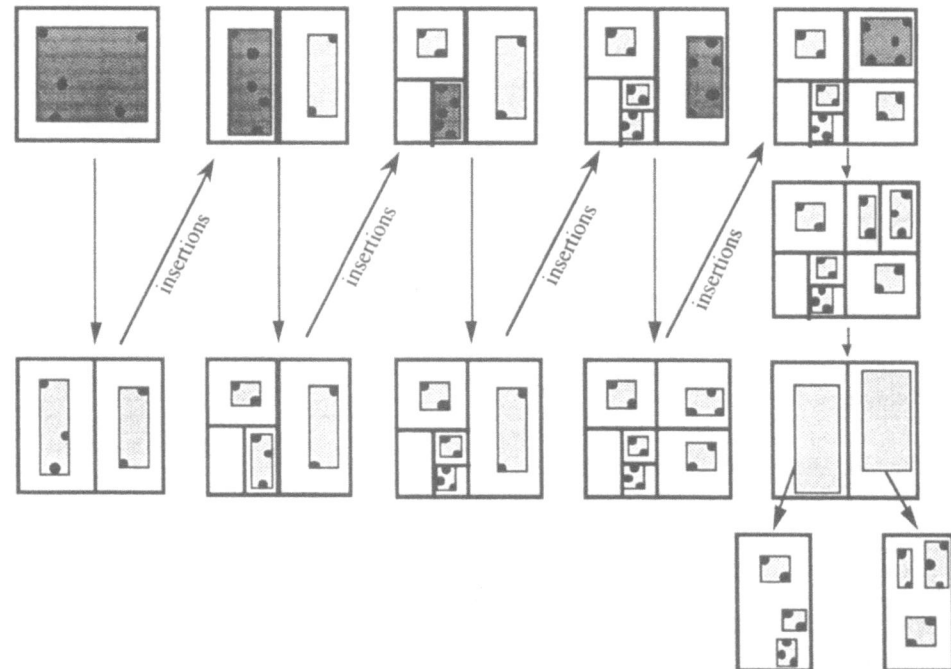

Fig. 2.2: Development of the buddy-tree

Additionally to the above design properties let us emphasize that each of the directory rectangles is the minimum bounding rectangle of the points stored in the corresponding subtree.

Following these basic ideas a more formal description of the structure of the buddy-tree is presented.

The nodes of the tree-directory consist of a collection of entries $\{E_1, \ldots , E_k\}$, $k \geq 2$. Each entry E_i, $1 \leq i \leq k$, is given by a tuple $E_i = (R_i, p_i)$ where R_i is a d-dimensional rectangle and p_i is a pointer referring to a subtree or a data page containing all the records of the file which are in the rectangle R_i.

In order to achieve a good dynamic behavior, the rectangles have to fulfil several conditions which are described in more detail in the following:

Let (S, q) be an entry of an inner node of the buddy-tree where q refers to the node $\{(R_1, p_1),\ldots, (R_k, p_k)\}$, $k \geq 2$. Then we require that the set of rectangles $\{R_1, \ldots, R_k\}$ is a regular B-partition of B(S) which is defined as follows:

A set of d-dimensional rectangles $\{R_1, \ldots, R_k\}$, $k \geq 1$, is called a **B-partition** of the data space D, iff

$$B (R_i) \cap B (R_j) = \emptyset \qquad \forall\, i, j \in \{1, \ldots, k\},\ i \neq j$$

Such a B-partition is called **regular**, iff all B-rectangles $B(R_i)$, $1 \leq i \leq k$, can be represented in a kd-trie.

A kd-trie [10] is a binary digital tree where the internal nodes consist of an axis and two pointers referring to subtrees. In the leaves of the tree the rectangles of a B-partition are represented. Each internal node represents a B-rectangle and the root represents the complete region. In the left or right subtree of such a node, all rectangles are represented which are in the left or right half of the B-rectangle with respect to the corresponding axis, respectively. On the left hand side of figure 2.4 we have depicted a kd-trie corresponding to the B-partition of figure 2.3. Let us mention that there is no unique kd-trie representation of a B-partition. For example, the kd-trie on the right hand side of figure 2.4 represents also the B-partition of figure 2.3.

Considering regular B-partitions, we can also find a split axis which does not intersect with any rectangle of the B-partition. This can be done by using one of the axes denoted in the root of the kd-tries. The test, whether a B-partition is regular, costs quite a bit CPU-time and should not often be performed. The buddy-tree uses the test, if and only if two pages should be merged. After a split this test does not need to be executed, because in such a situation a leaf of the corresponding kd-tries is split into two and an internal node is added to the tree structure referring to these leaves. Let us

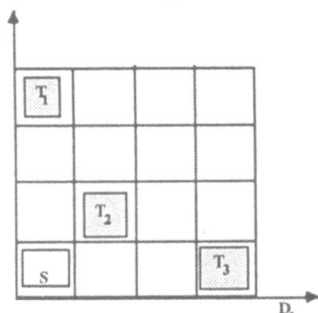

Fig. 2.3: For d=2 and L=5, we have illustrated the buddies T_1, T_2 and T_3 of S

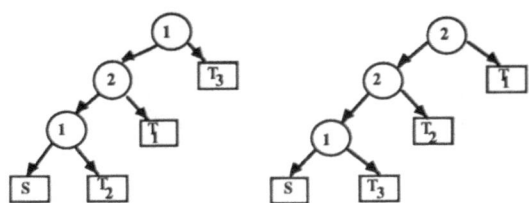

Fig. 2.4: Two kd-trie representations of the B-partition of fig. 2.3

mention that the grid file uses a very similar concept for detecting deadlocks. However, in case of the buddy-tree deadlocks cannot occur, because empty data space is not represented, i. e. rectangles without containing a record are not represented in the directory.

3. Increasing the Fan Out of the Directory Nodes

One shortcoming of the buddy-tree as well as of the R-tree is the relatively low fan out of the directory nodes, because both structures store sets of d-dimensional rectangles in their directory nodes. In this section, we suggest a representation of the rectangles which is similar to that of the so-called hash-trees such as the interpolation-based grid file [12]. The basic idea is to use a d-dimensional orthogonal grid with a dynamically varying resolution for each node. Only these rectangles are accepted which can be exactly mapped on such a grid. The rectangles are represented by two cells matching the lower left and upper right corner of the rectangles. The cells are addressed using a hashing function. Therefore, instead of two d-dimensional points, only two hash values are necessary for the representation of the rectangles. Thus the fan out will increase. For the representation of rectangles by hash-values we decided to use z-values [11].

Another important characteristic of the buddy-tree is that the grid belonging to a directory node does not partition the minimal bounding rectangle M in equal sized cells, but partitions the B-region of M. The partition of the minimum bounding rectangle by a grid would lead to severe problems. If we merge two nodes, a completely new computation of the new grid must be performed. More seriously, we cannot guarantee a unique identification of the rectangles in the merged node. However, if we partition B-regions, the grids of the two merged regions are part of the common grid. This property can be derived from the following principle of B-partitions. If V and W are B-partitions of their B-regions $B(V)$ and $B(W)$ with $B(V) \cap B(W) = \emptyset$, then V and W are also B-partitions of $B(V \cup W)$. For a unique identification of the rectangles in a B-partition, it is necessary that in any grid cell there are not two B-rectangles in common.

Obviously, a shortcoming of a grid representation is that we do not maintain the minimal property of the rectangles in the directory. As illustrated in figure 3.1 the rectangles in a directory node, indicated by the light fill pattern, only enclose the minimal rectangles. At first glance we will expect more disk accesses asking for retrieval operations. However, we have gained a high fan out in the directory nodes. For example, let us assume 2-dimensional keys where each component requires 4 Bytes. Then for an entry consisting of a rectangle and a pointer 4*4+2=18 bytes are necessary for the exact representation where 2 bytes are used for the pointer referring to the subtree. For a grid representation generally two bytes per z-value are sufficient. Therefore the fan out increases by the factor 18:6. This factor will be even better for higher dimensions. The improvement of the fan out is more important for

the performance of the buddy-tree than giving up part of the minimal property.

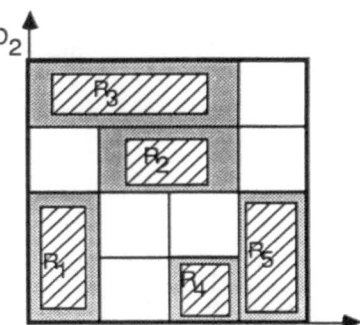

Fig. 3.1: Representation of the minimal rectangles $R_1,..,R_5$ in the buddy-tree

4. Performance Comparison

In the following we give a brief summary of our standardized testbed of PAMs described in detail in [7]. For justifying the choice of PAMs selected for our comparison we refer to the classification of multidimensional PAMs in table 1. Considering class C 1, the most promising structure definitely is the interpolation-based grid file [12]. However, this structure can be obtained as a special case of the buddy-tree by restricting the properties of the regions. Therefore this PAM need not to be implemented. We do not include the best multidimensional dynamic hashing scheme without directory, PLOP hashing [6], since it is efficient only for weakly correlated data, but not for strongly correlated data. From class C1 we selected the 2-level grid file because its efficient fine-tuned and well tested implementation by Klaus Hinrichs [4] is generally available which we thankfully acknowledge.

From class C4 we omitted the B⁺-tree storing z-values [11] from our comparison. Instead, we decided to implement the BANG file [2] and the hB-tree [8], because they are both improvements of the basic B⁺-tree storing z-values. Obviously, we decided to implement the buddy-tree (class C3) due to its non-complete partition of the data space thus avoiding to partition empty data space. Since the concept of the twin grid file [5], which is the only member of class C2, of organizing two dependent grid files at the same time is generally applicable to any PAM, we did not include it in our comparison. It might be worth investigating the application of this principle to the winners of our comparison. As a measuring stick we use our buddy-tree.

Our standardized testbed incorporates seven data files of 2-dimensional records following highly correlated and non-uniform distributions. Each data file contains about 100,000 records. For each data file we considered five query files each of them containing 20 queries. The first query files contain range queries specified by square shaped rectangles of size 0.1%, 1% and 10% relatively to the data space. The other two query files contain partial match queries where in one only the x-value and in the other only the y-value is specified, respectively. For all operations, we have measured the number of disk accesses per operation.

In table 4.1 for the parameters *stor* (average storage utilization) and *insert* (average cost for an insertion) we computed the unweighed average over all seven data files. As an indicator for the average query performance we present the parameter query average which is averaged (unweighted) over

	query average	store	Insert
hB-tree	164.1	68.6	2.80
BANG-file	131.9	67.9	2.49
grid file	148.5	58.3	2.56
buddy-tree	100.0	64.9	2.78

Table 4.1: unweighted average over all 7 distributions

all five query types for each distribution and then averaged over all seven distributions. The goal of this indicator is to help make things more clear, at first glance; however, we are aware that such an average implies a loss of information. For the detailed description of all experiments and all results the interested reader is referred to [7].

In order to keep the performance comparison manageable (we already had more than 2.7 million insertions), we have chosen the page size for data pages and directory pages to be 512 bytes which is at the lower end of realistic page sizes. Using small page sizes, we obtain similar performance results as for much larger file sizes, e.g. a doubling of the page size can accommodate an eight times higher file size within the same directory height for tree-based directories (BANG, file hB-tree, buddy-tree) . We want to emphasize that the grid file implementation [4] always keeps the 1st level grid directory in main memory whereas for the other PAMs only the root page of the directory is main memory resident. Since it was crucial to change the grid file implementation to allow only one root page of the directory in main memory, we accepted that the relative ranking of grid file is too good in comparison to the other structures. To clarify this: for one of our files the 1st level grid directory needed more directory pages in main memory than the complete BANG-file or buddy-tree in secondary storage. Thus the rating of grid file in a comparable environment would be considerably worse. Due to the main memory-resident directory increasing page size implies that the relative performance of the grid file will decrease in comparison to the other structures.

Considering table 4.1 the buddy-tree offers itself to be the winner of our comparison. It is interesting to observe that the buddy-tree does not fulfill the often cited rule "best storage utilization - best query performance". Summarizing we can state that the buddy tree clearly outperforms its competitors if at least one of the following two data characteristics occur:
(C1) densely populated and unpopulated areas vary over the data space,
(C2) sorted data is inserted.
Sorted insertions frequently occur in real-life applications, either sorted by some local ordering such as clusters or quadrants or by lexicographical ordering.

First results in a performance comparison with rectangles underline the superiority of the buddy-tree.

5. Conclusions and Future Work
In this paper, we proposed the buddy-tree, a new dynamic multidimensional access method. Contrary to previously suggested point access methods, the buddy-tree generates the rectangular regions in its directory as minimal as possible. Therefore, the data space is not completely covered by these regions. In particular empty data space is not reflected in the directory. Moreover, the buddy-tree avoids overlap in the directory nodes using a generalization of the so-called buddy-system. Additionally, we propose a general implementation technique for the directory increasing the fan out of the directory nodes. Using our standardized testbed, we present a performance comparison of the buddy-tree with other access methods demonstrating the superiority and robustness of the buddy-tree.

We are still working on some technical improvements of the buddy-tree. Because of the occurrence of underfilled nodes we integrate an pack-algorithm in our implementation for avoiding such nodes. Moreover, we investigate different representations for the directory nodes to improve the buddy-tree with respect to CPU-time.

Additionally, we consider applications for the buddy-tree, such as the organization of rectangles and more complex spatial objects, e.g. non-convex polygons in geographic data bases. Typical operations in geographic data bases such as the rectangle intersection query and the spatial join are efficiently supported by the buddy-tree.

References:
[1] N. Beckmann, H.-P. Kriegel, R. Schneider, B. Seeger: 'The R*-tree: An efficient and robust access method for points and rectangles, Proc. ACM SIGMOD Int. Conf. on Managment of Data, 322-331, 1990

[2] M. Freeston: 'The BANG file: a new kind of grid file', Proc. ACM SIGMOD Int. Conf. on Management of Data, 260-269, 1987

[3] A. Guttman: 'R-trees: a dynamic index structure for spatial searching', Proc. ACM SIGMOD Int. Conf. on Management of Data, 47-57, 1984

[4] K. Hinrichs: 'The grid file system: implementation and case studies for applications', Dissertation No. 7734, Eidgenössische Technische Hochschule (ETH), Zuerich, 1985

[5] A. Hutflesz, H.-W. Six, P. Widmayer:'Twin grid files : space optimizing access schemes', Proc. ACM SIGMOD Int. Conf. on Management of Data, 183-190, 1988

[6] H.P. Kriegel, B. Seeger: 'PLOP-Hashing: a grid file without directory', Proc. 4th Int. Conf. on Data Engineering, 369-376, 1988

[7] H.P. Kriegel, M. Schiwietz, R. Schneider, B. Seeger: Performance comparison of point and spatial access methods, Proc. Symp. on the Design and Implementation of Large Spatial Databases, Santa Barbara, Lecture Notes in Computer Science 409, 89-114, 1989.

[8] D.B. Lomet, B. Salzberg: The hB-tree: A robust multiattribute search structure, in Proc. of the 5th Int. Conf. on Data Engineering, Feb. 6-10, 1989, Los Angeles, also available as Technical Report TR-87-05, School of Information Technology, Wang Institute of Graduate Studies.

[9] J. Nievergelt, H. Hinterberger, K.C. Sevcik: 'The grid file: an adaptable, symmetric multikey file structure', ACM Trans. on Database Systems, Vol. 9, 1, 38-71, 1984

[10] J.A. Orenstein:'Multidimensional tries used for associative searching', Inf. Proc. Letters 14, 4, 1982, 150-157

[11] J.A. Orenstein, T.H. Merrett: 'A class of data structures for associative searching', Proc. 3rd ACM SIGACT-SIGMOD Symposium on Principles of Database Systems, 181-190, 1984

[12] M. Ouksel: 'The interpolation based grid file', Proc. 4th ACM SIGACT-SIGMOD Symposium on Principles of Database Systems, 1985

[13] J. T. Robinson: 'The K-D-B-tree: a search structure for large multidimensional dynamic indexes', Proc.ACM SIGMOD Int. Conf. on Management of Data, 10-18, 1981

[14] B. Seeger, H. P. Kriegel: 'Design and implementation of spatial access methods', Proc. 14th Int. Conf. on Very Large Databases, 360-371, 1988

Coupling the Complex-Relational Data Base CoReDB [*]
with the Object Management System OMS [**]

Thomas Bode **Armin B. Cremers** **Jürgen Freitag** **Thomas Lemke**

University of Dortmund
Department of Computer Science VI; P.O. Box 500 500; D-4600 Dortmund 50; Federal Republic of Germany
E-Mail: {bode,cremers,freitag}@exunido%unido.uucp; tl@anja.ls6.informatik.uni-dortmund.de

Abstract

The CoReDB/OMS approach consequently integrates mechanisms to handle very large logic programs in a data base system.

CoReDB extends the relational model by introducing two new attribute types. The model supports variables in terms and offers a unification operator at the database level. The complexity of the relational operators is enriched to manipulate terms. CoReDB is currently implemented as a main memory oriented system.

The object management system OMS supports complex objects and is extensible by new data types. Both features are considered important when choosing an efficient DBMS backend for CoReDB.

This paper describes a first CoReDB/OMS prototype, which joins the two approaches in a uniform database system.

1 Introduction

Motivated by the requirements of logic programming systems, we regard complex objects as arbitrarily structured data that might contain variables. While conventional database management systems lack the possibility of treating nested data, non standard database systems are not yet able to handle variables in data that is not structured in a uniform way.

The Complex-Relational Data Model (CoReDM) is an extension of the relational data model. A complex relation is a set of complex tuples, whose attribute values might be atomic values but also arbitrarily structured terms containing variables (and lists) in the way they are used in logic programming. This extension requires to enrich the relational algebra, mainly by the introduction of unification and access to subterms.

The CoReDM has been realized in the Complex-Relational Data Base, the CoReDB, as a main memory oriented system. For extending CoReDB by the yet missing secondary storage support, we chose the Object Management System OMS which is being developed at the University of Dortmund in a parallel project. OMS introduces two concepts which are considered helpful for our goal: OMS supports the mapping of complex objects to secondary storage and it is extensible by the means of embedding the implementation of new data types in its kernel. The first concept is particularly useful for modeling arbitrarily structured heterogenous objects which need not be uniquely structured. The second concept allows to move (parts of) the non standard operations of CoReDB to the database

system, thereby reducing the number of object exchanges between CoReDB and OMS.

This paper describes the coupling of CoReDB and OMS. In the following chapter, we give a brief overview of the Complex-Relational Data Model. Chapter 3 sketches the Object Management System and the differences of OMS to other systems supporting complex objects and/or functional extensions, while chapter 4 discusses topics of the coupling. Finally we draw some conclusions in chapter 5.

2 The Complex-Relational Data Model

In the relational model, an object of the "real world" is represented as a tuple of a relation containing objects of the same type. A tuple is described by the values of its attributes. Therefore, representing complex objects in a relational environment entails the introduction of complex tuples, being described by complex attribute values ("non-first-normal-form"). Consequently, we extend the relational data model by extending the complexity of the attribute types which in turn makes it necessary to enrich the complexity of the relational operators.

A similar approach has been taken by Zaniolo ([17]) in the framework of LDL ([16], [3]). The most important difference to his work is that we introduce variables in base relations. This seems to be an essential precondition for real database support of logic programming systems, and it is a necessity for supporting the management of large rule bases by relational database technology. The introduction of variables at the level of base relations leads us to the introduction of unification (cf. e.g. [10]) into the relational algebra. In the following, a brief description of the Complex-Relational Data Model is given. A precise definition can be found in [15] and [8].

2.1 The Notion of Complex Relations

The basic ideas of the relational data model remain unchanged with all their useful and reliable concepts. The simple attribute types like $INTEGER$, $STRING$ or $CHARACTER$ can further be used. We introduce two new attribute types $TERM$ and $RULE$. A complex relation is a set of complex tuples together with its schema. Each tuple consists of a fixed number of atomic or complex attribute values.

The attribute type $TERM$ is used to represent all terms which can be expressed in a standard logic programming environment, i.e. it allows the representation of structured terms, lists and variables. A term $t \in TERM$ can be

- a constant, i.e. an integer or an atom, or
- a variable, which must begin with an underscore (`_`), or
- a structured term $f(t_1, ..., t_n)$, where the functor f is an atom and the t_i, $i = 1, ..., n$, are terms, or
- a list of terms $[t_1, ..., t_m]$, where the t_i, $i = 1, ..., m$, are terms. The list might be the empty list [].

The attribute type $RULE$ is a restriction of $TERM$ to terms

---

[*]   Research supported by the European Community ESPRIT project P530 (EPSILON).
[**] Research supported by the German Research Council (DFG).

representing rules of a logic program in the form *rule(_Head, _Body)*, where *_Head* represents the head literal and *_Body* is a placeholder for the list of body literals of the rule.

We use a dot notation to access parts of a complex attribute value. In our formalization of the relational model attributes are numbered; the i-th attribute has the name *#i*. Each attribute name *#i* is an attribute part specification (APS) addressing the i-th attribute. If *S* is an APS and *n* is a number, then *S.n* is an APS addressing the n-th subterm of the structured value or the n-th element of the list being addressed by *S*. *S.0* addresses the functor of the value addressed by *S*.

For many operators of our Extended Relational Algebra (ERA), equality of terms and of tuples are basic mechanisms which have to be redefined according to the properties of variables. Two terms are defined to be equal when they are equal up to renaming of their variables. A consistent renaming can be realized by numbering the variables of a term from left to right by the position of their first occurrence. For example, $p(\_X, \_Y, \_X)$ and $p(\_a, \_b, \_a)$ will both be transformed to $p(\_1, \_2, \_1)$ and are considered to be equal. This mechanism is extended for the definition of the equality of tuples.

Increasing the flexibility of a data model also increases the possibility of errors. If a query containing APSs is evaluated over a set of complex relations, there might be some tuples where the position being addressed by a specific APS does not exist because not all values of an attribute have to be structured in the same way. In this case, the behaviour of a relational operator is determined by a mode parameter (e.g., "*error*": The result is not defined; or "*ignore*": Just ignore the tuple causing the error.). Together with other modes of operation, this parameter makes up the mode list (*ML*) given to most relational operators. Modes and extended equality are supported by the OMS operations, although this is not described in this paper for the sake of readability.

2.2 The Extended Relational Algebra

The Extended Relational Algebra (ERA) is built of ERA operators which can be used in a nested form to construct ERA trees. Basic ERA operators are "relation name" and "tuple constructor"; all other operators accept ERA trees as arguments.

Relation Name and Tuple Constructor
If *R* is the name of a relation, then $v(R)$ is an ERA tree. The evaluation of $v(R)$ yields the relation *R* itself. If $[a_1, ..., a_n]$ is a list of (complex) attribute values, then $\tau([a_1, ..., a_n])$ is an ERA tree. The evaluation of $\tau([a_1, ..., a_n])$ yields an n-ary relation containing only the tuple $<a_1, ..., a_n>$. All attributes of this relation have the type *TERM*.

Union, Intersection, Difference and Cartesian Product
The "simple" operators union, intersection, difference and cartesian product of two relations remain unchanged. Thus, if E_1 and E_2 are ERA trees that evaluate to relations of the same schema, then $E_1 \cup E_2, E_1 \cap E_2, E_1 \setminus E_2$ and $E_1 \times E_2$ are ERA trees with the common semantics.

Projection
If the projection list *PL* is a list of APSs and *E* is an ERA tree, then $\pi_{ML}(PL, E)$ is an ERA tree. This expression evaluates to a relation consisting of as many attributes as there are APSs in *PL*. The attribute values of the result tuples are the (sub-) terms of the relation yielded by evaluating *E* which are addressed by the APSs in *PL*.

Selection
A selection formula *SF* is formed by disjunction, conjunction and negation of selection atoms of the form $Op_1 \theta Op_2$, where each operand is a constant of any attribute type, an APS or an arithmetic expression, and θ is one of the usual comparison operators or the unification operator $\approx$. If *E* is an ERA tree, then $\sigma_{ML}(SF, E)$ is an ERA tree. In addition to *ML*'s use in possible error cases, a special mode determines the behaviour of unification. The evaluation of $\sigma_{ML}(SF, E)$ yields a relation of the same schema as the relation being associated with *E*, containing all the tuples of this relation fulfilling *SF*.

Selection & Projection
Selection and projection are combined to a new operator. The expression $\rho_{ML}(PL, SF, E)$ is an ERA tree being defined as an abbreviation for $\pi_{ML}(PL, \sigma_{ML}(SF, E))$.

Combination
A combination term (CT) is a term that might contain APSs as "leaves". If the combination list *CL* is a list of combination terms and *E* is an ERA tree, then $\gamma_{ML}(CL, E)$ is an ERA tree. The combination operator constructs a new relation having as many attributes as *CL* has CTs. Regarding one tuple of the result relation, the attribute *#i* has basically the form of the i-th combination term of *CL*, where all APSs are replaced by the terms that result from the APS's evaluation over a tuple of the relation associated with *E*.

Join
A join formula *JF* is basically a selection formula, a join combination list *JCL* is basically a combination list. They differ from the latter ones by containing join attribute part specifications (JAPS) replacing the usual APSs. A JAPS is an APS with a prefix *L.* or *R.* to identify the first (left) and the second (right) relation of the two operands of join. Thus, *L.#5* is the fifth attribute of the first relation. If E_1 and E_2 are ERA trees, then $\otimes_{ML}(JCL, JF, E_1, E_2)$ is an ERA tree. This expression is defined as equivalent to the ERA expression $\gamma_{ML}(JCL', \sigma_{ML}(JF', E_1 \times E_2))$, where *JCL'* and *JF'* are *JPL* resp. *JF* with the JAPSs being replaced by APSs according to the translation of the prefixes refering to attributes in E_1 or E_2 to the position of the appropriate attribute in $E_1 \times E_2$.

Arithmetic
An arithmetic expression *A* is constructed from (numerical) constants and APSs using operators like addition, subtraction, multiplication, division and aggregate functions to compute the minimum, maximum, sum, average and number of values of an attribute or an attribute part. If *E* is an ERA tree, then $\varphi_{ML}(A, E)$ is an ERA tree evaluating to a relation having one attribute more than the relation associated with *E*. For each tuple of *E*'s relation, the new attribute contains the result of evaluating *A* over this tuple.

ERA trees
ERA trees, the queries of the Complex-Relational Data Model, are built by the nested application of the operators of the Extended Relational Algebra. For example, $\pi_{ML}([\#2.1, \#3], \sigma_{ML}(\#1 = vienna, v(R)))$ is an ERA tree.

2.3 Support of Logic Programming

There are (at least) two ways the Complex-Relational Data Model is suitable for supporting very large logic programming projects. First, the facts of a logic program can be stored in complex relations, thus allowing structured terms and variables to appear in the fact base; second, the rule base itself can be kept in the data model.

Fact base management   The set of facts of a logic program might become very large making it useful to store it in a data base management system. Using the CoReDM, structured facts need not be spread over several relations, but each logic predicate is represented by one complex relation.

For example, the fact base of a library application, given in excerpts by

```
literature(1,book(author(Mellish),
    title(Programming in Prolog),year(_UNKNOWN))).
literature(2,article(author(Codd),title(Extending
    the Relational Model),year(1979)))).
```

can be represented in a relation Literature:

| 1 | book(author(Mellish),title(Programming in Prolog),year(_UNKNOWN)) |
| 2 | article(author(Codd),title(Extending the Relational Model),year(1979)) |

Modelling data in a relational way allows avoiding the tuple oriented execution strategy of standard logic programming systems. A query to the (fact or rule) predicates of a logic program can be translated to a (up to duplicate elimination equivalent) ERA tree, as long as the part of the rule set considered does not contain any recursion. E.g., given a rule and a query

```
books_of(_Author, _Title) :-
    Literature(_,
        book(author(_Author),
            title(_Title), _)).

?-books_of(Mellish, _Title).
```

the answers can be retrieved by evaluating the ERA tree

$$\pi_{ML}([\#2.1.1, \#2.2.1],$$
$$\sigma_{ML}(\#2 \approx book(author(Mellish), title(\_Title), \_),$$
$$\nu(Literature))).$$

The compilation of logic programs, including recursive predicates with function symbols, to programs containing ERA trees is described in [7]. The resulting programs simulate an efficient goal-driven, top down evaluation of logic queries.

Rule base management   In real life expert systems, not only the amount of facts, but also the rule base is expected to become very large. One possibility to cope with this is the administration of the rule base on secondary storage in a kind of rule base management system. The CoReDM offers a canonical mapping of logical rules to the attribute type *RULE*. The rule books_of described above might be stored in a relation Library_Queries collecting all query-like rules of the library application:

| 1 | rule(books_of(_Author, _Title), [Literature(_, book(author(_Author), title(_Title), _))]) |

Of course, further, e.g. textual, information can be stored together with the original rule. One option is to keep the translated rule, i.e. the ERA tree corresponding to the rule (which is representable as a term) in the same relation and to

use it when queries to the rule are posed. If such queries shall not be answered directly by the CoReDB but by the logic language interpreter, the rules needed for evaluation can be retrieved testing for the unifiability of the query literal and the head literal of the rule.

It should be noted, that the possibility of dividing the set of logical rules onto different relations is a means of supporting modularization of logic programs which is a useful mechanism for large knowledge bases and which is a critical topic in distributed knowledge based systems.

3 The Object Management System OMS

A major drawback of conventional database systems is their lack of support for special types and special functions needed in advanced applications. Quite a number of proposals try to solve this problem by mechanisms allowing to add new types and functions to a database system. Among others this approach is followed by the systems AIM-P ([9]), STARBURST ([11]), PROBE ([4]), and POSTGRES ([14]) .

In the OMS project we aim at the development of an extensible database kernel system. First, like [9] and [6] we are following the approach of externally defined functions (EDF) embedded in the query language of the kernel. These functions will be implemented in a programming language, as independent from the database kernel system as possible.

The interface between database kernel and EDFs is built by I/O functions. For instance, when an EDF is used within a selection formula, the database system prepares the call by passing the input object(s) from their internal database representation into the representation chosen within the EDF. Analogously, the results of a function are again converted into the internal database representation.

Where conventional database systems are only capable to deliver a (large) superset of a result needed in a non standard application, the expensive transfer of superfluous objects can be reduced by a suitable introduction of EDFs. But still a massive interchange of objects between EDFs and database kernel may take place. To avoid this, OMS additionally allows to integrate new internally embedded data types (IET) directly within the kernel. In contrast to EDFs the implementation of an IET defines its own database internal object representation, therefore there is no need to convert objects when an IET function is called. We will not only introduce atomic IETs this way, but especially polymorphic IETs (type constructors). Even the standard data types *set* and *tuple* are built in by IET implementations.   An important feature of these type constructors is that they can be applied to any other type known to OMS, which supports the modelling of complex objects. For instance we can construct an NF^2 structure since set valued attributes are allowed.

The central idea of the concept of IETs in OMS is that while the systems mentioned above paste functional extensions to finished kernels, we are experimenting with an architecture which is tailored to add modules representing new data types to the kernel at any time. However, we do not call for IETs instead of EDFs. Both concepts are needed: an EDF implementation will be more simple and easier to control, on the other hand we intend to gain efficiency by choosing an IET implementation within a tailored architecture.

The intended OMS kernel architecture (fig. 1) essentially consists of four system layers: the storage system, the storage object manager, the type layer and the object manager. Except for introducing page sets ([5]) to support accesses to large objects the storage system does not diverge much from conventional storage systems.

One problem to be solved when introducing a new IET is to implement an efficient object mapping to secondary storage. To simplify this task some general mechanisms should be provided by the kernel. In EXODUS ([2]), a toolkit to build application-specific database systems, a storage object manager offers bytestrings of variable length and sets of bytestrings (files) for this purpose. Files can be scanned and direct access to a bytestring within a file is supported by an identifier assigned to each bytestring. Moreover, the access to parts of a bytestring via an offset specification is supported, a concept which makes it possible to a certain extent to use bytestrings as container for composite objects. A similar approach has been chosen for a storage object manager within OMS. Atoms again are bytestrings, but instead of files lists and sets of objects are supported, and these two constructors may be used repeatedly to build hierarchically structured records, so-called storage objects. Therefore, even depth structured objects are directly supported by the storage object manager of OMS. An important feature is that the structure of objects within a list or set may differ. The storage object manager maintains an index to support the secondary storage access to the parts of a storage object, and it clusters each subhierarchy of a storage object on secondary storage.

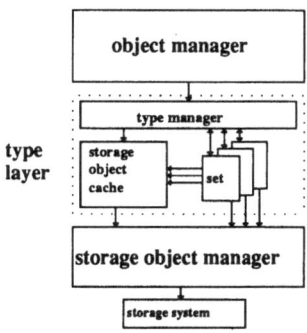

Figure 1: OMS kernel architecture

The type layer is decomposed into three parts: type manager, IET implementations and storage object cache. The storage object cache provides the same notion of a storage object as the storage object manager. Whereas the task of the storage object manager is to minimize the number of page accesses when retrieving a particular part of an hierarchically structured object from secondary storage, the storage object cache supports an efficient main memory management of (parts of) a storage object.

A first task in each IET implementation is to choose a storage object representation for its objects. The implemented functions will work on this internal database representation as far as reasonable. Polymorphic types are implemented independently from the component type(s). For example, a tuple implementation will know how to access an attribute within the storage object representation of a tuple, but it knows nothing about the storage object representation of the attributes. The current tuple implementation uses the list constructor of the storage object manager to map tuples to secondary storage, no additional address calculation to access attributes within a tuple is needed.

On the one hand, the type manager realizes the interface between type layer and object manager, on the other hand it serves as a link between the different type implementations. It allows the specification and execution of special operator graphs describing complex operations on (hierarchically structured) typed objects. These graphs are a generalization of traditional operator trees. For instance, the execution order is not defined by the graph structure but is controlled by the functions connected to the nodes. Additionally nodes may exchange messages. However, for the sake of readability we will use a functional notation instead of operator graphs in this paper.

The object manager provides the OMS kernel with a data model. Its task is to enrich the type implementations with important concepts like shared subobjects and inheritance. Currently the specification of a suitable OMS data model is still under way. A more detailed description of OMS is given in [1].

4 Coupling CoReDB and OMS

Our intentions in coupling CoReDB and OMS are twofold: OMS will provide the secondary storage support yet missing in CoReDB, and we will gain experience with a complex IET implementation in the OMS environment. Last not least, the Complex-Relational Data Model will realize a first data model for OMS, since the design of the OMS object manager is still subject to research.

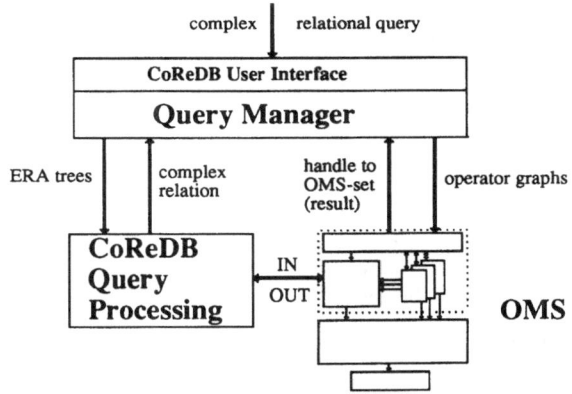

Figure 2: architecture of CoReDB/OMS

In our first prototype sketched in this paper we will not support the complete set of CoReDB operations by OMS: Unification is only partly supported within OMS. This is due to the fact, that a first secondary storage support for the management of large sets of facts and rules is quickly needed in CoReDB, and that we are tackling recursively structured objects (terms) in OMS for the first time. The experience gained with the prototype will influence its future replacement by a tight coupling, where each operator of the CoReDB data model is represented by a suitable OMS function.

The prototype will couple CoReDB with the type layer of OMS (fig. 2). We will use the standard IET implementations *SET*, *TUPLE*, *INTEGER*, *STRING* and *CHAR*, and we will integrate a new IET *TERM* to support the notion of terms in CoReDB. As already mentioned, the CoReDB operations are not covered completely, therefore a special query manager embedded between CoReDB and the OMS type layer resolves each query in CoReDB into a set of queries evaluated by OMS, and a remaining part, which is evaluated by CoReDB. Large intermediate results are stored within OMS again. Data transfer and transformation between CoReDB and OMS is executed by two special functions (*IN*, *OUT*), which will also enable a successive transfer in the case of large objects.

After describing the operations delivered by the IET implementations supporting CoReDB, we will outline, how ERA expressions are resolved into a corresponding set of OMS operations.

4.1 Modelling Complex Relations in OMS

To model the notion of complex relations in CoReDB, besides the standard IETs *INTEGER*, *STRING* and *CHAR* a realization of the types *RELATION* and *TERM* is needed in OMS. However, instead of implementing an IET *RELATION* explicitly, we will use the more general standard IETs *SET* and *TUPLE*, which support not only flat relations, like they are required by the CoReDB, but nested relations (NF^2 relations) too. To map terms to the standard OMS types would be rather forced and would lead to a huge amount of superfluous object transfer between OMS and CoReDB. Therefore we aim at additional support by a special IET *TERM*, thereby reaching the same performance as for the standard types mentioned above. We emphasize the description of *TERM* in this chapter, but previously we sketch à subset of operations of the IETs *SET* and *TUPLE* needed for CoReDB. *INTEGER*, *STRING* and *CHAR* are neglected here.

The IET *SET* The IET *SET* allows to model a collection of objects of any type known within OMS. Among others it supports the following operations, where $SET[X]$ denotes a set of objects of type X :

Union, intersection, difference:
$$\cup, \cap, \backslash: \quad SET[X], SET[X] \longrightarrow SET[X]$$

Selection:
$\sigma[i: P(i)]: \quad SET[X] \longrightarrow SET[X]$,
where the selection formula "$i: P(i)$" denotes a symbol i and a boolean function $P: ..., X, ... \longrightarrow BOOL$.

Iteration:
$I[i: T(i)]: \quad SET[X] \longrightarrow SET[X]$,
where the iteration formula "$i: T(i)$" denotes a symbol i and a transformation $T: ..., X, ... \longrightarrow Y$.

Selection&Iteration:
$\rho[i: P(i), T(i)]: \quad SET[X] \longrightarrow SET[X]$,
where the formula "$i: P(i), T(i$" denotes a symbol i, a transformation $T: ..., X, ... \longrightarrow Y$ and a boolean function $P: ..., X, ... \longrightarrow BOOL$.

Join:
$\otimes[i, j: P(i, j), T(i, j)]: \quad SET[X], SET[X] \longrightarrow SET[X]$,
where the join formula "$i, j: P(i, j), T(i, j)$" denotes symbols i and j, a transformation $T: ..., X, Y, ... \longrightarrow Z$ and a boolean function $P: ..., X, Y, ... \longrightarrow BOOL$.

Constructor:
$c_{SET}: \quad X, X, ... \longrightarrow SET[X]$

Aggregate functions:
$min[i: T(i)], max[i: T(i)], ...: \quad SET[X] \longrightarrow INTEGER$,
where the formulas "$i: T(i)$" denote a symbol i and a transformation $T: ..., X, ... \longrightarrow INTEGER$.

The functions are a generalization of the corresponding relational operations. For instance, iteration is used to realize the relational projection, but the transformation may be any other function, where input and output are of types X and Y respectively. The result of each transformation, one for each element in the set, is inserted into the result. Analogously a join is processed, where the transformation is applied to all qualified pairs of type X and Y.

The IET *TUPLE* A tuple of type $TUPLE[T_1, ..., T_n]$ is an ordered collection of objects of types $T_1, ..., T_n$, where T_i denotes any type defined within OMS. Among others the IET *TUPLE* supports the following operations:

Attribute projection:
$\pi[k]: \quad TUPLE[T_1, ..., T_k, ..., T_n] \longrightarrow T_k$

Boolean functions:
$=_{TUPLE}, >_{TUPLE}, ...: \quad TUPLE[T_1, ..., T_n], TUPLE[T_1, ..., T_n] \longrightarrow BOOL$

Concatenation:
$\times: \quad TUPLE[X_1, ..., X_n], TUPLE[Y_1, ..., Y_m] \longrightarrow TUPLE[X_1, ..., X_n, Y_1, ..., Y_m]$

Constructor:
$c_{TUPLE}: \quad T_1, ..., T_n \longrightarrow TUPLE[T_1, ..., T_n]$

Constructor and attribute projection are used within a set iteration to realize the relational projection. The order on tuples ($>_{TUPLE}$) is defined lexicographically.

The IET *TERM* Where the mapping of *SET*s and *TUPLE*s to storage objects is obvious, we should briefly describe this subject in the case of *TERM*s, since the structure of these objects varies and is defined recursively. We decided to map the entire structure of a term to a corresponding hierarchically structured storage object: functors and lists are mapped to lists of storage objects, integers, atoms and variables are represented as bytestrings. Since the operations need to identify the type of a term, a corresponding information is stored additionally. In the case of integers, atoms and variables the first byte is used for that matter, in the case of functors and lists the first list element contains this information. A functor name is stored as a bytestring in the second element of the storage object list. This mapping makes full use of the features offered by the storage object manager:

- A term and each part of a term is clustered on secondary storage.
- The secondary storage access to subterms is supported, since the storage object manager maintains a corresponding index.
- In spite of the support of subterm access the depth of a term structure is not limited.

The most important operations offered by the IET *TERM* are:

Subterm addressing:
$\pi[APS]: \quad TERM \longrightarrow TERM$,
where *APS* describes the path to the inquired subterm.

Boolean functions:
$=_{TERM}, >_{TERM}, ...: \quad TERM, TERM \longrightarrow BOOL$

Similarity:
$\cong: \quad TERM, TERM \longrightarrow BOOL$

Type transformation:
$INT_{TERM}: \quad TERM \longrightarrow INTEGER$
(partially defined function)

Term constructor:
$c_{TERM}[TC]: \quad \longrightarrow TERM,$
where TC is a constant $TERM$.

Functor constructor:
$c_{FUNC}[FN]: \quad TERM, TERM, ... \longrightarrow TERM,$
where FN is a functor name.

List constructor:
$c_{LIST}: \quad TERM, TERM, ... \longrightarrow TERM$

All CoReDB operations on terms except unification are directly represented in the IET $TERM$. "Similarity" serves as a weak unification: two terms are considered similar, if its constant subterms are equal, i.e., the comparison of a variable with a term is always evaluated to *true*.

The type transformation "term to integer" allows the application of the operations implemented by the IET $INTEGER$, for instance to evaluate arithmetic ERA expressions.

4.2 Evaluating ERA Trees using OMS

Coupling CoReDB and OMS on the level of query execution can be regarded as a two-step-process: First, all the ERA operators have to be supported by OMS functions so that a single ERA operator can be translated in an expression that can be evaluated by OMS. Second, there are several topics that have to be taken care of when an ERA tree consists of more than one ERA operator. Dependencies between the operator nodes have to be considered, especially in the case when there is a unification (which is not supported by OMS).

Relation Name and Tuple Constructor The relation name operator ν, applied to a relation name R, yields the relation R. This operator corresponds to the reference to an OMS object by using its name in an expression. The tuple constructor τ is supported by the successive use of OMS´s construction functions. The ERA tree $\tau([a_1, ..., a_n])$ is transformed to an OMS expression $c_{SET}(c_{TUPLE}(c_{TERM}(a_1), ..., c_{TERM}(a_n)))$.

Union, Intersection and Difference These operators are defined on sets of OMS objects and therefore can be directly used.

Cartesian Product OMS provides an operator to concatenate two tuples. The cartesian product of two relations has to be realized by an iteration of this operator over both relations.

Projection OMS offers a projection operator which is defined over a single tuple. This makes it necessary to use OMS´s iteration operator to execute a projection on a whole relation. Thus, a projection operator $\pi_{ML}([APS_1, ..., APS_n], \nu(R))$ becomes $I[t: c_{TUPLE}(APS_1´, ..., APS_n´)](R)$, where t is a tuple variable "scanning" the relation R. A "simple" APS of the form $\#i$ is transformed to $\pi_A[\#i](t)$, while a nested APS $\#i.path$ is translated to $\pi[path](\pi_A[\#i](t))$. In the following, APS´ denotes an APS which is translated according to these modifications.

Selection The CoReDB´s selection operator is supported with the exception of its unification facility. A selection formula without unification can be translated into an OMS selection formula using c_{TERM} for term constants, APS transformations for APSs and OMS´s equality and comparison operators and its facilities for logical connections (*and, or, not*) in a suitable way. Unification is not processed by OMS. It offers a similarity operator $\cong$ which succeeds when two terms are equal in their constants and so avoids the expensive operation of unification, especially its occur check part (see [13]).

Similarity is used instead of unification, so the evaluation of an OMS selection containing a similarity typically yields a superset of the result relation. The unifying part of the selection formula (i.e., the part containing unifications) has to be evaluated on this set (relation) by the CoReDB afterwards. Moreover, those comparisons of the testing (non-unifying) part which are coupled with the unifying part by shared variables, have to be executed by the CoReDB. For example, $\sigma_{ML}(\#2.3 \cong p(\_X)$ *and* $\_X > 1963$ *and* $\_X < 1990, \nu(R))$ has to be completely evaluated by CoReDB because splitting the selection formula would destroy the binding of $\_X$ to a value of R. Alternatively, the formula can be transformed to the expression $(\#2.3 \cong p(\_X)$ *and* $\#2.3.1 > 1963$ *and* $\#2.3.1 < 1990)$ which does not contain any unification and can completely be evaluated by OMS. Such strategies for eliminating unifications have to be further studied.

Selection & Projection The combination of selection and projection is realized by OMS´s ρ-operator. If the selection formula contains unifications, the same conditions as for the selection hold.

Combination The γ-operator can be understood as a counterpart to the projection in the sense that it allows to construct new values not being part of the database and thereby increasing the "breadth" of a relation while the projection typically decreases its "breadth". Thus, the combination is treated in a similar way. Using the iteration operator I, a suitable list of construction operations is repeatedly applied to each tuple of a relation. For example, the ERA tree $\gamma_{ML}([new(\#1), other(\#2, \#3)], \nu(R))$ is transformed to the OMS expression $I[t: c_{TUPLE}(c_{FUNC}[new](\pi_A[\#1](t)), c_{FUNC}[other](\pi_A[\#2](t), (\pi_A[\#3](t))))](R)$.

Join A join operator not containing any unification can be evaluated using OMS´s join operator. A join operator $\otimes_{ML}([CT_1, ..., CT_n], JF, \nu(R_1), \nu(R_2))$ is then transformed to $\otimes[t, u: JF, CT_1´´, ..., CT_n´´](R_1, R_2)$, where $CT_i´´$ is the combination term CT_i containing APSs $APS_j´$ (i.e., APS_j transformed using the modifications described earlier) evaluated on the tuple t of R_1 or u of R_2 respectively.

Evaluating nested ERA trees Due to the possibility of nesting OMS expressions, an ERA tree without unification can completely be evaluated by OMS in one step.

Selection and join formulas containing unifications are rearranged as far as possible in order to eliminate unifications

214

and to replace them by a combination of similarity and other comparison operators. If this succeeds, the resulting formula(s) can also be handled by OMS, otherwise (e.g., when two attribute values are to be unified), similarity is used taking into account that OMS will offer a superset of the "real" solution. For selection, this will result in one call to OMS, for a join operator it might be necessary to call OMS twice, so that in the general case there will be a sequence of OMS calls yielding intermediate result relations. These relations have to be postprocessed by CoReDB in order to evaluate unification.

For the compilation of ERA trees to OMS expressions the general topics of algebraic optimization hold. Especially when more than one OMS call is necessary, attention must be paid to not "cutting out" attributes which are needed in a later state of evaluation.

To be able to handle very large relations, OMS's output routine offers the possibility of accessing the tuples of a relation successively, while on the other hand the input routine allows storing a relation tuple by tuple. Final result of an evaluation of an ERA tree is a relation in CoReDB representation which can be written to OMS using *IN*, or an OMS relation that can be accessed via *OUT*.

5 Conclusion

Introducing the Complex-Relational Data Model, we have extended the relational data model by arbitrarily structured attribute values with variables. OMS supports the complex object structure needed for terms, and its extensibility enables the realization of the non standard operations of CoReDB as internal data base operations.

A system comparable to CoReDB/OMS is LILOG-DB ([12]). The data model of LILOG-DB offers features not directly covered by the CoReDB data model. On the other hand, variables are not supported in LILOG databases. Another important difference is that LILOG-DB is not developed as an extensible system.

The CoReDB has been implemented as a main memory oriented system and is currently running as a prototype. OMS has been implemented at the University of Dortmund too. Research on both systems is on-going; special attention is paid to the coupling of CoReDB and OMS. We aim at finishing the CoReDB/OMS prototype within the current year. Afterwards we intend to examine a complete covering of the CoReDB operations by OMS, thus replacing the CoReDB/Query processing component (fig. 2) by advanced IET implementations.

References

[1] Th. Bode, J. Freitag: *Mapping Complex Objects to Secondary Storage in the Object Management System OMS*. Technical Report.

[2] M. J. Carey, D. J. DeWitt, D. Frank, G. Graefe, M. Muralikrishna, J. E. Richardson, E. J. Shektia: *The Architecture of the EXODUS Extensible DBMS*. In: Proc. International Workshop on Object-Oriented Database Systems, 1986.

[3] Danette Chimenti, Ruben Gamboa, Ravi Krishnamurthy, Shamim Naqvi, Shalom Tsur, Carlo Zaniolo: The *LDL* System Prototype. In: *IEEE Transactions on Knowledge and Data Engineering* 2, 1 (March 1990), pp. 76-90.

[4] U. Dayal, F. Manola, A. Buchmann, U. Chakavarthy, D. Goldhirsch, S. Heiler, J. Orenstein, A. Rosenthal: *Simplifying Complex Objects: The PROBE Approach to Modelling and Querying Them*. In: Proc. BTW 1987.

[5] T. Härder (ed.): *The PRIMA Project - Design and Implementation of a Non-Standard Database System*. Universität Kaiserslautern, SFB 124, Report No. 26/88, 1988.

[6] L.M. Haas, H.-J. Schek, P.M. Schwarz, P.F. Wilms: *Incorporating Data Types in an Extensible Database Architecture*. In: Proc. Int. Conf. on Data and Knowledge Bases 1988.

[7] Günter Kniesel: *Compilation of Logical Programs for Parallel Set Oriented Evaluation in Distributed Knowledge Based Systems*. (in german). Diploma thesis, University of Dortmund, Department of Computer Science VI 1988.

[8] Thomas Lemke: *The Complex-Relational Data Model*. Technical report, manuscript in preparation.

[9] V. Linnemann, K. Küspert, P. Dadam, P. Pistor, R. Erbe, A. Kemper, G. Walch, M. Wallrath: *Design and Implementation of an Extensible Database Management System Supporting User Defined Types and Functions*. In: Proc. VLDB 1988.

[10] J.W. Lloyd: *Foundations of Logic Programming*. Berlin, Heidelberg, New York, Tokyo: Springer-Verlag 1984.

[11] B. Lindsay, J. McPherson, H. Pirahesh : *A Data Management Extension Architecture*. In: Proc. SIGMOD 1987, San Francisco, May 1987.

[12] Th. Ludwig, B. Walter, M. Ley, A. Maier, E. Gehlen: *LILOG-DB: Database Support for Knowledge-Based System*. In: Proc. BTW 1989.

[13] Alberto Martelli, Ugo Montanari: An Efficient Unification Algorithm. In: *ACM Transactions on Programming Languages and Systems* 4, 2 (April 1982), pp. 258-282.

[14] L. A. Rowe, M. R. Stonebraker: *The POSTGRES Data Model*. In: Proc. VLDB 1987.

[15] Petra Schöfer, Thomas Lemke: *Design and Implementation of a Data Model for the Representation of Complex Objects in Relations*. (in german). Diploma Thesis. University of Dortmund, Department of Computer Science VI, 1988. Submitted for publication.

[16] Shalom Tsur, Carlo Zaniolo: LDL - A Logic-Based Data-Language. In: Yahiko Kambayashi (ed.): *Twelfth International Conference on Very Large Data Bases. Proceedings*. Kyoto, 1986. pp. 33-41.

[17] Carlo Zaniolo: The Representation and Deductive Retrieval of Complex Objects. In: A. Pirotte, Y. Vassiliou (eds.): *Eleventh International Conference on Very Large Data Bases. Proceedings*. Stockholm, 1985. pp. 167-178.

Query Optimization in Object−Oriented Database Systems[*]

Wei Sun, Weiyi Meng, and Clement Yu

Department of Electrical Engineering and Computer Science
University of Illinois at Chicago
Chicago, IL 60680

Abstract

In this paper, query processing and optimization in object-oriented database systems (OODBs) in a centralized environment is discussed. The typical chain query processing and optimization in OODBs is investigated in detail. An algorithm with complexity of $O(n^3)$ to minimize the total cost is provided using dynamic programming, where n is the number of classes referenced by the query. Many issues are addressed and integrated into our basic formulation of the problem. These include sorted states of classes, local processing of selections and projections, allowing multiple intermediate results, arbitrary answer class, class hierarchy (which captures the IS-A relationship among objects), loop query (a simple cyclic query).

1. Introduction

Object-oriented programming has been introduced into database system recently. Several prototypes of OODBs have been and/or are being developed such as Iris [BEEC83, LYNG87], Postgres [STON86], Orion [BANE88, KIM87], Starburst [HAAS89], and Exodus [CARE88]. Many research results indicate that OODBs can be applied in various large-scale and complicated application domains [AFSA85,86, AHLS84, ATWO85, HARD86, LYNG84, NIER86, SPOO86, WOEL86, WOEL87].

In order to efficiently manage objects, to support generalization/specialization and to be conceptually simple and uniform, objects are grouped into *classes*. All objects of a class are defined by the same set of attributes. Objects that belong to a class are called *instances* of the class. *Class hierarchy* can be defined to capture the IS_A relationship among objects in different classes. A higher/lower level class is called a *superclass/subclass*. Attributes specified for a class are inherited (shared) by all its subclasses. More specific and additional attributes can be defined on lower classes. The *domain* of an attribute is a class. If the domain of attribute B in class C is class D, then an instance of C may take any instance from class D or one of the subclasses of D as value for attribute B in that instance of C. It is assumed that each object of a class is assigned a system-wide unique identifier (UID) [ULLM88]. A class can be a *primitive class* (e.f. string, integer, and boolean classes) or a conventional class with a set of attributes defined. The value of an attribute is a value of its domain if its domain is a *primitive class*, or a reference to (*object identifier* of) an instance of the domain class if the domain is a

non-primitive class. In the later case, the attribute is a *complex one*.

This paper will discuss query optimization in OODBs. We will use examples from Orion[BANE88, KIM90] to illustrate our approach. Since Orion, which has exploited many object-oriented characteristics such as class hierarchy, unique identification of objects, is a representative OODB, we believe our result is applicable to many other OODBs.

The following is an Orion database schema if class hierarchy is ignored [BANE88]:

Auto ──▶**Person** ──▶**City** ──▶**State**
Manufacturer   age   name   name
color   hometown ──┘ state ──┘ population
owner ──────┘

Figure 1.1: A Sample Database

Class *Person* is defined as the domain of attribute *owner* of class *Auto*; the domain of attribute *population* in class *State* is primitive class *integer*, and so on. *Auto-ID, Person-ID, City-ID,* and *State-ID* are unique object identifiers for classes *Auto, Person, City* and *State*, respectively. They are automatically generated and maintained by OODBs. An example query against this database schema is:

Example 1.1: Find all automobiles owned by persons who live in cities within states with population over 10,000. This query if using notations from [ZANI83] is:

> **select** Auto
> **where** owner.hometown.state.population > 10,000

Its query graph becomes [BANE88]:

Auto ──▶**Person** ──▶**City** ──▶**State**
owner ──┘ hometown ──┘ state ──┘ population

Figure 1.2: Query Graph of Sample Query

As we can see, attribute *owner, hometown,* and *state* are complex ones which take UID's of class *Person (Person-ID)*, class *City (City-ID)*, and class *State (State-ID)* as their values, respectively. The attributes *Person-ID, City-ID* and *State-ID* may be invisible to the users. If class Y is the domain class for attribute X of class Z, then we draw an arrow from X to Y. If we neglect the output and the selection, and properly rename some attributes, this query can be expressed as:

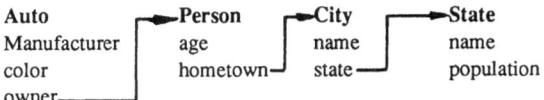

Figure 1.3: Query Graph of Sample Query

[*] Research supported in part by NSF under IRI-8901789 and in part by MCC.

This is an example of a typical query called a *chain query*. In a chain query, there is a common "chaining" attribute between adjacent classes, but there is no common "chaining" attribute between non-adjacent classes. We use R_i to denote an original class. For example, R_1 denotes the class **Auto**. Let R_{ii} represent the simplified class containing only the ID attributes which are chained to its adjacent classes as in Figure 1.4. For example, R_{22} is Person(Person_ID, City_ID). The general form of a chain query is:

$$R_{11} \quad R_{22} \quad ... \quad R_{ii} \quad ... \quad R_{nn}$$
$$ID_2 \text{———} ID_2 ID_3 \text{ ...———} ID_i ID_{i+1} \text{ ...———} ID_n$$

Figure 1.4: Query Graph of Generalized Chain Query

where ID_i is the attribute for uniquely identifying objects in class R_i, $1 < i \leq n$. In OODBs, the chaining from one class to another comes about naturally through the use of complex attribute as in *Example 1.1*. In this paper we will restrict ourselves to mostly chain query optimization. It can be observed that chaining of classes involved in a query graph corresponds to joining in relational database (this is referred to as a *functional join*[CARE88, ZANI83]). If class R_{ii} is considered as a relation, then attribute ID_i of R_{ii} becomes the "join" attribute between R_{ii} and $R_{i-1,i-1}$, and attribute ID_{i+1} of R_{ii} becomes the "join" attribute between R_{ii} and $R_{i+1,i+1}$, $2 \leq i \leq n-1$.

Let the natural join be ∞. Further, let

$$R_{ij} = R_i \infty R_{i+1} \infty \mathbin{\vdots} ... \infty R_j \ [ID_i, ID_{j+1}], \ 1 < i < j < n$$
$$R_{1i} = R_1 \infty R_2 \infty ... \infty R_i \ [ID_{i+1}], \ i \leq n-1$$
$$R_{in} = R_i \infty R_{i+1} \infty ... \infty R_n \ [ID_i], \ i \geq 2$$

where the two attributes within the brackets are the attributes of the intermediate results, R_{ij}, $i \neq j$. R_{1i} and R_{in} are special intermediate results that they only have a single attribute, since we only need to keep the join attributes which will be used in subsequent join operations (Attribute ID_1 in R_{1i} and attribute ID_n in R_{in} will never be used for subsequent joins. Therefore, they are abandoned). Furthermore, whenever a join has been performed, the attribute that participated in the join will be abandoned, so that the intermediate results R_{ij} only consist of UID pairs $[ID_i, ID_{j+1}]$. The definition for R_{ii}, $1 \leq i \leq n$, is also consistent with this notation. Obviously R_{1n} is the answer (if we ignore the target class), which can be obtained from $R_{1k}[ID_{k+1}] \infty R_{k+1,n}[ID_{k+1}]$ for some k, $1 \leq k < n$. This implies

$$R_{1n} = R_1 \infty R_2 \infty ... \infty R_n \ [ID_{k+1}].$$

We are interested in obtaining R_{1n} with the least cost.

Dynamic programming techniques have been employed by [CHIU84, DANI82, LAFO86, SELI79, YLCC82, YUOZ84] in relational query optimization. However, there are significant differences between the solution we propose and earlier solutions. We summarize these differences and our contributions as follows.

(1). The cost model in our formalism is much more realistic than those given by researchers.

(1a) **Local reductions (selections/projections):** In previous papers, local reductions are either not addressed [LAFO86] or always performed before joins [SELI79, DANI82]. However, it was demonstrated in [ABGL88] that performing local reductions before joins may not yield optimal results. In our formalism, there is no restriction on the order in which local reductions and joins are performed, that is, local reductions are allowed to be performed before joins, while performing joins, and/or after joins. In addition, reductions can be carried out by using indices or sequential scanning.

(1b) **Sorted state:** A base relation or an intermediate result is said in a sorted state if the tuples of the relation are sorted in ascending order of an attribute to be joined with some other base relations or intermediate results in subsequent joins. The cost of performing a join in which tuples are already sorted under the join attribute is different from that of joining relations with unsorted tuples. It is important to note that a certain nested-loop join may have higher join cost than another join method, but yields an intermediate result in a sorted state, which in turn may lessen the cost of subsequent joins. In most previous papers, the issue of sorted state is not addressed. [SELI79] briefly mentioned a distinction between a sorted relation and an unsorted one, but no detailed analysis is provided. In our formalism, sorted states of original relations as well as of intermediate results are taken into full consideration for query optimization.

(1c) **Base relation:** In [SELI79, DANI82], a join required that one relation be a base relation. However, such restriction may not enable an algorithm to yield an optimal result. In our formalism, joins between two intermediate results are allowed for a query execution plan. It is known that the strategy which only allows at most one intermediate result during a query processing may not necessarily yield an optimal result.

(2). In addition to the above situations, the algorithm is able to uniformly handle many other situations, including arbitrary answer class in a centralized environment, class hierarchies, and loop query processing. This demonstrates the usefulness and the flexibility of the algorithm. A single, yet uniform, algorithm capable of handling such a wide range of situations efficiently has not been reported.

(3). The algorithm is shown to require $O(n^3)$ time complexity, in minimizing total cost, where n is the number of classes involved in the query.

This paper is organized as follows: In *Section 2*, three basic join methods are discussed. Special attention is given to the sorted state of joining classes and intermediate results and their effects on the cost of subsequent joins. Dynamic programming technique is applied to obtain an optimal solution to the problem in *Section 3*. An algorithm with complexity $O(n^3)$ is provided, where n is the number of classes in the chain. In *Section 4*, local processing costs incurred by selections and/or projections are taken into consideration. In *Section 5*, the solution is extended to the case where an arbitrary answer(target) class is specified. *Section 6* deals with class hierarchy which captures the IS-A relationship. A simple cyclic query, the *loop query*, is investigated, and an algorithm with complexity $O(n^3)$ is obtained in *Section 7*.

2. Physical Access of Objects

It is assumed in Orion [KIM87, BANE88, KIM90] that each class is a physical file. Objects of classes are stored in ascending order of their ID's. However, an intermediate result

R_{ij} $[ID_i, ID_{j+1}]$, which is created during the processing of the query, may or may not be in the order of its ID_i, depending on how R_{ij} is created.

Nested loop (NL) and *sort merge (SM)* relational join methods [SELI79] can be used to construct the intermediate results and the final answer. Based on the choice of the inner and the outer relations (classes), a *nested loop* join is either a *forward nested loop(FNL)* join or a *reverse nested loop (RNL)* join. The two join methods yield different cost formulas. We now review them as follows:

(1) Forward Nested Loop (FNL)

$$R_{ik}[ID_i,ID_{k+1}]=R_{ij}[ID_i,ID_{j+1}] \overset{FNL}{\infty} R_{j+1,k}[ID_{j+1},ID_{k+1}],$$

$1 \leq i < k \leq n$. This is the *nested loop* join method with R_{ij} as the *outer* relation (class) and $R_{j+1,k}$ as the *inner* relation (class). For each object t of R_{ij}, a value $t.ID_{j+1}$ is obtained. Then $R_{j+1,k}$ is searched for $t.ID_{j+1}$ (say, by hashing). If $t.ID_{j+1} = s.ID_{j+1}$ for some object s in $R_{j+1,k}$ (note that at most one such s can be found because of the uniqueness of the class objects), then an object with the value pair ($t.ID_i$, $s.ID_{k+1}$) is constructed for R_{ik} whose schema is $[ID_i, ID_{k+1}]$ (the join attribute ID_{j+1} is abandoned). This process is repeated for all objects of R_{ij}. It is important to observe that if the objects of R_{ij} are in ascending order of ID_i, then the objects of the intermediate result R_{ik} are also in ascending order of ID_i. Thus, we have:

$$R_{ij}^s \overset{FNL}{\infty} R_{j+1,k}^* \to R_{ik}^s$$

where "$\to$" denotes *produces*, R_{ij}^s denotes R_{ij} sorted in ascending order of ID_i, and $R_{j+1,k}^*$ denotes $R_{j+1,k}$ in any state (sorted or not). And naturally we also have

$$R_{ij} \overset{FNL}{\infty} R_{j+1,k}^* \to R_{ik}$$

That is, the produced intermediate result R_{ik} is not in sorted form if its first joining class or intermediate result R_{ij} is not in sorted state. We also use FNL to denote the cost of applying the *forward nested loop* join method. Then,

$$FNL(R_{ij}^*, R_{j+1,k}^*) = F_1(|R_{ij}|, |R_{j+1,k}|)$$

where F_1 is a cost estimation function (which can be derived using standard techniques [YUCC84]). F_1 is independent of whether these two arguments are sorted or not because $R_{j+1,k}$ is accessed by ID's. |X| is the number of objects in class X.

(2) Reverse Nested Loop (RNL)

$$R_{ik}[ID_i,ID_{k+1}]=R_{ij}[ID_i,ID_{j+1}] \overset{RNL}{\infty} R_{j+1,k}[ID_{j+1},ID_{k+1}]$$

This is the *nested loop* join with R_{ij} as the *inner* relation and $R_{j+1,k}$ as the *outer* one. The processing is for each object of $R_{j+1,k}$ to match against the objects of R_{ij} (say, by index on attribute ID_{j+1} of the class R_{ij}). Since objects of R_{ij} are not uniquely identified by ID_{j+1}, accessing an object in R_{ij} with ID_{j+1} is more costly than that in $R_{j+1,k}$ when the FNL join method is used. Also the resulting objects of R_{ik} are not in ascending order of ID_i, irrespective of whether R_{ij} and/or $R_{j+1,k}$ are sorted or not. Thus,

$$R_{ij}^* \overset{RNL}{\infty} R_{j+1,k}^* \to R_{ik}$$

And the cost to apply RNL is

$$RNL(R_{ij}^*, R_{j+1,k}^*) = F_2(|R_{ij}|, |R_{j+1,k}|)$$

where F_2 is a cost estimation function which can be derived using standard techniques [YUCC84]. F_2 is independent of whether these two arguments are sorted or not. This method is likely to be preferable to FNL if $R_{j+1,k}$ is much smaller than R_{ij}.

(3) Sort Merge (SM)

$$R_{ik}[ID_i,ID_{k+1}]=R_{ij}[ID_i,ID_{j+1}] \overset{SM}{\infty} R_{j+1,k}[ID_{j+1},ID_{k+1}]$$

This is the standard sort merge method. If $R_{j+1,k}$ is not in ascending order of ID_{j+1}, sort it in that order (note that $R_{j+1,k}$ can be in ascending order of ID_{j+1} if it is an original class or an intermediate result obtained by the FNL join method whose first class is in ascending order). Sort R_{ij} in order of ID_{j+1}. (This is necessary, since no matter R_{ij} is an original class or an intermediate result, it is unlikely that the objects of R_{ij} can be automatically in ascending order of its second attribute.) Then merge these two classes by comparing the objects in the two classes as in the standard sort merge algorithm. Therefore, we have:

$$R_{ij}^* \overset{SM}{\infty} R_{j+1,k}^* \to R_{ik}$$

The obtained intermediate result R_{ik} will not be in sorted form, irrespective of whether R_{ij} and/or $R_{j+1,k}$ is sorted or not. The cost of SM method is:

$$SM(R_{ij}^*,R_{j+1,k})=Sort(R_{ij})+Sort(R_{j+1,k})+Merge(R_{ij},R_{j+1,k})$$
$$SM(R_{ij}^*,R_{j+1,k}^s)=Sort(R_{ij}) + Merge(R_{ij}, R_{j+1,k})$$

where Sort(X) is the cost to sort X on an attribute of X, and Merge(X, Y) is the cost to merge two classes which have been sorted on their join attributes. Deriving the estimating costs for Sort(X) and Merge(X, Y) is straightforward. For the SM method, if the second class is sorted, then the cost will be smaller because a sort operation on the second class is saved.

For each of the three methods, whether the first class is sorted in ID_i or not will not make any difference in cost estimation. However, if the first class is sorted on ID_i, FNL will produce an intermediate result in sorted form which may lessen the cost for some subsequent SM joins; the other two methods produce unordered intermediate results. Note that none of these methods will produce an intermediate result in ascending order of its second attribute. Initially, all original classes are sorted on their first attribute.

Let $jc(R_{ij}, R_{j+1,k}^t)$ be the minimum cost to join R_{ij} and $R_{j+1,k}^t$, where if t=s, then the second class is in sorted form. As discussed above, it is not necessary to have a superscript for the first class R_{ij} (no matter whether R_{ij} is sorted on ID_i or not, it makes no difference for join cost). Thus,

$$jc(R_{ij}, R_{j+1,k}^t) = min. \begin{Bmatrix} FNL(R_{ij}, R_{j+1,k}^t) \\ RNL(R_{ij}, R_{j+1,k}^t) \\ SM(R_{ij}, R_{j+1,k}^t) \end{Bmatrix}$$

$$= \min. \begin{cases} FNL(R_{ij}, R_{j+1,k}) \\ RNL(R_{ij}, R_{j+1,k}) \\ SM(R_{ij}, R_{j+1,k}^t) \end{cases} \quad (2.1)$$

Similarly, let $jc^s(R_{ij}^{t1}, R_{j+1,k})$ be the minimum cost to join the classes such that the obtained intermediate result R_{ik} is in sorted form R_{ik}^s. Then,

$$jc^s(R_{ij}^{t1}, R_{j+1,k}^t) = \min \begin{cases} jc(R_{ij}, R_{j+1,k}^t) + Sort(R_{ik}), \\ Sort(R_{ij}) + FNL(R_{ij}^s, R_{j+1,k}) \end{cases}, \text{ if } t_1 \neq s \quad (2.2)$$

$$= \min. \begin{cases} jc(R_{ij}, R_{j+1,k}^t) + Sort(R_{ik}), \\ FNL(R_{ij}^s, R_{j+1,k}) \end{cases}, \text{ if } t_1 = s \quad (2.3)$$

In *Formula (2.2)* (R_{ij} is in unsorted form), the first expression is for the situation where the required class R_{ik} is first obtained in unsorted form and then sorted explicitly; the second expression is for explicitly sorting R_{ij} first and applying FNL to obtain R_{ik}^s. The expressions in *Formula (2.3)* can be understood similarly.

3. Problem and Solution

In this section, we will give a solution to the problem of obtaining R_{1n} for a chain query of n classes, n>2, with the least cost under the following assumptions: (1). no local processing (selections/projections). (2). answer class is not considered. and (3). no class hierarchy. All these assumptions will be relaxed in the coming sections.

Our solution to compute R_{1n} with the least cost using dynamic programming consists of finding all minimum costs for computing R_{ij} and R_{ij}^s for all pairs of i and j such that (j-i)=k, $1 \leq i \leq j \leq n$, $0 \leq k \leq n-1$. Initially, k=0. In each iteration, k is incremented by 1 until j=n and i=1. Let C_{ij} and C_{ij}^s be the minimum costs for computing R_{ij} and R_{ij}^s, respectively. This is a bottom-up strategy as shown in *Figure 3.1*. The first row indicates the costs for computing R_{ij} for j-i = 0. The next row gives the costs for computing R_{ij} for j-i = k, which is one higher than the k value in the previous row. There is also a similar C_{ij}^s matrix which will be computed synchronously with the C_{ij} matrix, i.e., as soon as a row of C_{ij} is computed, the corresponding row of C_{ij}^s is computed. This is repeated until we reach R_{1n}. R_{ij} is formed by computing $R_{im} \infty R_{m+1,j}$ for some m, $i \leq m < j$ (note that in the computation of C_{ij}'s, the minimum costs for constructing R_{im} and $R_{m+1,j}$ are C_{im} and $C_{m+1,j}$ respectively which have been computed by the bottom-up algorithm). C_{ij} is obtained by choosing the m that yields the minimum cost. These are all possible ways in which R_{ij} may be formed (if cross product is avoided). Note that both R_{im} and $R_{m+1,j}$ can be in sorted form, but only the sorted state of $R_{m+1,j}$ may affect the cost of computing the join of R_{im} with $R_{m+1,j}$. Thus,

$$C_{ij} = \min_{i \leq m < j} \begin{cases} C_{im} + C_{m+1,j} + jc(R_{im}, R_{m+1,j}), \\ C_{im} + C_{m+1,j}^s + jc(R_{im}, R_{m+1,j}^s) \end{cases} \quad (3.1)$$

In order to compute R_{ij}^s, i.e., R_{ij} in sorted form, we may first obtain R_{ij} by using *Equation (3.1)*, and then explicitly sort R_{ij}; or we may compute R_{im}^s first and then apply FNL to join R_{im}^s with

$R_{m+1,j}^*$ (which can be sorted or not) to obtain R_{ij}^s directly.

$$C_{ij}^s = \min_{i \leq m < j} \begin{cases} C_{im}^s + C_{m+1,j} + FNL(R_{im}^s, R_{m+1,j}), \\ C_{ij} + Sort(R_{ij}) \end{cases} \quad (3.2)$$

Figure 3.1 gives all C's that need to be computed (there is also a corresponding C^s matrix). The order to compute them is row by row for both the C and the C^s matrices, starting from the first row. It is clear that when computing C_{ij} and/or C_{ij}^s, all C_{im}, C_{im}^s, C_{m+1j} and $C_{m+1,j}^s$, $i \leq m < j$, should have already been computed. Thus, each C_{ij} can be obtained in time proportional to j-i (which is the number of values m can take on). The same procedure applies to C_{ij}^s. Let k = j-i. The complexity of the computation of the row of $C_{1,k+1}$, $C_{2,k+2}$, ..., $C_{n-k,n}$ is O((n-k)(k)) $\leq$ O(n^2). There are n rows as indicated below (actually there are two rows for each row given below, one for C, the other for C^s). Thus, the total complexity is O(n^3).

$$
\begin{array}{ccccc}
C_{11} & C_{22} & \cdots & \cdots & C_{nn} \\
 & C_{12} & C_{23} & \cdots & C_{n-1,n} \\
 & & C_{13} & \cdots & C_{n-2,n} \\
 & & & \cdots & \cdots \\
 & & & & C_{1n}
\end{array}
$$

Figure 3.1: The Computation of all $C_{ij}'s$

By definition, $C_{ii} = C_{ii}^s = 0$ for all i, $1 \leq i \leq n$, since the original classes are assumed sorted. From the initial condition, *Equations (3.1) and (3.2)*, and the definition for jc/jc^s, it is easy to see that $C_{ij} \leq C_{ij}^s$ for all $1 \leq i \leq j \leq n$. *Equations (3.1) and (3.2)* are the foundation for our following discussions and extensions.

Example 3.1: There are four classes R_{11}, R_{22}, R_{33} and R_{44}.
Step 1: Construct R_{12} from R_{11} and R_{22}/R_{22}^s by (3.1) with m ∈ {1}, and then R_{12}^s from R_{12} (by sorting R_{12}) or from R_{11}^s and R_{22} by (3.2) with m ∈ {1}. R_{23}, R_{34}, R_{23}^s and R_{34}^s can be similarly constructed. These form the second rows of the two matrices in *Figure 3.2*.
Step 2: Construct R_{13} from either R_{12} joined with R_{33}/R_{33}^s or R_{11} joined with R_{23}/R_{23}^s by (3.1) with m ∈ {1, 2}. Suppose C_{23} = 100 and C_{23}^s = 200, that is, the minimum cost for having R_{23} in sorted form is more expensive than the minimum cost for having R_{23} in unsorted form. Suppose that in constructing R_{13}, sort merge turns out to be the cheapest and SORT(R_{23}) = 150. Therefore, we can see obtaining R_{23} using a more expensive method but with R_{23} in sorted form could yield the lowest cost for forming R_{13}. Construct R_{13}^s by (3.2) with ∈ {1, 2}. Similarly, R_{24} and R_{24}^s are constructed. These form the third row in *Fig. 3.2*.
Step 3: R_{14} is formed with m∈ {1,2,3} using (3.1).

$$
\begin{array}{cccc}
C_{11}/C_{11}^s & C_{22}/C_{22}^s & C_{33}/C_{33}^s & C_{44}/C_{44}^s = 0 \\
 & C_{12}/C_{12}^s & C_{23}/C_{23}^s & C_{34}/C_{34}^s \\
 & & C_{13}/C_{13}^s & C_{24}/C_{24}^s \\
 & & & C_{14}
\end{array}
$$

Figure 3.2: The Computations of all C_{ij}'s/C_{ij}^s's

4. Including Selections and Projections

In the previous sections, we assumed that there was no selection or projection. In this section, we take into consideration selections and projections in the formulation of the problem, i.e., our optimal query execution plan will determine when joins, selections and projections will take place. Let us call a selection or a projection a *reduction*. Many papers on query optimization suggest performing all reductions before joins. We believe that the strategy is not necessarily a good choice.

It is known that if there are a number of selections/projections to be performed on a class, it is cheaper to perform all such actions at the same time, instead of performing one at a time. Thus, we can assume that there is at most one such action per class.

Consider an intermediate result, say R_{im}, $m > i$, which is created during the processing of a query. We may assume that all reductions on the original classes R_i, R_{i+1} ,..., R_m have been performed by the time R_{im} has been created, because if the reductions were not performed, then the intermediate result would be bigger and indices or other data structures in support of efficient processing of selections (if they are not explicitly created) would not be available in the intermediate result. In fact, joins are performed to form the intermediate result. At the time joins are performed, it is relatively cheap to perform these local reductions if they have not already been done. Thus, there is no reduction that remains to be performed on intermediate results. In other words, the formulation of the problem given in the last few sections is applicable to intermediate results. It is sufficient to concentrate on how reductions and joins are performed involving original classes. Specifically, if there is a join between two original classes, one or both of them may have reductions to be performed, there are 4 different ways to execute the join and the reductions.

(1). Perform reductions on both classes before the join.
(2). Perform reduction on one class before join and while the join is being performed, execute reduction on the other.
(3). Same as (2) except the reductions are performed in the reverse order.
(4). Perform the join first and during the join perform the reduction. This is a possible since the join may be supported by fast access paths, and the reductions do not reduce the classes significantly and may not supported by fast access paths.

One reduction method may be more expensive than another but they leave the intermediate result in different states (sorted or not). For example, scanning a class in ascending order of UID and selecting the objects based on certain criterion is expensive but the obtained intermediate result is in ascending order of the UID, while performing the selection (in particular when involving inequality) using indices is less expensive but may leave the intermediate result unordered. Having the class ordered is useful in a subsequent join if the class is the second argument in the join operation (see *Section 2*). As discussed above, the state of an intermediate result (sorted or not) is important. Let $o\_red(R_i)$ and $n\_red(R_i)$ be the minimum cost to reduce R_i with the resulting classes ordered and not necessarily ordered, respectively. Let $rjc(R_{il}, R_{l+1,j})$ be the minimum cost to perform the reductions in the classes and the join between the classes. As discussed earlier in this section, if R_{il} and $R_{l+1,j}$ are intermediate results, then all reductions must have already been performed and therefore the following is true for all $m>i$ and $j>m+1$

$$rjc(R_{im}, R_{m+1,j}) = jc(R_{im}, R_{m+1,j}), \quad j-1>m>i \quad (4.1)$$

Now we proceed to consider the three cases that (1) both R_{im} and $R_{m+1,j}$ are original classes; (2) only R_{im} is an original class; and (3) only $R_{m+1,j}$ is an original class.

(1). Suppose R_{im} is R_i and $R_{m+1,j}$ is R_{i+1}. Then as discussed before, there are four possible cases for performing the reductions and the join, and the strategy with the minimum cost should be chosen.

$$rjc(R_i, R_{i+1}) = min \begin{cases} jc(R_i, R_{i+1}), \\ n\_red(R_i) + jc(R_{ii}, R_{i+1}), \\ o\_red(R_{i+1}) + jc(R_i, R_{i+1,i+1}^s), \\ n\_red(R_{i+1}) + jc(R_i, R_{i+1,i+1}), \\ n\_red(R_i) + o\_red(R_{i+1}) + jc(R_{ii}, R_{i+1,i+1}^s), \\ n\_red(R_i) + n\_red(R_{i+1}) + jc(R_{ii}, R_{i+1,i+1}) \end{cases} \quad (4.2)$$

where the first expression denotes the situation that the reductions are taken at the time of joining the original classes R_i and R_{i+1}; the second expression is for reducing the original class R_i to R_{ii} which is not necessarily sorted (whose schema becomes $[ID_i, ID_{i+1}]$) before the join is executed; the third expression is for reducing R_{i+1} to $R_{i+1,i+1}$ in ordered form before the join; etc. It should be noted that having the first argument in ordered form does not help in the join and therefore no such expression is in rjc.

(2). If the intermediate result is the second argument and the original class is the first argument in the join, then there is no reduction in the intermediate result and there is no need to have the first argument ordered. Thus,

$$rjc(R_i, R_{i+1,j}^t) = min \begin{cases} jc(R_i, R_{i+1,j}^t), \\ n\_red(R_i) + jc(R_{ii}, R_{i+1,j}^t) \end{cases}, \quad j>i+1 \quad (4.3)$$

where if $t = s$, then the intermediate result is sorted, otherwise, not necessarily sorted.

(3). If the intermediate result is the first argument and the original class is the second argument in the join, then we have

$$rjc(R_{i,j-1}, R_j) = min \begin{cases} jc(R_{i,j-1}, R_j), \\ o\_red(R_j) + jc(R_{i,j-1}, R_{jj}^s), \\ n\_red(R_j) + jc(R_{i,j-1}, R_{jj}) \end{cases}, \quad j-1>i \quad (4.4)$$

Finally, let rjc^s be the minimum join cost with the resulting class sorted while taking reduction into consideration. The equations for rjc^s are similar to those for rjc.

5. Extended to Arbitrary Answer (Target) Class

It is possible that a user will retrieve the ID's of any given class, called *answer (target) class* denoted as R_a, satisfying a given condition. In *Example 1.1*, the answer class is the "leftmost" class *Auto* in the query graph. But in general the answer class can be any class in the chain. This is the subject to be addressed in this section.

Example 5.1: Using *Figure 1.1*, the following is a valid query: *"Find all persons who own a red automobile"*.

select *Person* (X **ref** *Auto*)
   where X.owner = Person **and** X.color = "Red"

where (X **ref** *Auto*) defines the variable referencing class *Auto*, and the answer class is R_2. []

In *Section 3*, we computed R_{1n} without designating the answer class. Let R_{1n} be obtained from $R_{1m} \infty R_{m+1,n}$ for some m, $1 \leq m < n$. After obtaining $R_{1n}[ID_{m+1}]$, then in order to obtain the ID's in R_a as the answer, we need to *propagate* the result from $R_{1n}[ID_{m+1}]$ to $R_{a-1}[ID_{a-1}, ID_a]$, since the second attribute of R_{a-1} is ID_a, i.e., the desired result. Without loss of generality, assume a-1 $\geq$ m+1. The propagation from $R_{1n}[ID_{m+1}]$, denoted by $R_{m+1}^f[ID_{m+1}]$, to $R_{a-1}[ID_{a-1}, ID_a]$ consists of joining $R_{m+1}^f[ID_{m+1}]$ with $R_{m+1}[ID_{m+1}, ID_{m+2}]$ to yield an intermediate result on attribute ID_{m+2}. This is then joined with $R_{m+2}[ID_{m+2}, ID_{m+3}]$ to yield an intermediate result on ID_{m+3}. This process is repeated until $R_{a-1}[ID_{a-1}, ID_a]$ is joined to yield the answer on ID_a. Let the propagation from $R_{1n}[ID_{m+1}]$ to $R_{a-1}[ID_{a-1}, ID_a]$ be $P(R_{m+1}^f, R_{a-1})$.

An optimal algorithm to compute the answer while taking into consideration the propagation cost is as follows.

Compute C_{ij} and C_{ij}^s as in *Section 3* for all j-i $\leq$ n-2. Then at the last stage, C_{1n} is redefined to be:

$$C_{1n} = \min_{1 \leq m < n} \left\{ \begin{array}{l} C_{1m}+C_{m+1,n}+jc(R_{1m},R_{m+1,n})+P(R_{m+1}^f,R_{a-1}), \\ C_{1m}+C_{m+1,n}^s+jc(R_{1m},R_{m+1,n}^s)+P(R_{m+1}^f,R_{a-1}) \end{array} \right\}$$

We can see that if a = m+1, then the answer is $R_{1n}[ID_{m+1}]$ and $P(R_{m+1}^f, R_{a-1}) = 0$, that is, no propagation is needed in this case. We note that an alternate approach is to associate the UID's of the answer class R_a with all the intermediate results R_{ij}, $i \leq a \leq j$, that is, the scheme for all such R_{ij}, $i \leq a \leq j$, consist of $[ID_i, ID_{j+1}, ID_a]$; all others are unchanged. In this case, we do not need *propagation*, i.e., as soon as R_{1n} is obtained, the result can be obtained directly. With slight modification of basic cost estimation formulas, our dynamic programming approach is still applicable.

In estimating $P(R_{m+1}^f, R_{a-1})$, we note that some intermediate results, say R_{fg}, f $\geq$ m+1, g $\leq$ a-1, may have been computed during the computation of $R_{m+1,n}$. Thus, it is sufficient to propagate $R_{1n}[ID_{m+1}]$ to R_{fg}, join with R_{fg}, and then propagate to R_{a-1}. There may be more than one such R_{fg} during the computation of $R_{m+1,n}$.

6. Extend to Class Hierarchy

We assume that each class is stored in a physical file. Classes are organized into *class hierarchies* which capture the IS-A relationship between objects. A higher/lower level class is called a *superclass*/*subclass*, respectively. All attributes specified for a class are inherited by its subclasses. For example, VEHICLE, BIKE, AUTO, and MOTORBIKE are four classes as shown below, and VEHICLE is the superclass of BIKE, AUTO and MOTORBIKE classes.

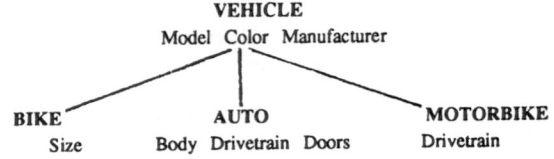

Figure 6.1: A Sample Class Hierarchy

Since attributes are inherited from their superclass, attributes *Model*, *Color* and *Manufacturer* of class VEHICLE are defined for classes BIKE, AUTO, and MOTORBIKE. It is assumed that if a UID of an object in the hierarchy is given, then this object as well as the class to which the object belongs is identified; if an index is created on an attribute, then it is established on the class hierarchy instead of on a single class. In other words, the objects which will be indexed are those objects in the classes on which this attribute is defined. This is called a *class hierarchy index* [KIM87]. The advantages, disadvantages and performance of the class hierarchy index can be found in [KIM87]. Here, we assume the use of the class hierarchy index. In query languages of OODBs [BANE88], it is usually possible to specify each node in the query graph as a single class or as the class hierarchy rooted at a specified class. For example, the following two queries specify *Vehicle* as class *Vehicle* together with all its subclasses.

Example 6.1: Find all vehicles (including all vehicles, bikes, automobiles and motorbikes) whose manufacturer is Ford.

   select *Vehicle**
   where Manufacture.Name = "Ford"

where *Vehicle** is the class hierarchy rooted at class *Vehicle*.

Example 6.2: Find all persons who own any kind of red vehicles. This query is the same as *Example 5.1*, except that X now refers to the class hierarchy including classes Vehicle, Bike, Automobile and Motorbike. []

   select *Person* (X **ref** *Vehicle**)
   where X.owner = Person **and** X.color = "Red"

In general, each class R_i in a query can be specified as the single class R_i or as the class hierarchy rooted at R_i (denoted by R_i^*). R_i^* is a subhierarchy, instead of the complete hierarchy that R_i is in, if R_i is not the root of the complete class hierarchy.

Now we proceed to see how the cost formulas and/or sorted states for R $\overset{FNL}{\infty}$ S, R $\overset{RNL}{\infty}$ S and R $\overset{SM}{\infty}$ S will be affected when R and/or S are specified as hierarchies. It is easy to see that no intermediate result will be in any class hierarchy. Therefore, it is sufficient to study the cost effect on original classes.

(1). R $\overset{FNL}{\infty}$ S: If R refers to the hierarchy rooted at class R, then we simply take classes from the hierarchy rooted at R, one at a time, to join with S. It is assumed that for any two classes within a hierarchy, all id's of one class are less than all id's of the other. Since objects in each class are in ascending order of their id's, it is possible to scan R^* in ascending order of uid by proper choice of one class after another from the hierarchy rooted at R. For each object in R or R^* with a certain id, say id_k, searching of the presence or absence of an object whose id is id_k in S^* or S can be done by hashing. Thus, the original cost formula for FNL, F_1, is unchanged (see *Section 2*).

RNL

(2). R ∞ S: This is similar to the RNL case given in *section 2*, except that no matter whether R refers to a single class or an hierarchy, a complete class hierarchy index on the join attribute is used, if available. Therefore in estimating the join cost, we need the correct index size which depends on the total number of objects to be indexed. The total number of objects to be indexed is the sum of the number of objects in the classes on which the index attribute is defined in the complete hierarchy (instead of in the hierarchy rooted at R). Thus, in estimating the cost of RNL, a third parameter, I(R), which represents the total number of objects to be indexed is added.

$$RNL\ (R^x, S^y)\ =\ F_2\ (\ |R^x|, |S^y|, |I(R)|\ )$$

where F_2 is the cost estimation formula given in *Section 2* and if x = * or y = *, then a hierarchy is present (see *Section 2*).

SM

(3). R ∞ S: If R refers to the hierarchy rooted at R, then there are two ways to make R^* sorted on the second attribute (as join attribute). One way is to sort each class in the hierarchy on the second attribute in ascending order, then merge them to form a R^* in ascending order of its second attribute. The second way is to concatenate all classes in R^* to construct R^* first, then sort R^* on the second attribute. Choose the way with the smaller cost.

If S refers to the hierarchy rooted at S, it is sufficient to concatenate one class after another so as to ensure that elements in S^* will be in ascending order of their uid's, as discussed in (1).

7. Extend to Loop Query

The following is a loop query example.

Example 7.1: Find the official car of the president of each company which manufactures the car. (It is assumed that the official car of an employee is unique.) Its query graph is:

Figure 7.1: Query Graph of *Example 7.1*

A general loop query graph is as follows:

Figure 7.2 Loop Query Graph

That is, $R_0 \infty R_1 \infty ... \infty R_{n-1} \infty R_0$ forms a loop. Note that the scheme associated with each class is a UID-pair. Let $r_{ij} = R_{ii} \infty R_{i+1,i+1} \infty ... \infty R_{mn} \infty ... \infty R_{jj} [ID_i, ID_{j+1 \bmod n}]$, $0 \le i, j \le$ n-1. If m > n - 1, then m = m **mod** n. Let r_{ij}^s be the sorted r_{ij}. We define $r_{ii} = R_{ii} \infty R_{i+1,i+1} \infty ... \infty R_{n-1,n-1} \infty R_{00} \infty ... \infty R_{i-1,i-1} \infty R_{ii}$. Note that r_{ii} is different from class R_{ii} and r_{ii} is what we want to compute.

Similarly, let C_{ij} and C_{ij}^s be the minimum cost to compute r_{ij} and r_{ij}^s, $0 \le i, j \le$ n-1, i ≠ j, respectively. We have the following equation based on *Equation (3.1)*.

$$C_{ij} \underset{0 \le i \ne j \le n-1}{\underset{0 \le m \le n-1}{=\ \min}} \begin{Bmatrix} C_{im} + C_{m+1 \bmod n, j} + \text{rjc}\ (r_{im}, r_{m+1 \bmod n, j}) \\ C_{im} + C_{m+1 \bmod n, j}^s + \text{rjc}\ (r_{im}, r_{m+1 \bmod n, j}^s) \end{Bmatrix}$$

where rjc takes both the local reductions and the join into consideration (see *Section 4*). C_{ij}^s can be defined similarly based on *Equation (3.2)*.

Initially, we have $C_{ii}=C_{ii}^s=0$, $0 \le i \le$ n-1, which is the minimum cost to have a copy of base class R_i. We start with computing all $C_{i,i+1 \bmod n}$ and $C_{i,i+1 \bmod n}^s$, $0 \le i \le$ n-1. There are n such $C_{i,i+1 \bmod n}$, instead of the n - 1 costs in a chain query. Then we proceed to compute all $C_{i,i+2 \bmod n}$ and $C_{i,i+2 \bmod n}^s$, $0 \le i \le$ n-1, and so on. After n - 1 steps, all $C_{i,i+n-1 \bmod n}$ and $C_{i,i+n-1 \bmod n}^s$, $0 \le i \le$ n-1, have been computed, that is, $C_{0,n-1}$, C_{10}, C_{21}, ..., $C_{n-1,n-2}$ (see *Figure 7.3*). Finally, we define $Cost_{ii}$ as the minimum cost to compute r_{ii} while taking the propagation to the answer class into consideration (see *Section 5*). According to the semantics of the query, the last join is performed by retaining only those tuples in $r_{0,n-1}[ID_0, ID_0]$, $r_{10}[ID_1, ID_1]$, ..., $r_{n-1,n-2}[ID_{n-1}, ID_{n-1}]$ which have the same values under both attributes (in practice, it is sufficient to keep one attribute). Let $Eval(r_{i,i-1})$ be the cost of performing such an action, the result of it is the fully reduced R_i, denoted by R_i^f. Finally, the minimum cost, MIN_COST, to process the loop query is:

$$MIN\_COST\ =\ \min_{0 \le i \le n-1}\ \{COST_{ii}\}$$

where $COST_{ii}=C_{i,i-1 \bmod n}+Eval(r_{i,i-1 \bmod n})+P(R_i^f, R_{a-1})$. R_a, a ≥ i - 1, is the answer class, and $P(R_i^f, R_{a-1})$ is the minimum cost to propagate the fully reduced R_i^f to R_a. It is easy to see that the complexity still remains to be $O(n^3)$.

$$
\begin{array}{lllll}
C_{00} & C_{11} & C_{22} & ... & C_{n-1,n-1} \\
 & C_{01} & C_{12} & C_{23} ... & C_{n-1,0} \\
 & & ... & ... & ... \\
 & & C_{0n-1} & C_{10} ... & C_{n-1,n-2} \\
 & & & Cost_{00} & Cost_{11} & ... & Cost_{n-1,n-1}
\end{array}
$$

Figure 7.3 Computing all C_{ij}'s and $Cost_{ii}$'s (C_{ij}^s's ignored)

Example 7.2: Using *Example 7.1*, classes *Auto*, *Company* and *Employee* are R_{00}, R_{11} and R_{22}, respectively. $r_{02}[ID_0, ID_0]$ can be computed as shown in *Section 3*. Let v_1 be an automobile object identifier and v_2 be the ID of the official car assigned to the president of the manufacturer of the automobile with ID v_1. Then uid-pair (v_1, v_2) should be in $r_{02}[ID_0, ID_0]$. According to the semantics of the query, only those v's such that $v_1 = v_2$ are retrieved, i.e., there is another *join* between these two attributes in r_{02} to be performed. The sum of the costs to obtain r_{02}, to perform the last join, and the propagation is $COST_{00}$. (Note that since the target class is R_0, there is no propagation involved if $r_{00}[ID_0, ID_0]$ is obtained.) Of course, it is clear that this last "join" can be performed physically at a small cost at the time r_{02} is formed. Furthermore, in order to obtain the answer, there are other choices involving the computation of $r_{10}[ID_1, ID_1]$ and $r_{21}[ID_2, ID_2]$. The optimal strategy should be the one with the least cost among the three. In each of these cases, the cost of performing the last "join" and the propagation cost should be added.
[]

8. Conclusions

In this paper, we provide an algorithm to process typical (chain) queries in OODBs in a centralized environment, using dynamic programming. An efficient algorithm taking into consideration numerous different situations is provided to process typical chain queries in OODBs. Our algorithm is capable of handling a wide range of issues, including local reductions, arbitrary answer class, the sorted state of classes and intermediate results, class hierarchies, and loop query processing. This demonstrates the usefulness and the flexibility of the algorithm in different situations. The uniformity of this algorithm under so many diversified situations strongly suggests the feasibility of yielding a practical query optimization system and the potential generalization of the algorithm to more general queries and in more complicated situations.

Future research includes the extension of the algorithm so that more general types of queries such as tree queries can be handled. And an application of the algorithm in a distributed environment is also an interesting research topic.

9. Acknowledgement

We are very grateful to Dr. Won Kim of MCC for comments and criticism on an earlier draft of this paper.

REFERENCES

ABGL88 Agrawal, P., D. Bitton, K. Guh, C. Liu and C. Yu, "A Case Study for Distributed Query Processing", *Int'l Symposium on Databases in Parallel and Distributed Systems, Dec. 1988*

AFSA85 Afsarmanesh, H., D. Knapp, D. McLeod, and A. Parker, "An Object-Oriented Approach to VLSI/CAD", *Proc. of Int'l Conf. on VLDB* , August 1985, Stockholm, Sweden

AFSA86 Afsarmanesh, H and Knapp D., "An Extensible Object_Oriented Approach to Data Bases for VLSI/CAD", *Proc. of Conf. on VLDB*, 1986

AHLS84 Ahlsen M., et al, "An Architecture for Object Management in OIS", *ACM Tran. on Office Information System*, Vol. 2 No. 3, July 1984, pp. 173-196

ATWO85 Atwood, T. M., "An Object-oriented DBMS for Design Support Applications", *Proc. IEEE COMPINT 85*, Montreal, Canada, pp. 299-307

BANE88 Banerjee, J., W. Kim, K. C. Kim, "Queries in Object-Oriented Databases", IEEE 4th Int'l Conf. on Data Engineering, Los Angeles, Feb. 1988, pp 31-38

BEEC83 Beech, D. and J. Feldman, "The Integrated Data Model: A Database Perspective", *Proc. 9th Int. Conf. on VLDB* , Florence, Italy, October 1983

BOOC86 Booch, G., "Object-Oriented Development", *IEEE Trans. on Software Engineering*, Vol. SE-12, No. 2, February 1986

CARE88 Carey, M. J., D. J. DeWitt and S. L. Vandenberg, "A Data Model and Query Language of Exodus", ACM-SIGMOD88, June, 1988, pp 413-423

CHIU84 Chiu, D. M., P. Beinstein and Y. C. Ho, "Optimizing Chain Query in a Distributed Database System", *J. of Computing*, SIAM, No. 1, Vol. 13, Feb. 1984, pp 116-134

COX86 Cox, B. J, "Message/Object Programming: An Evolutionary Change in Programming", IEEE Software 1986

DANI82 Daniels, D., et al, "An Introduction to Distributed Query Compilation in R^*", IBM Research Rep, RJ3497, June 1982

GOLD81 Goldberg, A., "Introducing the Smalltalk-80 System", *Byte*, VOL. 6, NO. 8, AUGUST 1981, PP. 14-26

GOLD83 Goldberg, A. and D. Robson, "SMALLTALK-80: The Language and its Implementation", Addison-Wesley, 1983

HAAS89 Haas, L., J. Freytag, G. Lohman, and H. Pirahesh, "Extensible Query Processing in Starburst", ACM SIGMOD 89, Portland, Oregon, 1989, pp. 377-388

HARD86 Hardwick, M. and G. Sinha, "A Data Management System for Graphical Objects", *Proc. of Conf. on VLDB* , 1986

KIM87 Kim, W., K. Kim, and A. Dale, "Indexing Techniques for Object-Oriented Databases", MCC TR134-87, May 1987

KIM88 Kim, W., H.-T. Chou, and J. Banerjee, "Operations and Implementation of Complex Objects", *IEEE Transaction on Software Engineering*, No. 7, Vol. 14, July 1988, pp 985-996

KIM90 Kim, W., Garza, J., Ballou, N., and Woelk, D., "Architecture of the ORION Next-Generation Database System", *IEEE Trans. TKDE*, No. 1, Vol. 2, March 1990, pp. 109-124

LAFO86 Lafortune, S. and E. Wong, "A State Transition Model for Distributed Query Processing", *ACM Transactions on Database Systems*, No. 3, Vol. 11, September 1986, pp 294-322

LYNG84 Lyngbraek, P. and D. McLeod, "Object Management in Distributed Information System", *ACM Trans. on Office Information System*, April 1984

LYNG87 Lyngbaek, P. and V. Vianu, "Mapping a Semantic Database Model to the Relational Model", *ACM-SIGMOD*, San Francisco, May 1987, pp 132-142

NIER86 Nierstrasz, OM and DC Tsichritzis, "An Object-Oriented Environment for OIS Applications", *Proc. VLDB*, 1986

SELI79 Selinger, P. G., et al, "Access Path Selection in a Relational Database Management System", *ACM-SIGMOD 79*, pp 23-34

SELI80 Selinger, P. G. and M. Adiba, "Access Path Selection in Distributed Database Management Systems", IBM Research Lab., San Jose, Cal., RJ2883(36439), August 1980

STON86 Stonebraker, M. and L. Rowe, "The Design of POSTGRES", *ACM SIGMOD86*, Washington, D.C., May 1986, pp 340-55

ULLM88 Ullman, J., "Database and Knowledge-based Systems", Computer Science Press, 1988

WOEL86 Woelk, D., W. Kim, and W. Luther, "An Object-Oriented Approach to Multimedia Databases", *Proc. ACM-SIGMOD*, Washington D.C., May 1986

WOEL87 Woelk, D., and W. Kim, "Multimedia Information Management in an Object-Oriented Database System", *Proc. VLDB*, Brighton, England, Sept. 1987

WOLF86 Wolf, W., "An Object-Oriented Procedural Database for VLSI Chip Planning", *Proc. of Design Automation Conf.*, 1986

YLCC82 Yu, C.,et al, "A Promising Approach to Distributed Query Processing", *Berkeley Workshop on Database and Computer Network*, 1982, pp 152-170

YUCC84 Yu, C. and C. Chang, "Distributed Query Processing", *Computing Surveys*, Vol. 16, No. 4, Dec. 1984

YUOZ84 Yu, C., M. Ozsoyoglu and K. Lam, "Distributed Query Optimization for Tree Queries", *Journal of Computer and System Science*, 1984, pp 409-445

ZANI83 Zaniolo, C. "The Database Language Gem", *ACM-SIGMOD*, San Jose, California, May 1983, pp 207 - 217

"Conceptual Retrieval" Using Object-Oriented Approach

T.C.Tan   P.Smith

Sunderland Polytechnic
School of Computer Studies and Mathematics
Priestman Building, Green Terrace,
Sunderland, SR1 3SD
United Kingdom

M.Pegman

Headway Systems Ltd.
28, Howard Street, Glossop
Derbyshire, SK13 9DD
United Kingdom

ABSTRACT

The emphasis today in information retrieval is leaning towards 'quality' rather than 'quantity'. This is due to new technologies such as artificial intelligence and expert systems. From these technologies, 'expert' data base systems have emerged. Not long after that enters object-oriented programming and another class of database called object-oriented data bases begin to appear. These new technologies have serious implications on information retrieval as a whole, changing the ways in which we can perceive and treat information. This paper describes how one can improve on the quality and the authoritativeness of retrieved information using 'conceptual retrieval', implemented via the object-oriented paradigm.

1. INTRODUCTION

The computers of today are about a quarter of a million times faster than their fore-fathers produced less than five decades ago. There are currently more supercomputers in the pipeline that will dwarf even these figures! Extra power, speed and storage capacity open up computing to applications that were previously thought not possible. Although the computer hardware has came a very long way in a relatively short span of time, its 'sister', computer software, has been lagging behind. However, recent times have seen the emergence of a number of technologies which look set to render new momentum to software technology. These technologies are artificial intelligence, expert systems, object-oriented programming, hypermedia and neural networks. These new technologies have very profound impact on information technology because they have changed the way in which we can perceive and treat information.

Previously people were more interested in the speed at which information could be retrieved and the quantity of information that can be stored. But now, since these are not quite so much a problem, people's attention is channelled into the quality and the authoritativeness of the information. In other words, the desire is for the process of retrieval of information to be more 'discreet', owing to the fact that there is a mountain of documents available and only a selected few of them will be useful and applicable to the enquirer's current situation. Thus the emphasis is now on the intelligent retrieval[1] of information.

2. THE PROBLEM WITH WORDS

The crux of the information retrieval problem is how to store information and to accurately retrieve it. The traditional approach to information retrieval can be shown as :

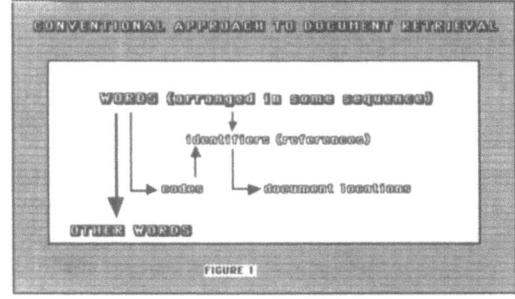

FIGURE 1

Information contained in documents is represented using keywords which are used to index the documents as a means for retrieval. This is the essence of traditional information retrieval and, perhaps, its main hindrance. Successful retrieval is solely dependant on the choice of the keywords used and even then the document retrieved may not be what the seeker wanted. This problem is well illustrated by Aristotle who once said :

"Spoken words are symbols of experience in the psyche; written words are symbols of

224

the spoken. As writing, so is speech not the same for all peoples. But the experience themselves, of which these words are primarily signs, are the same for everyone, and so are the objects of which those experience are likeness."

Memories can be classified into two categories : episodic and semantic[2]. Episodic memories are what people remember about individual things and events. Semantic memories store universal principles; things that are true no matter the circumstances (as observed by Aristotle). Sowa[3] relates episodic and semantic memory to the two aspects of word meaning (see Figure 2) : intension and extension.

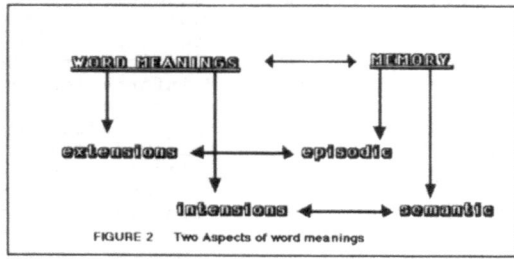

FIGURE 2   Two Aspects of word meanings

The intension of a word meaning is that part of meaning that follows from general principles in semantic memory and the extension of a word is the set of all existing things to which the word applies. Therefore the extension of a word varies from one individual to another depending on the experience and background of the individual. This can be illustrated by Figure 2A.

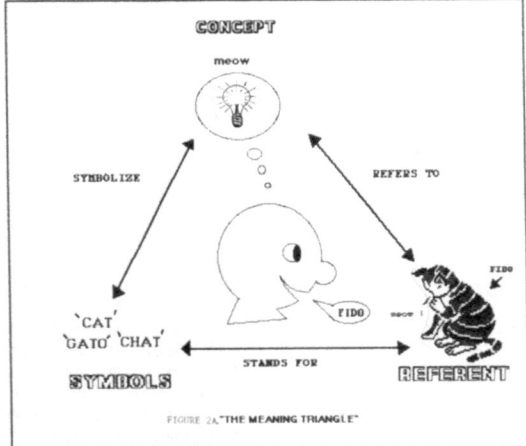

FIGURE 2A "THE MEANING TRIANGLE"

The left corner is the symbol or word, the apex is the concept, intension, thought, idea, or sense and the right corner is the referent, object, or extension. Hence if a person, who owns a

cat, hears the call of a cat outside the door, he/she will come to conclusion that it is 'Fido' (the name of his/her cat). If the person is English then the symbol used would be 'cat'. If could just as well be 'gato' if he is Spanish or 'chat' if he is French. Therefore traditional information retrieval is inherently inaccurate because of the ambiguity of using keywords alone.

When artificial intelligence and expert systems technologies arrived they have profound impact on information retrieval because they provide new techniques which can be applied to information handling. Basically, the key issues involved in artificial intelligence and expert systems are knowledge representation and the human-like approach to problem-solving. These issues, in fact, are relevant, if not related, to the issues of information retrieval. Consequently, information systems are slowly adapting to knowledge-base architectures as intelligent information systems[4] and expert data base systems[5] begin to appear.

3. KNOWLEDGE REPRESENTATION

KNOWLEDGE IS POWER !

Without knowledge of the application environment, the domain and the knowledge of the intended user(s), any system will not be able to 'comprehend' its functions (just like any human if he/she is lacking some knowledge about his/her environment). For this reason, it is imperative that for any system to exhibit some form of intelligence, it must contain, within itself, information about its environment and functionality. The majority of artificial intelligence research concerned such aspects of knowledge representation.

An efficient intelligent system often owns its efficacy to the superiority and flexibility of its representation of knowledge (whether it is knowledge about objects, knowledge about processes, hard-to-represent common sense knowledge about goals, motivation, causality, time, action etc.). Numerous knowledge representation paradigms have emerged to date and these can be broadly listed as follows :

1. semantic networks
2. first-order logic
3. frames
4. production systems

These should not be taken as the only approaches to knowledge representation but they do represent the more common techniques. However, each technique is only suited to a particular kind of problem domain (for example, frames are particularly useful for representing knowledge of certain stereotypical concepts or events and production systems originated as models of human reason etc.). Therefore the choice of representation is hampered by the various possibilities and also a lack of criteria.

When considering the choice of representation, two aspects of the problem of knowledge representation[6] must also be taken into consideration. They are :

1. expressive adequacy
2. notational efficacy

Expressive adequacy is concerned with the expressive power of the representation and notational efficacy has to do with the actual shape and structure of the representation as well as the impact the structure has on the operations of the system. The choice of representation becomes crucial especially for the knowledge of intelligent systems which has to characterise perceptual data.

One class of such systems are information systems. Because an information system functions in a fairly well defined environment, the view of its 'world' would consist of :

1. users
2. documents
3. itself (eg its function and purpose etc.)
4. domain knowledge of the information contained in the documents

To implement an intelligent information system would require representation of at least one of the above components. (The degree of intelligence and flexibility exhibited by the intelligent system would depend on the number of the components represented in the system). An intelligent document retrieval system called RADA[7] has been implemented which contains all of the above components. The following sections discuss the representation and implementation of component (4) and how retrieval is more effective in such a system.

4. CONCEPTUAL RETRIEVAL

Information is becoming more readily available to a wider spectrum of people. These "information consumers" are also becoming more sophisticated and as a consequence are more aware of the short-

comings of the conventional information retrieval systems, which are mainly based on keyword retrieval (the disadvantage of which is discussed in Section 2). Hence people began to seek better and more flexible ways in which any 'casual' user can obtain optimum results from the information system. They are also more critical about the 'quality' of the information that is returned to them. To increase the effectiveness with which the user can retrieve information, the concept of browsers[8] has been introduced. This has proved to be a useful tool for an information system to possess because a majority of users do not normally have a definite idea of what is it that they are looking for and where to actually start looking.

Semantic network notation, perhaps the most commonly used knowledge representation paradigm, is based on the ancient and very simple idea that "memory" is composed of associations between concepts. Concepts are more abstract than language (i.e. the words used in the language). They are considered to be discrete units and only discreet relationships are recorded in concepts. A concept acquires its meaning through a vast network of relationships that ultimately links them to concrete concepts :

> To discover the logical relations of a concept is to discover the nature of that concept. For concepts are, in this respect, like points; they have no quality except position. Just as the identity of a point is given by its coordinates, ..., so the identity of a concept is given by its position relative to other concepts .... A concept is that which is logically related to others just as a point is that which is spatially related to others.
>
> ---- WHITE[9]

Hence a combination of concepts are 'ordered structures'. The conceptual graphs[3] as defined by Sowa are based on linguistics, psychology, and philosophy and is used for interpreting sensory perception.

The idea of a 'conceptual semantic net' (CSN) is derived from the two basic ideas of the semantic network and the idea of conceptual graphs. The domain knowledge of the RADA information system is represented using 'conceptual semantic net'. Retrieval of information is facilitated by the use of the CSN and is called 'conceptual retrieval'.

4.1 CONCEPTUAL SEMANTIC NET (CSN)

The two major components of a CSN are :

1. concept nodes
2. conceptual relations/links

The major properties of the CSN are :

1. Concept nodes are used to group entities in the 'real world' which can be classified under the concept.
2. Conceptual relations are user to define the relationships between two or concepts and hence cannot exist on their own.
3. A CSN can consist of only one concept node. Such a CSN would be 'undefined' because it has no other concepts to relate with.

The purpose of the CSN, apart from being a browsing mechanism, is to deduce word meanings and associations in a specific context. It differs from the conventional semantic net representation because it is of a higher level of abstraction. This is illustrated by Figure 3.

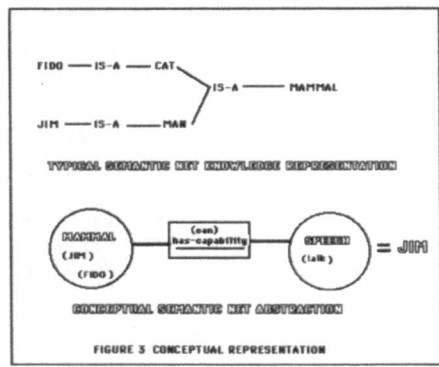

FIGURE 3 CONCEPTUAL REPRESENTATION

The abstract concepts acquire their meaning through the structure of the CSN which form a coherent piece of information (scenario). From the 'scenario', the system can deduce the possible meanings, thus prescribing the possible 'extensions' (see Section 2) or 'real world' entities. This eradicates the need for the user to use specific keywords to retrieve documents. The basic idea can be illustrated by Figure 4.

To effect retrieval of documents the user will have to define or 'conceptualise' his/her query using the CSN. This is necessary because of the user's anomalous state of knowledge[10]. Once this has been achieved, the information system can then proceed to retrieve documents based on the CSN. A typical CSN in RADA is shown in Figure 5.

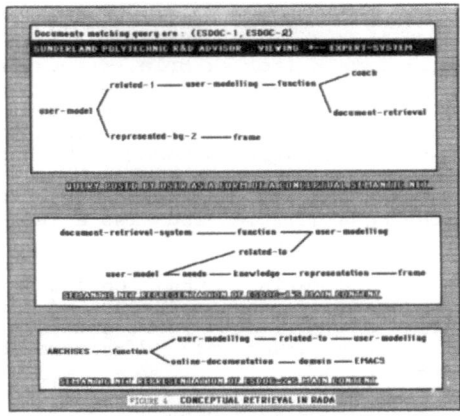

FIGURE 4 CONCEPTUAL RETRIEVAL IN RADA

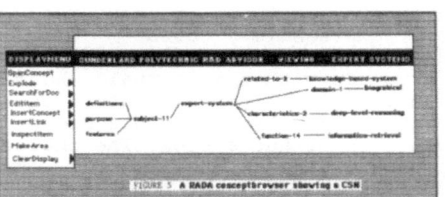

FIGURE 5 A RADA conceptbrowser showing a CSN

4.2 IMPLEMENTATION OF THE CSN

The object-oriented programming paradigm[11] has made the implementation of complex systems possible. The attraction of object-oriented programming is that entities, with their structures, operations and constraints, once represented as an object, can be treated as they are. This is where the power of OOPS lies - the high level of data abstraction. The higher the level of abstraction the closer will be the system in reflecting the problem domain and providing a solution that is more 'natural' and intuitive[12].

The CSN is implemented using the object-oriented paradigm. The two entities of the CSN, the concept and the link, are implemented as objects called classes. Classes can have subclasses which are specialisations of their parent classes called the superclasses. This is illustrated in Figure 6.

Each class contains characteristics from which members of the class assume values. These members are called instances and are themselves distinct objects. There are two kinds of characteristics in a class : class variables and the instance variables. Class variables hold values which are 'global' and every member of the class will have the same value. Instance variables are used by individual

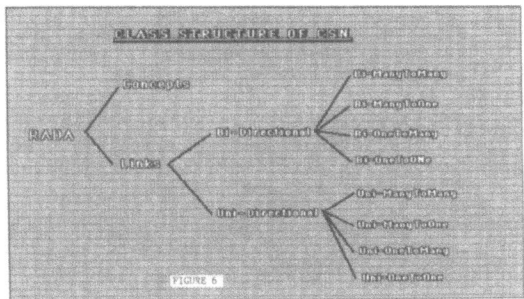

FIGURE 6

instances of the class to hold distinct values and are the mechanisms by which one instance object is distinguished from another. Classes also have methods. These methods are like functions and procedures and are invoked when one object sends a 'message' to another. Messages are the means by which objects communicate and the actions to be taken are dictated by the methods. The structures of the class 'Concepts' and 'Links' are shown in Figure 7.

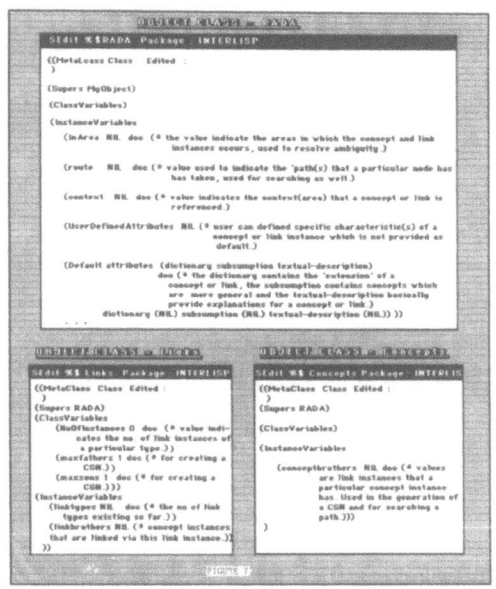

FIGURE 7

A CSN is created using instance objects of these classes. Examples of details of a couple of instance objects of Figure 5 are shown in Figure 8.

The object-oriented implementation enables a particular CSN to be created 'on-the-fly' which allows the user to slowly 'explode' the network in whatever way he chooses.

The dictionary-list of the concept object is used to hold 'extensions' related to the concept. These

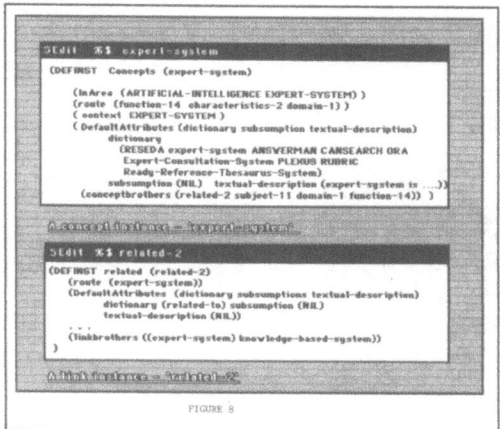

FIGURE 8

'extensions' are in fact words that occur in documents. To improve on the quality of the document(s) retrieved, the principle contents of the document is also represented as part of the document's surrogate[13] in the form of conventional semantic network(s). This is shown in Figure 9.

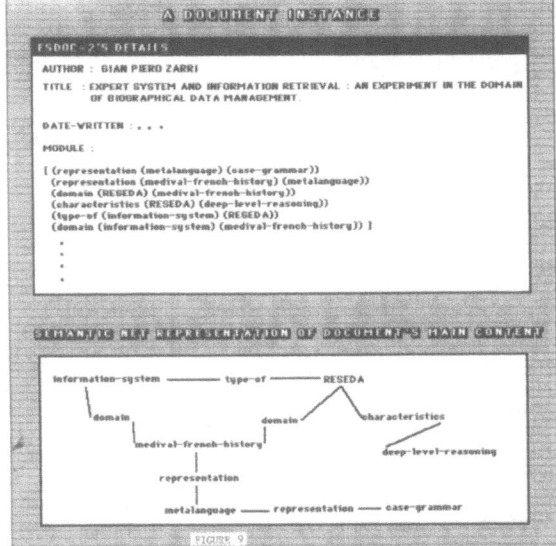

FIGURE 9

Conceptual retrieval is thus achieved by matching the CSN with the semantic network(s) of the document (Figure 10). This will ensure that the document(s) contains information that are close to the user's need. (Documents can also be ranked according to how close their semantic networks match the CSN. A threshold/degree of matching can be set so that any documents falling below that will be not be retrieved.)

228

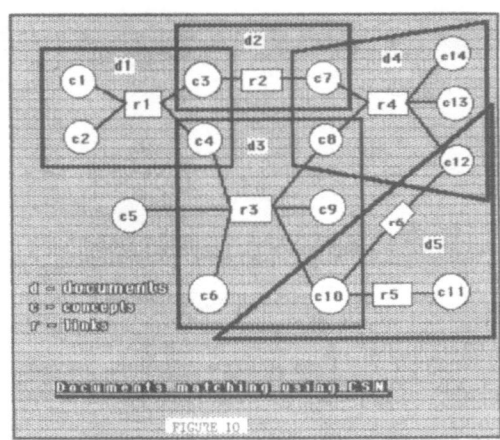

Documents matching using CSN

FIGURE 10

5. CONCLUSIONS

The objective of using 'conceptual retrieval' is to make information readily accessible to people. This implies that an information system should not impose its constraints on the user (except perhaps the ability of the user to use the keyboard or the mouse to communicate with the system). The authors propose that 'conceptual retrieval' is one of the many possible avenues, such as browsers, hypermedia and highly interactive graphic interface using mouse, windows and menus, that will bring that objective one step closer. In fact all these features have been implemented, to certain extent, into the RADA system.

One advantage of using the CSN is that apart from being a browser for users to glance through the information available in a certain domain, it is also a knowledge base for that particular domain and, as such, an expert system can also be built by simply incorporating an inference engine for the knowledge base thus creating two systems, an expert system as well as an information system. Because the implementation is object-oriented, the extensibilities are great. Another highly sought after enhancement to a system is user-modelling[14]. This is also implemented as a feature of RADA.

6. REFERENCES

[1]   Brooks,H.M.   Expert systems and intelligent information retrieval. Information processing and manage- ment,   Vol 23 No 4, 1987, pg 367 - 382.

[2]   Tulving,E.;Donaldson,W.(eds). Org- anisation of memory. New York : Academic press, 1972.

[3]   Sowa,J.F. Conceptual structures : Information processing in mind and machine. Reading, Mass., : Addison- Wesley publishing co., 1984.

[4]   Davis,R.(ed).   Intelligent information systems : progress and prospects. Chichester, W. Sussex, : Ellis Harwood Ltd., 1986.

[5]   Kerschberg,L.   Expert data base system.Computer   bulletin,   June 1987, pg 7-9, 16.

[6]   Woods, W.A.   What's important about knowledge representation? Computer, Oct. 1983, pg 22 - 27.

[7]   Tan, T.C. ; Smith, P ; Pegman, M. A knowledge based tool to support technical research and development. In : Proceedings of the first ESA world conference, J. Liewbowitz (ed), Paris 1989, iitt Int'l, pg 89 - 94.

[8]   Robertson,D.;   Muetzelfeldt,R.; Plummer,D.;Uschold,M.;Bundy,A. The ECO browser. Department of AI, University of Edinburgh, Scotland, U.K.

[9]   White,A.R.   Conceptual analysis. In : The Owl of Minerva, C.J. Bontempo & S.J. Odell (eds), New York : McGraw-Hill, 1975, 103 - 117.

[10] Belkin,N.J.;Oddy,R.N.;Brooks,H.M. ASK for information retrieval: Part I, Background & Theory. Journal of documentation, Vol 38 No 2, June 1982, pg 61-71.

[11] Stroustrup,B.   What is object- oriented programming? In : Proceedings of ECOOP '87, Paris, BIGRE (pub), June 1986, pg 139 - 144.

[12] Abbott,R.J. Knowledge abstraction. Communication of the ACM, Vol 30 No 8, August 1987, pg 664 - 671.

[13] Artandi,S. Document representation and representation. Annual review of information science and technology. C.A. Cuadra, 5 : 161, 1970, pg 143 - 167.

[14] Rich,E.   Users are individuals : Individualizing user models. In : R. Davis[4].

Logics and OO-Data Bases: a declarative approach

I.Ramos

Dept.Information Systems and Computation
Valencia University of Technology
46020 Valencia (Spain)

ABSTRACT

Three perspectives are adopted in the paper to define the Object Oriented (OO) Paradigm:the General System Theory principles adapted to Information Systems (IS)[1], the Abstract Object Types (AOT) or Objectual Logic (OBLOG)[2] and clausal or equational logics. In this approach the OO-Data Base (OO-DB) specification (the system view or Conceptual Scheme (CS)) is a formal theory in this blend of logics. Its model is the OO-DB extension. Two Object Definition Languages (ODL) are implemented: FMOL and RMOL. Two first order languages used as User Languages (UL) are associated with them. The operational semantics of the underlaying logic (implemented by deduction) together with some software sugar constitutes an OO-DB Management System.

1. INTRODUCTION

One of the tasks of the IS Analyst is to specify its system view of the object system in order to produce the Conceptual Model specification. Several models (relational, deductive, OO...)and different linguistic frameworks are used to perform this task. Historically the IS models have been associated with the data models. In the relational model the IS is viewed as a set of entities with attributes, relationships etc. in the Deductive Data Base (DDB) model as a first order theory. In both models nothing is said (inside the model) about the behavioral manner of the system.

In the OO-DB model the IS is viewed as a collection of interacting objects. Each object is a self-contained operational unit (the system behavior is specified at that level). A unique model is used for specifying structural and behavorial aspects; the semantic gap is also narrower than in the other two cases.

Once the system view and the model are fixed, a good linguistic framework is required to specify the IS Conceptual Model. What is good depends on subjective criteria but the following characteristics of the specification language are widely accepted: precise(formal), declarative (not imperative), executable (allowing prototyping)

We will use a blend of AOT (that captures the descriptive concepts of the IFIP WG8.1 approach in a precise way) and clausal logic in RMOL or equational logic in FMOL as the linguistic framework.

In Section 2 IFIP's descriptive concepts are presented.

To be precise: the language RMOL/FMOL is a blend at the semantic level of AOT and clausal/equational logic used as ODL to specify Open Passive IS (OPIS) following the OO model.

The underlying data model is:the Conceptual Model specification is a theory in this blend of logics. It has the OO-DB extension as model (declarative semantics) and the deductive mechanism as the operational semantics.

In RMOL/FMOL the OO-DB is implemented over the standard/initial model of the clausal/equational theory which is equivalent to the IS specification. The operational semantics is implemented by using SLDNF-Resolution/ Conditional Narrowing. If an OPIS specification is equivalent to a theory (we will see how this theory is built in Section 4), we can use its first order associated language as UL of the OO_DB. We define the ULs in Section 3 , with its ODL, and give some examples.We build an OO-DBMS by adding software sugar. Finally in Section 5 we make some concluding remarks and comment on future extensions of our work.

2. THE OO-MODEL

Let us give the descriptive concepts we use on the OO model following IFIP approach.

An _object_ is a self contained unit. Which will have _properties_ (attributes).

It will have an _state_ that is the state of the set of its attributes. When an object is _created_, it is brought into existence and when it is destroyed, it finishes its _existence_(life). Each object has a _name_ that identifies it during its existence. An object has _static_/ _dynamic_ aspects in the sense that it does not change/ changes its state over time. An object may be _active_/_passive_ if it is/is not involved as necessary for a change of state to take place.The _change of state_ concept is a very important one. The _creation_/_destruction_ of the object are strong cases of state changes. Weak changes occur when there is a change of state in an existing object which is not destroyed. We call _process_ the cause of a change of state of an object. It is limited in time. It has elementary parts responsible for a single unified change of state that we call events. An _event_ is an abstraction of a change of state in the object system. It is discrete, has no duration and occurs at a certain point in time. The event concept is relative to the abstraction level. We call _behavior_ the dynamic manner of an object. The object exists during a temporal period, its _life_, that is a limited coherent amount of time. It has a duration. Events happen in a certain _point of time_ (a period having no duration).

By means of the _abstraction_ mechanisms we put together objects in types.We call _class_ a set of properties all of which characterize certain objects. A class is a precise characterization of structural and behavioral properties which a collection(or type) of objects all share [3].

The operator _instance-of_ works on a class and yields a member of the corresponding type as the result.The operator _population-of_ yields the type for a class. We may have classes and _subclasses_ denoting types and _subtypes_.Subtype populations are subsets of the _supertypes_ populations. Subclasses are defined by adding more properties to the superclasses (_specialization_). We define _generalization_/_specialization_ as relations between classes and subc,lasses at the same abstraction level.

3. THE LINGUISTIC FRAMEWORK

Let us present our linguistic paradigm following the AOT approach and adapted to the previous descriptive concepts.

We will have a specification level of the Conceptual Scheme where RMOL/FMOL are used(they are the ODLs) and a user level with its corresponding ULs.The two levels share the same logic paradigm.

The object definition language (ODL)

An object class may be formalized as a 4-ple {X,A,T,ob} where X is the event set and A is the set of typed (classed) attributes.Their values at a given instant are the object state.When an attribute has no assigned value (at creation time for example) it takes the main constant of the type as the default value [4].T is the set of allowed lives (processes or _traces_) for the objects of the class.**ob** is the observation function.The **ob** domain is **T** and the codomain is the set of pairs {attribute,value}. We can say that the objects are observable processes.

Let us see an example. If the _system domain_ is a library where books are loaned to readers, they are returned after a period... and certain rules need to be respected like " it is not possible to loan a book which is not available", etc. We can specify the class of the books in the following way.

```
conceptual_scheme library;
    domains  nat(0), bool(false), string(" ");

  class book;

        constant_attributes
            code: string key;
            title: string

        variable_attributes
            available(b:book):bool;

            equations   r: reader
                available(b)=True if T=T1'newbook(b)
                                 else available(b) at T1;
                available(b)=False if T=T1'loan(b,r);
                available(b)=True if T=T1'return(b,r)
            end_equations;

            is_of_library(b:book):bool;

            equations
                is_of_library(b)=True if T=T1'newbook(b)
                                 else is_of_library(b) at T1
            end_equations;

        private_events
            newbook(b:book)

        shared_events (reader)
            loan(b:book,r:reader);
            return(b:book,r:reader)
    end_class; ...
```

In the example we easily identify the attributes and the events. We use preconditions to specify when an event is relevant. In this case it is concatenated to the old trace T1 to give the new one T: T=T1.newbook(b) if not-is-of-library(b). With trivial meaning if b is a book.Other events have similar treatment. Relevant events will change the state of the variable atributes according to ob. In the example: available(b)= true if T=T1.newbook(b) else available (b) at T1. The function ob is given axiomatically by using equational logic. When we use FMOL.Other classes will be specified in a similar manner, like class reader, etc. and combined by using the class operators for building complex classes. This process continues until we have completely specified the IS(the Conceptual Model will be the class specifyng the object system). Class instances are named by using object surrogates (in the example strings) following the key mechanism used [4]. '

A class may not contain events and variable attributes. It is a primitive class.Its type is an Abstract Data Type (ADT). Primitive classes denote the data subspecification. They are used as object surrogates and attribute classes.Their instances always exist, they are not created nor destroyed and they have not a changing state. For example: class Nat,Bool with obvious types {0,1,2,...},{true,false} If a class has events and variable attributes and is not built by using class operators,it is an elementary class like the class book. We call complex classes those defined by using class operators. At the moment we have only one kind of complex classes in our ODLs that we call relationships.

Objects interact by sharing events.A shared event (as a loan) for class book and reader(not specifyed) is a private event for the relationship has-book. Shared events will participate in the lives of the objects with the same name but different arity. An instance will be the pair {class,surrogate}.i.e:{book,"b1"}.

In this model an IS will be specified as a composition of interacting classes that is a class. Its type is a Society of interacting objects modelling the IS. This way of modelling allows a constructive and interactive manner of specifying IS.

Let us see how the system supports the OO principles: encapsulation is guaranteed by the fact that objects are only acceded by using their attributes (to observe their states) or their events (to change them). Attributes and events are two well defined interfaces of acceding to objects.

Objects instances persist in time changing their state. They are the OO-DB extension that is in the main memory when it is used and in the back memory when is idle.

Independence: the CM is specified in a very abstract way independently from any concrete representation of data or requirements.

Homogeneity:the same declarative model is used at any level. The underlying "data model" is always the same.

Communication: objects communicate by sharing events. More complex ways of communication will be introduced when we add OA (Open Active) IS facilities.

Inheritance is implemented by algebraic enrichment in FMOL and by adding the new properties in RMOL.

We have other "non-standard" characteristics like the class operators which allow the definition of abstraction mechanisms like agregation/part-of (by tupling/projecting) and others which are easily implementable in our model. We also have a deductive way of defining complex classes which will open the possibility of having Deductive OO-DB in a similar way to the DDB field[5].

User languages (ULs)

We will define the associated UL to RMOL in an inductive way:

syntax of the UL

Terms of primitive class t are:

  i.An instance of class t
 ii.A variable of class t
iii.Only i,ii are Terms

Terms-a of primitive class t are:

  i.If a is an attribute of class t,C is a class having a as attribute and kc as the class of the key attributes and ikc is one of their instances, then a(ikc) is a Terms-a of classe t. i.e: available("b1")
 ii.Only i. are Terms-a

Atom

    i.If C is a class with constant attributes a1..ar and t1..tr are Terms then C(t1,...,tr) is an Atom. Nat(0),book("b1","Hamlet")

    ii.If f,g are Terms or Terms-a of the same class then forg is an Atom. or are some relational operators:
       no-of-books(reader("r1"))<6

    iii.If e is an event with arity class ae and iae is one of its instances then e(iae) is an Atom:loan("b1","r1")

    iv.Only i,ii,iii are Atom

wff

    i.An Atom is a wff

    ii.If A,B are wff then not A A,B A;B A<-B are wff

    iii.Only i,ii are wff

semantics of the UL

We take the object surrogate types and the types of the primitive classes as the domain of the interpretation. In RMOL only two constructions need auxiliary interpretation: -let **lambda** be the semantic denotation function,C(v1,...,vr) an instance of a non-primitive class C then
lambda(C(v1,...,vr))=true if exists (C(v1,...vr)) **else** false
-let be e(v1,...,vn) an instance of the event e then
lambda(e(v1,...,vn))=true if happens(e(v1...)) **and** pre-cond(e(...))=true
         else false

exists is defined in the following way:
exists(C(...)):-new(C(...)),where **new** is the instance creating event.If we introduce a time-stamping [6], we have
exists(C(...,t)):-new(C(...,t1)),t1<t, not destroy(C(...,t2)),t2<t,t1<t2.
destroy is the instance destroying event.

happens(e(...)) means that the environment activates e(...) and **pre-con** is the event pre-condition (the event is relevant). Examples of wff are:
book(b,-,t),has-book(b,"r1",t),t=6

used as a query will give the number of books that reader r1 has at time instant 6.

reader(r,-,-),no-of-books(y,-)<6
used as an integrity constraint expresses that no reader will have more than 5 books.Obviously no-of-books will be a variable atribute of the class reader.

4. OO-DB AS THEORIES

Once the UL has been defined as a first order language for RMOL(in FMOL things happen in a similar manner), let us see how the equivalent clausal theory is obtained.

i.primitive class axioms

They incorporate the **primitive types**: nat(0), nat(1)...bool(true),...in an extensional or intensional way by using axioms. The most usual are predefined.

ii.elementary class axioms

Let kc be the constant attributes of an elementary class C. We add an axiom per class: C(kc,t):-exists(C(kc,t))

iii.complex class axioms

They implement how complex classes are defined.For example:
hasbook(b,r,t):-loan(b,r,t1),t1<t, not(return(b,r,t2)),t2>t1,t2<t1.

iv.relevant events

a)If e(...) is a relevant event then e(...) is an axiom: loan("b1","r1",15)
b)Event pre-conditions are added as integrity constraints: for loan(b,r,t) we have: is-of-library(b,t),avalaible(b,t), is-a-reader(r,t),no-of-books(r,t)<6

v.attribute axioms

For every object instance of a class we will add
a)An axiom per constant attribute.For ex.:
title("b1","Hamlet",-)
They are redundant but we add them to have a unified treatment of the attributes.
b)The clauses defining the variable attributes. For example:
no-of-books(r,n,t):-loan(b,r,t),
        no-of-books(r,n-1,t-1);
      return(b,r,t),
        no-of-books(r,n+1,t-1);
        no-of-books(r,n,t-1).

vi.Prolog axioms

They are implicit in the Prolog interpreters that are used.
Note: by using forward inference we will also add the object or attribute instances for axiom types ii,iii,vb. The underlying Deductive Data Base will then be redundant.
Let us see the equivalent theory for the example:

```
ii.elementary class axioms
   book(b,r,t):-exists(book(b,r,t))
   reader(r,n,t):-exists(reader(r,n,t))
iii.complex class axioms
   has-book(b,r,t):-loan(b,r,t1),t1<t,
   not(return(b,r,t2),t2>t1,t2<t)
iv.relevant event axioms
   new("b1","Hamlet",1)
   loan("b1","r1",27)
   ...
 v.attribute axioms
   title("b1","Hamlet",1..-)
   ...
```

This equivalent theory is the DDB which is used for the evaluation of the **wff** of the UL. It is automatically generated from the ODL specification by a translator. These translators, editors, and an interactive environment constitute an OO-DB Management System.
In FMOL we proceed in a similar way. The object theory for a FMOL specification is a presentation in AXIS[7] or RAP[8], two functional languages.In the object theory the classes are represented by sorts. For each Conceptual Scheme ec we add the sort ec as the last sort in the arity of each operator.This will be the interest sort.Its type is T (the set of traces). Attributes,events, event pre-conditions and relations will be represented as operators (the only expressive mean in a presentation). The corresponding UL will be defined in a similar manner (the only predicate is =); then the **wff** will be sets of equations with logical variables.

5.CONCLUDING REMARKS

The two specification languages R/FMOL represent a blend of logical paradigms with good specification properties,a declarative style of the IS Conceptual Model following the OO model. It has good locality properties and a deductive style [9].

These languages allow the specification of OPIS. The system runs on SUN 3/60 work stations.BIM_PROLOG [8] is used as the implementation language and the object language in RMOL (AXIS or RAP in FMOL).It includes editors, translators and prototypers.
We are already working on future extensions of our work: incrementing the language expresivity to specifying OAIS and introducing a more flexible way of axiomatizing time (it will be a declared class).
Now the prototyper acts as an OAIS modelling the global environment, but each class may be viewed as a prototyping environment. Blend FMOL and RMOL to have a powerful expressivity with the three emerging specification paradigms: objectual, relational and functional.
We are also implementing graphical and friendly environments.

REFERENCES

[1] P.Lindgreen ed."A Framework of Information System Concepts".FRISCO. Interim Report.IFIP WG8.TG.90.

[2] A.Sernadas "Abstract Object Types:a temporal perspective".Colloquium on temporal logic and specification. Springer Verlag 89.

[3] P.Deutsch.In records of a discussion on the type concept.SIGPLAN Notices vol.16 n°1.ACM 81.

[4] J.Goguen et al."Unifying Functional Object Oriented and Relational Program ming whith logical semantics". Research Directions in OO Programming. MIT Press 87.

[5] G.Gallaire et al."Logic and Databases:a deductive approach".Computing Surveys 84.

[6] R.Kowalsky."Logic as a Database language".New Generation Computing 87

[7] D.Coleman et al."The AXIS specification language".Tech.Rep.HP-Labs.88.

[8] A.Gesser et al."RAP".Tech.Rep. Univ.Passau 88.

[9] A.Olive."A comparison of the operational and deductive approaches to Conceptual System modelling".Proc.IFIP 86.

[10]BIM_PROLOG.ISS,Everberg.Belgium.

Visual Interaction with Electronic Art Gallery

Toshikazu KATO and Takio KURITA

Electrotechnical Laboratory
1-1-4, Umezono, Tsukuba Science City
305, Japan

Abstract

This paper describes the ideas of visual interaction and their implementations on an image database system. The visual interaction includes a query by visual example (QVE) and a query by subjective descriptions (QBD). The former provides a sketch retrieval function and the latter provides a sense retrieval function. This paper shows the detail algorithms of these functions developed on our experimental database system ART MUSEUM. These functions use a pictorial index created by image analysis and a personal index automatically learned as the user model. They formed visual interaction in a truly user-friendly manner. This paper also summarizes the requirements to a multimedia data model from a cognitive aspect.

1. Introduction

A visual interface plays an important role in multimedia information systems. We need a visual interface to enable flexible man-machine communication in the user-friendly manner. Especially we request the visual interface for image database systems to communicate the visual information to and from the system [1, 2, 3].

Modern engineering workstations provide visual interfaces using icons, menus and a mouse. Window systems also provide us with several drawing tools. In spite of visual presentations, the computer system receives only alphanumeric data as the result of an operator action, such as typing commands or selecting options from a window system device. Even though they provide a user-friendly interface, these systems do not interpret the visual information itself such as the meaning or similarity of the images. Therefore, the window systems do not provide enough facilities for visual interaction with a database.

What are needed in visual interaction? We can summarize the essential needs in visual interaction as follows [4, 5].

(a)   We want to process the visual information itself within the database.

(b)   We need to communicate this information to and from the database in a user-friendly manner.

We can answer these needs taking a cognitive approach. The cognitive approach integrates both image model and user model to interpret and operate the visual information semantically.

This paper describes the ideas of visual interaction from our cognitive aspect in Chapter 2. We will show our approach by typical user's query requests. A query by visual example (QVE) provides a sketch retrieval function and a query by subjective descriptions (QBD) provides a sense retrieval function. This chapter also introduces our experimental database system ART MUSEUM*. The algorithm for QVE is described in Chapter 3. The system automatically creates the pictorial index for sketch retrieval. This index describes the general composition of paintings. Chapter 4 describes the detail algorithm for QBD. We have designed this algorithm to refer the user model in sense retrieval. This model describes the correlation between the color feature of paintings and the subjective impression of each user. This chapter also includes the learning algorithm to build the user model. Chapter 5 discusses the requirements for the multimedia data model from our experience.

2. Intelligent Visual Database System

2.1 Visual Interaction and Visual Interface

"A picture is worth a thousand words." Visual information is a good man-machine communication media. We will regard visual information as not only image data itself but also linguistic data related to some image data. For example, a photograph and a hand-written sketch belong to the former category. Subjective remarks on an artistic painting belong to the latter category. We can

---

* Multimedia Database with Sense of Color and Construction upon the Matter of Art.

communicate the visual information to and from the system in the visual interaction process.

Several experimental image database systems provide visual interfaces. For example, the QPE system provides the schema of graphic data in a tabular form [6]. The image browser navigates a user tracing its hypermedia-like indexes [7]. In the icon-based system, icon is the key of an image as well as the element of the visual query language [8]. While these systems use graphic devices to show schema, icons and guidelines, their queries are only substitutes for the SQL-like query languages on alphanumeric information. These interfaces do not interpret the semantics of the visual information which we want to process.

We wish to process the semantics of visual information and to communicate the visual information to and from the database in a user-friendly manner. We expect image database systems to have good visual interfaces to enable such visual interaction.

2.2 Visual Interaction Facilities

Then, how do we organize such a visual interface? We will show our approach by typical user's query requests.

A user often wishes to see some painting which he keeps in his mind. Then, he has only to draw its rough sketch and show the sketch as a pictorial key to the system. We call this kind of visual interaction a query by visual example (QVE). QVE should evaluate the similarity between the sketch and the images in the database. Therefore, we have to define a similarity measure on a robust image model [9, 10].

Our second request to visual interaction is a query by subjective descriptions (QBD). A user often wishes to see several paintings which may leave him some artistic impressions. Then, he has only to describe such impressions by his own words to see several paintings which may leave him similar impressions. This kind of visual interaction is sense retrieval. Note that our impressions differ for each of us, even when viewing the same painting. Therefore, the system should analyze and learn the correlation between the subjective descriptions and the images with each user. Such correlation forms a user model. We have to develop a simple learning algorithm to adjust the model to each user.

Thus, we have to design a robust image model and a user model. These are the requirements and the technical problems associated with visual interface and visual interaction.

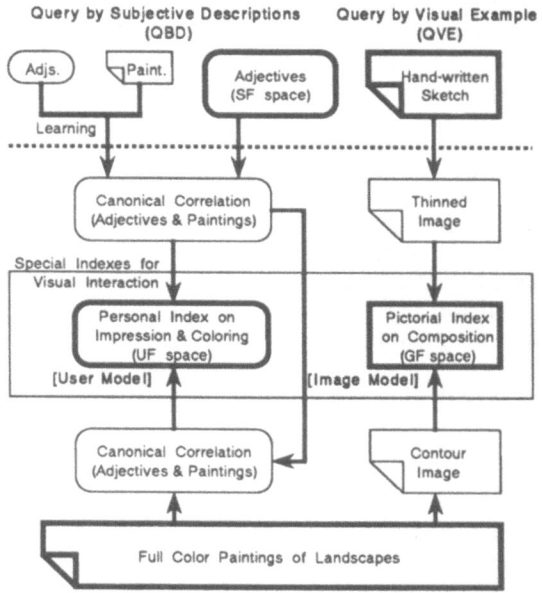

Figure 1. Overview of the ART MUSEUM System and Visual Interaction

2.3 ART MUSEUM System

We have been developing an electronic art gallery called ART MUSEUM [4, 5, 11] The ART MUSEUM is a collection of full color paintings of landscapes. The ART MUSEUM system provides both types of visual interaction. QVE is available for sketch retrieval using pictorial keys. QBD is also available for sense retrieval using some words from the user's personal view. Figure 1 shows the overview of the ART MUSEUM system. This system has two types of special indexes for visual interaction. One is a pictorial index and the other is a personal index.

We have assumed following image models to design the pictorial indexes. The general composition and the coloring characterize each full color painting.

A contour image roughly approximates the general composition of the painting. A user has only to draw a sketch of the overall picture as a pictorial key in QVE. The system searches for a similar composition on the pictorial index, comparing the parameterized graphic feature of contour images. Then, the system finds the target picture and presents it in a full color representation.

An artist paints with many colors. We can parameterize the coloring by the distribution of the RGB intensity values. The system refers this pic-

236

torial index to create the following user model and personal index.

We have also assumed a user model to design the personal index. The subjective descriptions of each user correlate with the coloring of paintings. The system analyzes such correlation between the set of words and the parameterized coloring feature on the several test samples. The system uses the correlation as the personal index for the user. The user has only to show several words in QBD. The system evaluates the most suited coloring to the words on the personal index. Then, the system provides the paintings of suited coloring.

3. Query by Visual Example

3.1 Pictorial Index

The general composition of painting is one of the major part in our impression. This chapter discusses an approach to the query by visual example (QVE). A user has only to draw a sketch of the overall paintings to retrieve several paintings of similar composition.

A contour image roughly approximates the composition of the original painting. The ART MUSEUM system has a pictorial index of contour images for QVE. We have developed the following differential filter on RGB space to get a contour image.

[Construction of pictorial index]
(1) Apply an affine transformation to normalize the image size into 256×256 pixels. Then, apply a median filter of 3×3 pixels window to smooth the RGB intensity values.
(2) Apply the following nonlinear differential filter to evaluate the edge rate.
$$\Delta S = \Delta I \, / \, I.$$
Where for each pixel m_{xy} and for each of its 8-nearest neighbors $m_{x'y'}$,
$$\Delta I = m_{xy} - m_{x'y'},$$
$$I = m_{xy} + m_{x'y'}.$$
(3) Choose higher edge rate points from the distribution of ΔS to get a binary contour image.
(4) Apply a thinning algorithm to the contour image.
(5) Calculate the number and the rate of edge directions p_i. (Currently, the edge directions are digitized into 36 patterns.)

Figure 2 shows an original color image and its contour image derived from this algorithm. The contour image approximates the general composition of the original color painting. Our differential filter satisfies Weber-Fechner's Law in visual psychology [12]. We will refer to the number and the rate of edge directions as the pictorial index of graphic feature (GF) vector on general composition.

Figure 2. Color Image and its Contour Image

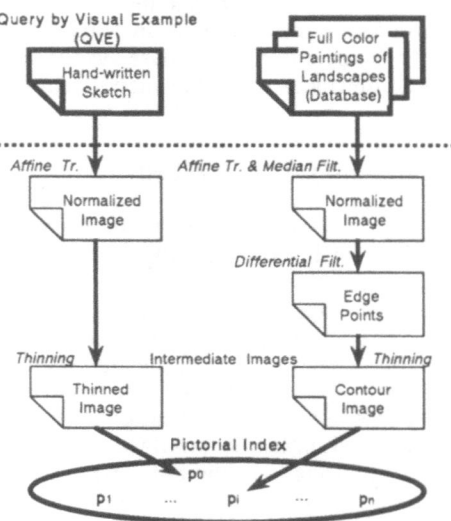

Figure 3. Sketch Retrieval in QVE

3.2 Sketch Retrieval

Let us show the sketch retrieval algorithm in QVE. Figure 3 shows the outline of this algorithm. The user has only to draw a sketch of the overall pictures. The sketch is thinned and referred to as a pictorial key. The system searches for a similar composition on the pictorial index. Then, the system provides the target picture with a full color representation.

[Sketch retrieval]
(1) Apply an affine transformation to normalize the image size into 256×256 pixels. Then, apply thinning algorithm to the image, and

237

calculate its GF vector p_0 of the number and the rate of edge directions.

(2) Choose the suited paintings whose GF vector p_i is near to the user's sketch.

We have experimented the sketch retrieval algorithm on our ART MUSEUM system. Figure 4 shows an example of sketch retrieval. A user has written down a sketch shown in the left side of Figure 4. The system searches the best matched painting on the pictorial index. The target painting of Utorillo is retrieved and shown in full color representation in the right side of Figure 4.

In the current stage of our research, we have assumed that the user can write down the detailed sketch. The development of a powerful matching algorithm for rough sketches is the next stage of our research.

4. Query by Subjective Descriptions

4.1 Impression and Color Feature

To retrieve some paintings which give us some impressions, key word indexes have been the popular approach. The indexer assigns several key words to each image as the index terms. The user retrieves some images by the preassigned key words. Even if the key word thesaurus is available, this approach has following two problems:

(a) The indexer has to assign some key words to every painting in the database, which costs much personnel expense.

(b) Such descriptions may differ for each person according to his cultural backgrounds, even when looking at the same painting.

Therefore, we have to model how each user feels as the user model. Art critics views paintings from several aspects. They take notice on motif, general composition and coloring. [13] reported that the dominant impression generated by paintings is coloring. From this aspect, we may expect there is a reasonable correlation between the coloring and the words in the reviews.

The ART MUSEUM system learns the correlation between such coloring and the subjective descriptions of the user's impressions. We may refer such correlation as the user model. In our current implementation, the artistic impressions are described by special 30 adjectives.

4.2 User Model and Personal Index

Let us show the algorithm for learning a user model. We cannot directly compare the words of subjective descriptions and the coloring of paintings, since they have different domains. Therefore, we have parameterized the words and the coloring into the subjective feature (SF) vector and the graphic feature (GF) vector at first. Here, the SF vector shows the weight of the adjectives for the user's impressions. The GF vector shows the distribution of the RGB intensity values. The SF vectors and the GF vectors make the SF space and the GF space, respectively. We adopted several test samples from the database to analyze the correlation

Figure 4. Example of Sketch Reteival in QVE
(left: hand-written sketch, right: original color image)

238

between the SF space and the GF space.

Figure 5 shows the outline of the learning algorithm. A user describes his impressions by several adjectives with each painting in the test sample, which gives SF vectors. The system extracts the GF vector of each painting. We need a unified feature (UF) space where the correlation between SF space and GF space is maximum. We can construct such a UF space by the canonical correlation analysis. The canonical correlation analysis is one of the multivariate analysis methods to correlate the distinct domains [14]. The algorithm to construct the UF space and the personal index is as follows. (See also Figure 5(a).)

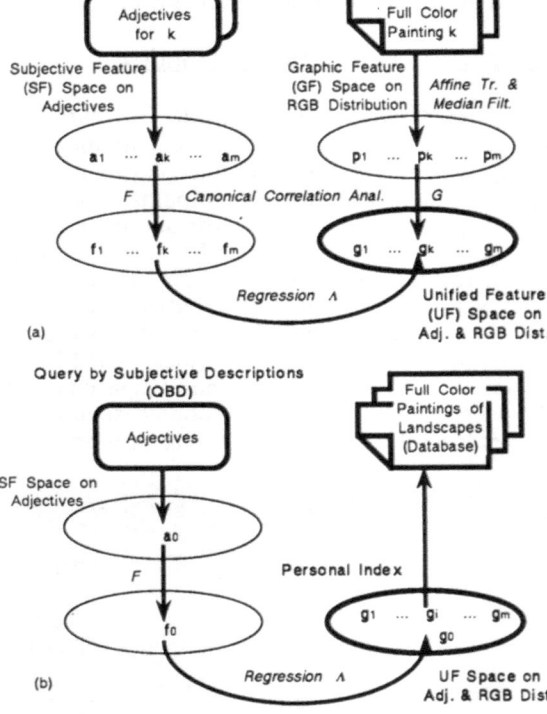

Figure 5. Sense Retrieval in QBD

[Construction of the UF space and personal index]
(1)   Sample arbitrary paintings from the database as a learning set P. The user gives his impressions by a_k to each painting $k \in P$. (The SF vector a_k shows the weights of adjectives.)
(2)   Apply an affine transformation to normalize the image size into 256×256 pixels. Then, apply a median filter of 3×3 pixels window to smooth the RGB intensity values [15].

Calculate the GF vector p_k of each painting $k \in P$. (The GF vector p_k is a histogram of RGB intensity values.)
(3)   Construct the linear mappings F and G to correlate f_k and g_k, applying the canonical correlation analysis.
$$f_k = F' a_k,$$
$$g_k = G' p_k.$$
(F' means the transposed matrix of F.)
(4)   Calculate the UF vectors with every painting in the database by $g_i = G' p_i$.

We will refer the UF space of g_i as the personal index. Note that we do not have to assign the adjectives a_n to every painting in the database. Once the system has learned the linear mappings F and G, it can automatically construct the personal index only from the GF vectors. This algorithm reduces the personnel expenses for indexing.

If we develop this image database system on the network, we can allocate the personal index on the local site for personal use. To the contrary, we had better place the image data and the pictorial index of coloring on the center site for common use.

4.3 Sense Retrieval

We may expect that the neighboring paintings on the personal index cause similar impressions with the user. (Of course, the test samples P must reflect the properties of the whole database.) The user describes the target paintings he wants to appreciate by several adjectives in sense retrieval. The system infers some coloring which makes him such feeling on the personal index. The system then shows suited candidates in the database. The algorithm for sense retrieval on coloring is as follows. (See also Figure 5(b).)

[Sense retrieval]
(1)   Apply the linear mappings F and L to the vector a_0 of denoted adjectives in the user's query.
$$g_0 = \Lambda F' a_0.$$
Where Λ is the diagonal matrix of canonical correlation coefficients.
(2)   Choose the neighboring paintings g_i on the personal index as candidates in sense retrieval.

The sense retrieval algorithm binds two attributes in different media. The one is the key words in linguistic media, and the other is the paintings in image media. Therefore, the sense retrieval algorithm seems to be a multimedia join operation between the linguistic media and the image media.

We have experimented the learning algorithm and the sense retrieval algorithm on our ART MUSEUM system. In this experiment, we used 50 paintings for the samples, while the whole database has 100 paintings. Figure 6 shows an example of sense retrieval. Figure 6 shows the first sixth candidates for the adjectives; clear, bright and clean. In this experiment, we have adjusted the user model to five young girls. Their subjective estimation was almost good. Therefore, we may expect that the personal index is useful for the sense retrieval on image databases.

Using the UF space, we can also retrieve several paintings which cause the similar impression on coloring by showing a painting. We can also infer suited key words for a painting, using the inverse mapping F^{-1} and L^{-1} as follows.

$$a_0 = F'^{-1} \Lambda^{-1} G' p_0.$$

5. Discussions on Data Model

5.1 Semantics of Image Database

From our experience described above, let us consider the requirements for the multimedia data model.

The major topics for spatial databases have been physical data structures for data compression and high-speed data access. An image model has a role to design a suited data structure and its file storage [16].

On the other hand for the schema designing of image database systems, we know semantic data models. These models describe the relationships among the entities and their attributes of images. An object-oriented model is a current topic for multimedia database systems [17].

Our experience on visual interaction suggests another aspect to an image database system. We may call it cognitive aspect. Visual interaction requires interpreting the contents of image data to operate them semantically. Such interpretation algorithms have to suite the visual perception process of the user, i.e. the user model. It belongs to a subjective human factor. We have to combine the image model and the user model to support visual interaction.

5.2 Requirements for Multimedia Data Model

Let us summarize the requirements for a multimedia data model from our cognitive aspect [18].

(a) Spatial independence: We want to provide the query by subjective descriptions in the user's view. User's view mechanism should manage the subjec-

Figure 6. Example of Sense Retrieval in QBD *(for clear, bright and clean)*

240

tive indexes. Of course, the system has to manage also the pictorial indexes to process the spatial relationships and graphic features of images.

(b) Media independence: We use many kinds of image data types suited to image compression and image processing. For example, a painting is stored as a matrix of RGB intensity values, a matrix of binary values, a series of run-length codes, and so on. We expect these data structures are transparent to the image processing algorithms. The abstracted data type is one of its approach.

(c) Application independence: We developed many image processing algorithms. These algorithms depend on their data type of domain and range, which makes the control mechanism complicated. Therefore, we have to abstract these algorithms by their classifications according to their functions. This idea is method abstraction, which is useful to manage the relationships among the image entity, its data type and image processing algorithms. This mechanism provides the flexible wake-up of image processing algorithms in object-oriented environment.

6. Summary

We have described the ideas and their implementations of visual interaction with an image database system. The ART MUSEUM system provides sketch retrieval in query by visual example and sense retrieval in query by subjective description. These functions formed visual interaction in a truly user-friendly manner, based on the use of the image model and the user model.

This paper also summarized the requirements to a multimedia data model from a cognitive aspect. Multimedia database systems require method abstraction and media transparency as well as data abstraction.

We would like to thank the colleagues in Electrotechnical Laboratory (ETL) and the students from University for Library and Information Science (ULIS). This research is supported by the national research and development project of *Interoperable Database Systems*.

References

[1] Chang, S. K.: "Image Database Systems", in "Hand Book of Pattern recognition and Image Processing", Young, T. Y. and Fu, K. S. (ed.), Academic Press, Chap.16, pp.371-393, 1986.

[2] Iyenger, S. S. and Kashyap, R. L.(ed.): "Image Databases", IEEE Trans on Software Engineering (special selection), Vol.SE-14, No.5, pp.608-688, May 1988.

[3] Grosky, W. I. and Mehrotra, R. (ed.): "Image Database Management", IEEE Computer (special issue), Vol.22, No.12, pp.7-71, Dec. 1989.

[4] Kato, T.: "Multimedia Interaction on Advanced Image Database System — Intelligent Personal Interface —", Proc. of Computer World'89, pp.174-181, Sep. 1989.

[5] Kato, T., Kurita, T. and Shimogaki, H.: "Multimedia Interaction with Image Database Systems", Proc. of Advanced Database System Symposium'89, pp.271-278, Dec. 1989.

[6] Chang, N. S. and Fu, K. S.: "Query-by-Pictorial Example", IEEE Trans. on Software Engineering, Vol.SE-6, No.6, pp.519-524, June 1980.

[7] Kasahara, H. and Abe, S.: "Image Mnemonics — Indexing and Communication —", Proc. of Advanced Database System Symposium'89, pp.293-300, Dec. 1989.

[8] Chang, S. K., Yan, C. W., Dimitroff, D. C. and Arndt, T.: "An Intelligent Image Database System", IEEE Trans. on Software Engineering, Vol.SE-14, No.5, pp.681-688, May 1988.

[9] Kato, T., Shimogaki, H. and Fujimura, K.: "TRADEMARK: Multimedia Image Database System with Intelligent Human Interface", Trans. of IEICE Japan, Vol.J72-D-II, No.4, pp.535-544, Apr. 1989 (in Japanese).

[10] Kurita, T., Shimogaki, H. and Kato, T.: "A Personal Interface for Similarity Retrieval on an Image Database System", Trans. of IPS Japan, Vol.31, No.2, pp.227-237, Feb. 1990 (in Japanese).

[11] Kato, T., Kurita, T. and Sakakura, A.: "Electronic Art Museum: Full Color Image Database with Visual Interaction on Color and Sketch", Tech. Rep. of SIG-IE of IEICE Japan, IE88-118, pp.31-38, Mar. 1989 (in Japanese).

[12] MacLeod, D. I. A. and Thomas, J. P. (ed.): "Basic Sensory Processes I", in "Hand Book of Perception and Human Performance (I)", Boff, K. R., Kaufman, L. and Thomas, J. P. (ed.), Sec.2, 1986.

[13] Chijiiwa, H.: "Chromatics", Fukumura Printing Co., Chap.5, pp.128-163, 1983 (in Japanese).

[14] Cooly, W. W. and Lohnes, P. R.: "Multivariate Data Analysis", John Wiley & Sons, Inc., 1971.

[15] Rosenfeld, A. and Kak, A. C.: "Digital Picture Processing (2e)", Academic Press, 1982.

[16] Ahuja, N. and Schachter, B. J.: "Image Models", ACM Computing Surveys, Vol.13, No.4, pp.373-397, Dec. 1981.

[17] Masunaga, Y.: "An Object-Oriented Approach to Multimedia Database Organization and Management", Proc. of the Int. Symp. on Database Systems for Advanced Application, pp.190-200, Apr. 1989.

[18] Kato, T. and Mizutori, T.: "Multimedia Data Model for Advanced Image Information Systems", Proc. of Advanced Database System Symposium'89, pp.113-120, Dec. 1989.

OMEN - An Object-Oriented Database Management System for Non-Standard Database Applications

H. Schukat   F.J. Schmid

SIEMENS AG
ZFE IS KOM34
Otto Hahn Ring 6, 8000 München 83

Abstract

Object-oriented Database Management Systems (ooDBMS) gain a lot of attention in the database research area, because they offer much promising facilities to support non-standard database applications like CAD/CAM, office automation, multimedia databases or data-intensive knowledge bases. Conventional database technology (i.e., relational or network) is not well-suited in these fields, because of their poor structural and behavioral modeling capabilities.

Object-oriented databases bring database functionality like persistence, transactions, recovery or concurrency to object-oriented systems, so that object-oriented modeling capabilities can be used to fulfill the requirements of non-standard database applications.

This paper presents concepts and implementation of an ooDBMS prototype, called **OMEN** (Object-Oriented Database Management System) which offers a C++-database extension for object-oriented database programming. The whole system is embedded in an interactive, graphical user interface management, based on the standard OSF/Motif for window management systems.

1. Introduction

In the last years, the object-oriented concept has received a lot of attention in the design and implementation of non-standard database applications, dealing with data of high complexity and complex application semantics, like CAD/CAM, CASE, office automation, multimedia databases or data-intensive knowledge based systems.

Conventional record-oriented database technologies have some inherent disadvantages ([18], [12]) in these application areas. To overcome this problem, object-oriented database systems (ooDBMS) [6] extend conventional database technology by combining database- and object-oriented concepts [20].

Object-oriented concepts [3] provide many advantages in designing non-standard databases, a few of them are:

- They provide a natural modeling of application semantics: real world objects are modelled in one-to-one correspondence into database objects. Objects are not mapped into flat record structures like in conventional DBMS. This mapping has great performance drawbacks for database application programs [8]. The behavior modeling of database objects is also part of the object-oriented concept.

- In ooDBMS there is no distinction between database and application programming, so that ooDBMS fill the "semantic gap" between database and application programming. Database programming is computationally complete.

- Inheritance mechanismn in ooDBMS allow stepwise refinement of conceptual entities and 'programming in differences'. The concept of inheritance forces the reusability of software components.

As mentioned above, ooDBMS support complex object structures and definition of application-specific operations for database objects modeling their behavior.

To differentiate between DBMSs which support only one of the two aspects, [6] introduces the terms **structural** and **behavioral** object-orientation. Only when both are supported, **full object-orientation** is obtained. Today the research on object-oriented database systems is characterized by the lack of formal foundations and hence of common data models, and further by a lot of experimental work. Most object-oriented database systems today are just prototypes ([10], [4], [17]). The main features and characteristics of ooDBMSs are still in discussion, as described in the position paper [1].

In this paper we present a prototype of a fully object-oriented database system which is embedded in an interactive, graphical programming environment. This prototype, called **OMEN** (Object-Oriented Database Management), is developed by upgrading the existing structural object-oriented system DAMASCUS (Database Mangement System for CAD using UNIX Stations) to full object-orientation [9]. DAMASCUS has been developed in a cooperation project between SIEMENS AG, Corporate Research and Development, Munich, and Research Center for Computer Science, Karlsruhe .

OMEN combines features of the structural object-oriented DBMS kernel with features of object-oriented programming like classes, inheritance and data encapsulation, by providing an object-oriented data definition language (ooDDL).

There are some other commercially available ooDBMS like VBASE+ [15] or Ontos (for C++) or GemStone [14] (for Smalltalk) which follow concepts also present in our prototype. But they lack the support of database features managed by a structural object-oriented DBMS.

In our approach we try to combine database programming with an interactive, graphical user interface management, based on modern trends and standards (OSF/Motif [16], [21]). Schema definition is provided by a structure editor which supports schema definition using semantic information.

In Chapter 2 we introduce the underlying concepts of our prototype implementation, namely how to upgrade an existing structural ooDBMS to full object-orientation. Chapter 3 is concerned with a short overview of our object model and the ooDDL. In Chapter 4 we give a quick look at the implementation, which is realized with the system Gandalf [11], a modern software generation tool for the development of interactive software environments. Chapter 5 closes with some concluding remarks.

2 Upgrading a structural object-oriented database to full object-orientation

The idea of our approach is to use an existing structural object-oriented database system and extend it to support object-oriented features to make it fully object-oriented. In fig. 1 we show, how a structural object-oriented database system [6] can be embedded in the overall architecture of an object management system fulfilling all object-oriented requirements.

The system consists of two main layers and DAMASCUS ([7], [8]) builds the underlying object administration kernel. The data model of DAMASCUS is called iODM (internal Object Data Model) and is an extended entity-relationship model supporting complex objects and n-ary relations between them.

The 'low level' (shaded parts) of the architecture in fig.1 are already provided by DAMASCUS. All higher level features like classes, inheritance, etc., are realized by the general object manager (GOM). The GOM may be coupled to programming languages following different programming paradigms. Details of this approach are given in [9].

This architecture has all features of an ooDBMS, whereas our prototype does not support all of these features: query language, multi user management, etc., are omitted (see chapter 4). The main question to be solved is the programming language interface.

In general, there are three ways to solve the interface problem:

- Design of a completely new language (like e.g. OPAL [14]). The same kinds of objects are used for programming as well as in the DBMS.

- Object-oriented data definition concepts are combined with various existing programming

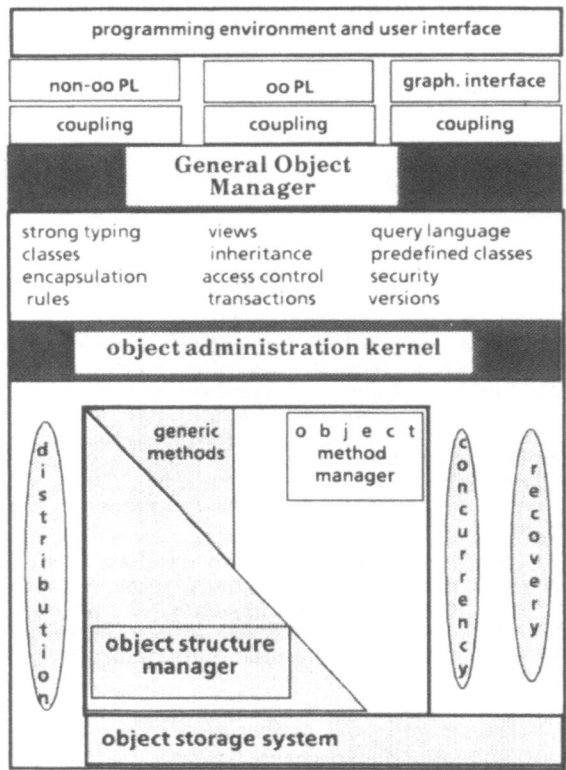

Fig. 1: Architecture of the General Object Manager

languages for method implementation and application programming (an approach chosen e.g. in O_2 [2]). The DBMS objects are made accessible inside the chosen programming language (for example C or Basic in O_2).

- An existing object-oriented programming language can be extended by the necessary database features (e.g. VBASE+ which extends C++ [15]). The objects defined in the programming language may directly become database objects, the structural definition and manipulation features are taken from the language.

We chose the last way to build a C++ - DBMS. In our approach, we design special language features for data definition and manipulation, whereas the methods and applications may be implemented by the user in C++ or C. The language designed for data handling will integrate the C++ class concept, so that the whole system can be considered as an extended C++ - DBMS. The next chapter presents the underlying concepts of our solution.

3. The object-oriented Data Definition Language (ooDDL)

3.1 The Object Model

The OMEN object model relies on concepts of object oriented programming languages. It allows the definition of types, which can be explicitly instantiated in form of objects. A type is the description of all object properties, structural as well as behavioral. Types with an explicit instantiate-operation are called classes. The notion of class also has extensional semantics and refers to a set of objects of a given type. The class specification consists of the following features:

- Attributes may have any type which is allowed in the iODM data model of DAMASCUS [8] and which can be described with a C++ - type [19].

- Methods are the functions or procedures applicable to the class instances. A class specification contains only the method headers.

- Further optional specifications: type invariants, consistency constraints, derivation rules, pre- and post-conditions of methods [13].

Classes may be arranged in an inheritance hierarchy. By this facility, the 'IS-A semantics' can be modelled. Already implemented methods may be reused and therefore redundancy is minimized. The OMEN object model should support multiple inheritance.

The root of any inheritance hierarchy in our data model is a predefined class called the 'superclass' OBJECT (see fig.2). OBJECT provides generic operations to copy or delete objects and operations to receive general information of objects like the total number of instances in the extension of a class.

To meet important requirements in respect to schema modifications and extensions, the object model provides the metaclass CLASS, whose instances are representatives of all currently existing classes. CLASS contains any operation which is valid for arbitrary classes and inherits the properties of OBJECT, so the conventional operations on instances may be used to express schema modifications. The modification of an instance of CLASS may have far-reaching consequences like recompilation and reorganization of the database. The existence of CLASS is also justified by the necessity to formulate queries involving several classes. The method QUERY will therefore be considered as a method of CLASS. By representing CLASS as an instance of its own extension, the user is enabled in a natural manner to formulate queries involving metadata, e.g., to select the number of classes, the names of all classes, the attributes of a given class, etc. A graphical visualization of the relationship between classes and objects is given in fig. 2.

To simplify schema design, more predefined classes than just CLASS and OBJECT may be provided (not shown in fig. 2). The most important of them is the class RELATION which can be used to model relationships between objects - a widespread feature in the database world -, but yet unusual in the context of object-oriented programming. Relationships are a powerful modelling concept to express associations between an arbitrary number of objects and to provide describing attributes for these associations.

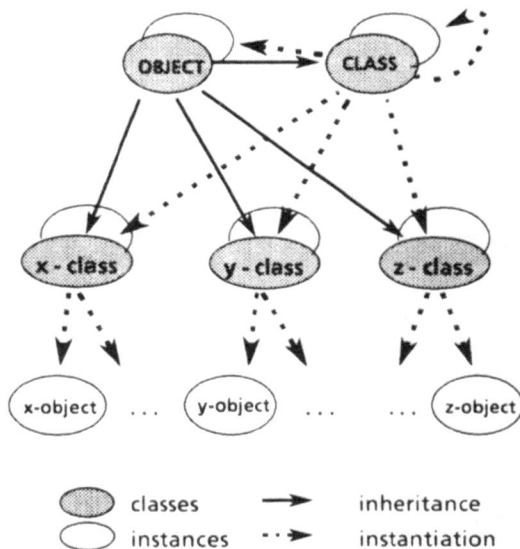

Fig. 2: Relationships between Classes and Objects

Among other features, relationships are automatically deleted, if one of the participating objects is removed. The user will not have to take care of them when implementing the delete operations of his object classes.

Another important predefined class in the area of engineering applications is the class VERSIONED-OBJECT which provides mechanisms for efficient version handling. A subclass *SUB* of class VERSIONED-OBJECT inherits the operations for version management like create-new-version, delete-version, get-version-nr, find-next-version, etc. Note that an object of class *SUB* represents a generic object with all its actually existing versions; every individual version is itself an object in its own right. A similar concept can be found in [22].

3.2 The object-oriented Data Definition Language (ooDDL)

The object-oriented Data Definition Language (ooDDL) combines features of the C++ type concept with features of the DAMASCUS-DDL. Thus complex object structures supported by the DAMASCUS-DDL are extended with object-oriented concepts like classes, inheritance, data encapsulation and methods. The object model described above is the foundation of our language definition. Database objects are made visible to an application programmer in C++ by an ooDDL schema, which is used to generate a DAMASCUS database schema and an equivalent C++ class structure.

A database schema in the object-oriented approach can be regarded as a set of classes. A class offers a structural and behavioral property description and has (or inherits) a constructor to create persistent objects at runtime. The ooDDL is a strongly typed language, i.e., each object belongs to a given class. A set of objects belonging to a class is called the extension of a class.

Classes are organized in an inheritance relation [1]. Class hierarchies with inheritance are used to model generalization or specialization (IS-A semantics). Inheritance supports property transfer from supertype to subtype, reducing redundancy of definition and implementation. For example, a display method may be defined for a class polygon and is inherited by all specialized classes like triangle, rectangle, etc.

An ooDDL schema must have (at least) one class which inherits from the super-class OBJECT. OBJECT and CLASS are predefined classes implicit defined for all ooDDL schemata. As described in chapter 3.1, OBJECT has all generic db-operations like read-object(), delete-object(), and further the object-constructor create-object(). User defined constructors, known from C++, are not allowed for database objects.

An ooDDL schema starts with a list of basetype definitions. Basetypes are not objecttypes, i.e., they must not have an extension, and are only used for abbrevation of type descriptions. They may be composed of simple and complex types.

A class definition is composed of an attribute definition part and a method definition part. The object structure is defined as an aggregation of attributes of simple or complex type. Several type constructors for complex domains are applicable. They allow the definition of sets, lists, tuples and vectors (i.e. arrays).

Built-in objects and references to objects are realized by attributes and can be combined with the domain constructors. Treelike object hierarchies are modelled with built-in objects, nets of objects of arbitrary complexity can be constructed by references.

Attributes are encapsulated, that means that only methods defined in the class have access to them. A simple attribute may be defined as a key-attribute for value based retrieval of objects.

The behavioral modeling of classes is realized in the method part of a class definition. Methods are specified there by their interfaces and are implemented elsewhere in an application program (in C++ or in C code). The keyword 'virtual' is a compiler option with the same semantics as in C + + : Methods marked as 'virtual' may be redefined (new implementation) in subclasses of the superclass (polymorphic functions [19], [5]).

Until now, we are only concerned with complex object structures and classes as modeling constructs. Relations between objects (as known from the Entity Relationship Model) are another important modeling construct. They are used as described in the object model.

4. OMEN System Architecture

We will now give a brief look to the prototype system architecture. OMEN is built of three layers, as shown in

fig.3, to realize some of the facilities of the general object manager:

- User Interface Management (UIM).
- ooDDL editor for schema definition (structure editor).
- Frame for application programming tools in C++ (browser, class library, etc.).

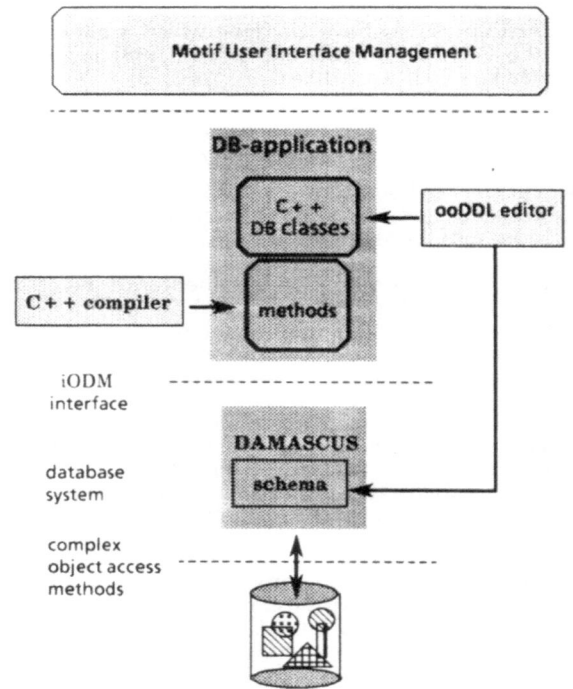

Fig.3: OMEN system architecture

The User Interface Management is based on the new industrial standard OSF-Motif [16] for window management systems. OSF/Motif provides an object-oriented toolkit for developing of portable, graphical user interfaces. It offers a "look and feel" with 3-D effects and a good usability. All system components of OMEN are embedded in this UIM interface.

The database schema definition is produced with an interactive structure editor (ooDDL editor), which is implemented with the system Gandalf [11] from CMU (Carnegie Mellon University). Gandalf is a modern software tool for generating interactive software development environments. The implementor of a structure editor has to specify syntax and semantics in a high level specification language which is automatically transformed into a C-program (code of the structure editor). The syntax specification is BNF-like and uses a procedural, tree-oriented language for semantic processing, for example to check for consistent schema definitons.

The output of ooDDL editor session is a C++ class structure and an equivalent DAMASCUS DDL schema, both are checked by the editor for inconsistent definitions. No compiler changes or additional programming tools are necessary. A standard C++ compiler can be used. Predefined classes like OBJECT and CLASS are provided for C++ database programming. A database application has to be compiled and linked to built an executable program.

5. Conclusion

In this paper we have presented the prototype of an ooDBMS. OMEN is still under development and first experiences are made. Several evident advantages are gained by placing full object-orientation on an existing structural object-oriented DBMS instead of a completely new development. The new system can rely upon a stable database kernel with advanced features well-suited for the planned non-standard applications. The evolutionary development makes use of existing system modules and interfaces, saving considerably implementation effort and providing upward compatibility. The use of existing application programs of the kernel DBMS is possible by using intermediate interfaces.

Other advantages in our approach are a good language acceptance (C or C++) for database application programming and the portability of the system.

But the upgrading approach in our prototype has also some inherent disadvantages, which come from coupling to existing systems. So one has to accept disadvantages of the C++ type concept and make them visible in the ooDDL. C++ classes are no objects, so schema evolution -like adding or removing classes- would cause the recompilation of a schema and reorganization of the database.

We are planning now working on concepts for extension of our prototype with respect to query language design, method management, and object-oriented distribution models.

6. References

[1] M.Atkinson, F.Bancilhon, D. DeWitt, K. Dittrich, D. Maier, S. Zdonik: "The Object-Oriented Database System Manifesto". Proc. DOOD89, Kyoto, Japan.

[2] F. Bancilhon et al.: "The Design and Implementation of O2, an Object-Oriented Database System." In [Ditt88].

[3] Banerjee,et.al.: "Data model issues for object-oriented applications". ACM TOIS Jan. 1987.

[4] M.Carey, D. DeWitt: "Object and File Management in the EXODUS Extensible Database System". Proc. VLDB, Aug. 1986

[5] L. Cardelli, P. Wegner: "On Understanding Types, Data Abstraction, and Polymorphism." ACM Computing Surveys, Vol. 17, No. 4, pp. 471-522, Dec. 1985.

[6] K.R. Dittrich: "Advances in Object-Oriented Database Systems." Proc. of the 2nd Int. Workshop on Object-Oriented Systems. Lecture Notes in Computer Science, Vol. 334, Springer 1988.

[7] K.R. Dittrich, A.M. Kotz, J.A. Mülle: "A Multilevel Approach to Design Database Systems and its Basic Mechanisms." Proc. IEEE COMPINT, Montreal 1985.

[8] K.R. Dittrich, A.M. Kotz, J.A. Mülle: "Database Support for VLSI Design: The DAMASCUS System." In: M.H. Ungerer (ed.): CAD-Schnittstellen und Datentransferformate im Elektronik-Bereich, Springer 1987.

[9] H.Dentler, M. Scheurer, F-J.Schmid, A. Kotz, B. Schiefer, K. Dittrich: "Upgrading a Complex Object DBMS to Full Object-Orientation: a Case Study." Proc. 2nd Conf. on Data and Knowledge Systems Gaithersburg, Md 1989, IEEE Computer Society Press.

[10] D. Fishman: "Iris: An object-oriented database management system ". ACM TOIS, Jan. 87

[11] Haberman, Ellison, Notkin, Kaiser, Staudt, Ambriola: "Special Issue on the Gandalf Project".The Journal of Software and Systems 5(2) May, 1985

[12] W. Kent: "Limitations of Record-Based Information Models." ACM Transactions on Database Systems, Vol.4, No.1, 1979, pp.107-131.

[13] B. Meyer: "Object-Oriented Software Construction." Prentice Hall Int. Series in Computer Science1988.

[14] D. Maier, J. Stein, A. Otis, A. Purdy: "Development of an Object-Oriented DBMS." Proc. OOPSLA86.

[15] Ontologic Inc.: "Vbase + - Object Database for C++ - Functional Specification." Bilerica, Dec. 1988.

[16] Open Software Foundation: "Application Environment Specification (AES)" Cambridge, Ma. 1989

[17] D. Schmidt, K. Bauknecht: "DB + - persistent objects for C++". Proc. BTW 89, Springer Verlag, IFB 204

[18] T.W. Sidle: "Weaknesses of Commercial Database Management Systems in Engineering Applications." Proc. Design Automation Conf., Minneapolis, Vol.17, June 1980, pp.57-61.

[19] B. Stroustrup: "The C++ Programming Language." Addison-Wesley 1985.

[20] D.C. Tsichritzis, O.M. Nierstrasz: "Fitting Round Objects into Square Databases." Proc. ECOOP, Oslo 1988, Springer Verlag.

[21] D. Young: "X Window Systems. Programming and Applications". Prentice Hall, Englewood Cliffs, New Jersey 1989.

[22] S.B. Zdonik: "Version Management in an Object-Oriented Database. "Proc. of an Intl. Workshop on Advanced Programming Environments, Trondheim 1986, Springer Verlag.

ARDITO: AN ADVANCED RELATIONAL DATABASE SYSTEM FOR IMAGE AND TEXT ORGANIZATION

F. Cesarini   G. Soda

Dipartimento di Sistemi e Informatica
Universita' di Firenze
Via S. Marta 3 - 50139 Florence - Italy
Phone +39-55-4796260; e-mail: GIOVANNI@IFIIDG.BITNET

ABSTRACT

This paper presents the main design and implementation features of a system for managing multimedia documents that are composed of texts and images. Besides having filing and retrieving facilities, this system is capable of defining and managing various kinds of links that can be established between several different documents and document components. Interactive display and navigation through the network are supported. The system architecture is based on a relational DBMS for storing data, network links, and control information.

1 - INTRODUCTION

In this paper, we present the main design and implementation features of ARDITO (Advanced Relational Database for Image and Text Organization), a system for managing multimedia documents.

The origin of ARDITO can be traced back to a project made for a system designed for cataloguing Artistic Goods in various environments, such as public offices or restoration laboratories. This system was intended for use by state officials or researchers who needed sophisticated cataloguing and consulting tools but were not necessarily experienced in computer techniques. The description of the catalogued objects had to follow the structure of the paper forms used by ICCD (the Central Institute for Catalogues and Documentation). These forms are quite complex and they take the form a dossier that provides various types of information, according to the object they refer to (buildings, gardens, ...). Therefore, some of our work has been focused on the conceptual modelling of these dossiers. The system also had to manage photogrammetric images of the catalogued objects and the user needed accessing forms and images in order to make correlations, comparisons, details, etc.

After we modelled this particular application, developed a prototype named GART, and used it, we redesigned the system in order to obtain both a model suitable for a wider range of applications and a kind of implementation more fully based on the underlying DBMS. ARDITO is the result of our efforts. Target applications refer to the manage-

ment of data, texts, and images in medical and artistic environments. The system is designed primarily for authoring.

The basic information unit of ARDITO is the dossier which is a collection of different kinds of data, i.e., formatted data, texts, and images. The structure of the dossier provides a flexible data organization that is suitable for many different applications. The system is characterized by the possibility of establishing links between entities stored in the database, and the network is created, manipulated and displayed interactively. The network capability allows the user to organize the database content in a dynamic and effective way, create information hierarchies, and define and use logical search paths.

Hypertext/hypermedia system technology [1] was taken as a reference point in the designing of ARDITO. In particular, information can be considered to be chunked in units that can contain various forms of data, such as texts, vector graphics, and bitmapped images. The units are interconnected by links, and navigation is supported by browsing mechanisms. However, ARDITO possess only a few of the features usually present in general hypertext systems because its application requirements mainly concern the database world rather than a hypertext one. For example, being able to build a report dynamically is not as important as being able to make inquiries within the stored information selectively.

ARDITO appears to be a tool with a certain number of integrated facilities for 1) database inquiring; 2) inserting, deleting, and updating data; 3) creating, deleting, and modifying links; 4) displaying and navigating through the network. The system is flexible and simple to use because the interface makes ample use of windows, icons, labels, and graphic symbols; the mouse is the main interactive device.

Our system architecture is based on using a relational DBMS for data managing and network storing. Images are known by the DBMS by means of their file name and some descriptive parameters that specify their type. Image display is performed by suitable graphic routines; the graphic library can be built incrementally as new kinds of images are managed. User interface, especially as regards network navigation, is implemented by using a system for graphic-based applications running within windows. Data and network management is controlled by a software layer that interfaces both the DBMS and the graphic application.

In section 2, we illustrate the basic information unit managed by the system: the dossier. Dossiers are collections of heterogeneous data [2]; our dossier model refers to texts and images and has a hierarchical structure.

The network is based on links connecting database units which can be heterogeneous; navigation is performed by travelling from one unit to another (see section 3).

Section 4 illustrates the navigation features. Navigation is based on through-document and within-document browsing mechanisms [3]. Partial network graphs around nodes are displayed in sequence, according to the user mouse movements; it is possible to display the content of nodes appearing on the screen at any time.

Section 5 illustrates the system implementation guidelines.

2 - THE DOSSIER

The **dossier** is the main information unit managed by this system; it is composed of various kinds of data that are organized into a hierarchy. The dossier structure is illustrated in fig. 1.

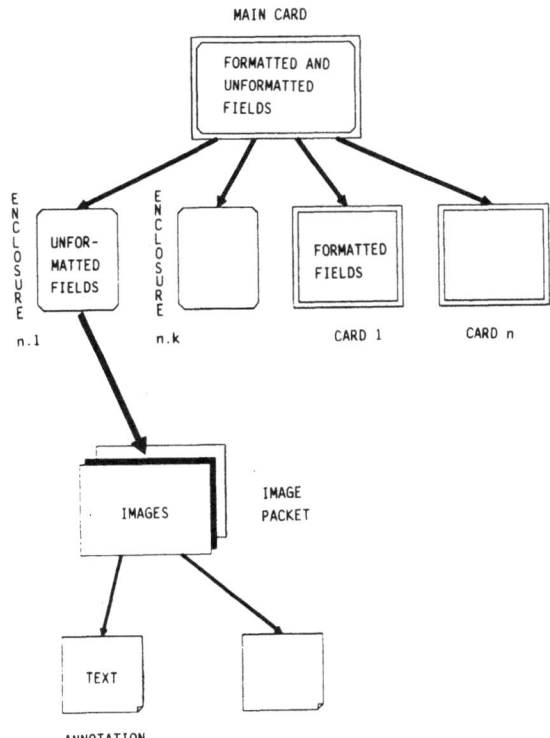

Figure 1 - The dossier structure

The **main card** is the root of the dossier and contains:
1) the code, 2) a set of formatted data used for containing the general information that appears in all the dossiers stored in the database, and 3) a text field usually used for brief descriptions.

For example, the main card of a patient record may contain the patient's registration data and some free notes. All other information is stored in cards and enclosures whose number can vary.

Cards contain formatted data. Since they can vary in number, they provide flexibility for storing multiple information about the subject; for example, the results of subsequent analyses can be represented in several different cards.

Enclosures collect information that is not treatable as formatted data, that is, texts and images. In particular, an enclosure can contain some free text information that doesn't follow a predefined structure and/or a pointer to an image packet. The enclosure is the means by which an image can be inserted into the database. Each enclosure can only point to one packet, but the number of enclosures per dossier can vary.

An **image packet** is a set of images the user also wants to be able to manage as a unique entity because they are correlated logically. There is no limit to the number of images that can be present in a packet and therefore it is possible to have packets with stand-alone images or a great number of images.

An image of the packet is called the **header** and the other eventual images are called **slaves**. This distinction is made because the packet is considered to be an environment that encompasses all aspects of the same object or phenomenon. For example, a photograph, an infra-red photograph, and a photogrammetric representation that all refer to the same object can belong to the same packet. In other cases, the user can correlate the different points of view referring to the same phenomenon. For example, an ECG signal image can be associated with other images representing arterial and ventricular pressure signals, all monitored at the same time. This is useful in hemodynamic monitoring because in the case of anginal episodes, it is useful to be able to examine these signals all together.

Therefore, we can consider a packet to be an equivalence class represented by the header image. For this reason, the header image's attribute set is richer than the slave images's set and it is important to note that only header images possess linking marks (see sec. 3.2).

Both header and slave images can be associated with several different **annotations**, i.e., texts that contain free information about the image. An annotation is associated with a specific area of the image and so it is possible to relate the annotations to the image content.

Since the dossier is complex, it is generally built in incremental way. The starting point is the dossier code definition. This crucial operation is carried out via main menu (see fig. 6); once its code has been defined, the dossier exists even if no other section is defined. The dossier sections are created in an interactive way under the control of suitable DBMS masks (see sec. 5). As far as the image packet input is concerned, the user has to define an enclosure and enter the header image code. After this operation, the dossier contains the definition of a new pair: "enclosure - header image". Slave image codes are then entered.

3 - THE NETWORK

Documents and images can be related to one another by means of links explicitly stated by the user. Therefore, it is possible to build a network over the database units that points out all the semantic relationships considered to be important. It is possible to establish links between main cards, between image packets and main cards, and between image packets.

3.1 - Links between main cards

Since the main card is the root of a dossier, a link between two main cards is considered to be a link between the dossiers they represent. Each dossier can be related to several dossiers.

These links can be motivated by an affinity existing between the dossier contents; for example, the links can be stated both, if some requests of comparative scanning are expected, and if it is useful to point out that several dossiers make up a single logical unit. From this point of view, it is possible to define a logical multi-dossier by collecting several different dossiers, and it is therefore possible to define a dossier having a more complex structure than the one directly provided by the system.

3.2 - Links associated with images

An image packet can be linked to other image packets and/or to some main cards by means of **marks** (see fig.2); in the former case, the marks are called **image marks**, while in the latter, they are called **dossier marks**.

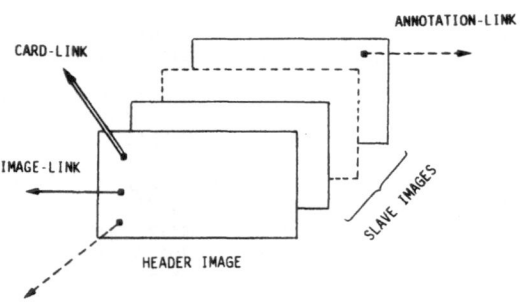

Figure 2 - Images and marks

While links between main cards relate whole dossiers to each other, a mark relates a specific point of an image to other database units. When some links originating from a certain image have to be established, the image is displayed, together with an eventual, previously-defined mark map over it; with the mouse the user points to the areas where the new marks have to be placed and enters the unit codes to be linked. The image and dossier marks created over an image are displayed

separately because the same point can be linked to both another image and a dossier.

In the linking process, the packet is represented by the header image and therefore marks can only be associated with the header image. This is not so as far as the annotations illustrated in section 2 are concerned; they can be associated with any image because they are designed for maintaining textual information with local significance. The mark map feature is also used for linking images to annotations and, in this case, the mark is called an **annotation mark**.

An image can be linked to other images that are logically related to it. For example, in the case of national monuments, the global image of a building can be linked to both the facade and park images.

A link to a dossier is established when it is necessary to associate the image with a set of structured and complex information that cannot be stored in a simple textual annotation. For example, in a medical environment an image point can be associated with a particular pathology described in a specific dossier.

Since it is possible to mark several zones of the same image, our system provides great flexibility and effectiveness for building an expressive network.

In figure 3, all possible link types are illustrated.

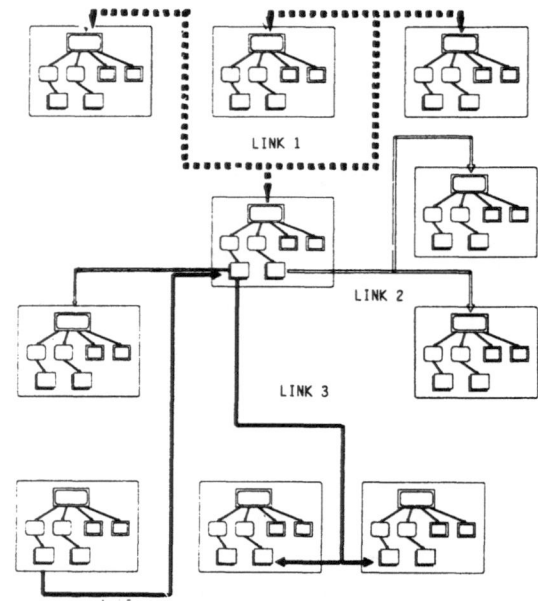

LINK 1: MAIN CARD-MAIN CARD
LINK 2: IMAGE-MAIN CARD
LINK 3: IMAGE-IMAGE

Figure 3 - Link types

4 - NETWORK NAVIGATION

The system network is created by means of the links defined in the previous sections and illustrated in fig.3.

Since the dossier is the basic unit of ARDITO, the network is structured as a set of nodes, each of which constitutes a single dossier. This network level is realized by means of links between main cards.

However, a more refined view of the network can be obtained thanks to the various kinds of links the system can provide. As a result, we can also refer to an image network in which nodes are image packets. The possibilrty of linking image packets to other image packets or main cards allows us to move through the image network or to switch from the image network layer to the dossier layer.

This system doesn't allow the user to display a global view of the network. This choice is also common to some other systems [4] because of the intrinsic difficulty of creating, updating, and displaying a global map that is a network (rather than a hierarchy) in a clear and effective way. As a matter of fact, it is only possible to display local maps.

Navigation is based on a **browsing mechanism**, described as follows:
- the network graph around a node is displayed;
- then, another node appearing in it can be pointed to and its graph displayed;
- and so on.

More specifically, when the user points to a dossier, its graph is displayed and shows all the links existing both within the current dossier and to all the other dossiers (see fig.4).

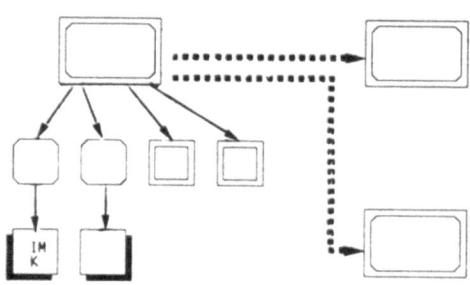

Figure 4 - Dossier node graph

When an image packet node is pointed to, its graph is displayed, i.e., all the links originating from the packet itself and arriving to it from other packets are displayed(see fig. 5). Furthermore, when the user looks at an image, it is possible to display the mark maps over it and therefore know what links originate from the image and the specific points they refer to; it is then possible to access the linked units.

We can distinguish between two kinds of navigation: intra-dossier and inter-dossier navigation.

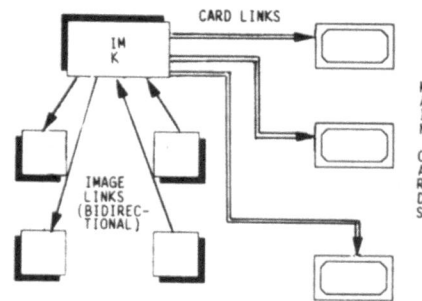

Figure 5 - An image node graph

4.1 - Intra-dossier navigation

Intra-dossier navigation makes it possible to move through all the various sections constituting a single dossier. Since the dossier has a complex structure, in many cases this kind of navigation is sufficient for obtaining all the information required. For example, in hospital applications we can find all the information concerning a patient within one dossier.

Navigation begins by displaying the dossier graph (see fig. 4). Image annotations are not indicated because they have a local meaning and can only be accessed after the image has been accessed and displayed. The displaying of some links from one dossier to other dossiers is also performed for inter-dossier navigation purposes (see sec. 4.2).

The user can continue examining the network by pointing to an image or dossier node with the mouse, or he/she can ask for the content of a dossier section (image or text). Each section has its own rules for moving from it to other linked sections, according to the links meaning.

Image links are bidirectional, so it is possible to walk through various images and then come back step by step. However, it is possible to switch to the dossier graph display at any time.

The dossier graph display is considered to be the root of intra-dossier navigation. This feature is particularly useful when the user walks through images because coming back through image displays can be time-consuming.

4.2 - Inter-dossier navigation

The passage from one dossier to another can be performed in three distinct ways by following:
1) a link established between two main cards;
2) a link established between an image packet contained in the dossier and another main card;
3) a link between an image packet contained in the dossier and another image packet contained in another dossier.

In the first case, we can move along the dossier network layer by pointing to one of the linked dossiers appearing in the dossier graph with the mouse (see fig. 4). An important feature of this environment is the possibility of maintaining a **session list** of traversed dossiers. This list is present in an icone and it makes it possible to reactivate any of the previously examined dossiers

250

at any time.

In the second case, it is possible to switch from the image network to the dossier network and to have access to complex information related to the current image. After switching from an image to a dossier, it is not possible to go back to the original image directly but it is necessary to access the owner dossier via the session list and then access the image.

In the third case, image network navigation is implemented and can be performed:

1) on the graph (i.e., by pointing to image nodes and displaying the new node graphs one after the other);
2) on the real image network (i.e., by displaying images, selecting marks, and displaying new images).

In the latter case, all the images that are displayed are also pushed into a temporary stack. As a result, forward accessing to other images is controlled by mark processing, while backward accessing is controlled by stack popping out. Slave images belonging to a packet can also be displayed. At any moment, it is possible to switch from an image to the dossier it belongs to, and to continue examining the network from the dossier graph on.

5 - IMPLEMENTATION

The prototype is implemented on a SUN 3/60 workstation and is based on SUNVIEW and on the Informix\ESQLC data base management system. An overview of the system functionalities is shown in fig. 6. SUNVIEW supports network management and navigation, while Informix\ESQLC supports data management and network storing. Inside the system, all database information retrieving is performed by means of some embedded SQL queries.

5.1 - Dossier implementation

Main cards, cards, and enclosures are mapped onto MAIN_CARD, CARD, and ENCLOSURE relations. The dossier unit is maintained by means of the main card code, and this also appears as an attribute of CARD and ENCLOSURE. Information that is not formatted appears in the relations as file names; files are created by the system and managed in a trasparent way for the user. The image packet is represented in ENCLOSURE by the image header code.

As far as the above-mentioned relations are concerned, the user interface is implemented in an integrated environment supported by Informix\ESQLC (see fig. 7).

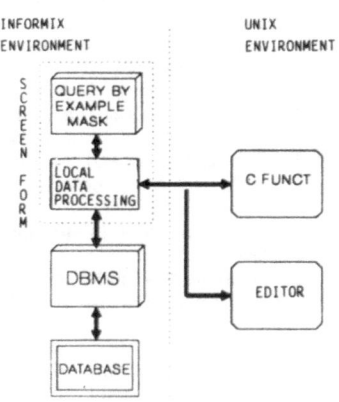

Figure 7 - Interaction environment with relations mapping main card, cards, and enclosures

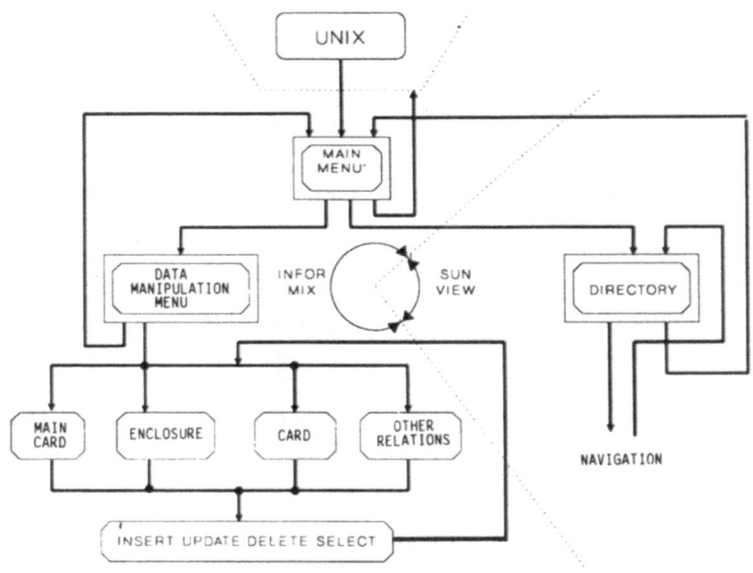

Figure 6 - Overview of system functionalities

Interaction with formatted fields is performed by means of screen forms that make data inquiring and manipulation possible in a Query By Example-like style. Screen forms also provide links between fields and procedures; this capability is used for linking free fields management to a system editor. At present, no inquirying is possible on texts because they can only be displayed and edited.

5.2 - Images

Images are managed by means of a graphic library that can be built incrementally; therefore, no a priori constraint exists concerning their type. For example, they can be vector graphics or bit map images. Image display is performed by library functions specifically related to the image type.

An image is represented in the system by means of a code. Image types that can be managed by the library have a code; the type code is associated with the corresponding library function. These associations are maintained in database relations and allow the system to satisfy display requests (see fig.8).

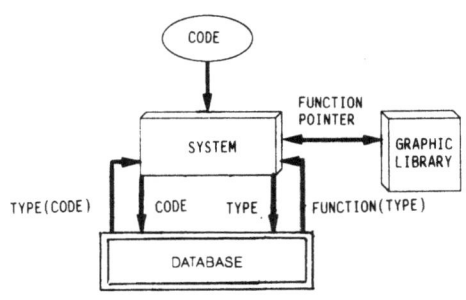

Figure 8 - Management of image display requests

Image packets and their contexts, i. e., the dossiers they belong to, are represented by means of:
1) a relation with attributes
   (HEADER_IMAGE_CODE,IMAGE_TYPE, DOSSIER_CODE)
   that stores data regarding the header image;
2) a relation with attributes
   (IMAGE_CODE,IMAGE_TYPE, HEADER_IMAGE_CODE)
   that maintains the packet structures.
   The DOSSIER_CODE is the code of its main card.

5.3 - The network

The links between main cards are maintained in a two-column relation whose attributes are the codes of "from" and "to" main cards.

As regards marks, we have a relation for:
1) image marks,
2) dossier marks,
3) annotation marks of header images,
4) annotation marks of non-header images.

All these relations have the same structure; for each mark they contain the code of the marked image, the mark position, and the linked unit identifier.

The linked units can be dossiers, packet images and annotations. Dossiers and images have their own code, which is known by the user. Annotations are identified by the file names assigned to them by the system and are not known by the user. As a matter of fact, the user only has access to an annotation only from the image the annotation is placed in.

The mark position is recorded by means of its co-ordinates.

5.4 - Network navigation

The functional scheme of navigation is sketched in fig. 9.

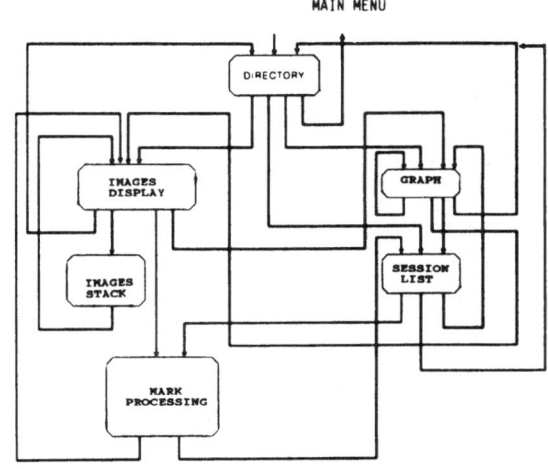

Figure 9 - Navigation functional scheme

The directory appearing in the figure is the entry point in the navigation environment: a list of dossier and image packet codes is shown and the user can select the point to enter the network at. The image display is based on the mechanism illustrated in sec. 5.2. The network graph display makes use of the information about the network structure that is stored in the database and retrieved by means of suitable queries. Mark processing also refers to information stored in database relations. Image stack processing is involved in subsequent image displays (see sec. 4.2). The role of the session list, too, is illustrated in sec. 4.2.

6 - CONCLUDING REMARKS

A first prototype based on some of the ideas presented in this paper was implemented on a OLIVETTI PE28 computer under MSDOS by using the QUICKSILVER version of DBASE III and C language [5]. Network and network navigation notions are present, but their implementation doesn't refer to the DBMS and is based on ad-hoc files directly managed by the program. Moreover, images are not collected in packets and are of a predefined type. At present, the prototype, named GART, is used for cataloguing artistic goods by means of dossiers equipped with photogrammetric images.

Our experience with the GART prototype emphasized the flexibility and effectiveness of the

following features:
1) using the dossier as the basic information unit for collecting heterogeneous data;
2) linking specific points of an image (rather than the whole image) to other database units;
3) both navigating through the network and accessing alphanumeric data and images, if desired.

On the contrary, system maintenance and updating turned out to be quite complex because the network implementation was totally C-based. Furthermore, users suggested extending the system for managing various kinds of images and grouping them according to various requirements.

ARDITO manages dossiers that are structured documents composed of sections of different types, i.e., formatted data, texts, and images of various kinds. As far as these heterogeneous data are concerned, formatted data can naturally be stored in DBMS relations, while unformatted texts and images are stored in separate files linked to database relations by means of codes. It is therefore possible to manage information developed separately from the application involved and stored in particular devices, such as optical devices for images.

A different approach can be found in gIBIS [6]. gIBIS is implemented on the top of a relational DBMS that supports an uninterpreted data type, i.e., a field that can contain any sequence of bits; therefore, all information is stored in relations. At any rate, this feature is not sufficient and gIBIS also needs to refer to external data and ad-hoc display procedures.

ARDITO implementation substantially relies on a relational database system. The database is not only used for managing user alphanumeric data, but also for storing and managing the network and other control information. This information is accessed by means of embedded SQL queries. The reliability and simplicity in using the DBMS is a great advantage in system coding, updating, and maintaining. Furthermore, it is possible to refer to a graphic library that is interfaced by means of specific database relations. In this way, the library is independent of the system and can be built up incrementally by simply adding some tuples to the relations.

Since ARDITO allows us to establish links between whole dossiers and/or sections of them, the various documents are organized in a hypermedia-like network. Let us examine some significative correlations and differences between hypermedia systems and our own.

It is worth noting that we explicitly make a distinction between different kinds of documents, that is, not only between texts and images, but also between formatted data and texts. This approach is different from the one used in other very general systems, such as KMS [1], in which a uniform frame type is managed and displayed. Our approach is more restrictive in that we deal with an assigned set of document types. On the other hand, this makes it possible to specialize operations and, therefore, to satisfy specific user requirements that are directly related to the kind of information stored. For example, our system supports queries on formatted data very

efficiently.

This system provides inquirying and browsing mechanisms. At present, inquiry is only used with formatted data, while text searching is in the process of being developed.

Browsing is based on intra- and inter-dossier navigation. As is also true fort other systems [7] [4], [8], navigation in ARDITO is performed both at a document and a network level. In the first case, we go from a displayed document to another; in the second, the user is provided with a graphical browser that deals with the network architecture.

Some facilities for orientation in both a temporal and spatial context [4], [9] are provided. Temporal orientation is supported by both back-tracking through previously examined image sections and maintaining a history trail of all the dossiers examined. The possibility of switching from a text or image section display to a dossier graph display can help the user in spatial orientation since it allows him to locate the section in its own context.

REFERENCES

[1] D. L. McCracken, E. A. Yoder - KMS: A Distributed Hypermedia System for Managing Knowledge in Organizations, Comm. ACM, vol. 31, n. 7, 1988.

[2] F. Rabitti - A Model for Multimedia Documents, in "Office Automation" (D. Tsichritzis ed.), Springer-Verlag, 1985.

[3] S. Christodulakis, M. Theodoridou, F. Ho, M. Papa., A. Pathria - Multimedia Document Presentation, Information Extraction, and Document Formation in MINOS: a Model and a System, ACM Trans. on Office Automation Systems, vol.4, n.4, 1986.

[4] K.Utting, N. Yankelovich - Context and Ortientation in Hypermedia Networks, ACM Trans. on Information Systems, vol.7, n.1, 1989.

[5] F. Cesarini, A. Mazzoni, A. Pampaloni, G. Soda - GART: un sistema per la catalogazione di beni artistici, proc. of AICA88, Cagliari, 1988.

[6] J. Conklin, M. L. Begeman - gIBIS: A Hypertext Tool for Exploratory Policy Discussion, ACM Trans. on Office Information Systems, vol. 6, n. 4, 1988.

[7] F. R. Campagnoni, K. Ehrlich - Information Retrieval Using a Hypertext-Based Help System, ACM Trans. on Office Information Systems, vol.7, n.3, 1989.

[8] N. M. Delisle, M. D. Schwartz - Contexts - A Partitioning Concept for Hypertext, ACM Trans. on Office Information Systems, vol.5, n.2, 1987.

[9] J. Nielsen - The Art of Navigating through Hypertext, Comm. ACM, vol.33, n.3, 1990.

Name Reactions in Organic Chemistry — a New Application Domain for Deductive Databases

Christoph Draxler
Kurt Bauknecht
Dept. of Computer Science
Zurich University

Abstract

Name reactions are reaction schemes that are used to plan chemical syntheses. We present the deductive database application **DedChem** that computes a synthesis tree for chemical substances from name reactions stored in a database using nonlinear recursive deduction rules.

At present **DedChem** is implemented in Prolog. A coupling of external relational databases is currently being developed, based on the new concept of accessing the database via the built-in set predicates of Prolog.

Keywords: Prolog database coupling, synthesis planning, deductive database application, nonlinear recursion, transitive closure

1. Introduction

DedChem is a database system that supports synthesis planning in organic chemistry. It is intended to be used in students' education and by experts.

DedChem successfully implements new concepts in the field of organic chemistry and database applications. Support tools for synthesis planning in organic chemistry exist so far only for reactions involving individual molecules. The approach of **DedChem** is completely different in that it employs the higher abstraction level of name reactions.

In the field of database applications **DedChem** opens a completely new application domain. The system incorporates nonlinear recursive tree-construction algorithms for the computation of the transitive closure of name reactions, and it implements a new concept of coupling relational databases with a logic programming language.

DedChem has been developed at the Department of Computer Science of Zurich University in collaboration with the Department of Organic Chemistry.

1.1 Terminology

Name reactions are reaction schemes that describe standardized reactions. Name reactions abstract from other reactions in that they are defined for substance *classes*, not individual molecules. Historically name reactions are *reaction prototypes* that have proven to be useful in practice. For mnemotechnical reasons name reactions are given the names of their inventors.

A *synthesis* is the production of a certain substance (*product*) through a chaining of single reactions. This reaction chain is a *synthesis tree*, its root is the substance that is to be synthesized, and its leaves contain the substances needed for this particular synthesis (*educts*). Synthesis planning is *retrosynthetic* if the planning starts with the product.

Substances belong to substance classes. The class memberships for a given substance are determined by its, possibly many, substructures. Name reactions contain only substance classes, therefore information about specific substances for a synthesis *cannot* be provided by the name reaction database. Synthesis plans generated by the system are thus only synthesis *proposals* which

254

have to be checked for their feasibility. Name reactions are thus *heuristics* that help to find solutions quickly.

2. Problem description

Name reactions are uniquely identified through their name and the substance classes involved. Some name reactions have one educt, others have two. Name reactions can be represented as directed graphs with labelled edges:

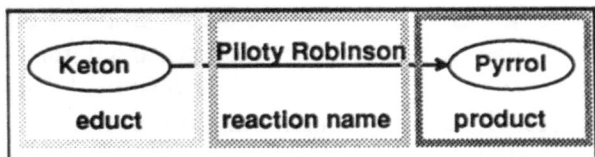

Fig. 1: name reaction with one educt

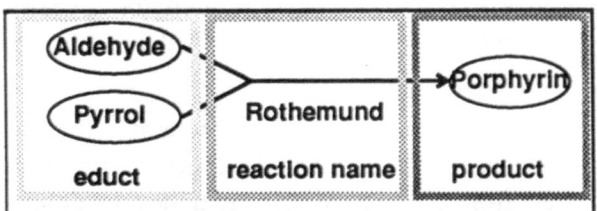

Fig. 2: name reaction with two educts

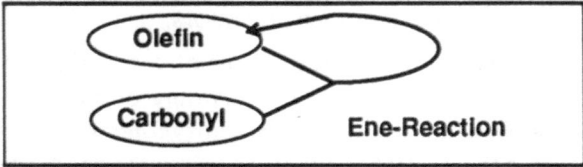

Fig. 3: cyclic name reaction

Name reactions may be chained, resulting in a synthesis tree. The product of a single name reaction is the educt of a reaction on the next higher level in the tree. Under controlled circumstances the tree may contain duplicate nodes and subtrees, i.e. in the case of cyclic name reactions or of name reactions appearing in more than one place in the tree (Fig. 4, Fig. 5).

There exist superclass and synonym relations between substance classes (Fig. 6). Substance classes are organized in a superclass hierarchy. As su-

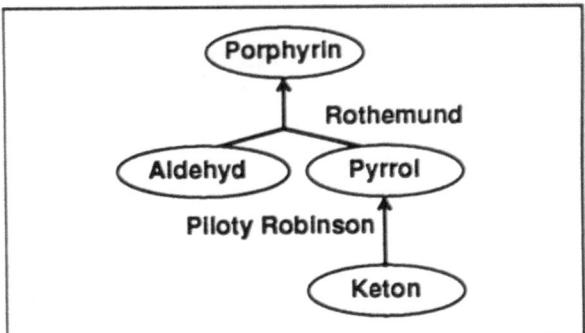

Fig. 4: synthesis trees

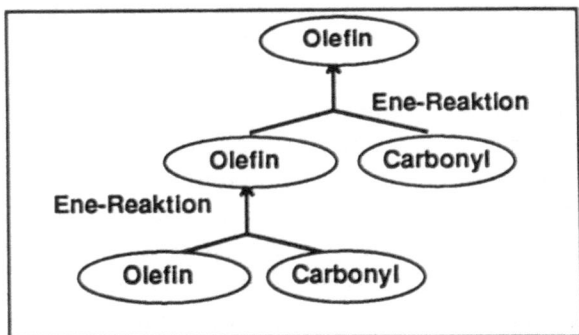

Fig. 5: synthesis trees

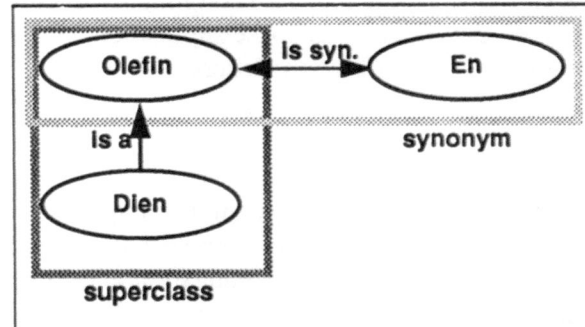

Fig. 6: synonym and superclass relationships

perclasses may share common subclasses this hierarchy is a directed acyclic graph.

2.1 Transitive closure

A synthesis tree is constructed by computing the *transitive closure* of name reactions. This computation must respect the specific properties of name reactions:

- Name reactions with two educts require the computation of the transitive closure for the *name reactions* of *both* educts.

- Synonym and superclass relations require the computation of the transitive closure for the *synonym* or the *superclass of a substance*.

If there is no name reaction that has a particular substance class as its product, then search has to be continued with the superclass of the current substance class.

An upper bound may be used to restrict the search. A synthesis tree will then always be lower than this bound. This is no limitation, however, as the bound may always be increased, e.g. until the set of solutions remains constant.

2.2 Requirements for a synthesis planning system

A synthesis planning system must meet the following requirements: It must be able to

- compute the transitive closure of name reactions,
- cope with cyclic name reactions,
- store name reactions with one *or* two educts, and
- deal with synonyms and superclasses.

Furthermore it must allow the construction of a tree structure for the synthesis tree.

These requirements cannot be met in the relational model:

- Recursion to compute the transitive closure is not available,
- Functions or structured terms which are needed to represent synthesis trees are not expressible, and
- Structured attributes which are needed to store name reactions with one *or* two educts violate the 1.NF.

Relational databases are thus not suited for our application. However, deductive databases consisting of a relational database coupled with a deduction component in a high level programming meet these requirements very well. Such a coupling of a relational database and a programming language is even powerful enough to handle tree

structures because of its capability of handling structured terms.

The quantitative requirements for a synthesis planning system are fairly low. The name reactions known to date number little more than 1000. As some name reactions are defined for more than one combination of substance classes, the total number may be slightly higher. Name reactions are never deleted from the database, so that their number steadily increases. There are approximately 1000 different substance classes. Again, this number is rather low from a database point of view.

Although the amount of data such a system will have to handle is rather small, a true database system should be used because of the known database security and integrity features and multi-user access.

3. Architecture of DedChem

DedChem is a deductive database that will be implemented as a coupling of a relational database and a logical programming language. Logic programming languages are particularly well suited for deductive databases because they offer a consistent language for all the system components.

A relational database can easily be implemented in a logic programming language because such a database is, ultimately, only a subset of predicate logic. A logic programming language is even more powerful than relational languages, so that extensions to the relational model can be implemented as easily [5, 6, 8].

A coupling or the integration of existing relational systems with logic programming languages is possible. There already exist implementations, such as DedGin* [9] or KB-Prolog [2]. Both these systems are *physically* and *logically tightly coupled* [1] (= integrated) systems. However, both systems have serious drawbacks: DedGin* is restricted to the Datalog language and thus unable to handle trees, and both systems can only access the built-in relational database.

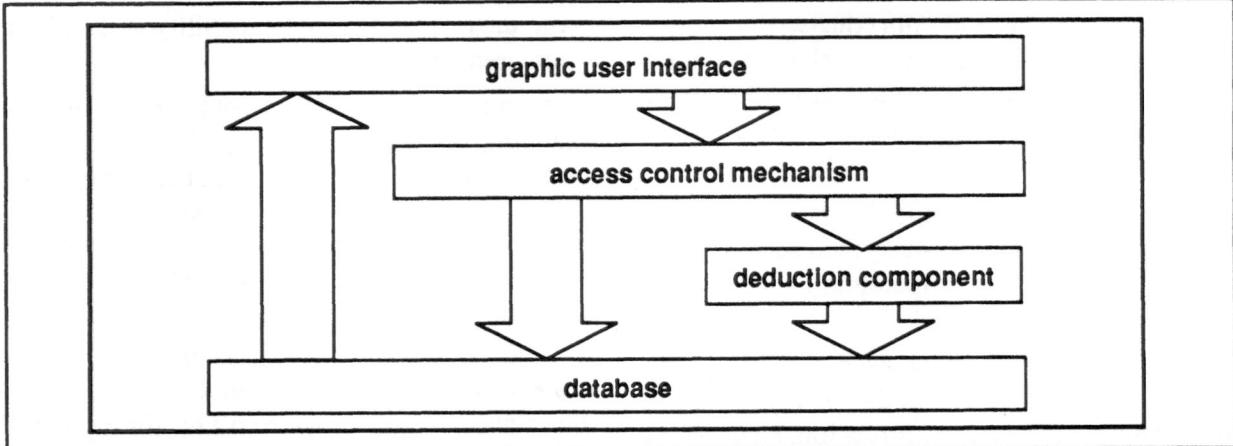

Fig. 7: architecture of **DedChem**

Most commercially available Prolog systems (e.g. Quintus or InterFace Prolog) feature database couplings. They usually access the databases through special database predicates. These systems usually are *physically* and *logically loose couplings* and thus give up on the principle of having one single language in the system.

DedChem thus utilizes a new approach to coupling Prolog with relational databases. This approach extends the Prolog built-in set predicates to access relational databases and is thus a *physically loose* and *logically tight coupling*. A brief description of this coupling is given in section 5.

3.1 Components of DedChem

DedChem is built in a modular way. The system consists of four main components: a relational database, a deduction component, an access control mechanism and the user interface.

The database stores name reactions and class relations. The deduction component contains the rules needed for the generation of synthesis trees. These rules operate on the facts stored in the database. The access control mechanism supervises database access requests: simple relational queries can be evaluated directly by the database system. Recursive queries are handled by the deduction component. The user interface allows in- and output on graphic terminals.

3.2 Schema

DedChem's database consists of the entity sets **substance_class** and **name_reaction**. The relationships are **is_superclass**, **is_synonym**, **is_product**, and **is_educt**. Name reactions are 1-1 and 1-2 relationships between substance classes. Superclass and synonym relations between substance classes are m-n relationships.

The conceptual model of **DedChem** is given in (fig8).

3.3 State of the implementation

DedChem will be implemented in Prolog coupled to an external relational database. Prolog was chosen because it is the most widespread implementation of a logic programming language, and because there exist very powerful implementations on a variety of machines.

In Prolog it is very easy to implement the access to relational database systems and the deduction rules needed for the computation of synthesis trees. Later extensions to the system like a knowledge base that contains criteria for an optimum choice of synthesis plans or meta-level control structures may be expressed naturally in Prolog. Although the amount of data required for the application can be handled by most Prolog systems we plan to couple Prolog with external relational databases so that any external relational database may be accessed. These databases may be either public or proprietary databases.

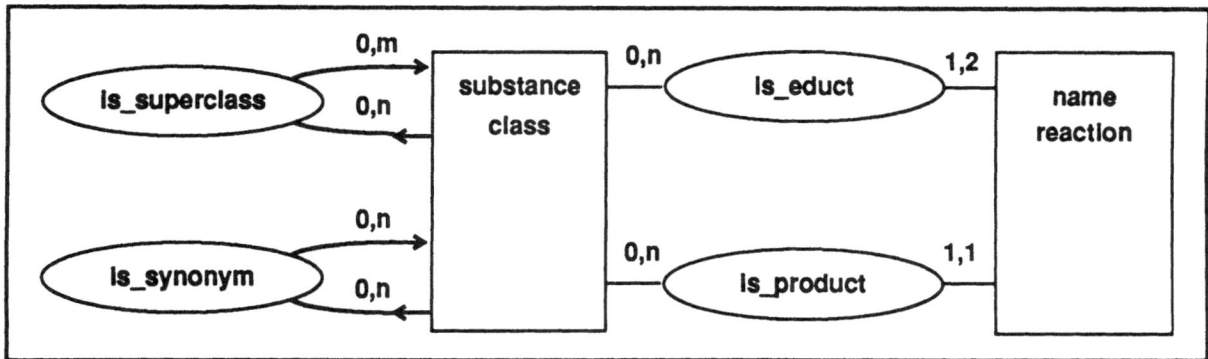

Fig. 8: ER - diagram of **DedChem**

DedChem is currently implemented as a protoype system with all its components written in Prolog. The database contains three relations: **substance class, name reaction** and **superclass** which also contains the synonyms. The user interface features database menus and dialogs, and has a graphics window in which the synthesis tree is displayed.

4. Implementation in Prolog

DedChem is written in LPA MacProlog on a Mac II. The strategy chosen in the chemical part of the system is retrosynthetic search. The search algorithm is the standard path finding algorithm for directed graphs extended to handle branching. Lists of visited substance classes are kept so that cycles in name reactions and synonym relations can be detected (note that certain forms of cycles are allowed). A synthesis tree is built which contains the reactions of each synthesis proposal.

4.1 Database

Name reactions are stored as Prolog facts. Name reactions with one or two educts can be stored using the same structure:

```
% reaction(Product,Educt,ReactionName)
```

```
reaction(pyrrol,keton,piloty_robinson).
reaction(porphyrin, (aldehyde, pyrrol),
  rothemund).
```

Substance classes are simple facts:

```
substance_class(olefin).
```

Superclass relations are 2-ary facts:

```
is_a(dien,olefin).
```

Synonym relations are simply symmetric superclass relations:

```
is_a(olefin, en).
is_a(en, olefin).
```

4.2 User interface

The user interface consists of input and output predicates. Input is entered via menus and dialogs. The synthesis tree is displayed in a graphics window (Fig. 9).

The computation of a synthesis tree is started through a dialog, in which the substance class that is to be synthesized is selected from all the possible substances. A substance class may be synthesized if there is at least one name reaction with this substance class as its product.

Some consistency control is already achieved through the interface: selection from available substance classes prevents entering an illegal substance class name.

4.3 Deduction component

The deduction component is the main component of **DedChem**. It is this component that contains the rules for the generation of the synthesis tree.

According to the retrosynthetic search, a specific substance class is the starting point for the computation. If there does not exist a name reaction for a given substance class, the computation terminates. If there exist name reactions for this substance, the substance becomes the root of the sub-

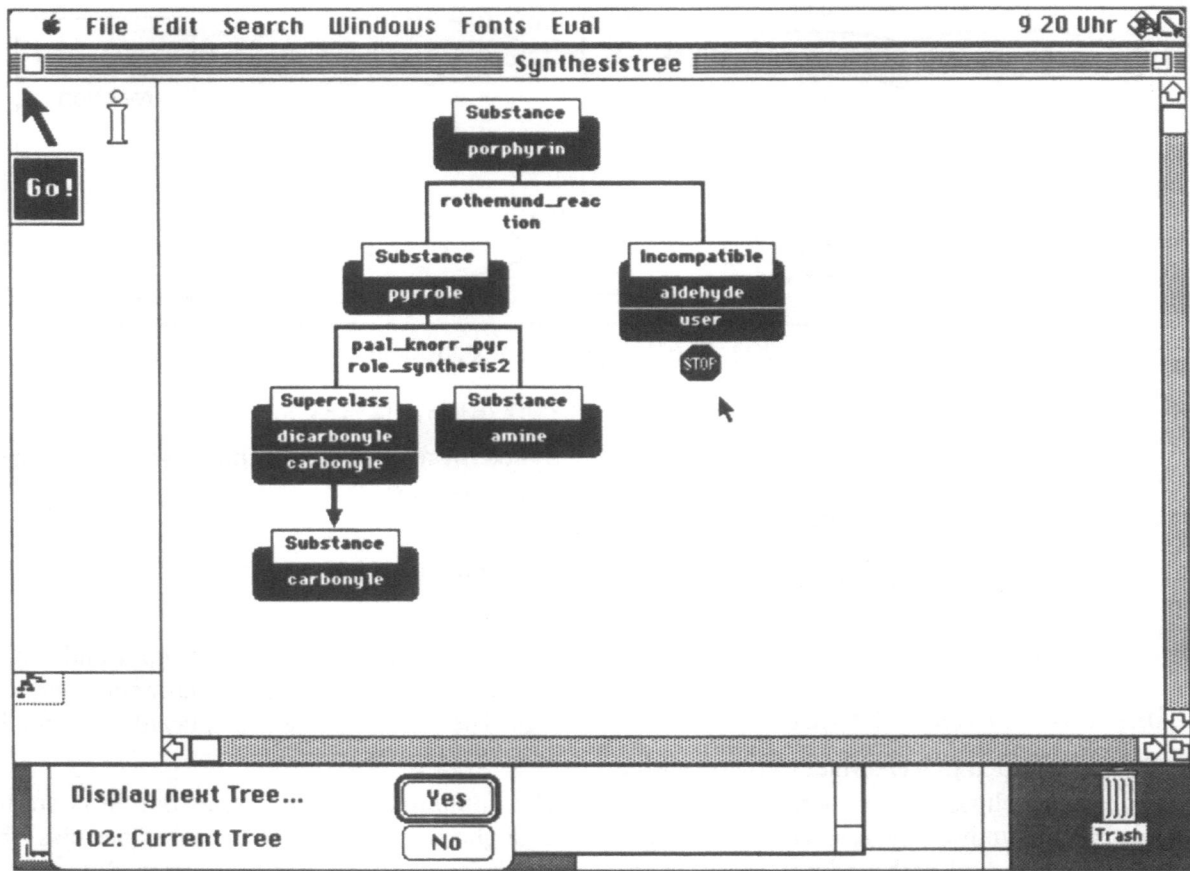

Fig. 9: Screen with graphic window

tree and the educts of the name reactions then have to be synthesized. The synthesis tree is thus being constructed recursively.

The synthesis tree must split into two branches for name reactions with two educts. If there is no name reaction for the current substance class then search will continue with a superclass or a synonym of this substance class. If there are no matching superclasses or synonyms stored in the database, the tree terminates in a leaf.

The cycles described in chapter 2 are not allowed to lead to nonterminating recursion. Thus it is necessary to keep track of the substance classes contained in the tree so far. For this purpose some bookkeeping effort is necessary. In the following code examples this is done by the predicate con-

trol/3 (control/3 calls simple list membership predicates)

The predicate synthesis builds the synthesis tree and implements the search strategy:

synthesis/5 is a nonlinear recursive predicate with two terminal and three recursive clauses (Fig. 10).

Recursion terminates successfully if there is no name reaction for the current product in the database. The synthesis tree terminates in a leaf containing only the substance class. The synthesis tree also terminates successfully if the maximum depth of recursion has been reached (clauses 1 and 2)

```
/* synthesis(Product,SynTree,R,Sup,Dep)

synthesis/5 constructs the synthesis tree for a given product in a top-down man-
    ner. R and Sup are two lists that contain the name reactions and superclass
    relationships used so far.*/

synthesis(Product,leaf(Product),_,_,Depth):-                              (1)
    Depth > 0,
    not reaction(Product,_,_).

synthesis(Product,stop(Product),_,_,0).                                   (2)

synthesis(Prod,node(Prod,Name,LSub,RSub),R,Sup,Depth):-                   (3)
    reaction(Prod,(Ed1,Ed2),Name),
    control((Ed1,Ed2),R,_),
    Depth > 0,
    Depth1 is Depth - 1,
    synthesis(Ed1,LSub,[r(Ed1,Prod,Name)|R],Sup,Depth1),
    synthesis(Ed2,RSub,[r(Ed2,Prod,Name)|R],Sup,Depth1).

synthesis(Prod, node(Prod, Name, SubTree), R, Sup, Depth):-              (4)
    reaction(Prod, Educt, Name),
    control(Educt, R, _),
    Depth > 0,
    Depth1 is Depth - 1,
    synthesis(Educt,SubTree,[r(Educt,Prod,Name)|R],Sup,Depth1).

synthesis(Prod,is_a(Prod,SuperClass,SubTr),R,Sup,Depth):-               (5)
    is_a(Prod,SuperClass),
    control(SuperClass,_, Sup),
    synthesis(SuperClass,SubTr,R,[s(Prod,SuperClass|Sup],Depth).
```

Fig. 10: synthesis/5 basic algorithm

The first two recursive clauses construct the synthesis tree with the current substance class (clauses 3 and 4).

The last clause of synthesis/5 is responsible for the change in substance classes: it selects either a superclass or a synonym of the current substance class. Note that the recursion depth is not decreased, as the substitution of a substance class is not a reaction step..

synthesis/5 is thus mainly an extension of the transitive closure algorithm to the nonlinear recursive case. In contrast to similar programs, e.g. the ancestor program, a tree structure is built which represents a branch of the synthesis tree.

Three implementation details are now described:

- The lists R and Sup contain the reactions and superclass substitutions that have been carried out to date. These lists are always instantiated, so that the member check for any element can be performed at any time. The lists are built in a bottom-up manner, except that the result variable that is usually associated with such an accumulator pair, can be omitted.

- In the nonlinear recursive case the lists are different for both branches of the subtrees. Each subtree thus only accesses the lists that are relevant for this subtree. The calls for the computation of both subtrees are shown below.

```
% --- left subtree ---------

synthesis(...,LeftSubTree, [r(Prod-
uct, Ed1, Name) | R], Sup,...)

% --- right subtree --------

synthesis(...,RightSubTree, [r(Prod-
uct, Ed2, Name)|R], Sup,...)
```

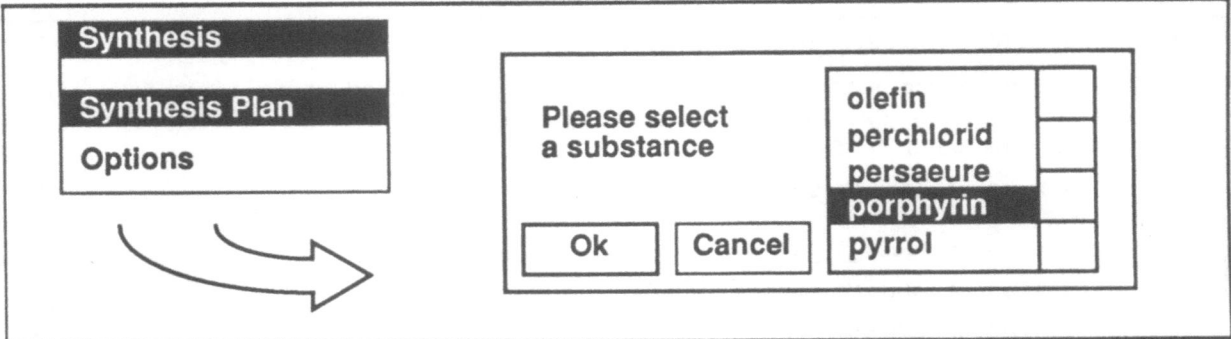

Fig. 11: Selection of porphyrin as synthesis product

• .The synthesis tree is being constructed top-down. A clause head contains a subtree schema that is only partly instantiated. In the linear recursive case there is one variable for the subtree, in the nonlinear case there are two such variables (for the left and right subtree) that will be instantiated further during the recursion:

```
synthesis(...,node(...,...,SubTree),
...)
```

```
synthesis(...,node(...,...,LeftTree,
RightTree),...)
```

The subtrees will eventually be instantiated in the terminal cases:

```
synthesis(...,node(Product),...)
```

4.4 Example

The substance class **porphyrin** is to be synthesized. We click on the command **Synthesis plan** in the **Synthesis** menu. In the dialog box that now appears we select the substance class **porphyrin** from the list of all known products (Fig. 11)

A few seconds later the first branch of the synthesis tree is displayed in the graphics window (Fig. 12).

The leaves of the tree carry labels that indicate how the substances were reached. Further branches ot the synthesis tree may be generated upon request.

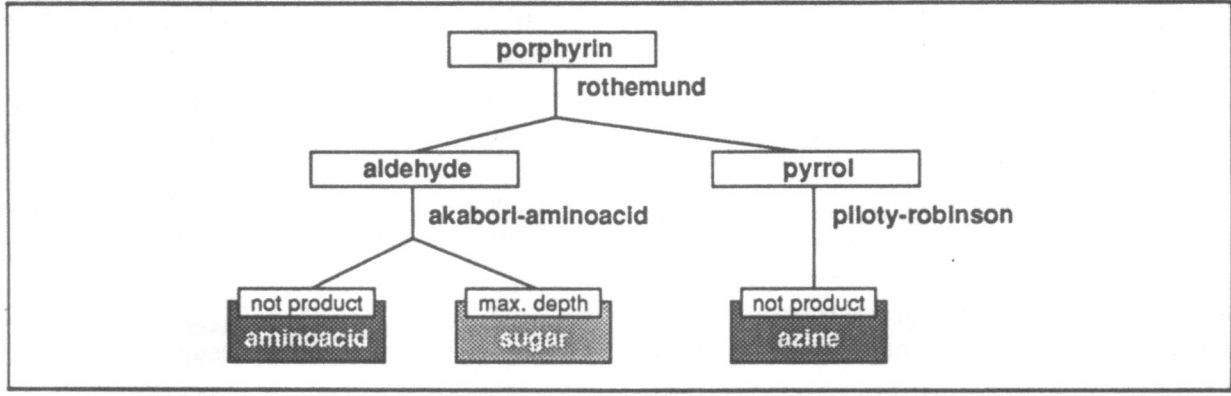

Fig. 12: synthesis tree for porphyrin

5. Future work

Future work will concentrate mainly on three areas:

- The order of solutions found depends on the order of facts in the database. It would thus be interesting to define meta-level rules that will compute "better" solutions first. Such a rule could be: "Take the name reaction with the highest yield first". Of course the criterion *yield* must then be part of the name reaction tuple.

  Meta-level rules require accessing not only one tuple, but a set so that the optimum tuple can be chosen. With the combination of set predicates and nondeterministic selection of an element an elegant integration of sets and tuples is possible:

  ```
  setof(reaction(Yield,E,P,N),reaction
  (P,E,N,Yield),SortRelation),

  member(SortRelation,reaction(OptProd
  ,OptEd,OptName))...
  ```

  `setof/3` generates a list that is sorted according to some criterion, and `member/2` selects one element from that list. Upon backtracking the next element is taken from the list. The search strategy of the program as a whole does not change, there is merely an intelligent ordering of the next steps to perform.

- To keep the search space small it is possible to store so called *incompatibilities* with individual name reactions. These incompatibilities automatically prevent the use of particular substance classes in the current synthesis. Furthermore it should be possible to exclude specific substances from syntheses altogether.

- **DedChem**'s user interface is to follow the Macintosh programming guidelines. This has been done to some extent already, but there remains a lot of interface design to do.

5.1 Coupling with external databases

We plan to couple **DedChem** to external relational databases to handle the increasing amount of data and to permit multi-user access to the system. These external databases not only contain the name reactions, but also structure diagrams, literature references and case examples.

This coupling will be implemented using an extension of Prolog's set predicates combined with the programming technique of nondeterministic selection.

Set predicates are of the form

```
predicatename(Term, Goal, List)
```

`List` contains all the instantiations of `Term` for which the `Goal` was proved. Any variable instantiation done by the evaluation of `Goal` is palced into the list datastructure in `List`.

We define database set predicates to be set predicates that can access external relational databases. The `Goal` is translated into the database DML and this query is transmitted to the database system where it is then evaluated. The resulting relation is returned to the Prolog system and placed in `List` of the database set predicate.

This particular kind of coupling implements a *physically loose* and *logically tight coupling*. It can be implemented with minor modifications of the Prolog system, and offers as its main advantages one language for both database and Prolog operations and a very elegant way around the traditional set-at-a-time versus tuple-at-a-time *impedance mismatch* [7] between relational systems and Prolog (see [3,4] for further details).

The abovementioned combination of set predicates and nondeterministic choice successfully can also be employed with database set predicates. Prolog is thus used to access external relational databases and as the application language for the system as a whole.

6. Conclusion

DedChem is a first step into a completely new application domain, namely that of name reactions in organic chemistry. The requirements of this application domain cannot be met with traditional relational database systems. We have shown that

262

these requirements can be successfully met with deductive databases if they provide a language which is more powerful than Datalog.

Using Prolog, a language based on predicate logic, it was possible to implement the whole system from database to meta-level rules in one single formalism. Future extensions, such as the coupling with expert systems or external databases will equally be feasible within this framework.

A **DedChem** prototype is currently undergoing tests at the Department of Organic Chemistry at Zurich University, and the first version of the final system will be available by Spring 91.

7. References

[1] J. Bocca: EDUCE - A Marriage of Convenience: Prolog and a Relational DBS. Proceedings of the Third Symposion on Logic Programming, Salt Lake City, 1986.

[2] J. Bocca, M. Dahmen, G. Macartney: KB-Prolog User Guide. Technical Report of 4.9.1989, ECRC Munich.

[3] C. Draxler: Redefining findall/3 for Accessing Relational Databases. ICLP Workshop Eilat, June 1990.

[4] C. Draxler: Using Prolog's Set Predicates for Accessing Relational Databases. Technical Report, Institut für Informatik, Universität Zürich, 1990 (to appear)

[5] H. Gallaire, J. Minker, J.M. Nicolas: Logic and Databases: a Deductive Approach. Computing Surveys, vol 16 No. 2, June 1984

[6] D.Li: A Prolog Database System. Research Studies Press, John Wiley & Sons Ltd., 1984.

[7] D. Maier: Is Prolog a Database Language? in: NYU Symposium New Directions for Database Systems, 1984 New York.

[8] A. Thayse: From Modal Logic to Deductive Databases (esp. Chapter 6)., John Wiley and Sons, Chichester, 1989.

[9] L. Vieille, A. Lefebvre: Deductive Database Systems and the DedGin* query evaluator. Invited paper for the 7th British National Conference on Data Bases, Edinburgh, UK, July 1989.

A Data Model for Engineering Design and its Implementation

using a Link-Oriented Database

Deepa Krishnan   Tosiyasu. L. Kunii

Department of Information Science
Faculty of Science
The University of Tokyo
7-3-1, Hongo, Bunkyo-ku
Tokyo 113, JAPAN

Abstract

A database that exploits the creativity of the designer is essential for CAD applications. A new model for efficiently organizing and manipulating shape meta-data is presented. Implementation by extending the DML of an existing database system and in the form of a visual interface is also discussed. Shape data can be created and viewed using the facilities in the interface. The advantages of this approach such as enhanced modelling capability, operational support for the design task, elimination of a complex query language and storage minimization are highlighted.

1. Introduction

A geometric modelling database is indispensable in a mechanical computer-aided design (CAD) environment. Contemporary geometric modelling databases are based on a boundary or set-theoretic three-dimensional (3-D) object representation. Extraction of machinable features from such a representation is computationally expensive. Hence, due to missing product information, such databases cannot be used to drive automated applications or process planning. On the other hand, a hierarchical representation which explicitly contains details of features that constitute the design would be more appropriate for CAD. A database environment more conducive to creativity in design is necessary. Extensive modelling capabilities are required to describe constraints, versions and other information associated with detailed components and assemblies.

An integrated data model which enables designers to create and manipulate detailed components and combine them into assemblies is presented. The model is based on a hierarchical feature-oriented representation and provides an environment which is more natural for a designer to work in. New features can be added and components created using the operations in the model. Storage is minimized by permitting topologies to be shared and the efficiency of operations is increased by separating topology and geometry descriptions in the model. This model is being developed so as to form a software front-end to G-Base, a DBMS based on the Graph Data Model [7]. In contemporary approaches, 3-D shape data is reduced to one-dimensional (1-D) relations for easy storage and manipulation. This complicates the understanding of 3-D shape data. Queries are also textual and difficult to formulate especially in the case of hierarchically-structured objects. Answers to queries are alpha-numeric and are not easily comprehended. We have developed an interface for the above-mentioned model that allows the designer to interactively create objects and visually formulate and view answers to queries. The model is user-friendly, can describe constraints, versions and other information related to objects and is supported by a theoretical foundation based on hypergraphs [5].

In section 2, a review of existing CAD databases is presented. Visual interfaces to databases are also examined. The model and its salient features are illustrated in Section 3. Section 4 discusses implementation aspects. Finally, conclusions and extensions are highlighted.

2. Contemporary Approaches: A Survey

A detailed survey of contemporary approaches to CAD databases is presented to emphasize the need for this model. Visual database interfaces that have been developed are also reviewed.

Approaches to CAD databases can be primarily classified into three types. The first approach recommends the use of commercially available DBMS to model CAD data. Relational databases and their variations have been widely used [3]. This approach suffers from drawbacks such as the need to map object structure into flat relations, syntactically complex textual queries, inefficient modelling of the hierarchical design process, and a lack of data operations that aid the designer. Semantic models were considered as an alternative approach. Models like SAM* provide rich constructs to model machine parts [11,14]. However, no operations have been defined to support the design task. For example, it is not clear how parametrization and instantiation of objects are supported or how object-specific topological and geometric operations can be defined. Object-oriented approaches [4] have proven to be by far the most promising. However, the input of methods requires the knowledge of a database or programming language which proves to be a disadvantage. In addition, the definition of solid modelling operations as methods is complex and error-prone. Further, the complexity of the methods that can be defined is limited. Also most of the above approaches do not incorporate a hierarchical feature-based representation and hence, extraction of the engineering meaning of the representation used is difficult [12]. The design environment is in general far from conducive. Only nominal geometry can be represented and variational information in the form of tolerances is lacking in the above databases.

One approach that uses form features is described in [12]. Our model differs from this approach in several ways. Firstly, the model proposed here is more general and can be used as a front-end to an existing database system. This has the advantage that one can rely on a fully implemented tested technology that is readily available. Further, our model is supported by a formal foundation based on hypergraphs [5]. Due to this, detailed component creation and manipulation is handled completely by the database. A solid modeller is required only for assemblies. In the above-mentioned approach [12], however, integration with a solid modeller is necessary even at the detailed component level. Our model also allows efficient sharing and manipulation of topologies and description of object-specific topological and geometric operations which is missing in the approach described in [12]. Lastly, an interactive environment for visualizing data goes with our model and allows more user-friendly interaction than in [12]. The basic structure of the model presented in this paper is derived from Managaki et al [9]. Managaki's model [9] suffers from drawbacks such as the lack of a formal foundation, the need for data operations to aid the designer, inefficient modelling of hierarchical feature-based design, and flexibility [5]. Our model is proposed as a solution to many of these problems.

A number of visual database interfaces have been developed in the recent years. These interfaces have been developed primarily to simplify the query formulation task. Interfaces such as SDBMS [2] provide browsing facilities for answering simple queries. TIMBER [13] also supports complex queries. Other interfaces based on semantic models [1, 15] have proven to be more effective. Another interface described in [8] enables the user to see the contents of the database as well as displays syntactic diagrams corresponding to the valid query language. This enables the user to learn the query language. However, none of these interfaces are suited for a special-purpose application such as engineering. Such an application requires:

* elimination of complex textual queries. Since, most queries are related to the structure of objects (topological queries), they often require a syntactic traversal of the hierachical structure.
* provision for visual answers to queries. For example, answers to geometrical queries in existing systems, are often in the form of relations that use alpha-numeric data to describe edge-equations, vertex coordinates etc. These are hard to visualize and understand.
* enabling easy input of 3-D shape and design data
* adequate browsing facilities.
* elimnation of the need to remember object identifiers. For example, multiple versions of objects often co-exist in CAD databases. It is difficult for the user to remember pathnames of versions while formulating queries.

A prelimnary version of the interface GRIN (GRaphical INterface) has been described in [6]. This version has been considerably extended to satisfy the above requirements and to provide increased user-friendly interaction. We describe the interface in detail in Section 5.

A brief review of related research was presented in this section. The next section discusses the data model and the characteristics that contribute to make it unique.

3. The Data Model

An initial version of the model was described in [5]. This model has been extended considerably. Some of the salient characteristics are summarized here.

The database consists of a set of features. The features may be versioned or non-versioned. Let T denote the set of topologies (connectivity relations among edges, faces, vertices and features) available in the database. Here, each topology is denoted by a hypergraph. Each hyperedge in the hypergraph denotes the connectivity between any two boundary elements, for example, face-edge or face-face relationships. Let T_OP represent all topological operations available and each operation modifies object structure. Also let G constitute the set of all possible geometric information (dimensions, vertex coordinates, edge equations etc.), and G_OP refer to all possible geometric operations available: operations that define and manipulate the geometry of an object. Let R describe all possible relationships between elements in the database, V denote the set of variables and C describe the constraint set.

Each version in the case of a versioned feature or the feature itself in the case of a non-versioned feature is represented as

$$(A, SHAPE\_TEMPLATE)$$

where A denotes a set of attributes not related to the shape and SHAPE_TEMPLATE describes shape-related information. Each such template is given as a 7-tuple,

$$\{ t, t\_op, g, g\_op, r, v, c \}$$

where,

t: $t \subset T$ and is represented as the 3-tuple:

$$(H, TE, F\text{-links}) \qquad (1)$$

where,

H - is a hypergraph [5], TE represents the set of tentacles (hyperedges required to attach this object to another when it is used as a feature) [5], F-links are feature-links which serve as pointers to features lower in the hierarchy and are given as pairs (t_i, E_d). Here t_i is a 3-tuple topology as described in (1) and E_d denotes the base object hyperedges to be deleted while inserting the feature ($t_i \subset T$, $E_d \subset E_P$, P is the set of parents of the feature in the hierarchy).

Two types of topological representations are possible. The first is explicit representation (E-rep), where the pointer to the F-links is NULL and the object topology is expressed in terms of the hyperedges of H, and connections involve tentacles (1). A feature with its tentacles marked is shown in Fig. 1. However, tentacle specification is optional. The second type is the implicit representation (I-rep) where topology is expressed as a hierarchy of features. Both kinds of examples are illustrated in Fig. 1.

t_op: $t\_op \subset T\_op$ and represents the set of topological operations associated with the object and is denoted by { top_1, top_2,..., top_n }. Each topological operation replaces a portion of one hypergraph by another using the feature-evaluation mechanism [5]. An operation is denoted as follows:

$$top_i : t_b \leftarrow F\text{-link}_i,$$

A new F-link is introduced into a base topology t_b. The F-link is subsequently defined. This is illustrated in Fig. 2b.

g: $g \subset G$. An explicit representation consists of geometrical information such as edge and face equations, face normals, edge lengths and angles between edges. Dimensions can be defined with reference to other surfaces. Geometry can also be represented implicitly as a sequence of primitive graphical operations.

g_op: $g\_op \subset G\_op$ and permits the specification of a set of geometric operations associated with the object { gop_1, gop_2,..., gop_n}. Each operation alters the geometry of the object and is expressed as a sequence of graphical operations.

r: $r \subset R$ and $r = r_1 \cup r_2 \cup r_3 \cup r_4 \cup r_5 \cup r_6$

$$r_1 = \{ (g, v) \mid g \subset G, v \subset V_1 \}$$
$$r_2 = \{ (t, v) \mid t \subset T, v \subset V_2 \}$$
$$r_3 = \{ (t\_op, v) \mid t\_op \subset T\_op, v \subset V_2 \}$$
$$r_4 = \{ (g\_op, v) \mid g\_op \subset G\_op, v \subset V_1 \}$$
$$r_5 = \{ (c, v) \mid c \subset C, v \subset V \}$$
$$r_6 = \{ (t\_op, g\_op) \mid t\_op \subset T\_op, g\_op \subset G\_op \}$$
$$r_7 = \{ (t\_op, c) \mid t\_op \subset T\_op, c \subset C \}$$
$$r_8 = \{ (f, v) \mid f \subset objects, v \subset V_3 \}$$

$r_m \cap r_n = \emptyset$ m, n= 1, 2,...,6 m=n

where V_1, V_2 and V_3 represent the geometrical, topological and the attribute variables respectively and $V = V_1 \cup V_2 \cup V_3$.

v: $v \subset V$ and denote variables essential for parametrization. These variables are of three types:

1) topology variables: variables related to F-links which are used for example, to indicate the number of holes on a surface. These include topological operation variables.

2) geometry variables: variables related to dimensions and geometrical operations.

3) attribute variables: related to other attributes of a feature.

c: $c \subset C$ represent constraints which are defined on the different types of variables.

Here, a "feature" refers to any topology: a set of boundary elements and their adjacency relationships. Each feature is represented as a hypergraph and a special set of hyperedges required to attach it to another feature. These hyperedges are called tentacles [5]. Features may be 'primary' or 'secondary'. Primary features form a major part of the shape and do not require tentacles. Secondary features are the alterations made to the major part of a shape and hence, tentacles are necessary. To add a feature to an object, the required feature is selected and the tentacles of the base object to be matched with those of the feature are defined. Hyperedges in the base object may be deleted if necessary. These pairs of tentacles are then matched using a process called hyperedge matching [5] to generate the resultant topology (Refer Fig. 1a) . Since the definition of a feature is not restricted to be those encountered in the design of machine parts, a wide variety of structural modifications on an object can be modelled. This contributes to the novelty of the model.

Fig. 1 shows a representation using this model. The geometry of an object is clearly separated from the topology definition.This would mean that operations (a local modification operation like tweaking) that alter geometry alone can be done independently without traversing the connections in the data structure. Topological operations are useful to model the changes in the structure of an object caused by machining operations and wear and tear. Unlike object-oriented approaches (see Section 2), no code has to be input to define these operations since they can be defined as hypergraphs. Further, parametrization and instanciation operations[5] help to enhance the reusability of designed objects. A detailed component or an assembly description in our model corresponds to a "complex object" or to "objects" in object-oriented databases. However, a feature is a unit object used to construct detail components or assemblies. The difference between "complex objects" and detailed components lies in the fact that specialized operators are required to create and manipulate detailed components. The parametric descriptions and the topology and geometry of individual features are effectively combined to generate a component[5]. Our model also provides adequate facilities to create, modify and query such special-purpose engineering objects. Variables represent design parameters. Constraints and variables are used to represent variational information such as tolerances, material, surface-finish etc.

The topology of an assembly is represented as an ordered sequence of detailed components and set operations in an implicit manner. An example is shown in Fig. 1c. However, to evaluate the E-rep, a solid modeller is required. Once the boundary of the resultant object is evaluated, it can be stored in the format specified above. Thus, a database using this model requires integration with a solid modeller to represent assembly objects.

The architecture of a system using this model is illustrated in Fig. 2. The I-rep of a feature can be converted to the corresponding E-rep by using the feature-evaluation mechanism as indicated in the Figure. Since, both representations may exist for the same feature, certain rules are required to maintain consistency. For example, while inputting an E-rep, the steps given below are followed:

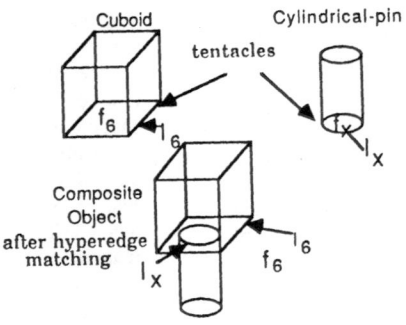

$$p= \{ g, g\_op, t, t\_op, v, r, c\}$$

g: $\{ l_1, l_2, l_3, rad, ht, a, rpt \}$

l_1 = length(e_2)= length(e_4) = length(e_{10}) =

length(e_{12})

$\vdots$

radius(e_x) = radius(e_y)

coordinates of vertices and other geometry can also be specified explicitly along with their relationships to variables.

g_op: $\{ \}$

t: $\{ f_1, f_2,...,f_z, l_1, l_2,...,l_z, e_1, e_2,...,e_z, v_1,...,v_z \}$

f_1 : (l_1)

$\vdots$

f_6 : (l_6, l_x)

l_1 : (e_1, e_2, e_3, e_4)

$\vdots$

e_1 : (v_1, v_2)

tentacles: $\{ f_z \}$

t_op : $\{ o_1 \}$

o_1: t_{cube} <- f_link_1

f_link_1 = (t_{round}, v)

v - $\{$ length, breadth, height, depth, radius, refpt,

axis, vedge$\}$

r - $\{ r_1, r_2 ...,r_8 \}$

r_1 = $\{$ length, l_1 $\}$

$\vdots$

r_2 = $\{$ breadth, l_2 $\}$

c - $\{ c_1, c_2,..., c_5 \}$

c_1: length > 0

c_2: breadth > 0

$\vdots$

c_5: vedge.type = V-L

Fig. 2a An example of an E-rep

1: check if explicit representation of the topology exists. If yes, terminate process, else step 2.
2: check if the implicit representation of the topology exists. If it does, the hierarchy is evaluated to generate the explicit representation and the user is not allowed to input. If no implicit representation exists, execute step 3.
3: allow user to input.
Similar steps are adopted while inputting an I-rep or while making modifications. For example, if an I-rep is modified, the corresponding E-rep that exists in the database is deleted. A new E-rep is then generated from the modified I-rep using the feature-evaluation operation discussed in [5, 6], Instances of features are also maintained in the database and can be directly used by designers when necessary. For frequently used components, the E-rep can be stored so that no time is wasted in evaluating an I-rep.

The classification of versions in this model is indicated by the hierarchy in Fig. 3. This tree is called a version-tree (v-tree) and is maintained for each shape. Level 1 indicates that the I-rep and E-rep representations are possible for a shape. Moving to the left subtree under

Refer Fig. 1a for diagram

$$p = \{ g, g\_op, t, t\_op, v, r, c \}$$

g: $\{ g_1, g_2 \}$

$\quad g_1$: CUBOID(o,l_1, l_2, l_3)

$\quad g_2$: CYCLN(o,r, h, a, rpt)

g_op: $\{ gop_1 \}$

$\quad gop_1$ (tweak): CHANGEVERTEX(v, x, y, z)

t - $\{ o \}$

$\quad$ o: Null <- f_link$_1$

$\quad\quad$ f_link$_1$ = (t$_{cube}$, NULL)

$\quad\quad$ t$_{cube}$ <- f_link$_2$

$\quad\quad$ f_link$_2$ = (t$_{cyclnpin}$, NULL)

t_op - $\{ o_1 \}$

$\quad o_1$: t$_{cube}$ <- f_link$_x$

$\quad\quad$ f_link$_x$ = (t$_{round}$, v)

Note: The rest of the representation remains the same except for the addition of a relationship between the topological operation o and the geometric operations g_1 and g_2. The required tentacle is implicitly specified while evaluating the feature.

Fig. 1b An I-rep example

E-rep, level 2 represents equivalent versions, where in each case a different set of hyperedges are chosen to represent the same shape. Woo [16] classified boundary data structures based on the adjacency relationships chosen to represent an object. In correspondence with each of these data structures, different sets of hyperedges are chosen for each shape. The types of hyperedges contained in each version is indicated by a 16-bit code. These representations are essentially equivalent because, one can be derived from the other if necessary. Design is an incremental process, wherein a designer should be given the freedom to store an incomplete task and continue at a later stage from where he left off. Level 3 in the left subtree represents stages of a design task ordered linearly according to the time of creation. The last level in the same subtree denotes revisions to each stage again ordered as per the time of creation. Revisions could denote versions which have changes made to shape-related data such as constraints, variables or operations. Versions encountered under the subtree marked I-rep are now considered. Different combinations of features can be used to generate the same shape. Various feature hierarchies representing the same shape are indicated by level 2. The next 2 levels denote stages and revisions as in the case of the left subtree. The classification of versions is governed by the representation scheme adopted for shape description. Details on version management are omitted for brevity.

For brevity, operations in this model are not described in this paper. Operations for manipulating

topology are based on primitive hypergraph operators[5]. The next section, describes the implementation.

4. Implementation

Two approaches are adopted for implementing this model. In the first approach, the Data Manipulation Language (DML) of an existing database system is extended to incorporate the operations described in Appendix A. In the second approach, a portion of the database is read into the data structures of a visual interface and the commands in the interface are then used to interactively manipulate data. The data can then be re-stored in the database after a design session. Both these approaches are described here.

4.1 Extending the DML

The DML of a link-oriented DBMS G-Base was extended to incorporate the operations in the model. The model underlying G-Base is the Graph Data Model (GDM) which was developed by H.S. Kunii [7]. We chose G-Base for two reasons. Firstly, this system allows an explicit representation of relationships between entities. This increases the expressive power of the database and G-Base schemas are easier to understand and formulate than relational schemas. The use of links as logical access paths in the specification of queries (explained later in this section) simplifies the query formulation task. The other reason is because the DBMS was easily available in our laboratory.

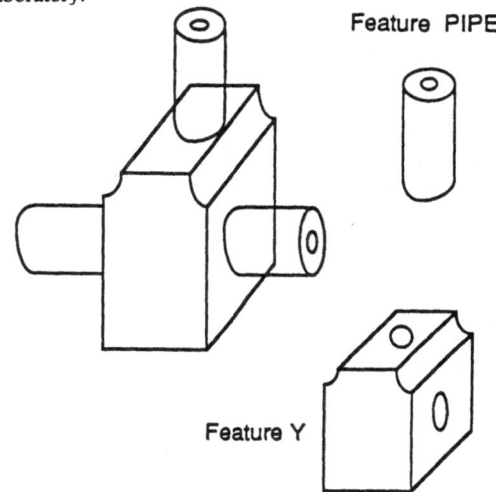

Feature PIPE

Feature Y

PIPE (S_1, d_1, d_2, h)

Y (S_2, l, b, h, fillets, r_1, r_2)

UNION(P, S_1, S_2)

SCALE(S_3, S_1, x, y, z)

TRANSLATE(S_4, S_3, dx, dy, dz)

ROTATE(S_5, S_4, rx, ry, rz)

UNION(P, S_5)

Fig. 1c Representation of a simple assembly

268

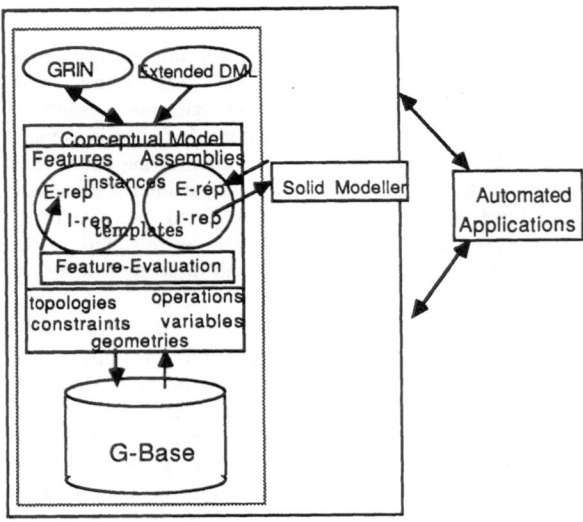

Fig. 2   System Architecture

A GDM schema is a set of *record* and *link* types [7]. Each *record* type represents an entity in the real world and is characterized by a list of attributes. Each record type is identified by a Unique Record Identifier (URI) and corresponds to a relation scheme. A binary association between two record types is denoted by a *link* type. Formal definitions of record and link types are given in [7]. GDM supports two types of links. The value-based representation of relationships (based on common attributes)[7] denoted by *virtual* link types in GDM. Virtual link types are typically used to express many-to-one or one-to-many relationships, if the attribute in consideration is the primary key of one of the records involved. Relationships between record types could also be represented explicitly using *real* link types. The occurrences of a real link type are stored independently of the record types involved. Each occurrence is identified by the URI's of the records involved in the link type. Real links are commonly used to represent many-many relationships. Recursive (defined only on one record) and parallel (many links between the same pair of records) real link types can be defined. G-Base creates inverses for each link automatically. Languages like SQL do not maintain the intermediate results of queries for further processing. However, GDM provides a structure *record list* to store intermediate results [7]. This is very useful in most applications. N-ary links between record types can also be simulated using the record list structure and n binary link types. GDM algebra includes relational algebra and incorporates operators to

manipulate link types. For more details about G-Base and its operations, the interested reader may refer [10].

Initially, a graph schema was developed for this model. The DML compiler's C language interface was used to develop the operations [5,6] which use the above schema. An example of operation "delete_edge" is shown in Fig. 4. These operations are maintained in a library and can be used in a DML program which can then be compiled and executed. We have also defined a high level DML for this model. We hope to develop an interpreter soon to facilitate better interaction with the model.

4.2 The Visual Interface

The GRIN interface has been developed to enable high-level interaction with the model described earlier. It enables the viewing of shape meta-data, and at the same time eliminates complex textual queries. This isolates the user from concepts such as clauses and projections and simplifies the understanding of 3-D shape data. When GRIN is used, a portion of the database can be loaded into the data structures of the interface before or during a design session. A prelimnary version of GRIN was described in [6]. The facilities available in the presently available version are described in this section.

4.2.1 Queries

Queries come in three kinds. The most commonly encountered queries are topological queries which are again of two types. Queries that explore the connectivity relationships among boundary elements such as vertices, edges and faces constitute the first type. "what edges form

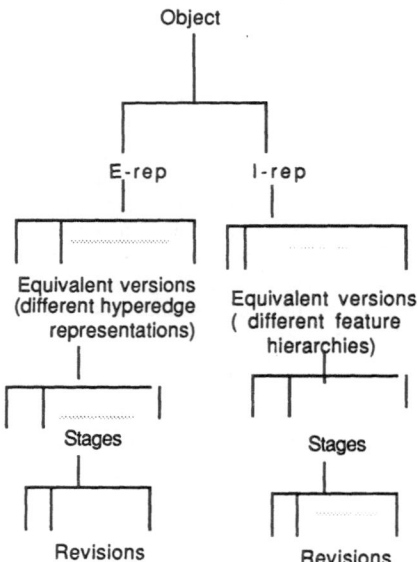

Fig. 3 The Version Hierarchy

```
delete_edge()
{
        char pattern[MAXNAME];
        $var xhname,xcname,xtname;
        int p;
        $target t E_rep order E_rep.hname;
        printf("Please enter topology identifier0");
        scanf("%d",&p);
        printf("Please enter hiedge name0");
        scanf("%s",pattern);
        dbSetI(xtname,p);dbSetS(xhname,pattern);
        $find t=E_rep[tid=xtname and hname match xhname];
        ERR_CLOSE;
        $reset t; $skip t;
        $while (not eof(t)){
                $for current t $set xcname=E_rep.cname;
                /* delete each blob and related entities */
                ERR_CLOSE;
                $transaction;
                $for  blobs[tid=xtname  and  bname  match  xcname]
                ../parent_of/.. E_rep
                delete E_rep;
                ERR_ROLLBK;
                $transaction;
                $for blobs[tid=xtname and bname match xcname] delete
                blobs;
                ERR_ROLLBK;
                /* delete the blob in instances of a topology */
                $transaction;
                $for celement[tid=xtname and cname match xcname]
                delete celement;
                ERR_ROLLBK;
                /* delete the hyperedge in instances */
                $transaction;
                $for hiedge[tid=xtname and hname match xcname] delete
                hiedge;
                ERR_ROLLBK;
                $transaction;
                $for E_rep[tid=xtname and cname match xcname] delete
                E_rep;
                ERR_ROLLBK;
                $skip t;
                }
```

Fig. 4 The procedure *delete_edge* written in the embedded DML

a part of face F_1 of feature A?" is one example of such a query. The second type of topological queries deal with the hierarchical structure of an object. For example, "what primitive objects compose object A?". For the first kind of topological queries, GRIN provides facilities for viewing and manipulating boundary hypergraphs of objects. Hypergraphs can be viewed at various levels. The vertex-face level for example, illustrates the connectivity relations between vertices and faces of a feature. Viewing operations that extract partial and sub-hypergraphs or perform set operations on hyperedges can extract answers to specific queries from displayed hypergraphs. Feature tree displays answer topological queries of the second type. Such trees indicate the hierarchical composition of a machine part in terms of features such as holes, steps and grooves. Version trees can also be displayed. Picking and highlighting facilities eliminate the need to remember object identifiers. Answers to some such queries are indicated in Fig. 5. The second kind of queries concern the geometry of an object. For example, "what is the geometry of instance X of feature A?". In conventional databases, the answer is usually in the form of alpha-numeric data describing vertex coordinates, edge equations etc. Shaded colour displays of shapes (refer Fig.5) provide answers to such queries in GRIN. Such displays can be transformed and viewed from any direction. More specific queries such as "what are the coordinates of vertex V_1?" are also possible. Queries that examine other meta-data form the last type. Queries such as "What are the variables associated

with a rectangular slot?" can be answered. To view the details of each variable, the user can enter the picking mode and click on the vertex denoting the appropriate variable. A window opens and indicates the details of the variable (Fig.5). Queries can can deal with multiple representations of the answers. For example, variable values can be represented textually or in the form of a dimensioned drawing. The result of a query can be modified and stored to be reviewed later if necessary. Dynamic animation facilities are provided to review how a design was constructed. The screen display of a query can also be altered by changing the colors or eliminating unwanted objects to make it more pleasing to the eye. Answers to complex queries are viewed by using multiple windows simultaneously.

4.2.2 Input and Manipulation

Both implicit and explicit topologies can be directly read in from files. GRIN maintains a temporary database to support the trial and error design process. Objects hierarchies can be created in the temporary database by adding and deleting features. A command "evaluate" is used to derive the E-rep from a hierarchy. The hierarchies can be either partially (lazy-evaluation) or fully evaluated and the corresponding E-rep stored in the database. Thus, it is possible to input new topologies using this method too. A sample session is illustrated in [6]. A graphical editor GLEE is used to input and view geometrical information. Explicit geometry can be read in from files. Geometry can also be expressed as a sequence of graphical operations (see Ref. 6). Facilities are provided to translate, rotate, scale and view shapes from all directions. Once, the geometry of the object has been determined the corresponding operation sequences are automatically stored in the database. The designer can also formulate these sequences by selecting the operations from a menu. All the stored data can be modified interactively. Variables, constraints, relationships and versions can be defined by clicking on boxes in the appropriate windows (Fig. 5). Constraint graphs are displayed to indicate the connections between the constraints of an object.

4.2.3 Advantages

The data created during a design session using GRIN can be incorporated into the database at any time before exiting GRIN. The interface is designed to minimize the textual input. Most of the interaction is done using a mouse. The user need not remember pathnames of versions or pathnames in the feature tree of an object. Operations can be executed by clicking on appropriate nodes in the tree structure. Also, memory is optimized by allowing objects to share topological data. In contemporary approaches, much of this is not possible. To minimize the execution speed the user is allowed to operate over sections of the database. Since CAD databases are very large, this results in a significant performance improvement. The geometry of the shape is separated from its topology and hence, geometrical manipulations can be easily performed without traversing complex topological interconnections. Modifications made

270

using this interface are easily verifiable and are kept consistent by the underlying model. A prototype of the interface is implemented on the personal IRIS workstation in the C programming language and has about 5000 lines of code.

Our visual interface presents an effective way to organize and view shape information from a database point of view. Conventional databases do not incorporate many of the facilities described above and are in that sense inadequate for engineering applications.

5. Conclusions

A data model for storing and manipulating shape meta-data was presented. The model is complete and can be used for describing components and assemblies. Unlike existing CAD databases, this model represents shapes efficiently, offers operational support for the design task, eliminates the need for a complex query language and allows user-friendly interaction. Storage is also minimized by sharing topological information and performance is improved by separating topology and geometry descriptions. Further the model is supported by a formal foundation based on hypergraphs [5]. A visual interface to this model was also discussed. A number of facilities are available for browsing, exploring, defining and manipulating shape data. The integration of G-Base and the interface is being done on the Sun4 SPARC workstation. Based on our experience with GRIN, we have developed a high-level graphical query language for interrogating a

link-oriented schema. This will be described in a later paper. Efficient methods for retrieving and organizing data are also being explored.

Acknowledgements
We are grateful to Dr. Hideko S. Kunii of the Ricoh SRC for the G-Base system and to Silicon Graphics, Japan for the personal IRIS workstation. We would also like to thank Mr. Arashiba of Famotek for providing us with the HOOPS graphics software.

References
[1] Goldman K. J., Goldman S. J., Kanellakis P. C. and Zdonik S. B., ISIS: Interface for a Semantic Information System, in *Proceedings of SIGMOD*, Austin, 328-342 (1985).
[2] Herot C. F., Spatial Management of Data, *ACM Transactions on Database Systems*, Vol. 5, No. 4 , 493-514 (1980).
[3] Kemper A. and Wallrath M., "An Analysis of Geometric Modelling in Database Systems", *ACM Computing Surveys*, Vol. 19, No. 1, March 1987, pp 47-91.
[4] Ketabchi M. A., Berzins V. and March S. T., "An Object-oriented Semantic Data Model for CAD Applications", *Information Sciences* 46, pp109-139, 1988.
[5] D. Krishnan and T. L. Kunii, "Parametric model: A conceptual framework for geometric modelling database", in the *Proc. of the Second International Conference on Data and Knowledge Systems for Manufacturing and Engineering*, Maryland, October (1989).
[6] Krishnan D. and Kunii T. L., " A Graphical Interface for a Geometric Modelling Database". in *Human Machine Interactive Systems* ed. by A. Klinger, New York, Plenum Press, to be published.
[7] Kunii H. S., "Graph Data Language: A High Level Access-Path Oriented Language", Doctoral Thesis, The University of Texas at Austin, May 1983; a monograph version is available from Springer-

Verlag "Graph Data Model- Theory and Implementation-", 1990.
[8] Larson and Wallick, "An Interface for Novice Infrequent Database Management Users", in *Proceedings of the National Computer Conference* 1984, pp 523-529.
[9] Managaki M. and Kawagoe K., "A Parametric Man/Machine Interaction with Semantic Data", *Computers and Graphics*, Vol. 7, No. 3-4, 1983, pp 233-242.
[10] Ricoh Co., *G-Base User's Guide*, in Japanese,1988, and in English , 1990.
[11] Roy U. and Liu C. R.,"Establishment of Functional Relationships between Product Components in an Assembly Database", *Computer-Aided Design*, Vol. 20, 10, December 1988, pp 570-580.
[12] Shah J. J. and Rogers M. T.," Expert Form Feature Modelling Shell", *Computer-Aided Design*, Vol. 20, No. 9, 1988.
[13] M. Stonebraker and J. Kalash, TIMBER: A sophisticated relation browser, in *Proc. of the 8th VLDB* Mexico City, 7-10 (1982).
[14] Su S. Y. W., "Modelling Integrated Manufacturing Data with SAM*", *IEEE Computer*, Vol. 19, No. 1, Jan. 1986, pp 34-49.
[15] Wong H. K. T. and Kuo I., GUIDE: graphical user interface for database exploration, in *Proc. of the 8th VLDB*, Mexico City, 22-32 (1982).
[16] Woo T. C.,"A Combinatorial Analysis of Boundary Data Structure Schemata", *IEEE Computer Graphics and Applications*, March 1985, pp 19-27.

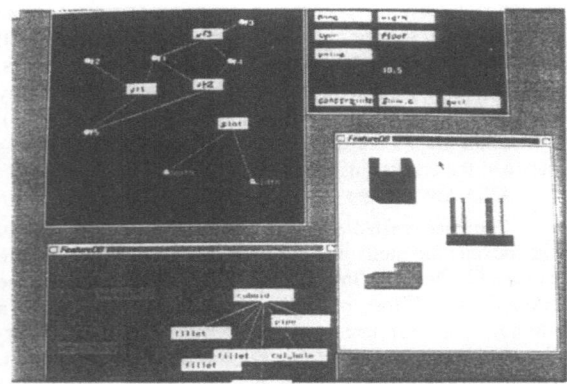

Fig. 5 A View of the GRIN screen

Implementation of a historical/geographical database with support of imprecise dates

O. Signore, R. Bartoli

CNUCE - Institute of CNR - via S. Maria, 36 - 56126 Pisa (Italy)

ABSTRACT

Art history data management leads to express dates in a "fuzzy" way, which is not suitable for electronic processing.
A standardized, easy to use, way of coding dates, mantaining all the semantics of the "natural" format, has been defined. Each date is therefore expressed (in the extended way) as a string of characters, with a well defined syntax, while it is really managed as a set of fields, which contain, in a coded way, the same information that are contained in the extended format.
The coded format of dates is easily and transparently managed by every DBMS, thus allowing selection by exact values or by ranges.
This conventional way of managing dates has been tested in the implementation of a DBMS based historico-geographical authority file.

INTRODUCTION

Anyone involved in historical research is constantly faced with the need to make reference to a historical "geography" that differs sharply from present-day geography. This is because historical geography is the cumulation of historical phenomena which have followed one another in an uninterrupted sequence of events since time immemorial.
As happens with every type of historical development, in historical geography we encounter "long-range," structural patterns, or else we encounter circumstances that are intimately bound up with clear-cut, individual "events."
This is an issue which contemporary historiographers have raised time and time again, without actually coming up with any practical solutions to the problem, such as the design for a "historical atlas" that is at once both comprehensive and *dynamic* (in the sense that it could be constantly updated to accomodate the latest developments in historical research).
Nor has this problem escaped the attention of archaeologists and art history scholars. However, the solutions proposed to date have always been either empirical in nature or limited to specialized academic disciplines.

Therefore, the question has been raised as to how best to use data-processing resources to produce a data archive encompassing historical, geographic and toponymical data on a particular site, in relation to the timespan in question and with bibliographical source

material being specified. For instance, we may infer from the available literature that the town today known as *Sezze* was called *Setia* from 382 B.C. until the 11th century; *Castrum Sitiense* from the 13th century up to a period prior to the 16th and 17th centuries; *Secia* from 1478 until (presumably) the 16th century.
The literature further reveals that Sezze belonged to the *Papal States* from the 10th/11th century up to a date prior to 1404, at which time it passed into the *Kingdom of Naples* until 1414, the year in which it once again became part of the *Papal States* up until 1870.
We want to be able to use data-processing resources to find answers to questions such as: what was Sezze called during the period in which it came under the jurisdiction of the Kingdom of Naples, or else which status did Sezze hold in the region in the 13th century? We also have need to obtain maps, e.g. a chart showing the situation of the Kingdom of Naples in 1404, identifying its constituent towns and villages, shown with the names in use at that particular moment in history. The research which we conducted was designed with these needs in mind.

The conceptual model of the world of interest is represented by the following Entity-Relationship ([1], [2]) diagram, where each relationship has two "time attributes" (beginning date, ending date):

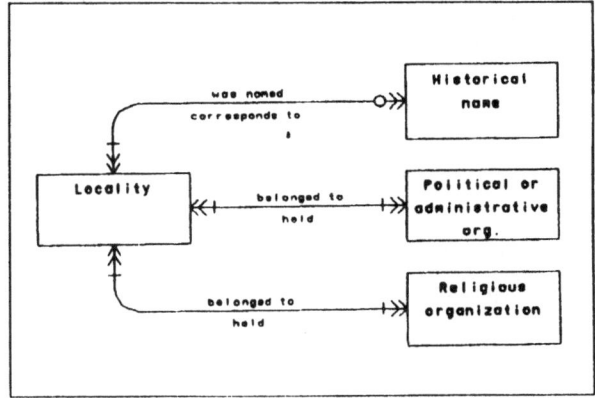

Fig. 1: The conceptual schema

It should be noted that the various pieces of information (administrative or ecclesiastical belonging and his-

torical name) are completely **independent**, and may be got from different sources in different times.
A liaison between them may only be established on the basis of the *time*.

SUPPORT OF IMPRECISE DATES

It is important to remember that the "time" coordinate is something that is always present, as a lot of information are dependent on the time.
In fact, not only names of the places, or administrative boundaries or ecclesiatical jurisdiction, are time dependent, but also some other information that, at first glance, seem to be invariant, as watercourses, lakes (artificial ones may born, others may be dried), roads, marshes, etc. may vary as the time goes on.

The traditional approach

In managing art history data, the user is frequently faced with dates expressed in a fuzzy way (i.e. *century, before, after, circa*, etc.), while sometimes it is required to find the information referring to some specific year, or range of dates. In addition, it may happen that the date itself is known with a certain approximation (i.e. *certainly after 338 B.C. and before 314 B.C.*)
However, even if dates expressed in this traditional way are meaningful to the scholars and easy to specify, nevertheless they present some disadvantages. In fact, they are language dependent and hardly managed by computer programs. As a matter of fact, when dates are expressed in the traditional way, it is impossible to join different information on the basis of the time span they apply.
On the other hand, it is well known that DBMSs do not provide effective ways for management of dates. The SQL ISO standard ([8]) is considering only numbers and characters as data types. Even the recently proposed "date" data types ([3]), and the "datetime" data type defined in the ISO SQL2 standard ([9]), do not allow to preserve and represent the semantic richness of the traditional way of expressing dates. They seems more suitable for the business environment. Consequently, it has been decided to implement a special "data type," based on an appropriate aggregation of the elementary existing data types, adopting an approach similar to that suggested in [10].

The extended format syntax

The main goal in defining a syntax for dates has been to preserve the semantic richness of the traditional fuzzy format, retaining the maximum degree of flexibility, without introducing any useless or innatural formalism.
The decision has been made to express every date in three possible ways:

- as a simple date;
- as an interval: $(Date_{min} - Date_{max})$
- as an interval, with indication of a probable date: $Date_{prob} (Date_{min} - Date_{max})$

The first form is the correct one of a date known with certainty. The second is used when the scholar is not able to determine a probable date between the minimum and maximum date. The third case comes up when, together with a probable date, there is present conflicting information, but from reliable source.
The preferable forms are, obviously, the first and the third. There are, however numerous cases where it is not possible to suggest a probable date in that any hypothesis would have little substantiation.
Similarly, there exist cases in which it is not scientifically correct to guess at limits for a date qualified as "circa" (about).

Consequently, after several attempts at formalization, it has been considered opportune to use a series of conventions to represent, in the most natural way for the scholar, the possible forms to give to dates. The extended format syntax has been developed for *italian language*, but it is evident that a similar approach may be developed for any language.
On the basis of this convention, every date is expressed in one of the forms recorded above, where $Date_{prob}$, $Date_{min}$ and $Date_{max}$ all have the same format, which can be one of the following:

- a **number**, preceded by the expression *anno* (if the date is known with certainty) or the expression *circa* (if it is approximate);
- a **roman numeral** preceded by the expression *sec.* or *inizio* or *meta'* or *fine*.

They will be followed by the expression *a.C.* or the expression *d.C.* (or nothing) depending if the date is before or after Christ.
In the case in which the date is merely hypothetical, and is recorded only for the purpose of avoiding inconsistent answers, the expression is followed by "(?)."
The expression *oggi* indicates the present year.

The coded format

In a database approach, processing and sorting of dates can easily be done if dates are stored as signed numbers: the dates before Christ may be recorded as negative numbers.
As each date is expressed (in the extended way) as a string of characters, with a well defined syntax, the basic problem has been to translate every date in a set of fields, which contains, in a coded way, the same information that are contained in the extended format.

In the data entry phase, the operator enters the dates in the extended format. After loading the database, the whole database is processed in order to update the fields that contains the coded form of the dates. At the query stage, all the processing is performed using only the coded format, while the results are showed using the extended format.
This approach has been adopted only for speeding up the first pilot phase, in order to check the effectiveness of the adopted solutions. A routine which translates the coded form into the extended format, so allowing different languages (*english, french, german and italian*) to be used, has been implemented. Consequently, the column containing the date in the extended format has been deleted from the database, so allowing a considerable saving in space and a 3NF design of the database.

To be clearer, each date is split into three triplets:

1. D_p_type D_p_QM D_p_num
2. D_{min}_type D_{min}_QM D_{max}_num
3. D_{max}_type D_{max}_QM D_{min}_num

which represent, respectively, the probable date, the minimum date and the maximum date.

The various fields have the following significance:

- **D_x_type**

  Indicates whether the date is known with certainty, or is approximate, or is simply a century (possibly a fraction of a century) and may have the value:

  Y when the date (understood as a year) is known for sure (e.g. *definitely in 1820*)
  A when the date is approximate (e.g. *circa 1530*)
  S when the date is provided as a century or as a fraction of a century (e.g. *century XVI*)
  C when the date has been calculated on the basis of information provided (e.g. the minimum and maximum for an exact date, or the probable date for a date provided only as a minimum and maximum).

- **D_x_QM**

  Indicates whether the date has been gleaned from a source or is simply a hypothetical date. In this case, the field takes on the value "?."

- **D_x_num**

  Is the equivalent numerical value for the date and is simply a binary number, less than zero in the case of B.C. dates. When a date is expressed as a century or fraction of a century and thus indicates an interval (e.g. *cent.* IV indicates the period from 300 to 399), the value is made equal to the minimum or maximum for the interval of values, depending upon whether the date is a *From* date or a *To* date (e.g. *beginning* III B.C. is made equal to -299 if it is a *From* date, and equal to -290 if it is a *To* date).

In the following table, a sample of the equivalence between extended format and coded format is reported.

Date (extended format)	DP	DMIN	DMAX
sec. VIII a.C.	S -750	S -799	S -700
(sec. VIII a.C. - sec. VII a.C.)	C? -699	S -799	S -600
(meta' VII a.C. - meta' VI a.C.)	C? -599	S -654	S -544
sec. VI a.C.	S -550	S -599	S -500
(sec. VI a.C. - sec. V a.C.)	C? -499	S -599	S -400
inizio V a.C.	S -494	S -499	S -489
sec. V a.C.	S -450	S -499	S -400
(sec. V a.C. - sec. IV a.C.)	C? -399	S -499	S -300
(anno 497 a.C. - anno 492 a.C.)	C? -494	Y -497	Y -492
(anno 495 a.C. - sec. IV a.C.)	C? -397	Y -495	S -300
anno 492 a.C.	Y -492	Y -492	Y -492
fine IV a.C.	S -304	S -309	S -300
(circa 211 a.C. - circa 90 a.C.)	C? -150	A -211	A -90
(sec. VII (?) - sec. VIII (?))	C? 699	S? 600	S? 799
(sec. VII - sec. VIII)	C? 699	S 600	S 799

THE DATABASE

As a test bed for the proposed formalism for the representation of dates, an historico-geographical authority file ([5], [6], [7]) has been implemented, where, for each locality, information about historical names, historico-political and ecclesiastic structures the locality was belonging to, are separately recorded.

At present, only the region Lazio, with province of Latina in full (31 Communes and 269 Localities), other provinces partially, is covered. In total, 738 localities are covered, with 2676 notices and 3543 references to sources. For each information, it is recorded the period (from-to) the information apply, and the sources the information comes from. These information may be easily correlated, so allowing the production of indexes and of historical atlases for any arbitrarily chosen year (for each locality, the present boundaries are available in digitized form, so that maps may be produced).

A set of application programs can produce various printed indexes of high quality, which are considered by the scholars an essential instrument of work. The following indexes are presently available:

- *Topographical index* where for every Comune, and for each locality, all collected data, in chronological order and with indication of source, are reported, grouped by historical names, ecclesiastical jurisdiction, historico-political situation.
- *historical names index* where, for each historical name, the time span and the corresponding present toponym are reported;
- *ecclesiatical jurisdiction index* where, for each diocesi, present toponym names, accompanied by the historical names got in the period they where belonging to the diocesi, are reported;
- *historico-political situation index* where, for each historico-political situation, present toponym names, accompanied by the historical names got in the period they where belonging to the historico-political situation, are reported;
- *sources*

Needless to say, almost every casual query may be satisfied using the query language of the DBMS (SQL/DS). Some parametric queries have been defined.

In addition, maps showing historical administrative or ecclesiastical entities, together with historical names of localities, may be easily produced.

A complete description of the project, and all indexes and maps produced, are in [4].

This approach has been tested for a different area in a totally different technical environment (IBM PS/2 and ORACLE), and has been found absolutely satisfactory. Selected sites in Texas were chosen, because Texas has had a complex and varied history beginning with the Spanish colonization in the sixteenth century. The area of a present state of Texas experienced a variety of political and ecclesiastical jurisdictions during its colonial status, during its existence as an independent republic, and as state of the U.S. There were numerous additional administrative changes as well as alterations in ecclesiastical jurisdictions.

As might be anticipated, both the current and historical political/administrative structure for Texas differ from that of Italy. The Italian entities were slightly modified to accommodate structures peculiar to Texas. A major difference between Texas and Italy concerns the matter of dating. Before Christ dates (BC) are not relevant. Its history (as defined by this system) does not begin until a much later date. Texas was populated by various Indian peoples prior to Spanish occupation, but these occupations were not considered in this project. In Texas dates tend to be better known and more specific than in ancient Italy, or unknown (i.e., when a historical name fell into disuse).

OUTSTANDING PROBLEMS

Even if the general approach appears to work very well, especially for dates management, there are, however, some outstanding problems for which we may envisage some possible solutions.

- For unlocalized toponyms, a possible solution is to give coordinates with uncertainty, specifying them as a rectangle, or as a circle.
  In both cases, the structure of the database should be modified.
  The preferable solution seems to be the second (supplying center and radius).

- Linear elements (rivers, roads, lake boundaries) could be digitized together a date (from-to), so allowing the choise of the correct data depending on the date the historical map is referring to.

- Physical data may be useful for defining hypothetic boundaries, as all data are collected as points, and it seems to be incorrect to rely on present boundaries.
  An approach similar to that adopted for the linear elements may appear feasible, but it is difficult to establish at which level of detail we have to store information. Also, it is not definite where to guess boundaries, as some concepts may be not well defined. Typically, what we have to consider to be a mountain, that could have probably determined a boundary between two different administrative entities? (Webster's dictionary defines a hill as being *lower than a mountain*, and a mountain as being *higher than a hill!*).

- The upward-downward extension to countries in one direction, and to towns and streets in the other, appears possible, but costly, and would require an in depth historical research. The cost/benefit ratio of a similar extension should be carefully evaluated.

CONCLUSION

As a conclusion, we may notice that the extended format is understandable and easy to use, and the coded internal format:

- performs very well;
- allows a very compact.representation (only 12 bytes) for every date;
- may be easily extended to century fractions and to more precise dates, where the month or the day are specified (it is only a matter of defining an appropriate wording in the extended format);
- is a convenient way for exchanging data and may be adopted as a standard;
- has been proved suitable in overcoming differences in languages;
- may be useful in building a true "date expert."

ACKNOWLEDGEMENTS

This work has been carried out by the TAU group, funded by J.P. Getty Trust Art History Information Program, under the supervision of the Comite' International d' Histoire de l' Art (C.I.H.A.)

The data have been collected by G. Grita (University of Roma). General advice was given by O. Ferrari and S. Papaldo (ICCD, Roma).

Maps were produced by I. Campari and C. Magnarapa (CNUCE, Pisa).

References

[1] Chen, P.P.: *The Entity-Relationship Model: Toward a Unified View of Data*, ACM TODS 1, n.1, 9-36,1976

[2] Chen, P.P.: *The Entity-Relationship Model: A Basis for the Enterprise View of Data*, National Computer Conference, 77-84, 1977

[3] Date C.J.: *Defining Data Types in A Database Language*, ACM SIGMOD RECORD, Vol. 17, N. 2 (June, 1988)

[4] Papaldo S., Signore O.: *A methodological approach to producing a historical/geographical databank*, Multigrafica Editrice, Roma 1989 (ISBN 88-7597-105-6)

[5] Signore O., Campari I., Magnarapa C., Ferrari O., Grita G., Papaldo S.: *Schema di realizzazione ed elaborazione cartografica di un thesaurus Storico-geografico* CNUCE - Internal report C88-14, March 1988, Pisa

[6] Signore O., Bartoli R.: *Controlling geographic descriptions: a case study for historico-geographical authority*, International Conference on Terminology for Museums, 21-24 September 1988, Cambridge, UK

[7] Signore O., Bartoli R.: *Managing art history fuzzy dates: an application in historico-geographical authority*, Historical Social Research, Vol. 14 (1989) No. 3

[8] ISO/TC 97/SC 21/WG 3: *Information Processing Systems - Database Language SQL* ISO Standard 9075 (1989)

[9] ISO/IEC JTC 1.21.3.3: *Database Language SQL2* SC21/WG3 N745

[10] Overmyer R., Stonebraker M.: *Implementation of a Time Expert in a Data Base System* ACM SIGMOD RECORD, Vol. 12, N. 3 (April, 1982)

DEFINITION OF CIGALES[†] : A GEOGRAPHICAL INFORMATION SYSTEM QUERY LANGUAGE

Michel MAINGUENAUD

Institut National des Télécommunications
9, rue Charles Fourier
91 011 EVRY
email: MAINGUENAUD@FRINT51.BITNET

Marie-Aude PORTIER[††]

Paris VI University - Laboratoire MASI
45, avenue des Etats-Unis
78 000 VERSAILLES
email : portier@zeus.ibp.fr

Abstract

In this paper we present a graphical query language for Geographical Information System. This language is based on a graphical Query-By-Example-like (QBE) philosophy. A set of graphical primitives (icons) represent data or operations such as inclusion, intersection, etc. The user-defined query is made by composition of these icons. The application of the icons defines the query as the data are supposed to be. This graphical query is then transformed into a functional-based-language query. This expression is compiled into specific Data Management System orders or graphical operators. The main contributions of this language are its simplicity to express a query and its representative power.

Keywords : Geographic Information System, Data Manipulation Languages, User-Interface

1 - INTRODUCTION

Nowadays, Geographical Information System (GIS) need large investments in time and human resources. Various domains such as urban planning, remote sensing, military organizations, travel agencies, etc use geographical data.

A Geographical Database is a collection of two typed data : 1) spatial data (generally referenced as point, line and area) and 2) alphanumerical data (i.e. names of towns, population). To manipulate these data, GIS designers have to define a new Data Manipulation Language (DML) which can take heterogeneous data types into account. Numerous approaches were based on a SQL-like language able to deal with new operators [1]. Other approaches were based either on a logic programming language [2], on an object oriented paradigm [3] or on an algebraic approach [4]. The main drawback for these different approaches is the lack of user-friendliness. Furthermore, all these approaches, except the deductive approach, do not allow to express all kinds of geographical queries [5].

The first aim of Cigales is to increase the user-friendliness. To do so, we define a graphical language which is an easier and more natural way of manipulating geographical data. We use a

simplified data model independent from the physical representation. A graphical representation is more complex but richer than a lexical one. Our second aim is to increase the expressing power allowing to manage a great number of geographical queries.

This paper presents in section 2, the user-interface of Cigales. Section 3 defines the semantic of this language. Section 4 presents the results of queries. Section 5 describes the architecture of the system and section 6 deals with the conclusion and further works.

2 - USER INTERFACE OF CIGALES

In this section, the definition of a graphical query and the alphanumerical data associated are presented.

2.1 Definition of a graphical query

Query construction is performed by a specialized editor shown in Figure 1. This editor provides query construction facilities (mainly using pop-up menus).

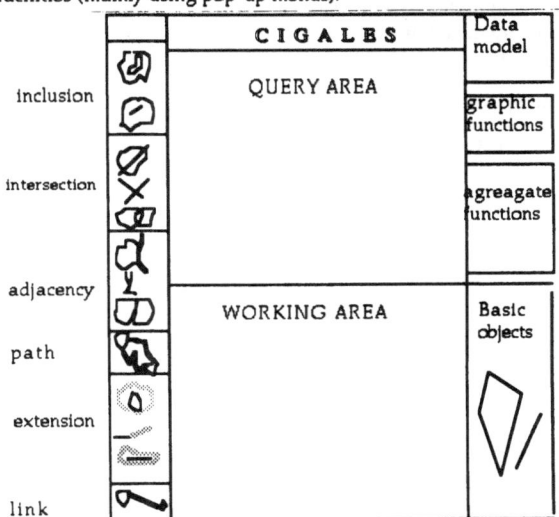

Figure 1

A set of icons representing all the available operators (inclusion, intersection, etc) is displayed. A query is a combination of different operators. We introduce the notion of

---
[†] CIGALES stands for Cartographical Interface Generating an Adapted Language for Extensible Systems.

[††] This work has been partially financed by CGI / Fleximage

current objects in order to realize these combinations. The user makes a choice of an object (either a previously-defined object or a basic object) then a choice of an operator (in case of unary operator such as extension - see section 3) or a choice of a second object and an operator to be applied to the selected objects. The rule for labelling the objects is defined in section 2.2. Two working spaces are defined : the query area and the working area. The first one contains a query at each step of its construction. Current objects will be selected in this area by the user. The second one is used to define new objects which can be combined, by application of an operator to the current objects. Aggregate functions (Min, Max, etc) can be applied to one or several objects or operators.

2.2 Definition of an alphanumerical query

An important issue of Cigales is to be independent of the physical storage of data. Therefore, alphanumerical data are modelized with an object-oriented methodology. We now only consider a classical object-oriented model relying on hierarchical concepts (simple hierarchy). A set of information is associated to each thematic object (attribute such as name and method such as length for the link operator).

An alphanumerical query is the definition of a label. A label may be defined on an object or on an operator. A label defined on an object is built from a set of information I_i of the data model for an object of type i. A label defined on an operator is built from a set of information I_j specified for this operator (or defined by the conceptor for dynamic operator such as extension). A labelling function L_i defined for each type T_i of object or operator allows to define an alphanumerical query :

$$L_i \quad : \quad T_i \quad -> \quad D1 \times ... \times Dn$$

where D_i is the domain of elements of I_i or I_j. A label can be seen as a tuple.
A label is defined as a list [s1, ... , sp] of selection criteria attached to an object or an operator. An attribute of the user-defined data model takes its value in a domain. A constant is an element of this domain. All selection criteria defined on elements are organized using a Regular Expression (R.E.). A R.E. is recursively defined as :

Manipulations of attributes :

Let a_i be an attribute of the user-defined data model
Let c be a constant of the domain of a_i
Let cp be a comparator ($<, >, \geq, \leq, =, <>$)
Let f be an aggregate function (Min, Max, ...)

Mono-valued attributes :

1) a_i cp c is a R.E.

Multi-valued attributes :

2)   Let c1, ... , cn be constants of the domain of a_i then
       a) a_i = c1,.... , cn   (c1 and c2 ...) is a R.E.
       b)   f(a_i) cp value is a R.E.

Manipulation of expressions :

3)   Let E1, E2 be R.E. then E1 $\vee$ E2 (E1 or E2) is a R.E.
4)   Let E1, E2 be R.E. then E1 $\wedge$ E2 (E1 and E2) is a R.E.
5)   Let E1 be a R.E. then $\neg$ E1 (not E1) is a R.E.
6)   Let E1 be a R.E. then $(E1)^+$ (repetition of E1) is a R.E.

The label of an operator is defined using a R.E. The semantic defined for the operators is a default multi-valued semantic (see section 3.2). Rules 1, 2, 3, 4 are defined as selection criteria in the relational model. For set-oriented operators the order of definition is not important for rule 2a. But this order is important for non-set-oriented operator. Rule 6 allows to define a connected or non-connected result for an operator. These rules can be applied either on objects or on operators.

Example :   The label defined for the object "Town of Paris" is :

Let s1 = Type and s2 = Name

Application of rule 1 :   Type = Town
Application of rule 1 :   Name = Paris

Thus the label defined for the object which symbolizes Paris is [Type = Town, Name = Paris]

In this paper we limit the presentation of Cigales to this point. We shall not present an introduction of variables and the consequences. Informally a variable is a set of homogeneous values (selected data under constraints). A variable can be seen as a set of values an attribute can take within a query.

3 -   SEMANTIC OF CIGALES

3.1 The functional langage

Many propositions concerning models for thematic maps can be found in the literature [4, 6, 7]. We will consider a subset of the operators defined in these approaches (only logical level operators). We do not consider operators such as map overlay because we are not interested here in physical data manipulation but in user defined query. The formalism is based on a functional language approach which provides composition of operators.

A basic object (O_i) is a graphical-typed object (G-type) : either a line (L) or an area (A). A point is considered as an area with a null surface. Each operator (op) is defined in a standard way :

$$op: \quad O_i \quad \times \quad O_j \quad -> \quad \{O_k\} \text{ for binary operators}$$
$$O_i \quad\quad\quad -> \quad \{O_k\} \text{ for unary operators}$$

O_i and O_j represent objects which are instanciated during query evaluation ; $\{O_k\}$, the query result, is a set of objects.
Two kinds of operators are defined from the user's point of view : Static operators rely on existing data while the dynamic operator (extension) is based on user-defined rules and existing data to compute a specific result (i.e., What is the extension of a fire initiated at 50 km of Toulon with a S-S-E force 6 wind ?). Two operators are available from the system point of view to be able to manage the notion of current object.

From the user's point of view, the operators are the inclusion, the intersection, the adjacency, the path, the link and the extension. They are defined by the following rules :

Inclusion :   C (O_1, O_2)   = O_1 if O_1 C O_2
                              = $\emptyset$ otherwise

Integrity constraint : G-type (O_1) = A => G-type (O_2) = A

Intersection : $\cap$ (O_1, O_2) = $\{O_k\}$ if there is a geometrical intersection between O1 and O2 (this intersection may or not be connected)

                              = $\emptyset$ if O_1 and O_2 do not intersect

Adjacency : $\square$ (O_1, O_2) = $\{Ok\}$ if there is a common geometrical element for O_1 and O_2 (coordinates)

= $\varnothing$ otherwise

Integrity constraint : G-type (Ok) = L

Path : -> (O_1, O_2) = $\{Ok\}$

Integrity constraint : $\cap (O_1, O_2) = \varnothing$ and G-type (Oki) = L $\wedge$
$\exists$ k1 / $O_1 \cap$ Ok1 $\neq \varnothing \wedge \exists$ k2 / $O_2 \cap$ Ok2 $\neq \varnothing$
A path is set of lines allowing to go from O_1 to O_2

Link : $\sqrt{}$ (O_1, O_2) = Ok

Integrity constraint : $O_1 \cap O_2 = \varnothing$

G-type (Ok) = L where L is a (logical) line with the minimal distance between O_1 and O_2.

Extension : ->> (O_1) = $\{Ok\}$

Integrity constraint : G-type (O_1) = A => G-type (Ok) = A

From the system's point of view the operators are the union and the difference :

Union : $\cup (O_1, O_2)$ = $\{Ok\}$ (geometrical union)

Difference : $\Delta (O_1, O_2)$ = $\{Ok\}$ (geometrical difference)

Integrity constraint : G-type (O_1) = G-type (O_2) = A

The language is enhanced with a Composition operator to construct a query. Classical relational algebra operator (selection: σ), and aggregate functions (sum, min, max, avg, count) are available to define a label. The grammar which defines a query has been developed in [5].

3.2 Semantic of operators and queries

Each geometric operation is assumed by default to give back a set of objects. Yet, an unicity constraint can be explicitly specified by the user. Figure 2 is the graphical representation of the following query (query area window) : What are the roads crossing the TGV railway between Paris and Lyon ? No unicity constraint is defined on this query. So, (1) the roads may cross the TGV railway one or more times, and (2) several roads may also cross this railway. Figure 3 represents a possible result (result area window).

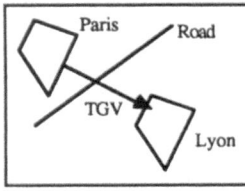 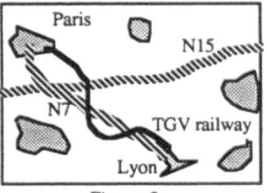

Figure 2   Figure 3

Two roads (N15 and N7) cross the TGV railway, and N7 does it several times.

Defining a semantic leads to set a default semantic. The default semantic will be the independence between two operators unless it is explicitly modified by the user. The default semantic

is supposed to be known by the user, and the possibility to modify this semantic is offered. A graphical solution is adopted to indicate the modified semantic (use of different textures, etc).

For example the following graphic (Figure 4) represents an intersection between two areas A and B, and the intersection of the path between two areas C and D and the previously defined object A :

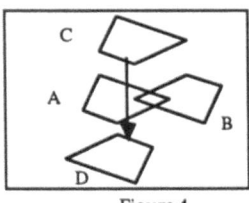

Figure 4

Two interpretations are possible :

1) intersection between the path from C to D and the object A without the intersection between A and B :

Composition ($\cap$ (A, B), $\cap$ (-> (C, D), Δ (A, B)))

2) intersection between the path from C to D and the object A (ignoring the object B) :

Composition ($\cap$ (A, B), $\cap$ (-> (C, D), A))

The default semantic is the second interpretation.

3.3 Example of queries

We now give some examples of queries translated into the functional language and their graphical representation :

Query 1 : What are the names of the towns bigger than 50 000 inhabitants of Var county ?

Composition (C (σ_{F1} (A1), σ_{F2} (A2)))

σ_{F1} : [Type = Town, Population > 50 000]
σ_{F2} : [Type = County, Name = Var]

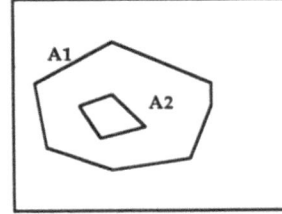

object A1:

type = county
name = Var

object A2:

type = town
pop> 50 000

Query 2 : What are the forests which distance from the town of Fougeres is less than 5 km ?

Composition (σ_{F3} ($\sqrt{}$ (σ_{F1} (A1), σ_{F2} (A2))))

σ_{F1} : [Type = Forest]
σ_{F2} : [Type = Town, Name = Fougères]
σ_{F3} : [Distance < 5 km]

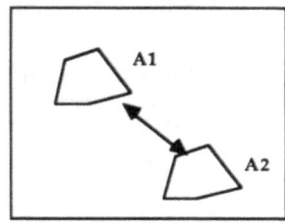

object A1 :

type = forest

object A2 :

type = town
name = Fougères

operator √   :
distance < 5 km

Query 3 :   What would be the radioactivity field if an incident happens in the St-Laurent-des-Eaux nuclear reactor ?

Composition (σ_{F2} ->> σ_{F1} (A1))

σ_{F1} :   [Type = nuclear reactor,
                 Name = St-Laurent-des-Eaux]
σ_{F2} :   [Intensity = 6 , Direction = South-west]

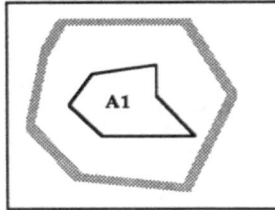

object A1 :

type= nuclear reactor
name= St-Laurent-des-Eaux

operator ->> :
parameters:
wind : intensity 6
direction : south-west

4 -   RESULTS OF A QUERY

A query result is composed of a set of objects which represent an elementary result. An elementary result is an instanciation of each object and each operator of the functional expression. These results verify the properties defined by the user and may be multi-valued (i.e. the intersection between a road and a TGV railway may or not be unique).

Consider the following query : What are the roads croosing the TGV railway between Paris and Lyon ? The graphic query is represented figure 5 :

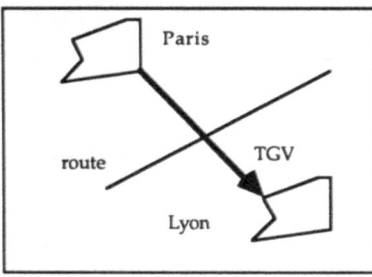

Figure 5

The result is composed of a set which contains two elements (figure 6 and 7) :

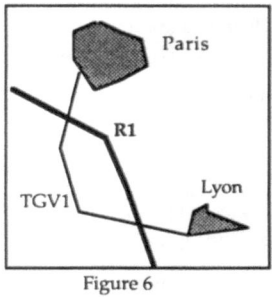

Figure 6

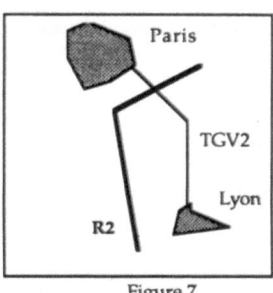

Figure 7

Several roads can cross a TGV railway, and a road may cross several times a TGV railway.

A result can be multi-valued. We explain this notion. Consider the following query represented figure 8 : What are the counties which intersect the forest of Laval ? Figure 9 and 10 give two results. The first one is a multi-valued result (composed by two areas), and the second one is mono-valued.

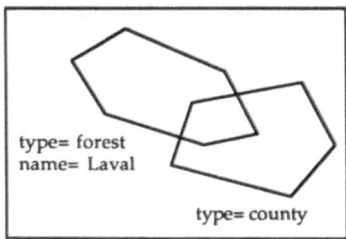

Figure 8

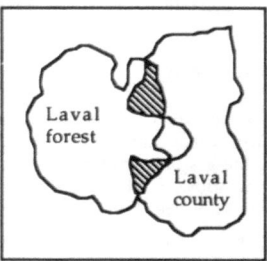

Figure 9

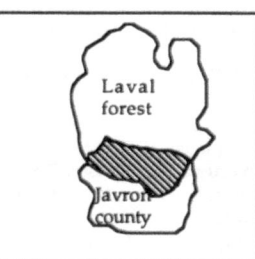

Figure 10

A query result is a set of lines and areas. This result is stored in a graphical expression.

Manipulations on a query result are made using : zoom, clipping and point location functions, but other useful functions such as : object modification, surface object measure, etc are defined.

Two possibilities are defined for the *zoom* function : (1) scale variation will increase the number of displayed information , and (2) zoom without scale variation will enlarge a particular area of the map, specified by the user (lens effect). In the second case, no acces to the database is required. The zoom function may be useful in the case of a research by *refinements*.

Clipping and point location functions allow the obtention of the characteristics of the selected objects. These functions need : (1) to take account of point location errors (by the definition of a margin of error for each object) and (2) a geometric index [8] to provide a reasonable response time.

To summarize, the user can define a Cigales query with the graphical language, specify a particular display (i.e. display in red all the main roads crossing the National Parc of Mercantour), visualize the result, zoom, etc.

5 - THE ARCHITECTURE

The introduction of new functionalities in a DBMS leads to different solutions of architecture : Extended DBMS, new DBMS or definition of a new layer on a top of a DBMS. In the first approach, new components (operators, domains, ...) are added to the system kernel [9], the second imply a complete modification of the DBMS [10] (this operation may be time consuming and costly). In the third approach, the DBMS is not modified : a layer is added at the user interface level to perform new functionalities ; the Data Manipulation Language and the external model of the DBMS are used as an entry point.

Our aim is to validate a new query language and not a complete system, so we adopt the third approach, the definition of a new layer, which is a more simple and realistic solution. In a first version, we are fully aware that our prototype will suffer from some weaknesses for the optimization (global graphical and alphanumerical optimization), but will offer a very user-friendly interface for geographical applications.
The main vocation of Cigales is to be independent of physical data management. Figure 5 represents Cigales architecture :

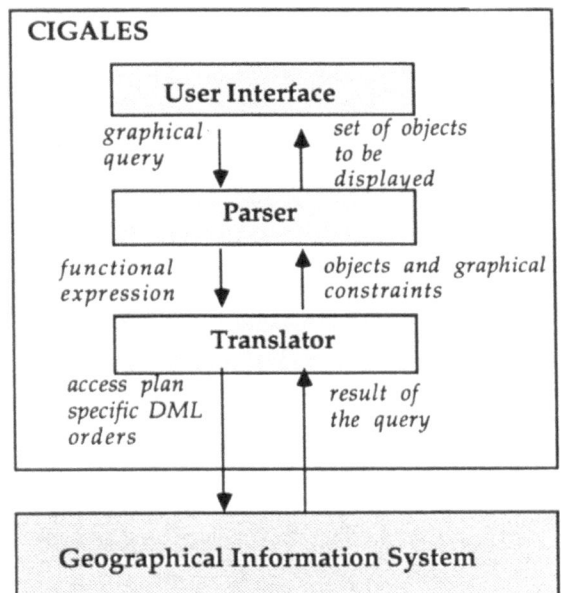

Figure 11

We now briefly describe the components involved in the architecture : the query is defined by the user with a graphical interface. The parser compiles this graphical query into a functional expression using Cigales operators ; logical optimization is performed on this expression to avoid redundancy and useless computation of expressions. The functional expression is then translated into specific DML orders according to the physical storage of data : Extended Relational Data Base System [11], Object Oriented Database [10]. The query result is transmitted by the Physical Data Management System to the

translator module, formatted into data structures associated to the logical query expression. Information about graphical display constraints defined by the user are also included in these structures. The result of the query is then transmitted to the user interface by the parser.

The main advantage of this architecture comes from the independence of the physical data management. The translator is the only module concerned with physical data storage.

A first prototype is currently under implementation on Sun workstation using an extended RDBMS [11] and a user-interface generator [12].

6 - CONCLUSION AND FURTHER WORKS

Geographical DMLs suffer from a lack of friendliness, and are too dependent of physical data representation. As relational DBMS introduced the concept of independence between physical and logical information, we need to introduce the concept of independence between logical (point, line and area) and physical (coordinates) geographical data. Abstract Data Type (ADT) is an attempt to provide this functionality. Furthermore, it seems necessary for semantic objects (town, road, etc) to be independent from their logical representation (point, line and area).

The approach we use for this new language is based on a graphical philosophy. The user defines a query with the help of a set of graphical primitives which modelize intersection, inclusion, etc. The graphical query is translated by a parser into an optimized functional expression using geometrical and classical alphanumerical operators. This functional expression is then translated into DML orders which are specific of a DBMS (extended DBMS, Object-oriented DBMS,...) in charge to manage physical data.
This architecture do not perform a global optimization of classical and geometrical operators in a first version. Our main contribution is to define and realize a graphical tool for a Geographical DBMS, independent of physical data storage.

The main advantages of Cigales are its ease-of-use and its expressive power. The ease-of-use is due to a natural approach to define a query by graphical specifications. The user defines the properties that must be verified by an object. This language is a new approach of geographical DML, and can be seen as a good complement to a language such as SQL for these applications. In further works, we will study the introduction of negation in our language and the various ways to optimize the query evaluation from the physical point of view.

REFERENCES

[1] A. Franck, MAPQUERY : Database Query Language for retrieval of geometric Data and their graphical representation, Computer Graphics, Vol 16, n° 3, July 1982

[2] E. Jungert, Inference rule in a Geographical Information System, IEEE Workshop on Language for Automation, New-Orleans, USA, November 1984

[3] JR Herring, Tigris : Topologically Integrated Geographical Information System, Proc. of the AUTOCARTO Conference, Baltimore, Maryland, USA, 29 March - 3 April 1987

280

[4] R.H. Güting, Gral : an Extensible Relational Database for Geometric Applications, Proc. of the VLDB Int. Conference, Amsterdam, The Netherlands, 22-26 August 1989

[5] M. Mainguenaud   M.A. Portier, Cigales : a Graphical Query Language for Geographical Applications, To appear : 4th International Symposium on Spatial Data Handling, Zurich, Switzerland, 23-27 July 1990

[6] B. David, Le modèle Spatiarel, 4èmes Journées Bases de Données Avancées - INRIA, Bénodet, France, 17-20 May 1987

[7] M. Scholl   A. Voisard, Thematic map modelling, Symposium on Large Spatial Data Bases, Santa-Barbara, USA, July 1989

[8] A. Guttman, R-Tree : A Dynamic Index Structure for Spatial Searching, Proc. of the ACM SIGMOD Conference, Boston, USA, 1-3 June 1984

[9] L. Rowe   M. Stonebraker, The Design of Postgres, Proc. of the ACM SIGMOD Conference, Washington, USA, 26-30 May 1986

[10] F.Bancilhon, G.Barbedette, V.Benzaken, C.Delobel, S.Gamerman, C.Lecluse, P.Pfeffer, P.Richard, F.Velez, The Design and Implementation of O_2, an Object Oriented Database System, Proc. of the OODBS II Workshop, Bad-Munster, FRG, September 1988

[11] G.Gardarin, M.Jean-Noël, B.Kerherve, F.Pasquer, D.Pastre, E.Simon, P.Valduriez, L.Verlaine, Y.Viemont : Sabrina * : a Relational Database System developed in a research environment, TSI, Vol 6, n° 3, 1987

[12] Aida : User's Guide

EXPERT SYSTEM AND DATABASE INTERACTION IN THE LEGAL DOMAIN

Rosa M. Di Giorgi, Elio Fameli, Roberta Nannucci

Istituto per la documentazione giuridica del Consiglio Nazionale delle Ricerche

Summary:

1. Project Objectives and General Features - 2. System Interaction: The Relational Database - 3. Database Documentary Coverage - 4. Database Management - References.

1. Project Objectives and General Features

It is sometimes necessary for expert system users to directly access documentation during a search, both to verify the outcome of the search and to have material at their disposal which can be used later according to their needs.

It, therefore, seems very useful to enrich expert system potentialities, permitting the different user groups to have access to documentation through interfaces which, starting off from the expert system, allow information stored in remote data banks or data banks constructed ad hoc and installed in the same tool in which the E.S. runs to be retrieved.

The possibility of fusing "documentation" and "decision" to create a unique, complex tool with logical structures capable of making use of data stored in external databases, and to interact suitably with them, is therefore of fundamental importance for building expert systems in specific domains.

It is in this context that the Istituto per la documentazione giuridica of the Italian National Research Council in Florence has undertaken to build an expert system in the field of the legal protection of the environment linked with a database.

The system, called ELP (Environmental Legal Protection) Advisor comprises, besides national and/or regional legislation and regulations (laws, decrees, Ministerial circulars), the necessary references to legal authority, case law and international law (EEC directives and regulations, agreements, conventions, treaties).

Choice of this particular application domain was based, on the one hand, on the importance vested in environmental problems in recent years and, on the other, on the decisive role of information technology as an instrument for the information dissemination and for natural resources management.

Organizing environmental legislation in a complete and comprehensive fashion appears to be more than simply useful, since legislation in the field generally covers only sectorial aspects giving rise to a muddled and fragmentary corpus which, in light of current importance of environmental questions, lacks an adequate general framework.

Environmental protection measures will therefore become more effective as the ease with which complete information may be accessed increases; not only on the legal level (from collection of the sources of law to legal authority and case law) but also on a more strictly technical level, enabling initiatives to have a solid scientific basis.

Appropriate and intelligent use of informatics would not only allow the legal professional to rapidly obtain information on what law to apply in his specific instance, but would also permit him to familiarize himself more easily with the different approaches taken in legal authority to his subject and with the different solutions adopted in cases analogous to his. All this would contribute to raising the quality of public intervention and to giving the discipline a more organized framework.

The present application of the ELP Advisor is the result of an exploratory study conducted on the scope of existing Italian laws on the protection of assets of outstanding natural beauty.

For this experimentation, a shell which, for its logical characteristics and considerable user friendliness, seemed particularly suitable for application to the legal domain, was chosen. It is a product expressly designed for use in expert system building. Written in the C programming language and possessing a structure capable of representing specialized knowledge in a manner easily accessible to even non-computer users, it is a general-purpose, domain-independent tool, and its structure is based on production rules, which are later processed by the inference engine, using a forward-chaining strategy. It runs on personal computers.

The present level of development of the ELP Advisor application (see Table 1) allows the expert system to be linked to a relational database which stores documents relating to legislation, case law and legal authority considered useful for hose users who want a more exact framework of the domain covered by the expert system.

A specially built interface allows direct access to documents in the database activating the link-up with keywords or with a thesaurus of terms pertinent to the expert system domain and with a specific classification table.

A special procedure allowing the documents retrieved in the database to be printed out is also planned. The documents can be printed either in data-profile form (cards containing the important data in each document) or in their complete form (full text).

Another option of the system provides a series of standard forms (petitions, appeals, etc.) which may be useful to those users who, after completing their search of the expert system, decide to use them as a basis for some kind of action against the Public Administration.

The final system architecture (see Table 2) plans to link the expert system up to other expert systems. These include advisory systems which cover pertinent domains, expert systems for intelligent information retrieval which are, in turn, linked to national and international legal or technical data banks, expert systems to assist in the drafting of legal acts or in the compilation of the forms it makes available to the user at the end of a search.

In this perspective, the portability of the packages on which the various expert systems and local databases are implemented becomes very important.

2. System Interaction: The Relational Database

The choice of linking a relational kind of DBMS to the expert system appeared advisable for several reasons.

Relational DBMS consider each database as a set of data tables or units, virtually independently of the data's physical organization. This feature makes the system very transparent in as far as the way data is accessed remains hidden from the user, who comes into contact with the data directly and in a much more simplified manner, as compared with other types of DBMS (hierarchical or reticular). The data is structured in bidimensional tables (R-tables) and the user formulates his queries on the basis of a simple understanding of the three main coordinates: the name of the table, the line and the column.

The tool employed here (Oracle 5.1B) is one of the first RDBMS packages to have used SQL (Structured Query Language). It is made up of a series of modules which by completing the commands offered by the SQL engine contained in the system core (SQL*Plus), make the package suitable for developing this particular application.

From the technical point of view, one of the main aims of the ELP Advisor project was that of "link-up capacity", that is, the ability to access databases stored in other machines from any microcomputer or workstation (through a local network) using only one tool and with the same interface. ORACLE satisfies this need through its SQL*NET module which, through special protocols, permits the user to link his computer to either a local or distributed network.

The step is taken towards a distributed processing environment, with the possibility of linking up to more than one database at the same time localized in different nodes of the network, through procedures which are transparent for the end user. This becomes extremely important if we consider the numerous difficulties that information system users meet in acquiring an overall view of the patrimony of information available.

3. Database Documentary Coverage

The documents which constitute the ORACLE database in the ELP Advisor application, have been subdivided into several tables storing, respectively, the strings referring to subject matter of different kinds (legislation, case law, legal authority).

Each documentary unit has been given a significative title and contains a series of keywords, apart from the name of the word processing file with the full text of the documents. The texts, written with any WP system - in our case WORDSTAR was used - can be transferred in ASCII to guarantee their portability from one operating system to another. As a future development in the system, we are, in fact, planning to add, transfer and search data between different hardware tools (PCs, workstations and mainframes).

The documents in the legislation file are made up of single sections of laws, decrees, regulations and circulars; those in the case law file, of "massime" (summaries of the cases) and decisions; and those in the legal authority file of bibliographical references also containing an abstract. The available typology of documents is very articulated. Various categories have been identified for the legislation file. For international legislation these include: agreements, conventions and treaties; for Community legislation: directives, regulations, agreements, treaties and conventions; for national legislation: laws, decrees, regulations and ministerial circulars; for the national legislation of other States: laws, decrees and regulations.

The decisions of the European Court of Justice, the Italian Constitutional Court, the Council of State, the Court of Cassation, the courts of first instance and the Regional Administrative Courts have been taken into consideration for the case law file.

Finally, the legal authority file is made up of documents which contain the bibliographical details relating to articles and papers taken from journals, books, miscellaneous works and grey literature.

Document management varies according to whether the user has a password - in which case he is given the possibility of adding, changing, searching or cancelling data - or not - in which case he can only have access for consulting the data.

Once the pertinent document has been identified, a functional key in ORACLE permits the user to pass from the reference file to the file storing the full text of the document. This passage requires two different access ways: through using a word processor, for users with a password, or through a simple display function, for those without a password.

4. Data Management

The database management is divided into various phases:

Data Acquisition. A special module manages the acquisition phase of that data which constitutes the document profile. The relative file is organized in documentary units with the following fields:

- the name of the text/file (name given to the file containing the document in full text);
- the documentary typology (L = legislation, G = case law, D = legal authority, with additional letters for the various document classes);
- the title of the document (significative title given to the document);
- the keywords (important words which identify the document).

The various key functions allow the user to move about in the document and to shift from one document to another, to return to the main menu once the data has been added, to display the available help keys, to insert or delete a new documentary unit, to duplicate records from one unit in another, to confirm a group of operations, to display the corresponding full text, to delete fields and records, and to obtain a list of available units.

Document Typology Table Management. After the typology of the legal documents has been identified (as far as legislation, case law and legal authority are concerned), a table has been designed to assist in giving the right letter corresponding to each document in the data acquisition phase.

The table is managed through a series of functional keys which enable all the operations relating to adding, deleting or displaying data to be performed within it, as well as search functions for obtaining value lists. Querying the Data Files. The function which permits the files to be queried in conjunction with the expert system is the core of the ELP Advisor application. Once the user has decided on the topic he wishes to examine by utilizing the documentation in the database, this function takes the step from the expert system to the database until finally displaying the full text of the document.

Thanks to the SQL language, the user can formulate his queries in a reasonably free form without resorting to the special codes commonly required by traditional query languages; the documents are retrieved on the basis of the words found in the fields relating to the title and keywords. At this point, therefore, the thesaurus, classification table and semantic network functions may be inserted. The thesaurus management system is only activated at the user's request.

The utility of being able to rely on a well-defined semantic structure which enables the search to be expanded to additional syntagma or to limit it only to one or more relations between them (BT, RT, NT) is

evident. It is obvious that the more complete the thesaurus is in relation to the topic about which the query is made in the expert system, the better the results will be. Each syntagm appears on the screen with the network of its relations. Not only are the documents indexed with chosen syntagma automatically identified, but also those containing other syntagma which appear in that particular semantic structure. This option means that the search is wider than is often useful and sometimes it can result in a certain redundancy making subsequent searches necessary.

The classification table management system, also only activated at the user's request, operates similarly to that described earlier. The search is begun on the basis of the significant terms or syntagma identified by the user contained in the various headings and subheadings of the classification table. Also in this case, all the documents classified under those headings of the classification table which contain the original term or syntagm are retrieved.

The semantic network, instead, is used for organizing those concepts requiring a procedural approach. By using the various system functions (free searching by keyword, thesaurus, classification table and semantic network) more effective results can be obtained and wider and richer information. Printing the Documents and Standard Forms. By starting off from the list made up of the profiles (typology, significant title, key words, name of the text file) of the documents retrieved in the database, the user can display the full text of the document (sections of laws, summaries of cases or abstracts of legal authority) and then return to the expert system at the point where he started his search in the database.

Whenever the suggestion is made to the user, during the search, to use a standard form, the system sees to printing the form chosen for his particular needs. The user only has to fill out the sections relating to his personal data and then, eventually, send it to the Public Administration.

Table 1 - Expert System Database Interaction

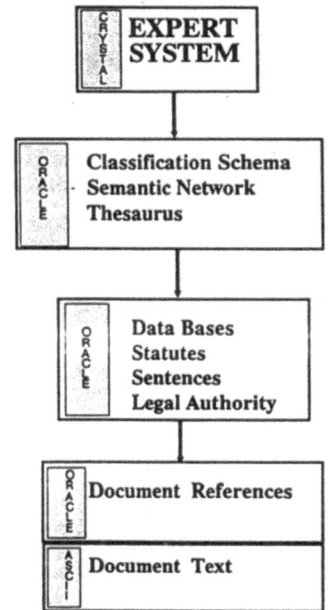

Table 2 - System Architecture

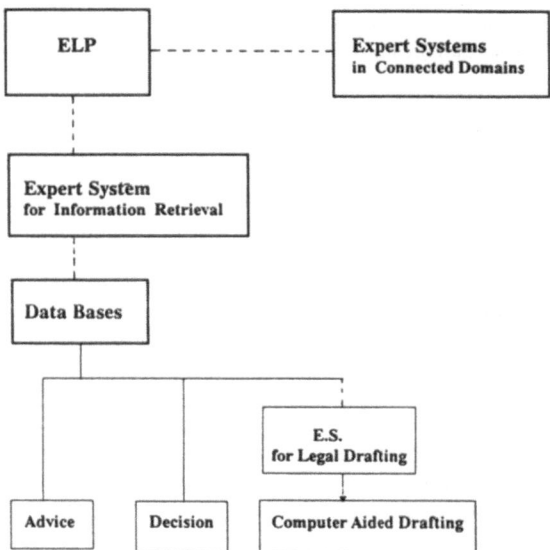

REFERENCES

ADDIS T.R., Expert Systems: An Evolution in Information Retrieval, in "Information Technology: Research and Development", 1982, 1(4), pp. 301-324.

ASLIB (ed.), Informatics 8: Advances in Intelligent Retrieval, "Proceedings of a Conference Jointly Sponsored by Aslib, the Aslib Informatics Group, and the Information Retrieval Specialist Group of the British Computer Society", 1985 April 16-17, Oxford (England), Aslib, 1985, 314 pp.

BELKIN N.J., CROFT W. Bruce, Retrieval Techniques, in Williams Martha E. (ed.), Annual Review of Information Science and Technology, Vol. 22, Amsterdam (The Netherlands), Elsevier Science Publishers B.V. for the American Society for Information Science, 1987.

BELKIN N.J., VICKERY ALINA, Interaction in Information Systems: A Review of Research from Document Retrieval to Knowledge-Based Systems, London, England: British Library, 1985, 250 pp. (Library and Information Research Report 35).

BELL D.A., An Architecture for Integrating Data, Knowledge, and Information Bases, vedi ASLIB (ed.), pp. 240-257.

BRODIE Michael L., MYLOPOULOS John (eds.), On Knowledge Base Management Systems: Integrating Artificial Intelligence and Database Technologies, New York (NY), Springer-Verlag, 1986, 660 pp.

BROOKS H.M., DANIELS P.J., BELKIN N.J., Problem Descriptions and User Models: Developing an Intelligent Interface for Document Retrieval Systems. Advances in Intelligent Interface for Document Retrieval Systems. Advances in Intellinget Retrieval, in "Proceedings of Informatics - 8", London, Aslib, 1985, pp. 191- 214.

DANIELS P.J., The User Modelling Function of an Intelligent Interfaces for Document Retrieval Systems, in "Proceedings of Sixth International Research Forum in Information Science (IRFIS 6): Intelligent Information Systems for the Information Society", 1985 September 16-18, Frascati (Italy), Amsterdam, North Holland, 1986, pp. 162-176.

EVENS M., VANDERDORPE J., WANG Y.C., Lexical Semantic Relations in Information Retrieval, in William S. (ed.), Humans and Machines: the Interface through Language, Norwood (NJ), Ablex, 1985, pp. 73-100.

SALTON G., Recent Trends in Automatic Information Retrieval, in "Proceedings of the 1986 ACM SIGIR Conference on Research and Development in Information Retrieval", 1986 September 8-10, Pisa (Italy), New York, ACM, 1986, pp. 1-10.

SALTON G., MCGILL M.J., Introduction to Modern Information Retrieval, New York, McGraw-Hill, 1983.

SPARCK JONES K., Natural Language Interfaces for Expert Systems: An Introductory Note, in "Research and Development in Expert Systems: Proceedings of the Fourth Technical Conference of the BCS Specialist Group on Expert Systems", 1984 18-20 December, Warwick (England), Cambridge (England), Cambridge University Press, 1985, pp. 85-94.

VAN RIJSBERGEN C.J., A New Theoretical Framework for Information Retrieval, in "Proceedings of the 1986 Annual International ACN SIGIR Conference on Research and Development in Information Retrieval", 1986 September, Pisa (Italy), New York, ACM, 1986, pp. 194-200.

WILKINSON Julia, Database in Artificial Intelligence, in "Online Review", 1986 October, 10(5), pp. 307-315.

WILLIAMS M.E., Transparent Information Systems through Gateways, Front Ends, Intermediaries, and Interfaces, in "Journal of the american Society for Information Science", 1986 July, 37(4), pp. 204-214.

WILLIAMS M.E., KINNUCAN M., SMITH L.C., LANNOM L., CHO D., Comparative Analysis of Online Retrieval Interfaces, in "Proceedings of the Forty-Ninth Annual Meeting of the American Society for Information Science", 1986 September 28 - October 2, Chicago (IL), Medford (NJ), Learned Information, 1986, pp. 365- 370.

A SIMPLE INTELLIGENT INTERFACE TO DATA BASES ON ENVIRONMENTAL LAW

P. Guidotti*, L. Lucchesi**, P. Mariani*, M. Ragona*, D. Tiscornia*

*Istituto per la Documentazione Giuridica del CNR   **Systems & Managements s.p.a.
Via Panciatichi 56/16, Florence (Italy)   Vicolo S. Pierino 2, Pisa (Italy)

ABSTRACT

This article features some solutions adopted to develop an interface to data bases on environmental law which adopts string search methods. Emphasis is placed on the structure of the semantic network used for knowledge representation of the domain and an explanation is given of its use.

INTRODUCTION

Interest in problems related to ecology and, more generally, to the "environment" has been growing in our society in recent years. These issue have also become very important within the panorama of legal science: there have been numerous legal studies on the environment and it is now possible to talk about "environmental law".

Although those involved in this field are interested in being able to have rapid and easy access to environmental law documentation, the situation regarding information retrieval systems in this sector in Italy cannot be considered satisfactory. Whilst, in fact, many data banks exist with an enormous overall total number of documents on-line, such as those for example in the data banks of Italgiure system, environmental law information is currently spread throughout many different data banks and is almost always organized under the classifications found in standard legal sources (national legislation, regional legislation, civil "massime" (summary of the principles in a case) of the Italian Corte di Cassazione, criminal "massime" of the Cassazione, etc.), held at different documentation centres (Italgiure, Celex, IUCN, etc.).

The difficulty is not, therefore, related to the lack of information but rather to being able to have easy access to it. The user who wishes to obtain information by on-line searching faces the following problems:
- the proliferation of data banks,
- the structural differences in the individual data banks (full text or only reference data banks),
- the absence of standardization in link-up procedures,
- the diversity of query languages,
- the muliplicity of conceptual retrieval tools (thesauri, classifications, etc.).

The purpose of our research, supported by Environment Committee of Italian CNR, is to build a system which facilitates user/computer interaction during the search of environmental data banks, thereby overcoming the problems discussed above. It should, therefore, give the user the possibility of searching the documents stored in different data banks in a logically uniform way and it should aid him in formulating his query and search strategy.

Although there are various expert systems implemented for I.R. described in recent publications [1-8], there are no such applications in the legal field. In this field many papers [9-11] stress that conceptual retrieval techniques must be used in the legal area if an efficacious selection of documents, by using their semantic content, is to be made. It goes without saying that the documents must be interpreted if they are to be given a semantic representation which can be employed by these search techniques. In our case, as it is not feasible to modify the structure or the classification of the documents, which are already largely stored in existing data banks, we are forced to use the string search method found in on-line systems.

We will illustrate the main features of the system in this paper and will, therefore, pay special attention to the A.I. technology utilized for permitting the user to search for documents according to their domain, while retaining the string search structure under which they are stored.

FUNCTIONALITY AND STRUCTURE OF THE SYSTEM

In order to define the required functions of the system, it is useful to analyze the task carried out by a human intermediary who helps the user satisfy his information needs. In brief, he carries out the following tasks:
a) he understands the user's request: he talks to the user until

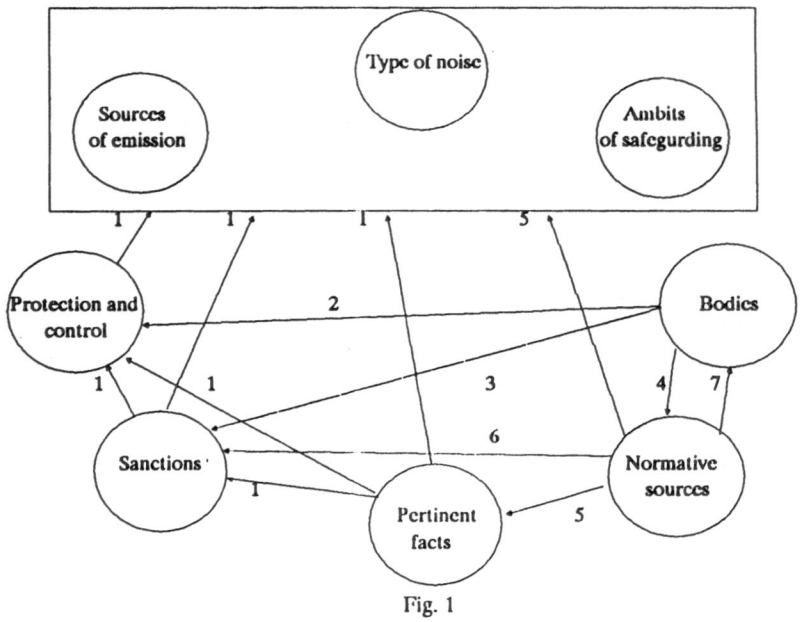

1 relating to
2 competent
3 inflicting
4 delegating
5 identifying
6 providing for
7 enacting

Fig. 1

he eliminates any ambiguity in the request;
b) he translates the user's request into the formal data base query language and defines a search strategy;
c) he analyses the results.

The proposed system, called CABALA (Consultazione Assistita di Basi Dati di Leggi Ambientali) has four main features which enable it to perform some parts of the previously listed tasks:
- navigation on a semantic network,
- management of the dialogue with the user,
- construction of the query,
- definition of the search strategy.
Its main aim is to display the conceptual structure of the data base described by a semantic network, and to assist and guide the user in navigating it so that he can formulate his queries properly. The query is then translated into a suitable form for the specific information retrieval system involved.

CABALA can be divided into three main logically independent parts which communicate amongst themselves only by exchanging messages:
- Query Generator,
- Data Base Query Manager,
- Data Bases.
In this paper, we are only going to take into consideration the Query Generator, currently the only part under development.

The objective of the Query Generator is to enable the user, regardless of his experience in the domain, to easily formulate a valid query from both the legal and common sense points of view. Once the user has formulated his query, this is translated into an intermediate language and both its correctness and efficacy are evaluated. The Query Generator is, therefore, subdivided into three modules:
- the Navigator,
- the Query Constructor,
- the Query Evaluator.

The three modules act simultaneously, supplying, during any step, the query equivalent to the specifications supplied by the user and its evaluation. This enables the user to immediately check the work done during the search session. This operational procedure is achieved through a blackboard-like architecture.

DOMAIN KNOWLEDGE FORMALIZATION

The basic criterion used for the choise of the domain knowledge formalization is the facility to codify due the width of the filed taken in consideration. In our system deep models are not necessary as for the advisory systems in fact more complex formalisms such as production rules have been rejected, and a semantic network as the representation framework has been adopted.

In pratice a thesaurus has been created by extracting a series of significant terms from legal texts, representing the nodes in the network. The choice has also been suggested by the fact that another equipe at IDG was already working on the classification of environmental law. Anyhow the relations, which we use, are semantically enriched whereby we prefere to consider it a semantic network. The first relation defined between the terms is the Broader Term relation (BT); which is transitive. The BT relation lays down hierarchies (trees) among terms, each belonging to a specific argument that arises in the definition of the hypothetical case or defines legal aspects pertaining to the domain. In the field of noise pollution, the subdomain chosen for building the prototype, the identified BT hierarchies are illustrated in Fig. 1. In fact, these hierarchies constitute a classification of the conceptual domain stored in the databases below mentioned.

It must be noted that the BT hierarchies point out the basic concepts that make up the query. Then the hierarchies, representing the nodes of a graph, may be linked by oriented arcs, identifying the relations existing between them. Fig. 1 illustrates the hierarchies graph (HG graph) related to noise pollution. Through the HG graph it is possible to capture the semantic of the user's queries. Let us suppose that the user selects terms in more than one hierarchy: the path on the HG graph that links the hierarchies univocally identify the query. For example, on the basis of the terms used and on the relations between hierarchies, it is easy to capture the meaning of the following questions:

- Which judicial bodies are competent to control and prevent noise pollution?

- Has the judge the power to verify the tolerance level of the noise?

We use another class of relations to codify knowledge resulting from a partial interpretation of the norms and from the case law found in the data bases. We call a relation of this class a Related Term (RT) because it is used by the Query Constructor as it was symmetric and transitive, but all RT relations between terms of two hierarchies take the name and the direction of the relation between the hierarchies on the HG graph. An example of this type of knowledge is:
in the case of noise pollution, only fines and arrests can be inflicted as sanctions by the judge.

Moreover, this relation enables the representation of general knowledge on law and legal authority of the type:
the ordinary courts inflict criminal sanctions,
the administrative bodies inflict administrative sanctions.

These examples underline two meanings of the RT relation. The former is only valid according to the context of the case in question: in the case of noise pollution the sanction is inflicted by the judge. In the present state of our research, the context is represented by the type of pollution. Let us, therefore, consider RT relations as being divided into two groups:

- primaries: validity is independent of the context,
- secondaries: validity depends on the context.

As an example of the knowledge which can be extracted and formalized in this way, see Fig. 2 in which some parts of the hierarchies relating to the Bodies and Normative Sources are represented according to the RT relations existing between them.

USE OF THE SEMANTIC NETWORK

The semantic network is utilized by both the Navigator and the Query Constructor.

The Navigator allows the conceptual structure of the documents stored in the data base to be visited: the user specifies his query from the menu in which he selects some pre-defined terms (items). The menus are derived from the hierarchies defined by the BT relation, which means that specifying the query is the same as selecting nodes in those hierarchies.

In this way, the set of hierarchical nodes performs the role of the system's vocabulary. This considerably simplifies the user-system interaction: the system, in fact, never has to analyze an unknown term as may occur by freely interacting in natural language. The method which is adopted, however, leaves it up to the user to express his query in the terms of the system's vocabulary. This is counterbalanced by the fact that being hierarchically organized terms, the user is offered a classification table of the domain which acts as a map of the conceptual structure of the data base. We left the user the possibility to select the hierarchies without any predefined order informing him, however, about the hierarchies correlated to the selected one.

The RT relation is utilized by the Navigator for displaying the related terms and for guiding the user in formulating his query.

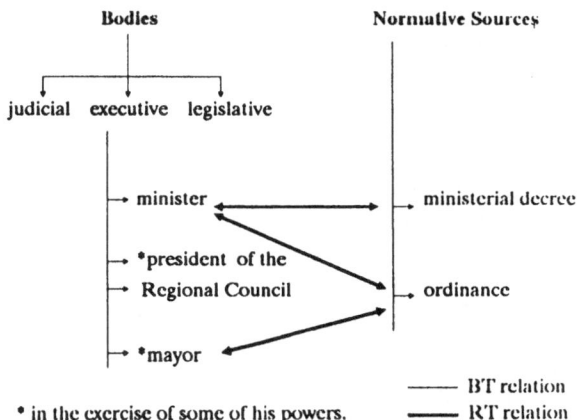

Fig. 2

It should, also, be noted that additional information is given by the absence of a RT relation between two selected terms. In fact, if two terms belong to hierarchies having RT relations but they are not linked by a RT relation or do not belong to sub-trees whose roots are linked by RT arcs, an error in the selection can be assumed and the user can, therefore, be informed about it. This is the case, for example, where the user selects "mayor" and "ministerial decree", see Fig. 2.

In the Evaluator implementation, we thought that it was more suitable to use simple heuristic criteria like those generally followed in developing the system, which can be set up in an easier way than statistical models. The latter are more reliable but more complex and need a large amount of data.

The Evaluator, as said above, has the task of verifing the validity and the efficiency of the query. Therefore, the first thing that the Evaluator has to do is to verify whether it is possible to find a path linking the selected hierarchies on the IIG graph, if not the Evaluator suggests how to complete the path. Anyhow, it is always possible to force the system to process the query.

It's more difficult to evaluate the query's possibility of success with our model. Particularly, we think it is very difficult to evaluate query precision, a standard which measures the intermediary's capacity to reject non pertinent documents. Anyhow it is easier to evaluate query recall, a standard used to measure the intermediary's capacity to retrieve all documents pertinent to the query. For example, the documentation on noise pollution is poor and fragmented, therefore very specific queries may not have any answer.

We can use the deepness of the selected terms from the hierarchy's roots as a measure of the specificity of the query. Since the various types of normative action and the bodies competent to carry them out are common to all sector of environmental law, the most significant elements seem to be those related to areas where regulations are applied, i.e. Sources of Emission, Types of Noise, Ambits for Safeguarding. Therefore it is natural to allow more specificity in the selection of terms for these hierarchies than for the others.

To accomplish this, we assign a weight to each hierarchy, which multiplied by the deepness of its selected terms, gives a number that we use to find a pounded measure of the specificity. The sum of the numbers calculated for each selected hierarchy must be lower than a fixed number.

The Query Constructor accepts the selection about the hierarchies made by the user and transforms it into a query for the textual data base.

Let us analyze a series of examples of the method for constructing a query of the following kind:

give me all the documents which contain <expr>,

where *<expr>* represents the set of terms generated by the Constructor starting off from the selection made by the user.

Let us assume that we have one hypothetical textual data base in which the query language represents the system's intermediary language.

In order to understand the use of the BT relation, let us consider the case where only one node in the hierarchy has been selected. There are two alternatives: either the node is a leaf or the node has children.

In the former case, the node represents itself and is picked up immediately. In the latter case, we will use all the sub-tree which has the node selected as its root in the query construction. Let us call N the set of nodes we obtain by visiting the tree of the root n.

If the user selects the nodes n_1 and n_2, with the same sub-trees N_1 and N_2, in the same hierarchy, the set M of terms used for constructing the query is reached by uniting N_1 and N_2. The elements of the set M, linked by the logical operator *or*, form a term of *<expr>* relating to the activated hierarchy; it is equivalent to the following query:

give me all the documents which contain one or more elements of M.

The terms generated by the sets $M_1, . . , M_n$, belonging to different hierarchies, are linked through the logical operator *and* ; that is equivalent to the following sentence:

give me all the documents which contain
one or more elements of M_1

....

one or more elements of M_n

The RT relation is, instead, utilized by the system for completing and making the query formulated by the user more exact. In order to understand it, let us look at the parts of the hierarchies illustrated in Fig. 2, relating to the Bodies involved and to Normative sources.

Let us assume that the user has selected the node "minister" in the hierarchy relating to Bodies, which we can, therefore, say has been activated. The information given by the RT arcs is that the minister issues ordinances and ministerial decrees. In order to broaden the system's retrieval capacity, we can include the terms "ordinance" or "ministerial decree" in the query; this improves the system's recall. The risk is, however, to retrieve a large number of non pertinent documents, for example, those relative to mayoral ordinances: it is, therefore, necessary to exclude documents in which the terms "ordinance" and "mayor" appear; this increases the system's precision.

Finally, let us consider the case where a RT arc links a selected term to another term belonging to an activated hierarchy. In this case we cannot utilize the latter term because we distort the user's intention. Let us, in fact, assume that the user has selected the terms "minister" and "ordinance" in the two hierarchies represented in Fig. 2 or, in other words, that he has requested documents where both "minister" and "ordinance" appear. It is, obviously, wrong to add the term "ministerial decree" to the query, in this case. Therefore, the more hierarchies activated by the user the less the system will use the RT arcs, which will be completely unutilized, in the query construction, if the user has selected a node for every hierarchy.

ALGORITHM OF THE QUERY CONSTRUCTOR

We can define the algorithm for the Query Constructor in a final summary which utilizes both types of knowledge simultaneously. Firstly, let us formalize the construction of the term related to an activated hierarchy.

Let $n_1 ... , n_m$ be the nodes selected in the k-th BT hierarchy and $N_1 ... , N_m$ be their respective sub-trees. We presume:

$$M_k = \bigcup_{l=1}^{m} N_l$$

Let $[f_1,...,f_n]$ be terms, belonging to non activated hierarchies, obtained from the nodes in M_k following the RT arcs and let $[b_{i1},...,b_{1h}]$ be terms related through the RT relation to f_i so that every $b_{ij} \notin M$. Let us indicate by F_i the sub-tree of f_1 and by B_{ij} the sub-tree of b_{ij} so that $B_{ij} \cap M_k = 0$. Let us assume $B_i = B_{i1} \cup B_{i2} ... \cup B_{ih}$ and let us construct the term B_1 of $<expr>$ by linking the elements of the set through the *or* operator. We will recursively construct the term:

$$A_k = F_1 \ and\text{-}not \ B_1 \ or \ldots or \ F_n \ and\text{-}not \ B_n.$$

where F_1 is obtained by applying the procedure we have just seen for M_k to each F_i and setting activated the hierarchy of F_i. Let be

$$T_k = M_k \ or \ A_k,$$

where M_k is the term obtained by linking the elements of M_k through the *or* operator.

For each M_k we will construct the related term T_k, as explained. The query will be:

give me all the documents which contain $<T1$ and $T2$ and $\ldots$ and $Tz>$.

The conceptual Query Constructor's algorithm is, therefore, completely specified.

CONCLUSION

One of the most important aspects in definig a knowledge-based interface to retrieval systems is to decide the level of "deepness" at which knowledge must be represented. This means identifying all the concepts for ensuring the completeness of the retrieval which are necessary and sufficent in order to avoid transforming the system into a decision-support system the semantic network has, in this sense, the advantage of providing a great deal of elasticity in definig the deepness level.

The functions of the evaluator can undergo further developments. Particularly we think that the comprehension of the query by the evaluator can furtherly be used allowing a dialogue with the user. Such situation till now is not provided. We also plan to use the HG graph in the Query Constructor in order to improve the query's precision.

At present, a CABALA prototype, including the functions of the Query Generator described here, is being implemented. The tool used to implement it is Epsilon, an expert system shell based on Prolog, which enables a partition of the knowledge into various modules, each with its own deduction mechanism [14-15].

REFERENCES

[1] Anderson R.H., Gillogly J.J., *Rand Intelligent Terminal Agent (RITA): Design Philosophy*, Rand Report n. R - 1809 ARPA 1976

[2] Bennet J.S., Englemore R.S., *SACON: A Knowledge-based Consultant for Structural Analysis*, in: Proceedings of 6th International Joint Conference on Artificial Intelligence, Tokyo - Japan, pp. 47-49, 1979

[3] Marcus R.S., Reintjes J.F., *A Translating Computer Interface for End-user Operation of Heterogeneous Retrieval Systems: Design*, Journal of the American Society for Information Science 32, 4, pp. 287-303, 1981

[4] Meadow C.T., Hewett T.T. e Avesa E.S., *A Computer Intermediary for Interactive Database Searching: Design*, Journal of the American Society for Information Science 32, 5, pp. 323-332, 1982

[5] Vickery A., *An Intelligent Interface for Online Interaction*, Journal of Information 9, pp. 7-18

[6] Tong R., Askman V. e Cunningham L., *RUBRIC: An Artificial Intelligent Approach to Information Retrieval*, Proceeding 1st International Workshop on Expert Database Systems, 1984

[7] Ceri S., Gottlob G., Tanca L., *Logic Programming and Databases*, Atti della Giornata di Studio "Evoluzioni dei sistemi per basi di dati e di conoscenza", AICA, Milano, 1988, pp. 3-24

[8] Zarri G.P., *Conceptual Representation for Knowledge Bases and 'Intelligent' Information Retrieval Systems*, Proceedings of the Eleventh International ACM Conference on Research and Development in Information Retrieval, Presses Universitaires (PUG), Grenoble, 1988

[9] Hafner C.D., *Conceptual Organization of Case Law Knowledge Bases*, Proceedings of 1st International Conference on Artificial Intelligence and Law, Boston, May 1987, pp. 35-42

[10] Hafner C.D., *An Information Retrieval System Based on a Computer Model of Legal Knowledge*, Ann Arbor, UMI Research Press, 1981

[11] Bing J., *Designing Text Retrieval Systems for 'Conceptual Searching'*, Proceedings of the 1st International Conference on Artificial Intelligence and Law, Boston, May 1987, pp. 43-51

[12] Brajnik G., Guida G., Tasso C., *User Modeling in Intelligent Information Retrieval*, in "Information Processing & Management", Vol. 23, 1987, No. 4, pp. 305-320

[13] Rabitti F. (ed.), *Research and Development in Information Retrieval*, Proceedings of the ACM Conference, Pisa, 1986, 249 pp.

[14] Coscia P.,Djennaoui S., Franceschi P.,Kouloumdjian J.,Levi G., Lei L.,Moll G-H.,de San Victor I.,Sardu G.,Simonelli C., Torre L., *The Epsilon Knowledge Base Management System: Architecture and Data Base Access Optimization*, Worshop on Logic Programming, Venice, August, 1988

[15] Mariani P., Ragona M., Tiscornia D., *An Intelligent Information Retrieval System for Environmental Law*, Proceedings of the International Conference "Expert Systems in Law", Bologna, 3-5 May, 1989

The prototype work payment claim (ARPO), as the first step towards the construction of an aid program for legal decisions.

F. Galindo   E. Albertos

Seminario de Informática y Derecho
Universidad de Zaragoza
50009 Zaragoza (Spain)

ABSTRACT

The explanation of the knowledge used by professionals as the jurists, not accustomed to use formal languages, makes necessary to develop estrategies for capturing and storing these knowledge by computers. This action needs eventuality the work in special programs using standard resources. This is made in the program ARPO, using an expert system and a data base in order to explain the jurist's knowledge. The paper speaks about the steps made in this sense from the experiences of ARPO

The field of law tends itself especially to development of data base and expert system applications [3], despite the fact that, paradoxically, those formed up to date have not been satisfactory. On the one hand this has been due to the fact that legal problems to be solved by computers have not in general been posed correctly, starting with the acceptance of all its complexity, and on the other hand it has been due to the scarcity of the technical possibilities available up to now in order to solve them [9]. To resolve such difficulties, the experimental prototype ARPO (in spanish: "Acción de reclamación del pago de la obra", work payment claim), has been constructed and at the moment it is being transformed into an aid program for legal decisions, the so-called SIREDOJ ("Sistema inteligente de recuperación de documentación jurídica") or intelligent system of legal document retrieval. From the legal point of view, the prototype helps a lawyer to discover by means of a dialogue if it is possible to exercise a legal claim relative to the work contract for the case being presented to the computer, what is such a claim, the process to follow and the legal documents to be used (statutes, sentences and bibliographical references) to lay the foundations of such activities. For these reasons the purpose of the prototype and the program is to explain the jurist's knowledge. This is the same to say that the problem here is to produce useful

theories, principles of practice and tools for the knowledge acquisition.

The prototype ARPO is the product of the research carried out in the course "Design of a computer system as an instrument of access to legal documents and to the solution of problems of a civil nature" (1988-1991)[*] , which is the continuation of the so-called "Intelligent legal thesaurus" (1985-1988)[**] . It is a program which accedes to a system of retrieval of legal documents (legal -statute- texts, sentences references and bibliographical references, in work contract subject matter) [4]. At the moment it is constituted by an expert reasoning system directed by the objective, constructed due to the intervention of the shell Crystal. The data bases and the program which links to the expert and to the data bases have been coded in Pascal language.

In this paper the process followed in the prototype building (I) is described, the accounts and limitations of the current implementation are taken into account (II), and the initial steps which are being taken to convert the prototype into the SIREDOJ program (III) are briefly explainied.

I
The prototype design

During the research carried out after 1984, in the first place the legal and computer problem characteristics to be solved were established. The problems centred on the theoretical and technical fixing of the precise steps so that a computer program could propose a argument in certain easy cases, put to it by a lawyer, at the request of the program, so that the said lawyer can document his legal position to the proposed case, with a view to his allegation in a trial.

The first step was centred on establishing the

[*] For this research funds have been received from the Spanish General Offices of Research, Science and Technology (DGICYT). Project PB87-0632. Also from IBM

[**] For this research funds have been received from the Advisory Board of Research of Aragon. Project CHS-7/85

hypothesis that a lawyer, in order to establish the defense of his client, is used to expressing a case in the following fashion: "A person has entrusted the construction of a building to a contractor. Once it has been built, and no having received payment, can the contractor claim the arranged price and from whom must he claim it? Other information necessary is the statutes, sentences and biblliography which can support such a claim". This in spanish is: "Una persona ha encargado a un contratista la realización de una obra consistente en una edificación. Una vez realizada la obra, y no habiendo cobrado, se quiere saber si el contratista puede y a quién tiene que reclamar el precio acordado. También se quiere conocer la legislación, jurisprudencia y bibliografía que puedan apoyar a dicha pretensión". The reply expected from an automaton to this case was summarised in a elemental way and in an illustrative capacity only, as follows:

1)

> Se puede ejercitar la acción de reclamación del precio de la obra

2)

ACCION DE RECLAMACION DEL PRECIO DE LA OBRA
===

-Fecha de prescripción de la acción: 01/01/2005
 * Es posible ejercitar la acción de reclamación del pago de la obra hasta 15 años después de la fecha de entrega de la obra (01/01/1990) o la de recepción de la obra (01/01/1990) (Art. 1591 Cc) -El trámite procesal a seguir es el del juicio declarativo de menor cuantía. La cantidad reclamable está comprendida entre 500.000 y 100.000.000 de pesetas.

-------------Fundamentación Jurídica--------------------
 -Artículos 1544, 1591 y 1599 del Código Civil
 -Artículos 680 al 714 de la Ley de Enjuiciamiento Civil
 -Jurisprudencia: Sentencias del Tribunal Supremo ....
 -Bibliografía: ....

(Seleccione palabras clave con el cursor)

The ARPO prototype allows in effect that the input-case, introduced through a dialogue held between the lawyer and the program, and the output-reply fit into the hypothesis-question-input described, just expressed.

In order to achieve this in the first place it was necessary to study the behaviour pattern of the jurists when adopting a stand in a lawsuit directed to a judge or in court, with the aim of obtaining a favourable verdict for their client. This problem was solved with the help of the suggestions made by the Sociology and Philosophy of Law during the last few years. These suggestions have expressed in detail the range of the "justification" of the legal decision, indicating that although it is guided in the last instance by the freedom of the concluder, it moves within the framework signalled out by the characteristics of the scope of the communication of the context: the so called legal argument, integrated by determined formal and political standards. Various papers have been dedicated to describing this model [6].

Considering the potentiality of computers and programs, and after taking the necessary steps to specify the contents of a legal example to be carried out, which was chosen eliminating as far as possible the difficulties limiting for the moment the construction of the program, it was decided that the example to solve the prototype be constituted by the solution of various typical cases relative to the work contract.

From a computer perspective the following block diagram was designed for the construction of the prototype, which explains the essential elements or modules to be integrated in the prototype (Figure 1).

Following this diagram the construction of the modules began in successive phases. The trail up to now has had relation with the construction of the knowledge base, the documentary data base and the necessary interfaces to establish necessary communication between the said modules and the lawyers using them. The work relative to the language processor module has not been started.

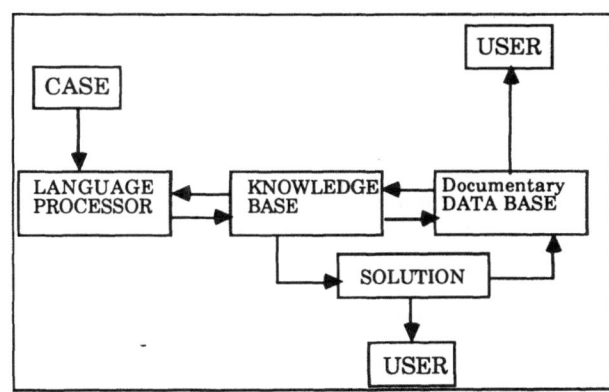

Figure 1

The main work has been set out in the construction of the knowledge base relative to the work contract. This was constructed starting from the structurization of the said knowledge in various of the multiple actions or claims or elements which could be integrated. From the legal perspective each object was integrated by the necessary elements to construct a lawsuit relative to the case about which criterion are required.

As concerns the legal form of producing this structurization, there is a concrete reference to the necessary steps for the systematization of the legal decision in order to construct a computer program as an aid in the sense that is indicated in the following suggestions, relative to difficult cases by Lombardi [8] : "individualize the solutions positively legal and sociologically possible based on all the permitted types of interpretation and on a dynamic effectiveness prospective; investigate the possible incidental causes, individual and universal; within the scope of the latter two, investigate before anything else an 'absolutely ideal' solution as well as a 'sectorial' one scouring 'outside systems' for the range of specific solutions proposed up to now and choosing a 'solution in pectore'; examining the problem after from some of the main metapositive systems of reference (catholic, radical-liberal, marxist, psychoanalytical, orientalascetic, etc.), taking into consideration if the authority of the systems themselves and the confrontation between them do not retouch the first solution; finally confront the ideal solution adopted with the positively and sociologically legal possibles, and choose the final legal solution".

To be exact and for cases like the one mentioned above, for the jurists expert in the respective field, the following object or "typical" solution relative to the claim of the payment of the price of the work, was constructed:

Supuesto de hecho.- Existe un contrato de obra
Se ha realizado la obra
Se ha entregado la obra (en determinada fecha)
Se ha recibido la obra (en determinada fecha)
No se ha cobrado el precio de la obra
El sujeto activo de la acción es el contratista
El sujeto pasivo de la acción es el propietario

Consecuencia jurídica.- Acción de reclamación del precio de la obra
Juicio declarativo
Arts. 1544, 1591 y 1599 del Código Civil
Arts. correspondientes al juicio de la Ley de Enjuiciamiento Civil
Sentencias relativas al caso
Bibliografía relativa al caso

As for the documentary data base, it was integrated by the Civil Code, the Civil Procedural Law, sentences references and bibliographies relative to contract work selected by jurists expert in the matter.

Starting from these hypotheses, the introduction of the prototype was passed on to. This introduction's only aim was to build a program which could check the effectiveness of the model developed for use of the jurist.

II
The current implementation

For the above mentioned aims, the ARPO system was built. This system has been built using the possibilities offered by a shell capable of constructing expert systems like Crystal. The choice of this shell among all the many on the market was due to the fact that it had been used in the common law sphere, in an example documented as the one relative to "Latent Damage Law - the expert system" [5]. A documentary data base has also been constructed as an experiment, in Pascal language, in which the documents relating to the work contract are contained.

The ARPO system is constructed by it, from a legal point of view, by the system of guide lines by the objective which provides the possibility that for a case introduced by an operating jurist, in conversation with the program, the mentioned system gives him a reply in the manner mentioned above. The ARPO claim explained above from a legal perspective, is expressed in Crystal by the following rules:

[78] Reclamación del precio de la obra
+ IF   [21] Existe un contrato de Obra
+ AND [81] Se ha realizado la Obra
+ AND [80] Se ha entregado la Obra
+ AND [82] Se ha recibido la Obra
+ AND [79] NOT se ha cobrado el precio de la Obra
+ AND [86] Sujeto activo: Contratista
+ AND [90] Sujeto pasivo: Propietario+Comitente
+ AND [68] Obra entregada o recibida en los últimos 15 años
+ AND [2] Acción de Reclamación del Precio de la Obra
+ AND [12] Cantidad adeudada
+ AND [29] Juicio Declarativo

Entering into the computer description of the prototype, it is necessary to say that we are dealing with a small expert system as an aid to finding legal documents via the solution to the case introduced by the user. The prototype only solves determined cases relating to the work contract.

The computer objectives of the prototype have been three: in the first place, state the versatility and the problems which the chose of the shell

Crystal can cause as an expert system development tool in the law sphere perteining to continental or romanic tradition countries; in the second place, design a documentary data base suitable for the necessities of the problem; and lastly, design the user interface, trying to make this communication as friendly as possible, keeping in mind the characteristics of the language used, the ways of introducing the information and the presentation of the product to the jurist in question. To these ends, and as a complement to shell Crystal -the Crystal III version has been used- two programs have been developed: the F1_Aid, which helps the operator when he presses F1, and Consult, which is a specially carried out documentary data base for full text. The prototype works in personal computers with hard disk and under DOS 3.3.

Shell Crystal III

Crystal III (Intelligent Environments) is a program to develop expert systems. The expert systems are built with rules which are stored in the knowledge base. The program, furthermore, contains different commands which make uses easy: showing the text on the screen, consulting the user and carrying out determined operations with different type of data, numbers, strings and dates.

In the development of the ARPO system the absence of various elements in the Crystal III program have been noted. If they have been implemented in the example in question, their potentiality would increase and this would not diminish their easy use. Among other elements or characteristics, we have especially noted the following:

1. The rules do not allow recursivity, which makes the introduction of a language analysis module, very useful in this type of system, somewhat difficult.

2. The concept of a local variable to the rule does not exist and this makes difficult that various people work together on the project.

3. The only type of data admitted are real numbers, strings and their vectors; this is sufficient to work with but it does not allow a comfortable programming.

4. Parameters cannot be passed to a rule except by means of global variables.

5. Rules cannot be passed to another rule. The concept of metarule does not exist, it is simulated by alternative combinations with the OR connector. From this point of view it can be said that all the rules built into Crystal are metarules.

6. The system does not learn. There is no way of increasing or modifying the knowledge base from the program created.

7. The access to the Ascii files and to the data bases is carried out through the so-called interfaces, routines written in the C programming language and compiled with Lattice C or Microsoft C.

8. The interface supplied for the files of DBase III, do not allow access to the "memo" type records, variable length text records.

9. The construction of loops is quite awkward, two rules are necessary, one containing the initiation part and the other containing the loop itself.

10. The rule documenting as it is done with traditional languages is practically impossible; this is solved by connecting them with the operator AND (including rules that are always true or those that are always false, by connecting them via the operator OR).

11. It is not possible to return to a previous consultation without first doing a "Special" type rule. This means that the rule is repeatedly evaluated every time it is used. Even in this way returning to a previous consultation requires the storing of the path, or at least that of the last rule evaluated by the program. It would be good to be able to define different worlds with their own variables.

12. The ARPO prototype has been the victim of some of these missing elements. Therefore in the end it is more certain to speak about it as a decision table driven algorithm than of a true expert system.

Crystal lacks many implements, the concordance between rules for example, which would help the development and the testing of the project, among other things. It is true that these characteristics can be implemented by means of routines and outside programs, but the cost of programming is too high. It must be said that it is quite simple for the Crystal programmer to represent the knowledge in such a way as for it to be more useful for the jurist. Furthermore, in a way that the jurist is capable of understanding the representation without having to learn a language very different from that used everyday.

F1 Aid

The F1_Aid is a small program which indicates the user where he is, showing him the way he has followed during the consultation. The indications are given in a language that is similar to the jurist's, and are not given in the Crystal fashion which show the rules checked and those not, something which tends to shock the user not familiar with the Crystal programming. In order to avoid the programming to check that the F1_key has been pressed when necessary, it has been thought to construct a program running simultaneously with Crystal. Since this is not possible under DOS 3.3, it has been decided to develop a TSR (Terminate and stay resident program) which initially redirects the keyboard interrupt vector to its own keyboard control routine, detecting in this way that the F1-key has been pressed, assigned to the routine which shows where and why the user is.

The Consult program. The data base

Another program independent of the Crystal one has been developed, which allows the consulting of the Spanish articles in the Civil Code and the Civil Procedural Law. The consulting program can be used independently or be called from the prototype created with Crystal when the user requieres some information about those two texts.

The data base is composed of the complete texts of the Civil Code and the Civil Procedural Law. The texts have no marked additions on them. For access to the information, the user must introduce a phrase in the form of connectors and keywords, after this the system tries to find those parts in the text where the words have a certain proximity within the text.

During the search the system isolates the consulting words and look to see if they exist in the synonym dictionary. If this is the case, a category is associated to the word, reference lists of the words are then obtained and the specific links and intersections for the connectors are carried out in order to obtain the list of the parts of the text where a proximity is observed between the specified words for the operator.

In the developed system two words are close to each other if both belong to the same page. The problem is how to define a page. After a brief study of the texts being worked with, it is easy to see that a structure exists in the same ones: at a conceptual level as well as in the composition of the text. Therefore as far as the texts of the two laws which make up the data base up to now are concerned, the said laws contain articles so that in order to number the pages of the text, it is enough to teach the structure of the text to the system. This can be carried out in the data base designed using a parser for each determined text [1] [10]. For example, faced with a structure like the following:

Art. 1025.- De los......................
....
....
....

Art.1026.- Cuando....................
....
....
....

the parser would take the following form, using production rules in BNF (Backus-Naur-Form):

<Libro>::=<Página>{Página}.
<Página>::=<ReferenciaArtículo>.- <Contenido>.
<ReferenciaArtículo>::=**Art._** l **art._**<Número>.
<Número>::=<Dígito>{<Dígito>}.
<Dígito>::=0 l 1 l 2 l 3 l 4 l 5 l 6 l 7 l 8 l 9.
<Contenido>::=<Letra> l <Dígito> l
<CarácterEspecial>.
<Letra>::=**A** l **B** l **C**.... l **Y** l **Z** l **a** l **b** l .... l **y** l **z**.
<CarácterEspecial>::=¿ l ? l , l . l _ l .... l º l ª.

This example is very simplified and few texts will fit this case. even so it gives and idea of the potential of the method. For example in the following text:

Art. 1025.- De los......................
....
.................según el art.345.............
....

the detection of the reference in the article to another article could be represented modifying the production rule of <Contenido> to:

<Contenido>::=<Carácter>{<Carácter> l
<ReferenciaArtículo>}

Of course the grammars obtained are not absolutely deterministic, but this does not complicate their use. Once the text structure has been defined, the numbering of the pages is automatic and the proximity of two or more words in the text is determined by their belonging or not to the same page of the text.

In order to make the searches easier a structure of inverted files has been implemented [7], on the one hand the words are stored without empty words, in the B-tree [2] and via a pointer points to a list of references to them on the text. The references are really references to the pages defined by the parser, in this way the proximity function is even more simplified: it only remains to compare the stored references.

The inverted file creation process is constructed through the following phases:

1. The isolation of a new symbol in the text to be worked on.
2. Look to see if the symbol belongs to the set of empty words. If it is go to 6, if it isn't go on.
3. Determining of the page on which the symbol is found.
4. Search for the symbol in the synonym dictionary.
5. Add the symbol or the category obtained with the page in which the inverted file was found.
6. If there are any symbols left go back to No. 1.

The set of empty words is formed by all those words which do not have a special meaning in the search. It must be said that in Spanish also and in the context of information retrieval in legal texts, the one or two letter words don't help a lot in a search, and are therefore automatically classified as empty without the need to check their inclusion in the set.

When a symbol has synonyms a category is associated to it and this is what is added to the inverted file, in this way there are less accesses to the disk than if it had been thought to restore the synonym list, since most of the accesses to the disk are used to accede to the symbols in the B-tree. Unfortunately this means more work if new synonyms are added to the dictionary. Fortunately, the adding of synonyms operation is less frequent than the really essential one of searching in a text. Therefore it is not very important the fact that it takes quite a long time since it is less frequent. When adding a synonym, the following steps are taken:

1. Associate a category to the symbols which one of them belongs to already or a new one, depending on the dialogue with the user.

2. Obtain the symbol reference lists and add them to the previously assigned category.

The creation of the inverted file is quite costly, but it must be born in mind that the experiment carried out up to now has been with texts which have undergone few modifications during that time. In any case even if there are modifications, it will not be often necessary to reconstruct the whole inverted file, due to the fact that a logical and not physical page structure has been carried out, and it will be enough to reorganise the modified text page structure, add the new symbols and eliminate the erasures. The reorganising of the page system does not require reanalysing the texts, it is only necessary to add up the difference between the added characters and those erased to the physical references of the following pages in the page list. When adding the text to the end of the book, it will only be necessary to add the new symbols to the inverted file and the new pages to the page list.

The intention is that the user interface be as friendly as possible, so that he can go to the following or previous page or to the references made to other pages within the text, by only pressing a key. A list of the last consultations is also stored, and they can be returned to in sequence. In this way it is possible to consult all the referenced articles without having to repeat the initial search, only through requesting the previous search, or the one before that, etc...

III
The next steps to take (preliminary)

The next steps will centre on the complete development of the data base, and check its potentialities with relation to the expert system and the language analyst which provides an artificial intelligence tool like KEE. With all this the program to be called, for the moment, the intelligent system of legal document retrieval (SIREDOJ), will be constructed.

REFERENCES

[1] AHO, A.V./ HOPCROFT, J. E./ULLMAN, J.D., The design and analysis of Computer Algorithms, Massachusetts, 1974, pp. 318ss

[2] BAYER, R./ MC CREIGHT, E., Organization and Maintenance of Large Ordered Indexes, in Acta Informatica, 1, No. 3, 1972, pp. 173-189 passim

[3] BERMAN, D.H. / HAFNER, C.D, The potential of artificial intelligence to help solve the crisis in our legal system, in Communications of the ACM, vol. 32, 8, 1989, pp. 928-938, p. 937

[4] BING, J., The Text Retrieval System as a Conversion Partner, in Yearbook of Law Computers & Technology, vol.2, London, 1986, pp. 25-39, p. 38

[5] SUSSKIND, R. E., The Latent Damage System: a jurisprudential analysis, in Proceedings of the Second International Conference on Artificial Intelligence and Law, June 13-16, 1989, Vancouver, 1989, pp. 23-32

[6] GALINDO, F.,PIDCA, a methodological prototype to build legal software, in III International Conference on Logica, Informatica, Diritto, vol. II, Florence, 1989, pp. 419-438, pp. 435s.

[7] KNUTH, D. E., The Art of Computer Programming, vol. 3, Sorting and Searching, Massachusetts, 1973, pp. 552-559 passim

[8] LOMBARDI VALLAURI, L., Informatics and "Political" or Value Criteria of the Legal Decision, in Artificial Intelligence and Legal Information Systems, vol. I, Armsterdam, 1982, pp. 61-72, pp. 71s.

[9] SVOBODA, W.R., Die Zukunft der juristischen Informationssysteme, in Computer und Recht, 12, 1987, pp. 905-911, pp. 906s.

[10] WIRTH, N, Algoritmos + Estructuras de Datos= Programas, trans. Angel Alvarez Rodríguez, José Cuena Bartolomé, Madrid, 1986, pp. 300-306

An expert system for drafting contractual documents in Public Administration Procurement Operations

Dominique BROUWERS   Jacques GERARD   Etienne MONTERO

Centre de Recherches Informatique et Droit, Facultés Universitaires Notre-Dame de la Paix,
Rempart de la Vierge, 5   5000 Namur Belgium
Tél. 32 - 81.72.47.71 Telex FAC.NAM.B 59222 - Fax 32 - 81.22.88.58

Abstract

This paper present a research project involved in legal expert system. The expertise domain concerns Public Procurement Market (PPM) in software acquisition. A very few civil servants have the necessary skill to combine public procurement regulations, data processing and computer law knowledge. The system should assist the Belgian administration in writing legal documents. During the consultation, the user can call several help-modules such as concept definition, reasoning justification power or can access a legal sources base.

Introduction

If the Belgian State plans to undertake public works (road, bridge, edifice,...), to acquire material (planes, office supplies,...), or services (engineering, architecture, ...), it must use a specific regulation. A statute (1976-07-14) defines the procedural and contractual rules in the elaboration and allocation of the Public Procurement Market (PPM).

The PPM may be considered as a written contract concluded by the administration to get the benefit of works, goods and services from a private company. The PPM regulation is based upon some fundamental principles : the obligation of advertising in order to allow free competition, the equality between tenderers, contract price, etc.

The statute of 1976 defines three procedures to conclude PPM :"adjudication" , "appel d'offres", "gré à gré". Only the last one permits the tenderer to negotiate. Furthermore, standard clauses must be included into the agreement, according to the statute.

Expertise domain : software acquisition

In practice, the publics administrations that want to computerize any activity are often unaware of some legal aspects. Three serious difficulties arise. The first difficulty includes three points (i) (ii) (iii) :

(i) The PPM regulations are relatively unsuited for data processing market. The 1976 Statute is particularly appropriate for public works market because they are the more frequent operations. So the purchasers have an experience which is unsuited for the software market.

(ii) Softwares have such specific qualities that rules governing goods and services PPM do not fit in this area. Specifications about conventional goods and services (a bridge construction, helicopter purchase, guarding activity) are pre-established. Instead, in the area, tenderers are required to propose a solution to some problem (automatization of book-keeping, ...). Thus, it is not up to the administration to specify the technicalities of the problem solving.

(iii) Some procedures are ineffective as well. Only the most flexible procedure can be used.

So there is a need to examine how the rules of public procurement -especially the rules of procedure- can apply to data processing procurement.

A second difficulty lies in the specificity of software acquisition. The clauses of the legal document are not sufficient for the administration. It must get a range of legal guarantees by the inscription of adequate clauses in the contract. Without the expertise in computer law, the administration is often forced to accept models of contract imposed by the software houses. The system proposes such adequate clauses to help the administration in concluding software contracts.

Of course, it is very important that the contract includes all the guarantees, combined with the technical and functional specifications.

The third problem is the difficulty to merge the different expertises which are : theoretical and practical public procurement knowledge, technical knowledge and computer law.

The "Centre de Recherches Informatique et Droit" has the necessary knowledge to undertake and develop an expert system in data processing PPM. Lawyers and computer scientists work together in study and development of legal expert systems.

Thanks to the numerous consultations, provided for administrations these last years, we acquired a good experience in data processing PPM.

Formalization

The knowledge embodied into the base of the expert system was already partly formalized. A practical guide has been written by a lawyer [Mont 90], at the request of the Belgian administration. It includes a series of clauses that will be the starting point during the conception of the facts base.

The set of the questions to be examined when a public purchaser is preparing the contractual documents has been divided into 21 topics such as software performance, duration of the operations, maintenance, documentation, warranties, intellectual property,... During a complete consultation, every topic is inspected. However, the user can make the choice to consult only one or a few modules.

The system flexibility

The typical user of the system is supposed to be a civil servant occasionally involved in the drafting of documents concerning a software PPM. It is likely that the user will neither be a lawyer nor a data-processing expert. But experienced writers will be helped by the system as well. For this kind of users, it works as a support of conception, thus accelerating the writing process of documents.

In general, the expert system is requested to be really flexible regarding the user's skill. As it will be shown in the following example, different help features are provided concerning questions or suggested clauses.

Here is an excerpt of a consultation, when the system is dealing with the problem of software maintenance :

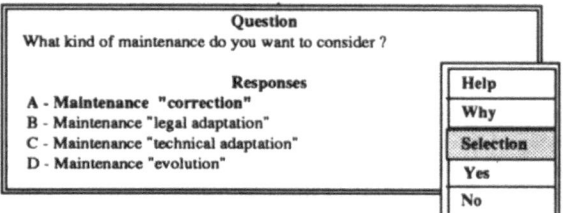

The system's user asks for an explanation about the responses

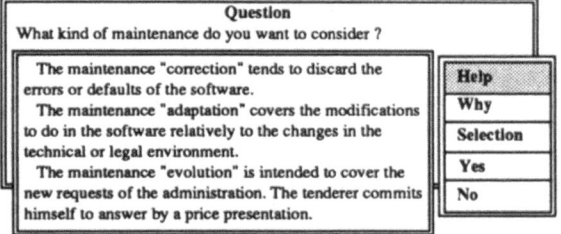

The maintenance "correction" has been chosen; then the system proposes to insert into the contract document the following clause

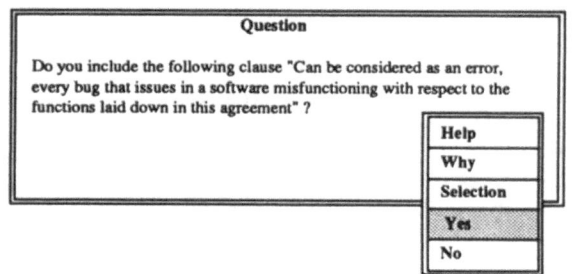

At any moment, deductions that have led up to a question or a result (clause) can be shown to the user

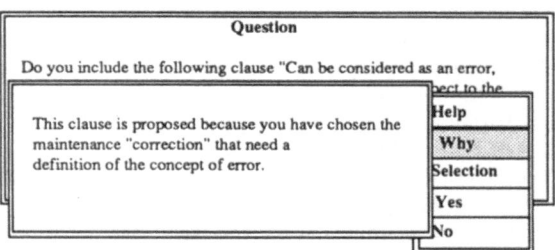

The user can ask for an explanation about the concept of "error"

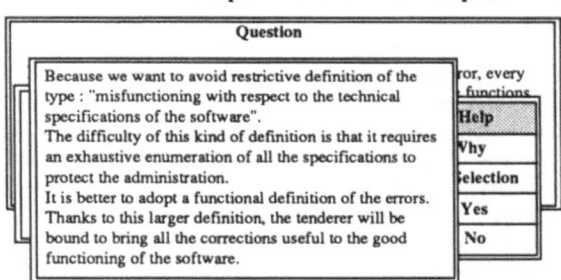

At this stage, if the first explanation of a concept does not satisfy the user, he can consult the legal documentation (statutes, jurisprudence, doctrine). For this purpose, a data base containing all the relevant documents can be accessed at any time during the consultation. Then, it is up to the user to find the meaning of the debatable concept and therefore to make up his mind about selecting or rejecting a proposed clause. This way of working with the expert system is really close to the traditional lawyer's method who consults a range of reference texts before deciding to give any value or meaning to an ambiguous term. However, the preliminary search in the library, that can be tedious and time consuming, has already been done by the experts and the results are immediately accessible. The only remaining task for the user is to interpret the documents found into the data base. If the user has no law qualification, it can be dangerous to work with such a method because that task goes out of his depth. For that reason, a whole consultation can be carried out without going into the documentation base, just by following the first explanation. This one contains the interpretation considered as the mostly appropriate by the expert.

Conception and updating

The shells used for expert systems are written for the applied domain and to the knowledges for which they are conceived. Furthermore, the limits fixed by the real world represented infer restrictions in the shells forms. It is not easy to abstract all the knowledge of a domain, even limited, and especially to precise the boundaries.

The legal domain in which we work does not differ. The implications of this arbitrary cutting are very difficult to assess. In fact, the representation of all the connections between the specified do-

298

main and the outer world will tend towards a complete real explanation.

We built a prototype with a shell written in Pascal. This shell was conceived to be used in an other legal activity, to determine public subsidies for companies [Scha 88, page 81]. This shell did not fit really well our new project because of the lack of text generation utilities. To realize the real system, we plan to write our own shell using the PROLOG language.

The "transfer" step of knowledge between experts in law and computer scientists, as enlightened before, takes a big part of the conception and realization time. The legal knowledge about contracts is quite easy to transform in logic rules of the second order, which need to be split up into Horn rules. These rules will be used for the real achievement. A team of both jurists and computer scientists carry out this part of the work to ensure a splitting which does not alter legal clauses. Only the lawyers can establish if a separation need induced logical rules (such as compatibility or exclusive rules, ...).

The aim of splitting is twofold : an easy conception and a rational maintenance. By maintenance, we mean suppression, change of clauses or rules, adding new clauses or new rules which are induced by a modification of the showed real, updating the helps and the legal documentation.

No "self-maintenance" is considered for consistency reasons of the legal clauses.

Here is the decomposition which appears to be the most efficient for the shell construction:

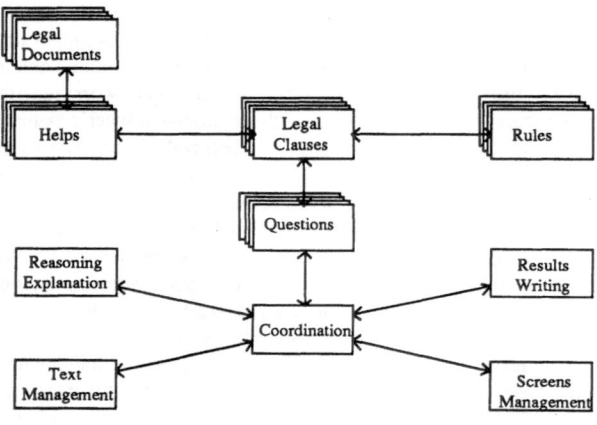

The 21 legal topics fit with the modules outlined by several superimposed rectangles. Only this multiple modules must be modified in case of adaptation.

The PROLOG representation of the legal clauses is as follows :

clse(X, Text, Modification, Help_list, Documentation_list).
<X> is the clause name (must be identifier),
<Text> is the legal text of the clause,
<Modification> is a flag defining whether the clause belong to the base of facts or whether the original text was modified,

<Help_list> is the list of helps available for the clause and,
<Documentation_list> represents the list of "legal documentation" facts relative to the clause (basically jurisprudence). The *legal clauses* module is formed by the set of facts *clse.*

The helps and legal documentation are satisfied by 2-arity facts where the first argument is an identifier and the second, the text of help or documentation.

The rules govern the applicability of the different legal clauses and the questions allow to select applicable clauses by facts and rules adjunction in the work base. Every rule of compatibility between the existing clauses is embodied in this module. Using this method, the consequential effects of an incompatibility is inherent to the system.

The five simple modules can be used as soon as one of the 21 legal topics is designed. Firstly, the links between the legal parts can be simulated by a new set of questions which emerge from the facts that would be supposed to be imported from other modules.

These five modules compose the centre of the shell. They are partly independent of the subject. The mechanism required for a total and correct justification of the results issued from the system, is concentrated in the *reasoning explanation* module. The *text management* module allows the user an "a posteriori" modification of the clauses text that have been picked up. The two *results writing* and *screen management* modules are not specific to the expert systems. The nucleus of the shell is the *coordinating* module. It controls the consultations.

Bibliography

FLAMME, M.-A., *Traité théorique et pratique des marchés publics*, tome I, Bruxelles, Bruylant, 1969, 1100 pages.

FLAMME, M.-A., *Traité théorique et pratique des marchés publics*, tome II, Bruxelles, Bruylant, 1969, 1100 pages.

FLAMME, M.-A., FLAMME, Ph., et MATHEI, Ph., *Commentaire pratique de la réglementation des marchés publics*, Bruxelles, Confédération des marchés publics, 1986, 1226 pages.

KOERS, A.W., KRACHT, D., SMITH, M., SMITS, J.M. et WEUSTEN, M.C.M., *Knowledge Based Systems in Law*, Kluwer, Deventer, 1989, 190 pages.

KOWALSKI, R., SERGOT, M., KRIWACZEK, F., HAMMOND, P., CORY, H., SADRI, F., The British Nationality Act as a Logic Program, *Communications of the ACM*, 1986, page 370-386.

MONTERO E., *Les marchés publics d'acquisition de logiciels*, à paraître, 185 pages.

SCHAUSS, M., *Systèmes experts et droit*, collection des Précis et travaux de la Faculté de droit de Namur, E. Story-Scientia, 1988, 182 pages.

STERLING, L. et SHAPIRO, E., *The art of PROLOG*, MIT Press, Cambridge, Massachusetts, 1986, 427 pages.

SUSSKIND, R., *Expert systems in law*, Clarendon Press, Oxford, 1987, 300 pages.

VON DER LIETH GARDNER, A., *An artificial intelligence approach to legal reasoning*, MIT Press, Cambridge, Massachusetts, 1987, 225 pages.

ESQL : An Extended SQL with Object and Deductive Capabilities[1]

Georges GARDARIN & Patrick VALDURIEZ

INRIA
BP.105, 78153 Le Chesnay-Cédex, France

ABSTRACT

ESQL is an SQL upward-compatible database language that integrates in a uniform and clean way the essential concepts of relational, object-oriented and deductive databases. ESQL is intended for traditional data processing applications as well as more complex applications such as large expert systems. Therefore, ESQL's salient features are: a rich and extendible type system based on abstract data types (ADTs) implemented in various programming languages; complex objects with object sharing by combining generic ADTs and object identity; the capability of querying and updating relations containing simple or complex objects using SQL-compatible syntax and semantics; and a DATALOG-like deductive capability provided as an extension of the SQL view mechanism.

1. INTRODUCTION

The relational database approach has gained wide acceptance in traditional data processing (i.e., business) mainly because it increases user productivity and enables automatic optimization of database accesses and updates. This approach is highly promoted by the existence of the standard relational query language SQL [ISO86] which provides a uniform interface to database administrators, application programmers and end-users for data definition and data manipulation. As a result, SQL is becoming the common language for exchanging data in centralized, decentralized and heterogeneous environments.

Current relational database systems have been designed for traditional data processing applications. Therefore, they do not support well emerging database application domains such as computer aided design (CAD), office information systems (OIS) and knowledge-based systems (KBS), in particular expert systems. These applications express new requirements such as user-defined data types (incorporating both data structures and their associated operations), complex objects (identified values of rich type or complex structure) and rule-based knowledge management. Research aimed at supporting new application requirements in a more integrated way led to two new approaches : object-oriented databases and deductive databases [Gardarin89].

Object-oriented databases aim primarily at supporting user-defined data types and complex objects. Their salient features are abstract data types (ADTs) [Guttag77], object identity, type inheritance and persistence independence [Bancilhon88]. ADTs enable the encapsulation of data and their associated operations (called methods) while hiding implementation details. Object identity [Khoshafian86] provides referential object sharing

[Khoshafian87] to model complex (graph-structured) objects without replication. Type inheritance enables objects of different types to share the operations pertinent to their common supertypes thereby encouraging reuse of code and reducing the size of application programs. The object-oriented database approach combines object-oriented programming, as exemplified by C++, and database technology. Therefore, database applications can be entirely written in a single database programming language (e.g., as opposed to SQL embedded in a programming language).

Deductive databases focus on integrating within the database the knowledge typically embedded in application programs. With better sharing, control and management of knowledge, typically represented by assertions and deductive rules, deductive databases can reduce significantly the size and complexity of application programs. The deductive database approach combines logic programming, as exemplified by PROLOG, and database technology. Therefore, it provides a highly expressive database language which allows powerful queries such as recursive queries.

These approaches bring definite advantages over relational databases. However, they generally come with what is perceived by traditional database users as a new language (although it is more a significant extension of an object-oriented or logic programming language). This hampers the acceptance of these technologies by data processing users who could also benefit from their advanced features. Furthermore, albeit it is Turing-complete, a new language does not necessarily solve the infamous "impedance mismatch" problem [Copeland84] for the simple reason that there will always be users who want to access the database from their favorite programming language. In other words, the impedance mismatch is not a model or language problem, but must be dealt with by the database system.

A more conservative approach capitalizes on relational database technology and extends it in a way that the advantages of object-oriented databases and deductive databases can be gained. The rationale behind this approach is that the relational model provides a stable platform with simple concepts open for such extensions. The concept of nested relation [Ozsoyoglu87] is useful to model hierarchical structures and manipulate them with a SQL-like language [Schek88]. The concept of domain, not constrained in its original definition, can be defined as ADT [Stonebraker83, Gardarin89b], query or procedure [Stonebraker86], or object [Carey88, Danforth88]. In addition, a relational query language can be given sound functional semantics, e.g., OSQL [Beech88] and FSQL [Valduriez89a], and thus support powerful user-defined functions. Each of these extensions provide some generality over the relational model. However, they have been proposed independently and in various contexts, thereby making their integration difficult.

[1] This work is sponsored by ESPRIT project EDS

The contribution of this paper is to integrate in a uniform and simple way the key concepts of object-oriented databases and deductive databases within the SQL framework. The result is ESQL (for Extended SQL), an SQL upward-compatible query language supporting rich types, complex objects and derived relations. For instance, these capabilities are essential for large expert system applications that typically require inferencing (deduction) on complex objects. Rich type support is provided by a generic ADT capability allowing multiple implementation programming languages. Complex object support is provided by structures that may contain arrangement of values of any types. Finally, recursive derived relations are supported through an extension of the SQL view mechanism. Furthermore, ESQL's functional semantics [Gardarin90] make uniform and simple the manipulation of ESQL data and should ease the development of an ESQL compiler [Valduriez89b]. Finally, ESQL's relational basis favors reuse of known query optimization techniques [Valduriez89c].

The following presentation concentrates on the most powerful concepts of ESQL. Section 2 gives an overview motivating the design of ESQL. Section 3 introduces a powerful ADT model with ADT inheritance and ADT constructors. This model provides a solid basis for supporting efficiently objects of rich type and complex structure. Section 4 illustrates the data definition and data manipulation facilities of ESQL. Section 5 presents the ESQL derived relation capability.

2. ESQL OVERVIEW

ESQL is intended for traditional data processing applications written in standard SQL as well as non-traditional data intensive applications. To promote the access of SQL users to ESQL's new functions, the language extension is provided with minimal impact to the SQL syntax. The main advantages provided by ESQL over SQL are strong support for abstract data types specified in different programming languages, complex objects with object sharing, and a deductive capability to infer new data from stored data.

The support of ADTs provides a rich typing capability. It makes the fixed set of system-defined types extendible by the users to accommodate their application specific requirements. An ADT is a new type together with methods applicable to data of that type. The value of any ADT (e.g., map) can be stored in the database system and manipulated using the associated methods (e.g., map intersection). ESQL supports this ADT capability by extending the notion of domain traditionally supported by relational database systems. The goal is to allow ADTs to be implemented in various languages such as C, C++, LISP and PROLOG. For each ADT implementation language supported, the database system must provide routines to convert between the language data structures (e.g., list in LISP) and a supporting database system type (e.g., string).

ESQL's support for complex objects includes object identity, which enables objects to be referentially shared, and permits the construction of complex structures (e.g., hierarchy, graph). Complex objects such as office automation objects or CAD design objects can be modelled and manipulated in a natural way, while giving an ESQL compiler opportunities to optimize the access to such objects. The relational data model only supports values, imposing the use of key values to identify objects. ESQL supports both values and objects. A value is an instance of an ADT while an object has a unique identifier with a value bound to it. Data not declared as objects are values by default as in the relational model, which means that they have no system identifier. Therefore, ESQL data are divided between objects and values, and only objects

may be referentially shared using object identity. The relational data model supports flat values using the tuple and set constructors at one level. To support complex values, ESQL generalizes the relational model with a library of generic ADTs which may be combined at multiple levels. Generic ADTs are higher-order constructors that take as arguments values or objects of any type. The primary generic ADTs are tuple, set, bag, list and array. Others useful constructors are ordered sequence and graph. By combining objects and generic ADTs, arbitrarily complex objects can be supported.

A deductive capability enables one to abstract in a rule base the common knowledge traditionally embedded with redundancy in application programs. The rule base provides centralized control of knowledge, and is primarily useful to infer new facts from the facts stored in the database. ESQL provides this deductive capability as an extension of the SQL view mechanism. This gives the ESQL user the power of the DATALOG logic-based language using statements already available in SQL.

The ESQL data definition language (DDL) augments the SQL DDL in three major ways. First, it includes a type language to create and manage ADTs with related methods, and generic ADTs. Second, it extends the table creation statement to deal with nested relations and objects. Third, it adds a statement to create derived relations defined by general rules, including recursive rules.

The ESQL data manipulation language (DML) generalizes the SQL DML in several ways. The most significant advantages are the possibility of ADT operations in SQL statements, the manipulation of shared objects by extending the dot notation, the manipulation of nested objects through nested statements and the possibility of deductive queries. Data manipulation in ESQL is more regular than SQL, much in the way of SQL2 [Melton89].

3. ABSTRACT DATA TYPE DEFINITION

3.1. Overview of the Data Model

The data model of SQL is relational in nature, and therefore based primarily on two concepts : domains of values and relations on domains. The data model of ESQL is the relational model extended with abstract data types (ADTs), which generalize the domains of values. Thus, a domain of value in a relation is defined either as an elementary data type or as an ADT. An elementary data type provides a domain of values directly supported by standard SQL2 (i.e., character strings, numbers, enumerated types, dates, times, intervals and nulls) and comes with operations applicable to values of that type, for instance, arithmetics on numbers. Similarly, an ADT defines a domain of values, for instance, text or triangle, and comes with user-defined operations, for instance, extract the title from a text or compute the surface of a triangle.

An ADT is viewed as a set of methods (or functions) that operate on values of the defined type. Thus, an ADT encapsulates the type structure within a set of operations so that the implementation details are hidden from the ADT user who only sees the interface methods. Values of a given ADT are manipulated through functions (known as methods). Public methods can be invoked within DML statements, both in the definition of query results, query qualification and update actions. A specific command (CREATE TYPE) is added to SQL to enter the abstract data type definition toolbox and define a new ADT.

An ADT structure is built by combining elementary data types or other ADTs using generic ADTs (i.e., generalized constructors). The primary generic ADTs needed to achieve functionalities required by engineering or office applications are supplied by a system tool box to define ADTs. This includes the tuple, set, bag, list, array generic data types (sequence and graph could also be added). All user defined ADTs are built from this set of generic ADTs and a base set of simple type. The usual notion of type inheritance is supported : an ADT can be a subtype of another ADT; it then inherits all the methods of the generic ADT. Further, new attributes can be added to a tuple inherited type. In general, methods can be redefined (i.e., overloading is permitted) or added to a subtype. For instance, triangle may be a subtype of polygon. A height attribute can then be added to the triangle subtype; heights should then be updated by user programs. An alternative is to define height as a method that computes the triangle height from the sides.

3.2. Generic Abstract Data Types

An ADT specification is a representation independent functional definition of each operation of an ADT. This specification will be the only visible part of the ADT in SQL. Thus, the complete design of an ADT would proceed by first giving its specification, followed by an implementation that agrees with the specification.

ESQL includes a set of generic ADTs to specify and implement ADTs. Generic ADTs are useful for specialization. Generic ADTs are typically parametrized by one or more types. A generic ADT capability is a powerful tool for constructing new ADTs; it offers a homogeneous implementation of constructors as tuple and collections. Collections may be specialized in sets, bags, list, or vectors, which are specific generic ADTs of most object-oriented database systems.

In the following, we define the signature of specific generic ADTs. For this purpose, we introduce a few notations. The notation "[a]" indicates that a is optional. The notation "a l b" indicates that a or b must be chosen. The notation "(a)... " indicates that a is repeated one or more times. A function is defined as F(x,...) --> y, where x,... specifies the arguments type and y the result type. ø is the empty type, which means no element.

A simple example of ADT is the tuple ADT. Denoting by a1, a2, ... values of type Type1, Type2, ..., denoting by A1, A2, ... the attribute names and assuming that Formula is a logical formula on A1, A2, ..., the tuple ADT may be specified as follows :

```
ADT TUPLE OF (<A1> : <Type1> [ { , <A2> : <Type2> } ... ] )
    FUNCTION :
        MAKETUPLE(a1 [ {, a2} ...] --> Tuple
        EQUAL(Tuple,Tuple) --> Boolean
        PROJECT(Tuple, A1, A2 ...) --> Tuple
        ASSIGN(Tuple,A1,A2,..., a1,a2,...) --> Tuple
        CHECK(Tuple, Formula) --> Boolean
        PRODUCT(Tuple,Tuple) --> Tuple
    END TUPLE ;
```

MAKETUPLE creates a tuple of the generic type with initial values. EQUAL checks the equality of two tuples. PROJECT is the projection function. ASSIGN assigns the given attribute values to the corresponding attributes of the tuple. CHECK checks whether a given tuple satisfies the parameter formula. PRODUCT performs the Cartesian product of two tuples.

In ESQL, special attention is given to the support of collections. Collection is a built-in generic ADT in the language. Collections are organized in an inheritance hierarchy whose root is Collection and subtypes are bag, set, list and vector (see Figure 1). Certain functions, such as COUNT, ISEMPTY, EQUAL, INSERT, REMOVE

are general and act on any type of collections: they are attached to the root of the hierarchy. MAP is also a function attached to any collection : MAP(C,f), where C is a collection and f a function defined on the elements of C, applies f to each element of C. MAP is a powerful function for processing all elements of a collection. Other functions are specific to a collection subtype (e.g., set). For each subtype of collection x, there exists a conversion function translating a collection y in that subtype of collection : the name of the function is Tox (e.g., ToSet, ToList, ToVector). For example, ToSet(y), where y is a bag, transforms the bag y in a set (thus, it removes duplicate from the bag). There exists also a Make function, which creates a collection from an enumeration of elements (e.g., MakeSet).

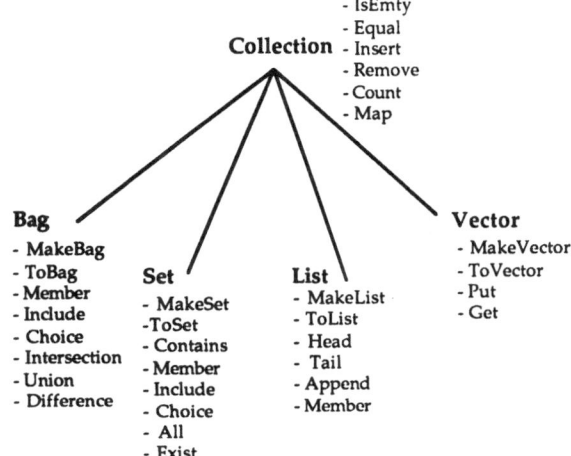

Figure 1 : The Collection generic ADT hierarchy

A good example of a generic ADT subtype of collection is the set ADT. Denoting "Element" a value of type <Type> and given a function "Function" defined on elements of type <type>, it may be specified as in Figure 2 (including inherited functions).

```
ADT SET OF <Type>
    FUNCTION :
        ISEMPTY(Set) --> Boolean
        EQUAL(Set, Set) --> Boolean
        INSERT(Set, Element) --> Set
    REMOVE(Set, Element) --> Set
        COUNT(Set) --> Integer
        MAP(Set, Function) --> Set
        MAKESET(Element [ {,Element}...]) --> Set
        TOSET(Collection) --> Set
        CONTAINS(Set, Element) --> Boolean
        MEMBER(Element, Set) --> Boolean
        INCLUDE (Set, Set) --> Boolean
        CHOICE(Set) --> Element U ø
        ALL(Set, Formula) --> Boolean
        EXIST(Set,Formula) --> Boolean
    END SET ;
```

Figure 2 : The SET generic ADT

Note that this ADT specification defines any set of data elements and encapsulates it within the given functions. The first functions, up to MAP, are inherited from the collection type. MAKESET is the creation function while TOSET converts a collection into a set. The other functions respectively check whether a given set contains a given element, whether an element is in a set, whether a set is included in another set. The CHOICE function reduces a set by withdrawing an element at random. The ALL function checks whether all elements of a set satisfy a given formula. The EXIST function returns True if one element in the set satisfy the given formula, and False otherwise. Other functions can be added (e.g., union, intersection and difference of sets). The set generic ADT can be used to define, for example, a set of integers, a set of tuples or a set of complex objects. All these functions can be invoked in ESQL queries as shown below.

3.3. Constructed Type Definition

The specification of a new type in ESQL requires the use of the CREATE TYPE statement. This statement is built from generic types, which are specialized and nested. It introduces a new type by associating a name to a possibly nested type structure. Nesting is possible by value or by reference. Also, a type can be implemented in a relation as a value or an object identifier; in the latter case, objects are stored in an object store associated with the object type. In the case of an ADT that is a specialization of a previously user-defined ADT, the user must provide its supertypes. Additional attributes may be given when the ADT is a specialization of a tuple type. A simplified syntax of the CREATE TYPE command is given in Figure 3. Note that VALUE is the default option for a type specification (type clause) while TUPLE OF is the default option for a structure specification (structure clause).

```
<type definition>    ::=    CREATE TYPE <type name>
    [SUBTYPE OF <type name> , [[<type name>]...] ]
    [ <type clause> ]

<type clause>    ::=    [VALUE] <structure clause>
    |  OBJECT <structure clause>

<structure clause>    ::=    [TUPLE OF]
    ( <column name> <type spec>,
    [ { <column name> <type spec> } ...] )
    |  <generic type> OF <type clause> [ (, <type clause> }...]
    |  < data type >

<generic type>    ::=    SET | BAG | LIST | VECTOR
    |  <identifier>

<data type> ::= <character string type>
    |  <exact numeric type>
    |  <approximate numeric type>
```

Figure 3 : Syntax of the type definition command

The following example defines two tuple types ITEM and CUSTOMER, a set type ORDERED. We assume that the ECU type is simply a sub-type of FLOAT. Note that CUSTOMER is an object type, which means that customer instances may be referred to by object identifiers in relations. Objects may be referentially shared between multiple relations.

```
CREATE TYPE ITEM
    (INUM INT, INAME ARRAY OF CHAR, PRICE ECU) ;

CREATE TYPE CUSTOMER OBJECT
    (CNUM INT, CNAME ARRAY OF CHAR,
    CPHONES SET OF INT) ;

CREATE TYPE ORDERED
    SET OF (OITEM ITEM, QTY INT) ;
```

The next example defines a polygon type as a tuple object composed of a numerical identifier (PID) and a vertex attribute itself composed of a list of points, and then a triangle type as a subtype of polygon with a height. The addition of a new attribute

to a subtype of a tuple type is illustrated with the height example. Note that an integrity constraint should specify that a triangle has only three vertices.

```
CREATE TYPE POLYGON OBJECT
    TUPLE OF (PID INT, VERTICES LIST OF POINT) ;

CREATE TYPE POINT
    (X FLOAT, Y FLOAT) ;

CREATE TYPE TRIANGLE
    ISA POLYGON
    (HEIGHT FLOAT) ;
```

The next example is more involved. It defines a text as a tuple composed of a title, a set of author names defined as arrays of characters (an alternative is to use the CHARACTER VARYING type of SQL) and a content defined as a list of sections. A section is defined as a number, a title and an array of paragraphs, each represented as a list of phrases. A phrase is a list of references to words in a dictionary. Words are simply arrays of characters.

```
CREATE TYPE TEXT
    TUPLE OF (    TITLE PHRASE,
        AUTHORS LIST OF ARRAY OF CHAR,
        TCONTENT LIST OF SECTION ) ;

CREATE TYPE SECTION
    TUPLE OF (    NUMBER INT,
        TITLE PHRASE,
        SCONTENT ARRAY OF LIST OF PHRASE) ;

CREATE TYPE PHRASE LIST OF WORD ;

CREATE TYPE WORD OBJECT ARRAY OF CHAR ;
```

3.4. Implementation of ADT Functions

A user constructed type is a specialization of a generic type. As such, it inherits all the functions of the generic types. For example, the type TEXT being a tuple, it inherits the projection function. If t is a text, then TITLE(t) is a phrase and AUTHORS(t) is a list. By applying the FIRST function to the list AUTHORS(t), we obtain FIRST(AUTHORS(t)), which delivers an array of characters or the empty value. This capability of specializing generic types provides a powerful functional language to manipulate nested objects. However, it is not sufficient to express general functions, which should be provided by a general-purpose programming facility.

The support of multiple languages to specify ADTs is provided by the concept of ADT view. An ADT view is a data structure accessible from a programming language, which represents the constructed database ADT as seen in the considered programming language. Of course, the functions inherited by the ADT structure (e.g., TITLE, AUTHORS and FIRST) are callable from the considered programming language.

The general command to define a new function is as follows :

```
CREATE FUNCTION <function name>
(<operand data type list>)
RETURNS <result data type>
LANGUAGE <language>
```

While language can be C++, LISP, PROLOG or C, a function specification is a function name followed by the parameter types, the key word RETURNS and the result type. For example, the addition of the surface function (returning a float) to the TRIANGLE data type requires the command :

CREATE FUNCTION SURFACE
(TRIANGLE)
RETURNS FLOAT
LANGUAGE C++ ;

3.5. Type Alterations

The ALTER TYPE statement enables one to modify an existing named type, for instance, adding a new attribute to a tuple type. In the case of an ADT, the user can change existing operations or modify the subtype relationship. It can also drop a function using the DROP FUNCTION statement or delete an existing type using the DROP TYPE statement.

4. TABLE CREATION AND MANIPULATION

4.1. Table Creation

As previously mentioned, the basis of the ESQL data model is relational, generalized for supporting collections of objects and values. Collections of objects or values are recorded in set of tuples (i.e., relations), which are the first level constructs (in other words, relations are first class citizens).

The CREATE TABLE statement of SQL is generalized to allow a table to be defined as a collection of tuples of attribute names of possibly complex types. To support referential object sharing, a value type in a tuple definition can be replaced by an object type.

Object type is defined at type creation time using the OBJECT keyword. The general syntax of the CREATE TABLE statement is as in SQL2. Note that table inheritance is supported in SQL2. We give here a simplified syntax for it.

<table definition> ::=
    CREATE TABLE <table name>
        [**SUBTYPE OF** <table name> [(, <table name>)...]]
        [(<table element> [, <table element>) ...])]

<table element> ::=
            <column definition>
    | <table constraint definition>

<column definition> ::=
        [<column name>] <data type>
        [<column constraint definition>]

The CREATE TABLE statement of SQL is basically unchanged. The only modification is that a data type can now be an ADT (user-defined or built-in) and attribute names in column definitions are optional. Note that a table can inherits attributes from existing tables. Also, attribute names can be omitted in the case of a tuple data type. Attribute names are then inferred from the tuple attributes.

Examples of table creation are given below :

CREATE TABLE ITEMS
(ITEM)
KEY IS INUM ;

CREATE TABLE CUSTOMERS
(CUST CUSTOMER)
KEY IS CUST ;

CREATE TABLE ORDERS
(ONUM **INT**, CUST CUSTOMER, ORDER ORDERED)
KEY IS ONUM ;

CREATE TABLE NEWORDERS
    SUBTYPE OF ORDERS
(PRIORITY **INT**) ;

Note that the CUSTOMER object tuples can be referentially shared between the CUSTOMERS relation and the ORDERS relation. The ORDERED set is nested by value within the ORDER relation. NEWORDERS inherits the ORDERS attributes and is extended with a priority attribute.

CREATE TABLE TEXTS
(CONT TEXT)
KEY IS TITLE(CONT) ;

creates a relation of texts stored by value. Note that the key is defined using a function applied to the text type. In the next section, further use of functions will be exemplified.

CREATE TABLE TRIANGLES
(RNUM **INT**, COLOR **STRING**, SHAPE TRIANGLE)
KEY IS RNUM ;

creates a relation of colored triangles whose shape is stored by reference.

4.2. Querying tables with Single-valued Attributes

The ESQL language is an upward compatible version of SQL. The user sees relations and can manipulate them using SQL. However, since relations may be defined over complex domains, it is also possible to manipulate data inside a complex structure using the ADT functions. Thus, the first significant extension is the possibility of ADT operations. Complex structure instances are encapsulated by their functions as specified in the type definition. In general, any function attached to a given type may be applied to an element of that type. If A is of type T1 and F is defined over type T1 as producing type T2 (i.e., F(T1) --> T2), F(A) may be used in any expression of type T2. If G is defined over type T2 as producing type T3, G(F(A)) may be used in expressions of type T3. Thus, SQL2 expressions are generalized to include the possibility of applying ADT functions at various levels. Expressions and sub-expressions must be correctly typed. Of course, functions that update objects or values cannot be used in queries (SELECT statement) but only in updates (UPDATE statement).

ESQL data manipulation using user-defined or generic functions is now illustrated. For example, let FRANCS be an ADT user function converting ECU into French francs expressed in the float data type (FRANCS(ECU) gives FLOAT). The following query on the ITEMS relation lists all items for which the price is less than 100 francs.

SELECT   *
FROM   ITEMS
WHERE   FRANCS(PRICE) < 100 ;

To deal with objects, a VALUE function is necessary to read through an object identifier. However, this function can be implicitly applied by the system to get the correct typing. Consequently, the following query returns the name of the customer whose order number is 10.

SELECT   CNAME(CUST)
FROM   ORDERS
WHERE   ONUM = 10 ;

304

This is a short notation for :

    SELECT   CNAME(VALUE(CUST))
    FROM   ORDERS
    WHERE   ONUM = 10 ;

Conversely, the manipulation and updating of object identifiers may require accessing the reference of an object X using the OID function. OID(X) gives the object identifier of X. The OID function makes precise the distinction between object equality and object identity. Given objects O1 and O2, O1 = O2 will return true if the value of the objects are equal whereas OID(O1) = OID(O2) will return true if they both refer to the same object identifier.

4.3. Querying Collections of Objects

Built-in functions can be used to manipulate collections of objects, which are specific generic ADTs instances. Functions can be composed in expressions. To simplify the handling of collections in ESQL, a function F defined on a type T and not defined on a collection of T (denoted here Collection(T)) can be directly applied to a collection of T in ESQL queries. The semantics of such an application is to apply F to all elements of the collection and return the collection of results. Thus, F(Collection(T)) is simply Collection(F(T)). This corresponds to an automatic generation of the MAP function; formally, F(Collection(t)) is rewritten into MAP(F, Collection(T)). For example, the following query lists the names of the customers which order a disk. Note that an attribute function is applied directly to a set of tuples having that attribute ; such an application returns the set of attribute values of the tuples in the set.

    SELECT   CNAME(CUST)
    FROM   ORDERS
    WHERE   CONTAINS(INAME(OITEM(ORDER)), "Disk") ;

Note that CONTAINS is the Boolean function defined on sets to determine whether an element (here "Disk") belongs to the set. OITEM and INAME are projection functions directly applied to set of tuples.

Assuming that the list data type can also be manipulated using a MEMBER function (i.e., MEMBER(Element, LIST) --> Boolean), the following query retrieves the first author of all texts containing the word "Database" in the title.

    SELECT   FIRST(AUTHORS(CONT))
    FROM   TEXTS
    WHERE   MEMBER(,"Database",TITLE(CONT)) ;

Note that the query assumes an implicit translation of OIDs to values, as TITLE(CONT) is in fact a list of word identifiers. A complete qualification without implicit notations would be :
    MEMBER("Database", VALUE(TITLE(CONT))).
The value function is useless since an automatic translation from OIDs to values is assumed when necessary.

Collection handling requires the ability to transform single-valued attributes to collection, according to a grouping criteria. This is the classical "nest" operation, generally implemented by a group by in SQL. In ESQL, we maintain the GROUP BY clause. However, the result of a group by does not require applying an aggregate function (e.g., SUM) : it can simply be a collection. By default, we assume that the bag collection is specified. Thus, the following query gives a bag of large triangles (surface greater than 10) for each color :

    SELECT COLOR, SHAPE
    FROM TRIANGLES
    WHERE SURFACE(SHAPE) > 10
    GROUP BY COLOR

To get another type of collection (e.g., a set), a conversion function (e.g., TOSET) must be applied. Thus, the following query returns set of large triangles per color :

    SELECT COLOR, TOSET(SHAPE)
    FROM TRIANGLES
    WHERE SURFACE(SHAPE) > 10
    GROUP BY COLOR

It is also possible to unnest a relation with a multi-valued attribute, according to an ungrouping attribute. This is performed by an UNGROUP clause, similar to the GROUP BY clause of SQL. For example, the following query gives each product ordered for each customer. :

    SELECT CUST, ORDER
    FROM ORDERS
    UNGROUP BY CUST

4.4. Updating Tables

The UPDATE command of SQL can now be used to modify objects. For example, one can add "John Doe" as author of all texts containing the database keyword in the title using the following command. Note that the "=" of SQL is replaced by ":" as the command does not assign a new value to a complex attribute (here CONT), but rather applies a function to it.

    UPDATE TEXTS
        SET CONT : INLIST(AUTHORS(CONT), ["John Doe"])
        WHERE   CONTAINS(TITLE(CONT), W)
        AND   VALUE(W) = "Database" ;

In summary, the nesting of ADT functions in ESQL expressions provide a concise and powerful tool for manipulating any nesting of generic or user defined ADTs. It is a regular extension of SQL, which reduces to the normalized version for flat tables.

5. DERIVED TYPES AND RELATIONS

Much work has been devoted to extending relational databases to deductive databases. The so-called DATALOG language allows the user to derive virtual relations from the database. DATALOG has the power of relational algebra plus recursion. It may be extended to support negation and functions. Unfortunately, the syntax of DATALOG does not fit well with that of SQL. However, given their importance, recursive queries have been introduced in SQL3 but are not easy to express.

ESQL supports deductive capabilities through derived relations defined as generalized views. We simply extend the view concept of SQL2 with recursion, by allowing a view to be defined from itself. Deriving a relation from a relation using a query expression referencing this relation is a powerful functionality. As an example, consider the type PARTS(PART ITEM, COMPONENT ITEM). The following recursive view definition specifies the transitive closure of the PARTS relation :

```
CREATE VIEW SPARTS AS
    SELECT *
    FROM PARTS
UNION
    SELECT P1.PART, P2.COMPONENT
    FROM SPARTS P1, PARTS P2
    WHERE P1.COMPONENT = P2.PART ;
```

The form of the relation derivation statement which gives the power of standard DATALOG is :

```
CREATE VIEW <table name> [<column name>]...
    AS <query>
    [ UNION <query> ] ... ;
```

where <query> is an SQL query. The query can refer to the derived table, thus allowing the database administrator to define recursive relations. Furthermore, ADT functions can be used in queries, thereby giving ESQL the power of DATALOG with functions.

Let us assume a ROADS relation, representing the roads between large cities in EUROPE, created as follows :

```
CREATE TABLE ROADS (  #R INT, SCITY STRING,
    TCITY STRING, LENGTH FLOAT ) ;
```

An example of a derived table with functions is a PATHS relation, which gives all paths from one city to another with their lengths. It is defined as follows :

```
CREATE VIEW PATHS (SCITY, TCITY, LENGTH) AS
    SELECT SCITY, TCITY, LENGTH
    FROM ROADS ,
UNION
    SELECT P.SCITY, R.TCITY, P.LENGTH + R.LENGTH
    FROM PATHS P, ROAD R
    WHERE P.TCITY = R.SCITY ;
```

To support negation as in certain versions of DATALOG, we use the EXCEPT command of SQL2. For example, if one wants to avoid all paths going through special roads recorded in a FORBID relation, we can define the following view :

```
CREATE VIEW PATHS (SCITY, TCITY, LENGTH) AS
(    SELECT SCITY, TCITY, LENGTH
    FROM ROADS
EXCEPT
    SELECT SCITY, TCITY, LENGTH
    FROM FORBID  )
UNION
    SELECT P.SCITY, R.TCITY, P.LENGTH + R.LENGTH
    FROM PATHS P, ROAD R
    WHERE P.TCITY = R.SCITY ;
```

ESQL supports stored queries within relations [Stonebraker86] by allowing a type to be defined as a query. Deriving a type enables the database administrator to create a new type from a more or less complex query. The syntax of the type derivation statement is :

```
CREATE TYPE <type name> AS <Query> ;
```

It can be used for example to implement truly nested relations as in the following example :

```
CREATE TYPE NORDER AS
    SELECT  *
    FROM ORDERS
```

and then :

```
CREATE TABLE NESTEDORDERS
(NUM : INT, TAB : NORDER) ;
```

6. CONCLUSION

In this paper, we have extended standard SQL for better supporting new application domains. The main extensions are twofold : the support of abstract data types and the support of recursive rules as extended views. This demonstrates the integration in a common abstract data type framework of the relational, object oriented and deductive paradigms. The integrated approach is based on the introduction of nested generic abstract data types, the relation abstract data type being the first visible data type. Compared to previous proposals [Beech88, Carey88, Gardarin89b, Scheck88, Valduriez88a], ESQL goes further in terms of nested data types, object oriented and deductive capabilities. Furthermore, the integration of object oriented features is only based on a generic ADT framework, which is easy to implement.

In [Gardarin90], we introduced a functional operational semantics for ESQL. This semantics gives a first translation of a query into a functional program. This program could be used as a basis for query optimization using transformation rules. Other techniques are possible for query optimization [Valduriez89c].

ESQL is the interface to the database server of the European Declarative System (EDS) developed in an ESPRIT.II project (1989-1992). ESQL is to be compiled and optimized for parallel execution on the EDS highly parallel data server. ESQL applications primarily include both on line transaction processing queries and complex decision support queries for large expert systems.

Further enhancements to ESQL are planned in a near future. This includes the addition of conditional and loop statements to program multi-statement procedures and perform explicit loops on set elements. Another planned extension is triggers to manage active databases. We also plan to add good support for integrity constraints, both on tables and ADTs.

ACKNOWLEDGMENTS

We would like to thank all our colleagues of the EDS ESPRIT project for their helpful comments and suggestions on earlier drafts of ESQL.

REFERENCES

[Bancilhon88] F. Bancilhon, "Object-Oriented Database Systems", *Int. Symp. on PODS*, Austin, Texas, March 1988.

[Beech88] D. Beech, "A Foundation for Evolution from Relational to Object Databases", *Int. Conf. on EDBT*, Venice, Italy, March 1988.

[Carey88] M.J. Carey, D.J. DeWitt, S.L. Vandenberg, "A Data Model and Query Language for EXODUS", *ACM SIGMOD Int. Conf.*, Chicago, Illinois, June 1988.

[Danforth88] S. Danforth, P. Valduriez, "The Data Model of FAD, a Database Programming Language, Rev.1", MCC Technical Report ACA-ST-059-88, June 1988, to appear in *Information Sciences*.

[Gardarin89a] G. Gardarin, P. Valduriez, "Relational Databases and Knowledge Bases", Book, *Addison-Wesley*, 1989.

306

[Gardarin89b] G. Gardarin et al., "Managing Complex Objects in an Extended Relational DBMS", *Int. Conf. on VLDB*, Amsterdam, August 1989.

[Gardarin90] G. Gardarin, P. Valduriez, "ESQL : an Extension of SQL Combining Deductive and Object-Oriented Capabilities", *Research Report* No.1185, INRIA, France, March 1990.

[Guttag77] J. Guttag, "Abstract Data Types and the Development of Data Structures", *Comm. of ACM*, Vol. 20, No. 6, June 1977.

[ISO86] ISO ANSI, "Database Language SQL", ISO/DIS 9075, *International Standard*, 1986.

[Khoshafian86] S. Khoshafian, G. Copeland, "Object Identity", *Int. Conf. on OOPSLA*, Portland, Oregon, September 1986.

[Khoshafian87] S. Khoshafian, P. Valduriez, "Persistence, Sharing and Object Orientation: a database perspective", *Int. Workshop on Database Programming Languages*, Roscoff, France, September 1987.

[Melton89] J. Melton, " Database Language SQL2 and SQL3", *ISO-ANSI working draft*, ISO DBL CAN-2b, May, 1989.

[Ozsoyoglu87] Z.M. Ozsoyoglu, L-Y. Yuan, "A New Normal Form for Nested Relations", *ACM TODS*, Vol. 12, No. 1, March 1987.

[Schek88] H. Schek, "Nested Relations, a Step Forward or Backward", *IEEE Data Engineering*, Vol. 11, No. 3, September 1988.

[Stonebraker83] M. Stonebraker, B. Rubenstein, A. Guttman, "Application of Abstract Data Types and Abstract Indices to CAD Databases", *ACM -SIGMOD Int. Conf.*, San Jose (California), May 1983.

[Stonebraker86] M. Stonebraker, L.A. Rowe, "The Design of POSTGRES", *ACM-SIGMOD Int. Conf.*, Washington, D.C., May 1986.

[Valduriez89a] P. Valduriez, S. Danforth, "Functional SQL (FSQL), an SQL Upward Compatible Database Programming Language", MCC Technical Report ACA-ST-045-89, February 1989, to appear in *Information Sciences*.

[Valduriez89b] P. Valduriez, S. Danforth, B. Hart, T. Briggs, M. Cochinwala, "Compiling FAD, a Database Programming Language", *Int. Workshop on Database Programming Languages*, Portland, Oregon, June 1989.

[Valduriez89c] P. Valduriez, S. Danforth, "Query Optimization in Database Programming Languages", *Int. Conf. on Deductive and Object Oriented Databases*, Kyoto, Dec. 1989.

A Proposal for Integrating Artificial Intelligence and Database Techniques

Gian Piero Zarri

Centre National de la Recherche Scientifique
CERTAL - INALCO
2, rue de Lille
75007 Paris, France

ABSTRACT

This paper describes some aspects of a current, interdisciplinary project carried out at the French National Center for Scientific Research (CNRS), and centered around a proposal concerning the integration of Artificial Intelligence (AI) and Database (DB) techniques. Our aim is to establish a sound methodology for the construction of Large Knowledge Based Systems (LKBSs) by combining the high-level information modeling features, the deductive capabilities, and the flexibility of the AI Knowledge Representation Languages (KRLs) with the characteristics of efficiency, security, concurrency, recovery and persistence of data provided by the Data Base Management Systems (DBMSs). We give in particular a succint description of the work already accomplished within the project in the knowledge representation area (set up of a powerful "hybrid representation system").

1. INTRODUCTION

This paper describes some aspects of a current, interdisciplinary project in the Artificial Intelligence (AI) / Database (DB) integration field carried out at the French National Center for Scientific Research (CNRS). The aim of this project is the definition of a sound methodology for the construction of those Large Knowledge Based Systems (LKBSs) which will supercede the actual generation of DBs whenever advanced applications must be set up - implying, for example, complex inference operations making use of very powerful data/knowledge models. Our proposal draws its strength from trying to merge the best characteristics of the AI and DB approaches to the information management problem, i.e. trying to combine the high-level descriptive features, the deductive capabilities, and the flexibility of the AI Knowledge Representation Languages (KRLs) with the characteristics of efficiency, security, concurrency, recovery and persistence of data provided by the Data Base Management Systems (DBMSs). In other words, the project relies on the results obtained in the DB field in order to deal with all the problems concerning the "architecture" of the LKBSs and, more in general, their information engineering aspects, and on the AI results as regards to all the "domain modeling" aspects.

With respect to this last point, an important feature of the project is that, as with the hyper-semantic data models developed in a DB context, see 2.11, our knowledge representation model makes no real distinction between "data", and "knowledge" or "rules" ("knowledge/data transparency"). This unified approach avoids, amongst other things, those consistency problems ("semantic mismatch", "granularity mismatch"..., see 2.22) that bother so much the scholars who are working on the "classical" road towards the construction of LKBSs, i.e. trying to integrate Expert Systems (ESs) and DBs while still maintaining their autonomy. On the other hand, the considerable descriptive power of this model (an "hybrid representation system", see 4.) will help overcome the expressive limitations of the traditional relational model ("loss of information"), while permitting all sort of non-deductive (abductive, inductive, nonmonotonic, analogical etc.) strategies of reasoning to be applied when necessary.

Section 2. of this paper will give a description of the "state of the art" in the field of the AI/DB integration, which will permit us (Section 3.) to better frame and justify the approach outlined before. In Section 4., we will give a succint description of the work already accomplished within the project in the knowledge representation area. Given the "introductory" characteristics of this paper and the space limitations, I will refer the interested reader, for more technical details, to other papers already published about the project, see for example [20].

2. STATE OF THE ART

The attempt to merge AI and DB techniques is by no means a new concept : we can class the efforts towards the discovery of better ways of dealing with large quantities of information into two categories : a) efforts originated in a prevailing DB context ; b) efforts orginated in a prevailing AI context.

2.1 Efforts originated in a prevailing DB context

Data Base Management Systems (DBMS) are an essential part of the software environment used in the construction of almost all information systems. However, numerous additional technical challenges arise for DB technology, as attempts are made to apply this technology in many new applications that have different requirements and constraints from those involved in traditional business data processing field. Examples of such applications occur in industrial automation, Computer Aided Design and Manufacturing (CAD/CAM), office applications, Computer Aided Software Engineering (CASE), military command and control, information retrieval from textual data, and cartography. We can classify the extensions to the current DB technology into two categories, where the first refers to extensions which concern primarily the enlargement of the expressive power of traditional data models ("static extensions"), while the second is more related towards the attempts to introduce some limited reasoning capabilities inside the DMBSs ("dynamic extensions").

2.11 Augmenting the expressive power of the traditional data models ("static extensions"). Several recent developments in DB research have centred around the study of new structuring principles capable of overcoming the limited modelling capabilities of the traditional relational paradigm : being forced to model everything as (flat) relations containing only atomic attributes because of the the "first normal form" restriction often leads to awkward database designs and unnecessarily complicated queries also in the case of the "traditional" data processing applications. A major trend in the database field has therefore been to relax the first normal form constraint, permitting the use of more powerful data structures like "nested relations" or "complex objects". In a nested relation (NF^2, Non First Normal

Form Relations) attribute values are not necessarily atomic, but they can be relations themselves ; a relation valued attribute may, in turn, have relations as attributes and so on, see [14, etc.]. Examples of research prototypes based on this approach are the AIM-P project at IBM Heidelberg and the VERSO system at INRIA. Nested relations have been often criticized as a step back to the old world of hierarchical databases or, more seriously, as flawed by the lack of support for shared subobjects, $n : m$ relationships and recursive data structures. In his presentation for the panel discussion on "Nested Relations" at the 1988 ACM SIGMOD Conference, H.-J. Schek demonstrated that this criticism is ill-founded if, as in the DASDBS (Darmstadt Database) kernel system, the starting point for implementing a nested relational model is not a "static" nested relational schema but rather a "recursive" relational schema definition. From the point of view of our own approach, the most interesting feature of this demonstration is that what Schek defines as "recursive nested relations" correspond directly to the definitions of "generic concepts" in Brachman's KL-ONE [4], as emphasized by Schek himself ; as well known, KL-ONE is a pure AI product, one of the most popular Knowledge Representation paradigms.

Traditional data models are basically record-oriented models : for example, in a relational DMBS, the tuples in a relation correspond to the records in a file. Trying to model a variety of situations with just one modelling construct typically results in the loss of the exact meaning of the relationship : "semantic data models" [11] were developed to provide a higher level of abstraction for representing the data and the relationships between them. Typical abstraction constructs provided by these models include "generalization" (see the "is-a" link of semantic networks), "aggregation" ("part-of") and "grouping" ("element-of") ; "aggregation" and "grouping" are the two main "type constructors". A fundamental notion linked with the semantic models is that of "relationship" amongst object classes : the relationship construct may be realized under several forms, basically as "attributes" (functions), or by using explicit type constructors. Semantic data models can be classified into three general categories : "relational models" (e.g. Chen's Entity-Relationship, ER, Model), "functional models" (e.g. the Functional Data Model, FDM, introduced in 1976 by Kerschberg and Pacheco), and the "semantic-networks models" (e.g. the Semantic Database Model, SDM, by Hammer and McLeod). Models in the relational category are basically extensions to the relational data model, like the nested relations examined above. The functional models have a strong mathematical flavour. Their operation mode is centered around the specification of the relationships among objects through the use of "functional definitions" (attributes) which can be used to manipulate the objects : applying, for example, the ENROLLED-IN function to a particular student returns the set of courses that the student is currently enrolled in. The semantic-networks data models have a close relationship to the IA languages in the semantic network style : a structural approach is used to organize knowledge using "nodes" and "arcs" to represent, respectively, "objects" and "relationships". Well-known systems based on semantic models are ADAPLEX (functional, Computer Corporation of America), GALILEO (hybrid, University of Pisa), GEM (relational, Bell Laboratories), TAXIS (hybrid, University of Toronto).

Recently, the semantic data modelling approach (and, in particular, the functional approach) has received increased attention because of some strong similarities with the "object-oriented" approach which is now so popular. Although there is not yet universal agreement on what exactly is meant by object-oriented languages, a minimal consensus exists in order to qualify a language having the following characteristics as object-oriented : a) it should support "data abstraction" ; b) it should provide an "inheritance" mechanism ; c) it should enforce "encapsulation". To meet the first criterion the language must have a primitive construct for defining a "class" (a "type") with associated "methods" (procedures proper to this particular class) : every object, combining both "data structures" and "procedures", is an "instance" of a class (a type). To meet the second criterion the language must provide for "hierarchical class definition" (allowing a subclass to inherit data and methods from its superclasses, i.e. types (classes) are specialized through type inheritance). The third criterion describes the fact that the concrete implementations of data-representation and method-routines of an object are not directly accessible : to obtain the value associated to a particular property of an object the designer of the corresponding class would have to implement a specific method for the class which would return that value when called. Consider now the corresponding features on the semantic models side : a) any entity is identified as an "object" ; b) objects are organized into object-types or classes ; c) object-types are organized via generalization, aggregation, grouping and user-defined relationships ; d) property inheritance is allowed within generalization hierarchies. A first distinction between these two approaches concerns the fact that object-oriented models do not typically embody the rich type constructors of semantic models (consider, however, the functional models, where type constructors are not used). A second, more important difference, is linked with the presence of "methods" in object-oriented languages, and with the fact that the "inheritance of a method", since it is a behavioural property, can be between (seemingly) different types : in a semantic model, the "inheritance of attributes" is only between types where one is a subset of the other. Making abstraction, however, from the "methods" aspects, the similarities between the two approaches are striking.

It is not really surprising, therefore, that DB researchers have adopted this approach as another way which can be used to realize extensible data models. All extensible DBMSs require some way to specify the semantics of predicates and operations defined for the new data types : in the Object-Oriented Database Management Systems (OODBMSs) approach, both the data and the procedures on the new types are encapsulated in the definition of abstract data types. An OODBMS is defined as including an object-oriented data model characterized by the properties examined above (object identity, object state and behaviour, classes/instances, inheritance, etc.), facilities for data definition and query, permanent storage, mechanisms for database control, and support for versions and long transactions. Commercial examples of OODBMS are G-base (Graphael), Vbase (Ontologic), GemStone (Servio Logic).

Even if nested relations, semantic data models and object-oriented data models represent a notable advance in what concerns the possibility of an adequate representation of real world situations, a new class of models have recently appeared in the DB arena, the "Hyper-semantic data models"[15]. These models extend the capabilities of semantic models by incorporating more features characteristic of the Knowledge Based Systems field, e.g. by including explicitly "inference", "uncertainty", "constraints" and other AI features amongst the concepts to be used inside a DBMS. For example, in the Knowledge/Data Model (KDM) developed by Potter and Kerschberg, three new "abstraction constructs" are added to the usual ones of semantic models, namely the "constraint", "heuristic", and "temporal" constructs. With the "heuristic" construct, an information derivation mechanism of the "inference" type is associated to the relationship "is-heuristic-on", allowing, for example, the courses to be taken next term by a student to be inferred from the courses required for the student's degree program, the courses already taken by the student, and those being offered next term. Constraints, heuristics, and temporal objects may be generalized, aggregated, or considered as higher level abstract objects by using another abstraction mechanism. An important feature of hyper-semantic data models is that, regardless of the kind of "data" or "knowledge" ("rules") to be addressed, the access and representation formalisms are the same ; in this type of systems, there is practically no partition between a "database" and a "knowledge base" ("knowledge/data transparency"). The representational scheme in KDM follows the <Attribute, Object, Value> paradigm. We can object that a "pure" associative triple approach for Knowledge Representation is a bit oversimplified ; we must nevertheless acknowledge that, with regards to the recent developments inside the DB world, hyper-semantic data models seem to be the nearest to the general philosophy of our approach.

2.12 Attempts to introduce some reasoning capabilities inside the DMBSs ("dynamic extensions"). Hyper-semantic data models are characterized by the presence of inference capabilities, and therefore permit a good transition to those studies which concern the definition of "rules" or "triggers" mechanisms for DBMSs.

Traditional DMBSs are passive, i.e. queries or transactions are executed only when explicitly requested. Many applications, such as inventory control, cooperative processing, and factory automation are not well served by passive DBMSs : these applications require automatic monitoring of conditions defined over the database state and a capability to take actions when the state of the underlying database changes (transaction-triggered processing). A database augmented with such capabilities can be described as an "active database" : an active DBMS monitors "conditions" triggered by "events" representing database updates or external occurrences, and if the condition is evaluated to true then an "action" is executed. In the literature, "alerters", "triggers", "daemons", "active objects" and "situation-action rules" have been used to modelling active DBMSs.

The studies concerning rule specification and processing in order to build genuine "Expert Data Base Management Systems" (EDBMSs) can be considered as a development of the researches on active databases, and for this reason they are examined in this Section. In this type of systems, "rules" means normally "AI-type production rules (*if* X *then* Y)" ; systems of production rules have been integrated into EDBMSs according to two basic strategies : a) extending relational DBMSs in order to include a production rules facility ; b) using DB technology to efficiently implement OPS5-like production rules languages. An example of the first category is a system [19] actually under development at the IBM Almaden Research Center as an extension of the STARBUST enhanced DB product. In this system, the production rule facility is compatible with the SQL language ; rule activation results from user-generated or application generated DB operations. In contrast with the usual technique of "instance-oriented rules" (rules that are applied once for each data item satisfying the condition part of the rule), in this system the rules are "set-oriented rules" (rules that are triggered by sets of changes to the database and may perform sets of changes by using "operation blocks") ; this is in good agreement with the set-oriented approach of relational DBs. The best-known system in the second category is probably RPL (Relational Production Language), by Lois Delcambre and her colleagues [8]. RPL uses the "relational data model" as the basic framework of a "production system". In this way, on the one hand, Expert Systems (ESs) written in RPL have direct access to conventional DBs because RPL relies on a relational query language to express rules ; on the other, ES inferencing power immediately enriches conventional database systems. RPL's architecture is based on a two-level database hierarchy, in which the system's outer level comprises conventional databases, and the inner level contains an RPL interpreter employing a memory-resident relational database to replace the "working memory" normally associated with production systems. The system uses RPL rules to express and control data exchange between levels ; once a situation that requires inferencing has been identified, an RPL rule can load from the outer level data necessary for inferencing into the working database. Given that RPL views the working memory as

a relational database, the fundamental functions of the production system interpreter can be realized with DBMS assistance. In particular, an RPL program contains a production rule set in which each rule's LHS ("left hand side") is a relational query, profiting from the fact that the LHS of a production rule is essentially a limited form of database query. The RHS ("right hand side") comprises normal actions supported by OPS5, like "make", "modify" and "remove", slightly modified in order to conform to SQL syntax. Similar work is developed at Bellcore, INRIA, MITRE Corporation, etc.

A system like RPL is subject to two forms of criticism. The first one, as Delcambre herself acknowledges, concerns the poor performances of the system because of the overhead involved in the exchanges between memory- and disk-resident DBs. The second, which leads us to qualify this type of systems as "short-term solution" to the problem of discovering better ways of dealing with large quantities of information, is linked to the expressive limitations of both the relational and the OPS5 data/knowledge models.

2.2 Efforts originated in a prevailing AI context

Knowledge Based Systems (KBSs) differ considerably from conventional DB systems. The most outstanding difference is that KBSs typically contain explicitly represented "rules" as well as simple facts, and components which can make inferences over the "Knowledge Base" (KB, rules + facts), thereby providing a deductive retrieval facility. KBS software ranges between two basic possible forms :

• Pure "rule-based representations" supporting inference by resolution ; inside this first pole, is at least pragmatically useful to distinguish between the the systems developed in a "logic programming" context and the simplest "Expert Systems shells" based on the production rules paradigm.

• Pure "frame- or object-based representations" supporting inference by inheritance, defaults and procedural attachment.

Logic programming has grown out of research into automated inference, and especially of the work on resolution inference that followed the publication of Robinson's [16] seminal paper ("resolution principle"). It refers to a programming style based on writing programs as sets of assertions in predicate logic ("clauses"), which have a "declarative meaning" as descriptive statements about entities and relations and, in addition, derive a "procedural meaning" by virtue of being executable, thanks to the resolution principle, by an interpreter. Resolution principle tries to prove that a "theorem", i.e. a clause whose truth value is yet unknown, can be derived from a set of "axioms", i.e. clauses that are assumed to be true : it is based on the notion of contradiction, i.e. a clause and its negation can not both be true. Restriction to a resolution theorem prover for the "Horn clauses" subset of logic ensures to PROLOG and to its derivatives a relative tractability of deductions ; Horn clauses are disjunctive formulae with at most one positive (unnegated) "literal". Of a particular interest from the point of view of the connections between logic and databases is the DATALOG language [6], specifically designed for interacting with large DBs, thanks to the possibility of translating DATALOG programs in terms of (positive) relational algebra expressions. From a "syntactical" point of view, DATALOG, a very restricted subset of first-order logic (a pure Horn clause language), is also a subset of PROLOG. However, DATALOG and PROLOG differ in their "semantics" : while DATALOG has a purely "declarative" semantics, the meaning of PROLOG programs is defined by an "operational" semantics, i.e., by the specification of how PROLOG programs must be executed. Notwithstanding its very nice formal properties linked to its clean declarative style, DATALOG is little more than a toy language, a "pure" computational paradigm which does not support many ordinary, useful programming tools.

Well-known ordinary ES shells typically provide a uniform rule-based language which allow the construction of a "rule base" composed of a modular set of production rules of the form "situation ---> action", and a mechanism ("inference engine"), essentially a form of theorem prover, allowing (in forward-chaining mode, backward-chaining mode ...) the manipulation of these rules to form inferences, make diagnoses, etc. In this respect, a simple ES shell for rule-based reasoning can be seen as a special case of a system based on logic. Normally ESs provide also a standard user interface for initiating consultation queries, and some (rudimentary) "explanation facility".

In "pure" frame- or object-based systems, the representation scheme is, fundamentally, a labelled binary relationship model, where labels provide the "intensional" (definitional, classificatory) component of the representation and values the "extensional" (concrete) data. Distinguished labels denote the classification of objects, default values, and attached procedures ("methods" and "active values"). Rather than a general purpose inference mechanism, property inheritance from superclasses is provided as an useful but restricted form of inference, and active values permit lazy evaluation or update-triggered processing ; in their most abstract form, these system typically lack the unification and resolution capabilities of ESs and logic programming systems.

In reality, as commercial realizations of frame- and object-based systems are configured as independent but sufficient software environments for application development, it is always possible for them to make available alternative inference methods and representation schemes. An example is that of KEE (IntelliCorp), a well-known frame-based system which adds to the two standard forms of procedural attachment, methods and active values, the possibility to use frames in order to represent production rules, and makes use of the powerful frame-based representation facility as a means of organizing and indexing modular collections of production rules [9]. We shall refer in the following to this class of powerful "hybrid" systems as the Knowledge Engineering Software Environments (KESEs).

Coming now to the problems linked with the "intelligent" processing of large quantites of knowledge and data, several problems exist which affect all possible types of KBSs and which make them just as inadequate as conventional DBMSs for supporting the new data/knowledge-intensive applications. They can be summarized as follows :

• KBSs usually deal with Knowledge Bases (rules + facts) of small size, with the KB residing only in volatile memory ;

• KBSs provide limited services for recovery, protection, concurrent access to distributed knowledge bases, etc., if any is provided at all.

As a result, there has been in the last few years a growing interest in coupling KBSs with DBs : DBs are supposed to supply the KBSs with the correct quantity of data required to drive their inferencing mechanisms, while still preserving their basic functions which (for example) avoid losing data or accessing inconsistent information in case of concurrent applications. This coupling has been realized using all possible forms of association between DBs and KBSs, all sort of "loose" or "tight" coupling : in the following, we will limit ourselves to mentioning the two most popular classes of systems developed in this context, i.e. the solutions ("deductive databases") created in a logic programming environment, and those concerning the co-operation of DBs with KESEs and ES shells where the two types of systems preserve their autonomy.

2.21 Deductive databases. In order to understand the mechanisms of deductive databases, it may be useful to introduce a general distinction between "extensional" (EDB) and "intensional" databases (IDB). Accordingly, the EDB component of a whatever DB system contains base relations stored explicitly in secondary storage. Information which does not need to be explicitly stored but can be derived from base relations is labelled as "virtual relations" ; definitions deriving virtual relations are stored in the IDB component. In a relational DB system, virtual relations are created by data retrieval statements (such as those typical of SQL) which can be embedded into applications programs ; in a deductive DB system, definitions which deduce virtual relations are represented as logic formulae, and extensions of virtual relations are derived from base relations using the intrinsic inference mechanisms provided with logic. This means that definition of virtual relations can be considered as "declarative" in the deductive databases, whereas this definition is "procedural" (see SQL) in the traditional, relational databases. Cooperation between intensional (logic formulae) and extensional database can be activated according to a "homogeneous approach", in which a single, integrated system is used to manipulate both EDB and IDB and to perform deductive reasoning over them, or according to a "heterogeneous approach", in which a relational DB is used to manage the extensional database, and a logic-programming system is used to perform deductive reasoning based on the intensional one [12].

In the homogeneous approach, the same programming system (for example, PROLOG) is used to represent both rules and facts. In a "pure logic system", facts and rules reside on secondary storage ; they are loaded into main memory prior to system execution and must remain there while the system is executing. When a query is being answered, unification is performed on the clauses stored in main memory ; little or no access to secondary storage is made. A "pure system" like this has serious drawbacks. Representing facts and rules in exactly the same way is only apparently an optimal solution : facts and rules differ in size as well in the ways they are used ; thus, representing and accessing them separately may achieve better performance. A second drawback is that storing all rules and many facts in the main memory severely limits the size of the database the system can handle. In concrete situations the homogeneous approach is, therefore, often realized by using "enhanced logic systems" which have data management functions built into a logic system. These functions can manage, in particular, data residing on external storage, so that facts in the external DB can be accessed from the logic system when needed. They are realized by implementing in a logic language (PROLOG) some concepts developed in the DB domain (e.g. indexing techniques, query optimization), and incorporating them into the logic system.

The heterogeneous approach uses two separate subsystems, a Logic System (LS) and a DBMS. The LS can be considered as a front end where the rules are stored and the inference performed ; the DBMS can be viewed as a back end to the LS, which returns results to the LS in response to LS requests. Heterogeneous systems can be categorized as "compiled" or "interpreted" (with some variations on the theme), depending on the granularity of the interaction between the two subsystems (Leung and Lee [12]). The "compiled" approach consists of two distinct phases, "compilation" and "execution". In the first phase, the LS compiles the user query and the rules into an iterative or recursive DB program that references only base relations. In the execution phase, the DBMS executes the program as a single unit, generates all answers using the extensional database (EDB) only, and finally returns the answers to the LS. Interaction between the LS and the DBMS is at a "large granularity" (interaction between the two subsystems is infrequent) : the request is a program able to retrieve all answers from the database ; the response from the

DBMS is the complete answer set. In an "interpreted" approach, facts are retrieved from the DBMS whenever the interpreter needs them to continue a computation in the LS (this approach is, therefore, defined as "tight" by some author). The interaction is frequent and of a "small granularity", as most requests are for single facts. However, this approach will incur a lot of interaction between the two subsystems and cause, therefore, communication overhead. Furthermore, since single requests rather than batches of subqueries (as in the compiled approach) are sent to the DBMS, global optimization within the DBMS becomes less effective. The merit of this approach is that it allows more flexibility in controlling the search process.

A well-known example of a deductive DB system based on the heterogeneous approach is PROSQL [7], which associates PROLOG as a front-end to a SQL/DS relational back-end. Basically, a PROSQL program is a PROLOG program that uses the special predicate "SQL" to create tables and views and to insert and delete tuples to and from the DB system ; the SQL predicate contains as its argument a legal SQL statement that is passed to SQL/DS for execution. PROSQL can operate in either compiled or interpreted mode. PROSQL inherits most of PROLOG's limitations, e.g., the clause-at-a-time computation model of PROLOG which is substantially different from the set-at-a-time model of the relational model. An interesting, new project in the deductive field is the LDL (Logic Data Language) project at MCC (Microelectronic and Computer Technology Corporation, Austin, Texas). LDL [17], a DATALOG extension, is based on Horn-clause logic but enriched with features not found in languages of the PROLOG class ; one significant improvement is the way LDL handles sets and negation. Unlike PROLOG, which emulates sets with lists, LDL allows users to use sets as data primitives. Negation is based on set difference ; this formulation replaces the notion of "negation by failure" employed in PROLOG and the relational data model.

Deductive database systems have been designed and intensively studied over the last years ; their main interest seems to reside, as usual in a logic programming context, in the possibility of an elegant, sound and exhaustive definition of their syntactic and semantic features. Their practical utility as commercial tools is more subject to caution ; we can mention, in this context, the provocative title of a panel programmed at the "2nd International Conference on Extending Data Base Technology" (Venezia, March 1990) : "Why are Object-Oriented Folks Producing Systems, while Deductive Folks are Producing Papers ?".

2.22 Coupling Knowledge Engineering Software Environments and Expert Systems Shells with DB Systems. As already said, we will examine, here, the architectural solutions based on the notion of two co-operating but separated "front end" and a "back end" subsystems [2 ; etc.], as for the "heterogeneous approach" in a deductive database framework.

In our case, the front end, the KESE or ES, serves as the repository for the domain-specific knowledge as well as the implementation of the reasoning mechanisms required for user tasks. The back end is a general-purpose DBMS containing facts required for front-end reasoning. The coupling is realized by providing the reasoning mechanism of the front end with some sort of direct access to the DBMS, basically by using two different techniques. In the first case, there is no "dynamic link" between the two subsystems : data are downloaded from the DB to the front end, as a snapshot, before the reasoning mechanism (inference engine) is activated. Alternatively, a dynamic link is set, and data are retrieved from the DB only when required during the operations of the front end. The main advantage of this type of architecture resides in the fact that, given the two subsystems conserve their independence, the operational data required by the front end are already available from an existing, online DB,

without any necessity of restructuring and recoding the database information. Therefore, it is not surprising that there exist several commercial systems which implement this type of coupling. A well-known example is given by IntelliCorp's "KEEConnection" product, which allows the KEE shell to access DB information as it was part of the KEE Knowledge Base, automatically generating SQL queries to move data between the DB and the KB.

However, such systems have some serious drawbacks, and cannot be considered as the archetype of the new generation of database/knowledge base systems. The criticisms usually advanced against this particular solution are the following :

•   The main criticism concerns the fundamental "mismatch" between the two types of subsystems ; this mismatch takes several forms. A first one concerns the knowledge representation aspect ("semantic mismatch") : "pure" relational algebra and "flat" relations are not really compatible with the frames and semantic networks typical of KESEs, to say nothing of the *ad hoc* ways of structuring the fact base which are current in the ES shells. Severe performance problems arise from this mismatch, requiring, amongst other things, the use of redundant data descriptions to make data exchange across the interface possible. A second type of mismatch concerns the "granularity" of the data to be handled ("granularity mismatch"). An AI reasoning mechanism makes use of data in order to instantiate its variables ; therefore, it requires some data during each inference, and under an "atomic form". On the contrary, a relational DBMS answers a query by returning results as "sets of tuples". Accordingly, when the front end breaks down a query into a sequence of queries on tuples, each of them incurs a heavy back end performance overhead : we lose, therefore, the benefits of the set-oriented optimization the back end was designed for.

•   The second criticism, of a more fundamental nature, concerns the "loss of information" linked to the limited modeling capabilities of the relational paradigm used to implement the back end, i.e. the use of formatted data in the form of files of records to represent an original information which is often extremely rich and structured, see also the discussion at the beginning of 2.1.

3.   THE MAIN CHARACTERISTICS OF OUR PROPOSAL

As already said, the main impetus behind the project described in this paper is the willingness to combine the high-level information modelling features, the deductive capabilities, and the flexibility of AI-based systems with the efficiency, security, and concurrent access provided by DB systems over large sets of information. This will be fulfilled by realizing an advanced environment for the construction of Large Knowledge Based Systems (LKBSs). According to the "normal" DBMS standards, our LKBSs must be able to concurrently support a) requests issued by users operating interactively through a query interface ; b) requests issued by application programs. According to the features of the most advanced KESEs or ES shells, the knowledge handling needed to satisfy these requests will be realized by making use, in case, of powerful reasoning strategies which capitalize on the high-level knowledge representation paradigm adopted, see next Section, 4.

Given the analysis we have accomplished in 2., we can now detail the desirable properties of our LKBSs :

•   like a DBMS, our LKBSs cater for "persistent storage management" with physical and logical "data independence" ;

•   like a DBMS, they can be configured as a "server", enabling embedding within end-user applications ;

•   like a (relational) DBMS, they provide a powerful general "query and update language" ;

- like a DBMS, they use appropriate "indexing" and "query optimisation" techniques for efficiency ;

- like a DBMS, they permit enquiries and updates concurrently from "application programs" and "end users" alike, protecting the extensional database from concurrent update anomalies, catering efficiently with multiple users by re-entrancy ;

- like a nested relation system, they can use "attribute values" which are not necessarily atomic, but can be "relations" themselves and, more in general, enable a "recursive" style of schema definition ;

- like semantic data models and object-oriented systems, they structure an application domain into "object-types" or "classes", where object-types are organized via generalization, aggregation, grouping and user-defined relationships ;

- like semantic data models and object-oriented systems, they allow "property inheritance" within generalization hierarchies ;

- like hyper-semantic data models, they make no real distinction between "data" and "knowledge" (rules) ;

- like a rule-based control system or active database, they have the capability to take actions when the state of the underlying database changes ("transaction-triggered processing") ;

- like an advanced KESE (Knowledge Engineering Software Environment), they enable "non-deductive", e.g. abductive, inductive, nonmonotonic, probabilistic, analogical, reasoning to be applied if licenced by the enquirer ;

- like any state-of-the-art DBMS, ES shell or KESE, they provide sophisticated user interfaces as well as knowledge- and application- engineering tools, bootstrapped using their representational and inferential capabilities rather than being independently created by *ad hoc* means ;

- like the more "advanced" KBSs, they use a "hybrid" Knowledge Representation Language (KRL), see 4.

4. DEFINITION OF THE KRL

In defining our Knowledge Representation Language (KRL), we have maintained the differentiation introduced by Newell between "Knowledge" and "Symbol" level [13]. Accordingly, we can say that :

- At the Knowledge Level, which concerns the "semantics" of the KRL, we have decided the adoption of neatly differentiated representational instruments in order to describe the "descriptive (assertional) knowledge" ("Snoopy is Charlie Brown's beagle") and the "definitional (terminological) knowledge" ("A beagle is a sort of hound / a hound is a dog..."), see for example Zarri [20] . This approach can, therefore, be casted within the family of "hybrid representation systems", which has proved to be fruitful enough to give rise to the latest generation of KRLs, see [5, 18, etc.].

- At the Symbol Level, data structures suitable for the representation of the KRL expressions must be devised, along with the algorithms for carrying out the manipulation of the knowledge primitives. In what concerns some "static", passive aspects of the KRL, as the definitional hierarchies (see 4.2), a good candidate as an implementation vehicle could be some sort of "object-oriented representation" given the importance of the inheritance properties. On the other hand, as our KRL shares many characteristics of a purely declarative language, a "logic-oriented" computational framework may present some additional

advantages. We have reconciled the two points of view through the realization of a sort of theorem-prover centered around the use of a powerful "Filtering and Unification Module" (FUM), i.e. an unification algorithm in which the classical "resolution algorithm" (see 2.2) is modified in order to take into account directly the definitional hierarchies. This means that some simple deductions ("level zero inferences") can be done at the unification level rather then at the resolution level, see also [1].

4.1 Descriptive Component of the KRL

We shall refer to the "descriptive component" of the KRL as that part of knowledge which concerns the representation of detailed, particular facts about individual things, characters and events. Therefore, an information such as : "On the 21st and 22nd October, 1988, the Bluefields town on the Atlantic coast of Nicaragua has been ravaged by the cyclone Joan" will be represented using the "descriptive" tools ; information such as : "a cyclone is a storm or a system of winds that rotates around a center of low atmosphere pressure ...", as well as the definition : "a beagle is a sort of hound / a hound is a dog of any of various hunting breeds / all dogs are animals" in the Snoopy's example will be in the domain of the KRL's definitional component.

Brachman and his collegues have proposed [5], for the corresponding component of KRYPTON (ABox, "assertional component"), a language structured compositionally like a first order predicate calculus language where the sentence-forming operators are the usual ones, "Not", "Or", "ThereExist", and so on. We can notice that the generality of this language makes it inherit all the intractability results that hold for predicate calculus, and that a drastic improvement can be obtained, as usual, by "limiting" the form of the assertions that can be constructed using the descriptive (ABox) tools. In our case, we must, in particular, take into account the imperatives linked to the necessity of dealing

with large quantities of knowledge and information. This means that we must be able to structure efficiently the Knowledge Base (KB), i.e. that we must use powerful "conceptual indexing" schemata : as previous results demonstrate, see for example [21], conceptual indexing can be easily realized by choosing some "significant", "expressive" characteristics (some "key slots" for example) of a knowledge representation system where the basic syntactic constructs are given under the form of "structured objects".

We make therefore use, for the descriptive component of the KRL, of structured objects built according to a "canonical" approach consisting in the use of a well-balanced mix of "primitive" and "higher-level" conceptual objects. Accordingly, the coding of an elementary event using the KRL's descriptive tools gives rise to a "conceptual unit", a structured object organized around a semantic predicate identifying the "basic" type of action, state, situation etc. which is described in the event. The entities (normally some "instances") which are mentioned in the elementary event and which are, at least partly, proper to a particular application domain fill the peculiar "roles" (slots, facets, cases) associated with the semantic predicate ; the entities are, therefore, the arguments of the predicate. The semantic predicate, the arguments and the conceptual unit as a whole may be characterized by determiners (attributes) which give details about their significant aspects. For example, the predicate may be accompanied by "modulators" that are there to refine or modify the original semantic meaning of the predicate (an obvious example is the "negation" modulator which allows the happening of an elementary event to be denied : "Mary did not get the book from John"). Determiners which are associated with the arguments are the "location attributes" ("Mary, in Pensacola, got a book from John, in Kansas City"). Structured arguments ("expansions") can be created in many ways, for example, by associating to the entities (the instances) some "quantifying" ("some", "all", "329"...) or "qualifying" ("red", "powerful"...) attributes. Determiners associated to the whole conceptual unit are the "temporal attributes", which quantify time duration or frequency of an event, or the "identification attributes", giving the origin of the piece of information relating this event, etc. Roles are primitives. The entities of the domain, i.e. the arguments of the semantic predicate are, on the contrary, high-level conceptual objects which are freely chosen according to the necessities of the particular application(s) at hand and which are not decomposed into primitives ; their definitions are given by the definitional component of the KRL. The semantic predicate can be chosen according to any "deep" or "surface" option. This type of coding takes the name of "predicative occurrence". The general appearance of a predicative occurrence is shown in Fig. 1.

```
{ PREDICATE :   [ modulators ]
                ROLE - 1  { < argument > : [ location ] } }
                ROLE - 2  { < argument > : [ location ] } }
                 .
                 :
                ROLE - n  { < argument > : [ location ] } } }
                 .
                 :
                [ temporal attributes ]
                [ identification attributes ]
                 .
                 :
```

Figure 1

Being able to represent the elementary events in predicative occurrences is not enough to translate the original information completely. It is, in fact, necessary to represent also the logico-semantic links which exist between the events, for example between the two halves of the information : "John went to the post office in order to send a book to Mary". In our KRL, we solve this problem by making use of (recursive) nested relations, see 2.11, which will give rise to a new type of conceptual units, the "binding occurrences", see [20] for some details.

4.2 Definitional Component of the KRL

On the "definitional component" side, the knowledge to be represented concerns that sort of general information which can be associated as a definition to :

• the patterns ("templates") that subsume and generalize the specific "occurrences" which translate the elementary events of the descriptive component, see Fig. 1, and their links ;

• the "classes" (cyclone, beagle, hound...) representing the "general categories" to which can be reduced all the specific "instances" (cyclone_Joan, Snoopy...) of the application domain.

All these definitions are given by making reference to "specialization hierarchies", ("is_a" hierarchies), which (in general) are represented by an oriented graph characterized by the inheritance of properties and behaviors. The specialization hierarchy concerning the templates takes the name of H_TEMP hierarchy, or "grammar" ; the hierarchy concerning the classes is the H_CLAS hierarchy, or "lexicon".

The elements of the lexicon (H_CLAS) can be defined according to several strategies. For example, it is possible to derive a definition of these elements simply by determining their position inside the graph, i.e. by determining, following the "is_a" links, the ordered set of their "generic" terms. In this way, "beagle" is defined only by the fact of being a specific term of "hound" (the "supertype" of "beagle" is "hound", i.e. "beagle" pertains to the

type "hound") ; "hound" is a specific term of "hunting_dog", etc. ; all these terms pertain to the sub-graph which has "animal" as the top-level node. On the other hand, the definition of entities (classes) which are of particular importance from the point of view of a given application cannot be given satisfactorily by this type of representation only, and must be "augmented" by a formal description of their outstanding characteristics. The simplest way to furnish this description is to use some sort of "attributes", i.e. to associate a "frame" (another form of structured object) to the nodes of the oriented graph. Frames are well-known semantic structures used in the knowledge representation domain, see [9, 10, etc.], and it is not necessary to dwell excessively about this argument. We will only mention the fact that, in order to obviate the current criticism concerning the arbitrary choice of the slots which is characteristic of frame systems, we have taken in consideration the proposals, see [10] for example, suggesting to associate to each slot an (once again) explicit, structured object which can be named "metaslot" and which specify the "semantics" of the slot. Finally, a complete characterization of an entity can be obtained if the description of its typical "behaviour" ("behavioural rules") is added to the normal, "static" attributes. In conformity with the general characteristics of the KRL, these procedures are implemented in a declarative style using the "templates" of the H_TEMP hierarchy, see below.

With regards to the general philosophy underlying the set up of a H_CLAS hierarchy, we must strongly emphasize that the basic building block of this hierarchy is the "is_a" relation, to be interpreted as an operator giving rise to universally quantified sentences ("if someone is an employee, then he necessarily is a person"). This suffices to rule out a lot of very speculative problems such as those discussed by Brachman in some well-known papers [3, etc.], and originated by the use of examples in the style of "bird is_a flying_thing" which, of course, cannot be read as universally quantified sentences. This postulate about universal statements, which is valid for the relationships between the nodes of the hierarchy, does not apply to the sets of slots and fillers to be associated with these nodes, and translating our knowledge about some interesting properties of the entities of the domain. The values assumed by these properties can, therefore, be overridden. The value "can_fly", which would normally be inherited by "ostrich", is explicitly cancelled for this particular class ; this has no consequence on the relationships between "ostrich" and his parent-node "bird", because "ostrich" is still necessarily a "bird".

The hierarchy concerning the predicative and binding occurrences (H_TEMP, or "grammar") defines the general properties of the syntactic structures used in the descriptive component ; H_TEMP is simply a "tree", i.e. multiple inheritance should not be admitted here. An important characteristic of this specialization hierarchy is that one of the main aspects of the "defining information" associated with the nodes (templates) of this tree is given by the "constraints" which delimit the validity domain of the templates, i.e. which are used to specify the legal set of values (normally, "instances" of the "Snoopy" type), and their syntax, to be used in the construction of the concrete occurrences of the Descriptive Component. Given that the formal expressions implementing these constraints can be really complex, very often constraints are only indirectly inserted into the definitions under the form of an association with some "explicit variables", "x", "y", etc ; variables and constraints are also used in the H_CLAS component. For example if, in constructing the occurrences of the descriptive component, we make use of a "deep" predicate of the "MOVE" type in order to represent the displacement of a person or a group of persons, we can think of the corresponding "person_displacement_template" under the form of a conceptual unit like that of Fig. 1, where the "PREDICATE" is "MOVE", "ROLE-1" is "SUBJECT" or "AGENT", and the corresponding "argument" is something like " x : [<departure_location>] " ; the

314

"parent node" of this template in the H_TEMP hierarchy will be the generic "displacement_template". A (simple) constraint of the type "$x = $ <human_being> | <person_group>" should be associated to the variable "x". We have therefore developed a powerful "constraint satisfaction system" which can compute all the globally consistent assignments for a set of variables by using local propagation, tentative assumptions and backtracking.

Besides the creation of the predicative and binding occurrences, and in accordance with the principle of the "knowledge/data transparency" which is one of the theoretical basis of the project, the templates will be also used in the definition of a powerful class of conceptual inference procedures to be inserted in the "rule base" part of the LKBSs. They may also be used in the definition of the elements pertaining to the H_CLAS (lexicon) hierarchy, (behavioural rules, see above), in the construction of complex conceptual structures "à la Schank", etc.

4. CONCLUSIONS

In this paper, I have described some aspects of a current, interdisciplinary project carried out at the French National Center for Scientific Research (CNRS), and centered around a proposal concerning the integration of Artificial Intelligence (AI) and Database (DB) techniques. Our aim is to establish a sound methodology for the construction of Large Knowledge Based Systems (LKBSs) by combining the high-level information modeling features, the deductive capabilities, and the flexibility of the AI Knowledge Representation Languages (KRLs) with the characteristics of efficiency, security, concurrency, recovery and persistence of data provided by the Data Base Management Systems (DBMSs). In other words, the project relies on the DB results in order to deal with all problems concerning the architecture of the LKBSs and, in general, their Information Engineering aspects, and on the AI results with regards to all the domain modeling aspects (concerning both knowledge and data). After a description of the "state of the art" in the field of the AI/DB integration, devoted to better frame and justify our approach, I have given a succint description of the work already accomplished within the project in the knowledge representation area (set up of a powerful "hybrid representation system").

ACKNOWLEDGMENTS

I wish to thank Bill Black (UMIST Manchester, UK), who gave a precise formulation of many of the points expressed in Section 3. of this paper.

REFERENCES

[1] AIT-KACI, H., and NASR, R. (1986) "LOGIN : A Logic Programming Language with Built-in Inheritance", The Journal of Logic Programming, 3, 185-215.

[2] AL-ZOBAIDIE, A., and GRIMSON, J.B. (1987) "Expert Systems and Database Systems : How Can They Serve Each Other ?", Expert Systems, 4, 30-37.

[3] BRACHMAN, R.J. (1985) " 'I Lied about the Trees' Or, Defaults and Definitions in Knowledge Representation", AI Magazine, 6, n. 3, 80-93.

[4] BRACHMAN, R.J., and SCHMOLZE, J.G. (1985) "An Overview of the KL-ONE Knowledge Representation System", Cognitive Science, 9, 171-216.

[5] BRACHMAN, R.J., FIKES, R.E., and LEVESQUE, H.J. (1985) "KRYPTON : A Functional Approach to Knowledge Representation", in Readings in Knowledge Representation. San Mateo: Morgan Kaufmann.

[6] CERI, S., GOTTLOB, G., and TANCA, L. (1989) "What You Always Wanted to Know About DATALOG (And Never Dared to Ask)", IEEE Transactions on Knowledge and Data Engineering, 1, 146-166.

[7] CHANG, C.L., and WALKER, A. (1986) "PROSQL : A PROLOG Programming Interface with SQL", in Expert Database Systems - Proceedings from the First International Workshop, Kerschberg, L., ed. Menlo Park: Benjamin/Cummings.

[8] DELCAMBRE, L.M.L., and ETHEREDGE, J.N. (1988) "A Self-Controlling Interpreter for the Relational Production Language", in Proceedings of the 1988 SIGMOD Conference, special issue of ACM SIGMOD Record, 17, n. 3, 396-403.

[9] FIKES, R., and KEHLER, T. (1985) "The Role of Frame-Based Representation in Reasoning", Communications of the ACM, 28, 904-920.

[10] GREINER, R., and LENAT, D.B. (1980) "A Representation Language Language", in Proceedings of the First National Conference on Artificial Intelligence - AAAI/80. San Mateo: Morgan Kaufmann.

[11] HULL, R., and KING, R. (1987) "Semantic Database Modeling : Survey, Applications, and Research Issues", ACM Computing Surveys, 19, 201-260.

[12] LEUNG, Y.Y., and LEE, D.L. (1988) "Logic Approaches for Deductive Databases", IEEE Expert, 3, n. 4, 64-75.

[13] NEWELL, A. (1982) "The Knowledgbe Level", Artificial Intelligence, 18, 87-127.

[14] OZSOYOGLU, Z.M., ed. (1988) IEEE Data Engineering - Special Issue on Nested Relations, 11, n. 3.

[15] POTTER, W.D., TRUEBLOOD, R.P., and EASTMAN, C.M. (1989) "Hyper-semantic Data Modeling", Data and Knowledge Engineering, 4, 69-90.

[16] ROBINSON, J.A. (1965) "A Machine-Oriented Logic Based on the Resolution Principle", Journal of the ACM, 12, 23-41.

[17] TSUR, S. (1988) "LDL - A Technology for the Realization of Tightly Coupled Expert Systems", IEEE Expert, 3, n. 3, 41-51.

[18] VILAIN, M. (1985) "The Restricted Language Architecture of a Hybrid Representation System", in Proceedings of the Ninth International Joint Conference on Artificial Intelligence - IJCAI/85. San Mateo: Morgan Kaufmann.

[19] WIDOM, J., and FINKELSTEIN, S.J. (1989) A Syntax and Semantics for Set-Oriented Production Rules in Relational Database Systems (IBM Research Report). San Jose (Calif.): IBM Almaden Research Center.

[20] ZARRI, G.P. (1989) "A Knowledge Representation Language for the Construction and Use of Large Intelligent Systems", in Proceedings of the 1989 Annual Conference of the Associazione Italiana per l'Informatica ed il Calcolo Automatico (AICA). Milano: AICA.

[21] ZARRI, G.P. (1990) "Temporal Knowledge Denotation in the Context of the Descriptive Component of a Knowledge Representation Language", in Computational Intelligence, II, Gardin, F., Mauri, G., and Filippini, M., eds. Amsterdam: North-Holland.

Knowledge Systems: A Synthesis of Database Systems and Expert Systems Technologies

John K. Debenham

Key Centre for Advanced Computing Sciences,
University of Technology, Sydney, Australia.

ABSTRACT

Traditional database technology includes rigorous, formal techniques for the analysis, design and subsequent maintenance of the "information component" of database applications. By contrast, the database rules tend, in practice, to be handled by ad hoc methods. However, research in Expert Systems technology has generated techniques for handling rules in a systematic, rigorous way. We propose that these two technologies can benefit greatly from the other and can be effectively synthesized into one; thus leading to "knowledge systems".

Introduction

We promote "knowledge systems" as a synthesis of database systems and expert systems. In particular we show that rigorous techniques developed for handling the rules in Expert Systems technology may be employed together with the established modelling techniques for handling the information in database technology to give an integrated method for analyzing, designing and maintaining expert database systems, or knowledge systems.

Techniques such as Entity-Relationship or Binary-Relationship modelling are widely used to support the analysis, design and maintenance of the information component of database applications. By contrast the database rules are usually treated, in practice, in an ad hoc way and are represented as programs in some, usually imperative, host programming language. Consequently the effective maintenance of the knowledge embedded in these rules tends to be a complex issue. However, research in Expert Systems technology has developed systematic modelling techniques for handling rules. We propose that both of these technologies have something to learn from the other and that they can be synthesized into what we refer to as "knowledge systems". Our approach is based on formal modelling of the application, including the rules in the application, and on a process of normalisation which is applied to the entire model. The over all objective is to generate systems, either database systems or expert systems, that are maintainable.

From the database point of view, our major advances, which are drawn from our work in knowledge processing [7], are a notation for modelling knowledge and a set of normal forms for knowledge which are compatible with the traditional normal forms for information. Thus we promote two specific skills for the knowledge systems analyst:

- The skill to be able to represent and analyze rules effectively in a form that is not committed to any particular Expert Systems shell, programming language or database management system.
- The skill to be able to process the rules component so that it is then designed for maintenance. This process we will call "normalisation".

Still from the database point of view, failure to exercise these skills will mean that:

- Valuable knowledge is being gathered and is being represented usually in a procedural programming language. Thus, in effect, expensive, declarative knowledge is being represented as the specifications for particular, imperative programs. If there were a need to move to a new database management system with a different procedural host language then very substantial re-design costs could be incurred.
- The knowledge, or rules, will be represented as they are; that is, they will be represented in the host language more or less as the domain expert has pronounced them. The effect of this on maintenance can be quite serious, because, as we will see, chunks of knowledge can "overlap" in which case if "one chunk" is modified then "any overlapping chunks" may have to modified too. Furthermore, a small portion of knowledge may be represented, within other portions of knowledge, in a number of different places; if the small portion of knowledge should change, then all the different representations containing it will have to be altered.

Our experiments in designing expert, knowledge-based systems were first reported in [4]. Since that time we have come to realize the significance of constructing a "normalized" model, but not necessarily a normalized implementation, of the rules if the system is to be maintained effectively [5]. Difficulties with the maintenance of early expert systems are now well understood [13]. However little has been done to promote design techniques which prevent these difficulties from occurring [17]. We will discuss here the two skills referred to above which, we believe, are key, practical skills associated with the general business of preserving the accuracy of the rules. These two skills also receive extensive coverage in the recent text [7].

As a general preamble to our discussion we first clarify precisely what is meant by the "data", "information" and "knowledge" in an application. The *data* in an application is the fundamental, indivisible objects in that application; in simple terms, the data is the set of objects which are represented by populations and labels. The *information* in an application is

316

those relations between data items which cannot be represented by a succinct, general rule. The *knowledge* in an application is those relations between data and/or information items which can be represented by a succinct, general (computable) rule.

A special sort of knowledge is those rules which define the tuples which satisfy one relation in terms of the tuples which satisfy a number of other relations. Knowledge of this form can be represented directly in an "if-then" notation such as Horn clause logic. For example, suppose that the tuples which satisfy binary relation P are uniquely and explicitly determined by the tuples which satisfy the two binary relations Q and R. In general, a collection of Horn clauses will be required to represent a relation of this form; such a collection is called a *clause group*. In this example, this might be achieved by the two clause, clause group:

$$P(\underline{x}, y) \leftarrow Q(\underline{x}, z), R(z, y)$$
$$P(\underline{x}, y) \leftarrow P(\underline{x}, z), R(y, z)$$

We will illustrate our discussion with Horn clause logic, but note that we are not promoting Horn clause logic as a practical language for representing rules. However, as a declarative language, it is certainly preferable to traditional, imperative languages. The important point is that, as far as ease of maintenance is concerned, it really doesn't matter what language is used to implement the knowledge as long as the knowledge has been modelled rigorously and as long as this model of the knowledge has been normalized, is maintained and is used to drive the system maintenance process.

As we will see, in general, knowledge is not necessarily in an "if-then" form; in general, a chunk of knowledge will be represented by a collection of clause groups. We will refer to such a collection as a "cluster".

Modeling knowledge

We now discuss the first of our two skills, which is concerned with the ability to represent and analyze rules effectively in a form that is not committed to any particular Expert Systems shell, programming language or database management system. Techniques for preserving independence of the information in database applications from particular database management systems are well understood; these techniques rely heavily on the construction of a formal model of the application. In other words, these techniques cope adequately with data and information. Here we will refer to one such technique and will show how it can be employed together with our technique for modelling knowledge. See also [9, 15].

The knowledge in an application is those relations between data and/or information items which can be represented by a general (computable) rule. Consider the rule, "the selling price for spare parts costing less than $20 is the cost price marked up by 30 percent, and the selling price for spare parts costing $20 or more is the cost price marked up by 25 percent". The information in this example can be represented using the B-R notation [16] as shown in the diagram in Figure 1. However, this example also contains some knowledge. The knowledge in this example can be represented using a "dependency diagram". The dependency diagram for this example is shown in Figure 2. The dependency diagram notation should be read as "the information in the relation:

spare-part/sale-price:$

may be deduced from the information in the relation:

spare-part/cost-price:$

using the group named (A)".

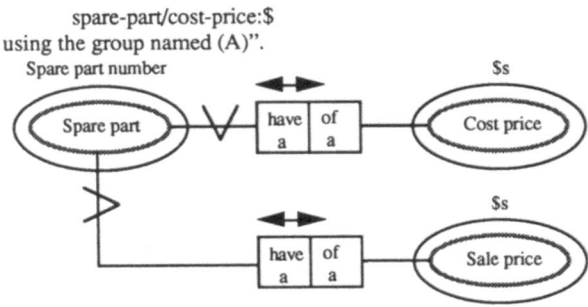

Figure 1 Information in the example

Figure 2 Knowledge in the example

As we will see, as the line shown in Figure 2 connecting the two circles is not annotated in any way this indicates that *all* such information may be deduced using group (A). The group (A) associated with the dependency diagram shown in Figure 2 is:

$$\text{spare-part/sale-price}(x, y) \leftarrow$$
$$\text{spare-part/cost-price}(x, z),$$
$$z < 20, \ y = z \times 1.3$$
$$\text{spare-part/sale-price}(x, y) \leftarrow$$
$$\text{spare-part/cost-price}(x, z),$$
$$z \geq 20, \ y = z \times 1.25 \qquad (A)$$

In general, a *dependency diagram* for a group with group name (G) and head predicate P is a directed tree. In this tree there is a node labeled (G). There is a directed arc from this node labeled (G) to a node labeled P. There is a node for each body predicate; these nodes are labeled with a body predicate name. There is a directed arc from each node labeled with a body predicate to the node labeled (G). By convention, the nodes of the dependency diagrams are labeled with the names of thing-populations. Thus, dependency diagrams could form the basis of an abstract modeling tool for knowledge but this lies beyond the scope of our discussion here. In other words, our present interest in dependency diagrams is purely as a pragmatic tool for designing the rules component of database applications.

If a group enables *all* the information in its head predicate to be deduced from the information in its body predicates it is called a *categorical group*. If the group (G) with head predicate P is *not* a categorical group then the arc from the node marked (G) to the node marked P is marked with a "flash" as shown in Figure 3.

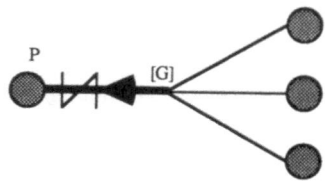

Figure 3 Diagram for a non-categorical group

For example, the group:

spare-part/sale-price(x, y) ←
        spare-part/cost-price(x , z),
        z ≥ 20 , y = z × 1.25   (A')

is not categorical. Its dependency diagram is shown in Figure 4.

Figure 4 Dependency diagram for non-categorical example

On occasions it is not possible to express a rule using a single clause group; the expressive power of logic simply may not be strong enough. In such a case, the expressive power of logic can be enhanced by introducing "internal predicates" which are predicates used in the phrasing of the clause group which are of purely computational significance. Internal predicates are *not* shown on the dependency diagram.

Consider the statement "the selling price for all spare parts is the product of the cost of the spare part and the mark-up-factor, where the mark-up-factor is determined by the type of the spare part". This rule could be represented by the single clause group:

spare-part/sale-price(x, y) ←
        spare-part/cost-price(x, z),
        spare-part/part-type(x, v),
        part-type/mark-up-factor(v, w),
        y = (z × w)   (B)

the dependency diagram for this group is shown in Figure 5. Note that the arc to the root node:

        spare-part/sale-price:$

has *not* been marked with a flash because we have been told that *all* the information in:

        spare-part/sale-price:$

can be obtained in this way.

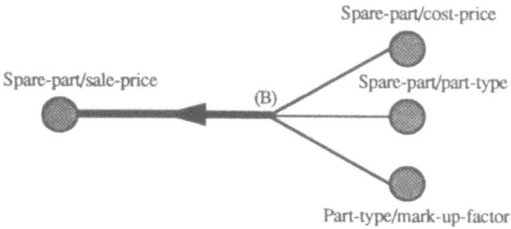

Figure 5 Dependency diagram for group (B)

In [7] it is shown how the dependency diagrams can be annotated to cope with "modalities". (*Modalities* are statements of probability, plausibility, belief and so on.)

We will now introduce the "cluster". A *cluster* for a collection of predicates consists of a set of groups where each group has one of the predicates from the collection as head and the body of each group will be a subset of the collection of predicates. For example, consider the set of predicates as in (B) above:

        spare-part/sale-price
        spare-part/cost-price
        spare-part/part-type
        part-type/mark-up-factor

In addition to group (B) it would be no surprise to find that "the cost price for those spare parts which are purchased for sale is the quotient of the sale price of the spare part and the mark-up-factor, where the mark-up-factor is determined by the type of the spare part". This rule could be represented by the single clause group:

spare-part/cost-price(x, z) ←
        spare-part/sale-price(x, y),
        spare-part/part-type(x, v),
        part-type/mark-up-factor(v, w),
        y = (z × w)   (C)

The dependency diagram for this group is shown in Figure 6.

Figure 6 Dependency diagram for group (C)

Furthermore, we would not expect that the predicate spare-part/part-type could be deduced from the other three predicates unless "mark-up-factor" determined "type" which, we will assume, is not the case. Finally, we assume that the predicate part-type/mark-up-factor cannot be deduced from the other three. At first glance it might appear that the predicate part-type/mark-up-factor could be defined by:

part-type/mark-up-factor(v, w) ←
        spare-part/part-type(x, v),
        spare-part/cost-price(x, z),
        spare-part/sale-price(x, y),
        y = (z × w)

but this group will only work if there is at least one part number in the system for each type. Hence, we reject it. Thus, the cluster for these four predicates consists of the two groups (B) and (C); we call this cluster "(D)".

It is often useful to represent the knowledge-dependency structure of an entire cluster; this may be achieved in an obvious way by drawing the "cluster group diagram". The *cluster group diagram* shows all the groups in the cluster on one "dependency" diagram. For the cluster (D) above, the cluster group diagram is shown in Figure 7. If, furthermore, it is required to represent the way in which these knowledge-dependencies are established, then this can be achieved by simply quoting the clauses which make up the groups in the cluster.

The cluster group diagram contains an unnecessary amount of information for use in system design. Thus, we introduce the "cluster diagram" for a given cluster. Given a cluster for a collection of predicates, the *cluster diagram* is a directed graph. There is a node for each predicate which is marked with that predicate's name. There is a single "central node" which is marked with the cluster's name. We usually draw the central node as a large circle. There is an arc between the central node and each of the nodes which are marked with a predicate's name. In addition, these arcs are marked as follows: if the arc is

318

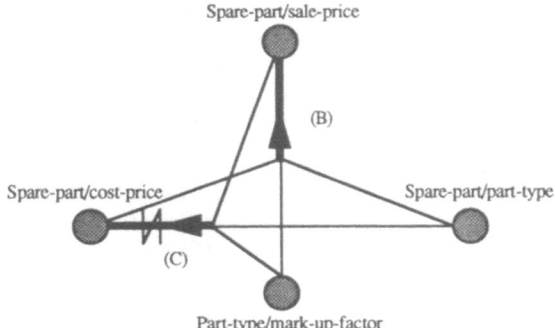

Figure 7 Cluster group diagram for cluster (D)

connected to a predicate which is the head of one of the groups in the cluster, then the arc is marked with the name of that group and with a "flash" if the group is so marked. Otherwise, the arc is marked with an arrow *from* the predicate node *to* the central node. For example, the cluster diagram for the above example is shown in Figure 8. The cluster diagram represents an "executive view" of the knowledge-dependencies in the component groups.

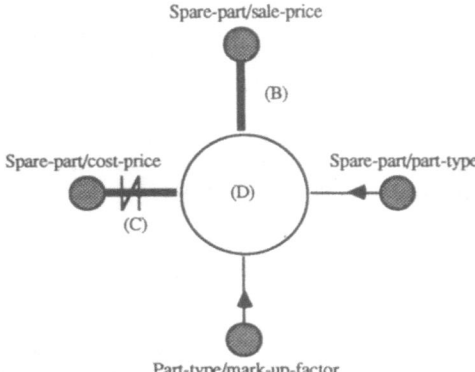

Figure 8 Cluster diagram for cluster (D)

We are particularly interested in two properties of clusters; they are "complete" clusters and "consistent" clusters. If a cluster for a collection of predicates consists of categorical groups, such that for each predicate in that collection there is one group with that predicate as its head, then the cluster is called a *complete cluster*. For example, cluster (D) is *not* complete because it does not contain a categorical group with "spare-part/part-type" as head, and it does not contain a categorical group with "part-type/mark-up-factor" as head. The idea behind a *consistent* cluster is that the knowledge in such a cluster should not permit the derivation of a contradiction. The demonstration of consistency is extremely complex in general. Instead, we introduce the notion of "information model consistency". To demonstrate "information model consistency", we associate a set of tuples with each predicate; these tuples are seen as satisfying that predicate at some particular time. All of these tuples, associated with each predicate in the cluster, are called an "information model of the cluster". A cluster is called *information model consistent* if, for each predicate, this

associated set is precisely the set which can be deduced from the group in the cluster which has that predicate as head. This notion of consistency is very crude but, nevertheless, it can be computed. Its principal weakness is that it depends on the construction of a good information model of the cluster. This notion of consistency demonstrates that the groups in a cluster are consistent with a particular model only of the information in that cluster.

Normalizing Modelled Knowledge

We now consider the second of our two skills which is concerned with the ability to process the rules component so that it is designed for maintenance. It is our observation that, in practice, the rules component of database applications is assembled and maintained by ad hoc means. We believe, therefore, that, in general, much of the cost of maintaining database applications is attributable to the maintenance of the database rules. Techniques for ensuring that the information component of database systems are, at least in theory, maintainable are well understood; these techniques rely heavily on the concept of the normalization of the model of the application. In our work on the design of expert systems for maintenance we have extended these ideas to include the normalization of knowledge, see [7] for a full account. Here we will illustrate the business of normalizing knowledge with some simple examples.

To illustrate our discussion here, we will consider a simple version of one of these new normal forms for knowledge. Suppose that two rules (A) and (B) have dependency diagrams as shown in Figure 9. If rule (A) could be expressed as shown in Figure 10 **then** rule (A) is said to violate this normal form and should be replaced by the form in Figure 10.

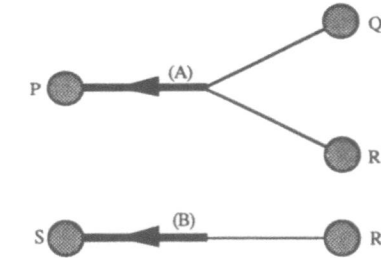

Figure 9 Rules (A) and (B)

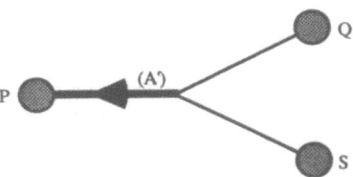

Figure 10 The normalized rule (A')

The wisdom behind the above rule for normalization is that rule (A) contains rule (B) implicitly embedded within it. In other words, if rule (B) were to change then, to preserve consistency, rule (A) may have to be changed as well. It should be clear that rule (B) and rule (A') are not likely to suffer from this difficulty.

Thus the goal of normalization for knowledge (and information and data) is that if one real "thing" changes in the application then only one modification will have to be made to the model of the application . The rule just discussed parallels something of the spirit of the third normal form rule for information [11]. We now discuss an example to illustrate this rule for normalizing knowledge. Consider rule (B) introduced above which is reproduced again below:

> spare-part/sale-price(x, y) ←
> > spare-part/cost-price(x, z),
> > spare-part/part-type(x, v),
> > part-type/mark-up-factor(v, w),
> > y = (z × w)　　　　　　　　(B)

Buried within this rule is the rule that "the mark-up factor for a spare part is the mark-up factor associated with that spare part's type". This rule could be represented as:

> spare-part/mark-up-factor(x, y) ←
> > spare-part/part-type(x, z),
> > part-type/mark-up-factor(z, y)　　　(F)

the dependency diagram for this rule is shown in Figure 11.

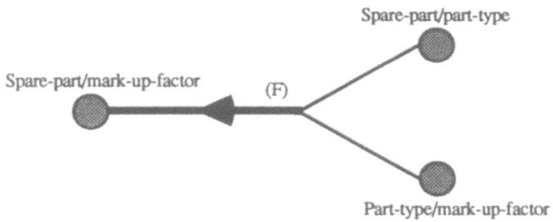

Figure 11 Dependency diagram for group (F)

Now it should be clear that rule (F) is buried within rule (B), and that rule (B) should thus be re-expressed as:

> spare-part/sale-price(x, y) ←
> > spare-part/cost-price(x, z),
> > spare-part/mark-up-factor(x, w),
> > y = (z × w)　　　　　　　　(B')

The dependency diagram for this group is as shown in Figure 12.

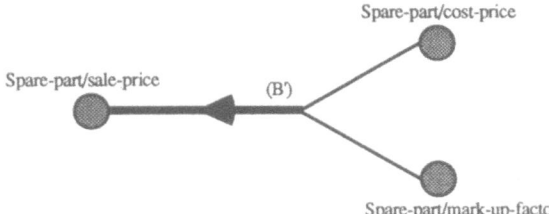

Figure 12 Dependency diagram for group (B')

The normalization rule discussed above is concerned with one rule being buried within another. A more subtle, and more general, case is the situation when two rules share an, as yet unstated, sub-rule between them. This situation is clearly undesirable because if the knowledge implicit in the sub-rule should change then both of the rules will have to be re-expressed. For example, consider the rule "the sale price of an item is calculated by taking the cost price of that item, marking the cost price up by the profit margin for that item and adding

sales tax at the correct rate for that item". This rule could be expressed as:

> item/sale-price(x, y) ← item/cost-price(x, z),
> > item/sales-tax-rate-%(x, v),
> > item/profit-margin-%(x, w),
> > u = (1 + w ÷ 100) × (1 + v ÷ 100)
> > y = u × z　　　　　　　　(G)

The dependency diagram for this group is as shown in Figure 13.

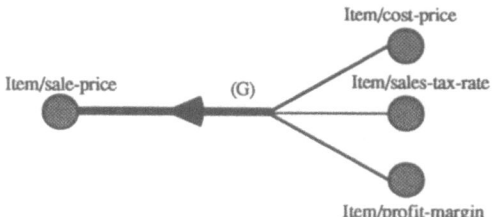

Figure 13 Dependency diagram for group (G)

Consider the rule "the value added tax payable on an item is the product of the value added tax rate for that item and the difference between the pre-sales tax sale price and the cost price of that item". This rule could be expressed as:

> item/value-added-tax(x, y) ← item/cost-price(x, z),
> > item/profit-margin-%(x, w),
> > item/value-added-tax-rate-%(x, v),
> > y = (z × w × v) ÷ 10,000　　　(H)

The dependency diagram for this group is as shown in Figure 14.

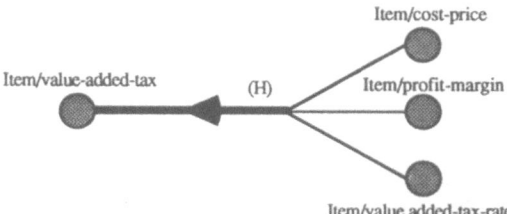

Figure 14 Dependency diagram for group (H)

The problem with groups (G) and (H) is that buried within both rules is the sub-rule that "the pre-sales tax selling price of an item is the cost price of the item marked up by the profit margin for that item per cent". This rule could be expressed as:

> item/pre-sales-tax-selling-price(x, y) ←
> > item/cost-price(x, z),
> > item/profit-margin-%(x, w),
> > y = (1 + w ÷ 100) × z　　　(J)

The dependency diagram for this group is as shown in Figure 15. Now suppose that rule (J) were to change, and to be replaced by the rule "the pre-sales-tax selling price of an item is a fixed $5 charge plus the cost price of the item marked up by the profit margin for that item per cent". This new rule could be expressed as:

> item/pre-sales-tax-selling-price(x, y) ←
> > item/cost-price(x, z),
> > item/profit-margin-%(x, w),
> > y = 5 + (1 + w ÷ 100) × z　　(J')

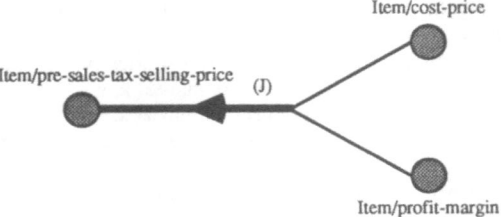

Figure 15 Dependency diagram for group (J)

The problem is that rules (G) and (H) will both have to be re-expressed as both depend implicitly on the notion of the "pre-sales tax selling price". Actually the problem is more serious than this because the implicit dependence of rules (G) and (H) on the concept of "pre-sales tax selling price" is not at all clear from the expression of those rules in logic. In other words we identify a potential "maintenance hazard" in the expression of the two rules (G) and (H). This hazard could have been avoided by identifying the sub-rule defining "pre-sales tax selling price", extracting this sub-rule from the rules as expressed in (G) and (H), and then re-expressing these two rules as:

item/sale-price(x, y) ←
        item/pre-sales-tax-selling-price(x, z),
        item/sales-tax-rate-%(x, w),
        $y = (1 + w \div 100) \times z$ (G')

with dependency diagram as shown in Figure 16, and:

item/value-added-tax(x, y) ←
        item/pre-sales-tax-selling-price(x, z),
        item/cost-price(x, w),
        item/value-added-tax-rate-%(x, v),
        $y = (v \div 100) \times (z - w)$ (H')

with dependency diagram as shown in Figure 17.

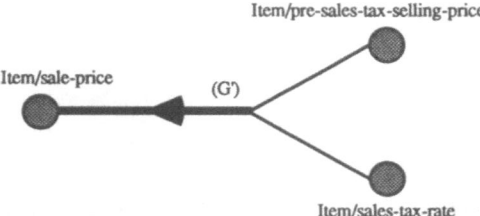

Figure 16 Dependency diagram for group (G')

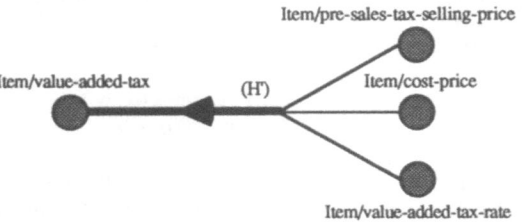

Figure 17 Dependency diagram for group (H')

It should be clear that the two rules as expressed in (G') and (H') are not now insulated against changes in the definition of the "pre-sales tax selling price".

Conclusion

We have promoted knowledge systems as a synthesis of database systems and expert systems. Our approach is based on the construction of a formal model of the application which includes the rules in the application, and a process of normalisation which is applied to this entire model. The over all objective is to generate expert database systems systems that are maintainable.

We have promoted two specific skills for the knowledge systems analyst:

- The skill to be able to represent and analyze rules effectively in a form that is not committed to any particular Expert Systems shell, programming language or database management system.
- The skill to be able to normalize the rules component so that it is then designed for maintenance.

A prerequisite to mastering these two skills is a clear understanding of the meaning of the terms "data", "information" and "knowledge"; these terms have been briefly discussed. Modelling knowledge using dependency diagrams and cluster diagrams has been promoted as an effective way to represent knowledge which ensures independence of any particular programming language or database management system. Finally the important issue of maintainability of rules has been examined and two normalization rules for knowledge have been illustrated.

References.

1. ADDIS, T.R., "Designing Knowledge-Based Systems", Kogan-Page, 1985.
2. DAHL, V., "On Database Systems Development Through Logic", ACM Transactions on Database Systems, Vol 7, No 1, 1982, pp 102-123.
3. DATE, C.J., "An Introduction to Database Systems" (4th edition) Addison-Wesley, 1986.
4. DEBENHAM, J.K. and McGRATH, G.M., "The Description in Logic of Large Commercial Data Bases: A Methodology put to the test", Proceedings of the Fifth Australian Computer Science Conference, 1982, pp. 12-21.
5. DEBENHAM, J.K., "Knowledge Base Design", Australian Computer Journal, Vol 17, No 1, 1985, pp 187-196.
6. DEBENHAM, J.K., "Style in Logic Programs", in Proceedings Australian Computer Conference, Gold Coast, Australia, 1986.
7. DEBENHAM, J.K., "Knowledge Systems Design", Prentice Hall, 1989.
8. GAINES, B.R., "Foundations of knowledge engineering", in (M.A. Bramer, Ed.) "Research and Development in Expert Systems III", Cambridge University Press, 1987.
9. GRAY, P.M.D., "Expert Systems and Object-Oriented Databases: Evolving a New Software Architecture", in "Research and Development in Expert Systems V", Cambridge University Press, 1989, pp 284-295.
10. HOGGER, C., "Introduction to Logic Programming", Academic Press, 1984.
11. KENT, W., "A Simple Guide to Five Normal Forms in Relational Database Theory", C. ACM, Vol 26, No 2, Feb 1983, pp 120-125.
12. NAPHEYS, B. and HERKIMER, D., "A Look at Loosely-Coupled Prolog/Database Systems", in Proceedings Second International Conference on Expert

Database Systems, George Mason University, 1988.

13. STEELS, L., "Second Generation Expert Systems", in (M.A. Bramer, Ed.) "Research and Development in Expert Systems III", Cambridge University Press, 1987.

14. STONIER, T., "What is Information", in (M.A. Bramer, Ed.) "Research and Development in Expert Systems III", Cambridge University Press, 1987.

15. TWINE, S., "Towards a Knowledge Engineering Procedure", in "Research and Development in Expert Systems V", Cambridge University Press, 1989, p 90-102.

16. VERHEIJEN, G.M.A and VAN BEKKUM, J., "NIAM: An Information Analysis Method" in "Information Systems Design Methodologies: A Comparative Review", (T.W. Olle and A.A. Verrijn-Stuart, Eds), IFIP, North-Holland, 1982.

17. WALKER, A., KOWALSKI, R., LENAT, D., SOLOWAY, E. and STONEBRAKER, M., "Knowledge Management", in (L. Kerschberg, Ed.), "Proceedings from the Second International Conference on Expert Database Systems", Benjamin Cummings, 1989.

An Expert System Approach to Database Design

Branka Tauzovich

Cognos Inc., Research Division
3755 Riverside Drive, P.O. Box 9707
Ottawa, Ontario, Canada K1G 3Z4

ABSTRACT

Although numerous methodologies, techniques and automated tools have been developed specifically to improve application database designs, this task still remains complex and demands a high level of skill on the part of the designer. Its judgmental nature makes it a type of task that can benefit greatly from the application of expert system technology. This paper describes an effort in that direction. We present expert systems for conceptual and logical database design which have been developed as integral parts of a next generation CASE tool.

INTRODUCTION

In the past several years, a number of computer-aided software enginnering (CASE) tools have appeared on the market. They increase the productivity of systems designers and improve the quality of software produced. Most of them, however, are little more than automation of relatively old design techniques. At best, these tools provide convenient graphics interfaces, help keep track of design components, and ensure that the design conforms to a given methodology. What they do not provide, however, is active help in making design decisions. Expert system technology can be used to develop a new generation of CASE tools capable of giving advice to the system designer, of proposing alternative solutions, and of helping to investigate the consequences of design decisions. By trying to capture, represent, and effectively use design knowledge, a knowledge-based design tool can help create a much better application database design than one created with traditional tools. Moreover, if the system can explain its reasoning, which is an essential requirement of an expert system, its decisions are more likely to be accepted by the user, and it can teach its less experienced users while assisting them in their work. To date, only a relatively small amount of effort has been invested in applying expert system technology in commercial CASE tools [1].

In this paper we describe the Modeller, an intelligent database design assistant which is an integral part of a next generation CASE tool being built by Cognos Inc. Its architecture (shown in Figure 1) comprises three levels, one for each of the three traditional steps of the current consensus approach to database design [2]. At the top level, there is a conceptual design expert; there is a logical design expert at the intermediate level; and, a physical design expert for each target Database Management System (DBMS) at the bottom. We acknowledge but do not currently address the network model which is sometimes interposed between the logical and physical levels.

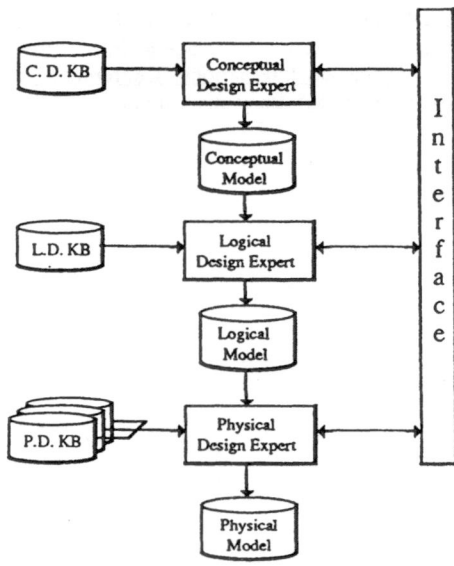

Figure 1. The 3-tier architecture of the Modeller

The top level expert takes initial requirements, a description of the *enterprise* (also called the *universe of discourse*) being modelled as input, and creates a high level, DBMS-independent model of the enterprise called the *conceptual model*. The logical design expert takes the conceptual model as input, and creates a *logical model* (in our case, based on the relational approach), allowing certain types of modifications to be done to the model. Finally, the physical design expert converts the logical model into a *physical model* for a particular DBMS. In performing its task, each expert system accesses the corresponding knowledge base and uses its rules for reasoning about and refining the evolving model. Expert systems communicate with the user through an interface that offers a combination of text-based and diagrammatic representation and manipulation of the evolving model [3]. Textual input to the Modeller, external knowledge representation, and the textual model presentation are all given in an English-like, general purpose knowledge acquisition language [4] used in the development of several expert systems [5, 6].

In the rest of the paper we will give an overview of the conceptual and logical design expert systems of the Modeller.

CONCEPTUAL MODELLING EXPERT

Conceptual modelling is a an intellectually-challenging and time-consuming task which consists of extracting, combining, refining, and representing knowledge about the enterprise. The result of this process is a conceptual model, a representation of the enterprise based on a set of abstractions. Because of its rather judgmental nature, it is a subject suitable for the application of expert system technology. Some results in this area have been reported in [1, 7, 8, 9, 10].

We have adopted and extended the entity-relationship (ER) approach which is the most widely, and best understood approach to semantic data modelling today [11]. Using this paradigm, the designer creates a diagrammatic model of an enterprise in terms of *entities* (which represent classes of individual things, persons, places, organizations, etc. considered to be of relevance to the enterprise), *relationships* (semantic connections) that exist among them, and *attributes* that further describe entities and relationships. We have extended the ER approach by specializing the types of basic concepts in a number of different ways (e.g., 'independent entity' and 'association are specializations of entity, 'role-of' and 'characteristic-of' are specializations of relationship). This resulted in a rich taxonomy of concepts for modelling the structure and (to some extent) the behaviour of an enterprise. We will not discuss this taxonomy here (this topic is explored in [12]), but will give a small example that illustrates the use of some of the concepts. Figure 2 shows the extended entity-relationship (EER) diagram described by the following set of Modeller statements:

> subproject is a characteristic of project
> min cardinality of project to subproject is 1
> task is association of subproject and activity
> min cardinality of subproject to activity is 2
> min cardinality of activity to subproject is 1
> max cardinality of activity to subproject is n
> project-manager is a role of employee
> min cardinality of project to project-manager is 1
> max cardinality of project to project-manager is 1
> min cardinality of project-manager to project is 1
> max cardinality of project-manager to project is n
> max cardinality of task to employee is n
> employee-name is an attribute of employee

subproject-number is a subkey_attribute of subproject within project
address is an attribute of employee
address is an aggregate of apt-no street city postal-code
skills is an attribute of employee
skills is a set of skill
employee-number is a key_attribute of employee
task-code is a key_attribute of task

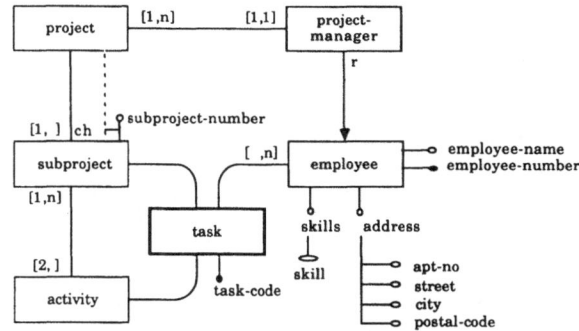

Figure 2. EER Diagram: An Example

In the Modeller, conceptual design knowledge is represented by several groups of rules. *Definition* rules are typical if-then rules that state that if (for some instantiation of variables) the antecedent is true, then the consequent is also true.

CASE tools typically force the user to explicitly supply each and every piece of information in order to perform some task. An intelligent tool should be able to reason even with incomplete information. The Modeller has a set of heuristic rules called *default rules* that allow the system to fill in gaps in the evolving model of the enterprise. For example, the following rule sets max cardinality from 'subproject' to 'activity' to n (many), because min cardinality is greater than 1 (cardinality from entity X to entity Y indicates the number of instances of Y related to any specific instance of X):

> IF
>> min cardinality from X to Y is C AND
>> C > 1 AND
>> max cardinality from X to Y is not specified
> THEN
>> set max cardinality from X to Y to n.

Contradiction rules are declarative rules that embody incompatibility constraints. They identify pairs of of statements that contradict each other. For example, the following rule states that an attribute of an entity cannot be both mandatory

324

(value required to be present in the database) and optional (value not required) at the same time:

CONTRA

    attribute X of Y is mandatory

AND

    attribute X of Y is optional

Full modelling of the behaviour of an enterprise requires representation formalisms and reasoning mechanisms that are mostly different from those used in the modelling of structure. The structure and behaviour are, however, two aspects of the same object (the enterprise) and thus reflect each other in many ways. Consequently, many facts about the behaviour of an enterprise can be inferred by examining a representation of its structure alone. These inferences pertain to a predefined set of generic operations on instances of entities. We use *causal* rules to reason about structure-implied behaviour.

The Conceptual Modeller is capable of reasoning about the implications of an individual change to the evolving model, as well as about the model as a whole. While the user is constructing the model by manipulating assertions, the system explores the consequences of each change being made and helps the user maintain the consistency of the model at all times. Reasoning about the model as a whole is done whenever the user wants the system to globally evaluate the model and to complete it in certain ways. The completion of the model involves the elimination of many-to-many relationships (by transforming them into two one-to-many relationships which simplifies the model), and the assignment of default cardinalities. Figure 3 shows the example diagram completed through application of these heuristics by the Modeller.

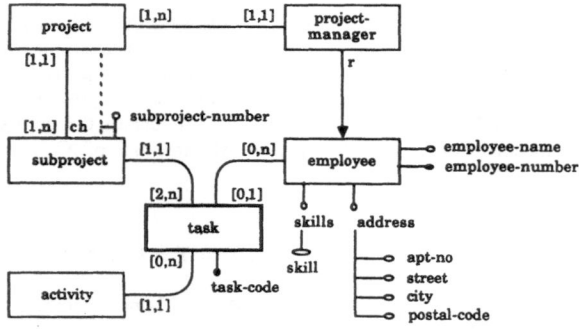

Figure 3. Completed EER Diagram (Example)

Global evaluation consists of the detection of subtle semantic errors (e.g., an existential dependency loop in the EER graph)

and potential problem areas of the model (e.g., the existence of an entity which is not related to any other entity).

Reasoning combines forward chaining of rules, generalization and simulation.

The system environment provides a variety of commands for building, refining, and documenting models. An important factor in the acceptance of an expert system is the mode in which it interacts with the user. It should not interrupt or distract the user's work unless it is senseless to continue under the circumstances. Neither should it rely on the user to provide all the pieces of the specification in order to be able to arrive at certain conclusions. The Modeller quietly but carefully watches while the user develops his/her ideas in any order, and provides most of the assistance only when the user is ready to accept feedback. The Conceptual Modeller is fully described in [13].

LOGICAL DESIGN EXPERT

The expert system for the second phase of database design takes as input a conceptual model produced by the Conceptual Modeller and produces a logical database design. This design is generic in the sense that it is based solely on relational concepts (e.g., relation, column, primary key) [14] without any consideration of the physical implementation issues (e.g., indexes for efficient data access).

There are three requirements that a conceptual model must fulfill before it will be accepted as valid input to the logical design: (a) the model must not contain any of the errors which can be detected in the Conceptual Modeller, (b) all many-to-many relationships must be resolved into one-to-many relationships (in our example, the many-to-many relationship between 'subproject' and 'activity' is resolved via the association 'task'), and (c) all cardinalities must be assigned (by the user and/or default rules). Logical design is performed in three phases: relational design, design optimization, and schema preparation. A trace of the logical design for our example is shown in Appendix A.

Relational Design. This phase consists of four steps. First, the initial set of relations is generated. For every entity in the conceptual model, a corresponding relation is created. Our paradigm allows attributes to be defined on structured domains, namely aggregates and sets (as illustrated by the example). In order to ensure that the initial relations are already in the first normal form, we create additional relations through the following rule (it is applied in the creation of the 'employee&skills' relation):

IF

    A is an attribute of entity E AND
    A contains a set

THEN

    create relation for E and A.

Columns are assigned to relations based on a variety of conditions reflected in a given EER diagram. At this abstract level, columns are actually pointers to corresponding attributes and other relations. In the next step, candidate keys are determined for each relation. A key is formed either from a single column or as a combination of two or more columns. For example, the following rule assigns 'project' and 'subproject-number' together to be a candidate key for the 'subproject' relation (in our taxonomy A is a subkey attribute of X within Y if it is an attribute of X that alone does not uniquely identify an instance of X but its combination with related instance of Y does so):

> IF
>
> > A is a subkey_attribute of X within Y AND
> > A does not contain a set AND
> > Xr is the relation of X
>
> THEN
>
> > make [Y,A] a candidate_key of Xr

In the last step of the relational design, the system designates one of the candidate keys of each relation to be its primary key. For example, the following rule designates 'employee-number' as the primary key of relation 'employee' (values of a key attribute uniquely identify instances of the entity):

> IF
>
> > Xr is the relation of X AND
> > Xr does not have a primary_key assigned AND
> > Y is a candidate_key of Xr AND
> > Y is a key_attribute of X AND
> > Y is not an optional attribute of X
>
> THEN
>
> > make Y a primary_key of Xr.

For those relations that do not have any candidate keys after the previous step is completed, primary keys are generated by the system (e.g., 'project-Id').

Design Optimization. In this optional phase, the system performs design optimization according to generic rules that apply regardless of the target DBMS. Typically, this pertains to the elimination of what we term "no-data" relations, i.e., relations that turned out to be redundant. The following rule, for example, eliminates relation 'project-manager' from the design:

> IF
>
> > X is an entity AND
> > Xr is the relation of X AND
> > X has 1 relationship AND
> > X is related to Y AND
> > Yr is the relation of Y AND
> > X is a column of Y AND
> > X is not a subclass AND
> > X is not an independent entity
>
> THEN
>
> > eliminate Xr.

Schema Preparation. It is only in this phase that all columns and keys defined on aggregate domains are exploded into their non-structured parts (e.g., column 'address' of relation 'employee' is replaced by columns 'apt-no', 'street', 'city' and 'postal-code'). In addition to that, unique names are assigned to columns. Because the Modeller has a rich set of abstractions and heuristic design rules, and because the relational design is performed at a rather abstract level, it often happens that two or more columns of a relation refer to the same entity or domain. For example, the Modeller has concepts which allow domains be defined in terms of other domains. According to this, both 'home-address' and 'business-address' could be defined on an aggregate domain 'address'. Should a relation have both of these as its columns, their components would have to be given qualified names to avoid ambiguity. A number of rules govern the name assignment process in order to produce as short and as meaningful names as possible under the given circumstances.

The result of the logical design is presented to the user in an SQL-like form which we term the *generic relational schema*. The schema for our example is shown in Appendix B. An explanatory facility that relates any relational object to its origins in the conceptual model is also provided.

The internal form of the model is passed on to the Physical Modeller for further optimization and detailed physical design based on restrictions and requirements of the target DBMS implementation.

CONCLUDING REMARKS

The paper presents an an application of expert system technology to both conceptual and logical database design. The conceptual modelling expert system allows the user to explore ideas in any order, without interrupting or requesting additional information. It uses a taxonomy of modelling concepts and a variety of rules to reason about individual pieces of information supplied by the user, to extend the evolving model through heuristics, to maintain the consistency of the model, and to detect those parts of the model that might need further revision. The logical modelling expert system uses a novel, three-phase approach that clearly separates abstract relational design from the issues of design presentation. Both expert systems can justify their conclusions and decisions by explaining the reasoning behind them.

A fully operational, stand-alone prototype of the system has been implemented in Arity Prolog on a Compaq 386/20 workstation. The scope of the present version of the system is limited to structure modelling. We are presently working on a behaviour modelling component. It is our intention to extend the functionality of the tool to the full application systems design area, including the reverse engineering process, as well as to add machine learning mechanisms for the refinement and customization of the knowledge base.

REFERENCES

[1] Bouzeghoub, M., and Metais, E, "SECSI: An Expert System Approach for Database Design", *Information Processing 86*, edited by H.J. Kugler, North-Holland, 1986, pp.251-257.

[2] Navathe, S. B., *Conceptual and Logical Database Design*, Tutorial, 7th Int. Conference on Entity Relationship Approach, Rome, Italy, Nov. 1988.

[3] Dudley, T., "A Visual Interface to a Database Modelling Tool", Proceedings of the IEEE Workshop on Visual Languages, Rome, Italy, 1989.

[4] Skuce, D., "The LESK Tutorial", TR-83-03, Department of Computer Science, University of Ottawa, July 1983.

[5] Tauzovich, B., Matwin, S., Oppacher, F., Skuce, D., and Szpakowicz, S., "An Expert Advisory System for Government Regulations: Knowledge Acquisition Methodology", in *Artificial Intelligence in Economics and Management*, edited by L. F. Pau, North Holland, 1986, pp.205-212.

[6] Skuce, D., Stanley, R., and Tauzovich, B., "An Expert Advisor that Answers Coding Questions about Commercial Fourth-Generation Software", *International Journal of Expert Systems 1*, No.3, 1988, pp.217-235.

[7] Briand, H., Hebrias, H., Hue, J-F, and Simon, Y., "Expert System for Translating an E-R Diagram into Databases", *Proceedings of the Fourth International Conference on Entity Relationship Approach*, Chicago, Oct. 1985.

[8] Furtado, A.L., Casanova, M.A., and Tucherman, L., "The CHRIS Consultant", in *Entity-Relationship Approach*, *Proceedings of the Sixth International Conference on Entity-Relationship Approach*, edited by S. March, North-Holland, 1988, pp.515-532.

[9] Rolland, C., and Proix, C., "An Expert System Approach to Information System Design", *Information Processing 86*, edited by H.J. Kugler, North-Holland, 1986, pp.241-250.

[10] Springsteel, F.N. and Chuang, P-J, "ERDDS: The Intelligent E-R-Based Database Design System", *Proceedings of the Seventh International Conference on Entity Relationship Approach*, Rome, Italy, Nov. 1988, pp.211-230.

[11] Chen, P., "The Entity-Relationship Model - Toward a Unified View of Data", *ACM Transactions on Database Systems 1*, 1 (Mar), 1976, pp.9-36.

[12] Tauzovich, B., and Skuce, D., "A General Taxonomy for Conceptual Data Modelling", submitted to the 9th International Conference on Entity Relationship Approach, Lausanne, Switzerland, 1990.

[13] Tauzovich, B., "An Expert System for Conceptual Data Modelling", *Proceedings of the 8th International Conference on Entity Relationship Approach*, Toronto, Canada, Oct. 1989, pp.329-344.

[14] Codd, E. F., "A Relational Model of Data for Large Shared Data Banks", *Communications of the ACM 13*, 6 (June), 1970.

APPENDIX A: Logical Design Trace

```
PHASE I: Relational Design

 Determining relations  --
    employee is a relation
    project is a relation
    project-manager is a relation
    activity is a relation
    subproject is a relation
    task is a relation
    employee&skills is a relation

 Determining columns  --
    employee-name is a column of employee
    address is a column of employee
    project-manager is a column of project
    project is a column of subproject
    task is a column of employee

 Determining candidate keys  --
    employee is a candidate key of project-manager
    [subproject,activity] is a candidate key of task
    [employee,skills] is a candidate key of employee&skills
    [project,subproject-number] is a candidate key of subproject
    employee-number is a candidate key of employee
    task-code is a candidate key of task

 Determining primary keys  --
    employee is the primary key of project-manager
    [project,subproject-number] is the primary key of subproject
    [subproject,activity] is the primary key of task
    [employee,skills] is the primary key of employee&skills
    employee-number is the primary key of employee
    project_Id is the primary key of project
    activity_Id is the primary key of activity

 Phase II: Design Optimization

    del: activity is a relation
    del: project-manager is a relation

 PHASE III: Schema Preparation

    apt-no is a column of employee
    street is a column of employee
    city is a column of employee
    postal-code is a column of employee
```

APPENDIX B: Generic Relational Schema

```
RELATION  employee
      ( employee-number                              NOT NULL,
        employee-name,
        apt-no,
        street,
        city,
        postal-code,
        project_Id          PART_REF  task,
        subproject-number   PART_REF  task,
        activity            PART_REF  task
      PRIMARY KEY (employee-number) ) ;

RELATION  project
      ( project_Id                                   NOT NULL,
        project-manager     REF  employee            NOT NULL
      PRIMARY KEY (project_Id) ) ;

RELATION  subproject
      ( project_Id          REF  project             NOT NULL,
        subproject-number                            NOT NULL
      PRIMARY KEY (project_Id, subproject-number) ) ;

RELATION  task
      ( project_Id          PART_REF  subproject NOT NULL,
        subproject-number   PART_REF  subproject NOT NULL,
        activity                                 NOT NULL,
        task-code                                NOT NULL
      PRIMARY KEY (project_Id, subproject-number, activity)
      ALTERNATE KEY (task-code) ) ;

RELATION  employee&skills
      ( employee-number     REF  employee        NOT NULL,
        skill                                     NOT NULL
      PRIMARY KEY (employee-number, skill) ) ;
```

Concepts for intelligent database front-end systems

A. J. Tulp

Royal PTT Nederland NV.
PTT Research division Tele-informatics
Groningen - The Netherlands

Abstract

In many cases it is quite diffucult to retrieve information from databases in a heterogeneous database environment. In this paper I present some concepts which can be useful in a database font-end system in order to guide a user to the necessary information. To support the user in making the appropriate choices in the information retrieval process, the font-end system has to carry out some knowledge processing and - according to the results of this reasoning - to advise the user.

1. Introduction

Within PTT Research a prototype front-end system has been developed as an automated intelligent intermediary between the user and a number of bibliographical databases. In this paper we will present four concepts which are applied in this prototype database front-end system. The aim of this article is to consider whether the concepts on which this prototype is based can be generalised to other types of intermediary systems for databases. Firstly we will define the problem and describe the concepts on which this prototype has been developed. After describing some general aspects of an intermediary system we will finally try to apply the presented concepts in intermediary systems for accessing business oriented databases.

2. Problem description

In the last decade it has become clear that the supply of information is of vital importance for managers within organisations. Several authors [1,2,4] pointed out already that - beneath capital, human power and raw materials - information can be considered as an additional vital resource for organisations. Business databases play an important role in the supply of information in an organisation. When someone regularly uses a few or more databases for information retrieval he or she will not meet many problems. Because of regular use of the databases the user has built up enough experience to know how to retrieve information. When a person wants to get information out of a database which is only occasionally used the situation is quite different. Each database has its own specific access method and data manipulation language. For this reason there is often a need to ask a human expert on database retrieval for help. In the librarian world it is usual to consult an intermediary person for information retrieval concerning information from several different bibliographical databases.

Williams [5] offers us a distinction which defines three different kinds of activities in the search process:

1. pre-search functions, such as defining the required information and the selection of the database;

2. search related functions, these concern the choice of the right terms in the search profile and the query action in the database;

3. post-search functions, which is related to the evaluation of the search and the presentation of the search results to the user (printing or presentation on the computer screen).

As a foundation for defining the tasks of an intermediary, we adopted this classification. Because the goal of the project was to create a database front-end system which should be able to take over as many as possible tasks of a human intermediary . For our intermediary system for searches in bibliographical databases we defined 5 tasks:

- formulation of the search profile (search related);
- selection of a database (pre-search);
- truncation of terms and morphological extension of the search profile (search related);
- the database query itself (search related);
- evaluation of the query results (post-search).

The sequence of this list is the same sequence in which the functions are performed in our prototype system. This is presented in the diagram below. In the prototype all these intermediary functions are implemented although some of them are implemented in quite a rough manner.

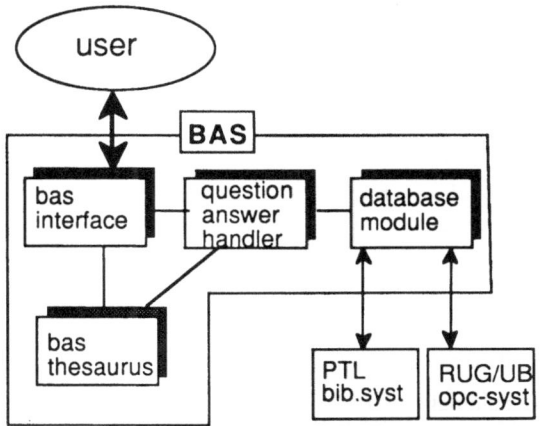

fig.1 the functions of the BAS-prototype...

3. Concepts used in an intelligent

front-end prototype

Between September 1987 and January 1989 one of the research-projects of PTT Research Groningen investigated the technical possibilities of the development of an intelligent database front-end system.

As a result the project delivered a prototype front-end system for accessing a number of bibliographical databases. This intermediary system - called BAS, an abbreviation of "Bibliotheek Assistent Systeem" (Library Assistant System) - is now used as an intermediary support for searches in bibliographical databases within PTT Research itself. In this section we will describe the concepts which have been applied in the BAS-prototype. For a better understanding of these concepts we give a short overview of the architecture of the BAS-prototype.

3.1 The BAS-architecture

The system is devided in three modules: the BAS-interface, the Question-and-Answer Handler and the Database Module. The BAS-interface concerns the communication between the intermediary system and the user. One of the main features of the BAS-interface is the interactive support of the search profile definition. The Question-and-Answer Handler is the expert part of the architecture and generates database advise as well as advises regarding the evaluation of a database query. In the Database Module the communication between BAS and the linked databases is handled. This means automatic logon and logoff procedures and the translation of the search profile into the syntax of the chosen data-base system. The search profile is represented in an intermediary language (CCL) for communication within the intermediary system. As most important knowledge base a thesaurus has been designed in the architecture of the system. This thesaurus contains knowledge on synonyms and related terms which can be used in the search profile. The architecture of the BAS-prototype is shown in the figure below.

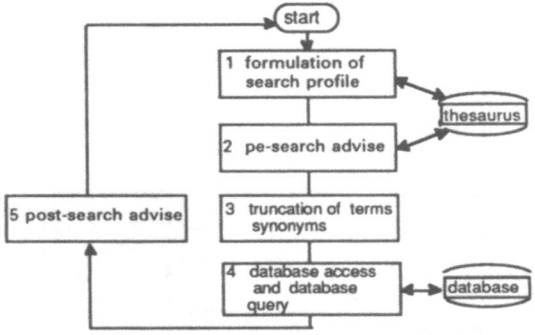

fig. 2 the architecture of the BAS-prototype

The ultimate prototype of the intermediary system has been implemented on a SUN 3/60 UNIX-machine using the AI-programming environment POPLOG, which contains a set of programming languages: Lisp, Prolog and POP11. In the BAS-prototype all these programming languages have been used.

In the sections which follow we want to make clear the

concepts applied in the BAS-prototype; these concepts are:

1. the thesaurus function (section 3.2)
2. user modeling: a context mechanism (section 3.3)
3. the expert function (section 3.4)
   including the pre-search and post-search advise
4. the intermediary language (section 3.5).

These concepts have been described earlier in [6] which has been presented at the "AI-applications" conference, November 1988 in The Hague.

3.2 The thesaurus function

3.2.1 The thesaurus as knowledge base Originaly a thesaurus is a collection of preferred or permitted terms and their mutual relations. A thesaurus can be used to assign preferred terms to library documents, in order to offer possibilities in searching bibliographical databases for documents on a specified subject. Another function of a thesaurus is to support the user who wants to do an online search in a bibliographical database. The classical way of use of a thesaurus offers two disadvantages:

- retrieval with selected terms is not always possible in databases in which the user wants to search and
- the thesaurus is not often available as an online service.

In the BAS-prototype we applied the thesaurus in a different way. The thesaurus represents all possible terms which can be used in searching in the underlying databases. In fact the BAS-thesaurus generates ideas for the user to select search terms that match with the problem definition of the user. Therefore the thesaurus of the BAS-prototype has been extended and contains many

more terms than an ordinary thesaurus. Also the BAS-thesaurus is always online available in the BAS-prototype and can be consulted by the user.
There may be some discussion as to whether an intermediary system should use its own (centralised) thesaurus or the local thesaurus of specific databases. There are reasons - e.g. maintainability - to use the local thesauri of the underlying databases. As far as the BAS-prototype is concerned we have chosen for the solution of one thesaurus in the intermediary system. In fact the function of the thesaurus has been extended: the thesaurus has become the knowledge base of the BAS-prototype containing meta knowledge about the linked databases.

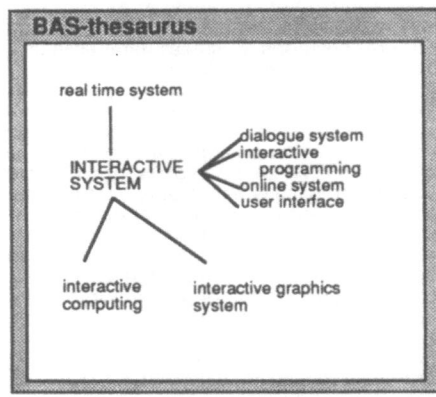

fig. 3 the graphical presentation BAS-thesaurus

The thesaurus covers knowledge about the databases. For each term the number of references in the distinguished databases is represented in the thesaurus. The information concerning the number of references is needed to generate a database advice (see section 3.4.1).As shown in the diagram above one of the main features of the interface of BAS is the graphical presentation of the thesaurus. By means of the graphical presentation and mouse manipulation the user is able to choose the terms which are most suitable for his or her search profile. Because of this facility the BAS intermediary system is especially suitable for users who do not already have an exact defined search profile to search with in a bibliographical database. The graphical presentation of the thesaurus helps the user to find the right terms to match his or her own (not exactly defined) ideas.

3.2.2 The general applicability of the thesaurus function
The concept of a thesaurus is not only limited to applications in the bibliographic context. The thesaurus concept can also be applied in more business oriented databases. In a general database environment the thesaurus concept can be related with a data dictionary. A datadictionary is the logical representation of the data model and according to this the data dictionary presents the contents of the database. When the data dictionary is used in a multi database front-end system we prefer to speak of a meta data dictionary because a datadictionary implemented in a front-end system has to cover the contents of a number of databases. The meta data dictionary also contains the access paths to the connected databases. In this context a meta data dictionary may be viewed as a "signpost" to inform the user in which of the connected databases the necessary information can be found.

In a multiple database environment the problem of information retrieval is more complex because in separate databases different (but synonym) terms may be used for the same data. When we create a list of synonym terms which covers all used terms in the underlying databases a kind of semantic presentation will be established. Terms with a similar meaning indicate one conceptual object about which data is available in the underlying databases. The list of synonyms should be implemented in the intermediary system and is linked with the meta datadictionary. The synonyms will be matched with usable terms (data elements) in certain databases as registrated in the meta datadictionary. In this context the list of synonyms adopts the function of the thesaurus as we applied in the BAS-prototype.

3.3 User modeling: a context mechanism

As stated earlier the BAS-thesaurus contains a lot of terms. In order to bring some additional structure in the thesaurus a context mechanism has been developed. The context mechanism offers a set of (pre-defined) user contexts which can be choosen in searching terms in the thesaurus. In this paper we will explain the principles of this mechanism by some general examples.

With the context mechanism within the BAS-prototype we wanted to reach two goals. On the one hand this mechanism has to limit the number of thesaurus terms on the screen of the user. This means that the graphical presentation of the thesaurus contains only the relevant terms for the user. In the user interface of the BAS-prototype the user is able to choose his (or her) own context by means of a specified menu in a separate window. Because of this choice of the user the intermediary system knows the context on which the system

has to interpret the input of the user. Suppose a user works as a software engineer specialised in object oriented languages. He or she wants to have references about the term "procedural languages". Without activating any context BAS would generate a tree of more than 20 different languages on the screen. If the user would choose the context "object oriented" the system would only generate a tree with a limited number of languages such as SIMULA, POOL-T, Smalltalk etc.. The context mechanism makes use of global user profiles which have been implemented in a separate knowledge base.

As second goal the context mechanism contributes to solve the problem of ambiguous terms. A given term in the thesaurus can be interpreted differently by different users (or usergroups). This is due to the fact that the context of these users is different. For example in the context of users who are interested in human factors the term "interface" has the meaning of user interface. In the context of someone who is interested in networking between several computer systems the same term has a different meaning; in this context the term "interface" means an interface between systems. The BAS-prototype offers possibilities to generate synonyms of given terms. The contribution made by BAS towards solving the problem of ambiguity consists of generating synonyms that match with the context of the user. Synonym for "interface" in the context of human factors may be the term "user interface"; in the other context (networking between systems) a synonym for "interface" may be the terms "system interface" or "system connectivity".

3.4 The expert function

As stated in section 2 the intermediary system takes over the function of the human expert in database access and information retrieval. This implies that knowledge of the human expert has to be implemented in the intermediary system.
Regarding the knowledge of a human expert we can distinguish two kinds of knowledge. Firstly we distinguish the knowledge which the user needs concerning the choice of the database. Secondly we indicate the knowledge which is needed to evaluate the results of retrieval actions of the intermediary system. We will use here the terms "pre-search" and "post-search" similar to Williams as mentioned in section 2.

Before we discuss both forms of advise giving we want to point out the role of the expert function within the intermediary BAS-prototype. The development of an intermediary system means that a lot of activities can be carried out automatically by the intermediary system, such as login and logout procedures and conversion of the syntax of the search profile. Even the choice of the database, the evaluation of search results and the initiative for a new database search may be an autonomous actions of an intermediary system. Regarding the development of the BAS-prototype we hesitated to let every activity be handled by the prototype itself. In fact we decided allowing the user to keep the ultimate responsibility for the whole information retrieval process. Besides for each database query certain costs will be charged and in the case of users responsibiblity concerning the whole retrieval process these costs can be kept under control. In this scenario the user has to choose the database in which he wants to search. Even if the expert function of the intermediary system advises a specific database the user should have the possibility to choose otherwise. Considering the expert function as knowledge processing aid for the evaluation of the search results (the post-search advise) the same idea has been applied: the expert function has been viewed as an advise giving part of the intermediary system.

The pre-search advise is mainly focused upon the choice of the database in which to search. Based on the formulated search profile the BAS-prototype advises the user to search in one of the available databases. This advise is generated on basis of knowledge stored in the thesaurus. As stated in section 3.2.1 for each term in the thesaurus the number of references in each of the available databases is registrated in the thesaurus. In the Question and Answer Handler of the prototype a number of rules have been applied to analyse the search profile and generate the right advise. An example of such a rule is:

If two term in the search profile are combined with OR operator then add the numbers of references and take the result as the estimated number in the advise.

This is of course a very simple rule to apply. One of the conclusions of the knowledge elicitation process was that the knowledge a human intermediary needs to select the rmost appropriate database is not as strictly defined as one might suppose. In more difficult cases - in which AND and OR operators are combined - we did not have enough knowledge about how to construct valid rules. In these cases we applied some heuristic rules.

The post-search advise is related to the interpretation of the search results. The results of a database search are compared with the original search profile and the constraints which the user defined earlier in the session. For example the user may have indicated that he or she wants no more than 25 references as a constraint to the database search. But when the same user selected only one thesaurus term to use in his or her search profile the result of the search may be 100 references. In this case the expert function of the intermediary system has to evaluate the number of references and to advise the user to narrow the search profile. This means that the user should choose one (or more) term(s) in the thesaurus which are narrower terms compared with the term used in the profile. The post-search advise supports the user in continuing (or stopping) the session with the intermediary system. To give an idea of a post-search advise we present the following rule:

If the difference between references wanted and the references found is more than 15
And the user wants a "state of the art" review
And there is no criterium for time of appearance

Then search for the latest review article
• search criteria: number of pages more than 10;
 number of references in the article
 more than 10;
And select this review article and all articles which appeared afterwards.

Note that the criteria and the numbers mentioned in this example are strictly random and have no relation to empirical evidence.

3.5 The intermediary language

Whether information retrieval by means of a database front-end system will be successful is dependent on how different the underlying databases are. As far as the connected databases are more or less of the same kind (say relational) but only differ in query language, the intermediary system has to convert the syntax of the search profile into the syntax of the chosen database. In a more heterogeneous database environment information retrieval by means of a front-end system will be more difficult (see also section 4.2). The syntax of the search profile is called the intermediary language. Also the format in which the database results are defined has to be converted into the syntax of an intermediary (internal) language. We applied this concept of an intermediary language in order to be able to develop a different user interface or to add a new database without changing the entire system. In the interface the formulated search profile (in menu form e.g.) will be converted into the syntax of the intermediary language of the front-end system. At the other end of the line the search profile represented in the intermediary language will be converted into the syntax of the query language of the database. In fact there are two kinds of syntaxes which have to be defined: firstly a syntax in which the search profile can fit, secondly a syntax to communicate the results of a database query. In the BAS-prototype we used the syntax of the Common Command Language (CCL) for the definition of the search profile. For the database results we defined another internal format to represent the results to the user.

4. Types of database front-end systems

In this section we want to identify a number of different types of intermediary front-end systems for the benefit of database access and information retrieval. First of all we can distinguish single database front-end systems and multi database front-ends. This distinction is of course very obvious but it is important in relation with the position and the role of intermediary front-end systems. In this section we will have a closer look at two kinds of interfaces which determine database front-end systems: the usergroup(s) of a front-end system and the databases which are connected with a specific front-end system. For each type of front-end system - single database front-end system and multi database front-end - we will describe types of users and usergroups and different kinds of databases. The aim of this description is to give a picture of different environments (databases and users) in which an intermediary front-end system can be placed. In section 5 we will generalise the concepts of the prototype and match them with the types of intermediary front-end systems as we describe below.

4.1 Users and usergroups

One of the main goals for the development of intermediary front-end systems is to relieve the user of knowledge concerning methods of access in databases and the way in which a search profile should be formulated. In other words: an intermediary system should offer the user opportunity to search in a transparent manner in one or several database(s). In case of a multi database front-end system the user ought to have the idea to search in one virtual database instead of accessing several databases in perhaps a number of sessions.

Users of intermediary database services can be divided into two main groups: closed usergroups and open usergroups. The identification of a usergroup is most important for the definition and use of concepts in a intermediary system. We will give a short impression of each kind of groups. A closed usergroup can be chararised by two attributes:

• a common goal which can be defined for the activities of the usergroup; derived from this goal the use of an intermediary (database) information service can be defined;

- the domain of the information (and knowledge) which users of the usergroup need for the performance of their task is well known;

Talking about intermediary information services for an open usergroup we focus on public information services. Regarding an open usergroup there is less certainty about the goal of users and the domain of information in which they are interested. On the contrary: there is no detailed information about potential users and their interests. In fact everybody can be a client of a proposed public information service. At best there may be some estimations about the domain of information in which "everybody" is interested.

In comparison with a public information service a closed usergroup offers advantages regarding the development of an intermediary information service. Firstly it is very important that potential users are known and eventually can be involved in the specification of the system requirements of an intermediary information service. Secondly developers of the intermediary service are able to estimate the degree of automation within companies that want to make use of the intermediary service. This aspect is important for choosing the technical environment for which the intermediary system will be developed.

As a final point in this section we want to make a distinction between experienced users and novice users. We define experienced users as people who are familiar with working with computers in general as well as with retrieving information from databases specifically. On the other side we define a novice user as a layman in the field of computers and information retrieval. Of course reality is not as black and white as we define here. For instance users can be experienced in the use of one specific database but not in any other database. It may be especially annoying for experienced users if the interface of an application must be approached by the user as if he were a novice. Perhaps a user is well acquainted with the command language within the intermediary system. In that case the interface of the intermediary system should offer experienced users the possibility of using the command language directly. In other words: the interface of an information service by means of an intermediary system has to be adaptive regarding the degree of experience of the user.

4.2 Types of databases

One of the main advantages for the user of using an intermediary database front-end system is the possibility to access one (or more) database(s) without the need for knowledge about technical features of database access. Apart from accessibility to databases, databases may be heterogeneous because their data model as well as their implementation can be quite different. On the other hand information can be stored in special purpose database environments like hypertext or videotex systems. This variaty of database implementations causes many problems to retrieve information in a heterogeneous database environment. Perhaps a user wants to get information from a videotex database concerning weather forecast information as well as from a hypertext database with tourist information. It will be clear that information retrieval from (conceptual and technically) different databases is a very hard problem to solve regarding the intermediary task of a database front-end system. As far as the underlying databases are more or less of the same kind (relational or text oriented) an intermediary system has to be able to convert a formulated search profile into the different query language for information retrieval in a specific database.

4.3 Single database front-end systems

Database front-end systems can be suitable to solve some problems concerning the access and information retrieval in one database. One may argue that an intermediary front-end to one database is not relevant to use. For if an intermediary system is needed as a front-end to one database the interface of the database might prove a lack on functionality or the interface might offer more convenience in the use of the system. We think however that a single database front-end system may be useful as an intelligent interface to the database. Such a front-end system may be an important tool, especially when:

- the database is to be used by quite a lot of different people
- access and search possibilities require special knowledge
- each individual user does not use the database frequently.

In fact the intermediary system replaces an intermediary person to guide the user in the information retrieval process in the database. Without pretending to present an exhaustive list we mention models which can be defined for single database front-end system as an "intelligent" user interface:

- **the datamodel** of an "intelligent" interface contains knowledge about the contents of the database and its database representation. To use a general purpose database the user wants to have a clear idea of what he or she can search for in that database. The datamodel of the single database front-end system can be useful to present the contents of the database. Of course the datamodel will be based on the datamodel of the database. The intermediary system can be viewed as a tool to present the datamodel in a convenient way to the user. A very simple form of presentation of semantics is a list (menu) with several permitted keywords which the user can use. An more advanced form may be a graphical presentation as implemented in the BAS-prototype.

- **the contextmodel** represesents the contex in which the input of the user - in relation with the data in the database - has to be interpreted by the interface itself. In this paper we will make this clear with one example. In financial databases data have a strong dependency on time. For instance: the turnover results of a company, depreciation figures and the cost figures are all items which are related to a certain period in the past. On the other hand planning data are related to periods in the future. In the process of information retrieval the "intelligent" interface should be able to judge whether the user wants information about a valid period. When a user wants turnover figures about the first 6 months of last year and he types 1999 instead of 1989 the intermediary system should be able to interpret that correctly as an improper period. In most database systems such a typing error causes a retrieval operation in the database with no result.

- **the usermodel** is an essential part of an "intelligent" interface. The use of user models makes an intermediary system flexible to use. By means of these models - or context mechanisms (section 3.3) - the intermediary system unburdens the user of actions such as identifying areas of interests, account information or level of experience (novice/expert).

Of course these elements are also relevant to multi

database front-end systems. We emphasize them here to make clear that a single database front-end system may have relevance to the user. However, the domain and complexity as well as the kind of users are of decisive importance as to whether an intelligent front-end system to one database is useful.

4.4 Multi database front-end systems

Regarding this category of database front-end sytems we can be brief. In fact we are talking about systems like the BAS-prototype described earlier in this paper. In this section we want to point out that a multi database front-end system may act on different levels of functionality. We distinguish the folowing levels:

a. Technical level:
   the intermediary system gives support for basic operations like automatic logon and logoff procedures, filing etc..

b. Syntactical level:
   the intermediary system acts as (a) and also converts the (standard) syntax in which the search profile is formulated into the query language of the chosen database system.

c. Semantical level:
   the intermediary system acts as (b) and presents also the search possibilities (semantics) of available database.

As stated earlier a list of synonyms based on the meta data dictionary may have the same function in an intermediary system as a thesaurus. The meta data-dictionary can be viewed as a knowledge base which may contain knowledge about:

- the search tree: which possible search paths are defined to search in the underlying databases;
- how to retrieve data elements from each underlying database;
- the access methods to each database;
- the contents (and eventually semantics) of each database.

Depending on the kind of intermediary service also knowledge for the benefit of accounting of the information service may be included in the meta datadictionary. As we see here the meta data dictionary is the most important part of a multi database front-end system.

5. Conclusions

In this concluding section we will match the concepts of BAS presented in section 3 with different users/usergroups and types of databases. For each concept we will give an answer to the question of whether the concept can be used in a single database or multi database front-end system. In the same way we will see whether each concepts can be useful for a convenient interaction between users and intermediary system. In section 5.5 we will give some general conclusions.

5.1 The thesaurus concept

In the previous description of the thesaurus concept we put forward that in the context of business oriented databases a list of synonym terms can have the same function as a thesaurus to bibliographical databases. In this section we only focus on databases and the use of a list of synonyms and the meta datadictionary.

The use of a meta datadictionary in an intermediary

system implies application of a database dependent concept. For the use of the meta datadictionary it does not matter whether the system is used by a closed or open user group. The meta datadictionary not only includes definition of relations and fields but in this context also represents the contents - and therefore also the search possibilities - of the underlying databases. That is why the meta datadictionary is the most important part of an intermediary system: it produces the elementary data for constructing a list of synonyms. In fact the list of synonyms of the intermediary system represents an abstract from the meta datadictionary to the user. The user can choose one term of the synonym list and use it in the search profile. An additional important feature of the intermediary system to the user is the support of the search profile formulation. Not every user is familiar with boolean algebra, so the intermediary system has to explain and support the use of AND, OR and NOT operators in the search profile.

5.2 The concept of user modeling

User modeling as a support tool in an intermediary system is a typical user bound feature. The context mechanism as described in section 3.3.1 is one aspect of user modeling. The context mechanism as implemented in the BAS-prototype is only meant for a limited number of user groups. The idea of an context mechanism can be extended by defining personal contexts (usermodels). For each user the intermediary system knows background, experience and interests on which the intermediary system can anticipate in the interaction with the user. It is even possible to think of dynamic contexts by including some constraints which are applied for users for a certain period of time.

When we look at the distinction of open usergroups versus closed usergroups we can conclude that user modeling is almost exclusively applicable for closed usergroups, because the definition of contexts for different user groups or individual users requires knowledge about the users of the intermediary system. The application of a context mechanism is especially relevant when a number of well defined subgroups of users can be distinguished within the (closed) usergroup of the intermediary sytem. To account for open user groups implementation of a context mechanism in the interface of an intermediary system would offer too little added value because "everybody" may be a user of the system.

Based on the above reasoning we conclude that user modeling has no direct relation to a single database or multi database environment.

5.3 The expert function

The expert function implies the pre-search and post-search advise and is the most general concept which can be applied in an intermediary system. An expert function in an intermediary system may be relevant for open as well as for closed usergroups but also for each type of database front-end system we described earlier.

It is important to realise that the more knowledge is implemented in the intermediary system, the easier it is for the user to carry out search actions in (connected) databases. As we described earlier we distinguished two kinds of advise in the BAS-prototype: pre-search advise and post-search advise. In the pre-search process as well as in the post-search process the user needs support. In the pre-search phase the user may need support to formulate his or her search profile, after the search has taken place the user may need advise how to proceed with database searches.

As we stated in section 3.4 the obvious solution is not always to implement an intermediary system which takes over all search tasks and choices from the user. In this paper we will argue that an advise giving database front-end system is much preferable. It implies two advantages: the user keeps his or her responsibility for database searches, and the costs for information retrieval can be kept under control.

5.4 The concept of an intermediary language

It may be obvious that the implementation of this concept is only relevant in an intermediary system for multi database access. Within the intermediary system the developer has to choose a syntax in which the search profile as well as the database result can be defined. One of the main tasks of the multi database front-end system is the conversion from syntax of the intermediary language into the query language of the chosen database. Of course a multi database intermediary system has to offer the most suitable interface for connecting several technically different databases. Therefore it is advisable to consider an intermediary language which has connection with an international standard like the ISO-standard for SQL.

5.5 General conclusions

When we review the conclusions above there is one combination of database front-end type and usergroup type which gives the most advantages for creating an intermediary database service including the concepts we discussed in this paper. An intelligent intermediary system can be developed most effectively for a closed usergroup for the benefit of multi database access.

Regarding the closed usergroup we want to remark that unless there is a defined group there may be a lot of difference between individual users or even between various subgroups of users. Also there may be differences in the degree to which a user (or usergroup) already knows exactly what he or she wants to search for. If users can define precisely what they want there is less need to support users in formulating the search profile concerning the contents of the search. In the case of users who only have a vague idea of what they want to search for, an intelligent support as implemented in the BAS-prototype may be suitable.

Concerning databases which can be accessed by the intermediary system we remark that not every type of database (in the technical sense) is suitable to connect with an intermediary system. For instance a hypertext database has such a specifically defined user interface that it is useless for connecting this type of database with an intermediary system.

Finally we conclude that an intelligent intermediary services promise an improved accessibility and use of general purpose databases.

Acknowledgement

I want to thank here some of my collegues for their contributions to this paper. Their critisism and suggestions for alterations have been of much value in finishing this paper.
Especially I am very grateful to Ms M.R.J. Koopman with whom I discussed a number of subjects mentioned in the paper. Last but not least I have to thank members of the ASI study group "Intelligent Interfaces" for discussions on this subject.

Reference list

[1] Davis, G.B.,Olson, M.H., Management Information Systems McGraw-Hill 1984 (second edition).
[2] Parsaye, K. (et al), Intelligent Databases John Wiley & Sons Inc 1989.
[3] Pollit, A.S. , An expert system as an online search intermediary, Proceedings Int. Online Meeting Londen, December 1981.
[4] Pollit, A.S. ,Information storage and retrieval systems Ellis Horwood LTD 1989
[5] Williams, M.E., Transparent information systems through gateways, front-ends, intermediaries and interfaces,
Journal of the American society for information science 37(4) 1986.
[6] Boonstra H., Koopman M.R.J., Tulp A.J., BAS: een front-end systeem voor bibliografische databases (written in Dutch),
Proceedings "AI-toepassingen " conference, The Hague 1988.

Knowledge-Based Applications in Office Information Systems: An Integration Approach

Klaus Faidt   Dimitris Karagiannis

Forschungsinstitut für anwendungsorientierte Wissensverarbeitung (FAW)
P. O. Box 20 60
D-7900 Ulm / Donau (F. R. G.)

ABSTRACT

A system is being developed for supporting the integration of knowledge-based systems into a distributed and heterogeneous office environment by making available the functionality of existing basic office systems. For this purpose, abstract office procedures are defined to provide the knowledge-based systems with independence from the basic office systems actually used. Control mechanisms interpret these procedures and execute them falling back on the available office system functionality.

1   Introduction

Generally, conventional systems for supporting office applications are restricted to elementary domains like text processing, establishing of documents, retrieval and communication functions. The integration of these applications leads to so-called office information systems. However, by developing knowledge-based systems the methods of artificial intelligence offering a farther-reaching cooperative support also in the office area shall be made available.

The present approach starts from a system architecture that comprises as a decisive factor the inclusion of certain functionalities of already available basic office systems [5]. For the administration and distribution of requirements arising while processing office tasks, in this approach — that is based on the philosophy of the Flexible Office Systems (FOS) [5] — a *virtual office system* (VOS) is developed which unifies the functionalities of the basic office systems and represents them in an abstract form as *office processes*. The VOS takes over the administration and distribution of these requirements among the available system components and basic office systems. Thus it is possible to abstract from the special interfaces of the single basic office systems and to concentrate on special themes concerning the development of knowledge-based office components, but nevertheless staying within the conception of prototypes to be established to treat the complete functionality of an office system. Moreover, problems with heterogeneity and the distribution of the office environment are fixed to a concrete level, and a realistic orientation towards typical facts in the application area is assured.

In the following section, the chosen approach is explained with the prototype developed in the OSSY (Organisation Support System) project. In the third section, the representation of requirements to this system and the methods used for their processing are described. In the fourth section, the possibilities for further developing the concepts used are referred to. Finally, in section 5 the experiences gained and resulting consequences for the further proceeding are described.

2   The Integration Approach

The basic concept of the VOS approach comprises abilities for the knowledge-based interpretation of the requirements posed. In order to provide the necessary functionality, semantic information on the possible requirements and on the call-off possibilities of the knowledge-based application systems as well as of the basic office systems have to be available.

The VOS receives as input the description of the *requirements to the office system* placed by the knowledge-based office application systems. Beside the indication of the office process certain marginal conditions on predefined sequences, time functions and causal dependencies have to be considered. The office processes are not directly called off as *elementary actions*, but are equipped with a context that describes initialisations, starting / final conditions, reprocessings and other modifications of the office process. Thus the user may, for example, specify a survey on deadlines in order to make arrangements, if necessary. The office process may also be provided with a *prolog* that takes care of a realization of the suppositions of a process or puts additional preconditions to the process execution. An *epilog* may cultivate the results of a finished office process or activate adequate follow-up actions.

A further source of information is the *specification of the functionality of the available basic office systems*. The information on the semantics of the provided functions and their syntax as well as the meaning of eventual responses must be available.

The execution of the requirements posed may be subdivided into three essential steps:

- Requirement Analysis

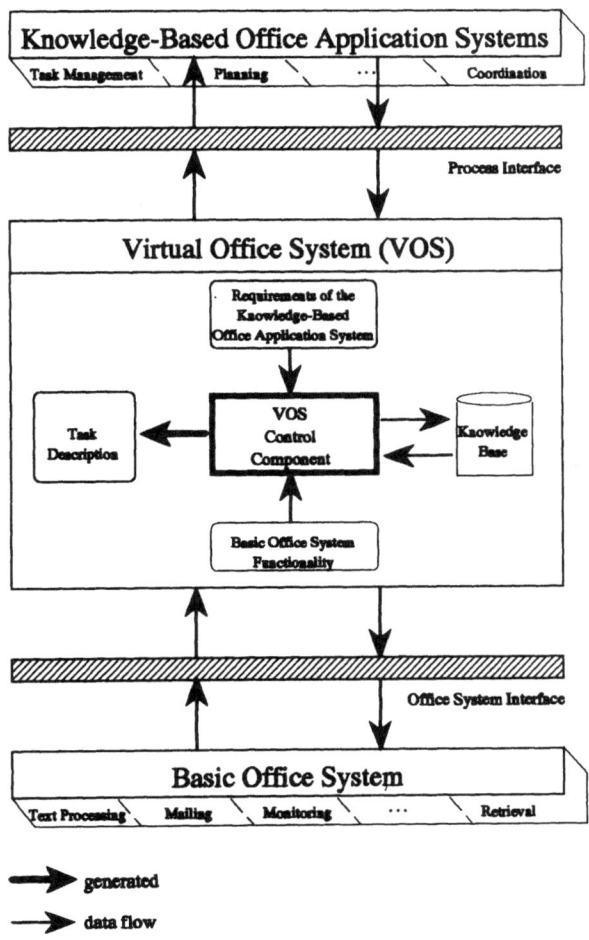

application systems and basic office systems is the process interface or the office system interface, respectively. These allow the transfer of requirements posed and results in both directions. Fig. 2 shows a VOS extension that was implemented in the OSSY project.

An important fact regarding the control flow within the OSSY system is that in general the single components may not communicate with each other directly, but that inquiries and orders are passed on by the OSSY-VOS. Thus the components of the OSSY system are joined by the OSSY-VOS (star architecture, see fig. 2).

3   The VOS Concept in OSSY

The practicability of this approach was shown in the OSSY project of the FAW by a prototype demonstrator. As knowledge-based office application systems, components for supporting special applications like communication, document retrieval and task management were developed [3,4]. However, these components do not realize these applications on their own, but in accordance with the approach mentioned their task is possibly even to create the necessary framework in which the concrete application may be supported. Finally, the executing components use this framework in order to facilitate the concrete support of the user.

Example: In order to support the action "invitation of a guest speaker" and using organizational guidelines and data on the organizational structure as well as on the concrete instantiation of edges of this structure, an event-processing component creates a plan showing how — starting from the actual situation — the invitation may be supported [4]. Falling back upon this plan adequate office procedures are compiled and passed on to the VOS component for processing.

The interface of the implemented VOS extension to these components is formed by the so-called OSSY procedure interface by which the activation of procedure calls in both directions is facilitated. The VOS receives the requirements of the other components in form of such office procedures. These requirements are analyzed and, eventually after a stay in a queue, the respective procedures for fulfilling these requirements are executed. As a consequence every execution can now have orders for the components of the basic office level, the organization description level and the user interface.

The OSSY task management component [4] creates a plan for the selected application "invitation of a guest speaker" that contains actions like "fill in application", "agree" etc. The OSSY-VOS offers a number of so-called OSSY procedures as VOS office processes for the realization of such partial actions. Among them are, for example, the activation of components of the OSSY system or editing data files. These are mapped by the OSSY-VOS on functionalities provided by the OSSY system itself or by basic office systems.

Figure 1: Basic Concept for the Integration Approach

This comprises the evaluation of the context information provided together with the requirement and the respective selection and combination of procedures for the realization of the office process. For the execution of these procedures data might have to be adapted from the context information.

- Interpretation
The procedures chosen and combined according to the requirements describe a control mechanism that has to be interpreted taking into consideration the available resources.

- Control
If during the interpretation a real office system functionality is required, this has to be transformed into control directions for the basic office systems or the knowledge-based office application systems.

The interface of the VOS to the knowledge-based office

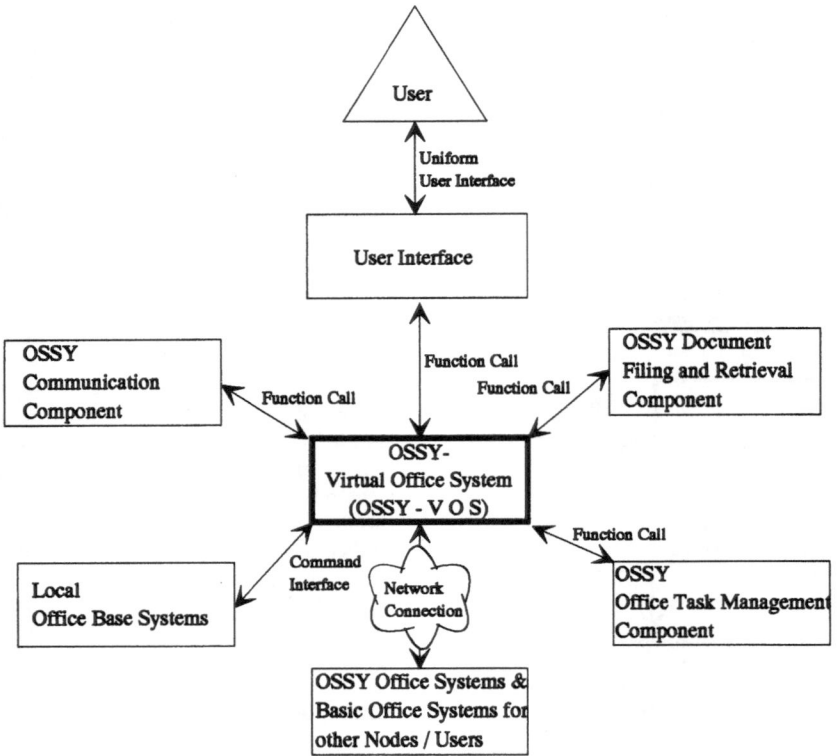

Figure 2: The OSSY-VOS environment

The following subsection cover some details of the object-oriented implementation of the OSSY-VOS. For example, it is described how to activate the OSSY-VOS. Further, the task management carried through by the OSSY-VOS and features resulting from the parallelism inherent in distributed systems are regarded.

3.1 Syntax

According to the explanations mentioned above, a simple syntax is available:

$$\text{(call-tmk } 'x)$$

The function **call-tmk** via which the OSSY-VOS (called T̲ask M̲anagement C̲omponent in the prototype demonstrator) is activated has one evaluated argument. Its value has to be an instance of the class COMPONENTINTERFACE (or a subclass of it) that specifies the OSSY procedure to be effected and its context.

3.2 The OSSY Processing

The agenda manager of the demonstrator only consists of a dispatcher and a task-specific queue administration. Requirements to be executed by the OSSY-VOS ("tasks") are

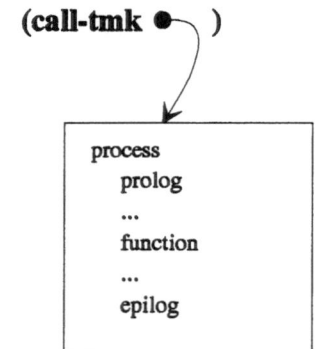

Figure 3: The OSSY-VOS Call

administrated with the help of instances of subclasses of the class TASKAGENDA. These instances can be distinguished from each other by different priorities of the tasks administrated by them, by different control strategies, fairness characteristics etc.

Example: Due to the fairness characteristic in the actual system the execution of a task with low priority cannot be prevented by the fact that the system is already working to capacity with tasks of high priority. Therefore after the activation of a certain number of tasks of high priority a queue of lower priority is compulsorily activated.

If a requirement represented by an instance of the class COMPONENTINTERFACE is chosen for processing, one can conclude from this instance which OSSY procedures impose on it and afterwards call the respective component by activating the corresponding OSSY procedure. Relevant parameters may be taken from the task instance that is substituted as a parameter to the OSSY procedure.

An incoming requirement is at first — depending on the priority specified by its sender — assigned to a subordinate queue or a queue administration, respectively, that is controlled by the dispatcher assigned to the input buffer of the sender.

The queue administrations may allocate a new requirement to special queues or queue administrations assigned to them. So there is, for example, a queue administration class for requirements tied by schedules whose instances may sort the requirements linearly according to the given schedules and thus administrate them more efficiently than the instances of more unspecific queues / queue administrations could. At last every requirement gets into an adequate queue. Several subclasses of the standard queue class are defined, e.g., for one-element queues or for the administration of periodic requirements. The hierarchy of queue administrations, queues and requirements is shown in a KEE output window on calling the OSSY-VOS from the OSSY desktop in. There this hierarchy may be inspected and modified.

3.3 Use of Parallelism

Due to the used development environment that is based on KEE and Common-Lisp, there is no multi-tasking available for the OSSY programmers to deal with process management. Context switches can only be used with the window system Common-Windows used by the KEE implementation; they may be released by interrupts (for example, mouse clicks).

With regard to the distribution of the OSSY system and to the UNIX operating system used on the workstations, we may at least start for a multitasking approach as far as activating the basic office systems is concerned. The respective calls only activate components; results are only available later. This behaviour is transferred into the OSSY system by the OSSY-VOS: Requirements are only registered in the input buffer by the function *call-tmk*. These requirements are processed when the OSSY-VOS receives control. However, for this purpose it is necessary that the requiring component terminates, which — when waiting for the result of a requirement — may conceptionally be compatible only with difficulty with a functional Lisp programming style.

4   Perspectives

Due to the experiences with the OSSY system, the concept of the virtual office system has to be enlarged in many respects.

- Possibilities of plan interpretation for control and simulation

- Inclusion of dialogue possibilities with the users

- Exchange of information

4.1 Use of Plans

The purpose of the OSSY-VOS is to convert application-oriented OSSY-procedures into a sequence of instructions for a basic office system. This sequence can also be non-linear, due to the prolog / epilog functions and a schedule survey. The realization of the OSSY-VOS led to special and always reusable program forms, when the OSSY-procedures were implemented. These program forms express above all the creation of partial tasks to be processed first and the continued processing of the original task in the following. The basic schemes may be standardized and combined to a control language in its own right. The next step is to use such a language not only for describing the transfer of OSSY procedures, but even to represent tasks created by an event-processing component that, however, could be classified to be completely rigid regarding the organizational environment.

If such a control language is enlarged by language features for describing control alternatives, knowledge relevant for controlling the processing of a task could be represented in this language and then passed in a well-defined form to a control component for the complete execution or only for simulating certain alternative partial processes [2]. Thus the control language becomes a plan description language.

4.2 User Modelling in Plans

One could even go further and represent also the user actions expected by the system in such a language. By comparing the represented plans with the really effected user actions the user behaviour may be classified, and even active help systems may be implemented. Conversely one could try to determine the underlying plans by analyzing the given action sequences for solving certain problems (learning by example).

4.3 Object-Oriented Examination of the Information Exchange

Abstracting from the application environment of the OSSY-VOS and examining the call of components as a delivery of messages, an analogy between the OSSY-VOS and a delivery service may be stated: Incoming messages are analyzed, and the adressees are determined. Then the messages might be modified and duplicated. Finally, they are passed to the adressee whereby difficulties may arise. Adressees like, for example, printer spoolers might possibly not be found or are already occupied otherwise and refuse the information.

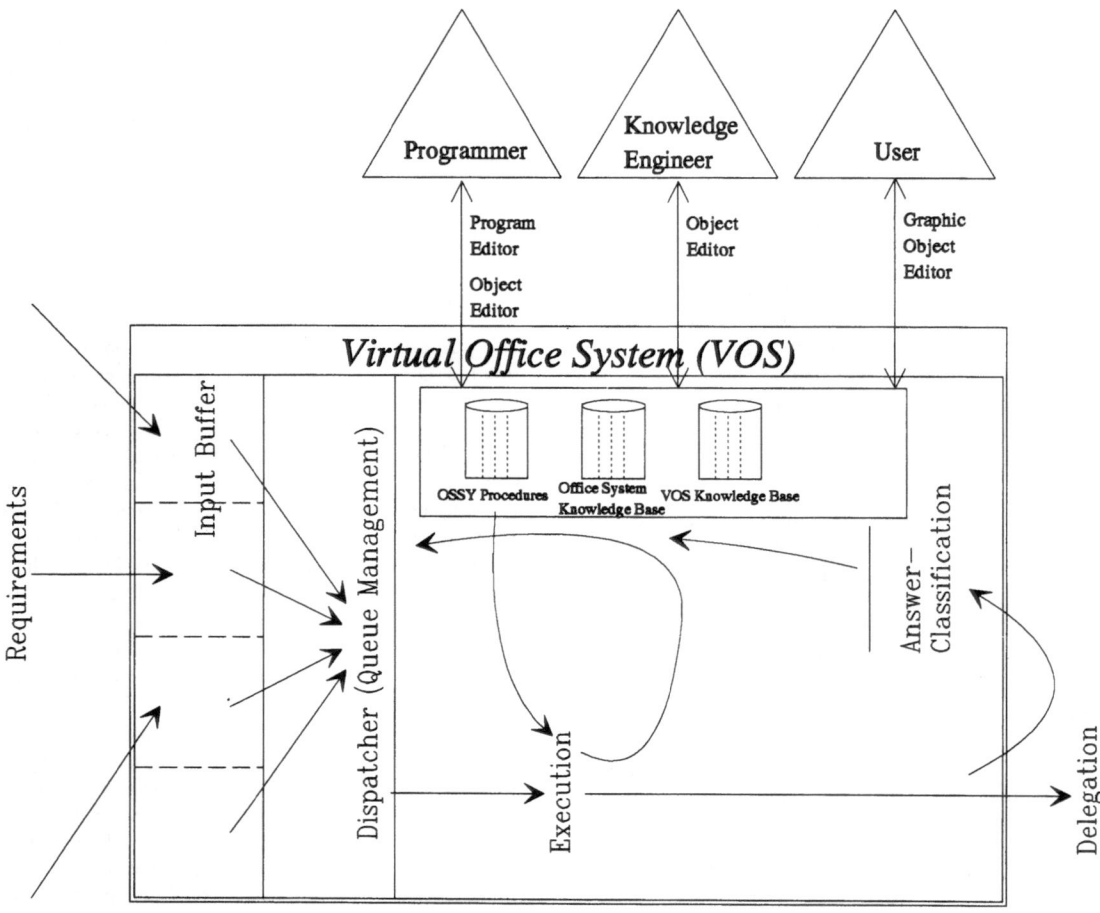

Figure 4: OSSY-VOS: Transformation Process and Information Processing

Then the delivery service must find a new adressee. Due to syntactic mistakes the message might also be not delivered to the presumed adressee which may lead to a return to the sender or activate an automatic correction of the mistake. Requirements concerning the delivery service could also be vague so that form and content of the messages also have to be considered in delivery attempts .

Nearly the same analogy may be drawn regarding the enlarged communication of the ObjTalk system [1] so that approaches used there for object recognition, correction of mistakes, refusal etc. may also have a certain relevance for the OSSY-VOS.

5 Conclusions

The practicability of the VOS transfer functions between the conceptional application-oriented office procedures and the interfaces of a basic office system have been shown with the OSSY demonstrator. However, a knowledge-based solution of this transfer also requires the explicit representation of the semantics of the requirements to the VOS which are only represented symbolically by OSSY procedures, prolog/epilog clauses and Lisp predicates. Also, Representations of the control semantics of the basic office systems and of the offered functionality of the knowledge-based components are required. For this purpose, as a first step the development of a formal semantic description for the used language utilities seemes to be useful. It should also be verified to what extent a language could be used for the control for which a formal semantics is already defined.

REFERENCES

[1] K. Faidt. *ObjTalk System, Version 5.0*. WISDOM-Forschungsbericht FB-INF-87-29, Forschungsgruppe INFORM, Institut für Informatik, Universität Stuttgart, September 1987.

[2] K. Faidt. *Ein interaktives Hilfsmittel zur Verifikation temporaler Aussagen über verteilte Systeme.* Diplomarbeit 241, Universität Stuttgart, Institut für Informatik, April 1984. Revised in October 1989.

[3] H. Heller, K. Faidt, H. Grünberger, K. Hinkelmann, D. Karagiannis, W. Salzmann, and S. Schebiella. *Organisation Support System (OSSY) — Der Demonstrator.* Projektbericht, FAW, Ulm, February 1990.

[4] K. Hinkelmann, D. Karagiannis, and W. Salzmann. *A Flexible Generation of Office Tasks.* FAW-Technical Report TR-FAW-90-014, Ulm, 1990.

[5] D. Karagiannis. Flexible Bürosysteme (FBS) — Architektur und Einsatzmöglichkeiten. In S. Fuhrmann and T. Pietsch, editors, *Praktische Anwendungen moderner Bürotechnologien, Band 12,* Erich Schmitt-Verlag, 1989.

A Terminological Approach to Business Domain Modelling

Maria Damiani   Sandro Bottarelli

Datamont R&D Centre
Datamont SpA - Gruppo Ferruzzi
Viale Restelli 1/A, 20124 Milano (Italy)

Abstract

We describe an application in the business management area developed using an experimental object based representation system relying on the KL-ONE terminological paradigm. For complex applications entailing a large amount of domain knowledge, efficient mechanisms for knowledge storing and retrieval are necessarely to be incorporated in the representation system. A general approach to the problem is proposed.

1. Introduction

Domain modelling aims at providing a high level, conceptual representation of application specific knowledge. The different approaches to modelling mainly pursued in the Database and Artificial Intelligence fields (through, respectively, semantic data models and knowledge representation formalisms) share the fundamental objective of providing highly expressive representation constructs close to the way in which reality is conceptualized [HK 87][BGN 89]. In general, semantic data models focus solely on the issue of representational adequacy while rarely are fully operational. Recent Object Oriented DBMS [ABDDMZ 89] overcome these limitations while lacking of inferential features. Knowledge representation formalisms, on the other hand, stress, in addition to "descriptive naturalness and richness", the inferential capability of the underlying computational model. Nevertheless, knowledge representation formalisms often lack a strong formal basis as well as powerful mechanisms for uniformly accessing and manipulating domain description.

The above features are indeed extremely relevant for modelling the business domain under consideration, concerning the social_structure/legal_organization of a very large Italian Company Group. The major goal of the application is the realization of a knowledge base describing the Group's overall organization, in the administrative, financial, legal and business aspects. Application requirements suggest an operational model and thus a representation formalism with high structuring power, able to capture the rich terminology of the domain, formally sound,

provided with deductive capabilities and a high level description interface for information manipulation and querying.

The class of representation formalisms based on of KL-ONE approach [BS 85] and centered on the so called terminological paradigm offers the representational features fullfilling the above descriptive needs. Nevertheless these systems, while intensively investigated at research level [BGN 89] [BFL 83] are still scarcely experimented on the field. Main purpose of our activity is to assess the adequacy of the terminological representation paradigm for the modelling of complex real domains as well as the level of usability of these systems in view of a practical and industrial relapse of the research effort.

The specific terminological system we have used for modelling the business domain is BACK [LNet 87] [Ne 87] [Ne 88] [PSet 89], one of the most successful KL-ONE like representation systems being actually available as running prototype. BACK is object-based in the tradition of frames and semantic nets, yet differs from these in being provided with logic-based formal semantics, making the language simpler to use and behaviourally sound and reliable. Analogously to KL-ONE, BACK introduces a sharp distinction between terminological (TBOX) and assertional (ABOX) knowledge under the cognitivistic assumption of relying world knowledge on a priori domain terminology acquisition [BS 85] [Ne 88]. Terminological knowledge captures the intensional aspects of the description and consists of a set of *concepts* and *roles* (concept properties) organized in subsumption taxonomies. Assertional knowledge consists of terminological object instances. A distinguishing feature of the language is the possibility of specifying *definitional* properties for concepts (i.e. properties expressing necessary and sufficient conditions for an individual to be a concept instance). Through *classification* inference concepts are placed automatically in the net of terminological descriptions depending on the specified properties, while instances are automatically completed with the best, i.e. most specific, description.

In this paper we report the results of the concrete application of BACK on field. We show how the terminological approach fits with the descriptive requirements of the domain while arguing the necessity of developing additional components and tools for making the representation system more usable in the practice of

---
This work was partially supported by the EEC. It was part of the ESPRIT project 311 (II phase), which involves the following partecipants: Nixdorf, Datamont, Olivetti, Technische Universitat Berlin, Quinary and Universitat Hildesheim.

real information systems. In particular the need of representing in a performant way a remarkable amount of knowledge has motivated the prototypical definition of a conceptual coupling between the representation system and a RDBMS for efficiently storage and retrieval of the assertional component. Moreover, in order to further support the end user in querying the information base, a friendly graphical interface on top of a hypermedia environment has been proposed.

In the following, requirements of the application are first outlined; then the BACK domain model is presented; finally the overall architecture of the system comprehensive of the additional components is described.

2. The business application domain

A relevant problem, quite common in very large Company Groups, is the maintenance of an updated view of the societary structure, evolving in time due to company acquisitions, disposals and share transfers. Such a view is fundamental for the top management in charge of defining and supervising the economic profile of the Group as well as for company shareholders. Commonly the overall knowledge is maintained by people very close to the top management, split among several offices with different tasks, often duplicated and stored on paper. In general access to this bulk of information is not simple; complex requests need often be decomposed in subqueries to be turned to the competent offices. The application we have investigated and prototyped, in strict cooperation with the user, focuses on the development of a knowledge base as the central repository of the societary structure of one of the most important private Industrial Groups in Italy. The societary structure is quite complex and heterogenous. It amounts to over 1500 companies operating in different countries, thus subject to different regulations depending on the legislation of the host nation, as well as engaged in diversified businesses in several economic areas. As a consequence, legal and financial terminology as well as jargon specific to the Group is extensively used both by experts in specifying and users in accessing the domain description. In some cases terminology is precise and stable; in others it is ambiguous and not fixed. In general, terminology acquisition is quite a complex and time consuming activity, while essential for the soundness of domain model. It leads to the identification of relevant conceptual entities in the domain and to the specification of their features including relationships with other entities. The result is the so called terminological model.

2.1 Requirements for a terminological model

Terminology in highly structured domains such as the one under consideration, presents specific features that it would be desirable to capture in the model and thus in the representation formalism:

• *description equivalence*. Often the same conceptual entity can be referred to either by using the specific terminology or through properties which univocally identify the object. For example the queries, taken from the domain:

i)Which are the Italian companies listed on New York Stock Exchange?
ii)Which are the "Spa" [1] listed on New York Stock Exchange?

have an identical answer, i.e. the set of companies that are formally declared located in Italy, with capital subdivided in shares, with shares of the specific type that make them quotable on a Stock Exchange and that are listed in New York; this set of properties can be synthesized using the proper terminology and inferences can be applied on the definitions of terms. For example given query i) we can derive, reasoning on the terminology, that the answer consists only of companies with juridical status *Spa*. In fact companies that can be listed on the Stock Exchange are only those whose capital is subdivided in shares and the italian companies with such property are only *Spa* companies. Viceversa, given query ii) and reasoning on the definition of *Spa* we can infer that the answer consists of the companies that are located in Italy with their capital subdivided in shares of a specific type. In synthesis, some terms can be identified by both necessary and sufficient properties. We can assert or retrieve a specific entity either through the proper domain term, i.e. a *Spa* company, or definitely through the distinguishing properties, i.e. an italian company with...., in turn relying on further terms. A knowledge base exhibiting behaviour as described above must thus incorporate both an accurate definition of domain concepts and an inferential engine for reasoning on the properties specified at the structural level.

• *consistency of term interdipendencies*. Domain terms can be strictly interrelated. For example, to remain in the legal area, the juridical status of a company determines the form of its administrative apparatus (i.e. Board of Auditors, Secretary Board..) and constrains the set of administrative/financial events the company is subject to (i.e. capital addition, share participation transfer..), the financial asset, the type of business activity of the company [Ga 86].Consequentely an assertion such as the following:

the company X had a capital addition of 10ML\$ in ordinary shares

is meaningful only if the company X has a juridical form for which the formally declared capital can be increased and such capital consists of *shares* that in turn can be *ordinary*. If, for instance, X is a non profit company, the assertion is wrongly formulated because by law, i.e. by definition, it is nonsensical. The inconsistency can be detected only if juridical terms are properly correlated to the concepts of *capital addition* and, consequently, *capital* and *share*. In that hypothesis, the resulting description is a complex net of term definitions, one strictly depending on the other. For the description to be sound, overall consistency has to be guaranteed. A knowledge base fullfilling that requirement has thus to incorporate proper consistency checking mechanisms.

• *taxonomic organization*. In the domain, terminology is often inherently structured in a taxonomy. It is quite common, both in legal clauses and in the jargon of the Group, to find terms ordered

----

1 SpA is a specific italian juridical form , acronym of "Società per Azioni"

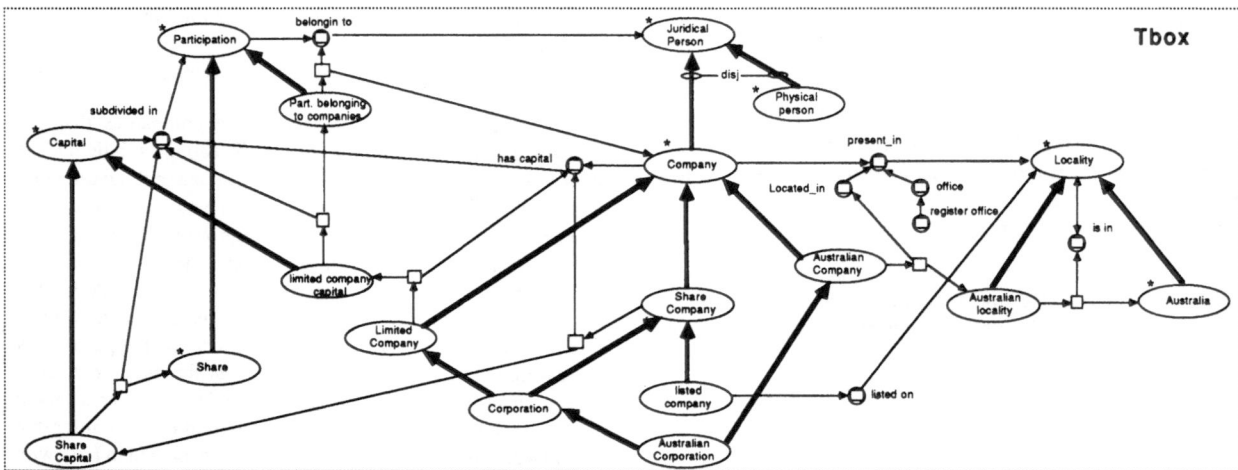

fig 1: graphical description of a sample terminology

in a hierarchy of abstractions. For example, with respect to the economic activities of companies, these are presented by management as grouped in increasingly specialized areas. So for instance the *agroindustry* business consists of activities of *transformation of agricultural products*, that can in turn be further specialized on the basis of products, i.e. *transformation of sugar...*; *trading* that can be further specialized depending upon the forms of trading; and so on.

• *inference on terms definitions*. For a sound representation, the positioning of a given object into the taxonomic description must respect the terminological definitions so far introduced. For example, given the economic activity of *growing*, defined as a type of *production* limited to the *agricultural sector*, if a company is engaged in *soy bean production*, it necessarily will be involved in the growing business as well. In this case the positioning of *soy bean production* is the result of an inference on term definitions.

• *retrieval facility and model scalability*. The terminological model has to be accessed not only for updating but above all for querying purposes. In general, articulated queries require a complex navigation of the model and consequently powerful mechanisms of query interpretation; the amount of information to be represented can be extremely large. In this domain, the dimension of the Group (1500 companies) and its great heterogenity entails a remarkable quantity of terminology to be modelled. In the realization of such a model, scalability is thus a fundamental aspect to be taken into account.

3. The BACK domain model

BACK's descriptive and inferential aspects are well suited for terminological modelling and most of the above requirements are fullfilled by the features of the representation formalism. The language is centered around very few representation constructs: concepts, roles, assertions, yet proven to be extremely powerful in capturing the semantics of the domain. In the modelling practice, we have used *concepts* to intensionally collect relevant entities of the domain; *roles* to specify properties of the elements of the concepts and thus model the relationships between concepts; *assertions* to specify the extension of a concept. If we declare the properties of a concept being necessary and sufficient we introduce in the model equivalent descriptions. With reference to a previous example, if a "SpA" concept is specified to univocally denote all and only the companies of Italian nationality with a capital subdvided in quotable shares, then a specific company can be equivalently described either as an element of the concept "SpA" or through the characterizing properties. Formally the "SpA" concept is described by the following expression:

$$spa := \text{'limited company' and}$$
$$\quad all(\text{'has capital', capital and}$$
$$\quad\quad all(\text{'subdivided in', 'quoted share')) and}$$
$$\quad all(\text{'located in', all('is in', 'Italy'))}$$

This example highlights one further representational feature of the terminological knowledge, i.e. the taxonomic ordering of concepts and even of roles with respect to set inclusion (subsumption) relation. In the example "SpA" concept is subsumed by "company" and this in turn can be subsumed by "Juridical person". In this way the formalism offers the structuring mechanisms of specialization, but differently from object oriented and frame based approaches it can be applied also to concept properties. With respect the above mentioned requirement of preserving the soundness of the overall description, the *classification* inference serves to identify the correct positioning of new TBOX/ABOX objects in the overall knowledge base net providing consistency checking mechanisms and deductive inferencing on term definitions. Finally, the requirement of supporting knowledge assertion and retrieval is fullfilled by a powerful *Tell/Ask* interface language defined on both the TBOX and the ABOX named respectively, BTL (Back Tbox language) and BAL (Back Abox language)[PSet 89].

We sketch the domain model organization and give a more tangible flavor of the representational and inferential capabilities of BACK through examples taken from the developed knowledge base. The implemented model encompasses the following types of information: juridical knowledge about the juridical status of companies; legal knowledge concerning the financial status as well as relationships with other companies; geographic knowledge; organizational apparatus internal to companies (bodies, charges, powers); knowledge about relevant events in specific companies. In Figure 1, a sample company description is depicted[2].

In brief the example describes the following aspects :

the central *concept* is "company", introduced as a *primitive concept* (i.e. only necessary conditions can be defined on it) which is a specialization of "juridical person" but *disjointed* from "physical person". Relevant properties for the "company" are expressed by the following roles:

• "has_capital" with *range* "capital"; the *role* of "capital", "subdivided_in" (and its related chain), expresses the property of "capital" to be subdivided in "participations" belonging to "juridical person";

• "present_in" with *range* a "geographic locality"; this *role* can be further specialized in the roles: "located_in", "office", "registered office", and describes the location - in its different forms - of a company.

The "Company" *concept* subsumes the *defined concepts*: (necessary and sufficient conditions can be defined on it): "Limited company", "Share Company", "Australian company", introduced as *value restrictions* of roles.

Given the above description, the insertion of a new company with, for example, its registered office in Sydney, listed on New York, and with Montedison as its major owner, is realized by the BAL expression:

X = company
with registered_office: 'Sydney' [3]
andwith listed_on: 'New York'
andwith has_capital: (Y = capital
   with subdivided_in:
      (Z = participation
         with belonging_to: 'Montedison')))

The above assertion entails the following set of classification inferences:

a) the company has a *registered office* in Sydney, and is therefore *located in* Sydney; b) Sydney is an Australian locality and the company is thus an *Australian Company*; c) The Australian company is *listed on* a Stock Market and is therefore a *listed company* and, as consequence, a *share company*, d) The company

----

2 In the used graphical notation an ellipse represents a concept (primitive concept are marked with asterisks). Wide arrow denotes the subsumtion link. A role is represented by a little box into a circle with arrows from the domain concept and to the range concept. The simple boxes denote value restriction. For an exhaustive description of BACK terminology see [PSet 89].

3 Sydney, New York and Montedison are alias of pre-existing abox instances

has a *participation belonging* to another company, hence it is a *limited company*; e) Australian limited companies with capital subdivided in shares can only be *Australian Corporation* companies. The company is thus inferred to be an *Australian Corporation* and consequently positioned in the knowledge base net as element of that concept. In this way, instances can be only partially specified and the insertion of an entity as new element of a concept is left to the inferential engine.

Finally we report an example of Abox query expressed in the powerful declarative formalism AQL (Abox Query Language) [Pset 89], one of the most remarkable and advanced features of BACK with respect to related approaches :

%which are the names of the chairmans of all italian companies engaged in both the chemical and agricultural sectors and that have some installation in a nation in which a company participated by Montedison is also present ?

[rf(firstname),rf(surname)] for
getall physical_person with inv has_in_office:
   some(chairman with inv has_body:
      some(italian•company with engaged_in:
         some(chemical_area) and some(agricultural_area)
      andwith installation:
         some(nation with inv present_in:
            some(company with has_capital:
               some(capital with subdivided_in:
                  some(participation with belonging_to:
                     some(company with named:
                        'Montedison')))))*

3. System usability issues

The knowledge base we have built consists of about 500 TBOX concepts/roles. The effectiveness of BACK in capturing the domain semantics and the powerful mechanisms it provides for accessing the description have greatly simplified and sped up the design of the model. From a representational point of view, BACK thus turns out to be a valid alternative to semantic data models and object oriented approaches in applications characterized by complex descriptions and rich deductive interrelations. Conversely, from an operational point of view,

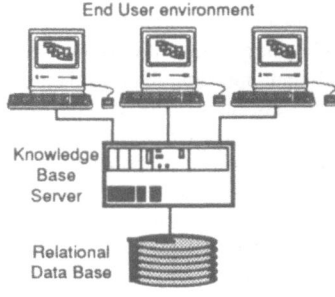

fig.2: application architecture

BACK proves not to be fully adequate because of the unsatisfactory performance. The system is practically unusable when a large amount of terminology especially of ABOX instances is to be managed. In this sense the mentioned requirement of model scalability is not actually fullfilled. One fundamental source of inefficiency is the algorithm for the ABOX_network navigation underlying the assertion classification and query expressions interpretation. The algorithm follows a *tuple* or *instance oriented approach*, i.e. operations on data are applied to single instances instead of sets (*set oriented approach*). To exemplify, the retrieval of a set of instances for a concept satisfying a whatever complex condition is realized through a filtering of the single instances of the concept extension. Of course, for very large extensions the approach is absolutely inefficient. To overcome this problem we propose a set oriented approach realized by coupling BACK with a relational database for efficient storage and retrieval of ABOX instances.

One more reason of scarce usability of BACK is its inherent complexity that makes the interaction with the system quite hard for an unskilled programmer/user. The need of providing a comfortable interaction environment especially to an application user is being approached by a hypertextual based interface to the BACK knowledge base.

The general architecture we have developed for the whole business application incorporating the facilities introduced above is depicted in figure 2.

4.1 Coupling BACK to RDBMS

Considerable attention has been only recently paid by the research community to the problem of integrating terminological formalisms with databases [BGN 89]. The research is still at the initial stages, and few results can be currently reported [WTS 89]. Our approach to this problem has focused on the following major aspects :

i) definition of a schema mapping strategy for the translation of the TBOX schema into relational tables
ii) BACK query optimization
iii) translation of BACK assert operations into transactions

i) BACK *concepts* and *roles* have a very straighforward semantics denoting nothing but sets of individuals/couples_of individuals. TBOX entities can thus be "naturally" associated with relational data structures. How to aggregate information in order to efficiently handle retrieval and updating requests is the basic issue. Unfortunately, general optimization criteria for scheme design seem difficult to define. The characteristics of a particular domain may, in fact, strongly influence the amount of data placed in relations and their layout. If we decide to adopt as an optimization strategy the reduction of the number of relations constituting the relational schema, we are able to design a schema grouping all available information together and storing facts concerning respectively concepts, role filler values and cardinalities in only three tables. If, conversely, the knowledge base defines concepts having a large number of instances, the use of few relations may

waste time, for example, when searching a great amount of non related information to determine all the instances of a concept. This last condition may be better handled by fragmenting the schema in a larger number of relations, one for each concept having as many attributes as the number of roles introduced for the concept. This strategy optimizes relation size as well as the number of joins, in case of queries containing several predicates. However which strategy is the best depends on the particular knowledge base's characteristics: number of concepts, roles, instances and access patterns. Intermediate strategies are therefore more appropriate consisting in a partition of the whole knowledge base into various concept clusters and using mapping strategies specifically adapted to each cluster.

ii) Given a Relational DBMS having SQL as its data definition and manipulation language, query optimization can be realized through translation of ABOX query expressions into composite SQL expressions (containing for example joins and subqueries), that are optimized by the DBMS. It has been demonstrated that an AQL query can be mapped directly onto a single relational SQL query or onto a small sequence of queries [BR 90]. Furthermore query execution performance can be improved by using storage and access techniques provided by the DBMS, such as clusters and indices. The complexity of query translation greatly depend on the strategy being used for the implementation of the instance classification inference (realization). If realization is performed at query time, as in the current version of BACK, the interpretation function for the query is quite complex as it needs also to access the intensional description (TBOX) to infer properties on assertions.

In such a case inference can be performed using SQL statements for manipulating concept extensions. If, conversely, the inference rule is applied at assertion time then the translation is quite straighforward and the additional cost induced by the deductive apparatus is moved to the operation of ABOX insertion.

iii) Insert operations are extremely costly, as - indipendently from the strategy of *realization* being used - consistency checks need anyway to be performed on the knowledge base to validate the new assertion. To that extent, transactions embedding set manipulation operations on concept extensions can be used for testing constraints on extensional descriptions. This aspect, not yet deeply analyzed at this stage, does not seem excessively complex, being the steps to be performed resembling the *realization* procedure.

4.2 An end user interface for accessing a BACK knowledge base

Usually, both in relational databases and in advanced representation contexts little attention is paid to end-user interaction; complicated query languages are at best made available at the interface level. This constitutes a barrier for the casual end user wishing to consult the information base, and consequently a large amount of informative potential is often wasted. The BACK data model seems to be too complex for the end user's perpective of the world and a simplified version of it , excluding for example defined concepts, may be more appropriate. Moreover, the BACK query language is a quite sophisticated formalism incomprehensible to an end user not already acquainted with the representation paradigm. It is therefore inconceivable for an unskilled user as a manager or business professional to interact directly with the knowledge base as well as be bothered with the low level details of the domain description, introduced as pure implementative choices or as heuristic shortcuts. The need for a high level and easy to understand visualization of the knowledge base content has motivated the development of a hypertextual interface for information querying and navigation centered on the concept of BACK view.

Very roughly a *BACKview* consists of "virtual" concepts and roles defined in terms of knowledge base actual structures and denoted by AQL expressions. For example , with reference to the business domain, we can introduce at view level the concept "company with positive balancesheet" and define it as the set of ABOX instances satifying the specific condition. View concepts are displayed through *graphical frames* defined as visual structures consisting of a set of slots for concept roles. The intensional part of the view can be naturally represented as a graph of linked graphical frames (*hyperframe*); the extensional part as a graph of *frames instances*. The fundamental operations the user can perform through the interface are view querying and navigation. The approach being used for supporting retrieval basically consists in graphically defining a query through a set of linked graphical frames or hyperframe, partially filled in, constituting the pattern to be matched by the requested instances. The set of instances resulting from the query can be freely inspected through the navigation utility exploiting the links between the frame instances for moving from one instance to its related entities in hypertextual manner .

A first prototype of interface has been developed in Hypercard™ on Macintosh™. The positive results we have obtained encourage a deeper investigation of the problem and a more careful analysis of the BACK view data model.

5. Conclusions

We have presented a terminological knowledge base developed for a business application, and have argued the suitability of the terminological approach in highly structured domains requiring inferential capabilities. Finally, the necessity of both adequate support for end-user interaction and efficient knowledge storage for the development of real-world complex applications has been emphasized.

The application we have developed can be used in various environments such as decision support systems, office procedures, computer supported cooperative work (CSCW). In particular, in the area of the CSCW [CSC 88] the terminological knowledge based system could support the users in cooperative access to shared information through particular views and by using different terminologies.

™ HyperCard and Macintosh are trademarks of Apple Computer, Inc.; Sun is a trademark of Sun Microsystems, Inc.

6. References

[ABDDMZ 89] M.Atkinson, F.Bancilhon, D.DeWitt, K.Dittrich, D.Maier, S.Zdonik, *The Object-Oriented Database System Manifesto*, Proc. of the First International Conference on Deductive and Object-Oriented Databases, Kyoto (J), December 4-6,1989.

[BGN 89] H.W.Beck, S.K. Gala, S.B. Navathe, *Classification as query process techique in the CANDIDE semantic data model*, Proc.IEEE Conf. on Data Engineering, Los Angeles (Cal.), February 1989, pp.572-581

[BFL 83] R.Brachman,R.Fikes, H.Levesque, *KRIPTON: A functional approach to knowledge representation*, IEEE Computer 16(10), 1983.

[BR90] E.Bertino, P.Randi, *Mapping AQL into SQL programs* Datamont spa technical report,May 1990.

[BS 85] R.Brachman, J.G.Schmolze, *An Overwiew of the KL-ONE Knowledge Representation System*, Cognitive Science 9(2): 171-216, April-June 1985.

[CSC 88] AA.VV., *CSCW 88*, Proceedings of the Conference on Computer-supported Cooperative Work, ACM, Portland, September 1988.

[DP 89] J.Doyle, R.S.Patil, *Two dogmas of knowledge representation*, Report MIT/LCS/TM-387.b Laboratory for Computer Science MIT, Massachusetts USA, September 1989.

[Fi 88] R. Fikes, *Integrating Hypertext and Frame-based Domain Models*, Proc. AAAI-88 Workshop AI and Hypertext: Issues and Directions, May 1988.

[Ga 86] F. Galgano, *Diritto Commerciale*, Le Società, (In Italian), Zanichelli Ed., Bologna (I), 1986.

[HK 87] R.Hull, R.King, *Semantic Database Modelling: Survey, Applications and Research Issues*, ACM Computing Surveyes, Vol.19, No.3, September 1987.

[LI 87] P .Lynback, V.Vianu, *Mapping a Semantic Data Model to the Relational Model*, Proceedings of ACM Special Interest Group on Management of Data, San Francisco, May 1987

[LNet 87] K.v.Luck, B.Nebel, C.Peltason, A.Schmiedel, *The Anatomy of the Back System*, KIT Report 41, Technische Universitat Berlin, January 1987.

[MAet 87] E.Mays, C.Apté, J. Griesmer, J.Kastner, *Organizing Knowledge in a Complex Financial Domain*, IEEE Expert, fall 1987 pp. 61-70, 1987

[Ne 87] B.Nebel, *Computation Complexity of Terminological Reasoning in BACK*, Artificial Intelligence, Vol.34, No.3, pp. 344-348, April 1988.

[Ne 88] B.Nebel, *Hybrid Reasoning in BACK*, Proc. Methodologies for Intelligent Systems, 3, Ed. W.Ras, L. Saitta, Turin (I), October 1988.

[NI 87] B.Nixon, L.Chung et al., *Implementation of a Compiler for Semantic Data Model: Experiences with Taxis*, Proceedings of ACM Special Interest Group on Management of Data, San Francisco, May 1987

[P311 89] *ADKMS (Esprit Project 311) Deliverable 1*, May 1989.

[PSet 89] C.Peltason, A.Schmiedel, K.Kindermann, J. Quanz, *The Back System Revisited*, KIT Report 75, Technische Universitat Berlin, September 1989.

[SPet 86] A.Schmiedel, C.Peltason, B.Nebel, K.v.Luck, *Bitter Pills - A Case Study in Knowledge Representation*, KIT Report 39, Berlin: Departement of Computer Science, Technische Univeritat Berlin, August 1986.

[SG 88] G.Spinelli, S.Gaglio, M.Costa, M.Frixione, M.Traversa, M.Zoletti, *Was King ARThur a King by Definition?*, AICOM 1(1), January 88.

[WTS 89] AA.VV., *Statements of Interest for the Workshop on Term Subsumption Languages in Knowledge Representation*, Workshop on Term Subsumption Languages in Knowledge Representation, Thorn Hyll, New Hampshire, USA, August 198.

An Organization & Resources Model for Adapting Office Systems to Organizational Structures

Walter Rupietta

Nixdorf Computer AG, PSD–D7,
Fürstenallee 7, D–4790 Paderborn

ABSTRACT

Office systems have to conform to organizational structures governing work in an enterprise. This means they have to be configured according to these structures and must obey the rules defined explicitly or implicitly by the enterprise organization. The Organization & Resources model (OR) defines a conceptual data model for representing organizational structures and resources controlled by an office system. Its implementation is a database containing a representation of the organizational structure of a company, it's actors and resources. This database provides the information necessary to adapt services of an office system to organizational requirements.

With its dialog interface, the OR model provides an electronic organization reference manual. To make this information available to application systems, an application programming interface (API) is supplied. The OR model provides a means for adapting office software systems to a company's static and dynamic organizational structure. It comprises a representation of office objects and their relations that are maintained by the underlying office system.

INTRODUCTION

This paper is structured a follows: The introduction gives a motivation for starting the OR model project and discusses related work. The main part presents our conceptual data model. A short description of the software architecture concludes the paper.

Office Systems and Organizational Structures

Today's perspective for office systems is a network connecting multiple personal workstations and one or more server systems. Applications in such an environment apply a client/server architecture. Office workers are expected to use client programs running on their workstation, which may require and access services provided by another program running on a remote server system. System users may communicate and cooperate by using the services provided by the system.

Organization is an essential determinant of work in an office environment. Cooperation of people in an office is governed by static and dynamic organizational structures. **Static organization** is determined by organizational units and their (hierarchical subordination) relations. The assignment of resources is another part of the static organization. **Dynamic organization** comprises the procedures used to do the work. The organizational unit a member of an enterprise belongs to defines his position and his tasks within the organization's work procedures.

The OR model defines a conceptual model for the description of organizational structures including resources. It provides interfaces for applications to access organization related information. By observing these interfaces, all applications within a system environment can make consistent use of organizational structures. We have identified three issues where such a model is concerned in an office system architecture as the one described above:

– **Cooperative office procedures** are *"processes involving a group of persons where each person is responsible for a certain action or certain actions in the procedure"* (from [6]).

   The **responsibility** of an actor is inferred from the role this actor is assigned within an organization. Monitoring of ongoing office procedures requires information on the organizational structure and the roles of actors as well as information on the processing steps to perform. The OR model is intended to provide the organization related information.

– **Addressing** is a critical issue in computer system networks: users need to address other users and services on different machines. But electronic mail and network addresses are mostly designed to meet technical requirements, not the users' needs and capabilities and not organizational requirements.

– **Access Control** is an important feature of systems for cooperative processing. Cooperation of multiple system users results in parallel and independent use of system resources. Access to such resources has to be controlled in order to avoid conflict and corruption of data.

   Access rights depend on the assignment of system resources to organizational entities such as actors, roles or organizational units. Access rights for individual actors are defined implicitly by organizational structures and may be inferred from the placement of an actor within the organization.

The OR model addresses all three issues: Cooperative office procedures are provided with information on organizational structures and responsibilities. Actors and resource descriptions can be addressed by names or by pursuing organizational relations (like "superiorOf"), retrieving electronic mail or network addresses from the description. The OR model also comprises an access control scheme based on organizational structures and the assignment of resources to organizational entities like actors, roles or organizational units. The combination of these features in the OR model allows to build integrated application environments that are adaptable to the needs of enterprise organizations.

Related Work

The model of an organization described by Ang in [1] is part of a more general office model also covering dynamic aspects (office procedures). Ang's active and passive office objects correspond to our distinction of organizational entities (actor, role, organizational unit) and resources, but his passive objects do not cover application programs. The paper describes a concept, not an implementation.

The "electronic organization manual" described in [2] is a knowledge base on structures, procedures, co-workers, products or services of an organization. The knowledge base is structured into four layers named taxonomy (concepts, object classes), organization (concrete organization model, instances), tasks and procedures. The procedures layer defines rules and guidelines for the execution of office procedures. The system was implemented as LUIGI knowledge base on a Symbolics Lisp-Machine.

[3] contains a description of an organization knowledge base modeling the specific organization of a research institute. This description is used for generating and executing office procedures. The paper describes a prototype implemented in KEE, that only handles a very limited set of procedures. The knowledge base contains representations of persons, work areas, work fields, rooms, technical equipment and relations between these objects. Work areas correspond to organizational units.

The Office Model One from [4] is a knowledge base containing representations of office procedures, organization structure and resources (like documents, files etc.). The model was implemented as a prototype on a Symbolics Lisp-Machine.

The paper from Kreifelts and Seuffert [6] is concerned with addressing in the office procedure system DOMINO. Their main issue is an organizational addressing scheme, which is necessary because DOMINO relies on electronic mail for coordination among office workers.

Karbe and Ramsperger [5] describe an office procedure system based on "electronic circulation folders". Each folder contains a "migration specification" describing possible migration routes of the folder through the organization. An electronic form of organizational handbook is split into the organizational structure and the migration specification. The system is implemented employing a relational database system providing distributed transactions.

All these organization models are concerned with office procedures requiring information on organizational structures. Most of the systems are research prototypes using some kind of knowledge representation mechanism to implement the organizational model. The organizational structures modeled differ, but all models at least allow to represent hierarchical static organizations. Only one system uses a relational database with nonstandard features (distributed transactions).

Our approach is to use a "standard" relational database for implementation. To clarify requirements and to define the conceptual model we started our project by building an object oriented prototype in Smalltalk as part of the system specification process. The prototype uses concepts of object-oriented knowledge representation to experiment with different structures and relations. We have restricted ourselves to model a limited set of organizational structure concepts, but included an access control scheme.

CONCEPTUAL DATA MODEL DESIGN

The conceptual data model of the OR model is defined using concepts of object-oriented design. It is developed by building an object-oriented prototype in Smalltalk. This prototype is the basis for the specification of the conceptual data model, which is presented here as an object class hierarchy.

The OR model comprises various basic object classes, namely actors, roles, tasks and resources, organizational units. **Actors** represent the office personnel, the users of the office system, which play certain **roles** within the organization. **Organizational units** are the building blocks to represent the static organization. **Resources** describe objects controlled by the office system

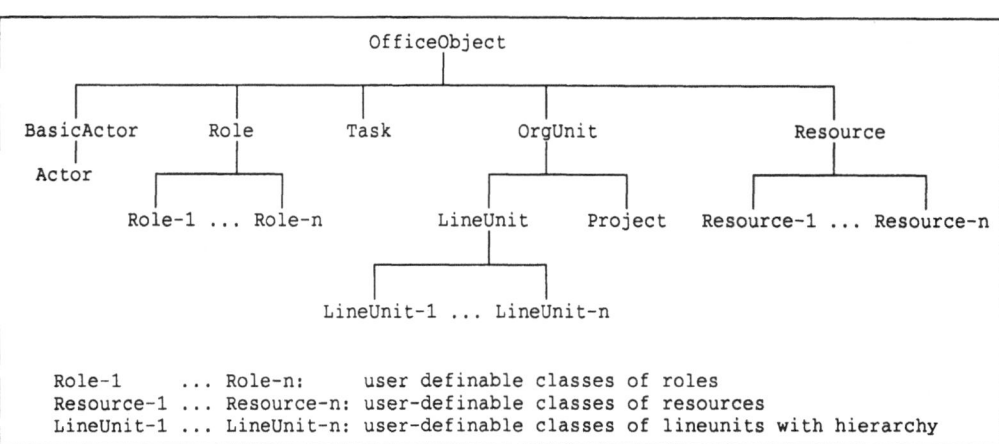

Figure 1: Object class hierarchy of the OR model

348

(like workstations, printers, filing systems, application programs etc.) and **tasks** are processing steps within office procedures. The exact naming and hierarchy will be defined in a comprehensive model specification.

Object classes in the hierarchy tree (see Figure 1) represent the data structures used within the model. The leaves of the tree above are the classes instantiated for describing a concrete organization and its resources. All the other classes are used for conceptual structuring. The OR model holds tables of all actors, roles, tasks, organizational units and resources. Each object can be addressed through the table for its class or by pursuing some relation from another object under consideration.

Actors

An actor is described as follows:

```
OfficeObject subclass: #Actor
    instanceVariableNames:
    'familyName              "family name of
                             actor"
     preName                 "prename of actor"
     title                   "title"
     personalID              "unique personal
                             number"
     phoneNumber             "phone number"
     assignedPositions       "positions assigned
                             to the actor"
     assignedResources       "list of directly
                             assigned resources"'
```

This is the basic actor description. Additional user-defined information (like electronic mail address, system user ID, system password etc.) may be attached to an actor description depending on the actual system configuration and requirements.

Roles and Tasks

The object class *Roles* is a generic definition of a role concept which has to be specialized into user-defined subclasses. A role subclass is used for defining groups of similar organizational roles like managers, clerks, consultants etc. Instances of such a subclass are the roles specific to an organization (for example credit clerk, securities clerk as instances of clerk). A role is described a follows:

```
OfficeObject subclass: #Role
    instanceVariableNames:
    'longName                "name of the role"
     assignedPositions       "list of assigned
                             positions"
     assignedTasks           "list of assigned
                             tasks"
     assignedResources       "list of directly
                             assigned resources"'
```

The object class *Task* is used to assign **responsibilities** for certain actions to an organizational role.

```
OfficeObject subclass: #Task
    instanceVariableNames:
    'longName                "name of the task"
     assignedRoles           "list of roles
                             responsible for
                             this task"'
```

An office procedure monitoring system has to determine a person responsible for a processing step (i.e. a task) as part of a predefined procedure. The OR model provides retrieval functions which – given a task – find the responsible roles. These roles are then used to find the assigned actors. It is also possible to attach a list of resource requirements for a task which allows to check whether a responsible actor is equipped with the necessary access rights for the required resources.

Organizational Units

The organizational units class is divided into **line units** and **projects**. Line units enable the description of strictly hierarchical organizations while projects allow to define rather arbitrary configurations. The user-defined subclasses of class LineUnit are ordered to allow control of hierarchical relations between line units. These subclasses are defined at installation time. Organizational units are defined as follows:

```
OfficeObject subclass: #OrgUnit
    instanceVariableNames:
    'longName                "name of the OrgUnit"
     unitManager             "head of the OrgUnit"
     deputyManager           "deputy of the head"
     costCenter              "unique cost center"
     unitPositions           "list of positions
                             within the unit"
     superiorUnit            "superior OrgUnit"
     subUnits                "list of subunits"
     assignedResources       "list of directly
                             assigned resources"'
```

This basic structure is inherited both by line units and by projects. In addition, projects contain a verbal description of themselves. Each subclass of a *LineUnit* is assigned a hierarchy index that determines its level within the organizational hierarchy. Subordination relations between instances of *LineUnit* subclasses are governed by the hierarchy indices of the subclasses. An instance α of a *LineUnit* subclass A may be subunit of an instance β of another *LineUnit* subclass B, if and only if the hierarchy index of A is less than that of B.

A **Position** in an organizational unit is defined as a triplet associating a role, an actor and the organizational unit. This is done to reflect the fact that each actor plays a (more or less well defined) role in the organizational unit he is assigned to. An actor does not play a role without any connection to the organization and is not associated to an organizational unit without specifying his role. An actor may be assigned different roles within different or within the same organizational unit.

Resources and access control

Resources controlled by an office system may be work objects like documents, files etc. or tools like application programs. Resources may be compound entities like a filing cabinet, consisting of multiple folders. Different types of resources can be modeled by different user–defined subclasses of class *Resource*. The structure of the basic resource class is presented below:

```
OfficeObject subclass: #Resource
  instanceVariableNames:
    'longName          "description of
                        resource"
     accessPath        "accessPath (network
                        address)"
     isPartOf          "resource, this one is
                        part of"
     subParts          "subparts of this
                        resource"
     accActors         "list of assignments
                        for actors"
     accRoles          "list of assignments
                        for roles"
     accOrgUnits       "list of assignments
                        for organizational
                        units"'
```

Access restrictions for resources may be specified by attaching an access right to an organizational entity like an actor, a role or an organizational unit. The OR model does not specify semantics for access rights (like read access, write access), but only maintains the assignment of access rights. The interpretation of a fact like *"actor A has access right B for resource C"* is left to the application programs maintaining the resources.

The variables *accActors*, *accRoles* and *accOrgUnits* contain lists of actors, roles and organizational units with their directly assigned access rights for this resource. Only one direct assignment for an organizational entity is allowed.

The basic OR model policy is to make access rights dependent on organizational structures: Resources are assigned to organizational units and all members of an organizational unit inherit its access classes. To provide for more flexibility, different access classes may be assigned to subunits, roles or actors. It is also possible to explicitly deny specific access operations for an organizational entity.

An **access right** is composed of two 32 bit values, each bit representing an access operation for the resource. One of the values is called *assigned rights*, the other *denied rights*. The *effective access right* ER of an organizational entity is determined by combining its assigned right AR, its inherited right IR and its denied right DR (¦ signifies the logical "or" operation, & the logical "and" operation):

$$ER = (IR \mathbin{\vert} AR) \mathbin{\&} DR$$

The *inherited access rights* of an organizational entity are derived according to the following rules:

– Organizational units inherit the effective access right of their immediate superior unit.

– Roles do not inherit access rights.

– Actors inherit the effective access rights from their roles and from the organizational units they are assigned to. As actors may be members of different organizational units,

their inherited access rights are a superset of all inherited access rights.

In some application contexts, inheritance for actors may be restricted to an *active role* within a specific organizational unit. The intention of this access control scheme was to eliminate the need to specify explicit access rights for each individual actor, favouring the deduction of access rights from organizational structures. This principle simplifies and partly automates the administration of an OR model for example in case of organizational restructuring.

The OR model provides an access control scheme but does not actually control access to resources. Control has to be implemented by application programs. The API of the OR model provides functions for checking access classes and thereby enables the implementation of access control monitors.

An example for the application of resources and the access control scheme is a menu system where each menu entry represents an application program. Each of these application programs is monitored by a resource description that determines which actors are allowed to execute it. The menu system may use the OR model API to check access rights while the OR model dialogue interface may be used for administration.

SOFTWARE ARCHITECTURE

The software architecture (see Figure 2) is based on a relational database with an SQL interface. We assume that the database is located on a server system. Database access may happen through a local area network from different workstations.

In the conceptual data model defined by our prototype, organizational entities together with their relations to other entities are agglomerated into a single object, following the principles of object–oriented design. Mapping this model to a relational data base results in a different structure where information pertaining to a specific object is split across several database relations. Organizational relationships defined implicitly (and redundantly) in the different object classes have to be extracted and explicitly modeled as data base relations. In the API and dialogue interface, we aspire to hide this implementation effect.

As we expect to use different databases, we mask the database access interface by defining a **logical access interface** for the OR data. This interface is an intermediate layer separating the external interfaces (dialog interface and API) from the implementation of data management for the OR model. The separation allows us to replace the database by integration of different data management systems.

The **dialog interface** is developed using the OR logical access interface routines. It will be implemented using a window system and is intended to serve as an administration tool for the OR model. Organizational relationships will be visualized graphically. The dialog interface makes the OR model useful as a kind of electronic organization reference manual, address– or telephone directory (provided the model is kept up to date).

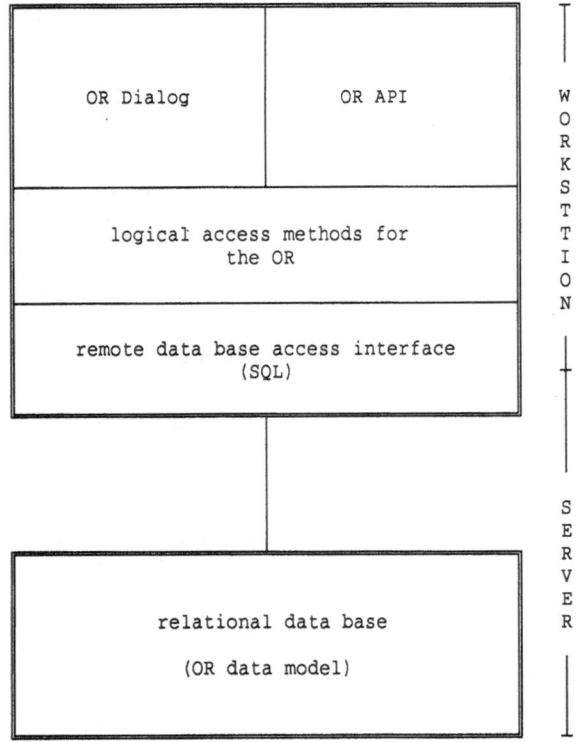

OR Dialog	OR API
logical access methods for the OR	
remote data base access interface (SQL)	

W
O
R
K
S
T
I
O
N

S
E
R
V
E
R

relational data base

(OR data model)

Figure 2: Software architecture

An application programming interface (**OR API**) is also based on the logical access interface. The API provides functions for retrieving information from the OR model and to manipulate data in the OR model. While the OR API is intended for application programmers, we also plan to integrate some of its functionality into a higher level language available at the user level. This language will serve to specify the model contents with **OR definition files** in a batch mode. OR definition files allow the partial definition and distribution of standard organizational structures.

SUMMARY

The OR model defines a conceptual framework for representing organizational structures and resources but is not an active component of an office system. It defines and implements an interface for accessing and maintaining organizational structures and an access control scheme based on the organization.

Aspects not covered by the OR model are organizational rules, that are not part of the static structure, but specify how certain procedures are carried out depending on dynamically changing conditions. (Like: Actor A is allowed to deputize for actor B for the tasks of signing form C from June, 1 to June 26. If the manager of unit D is absent, each manager of another unit within the same superior unit at the same hierarchy level than D is allowed to sign applications for leave.)

The model enables integration of software components through the use of a common organizational context including an access control scheme. Its main application area will be office procedures, but we expect that other components of an office system – like a desktop or a menu system – will at least make use of the access control scheme. An electronic mail system may use information from the OR model for generating distribution lists for documents according to document type and to organizational regulations.

Office systems combine the functionality of numerous individual software products. Office procedures involve multiple users and use several individual programs. Integration is achieved by special components such as desktop or menu systems that are used to combine individual software products and to standardize their handling – at least to a certain degree. If all applications and services within such an environment rely on a single source for organization and user related information, overall consistency may be greatly improved. The OR model is an attempt to provide a general concept for maintaining organizational structures.

REFERENCES

[1] Ang, J.: A Comprehensive Office Modeling Framework for ITHACA. ITHACA, Bull, 89, D9, #1, Version 0, June 1989.

[2] Chrapary, H.-J., Rosenow-Schreiner, E., Waldhör, K.: Das Elektronische Organisationshandbuch. Preprint. TA Triumph-Adler AG, 1989.

[3] Faidt, K., Grünberger, H., Heller, H., Hinkelmann, K., Karagiannis, D., Salzmann, W., Schebiella, S.: Organisation Support System –OSSY–. Der Demonstrator, Projektbericht. FAW Ulm, February 1990.

[4] Ishii, H., Kubota, K.: Office Procedure Knowledge Base for Organizational Office Work Support. In: Office Information Systems: The Design Process. Working Conference, IFIP WG 8.4, August 15–17,1988, Linz, Austria, p. 40–57.

[5] Karbe, B., Ramsperger, N.: Electronic Circulation Folders – Functionality and Implementation. Preprint from: Office Automation, Athens, October 1989.

[6] Kreifelts, Th., Seuffert, P.: Addressing in an Office Procedure System. In: Speth (Ed.): Message Handling Systems. Elsevier (North-Holland), 1988, p. 117–127.

[7] Röthig, .: Grundbegriffe der Organisation GBO. Akademie für Organisation, Giessen, 1985.

COMPUTER-AIDED INTERPRETATION OF ROUTINE HEALTH EXAMINATIONS

P. LEDUC   J. ZANAZAKA   J.P. MONNEAU

University of Sherbrooke, QC-J1K2R1, Canada
Center for Preventive Medicine, 54000 Vandoeuvre, France

Abstract

The Center for Preventive Medicine (CMP) carries out 60 000 routine health examinations each year. An "expert system" is being developed to assist doctors in interpreting these check-ups : it discerns anomalies, compiles them, determines risks and diagnoses, proposes investigations and questions to be asked to patients, indicates behavior modifications and desirable actions. For this, we use a rule-based system generator using a forward chaining inferencing scheme. The usefulness of the system has to do with the great diversity of disorders encountered because the system can access knowledge, that exceeds that of the doctor, who cannot be a specialist in every field. Above all, the system turns to account reference values and numerous factors of variation, in particular, medicational, much more precisely than a doctor would be able to do. The current prototype is being expanded, since it presently exploits only a part of the results.

The social security legislation in France gives its members and their dependants the right to regular medical check-ups. At the CMP, there are two stages to the ckeck-up :
- the pre-clinical examination, both biological and functional
- the clinical examination, two weeks later, leading to the doctor's synthesis of the complete medical results.

The check-ups are carried out in a family setting : father, mother and children are invited to attend. The proposed system is aimed at assisting the practitioner in the interpretation of the biological and functional examinations in order that he may arrive at a syntheses.

Action of the medical expert

For each patient, the doctor's synthesis traditionally requires several tasks :
- several readings of the biological and functional results and of the answers to questionnaires
- readings of possible prior medicals as well as of those of family members
- information gathering by personal questioning and by clinical examination
- the actual synthesis and its expression in lowest terms
- recommending adapted preventive action (fig. 1).

Studying entire personal medical histories demands much time of practitioner. Moreover, such work highlights neither salient details nor those which depend on several simultaneous factors.

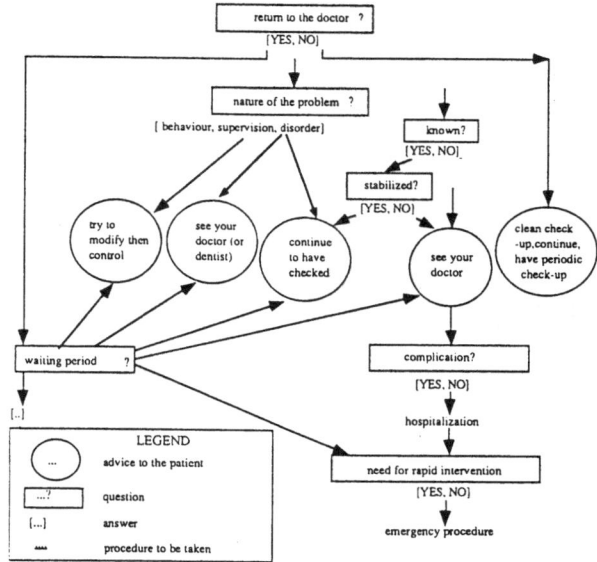

Figure 1 : recommending adapted preventive action

A rough outline of a medical synthesis by the computer could bring out significant or unexplained disorders and reveals syndromes. Doctors need spend less time going through the results and can thus more fully devote themselves to deriving the synthesis and to contacting the patient (notably in order to explain the check-up results and to better transmit the ensuing intructive message). After the check-up is completed, the doctor reviews any problems encountered and poses several questions for each one.

It is necessary to :
- remedy a behavioral error ?
- correct a lack of supervision ?
- treat a disorder ?

If yes, is the disorder already identified and controlled, or, to the contrary, is it new or uncontrolled ?

Should that the patient be advised to see his doctor ?

The doctor should be aware of the seriousness and nature of any anticipated investigations or interventions, as well as of the urgency of the situation.

Improvements achieved with the system

The system will save some practitioner's time. Above all it will allow him to take advantage of knowledge that is otherwise virtually inacessible to him, since no doctor can be a specialist in every field. Further, the doctor doesn't have the time necessary either to consult various reference charts (by age and sex), or to realize all the known variation factors of the results (medication, pregnancy, etc...) ; but the system has precise thresholds of decision and the updating of these limits is more easily accomplished in the computer memory than in the human experts. Finally, a greater uniformity of conclusion can be expected from the users of the system.

General characteristics of the system

Inference engine

A routine check-up must be fully carried out. No single, constant goal exists other that to derive all available pieces of information. For this reason, a rule based system using a forward-chaining inferencing scheme is used [2,3].

Knowledge modelling

The rules are divided into several categories. The first are used to compare the data (fig. 2) with the reference values, principally given by age and sex. The result is expressed by classification : high or low intra-or extra-reference value (fig. 3). Other rules refine the classification, taking into account known factors of variation : pregnancy [5], toxic, and medication [6]. These rules determine fundamental deviations.

The following rules compile the deviations to constitute syndromes or to point towards disorders. At this stage, the difficulty of having to deal with uncertainly is encountered. For example, we need to know how strongly a deviation should be taken into account in the prediction of a disorder. We may use the *predictive value of the deviation* (pv) for that. It is deduced from the frequency of the pathology (p) in the considered population, from the *sensitivity* (se, aptitude of the test to detect illness) and from the *specificity* (sp, aptitude of the test to detect healty people), according to the formula :

$$pv = se.p/[(1 - p) . (1 - sp) + se.p]$$

In practice, however, there is rarely enough reliable data to be able to apply this calculation.

Another difficulty lies in the manner of reinforcing a conclusion that is supported by several factors. There is no solid base available to combine the confidence weights of several premises. Thus we must be satisfied with recalling the obtained conclusions and classifying them by decreasing order of likelihood, without indicating the obtained values.

The Center for Preventive Medicine of Vandoeuvre
2, avenue du doyen J. Parisot P.O. Box 7 54501 Vandoeuvre Cedex Tel 83 44 44 15

Family name :   Individual n° :
First name :   Lab n° :

age :   year   month   date of visit :   sex :

biological rule-out

aspect of serum : normal   time of collection : 08h 00 mn   condition : fasting

test	unit	method	values low	normal	high	normal values		values old units
				tests on serum				
uric acid	umol/l	(1)			457	225	430	77mg/l
urea	mmol/l	(1)		5.78		3.60	8.50	0.35g/l
creatinine	umol/l	(1)		95		70	125	11mg/l
glucose	mmol/l	(2)		6.43		4.50	6.85	1.16g/l
cholesterol	mmol/l	(1)		5.66		4.20	7.70	2.19g/l
triglycerides	mmol/l	(1)		0.51		0.40	2.00	0.51mmol/l
total protein	g/l	(1)		68		64	82	68g/l
albumin	g/l	(1)		43		35	47	43g/l
total calcium	mmol/l	(1)		2.43		2.21	2.60	96mg/l
phosphatase	mmol/l	(1)		0.97		0.70	1.30	30mg/l
alkaline phosphatase	U/l	(1)		56		35	130	56mU/ml
bilirubin	micromol/l	(1)		12		2	30	7mg/l
GPT	U/l	(1)		20		12.0	60.5	20mU/ml
GOT	U/l	(1)		20		10.0	45.0	20mU/mlg
GGT	U/l	(1)		60		10.0	75.0	60mU/ml
etc...								

Figure 2 : a sample of biological medical results from a check-up at the CMP

REGLE : dérive élémentaire

SI

Est-un	(E)	=	Examen
Mesure	(E)	=	(VM)
Réf-975	(E)	< = =	(VM)

ALORS

| Dérive-basse | (E) | <-- | Haut |

FR

Figure 3 : example of a rule

Facts data base

The facts are represented by variables divided into several categories :
- the variables giving the decision thresholds, taken from reference charts (fig. 4)
- the observed quantitative and qualitative variables
- the results from the synthesis which are groups of observed variables and statements.

Implementation

Data from individual check-ups is implemented in no particular order. However, the medical history of the patient and his family is not researched unless long term of family disorders are perceived. The absence of an interactive phase makes the method of questioning useless.

The system involves several phases :
- acquiring the check-up data
- calculating the decision thresholds
- determining the fundamental deviations
- combine the various deviations to find possible disorders
- conclusion and statement of results

Following the final statement, the system provides the doctor with additional clinical and para-clinical examinations which may confirm or invalidate the results.

Results and perspectives

The system is still a prototype under development.

It does not yet take into account all the medical data, in particular the questionnaires which involve several tens of replies. As well, the layout of the results has to be refined. Such a system can only be useful to doctors once it is able to save them time, once it can properly interpret virtually all of the first part of the check-up.

For the moment, the most interesting positive results are the use of the reference charts and the inclusion of variation factors in the results, particularly, pregnancy, alcohol, and medication.

The present development progressively adds to the number of interpreted parameters. The problem of a high number of rules leaded us to reprogram from Prolog to Snark [1] the very repetitive rules of comparison. We dividing foresee the knowledge base into successive modules.

This system of interpretation is summoned to develop viably. Its application is possible throughout the computerized medical examination centers, with possible extension to other types of routine check-ups, for example, in occupational and sports medicine.

P-creatinin (mmol.$^{l-1}$), centiles 2.5 and 97.5

Age (years)	Men 2.5	97.5	Women 2.5	97.5
04-09	31.0	74.0	28.5	72.0
10-13	39.5	84.0	40.0	82.5
14-17	50.5	105.0	46.0	95.5
18-54	65.0	120.0	50.0	100.0
55-99	66.5	128.0	60.0	98.0

Figure 4 : Example of reference chart [4]

References

[1] "Snark-Open user's and reference guides", *SINAPSE*, Paris, 1988
[2] Laurière JL, "Intelligence artificielle - Représentation des connaissances : le cas de Snark", 2, *Eyrolles*, Paris, 1988
[3] Laurière JL, Vialatte M, "Snark, a language to represent declarative knowledge", *IFIP*, North-Holland, 811-816, 1986
[4] Siest G, Henny J, Schiele F, "Interprétation des examens de laboratoire, valeurs de référence et variations biologiques", *Karger Verlag*, Basel, 1981
[5] Monneau JP, Henny J, "Modifications du profil biologique au cours de la grossesse, établissement des limites de référence", *Centre de Médecine Préventive*, F-Vandoeuvre, 1988
[6] Siest G, Galteau MM & al., "Examens de laboratoire et médicaments, interférences analytiques et variations pharmacologiques", *Expansion Scientifique Française*, Paris, 1985

TEMPORAL ASPECTS OF A KNOWLEDGE BASED SYSTEM FOR THE MANAGEMENT OF HOSPITAL PATIENTS

Paul Soper and Geetha Abeysinghe
Department of Electronics and Computer Science,

Charles Ranaboldo
Department of Vascular Surgery,
Royal South Hampshire Hospital,

University of Southampton

Abstract

This paper considers temporal aspects of a knowledge based system which holds information on patients as they progress through their treatment in a vascular surgery department. It is argued that there are advantages to be gained by adopting a general temporal reasoning framework because it can be extended to support various medical and administrative tasks. It is shown how Kowalski and Sergot's event calculus, a formalisation of time and events in first order logic, can be used to describe a simple model of the clinical pathway. The resulting formalisation can be executed as a logic program. Medical knowledge about investigation and treatment options is added to the model so that the resulting system can recommend the options which are appropriate at any particular time. The additional detail needed to develop a system of realistic scale is outlined in relation to current audit practice.

1 Introduction

This work arose from a design study for a support environment to assist with the management of hospital patients in a vascular surgery department. A central component of the proposed system is a knowledge base containing static knowledge, medical and organisational, and dynamic knowledge of patient records. In this paper we explore a formalisation in first order logic, as a deductive database [1,2,3], and in particular propose the event calculus [4] as a way of reasoning about the time-dependent aspects of the system.

The event calculus represents change by adding the descriptions of new events (occuring at particular though not necessarily specified times) to the knowledge base which, therefore, comprises an historical record of changes in the domain model. This contrasts with an approach to updating which keeps the contents of a database in conformity with the current state of the domain model, reference to time being implicit through the time of the updates (see [5,6] for a classification of the temporal aspects of databases). Such databases may store temporal information and extract or impose specialised temporal relations, but cannot provide general temporal reasoning. The formalisms of Allen [7] and Lee et al [8] support general temporal reasoning in classical first order logic and in [9] it is argued in detail that they have much in common with the event calculus. Executable temporal logic

[10] would be an alternative approach.

Our motivation for using a more general temporal framework is to provide a basis for extension of the system to support various medical tasks. The basic system should provide flexible assimilation and retrieval of the information at present recorded in patient notes, and useful extensions to this might include support for diagnosis, planning investigation and treatment, audit and research (see [11] for a recent discussion of medical decision making). We have focused on support for planning investigation and treatment because, in vascular surgery, there are delimited sets of options at any time.

We have two main aims in this paper. Firstly, to show how the event calculus can represent a simplified model of the clinical pathway in which specialists review patients at variable intervals depending on how the results of investigations and consultations are progressing. In *Section 2* and *Section 3* we describe and formalise, introducing the minimum of detail needed for illustration, a part of the clinical pathway for the arterial side of vascular surgery. The resulting formalisation is executable as a logic program. In *Section 6* we outline the additional detail which would be needed for a realistic system.

Our second aim is to show how a useful support function can be built up on the basis of this formalism. In Section 4 and Section 5, building on the simple formalisation already presented, we provide the system with a partial model of the clinical options which arise in the treatment of patients during their stay in hospital. This system can recommend appropriate options at any time, as well as performing the role of patient notes. We consider a series of typical examples formalising the event calculus rules needed to deal with these cases.

2 A simplified clinical pathway

A particular patient admitted for vascular surgery might progress through the following typical stages:

interview	The patient's history and examination is recorded by a (usually) junior doctor and an initial diagnosis is produced (eg occlusive arterial disease)
investigation	Further tests are carried out by a specialist (eg arteriogram by radiologist) and a more specific diagnosis is produced (eg femoral arterial stenosis)
management plan	The clinicians concerned with the patient review the case with the responsi-

ble consultant and decide on treatment
(eg bypass operation)

treatment   Recommended treatment is carried out
(eg surgeon carries out the bypass
operation)

The patient may be directed back to an earlier stage (eg
for further tests at the plan stage, or to interview and tests
at the treatment stage). Since the stages represent increasing degrees of commitment, intermediate stages will only be
skipped in unusual circumstances (eg in an emergency). Communication between stages takes place, at present, by passing along the patient's notes. One of the aims of the support
environment is to enhance the communicative function of the
notes at the point when each clinician assesses the requests of
the previous stage and reports the results/recommendations
of the current stage.

3 Event calculus

In the event calculus knowledge is formalised in terms of
events and the relations which they initiate and terminate.
For example "John is admitted to hospital" might be described
as an event which initiates the relation *hospitalised(John)*.

Three levels of knowledge can be distinguished: particular event descriptions such as John's admission; domain dependent knowledge about what types of events affect what relations; domain independent knowledge concerning very general properties.

3.1 Domain independent knowledge

Here we adopt a simplified form of the event calculus which
has two domain independent axioms:

```
holds_at (U, T) <-
        initiates (E, U),
        E < T,
        not interrupted (E, U, T).

interrupted (E, U, T) <-
        terminates (E', U),
        E < E' ≤ T.
```

The first expresses the assumption that relation U holds
at time T if a prior event E initiates U and it cannot be shown
(the *not* denotes negation by failure) that U is interrupted
between the occurence of E and T, and the second that U is
interrupted between E and T if there is an intervening event
E' which terminates U. (For notational brevity we have used
the name of an event to denote its time in temporal ordering
relations.)

Together the axioms express default persistence: once initiated a relation continues to hold unless an event is known
to terminate it. The domain independent theory can be extended in many ways, for example by including: start and end
points of relations and intervals over which they hold; persistence of relations backwards, as well as forwards, in time [4];
transaction time [12]; processes as well as events [13]. Such
extensions are not needed for our simple exposition, but their
feasibility is a strong argument for using the event calculus.

3.2 Domain dependent knowledge

Domain dependent knowledge is expressed by giving rules
which describe the relations initiated and terminated by the

types of events encountered in the domain. We need to:

  i describe the types of events encountered in the domain

  ii describe the relations initiated and terminated by these
types of events

We give the generic name *task* to the types of event which
can occur in the clinical pathway domain. Typically a task is
an event which might be recorded on the patient notes.

Fig. 1 shows a provisional and incomplete hierarchy of
tasks. We take up the question of a realistic domain model in
Section 5. For the time being this hierarchy of tasks together

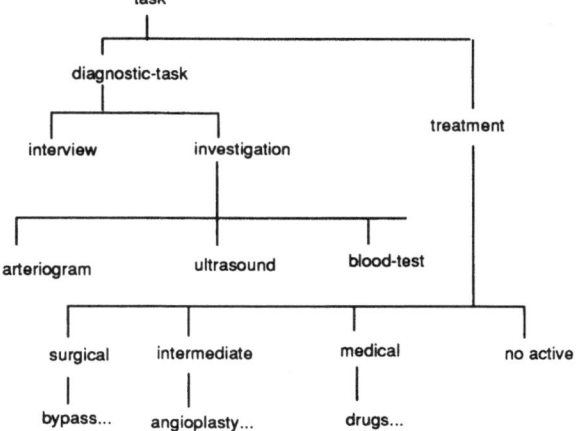

Figure 1: Task hierarchy

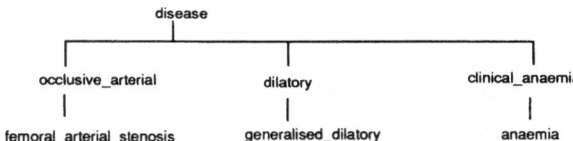

Figure 2: Disease hierarchy

with the small hierarchy of diseases shown in Fig. 2 will
be sufficient for the following illustrations. These will be
constructed in terms of a single (base) relation, *diagnosis (D)*,
which holds when the patient has been diagnosed as having
disease D. Naturally in a real system there would be further
arguments for the patient's name, the clinician, and so on,
and further base relations directly affected by events.

The following rules express the idea that the occurence
of a diagnostic task leads to either a specialisation of the
diagnosis or an additional diagnosis:

```
initiates (E, diagnosis(D)) <-
        inst (E, Etype),
        kind_of (Etype,diagnostic_task),
        result (E, D).

terminates (E,diagnosis(D)) <-
        initiates (E, diagnosis(NewD)),
        specialisation (NewD, D).
```

where *kind_of* and *specialisaion* are defined in a natural way

356

over the hierarchies.

In addition to base relations that are directly affected by events (eg *diagnosis*) other, so-called, *ramifications* can be expressed through the *holds_at* relation. For example that a treatment option is a ramification of the diagnosis can be expressed by

```
holds_at (recommended_test(arteriogram), T) <-
        holds_at (diagnosis(occlusive_arterial), T).
```

and that any outstanding tests should be completed before proceeding by

```
holds_at (awaiting(investigation), T) <-
        holds_at (recommended_test(X), T).
```

We envisage that much of the detailed medical knowledge needed by the system can be expressed as ramifications.

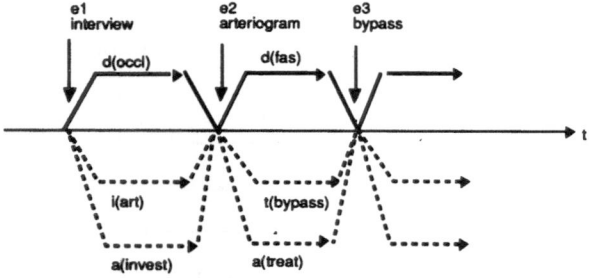

Key: a = awaiting, d = diagnosis, i = recommended_test, t = recommended_treatment]

Figure 3: See description of Case (i) in text

3.3 Case specific knowledge and queries

Finally there is case specific knowledge which is entered into the system as event descriptions. For example the following events might be entered for a particular patient during hospitalisation:

```
inst (e1, interview).     time (e1, monday).
result (e1, occlusive_arterial).

inst (e2, arteriogram). time (e2, wednesday).
result (e2, femoral_arterial_stenosis).

inst (e3, bypass).        time (e3, friday).
result (e3, bypassed_stenosis).
```

Given a knowledge base along the above lines, we can ask for information about what relations hold at what times. For example the query

```
<- holds_at (U, tuesday)
```

would give for U :

```
diagnosis (occlusive_arterial)

recommended_test (arteriogram)

awaiting (investigation)
```

For this simple case, referred to below as case (i), we can display the temporal information diagramatically as in Fig. 3 (base relations are shown by solid lines and ramifications by

dashes).

We could describe this patient's case as an 'expected' pathway, because the initial diagnosis is confirmed and the recommended tasks are actually carried out. In practice patients may be found to have unexpected conditions and specialists may take their own autonomous decisions about which tasks to carry out. Our system must be able to accept and make sense of such 'unexpected' event descriptions.

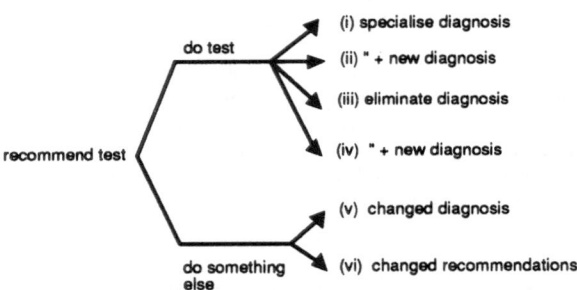

Figure 4: Possibilities arising when clinician responds to a recommended test

4 Classification of options

In general the main points of interaction between a clinician and the system are to review the case *before* a task is undertaken and to report the results of a task *after* it has been completed. In this section we examine systematically the options available to a clinician responsible for carrying out a recommended test on a patient who is awaiting investigation. We first enumerate the main options and then illustrate each with an example.

Initially the clinician responsible for a particular test can consult the system to find the patients for whom that test is recommended. Having selected a patient the main possibilities *(i)–(vi)* are shown schematically in Fig. 4.

The clinician reviews the case and decides whether or not the recommended test is appropriate. If the test is done its result may confirm the line of investigation giving a specialisation of the current diagnosis or it may eliminate that diagnosis. The test may also reveal new unrelated pathologies. If the test is not done there should be some reason given for cancelling or postponing the recommendation. The chief possibilities are that the patient's condition has changed, here signified by a new diagnosis, or that the clinician's interpretation of the case differs from the system's in which case a contrary recommendation is made.

The following series of examples illustrate *cases(i)–(vi)* focusing on options which would be available to a radiologist faced with a patient who has a diagnosis of *occlusive arterial* disease and an *arteriogram* recommended.

Case (i) This corresponds to the 'expected' pathway shown in the previous section (see Fig. 3): the radiologist carries out the arteriogram *e2* confirming the diagnosis. *Cases(ii)–(vi)* illustrate other possibilities for *e2*.

Case (ii) The Arteriogram *e2* shows *femoral arterial stenosis*, confirming and specialising the current diagnosis, but in addition it shows *dilatory disease*, an unrelated

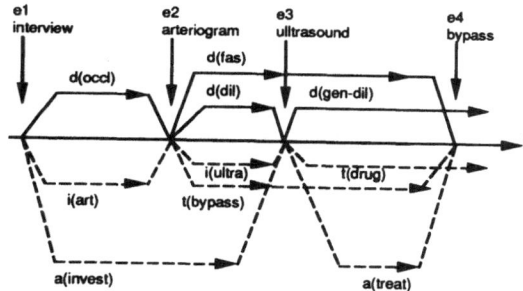

condition. The latter is investigated with ultrasound *e3* revealing *generalised dilatory* disease. The stenosis is treated by bypass operation *e4*. Assuming we have defined straight-forward ramifications recommending ultrasound to investigate dilatory disease and drug treatment for generalised dilatory disease, Fig. 5 results.

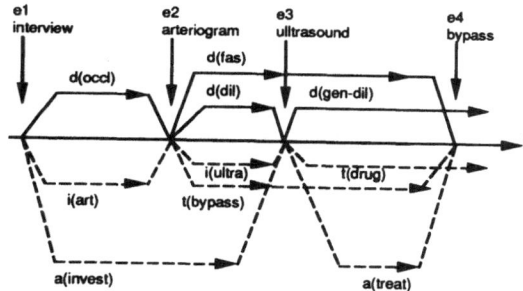

Figure 5: See description of Case (ii) in text

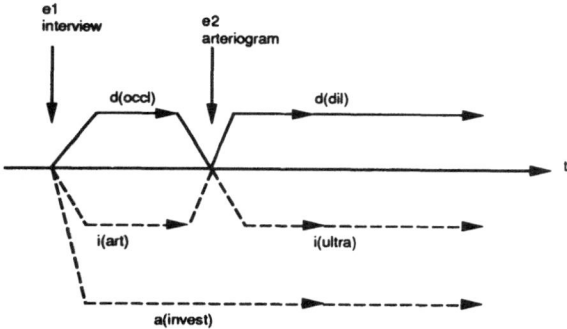

Figure 6: See description of Case (iv) in text

Comparing with *Case (i)* we see that the discovery of dilatory disease leads to an extended investigation stage. Only after the ultrasound test is the patient assigned to await treatment and a bypass operation carried out. (Note that the system has no preference for bypass rather than drug treatment.)

Cases (iii) and (iv) The arteriogram eliminates the *occlusive arterial* hypothesis and may introduce the independent diagnosis *dilatory* disease. Fig. 6 corresponds to *Case(iv)*.

The complete elimination of a diagnosis depends on the clinician deciding that the result of the test is definitive for that diagnosis. We assume here that the result of the arteriogram *e2* is judged to be definitive for occlusive arterial disease, and that the clinician enters

```
eliminates (e2, occlusive-arterial).
```

as part of the event description.

The behaviour shown in Fig. 6 can then be achieved by an additional terminates rule:

```
terminates (E, diagnosis (D)) <-
    inst (E, Etype),
    kind_of (Etype, diagnostic_task),
    eliminates (E,D).
```

It should be noted that tests are not necessarily definitive for the diagnoses they test. For example, an ultrasound may give a null result for suspected dilatory disease and then be followed by an arteriogram to determine the full extent of any pathology.

Case (v) On reviewing the patient, the radiologist decides that an arteriogram is inappropriate at this time because the patient appears to be anaemic. Presumably the patient's condition has changed between the first interview *e1* and this second interview *e2*. The radiologist enters a new diagnosis of *clinical anaemia*. A blood test *e3* reveals that the patient is indeed anaemic and this is treated by blood transfusion *e4*. Only then is the occlusive disease investigated further *e5* and treated *e6*. Fig. 7 depicts this sequence of events.

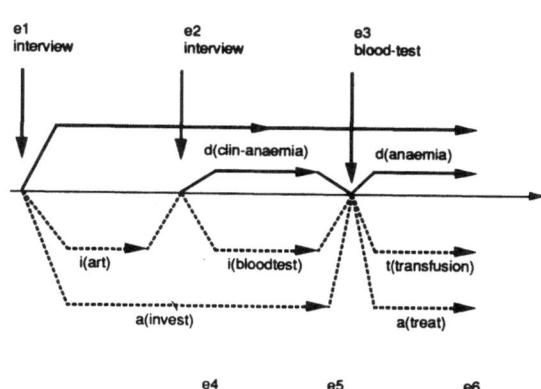

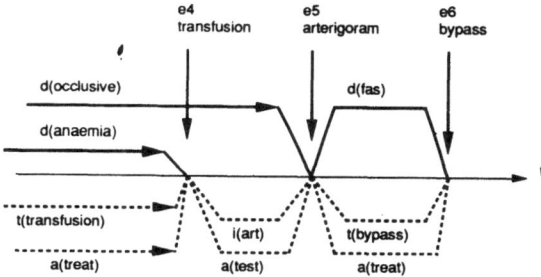

Figure 7: See description of Case (v) in paper

The ramifications shown require straight-forward rules associating blood test with clinical anaemia and blood transfusion with anaemia. We also need to modify the rule given in *Section 3.2* for recommending an arteriogram to:

```
holds_at (recommended_test(arteriogram), T) <-
    holds_at(diagnosis(occlusive_arterial), T),
    not ( holds_at (diagnosis(D), T),
            kind_of (D, clinical_anaemia)).
```

Another way to express such modifying conditions is to

leave the ramification rule alone, include the integrity constraint,

```
<- holds_at (recommended_test(arteriogram), T),
       holds_at (diagnosis(D), T),
       kind_of (D, clinical_anaemia).
```

and then check integrity when additions are made to the knowledge base [14]. This approach is more expressive when combined with abduction [15] and some of the problems of efficient implementation have been overcome [16], but we do not pursue the approach in this paper.

Case (vi) This case is essentially different. Although the clinician and the system agree on the patient's condition, they disagree on their recommendations. It would be interesting to model this disagreement in terms of the role and status of the clinician, but at present we propose only to maintain a distinction between system and clinician generated recommendations and to provide interactive explanation of the difference.

As an illustration, the radiologist may believe that all patients should have the result of their blood test before doing an arteriogram. This could lead to a diagram similar to *Case (v)* but with the blood test directly recommended and no diagnosis of clinical anaemia. A straight-forward way to exploit the divergence in recommendations for explanatory purposes is to allow *why* and *whynot* questions [17] at the time *e2* is entered:

why not holds_at (recommended_test (blood_test), T) ?

why holds_at (recommended_test (arteriogram), T) ?

5 Autonomous change

Sometimes we can predict that a relation will change autonomously, without new event descriptions being input to the system. For example the effect of a drug will vary with time in a fairly predictable way.

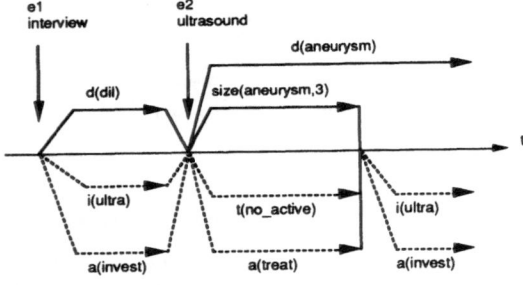

Figure 8: Example of autonomous change (see text)

A simple form of autonomous change can be modelled by the predicate *too_long_after* to constrain persistence in the domain independent axioms [4]:

```
holds_at (U, T) <-
     initiates (E, U),
```

```
     E < T,
     not interrupted (E, U, T),
     not too_long_after (E, U, T).

too_long_after (E, U, T) <-
     separation (E, T, I),
     life_time (U, I' ),
     I ' < I .
```

Example: Following an initial diagnosis of dilatory disease *e1* an ultrasound test *e2* shows a small aortic aneurysm, say of dimension 3, and no *active* treatment is recommended. However this recommmendation is only reliable for a limited time after which another ultrasound test should be carried out, as in Fig. 8.

The following are the additional rules needed to get the effect shown,

```
life_time (size (aortic_aneurysm, X), k/X).

holds_at ( recommended_treatment(no_active), T) <-
     holds_at ( diagnosis(aortic_aneurysm), T),
     holds_at ( size(aortic_aneurysm, X), T),
     X < critical.

holds_at ( recommended_test(ultrasound), T) <-
     holds_at ( diagnosis(aortic_aneurysm), T),
     not holds_at
          ( recommended_treatment(no_active), T).
```

We have assumed, as an approximation, that for small aneurysms the time over which the patient is safe varies inversely as the dimension of the aneurysm (k is a scale factor) and that the treatment of aneurysms with dimension greater than *critical* should not be delayed.

6 Outline for a realistic system

The vascular surgery record form used at the Royal South Hampshire Hospital [17] gives an indication of the detail needed in a realistic system. The complexity is limited by the range of investigations and treatments available, and by the outcomes possible. A crude estimate of the number of investigative possibilities can be obtained from the form which shows 8 possible test types, 6 locations, 8 routes and 8 outcomes. The treatment possibilities can be similarly estimated options are well-defined as indicated in the task hierarchy (see *Section 3.2*); and outcomes are classified as patient (improved, same, worse, died), vessel (patent, occluded), and 17 possible complications (general and surgical).

We are currently working on an event calculus representation at this level of detail. With each event type in the task hierarchy we associate semantic cases (a case frame) which are inherited by the tasks beneath them. For example the *bypass* task:

event type	cases
task	clinician, patient, time
treatment	diagnosis, outcome-patient, general-complication
surgical	location, outcome-vessel, surgical-complication

These case frames provide the basis for inputting case specific event descriptions and for defining domain dependent base relations.

7 Conclusion

The domain model we have presented has been kept to a bare minimum, but it shows how the simplified event calculus affords an elegant method for modelling the interdependencies of properties which change with time and for accessing historical information. In particular our model shows how the representation can be used to input, as event descriptions, some of information presently kept on patient notes, how this information can be accessed through the *holds_at* relation, and how some aspects of the timing of clinical tests and treatments can be modelled by ramifications. If transformations for improving efficiency were applied [19], such as reasoning forwards to derive initiates and terminates conclusions at the time event descriptions are entered, there are grounds for expecting that this simplified form of the event calculus can be implemented with an efficiency comparable to knowledge assimilation by destructive assignment.

We see two important directions for future development. Firstly the extension of the model, as outlined in the paper, to cover a more comprehensive area of vascular surgery, and the production of an efficient implementation. Secondly, the development of flexible interfaces to the system to support various clinical tasks. In the model of clinical options, we have suggested that disagreement on recommmendations between clinician and system provides a natural point of interaction. Although we restricted attention to the *holds_at* relation, information on time periods, start and end points, and time sequences is available for such interaction. To support these interactions we can also introduce extensions to the simple form of the event calculus. For example, valid time and transaction time can be distinguished [12] if it is important to know the order in which information about the patient became available.

References

[1] Gallaire H, Minker J and Nicolas J M *Logic and databases: A deductive approach* Computing Surveys, June 1984, pp153-185

[2] Lloyd J W and Topor R W *A basis for deductive database systems* J. Logic Programming, Vol 2, No. 2, 1985, pp 93-109

[3] Lloyd J W and Topor R W *A basis for deductive database systems II* J. Logic Programming, Vol 3, No. 1, 1986, pp 55-67

[4] Kowalski R A and Sergot M J *A logic-based calculus of events* New Generation Computing Vol 4, No. 1, 1986, pp 67-95

[5] Snodgrass R and Ahn I *A taxonomy of time in databases* in Proceedings of ACM SIGMOD International Conference on Data, Ed Navathe S. Association of Computing Machinery, Austin, Texas, May 1985, pp236-246

[6] Snodgrass R and Ahn I *Temporal databases* IEEE Computer, 19, No. 9, September 1986, pp35-42

[7] Allen J F *Maintaining knowledge about temporal intervals* CACM, Vol. 26, No. 11, 1983, pp 832-834

[8] Lee R M, Coelho H and Cotta J C *Temporal inferencing on administrative databases* Information Systems, Vol. 10, No. 2, 1985, pp. 197-206

[9] Sadri F *Three recent approaches to temporal reasoning* Department of Computing, Imperial College, DoC 86/23, revised 1986

[10] Gabbay D *The declarative past and imperative future: executable temporal logic for interactive systems* in Baneieqbal B, Barringer H and Pneuli A (eds), Temporal Logic Specifications, LNCS 398, pp 409-448, Springer, 1989

[11] O'Neil M, Glowinski A and Fox J *A symbolic theory of decision-making applied to several medical tasks* Imperial Cancer Research Fund, London; to be published in Proceedings of AIME, Lecture Notes in Medical Informatics, Springer-Verlag, 1989

[12] Sripada S M *A logical framework for temporal deductive databases* Proceedings of VLDB, Morgan Kaufmann, 1988, pp 171-182

[13] Bedford J M, Kowalski R A and Rosser B L *Representing change in air traffic flow management using the event calculus* in Colloquium on Temporal Reasoning, IEE, London, Digest No. 1990/024, pp 2/1-3, 1990

[14] Kowalski R A and Sadri F *Knowledge representation without integrity constraints* Department of Computing, Imperial College, December 1988

[15] Eshghi K and Kowalski R A *Abduction compared with negation by failure* Fifth International Conference on Logic Programming, MIT Press, 1989

[16] Kowalski R A, Sadri F and Soper P *Integrity checking in deductive databases* Proceedings of VLDB, Morgan Kaufmann, 1987, pp 61-70

[17] Hammond P and Sergot M *APES: augmented prolog for expert systems* Logic Based Systems Ltd, London, 1984

[18] *Edinburgh Surgical Audit* available from Department of Vascular Surgery, Royal South Hampshire Hospital, Southampton

[19] Kowalski R A *Database updates in the event calculus* Department of Computing, Imperial College, DoC 86/12 (revised 1989)

A Knowledge Representation Scheme and a Knowledge Derivation Mechanism for Achieving Rule Sharing among Heterogeneous Expert Systems

Stanley Y.W. Su   Jong H. Park

Database Systems Research and Development Center
Department of Computer Information Sciences
Department of Electrical Engineering
University of Florida

ABSTRACT

This paper presents a framework for integrating heterogeneous expert systems (ESs) on a complex domain, each of which has only partial knowledge with respect to the entire problem domain. It focuses on the types of knowledge that is expressed in the forms of intensional data such as rules and constraints. An integration approach by which the component ESs may exchange their expertises in an intertwined manner is presented. One advantage of this approach is that rules can in effect be shared among heterogeneous ESs. The knowledge representation scheme using both static and dynamic knowledge representation models, the query language, and the knowledge derivation mechanism for achieving such integration are described. This approach can be used as a basis for developing distributed database systems with explicit constraint management or heterogeneous distributed expert database systems, and for integrating multiple expert systems. A prototype system has been developed to verify the ideas presented in this paper. The implementation effort is briefly described.

1. Introduction

Our integration approach aims at environments where many Component Systems (CSs) have expertise on different aspects of a complex problem domain. They together form a "community" of Expert Systems (ESs) [1-2]. As an example, a company that does mechanical design uses three ESs: a structural analysis ES (SE), a material ES (ME) and a cost analysis ES (CE). Part of the knowledge of each ES is represented by a set of rules (or a knowledge base) as shown in Fig. 1-1.

Rule Set for Structural Analysis ES
SR1: If BEAM.LENGTH=x and BEAM.WIDTH=y
then BEAM.WEIGHT=x*y.
SR2: If BEAM.WEIGHT=x and BRACKET.WEIGHT=y
then SHAFT.WEIGHT=func1(x,y).
SR3: If BRACKET.WIDTH=x
then BRACKET.WEIGHT=10*x.
SR4: If SHAFT.WEIGHT=x then SHAFT.COST=100*x.
ST1: If UPDATE(SHAFT.WEIGHT) then EXECUTE SR5.
SR5: If SHAFT.WEIGHT>100 and COUNT(BRACKET)<5
then INSERT(BRACKET).

Rule Set for Material ES
MR1: If BRACKET.MATERIAL=x and BRACKET.WIDTH=y
then BRACKET.WEIGHT=func2(x,y).
MT1: If COUNT(BRACKET)>10 then EXECUTE MR2.
MR2: If SHAFT.WEIGHT>100
then BRACKET.MATERIAL="IRON"
else BRACKET.MATERIAL="COPPER".

Rule Set for Cost Analysis ES
CR1: If SHAFT.VOL=x then SHAFT.WEIGHT=10*x.
CR2: If SHAFT.WEIGHT=x and BRACKET.MATERIAL=y
then SHAFT.COST=10*x*y.

Fig. 1-1 Rule Sets of Member Expert Systems (ESs)

Each ES has its own inferencing mechanism to apply to, and interpretation scheme of, its rules, and also its own (implicit or explicit) underlying database (DB) so that it functions as an independent problem solver. It has full knowledge to solve problems within its own aspect. However, its knowledge is only partial with respect to the entire problem domain. To obtain a complete solution in this environment, partial solutions by the three ESs must be "patched up" in an ad hoc manner if an integrated system is not available. Such a manual compilation of partial results is inevitably an error-prone process. A more serious drawback is that the complete solution from such a process is not guaranteed to be the best solution within the knowledge available in the community.

To tackle the above problem, we develop an approach by which we can integrate heterogeneous ESs on a complex problem domain, each of which has only partial knowledge with respect to the entire domain. Specifically, this approach will allow preexisting ESs to share their heterogeneous knowledge at the rule level to derive the best global answer to a query.

The expertise of the member ESs of a community tend to be intertwined with each other along the phases and facets of the problem domain. Our approach allows such member ESs to undertake only their own aspects of problem domain and their single-aspect answers to be integrated into an optimal global answer. Specifically, SE, ME and CE in the example domain independently perform the structural analysis, the material and the cost analysis aspects of mechanical design processes, respectively, while the global controller resolves conflicts and assemble only the best parts of their local answers in a global perspective. This cooperation mode is analogous to the concurrent and interactive way in which a group of human experts usually work together, i.e., consulting each other, only if necessary for only required aspects of expertise. The resulting integrated system will provide the user with a unified, global view over the heterogeneous ESs as if the ESs were not independent systems but were a single system with a knowledge base equivalent to the union of the knowledge bases of those ESs. The advantage of this approach is that rules from independent ESs can be in effect shared despite their incompatibilities in inferencing mechanism and interpretation scheme.

There are several existing paradigms relevant to our approach. The heterogeneous Database Management System (DBMS) models take existing systems as their CSs [3-4]. But, they deal with only data, but not <u>knowledge</u> (i.e., extensional data as well as intensional data specified by rules and constraints.) even though they address many conventional issues required to handle the heterogeneity of CSs. Meanwhile, there has been a growing interest in incorporating rules with data under the name of Expert Database System (EDBS) [5-6]. Such a system shares some interests with our approach to the extent that it attempts to enhance the data management system into a knowledge derivation system by handling intensional data as well. However, main efforts in EDBSs are still grappling with issues on how to graft a standalone DB system with a rule processing system [7-8]. A few exceptions are found in [9-10].

Two models have been introduced in Artificial Intelligence (AI) to solve complex problems using multiple autonomous problem solvers. One model is called Distributed AI [11]. There are variations within the distributed AI in terms of cooperation methods, degree of

The development of this research is supported by the National Science Foundation grant #DMC-8814989, and the implementation is supported by the Florida High Technology and Industrial Council grant #UPN-88092237.

autonomy of CSs, or granularity of knowledge [12-13]. The other model has been developed as an extension of the conventional ES model [14]. The problem solving strategy of that model is to select the most appropriate inferencing mechanism among several ones according to the current conditions in the working memory. However, these two models are useful only to develop new systems, but not to integrate preexisting systems.

The Federated Information System [4][15] is emerging with the same objective as we are aimed at, that is, the integration of existing heterogeneous information systems. However, it can not achieve a "close" integration that our approach aims at, in that it considers the inputs and outputs of CSs as the only two contact points among them. It regards whole CSs as the atomic units of cooperation. Additional approaches with similar objectives are found in [16-18]. However, they are designed mainly to assist the user to identify the capabilities of existing information systems, rather than to take the primary responsibility of answering user queries.

The rest of the paper is organized as follows. The overall architecture of our system is presented in Section 2. Section 3 presents the types of global queries that are supported in our system. To process global queries, the knowledge representation scheme and query processing mechanism are developed in Section 4. An implementation is described in Section 5. Finally, a conclusion is drawn in Section 6.

2. Architecture of Integrated ESs

As shown in Fig. 2-1, our system structure is composed of two levels of managers, one Global Knowledge Administration Module (GKAM) and multiple Local Knowledge Administration Modules (LKAMs). As the global manager, the GKAM coordinates the activities of LKAMs in order to answer users' global queries. For this purpose, it manages the global information sources such as the global database schema and the dynamic knowledge representation structure, and uses them to make decisions required to process user queries.

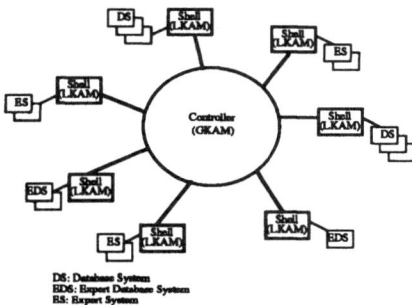

DS: Database System
EDS: Expert Database System
ES: Expert System

Fig. 2-1 Architecture of Our Integration Model

Each LKAM functions in effect as a foreman on behalf of the GKAM, invoking local CSs to process assigned subqueries. The roles of LKAMs are basically to manage their Local Knowledge Base Schemas and associated information to perform various mapping for exchanging information with the GKAM.

This topology is similar to those of heterogeneous DBMSs [3][19-20] and the Federated Information System models [15], but is a contrast to those of distributed AI models [11].

3. Global Query Types Supported in Our Approach

The general objective of our integrated system is to observe the "behavior" of local DBs (or virtual DBs for CSs with no underlying DBs) in a global perspective. According to the objective, our query is designed to allow the user to inquire into the global impacts caused by certain updates on local DBs. The resulting query:
(1) often reveals hypothetical nature [6].
(2) handles some non-determinism in that the parameters involved in the global impacts may not be determined when queries are issued.

(3) is equipped with some constructs for processing "repetitive" queries, which contains complex conditions that usually cannot be satisfied at one attempt.
(4) supports mixtures of retrieval and storage operations besides those traditional operations to meet the new requirements.

Specifically, The following four types of queries are supported in addition to the usual retrieval and update operations.
I. Get the impact on certain data items due to some conditions.
II. Get the entire impact due to some conditions.
III. Get the source conditions to satisfy some target conditions.
IV. Get all the data items to potentially affect certain data items, and their current values.

A language has been designed for querying the global knowledge base. However, for reader's convenience, queries are posed in English in the examples given in this section. Some example queries will be issued against our example problem domain, i.e., the mechanical design company. The example domain is represented in a knowledge base schema as shown diagrammatically in Fig. 3-1.

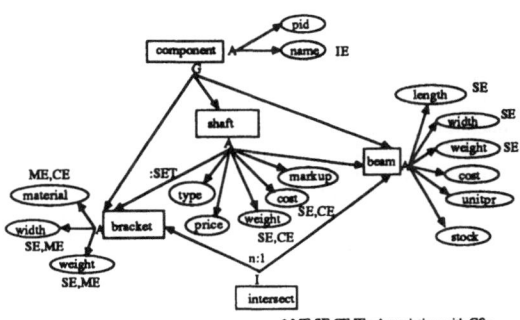

* ME,SE,CE,IE : Association with CSs

Fig.3-1 A Database Schema for Example Domain

The semantic diagram is based on Object-Oriented Semantic Association Model (OSAM*), which will be discussed in detail as our static data representation model. To explain the example domain briefly, the mechanical product that the company designs is SHAFT, which is defined by several attributes such as two object classes BEAM and BRACKETs and five domain classes, TYPE, PRICE, etc. The object classes, BRACKET, SHAFT and BEAM are organized into a generalization hierarchy with the superclass, COMPONENT (denoted by a G.) The class, INTERSECT, is used to represent an interrelationship that can exist between two object classes, BRACKET and BEAM, connected by an interaction association (denoted by an I.)

The type-I query allows the user to retrieve the values for a set of data items due to some update on another set of data items. The implication is that what would happen in the set of "target" parameters, if changes are made to the set of "source" parameters. A typical type-I query might look like, "What would be the COST of SHAFT be if the LENGTH of BEAM is doubled ?"

The global impacts due to a local update can be measured by the type-II query. In this case, the target parameters are unknown a priori, and not specified. This type of query is illustrated by the query, "Retrieve the value of each data item affected by the update that the STRENGTH of BEAM is increased by 10 percents."

The type-III query is designed to help the user find values of source parameters to satisfy some conditions. Consider the query, "Get the maximum WEIGHT of BRACKET such that the COST of SHAFT does not exceed 100 dollars." This query may need to go through more than one session of processing to obtain the desired value of source parameter, the maximum WEIGHT of BRACKET, to meet the given condition on the COST of SHAFT. Each session is roughly equivalent to a type-I query. For the query not solvable automatically, the user may peek into intermediate results of the query and modify the

362

conditions at the end of each session.

The type-IV query allows the user to identify the potential parameters that influence some designated parameters. This type of query is useful as a preliminary query to the other types of queries. A typical type-IV query might look like, "Find all entities and their current values that may potentially affect the PRICE of SHAFT."

4. Components of the Integrated ES

The integrated ES consists of three major parts: global knowledge representation scheme, global query language and global knowledge production mechanism. The global knowledge representation scheme is concerned with uniformly representing knowledge of heterogeneous component ESs. Based on the representation, the global knowledge production mechanism decides how to process global queries.

4.1 Knowledge Representation Scheme

As a global framework to unify the data distributed among CSs, our integrated system needs a global data representation model, like any heterogeneous DBMS [19]. Besides the data model (a static knowledge model), our system, unlike the other distributed DBMSs, needs a dynamic knowledge representation model (KRM) to capture dynamic aspects of knowledge to deal with knowledge specified in rules [21].

The dynamic aspects of knowledge in general refer to the information required to maintain the DB in consistent states after some operations, which may change the state of DB. An inferencing process in ESs can be viewed as a process to seek a global consistency among related data items through a chained firing of rules. Consequently, processing of a query to an ES usually involves data items not specified in the query as well. Thus, the consistency has to be considered between stored data and intensional data. In this light, the dynamic aspects of knowledge are essential information for representing knowledge in our approach.

The two aspects of global knowledge is represented in two tiers of conceptual schemas over the actual knowledge sources, member ESs, as illustrated in Fig. 4-1.

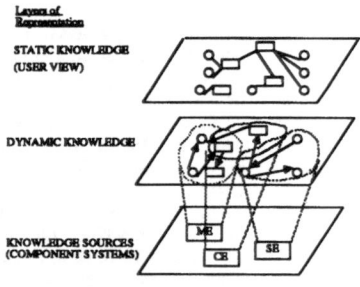

Fig. 4-1 Architecture of Knowledge Representation

The second tier of global knowledge representation is exclusively for integrating knowledge, while the global DB schema based on the static data model is a unifying global database schema as used in conventional DBMSs [3][19]. The global DB schema also provides the query issuer with a global user view over the entire problem domain.

4.1.1 Data Representation Model: A semantic data model, Object-Oriented Semantic Association Model (OSAM*) is chosen as our static data model [22]. In collaboration with its object-oriented concepts, its various association types offers an abundant menu of constructs for capturing a wide range of semantics. Thus, its inherent semantics could save efforts which would be required to represent complex problem domains with a conventional model. Refer to [22-23] for detailed discussion of this model. The associated CSs are indicated beside each data item in Fig. 3-1, meaning that those ESs

use the data item. The significance of this association is that, if there is at least one association set which two CSs are member of, e.g., ME and CE at BRACKET.MATERIAL, there is possibility of interaction between them. This idea will be utilized in the query processing later.

As the first step to become a part of the integrated system, each member ES must prepare an OSAM* version of its DB schema. ESs with underlying DBs need to translate their schemas into OSAM*, while the others have to create new schemas (for their virtual DBs). The resulting local schemas are integrated into a global DB schema [24].

4.1.2 Dynamic Knowledge Representation Model: The dynamics (or behaviors) of information systems have been attempted to be modeled in such ways as transaction modeling and behavior modeling [25-26]. But, such efforts have been directed to the development of new systems. In contrast, our model is designed to capture the behaviors of preexisting systems. We first describe how to represent each rule and then the rule bases of heterogeneous component ESs in a community.

Representation of Knowledge Specified in Rule: The dynamic aspects of knowledge specified in a rule essentially can be expressed in terms of data items used in the rule and dynamic relationships among them. The dynamic relationships refer to knowledge derivation paths and triggering conditions. The knowledge derivation paths specify what data items can be derived from, or dependent on, what data items. The triggering conditions indicate under what conditions to activate their associated knowledge derivation paths. Specifically, we represent the knowledge in a rule by a triplet of entity sets. A rule $R = (E_a, E_c, E_t)$, where E_a is the entity set in IF part of R, E_c is the entity set in THEN part of R, and R_t is the entity set in the triggering condition associated with R. An entity $e \in E_t$ may be either an attribute of an object class, an object class or a function associated with an object class. For data exchange among different CSs, we distinguish whether an entity is an I/O parameter in its underlying component system. Thus, an entity e = (id, type, mode) where id is name, type = attribute | object | function, and mode = EX (I/O parameter) | IN (internal entity.) The values of internal entity are derived as intermediate results inside inferencing chains which are not shown to the external world.

It is convenient to represent the above triplet by an edge with three vertex sets in a graph, i.e., $e = (W_a, W_c, W_t)$ where W_c is on the head of the edge, and W_a and W_t are on the two distinct tails (one on solid line and the other on dotted line.) An entity is represented by a vertex. A bold edge represents a rule with $W_t = W_a$ or W_c (depending on whether it is a forward or backward-chaining rule.) The three attributes of an entity is represented in terms of attached name, vertex shape and line thickness, respectively. The three types of entities are represented by a rectangular box, a circle and a diamond-shaped box, respectively. An I/O parameter is indicated by a bold vertex, e.g., SHAFT.COST. See Fig. 4-2 for the graphic representation.

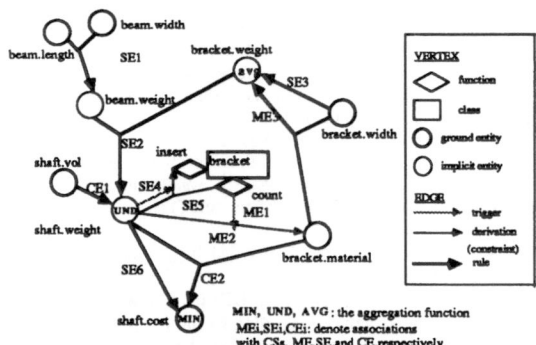

MIN, UND, AVG : the aggregation function
MEi,SEi,CEi: denote associations
with CSs, ME,SE,and CE,respectively.

Fig.4-2 A Function Graph for CSs: ME, SE and CE

For example, a rule SR1 of the forward-chaining SE, "If length of beam is l and width of beam is w, then weight of beam is l × w" is represented by an edge SE1 with three vertex sets, W_e and W_f = (BEAM.LENGTH BEAM.WIDTH) and W_a = (BEAM.WEIGHT).

Representation of Knowledge in Heterogeneous ESs: To represent the knowledge in an entire community of heterogeneous ESs, we merge all of the rules from the rule bases of the component ESs into a directed multi-graph (called the Function Graph.) Each rule has been represented by an multi-vertex edge. Edges corresponding to rules are connected via their common vertices. Specifically, two edges e_1 and e_2 are connected if $(W^1_a \cup W^1_e \cup W^1_f) \cap (W^2_a \cup W^2_e \cup W^2_f) \neq \emptyset$. In this merging, an additional information is attached to each edge to indicate its underlying inference mechanism or its associated CS. The edge CE1, for example, is associated with the member ES, CE, according to the obvious naming convention.

The Function Graph FG = (V,E) consists of a nonempty set of vertices V, and a set of edges E. For example, the FG shown in Fig. 4-2 represents a part of knowledge specified by the rule bases of ESs in our example domain. It is essentially a directed multi-graph. But, it is an extended multi-graph in that an edge has a set of vertices as its head or two tails.

Some important semantics of the resulting FG are described along with relevant terminology. A path in the FG is a sequence of edges of the form (W^1_f, W^1_e), (W^2_f, W^2_e), (W^3_f, W^3_e), ..., (W^n_f, W^n_e) such that $W^1_e \cap W^2_f \neq \emptyset$, $W^2_e \cap W^3_f \neq \emptyset$, and so on. For example, there is a path from the vertex, SHAFT.VOL, to the vertex, BRACKET.WEIGHT, through a sequence of edges, CE1, SE4, ME1 and ME3. A path from v_1 to v_2 means that the value of v_2 is derivable from the values of vertex set W such that $v_1 \in W$ by activating the rules corresponding to the edges on the paths in order. Two edges are connected if there is at least one path between them. A junction vertex denotes a vertex which is associated with more than one CS. For example, the vertex BRACKET.WEIGHT is a junction vertex that is associated with two member ESs, SE and ME. In particular, a confluent vertex is a junction vertex into which multiple edges converge. Hence, the vertex, BRACKET.MATERIAL, for example, is not a confluent vertex even though it is a junction vertex. Parallel paths denote paths whose ending vertices coincide. The existence of such paths implies different knowledge derivation paths on the same entities.

A vertex with two or more associated CSs reflects some commonality among the CSs. Such vertices provide the basis of our integration in that two edges with such a vertex on their heads or tails can interact with each other through the vertex. The edges, SE2, ME3 and SE3, for example, in Fig. 4-2, are meshed through their common vertex, BRACKET.WEIGHT. The FG resulting from such meshing of edges from different ESs represent all possible knowledge derivation paths <u>across</u> those heterogeneous ESs. Such paths represent <u>global</u> knowledge derivation paths available in the whole community of heterogeneous ESs.

The FG contains two more global components in addition to its associated CS. One is some metrics for evaluating parallel paths to select the best of them. For this purpose, Accuracy Factor (AF) and Efficiency Factor (EF) may be attached to edges to quantify their performances (by a global knowledge administrator.) The EF for an edge e_i with no embedded function, EF_i, is computed as below. $EF_i = E^s_i \times [\Sigma_j(E^c_j)]$ where E^s_i denotes the system performance factor (including efficiency of inferencing mechanism) of the component system underlying e_i, and E^c_j denotes the efficiency factor of unit clause c_j ($E^c_j \propto$ # of entities involved in c_j.) While, the AF does not hinge on the system performance; rather it depends only on the algorithms used in the rule. The AF for an edge e_i, $AF_i = \Pi_j A^c_j$ where A^c_j denotes the accuracy factor of unit clause c_j.

The other one is the aggregation function that may be attached to a confluent vertex (also by a global knowledge administrator.) The function is used to resolve possible conflicts among values on such a vertex derived by multiple paths converging on the vertex. The three available options are maximum, minimum, average and undecided, which are labelled as MAX, MIN, AVG and UND (also the default option), respectively, as shown in Fig. 4-2.

4.2 Global Knowledge Production Mechanism

The knowledge production refers to the mechanism to process global queries. Users issue queries in reference to the global DB schema into which the knowledge in the member ESs have been integrated based on the unifying data model, i.e., OSAM*. Through the global DB schema, however, the user sees only the static aspects of knowledge (or data), though the new types of queries supported in our approach involve various dynamic knowledge as well. Thus, the query processor is responsible for applying the dynamic knowledge captured in the FG, which is not visible to the user.

A query is executed in four global steps: query translation, searching for required functionality, query decomposition, and query execution. The four steps are handled by the Query Translator (QT), Query Evaluator (QE), Task Scheduler (TS), and Transaction Manager (TM), respectively. The control flow is shown in Fig. 4-3.

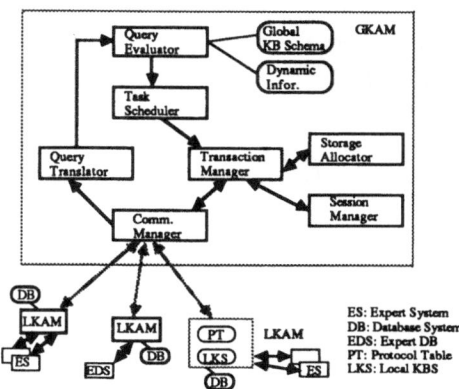

Fig.4-3 Control Flow Of The System

1) The query translation step takes a global query as input, and produces as output a tokenized query with reference to the global DB schema.

2) The functionality searching step performs the search of the FG for rules and constraints required for answering the query with no regard to their underlying CSs. Automatically the feasibility of the query is also decided with respect to the knowledge of the ES community as a whole.

3) The query decomposition step identifies which member ESs must be activated in what order to solve the query based on the results of the "global" search in the preceding step. As a result, the global query is partitioned into single-site queries, or tasks, which can be answered by individual ESs. The tasks are scheduled in a proper order to draw a global query execution plan.

4) The query execution step supervises the execution of the query according to the plan from the query decomposition step. The major functions of this step are the assignment of the subqueries to CSs, the compilation and evaluation of their results and the combination of such partial answers into a global answer.

A global query is translated into basically 1) query type, 2) source parameters and 3) target parameters in the query translation step. A query, for example, "What would be the PRICE of SHAFT be if the LENGTH of BEAM is doubled ?" will be translated basically into three items, i.e., **query type**: 1, **source parameter set**: BEAM.LENGTH and **target parameter set**: SHAFT.COST. (The actual value of parameter BEAM.LENGTH, will be required later in the query execution step to assign the tasks to CSs.) Hence, the query will be represented by its source and target parameter sets in the subsequent discussions. In a query of type II or IV, however, the source or target parameter set is initially empty, meaning that the parameters cannot be determined at this step. We shall describe our query processing mechanism mainly for the type-I query as the basic type. For the other types of queries, only unique issues will be discussed whenever necessary.

364

4.2.1 Searching for Required Rules: Given the two sets of parameters corresponding a global query, this step decides in a global perspective which rules and constraints to be involved in what order according the query type. The global DB schema and FG are two primary sources of information for this step of query processing.

This decision in essence depends on a search of the FG for paths, $\{P_1, P_2, ...\}$, from the source vertex set W_s to the target vertex set W_t along triggering edges. Consider the FG shown in Fig. 4-2. With a source parameter, W_s = {SHAFT.WEIGHT}, a target parameter, W_t = {BRACKET.MATERIAL}, and query type I, for example, a path P would be found along a sequence of edges and vertices, SHAFT.WEIGHT, SE4, SE5, BRACKET.INSERT, BRACKET, BRACKET.COUNT, ME1 and BRACKET.MATERIAL. Notice that there is no direct path through ME2, a derivation edge. The output of the search would be $\{P_i| i = 1,2,..\}$ = {SE4, SE5, ME1} in the form of a graph. The graph of edges represents the **required rules and constraints** (corresponding to those edges) and their **execution sequences** (in which they are activated) to answer the query. In case no path from the source to the target vertices is found, the query processing immediately terminates with "no impact" as the final answer of the query.

Recall that the source or target parameters, W_s and W_t, are not specified in queries of types II and IV, so they have to be decided by the query processor. For a type-II query, the W_t are all the vertices that are connected from any member of W_s given in the query. Consider the FG shown in Fig. 4-4.

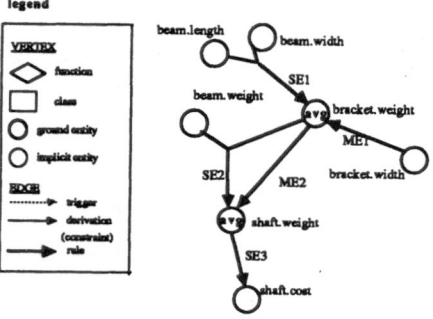

Fig.4-4 A Function Graph for CSs, ME and SE

A type-II query with BEAM.WIDTH as its source parameter, for example, will identify as its target parameters, three vertices: BRACKET.WEIGHT via SE1, SHAFT.WEIGHT via SE1 and SE2 or ME2, and SHAFT.COST via SE1, SE2 or ME2, and SE3. The output of the search will be represented by the graph of SE1, SE2, ME2 and SE3. That is, W_t = {BRACKET.WEIGHT, SHAFT.WEIGHT, and SHAFT.COST}, and $\{P_i| i = 1,2..\}$ = {SE1, SE2, ME2, SE3}.

By the same token, W_s of a type-IV query will contain all the vertices connected to the target vertices given in the query. However, the search for paths in this case is directed backward, that is, from W_t to W_s. The search for a type-IV query with SHAFT.WEIGHT as its target parameter, for example, starts at SHAFT.WEIGHT and finds BEAM.WEIGHT via SE2, BRACKET.WEIGHT via SE2 or ME2, BRACKET.WIDTH via ME2 and ME1, BEAM.WIDTH and BEAM.LENGTH via ME2 and SE1, as its source parameters. The output of search is a graph of edges, SE2, ME2, ME1 and SE1.

Besides the basic search mechanism illustrated above, we also need to address additional issues such as parallel paths and cyclic path, which involve more complex searches.

Parallelism in Path: Parallel paths reflects different ways of solving the same problem. The accuracy factor AF and efficiency factor EF attached to edges are used as the measures for the evaluation of such alternative paths. If the user specifies an option in the query in favor of efficiency, for example, the best path is the most efficient path

judged in terms of the EFs of the parallel paths (the composite EF of an entire path = Σ_i EF_i where EF_i is EF of edge e_i on the path, and the composite AF = Π_i AF_i where AF_i is AF of e_i.) Due to their natures, however, paths including edges with dependency semantics (i.e., representing constraints) are unconditionally selected regardless of their efficiencies. Specifically, such an edge is distinguished by a value of ∞ on its AF.

Cyclic Paths: In our system, the cycle is defined to be a path of length at least one whose starting and ending vertex sets intersect with each other [29]. Specifically, P = {e1, e2,...,en} is a cyclic path if $W^1_t \cap W^n_e \neq \emptyset$. As shown in Fig. 4-2, a cycle is detected along the path consisting of SHAFT.WEIGHT, SE4, BRACKET, SE3, ME1, ME2, BRACKET.MATERIAL, ME3, BRACKET.WEIGHT, SE2 and SHAFT.WEIGHT. In this step, cyclic paths are just identified for their processing in subsequent steps.

4.2.2 Decomposition of Query: The preceding step of query processing identified the required rules (and constraints) in a global perspective, that is, without being concerned with their underlying CSs. In general, those identified rules (corresponding to a global query) belong to several CSs. Thus, they have to be partitioned into multiple rule groups (corresponding to subqueries) according to their association with CSs before they can be executed.

Specifically, a graph of edges output from the preceding step is vertex-partitioned according to their association with CSs into subgraphs (called segments), which represent independently processable subqueries. These subgraphs are ordered by their dependencies via common vertices on their boundaries.

Partitioning of Query into Tasks: A task is the basic unit of job, which is expected to be performed by one of CSs without interactions with the other CSs. It refers to a segment complete with the input and output parameter sets.

A segment is basically a largest subgraph that meets two conditions:
1) all the edges in a segment S belong to the same CS, that is, $CS(e_m) = CS(e_n)$ if $e_m, e_n \in S$,
2) all the edges in S have the same sequence of preceding segments, that is, $S_i = S_j$ if $e_m, e_n \in S$, $S_1 = \{e| e >> e_m\}$, i.e., e is an ancestor edge of $e_m\}$ and $S_2 = \{e| e >> e_n\}$.

Given a path of SE1, SE2 and CE2, for example, in Fig. 4-2, a set of edges SE1 and SE2, and the edge CE2, form the two segments, S_1 and S_2, respectively. For example, S_1 becomes a task with BEAM.LENGTH, BEAM.WIDTH and BRACKET.WEIGHT as the input parameters, and SHAFT.WEIGHT as the output parameter.) A task is defined as T = (cs,IN,OUT,S) where cs denotes the underlying component system, IN and OUT denote input and output parameter sets, respectively, and S denotes the corresponding segment. IN_i represents data to be provided to start T_i and OUT_i represents data to be output as the result of T_i.

Ordering of Tasks: Adjacent tasks, e.g., tasks sharing some of their I/O parameters, are interconnected via their common parameters. Specifically, T_1 precedes T_2 if $IN_2 \cap OUT_1 \neq \emptyset$. As a result, two tasks may be interrelated in one of the three patterns such as precedence, parallelism and no relation.

To represent the orders among tasks, we extend the acyclic Precedence Graph [30] to a general graph. In the extended Precedence Graph, each task makes a node. The precedence between two adjacent tasks is represented by a directed edge from the preceding task to the trailing task. Then, tasks are scheduled along the edges. Consider the FG in Fig. 4-5. A path from BEAM.WIDTH to SHAFT.COST, for example, would result in five tasks: T1 composed of SE1, T2 of ME1, T3 of SE3, T4 of SE2, SE4 and SE5, and T5 of CE1. Each of the tasks becomes a node in the Precedence Graph. The order would be (T1, T2, T3), (T4), (T5) where tasks in the same parentheses are executable in parallel.

4.2.3 Execution of Query: A global query has been partitioned into tasks, and they have been ordered in the query decomposition step. The duty of Transaction Manager is to coordinate the execution of tasks in order to obtain a global answer to the query. One or more sessions are established for a query. A session denotes one execution of all the tasks for a query as scheduled.

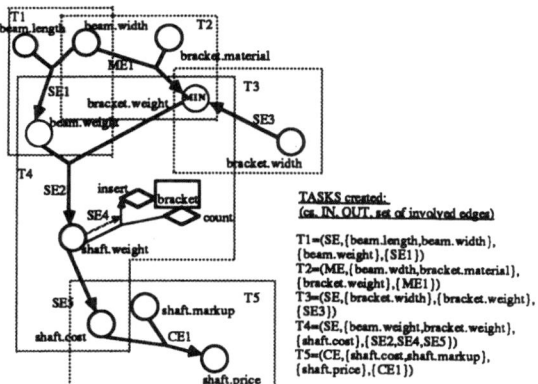

TASKS created:
(cs, IN, OUT, set of involved edges)

T1=(SE,{beam.length,beam.width},
{beam.weight},{SE1})
T2=(ME,{beam.wdth,bracket.material},
{bracket.weight},{ME1})
T3=(SE,{bracket.width},{bracket.weight},
{SE3})
T4=(SE,{beam.weight,bracket.weight},
{shaft.cost},{SE2,SE4,SE5})
T5=(CE,{shaft.cost,shaft.markup},
{shaft.price},{CE1})

Fig.4-5 Query Decomposition

At first, the general procedure of session is described as follows.

1) The adequate amount of storage is secured to buffer intermediate values returned from CSs executing tasks.

2) The tasks $T_i = (cs_i, IN_i, OUT_i, S_i)$ at the top of the schedule, e.g., T1, T2 and T3 in Fig. 4-5, are assigned with the values of IN_i, and the entity names of OUT_i to corresponding CS_i through associated LKAMs. Assigning tasks, it is checked if they are processable in a concurrent fashion.

3) The local queries are processed and the values of OUT_i are returned.

4) The values of OUT_i are evaluated to resolve conflicts on junction vertices, if one exists.

5) Repeat Steps 2) and 4) if the resolved values of OUT_i constitute the valid inputs IN_j to tasks T_j next on the schedule, i.e., $IN_j \subseteq \cup_i OUT_i$ where T_i represents all tasks that have been already executed.

6) The values of the output parameters of the last tasks are compared with the existing values (stored in underlying DBs), if needed, and formatted accordingly as the final answer to the query.

With outputs of tasks, the Transaction Manager deals with three kinds of conflicts such as confluent edges, cyclic paths and recurrent queries. At each confluent vertex, values returned from different CSs are evaluated by applying the aggregation function to those values. On the confluent vertex, BRACKET.WEIGHT, for example, in the Fig. 4-5, two CSs, ME and SE, will derive two competing values, v_1 and v_2, by performing the two tasks, T2 and T3, respectively. According to the attached option, MIN(v_1,v_2) will be the best value of the corresponding attribute, BRACKET.WEIGHT. With a UND option specified, however, the user interaction mode is called in to let the user decide on the selection of the best value on the vertex.

For a cyclic path, a sequence of values are derived on a reference vertex of the path, and analyzed to detect a trend in those values. Consider, for example, the cycle of SE4, SE5, ME1, ME2, ME3, and SE2, that is encountered in a path of SE1, SE2 and CE2. After the Transaction Manager has obtained the results of the task of SE1 and SE2 from SE, it attempts to detect possible trend on the reference vertex, SHAFT.WEIGHT, before it continues to assign the task of CE2 to CE. If the trend is decided converging after such an initial analysis, the execution of the cyclic path is reiterated a number of times to reach, if possible, an equilibrium in the values, i.e., $|v_i - v_{i+1}| < \Delta$ where v_i denotes the value from i-th iteration and Δ denotes a tolerance. If diverging, the cycle is concluded as nondeterministic. The third and last possible trend is no change in the value [27]. Then, the Transaction Manager simply stops repeating the cycle and departs it with the current value as its final value on its reference vertex.

A type-III query is answered in a recurrent fashion. That is, the Transaction Manager goes through multiple sessions to get an answer to such a query. The query, "Get the maximum WEIGHT of

BRACKET such that the COST of SHAFT does not exceed 100 dollars," for example, is not expected to be answered at the first session. The conditions given in the query may be refined each session according to the outputs of the preceding sessions.

In this type of query, the two available options differ in the degree of user intervention in the query processing. With the AUTO option specified in the query, the conditions are adjusted with no user intervention in an attempt to meet the given conditions. For this adjustment, the increment on a source condition value can be chosen as follows: suppose, by applying an increment δ to the source parameter s, we have obtained a series of values $v_1 > v_2 > v > v_3$, where v_i = value from i-th session, v = target value. Then, $-\delta/2$ would be a plausible increment for s in the next session. The MANUAL option allows the user to modify the conditions in the query in the way he/she believes to be optimal.

4.3 Execution of Tasks in Component Systems

Once a task is assigned to the corresponding LKAM, the Transaction Manager simply waits until its output is returned from the LKAM. Thus, the LKAM is responsible for attaining input data to activate the designated CS for the assigned task and shipping their output back to the Transaction Manager after proper formatting. First, more than one task that are in the same session and assigned to the same CS, are merged into one task because they all belong to one inferencing process. Second, the merged tasks are translated to a local query. Third, the CSs are activated and their outputs are collected.

4.3.1 Scheduling of Tasks in a CS:
In each CS, multiple tasks in the same session are merged into one task with offsetting I/O parameters corresponding to such vertices W = $IN_i \cap OUT_j$, where i ≠ j. The two tasks, T1 and T4, in Fig. 4-5, for example, will be combined into one task with two starting entities, BEAM.LENGTH and BEAM.WIDTH, via the common entity, i.e., BEAM.WEIGHT (an output parameter of T1 and input parameter of T4.) Unless T3 and T1 are translated to different entry points of the CS, SE, all of the three tasks T1, T3 and T4 will be translated to one query with three initial entities, i.e., BRACKET.WIDTH, and the above two starting entities of both T1 and T4.

4.3.2 Translation of Tasks into Local Queries:
To use preexisting information systems in general, one has to abide by their predetermined input and output procedures. For querying ESs (without query languages), a table is needed to register the "initial" entities of its member ESs. The initial entities of an ES refer to such data items that need to be instantiated to start inferencing process in the ES, e.g., name, age, sex and race, of MYCIN [27]. The mapping table allows a merged task to be translated into a local query in the form of entity set, i.e., IN → {initial entities}.

4.3.3 Data Exchange Channels between Global Query Processor and Component Systems:
The values of parameters in CSs are usually requested and accepted through the screen and keyboard (or the standard input/output devices) of a terminal. Those devices can not directly be used to exchange data among independent CSs, so they need to be redirected into sharable devices (e.g., disk files.) With such a redirection by means of, e.g., the redirection facilities supported in the UNIX system [14], the CS can accept input data from files instead of the keyboard and give output data on files instead of the screen. Then, the data exchange among CSs can be preformed with minimum (or no) user intervention.

For data exchange with another CS, i.e., ME, the vertex BRACKET.WEIGHT of the edge SE2 was originally designed as an implicit entity in the CS, i.e., SE, and must be converted to a ground entity. In ESs, such entities by design are convertible to ground entities by simply modifying rules to redirect I/O operations [13].

5. Implementation

We have completed building a prototype system for integrating heterogeneous expert systems based on the approach described in the preceding sections. The system is developed in C language and running on a SUN workstation. Its component systems are three independently developed expert systems with different inferencing mechanisms and rule formats. The first system is a backward-chaining system for cost analysis, while the second and third systems are forward-chaining expert systems for structural analysis and material engineering, respectively.

For searching the FG, a multi-vertex multi-graph, we extended the general graph search algorithm. Also, precedence algorithms have been modified to represent and process cycles across tasks. The parameter values required by CSs are incrementally provided on demand.

In this implementation, we focused on issues that are unique in our approach, and minimized conventional issues in general distributed systems. For example, general communication problems have been minimized by using pipe facilities among different processes (corresponding to component systems) on UNIX. Also, the usual lexical problems in query translation have been reduced by using common I/O protocols.

Through this implementation, we verified that the knowledge representation scheme is sufficient for the query processor to identify proper component ESs and decide proper execution orders among them. Our processing mechanism have been validated by obtaining the expected results from parallel and cyclic knowledge derivation paths as well as sequential paths. We also demonstrated that preexisting ESs need not be compromised in terms of their original inferencing mechanisms for this rule-level integration, except modifying some of their rules for I/O redirections.

6. Conclusion

We have developed an approach by which heterogeneous ESs can be integrated. As opposed to the existing heterogeneous DBMS, the CSs in this approach are not mere data retrieval systems. Rather, they derive knowledge by applying rules to data. This integration approach pursues a <u>tight</u> integration of such CSs. The resulting integrated ESs give a unified global view as if the heterogeneous ESs were not independent systems, but were one system.

Specifically, this approach allows independent expertises to be utilized on demand in an intertwined fashion. That is, the interactions among CSs occur in the rule level as opposed to the CS level. Thus, the rules and constraints can in effect be shared among heterogeneous ESs. To embody this approach, the knowledge representation scheme was designed to be neutral to the control mechanisms of particular CSs. The global knowledge manipulation language has a declarative nature with sophisticated semantics. The focus of the global language is to allow the user to observe the behavior of ESs from a global viewpoint. The system architecture is based on a hybrid central control to allow the CSs to maintain their autonomies after their integration.

Our approach achieves a control independency. That is, the heterogeneous CSs can interactively exchange their expertise regardless of their internal control mechanisms. This property leads to two desirable features in distributed systems: data independency and distribution transparency. Here, the data independency is elevated to knowledge independency. This approach directly applies to other rule-based systems such as constraint management systems and expert DBSs.

REFERENCES

[1] Freksa C., "Knowledge Representation for Interactive Aircraft Design," Proc. of the Tech. Assessment and Management Conf. of the Gottlieb Duttweiler Institute, Apr. 1985, pp.221-230

[2] Troeder C. and Naumann H.,"Expert Systems of Optimal Selection of Machine Elements," Proc. of the Tech. Assessment and Management Conf. of the Gottlieb Duttweiler Institute, Apr. 1985, pp.207-214

[3] Landers T. and Rosenberg R., "An Overview of MULTIBASE," Distributed Databases, H.Schneider ed., North-Holland, 1977.

[4] Heimbigner D. and Mcleod D.,"A Federated Architecture for Information Management," ACM TOOIS, Vol.3, No.3, July 1985.

[5] Missikoff M. et al.,"Toward a Unified Approach to Expert and Database Systems," Proc. First Int'l Workshop on Expert Database Systems, 1984, pp.186-206

[6] Golshani F.,"Tools for the Construction of Expert Database Systems," Proc. First Int'l Workshop on Expert Database Systems 1984, pp.442-455

[7] Kerschberg L. and Shepherd A.,"Constraint Management in Expert Database Systems," Proc. of the First Int'l Workshop on Expert Database Systems, Kiawah Island, South Carolina, 1984.

[8] Wong E. et al.,"Enhancing INGRES with Deductive Power," Proc. of the First Int'l Workshop on Expert Database Systems, Kiawah Island, South Carolina, 1984.

[9] Wilson G. et al.,"Distributed Database Considerations in an Expert System for Radar Analysis Intelligent Database Interfaces," Proc. First Int'l Workshop on Expert Database Systems, 1984, pp.586-602

[10] Su S. and Raschid L.,"Incorporating Knowledge Rules in a Semantic Data Model: An Approach to Integrated Knowledge Management," IEEE Conference on Artificial Intelligence Applications, Miami, Florida, Dec. 1985.

[11] Sridharan N.,"1986 Workshop on Distributed AI," AI Magazine, Fall 1987, pp.75-85

[12] Smith R. and Davis N.,"Frameworks for Cooperation in Distributed Problem Solving," IEEE Trans. Systems, Man, Cybernetics, Vol. SMC-11, No.1, Jan. 1981.

[13] Gerring P. and Shortliffe E., "The Interviewer/Reasoner Model: An Approach to Improving System Responsiveness in Interactive AI Systems," AI Magazine, Fall 1982, pp.24-27

[14] Tomada D. et al.,"A Framework of Expert System with Strategic Knowledge," Proc. of Int'l Conf. on Data Engineering, IEEE, 1986, pp.236-243.

[15] Navathe S. et al,"A Federated Approach to Loosely-Coupled Integration of Multiple Information Systems," Univ. of Florida, DBS R/D Center, Tech. Report, Apr. 1989.

[16] Larson J. et al.,"ATOZ -- A Prototype Intelligent Interface to Multiple Information Systems," Proc. IFIP Working Conference, Rome, Sep. 1985

[17] Marti R.,"Integrating Database and Program Descriptions Using an ER Dictionary," Journal of Systems and Software, Vol.4,No.2 and 3, Jul. 1984, pp.185-195

[18] Kaemmer W. and Larson J.,"A Graph-Oriented Representation and Unification Technique for Automatic Selecting and Invoking Software Functions," Proc. of AAAI, 1986. pp. 825-830.

[19] Ceri S., Pelagatti G., Distributed Databases-principles and systems, McGraw-Hill, 1985, pp.361-385.

[20] Su S. et al.,"The Architecture and Prototype Implementation of an Integrated Manufacturing Database System," Proc. of the COMPCON, Spring, 1988.

[21] Thompson B.,"Knowledge + Control = Expert Systems," AI Expert, 1, 3, Nov. 1986, pp.25-29.

[22] Su S.,"Modelling Integrated Manufacturing Data with SAM*," IEEE Computer, Jan. 1986, pp.34-49.

[23] Su S. et al,"An Object-Oriented Semantic Association Model (OSAM*)," in Artificial Intelligence: Manufacturing Theory and Practice, S.Kumara et al (eds), Industrial Management Press, Norcross, GA, 1989.

[24] Navathe S. et al.,"Integrating User Views in Database Design," IEEE Computer, Jan. 1986, pp.50-62

[25] Sakai H.,"A Method for Entity-Relationship Behavior Modeling," Entity-Relationship Approach to Software Engineering, C.Daviset al.(eds), Elsevier Science Publishers B.V. (North-Holland) pp.111-129

[26] Brodie M.,"On Modeling Behavioral Semantics of Databases," Proc. 7th VLDB, pp.32-42

[27] Buchanan B. and Shortliffe E., Rule-Based Expert Systems, Addison-Wesley, 1985, pp.314-328

[28] Brown L. et al, Programming Expert Systems in OPS5, Addison Wesley, 1985, pp.51-60.

[29] Aho A., Hopcroft J. and Ullman J., The Design and Analysis of Computer Algorithms, Addison-Wesley, 1974, pp.50-52.

[30] Peterson J. and Silverschatz A., Operating System Concept, Addison-Wesley Book Company, 1983, MA, pp.307-406.

[31] Kernighan B. and Pike R., The UNIX Programming Environment, Prentice-Hall, Inc., 1984, pp.29-31.

Toward a Knowledge model of problem solving

Z.Bellahsene

CRIM, 820 rue de Saint Priest
34090 Montpellier, France
e-mail :bellahsene @crim.fr

O. Massiot

LISAN-CNRS, Rue A.Einstein,
Sophia-Antipolis
O6560 Valbonne, France

Abstract

The model proposed in this paper belongs to a new class of data models that are characterized by the ability to capture both data semantics (description of entities) and knowledge (inferential and operational capabilities). Our approach attempts to extend the capabilities of semantic data models by incorporating features taken from the knowledge based systems area such as inferential capabilities. Its main contribution includes a mechanism that allows abstract knowledge typing by handling all concepts : heuristics, properties, relationships and constraints as objects. It also proposes an approach to reasoning process modelisation and presents concepts and mechanisms for problem solving simulation.

Key Words : data base, object oriented data model, knowledge based systems, problem solving, reasoning process...

1. Introduction

The topic of combining data base systems and Artificial Intelligence has been among the favoured subjects of recent research [1]. Usual database systems have a small schema filled with an important volume of instances whereas knowledge systems are characterized as having a large schema with many specific instances.The aim of our approach is enriching the database systems with inferencial capabilities and providing the knowledge systems with a large data capability.

The major purpose of this work is also to provide a complet model of data and knowledge in a unified way. While there is perhaps no general agreement about the major unresolved issues in knowledge representation,there is a definite trend towards more formal and conceptual investigations of representation schemes.
Classical models for conceptual design are often suggested as potentially robust approaches to built up new models for knowledge representation.

A brief review of traditional models should begin with the first record-oriented models : the hierarchical and the network and carry on with the development of the relational model [2] which provided more user-oriented modeling flexibility in expression and manipulation. Some models proposes a data representation which is the result of the relationship decomposition in homogeneous properties group. They are called Entity Relationship models [3] (hereafter E/R).

Some extensions of relational model : NF2 [4], V-relational [5], B-relational[6] also enable to represent complex objects by allowing attributes to be themselves relations. Further more some semantic data models [7] provide more powerful abstractions for the specification of database schemes and namely take into account the 'is - a' link beetween objects.

Recently, some models, called object oriented data models issued from object oriented languages have been proposed [8], [9]. The aim of their approach is to combine organisation features of semantics data models with the operational features of object-oriented programming languages. A second difference from previous approaches is the use of the notion of object identity : an object has an existence which is independent of its value [10]. That permits object sharing and update propagation : an object can be modified without changing its identity.

Disadvantages of the E/R model include its lack of support for semantic relativism in particular representation of all structural aspect of objects. In the other side, the major drawback of most semantic data models is that they essentially deal with structural links which correspond to generalisation and aggregation.They do not provide means to express in explicit way most of relationships. So to give a complet representation of the elements which interfer in our vision of the world, we had to define a new abstraction that would allow accurate modeling of relationships.
We must then notice the similarity in basic goals between Knowledge representation in object-oriented modelling and research on data models. In all two cases the aim is to provide tools for the development of description of slice of reality which correspond directly and naturally to our conceptualization of objects of real world. For the purposes of this paper, a knowledge base is considered as a representation of a world/entreprise/slice of reality.
Further more our model is an extension of the semantics data models combining their organisational features with those of object oriented models : the notion of classes of entities, property inheritance within class-subclass hierarchies, events or actions attached to each object, and emphasing the incorporation of inferential mechanism that allows knowledge representation (handling constraint, relations and rules as objects). This trend will help to bridge the gap between static data (without effects on processing) and active objects, between data models and knowledge systems.

The model proposed here is presented as natural extension of the use of E/R and semantic data models concepts for modelling operational properties of entities and their dynamics in problem solving context.The unified knowledge/data modeling features discussed in this paper combine Artificial Intelligence and database management.

techniques to establish the foundation for expert database system.

The aims of a knowledge representation system in resolving an expertise problem in a specific domain are :
-to give a structural and brief representation of the elements which interfer in our vision of the domain of study,
- to classify theses elements and to define the relationships among them in due to organise knowledge,
-to capture the type of reasoning process and analysis that the expert uses to solve a problem in the domain.
These first two points are discussed in the section 2 of this paper. The section 3 provides enhanced modeling primitives such as object behavioural properties, heuristics and model inferential relationships in due to represent the primitives of the expert capacity in resolving problems. While the section 4 gives a metadefinition of reasoning process based on psychological concepts.

2. Declarative aspect of knowledge

2.1 Complex objects

In a relational formalism, one object doesn't exist by itself, but only as a participant of a set of dispersed statements. At contrary, in the object formalism, the entities have got a real existence and their own space. And the model gives at the same time an image of things and behaviours. Our approach focus on how one could represent complex objects in knowledge base.

A complex object is usually defined as a hierarchy of records or objects.
An object will be said to be structurally complex if it is built up with other objects forming parts of it and if it can be manipulated as a whole. The representation mode must contains all the features to encode the structural aspect of complex objects that embody the expert knowledge. These features are :
- manipulating a structural concept : the "object", to represent any concept or thing.
- organising objects in objects-types (i.e classes) by creating partial hierachies from general to specific and discriminating object-types and object-intances
-characterising objects by attributes and organising objects-types via aggregation

Our model supports also additional modeling constructs on complex object-types that concern their behavioural properties and the inferential relationships between objects.

2.2 Introducing the concept of "relational link"

In fact, the object-type concept is not sufficient to handle the knowledge semantics. Therefore we add to it another modeling construct called a "relational link". A relational link is a relation, in the mathematical sense, defined between two sets of objects. For example, the links "grand-father", "loves", "married_with" are relational links.
The description or definition of a concept can't be limited to its immediate properties. We must be able to give to it a place to "spread out" and to link up to other concepts. The "relational link" is the basic feature of object context representation. It is considered as an abstraction , stating that some instance-objects are associated in the same way.

The first advantage is that new relational links can be added without modifying the object-type. Therefore it must be a modeling construct in the same footing with the object concept. Intuitively, a complex object regroups objects having the same

properties and behaviours and being structurally linked together; while the relational link modelise the interactions between objects. Generally speaking, the externalisation of inter-objects references into relational links permits to use them as semantics constructs of the same importance of the object concept.

Finally, object and relation are natural means for knowledge specifying and besides the notions of structural link and relational link are well known in the cognitive science domain.

2.3 The schema level

In usual object oriented models, the representation of relational links is carried out thanks to attributes having as value a reference to other object. No mean is provided to express relational links directly.
The principle of our approach is to consider that a relational link is an abstraction on its own. It is a more symmetrical form than reference.
So there are two types of predefined objects in our model : the E-object-type (E stand for Entity) and the R-object-type (R stand for Relation). The former one is used for entity représentation while the second one is dedicated to the relational link representation. All concept is an object in object oriented sense : each object has an identity which is independent from his value.The following figure shows the object-type hierarchy.

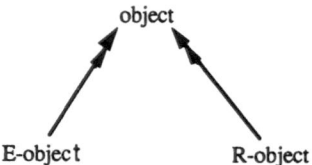

fig.1 Object hierarchy

E-object-type :
An E-object type is a collection of objects having same characteristics. For instance, a person, a employe, a constraint are E-objects-types. A property of an object is called in term of modelisation an attribute. For example, the name, address and salary are attributes of the E-object-type employe. Objects can be used as components of others objects. This type of object is referred as a composite or complex object
The specification of an E-object-type is shown by the figure2.

E-Objet-type : E-object-type name
    [Attributes :
    Composite_Attributes :
    Computed_Attributes :]
    [Defined by : { rules that define intensionally the E-object-type}]
    [Methods:]
    inherits from : object
End E-object-type

fig. 2 E-object-type specification

The E-object-type specification involves the attributes specification which is done by identifying each attribute name and the type of its value. An attribute may be single valued or multivalued (set or list type). The "computed" clause indicates that the value of the attribute will be generated by application of aggregate functions(sum,count,...) used in database systems or of a built-in operation relating others attributes. The "defined by" clause introduce the intensional definition of the object-type. In that case, the instances are not stored in the data base but inferred (see section 4). In term of implementation, it can be expressed in rules *à la* PROLOG. While the operational aspect of the object-type is described in the "methods" clause, the super-types will be specified in the last clause.

R-object-type

An R-object-type represents information about associations among different E-objects-types. It can be defined either extensively as a set of tuples or it can be defined in an intensional (i.e inferred way) by first-order predicates (see section 4). If a R-object-type is defined according to the latter way it would allow deduction.

The R-object-type can be view also as a mechanism for specifying classes of instance-objects satisfying specific properties corresponding to the related relational link.

The specification of its context is done by identifying the E-objects-types which are relationally linked and their own roles. The specification of the cardinality of each object-type is useful in tightening semantics. The figure 3 gives the R-object-type specification.

R-Objet-type : R-Objet-type name
  [Attributs : {attributes names and their data type}]
  [Context : <role 1 : E-Objet-type1 (min, max),...,rolek : E-Objet-typek(min,max)>]
  [Defined by : {rules that define intensionally the R-objet-type}]
  inherits from : object
End R-object-type

Fig.3 R-Objet -type specification

The R-Objet-type specification involves its own attributes specification including their names and the type of their values. The instances are defined extensionally by the "context" clause and intensionally by the "defined by" clause. This last can be expressed in terms of implementation under form of PROLOG's rules.

2.4 An example

In the figure 4 is given a schema of social service which is composed of nine E-object-types and five R-objects-types. "Person"isthe generic type of "child", "unemployed" and "employed". The "grand-parent-of" is an example of an intentionally defined R-object-type.

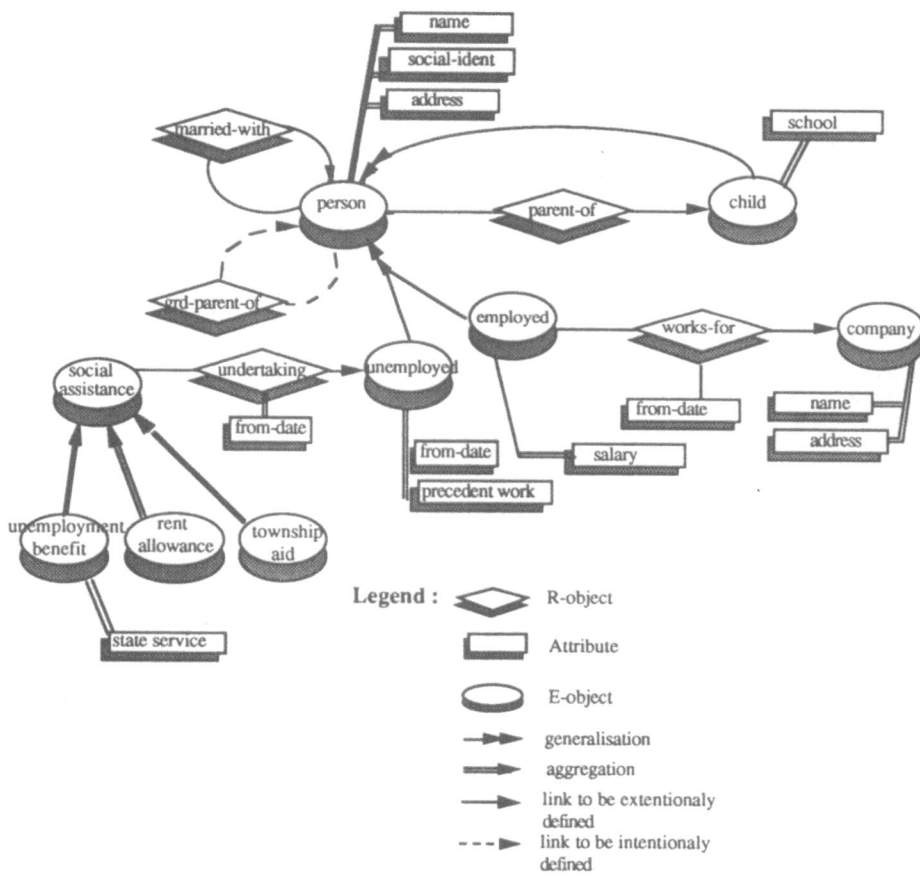

Fig.4

```
E-object-type : company
    Attributes :
        name : string;
        address : text;
end company

E-object-type : social-assistance
    Is composed of :
        unemployment-benefit;
        rent-allowance;
        township-aid;
end social-assistance

E-object-type : unemployment-benefit
    Attributes :
        state-service-id : string;
end unemployment-benefit

E-object-type : rent-allowance
    Attributes
        flat-surface : real;
        lodger_number : integer;
        flat-rent : real;
        allowance_amount =
    compute_amnt(flat-surface,logde_number,...)
    (*This procedure computes the amount *)
    Methods :
        allowance_right = comput_right(salary,
                    child_number, flat_rent)
    (*This procedure computes the right to allowance*)
end rent-allowance

E-object-type : township-aid
    attributes :
        amount : real;
end township-aid

R-object-type : parent-of
    context :
        <parent : person(1,1), child : child(1,n)>;
end parent-of

E-object-type : person
    Attributes :
        name : string;
        address : text;
end person
```

```
E-object-type : child
    Attributes :
        school : text;
        inherits from : person;
end child

E-object-type : employed
    Attributes :
        salary : real;
        inherits from : person;
end employed

E-object-type : unemployed
    Attributes :
        from-date : date;
        precedent-work : text;
        inherits from : person;
end unemployed

R-object-type : works-for
Attributes
    from-date : date ;
context :
        <employe : employed(1,1),
        firm : company(1,n)>;
end works-for

R-object-type : grand-parent-of
    context :
        <gd_parent : person(1,1), gd_child
            child(1,n)>;
    defined by :
    grand-parent-of(x,y) :- parent(x,z),
    parent(z,y);
end grand-parent-of

R-object-type : undertaking
Attributes :
        from-date : date
    context :
        <social-service :social-assistance(1,1),
        unemploye : unemployed(1,1)> ;
end undertaking
```

3. Behavioural aspect of knowledge

The most important features recently integrated in the data models are those of the operational aspect of the object concept. To take in account the dynamic properties of objects in their representation of world, they borrowed some tools from object oriented languages.

3.1 Procedural attachments

The major difference between an object and a record or tuple of database systems is that the first one can be active using object-associated procedures. The last ones provide facilities for procedural attachment that can be divided along two dimensions. The first one correspond to whether the procedure is associated with an object-type or with one of its attributes.

The second dimension is based on when and what for the procedure is intended to be used : integrity control or behavioural representation.

Procedural level : object or attribute

Some models attach procedures only at object level, others at attributes level or both. This type of attributes are reffered to in the litterature as derived attributes. For example in Postgres [11], it is allowed to define attributes as Quel expressed queries, while in the object oriented called models as O2 [7], and EXTRA [8] , the procedures are done only at object level.

In our model, we allow attributes to be computed : their values are not stored but are determined when needed via some procedure statements. The object can also have its proper procedures.

Behavioural representation

- The behaviour of an object is completely defined by procedural attachments. The aim is then to give to objects their proper deductive capacities in due to drive problem solving. "Methods" are parts of what is called object-oriented programming. Each method is a procedure attached to an object-type and describes one of its behavioural aspect. The dynamic can also be distributed on attributes. In the object internal structure, procedures are associated to each attribute and make a fast and direct mechanism of reasoning and analysis when the state of the attribute is modified. They "know" how to update the attribute value and they answer in an appropriate way to this modification. But they are only punctual jobs and unable to make a global reasoning.

3.2 Inter-object coherence constraints

Procedure can also contain automatic control for semantic integrity constraints.
Object-associated procedures provide the only means of altering an object. This ensures the semantic integrity of an object since all constraints on the object must be satisfied by all attempts to alter it. The procedures manage the object, control the coherence constraints and detect incompatibilities or contradictions that the presence of an instance object may induce. They are also expressed in two way : procedure attachment to object or procedure attachment to its local links (as it is described in next paragraph).

3.3 Actions and heuristics representation

Actions and heuristics are conceptual level application-oriented operations. They are traductions of relationships among elements of the domain. They participate in the dynamic aspect of the objects. Actions represent agents or actors of the world and heuristics expert rules. But they two, like all modeling concepts, are based on abstract object-types. Each is represented by an object.
Actions and heuristics are designed to only be active on a specific invocation context. Before certain preconditions must be necessary. The premisses and conclusions of actions and heuristics are attributes and directly act on attributes of other objects.
The action or heuristic local scope includes the object of interest and all objects immediately related by structural or relational links.
Because heuristics and actions are objects, they can be organised in classes hierarchy to benefit of the clearness of a constructed and controled search. This hierarchy enables to control the rules set and to participate in the system functionalities : choice of strategies, reasoning control, etc...

To conclude, the behavioural properties and structural links constitute an abstraction that completely defines the semantics of the object. The result of conceptual modelling, the conceptual model of the expert domain, is a network of abstrations related by the three defined forms.

4. From representation to reasoning simulation

The three constituent parts of our knowledge system proposed in this paper find some correspondance in problem solving models developed in the field of cognitive science.
The basic assumptions made by our model are :
1) -the knowledge of the subject expressed in a great diversity of forms: entities, relationships, knowledge schemes procedures and knowledge management mechanism
        -> knowledge base
2) -the problem and context representation made progressively by the subject from data and inferences
        -> data base instances
3) -a control part which makes regulation between representation of environnement/context of the problem to solve and the internal knowledge representation
        ->inference procedures and reasoning control.
Described in term of strategies, this structure is an attempt to capture some of the general features of the reasoning activity and to tie them into the larger scope of a complet model.

We refer here to "problem solving" as knowledge and inference procedures used to perform at such a level that they can be thought of as a model of the expertise of the practitionners of the field. So the word "expert" will mean a individual or a system who is widely recognized as being able to solve a particular type of problem that most other people cannot solve nearly as efficiently or effectively. By insisting on general agreement about meaning of "expert problem" we are focusing on performance and thus justifying the importance of reasoning activity simulation.
The concepts introduced in this section are fundamental in our approach since they form a set of assumptions that underlie our model representation of reasoning activity :
-inference procedures on objects, relational links, actions and heuristics,
-knowledge schemes,
-control of reasoning process and strategies.

4.1 Drawing inferences

Each chunk of domain-specific heuristic information with all its myriad associations can be retrieved, examined and utilized at will. Inference tools and procedures are associated with each abstraction defined in the preceeding sections.

4.1.1 Extentional and intentional definitions

Notions of extensional and intentional definition are introduced here to define the bases of inferential progress on E-objects and R-objects. The former one contitutes the extentional database while the intensional definition stands for the inference rules of deductive database.
Extentional definition -> extentional database : it describes the context by an exausted enumeration of all instances being elements of context-representation. To an E-object-type is associated a set of tuples of E-objects identifiers which defines the class contents.
Intentional definition -> inference rules od deductive database : it consists in defining E-objects-type or R-object-type by using rules or formulas in order to calculate their values. For example, the "grand-father-of" link can be defined intentionaly with the "father-of" and "parent-of" links as follows:
Grand-father-of (x,y) :- father-of(x,z) , parent(z,y)

4.1.2 Intrinsic properties of R-objects

A relational link may own logical properties such as transitivity which would allow deduction. An intrinsic property is a property which characterises a relational link without referencing other relational links. There are :
-Transitivity : $O_i L O_j$ and $O_j L O_k$ -----> $O_i L O_k$
    (example, O_i left_of O_j)
- Symetry : $O_i L O_j$ ----> $O_j L O_i$ (example, O_i beside-of O_j)
- Antisymetry : $O_i L O_j$ ----> $O_j L O_i$ then $O_i = O_j$
    (example, O_i contains O_j)
where O_i and O_j are objects identifiers

These properties can be described by rules which, added to the intentional definition, enrich the inference process. For example,a generic definition of transitivity can be added to the proper intentional definiton of a relational link R beetwen objects x and y , as follows :

R(x,y) :- R(x,z) , R(z,y)

Although the semantics of relations have been described for relations with any arity, only binary relations are such mathematical objects which can own binary logical properties.

4.1.3 Inference procedures manipulation

Let us see now how theses tools can provide deduction. The first attempt is done on extentional definition. When the extentional data is not enough to answer a query, the inferential process will be activated and therefore will exploit the rules of intentional definitions and if needed the logical properties of the relational links.

Extentional manipulation : in addition to the methodes proper to each E-object-type, operators of set type are defined in order to manipulate sets of objects like in relational database systems. The R-objects can also be processed by specific operators such as composition and reverse. The first one allow to compute the transitive closure of query referencing a R-object whereas the reverse operator is very useful in some applications. For example, the reverse operator defined on "parent-of" R-object is :

Reverse (parent-of) = child
i.e child (x,y) :- parent(y,x)

Intentional processing : the structuration of the relations under the form of objects allows to avoid the sequential reading of the rules. This is because all the properties concerning a link : intentional definition and logical properties, are gathered in an R-object -type.

The circulation in the network is done from E-object instance to E-object instance using links of R-objects if extensionaly defined. If not, the logical properties of each R-object-type are potentially generating rules which added to the intentional definition can be exploit by inference process to progress to the determination of the result.

Object behaviour simulation

Definition of expert problem, queries, intentional definition of R-objects can reference E-object-attached behavioural procedures. By that way you can realise simulation of E-object.

Action and heuristic activation :

Action and heuristic are dynamic objects which can also be involved in reasoning process.

4.2. Knowledge schemes

It is by more tiny connections between data structures (which convey information) and between inference procedures (which manipulate them) that we can give meaning to knowledge. Further more when the system has to manage a great quantity of data, the most important is to determine which chunks of knowledge can be applied and which links will enable to associate data and problem solving.

In problem solving situation, when the cognitive system move from conceptualizing a problem in terms of a mental model to thinking about it in symbolic terms, it search for a whole scheme of objects linked by multiple associations and which correspond to the stated problem.

This new terminology (knowledge scheme) allows for a more precise definition of problem solving. It is the process of starting in an initial state searching through the problem space guided by a knowledge scheme in order to identify and realise the sequence of operations or actions that will lead to a desired goal. So running through the network is limited to a predefined set of E-objects-types and R-objects-types. The root of scheme is known and used to start processing.

4.3. Control of dynamic process

The basic functions of the control part of model are :

1)- **activation** of knowledge entities and procedures according to the situation and context .The current object becomes an active entity and behaves in its context using all its behavioural procedures and all its links towards objects of its neighbourhood. In fact all the object properties are liberated and activated. So the active object becomes autonomous and has to provide the control of its own activity in the scope of its tasks.

2)- **evaluation** of the result of activation due to start an other reasoning process. All links in which the E-objet is implicated are evaluated. In the second step the links of the object to its immediate context are evaluated. The values so obtained will be conditions to the reasoning advance.

3)- **Anticipation** of he variables fixed by the preceeding step enable the selection of the next activation impacts. The control and dynamic will be delegated to the choosen E-objects. The reasoning process will follow new directions.

4.3.1 strategies

The inference and control strategies guide the knowledge system in using the facts and rules stored in its knowledge base and the information it acquires from the user. They give all matters to realise the three states of the process and also describe how to encode and store information and recall it from knowledge base.

4.3.2 Plannification, image of running process and finalities

The central executive of reasoning activity is based on an agenda of runnable processes and a scheduler for running them in a systematic order. This structure contains an image of future plans and tasks and is permanently kept to date.
Goals are not allways stated explicitly but can be represented by a set of facts and rules itselves described in terms of objects. This abstraction is called "finalities".

5. Concluding remarks

We have presented an extension of semantic data models which incorporates from database theory as well as mothods developped in IA research.We emphasize on the representation of knowledge semantics by offering a mechanism to handle them as objects. An object-oriented model combining the semantic data features with the inference capacities is presented. It also provide concepts and mechanisms for reasoning process control. All features have been built in an object-oriented way to enrich complex objects with all behavioural and inferencial capacities.

The proposed model is at an evaluation stage and a prototype has be made of it in Lisp and with the support of knowledge representation langage.

References

[1]   R.P Van de Riet, " MOKUM : An Object-oriented Active Knowledge Base System", Data & Knowledge Engineering, North Holland, 1989, PP.21-42

[2]   Codd E.F, "A Relational Model for Large Shared Data Base", ACM Vol. 13, n°6, June 1970, PP. 377-387

[3]   Chen P. P., "The Entity-Relationship Model Toward a UnifiedView of Data", ACM Transactions on Database Systems, vol. 1, N°1 , March 1976, PP 9-36.

[4]   Schek H.J, Pistor P., "Data Structures for an Integrated Data Base Management and Information Retrieval System", Proc.inter. conf. on VLDB, Mexico, 1982,PP 197-207.

[5]   Abiteboul S., Bidoit N., "Non First Normal Form Relations to Represent Hierarchically Organised Data", Proc. of ACM Symposium on Principles of Database Systems, Waterloo, April 1984., PP191-200.

[7]   Abiteboul S., Hull R., "IFO : A Formal Semantic Database Model", ACM Transactions on Database Systems, vol.12, N°4, Dec 1987, PP 525-565.

[6]   Miranda S., Le than N., Bellahsene Z., "The B-relational model : Towards a unified view of semantics", Int. Workshop on theory and application of nested relation and complex objects, Darmstadt, West Germany, 6-8 April 1987.

[8]   Lécluse C., Richard P., Velez F., "O_2, An Object Oriented Data Model", Rapport technique Altair 10-87, 15 Sep 1987.

[9]   Carey M. J., Dewitt D. J., Vadenberg S. L., "A Data Model and Query Language for EXODUS", ACM 1988, PP 413-423.

[10] Beeri C., "Formal Models for Objects Oriented Databases", Proc.DOOD89, Kyoyo, Japan, Dec. 1989.

[11] Rowe L.A., Stonebraker M. R., "The Postgres Data Model", Proc. 13th VLDB Conference, Brighton 1987.

USING ARTIFICIAL INTELIGENCE TECHNIQUES TO FORMALIZE THE INFORMATION SYSTEM DESIGN PROCESS

G. Grosz

C. Rolland

Laboratoire MASI,
Université Pierre et Marie Curie
4, place Jussieu, 75005 Paris, France
email : grosz@litp.ibp.fr

Université Paris 1 - Sorbonne
17, rue de la sorbonne
75231 Paris Cedex 05, France

ABSTRACT

The design of large and complex Information System (IS) is nowadays supported by Computer Assisted Software Engineering (CASE) tools. However, the current generation tools restrict their help to the management of the IS specifications. The goal of more advanced CASE tools is to support effectively designers during the design process itself and the production of the IS specification. The expert design tool OICSI, discussed in this paper, belongs to that perspective. The kernel of OICSI is a knowledge base homogeneously composed of design knowledge triplets. A triplet is a combination of a situation, a decision and an action. In order to define various triplets, we have experimented automatic learning techniques. The paper focuses on the presentation of the triplet notion and the use of learning techniques to find out triplets. Both are exemplified on a precise design task.

1 INTRODUCTION

As users requirements are becoming more sophisticated, the design of large Information System (IS) is becoming more difficult. IS design methods provide an essential, but incomplete, solution to this problem. Each method consists of (1) models for system specification, (2) a process for driving the construction of the specification and, for some of them, (3) a set of Computer Aided Software Engineering (CASE) tools to assist designers. During the last decade, methods developers have paid a particular attention to the definition of semantic models. They allow the expression of conceptual schema using a rigorous and powerful formalism.

Semantic models, such as SHM [1], SHM+ [2], SDM [3], THM [4] and TAXIS [5], propose concepts centred around the structural properties of IS. Knowledge representation techniques, and more precisely semantic networks, have strongly influenced these models. Dynamical models, such as REMORA [6] and TAXIS [5] allow to integrate the specification of both the structure and the behaviour of an IS in a conceptual schema. Within these models, CIAM [7], OBLOG [8] and THM [4], propose a formal specification based on logical formulæ in order to be able to reason about the specification.

These models provide undisputed advantages to specify IS conceptual schema. However, the applied process is not formalized and human controlled in a linear and stepwise manner. Here stands the remaining problem. Recent CASE tools do not give an efficient solution to this problem. Most of them are built around a data dictionary. They allow (1) the definition of the IS specification using the dictionary, (2) the documentation of the specification, (3) some automatic consistency checking, and eventually (4) prototyping and (5) performance simulation.

In order to support efficiently the design process itself, CASE tools must evolve from simple managers of IS specifications to more intelligent tools. They must be able to guide the designer to reach effective solutions, taking into account his decision, and proposing the most appropriate action. The design of these new tools must include a new formulation of the design process. This new formulation must take into account all the modelling tasks and the linking of these tasks. A formalization of this process, entirely based on AI techniques, enligthens a new perspective to the design of these tools which belongs to the Software Engineering approach [9].

This paper aims to show how AI techniques, and particularly automatic learning techniques, can help in the design of CASE tools. The expert design workbench OICSI [10] (a French acronym for intelligent tool for IS design), partially presented in this paper, belongs to that perspective.

The next section gives an overview of OICSI and underlines the problems we were faced with while building its Knowledge Base (KB). We introduce the notion of knowledge triplet and discuss its components. Section 3 presents how learning techniques aided us to define the notion of triplet. We illustrate both the definition and the use of triplets in a particular design problem. It consists in defining all possible structures in order to represent a relationship between two objects according to the cardinality values.

2 OICSI

OICSI is an expert system to help the IS design. More precisely, its goal is to assist the designer in building a conceptual schema. The provided help is developed in four directions:
- to highlight errors in the specification;
- to help the designer when correcting them by offering valid solutions;
- to propose choices in order to represent relevant real word phenomena;
- to drive progressively the designer from the requirements to the conceptual schema.

2.1 AN OVERVIEW

OICSI acts as a designer; it drives the design process, guides the designer to a solution and automates some tasks.

At all times, the *fact base* reflects the current state reached by the designer while modelling the system. Three levels of facts are embedded in the OICSI fact base:
- the requirement level; it corresponds to the facts as they exist in the real world; they are provided by the designer in natural language (French until now);
- the real-world model level; it corresponds to a description of relevant real-world entities, operations, events types and some constraints on these types. It also includes the description of binary relationships between these types;
- the conceptual schema level : it is a structured expression, based on an object oriented model [11]. It contains the definition of all the objects which will be really used by the operational IS. Any object definition integrates its structure and behaviour specification. Static modelling supports the structuration of complex objects based on the three well known abstraction constructors of semantic data models, namely : aggregation, generalization and set. As in the REMORA approach [6] , the dynamic modelling is based on two concepts : operation (an operation modifies the state of only one object) and event (a particular state change of only one object which triggers operations, eventually under some conditions).

These different levels of specification coexist, the designer can manipulate one or the other, whenever he wants.

The *rule base* defines how to drive the design process. More precisely, it is used for:
- making design decisions;
- automating modelling activities;
- interacting with the designer when it needs his decision;
- reasoning on specifications to point out undesirable properties such as ambiguity, contradiction and redundancy in the requirements;
- tolerating inconsistency and incompleteness and driving the designer in the way to solve them;
- enabling the designer to choose the level of specification he wants.

2.2 PROBLEM WHILE CODING OICSI

The major problem, while coding OICSI, was to build the KB. We initially followed a pragmatic approach based upon the simple idea that, after some formalization, the KB must reproduce the design actions as performed by an expert designer. We also respect the linear and stepwise view of current design process which, in our case,leads to the three basic steps:
- acquisition of the requirements describing the IS (natural language sentences);
- transformation of these requirements into the real-word model;
- construction of the final conceptual schema.

For each step, we defined rules such as:
- interpretation rules;
- mapping rules;
- validation rules;
- refinement rules.

The global result was a KB which was difficult to manage, mainly because of its heterogeneity. Its consistency and completeness became hard to validate. In fact, we were faced with the classical problem of knowledge acquisition: how to put the know-how of an expert (in this case a designer) into a KB. This is a long, tedious and costly work. In [12], this problem is described as the "knowledge acquisition bottleneck". As suggested by some AI specialists, we attempted to solve the problem in a more automatic way, by using automatic learning techniques. The next section details the work we did using this technique. However, before this, let us summarize the major results that we achieve as follows:
- we find out that the design process must be regarded as a decision process;
- this help us to find a common frame for knowledge representation: the *knowledge triplet*. Thus, while re-formulating the KB, using the notion of triplet, we obtain a totally homogeneous KB;
- the definition of the triplets, using the learning technique, leads to a better control of the consistency, non-redundancy and completeness of the whole KB.

2.3 THE KNOWLEDGE TRIPLET

A triplet is a set of three elements:
< SITUATION, DECISION, ACTION >.
It can be seen as a rule, but an important dichotomy is made in the premise: the *situation* part and the *decision* part.This distinction is useful because it shows precisely what is concerned by the application and what is a design decision.

A *situation* is a set of instantiated properties which are totally application dependent. It is a relevant or meaningful part of a specification (whatever its abstraction level is). For example, a situation can be a natural language sentence representing some requirements, a part of the real-world model or the global state of the design process at a given point of time.

A *decision* reflects the choices that a designer has to make during the design phase. It is design dependent but not application dependent. We have identified three types of decisions: *modelling*, *quality insurance* and *correctness* decisions.

Modelling decisions deal with the construction of elements of a specification whatever its level is. A modelling decision depends on the model underlying the specification. Examples, in OICSI, are elicitation and interpretation of requirements and structuration of the conceptual schema elements.

Quality insurance decisions deal with the characteristics that a schema must conform to, such as non redundancy, atomicity, etc. For instance, we consider that non redundancy of an IS conceptual schema is required for data structure as well as for operation and event structures.

Correctness decisions deal with the correctness of the design specification in relation to the used model; in OICSI, these decisions allow us to assure consistency, completeness and accuracy of the conceptual schema.

An *action* modifies the specification (whatever its level). It is model dependent. An action is performed in a given situation, with respect to some decisions and modifies the specification. Actions are of a unique type: they induce transformations of the current IS specification. However, they can be classified as to whether or not they change the abstraction level of the specification. We distinguish intra-level actions and inter-level actions. For example, mapping requirements onto elements of the real-world model will be called an inter-level action whereas improving the structuration of conceptual objects is considered as an intra-level action. Notice that an action may be associated with different types of decisions. For example introducing a new generic type in a hierarchy of objects can be the consequence of a modelling decision as well as justified by a quality insurance decision.

In summary, it can be said that the triplets represent the relationships between situations, decisions and actions. A triplet is an elementary piece of design knowledge. The assumption, we have made, is that all the knowledge needed for IS design can be decomposed into a collection of these atomic pieces of knowledge. In addition, we found that the meta-rules, to implement the design strategy, can be also expressed through triplets.

In this design perspective, AI techniques, as used in expert systems, are useful in order to implement the design process. The OICSI knowledge base is composed of rules (implemented as Prolog clauses) that represent the various triplets we have defined to deal with modelling, quality insurance and correctness decisions required by the design of conceptual schemas. Using this KB, the Prolog inference engine allows the view of the design process as a deductive process where:
- the semantics of requirements uttered in natural language are extracted and represented through the real-world model;
- elements of the conceptual schema are deduced from the real-world model;

- transformations of a current version of the conceptual schema required by the insertion of new requirements are automatically inferred.

3 LEARNING TECHNIQUES FOR TRIPLET DISCOVERY

We have chosen a learning technique based on examples. We, first, present a rapid overview of possible techniques and justify the one we chose. We highlight the major problem inherent to the technique we used. Then, we briefly introduce the learning tool that we used. Finally, we detail a precise use of the tool for defining the set of triplets required to properly structure two related objects.

3.1 A RAPID OVERVIEW OF LEARNING TECHNIQUES

Explanation based learning is a form of deductive learning, which uses formal proof to structure knowledge (see for instance [13]). In this case, a complete theory of the domain must exist to allow to automatically build formals proofs.

Learning by analogy involves transforming or extending existing knowledge applicable to one domain in order to perform similar task in another domain. This approach is described in [14]. In this case, the system must have, as prerequisites, a KB of concepts and resolution formulas to problems similar to the ones it will solve. It must also be able to recognize similarities between a new problem and the older ones. Unfortunately, these two forms of deductive learning cannot fit our problem. Mostly because the design process is not fully formalized. In fact, expert designers are not able to express a complete theoretical knowledge about IS design. They even have difficulties in giving the explicit structure of their knowledge.

Learning from examples is a form of inductive learning. Given a set of examples, and optionally counter examples, the system induces rules to classify the examples according to a given concept. The induction process is a generalization process. It can be implemented in different ways (see [15] or [16]). Expert designers can easily express examples. They can tell what they do in a specific context.

Learning by observation and discovery is another form of inductive learning. It includes a variety of processes, such as creating classifications, discovering relationships within the observations or forming theory. The system does not need any description about what to learn. The observations do not have to be classified as positive or negative, they may cover more than a single concept. Nowadays, this method is used with numerical observations [17], but not yet with qualitative ones. Knowledge design cannot be expressed using only numerical observations.

Thus, the assumption we made is that, for the expert designers, the easiest way to express their knowledge is by examples.

3.2 USING "LEARNING BY EXAMPLES" TOOLS TO FORMALIZE THE DESIGN PROCESS

The main problem, when using this kind of tool, is to decide what is an example and then to build all the meaningful examples. The validity of the induction depends on the completeness of the set of examples. It must cover all the relevant cases since otherwise the set of the generated rules will be incomplete. In most tools, an example is a set of instantiated attributes. In our case, while defining an example, we have to choose the relevant attributes to describe the design process. We can imagine two extremes solutions: an example can be a complete application (the specifications and the final conceptual schema) or an indivisible item in the specification and its associated description in the conceptual schema. The former requires a huge, even impossible, work to collect all the possible examples, i.e. to enumerate all the applications a designer can deal with. Further more, in this case, the size of an example should be simply enormous. The later, on the contrary, leads to define a lot of small different types of examples. For each type, a set of rules has to be induced. Then another work has to be performed: the chaining up of all these different set of rules.

On the other hand, the design process involves many different activities, for instance, the collecting of the specifications, their mapping into a conceptual model, the IS validation, etc. Thus, we chose to divide the design process into sub-tasks to reason on each sub-task separately and finally to integrate the set of generated triplets for each sub-task. Thus, we built the examples according to a single task. For instance, we have examples to describe:
- the recognition of pattern in French sentences and their associated roles;
- the structuration of a static or dynamic relationship between two objects;
- the mapping of the static schema into an object oriented data base, according to the O^2 DBMS [18].

The learning tool CHARADE [19] was selected. We briefly introduce it in the next paragraph.

3.3 THE LEARNING TOOL CHARADE

CHARADE is an example based learning tool. It builds a KB using :
- a description language with typed attributes;
- a set of examples described using the description language;
- a description of the target system functionality.
Its major features are :
- the use of axioms to state precisely the semantic of the domain;
- the measurement of certainty for each generated rule;
- the use of the target system functionality to build generalization heuristics;
- the possible direct use of the generated rules by a common inference engine.
CHARADE empirically looks for regularities which are present in the set of examples. To do so, the set of examples and the set of descriptor conjunctions are represented by two boolean lattices. The properties of these lattices are used in the learning process to facilitate the detection of regularities. In fact, the regularities correspond to a correlation empirically observed in the set of examples. The principle of induction used in symbolic learning consists of a generalization of this correlation to the whole description space.

3.4 A PRECISE USE OF CHARADE

We present in this section how we obtained the list of triplets from examples using CHARADE. We limit our presentation to the structuration sub-task for binary relationship between objects. This sub-task is introduced in the next paragraph. We follow by presenting the inputs of the tool, (examples and other features). We come up with what it indirectly generates : the triplets . Then, we describe the use of the triplets by an example. We end with some comments.

3.4.1 THE STRUCTURATION SUB-TASK

The goal of the structuration sub-task is to transform a binary relationship between two objects defined in the real-world model to the appropriate structure in the conceptual schema, within a hierarchy of aggregation, generalization and association. The model we use is defined in [11]. To solve this problem, we add, to each binary relationship, a set of cardinalities. The notion of cardinality has been extensively used in database models, for instance in the entity relationship model [20]. However, we propose to extend this notion in the following way. We define a relationship function f between two objects (A and B) and the inverse one f^{-1} between B and A. These functions have totalness, valuation and permanency as properties. These properties are our cardinalities.

Totalness : a function f (or f^{-1}) is total , iff each instance of A is associated with at least one instance of B at any point of time, otherwise f is partial .
Valuation : a function f (or f^{-1}) is simple , iff each instance of A is associated with at most one instance of B at any point of time, otherwise f is multiple .
Permanency : a function f (or f^{-1}) is permanent, iff each instance of A is always associated with the same instance of B, if not f is variable . (Note that when f is variable, f^{-1} is also variable and the same when f is permanent).

Let us illustrate this with an example. Suppose that the designer wants to represent the association between a person and his car; between these two objects, the cardinalities should be:
from person to car :
    partial (a person may not have a car)
    multiple (a person can have more than one car)
    variable (a person can change his car)
from car to person :
    total (a car is always owned by someone)
    simple (a car has one, and only one, owner)
    variable (the owner can change)

378

For this task, some decisions have to be stated:

- *the use of a generic type*. For instance, in the previous example, the designer has to decide if it is useful to consider the person as a generic object in order to make the differentiation between those who own car and those who do not. This decision will be denoted G(person). If this distinction is not useful then the decision will be denoted ¬G(person).

- *the necessity to see a set of objects as a whole*. In the example, the designer can consider the set of cars associated to a person (denoted S(car)) or stress the fact that a car is owned by only one person (denoted ¬S(car)).

- *the need to journalize an association* (only when it has been defined as variable) between two objects. In our example, it is a design decision to stamp and memorize all the cars owned by one person. In this case the decision will be denoted Stamp(car,person) otherwise, it will be denoted ¬Stamp(car,person). When an object A is seen as a set (S(A) is true) another decision can be to stamp the evolution of the set (Stamp(S(A)) is true) or to consider a set with stamped instances (Stamp(S(A) is false)).

- the choice, when a situation (A associated to B) is symmetric, to decide *which object takes place A* in the situation (denoted Up(A)).

3.4.2 INPUTS
CHARADE needs different inputs to generate rules, namely : descriptors, axioms, examples, and structuration constraints. We define each of these, taking examples related to the structuration sub-task.

The descriptors
They are typed attributes. The types are define by their domain and the operators we can apply on them. An example is an instantiated conjunction of some of these descriptors. Some of the twenty descriptors we defined are presented in figure 1.

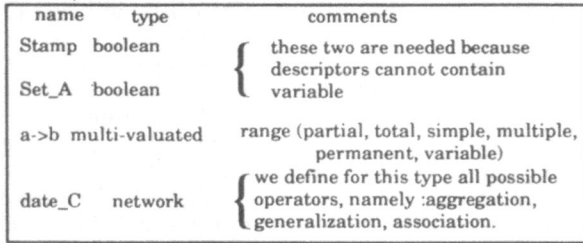

Figure 1 : some descriptors and their types

The axioms
They are rules which express logical relations between different descriptors. For instance, when the expert says that : "*when a relationship between two objects is permanent, there is no need to journalize*" we translate it to the following axiom :

    if a->b = permanent
then Stamp = false

Following the same way, we can express that "*when the permanency, for a relationship is stated for a to b, it is the same for b to a*" using the two following axioms:

if a->b = permanent   if b->a = variable
then b->a = permanent   then a->b = variable

The examples
The set of examples defines all the combinations of <descriptor,operator,value> which describe all possible and relevant cases, according to our IS design experts. To define the relevant set of examples for the structuration sub-task, we asked our experts to define all the meaningful relationships between two objects (in the real-world model) and their representation in the conceptual schema. Then, translating them in the CHARADE formalism, we obtained 41 examples. One of them is illustrated in figure 2 providing its two descriptions (the expert description and the CHARADE one).

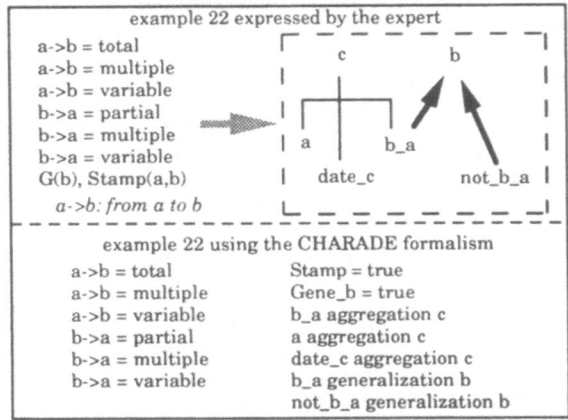

Figure 2 : an example used by the learning tool and its descriptions

To summarize, an example, for the structuration sub-task, is made by :

- a fully instantiated situation, i.e. the six cardinalities are stated;

- the relevant decisions; [note that they depend on the situation; some decisions do not have to be considered in some situations. For instance, let us suppose that an relationship between two objects A and B is total (from A to B), it has no sense to consider the generalization decision for A];

- a set of appropriate actions which defines how a designer map the initial situation, regarding the decisions, into the conceptual schema model.

The structuration constraints
Before starting the induction process (all descriptors, axioms and examples are entered), CHARADE allows to specify a hierarchy among descriptors. Using this functionality, we were able to express the advantages brought by the triplet's formalism. We classified the descriptors in three levels. The higher level contains the descriptors used in the description of a situation (a->b, b->a), the middle one contains those used to describe the decisions and the lower one those used by actions.

3.4.3 OUTPUTS
The induction process produces a set of 35 rules, in a

classic "if... then..." form. These rules summarize all the regularities found by CHARADE within the examples and allow us to state the 11 triplets listed below. Unfortunately, an elicitation had to be performed to reach the triplets. A lot of rules were similar: for equivalent decisions (set_a, set_a_b...) similar actions are stated (aggregation(a,c), aggregation(a_b,c)). We grouped rules with equivalent premise and action, i.e. when the differences, in the premise, imply the same differences in the action. Some rules also described some relationships between a subset of cardinalities and some decisions. Thus, we had to rearrange the generated rules. We finally recognized the eleven following triplets.

3.4.4 THE TRIPLETS
To be concise, the following notation is used :
p : partial, t : total, s : simple, m : multiple, p : permanent, v : variable.
A_B : refers to the instances of A which are related to B;
B_A : refers to the instances of B which are related to A;
Not_A_B : refers to the instances of A which are not related to B;
Not_B_A : refers to the instances of B which are not related to A;
C : refers to the relationship between an instance of A and an instance of B;
$date\_C$: is the time stamp property of the relationship;
set_A : refers to the set of A instances as a whole;
Note that the "_" (underscore) is used with the same meaning as it is in Prolog. It expresses that the value of this part of the situation is immaterial in the triplet.

List of triplets used in the structuration sub-task :
1 : <(p_,___), G(A),Generalization(A_B,Not_A_B,A)>
2 : <(___,p_), G(B),Generalization(B_A,Not_B_A,B)>
3 : <(_v,_v), Stamp(A,B) , Aggregation(date_C,C) >
4 : <(_m_,_m_), Ø , Aggregation(A,C) and Aggregation(B,C)>
5 : <(_s_,_s_), ¬Stamp(A,B) and Up(A), Aggregation(A,B)>
6 : <(_sv,_sv), Stamp(A,B), Aggregation(A,C) and Aggregation(B,C)>
7 : <(_s_,_m_), ¬Stamp(A,B) and ¬S(A), Aggregation(A,B)>
8 : <(_s_,_m_), ¬Stamp(A,B) and S(A), Set(A,B)>
9 : <(_sv,_mv), Stamp(A,B) and ¬S(A), Aggregation(A,C) and Aggregation(B,C)>
10 : <(_sv,_mv), Stamp(A,B) and S(A) and Stamp(S(A)), Set(A,set_A) and Aggregation(set_A,C) And Aggregation(C,B)>
11: <(_sv,_mv), Stamp(A,B) and S(A) and ¬Stamp(S(A)), Set(C,set_C) and Aggregation(A,C) and Aggregation(set_C,B)>

3.5 THE USE OF THE TRIPLETS
We illustrate, now, the use of the triplets on the example we have previously introduced, i.e. the binary relationship between person and car. Cardinalities are (partial, multiple, variable) from person to car and (total, simple, variable) from car to person .

```
repeat
    find a matching triplet using item 1
    repeat
        find the matching triplet using item 2
        repeat
            do the actions part in item 3
        until no more matching triplets
    until no more matching triplets
until no triplets match the situation
```

Figure 3: algorithm for processing a situation

The algorithm for processing a situation, using a set of triplets, is shown in figure 3. Note that the processing saturates the triplet space.

In our example, triplets 2, 3, 7, 8, 9, 10 and 11 (with A as car and B as person) can be applied. Thus, Generalization(person), Set(car), Stamp(Set(car)) and Stamp(person,car) have to be stated. Let's suppose that all these decisions are true except Stamp(Set(car)) - we consider as relevant to define the set of cars that a person owns and has owned during his life span . So, the part action of the triplets 2,3,11 has to be fired. Note that the result does not depend on the firing order.

Triplet 2 is the first to be fired. The designer has to tell what B_A and Not_B_A are. That means to label the two disjoint sets containing those A which are associated with B and those who are not . In our example, B_A refers to the person who owns cars and Not_B_A to the one who does not. As every requirement is stated, actions can be applied . This leads to the partial structure :
 Generalization(person_with_car,person)
 Generalization(person_without_car,person)

Then triplet 3 is fired. The designer must state the C label , which represents the label of the relationship between A and B. In our example, it is "owned_car". The same is done for $date\_C$ which is labelled by "date_of_purchase". The action part of this triplet leads to add to the previous partial structure :
 Aggregation(date_of_purchase, owned_car)

Finally, triplet 11 is fired . Every required label is known. This leads to a final structure by adding those marked with * :
* *Set(owned_car,set_of_owned_cars)*
* *Aggregation(set_of_owned_cars,person_with_car)*
* *Aggregation(car, owned_car)*
* *Set(set_of_owned_cars,owned_car)*
Aggregation(date_of_purchase, owned_car)
Generalization(person_with_car,person)
Generalization(person_without_car,person)

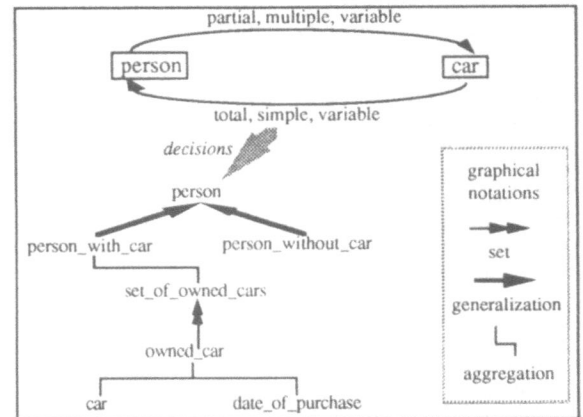

Figure 4 : The graphical representation of both initial and final result

The graphical representations of both the initial and the final result are showed in figure 4. The gap between these two expressions illustrates how the tool OICSI can progressively, in an automatic way, using decisions, infer a more and more sophisticated specification of objects of the future IS.

3.6 DISCUSSION

The experience with CHARADE was positive. CHARADE is:
- more efficient than human experts to find regularities in the design process,
- able to insure completeness and consistency of a set of triplets related to a global design situation,
- more effective in producing the results.
However, some problems remain:
- the pertinent use of the tool requires an important investment,
- the definition of examples requires a good expertise, on both the learning tool and IS design
- if significant examples are missing, the results will be incomplete.

4 CONCLUSION

The paper describes how some automatic learning techniques helped us in the construction of the knowledge base that serves as kernel of an expert design tool. Starting from a construction based upon the unformalized transposition of expert designers know-how, we reached the conclusion that we needed a more structured approach. Learning based on examples helped us to discover a general structure for all types of design knowledge (abstraction, validation, transformation, etc). This structure is the triplet < situation, decision, action >. This leads us to re-build entirely the OICSI knowledge base in a more homogeneous form. In addition, the triplet notion is used to structure the whole knowledge base into levels of abstraction; we mean that meta-rules, which fire sub-set of rules, in specific situation, are also structured according to the triplet frame.
Future work will be developed into two major directions :
- improving the use of the learning tool CHARADE and adapting it to our problem in order to minimize the gap between the generated rules and the triplets.
- extending the scope of OICSI. Until now, it covers the IS life cycle, from requirements to conceptual schemas. Existing solutions can be improved, specially to extend the reasoning capabilities of the tool.
In addition, we are studying the mapping of the conceptual schema elements onto both relational database schema and an object oriented database schema according to the O^2 DBMS [Bancilhon 88].

REFERENCES

[1] J.M. Smith and D.C.P. Smith : "Data Base Abstractions: Aggregation and Generalization", ACM TODS, Vol 2, No 2, 1977.

[2] M.L. Brodie, J. Mylopoulos and J.W. Schmidt (eds) : "On Conceptual Modelling", Springer-Verlag, New York Berlin Heidelberg Tokyo, 1986.

[3] M. Hammer and D. McLeod : "Database Description with SDM: A Semantic Model", ACM TODS, Vol 6, No 3, 1981.

[4] U. Schiel : "An Abstract Introduction to the Temporal Hierarchical Model (THM), 9th VLDB Conf., Florence, 1983.

[5] J. Mylopoulos, D. Yang and J.P. Fry : "A Language Facility for Designing Interactive Database-Intensive Applicatians", ACM TODS, Vol 5, No 2, 1980.

[6] C. Rolland and C. Richard : "The Remora Methodology for Information Systems Design and Management" in [22].

[7] M.R. Gustafson, T. Karlsson and J. A. Bubenko : "A Declarative Approach to Conceptual Information Modeling", in [22].

[8] A. Sernadas, C. Sernadas and H.D. Ehrich : "Object-Oriented Specifications Databases: An Algebraic Approach", Proc. of the 13th VLDB Conf.,1987.

[9] G. Arango, I. Baxter and P. Freeman : "A Framework for Incremental Progress, the Application of AI to Software Engineering",Research Report,Department of Information and Computer Science,Univ. of California, Irvine, USA, May 1987.

[10] C. Cauvet, C. Rolland and C. Proix : "Information Systems Design: an Expert System Approach" in Proc. of the Int. Conf. on Extending Database Technology,Venice,March 1988.

[11] C. Rolland, C. Cauvet and C. Proix : "A Design Methodology for Object-Oriented Database" in Proc of the International Conference on Management of Data, Hyderabed, India, 1989.

[12] E.A. Feigenbaum: "Expert Systems in the 1980s" in Bond (ed), State of the Art Report on Machine Intelligence, Maidenhead : Pergamon,Infotech, 1981.

[13] T.M. Mitchell , P.E. Utgoff and R. Banerji : "Learning by Experimentation : Aquiring and Refining Problem-solving Heuristics", Chapter in [21].

[14] J.G. Carbonell : " Learning by Analogy : Formulating and Generalizing Plan from Past Experience",Chapter in [21].

[15] R.S. Michalski, N. Hoof, R.E. Stepp: "INDUCE 2: A Program for Learning Structural Description From Examples", Technical Report, Department of Computer Science, University of Illinois, Urbana, September 1983.

[16] J.R. Quilan : "Learning Efficient Classification Procedure and thier Application to Chess End Games",in [21].

[17] P. Langley, G.L. Bradshaw, H.A. Simon : "Rediscovering Chemistry With the BACON System"in [21].

[18] F. Bancilhon et al : "The Design and Implementation of O^2, an Object Oriented Database System", Proc of 2 nd International Workshop on Object Oriented Database Systems, K. Dittrich (ed), Bad-Munster, FRG, September 1988.

[19] J.G. Ganascia : "AGAPE et CHARADE, deux mécanismes d'apprentissage symbolique appliqués à la construction de bases de connaissances", thèse d'état,Université Paris 11, Mai 1987.

[20] Y. Tabourier and D. Nanci : "The Occurences Structure Concept" in Entity-Relationship Approach to Information Modeling anf Analysis, P.P. Chen (ed), E-R Institute, 1981.

[21] Machine Learning: An Artificial Intelligence Appraoch, R.S. Michalski, J.G. Carbonell and T.M. Mitchell (eds), Tioga Publishing Compagny, 1983.

[22] T.W. Olle, H.G. Sol and A.A. Verryn-Stuart (eds) : "Information Systems Design Methodologies: A Comparative Review" North Holland (pub), 1982;

The rule language RL/1

Sieger van Denneheuvel & Peter van Emde Boas[*]
Department of Mathematics and Computer Science, University of Amsterdam
Plantage Muidergracht 24, 1018 TV Amsterdam

Abstract

In this paper we introduce and illustrate the rule language **RL/1**. This language was designed as an intermediate step towards implementing the more extensive rule language **RL** intended to become a tool for integrating logical and functional programming and constraint solving with relational databases into a relational framework.

1 Introduction

The language **RL/1** described in this paper is intended to be an illustrative prototype and an intermediate step towards implementing the declarative rule language **RL** (see [7], [8] and [9]). The language represents an effort to integrate logical and functional programming with constraint solving and relational databases. Towards the user, the free use of equational constraints together with the ease of logic programming constitutes a declarative and user friendly framework for expressing a knowledge base. On the other hand query processing should be executed with help of an existing relational database system; knowledge and queries expressed in **RL/1** are to be preprocessed by a constraint solver, and to be compiled into a database query language in order that large amounts of data can be processed effectively. In the current prototype **RL/1** we do not focus on recursion as is done in the NAIL! system [6] and the **LDL** logical database [5] but rather on the integration of a subsystem solving (numeric) constraints with a relational database system; the architecture for such an integrated system has been presented elsewhere [2].

This paper intends to illustrate the user perspective of our intended system by providing some illustrative syntax and semantics for the prototype language **RL/1** and some examples of **RL/1** modules. A compiler for the language **RL/1** has been implemented in a prototype system. All examples presented in this paper were processed successfully by this compiler in combination with a constraint solver and a relational database coded directly in **Prolog**. A version of the compiler producing standard **SQL** is currently being developped.

---

[*] also CWI-AP6, Amsterdam

2 Logical objects in RL/1

In the **RL** language design a program consists of modules, each module describing a system of relations. Relations are described using expressions originating from the worlds of relational databases, logic programming and equational logic. Atomic relations can be combined using operators originating from these worlds, providing maximal freedom and full conceptual transparence to the user. Syntactic categories are introduced to keep track of the origin and nature of the various relational expressions. A query in the **RL** language consists of a relational expression which is to be evaluated in the context of an existing program, the result of which is shown to the user.

The **RL/1** language was designed to become an implemented prototype for the full **RL** language, which eliminates some amount of syntactic and semantic complexity while preserving the main ideas of integrating relational databases with logic programming and algebraic constraint solving.

In **RL/1** relations, called logical objects, come in four types: tables, maps, clauses and functors. A property that logical objects share is that they have attributes and denote a relation. From the logical objects tables and maps are *extensional objects* in the sense that the relation denoted by the object is stored explicitly in the relational database. Clauses and functors on the other hand are *intensional objects* whose relations can be materialized by evaluation of the definition of the object.

A second distinction for logical objects is that they are either relational (undirected) or functional (directed). Tables and clauses are *relational objects* and therefore comparable to tables and views of a relational database. Maps and functors on the other hand are *functional objects*, where conceptually one attribute is considered to be dependent of the others (where dependence doesn't exclude that the function may be multivalued). They are invoked in scalar expressions, whereas relational objects are used in rule expressions. The difference between functional and relational objects therefore is primarily a matter of syntax; the first kind is used in functional notation and the latter is invoked as a predicate. For evaluation of rule expressions the SHOW query is available and for scalar expressions the PRINT query. The above properties are summarized in Figure 1.

logical-obj	relational-obj (rule-exp)	functional-obj (scalar-exp)
extensional-obj (EDB)	table	map
intensional-obj (IDB)	clause	functor

Figure 1: Classification of logical objects.

3 The data language DL

Each language in the **RL** family contains a sublanguage **DL** called the *data language* which is intended to reflect the nature of the underlying database system. In this sublanguage values and relations are expressed which are intended to be evaluated directly by this database. The operators from the data language **DL** need therefore to be supported by the corresponding relational database language. On the other hand the language **DL** should be rich enough so that features which are provided by the database can be accessed from the **RL/1** system directly.

Given the fact that in our **RL/1** prototype the database is implemented in **Prolog** an ad-hoc language **DL** has been designed for **RL/1**: This language **DL** has two scalar types, namely NUMBER with constants from category 'num-val' and STRING with constants from 'str-val'. The syntax of scalar expressions and constraints is defined in Figure 2 (predicates are not listed). In the grammar 'functor-inv' and 'map-inv' are invocations to functional objects which are described in the sections below. The grammar is incomplete with respect to the categories 'str-func' and 'num-func'. In our grammar notation below 'x-list' is a category consisting of a comma separated list of one or more 'x's. Similarly 'x-colonlist' is a category consisting of a colon separated list of 'x's.

4 The rule language RL/1

In contrast with the data language the rule language is independent of the underlying relational database. The rule language has a declarative nature providing various means to express what is known about a domain of interest. It does *not* specify how the knowledge is to be used for evaluation of a particular query. The compiler for the rule language will compile this query in the context of the **RL/1** program into a program which can be optimized and evaluated by the database.

As indicated before there are extensional and intensional objects. In **RL/1** an extensional object can be initialized by an explicit listing of its value when it is first created. This value consists of a set of tuples. A tuple is represented by the syntactic category 'row' and consists of a list of values. The category 'relation' stands for a set of tuples. A 'column' is a set of tuples consisting of one value

```
num-fac
  ::= [ - ] { num-val | functor-inv }
   |  [ - ] { map-inv | num-func }
   |  [ - ] { variable | ( num-exp ) }
num-term
  ::= num-fac | num-term { * | / } num-fac
num-exp
  ::= num-term | num-exp { + | - } num-term
str-term
  ::= functor-inv | map-inv
   |  str-func | variable | str-val
str-exp ::= str-term | str-exp CAT str-term
scalar-exp ::= num-exp | str-exp
```

```
comp ::= { = | < | > | ≤ | ≥ | ≠ }
constraint-fac
  ::= [ ¬ ] { predicate | ( constraint ) }
   |  [ ¬ ] num-exp comp num-exp
   |  [ ¬ ] str-exp comp str-exp
constraint-term
  ::= constraint-fac
   |  constraint-term ∧ constraint-fac
constraint
  ::= constraint-term
   |  constraint ∨ constraint-term
```

Figure 2: Scalar expressions and constraints.

```
val ::= num-val | str-val | NULL
row ::= "[" val-list "]"
column
  ::= "[" val-list "]" | val | EXTERN
relation
  ::= "[" row-list "]" | row | EXTERN
```

Figure 3: Object extensions.

only. All values in a column are of the same type (either NUMBER or STRING). In case a relation or a column has only one tuple or value a pair of square brackets may be omitted. Both relations and columns can be declared external indicating that the extension of the object is already stored in the database. The syntax of extensions is given in Figure 3.

In **RL/1** an intensional object is defined with use of the rule expressions in Figure 4 (the categories 'table-inv' and 'clause-inv' are described below). The declarative AND and OR operators used in rule expressions are more general than the corresponding operators join and union in relational algebra (see also [3]) since their operands are not restricted to be finite relations as is the case in relational algebra; instead these operands may be constraints or clause invocations that, by themselves, can represent intensional objects and thus potentially infinite relations. The question whether a rule expression as a whole represents a finite or infinite relation is in general undecidable;

```
rule-fac
  ::= [ NOT ] { clause-inv | table-inv}
  |   [ NOT ] { constraint | ( rule-exp ) }
rule-term
  ::= rule-fac | rule-term AND rule-fac
rule-exp
  ::= rule-term | rule-exp OR rule-term
```

Figure 4: Rule expressions.

```
assignment ::= attribute = scalar-exp
positional-arg ::= scalar-exp | #
attribute-arg ::= assignment | attribute
arguments
  ::= positional-arg-list
  |   "[" attribute-arg-list "]" | *
```

Figure 5: Grammar for arguments.

partial information about this question is obtained with help of a constraint solver (see [2]).

4.1 Object invocations

Both *positional notation* and *attribute notation* (Figure 5) can be used to supply arguments for invocations of extensional and intensional objects (cf. the language **LDL** in [5] where attribute notation can not be applied on intensional objects). This enables the user to use positional notation for objects with few attributes whereas for objects with many attributes, attribute notation may be preferred. In positional notation the positions of the invocation arguments should match the attribute positions in the object definition. In attribute notation the number of arguments supplied in an object invocation may be less than the number of attributes in the definition of the object. With each argument in the object invocation also the name of the substituted attribute is given.

In both notations substitutions of general scalar expressions for object attributes are allowed. In Figure 6 positional queries are shown next to equivalent queries in attribute notation ('t' is a relation with attributes <a,b,c> and one tuple [1,2,3]). In query (c), 1 was subtracted from the attribute value for attribute 'a' to yield the correct answer for 'x'. In (d) the substituted value 3 for attribute 'a' functioned as an implicit selection and the answer relation is empty.

4.2 Module definitions

In **RL/1** each identifier appearing in the module is declared either to denote a value of the types NUMBER or STRING, or to represent a logical object (see Figure 7). In the last case the type is determined by this logical object (see the section on domain objects below). In addition to a type declaration, a variable can have one or more property declarations. The property declarations listed in

	Positional	Attributive	Relation
(a)	t(*)	t([a,b,c])	<u>a b c</u> 1 2 3
(b)	t(x,y,#)	t([a=x,b=y])	<u>x y</u> 1 2
(c)	t(x+1,y,#)	t([a=x+1,b=y])	<u>x y</u> 0 2
(d)	t(3,y,#)	t([a=3,b=y])	<u>y</u> void

Figure 6: Positional and attribute notation.

```
domain-decl
  ::= NUMBER : variable-colonlist
  |   STRING : variable-colonlist
  |   logical-obj :  variable-colonlist
property-decl
  ::= KEY : variable-colonlist
  |   NOTNULL : variable-colonlist
  |   PRIVATE : logical-obj-colonlist
  |   USING : module-colonlist
decl ::= domain-decl | property-decl
module-decl
  ::= MODULE module ( decl-list )
```

Figure 7: Module declarations.

the grammar for variables are useful for the definition of tables and maps. The USING declaration allows logical objects defined in other modules to be imported, so that they become available in the declared module. For encapsulation the PRIVATE declaration applied on a logical object ensures that the object is only visible inside the module. Other modules are not allowed to use or modify private objects.

5 Tabular and map objects

Tabular and map objects are extensional objects corresponding to base tables of the underlying relational database. The TABLE command creates a table with attributes in the order of the given attribute list. The new object is initialized with a relation; in case the relation is omitted the object is left empty. A table (or map) can be declared as an external relation by using the EXTERN option so that the object may already be filled with a large number of tuples:

```
table-def ::=
  TABLE table ( attr-list ) [ = relation ]
table-inv ::= table ( arguments )
map-def ::=
  MAP map ( attr-list ) [ = relation ]
map-inv ::= map [ ( arguments ) ]
```

```
MODULE maps(NUMBER:x:v1:v2,STRING:y).
MAP map1(x,y) = [[1,red],
  [2,green],[2,yellow],[3,blue]].
MAP map2(x,y) = [1,red].
MAP map3(x,y) = EXTERN.
VECTOR v1 = 2.   VECTOR v2 = [2,3].
PRINT map1(1).  % yields red
PRINT map1(2).  % yields green,yellow
```

PRINT v1	PRINT 2*v2
2	4
	6
(a)	(b)

PRINT v2*v2	PRINT pow(v2,2)
4	4
6	9
9	
(c)	(d)

Figure 8: Map and vector objects.

```
MODULE arrays(NUMBER:i:j,
  NUMBER:a2:a3:a4, STRING:a1).
ARRAY a1(i) = [[1,red],
  [2,green],[2,yellow],[3,blue]].
ARRAY a2(i) = [[1,10],[2,20]].
ARRAY a3(i,j) = [[1,1,100],[1,2,200],
  [2,1,300],[2,2,400]].
ARRAY a4(i) = [[1,10],[33,20],[53,30]].
```

PRINT a1(2)	PRINT a2(i)+a3(1,i)
green	110
yellow	220
(a)	(b)

PRINT a2(i)+a3(i,1)	PRINT a2(i)+a3(i,j)
110	110
320	210
	320
	420
(c)	(d)

Figure 9: Arrays

The MAP command creates a map object with attributes in the order of the attribute list. The last attribute of the list is the return variable which yields the function value of the map. A map that is defined with n attributes is called in a map invocation with $n - 1$ arguments. Figure 8 lists some examples of maps (the PRINT query evaluates scalar expressions). Both tabular and map objects are defined with a *single* definition.

5.1 Vectors and arrays

Vectors are maps consisting of one column only; moreover this column has no attribute name. The syntax is as follows:

```
VECTOR map [ = column ]
```

The vector name is declared in the module declaration together with the type of the vector (NUMBER or STRING). A vector is internally compiled as a map with one attribute which serves as the return variable. Vectors can be used in the same way as variables in programming languages. Consider the definitions of vectors in Figure 8. The PRINT query (a) lists the value of vector v1. In (b) all values of v2 are multiplied by two. In query (c) v2 is multiplied by itself, yielding three different values (duplicate values are removed from the answer relation). Note that the answer relation in (c) is different from that of (d) because v2 itself has more than one value.

In analogy to vectors arrays are maps where the last attribute name is omitted.

```
ARRAY map ( attr-list ) [ = relation ]
```

The type of the return value of the array is determined by the type listed for this array in the module declaration. An array with n attributes is internally compiled as a map with $n + 1$ attributes. The extra attribute is the return variable of the map. Some examples are given in Figure 9. The query (a) lists two return values for the index 2. In (b) and (c) the index i occurring in the invocation of a2 and a3 limits the number of tuples in the answer relation. Query (d) lists four tuples because now all indexes are variables. Choosing all index variables different in (d) would give the full cartesian product (eight tuples).

An array object may have a non-dense index (i.e. not for all index values in the index range the array object needs to have a return value) as illustrated in the object a4. In this respect array objects behave like tables in the 'B' language (see [4]). Also the type of an array index is not restricted to be numeric (as in the above examples) but string indexes are also allowed.

6 Clausal objects

Clausal objects are defined with one or more clause rules:

```
clause-rule
  ::= CLAUSE clause [ ( attr-list ) ]
        WHEN rule-exp
  |   CLAUSE clause ( * ) WHEN rule-exp
  |   CLAUSE clause ( / ) WHEN rule-exp
clause-inv ::= clause [ ( arguments ) ]
```

In the first defining form the attribute may be omitted when empty; consequently the constants TRUE and

```
CLAUSE p(x) WHEN x=1.   CLAUSE p(x) WHEN
CLAUSE p(x) WHEN x=2.   x=1 OR x=2 OR x=3.
CLAUSE p(x) WHEN x=3.
          (a)                    (b)
```

Figure 10: Extending a clausal object in a module.

FALSE can be defined as clausal objects. In the second (short) defining form, the attributes of the new clausal object are all the variables occurring in the rule expression. Since no specific order of attributes is enforced by the '(*)' notation, clauses defined by the second form can only be accessed in attribute notation. The third defining form can be used if a clausal object is defined by multiple clause rules. In this case the clause rule has the same attributes as the rule that was previously compiled for the object and the attributes need not be restated. Specifying a clausal object with several clause rules expresses *disjunction* between the clause rules. Using the OR operator, the definitions (a) and (b) in Figure 10 for 'p' are equivalent.

The definition of a clausal (or functor) object may span *several* modules. Suppose a clause is defined by clause rules in both module A and module B. If module A is imported in module B, the definition of the object is the disjunction of the clause rules in A and the rules in B.

6.1   Domain objects

In creating modules it is sometimes useful to introduce a subtype by restricting the domain of a variable. In **RL/1** this is achieved by defining a domain object representing the restrictions for the domain. A domain object is a logical object which has only one attribute. For each occurrence of a variable in the rule expression, an invocation of such a domain object can be used to restrict the domain of the variable. However, in order to relief the user from repeatedly specifying domain restrictions in a rule expression, it is allowed to immediately declare the domain restrictions for a variable in the module declaration (see the section on module declarations above). For each restricted variable its domain object is compiled automatically into the rule expression. The type of the variable (NUMBER or STRING) is inferred from the domain of the (only) attribute in the domain object. Vectors are appropriate to serve as a domain object since they are created as extensional objects with only one attribute.

As an example consider the declaration of the domains 'sizes' and 'colors' in Figure 11. Due to the domain specification the compiler adds domain restrictions to the rule expression 'prod(name,size,color)' in the definition of the clause 'p' so that the original clause is replaced by the following:

```
MODULE domains(STRING:x:y).
CLAUSE sizes(x) WHEN
  x='small' ∨ x='medium' ∨ x='large'.
CLAUSE colors(x) WHEN
  x='red' ∨ x='green'.
MODULE products(USING:domains,
  STRING:name, sizes:size, colors:color).
TABLE prod(name,size,color).
CLAUSE p(name,size,color) WHEN prod(*).
```

Figure 11: Domain Objects.

```
CLAUSE p(name,size,color) WHEN
  prod(name,size,color)
AND sizes(size) AND colors(color).
```

7   Functor objects

Functors add new functions to the set of standard functions already available in the system. Functor objects are defined with use of rule expressions and as a consequence they may involve invocations to other logical objects:

```
functor-rule
  ::= FUNCTOR functor ( attr-list )
          WHEN rule-exp
  |    FUNCTOR functor ( * , variable )
          WHEN rule-exp
  |    FUNCTOR functor ( / ) WHEN rule-exp
functor-inv ::= functor [ ( arguments ) ]
```

In the first defining form the last attribute of the attribute list is the return variable of the functor and the other attributes represent the arguments of the functor. Functor definitions that have only one attribute (i.e. the return variable) are allowed. In the second (short) defining form, 'variable' is the return variable of the functor. All variables occurring in the rule expression, besides the return variable, become attributes of the newly defined functor. The third defining form can be used in case a functor object is defined by several functor rules or the definition spans more than one module. As for clauses the first defining form can also be used for extending a functor object. Some examples are given in Figure 12.

The full expressiveness of rule expressions is available for functors also, so functors are not restricted to yield only one function value for an assignment of argument values. For example a functor yielding a value x for given values of a, b and c such that $a * x^2 + b * x + c = 0$ can be defined as in Figure 12. The OR operator in the functor definition results in two x values for each assignment of values to variables a,b and c, since the conditions $d \geq 0$ and $d > 0$ are not exclusive:

```
MODULE functors(NUMBER:a:b:c:d:e:x:y:z).
FUNCTOR int(x,y) WHEN y=integer(x).
FUNCTOR sum(x,y,z) WHEN z=x+y.
FUNCTOR abs(x,y) WHEN
  y=x AND x≥0 OR y=-x AND x<0.
FUNCTOR pi(x) WHEN x=3.141.
SHOW x=sum(sum(1,2),3). % yields 6
SHOW x=abs(-10). % yields 10
SHOW x=pi+5. % yields 8.141
TABLE data(a,b,c)= [[1,8,7],[1,4,0]].
FUNCTOR quad(a,b,c,x) WHEN x=(-b+e)/(2*a)
AND d=b*b-4*a*c AND
  ( e=sqrt(d) AND d≥0
    OR e=-sqrt(d) AND d>0 ).
```

Figure 12: Functor objects.

```
MODULE convs(NUMBER:x1:y1:x2:y2,
  NUMBER:xc:yc:wc:hc, STRING:name).
TABLE rectdata(name,x1,y1,x2,y2)=
  [[ra,0,0,4,4],[rb,2,2,7,7],
  [rc,6,3,9,6]].
CLAUSE conv(x1,y1,x2,y2,xc,yc,wc,hc)
  WHEN x1=xc-wc AND y1=yc-hc
  AND x2=xc+wc AND y2=yc+hc.
```

Figure 13: A conversion rule.

```
SHOW data(a,b,c) AND x=quad(a,b,c)
```

x	a	b	c
0	1	4	0
-1	1	8	7
-4	1	4	0
-7	1	8	7

8 Examples

Logical objects are declarative representations of knowledge; therefore it is not known beforehand how the attributes of an object are invoked. A single logical object may in fact be used in many different ways.

For instance suppose rectangles are stored in a table with four numeric attributes x1,y1,x2,y2, the pair (x1,y1) denoting the origin and (x2,y2) denoting the corner. A user might want a list of these rectangles in an alternative representation system with center points (xc,yc) and size pairs (wc,hc) giving the distance between the center and the origin. The alternative center representation for rectangles could then be calculated with use of the clausal conversion rule given in Figure 13.

The conversion of point representation ((x1,y1), (x2,y2)) to center representation ((xc,yc), (wc,hc)) re-

quires solving the constraints x1=xc-wc, y1=yc-hc, x2=xc+wc and y2=yc+hc for the variables xc, yc, wc and hc. The constraint solver takes care of the solving process:

```
SHOW rectdata(#,x1,y1,x2,y2)
  AND conv(x1,y1,x2,y2,xc,yc,wc,hc)
```

x1	y1	x2	y2	xc	yc	wc	hc
0	0	4	4	2	2	2	2
2	2	7	7	4.5	4.5	2.5	2.5
6	3	9	6	7.5	4.5	1.5	1.5

Another user might want to know for a center point (7.5,4.5) and a size pair (1.5,1.5) the associated rectangle in origin and corner representation. For this query the same clause can be used since the rule states declaratively what is known to be true about the representation systems:

```
SHOW conv(x1,y1,x2,y2,7.5,4.5,1.5,1.5)
```

x1	y1	x2	y2
6	3	9	6

A second example: one of the most spectacular events in astronomy is the passage of a comet. The orbit of a comet is usually available to observing astronomers in the form of tables listing the right ascension (RA for short) and the declination. These two dimensions together constitute the location of the comet in the sky. A problem with this tabular description of orbits is that for most comets the RA and declination are not given for each day during the period of visibility. It is up to the astronomer to compute the intermediate right ascensions and declinations for the missing days. What makes the problem nasty is that the RA's are given in a h-m-s notation and consequently need to be converted to seconds. After computation of the interval values has finished the seconds are converted back to h-m-s notation so that the telescope can be directed.

In the case of the comet Austin, which was visible in May 1990 in Holland, a table was available with positions given for each five days. The module in Figure 14 lists an application to compute the missing days. A clausal object 'interval' creates from the table 'cometdata' a new table with an RA and associated next RA in one tuple. The table 'intervaldays' is used to vary over the five days of the interval. Finally the 'ra' object lists the requested RA in h-m-s notation together with the number of the observation day:

```
list ra
```

d	h	m	s
0	1	21	2
1	1	16	27
2	1	11	52
⋮	⋮	⋮	⋮
14	0	12	25

An unexpected application is the use of multivalued functors to represent type hierarchies. If types are interpreted as subsets of a value domain, it is quite natural

```
module stars(number:i:t:t1:t2:t3:h:h1:h2:
  h3:m:m1:m2:m3:s:s1:s2:s3:d:d1:iday).
table cometdata(i,h,m,s)= [[0,1,21,2],
  [1,0,58,8],[2,0,34,1],[3,0,7,2]].
table intervaldays(d)=[[0],[1],[2],[3],[4]].
clause interval(i,h1,m1,s1,h2,m2,s2)
  when cometdata(i,h1,m1,s1)
  and cometdata(i+1,h2,m2,s2).
functor time(h,m,s,t) when t=s+60*m+3600*h.
clause hms(t,h,m,s) when s=mod(floor(t),60)
  and m=mod(floor(t/60),60)
  and h=mod(floor(t/3600),24).
clause calcra(h1,m1,s1,h2,m2,s2,d,d1,h,m,s)
  when t1=time(h1,m1,s1)
  and t2=time(h2,m2,s2)
  and t3=t1-((t1-t2)*d1)/d
  and hms(t3,h,m,s).
clause ra(d,h,m,s) when
  d=i*5+iday and interval(*)
  and calcra(h1,m1,s1,h2,m2,s2,5,iday,h,m,s)
  and intervaldays(iday).
```

Figure 14: Interpolation of RA values.

```
MODULE types(STRING:x:herbivore:
  carnivore:bird:fish:invertebrate).
VECTOR herbivore= [elephant,kangaroo].
VECTOR carnivore= [dog,bat].
VECTOR bird= [duck,eagle,ostrich].
VECTOR fish= [shark,dogfish,plaice].
VECTOR invertebrate= [hydra,sponge].
FUNCTOR mammal(x) WHEN
  x=carnivore OR x=herbivore.
FUNCTOR vertebrate(x) WHEN
  x=mammal OR x=bird OR x=fish.
FUNCTOR animal(x) WHEN
  x=vertebrate OR x=invertebrate.
MODULE animals(USING:types, STRING:x).
CLAUSE warm_blooded(x) WHEN x=mammal.
CLAUSE warm_blooded(x) WHEN x=bird.
CLAUSE cold_blooded(x) WHEN x=fish.
```

Figure 15: Functional objects in a type hierarchy.

to establish a partial ordering among types based on set inclusion: this is the key idea underlying type hierarchies (see [1]). As a consequence a type t is a subtype of another type u when all the values of t are also values of u. Figure 15 declares a (rather incomplete) type hierarchy of animals with use of vectors and functors as domain objects.

The functional objects bird and fish represent sets of animals and are subtypes of vertebrate. Vertebrate itself is a subtype of animal. Query (a) below shows that indeed a duck is warm blooded. The same question for birds in (b) is answered positively because there are warm blooded birds.

```
SHOW                 SHOW
warm_blooded('duck') warm_blooded(bird)
yes                  yes
        (a)                  (b)
```

Since functional domain objects are allowed at the same locations as normal constants the question whether there are animals that are both a mammal and a bird can be stated as in (a) below. The same question for mammals and carnivores is represented as in (b):

```
SHOW mammal=bird  SHOW mammal=carnivore
no                yes
        (a)                  (b)
```

References

[1] Albano, A., Giannotti, F., Orsini,R., Pedreschi,D., *The Type System of Galileo*, Data Types and Persistence, (Eds. Atkinson, Buneman, Morrison), Springer-Verlag 1988, 102-119.

[2] van Denneheuvel, S. & van Emde Boas, P., *Constraint solving for databases*, Proc. of NAIC **1**, 1988

[3] Hansen, M.R., Hansen, B.S., Lucas, P. & van Emde Boas, P., *Integrating Relational Databases and Constraint Languages*, in Comput. Lang. Vol. **14**, No. 2, 63-82, 1989.

[4] Meertens, L., *Draft proposal for the B programming language*, MC Series, printed at the Mathematical Center, Amsterdam, 1981

[5] Naqvi, S. & Tsur, S., *A Logical Language for Data and Knowledge bases*, Computer Science Press, 1989.

[6] Ullman, J.D., *Principles of Data and Knowledge - Base Systems*, Volume II: The New Technologies, Computer Science Press, 1989.

[7] van Emde Boas, P., *RL, a Language for Enhanced Rule Bases Database Processing*, Working Document, Rep IBM Research, RJ 4869 (51299)

[8] van Emde Boas, P., *A semantical model for the integration and modularization of rules*, Proceedings MFCS 12, Bratislava, August 1986, Springer Lecture Notes in Computer Science **233** (1986), 78-92

[9] van Emde Boas, H. & van Emde Boas, P., *Storing and Evaluating Horn-Clause Rules in a Relational Database*, IBM J. Res. Develop. **30** (1), (1986), 80-92

Design and Implementation of Substantive Applications in Criminal Law: Beyond A Court Management Perspective

David E. Woodin, Esq.

Associate Law Assistant, Trial Part, Greene County Court
New York State Unified Court System
Greene County Courthouse, Catskill, New York 12414

This paper describes the experience of one New York court in extending its uses of microcomputers beyond the records management functions initially contemplated, to encompass substantive applications serving the judiciary in an advisory role. The applications described include a rule-based expert system in case disposition, and a system for the detection of ethical conflicts in the selection of assigned counsel. These substantive applications are seen to significantly extend the utility of the standard database functions typically encountered.

Microcomputers have been employed in the management of the court system of the State of New York for several years. As envisioned by the N.Y.S. Office of Court Administration (OCA), their primary functions have been to assist with indexing, scheduling, docketing, inquiry, and statistical reporting with respect to caseload processing.[1] As such, their users have been primarily non-judicial and clerical personnel. Impact upon judges has been indirect, through the reports generated in response to demand for case status information. The question has been raised whether there is not a more immediate role for the computer as a direct support to judicial decisionmaking. Several prototype systems have in fact been developed in other jurisdictions with respect to various judicial tasks.[2] The goal of the current work is to amplify the ability of existing database applications to support judicial functions, through the application of intelligent tools loosely coupled to existing database systems.[3] The benefits of this approach are modularity of design, and achievement of practical implementations. Its drawbacks include redundancy in information representation. The result, hopefully, will be the development of integrated systems able to directly support the judiciary as well as to perform ministerial recordkeeping tasks. Two examples are presented: a fully implemented system dealing with legal issues of case disposition, and a prototype system for the detection of ethical conflicts in the assignment of counsel in criminal cases.

In order to pursue the application of the computer as a tool to assist judges and law clerks in the substantive work of the courts, it is necessary first to consider the proper role of the computer in the judicial process. The process of "what judges do" when they decide a case in fact involves multiple processes. At present only a few of these processes are sufficiently well understood for an analytic model to be attempted. Roughly stated, they comprise those processes by which it is possible to solve "easy", or deductive cases.[4] Other processes involving intangible factors such as the exercise of moral judgment, may forever remain computationally intractable.[5]

Even restricting the analysis to so-called "easy" cases, there is considerable reason to hope for the successful application of substantive systems. A judge considering a case must be familiar with a wide range of rules and the conditions of their invocation. He must be alert to facts elicited from the parties which may trigger little used rules. He should consider the effect on the legal outcome of every relevant legal fact in the case being established or not established. He must know the effect of recent precedent on existing doctrines. The increasing number of statutes and regulations, the increasing factual complexity of litigation, and the burgeoning volume of case law all combine to make these formidable tasks indeed. It appears, therefore, that there is room for substantive systems in law which will solve "easy" cases and, by elimination, identify "hard" ones.[6] Because of the potential existence of intangible factors entering into every judicial decision, such systems should be seen always not as a substitute for the judge, but as a technical advisor to him or her. This premise underlies all phases of the present work.

The disposition of criminal cases in New York State typically involves tension between judicial or prosecutorial discretion and legislative regulation.[7] This tension is encountered at every stage of the proceedings, and is especially felt in the areas of sentencing[8], plea bargaining[9], consideration of lesser included offenses[10], initial charge[11] and indictment.[12]

The serious consequences[13] which may result from the failure to observe these limitations on discretion raise two challenges for the courts. The first is to recognize the circumstances in a given case which may invoke application of the various limiting statutes. The second is to accurately implement a statute whose application has been triggered by the facts of a given case. The need for powerful tools to assist judges in meeting these challenges is manifest. The solution proposed entails consultation of an expert system which is adept at recognizing the existence of the above issues, and suggesting routes to their resolution. Such a system should attempt to incorporate both the knowledge contained in the original written sources, and the experience of persons who have thoroughly studied the domain and who frequently deal with it. The system should be designed so as to be easily integrated into the existing database system of the court. Such a system dealing with the above issues has been constructed, and is described below.

The Expert System: An Overview

The expert system employed is an interactive MS-DOS PC-based substantive system, written in Turbo Prolog 2.0.[14] The program is compiled and is distributed commercially as a stand-alone product under the product name *Gunga Clerk*.[15]

When consulted independently of the database system, a typical work session commences with selection of a particular offense by section number from a menu displaying all offenses loaded into memory. The title of the offense, its classification, and a summary of its elements are displayed for confirmation. Returning to the main menu one may elect to investigate sentencing options, plea bargains, or lesser included offenses with respect to the selected offense. Input is requested from the user during the course of a consultation through pop-up "Yes/No" menus. Selections are made by highlighting the chosen item and pressing "Enter." The response selected from the menu is incorporated into the output text. Output text may be echoed to the printer or to a disk file for later editing using a word processing program. The use of a disk file for storage of results is a key aspect of the program's integration into the overall database system, as will be seen.

The program prepares a list of all legal sentencing alternatives, together with detailed statutory authority for each potential sentence, by first generating every possible potential sentence, and then testing it against conditions for legality as expressed in the program's rules and accumulated facts input by the user. The program requests information concerning the defendant and the crime, as needed, to calculate the range of available sentences. The answers to questions posed by the program are incorporated into the report being generated, to provide a record of the consultation. Varying the responses to the questions posed, one observes the effect upon the available sentencing options.

With respect to plea bargains, the program first determines what, if any, statutory restrictions apply to the offense selected for analysis. Input from the user is requested as needed by the rule being executed. The program then displays the controlling statutory restriction, giving a detailed citation to its location, and explains why the restriction applies based on the information provided. Finally, it prepares a list of suggested offenses which satisfy the statutory plea bargaining conditions and which are potential lesser included offenses of the selected offense for purposes of plea. The user may select an offense from this list and immediately return to the sentencing module to learn the potential benefits of a plea of guilty to the lesser offense.

The program can generate two reports with respect to lesser included offenses. The first contains a list of offenses which are arguably potential lesser included offenses of the selected offense. A lesser offense may be added to this list under New York law when it is theoretically impossible, under any circumstances, to commit the selected offense without by the same conduct committing the lesser offense. The legal analysis is performed by comparing the elements of the two offenses, and by applying rules of legal inference between elements. The program collects offenses whose elements are all elements of the selected offense, or whose elements are legally implied by the elements of the selected offense. Where a conclusion depends upon such a chain of legal inferences, the chain of reasoning leading to the conclusion is explicitly displayed, along with supporting authority for each step drawn from statute and case law.

The second report contains a list of offenses which arguably are not lesser included offenses of the selected offense, regardless of their apparent similarity under the facts of a given case. An offense is added to this list when there is existing legal authority to the effect that the lesser offense is not a potential lesser included offense of the selected offense, because it fails the "impossibility" test mentioned above. This "non-included" list is obtained by extending the preceding method to include chains of reasoning containing links which have been held by case law to be invalid or false inferences. The list is then restricted to contain only offenses derived from the selected offense by a process of reasoning which includes one or more of these legally invalid inferences. The report produces the list of these offenses, along with the argument by which each was derived. The steps in the argument are explained and supported step by step as above, with the false or invalid links in the argument explicitly identified.

The final major feature of the program is a data-driven, forward-chaining process, in contrast to the diagnostic, backward-chaining process of the previous sections. Instead of selecting an offense by its Penal Law citation and analyzing it, the user may compare the facts of his case to an alphabetically sorted list of elements of offenses and highlight any group of these elements. The program will combine the elements selected, (and any other elements legally implied by those selected) building as many offenses as possible from the given set. This function assists in comparing the elements of the offense charged against the proof actually produced before the grand jury or at trial.

The Database System

The case records of the court are maintained in a relational database managed by a compiled Clipper[16] program. Separate files are maintained for case records, attorneys, diary information, counts of each indictment, and offenses. The database system is used for all of the case management tasks initially alluded to, including preparation of calendars and reports. The link from the database system to the expert system is accomplished by a simple modification to each program which allows one or more items of information, such as the citation of the offense under investigation and the type of analysis requested, to be passed as command line parameters. The code in the database program to call the expert system with parameters, and the extra code added to the system to allow it to receive, parse and process the parameters is relatively simple. The system need only recognize which of its data files must be loaded into memory, based on the citation of the offense being considered and the function being requested, and activate its various modules accordingly.

The return of information to the database is equally simple. The results of a consultation produced by a parameterized call to the expert system are automatically echoed to a standard log file, which upon return to the database program is read and appended to a text memo file attached to the current case record. These memo records in turn are utilized by the database system in preparing a summary report of each case upon demand for insertion in the court file, for review by the judge.

Selected Computational and Design Issues: A Grammar for the Generation of Sentencing Alternatives

A frequently documented application of Prolog is its use to implement parsers or generators of a given language. The structure of well-formed expressions in the target language is quite easily represented by a series of Prolog rules, which specify the ways in which the basic units of the language may be combined into complex phrases. Contemporary work illustrates the power of this technique applied to the generation of so-called "grammars of law."[17] Examination of the structure of New York sentencing law suggests a similar approach, the target "language" to be parsed being the taxonomy of authorized sentences. Article 60 of the New York Penal Law establishes a comprehensive sentencing scheme, organized hierarchically by type of sentence (see **Figure 1**). A simplified outline of the sentencing generator syntax is shown in **Figure 2**. Its associated Turbo Prolog code is shown in **Listing 1**.

According to New York law, a sentence (*S*) may be either revocable (*REV*) or irrevocable (*IRREV*). A revocable sentence may be simple (*SIMPREV*) or compound (*COMPREV*). A compound revocable sentence consists of a fine plus a simple revocable sentence (*fine + SIMPREV*), and so on, until one reaches the "atomic" terms of the sentence referring to fines (*fine*), probation (*p*), indeterminate imprisonment (*ind*), etc. This basic model generates in every case a list of all constructible sentences, without regard to their legality. The next step is to add predicates such as the *ok(X,Y)* predicate in **Listing 1** at appropriate points in the program to test and filter the output of the sentence generator against the legal restrictions, and to calculate various specific parameters of the sentence being generated, such as minimum and maximum periods of incarceration, probation, etc. The code in **Listing 1** depicts the general structure of the program, omitting clauses for *ok(X,Y)* and other filtering predicates.

```
PL 60.01. Authorized dispositions; generally.

1. Applicability. Except as otherwise specified, ... the court must impose
a sentence prescribed by this section.

2. Revocable dispositions.
(a) The court may impose a revocable sentence as herein specified:
        (i) the court, ... may sentence a person to a period of probation
or to a period of conditional discharge ...; or
        (ii) the court ... may sentence a person to a term of intermittent
imprisonment....
(b) • • •
(c) In any case where the court imposes a sentence of probation,
conditional discharge, or a sentence of intermittent imprisonment, it may
also impose a fine authorized by article eighty.
(d) In any case where the court imposes a sentence of imprisonment not
in excess of sixty days, for a misdemeanor or not in excess of six months
for a felony or in the case of a sentence of intermittent imprisonment not
in excess of four months, it may also impose a sentence of probation or
conditional discharge ....

3. Other dispositions. When a person is not sentenced as specified in
subdivision two,... the sentence of the court must be as follows:
(a) A term of imprisonment...; or
(b) A fine ...; or
(c) Both imprisonment and a fine; or
(d) Where authorized,... unconditional discharge....
```

Figure 1.

```
Adult Sentencing Parameters – BNF Syntax For Rewrite Rules

S ::= REV | IRREV
REV ::= SIMPREV | COMPREV
    COMPREV ::= fine + SIMPREV
    SIMPREV ::= PUREREV | SPLITREV
        PUREREV ::= int | REVLIB
        SPLITREV ::= def + REVLIB | int + REVLIB
            REVLIB ::= cd | p
IRREV ::= ud | fine | IMP | fine + IMP
    IMP ::= def | ind

                    Key to Terms

S–sentence.  REV–revocable sentence.  IRREV–irrevocable sentence.
SIMPREV–simple revocable sentence. COMPREV–compound revocable
sentence. PUREREV–pure revocable sentence. SPLITREV–split sentence.
REVLIB–sentence of revocable liberty. IMP–sentence of imprisonment.
fine–a fine.  int–intermittent imprisonment.  def–definite sentence of
imprisonment. cd–conditional discharge. p–probation. ud–unconditional
discharge. ind–indefinite term of imprisonment.
```

Figure 2.

```
sentence(S,R) :- rev(S,R).
sentence(S,R) :- irrev(S,R).

rev(S,R)       :- simprev(S,R).
rev(S,R)       :- comprev(S,R1),
                  append(["PL 60.01(2)(c)"],R1,R).

comprev(S,R) :- simprev(S1,R1),
                concat(S1,"plus",S2),
                fine(S3,R2),concat(S2,S3,S),append(R1,R2,R).

simprev(S,R) :- purerev(S,R).
simprev(S,R) :- ok(splitrev,[]),splitrev(S,R1),
                append(["PL 60.01(2)(d)"],R1,R).

purerev(S,R) :- ok(intermittent,R1),
                intermittent(S,R2),append(R1,R2,R).
purerev(S,R) :- revlib(S,R).

splitrev(S,R) :- charge_is_a(felony),ok(definite,R0),
                 revlib(S1,R1),append(R0,R1,R),
         concat("Definite sentence up to 6 months plus ",S1,S).
splitrev(S,R) :- charge_is_a(misdemeanor),not(test(vtl1)),
                 revlib(S1,R),
         concat("Definite sentence up to 60 days plus ",S1,S).

revlib(S,R)    :- ok(cd,R1),cd(S,R2),append(R1,R2,R).
revlib(S,R)    :- ok(probation,R1),
                  probation(S,R2),append(R1,R2,R).

irrev(S,R)     :- ok(ud,R1),ud(S,R2),append(R1,R2,R).
irrev(S,R)     :- ok(fine,R1),fine(S,R2),append(R1,R2,R).
irrev(S,R)     :- imprisonment(S,R1),
                  append(["PL 60.01(3)(a)"],R1,R).
irrev(S,R)     :- imprisonment(S1,R1),fine(S3,R3),
                  concat(S1," plus ",S2),concat(S2,S3,S),
                  append(R1,["PL60.01(3)(c)"],R2),
                  append(R2,R3,R).
```

Listing 1.

Detection of Lesser Included Offenses: A Problem in Searching Directed Graphs for Shortest Acyclic Paths

The problem of determining lesser and non-lesser included offenses involves the problem of finding the shortest acyclic path between two nodes in a directed graph. A directed graph may be defined as a set of nodes connected by links, each of which may be traversed in one direction only. A graph is represented visually as a collection of points, representing the nodes, connected by arrows, representing the links. (See Figure 3(A).) A graph may be represented in Prolog by a collection of statements of the form,

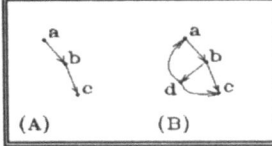

Figure 3.

imp(a,b). imp(b,c). imp(b,d). imp(d,c). imp(d,a).

where each such statement is to be interpreted as, "Node a implies node b", etc.

Such a structure is useful in the analysis of various legal domains, if the nodes are taken to represent atomic legal concepts. A directed link is drawn between two nodes whenever the legal relationship between their associated legal concepts is such that the presence of one necessarily implies the other. If a node, a, is considered to represent the legal element, "dwelling", the node b represents "building", and another node, c, represents "premises", the problems are (1) to recognize there is a connecting path between them, (a-b-c, representing *dwelling-->building-->premises*) (2) to construct or retrieve the path, (3) to select the shortest such path (rejecting paths such as *a-b-d-c*), (4) to avoid cyclic paths (*a-b-d-a-b-c, a-b-d-a-b-d-a-b-c*, etc.) (See Figure 3(B).)

The problems of recognizing and constructing a path are easily solved in Prolog. The additional condition of avoiding cycles in the graph adds only slight complications. A code fragment that constructs an acyclic path from any start node to any given goal node in a general graph connecting legal concepts is included in **Listing 2**, which is also an outline of the code used to compute lesser included offenses.

In the predicate *path(A,Z,P)*, *P* is a list of links between nodes each having the structure *l(Node1,Node2,Truthvalue,Rationale)*. Nodes such as *Node1, Node2* exist as arguments within the database of clauses *imp(Node1,Node2,Truthvalue,Rationale)*. The argument *Truthvalue* is here always assumed to be equal to the string "*yes*", indicating a positive implication between nodes. The extension to negative implications is given below. The argument *Rationale* is included to allow collection of explanatory text during path construction.

The predicate *gpath(G,E,P)* constructs through backtracking all paths from a given list or set of nodes, *G*, to a given node, *E*. A set of nodes, *G*, is said to "imply" a node, *E* along path *R* (*set_implies(G,E,R)*) if *R* exists and is the shortest of all paths from a node within *G* to *E*. The highest level predicate, *set_implies_set(G,L,R)*, succeeds if every element of *L* is "implied" by the set *G*, with *R* being the list of shortest paths from elements of *G* to each element of *L*. Offenses are stored in the structure (abbreviated here as) *off(section(Cite),Class,Elements)*. An offense cited as *section(L)* is a lesser included offense of an offense cited as *section(G)* if its classification *CL* is lesser in grade than that (*CG*) of *section(G)*, and if every member of the list *EL* of its elements is obtainable from the list *EG* of elements of *section(G)* according to the relation *set_implies_set(EG,EL,PL)*. An explanation for the result may be generated by examining the list of explanatory texts gathered in *PL*.

Nothing which has been said thus far deals with the general problem of finding the shortest path between two nodes. Algorithms for this purpose exist[18]; however, for this version of the program a naive brute-force method has been followed, namely that of simply computing all possible paths, and then selecting the shortest one. As the graph increases in complexity due to updates and upgrades to the program, it is likely that this method will have to be abandoned, to avoid combinatorial explosion in the number of possible paths which must be examined.

The above concept may be easily extended, however, to include "negative" inferences, by utilizing the *Truthvalue* argument mentioned above. Each indicated link between nodes is now labeled according to whether it is true or false. (A link is considered "false" in this sense if there is affirmative legal authority to the effect that the implication between the given nodes does not follow.) The predicate *i_path(A,Z,P)* succeeds if there is a path *P* from node *A* to node

```
/* Lesser Included Offenses */

lio(section(L),section(G),R) :-
    off(section(G),CG,EG),!,
    off(section(L),CL,EL),...,
    classorder(CL,CG),
    set_implies_set(EG,EL,PL),....

/* Affirmative Set Predicates */

set_implies_set(_,[],[]).
set_implies_set
    (G,[H|T],[RH|RT]):-
    set_implies(G,H,RH),!,
    set_implies_set(G,T,RT).

set_implies(G,E,R):-
    findall(P,gpath(G,E,P),PL),
    minlist(PL,R).

gpath(G,E,P):-member(X,G),
    path(X,E,P).

path(A,Z,P):-path1(A,Z,[A],P).
path1(A,A,_,[l(A,A,yes,[])]).
path1
(A,Z,[A|P1],[l(A,X,yes,R)|P2]):-
    imp(yes,A,X,R),
    not(member(X,P1)),
    path1(X,Z,[X,A|P1],P2).

minlist([X],X):-!.
minlist([H|T],H):-
    minlist(T,M),
    listlen(H,HN),listlen(M,MN),
    HN<MN,!.
minlist([_|T],M):-minlist(T,M).
```

Listing 2.

```
/* Non-Lesser Included Offenses */

n_lio(section(L),section(G),R):-
    off(section(G),CG,EG),!,
    off(section(L),CL,EL),
    classorder(CL,CG),
    set_n_implies_set(EG,EL,PL),....

/* Indifferent and Negative Set
Predicates */

set_n_implies_set(G,L,R):-
    set_i_implies_set(G,L,R),
    member(P,R),
    member(l(_,_,no,_),P).

set_i_implies_set(_,[],[]).
set_i_implies_set(G,[H|T],[RH|RT]):-
    set_i_implies(G,H,RH),!,
    set_i_implies_set(G,T,RT).

set_i_implies(G,E,R):-
    findall(P,gi_path(G,E,P),PL),
    minlist(PL,R).

gi_path(G,E,P):-member(X,G),
    i_path(X,E,P).

i_path(A,Z,P):-i_path1(A,Z,[A],P).
i_path1(A,A,_,[l(A,A,yes,[])]).
i_path1(A,Z,[A|P1],[l(A,X,T,R)|P2]):-
    imp(T,A,X,R),
    not(member(X,P1)),
    i_path1(X,Z,[X,A|P1],P2).
```

Listing 3.

Z irrespective of the *Truthvalues* encountered along the way. *G_i_path(G,E,P)* finds such a path P from a member of the set of nodes G to the node E. *Set_i_implies(G,E,R)* succeeds if R exists and is the shortest such path. *Set_i_implies_set(G,L,R)* succeeds if every node in L is so connected to a node in G by a path in R. *Set_n_implies_set(G,L,R)* is now defined as succeeding if *set_i_implies_set(G,L,R)* succeeds, and there is a path P in R which contains a link having a *Truthvalue* of "*no*" (see **Listing 3**).

Selection of Assigned Counsel

We turn briefly to a problem involving ethics as opposed to substantive law, and consider the potential for systems associated with a database capable of advising on ethical questions.

An indigent defendant charged with a crime is entitled to be represented free of charge by an attorney assigned by the court. The usual procedure is to assign the public defender. Not infrequently, the public defender is precluded from undertaking the representation due to a conflict of interest, resulting, for example, from multiple defendants having adverse penal interests. In such cases the court must select an attorney from the community to undertake the defense. In a small county, most attorneys hold one or more public positions which may conflict with the performance of assigned criminal representation, either in all cases or under the circumstances of a particular case. The court must avoid assigning an attorney to the case who has an impermissible conflict of interest. In addition, even those attorneys not directly disqualified may be disqualified by association. The prevailing rule is that all partners or associates of an attorney are disqualified if the attorney is disqualified.[19] The court must accordingly consider, not only conflicting interests of the attorney it contemplates assigning, but those of his or her partners and associates as well. A Prolog program has been designed which assists in the analysis of this issue, and in the rotation of assignments among eligible attorneys in an evenhanded manner. Communication between the database system and this rule-based program is accomplished in the same manner as described above, the unique identifier of the attorney being passed as a parameter to and from the Prolog program. Portions of the Prolog code are presented in **Listing 4**.

Information pertaining to attorneys is stored in a structure (here abbreviated as) *attorney(Identifier,Attributelist)*. An attorney referenced by identifier A is considered a candidate for assignment in a case arising out of location Loc according to *possible(Loc,A)*, provided no disqualifying relation *dq(A,Loc,_)* is found. A general disqualification *general_dq(A,Exp)* may exist with explanation Exp, either because an element X of the attorney's attribute list L satisfies *holds_incompatible_office(L,Exp)*, or because this state of affairs exists with respect to another attorney B with respect to whom *associate_of(A,B)* is satisfied. Associates are identified as attorneys who each have the item *firm(F)* as a common element of their respective attribute lists. A disqualification *loc_dq(A,Loc,Exp)* due to the circumstances of a given case can occur, where the case arises out of or in some way involves a locality Loc, and the attribute list of attorney A indicates he is a municipal attorney *ma(Loc)* or a local part time judge

judge(Loc) for that locality. As before, locality based disqualifications propagate to all members of an attorneys firm. Further extensions are easily imagined.

```
possible(Loc,A):-attorney(A,_),not(dq(A,Loc,_)).

dq(A,_,Exp) :- general_dq(A,Exp).
dq(A,Loc,Exp):-location_dq(A,Loc,Exp).

general_dq(A,Exp):-attorney(A,L), holds_incompatible_office(L,Exp1),
            concat(A,Exp1,Exp).
general_dq(A,Exp):-attorney(A,_), associate_of(A,B),
            attorney(B,L),
            holds_incompatible_office(L,Exp4),
    concat(A," is disqualified because associated with ",Exp1),
    concat(Exp1,B,Exp2), concat(Exp2,", who",Exp3),
    concat(Exp3,Exp4,Exp).

holds_incompatible_office(L,Exp):- member(X,L),
    incompatible_office(X,Exp1),
    concat(" is disqualified because ",Exp1,Exp).

incompatible_office(da, "a member of the District Attorney's office.").
incompatible_office(pd, "a member of the Public Defender's office.").
incompatible_office(ca, "a member of the County Attorney's office.").
incompatible_office(leg,"a member of the County Legislature.").
incompatible_office(judge("Greene County Supreme Court"),
            "a Judge of the Supreme Court.").
incompatible_office(judge("Greene County Court"),"a Judge of County Court.").


location_dq(A,C,Exp):-location_dq2(A,C,Exp1),
    concat(A," is disqualified, being ",Exp2),
    concat(Exp2,Exp1,Exp3), concat(Exp3,", and the case involving ",Exp4),
    concat(Exp4,C,Exp5),   concat(Exp5,".",Exp).
location_dq(A,C,Exp):--associate_of(A,B),
            location_dq2(B,C,Exp1),
    concat(A," is disqualified, being associated with ",Exp2),
    concat(Exp2,B,Exp3),   concat(Exp3,", who is ",Exp4),
    concat(Exp4,Exp1,Exp5), concat(Exp5,", and the case involves ",Exp6),
    concat(Exp6,C,Exp7),   concat(Exp7,".",Exp).

location_dq2(A,Loc,Exp):-attorney(A,L),
            member(X,L), location_dq3(Loc,X,Exp).

location_dq3(Loc,judge(Loc),Exp):-concat("local judge for ",Loc,Exp).
location_dq3(Loc,  ma(Loc),Exp):-concat("municipal attorney for ",Loc,Exp).

attfirm(A,F):-attorney(A,L),member(firm(F),L).

associate_of(X,Y):-attfirm(X,F),
            attfirm(Y,F),not(X=Y).
```

Listing 4.

Conclusion

Two examples of substantive rule-based extensions to conventional legal database systems have been shown. The applications were developed independently of the database system and of each other; communication between the applications and the database system is accomplished by passing required parameters via the command line or text files. The potential uses of substantive systems in the Courts are just beginning to be explored.

David E. Woodin, Esq. is a member of the bar of the State of New York. He is presently Associate Law Assistant, Trial Part, to the County Court of Greene County, New York, where he has served the New York State Unified Court System since 1982. He is also a freelance programmer and consultant, and sole proprietor of Due Process Software. He holds the degrees of J.D. from Albany Law School, M.A.T. in science and mathematics from Reed College, and B.A. in physics and music from Williams College.

References

[1]. Stout, Ronald M. and Seward, Ronald G. (1985) "Microcomputers: Information Managers in the Courts," 10 *The Justice System Journal* 97.

[2]. *See, e.g.*, Mulder, Richard V. and Gubby, Helen M., "Legal Decision Making By Computer: An Experiment With Sentencing", IV *Computer/Law Journal* 243 (1983). Pethe, Vishwas P., Rippey, Charles P. and Kale, L.V., "A Specialized Expert System For Judicial Decision Support", *Proceedings of the Second International Conference on Artificial Intelligence and Law*, p. 190. Simon, Eric, "ASSYST - Computer Support for Guideline Sentencing", *Proceedings of the Second International Conference on Artificial Intelligence and Law*, p. 195.

[3]. *See* Kerschberg, Larry, *Expert Database Systems, Proceedings From the First International Workshop*, The Benjamin/Cummings Publishing Company, Inc., Menlo Park, California (1986), Preface, p. iv.

[4]. See, Susskind, *Expert Systems in Law, A Jurisprudential Inquiry*, Clarendon Press, Oxford (1987); Gardner, *An Artificial Intelligence Approach to Legal Reasoning*, The M.I.T. Press, Cambridge (1987). Ciampi, "Artificial Intelligence and Legal Information Systems", in *Artificial Intelligence and Legal Information Systems, Volume I*, C. Ciampi (ed.), North-Holland Publishing Co., 1982, p. 49; Finan, "Lawgical: Jurisprudential and Logical Considerations", 15:4 *Akron Law Review* 675 (Spring, 1982); Meldman, "A Structural Model for Computer-Aided Legal Analysis", 6 *Rutgers Computers & Law* 27 (1971); Frank, *Courts on Trial*, Princeton, Princeton University Press (1949), pp. 206-208.

[5]. See, Tito, "Artificial Intelligence: Can Computers Understand Why Two Legal Cases Are Similar?", 7 *Computer/Law Journal* 409 (1987).

[6]. Susskind, *Expert Systems in Law, A Jurisprudential Inquiry*, Clarendon Press, Oxford (1987); Gardner, *An Artificial Intelligence Approach to Legal Reasoning*, The M.I.T. Press, Cambridge (1987).

[7]. See, e.g., *People v. Maderic*, 142 AD2d 892, 893 (3d Dept., 1989).

[8]. See New York State Criminal Procedure Law (CPL) 390.20, 390.30, 390.40, 400.10. New York State Penal Law (PL) Articles 60-85; *see esp.*, PL 60.01, 60.05, 60.11, 70.02-70.10.

[9]. CPL 220.10, 220.30.

[10]. *People v. Glover*, 57 NY2d 61; *People v. Green*, 56 NY2d 427.

[11]. CPL 100.40(1)(c), 200.50(7)(a).

[12]. CPL 170.35(1)(a), 210.20(1)(a), 210.25(1).

[13]. CPL 210.20(1)(a), 210.25(1)). *People v. Bartley*, 47 NY2d 965; *People v. Maderic*, 142 AD2d 892; *People v. Cook*, 93 AD2d 942; *People v. Hicks*, 79 AD2d 887; *Matter of Wadsworth v. Mogavero*, 71 AD2d 157. *People ex rel Gray v. Tekben*, 86 AD2d 176, *affd.* 57 NY2d 651, *see People v. Williams*, 95 AD2d 726. CPL 440.20(1), 440.40(1). CPL 470.15(2)(c), 470.45.

[14]. *TM Borland International*, 1800 Green Hills Road, P.O. Box 660001, Scotts Valley, CA 95066-0001.

[15]. *Gunga Clerk, version 1.2.* Copyright (C) 1988, 1989, *Due Process Software*, 340 Main Street, P.O. Box 433, Catskill, New York, 12414.

[16]. *TM Nantucket Corporation*, 12555 W. Jefferson Blvd., Suite 300, Los Angeles, CA 90066.

[17]. Koers, A.W., et al., *Knowledge Based Systems in Law*, Kluwer Law and Taxation Publishers, Deventer, The Netherlands, 1989, pp 58-68.

[18]. See Bratko, Ivan, *Prolog Programming for Artificial Intelligence*, Addison-Wesley (1986), pp. 262-273.

[19]. *A.B.A. Code of Professional Responsibility*, DR 5-105(D). "If a lawyer is required to decline employment or to withdraw from employment... no partner or associate of his or his firm may accept or continue such employment."

A HISTORICAL DATA BANK OF ITALIAN LEGAL LANGUAGE

Paola Mariani, Daniela Tiscornia

CONSIGLIO NAZIONALE DELLE RICERCHE
Istituto per la Documentazione giuridica   Firenze, Italy

Abstract

The article illustrates a research project, carried out at the Istituto per la documentazione giuridica del Consiglio Nazionale delle Ricerche, aimed at transforming an immense documentary patrimony in an historical data bank of the italian legal language. In the development of the project, the greatest problems arise from the different tecniques of storage, that (about twenty years ago) were adopted in bilding up the historical archives. The objective is to obtain an homogeneus information retrieval system, without lossing the richness of informations.
The historical data bank will be the widest source of documentation about the historical development of the italian legal language, since its beginning (960) up to the present time.

1. Introduction

There is no linguistically technical, historically and authoritatively complete dictionary in Italian legal literature. In order to fill this gap, the Consiglio Nazionale delle Ricerche, or C.N.R. (the Italian National Research Council), began a project, in 1964, at one of its institutes (the Istituto per la Documentazione Giuridica of Florence, or I.D.G.) aimed at drafting the "Vocabolario Giuridico Italiano", or "V.G.I.", an Italian Legal Dictionary. The initial phase of the work , namely, the study, research and collection of the sources through lexicographical criteria and the exploitation of the documents with the aid of informatic techniques, was concluded in less then ten years. This was not an easy task both due to the large number of works scanned and because its objective (to which this selection was directed) was to cover enough representative documentation from the point of view of time (historical periods), space (cultural areas) and stratification (in accordance with the twofold aspects of the various sources and the different branches of law).
After the work on the VGI had been suspended(1), an immense documentary patrimony, unique in Italy, was left which is currently being transformed into a data bank. It is our aim, in this article, to describe the methodology followed in building this data bank as well as the methodology being defined at present for putting it on line. This is aimed at overcoming the problems posed by the characteristics of the material, filed largely according to by now out dated techniques and at providing efficient and accurate tools for the retrieval of the documents. The completion of the project should make a legal-historical Data Bank available containing globally approximately 25,000,000 occurences, divided into three on line data bases, corresponding to the three legal-historical archives created at IDG. The two main data bases contain the material archived for the drafting of the Historical Dictionary of Italian Legal Language (VGI). The documentation contained in it was completed with a bibliographical data base: Bibliography of Old Legal Editions in Italian (BEGA - "Bibliografia delle edizione giuridiche antiche in lingua italiana").

2. The V.G.I. Data Base

The data base, which documents the language from its origins (960, Placito di Capua) until the present day, covers only printed texts, where possible, in the first edition for texts relating to legal authority and in the official version for legislative texts.
The material was selected not only for giving a merely technical explanation of strictly legal terms but for the purpose of pointing out that special language of the law which, in the Italian linguistic system, is distinguished from natural language both at a terminological and syntactical level.
The documents, that will constitute the VGI data base, were originally stored in two different ways: given the large amount of material considered, researchers adopted two different processing techniques - full-text storage (carried out electronically) and selective storage (carried out by hand and xerographically), both of which have advantages and disadvantages. The electronic technique guaranteed documentary completeness in the corpus but, in the drafting phase of the Dictionary, it would have drowned the editors in a sea of legally unimportant words (conjunctions, articles, prepositions) whilst the examples obtained by computer scanning on the basis of a given length, was not very suitable for those works (especially legal authority) in which the length of the examples needed regulating according to the requirements dictated by the clarity of interpretation. The selective technique allowed the lexicographer to be more agile in interpretation, by enabling him to immediately point out legal data, but it had the defect of not being exhaustive, of not providing any certainty that the choice was complete.

It was, therefore, decided to examine the great works which mark the fundamental steps in Italian legislative development by utilizing the former technique whilst current legislation, not such fundamental legislation, legal authority and procedure were examined using the latter technique. In this way, the enormous framework constructed by the full-text storage of these works was slowly filled in by the selected documentation, making way for the development of two separate sub-bases - one complete and one selective. Full-text storege was limited to the Statutes of Lucca of 1539, all the constitutions in Italian from 1600 until the present day, the main preunion codes, all the codes which were and are in force in unified Italy, regional statues in force and other laws thought worthy of attention for one reasons to another.

2.1. The Legislative Data Base Submitted to Full-text Storage

Computer procedures in use for linguistic analyses were adapted, in collaboration with the Istituto di Linguistica Computazionale (Computational Linguistics) of the C.N.R. in Pisa, to the particular requirements of processing legislative texts. This applied mainly for citations: systematized citations (section, subsection, etc.) had to be introduced along with topographical citations (page and line). It was, furthermore, considered opportune to provide brief indications, but able, on an initial reading, to identify, the special parts of a statute (initial and concluding formulae, headings, enactment, etc.). These details, in the advanced processing phase, allow us to go back from a single word to its whole context, independently of the official edition, which is often difficult to consult.

The data base is made up of a total of 3,033,673 occurences, resulting from the merging of the 102 processed texts. For the purposes of the drafting of the Dictionary, alphabetical concordances by form were provided with particularly long contexts. This does not mean that they cannot be processed or utilized in other ways (in print or on line): from concordances by lemmata (1) to automated lemmatization, to different frequency lists according to the user's needs.

The data bank generation did not present particular problems, apart of the choice of a suitable retrieval system (see below).

The structure of the original document was mainteined : the documentary unit is the sub-section, with the addition of predefined fields which contain: Date of Publication + Title + Systematical and Topographical Citations.

Examples of the structure of document:

DANNO

1539 Statuto di Lucca l.IV, carta 245v, rigo 26:

Negli precedenti tre capitoli Provisto habiamo della pena di quegli che fanno negli altrui beni **danno**, come suole spesso accadere.

1771 Codice Leggi e Costituzioni, l.5, tit.9, art.6:

In tutti i predetti casi oltre l'incorso delle pene   rispettivamente prescritte sarà il Reo tenuto all'emendazione del **danno** cagionato dall'incendio.

2.2. The Data Base Submitted to Selective Storage

Selective storage concerned a series of texts chosen in the field of four main nuclei - legal authority, jurisprudence, legislation, procedure and customary law - taking into account, where possible, how the texts correspond to the originality, systematic unity and representativeness of the various legal, chronological and - for pre-union Italy - geographical fields. Case law has not been included in the data base as Italian users already have access to it through the Italgiure system, developed and distributed by the Italian Supreme Court.

Only legally important words in their most intelligible context were chosen from the works but without neglecting the syntactical structures peculiar to the linguistic system considered. The passages were transferred onto cards ready for punching, headed with the words chosen from within the context (a card with a copy of the same context corresponds to every selected word) written in lemmatized form and with the addition of bibliographical details.

The different legal sources are represented as follows:

1) legislation: that of the preunion states, including the statutes of communes, associations and guilds, and the laws of the old Italian states from 1200 to 1861; the legislation of unified Italy from 1861 to 1955;

2) legal authority and jurisprudence: the selection covers works in Italian from 1500 to 1975;

3) procedure: including notarial forms and other documents of a varied nature in the administrative, civil, and procedural fields from 960 up until the present day;

4) customary law: this is a separate data base, made up of approximately 29,000 unpunched cards, resulting from the scanning of the provincial collections of customary law and a part of legal literature from the union of Italy up until today.

The data base consists of approximately 900,000 lexical cards, placed into order by author (about 400) as well as in alphabetical order for the lemmata under each author. Of the data recorded on each card, only the lemma (2), the date and the code number corresponding to the author were punched and stored. Alphabetical lists of the lemmata with their frequency, given classes of sources and actual position in the data base will be produced by the data processing.

Generating the on line version of this data base has created a series of difficulties, which are currently being studied. A feasibility study has been made which provides for the storage of the contexts appearing in the cards and of the citations contained in them. In this way, the search will be extended to the whole context and not only to the important words for which the the passage was identified. It has been considered advisable to save the large amount of work in selection done originally, by providing, in the structure of the document to be put on line, a specific field which will contain key words, or in other words, the lemmata which make up the heading of the cards, permitting two levels of research during retrieval, a wider level which, through a textual search, will identify all the contexts where the term appears and a more specific one, which will identify only the contexts that are more important for understanding, defining and interpreting the term (3).

The documentary unit will have the following structure: Date on which it was written + Date of Publication + Author Name +
Title + Systematical and/or Topographical Citations + Context + Key Words (most important lemmata).

Example:

TESTATORE

1673 DE LUCA Gio.Battista, Il Dottor volgare, l.IV, pt.I, p.36: Nelli suddetti et in altri casi, nelli quali detto usufrutto   non si acquisti al padre; Nasce la questione se almeno se ne   acquisti la comodità; Et in ciò si distingue, che se tal   proibizione nasce da volontà del testatore, per odio del padre,   et in tal caso non se ne acquisti ne meno la comodità.

Key Words: **Acquistare, comodità, proibizione, odio.**

An alternative methodology for data processing involves reproduction by using a scanner: the typographical characters of most of the documents taken from antique texts have excluded their further transformation into characters. The reproduction of images will be integrated by storing the elements necessary for identifying the documents: bibliographical and topographical details, terms selected in the form in which they appear in the text. This data will constitue a reference data bank which will allow searching by form and, by using programs for automated lemmatization, by lemmata.

2.3. The Bibliographical Data Base

A bibliographical data base constituting the Index of the texts selected for the Dictionary was created at the same time as the lexical data base. This data base is made up of about 2,000 documents on line, which contain information of a bibliographical and statistical kind. In fact, information about the date on which it was written, its full bibliographical reference, its abbreviated reference, its source class, the type of scanning, the number of pages, the consistency of the documentation in terms of the cards for the selective storage and occurences for full-text storage is given for each selected text. In the printed version, the Index is appears in four different lists: in chronological order, alphabetical order, by source class.

Example:

Lemma	Author Code	Date	D	L	G	C	P	V	Freq.
TESTATORE									
	306	1377	1						
	480	1410		4					
	312	1427	1						
	480	1553		2					
	....	....							
	14	1673	27						
	....	....							
	227	1781				1			
	....	....							
	124	1875	1						
	438	1891	1						
	....	....							
	281	1929	1						
									132

Legenda: D:Legal authority and jurisprudence; L:Legislation; G:Cases; C:customary law; P:procedure; V:other sources.

3. The Bibliography of Old Legal Editions

When work began on the Italian Legal Dictionary, a Philological Department was set up whose specific task was to research and select the texts for scanning. This starting point should be remembered as the initial nucleus of the work out of which the bibliography grew was that selected for an historical dictionary of legal language, defined as the development of legal institutions and concepts and not simply as proof of the existence of terms. The history of legal language is also documented by the texts that contain it independently of their literary nature. The legal content of the text is recuperated through key words already existing in the title or introduced in the notes by the document's author. The Bibliography of Old Legal Editions in Italian began in this way in 1970 and comprises a "Major" series (statutory texts and legal authority from 1400 to 1800) and a "Minor" series (a collection of legislation of all the old Italian States: Tuscany, Venice, Milan, Turin, Rome, Naples). In selecting the texts, the need was felt to trace the birth and evolution of Italian legal language, wherever it may have been manifested, even in texts mainly written in Latin or in moral, political, religious, historical or philosophical texts when they contained norms or discussed norms in some way.

The bibliographical archive for 1400-1700 is currently available in print (4) and is a data base storing approximately 4,500 bibliographical units. The period 1701-1800 consists in about 12,000 bibliographical units; a printed publication is forthcoming.

The Bibliographical File relating to the Minor Series (legislation of the preunion States, 16th-18th centuries) is being constructed: a card index of approximately 30,000 bibliographical units is estimated.

The structure of the document for the data bank contains: Date of Publication + [Author] + Title + References (libraries, repertories, annotations, citations, etc.) + Key words (guide to cataloging by subject-matter).

Example:

1539 Gli **Statuti della città di Lucca** nuovamente corretti et con molta diligentia stampati.[Trad.Tobia Sirti].
Lucca, per Giovanbattista Phaello Bolognese, 1539,cc.[5], CCCXXXV, [1], cm 33.
Biblioteca di giurisprudenza dell'Università di Firenze, C.6.131, esemplare mutilo: cfr. Catalogo Senese Iv, 124.
key-words: **statuto, legislazione, Lucca.**

4. Retrieval System

The three data bases will be stored separately in the data bank, but will be able to be searched by using the same retrieval system, in such a way that they will provide global documentation.

The Legal Texts Data Base (L.T.D.B.) is the retrieval system, developed by E. Picchi at the Istituto di Linguistica Computazionale (I.L.C.) of Pisa. The system was designed keeping in mind the features of the complete archives and Bega which had already been electronically processed at I.L.C. as well as the texts prepared for the Italian Legal Dictionary. It is, consequently, particularly suitable for processing archives of historical and linguistic interest.

The information retrieval program is very elastic in the data implementation phase, both due to the (free) length of the document and the definition of the citation-fields. It is, in fact, possible to define an unlimited number of fields, utilizing codified identifiers. This allows the wealth of information contained in the citations on the cards due to the variety of documents in the data base (letters, announcements, inventories, wills, contracts, etc.) to be retained.

Document retrieval is full text whilst other research tools can also be utilized such as computer dictionaries, thesauri, etc. The indexing of the document in the full text mode allows the logical structure of the form to be used (that is, the search can be extended to all the document or selected fields, for example, author, title, etc).

It is planned to place the data bases on line both by using personal computers (CD-ROM) and on main frames.

For the main frame version, it will be possible to search the data base through the Scientific Node of the Italian National Research Council, through the Computer Centre of I.D.G.

Notes

(1) After the initial editing phase which resulted in the production of a special issue, working groups were organized whose scope it was to seek the views and proposals of eminent experts in the field of Italian legal lexicography expressly relating to commencing the project. In fact, some concern had arisen about the development of a project based on traditional techniques for lexicographical drafting; on the one hand, concern of a practical kind (keeping in mind the number of editors employed in the task, the work would have required, in order to reach its conclusion, a period of not less than 60 years) and concern of a scientific kind, on the other, which, on the basis of the new possibilities offered by computer science, favoured simply documenting the historical development of legal language rather than the lexicographer defining and interpreting that development.

See: Gli archivi del Vocabolario Giuridico Italiano, in Proceedings of the II International Conference "L'informatica giuridica al servizio del paese", Rome, 1978, I/29; "Vocabolario giuridico italiano", Special Issue, Firenze, I.D.G., 1979;

(2) We mean with the term "lemma"(pl. "lemmata") the standard form in which words are registered in dictionaries. "Lematization" means the process through which all forms of the words are reduced to "lemma". (see: D.M. Burton, Automated concordances and word indexes: the Fifties, in Computers and the Humanities, vol.15, 1981, North-Holland).

(3) The stored data is estimated to be from a minimum of 120 million characters up to a maximum of 240 million characters. This means that the man hours necessary for storing the documents vary from between a minimum of 6 to a maximum of 10 man years, keeping in mind the exacting work required in carefully revising the stored data. In fact, a large part of the documents is in old Italian which makes automated spelling correction programs almost useless.

(4) Bibliografia delle edizioni giuridiche antiche, vol.I,pte. 1, Testi statutari e dottrinali dal 1470 al 1700, Bibliografia cronologica, pte. 2, Indici alfabetici, Leo S. Olschki Editore, Firenze, 1978.

REFERENCES

M. Alinei, Lessicografia italiana con l'ausilio di macchine a schede perforate all'Università di Utrecht. Prime esperienze e prospettive, in: J. Shtindlovà and Z. Skoumalovà (eds.), Les Machines dans la Linguistique (Academia Editions de l'Académie Tchécoslovaque des Sciences, Prague), 1968, pp. 95-108.

A. Duro, L'Emploi de moyens électroniques pour la constitution du Fichier lexicographique général par l'Accademia della Crusca, in: J. Shtindlovà and Z. Skoumalovà (eds.), Les Machines dans la Linguistique (Academia Editions de l'Académie Tchécoslovaque des Sciences, Prague), 1968, pp. 201-220.

A. M. Bartoletti Colombo (ed.), La Costituzione della Repubblica italiana, Testi, Concordanze, Indici, Firenze, Istituto per la Documentazione Giuridica (I.D.G.), 1971, pp.XXX, 598.

Vocabolario giuridico italiano, Saggi di redazione, Firenze, I.D.G., 1975, pp. 65 (74).

P. Fiorelli, Vocabolari giuridici fatti e da fare, in Rivista Italiana per le Scienze Giuridiche, vol. I, 1947, pp. 293-327.

P. Fiorelli, Per un vocabolario giuridico italiano, in Lingua Nostra, VIII (1947), pp. 96-108.

P. Fiorelli, Il primo vocabolario giuridico italiano, in Scritti in memoria di Antonino Giuffrè, vol. I, Milano, Giuffrè, 1967, pp.(491)-500.

G. Salton, Automatic Information Organition and retrieval, Mc Graw-Hill, New York, 1968.

T. Gregory, European Intellectual Lexicon, Computing Medieval Data Processing, 5(2), pp. 23-27.

C.D. Paice, Information retrieval and the computer, McDonald and Jane's, London, 1977.

P. Fiorelli, "L'accademia della Crusca per il Vocabolario giuridico italiano", in Studi di Lessicografia Italiana, I, (1979), pp.(55)-81.

L. Lancaster, Information retrieval systems: characteristics, testing and evolution, John Wiley & Son, (second edition), New York, 1979.

D.M. Burton, Automated concordances and word indexes: the Fifties, in Computers and the Humanities, vols. 15 (1981) and 16 (1982), Amsterdam, North-Holland.

A. Zampolli, A. Cappelli (eds.), The Possibilities and Limits of the Computer in producing and publishing Dictionaries, Proceedings of the European Science Foundation Workshop, Pisa, 1981, in Linguistica computazionale, III, 1983.

G. Salton, A. McGill, Introduction to modern information retrieval, Mc Graw-Hill, Singapore, 1983.

E. Picchi, Problemi di documentazione linguistica. Archivio dei testi e nuove tecnologie, in Proceedings of the Conference "L'informatica giuridica e le Comunità nazionali ed internazionali", Roma, 1983, I/17.

P. Fiorelli, La lingua giuridica dal De Luca al Buonaparte, in Teorie e pratiche linguistiche nell'Italia del Settecento, Bologna, Il Mulino, 1984,pp. 127-154.

Glossario delle consuetudini giuridiche dall'unità d'Italia, voll. 4, I.D.G., Firenze, 1980 - 1986.

P. Fiorelli, Archivi locali, storia del diritto, storia della lingua, in Proceedings of the Conference "Archivi comunali toscani: esperienze e prospettive", Firenze, 1987, pp. 77-94.

398

R. Busa s.j., Fondamenti di informatica linguistica, Milano, Vita e Pensiero, 1987.

M. Ascheri, Storia giuridica e computer: talune esperienze, progetti e esigenze, in Proceedings of the II International Conference " Informatica e regolamentazioni giuridiche", Roma, 1988, II/14.

Pre-proceedings of the International Conference "Le Médiéviste et l'ordinateur", Paris, 1989.

K^E_LP: A Hypertext oriented User-Interface for an Intelligent Legal Fulltext Information Retrieval System

Wolfdieter Merkl[*], Stefan Vieweg[*], Ajrapet Karapetjan[#]

[*] Institute of Computer Science, Department of Information Systems
University of Vienna, Liebiggasse 4, A-1010 Vienna, Austria

[#] Polytechnical Highschool of Erewan, Department of Computer Science
Terjanstreet 105, SU-375009 Erewan, USSR

Abstract

This paper concerns the description of K^E_LP, an intelligent legal information retrieval system with emphasis on a Hypertext oriented presentation of retrieved documents. K^E_LP provides two distinct categories of descriptors for indexing the documents. An approach to term classification and a four level hierarchy of interdocument similarities is introduced. Cluster analysis based on these similarities and a hierarchy of subject fields provided by a knowledge base is performed to obtain document classification. The retrieved documents are presented in a graphical browsing system showing both similarities between documents and similarities between retrieved documents and query. The relationships obtained from indexing and classification, and the knowledge base are used to obtain automatically generated Hypertext links for a user-friendly presentation of documents.

1. Introduction

Rapid progress in science and technology in the last three decades has created a so-called "information explosion". This development makes it a tremendous task for information centers to provide users with up to date material on topics of their interest [3]. Computer methods for overcoming these problems have been discussed since the early sixties. This has led to the establishment of a seperate scientific discipline: Information Retrieval.
Information Retrieval (IR) deals with the representation, storage, organisation, and retrieval of information [5].

Due to the size of a document base (length and number of documents) the search for relevant information (i.e., the documents that match the query best) cannot be performed in the texts themselves. Therefore the documents are mapped to document descriptions which build the basis for the search process. These descriptions consist in keywords either extracted directly from the text (fulltext indexing) or from a controlled vocabulary.

In conventional IR systems with boolean retrieval logic a query is a predicate consisting of keywords and operators. These predicates are matched against document descriptions. By this approach only those documents can be retrieved that contain the terms contained in the query. These documents are presented sequentially. Relevant documents that do not contain this keywords are not considered.
K^E_LP is designed to overcome this problem by providing two distinct categories of document descriptors (keywords and citations of legal paragraphs). This by taking advantage of the special structure of its documents representing decisions of Austrian Supreme Court. Such documents are typically build up from words and cited legal paragraphs. The set of automatically extracted descriptors and a knowledge base about the relationship between subject fields and legal sections are used for term and document classification.

Another deficiency in conventional IR systems is that the retrieved documents are either presented in random order (pure boolean retrieval) or in respect to their similarity to the query (weighted boolean retrieval). In both cases the user gets no information about the similarity between the retrieved documents. To overcome this problem K^E_LP presents the retrieved documents according to the similarity of documents and of documents and query.
To provide a more user-frienly query formulation and presentation of retrieved documents, K^E_LP provides a graphical browsing system and a Hypertext presentation of documents with automatically generated links.

The paper is organized as follows. First we describe our approach to automatic indexing using keywords and legal citations. In Section 3 we discuss the K^E_LP-Knowledge-Base. In Section 4 we introduce an approach to term classification and a four level hierarchy for measuring the degree of similarity between pairs of documents. Section 5 describes the retrieval process as a clusterbased search. Section 6 deals with using the results of the classification phase to obtain automatically generated Hypertext links between documents and between document clusters.

2. Automatic Indexing in $K^E_L P$

$K^E_L P$'s status as a fulltext retrieval system requires document descriptors to be taken from the text without using any form of controlled vocabulary. $K^E_L P$ uses two distinct types of weighted descriptors. The first type is a set of extracted words (referred to as TERMs). This category is also used in conventional fulltext retrieval systems. The second type consists of references to (citations of) relevant legal paragraphs typically used in legal documentation (referred to as CITs).

The use of citations as an extension of simple word extraction has been proposed by [3], [7], and [8]. This approach leads to better retrieval results because citations provide a better relation between the documents and their covered legal domains.

2.1. TERMs as document descriptors

The following strategies have been chosen to reduce the number of TERMs:

(1) $K^E_L P$ considers only nouns as TERMs. This limitation is made possible by the special property of the German language. In German each noun begins with a capital letter which can be recognized easily by $K^E_L P$'s indexing component.

(2) This set of TERMs is further reduced by eliminating the word endings which originate from the declination of nouns. This elimination of word endings is performed by applying linguistic heuristics without using external knowledge about word stems.

This procedure is designed as an open system. The user may specify a set of TERMs which are not considered for the elimination of word endings.
For example the German word "Klagegrund" (cause of action) occurs in 50 randomly selected decisions about divorce in the following forms which are all reduced to "Klagegrund":

Noun	Occurrence	Radical	Occurrence
Klagegrund	4	Klagegrund	40
Klagegrunde	2		
Klagegrundes	16		
Klagegründe	4		
Klagegründen	14		

The aim of eliminating the word endings is to concentrate on radicals[*]. As a result $K^E_L P$ decreases the number of TERMs in the set of document descriptors for the whole database and increases the effectiveness of the weighting scheme (as described below).

Three tests with randomly selected disjoint subsets of 197 decisions about the suject field "divorce" showed the following results for the first two steps of reduction:

	Documents	Words	Nouns	Radicals	Reduction
Test1	16	15.697	837	682	95.6 %
Test2	14	13.306	957	807	93.9 %
Test3	17	17.731	1.008	849	95.2 %

---

[*] As $K^E_L P$ does not use additional linguistic knowledge to obtain radicals we point out that the term "radical" is not used in a strictly linguistic sense.

As a conclusion we see that using only radicals of nouns as document descriptors leads to a reduction of about 95 % from the original amount of words.

(3) The set of TERMs is weighted using term frequency (TF) and inverse document frequency (IDF) as proposed in [4]. These weights are applied to obtain a smaller set of TERMs by defining upper and lower boundaries for the frequency of TERM occurrences and to gain values for the importance of keywords.

2.2. CITs as document descriptors

In addition to TERMs $K^E_L P$ exctracts CITs from the text. CITs are selected from text using a simple parsing method based on the occurrence of special keywords in law citations. The parsing algorithm benefits of the fact that the way of citing legal paragraphs is strictly standardisized in Austria. There is a limited number of special keywords that indicate the presence of a citation of a legal paragraph in a text. For example the terms "§", "Abs.", and "lit." are such special keywords.
A legal paragraph can be regarded as a frame with one slot for each special keyword and a slot for the name of the legal section.

... wobei die im § 3 Abs. (2) Z. 2 und § 4 des Datenschutzgesetzes genannten Bestimmungen ...

In this example $K^E_L P$ finds "§" or "Abs." as special keywords and extracts the following citations:

§ 3 Abs. (2) Z. 2 Datenschutzgesetz
§ 4 Datenschutzgesetz

The result are two (not necessarily completely) filled frames (the symbol $<e>$ represents an empty slot):

NAME	Datenschutzgesetz	NAME	Datenschutzgesetz
§	3	§	4
ABS	2	ABS	$<e>$
Z	2	Z	$<e>$
LIT	$<e>$	LIT	$<e>$

The extracted CITs are weighted according to their occurrence frequencies in analogy to the above mentioned methods for TERMs.

2.3. The final document descriptors

$K^E_L P$'s indexing phase ends up with a document representation by pairs of descriptors and weights:

$$D_i \; \leftarrow \; ((\{(TERM_{i1}, WT_{i1}) \ldots (TERM_{ip}, WT_{ip})\} \\ \{(CIT_{i1}, WC_{i1}), \ldots, (CIT_{iq}, WC_{iq})\}))$$

D_i	Document i, $1 <= i <= n$
$TERM_{ij}$	TERM j of Document i, $1 <= i <= n, 1 <= j <= p$
WT_{ij}	Weight of $TERM_{ij}$, $1 <= i <= n, 1 <= j <= p$
CIT_{ij}	CIT j of Document i, $1 <= i <= n, 1 <= j <= q$
WC_{ij}	Weight of CIT_{ij}, $1 <= i <= n, 1 <= j <= q$

3. The $K^E_L P$-Knowledge-Base

Knowledge bases as used in expert system applications represent the knowledge of a problem domain.
In the field of IR different kinds of knowledge exist: knowledge of relationships between documents and their descriptions, knowledge of the database and its access mechanisms, knowledge of the user, knowledge of the users' problems, and knowledge of the subject domain underlying both the problems and the documents [1].

$K^E_L P$ uses a knowledge base of the subject domain. The domain (in this case Austrian Civil Law) is divided into sections (subject fields) with associated legal paragraphs. $K^E_L P$'s knowledge base mirrors the hierarchy of subject fields and the relationship between subject fields and its associated legal paragraphs. We point out that a legal paragraph may belong to more than one subject field.

For example the subject field "Pfandrecht" (law of liens and pledges) is divided into the sub-fields:

* Pfandverkauf
* Pfandvertrag
* Pfandwerbung
* Pfandschein
* Pfanddarlehen

The sub-field "Pfandverkauf is referred to by the following legal paragraphs:

* § 461 ABGB
* § 1371 ABGB

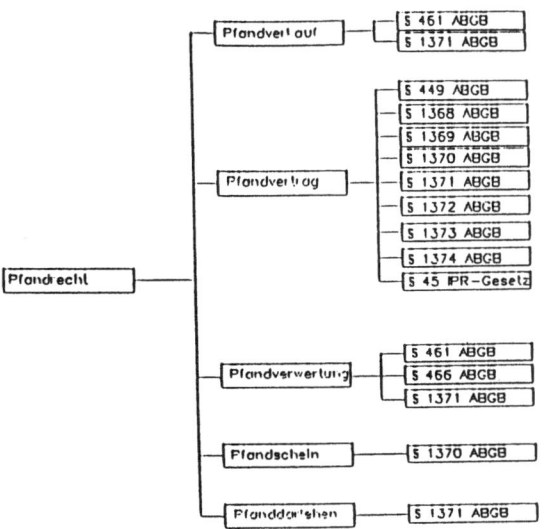

Fig. 1: Hierarchy for the subject field "Pfandrecht"

This knowledge base is used during the classification phase to increase the quality of the similarity coefficients for document clustering (as described in Section 4). Documents that cover the same subject fields are regarded to be more similar than documents covering other subject fields. These relationships can only be considered using citations because keywords usually do not relate to subject fields as strong as citations of legal paragraphs.

4. Automatic Classification in $K^E_L P$

$K^E_L P$ performs term classification to get a quasi synonym relationship[*) between TERMs, and document classification to obtain clusters of documents with similar properties.

4.1. Term classification[**)

For term classification $K^E_L P$ uses the output of the indexing phase. In detail $K^E_L P$ establishes a quasi synonym relation between TERMs which occur together with a specific CIT.
If a set of TERMs occurs with the same CIT, a coefficient for the occurrence frequency (COF) is computed by statistical means. For this coefficient a lower boundary is gained by heuristics and the TERMs with COFs exceeding this lower boundary are set synonym [6]. TERMs that are highly related to a CIT have a higher coefficient than TERMs that occur randomly together with a CIT.
The lower boundary can be seen as a threshold value for regarding TERMs as synonym.

The establishment of the synonym-relationship works as follows:

* A set of law-citations and a set of relevant documents in respect to those citations are intellectually chosen by an expert. This set of documents is then processed for the cooccurence of the specified law-citations.

* TERMs for this subset are extracted without regarding those that occur only once.

* Using n/N for TERMs in order to define a lower boundary for the synonym-set we obtain a set of keywords that are highly related to each other and that are likely to be synonym. Tests with other similarity functions are in progress.

As an example we have chosen the CIT "§ 480 ABGB" with 15 highly related documents.

TERM	n	OCC	NT	N	COF
Eigentumer	15	60	5525	15	1.0000
Liegenschaft	14	110	5525	15	0.9333
Dienstbarkeit	13	113	5525	15	0.8667
Feststellung	12	29	5525	15	0.8000
Grundstuck	12	195	5525	15	0.8000
Grundbuch	10	25	5525	15	0.6667
Frag	10	18	5525	15	0.6667
Servitut	10	22	5525	15	0.6667
Anspruch	9	30	5525	15	0.6000
Ausubung	9	22	5525	15	0.6000
Revision	9	28	5525	15	0.6000

n ... number of documents with TERM
OCC ... occurrence of TERM in the selected 15 documents
NT ... number of TERMs in the selected 15 documents
N ... number of documents
COF ... coefficient for occurrence frequency (n/N)

*) We point out that the term "synonym relationship" is not used in the same strength as in thesaurus applications.
**) On the basis of concepts developed by Werner Robert Svoboda within the EUREKA Project 359 - ITS 90 - funded by the Austrian Innovations- und Technologiefond (ITF).

4.2. Document classification

For document classification $K^E_L P$ computes similarity coefficients for each document pair, using the statistical information gained in the indexing phase and the knowledge provided by $K^E_L P$'s knowledge base. The statistical information consists of the relation between TERMs, the relation between CITs, and the relation between TERMs and CITs. $K^E_L P$'s knowledge base is used to determine documents that cover the same domain by citing the same legal sections.

The similarity function is based on four levels of similarity between parts of document descriptions ordered by their contribution-ratio to the final document similarity coefficient. This hierarchy mirrors the importance of co-occurrent descriptors for the similarity of pairs of documents.
Co-occurrent TERMs are less important for the similarity of document pairs than for example co-occurrent CITs. This is due to the fact that CITs represent a higher relationship between a document and a legal subject field.

Based on the above discussed idea we present four categories of co-occurrence of document descriptors in the order of their increasing contribution to the final document similarity function:

(1) Co-occurrent TERMs
(2) Co-occurrent CITs
(3) Co-occurrent TERMs and CITs
(4) Co-occurrent CITs covering the same subject domain

This leads to the final similarity function for pairs of documents:

$$SC(D_i, D_j) = SIM_{DOC}($$
$$SIM_{TERM}(T_i, T_j),$$
$$SIM_{CIT}(C_i, C_j),$$
$$SIM_{TC}((T_i, C_i),(T_j, C_j)),$$
$$SIM_{KB}(C_i, C_j))$$

$$T_i = \{(TERM_{i1}, WT_{i1}), ..., (TERM_{ip}, WT_{ip})\}$$
$$C_i = \{(CIT_{i1}, WC_{i1}), ..., (CIT_{iq}, WC_{iq})\}$$

SIM_{TERM}	...	similarity function between sets of TERMs
SIM_{CIT}	...	similarity function between sets of CITs
SIM_{TC}	...	similarity function between co-occurring TERMs and CITs
SIM_{KB}	...	similarity function between sets of CITs and domains
SIM_{DOC}	...	combination of similarity measures
SC	...	document similarity coefficient

SIM_{TERM}, SIM_{CIT} and SIM_{TC} represent those parts of the hierarchy that use only statistical information. Whereas SIM_{KB} incorporates knowledge from $K^E_L P$'s knowledge base.
SIM_{DOC} combines the four similarity functions whereby each single coefficient contributes to the final document similarity coefficient according to the above mentioned increasing order.

The SC coefficients are taken as base for a cluster algorithm to obtain hierarchical document clusters.
The result are clusters which consist of documents covering similar subject fields of the domain.
As $K^E_L P$ uses the knowledge base to compute similarity coefficients between documents the resulting hierarchical clusters mirror the hierachy of subject fields in $K^E_L P$'s knowledge base.

5. Clusterbased Search in $K^E_L P$

Clusterbased search in $K^E_L P$ is used for two purposes:

* to retrieve a homogenious set of documents
* to reduce the number of necessary comparisons to obtain this set.

$K^E_L P$ selects clusters from the hierarchy as superdocuments. These superdocuments are described by TERMs and CITs taken from the basic document descriptions. The query is matched against this superdocument descriptions. The documents contained in the best matching superdocuments are presented as the result of the retrieval process. The presentation of these documents is described in Section 6.

As an example we present the result of clustering nine documents in form of a dendrogram. The special feature of a dendrogram is the graphical presentation of similarity between document (or superdocument) pairs in form of different heights of the superdocument nodes.

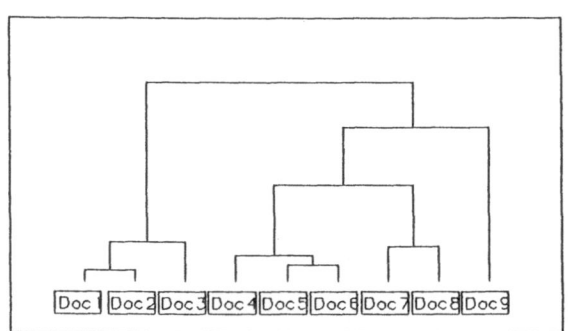

Fig. 2: Example for a cluster hierarchy

6. A Hypertext Approach for the $K^E_L P$ User-Interface

6.1. A graphical browser for the presentation of search results

In conventional IR systems the retrieved documents are either presented in random order (pure boolean retrieval) or in respect to their similarity to the query (weighted boolean retrieval). In both cases the user gets no information about the similarity between the retrieved documents.
$K^E_L P$ is designed to overcome this problem by providing a presentation of the retrieved documents according to the similarity between documents and between documents and query in form of a dendrogram.

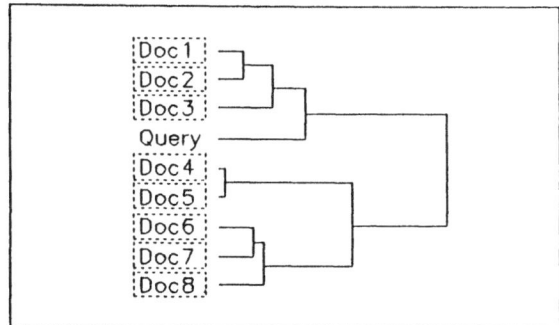

Fig. 3: Presentation of retrieved documents

The headers of the retrieved documents are presented in a graphical browsing system allowing the user to move directly to a document of interest by selecting the document header on the screen with a mouse.

To show the user the similarity of query and retrieved documents an icon representing the query is inserted into the hierarchy of retrieved documents according to the simliarity of the query to the retrieved documents.
Fig. 4 shows a very narrow query which is highly related to one special document (Doc1) wheras the query in Fig. 5 is very broad and is related only to the supercluster. Fig. 3 shows a query which represents a good description of the retrieved document clusters.

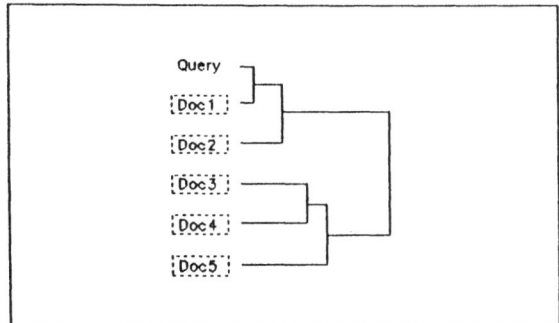

Fig. 4: Example for a narrow query

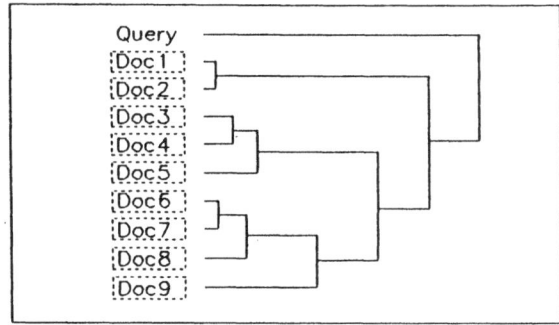

Fig. 5: Example for a broad query

6.2. A Hypertext presentation of retrieved documents

To make available the results of term and document classification to the user we have chosen a Hypertext approach for the presentation of documents. The document chosen by the graphical browser in the previous phase is presented on the screen.

The following relationships are interpreted as Hypertext links:

* CIT-CIT relationship, derived from the knowledge base (CITs belonging to the same subject field)
* CIT-subject field relationship, provided by the knowledge base
* TERM-document relationship, established in the indexing phase
* CIT-document relationship, established in the indexing phase
* CIT-TERM relationship, gained by the indexing phase (TERMs occurring frequently with the same CIT)
* TERM-TERM relationship, gained by term classification (quasi synonym relationship between TERMs)
* document similarities, resulting from document classification

In the presented document these links are made visible by marking the entry points (i.e. TERMs and CITs) of the Hypertext links. The user is optically aware of the positions in the presented document where from he may start browsing through the set of retrieved documents.

The user may use the following links to browse through the set of retrieved documents:

(1) Link to the presentation of all retrieved documents provided by the graphical browsing system.
(2) Link from the presented document to the most similar document (in both directions).
(3) Link from a TERM specified by the user to the most similar document containing this TERM.
(4) Link from a CIT specified by the user to the most similar document containing this CIT.
(5) Link from a TERM specified by the user to a list of synonym TERMs.
(6) Link from a CIT specified by the user to the according parts of the hierarchy of subject fields embedded in $K^E_L P$'s knowledge base.
(7) Link from a CIT specified by the user to the source text of this CIT.
(8) Link from a TERM specified by the user to a definition of this TERM.

The links (7) and (8) can be regarded as relations obtained from an additional external knowledge base which is not planned to be incorporated in $K^E_L P$ by now. Further the development of such a knowledge base could be useful to improve the results of the classification phase.

The usage of the above described links allows $K^E_L P$ to present the retrieved documents in non-sequential order. The user can easily "walk" through the document clusters by simply defining the entry points of the search. These entry points represent different levels of knowledge about documents and document groups.

404

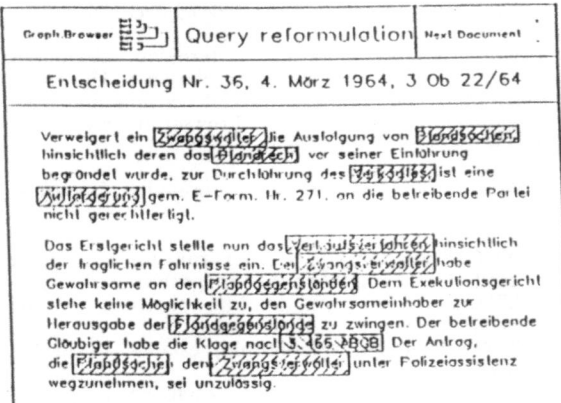

Fig. 6: Document presentation

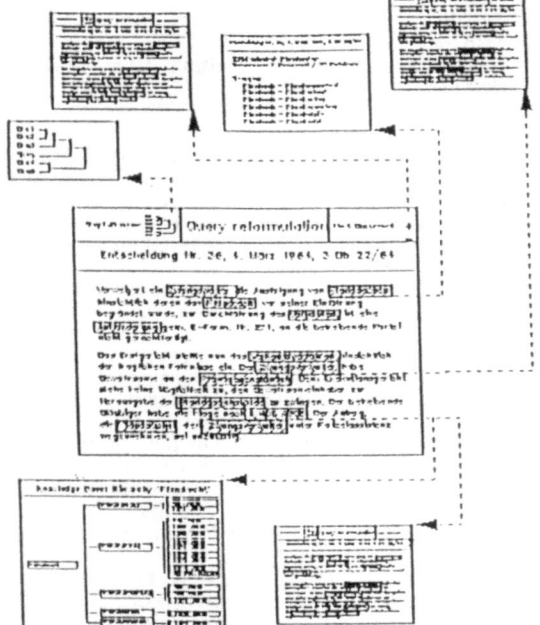

Fig. 7: Hypertext links

6.3. Assistance for reformulating queries in $K^E_L P$

As an extension to conventional IR systems $K^E_L P$ allows the user to reformulate a query while reading a retrieved document.

This by simply entering the pattern of the new query to a small query editor. For example the user may enter the following pattern:

$$(a \text{ AND } b) \text{ OR } (c \text{ AND } d \text{ AND } (\text{NOT } e))$$

The search variables are replaced by simply selecting TERMs or CITs with a mouse directly from the presented text.

The obtained new query is compared with the previously retrieved superdocuments. In case of increasing difference between the new query and the previously retrieved superdocuments the whole document base is taken as basis for a new retrieval process. Whereas in case of increasing similarity between the new query and a subset of the previously retrieved superdocuments only this subset is regarded as basis for the search.

This additional feature can be regarded as incorporating user feedback to the search process. The user may select new search criteria while reading previously retrieved documents. This provides a better retrieval results in respect to the user's definition of relevant documents.

7. Conclusion

$K^E_L P$, a prototype for an intelligent legal fulltext IR system has been presented. We have pointed out problems arising in conventional IR systems and described classification and a Hypertext oriented user-interface as ways to overcome these problems. Classification has been described as a tool to obtain semantically grouped documents. The results of the classification phase are proposed to be used to automatically generate links for a Hypertext oriented presentation of the retrieved documents. Furthermore a way for incorporating user feedback to the search process has been introduced. By this the user is assisted in retrieving relevant documents.

8. References

[1]   H. M. Brooks; Expert Systems and Intelligent Information Retrieval; Information Processing & Management 23(4), 1987

[2]   C. J. van Rijsbergen; Information Retrieval; Butterworth, London, 1975

[3]   G. Salton, M. Mc Gill; Introduction to modern Information Retrieval; McGraw-Hill, New York, 1983

[4]   G. Salton, C. Buckley; Term Weighting Approaches in Automatic Text Retrieval; Information Processing & Management 24(5), 1988

[5]   G. Salton; Automatic Text Processing: The Transformation, Analysis, and Retrieval of Information by Computer; Addison-Wesley, Reading; 1989

[6]   W. R. Svoboda; Zum Problem der Erstellung eines JURISTISCHEN THESAURUS (Automatisierte Erstellung von Kontextassoziationen); Entwicklungsunterlage MAJUS 10, GMD Institut für DV im Rechtswesen, 1976

[7]   C. Tapper; Citations as a Tools for Searching Law by Computer; in: B. Niblett (ed.); Computer Science and Law; Cambridge University Press; 1980

[8]   C. Tapper; An experiment with citation vectors; in: C. Campbell (ed.); Data Processing and the Law; Sweet & Maxwell, London, 1984

[9]   P. Willett; Recent Trends in Hierarchic Document Clustering: A Critical Review; Information Processing & Management 24(5), 1988

LEXIS: A LEGAL EXPERT SYSTEM FOR IMPROVING LEGISLATIVE DRAFTING

*Antonio Cammelli - *Fiorenza Socci

***Istituto per la Documentazione Giuridica
Italian National Research Council**

The prospective in which this research project has, in fact, developed, which we intend to illustrate here, is aimed at making a methodological contribution to the analysis and improvement of legislative drafting.

The awareness that a very inadequate legislative corpus has serious repercussions on society as a whole has, over the last few years, encouraged and prompted research and experimentation directed towards creating better laws from both the substantive and formal point of view [1].

SUMMARY

1. Introduction - 2. Expert systems for legal decision-making - 3. The LEXIS Project: the Xi plus system - 4. The LEXIS Project: the knowledge base - 5. The LEXIS Project: evaluation of the experiment.

1. INTRODUCTION

The rapid evolution in information retrieval systems and in artificial intelligence currently offers valuable tools for reaching this objective.

The utilization of these kinds of tools is now, in fact, indispensable for anyone currently engaged in the preparation of legislation or in the drafting of new codes or statutes.

The impact of such advanced technologies on a very frequently strongly conservative environment like that of the practicing lawyer, has never been, and is still not, without difficulties. Many of the tools made available to lawyers by computer technology have too often been underused, even if a greater awareness and education in this sector is gradually overcoming doubts and fears.

But along with this frequently emphasized factor, there is another consideration which must also be kept in mind.

Even if, on the one hand, it is unquestionable that computer science is useful (especially the more advanced applications of artificial intelligence), it is, nevertheless, possible that attention is mainly concentrated on the means rather than the end, with the result that the demands of computer technology rather than the law are met. Whenever the technological aspects are emphasized, any transformations in the law could give rise to complex issues partially overshadowing the constructive contribution of these methodologies.

It is, therefore, very important in this kind of research to constantly make the law, with all its specificity, the focal point if we are to avoid running the risk of reducing its role to that of a mere exercise.

The marketing of computer tools which are increasingly easy to understand and use enables the lawyer to keep his professional role.

2. EXPERT SYSTEMS FOR LEGAL DECISION-MAKING

Research and experimentation within the law is more and more frequently being dedicated to Artificial Intelligence and its possible applications to legal problem-solving.

As we described above, the rapid development in increasingly sophisticated software, on the one hand, and the evolution of the PC which is economically affordable and more user friendly, should have very important consequences especially for some categories of legal operators as systems designed to aid in decision-making lend themselves to becoming a valuable assistant for the expert.

Lawyers should welcome the possibilities offered by these new efficient decision-making aids. The ease and rapidity with which large quantities of information can be stored, thereby assuring the preservation and immediate utilization of a patrimony of ideas which allows, amongst other things, the high costs of professional consultation to be eliminated, are, furthermore, to be appreciated. The proper use of documentary legal information research and retrieval systems integrated with tools for legal decision-making permit the lawyer, in our opinion, to analyze and rationally exploit an enormous amount of data which would not otherwise be available to him.

As far as the structure of a legal expert system is concerned, although the role played by the inference engine is decisive, lawyers are now concentrating, and rightly so, on the knowledge base, that is, on the kind of data to be loaded and on the most appropriate techniques for its representation and organization. In this context, the need is felt for the most simplified dialogue possible between the user and the system: linguistic accessibility, reduced conventionality but, aboveall, transparency in the logical decision-making process. It is necessary that the "inexpert" user has a good interface at his disposal so he can always check the various phases at any point during a search and that the system is compliant enough to illustrate the hypotheses and subsequent paths of reasoning it is following. And, therefore, it is advisable that the capacity to enrich the documentation by listing the sources used in the various phases of the search or decision-making process is also added. Past experience and the need to keep the lawyer as the central figure in the process of building a legal expert system have directed the attention of experts to shells.

As the analyses and structuralization of knowledge bases is the first priority for the lawyer-computer scientist, shells appear to be the most appropriate tools due to their user friendliness and to the fact that it is not necessary, except in some specific cases, to possess particularly sophisticated hardware and because they are gradually becoming less expensive. Thanks to all these considerations and after some experimentation, we have focused our attention on a shell flexible enough for our needs which permits a complex universe to be represented whilst still guaranteeing the lawyer's central role.

3. THE LEXIS PROJECT: THE XI PLUS SYSTEM

Our choice was determined by evaluating the features of the tool in relation to the need to represent a knowledge base in the legislative field. It appeared to us that Xi plus produced by Expertech [2] unites ease in use and a user friendly interface with the capacity to represent even considerably complex knowledge structures, thanks to several facilities such as control rules, classes of knowledge, the possibility to alternate reasoning strategies through backward and forward chaining.

The knowledge base is divided into various elements: **rules**
(including **demons** or **when/then** rules), **questions, facts, queries.**

The rules express essential knowledge and are written in natural language with the "if...then" formalism ;

Example: if <identifier> is <value>
then <identifier> is <value>

The first term appearing after **if** indicates the object to which a value must be attributed, the verb identifies the relation and the last part is the value attributed to the identifier.

Although the system only provides some verbal forms: **is, is not** (for single values); **include, includes, is a, do not include, does not include, is not a** (for multiple values), any verbal form can be utilized as long as it is pre-defined by the user in the **language** sector. In the absence of any information about the values, pre-established values (defaults) can be used.

Demons are a special kind of rules expressed in the "when...then" form. They have precedence over normal rules and are activated by forward chaining, as soon as the conditions contained in them arise.

Apart from the rules which, along with the demons and the facts, organize the primary knowledge base, there are the questions which help to obtain information from the user about the values to be given to the identifier. They are made up of the same identifier appearing in the rules, of the values which have to associated with it (which may be single or multiple) and of a part in free text which will appear as a question to the user during the search.

The facts represent true assertions for all the conditions; this means that the assertion given as a fact is to be considered true in the whole domain of the knowledge base in question and is activated in the rules for integrating the data of the knowledge volunteered by the user in his answers to the questions.

The queries identify the objective. They contain the chosen identifier to which the system in the decision-making phase must attribute a value, once the inference engine is activated.

Besides these elements, some help and report facilities can be activated. The former can be utilized for obtaining additional information during the search. They can also be considerably long and stored in specific files which can be retrieved in order to complete the knowledge base. The reports can also be written directly in the knowledge base or in special files which can be used during the search phase completing, often in a very useful manner, responses which would otherwise be too concise or not exhaustive enough.

Apart from these facilities, there are also other more advanced facilities to which we have only briefly referred and would now like to describe in a little more detail, stressing their utility, especially when dealing with a very complex knowledge base.

These involve the capacity to activate meta-rules for checking and organizing complex sequences of rules. This is even more useful when it becomes difficult to check the paths of reasoning and to put the rules into order. The rigidity of inference in back chaining and of goal-directed research can be partially overcome by activating several special mechanisms such as forcing, forward chaining and the demons referred to previously.

It will, however, be mainly the job of the knowledge engineer to structure the database so that the best results can be obtained by getting around deficiencies in the tool.

This is not always an easy task when very articulated knowledge has to be represented (as in the case of many legislative texts).

Often several attempts and, therefore, more than one version are necessary before obtaining systems which function properly. This kind of effort is, however, a useful exercise in acquiring greater experience in this form of "programming". Furthermore, it is also an excellent test for evaluating the quality of the text. Our research has shown that the more difficult it is to transform a knowledge base into rules the more likely it is that the origin text was written badly or was inconsistent or muddled.

Furthermore, we can move from the formalized text to its rewriting by following the the logical structuralization followed and considerable benefits immediately flow from an exact and unambiguous choice of terms : for example, it is no longer necessary to go through the text jumping sections and subsections to get to the requested information (even when we are left with no information because the presence of gaps do not become evident from reading the text).

4. THE LEXIS PROJECT: THE KNOWLEDGE BASE

We chose for our research the conceptually uniform legislative corpus contained in Arts. 84-92 of the Italian Civil Code on the "Conditions Required for Contracting Marriage" and Law No. 898 of 1 December 1970 on the "Regulation of the Dissolution of Marriage" as recently amended by the Italian Parliament to which we then added Law No. 194 of 22 May 1978 on the voluntary termination of pregnancy, with which we are planning to end this initial cycle of experimentation.

The research group working on the "Automated Analysis of Legislation" [3] at "Istituto per la documentazione giuridica" of the Italian National Research Council had already for some time been experimenting on norms relating to marriage and this seemed to us to be a valid reason for evaluating whether this new trend in technology was capable of reaching better results. In this context, amongst other things, we chose the legislation relating to the dissolution of marriage which constitutes an extremely valid test thanks both to its formalization and its computer- aided reconstruction.

At this point, the normative text was subdivided into a number of conceptually uniform units denoting the various logically grouped conditions which, once they have been ascertained, compete to attribute the final value to the query identifier (for example, permitted, forbidden, etc.).

Now let us look, even if briefly, at the law on the dissolution of marriage: this phrase already illustrates how the language of lawyers is often a long way from reality. The term "divorce ", often heard in political debate, is perhaps more familiar to the man in the street. We will, however, examine sect. 3 of the Law which lays down the conditions for petitioning for the dissolution of a marriage.

Our choice has always been to substantially retain the terminology in the legislative text we will be examining, whereby the identifier in the query is "the dissolution of marriage".

Subsection 1 is important as it provides that one spouse can petition for the marriage to be dissolved on the grounds that the other spouse had been sentenced in a decision which had become final. The subsequent text describes this statement in detail: ss.1(a) life imprisonment or a 15 year prison sentence; ss.1(b) any prison sentence for serious offences (such as incest) but in this case the petition can only be filed by one of the injured parties; ss. 1(c) deals with cases of the second degree murder of certain persons and the attempted murder of a spouse. Subsection 1(d) provides that there must be two or more prison sentences for several types of offences. Even in this case, action can only be taken by a party who has clearly been injured. The final part of the text in subsection 1 ends with the statement that the petition for the dissolution of marriage cannot be filed by the spouse who has been convicted of complicity in the preceding offences or whenever the spouses have resumed living together.

The ordinary person is already faced with almost insurmountable problems in reading the subsection. The legislator, instead of specifying the various offences, lists them according to the articles in the Criminal Code. This is already a positive limitation to the easy understanding of a text intended for the public: all the offences have been listed in great detail in the formalization of the text thereby saving the non-expert reader a tiring search because we presume that not everybody has an updated version of the Criminal Code on hand.

However, moving on to subsection 2, the non-expert reader will think that the question about offences is closed, instead when reading ss. 2(a) it lays down, coming back to offences, that if the proceedings ended in an acquittal for total mental deficiency with regard to the offences provided for in ss. 1(b) and (c), then the petition can still be filed.

Furthermore, in subsection 2(c), the legislator goes back over the same offences allowing the action to be taken if the proceedings ended with the court finding it did not have to proceed because of the extinction of the offence. The offence of incest is expressly mentioned in subsection 2(d) affirming that the petition can be filed even if the proceedings ended with a release or acquittal due to the fact that the act could not be punished because there was no public scandal.

It becomes obvious from what has already been said that simply reading and interpreting the text is an extremely difficult and arduous task: in fact, if the legislator makes a prison sentence the premise for filing a petition we must conclude that there are offences where that approach is correct which are obviously so serious as far as the disso-

lution of marriage is concerned, to constitute, by themselves, the grounds enabling action to be taken. If we examine, for example, incest and we consider the descendent, including an adopted child, the injured party, the following grid regarding the possibility of filing a petition can be drawn up which, as we can see, goes far beyond the prison sentence. In fact:

If the offence is incest, action can be taken when there is:

a) any prison sentence (sect. 3(1)(a));

b) acquittal for total mental deficiency (sect, 3(2)(a));

c) not having to proceed because of the extinction of the offence (sect.3 (2)(c));

d) release or acquittal which states that the act cannot be punished because there was no public scandal (sect. 3 (2)(d)).

It would clearly have been desirable if the legislator had begun by describing the offences in detail and had made the prison sentences or other findings mentioned above subordinate to these and only these.

The need to formalize the text has forced us to work in this way and, therefore, we can state, without hesitation, that the text which was formalized for loading the data into the system is undoubtedly clearer and more legible than the examined text. By restricting ourselves to a single example, we can briefly write the rules regarding the example already given as follows:

IF the crime is yes
AND the offence is incest
AND the injured party is a descendant or adopted child
THEN the incest offence requirement is met

Another rule relating to eventual decisions regarding incest can be added to this first rule:

IF the incest offence requirement is met
AND the sentence is imprisonment, or acquittal for total mental deficiency or for not having to proceed because of the extinction of the offence or release or acquittal because there was no public scandal
THEN the sentence requirement is met

At this point the only thing left to do is write the rules:

IF the crime is yes
AND complicity in the offence is no
THEN the complicity offence requirement is met
IF crime is yes
AND marital cohabitation is no
THEN the cohabitation requirement is met

We are, therefore, able to write the final rule, reading the effects of the rules written above as:

IF the incest offence requirement is met
AND the sentence requirement is met
AND the complicity offence is met
AND the cohabitation requirement is met
THEN the right to bring the action is verified

Furthermore, if the spouse has petitioned the court and the judge has unsuccessfully attempted conciliation between the spouses, we can give the "possible" value to the "dissolution of marriage" query identifier and with this verify and close the search.

Further improvements can, in cases like this, be made to the terminology: the example we have given is of the conceptual utility of providing the exact measure of performance of the system's inference engine. However, the fact that the example taken from the legislative text is of great social importance but is difficult to read demonstrates how the subdivision of the text into distinct conceptual units which can be defined as "textual representation levels" is not only essential if the lawyer- computer scientist is to formalize the text but could also be the basis for redrafting it moving once again from the codified text to the free text keeping in mind all that was detected in the formalization phase.

5. THE LEXIS PROJECT: EVALUATION OF THE EXPERIMENT

As far as the tool we used is concerned, we are able to state that it has proved reasonably flexible and adaptable even for representing complex and articulated knowledge bases, such as those in the field of legislation. This judgment is based on the experience acquired during a long period of experimentation which has allowed us to build numerous knowledge bases as well as on advances in the Xi plus system which, in its present version, runs more quickly, has many more functions and an even friendlier user interface.

The logical structure of the "shell", which is necessarily rigid so that the deduction mechanism can subsequently be applied to it, has proved satisfactory in revealing inconsistencies, gaps and illogicalities in the normative text which do not always become evident, even through reading it carefully.

Sometimes formalizing the text with the often expressed intention to be absolutely faithful to that text would have either led to not giving the responses the user required (because of gaps in the text) or to giving conflicting answers. It is easy to fully understand, therefore, the importance of the role of the lawyer- computer scientist who, in these difficult situations, must perform his special task, namely to provide an integrative interpretation which even goes beyond the exact literary interpretation.

His intervention is not only necessary for allowing the system to reply but also for making a critical contribution to the interpretation of the text in question. To give an actual example of this, let us look at sects. 18 and 19 of Law No. 194. These sections lay down the punishment provided for causing the termination of a pregnancy without the consent of the woman. In sect. 18(5) it is stated that the punishment will be increased if the woman is less than 18 years old; sect. 19(5) talks about increasing the punishment in the case of women who are less than 18 years old or legally incapable. It would seem reasonably obvious, given the spirit of the law in question, that where a minor is mentioned this should also include a legally incapable woman. However, the problem can arise where the text does not define this inclusion (as far as the punishment is concerned) and it would, therefore, be advisable if the legislation were explicit on the matter.

Given the complexity of the problems faced and also for emphasizing the deficiencies in the text, we have, in some cases, made an integrative interpretation, relying on the spirit of the normative text in question as well as rules of common sense which complete the legal interpretation. It must, however, be pointed out that our work does not in any way aim at providing the "definitive" interpretation of the corpus we have examined and, indeed, we believe that this task is not amongst those to be performed by this tool. We are, nevertheless, of the opinion that our research should make all legal operators and, aboveall, the parliamentary draftsman think more carefully about how to restrict discretionality, as far as possible, especially where it is not necessary.

To give another example, if we consider sect. 19(5) which has already been cited (the text of which appears in Reference [4]), when it states that whoever causes the termination of the pregnancy of a minor or legally incapable woman will be sentenced to the punishment "laid down respectively in the preceding subsections". Referral to the preceding subsections using the adverb "respectively" cannot be interpreted in an unambiguous way because it can refer to more that one possible situation within the same section.

The formalization is, therefore, fundamental and also allows other expressive vagueness to be pointed out, demonstrating that the text, especially of the legislation in question, which is of great social impact, is in need of clarification. For example, as sect. 6(b) talks about "pathological processes", we believe that this expression should be explained better (also for the purpose of applying the law properly). The same can be said of sect, 7 (3) which talks about the "autonomous life of the fetus": in this case it would also be desirable that this formulation be clarified, even with scientific details, in order to avoid eventual disputes or forced interpretations.

For the purpose of completing and testing our research, it seems advisable to us, in this phase, to extend the experiment by furnishing the system with other kinds of knowledge such as case law and legal authority.

Our aim would be to, on the one hand, to offer the user a system capable of giving articulated and documented replies which are as complete as possible and, on the other, to verify, with a close degree of approximation, the interpretative effort we have made in the complex task of formalizing a normative text.

This evolution will, naturally, require experimenting with other computer techniques and studying the links that are possible with the tool we have utilized. This, therefore, means an articulated and careful experimentation keeping constantly in mind the needs of the lawyer who, as we have repeated on many occasions, must be the main beneficiary of this type of research.

REFERENCES

[1] Important research of this kind has been done by the Commission for Research into the Simplification of Procedures and the Feasibility and Enforcement of Legislation, chaired by Alberto Barettoni Arleri, described in a book by Arleri: "Fattibilità ed applicabilità delle leggi", Maggioli, Rimini, 1983. On the same topic, see G. Abagnale, "Tecniche legislative: prime riflessioni su alcune esperienze straniere", in "Le Regioni", Vol. XIII, 1985, March-June, Nos. 2-3, p. 241-255.

[2] The product works on an IBM Personal Computer or IBM compatible, requires at least 640 K of memory capacity and preferably a hard disk, is written in Language C. For a critical analysis of the potentiality of Xi plus see: R. Forsyth, "Expertech Xi plus", in: "Expert Systems", Vol. 4, 1987, February, No. 1, p. 48-51.

[3] With reference to this, see the Internal Report of the "Istituto per la Documentazione Giuridica" which collects several papers on the subject together: "Automated Analysis of Legislation, Trends in Research from 1981 to 1984", IDG, December 1984.

[4] Law No. 194 of 22 May 1978, sect. 19(5): "Quando l'interruzione volontaria della gravidanza avviene su donna minore degli anni diciotto, o interdetta, fuori dei casi o senza l'osservanza delle modalità previste dagli articoli 12 e 13, chi la cagiona è punito con le pene rispettivamente previste dai commi precedenti aumentate fino alla meta. La donna non è punibile".

"When the pregnancy of a woman who is less than eighteen years old, or who is legally incapable, is voluntary terminated, outside the instances provided for or without complying with the provisions in sections 12 and 13, the person who causes it will be sentenced to the punishment laid down respectively in the preceding subsections increased by up to a half. The woman will not be punishable".

"ARCHEO-NET" a Prehistoric and Paleontological Material Data Base
for Research and Scientific Animation

J. Fruitet, L. Kalloufi, D. Laurent

ITODYS - Université Paris 7, URA 34 CNRS, 1 rue Guy de la Brosse, 75005 Paris

L. Boudad, H. de Lumley

IPH - Museum d'Histoire Naturelle, UA 184 CNRS, 1 Rue René Panhard, 75013 Paris

ABSTRACT

With the increasing power of personal computers, archaeologists are provided with new means of treating the huge collections of data produced by major archaeological excavations. We describe here Archeo-Net, an archaeological data base (DB) coupled with an expert system (ES) containing graphical processing capabilities, developed at the the Institut de Palontologie Humaine (IPH) and the Institut de Topologie et Dynamique des Systèmes (ITODYS) in Paris for the management of paleontological and prehistoric data of La Caune de l'Arago, Tautavel (France) and many other archaeological sites of south of France.

INTRODUCTION

Modern archaeological excavation methods produce tremendous quantites of objects when applied to sites densely populated or used over long periods of time. Archaeologists, who routinely attempt to resolve enigmas for which keys have long been lost, are obliged to record even the most minute details about an excavation, knowing well that their investigations destroy the site, rendering it useless for any further study. Sophisticated analytical techniques furnish much diversified information about the multitude of objects recovered, all of which must be stored along with the pertinent data logged on site [1,2].

A) EXCAVATION METHODOLOGY

I. Archaeological excavation techniques

In order to understand the structure of the data base presented here, it is necessary to have some idea of excavation methods generally used in modern archaeology. Before any digging is undertaken, a rectangular grid system, most often with one meter spacing, is established on the site by means of wires oriented from south to north and from west to east. The position of each one-metre square, called a *zone*, is defined with respect to the origin of the coordinate system. The horizontal position of all objects found is indicated with a double set of coordinates, the position within the zone and the coordinates of the zone itself. The vertical position (depth) of large objects is measured directly with respect to an arbitrary zero level. Very small objects, recovered by screening, are referenced only to the zone and the average level of the layer treated.

Excavation proceeds with great care and the thickness of the various layers excavated is defined taking into account the homogeneity of the soil, its richness in objects and its hardness. Recovered pieces are numbered, recorded in the site log, drawn on a reduced-scale map and photographed.

An excavation campaign in a site like La Caune de l'Arago (Tautavel, France) generates more than 20,000 new pieces a year. At the present time, data on more than 300,000 objects have been acquired from the sites of La Caune de l'Arago - Tautavel (700,000/100,00 years BP), and La Grotte du Lazaret - Nice (200,000 BP).

II. Archaeological Data

Archaeological data are most often made up of linked pairs of data (O,T), where O defines the spacial origine of the object and T its most distinctive feature.

We should carefully distinguish between:

- Data accumulated on the site for a specified object;

- Data resulting from the study of an object in the laboratory. A systematic description system for stone tools and for fossil bones has been formulated by research groups at IPH, in collaboration with the anthropology and paleontology laboratories of the Museum d'Histoire Naturelle, under the direction of Professor Henry de LUMLEY.

Data are easily coded by alphanumeric strings. In some cases, the reference card for a particular object may be completed by the addition of photos, drawings, plans, transversal or longitudinal profiles of the site, etc.

For the data base organisation, we can propose the following diagram :

SITE LOG BOOK

(all registered objects)

Relation   'IS-A' BONE   'IS-A' TOOL

Bone description   Tool description

DESCRIPTIONS OF OBJECTS

III. Data Base Conceptual Diagram

A unique database is associated with each archaeological site, integrating information from the site log and descriptions of tools and fauna. In its relational form, the base can be schematized as:

Relation *rObjet* (zone,number,...) : site logbooks;

Relation *rFaune* (zone,number,...) : bones;

Relation *rOutil* (zone,number,...) : stone objects;

The *rObject* relation is relatively straightforward, in contrast to the *rFaune* and *rOutil* relations which are quite complex. This complexity is a result of the large number of attributes required in typology and in paleontology for the precise description of stone tools and fossils (between 30 and 300 per object) and the numerous functional dependencies existing between these attributes.

IV. Validity and Consistency of Data Bases.

Coexistence of static and dynamic relationships accentuates the problem of assuring the integrity of the data base and maintaining its coherence when acquiring new data. This latter problem was solved by developing pre- and post-processors in C language for checking the consistency of data input. They parse the input flow and passe on the validity of values affected to each field (domaine integrity) and the consistency of all cross references between fields. Other procedures provide on-line operator help for acquisition, modification and interrogation. In acquisition, default values are proposed, computations carried out automatically and some values suggested on the basis of pre-established rules.

B) **ES-ARCHEO**: EXPERT SYSTEM FOR

LITHIC TOOL RECORDING

Numerous tentatives of formalisation or modelisation of the reasoning processes in archaeology have been attempted in the past and easy acces to computers can't help but encourage these endeavors [3].

In this paper, we describe an ES coupled to a DB and using the relational form as the representation of knowledge. A relation between a Knowledge Base (KB) of AI and a the data base of a Data Base Management System (DBMS) offers the potential of permitting each part to benifit from the techniques proper to the other. The DB can take advantage of inferencing mechanism of the ES and take it as deductive component, and the ES can take advantage of the data management facilities available in the DBMS. Figures 1 to 3 describe the different kinds of relations between the DB and the ES [4,5,6,7,8].

412

Figure 1. Intelligent DB approach.

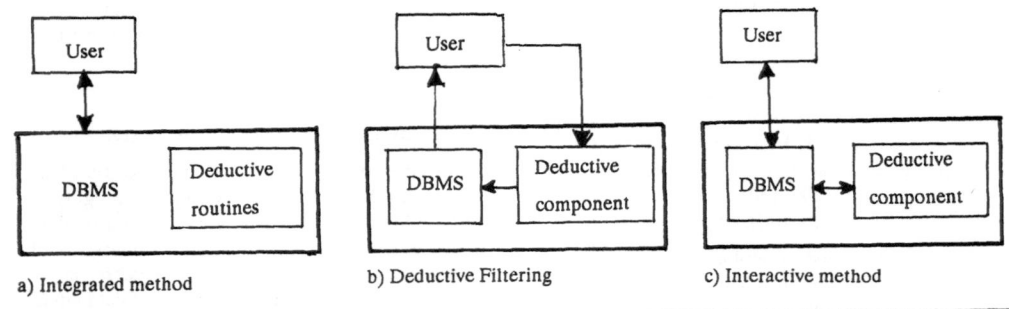

a) Integrated method   b) Deductive Filtering   c) Interactive method

Figure 2. Enhanced ES approach

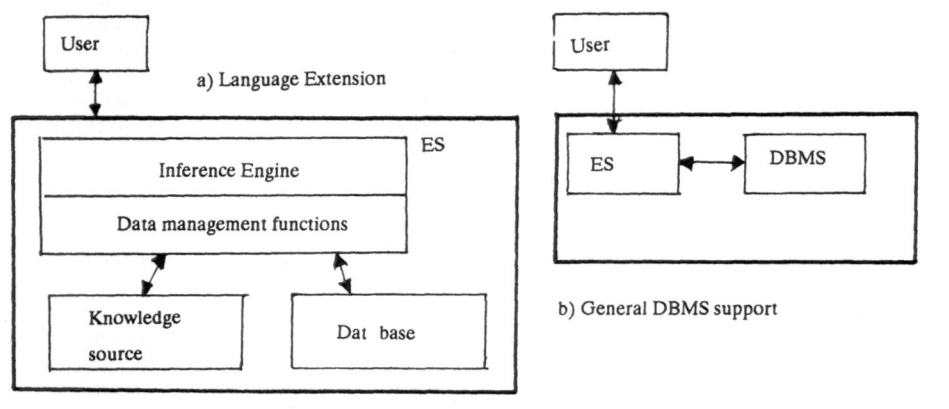

a) Language Extension

b) General DBMS support

Figure 3. Inter-system communication

a) Distributed processing   and control   b) Concentration of processing and control

c) Distributed processing and control
   by an independant subsystem

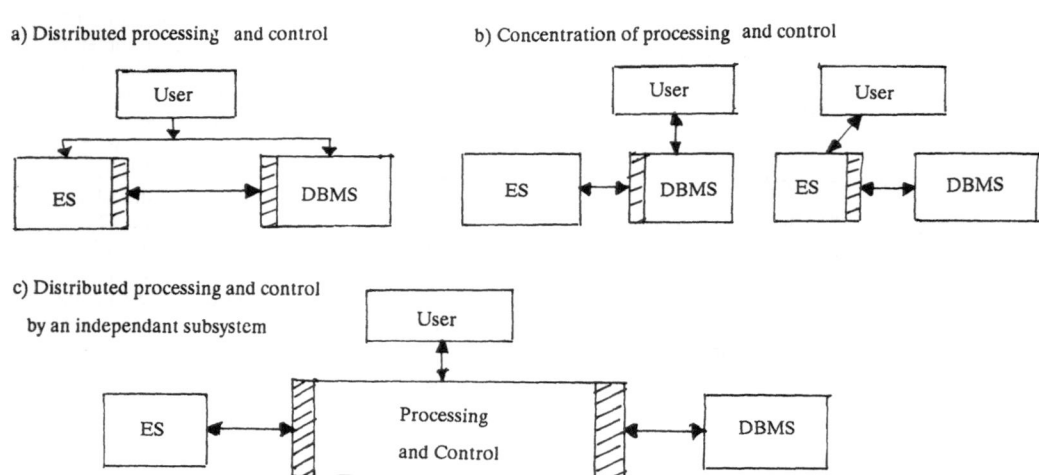

I. Expert System and Database Interaction.

The approach taken by ES-ARCHEO combines both possibilities of figure 3b. Each system has the means of communicating with the other but at any one moment, one of the systems dominates. The processor incorporated into the ES allows its access to the KB, represented as a relational DB, thus permitting it to benefit from all the facilities of a DBMS. The processor incorporated into the DB allows it to find the data necessary for the inference mechanism, to format them for the ES and the operator and to call up production rules when a control of the DB is necessary. This gives the appearance of having a deductive DB base when the operator works with that base and an expert system using a DB as a knowledge base when the operator uses the ES.

Since its initial structuring, our DB has greatly evolved in order to adapt itself to the precise needs of typologists. This has required frequent rewriting of the pre- and post- processing subroutines for controling data integrity. In order lessen that burden, we decided to implement control of the DB, the triggers and the most frequent requests as production rules, with the objective of:

- reacting to triggers more efficiently;

- permitting the inference of new data from the data existing explicitly in the data base;

- substituting production rules for rewriting of control procedures.

The problems of interaction between the ES and the DB and representation of knowledge are at the heart of our current research interests.

II. Representation of Knowledge

In our approach, the knowledge base is represented in the form of relations in a relationel data base. Let us first look at the knowledge base.   Facts are expressed by defining objets, their attributes and assigning values. An *object* can be a physical entity, like *a stone* as well as a concept, like *the width*. Associated with these objects are attributes permitting their identification and values adding precisions. In order to distinguish between such an expression and conventional data, we shall refer to the object-attribute-value triplet as *asserted data*.

Rationalization of this way of expressing facts can be accomplished by combining the object names and the attributes, transforming the triplet into a duo. This permits construction of a relational DB formed of tables composed of facts and rules. These tables are:

robject(**Name_object**, question, multivalued)
rvalue(**Name_object**, **value**, coef_certitude)
rpremise(**Name_rule**, **No_premise**,
        Name_object,value)
rconclusion(**Name_rule**, **No_conclusion**,
        Name_object, value)
rlegal(**Name_object**, value).

The **bold-faced** fields are the primary keys in the table. The *robject* table contains all the objects devined in the KB. An object has a name, can be multivalued and can have a question associated with it which can be posed to the operator at the time of inference if the value of the object is unknown (the fact doesn't exist).

The *rvalue* table contains the facts. The *rpremise* and *rconclusion* tables form the rules. The *rlegal* table contains permissible values for an object. Pointers have been defined between the *robject* table and the other tables, binding each object to the facts concerning it and to the premises and conclusions in which it participates.

III. The Different Kinds of Facts

There are three principal types of facts:

a - Simple facts that form the DB fields, that can be taken directly from the DB and used in production rules.

b - Composite facts that are deduced from several DB fields. Deduction of these facts is obtained by routines employed before starting the inference engine. This strategy aims to:

- reduce the number of production rules;
- diminish the complexity of expressing the rules;
- limit the chain of rules;
- avoid repeated accessing of the DB.

Consider the following wording: *If a tool has two simple lateral scrapers and if the junction of the scrapers is not pointed then the tool contains a convergent scraper.*

This can be translated in several ways:

If number_tool=2 *and*
If type_tool1=SCR *and*
If type_tool2=SCR *and*
If position_tool1=RLAT *and*
If position_tool2=LLAT *and*
If tool_contiguous=YES *and*
If pointed_junction=NO
Then composite_tool=CONVSCR

If such a rule is used, the DB must be accessed several times:

- in order to count the number of simple tools;
- to determine that two of these are scrapers;
- to verify that one scraper is right lateral;
- to verify that the other is left lateral;
- to determine that they are contiguous.

Numerous accesses to the DB result in long execution time and lengthy waiting for the deduction, especially when the failure of one rule results in an attempt with another. In order to reduce the number of accesses, and consequently the delai, the above rule can be formulated as follows:

If type_simple=SCR *and*
If position=LRLAT *and*
If tool_contiguous=YES *and*
If pointed_junction=NO
Then composite_tool=CONVSCR.

The first premise indicates both that the *simple tool* type is *scraper* and that their *number* is 2. The second indicates that one of the tools is *lateral right* and the other *lateral left*.

These routines access the DB, analyse the fields and construct the facts necessary for the different rules. That presupposes that we know at any given moment the finality of the operation, and hence, the rules and facts to be used. That is, these routines assume the role of metarules for they continually indicate the rule to be used and the necessary facts.

c - Facts supplied by the operator in response to a question.

IV. Inference Mechanism

The inference mechanism is an interpreter of production rules. Its goal is fixed by the name of the object. Using the *robject* table directly with *Name_object* as a key, and with the help of the pointer to the *rconclusion* table, it determines the entire set of rules having that object in the conclusion. If that set is empty, no rule has the object in its conclusion. If the set isn't empty, then only the pertinent rules are loaded into fast memory. In order to verify a fact, the *rvalue* table is accessed using the duo (object,value) as a key. The existence of a fact depends thus on the existence of a duo in *rvalue* having that key. Hence thanks to that representation and to the set of pointers, validation of a fact and hunting for pertinent rules is reduced to a direct access using a key and pointers.

V. Conclusion

As far as maintaining the integrity of very large data base of prehistorical material is concerned, we cannot insist too much on the importance of the interface with the user. This is particularly true when, as is often the case, data acquisition is confined to novice archaeologists, having rudimentry knowledge of the field and little experience with data processing. We hope that interaction between the ES-ARCHEO expert system and present data bases will result in better checking of data, easier use and more help to the novice in the definition of lithic objects.

C) ARCHAEOLOGICAL DATA TREATMENT

Once the data bases have been established, different types of treatment can be envisaged, either on the raw data or after preliminary processing.

- *Statistics and catalogs*. The data base from the Lazaret site [9] is being used for a systematic study of the distribution and proportions of various types of objects in the different levels.

- *Publication of profiles, plans and maps*. Using the spatial coordinates of the objects, it is possible to automatically plot their profiles (vertical projections along the North-South or East-West axes) as a means of showing eventual archaeological levels.

- *Numerical Archaeology: GR-Archaeo, an interactive and graphic approach*. A precise determination of the chronology of deposits conditions the study of the distribution of objects and their relationships. Programs we have written for personal computers permitting visualization of profiles in color on a screen show only too well the limits of purely graphical approach to the problem of strata. We are developing an interactive program that aids in the differentiation of levels.

While conserving an interactive graphical aspect, this program uses algorithms borrowed from image analysis and graph theory to utilise available data to a maximum. The archaeologist will be able to direct this program so as to obtain a series of proposals for homogeneous archeological levels. He can, if necessary, correct these proposals and finally visualize the results in 3-D on a screen and have the levels plotted. Queries are made in SQL on objects of the database and their spatial coordinates. ASCII files are generated and recovered by the visualization program. Data are reorganized in order to speed up graphic processing and at the same time, a micro-density map for each type of object is updated. Different algorithms are applied to the data of that map in order to distinguish closely associated components.

Using the hypothesis that levels of human occupation have certain specificities, we search for their presence in the data of the base using a series of transformations on the density values (filtering) and we connect together surfaces having the same properties while respecting certain topographical constraints (absence of holes, slope, etc.).

This treatment results in the establishment of a numerical terrain model (NTM) that is proposed to the operator in the form of a contour map. If it isn't satisfactory, the operator can interactively locally deform the model or chose other agregation criteria before having the NTM recalculated.

The results are recorded in ASCII files and plotted in large format (A0) using HPGL commands. The original DB is modified so as to mark objects identified as belonging to a same level and permit the use of this information in ulterieur processing. Coupled with efficient management of the data base, GR-ARCHEO constitues an important element in the treatment of archaeological data.

D) MATERIAL IMPLANTATION

The different laboratories associated in the constitution of a prehistorical material data base work on a dozen sites spread across southern France, Italy and Spain. This dispersion in the sites and the necessity of recording large volumes of data locally has imposed a decentralised acquisition system. This system operates under Unix using PC/AT compatible computers and is thus multi-user, multi-task.

If these systems have proven to be adequate for decentralized acquisition and validation of local data, they have shown themselves lacking sufficient power to managage all of the data from prehistorical sites in southern France. For this reason, the data are being transferred to an IBM mainframe linked to all of our laboratories. The whole data base will be available to all the users but acquisition and treatment will continue being carried out locally.

E) PERSPECTIVES

The use of data processing has obliged a very important effort of normalisation of terminology and classification criteria on the part of archaeologists. Archaeology was essentielly observational and descritive at the origine. Il will become more and more experimental and, in the near future, make use of the computer for simulating excavations and reconstructing prehistoric life. With the constitution of a computerized data base of paleontological and prehistorical material, the application of modern technologies to the understanding of fossil man is just taking its first steps.

Acknowledgement: The authors wish to thank J.A. MILLER, Ingénieur de Recherche at the ITODYS, for his helpful collaboration on this paper.

416

REFERENCES

[1] LUMLEY H. de "Exploitation automatique des données d'un site préhistorique" in "Les banques de données archéologiques", Editions du CNRS pp. 39-50, 1974.

[2] LEREDDE H., DJINDJIAN F. "Traitement automatique des données en archéologie," *Les Dossiers de l'Archéologie*, no. 42, pp. 52-69, 1986.

[3] LAGRANGE M.S., RENAUD M. "Simulation d'un raisonnement archéologique, description de l'application d'un système expert: le système SNARK" in *Panorama 1983 des Traitements de Données en Archéologie*. Edité par Henri Ducasse, Editions APDCA, pp. 31-64, 1983.

[4] AL-ZOBAIDIE A., GRIMSON J.B. "Expert systems and databases : how can they serve each other?", *Expert Systems*, pp. 30-37, vol. 4, no. 1, February 1987.

[5] BRACHMAN R.J., LEVESQUE H.J. "What makes a knowledge base knowledgeable ? A view of databases from the knowledge level " in *Expert Database Systems*, pp. 69-78, 1986.

[6] DECKER H. "Integrity enforcement on Deductive Database" in *Expert Database Systems*, pp. 381-395, 1987.

[7] RISCH T., REBOH R., HART P. and DUDA R. "A fonctionnal approach to integrating Database and Expert systems" in *Communication of the ACM*, pp. 1424-1436, vol. 31, no. 12, December, 1988.

[8] DELCAMBRE L.M.L. "RPL: An expert system language with query power" in *IEEE Expert*, vol. 3, no. 4, pp. 51-61, 1988.

[9] CANALS i SALOMO A. "Les niveaux archéologiques du Lazaret : Approche méthodologique de leur détermination", *Mémoire de DEA - Quaternaire: géologie, paléontologie humaine, préhistoire*, Museum National d'Histoire Naturelle, 1988.

A COMPREHENSIVE ENVIRONMENT FOR COMPUTER AID IN TECHNICAL SECURITY SYSTEM DESIGN

M. Kantardžić, M Jeftović, H. Glavić, A. Filipović, D. Gajić, N. Miličić

Faculty of Electrical Engineering in Sarajevo, Toplička bb, 71000 Sarajevo,
Yugoslavia

ABSTRACT

In this paper we present a realization of a software package for computer aided design of object and area technical security system. The system provides aid in various phases of design process: from technical security system component choice, system configuration, process simulation, to project documentation support. CAD system is based on tools and methods in areas of: artificial intelligence, computer graphics, data bases and computer-user interaction.

KEYWORDS: CAD, Technical Security Systems, Expert Systems, Expert System Shell

1. INTRODUCTION

This paper presents CAD software package for technical security systems (CSP-TSS). The CSP-TSS is a result of long-range research in Laboratory For Electronics and Computer Technique on Faculty of Electrical Engineering in Sarajevo.

1.1. CSP-TSS Goals

Analysis of a design process of computer based object and area technical security systems (TSS) introduced the following requirements on a CAD system in this area [3-9]:
- TSS component choice aid: sensors, communication lines, rails, control stations...
- components connection aid, in object to define the final TSS architecture;
- evaluation of performance of the designed TSS, based on simulation of processes in this system, as well as evaluation of efficiency and reliability parameters;
- aid in a choice of a particular TSS component manufacturer, considering availability of the component, price, delivery time, maintenance...
- aid in, and monitoring of a documentation design processes;
- capability of an education of CAD system users, as well as novices in the area of TSS.

1.2. Why AI?

After a serious and detailed consultations and interviews with a number of experts in TSS design, the conclusion arise that an AI methods are simply unavoidable if one wants to create a valid tool for TSS design aid. The type of knowledge the experts shared was a number of personal experiences in construction of some existing TSS-s, the stories of problems that had arise under certain environmental conditions. These were on one hand extremely difficult to describe by means of mathematical model, but, on the other hand, very suitable to formalization by means of IF - THEN rules. The other obvious lead towards ES based implementation of the module for TSS design aid was the fact that every time we have contacted a new expert (someone we had not talked to before), we encountered a new type of problem, a new story. In other words, the module must be quite opened, suitable to be changed and improved as the new experiences are gathered.

Shortly, the main indications of the necessity of AI methods implementation in the module for TSS design aid were:

418

- knowledge with unclear structure, based on experience of experts, difficult to be modeled;
- need for expandable system, adaptable to new experiences;
- knowledge suitable for formalization by means of IF - THEN rules.

2. ARCHITECTURE OF CSP-TSS

The CSP-TSS is realized in a modular manner, with large interaction degree between modules. Global architecture of the system is given on Fig.1.

The following chapters describe each of the modules in some more details.

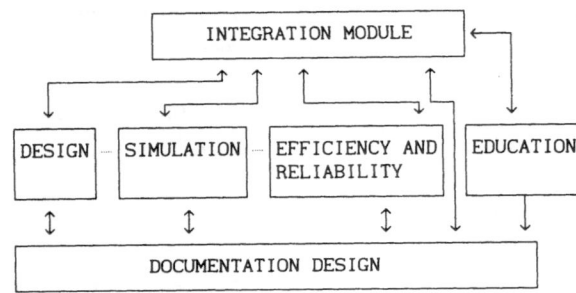

Fig.1. CSP-TSS System Architecture

2.1. Module for Technical Security System Design Aid

For the reasons given in chapter 1.2., the module for TSS design aid is realized as an ES, based on the knowledge of experts in this area. This module is implemented by means of an ES development tool DIPSY-E, also being a product of our laboratory, [1,2,10,11], using forward-chaining inference engine (FCIE) supported by the tool. An ES is connected to manufacturers-products data base, which can be approached independently, as a sub module of this module.

2.1.1. Formal Knowledge Description

The ES is rule based, due to the DIPSY-E manner of knowledge formalization [1,2,10]. The knowledge base is divided into two separate parts,

one containing the facts that describe the current state of the problem, an the other containing rules describing actions to be taken in a given state.

The facts in this particular case are some "objects" with their attributes, describing types of TSS components, characteristics of the object to be protected by TSS, characteristics of an environment, etc. For example, the environmental characteristics of a particular object are described as

geophysical_characteristics
    (climate_conditions = {snow rain fog},
    close_objects = {rail_road forest})

To show the rules formalism, the following rule means that if an attribute "climate_conditions" of a node "geophysical_conditions" does not contain a value "snow", and a kind of a land is not "swampy", a "sensor_type_x" can be added to the set of sensors which can be used.

IF
 geophysical_conditions (climate_conditions >!snow)
AND
    land(kind<> swampy)
THEN
    value
    exists(possible_to_use :+ {sensor_type_x})

2.1.2. Organization of the Rule Base

DIPSY-E tool offers several search and conflict resolution strategies [1,2,10,11]. A variant of the FCIE which divides the rule base into several segments, each dealing with a particular subproblem, is taken for this particular application. The "flow-chart" of the segments is given on a Fig.2.

The first segment interactively compiles the data necessary to determine all the constraints for the TSS implementation. The user is asked about technical characteristics of the (existing or future) TSS, geographical, climate and environmental characteristics of the location.

The next segment examines the same group of problems, but in the details connected to each of the etapes (the overall TSS is always divided into etapes, each covering the part with similar characteristics, eg. the river side of the object, the road side, ...).

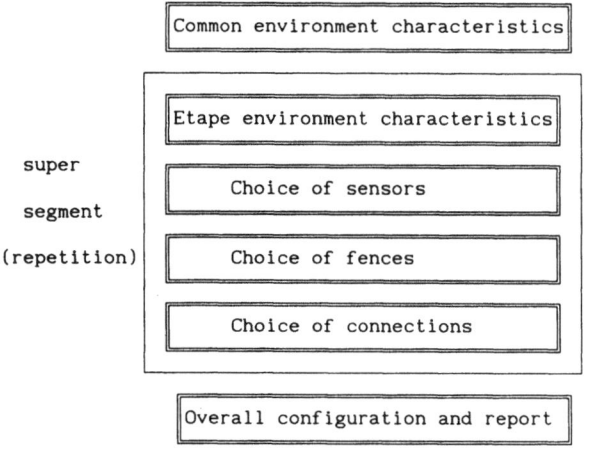

Fig. 2. Organization of the rule base

The following segments of the system offer recommendations on the TSS components choice, configuration of the TSS, and discuss and give recommendations on some special conditions for implementation of particular components for each of the etapes (e.g. one must not have a high snow when using particular types of sensors; if so, the snow must be regularly removed). Those recommendations could be also directly built into the project documentation. Example of a typical recommendation is as follows:

Since the object is surrounded with bushes and high grass, which might cause false alarms, if you decide to use radar_beside_the_fence, recommendation is:
- *to remove bushes on both sides of the fence, in the area of 2-5 meters,*
- *to mow the grass regularly during the system use.*

These segments are, together with the second segment, members of the structure in DIPSY-E called "super-segment". This structure enables group of segments to be repeatedly examined.

2.1.3. Manufacturers/Products Data Base

After the particular components are recommended, the more details on each of them can be found out by means of this sub module. It uses

the results of the ES analysis and for each recommended component it can provide manufacturers and products data bases retrieves, as well as a choice of a manufacturer considering the criteria of: price, delivery time, maintenance, availability, component reliability etc. This sub module can also ba approached independently, with no previous activation of an ES.

Fig. 3 shows an overall architecture of the design aid module.

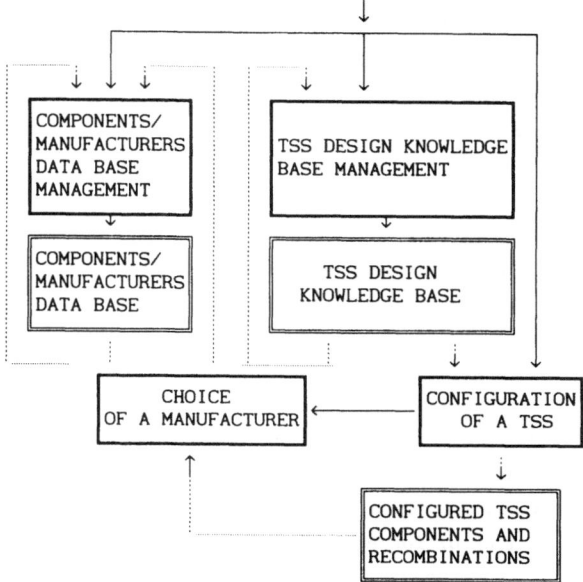

Fig. 3. Design Aid Module

2.2. Simulation

This module provides an aid in the following points of the TSS design process:
- Creation of a model of a computer based technical security system.
- Process simulation concerning failures and alarms enabling detection of faults in the defined technical security system architecture.
- Chronological evidence of events during the simulation process.

All the created models of TSS are stored into a model base, to be recalled when needed. The simulated events are stored in an event base. The bases can be used for reports generation. Reports can be generated either periodically or by request.

2.3. Reliability and Efficiency Estimation

The algorithm of this module relies on the data accumulated in the design (section 2.1.) and the simulation (section 2.2.) phase. In addition it uses some technical/economy aspects of price, quality and level of importance of the object [3,4,9].

The module enables analysis of reliability and efficiency parameters related to various changes of input parameters. Accordingly, it is possible to notice system failures, redundancy, influence of system structure change and component change [8]. This module can also be used with no interaction to other modules, to test previously implemented technical security systems.

2.4. Documentation

This module is based on principals of commonly known text processors [11], emphasizing comfortable computer - user interaction in following:
- Simple creation and connection of graphic and text documentation components;
- Possibilities to work with standard, software defined forms;
- Extended possibilities to work with document archives of former implemented technical security system designs;
- Possibility to use the archives during the new design documentation realization.

2.5. Education

This module introduces the user CAD system and manner of its use throughout comfortable menus. In fact, this is on-line user documentation.

It is possible to add new text files and appropriate menus, that enables the usage of the system in other, similar areas: sensors, communication etc.

3. CONCLUSION

The described implementation of a CAD software package for technical security systems (CSP-TSS)

has given two results: first, it was the first use of the DIPSY-E tool in area of design problems; second, it was a large project in creating the complete CSP-TSS. Functional requirements of the CSP-TSS, determined the necessary hardware components, as well as corresponding software. Computer configuration is based on microprocessor M68020, containing also TEK high-res. graphic terminal along with the mouse and tablet.

System software of the microcomputer is based on standard configuration:
- Operating system UNIX;
- Compiler for programming language C and Pascal;
- ES development tool DIPSY-E.

For the results, it is sufficient to mention that complete CSP-TSS is in operation, and the users are evidently generally satisfied. Yet, together with the results, the limitations arises. The DIPSY-E itself put some limitations (as any other possible tool would). Thus we have gathered significant experience and important information what to improve in the DIPSY-E itself (the described system is developed on DIPSY-E V2.x, while right now we are working on the V3.x).

5. REFERENCE

1. Kantardžić, H. Glavić, A. Filipović, Computer Aided Design Of Technical Security System: Approach Based On Knowledge Base, ETAN '88., Sarajevo, June 1988.
2. A. Filipović, M. Kantardžić, S. Osmanagić, Syntactic Editor DIPSY-E, Conference "Computer on University", Cavtat, May, 1986.
3. L. Kurai, Model For Analysis of Alarm systems efficiency Alarm 1-2 (2), 1983.
4. H. E. Morton, SENTRAX 1 - An Integrated Security Display and Control System, 1984 Carnaham Conference on Securtit Technology, Dentacky, 1984.
5. S. Hahn, Modern Electronic Security Systems, E. Hampton, New York, 1979.
6. R. Barnard, Intrusion Detection Systems, Butterworth publishers, London, 1981.
7. R. Healy, Design for Security, John Wiley and Sons, New York, 1983.
8. D.T. Chery, Total Facility Control, Butterworths publishers, London, 1986.
9. E.J. Henley, K. Kumamoto, Design for Reliability and Safety control, Simp. series No. 92., PSE '85, Cambridge, April, 1985.
10. M. Kantardžić, The Interference Engine in the DIP-E, Conference on Application of Artificial Intelligence IV, Insbruck, Austria, April, 1986.
11. M. Kantardžić, S. Kovačević, Intelligent Form Management System In "Networks in Office Automation", North-Holland, 1985.

AN OBJECT ORIENTED DATABASE FOR ARCHITECTURAL PROJECT MANAGEMENT

CARLO ARGIOLAS

Istituto di Architettura
Universita' di Cagliari
Piazza D'Armi,
09100 CAGLIARI (ITALY)

NICOLETTA DESSI

Centro Calcolo Elettronico
Universita' di Cagliari
Via Universita' 40
09124 CAGLIARI (ITALY)

ABSTRACT

Database support for architectural applications requires appropriate tools for managing graphical and textual informations. In this paper we propose the use of an object oriented database providing uniform access to diverse and autonomous information related to an architectural project. The presented approach supports the integration of heterogeneous data, some of which are under the control of a CAD system.

INTRODUCTION

Despite the recent advances in CAD systems, the commercial products technology is still based on obsolete paradigms approaching their limits in many situations.
In fact, graphic packages allow a workstation to function as an external representation medium of the design made by the user, but only geometric properties and few other quantificable attributes are represented by data models used in CAD systems [1,2,3].
These models place slight emphasis on the integration of heterogeneous data related to graphical images, whose existence involves numerical or textual informations (for example the client of a building project). Although CAD systems are not database management environments, they create another source of data that has the potential to be used with applications derived from design activities, such as bills of material, cost estimates, project schedules and so on [4].
As a result, a design should not be treated as a drawing whose sole purpose is for plotter output, but as an information element having graphical textual, and numerical components.
The access and the manipulation of these components must be integrated with the native drawing format, usually expressed by CAD system proprietary code.
To relieve designers of the above integration problems, many systems give users a glimpse into CAD database by including attribute capabilities. An

attribute is simply text that is assigned to a graphic symbol. The text can be extracted from the drawing in a tabular form and sorted or manipulated mathematically with a database or with specialized application programs.
It means that a drawing may be a good, but not excellent, database reference file, and as a reference file may be used by many proprietary products designed to address specifically its structure.

Within a CAD system, a traditional database (for easy data manipulation and retrieval) and a graphic database (designed generally to enhance the graphic viewing) are difficult to integrate for a number of reasons, including their diverse algorithms and data structures, and their application to different stages of the design process, from synthesis to maintenance [5].
If we consider a CAD drawing as a data file in DBMS environment, the integration requires drawing data to be mapped into data files and vice versa.

As a result, most designs created on computers are not transparent to the user, who perceives the design process and its management as the union of two logical levels of description: the graphic operations directly coming from an idea or an existing object and the textual data required to represent related informations. Obviously, from viewpoint of the designer, who thinks and designs different categories of operations, the quantitative, qualitative and graphical properties are semantically connected in the conceptual model of the project as involved in its description [6].

Ideally CAD users need to be able to manage graphics and texts interchangeably. The list of potential applications derived from the integration of graphic and associated textual information is unlimited, but one of compelling reasons to consider this integration, in the presented paper, is the need to organize an architectural CAD project and the many files associated with it.

We think it is possible to achieve the full and interactive integration of graphic and textual information only offering an opportunity for CAD drawing data to be a part of some common data pool, but this approach requires data modeling capabilities not supported by current implementation of database management systems.

The proposed methodology aims at solving the integration problem by merging object-oriented language concepts with those of database systems while providing a functional tool for managing and retrieving engineering drawings and technical documentation.

This is accomplished by the definition of a software environment that acquires modeling techniques from object-oriented paradigm and storage and retrieval methods from database technologies.

Each project is viewed as a collection of objects which are drawing files or textual information pertaining to the project.
Drawing are assigned to a project and may be located by the user defined features such as project name ,client, description etc.

THE DATABASE SCHEMA

Engineering project management information is defined once in the project configuration and then inherited completely or partially by other drawings or projects on a different level of abstraction. For example a project can be located according to project status, revision, client name etc.. but each of these fields can be custom taylored to user specific needs.
Good data management system lets the user store drawing files according to projects. The user can define and locate projects and drawing files according to his definition of them and other descriptors as client name or any other information the user want to connect to his work.
For the management of informations regarding CAD projects, we propose an object oriented database having the

following major purposes :

- To retrieve a CAD drawing according to the user desidered attributes while providing a working solution for handling people.

- To provide a general query front end with minimum limitations upon the user and allowing movement from database to CAD drawings at will.

Both purposes deal with the development of a general user friendly interface

combining different kinds of information which is not necessary of the same nature (text and graphics).
This form of integration is directly associated with logical data centralization, whose global schema is a highly-logical view of project information content. It does not require textual and graphical information is physically integrated.

In such an application environment, the object-oriented data models can provide constructs for capturing more of the semantics than is possible with a traditional data model. They mediate access and manipulation operations throghout a new form of conceptual schema.

The goal motivating the development of an object oriented database is to merge object-oriented language concepts with those of database systems.
We suggest that a project can be represented as a complex object, built by several more elementary objects, whose nature can be defined in a graphic or in a textual domain.
From graphical objects, the database acquires techniques for the graphical representation of the project.
From textual objects, the database acquires efficient methods for the storage and the retrieval of project informations.

A graphical object consists in a project drawing and expresses itself graphically through an interface built on top of an existing CAD system and acts as "read only object".
Each project consists of a set of drawings, which in turn consist of geometrical objects, representing data as well as geometrical operations to be performed by the user.

A textual object contains both information about the crucial parameters of the project and the set of operations allowed on that informations.

Each textual object is an istance of the following given object class:

- Project
- Drawing
- Client
- Typology
- Parameters

The set of all textual object instances can be partitioned on the basis of class-all objects belonging to exactly one class.

Following the Property Driven Model [7], an object is called entity and has attributes called properties.

There are two kinds of properties: terminal and structural.
A terminal property has an associated local value(i.e. the name of a project).
A structural property is a link to another entity (i.e. between a client and a project) and it is used to make a distinction between different types of relations. A relationship between two entities is defined in the form of pointers pointing from one entity directly to the other and viceversa.

Object properties are described by a set of instance variables, whose values define also the internal status of the object.
A terminal property is expressed by the value of an instance variable whose domain is a primitive class (real, integer, boolean etc..).
A structural property is defined by an instance variable whose value is a pointer to an instance of another class.
Fig.1 shows the object oriented database schema in terms of classes and instance variables .

Each of the classes Project, Drawing, Client, Typology,Parameters consists of its own set of instance variables, which in turn have associated domains.

For example, the domain of the "author" instance variable is the primitive string class and allows us to express a terminal property of the Drawing class.
The domain of the "client" instance variable is the class CLIENT and allows us to define a relation between clients and projects.
The instance variable "filename" takes values on the CAD system drawing directory.
For the purpose of semantic integrity, the proposed application requires the ability to define and manipulate a set of drawing objects as a single logical entity expressed by a project.
However, the instance variables cannot represent the IS-PART-OF relation, capturing the semantic meaning that a drawing is a part of a project.
We define a project as a "type" object [8] into which graphical and textual object are organized as objects whose existence depends and is owned by the project.
The binding objects to a type Project tells us what methods can be applied to or yield the object.
This means, for example, that an object of a constituent class (client, drawing,...) cannot be created unless the related project object exists.

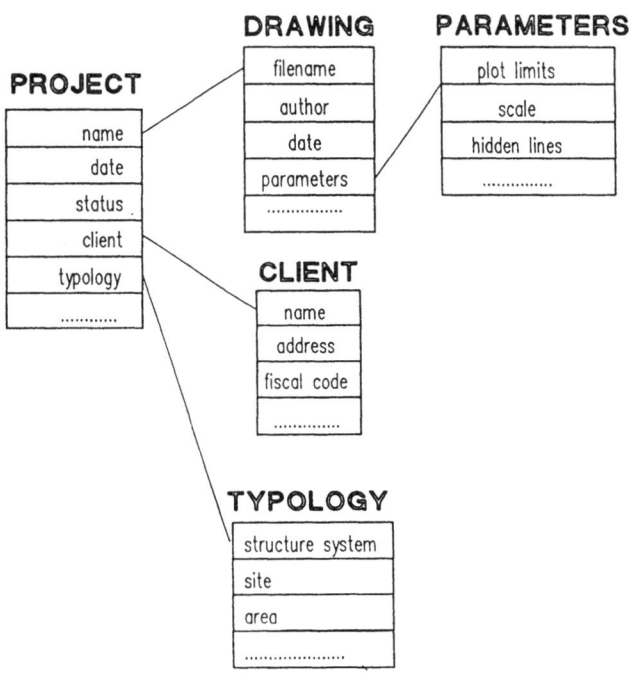

FIG. 1 THE OBJECT ORIENTED DATABASE SCHEMA

424

THE QUERY PROCESS

Against the presented object oriented
schema, a query is expressed in terms of
object properties by fetching all
instances of a class that satisfy certain
search criteria.

Each query appears formed by :

- A target part, giving a structural
description of the requested textual
objects.
- A condition part, giving the condition
to be satisfied by each requested entity.
This condition is a well formed first
order predicate, expressed against the
terminal property of an entity.

In the condition part, the instances of a
class may be restricted by specifying
predicates in the form of relational,
boolean, arithmetic and string operators.
In this context we may represent a query

(Fig. 2) as a graph where each node
represents a class. The root class is the
class whose instances are to be fetched
and each leaf node has only terminal
properties. An edge from node X to node Y
means that the class Y is the domain of a
structural property of the class X.

ARCHITECTURAL ASPECTS

From a functional viewpoint, the presented
database system resembles a complex frame
which provides the graphical images and
the textual information of a project.

Each data management process related both
to the conceptual schema representation
and to physical implementation (i.e.
presentation component) is performed by a
set of modules (Fig. 3), whose common
abstraction is that of objects.
The exchange of information is achieved
through the passing of messages.

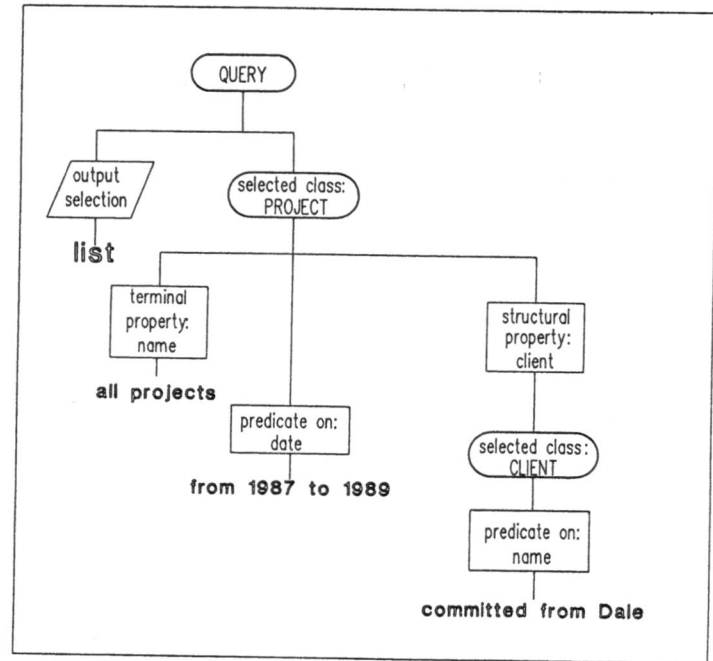

FIG. 2 THE QUERY PROCESS

The MONITOR module is executed first to establish the basic user session.The sessions associated to the project management are :

-Configuration session in which a user describes a new project.

-Query session in which the user formulates a query against the object oriented schema

-Drawing session, in which the user obtains the drawing representation .

The USER INTERFACE supports the user to system interaction.
The user looks at project information using the described object oriented schema. He works with an uniform graphical interface in which pieces of information about selected objects are presented in box-drawers and binders.
Using a mouse as a pointing device, the user configures a project or asks questions selecting objects and needed properties. By predicates, he declares conditions to be verified.

The DATA MODEL module contains the schema of textual and graphical objects as binded to a type represented by the Project class.

Each user operates in the context of a project in which the operations he may perform are applied to objects.

Generic operations are classified as :

Insertion and removal of an object in a class.
Inspection of instances of a class.
Operations on terminal properties including adding or removal of instance variable values, predicate definition, reading and writing object properties.

The concept of context is analogous to the concept of relational view. The relational view makes visible the data to which the user has access, the context makes visible objects and operations that apply to objects, by binding each object in Project type class.

Operations can be thought of as relations that express mapping from input arguments to output arguments [10].

That is, every operation is conceptually describable by a table where columns represent a specific combinations of terminal properties for which the operation is defined and each row represents an instance of some object class .

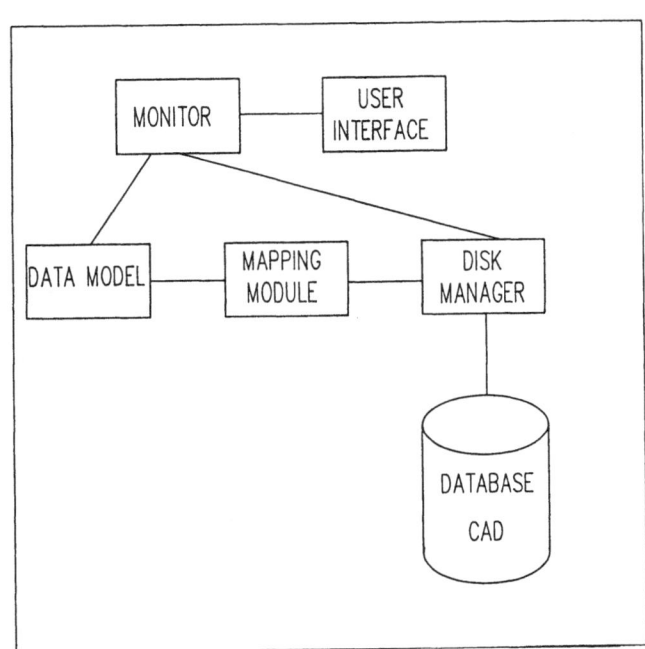

FIG. 3 THE FIRST LEVEL SYSTEM MODULES

426

This suggest that, by algorithm trasformations [9], a class of objects can be traslated into a relational representation where the attribute values of a t-uple in the relation correspond to terminal properties and structural properties are keys to access other relations.
Vice versa, a t-uple deriving from a relational table can be viewed as an object whose properties contain data value or pointers to other objects .

This way, we encoded the Project type definition into a relational schema and the state of any object of that type as a set of relational t-uple.

Due to the simple nature of a type object to the relation encoding process, a query formulated against the database schema can be translated in SQL language. That is accomplished by the MAPPING module that decomposes a query structured on object-oriented data base schema in a sequence of SQL propositions whose format is :

SELECT <attribute list>
FROM <relation list>
WHERE <propositional statement>

The relation list and the attribute list correspond the former to classes and the latter to terminal properties involved. The propositional statement defines a set of predicates expressed on terminal properties and linked by relational operators.

In order to make use of an exisisting technology , the DISK MANAGER is built on top of an available RDBMS and a commercial CAD system. This module is able to perform checkout or checkin operations on the CAD system and it is responsible for sending the queries, monitoring the execution. It receives the results and reformats them according to user interface. It is advantageous because a graphical object can be accessed in CAD system by its reference file and the state of a textual object can be retrieved into a relational representation.

CONCLUSIONS

In this paper we have proposed the use of an object oriented model for the integration of heterogeneous data.
A first system prototype is currently under development, with a substantial amount of the code written and running. It is written in Smalltalk/V and works on PC 80386 machines with at least 4Mbytes. The system currently supports a DISK MANAGER implemented on top of a CAD system , defacto standard for Personal Computers

[11], which allows interfaces with a relational database [12] supporting SQL.
The provision of a common interface to individual databases through an object oriented model plays a significant role: it makes feasible the project of user interfaces to a wide variety of engineering applications and creates the illusion of a single database which can be queried in a uniform manner.
However an important future direction is to allow a greater level of taylorability on the part of the user.

REFERENCES

[1] Berkhout E.E.,"Methodology of Intelligent CAD Systems",Intelligent CAD Systems, Eurographics Seminar, Springer Verlag (1987).
[2] Mostow J.,"Towards Better Models of Design Process", AI Magazine, 6(1), 44 (1985).
[3] Dessi N., Argiolas C.,"Towards an Expert Architectural CAD System", Proceedings of The First European Conference on Information Technology for Organizational Systems, Athens (1988).
[4] Dessi' N., Argiolas C., "How and Why an Intelligent User Interface in Architectural CAD", SAMT '89, Int. Conference on Advanced Manufacturing Technology, Sunderland, March,(1989).
[5] Rehem S. (and al.),"Support for Design Processes in a Structurally Object Oriented DatabaseSystem",Proc. 2nd Int. Workshop on Object-Oriented Database System,SpringerVerlag(1988).
[6] Flemming U., "Rule-Based Systems in Computer Aided Architectural Design" in Expert Systems for Engineering Design,Rychener(ed)Academic P.(1988).
[7] Barthes J. (and al), "Property Driven Data Base" , 6th IJCAI, Tokyo (1979).
[8] Won Kim (and al.), "Features of the ORION Object-Oriented DatabaseSystem" in Object Oriented Concepts,Database and Applic., Won Kim and Lochovsky (eds.) ACM Press (1989).
[9] Weiser S.P, F.H. Lochovsky, "OZ+ An Object-Oriented Database System ", in Object Oriented Concepts,Database and Applic.,Won Kim and Lochovsky (eds.). ACM Press (1989).
[10] Manola F.,"PDM: An Object Oriented Data Model", Proceedings of the International Workshop on Object Oriented Database Systems, (1986)
[11] Autocad,"User guide",Autodesk (1986).
[12] dBaseIV,"User Guide",AshtonTate(1988)

A Neural Net Learning Algorithm for Design of Cardiotocograph Signal Evaluation Expert System: MYDEARBABY 90/2.47

M. Umit Karakas, Ph.D. [1,2]* , Yoh-Han Pao, Ph.D. [2],

M. Sinan Beksac, M.D.[1], Kadir Ozdemir [1]

[1] Hacettepe University
Ankara, Turkey

[2] Case Western Reserve University
Cleveland, OH 44106

An Expert System (MYDEARBABY) for Evaluating Fetal Heart Rate (FHR) variations of an unborn baby has been developed using an ad-hoc Production Rule Technique (version 2.34) and Neural Network Technique (version 2.47). The training set contains 219 recordings from mostly at-risk patients. In Neural Netvork version of the expert system single layer Neural Net (functional link net) with 17 inputs, 1 output parameter are used.

The confusion matrix technique is used to determine the coincidence ratio of human medical expert and MYDEARBABY expert systems evaluations for classifying the normal, security, and danger zones of the cardiotocograph signal.

The discriminatory power of the new (90/2.47) expert system is based on neural net techniques found significant and advantages/disadvantages of the neural network based expert system over production rule/heuristic function based expert system are discussed.

In order to enhance the learning potential of the functional link net (neural net without internal layers), a input expansion based on fractional powers of the original input feature values is proposed. Other functional considerations encoding "OR" or "PLUS(+)" joint activations have also been explored.

1 . INTRODUCTION

A neural network techniques offer a new promise in the area of medical decision making where the number of features for a decision is frequently numerous. Moreover, most of the features in medical decision making is continuous in nature which is suitable for connectionist approach.

The neural network approach, an old topic in the history of artificial intelligence [1-4] has gained a new momentum with the recent work of other researchers in this field [5-9]. In recent years many successful expert system or learning system have been designed by using a neural network technique, including modelling to learn backgammon [10], sonar target identification [11], speech recognition [12], robotics [13,14], monitoring complex systems [15]. These demonstrations illustrate the unmatched capability of neural networks in modelling some aspects of human-like cognitive characterization in the performance of complex and ill-structured tasks. Such

successful applications of artificial neural-network computing have stimulated further widespread interest in such research, resulting in collaborative efforts bridging disciplines and in primary interest. The present paper is the result of a collaboration between from researchers spanning a broad range of backgrounds and research focus including medicine, medical information processing and neural network computing. This paper is also an application of our extension of a neural network previously devised by the Hacettepe group [16-19].

There are several existing medical expert systems have incorporated use of neural network techniques [20-22] and also a couple of expert systems for evaluation of cardiotocograph data [23-26], the latter do not use neural network computing. To the best of our knowledge MYDEARBABY 90/2.47 is the first expert system in the Fetal Monitoring area that uses neural network techniques.

For the benefit of the non-specialist we include brief statements of the salient points of the fetal monitoring task in Frame-1 .

1) After the 5th week of pregnancy a simple form of a heart is formed in the fetus and in each successive week of the pregnancy the heart of the fetus grows and matures. Heart beats are easily identifiable on medial ultrasound screens as small flashing points.

2) After 26th week of the pregnancy or cardiotocographs may be used to record Fetal Heart Rate (FHR) variations of the fetus on a special roll of paper. In a typical obstetric department or maternity hospital, doppler ultrasound based cardiotocographs are frequently available and traces are evaluated by medical doctors visually in order to assess the current state of the fetus.

3) The average heart beat of a healthy baby is around 141.5 bpm plus-minus 8.5 bpm and the average slightly varies over the 28 to 40th week of the pregnancy.

(a) Castillo, R., L Devoe, M. Arthur, J. Searle, and N. Searle, 1987. Computerized heart rate analysis of preterm fetuses, *Journal of Prenatal Medicine 15, Supplement 1*.

(b) Beksac, S., U. Karakas, S. Yalcin, S., K. Ozdemir, and E. Sanliturk. Computerized analysis of antepartum fetal heart rate tracings in normal pregnancies - Version 88/2.29, will appear in *European Jour. of Obst. & Gyn.*

4) The well respected, mostly used criterion (identification rules) in obstetric for healthy (reactive) baby is given in

(a) Rochard, F., B.S.Schifrin, F. Goupil, H., Legrand, J., Blottiere, and C. Sureau, 1976. Nonstressed fetal heart rate monitoring in the antepartum period, *American Obst. & Gyn.*, 126:699.

(b) Smith, C.V. and R.H. Paul, 1978. Antepartum cardiotocography, *Bailliere's Clinical Obst. & Gyn.* 1:17.

Frame-1: Some Definitions from Obstetric Practice

* This publication and MYDEARBABY 90/2.47 expert system version are prepared while Dr. Karakas was supported by Fulbright Scholarship at Case Western Reserve University, Center for Automation and Intelligent Systems Research.

(c) Manning, F.A., S. Menticoglu, C.R. Harman, I. Morrison, and I.R. Lange, 1978. Antepartum fetal risk assessment, the role of the fetal biophysical profile score, *Bailliere's Clinical Obst. & Gyn.*

as follows (or sample rules from the set of 15 to 20 rules):

. a baby is reactive (healthy) if a 10 minute recording frame has at least two acceleration and the signal is "undulatory", it is considered as that the baby is in good condition.

. a typical "acceleration" is at least 15 beats-per-minute (bpm) increase over the "baseline" and returns to the baseline within at most in 60 seconds.

Frame-1: Continue

The number of "rules" (or production rules in terms of artificial intelligence) to classify FHR tracing as reactive (health) or nonreactive (critical) varies 15 to 20 depending on the medical faculty, individual doctor or hospital. However, the situation is not so simple because of the complexities and variations in the visual or computerized feature extraction phase as it is seen in Figure 1. For example defining a baseline by 2 beats-per-minute

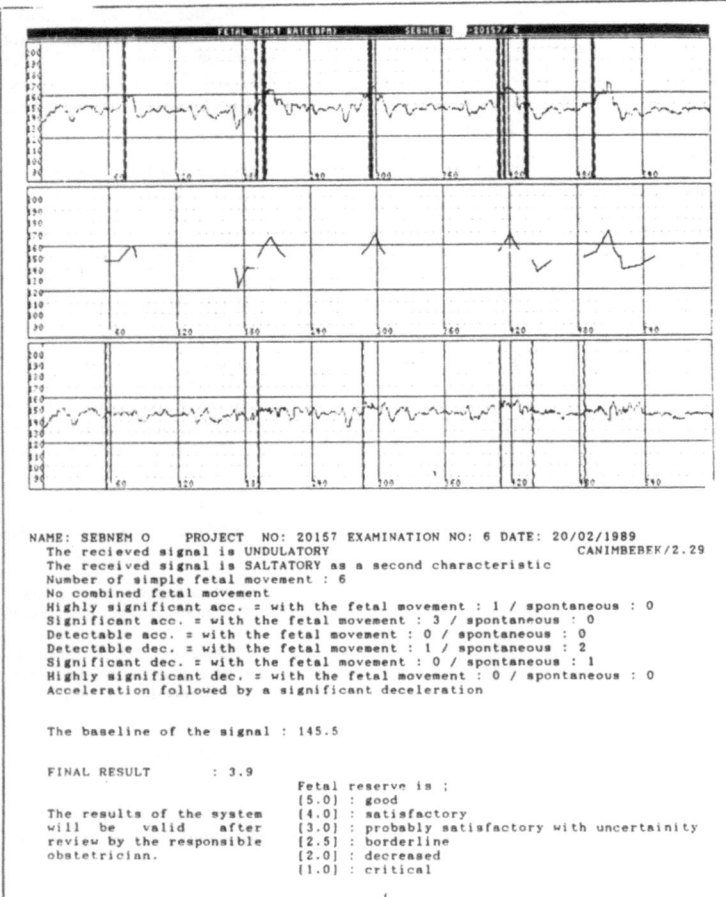

NAME: SEBNEM O   PROJECT NO: 20157 EXAMINATION NO: 6 DATE: 20/02/1989
    The recieved signal is UNDULATORY   CANIMBEBEK/2.29
    The received signal is SALTATORY as a second characteristic
    Number of simple fetal movement : 6
No combined fetal movement
Highly significant acc. = with the fetal movement : 1 / spontaneous : 0
Significant acc. = with the fetal movement : 3 / spontaneous : 0
Detectable acc. = with the fetal movement : 0 / spontaneous : 0
Detectable dec. = with the fetal movement : 1 / spontaneous : 2
Significant dec. = with the fetal movement : 0 / spontaneous : 1
Highly significant dec. = with the fetal movement : 0 / spontaneous : 0
Acceleration followed by a significant deceleration

The baseline of the signal : 145.5

FINAL RESULT   : 3.9

                            Fetal reserve is ;
                            [5.0] : good
The results of the system   [4.0] : satisfactory
will be valid after   [3.0] : probably satisfactory with uncertainity
review by the responsible   [2.5] : borderline
obstetrician.   [2.0] : decreased
                            [1.0] : critical

Figure 1. A Sample Fetal Heart Rate Display from MYDEARBABY 2.2x Software

(bpm) different (low or up) from the actual level will alter the type and meaning of the accelerations and decelerations in the signals. According to intermediate results of European Community Concerted Action Project on Fetal Surveillance in 1985 to 1987, these individual evaluation differences are identified in current practice. The level of agreement between visual evaluations of experienced obstetricians on 62 fetal monitor tracings varies 85% to 90% depending on the complexity situation when the number of outcome is chosen as 3 (reactive, borderline, critical) [27]. By using the features given in Frame-2, production rules for the rough grouping of the traces and heuristic function for fine evaluation a couple of different version of MYDEARBABY (CANIMBEBEK in Turkish) expert system is developed before this study [16-19]. This work is comparision of production rule based expert system design and neural network based expert system design.

2. USING NEURAL NET FOR FINE TUNING OF THE EXPERT SYSTEM

The previous expert system versions 2.14 and 2.29 has coincidence ratios 75% and 80.4% respectively [17,19], with human medical expert. Human medical expert has evaluated over two hundred traces twice in a way given below:

i) the first evaluation is done on the day of recording and the name of the patient is disclosed to medical doctor

ii) the second evaluation is done as a group after couple of months after the recordings. The name of the patient is not disclosed to medical doctor.

The number of non-identical evaluation between these two setting is 17 over the set of 200 traces on a 13 point (very good, good, borderline, reduced, critical and their combinations) scale. So, the interreferee consistency of a medical doctor in this study (who is our "trainer of the expert system") has attained 91.5% level with mixed set of patients (i.e., combined group of normal pregnancies and at-risk ones). Interreferee consistency (91.5%) on this study is perfectly acceptable on 13 point scale, when it is compared with intrareference consistency in fetal monitoring area (By using 3 point scale it is 85 to 90% depending on the type of the patients [27]). So, our aim is not to attain 100% coincidence with our "expert system trainer (Dr. Beksac in this study)", but to design a internally

1) Baseline value and its difference from weekly average.

2) The type of the signal representing macrovariability of the signal (1 to 21 Ankara Unit, will be published at Acta Reproductiva Turcica).

3) Acceleration and deceleration classified according to their height (6), width (6) and Relation to Fetal Movement Marker (2) resulting a map of 72 features.

4) The number of fetal movement marker indicating distinct number of movements of the baby (mother-to-be may press to the button more than once while same movement is in progress).

5) Decelerations following the accelerations.

Frame-2. Feature List of MYDEARBABY System that are Used on Production Rules

Table 1. Evaluation Ranges of Fetal Monitor Signal (Output Values)

Code (13 step scale)	Medical Doctor (discrete)	MYDEARBABY Version 2.47 (range)	Sematic of the Evaluation (five point scale)	Semantic of Evaluation (three point scale)
a	0.87	0.900 - 0.841	good	
ab	0.81	0.840 - 0.781		
ba	0.75	0.780 - 0.721		
b	0.69	0.720 - 0.661	satisfactory	good
bc	0.63	0.660 - 0.601		
cb	0.57	0.600 - 0.541		
c	0.51	0.540 - 0.481	uncertainty	
dc	0.45	0.480 - 0.421		security
de	0.39	0.420 - 0.361	uncertainty	
e	0.33	0.306 - 0.301	decreased	bad
ef	0.27	0.300 - 0.241		
fe	0.21	0.240 - 0.181	critical	
f	0.15	0.180 - 0.100		

consistent expert system.

In this study, leading to expert system version 2.47 a single layer neural net (functional link net) is used for training. The number of input parameters is selected as 17 (including macrovariability count of the trace, baseline difference from weekly average baseline, fetal movement count, excess fetal movement count, baseline shift types, and different types of acceleration over baseline and deceleration under baseline). The number of output parameter is selected as one and its values from 0.1 to 0.9 is

---

1) The input parameters are extracted from the cardiotocograph traces by using MYDEARBABY v.2.34 program. In order to identify a fine and critical line of loosing the baby (i.e., intrauterine exidus) almost all of the patients that are used were critical (at-risk) pregnancies. A few (2 out of 26) normal patients are included for training the good patterns. MYDEARBABY v.2.34 is extracting over 100 features from the cardiotocograph tracing including size, height and relation to fetal movement marker of the acceleration/decelerations. So, in order to reduce them to 17 input parameters some reclustering is done by the first author.

2) The single output parameter value is basically based on medical evaluations of the third author. In order to identify the most distinguishing parameters of the critical baby maximum 3 step distortion over 13 point scale (as given in Table 1) is applied on them. The distortions over "instantaneous evaluation of FHR trace by medical doctor (IFHRE)" is done as follows:

. if baby is found intrauterine exidus (died before born) after this trace within two days, then training value is reduced by 2 steps under IFHRE,

. if baby is found intrauterine ex. after this trace within four days, then training value is reduced by 1 step under IFHRE,

. if baby is survived at least 3 weeks after this trace then training value is increased by 2 steps over IFHRE,

. if baby is survived 20 to 10 days after this trace then training value is increased by 1 step over IFHRE,

. if mother-to-be has a "normal-health conditions" or "minor health problems that will not effect the fetus" then training value is not distorted due to "biophysical evaluations of the mother-to-be (BE)" but,

   if BE (mother-to-be) = "hypertensive" then - 1 step,

   if BE (mother-to-be) = "Diabetus Mellitus" then - 1 step,

   if BE (mother-to-be) = "Affected Rh" then - 2 step,

   modification is done in this step.

Frame-3. Heuristic Preprocessing for the Training Set of the Neural Net

---

divided into evaluation ranges from very good to very critical as it is shown in Table 1.

The input variables of the Neural Net Based Expert System(version 90/2.47) is patially prepared by previous production rule based expert system(version 89/2.34). The output variable for the training set is a combination of "instantaneous evaluation of FHR by medical doctor" and "the final outcome of the pegnancy" by using the heuristic rules given in Frame-3 .

After preparing 219 sets of input and output variables the AI WARE NNet 600 version 1.2 program is used to train and obtain the relative values of the 17 parameters. In order to obtain simple evaluation function at the first step a functional link net (single layer neural network) is used. The alpha value of the learning (feedback level from each case) is set to 0.065 (i.e., 6.5%), eta value is set to 0.96 and iterated by 6500 times on a microvax (approximate time is two hours) in order to find relative values of the features. The error level of the learned system with respect to "distorted-IFHRE" values has drop to 0.00732 from random distribution as a result of iterations.

The error level of the trained functional link net is very acceptable when it is considered the following facts:

i) Trainer (medical doctor) is using discrete evaluation scale over 0.10 to 0.90 with 13 different equally spaced outcome at most. The neural network program is using pseudo continuous scale (due to digital computer 10^{-7} internally), and part of error exist due to scaling differences between the trainer and the functional link net program.

ii) The trainer (medical doctor) has 1 or 2 step variability over 13 step scale in time (8.5% of the cases) due to many reasons including:

. knowing previous medical background of the patient,
. the personal mood of the doctor at the moment of evaluation.

The training results of the functional link net on 17 parameters and 219 pattern is discussed in detail as a part of the study. The significant ones from computer science area is summarized in the third part of this paper. The significant findings from obstetric medical practice point of view will be published elsewhere.

3. RESULTS AND PROPOSAL FOR FURTHER STUDY

In this study a functional link net (or neural net without internal layer) is used for training. In order to enhance capabilities of functional link net "joint activation" of the input parameters in the form of multiplication and "functional expansion" of the input parameters in the form of COS () and/or SINE() functions has been proposed explicitly previously [28] and are implemented in the program that we use [29]. The additive capabilities has proved its usefulness if the input parameters has interrelationship similar to the added expansion. On the other hand, our training results on this specific medical data and the analysis of the cases that are not coincede with medical doctor lead us that for better functional link net structure with medical applications must have these capabilities also:

i) input splitting around average value of a input parameter,

ii) Fractional power of the input parameter in the range of 0.4 to 1.6,

iii) Joint activation of the input parameters in the form of "OR" or "PLUS(mathematical function +)" joints.

We will comment on these proposals briefly before giving our results.

3.1 Necessity of Input Splitting

Most of the parameters, in the medical area has continuous values in nature. Moreover, many of them represent healthy individual on some well known range by medical doctors. On the other hand, in most of the cases both lower and upper values of the specific parameters represent some kind of non-normal outcome. So, input splitting (ie. dividing one input parameter into two input parameters representing values lover than average and higher than average) is frequently necessary with medical data on neural net applications and automating the input splitting by neural network program is advised.

3.2 Fractional Powers of Input Parameters

In medical area, if some of the biophysical parameter (for example trigliceride or collestrol) is slightly increased (for example +25 above 185 healthy limit) it may be considered slightly negative situation. On the other hand a +25 elevation from 240 is a kind of red alarm to the patient and doctor indicating the eating habit and lifestyle of the patient must be changed. For some input parameters of this type a fractional powers in the range of 1.1 to 1.6 seems necessary for better learning with neural nets. For example, in the Fetal Monitoring case healthy babies has signal macrovariability typically 10 to 12 Ankara Unit and if it is 9 to 7 it is considered slightly negative. Our database contains only 2 recordings that have 3 Ankara Unit and 1 recording has 2 Ankara Unit over the 3000. Those signals are recordings from the dead babies, which is expected to alarm the expert system. According to our analysis this can be done by using input expansion by fractional power 1.2 or more. The other edge is the necessity of fractional powers in the range of 0.4 to 0.9. If we give an example on fetal monitoring area, the case of having or one "fetal movement marker" indicating baby is moving and mother-to-be clearly notices it, is a positive information over no fetal movement marker at all. If there exist two or more markers the additional information supports the first positive information, but not double or triple the value of the first one. So we need fractional power expansion of the input in this case also. This necessity is pointed out by Cohen, et al. also [20].

Table 2. Confusion Matrix of the Expert System that Use the Production Rule Approach (214 recordings from normal patients, system v. 2.29)

Prenatal Expert v. 2.29	Normal Zone	Security Zone	Danger Zone
Normal Zone	167	8	1
Security Zone	15	1	2
Danger Zone	9	5	6

Table 3. Confusion Matrix of the Expert System that use the Neural Net Approach (219 recordings from at-risk patients, system v.2.47)

Prenatal Expert v. 2.47	Normal Zone	Security Zone	Danger Zone
Normal Zone	72	9	2
Security Zone	23	34	16
Danger Zone	0	12	49

3.3 Joint Activation of Parameters in the Form of OR or PLUS

Some input parameters represent groups in practice, in this case multilayered neural networks may be defined to handle this situation. However, to define a multilayered neural network is difficult (especially) to non-expert neural network designers. It may be made easier if OR or PLUS type of joint activation of input parameters are added to functional link structure. As an example, having a typical size acceleration with related to fetal movement marker is a positive point in fetal monitoring. The second, confirming information in this group may be (examples)

- two more typical acceleration with fetal movement marker.
- one small acceleration without maker.
- one big acceleration with marker and two small acceleration without markers.
- etc.

If there exist PLUS (+) type of joint activation between input parameters of the neural network (acceleration types with markers) then evaluation function would be easier and more accurate. Also, OR type of joint activation is found useful to identify the relationship between the accelerations with fetal movement marker and without it as a subset of "PLUS" joint activation.

The training sets of the two versions of the expert system are not directly comparable. The seventeen parameter, 219 pattern based version 90/2.47 of MYDEARBABY expert system has the coincidence ratio of 70.8% with the set of very critical patients. The previous expert systems 2.13 and 2.29 [17,19] has 75% and 80.4% coincidence with medical doctors for normal patients group. So, the results with neural net based one is promising and significant but the seventeen parameters without any input expansion is not enough to surpass the previous systems which was tested in the past. However, now there is a firm experience on this area in order to design better expert system around 30 input parameters. The confusion matrix of the version 2.29 with normal patients (Table 2) and confusion matrix of the version 2.47 with at-risk patients (Table 3) are given to demonstrate the level of current state of art in this area.

As a result, the advantages and disadvantages of expert system design with production rules and neural network is summarized below:

Technique	Advantages	Disadvantages
production rule and ad-hoc heuristic function	• flexible (possible to define ranges of variable with different evaluation value)	• fine tuning is difficult over the large number of samples
neural network	• learning capability • adaptability • accurate determination of relative values of parameters	• if the neural network program does not contain matching joint activation structure a manual preprocessing is necessary for training set

References

1. Rosenblatt, F., 1961. *Principles of neurodynamics, perceptrons and the theory of brain mechanism*, Spartan, Washington, D.C.

2. Nilsson, N.J., 1965. *Learning machines*, McGraw-Hill, New York, NY.

3. Minsky R.and S. Papert, 1969. *Perceptron: An introduction to computational geometry*, MIT Press, Cambridge.

4. Newell, A., 1983. *Intellectual issues in the history of artificial intelligence*, F. Machlap and U. Mansfield (Eds.), John Wiley and Sons, New York, NY.

5. Kohonen, T., 1982. Self organized formation of topologically correct maps, *Biological Cybernetics*, Vol. 43, pp. 59-69.

6. Kohonen, T., 1982. Clustering, taxonomy and topological maps of patterns, CH, IEEE, pp. 114-128.

7. Rumelhart, D.E., G.E. Hinton, and R J. Williams, 1986. Learning internal representations by error propagation, in *Parallel Distributed Processing: Explorations in the Microstructures of Cognition: Foundations*, Vol. 1, pp. 318-362, D.E. Rumelhart and J.L. McClelland (Eds.), MIT Press, Cambridge, MA.

8. Pao, Y.H., 1989. *Adaptive pattern recognition and neural networks*, Addison-Wesley, Reading, MA.

9. Hinton, G.E., 1989. Connectionist learning procedures, *Artificial Intelligence 40*, pp. 185-234.

10. Tesauro, G. and T.J. Segnowski, 1989. A parallel network that learns to play backgammon, *Artificial Intelligence*, Vol. 30, No. 3, pp. 357-390.

11. Gorman, R.P. and T.J. Segnowski, 1988. Analysis of hidden units in a layered network trained to classify sonar targets, *Neural Networks 1*, pp. 75-89.

12. Prager, R.W., T.D. Harrison, and F. Fallside, 1987. Boltzmann machines for speech recognition, *Compt. Speech Lang. 1*, pp. 3-27.

13. Pao, Y.H., D.J. Sobajic, and J.J. Lu, 1988. Neural-net implementations of pattern-based controls for robotic motion, *Proceedings of the IMACS World Congress*, Paris, France, July 18-22.

14. Sobajic, D.J., J.J. Lu, and Y.H. Pao, 1988. Intelligent control of the intelledex 605T robot manipulator, International Workshop NEURO-NIMES 88, Nimes, France, November 15-18.

15. Sobajic, D.J. and Y.H. Pao, 1988. Artificial neural-net based dynamic security assessment for electric power systems, IEEE/Power Engineering Society 1988 Winter Meeting, February 5, 1988, paper 88WM211-5, also published in the *IEEE Transactions on Power Systems*, Vol. 4, pp. 220-228, 1989.

16. Karakas, U., S. Beksac, S. Ergincan, F. Girgin, H. Koymen, and F. Tuzun, 1988. An obstretric database and cardiotocograph interface: MYDEARBABY v. 1.0, Seventh National Informatique Conference Turkey, September 22-24, 1988, Eskisehir, Turkey, pp. 23-334, in Turkish.

17. Karakas, U., S. Beksac, S. Ergincan, F. Girgin, H. Koymen, and F. Tuzun, 1988. Expert system for evaluating fetal monitor signals: MYDEARBABY v. 2.13, Third International Symposium on Computer and Information Sciences, October 29-November 2, 1988, Cesme, Izmir, Turkey, pp. 381-386, invited presentation.

18. Beksac, S, U. Karakas, S. Yalcin, K. Ozdemir, and E. Sanliturk, 1989. Computerized analysis of antepartum fetal heart rate tracings in normal pregnancies: version 88/2.29, presented by Beksac-Karakas at Vila Real, Portugal, Septemember 28 - October 1, 1989, EEC Concerted Action Project Workshop on Validity of Cardiotocography, will appear on *European Journal of Obst. & Gyn*.

19. Beksac, S., K. Ozdemir, U. Karakas, S. Yalcin, and E. Karaagaoglu. Development and application of a simple expert system for the interpretation of the antepartum fetal heart rate tracings, version 88/2.29, will appear on *European Journal of Obst. & Gyn*.

20. Cohen, M.E., D.L. Hudson, and M.F. Anderson, 1989. A neural network learning algorithm with medical applications, The 13th Annual Symposium on Computer Applications in Medical Care (SCAMC-89), November 5-8, 1989, Washington, D.C., *IEEE Computer Society Press*, 1989, pp. 307-311.

21. Meistrell, K.A. and K.A. Spackman. Evaluation of neural network performance by receiver operating characteristic analysis: Examples from the biotechnology domain, SCAMC-89, pp. 235-301.

22. Coffey, D. and G. Banks, 1989. A connectionist visual field analyzer, SCAMC-89, pp. 276-282.

23. Smith, J.H., K.S.J. Anand, P.M. Cotes, G.S. Dawes, R.A. Harkness, T.A. Howlett, and C.W.G. Redman, 1988. Ante-natal fetal heart rate variations in relation to the respiratory and metabolic status of the compromised human fetus, *British Journal of Obst. & Gyn*.

24. Searle, J.R., L.D. Devoe, M.C. Phillips, and N.S. Searle, 1988. Computerized analysis of resting fetal heart rate tracings, *American Jour. of Obst. & Gyn*., March, 1988, No. 71, pp. 401-411.

25. Caron, F.J., H.P. van Geijin, E.E. van Woerden, J.M. Swartjes, and R. Mantel, 1988. Computerized assessment of fetal behavioral states, *Journal of Prenatal Medicine (Berlin)*, No. 16, Vol. 4, pp. 365-372.

26. Mendez-Bauer, C., S. Schuman, B. Tran, A. Chun, M. Cheung, S. Porges, and U. Freese, 1987. Computer assisted interpretation of fetal monitor tracings, First World Symp. on Computers in the Care of Mother Fetus and Newborn, Wien, Austria, March 8-12, 1987.

27. Jongsmar, H.W., D.K. Donker, J.S. Duisterhout, and H.P. vanGeijn, 1987. A data base of visually described cardiotocograms, *Journ. of Perinotal Medicine (Berlin)*, No. 15, Suppl. 1.

28. Pao, Y.H., 1989. Functional link nets: Removing hidden layers, *AI Expert*, Vol. 4, pp. 60-68.

29. _____, 1989. N-NET Neural net development system user manual, AI WARE, Inc., 11000 Cedar Avenue, Cleveland, OH, 44106.

A HIGH PERFORMANCE CONCURRENCY CONTROL PROTOCOL
FOR MULTI-PROCESSOR TRANSACTION PROCESSING SYSTEMS

Shiwei Wang   Ugo O. Gagliardi

Aiken Computation Lab., Division of Applied Sciences
Harvard University, Cambridge Ma, 02138, USA

ABSTRACT   In this paper we have proposed a new concurrency control algorithm that consists of two phases of execution for centralized multiprocessor-based transaction processing systems. The proposed algorithm integrates optimistic concurrency control with back-shifting with pre-claimed locking schemes into two phases. It guarantees transactions to commit in two executions if access invariance holds for the second run. It also can offer superior performance than the existing concurrency algorithms by reduce the probability of aborts in the first phase, minimize the probability of blocking due to validation and the possible second phase. Furthermore, it is deadlock-free.

1. INTRODUCTION

Even though the existing concurrency control schemes can handle today's demand, technological trend will require the transaction processing systems to support much higher level of concurrency in the future. This increase in the demand for concurrency level can mainly be attributed to two factors. First is the increasing gap in the CPU speed the disk access speed. Also, because of the diminishing return of CPU speed vs. cost for the mainframe will move the architecture for future transaction processing systems from uniprocessor architecture to multiprocessor architecture. It can be estimated that the demanded concurrency level for transaction processing systems at the end of the decade will be ten time as that for today's systems. Based on the performance studies on the existing concurrency control schemes, we can infer that the existing concurrency control schemes cannot provide adequate response time under this level of concurrency when the "effective" size of the database is small due to hot-spot data contention [7]. Another deficiency for the existing concurrency control schemes has is the lack of a *single* concurrency control algorithm which can perform better than any other concurrency control schemes under all levels of data contention in every computing environment [3, 4, 6, 7].

The goal of this paper is to propose a concurrency control scheme, named two phase integrated concurrency control (2-PICC) which can meet the response time requirement under the concurrency level in the future transaction processing systems as well as provide better performance than any existing concurrency control scheme under all data contention levels in every computing environment. Furthermore, we would like this concurrency control scheme to have the desirable properties in various existing concurrency schemes such as the deadlock-free property in OCC and the transaction-starvation-free property in locking-based concurrency schemes.

Even through the generic 2-PICC scheme is suitable for both centralized and distributed system, this paper focuses on providing a general overview for the 2-PICC, its correctness proof, and its performance analysis in centralized multiprocessor systems. The organization of this paper is as the following. Section 2 depicts the system architecture and key data structures to be kept by the manager processors and by transactions. A detailed description of 2-PICC is provided in section 3. An quantitative comparison between 2-PICC and various existing schemes under different data and hardware environments is given in section 4. Section 5 gives proofs to the serializability of transactions executing under 2-PICC and demonstrates through formal proofs that 2-PICC is deadlock-free. Performance study through discrete event simulation is given in section 6. A conclusion is stated in section 7.

2. SYSTEM ARCHITECTURE MODEL AND KEY DATA STRUCTURES

A terminal complex is connected to the multiprocessor complex via a front-end machine which is responsible to route the transactions to appropriate processors. All the inter-processor communication is carried through a high bandwidth bus. Each processor has its own operating system and database manager. All the data blocks are shared at the disk level and are allowed to migrate from one processor to another throughout the system. That is, the database is *logically* partitioned among the the database managers but is *physically* shared by all the processors in the system. In addition, each processor node is assumed to have a stable semiconductor buffer and a volatile semiconductor buffer. These buffers are deemed as private storage space and are not shared by other processors. We assume that the transaction processing system supports a NO-FORCE policy for disk updates. The stable semiconductor memory buffers are used as database buffers to contain the modified data blocks before they are written back to the disks. Thus, when a transaction commits, it writes all the updates to the stable semiconductor buffer instead to the disks. This approach can reduce both the commit time required for a transaction and the data access time for any other transactions which are aborted because of data contention with this committing transaction. Also, a validity bit is associated with each entry in the stable semiconductor buffer to indicate whether the data content in that entry is valid. The updates are written back to the disks according to a LRU policy. The volatile semiconductor buffers function as the cache for the data blocks read in from disks or from other processors' stable semiconductor buffer. These data blocks remain in the buffer after the transaction commits and are available for future accesses. They are eventually replaced with a LRU policy.

Each transaction in the system must keeps track of a transaction ID, a read_set, and a write_set. The transaction ID is a concatenation of the processor ID and a process ID, and it uniquely identifies the transaction. The read_set contains the *address* and *version number* of each data block a transaction has read. Here, the *version number* is just the commit time of the transaction that produced the version this transaction has accessed. The write_set contains the address of each data block a transaction desires to update.

The key data structures kept by the manager processor of each partition of the data base include the owner field, the copy_set, the lock table, the lock waiting-list, the history_set, and the read time_stamp. Under the No-FORCE commit policy, the disks may not have the most up-to-date version for certain data blocks. Therefore the manager for each data block must keep track of which processor is the current owner of the most up-to-date version of the data block. The processor which was the host for the transaction that has most recently modified the data block is regarded as the "owner". In addition each manager keeps track of a *copy _set* for each data block. A copy_set contains the processor ID for each processor which has a copy of the most up-to-date version of the data block in its main memory buffer. Furthermore, the managers must keep a lock table for each data block in its partition. Each lock table in turn consists of two fields, one for the exclusive lock and one for shared lock. Each entry in the lock table contains the transaction ID for the transactions holding the locks. Also, each manger must keep track of a lock-waiting list for each data block in the partition. The lock-waiting lists are maintained and serviced in FIFO order. A history_set and a read time-stamp are associated with each data block. The history_set contains the write time-stamps of the transactions which have updated the data blocks, and the read time-stamp which indicates the commit time for the *most recently committed* transaction that has read it.

3. A DETAILED DESCRIPTION OF 2-PICC PROTOCOL

Transactions executing under 2-PICC scheme are illustrated in fig. 1a and 1b. Fig. 1a shows the case when a transaction can successfully commit after the first phase. In the fist phase, a transaction is executed initially under optimistic concurrency control. When it reaches the validation stage, the processor will broadcast a validation request to all the relevant processors in the system. The managers processors and the host processor will attempt to find an intersection for all the data blocks' valid intervals. If an intersection is found, the transaction can be allowed to commit without entering the second phase. Otherwise, the transaction will start the second phase and re-executed under the protection of the pre-claimed locks. Fig. 1b illustrates the case when a transaction fails to commit after the first phase and is re-executed in the second phase. The protocol of 2-PICC is described in detail in the following paragraphs.

(1) In the first phase of 2-PICC, transactions are executed under optimistic concurrency control. For any read operation in this phase, the host processor checks first checks if the desired data block is present in its main memory buffers (volatile an stable). If the desired data block is not found, a read request is sent to the manager processor of that data block. Upon receiving the read request, the manager checks its owner field to decide if itself is the current owner of the requested data block. If the manager is the current owner of the requested data block and the copy_set indicates that there is no outstanding copy of the most up-to-date version of it present in any of the processors' main memory buffers,

the manager will fetch a copy of the requested data block from disk and send it to the requesting processor. If the manager is the current owner but the copy_set indicates that a outstanding copy exists in a processor's main memory buffer, the manager will redirect the request to that processor. If the manager is not the current owner, it will redirect the request to the current owner. In all the above scenarios, the current write time-stamp of the requested data block is also forwarded to the requesting processor along the data block. The requesting transaction, in turn, will use the version number indicated by this time-stamp as the version for this data block. In addition, in all three cases, the manager will add the requesting processor's ID to its copy_set. For any write operation in the first phase, all the updates are written to its volatile memory buffer.

(2) When a transaction reaches the validation stage, the host processor for the transaction will broadcast a validation request message through the bus. This message contains the address, request for shared locks, and the version numbers for the data blocks in the transaction's read_set and address and request for *virtual* exclusive locks for data blocks in the transaction's write_set. This broadcast operation guarantees the same serial order is obtained for all the validation request at all of the processors in the system and, consequently, allows *Parallel* and *independent* validation at all processors. Upon arrival at a destination, if a virtual exclusive lock is held or pending on the desired data block, the lock request is appended to the lock waiting list and is processed in FIFO order. Deadlock is prevented since the all the lock requests are broadcast at once atomically so that same FIFO order holds for all the lock requests at all data blocks. Furthermore, note that the all the locks are pre-claimed in the validation step before a decision on whether or not a transaction can be allowed to commit is reached. If later the transaction is aborted, it can be re-executed under the protection of the pre-claimed locks without any additional work needed to obtain the locks. Comparing with the virtual execution scheme in [3], by integrating the validation and lock pre-claiming, we can reduce unnecessary computation for reobtaining the locks and avoid the possibility that more data blocks got updated by other transactions before all the locks can be obtained. Also, we can eliminate the extra work in checking a central FIFO queue every time a transaction in the second phase release the locks.

(3) When a lock request is at the head of the lock waiting list for a data block, the manager processor will grant the appropriate lock and attempt to find the *valid interval* for this data request. For any data block in the read_set, the valid interval is defined as the time interval between the version read by the transaction and commit time of the least recent (the oldest) transaction that has updated the data block after the read operation has taken place. This can be done by checking the write time-stamps in the history_set against the the version read by the transaction. For any data block in the write_set, the valid interval has the read time-stamp on the data block as the lower bound of the transaction, and the upper bound of the transaction is open. Each manager will then find the intersection for the valid intervals of the data blocks under its management which are in the transaction's read_set or write_set. Subsequently, the managers forward the intersections to the host processor. Upon receiving all the intersection, the host processor will attempt to find a global intersection for the received intersections. If the intersection can be found, the transaction can proceed to commit; the commit time is assigned somewhere in the valid interval. Thus, even if a data block in a transaction's read_set has been subsequently updated by another

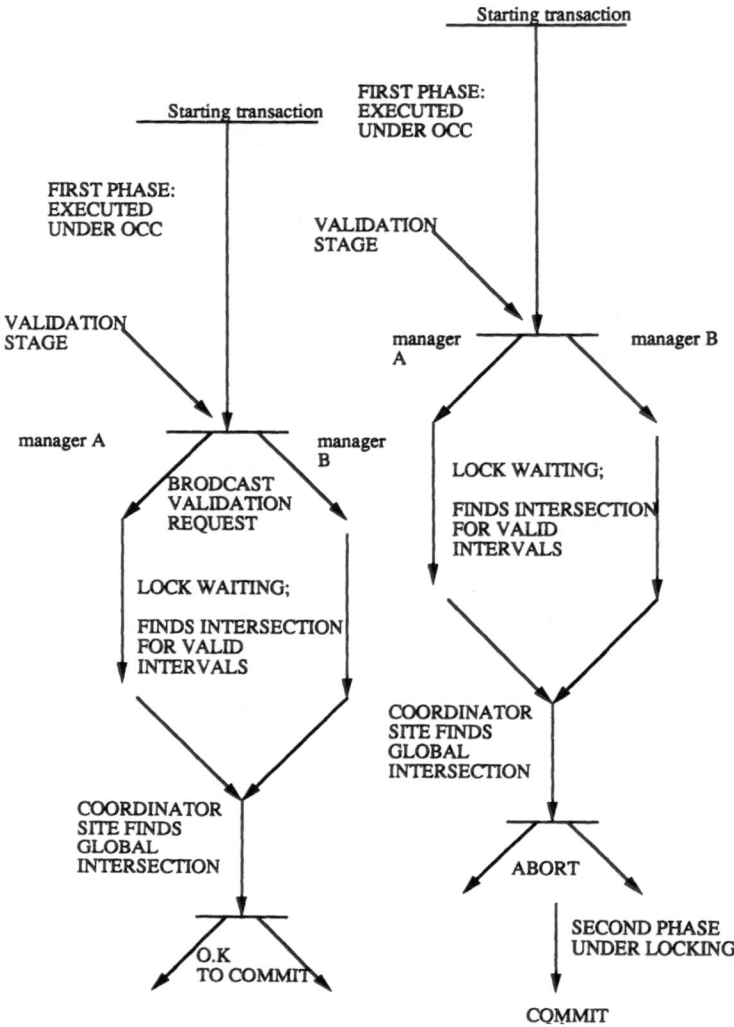

Fig. 1a

Fig. 1b

transaction before this transaction has reached its validation stage, the transaction can still commit if a global intersection .can be found. This, in essence, is shifting the commit to a time that is earlier than the time the transaction requests for validation. Otherwise, the transaction must enter the second phase for rerun under the protection of the pre-claimed locks. This procedure is illustrated by the examples in figure 2 and 3. The pre-claimed shared virtual exclusive locks blocks only transaction in the validation stage but not other transactions in the first phase of execution. The reason of allowing first phase transactions to access data blocks which are under virtual exclusive locks by other transactions is that, even though these first phase transactions would be accessing versions of data blocks which will later up-dated by the transactions holding the virtual exclusive locks, we can most likely able to allow them to commit by back-shift the commit time. This idea is somewhat similar to the transaction ID number reassignment described in [6] for the time-stamp ordering concurrency control algorithm.

In fig. 2, the example shows that a transaction has data blocks A, B, and C in its read_set with version numbers (time-stamps) 29, 15, and 30 respectively. Note that these time-stamps indicate the commit time of the transactions which produced the versions of data blocks A, B, and C read by the transaction in this example. The same transaction also has data blocks D and E in its write_set. Data blocks A and B are managed by processor site 1. The history_set of data block A contains time-stamps with version numbers 27, 29, and 33, and the the history_set of data block B contains time-stamps 15 and 37. Data block C is managed by processor site 2 and has time- stamps with version numbers 23, 24, and 30 in its history_set. Processor site 3 manages data block D which has time a read time stamp with a version number 31. Data block E is managed by processor site 4 and has a read time-stamp with version number 32. The valid intervals for the data blocks are indicated in the column on the right. The numbers in each of the brackets are the lower and upper bounds for each valid intervals. There, the infinite sign denotes for the open upper bound. The youngest lower bound of all the valid intervals now is 30, and an intersection, with 30 and 33 as the lower and upper bounds respectively can be found for the data blocks. Thus, a commit time can be assigned in between 30 and 33, and the transaction can be allowed to commit. In the second example, everything remains the same as example 3 except that now the version of data block A read by this transaction has changed to 33 and the read time-stamp on data block D has changed to 34. This results in a new lower bound with the time-stamp value of 34 and a new upper bound with the time-stamp value of 37 for the intersection. The transaction can be allowed to commit by assigning a commit time stamp in this new intersection.

From these examples we can see that a global intersection should have either the most recent (the youngest) read operation, as in example 1, or the commit time for the youngest transaction that has read a data block in the transaction's write_set, as in example 2, as the lower bound and the least recent (or the oldest) update on the data blocks in this transaction's read_set by another transaction as the upper bound. Note that the transactions both examples 3 and 4 would not commit in the conventional OCC-based schemes because some data blocks in their read_sets have been updated by other transactions before the transactions in the example reach the validation stage. They are, however, allowed to commit in these examples because we allow the commit time to back shift to a earlier time where a consistent view can be obtained for the database.

(4) In the commit procedure, at either the end of the first phase or the end of the second phase, the host processor will write all the updates to the stable semiconductor buffer and set the validity bit for those entries to valid. Also, a message is broadcasted by the host processor to all the relevant manager processors to inform them the transaction is allowed to commit. The commit time-stamp for this transaction is sent along this message and is written into the history_sets for the data blocks in this transaction's write_set. This commit time-stamp also becomes the read time_stamp for the data blocks in the transaction's read_set. The locks held by this transaction are subsequently released by the managers processors.

Comparing with the other optimistic concurrency control-based algorithms [1, 2, 3, 4, 5, 10], our approach can eliminate all the unnecessary aborts by paying minimum additional price in computing the valid intervals. Furthermore, our approach can also eliminate the blocking of transactions in the first phase, except for the ones in the validation stage, by the transactions holding locks. The overhead involved in finding the valid interval in our approach is negligible comparing with the potential advantage in minimizing the need for re-execution and the possibility of blocking. This is particularly true for the parallel processing systems in the future as the CPU speed continue to increase.

4.   QUALITATIVE COMPARISON WITH THE EXISTING ALGORITHMS

This section provides a qualitative comparison between 2-PICC scheme and the existing concurrency control algorithms under different levels of data contention in various computing environments. We will classify these environments into three groups: low data high contention but high hardware resource contention, high data contention, and main-memory resident data base systems with a large number of processors.

For the first group, locking-based schemes offer the best performance among all the existing concurrency control schemes [2, 7]. Locking-based concurrency schemes can guarantee the transaction to commit, unless deadlock occurs, and

READ SET : A (29), B (15), C (30);

WRITE SET : D, E ;

SITE 1		VALID INTERVAL
DATA BLOCK A	{ 27, 29, 33 }	(29, 33)
DATA BLOCK B	{ 15, 37}	(15, 37)
SITE 2		
DATA BLOCK C	{ 23, 24, 30}	(30, ∞)
SITE 3		
DATA BLOCK D	{ 19, 25}	(27, ∞)
	27	
SITE 4		
DATA BLOCK E	{ 28, 32, 34}	(26, ∞)
	26	

INTERSECTION : (30, 33)

Fig. 2   Example 1

READ SET : A (33), B (15), C (30);

WRITE SET : C, D;

SITE 1		VALID INTERVAL
DATA BLOCK A	{ 27, 29, 33 }	(33, ∞)
DATA BLOCK B	{ 15, 37}	(15, 37)
SITE 2		
DATA BLOCK C	{ 23, 24, 30}	(30, ∞)
SITE 3		
DATA BLOCK D	{ 19, 25}	(34, ∞)
	34	
SITE 4		
DATA BLOCK E	{ 28, 32, 34}	(26, ∞)
	26	

INTERSECTION : (34, 37)

Fig. 3   Example 2

therefore avoids any waste in CPU processing efforts. On the other hand under the existing OCC-based schemes, CPU may do wasteful work if the transaction is aborted. However, some of 2-PICC scheme can offset this advantage the locking-based concurrency control over the OCC-based schemes. First 2-PICC eliminates unnecessary aborts for the transactions in the first phase by allowing back-shifts in commit time. Also, 2-PICC allows transaction running in the first phase to access the data blocks under virtual exclusive locks and only blocks committing transactions. This will reduce the blocking that conventional locking may have. Also since either all or most of the needed data blocks will be main-memory resident, the lock holding time for the second phase of 2-PICC will be much shorter than the lock holding time of conventional locking schemes.

For the environment where the data contention is high, the schemes which offer best performance are the hybrid of conventional OCC and broadcast OCC scheme[2], the deferred locking scheme[4], and the virtual execution scheme [9, 3]. 2-PICC has the following advantages over the hybrid of conventional OCC and broadcast OCC. 2-PICC allows transactions in the first phase of execution (before they reach the validation stage) to access data blocks under the virtual exclusive locks. By allowing back-shifts in commit time, 2-PICC enhances the change for transactions to commit at the end of first phase. In addition, if access invariance holds, transactions are guaranteed to commit with at most two executions. Furthermore, 2-PICC also has considerable advantages over the deferred locking techniques. First, 2-PICC allows access to data blocks under exclusive locks, and, therefore, reduces blocking due to data contention. Compared with deferred locking techniques, by allowing 2-PICC eliminates the unnecessary aborts in the non-blocking phase if the transactions are executed under the deferred-locking scheme. Also, 2-PICC avoids the need for back-off time before restart by pre-claiming all the locks at the beginning of validation (before a transaction is known to be aborted). If access invariance holds, 2-PICC guarantees transaction to commit in at most two executions and to be deadlock-free. Even though both 2-PICC and deferred locking schemes are aimed to achieve better performance than existing concurrency controls under all the conditions, they differ significantly in the fundamental approaches. Performance of deferred locking techniques depends mainly on the actual position of the critical stage which is predetermined before runtime and cannot be adjusted dynamically in the runtime. However, 2-PICC is designed to offer superior performance in all data contention and computation environments by integrating features which give rise to superior performance in various environments. Despite of the similarity between 2-PICC and the virtual execution technique at the first glance, 2-PICC will provide better performance because of the following advantages. First, by allowing back-shift in commit time, 2-PICC enhances the chance for transaction to commit at the end of the first phase. Also, 2-PICC allows transactions in the first phase of execution (before they reach the validation stage) to access data blocks under the virtual exclusive locks. Moreover, with 2-PICC the locks are pre-claimed parallel to minimize the bottleneck resulting from central site validation. Furthermore, by pre-claiming the locks in validation, 2-PICC can avoid additional data blocks get invalidated by other transaction. Fifth, 2-PICC pre-claims the locks in validation stage without additional work needed.

For the environments where the database is main-memory resident and have a large number of processors with low computation power, broadcast OCC

protocol[5] offers the best performance among the existing algorithms [3]. The reasons behind broadcast OCC's success are that the transactions are aborted as soon as a conflict occurs and are starting over immediately and that no data contention due to locking can occur under this scheme. Features of 2-PICC that can offset these are the followings. First 2-PICC eliminates unnecessary aborts in the first phase. Also, 2-PICC allows transactions running in the first phase to access the data blocks under virtual exclusive locks and only blocks committing transactions.

5. FORMAL PROOFS

In this section we will prove that the protocol for the 2-PICC is serializable and any current state for the transaction governed by the 2-PICC scheduler is deadlock-free. For the proof on serializability of 2 - PICC will be demonstrated by establishing a partial order in commit times of the conflicting transactions first, and then use that partial order to show the serializability graph SG(H) is acyclic. We consider the case where the conflicting transactions are committed without back-shifts (in Lemma 1, 2, 3, and 4) and the case where at least one of the conflicting transaction committed with back-shift (Lemma 5).

Definition 1 Commit Projection: The committed projection of history H, denoted C(H), is the history obtained from H by deleting all the operations that do not belong to transactions committed in H.

Definition 2 Serialization Graph (SG) for history H over transaction T = { $T_1, \ldots, T_n$ }, denoted SG(H), is a directed graph whose nodes are the transactions in T that are committed in H and whose edges are all $T_i \longrightarrow T_j$ such that there exists conflicting operations $P_i[x]$ and $Q_j[x]$ such that $P_i[x] < Q_j[x]$.

Notation: $P_i[x]$, $Q_j[x]$, denotes for operations by transaction i and j respectively. $P_{li}[x]$ and $Q_{li}[x]$ are the lock operations associated with them. $P_{ui}[x]$, $Q_{uj}[x]$ are the lock-release operations associated with them.

Serializability theorem: A history H is serializable iff SG(H) is acyclic. Serializability theorem was proven in (8), and it is stated here without showing the proof.

Lemma 1 Let H be a history produced by the 2 - PICC scheduler. Any validation operation in H is bounded by the lock request operation and the lock release operation associated with it.

Proof: This lemma follows the definition of 2-PICC protocol directly.

Lemma 2 Let H be a history produced by the 2 - PICC scheduler. For transactions i and j which are both committed without having back-shifted the commit times, if $P_i[x]$ and $Q_j[x]$ (where i not equal to j) are conflicting operation in C(H), then either $P_{ui}[x] < Q_{lj}[x]$ or $Q_{uj}[x] < P_{li}[x]$.

Proof: Suppose we have two operation $P_i[x]$ and $Q_j[x]$ that conflict. The locks corresponding to these operation needed for the validation of the transaction must also conflict. By the definition of 2-PICC, only one of these locks can be held at a time. Therefore, the scheduler must release the lock corresponding to one of the operation's validation before it sets the lock for the other operation's validation. In terms of histories, we must have $P_{ui}[x] < Q_{lj}[x]$ or $Q_{uj}[x] < P_{li}[x]$.

Lemma 3   For any transaction in a complete history produced by the 2 - PICC scheduler, no lock can be by the transaction obtained after any lock is released by that transaction.

Proof: The fact that all the locks needed for a transaction are requested at once at the beginning of the validation in the first phase of the 2 - PICC and that every lock of a transaction is obtained before any lock is released will ensure the validity of this lemma.

Notation: P_Val_i [x] : the validation operation corresponds to $P_i[x]$. Q_Val_j [x] : the validation operation corresponds to $Q_j[x]$.

Lemma 4   For any two distinct transactions i and j in a history H produced by a 2 - PICC scheduler, if either if both i and j are committed without having back-shift in commit time, and T_i ---> T_j is SG(H), there must exist some data item x and conflicting operations $P_i[x]$ and $Q_j[x]$ in H such that the commit time assigned to i, C_i, is $<_H$ commit time assigned to j, C_j.

Proof: Since T_i ---> T_j , there must exist conflicting operations $P_i[x]$ and $Q_j[x]$ such that $P_i[x] < Q_j[x]$. For Q_Val_j [x] and P_Val_i [x], by Lemma 1 and the fact that 2 - PICC requires that the commit time is assigned before the locks are released, we have:

1) $P_{li}[x] < P\_validation\_i$ [x] $< C_i < P_{ui}[x]$ and

2) $Q_{lj}[x] < Q\_validation\_j$ [x] $< C_j < Q_{uj}[x]$

By lemma 2, either $P_{ui}[x] < Q_{lj}[x]$ or $Q_{uj}[x] < P_{li}[x]$. In the latter case, by (1) and (2) above and transitivity, we have $Q\_validation\_j$ [x] $< P\_validation\_i$ [x]. This implies $Q_j[x] < P_i[x]$, which contradicts $P_i[x] < Q_j[x]$. Thus, we have $P_{ui}[x] < Q_{lj}[x]$. Therefore, $C_i < P_{ui}[x] < Q_{lj}[x] < C_j$. Hence, we have the commit time assigned to i, C_i, is < the commit time assigned to j, C_j.

Notation: The notation $R_i[x]$ and $W_j[x]$ denotes for the time stamps associated with the read operation on x by transaction i and the write operation on x by transaction j, respectively. They are defined as equal to the commit time of the transaction. Ts (ValReq-i) is the time for validation request of transaction i.

Lemma 5   For a transaction i which is committed in the first phase of 2-PICC with a back-shift in commit time, for any edge T_i ---> T_j in the SG(H) where j is another transaction, we have $C_i <_H < C_j$. Furthermore, for any edge T_j ---> T_i in the SG(H), we have $C_j <_H C_i$.

Proof: For any data block x in the read set of transaction i, if T_i--- > T_j is in SG(H), then there is a conflicting operation $W_j[x]$ by a transaction j. Also, $C_j <_H$ Ts (ValReq-i) and $R_i[x] <_H W_j[x]$. By the definition of 2 - PICC, the commit time

must be within the intersection of all the valid intervals in which all the data blocks read by transaction i is valid. In this interval, the youngest read operation by transaction i and the oldest update operation on the data blocks in the read set of transaction i by other transactions are the lower and upper bounds of the valid interval of transaction i. Thus, $W_j[x]$ is either younger than or equal to the upper bound of the valid interval of transaction i. Also, since C_i is older than the upper bound of the valid interval and $W_j[x] = C_j$, we know, by transitivity, $C_i <_H C_j$.

The second case to be considered is that, for any data block x in the write set of transaction i, if T_i ---> T_j, there must be a conflicting operation $R_j[x]$ that is conflicting with $W_i[x]$. By the definition of 2-PICC, T_i must release all the locks before T_j's read operation on data block x can be granted. By the definition of 2-PICC, C_i < Ts (ValReq-i) < the time at which transaction i releases its locks. This implies that $C_i < R_j[x]$. Since $R_j[x] < C_j$, $C_i < C_j$ must hold for this case as well.

The two above scenarios together establish the validity of the first part of this lemma. We have demonstrated that, if T_i ---> T_j is in SG(H), then $C_i < C_j$ holds.

Next, for any data block x in the write set of transaction i, if T_j ---> T_i is in the SG(H), then there is a conflicting operation $R_j[x]$ by a transaction j. Let $C_i < C_j$, since $R_j[x] = C_j$, we have $C_i < R_j[x]$. However, according to 2 - PICC, C_i is younger than the lower bound of the valid interval which equals to youngest read time stamp *of all the data blocks* . This implies that C_i should be younger than $R_j[x]$. So we know that $C_i <_H R_j[x]$ is a contradiction to the 2 - PICC protocol. Therefore, the assumption that C_i ---> C_j must be false. Thus, we have C_j ---> C_i if T_j ----> T_i.

The last case to be considered is that, for certain data block x in the read set of transaction i, if T_j ---> T_i, then there must be a conflicting operation $W_j[x]$ that is conflicting with $R_i[x]$. By the definition of 2-PICC, the lower bound of the valid interval for transaction i must be either younger than or equal to the youngest of version number on the data blocks in the transaction's read_set and the commit time assigned to transaction i must be younger than the lower bound. In this case the version of data block x read by transaction i just equals to the commit time of transaction j. Thus, we can imply that $C_j < C_i$.

The two above scenarios together establish the validity of the first part of this lemma. We have demonstrated that, if T_j ---> T_i is in SG(H), then $C_j < C_i$ holds.

Lemma 6   For any two distinct transactions i and j, if T_i ---> T_j is in SG(H), there must be some data block x and conflicting operations $P_i[x]$ and $Q_j[x]$ in H such that the commit time assigned to i, C_i, is $<_H$ commit time assigned to j, C_j.

Proof: In Lemma 4, we have proven that what we stated in this Lemma holds if both i and j are committed without back-shift in commit time. From Lemma 5, we know what we stated in this Lemma 6 can hold if at least one of the conflicting transaction has its commit time back-shifted in order to commit. Putting them together, we can infer that Lemma should hold for all conflicting transactions i and j.

Theorem 1   If H is a history representing an execution produced by the 2 - PICC schedule, then H is serializable.

Proof: Consider SG(H). If $T_i \dashrightarrow T_j$ is an edge of SG(H), then there must exist "strongly" conflicting operations $P_i[x]$ and $Q_j[x]$ such that $P_i[x] < Q_j[x]$. Hence, by Lemma 4 and Lemma 7, $C_i < C_j$. If a cycle $T_1 \dashrightarrow T_2 \dashrightarrow ..... \dashrightarrow T_n \dashrightarrow T_1$ existed in SG(H), then by induction $C_1 < C_1$, a contradiction. So SG(H) is acyclic, and by the serializability Theorem, H is serializable.

Definition 3   Wait-For-Graph (WFG):   A directed graph whose nodes are labeled by transaction names, and that contains an edge $T_i \dashrightarrow T_j$ whenever T_j is waiting for T_i to release some lock (11).

Lemma 7.a   For a WFG produced by 2 - PICC assume $T_i \dashrightarrow T_j$ is in the WFG. Then, there exists a data block x and some conflicting operations $P_i[x]$ and $Q_j[x]$ such that $P_{ui}[x] < Q_{lj}[x]$.

Proof: Since $T_i \dashrightarrow T_j$, there must exist conflicting operations $P_i[x]$ and $Q_j[x]$ whose respective locks are conflicting as well. Since only one of the "strongly" conflict locks can be held at a time. Thus, we have $P_{ui}[x] < Q_{lj}[x]$.

Lemma 7.b   For a WFG produced by 2 - PICC, let $T_1 \dashrightarrow T_2 \dashrightarrow ..... \dashrightarrow T_n$ be a path in WFG where n > 1. Then, for some data block x and y and some operations $P_1[x]$ and $Q_n[y]$, $P_{u1}[x] < Q_{ln}[y]$.

Proof: The proof is by induction on n. The basic step, for n=2, follows immediately from Lemma 7.a. For the induction step, assume that the lemma holds for n = k for some k >= 2. We will show that it holds for n = k+1. By the induction hypothesis, the path $T_1 \dashrightarrow T_2 \dashrightarrow ..... \dashrightarrow T_k$ implies that there exist data block x and z, and operations $P_1[x]$ and $O_k[z]$, such that $P_{u1}[x] < O_{lk}[z]$. By $T_k \dashrightarrow T_{k+1}$ and Lemma7.a there exists a data block y and conflicting operations $O'_k[y]$ and $Q_{k+1}[y]$ such that $O'_{uk}[y] < Q_{lk+1}[y]$. In our 2 - PICC protocol, the fact that all the locks needed for validating a transaction and the possible second phase of 2 - PICC are pre-claimed at once before any lock is released. Hence, $O_{lk}[z] < O'_{uk}[y]$. By the last three precedence and transitivity, $P_{u1}[x] < Q_{lk+1}[y]$, as stated.

Theorem 2   Any current state of transactions produced by the 2 - PICC scheduler is deadlock-free.

Proof: From the definition of WFGs, we know that a WFG describes the current state of transactions which includes waits-for situations involving operations that may not be executed (due to abort). Suppose a WFG has a cycle: $T_1 \dashrightarrow T_2 \dashrightarrow ...... \dashrightarrow T_n \dashrightarrow T_1$. Each transaction is waiting for the next transaction in the cycle. By definition, deadlock occurs in a situation in which each transaction in a set of transaction is blocked waiting for another transaction in the set, and, therefore, none will become unblocked. Thus, a cyclic WFG implies deadlock. By Lemma 7.b, for some data blocks x and y, and some operations $P_1[y]$ and $Q_1[x]$, $P_{u1}[x] < Q_{11}[y]$. However, this contradicts the fact that all the locks are pre-claimed at once, no subsequent lock can be obtained after any lock is released. Thus, WFG produced by the 2 - PICC scheduler contains no cycle. Hence, any current state of transactions governed by 2 - PICC is deadlock-free.

6. PERFORMANCE STUDY

In the following study, we assume the following values for some of the crucial parameters: the average number of data blocks accessed per transaction =15; the number of data blocks in the database = 14,000; the number of instruction required in to set up a transaction =150K; the number of initial I/Os needed to set up a transaction = 5; the time required for disk access = 35msec; time required to access data blocks in other processor's main memory cache = 4msec; percentage of updates = 0.2; processor speed = 30MIPS; percentage of hot data block = 0.2; the number of instruction per stage in the first phase; the number of instructions per stage in the second phase = 90k. We first performed some initial experiments to determine a reasonable size on the history set of each data block to be tracked. The result we obtained suggested that by maintaining a history size of six gives results almost identical to the case with infinitely large history size. Therefore, in the following analysis, we will use a history size of six throughout. Also, we assumed that the CPU is released for each I/O. An Infinite server queue is used for the I/O. In the study we set the maximum tolerable response time to be 2 seconds and investigate the maximum number of transactions can be supported under this constraint.

In the first case, we assume the number of processor in the system to be two. Fig. 4 shows the average transaction response time versus transaction rate for stimulation result of 2 - PICC as well as conventional optimistic concurrency control. In this case, we intend to study the performance of our protocol in a resource contention environment (due to the relatively small number of processors in the system). In this figure, we see that the maximum transaction rate can be substantiated under our 2 - PICC is close to 30 percent better than that of conventional optimistic concurrency control.

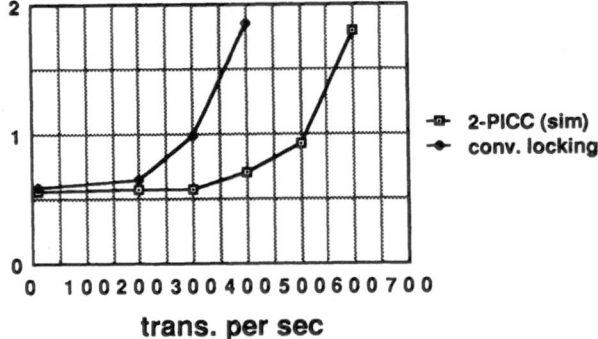

Fig.   4

In the second case, we increased the number of processors in the system to 12 while kept everything else the same. We intend to study our 2-PICC protocol's performance in an environment where the data contention rather the resource contention is the critical bottleneck. Fig. 5 indicates that the maximum transaction rate can be supported by using 2-PICC is more than 30 percent better than that of the conventional optimistic concurrency control. In fact, Fig. 5 shows that we can achieve a maximum rate of over one thousand transactions per second under the assume condition. Our study indicates that our 2- PICC protocol is robust and offers significant performance advantage over conventional optimistic performance under resource contention and data contention.

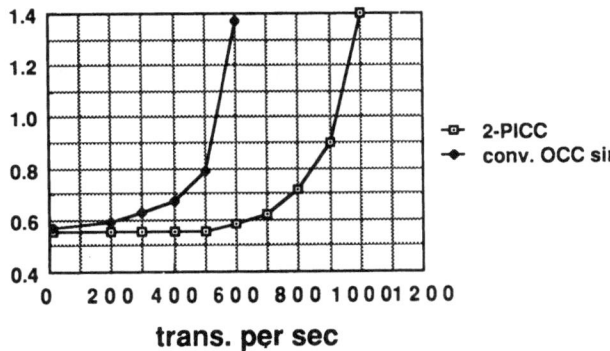

Fig. 5

7. CONCLUSION

In this paper we have proposed a new concurrency control algorithm for centralized multiprocessor-based transaction processing systems that consists of two phases of execution. The proposed algorithm integrates optimistic concurrency control with back-shifting and pre-claimed locking into two phases. It guarantees transactions to commit in two executions if access invariance holds for the second run. It also can offer superior performance than the existing concurrency algorithms by reducing the probability of aborts at the end of the first phase and minimizing the probability of blocking due to locking by transactions in the validation stage and the possible second phase. Furthermore, it is deadlock-free. We have demonstrated in this paper the correctness of this algorithm and its deadlock free property through formal proofs.

RERERENCE

[1] Kung and Robinson, "On Optimistic Methods for Concurrency Control," ACM TODS 6 (2), 1981, 213-226.

[2] Yu and Dias, "Performance Analysis of Optimistic Concurrency Control Schemes for Systems with Large Memory," Proc. ACM SIGMETRICS Conference, 1989.

[3] Franazek, Robinson, and Thomasian "Access Invariance and Its Use in High Contention Environments," Proc International Conf. on Data Engineering, 1990, 47-55.

[4] Yu and Dias, "Concurrency Control Using Locking with Deferred Blocking," Proc. Inter. Conf. on Data Engineering, 1990, 30-36.

[5] Robinson, "Design of Concurrency Controls for Transaction Processing Systems," Ph.D. thesis, tech. report, CMU-CS-82-114, CMU, 1982.

[6] Wang and Li, "The Precedence-agreement for Distributed Database Concurrency Control algorithms," Proc. ACM Symp. Principles of Database Systems, 1987, 119-128.

[7] Agrawal, Carey, and Livny, "Concurrency Control Performance Modeling: Alternatives and Implications," ACM TODS 12 (4) , 609-654.

[8] Gray, Lorie, Putzolu, "Granularity of Locks in a Shared Data Base," Proc. International Conf. on Very Large Data Bases, 1975, 428-451.

[9] Reuter, "The Transaction Pipeline Processor," Proc. International Workshop on High Performance Transaction Systems, 1985.

[10] Franaszek and Robinson, "Limitations of Concrrency in Transaction Processing," ACM TODS, March, 1985, 1-28.

[11] Holt, "Some deadlock Properties in Computer Systems," ACM Computing Surveys 4 (3), 1972, 179-196.

Font Cache Design Issues in a Distributed Electronic Publishing System for Japanese Language Documents

Atsushi Kawabata[(+)]   Dan C. Marinescu[(++)]

Computer Science Department
Purdue University
West Lafayette, IN., 47907, USA

ABSTRACT

In this paper, we investigate critical design issues for a distributed electronic publishing system for Japanese language documents. Several font cache organizations are evaluated and a new strategy, using shadow font cache directories, is proposed.

1 A Distributed Design Approach to an Electronic Publishing System

A desirable feature of the electronic publishing system is to allow the user to see on the screen of his/her graphics terminal or workstation the document as it would appear in printing. To achieve this result the document is processed and the output, usually in a bitmap format, is sent to the terminal. Clearly, the processing unit must have access to a font data base to replace every character in the page description with its corresponding bitmap according to the required style and size.

An electronic publishing system can be designed either as a centralized system with a set of graphics terminals connected to a processor or as a distributed system using workstations.

Distributed systems consisting of a set of workstations connected to a set of servers through a high-speed network is the environment of choice for many applications including scientific and engineering computing, instructional computing and many other areas. The main advantages of this approach are: good response time, convenience of use, low cost, incremental growth, and high availability. The reasons mentioned above apply to electronic publishing systems as well and make a distributed design approach attractive.

A distributed electronic publishing system consists of high resolution workstations connected to print servers and file servers. Figure 1 shows the typical configuration of a distributed electronic publishing system [1]. Of a particular concern to us are the font data sets, the data sets holding all fonts in all styles and sizes. To allow visualization of a document the workstation must have access to a font data set. When the size of the font data set is in the hundreds of Mbyte range it is impractical to store it on a local disk of a workstation and the font data sets must be shared. The file servers where font data sets are located will be called *font servers*.

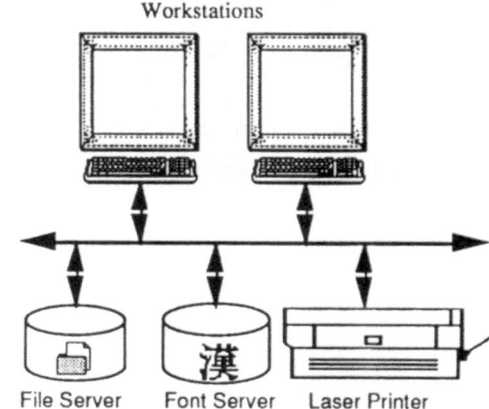

Workstations

File Server   Font Server   Laser Printer

Figure1 The Typical Configuration of Distributed Electronic Publishing Systems
Several workstations are connected with each others by a high speed local network and shared resources, like file server, font server, print server.

The main problem in a distributed system is to avoid overloading shared resources, different servers connected to the system and the interconnection network. The design of a distributed system depends heavily upon the workload of the system. Computationally intensive tasks benefit most from a distributed environment because they can use a dedicated processor rather than share a slightly faster processor with many other tasks. In case of I/O bound tasks which require frequent network access, a careful design of the system is necessary in order to prevent overloading the interconnection network. The delay throughput characteristics of the interconnection network show that at high load the communication delays increase drastically. For example

(+)   On leave of absence from Hitachi Ltd.
(++) Work supported in part by NSF grant NCR-8702115 and by ARO grant DDAL03-96-K-0106

diskless workstations need to have a substantial amount of local cache to avoid excessive paging to a file server.

Similar problems occur for font caches in a distributed electronic publishing system. Each workstation must cache fonts locally in order to avoid extensive use of the network and of the font servers. It is important to point out that a font cache is necessary even when the font data set is stored on a local disk. Otherwise the processor has to access the secondary storage device for every character or group of characters it has to process. Since the access time to data located on secondary storage is several orders of magnitude larger than the processing speed (tens of milliseconds as compared to microseconds) this solution is unacceptable.

2 Font Data Sets for the Japanese Language

This paper presents design issues pertinent to a distributed electronic publishing system for Japanese language documents. The Japanese language has a very large set of characters and the font data sets tend to be fairly large. There are about 7,000 characters in the Japanese language as defined by the Japanese Industrial Standard, JIS. The characters are divided into two groups, JIS-level 1 and JIS-level 2 standards. The JIS-level 1 standard contains Chinese and Kana characters, numbers, special symbols. The JIS-level 2 standard contains only Chinese characters.

To design a font cache, it is important to realize that the frequency of use of different Japanese characters varies widely. From the 7,000 characters, only a few have a relatively high frequency. The Kana character set contains only 169 characters but its frequency of use is over 50% while for the JIS-level 2 standard the Chinese characters, the frequency of use is very low. Table 1 presents the frequency of use of different characters. A typical Japanese monthly magazine, or a Japanese novel, typically contains 30K-70K characters. Table 1 shows that over 64% of characters in a typical Japanese book are Kana characters.

Table 1 Japanese Characters, Frequencies of use
This table shows the number of each type of character and the relative frequency of each group.

	Total Number	Frequency of use in a monthly magazine	Frequency of use in a novel
Kana	169	60.8%	64.8%
Non-Chinese Characters	412	12.8%	11.9%
JIS-1 Chinese Characters	2965	26.3%	23.1%
JIS-2 Chinese Characters	3388	0.1%	0.2%

To estimate the size of the font data set, it is necessary to discuss the font data formats. Two formats will be presented, the outline and the bitmap format. An outline format consists of the outline information of characters defined in normalized coordinates. Any sized characters or slanted characters are retrieved from one outline format by linear transformations. The outline format is independent of the resolution of the output device. However to display a character in outline format, a painting process is necessary, and displaying by painting takes 10-50 times longer than displaying by bit block transfer.

The bitmap format consists of bitwise information on dot-on, dot-off, and it is usually used directly to display characters on a bitmap output device. Clearly, the bitmap format depends upon the size of the character and upon the resolution of the output device. Typical resolutions for output devices are: 72 dots/inch for a dot-impact printer, 300 dots/inch for a laser printer, 2540 dots/inch for a typesetting device. Table 2 shows the size of the font data set for bitmap fonts for a 10 points, 7,000 character set.

Table 2 The Size of Font Data Sets for Different Resolution of Output Devices
The bitmap format depends upon the size of the character and upon the resolution of the output device.
This table shows the size of the font data set for bitmap fonts for a set of 10 points, 7,000 character set.

DPI: Dots Per Inch

Resolution (DPI)	72	300	600	2540
Size of font data	87KB	1.5MB	6.1MB	109MB

3 Font Cache Organization, Basic Concepts

In section 1, we have argued that in order to provide a good response time, a workstation must have a font cache. There are obvious analogies between the font cache and virtual memory and the terminology known from virtual memory will be extended to the font cache case. As long as the cache cannot hold the entire font data set, at times a font will need to be fetched from the font server. Such a situation will be called a *Font Cache Miss* (FCM). Whenever the font data is available in the font cache we have a *Font Cache Hit* (FCH). These two situations are illustrated in Figure 2. A document using only a fraction of the character set is said to have a good *locality of reference. The working set of fonts of a given document* is the set of fonts which are frequently used.

The organization of the font cache depends upon the size of the font data set and the frequency of use of different characters. Figure 3 shows the general structure of the font

442

cache for a workstation. Typically, the font cache consists of a directory and a data field. The directory holds the character code and a pointer to the bitmap representation of the character, stored in the data field portion of the font cache, [2], [3].

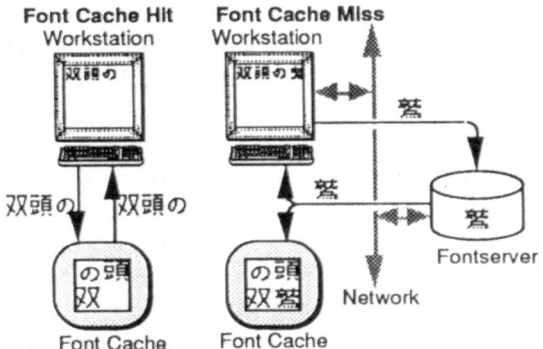

Figure 2 Font Cache Hit/Miss

Font Cache Hit: The font data is available in the font cache.
Font Cache Miss: The font data need to be fetched from the font server.

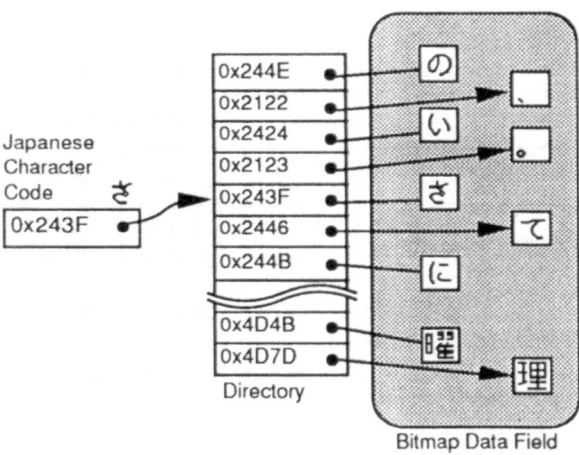

Figure 3 The Typical Font Cache

Typically, the font cache consists of a directory and a data field. The directory holds the character code and a pointer to the bitmap representation of the character, stored in the data field portion of the font cache.

Assume that a certain character in the input stream must be processed. At first, the font cache is searched. If the code corresponding to the character is found in the directory, the pointer to data field is retrieved and the bitmap representation of the character is copied to the output field. Let us denote by t_{fhit} the access time in case of a font cache hit, by t_{search}

the directory search time and by t_{copy} the time to copy the bitmap representation of the character to the output field. Then

$$t_{fhit} = t_{search} + t_{copy}. \qquad (1)$$

Note that t_{search} depends upon the size of the font cache and upon the font cache organization and t_{copy} depends upon the amount of data in the bitmap representation of a character which in turn depends upon the resolution of the output device and upon the point size.

If the required data is not found in the font cache, the font data is retrieved from the secondary storage and then transferred to a buffer in the memory of the processor. In case of a local disk, the transfer time is relatively short, while in case of a font server, this transfer implies the use of the interconnection network and the transfer time can be considerably longer. Then the character is displayed using the font data and at the same time, the font cache is updated. Let us denote by t_{fmiss} the access time in case of a font cache miss, by t_{access} the access time of the secondary storage device where the bitmap representation of the character is stored, by $t_{transfer}$ the transfer time from the secondary device to a buffer in the main memory of the processor and by t_{update} the time to update the directory of font cache. Then

$$t_{fmiss} = t_{search} + t_{access} + t_{transfer} + t_{update} + t_{copy}. \qquad (2)$$

Note that in case of a font server, t_{access} includes the waiting time for service at a shared resource, the font server, as well as the actual access time to the secondary storage connected to the font server. And $t_{transfer}$ includes the queuing delay for the interconnection network, data transmission time and propagation delay.

Let us call the ratio of cache hits to the total number of font references, *the hit ratio*, and denote it by *h*. To determine the average font access time, let us denote by t_{font} the average font access time, and as before, t_{fhit} is the access time in case of a cache hit and t_{fmiss} the access time in case of a font miss. Using the above notation the average font access time can be expressed as

$$t_{font} = h \times t_{fhit} + (1 - h) \times t_{fmiss}. \qquad (3)$$

Typically $t_{fmiss} \geq 10^2 \times t_{fhit}$. Simple arithmetic shows that when $t_{fmiss} = 10^2 \times t_{fhit}$ and the font hit ratio increases from 0.9 to 0.91 then the average font access time decreases by 10 %. When the hit ratio increases from 0.98 to 0.99 then the average font access time improves by 33%. These simple computations outline the significant impact of the font cache organization upon the overall performance of an electronic publishing system.

As in the case of virtual memory, several policies for font cache handling must be defined. The first policy is the *fetch policy* which determines when a new character is brought into the cache from the font data set. Typically a character not found in the font cache is brought in *on-demand*, namely when it is needed.

A second policy important for the organization of the font cache is the *replacement policy*, which determines what character from the font cache is purged when the font cache is full and a new font has to be brought into the cache because a font cache miss has occurred. A Least Recently Used, LRU strategy, is commonly used as a replacement policy.

To analyze the performance of a cache font replacement policy, we compare it with the *optimal policy* based upon the a priori knowledge of the input string. The optimal policy is to purge the character whose reference is the furthest in the future of any other character of the document.

4 Font Cache Organization for Japanese Language Characters

As pointed out in section 2, the Japanese language has a large set of characters and the font working set of a typical document is fairly large. To ensure acceptable processing speeds, the font cache must be large. But the physical size of the font cache memory is limited by cost considerations. In addition, searching a large font cache directory can become a source of inefficiency in itself and new strategies for font cache organization for Japanese language characters must be investigated.

In the following, we describe several new alternatives for font cache organization which depend upon the coding of the Japanese characters.

Throughout the paper, the case when the entire document uses the same point size is considered. Processing of documents when characters with multiple point sizes are needed adds additional complexity to the font cache design problem and it will be discussed only briefly.

As shown in Figure 4, the code of a Japanese character consists of 2 bytes, the high order byte and the low order byte. The high order byte indicates the group the character belongs to. We use the notation, x24, x25 for hexadecimal numbers. For example, if the high order byte is x24 or x25 the character is a Kana character.

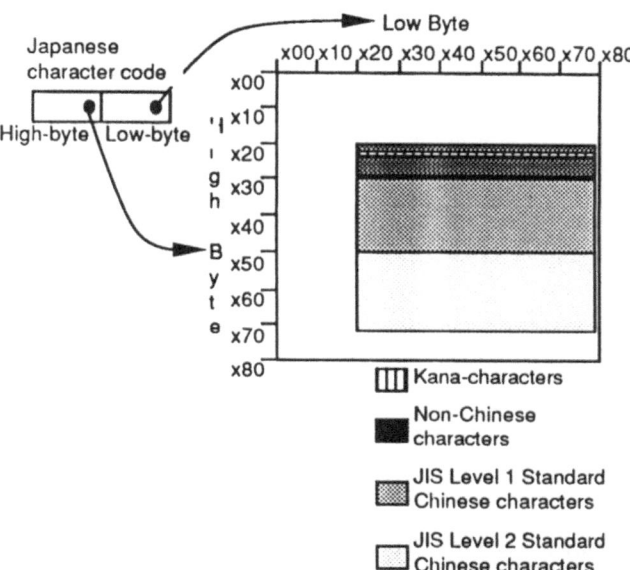

Figure 4 The Japanese Character Code Set

The code of a Japanese character consists of 2 bytes, the high order byte and the low order byte. The high order byte indicates the group the character belongs to.

Figure 5 shows an organization for the font cache based upon the *set associative* approach. The directory of the font cache is divided into several sub-directories. Each sub-directory contains characters with the same low order byte. The characters in a sub-directory are ordered by the high order byte. The number of sub-directories is determined by the range of the low order byte. In Japanese character code, the low orderbyte varies from x21 to x7E, hence the number of sub-directories is 94. The capacity of a sub-directory is called the set-associativity of the font cache. The capacity of the font cache is the product of the set-associativity of the font cache and the number of sub-directories.

Each sub-directory has a *tag* associated with it. The tag value corresponds to the low order byte of all characters stored in the sub-directory. An entry in a sub-directory contains the character stored as high order byte and a pointer to the bitmap field of the character.

To determine whether a given character's data is available in the font cache the following search procedure is executed

(1) Select the sub-directory, whose tag value corresponds to the low order byte of the character.

(2) Search the sub-directory using as a search argument the high order byte of the character. In case of a match, a font cache hit occurs and the font bitmap representation

444

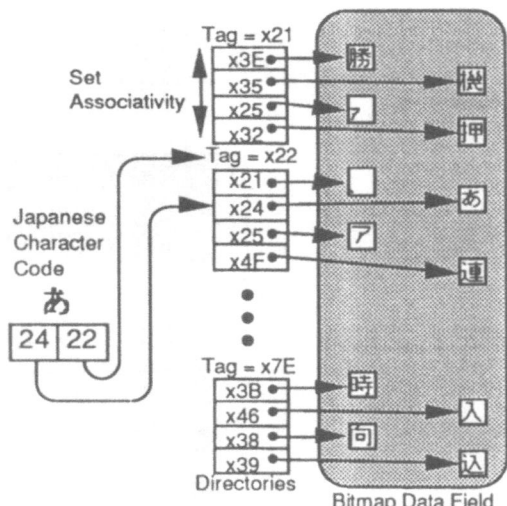

Figure 5 The Font Cache With Sub-Directories
The directory of the font cache is divided into several sub-directories. Each sub-directory contains characters with the same low order byte. The number of sub-directories is determined by the range of the low order byte.

is fetched from the corresponding field. Otherwise a font cache miss occurs.

In case of a font cache miss, the font cache is updated following the procedure described below.

(1) Select the sub-directory with a tag value equal to the low order byte of the new character.

(2) If the sub-directory is not full, the new character is stored in the sub-directory and the bitmap data is stored in the bitmap field.

(3) If the sub-directory is full, the least recently used character in it is purged and the new character is inserted.

This method scatters Kana-characters among sub-directories and allows efficient directory search. But the method leads to storage fragmentation, some sub-directories need more space, while others do not use all their entries. This method may cause unnecessary font faults. It is possible that a document has, in its working set, a group of characters with the same low order byte and the size of this group is larger than the size of the corresponding sub-directory. In this case, font faults will occur rather frequently.

Figure 6 shows an alternative font cache design. The directory of font cache is also divided into sub-directories but of different sizes. In other words, the set-associativity is different between sub-directories. Each sub-directory has tag values equal to the high order byte of the characters stored in

it. To determine whether a specified character's data is stored in the font cache, the following procedure is executed.

(1) Select the sub-directory with a tag value corresponding to the high order byte of the character.

(2) Search the sub-directory using as a search argument the low order byte of the character. In case of a match, a font cache hit occurs and the font bitmap representation is fetched from the corresponding field. Otherwise a font cache miss occurs.

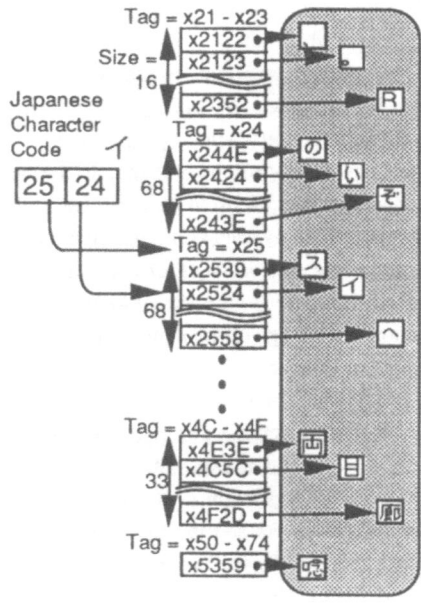

Figure 6 The Font Cache With Sub-Directories(2)
The directory of font cache is also divided into sub-directories but of different sizes. Each sub-directory has tag values equal to the high order byte of the characters stored in it.

In case of a font cache miss, a procedure similar to the one described for the previous case is used. As mentioned above, the high order byte shows the group which this character belongs to hence it indicates the relative frequency of the character. For example, if the high order byte is x24 or x25, the character is a Kana-character and its frequency of occurrence is relatively high. Using this information, the optimal size of a directory is estimated by the following method. Suppose that a font cache with a capacity of 500 characters is desired. At first, determine the most frequently used 500 characters in a "typical" document. This can be done using a priori knowledge about the frequency of Japanese characters. Divide the 500 characters among sub-directories according to the desired font cache organization and count the characters which belong to each sub-directory. Set the size of the sub-directory equal to the number of characters counted above.

Last, a font cache organization using the shadow directory concept is presented. Let us call a character with a low frequency of use a *Quite Unusual Character*, QUC. A QUC stored in the font cache is unlikely to be used. Typically a QUC is brought into the font cache, remains there for a random period of time δ, determined by the font replacement policy, without being referenced and then it is eventually replaced. In other words, during the interval δ, an entry of the font cache is unused. It follows that storing QUCs in the font cache leads to a waste of the font cache capacity and to an increase of font cache faults. To handle the case of QUCs, we introduce a shadow directory to font cache organization. In Figure 7 we observe a shadow directory in addition to the structures presented previously, a main directory containing the character entry (character code and a pointer to the bitmap field), and the bitmap representation. A shadow directory entry contains only a character entry without a pointer and a bitmap representation. Each character stored in the main directory has a flag, the QUC flag. The font directory search procedure in this case becomes:

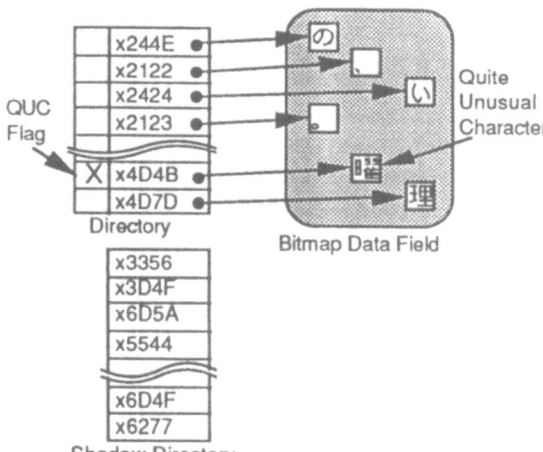

Figure 7 The Typical Font Cache With Shadow Directory

A shadow directory is added to the structures presented previously, a main directory containing the character entry (character code and a pointer to the bitmap field), and the bitmap representation. A shadow directory entry contains only a character entry without a pointer and a bitmap representation. Each character stored in the main directory has a flag, the QUC flag.

(1) At first, search the main directory. If the character is found, the bitmap data is retrieved and QUC flag is set to OFF. We call this a font cache hit.

(2) If the character is not found in the main directory, the shadow directory is searched. If the character is found in the shadow directory, the character is retrieved from the secondary storage, the main directory is updated and the QUC flag is set OFF. We call this case a font shadow miss.

(3) If the specified character is not found even in the shadow directory, the character is retrieved from the secondary storage, the main directory is updated and the QUC flag is set ON. We call this a font transient miss.

In case of a shadow miss or of a transient miss, when the main directory is full, the following procedure is executed.

(1) The least recently used character with the QUC flag ON is purged. The code of the purged character is stored in the shadow directory. The least recently used character in the shadow directory is purged from the shadow directory.

(2) If there is no character with QUC flag ON, then the least recently used character with the QUC flag OFF is purged. The code of the purged character is stored in the shadow directory. The least recently used character in the shadow directory is purged from the shadow directory.

The shadow directory can be used in conjunction with any of the font cache organizations described above. Using this approach the QUCs in the font cache tend to be purged quickly and the font hit ratios improve.

Finally, the application of shadow directory to the font cache design for the case when multiple font point sizes occur is discussed. Clearly the font working set of a document which needs different font point sizes is larger than the font working set of the source document using one font point size only.

It seems reasonable to assume that most document use a dominants point size and other point sizes will occur rather infrequently. This assumption is confirmed by the analysis of sample documents. But the shadow directory is designed to help precisely in the case when characters are used infrequently.

The experimental results to be presented in section 6 show that the benefits of a shadow directory occur precisely when the physical memory available for the font cache is in short supply. When the amount of physical memory available for the font cache is limited by cost considerations and the font working set of a document is increased because different point sizes are used, the system will operate in a region where the shadow directory leads to an improvement of the hit ratio.

As far as implementation is concerned, in case of multiple font point sizes, the font cache directory will identify a character by the character code and point size pair. The QUC flag is used to retain in the font cache only the most frequently used characters with the most used point size.

5 Performance Evaluation of a Distributed Electronic Publishing System

The numerical example presented in Section 3 shows the impact of the hit ratio upon the font access time. It can be observed that slight improvements in the hit ratio lead to significant reductions of the font access time and ultimately to significant reduction of the overall document processing time. The converse is also true, a slight decrease in the hit ratio will lead to a significant performance degradation. It follows that the first objective of a design study for a distributed or a centralized electronic publishing systems is to analyze the performance of different font cache organizations to determine their expected hit ratios for a typical workload.

At first, we evaluated the performance of the font cache designs. Three different designs and one technique were studied. These performances were measured by the font hit ratio. As mentioned above, the font hit ratio depends upon the design of the font cache and also upon the size of the font cache.

Several alternatives for such a performance analysis can be contemplated. The first possibility is to construct analytical models. But analytical models for a font cache are fairly complex, and based upon the analogy with virtual memory, it seems unrealistic to expect useful results from this approach.

Another alternative is to use *font traces* obtained from a "typical document" and to compare the hit ratios of different font cache strategies. A similar approach has been used successfully for cache evaluation for high performance computing systems, [4].

6 Experimental Results

The experimental results are discussed in this section. The simulation was carried out assuming the same point size for all characters on the input file. First, the relationship between the size of the font cache and the font cache hit ratio is presented for the techniques described previously. The input file consists of a Japanese novel which contains about 69,000 characters. The font cache is initialized using a priori information about the average frequency of Japanese characters.

Figure 8 shows the results of numerical experiments about font hit ratios for the three font cache organizations described above, namely (a) the font cache with a single directory, (b) the font cache with sub-directories of the same size, and (c) the font cache with sub-directories of different size. The fourth curve plots the font hit ratio for the optimal font cache replacement policy as defined in Section 3. The horizontal axis shows the capacity of font cache in multiples of 94 entries. As shown earlier in the Japanese character code, the low order byte varies from x21 to x7E, hence the number of sub-directories is 94. The inspection of the graphs in Figure 8 shows that the best performance is obtained for a font cache organization with sub-directories of different sizes, case (c).

Figure 9 shows the improvement in performance due to the addition of shadow directories for case (c). The graph shows the font hit ratios with and without the shadow directory. We observe that the shadow directory leads to a slight improvement in performance for relatively small sizes of the font cache.

The experiments presented in this section allow us to estimate the actual size of the font cache when a certain font hit ratio is desired. For example, when the font cache has multiple sub-directories of different sizes, a font hit ratio of 99% can be achieved when the cache has at least 16 x 94 entries, as shown in Figure 8.

If we assume that the output device has a resolution of 300dpi and that 9.6 point characters are required, then the size of each entry becomes

$$e_{300} = c + p + bm \qquad (4)$$

with

      c = the size of the character code, 2 byte
      p = the size of the pointer to the bitmap, 4 byte
      bm = the size of the bitmap, in this case 200 byte

The size of the font cache in this case is

$$F = 16 \times 94 \times e_{300} = 310 \text{ K byte} \qquad (5)$$

7 Conclusion

An electronic publishing system for Japanese language documents requires access to large font data sets. To reduce the processing time of a document, a carefully designed font cache is necessary.

In this paper, we present several alternative designs for the font cache and compare their performance characterized by the font cache hit ratio. To compare the different font cache organizations, we use input files obtained from small to medium size documents. This procedures show that for a given size of the font cache, the highest hit ratio is obtained for a font cache organization with multiple sub-directories of

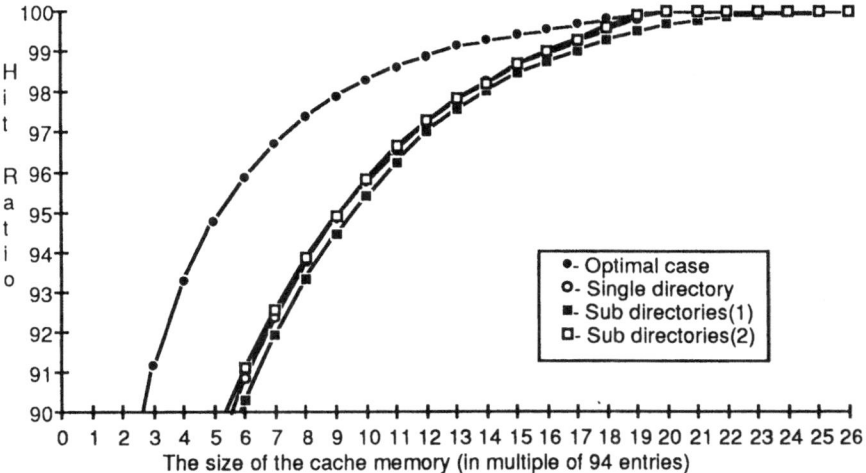

Figure 8 The Performance of Font Caches

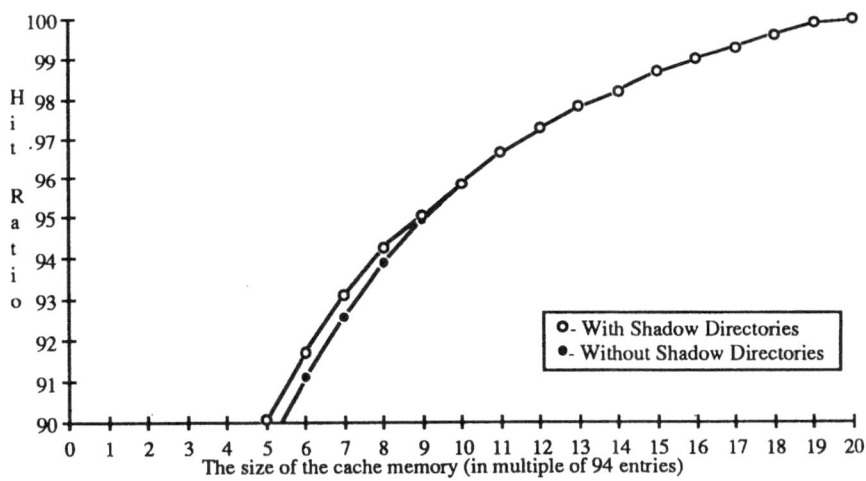

Figure 9 The Improved performance by the Shadow Directories

different sizes.

The characteristic obtained from the font hit ratio function of the font cache size can be used for the actual design of the system as follows. From the desired response time, the required hit ratio h can be computed from (3) after estimating t_{fhit} and t_{fmiss}. Then from these aspects, we estimate the size of the font cache.

We also propose an organization with a shadow directory and show that it improves the hit ratio when the amount of the font cache memory is limited.

8 Literature

[1] Schlichter, Johann H. and Miller, Leslie Jill:FolioPub: A Publication Management System, COMPUTER, Jan.1988, pp61-69.

[2] YAMAASHI, K., MIURA, S., KAWABATA, A., TAKI, Y., KOBAYASHI, Y.: Study of Character Printing Method for Japanese. Proceedings of the 37th Annual Convention Information Processing Society of Japan, 1988.

[3] Kobayashi, M. and Mima, Y.: Multi-font Handling for Large Character Set on Workstations, Proceedings of the IEEE Computer Society Office Automation Symposium in Gaithersburg, Maryland, 1987.

[4] Stone, Harold S.: High-performance Computer Architecture, Addison-Wesley Pub. Co., 1987.

[5] Becker, J.: Multilingual Word Processing, Scientific American, vol. 251, no.1, Jan. 1984.

[6] Jack Kai-tung Huang: The Input and Output of Chinese and Japanese Characters, IEEE Computer, Jan.1985,pp18-24.

[7] Becker, J.: Typing chinese, Japanese and Korean,IEEE Computer,Jan.1985,pp27-34.

The Design of a Logic Query Processor

Wen Yu Lu and Dik Lun Lee
Department of Computer and Information Science
Ohio State University
Columbus, OH 43210 USA

Abstract

We present the design of a logic query processor for linear recursive rules. Unlike the traditional methods which primarily use query information in query processing, our design makes use of both query information and program structure to achieve efficient query processing. The design of this processor consists of three major components: representation and classification, analysis, and compilation. The approach is to classify logic rules based on their structures and obtain quantitative information about the recursive expansions, and then combine the information with query instantiation to generate an efficient database program. This design suggests a sophisticated analysis phase before query processing. In return, it often yields a superior performance than other general processing strategies.

1 Introduction

The introduction of logic programming into database systems to provide database systems with deductive power has been under intensive study in recent years. The major effort in developing such extended database systems (called *deductive database systems*) has been on the efficiency in query processing. Many processing techniques have been proposed [2,7,15]. The *magic set method* is one of the well known methods [2,3]. It implements the optimization principle "retrieve only relevant facts via selection propagation" by rewriting rules using query instantiations and magic predicates. Although this strategy has the advantage of conceptual simplicity, it doesn't fully exploit the structure of the rules. Consequently, its per-

formance is not very impressive in many common cases [12,13,14,16].

In this paper, we propose a design of a logic query processor with a different approach. Our processor works as follows: when a logic query is input to the processor, the logic rule defining the recursive predicate is first classified according to its structure (*classification*); the knowledge about the structure of the rule and the recursive expansions are also encoded (*analysis*); then by combining the structural knowledge with query instantiations, an efficient database program is generated (*compilation*) to obtain answers for the query from the underlying database.

This approach is motivated by the observations that (1) for a given type of recursion, special-purpose algorithms significantly outperform general processing methods and (2) studies have shown that, in general, the information passing among variables of a recursive rule is highly periodic during rule expansions; these characteristics can be precisely encoded and utilized for developing efficient processing methods. Consequently, the database programs thus generated performs significantly better than the magic set methods in many common cases. Considering the facts that database relations are usually large and that searching and retrieving data from secondary storage is expensive, our approach is promising in improving the efficiency.

This paper is organized as follows. The rest of Section 1 introduces the preliminaries of logic query processing. Section 2 is the layout of the architecture of the processor. Section 3, 4 and 5 discuss in succession the functions performed by different components of the processor and the implementation algorithms. Section 6 discusses the feasibility of the design and the performance.

1.1 Preliminaries

A **deductive database** consists of an **extensional database (EDB)** and an **intensional database (IDB)** (a

This research is supported by NSF Grant IRI-881064. Any opinions, findings, and conclusions or recommendations expressed in this paper are those of the authors and do not necessarily reflect the views of the National Science Foundation.

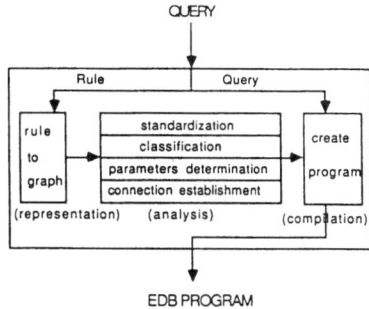

Figure 1: The architecture of the processor.

Figure 2: The information flow of the processor.

The architecture of the processor is illustrated in Fig. 1. The information flow of the design is illustrated in Fig. 2. In principle, our processor adopts the compilation approach of query processing, i.e., a query is first compiled into an EDB program which is then processed by the underlying database system. In accordance with the sequence of functions to be performed, the processor consists of three major components:

1. **Representation.** Given a linear recursive rule defining a recursive predicate, the component converts the recursive rule into a graph representation.

2. **Analysis.** This component has several functions: first, it classifies the rule into the proper class and determines the quantitative characterization of the rule. Then it establishes the connections of the expansions of the rule.

3. **Compilation.** The component uses the query constants to decide the processing plan and generate an EDB program for query processing based on the structural information obtained in the analysis phase.

In the following sections, we describe each component in detail.

3 Representation

To represent a linear recursive rule in a more manageable form, we use a V-graph, defined below, which is similar to those in [4,8].

1. Every variable in the rule is a vertex.

2. A directed edge (**D-edge**) connects vertex x to vertex y if y is in the head predicate and x is a variable in the same argument position in the recursive predicate in the body.

3. An undirected edge (**U-edge**) connects two variables which appear in the same base predicate. The edge is labeled with the name of the base predicate.

set of Datalog rules). Datalog is a logic programming language suitable for databases. A Datalog rule is of the format: $L_0 :- L_1, L_2, ..., L_n$, where L_i is of the form $P_i(x_1, ..., x_{k_i})$ in which P_i is a **predicate** and x_j is either a variable or a constant. j is the **argument position** of x_j in P_i. The left-hand side is the rule **head**, and the right-hand side is the rule **body**. A rule is **recursive** if its head predicate also appears in its body. Otherwise, it is a (nonrecursive) **exit** rule. A rule is **linearly recursive** if its head predicate appears exactly once in its body. The head predicate is the **recursive** predicate defining a virtual relation and the other predicates are nonrecursive (or **base**) predicates representing the base relations in a database. The variables of the head predicates are **distinguished variables**. A **query** to a recursive predicate R is of the form $?R(x_1, ..., x_n)$ where x_i is either a variable (inquisition), a constant (instantiation), or a "don't care" denoted by $-$. The answer to a query is the tuples of values for the inquired variables derivable from the EDB using the rules defining the recursive predicate. The **first expansion** of a linear recursive rule is the the rule itself and its **kth expansion** is the application of the rule to its $(k-1)$th expansion. This processor is designed to process linear recursions that consist of a linear recursive rule along with an exit rule, although it can be extended for more general recursions.

Example 1.1. The frequently cited linear recursion *Ancestor* is defined as follows:

$Ancestor(x,y) :- Parent(x,y).$

$Ancestor(x,y) :- Parent(x,z), Ancestor(z,y).$ (r1)

$?Ancestor(Bob,?y)$ is a query asking for all the ancestors of *Bob*.

2 Architecture And System Functions

450

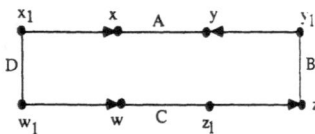

Figure 3: The V-graph of r2.

4. If a D-edge is encountered during a traversal, its weight is 1 if it is along the direction of the traversal, and is -1 otherwise. A U-edge has weight 0. The weight of a traversed route is the sum of the weights of the edges on the route.

Example 3.1.

$$R(x, y, z, w) :- R(x_1, y_1, z_1, w_1),$$
$$A(x, y), B(y_1, z), C(z_1, w), D(x_1, w_1). \quad (r2)$$

We use r2 as a running example throughout the paper. The V-graph of r2 is shown in Fig. 3.

The motivation of using such a graph representation is:

1. The intuition of graph representation is a great help in deriving the properties of the rules, which are hard to observe otherwise. In fact, the expansions of a rule can be precisely determined by traversing the V-graph [10].

2. Several common classes of linear recursive rules that can be efficiently processed have been identified using various graph representations (e.g., bounded recursions, transitive closure recursions and chain recursions).

3. The graph structure is easy to manipulate since many graph algorithms already exist.

4 Analysis

The most important component of the processor is the analysis phase. It collects and encodes all the information about the structures and properties of the rules. Specifically, it performs the following functions:

1. Standardization;
2. Rule Classification;
3. Parameter Determination; and
4. Establishing Rule Expansions.

We discuss the functions of this component separately (although they may not necessarily be implemented separately).

4.1 Standardization

A linear recursive rule is rewritten in a standard form such that

1. The rule head does not contain any repeated variables or constants;

2. The base predicates are simplified through projection, join and vectorization, etc.

The purpose of this subcomponent is to eliminate some superficial complexities of the rules so that they can be treated uniformly at later stages. The existence of a constant can be removed by replacing it with a variable and substituting the constant back in the query compilation phase. Repeated variables can be eliminated in the same way. The simplification of base predicate connections are thoroughly discussed in [4].

Example 4.1. The sequence of base predicates $A(x, y), B(x, z), C(z, w)$ in a rule can be rewritten as a new predicate as $D(y, w)$ if x and z do not appear anywhere else in the rule.

A linear recursive rule

$$R(x, y, z) :- R(x_1, y_1, w), A(x, x_1, y, y_1), B(z, w).$$

can be simplified to

$$R(u, z) :- R(u_1, w), A(u, u_1), B(z, w).$$

where $u = (x, y)$ and $u_1 = (x_1, y_1)$.

4.2 Rule classification

Rules are first classified into different classes according to the configurations of their V-graphs. Graph terminology is used here whenever there is no risk of confusion in doing so. The following additional definitions are needed for rule classifications.

Definition. A cycle is **unit** if it contains only one D-edge; **uniform** if all the D-edges go in one direction; and **nonuniform** otherwise. A cycle is **degenerate** if it contains no U-edges or **nondegenerate** otherwise. A **D-pair of level 1** on a path (or cycle) is two D-edges connected head to head by a sequence of U-edges on the path (cycle). A **D-pair of level i** on a path (cycle) is a D-pair such that all the D-edges between their heads are paired and their maximum level is $i - 1$. The unpaired D-edges on a path (cycle) are **uni-D-edges**. The **weight of a cycle**

is the number of uni-D-edges in it. The **level of a cycle** is the maximum level of all the D-pairs in it. The **length of a V-graph** (denoted by *len*) is the weight of the longest simple path in it and the **weight of a graph** (denoted by *w*) is the least common multiples of the weights of all the cycles in it.

The following is the classification of linear recursive rules.

1. trees;

2. cycles:

    (a) degenerate or has a zero weight;

    (b) nondegenerate and has a weight > 0;

3. connected components:

    (a) containing no degenerate cycles:

        i. containing no cycles of nonzero weight;

        ii. containing one cycle of nonzero weight;

        iii. otherwise;

    (b) containing degenerate cycles:

        i. containing no other cycles of nonzero weight after the degenerate cycles along with the adjacent U-edges are removed;

        ii. otherwise;

4. Disjoint components of class 1, 2 and 3:

    (a) each connected component is one of 1, 2.a, 3.a.i and 3.b.i;

    (b) each connected component is one of 1, 2, 3.a.i 3.a.ii and 3.b.i;

    (c) otherwise.

The purpose of rule classification is to further identify the properties of the rules. It is based on the following observations. Rules of the same class shares the same characteristics in their structures so they can be processed with the same strategy. Further, special classes of recursions lend themselves to special processing techniques which are more efficient than general methods [6,8,12,14,16]. In fact, many special classes of recursions of this nature have been identified using similar graph representation. In general, based on the nature of recursive expansions, we have the following definitions and proven results.

Definition. A linear recursive rule is **bounded** if it is equivalent to a finite number of nonrecursive rules. A

1, 2.a, 3.a.i, 3.b.i, 4.a	bounded
2.b, 3.a.ii, 4.b	simple chain recursion
3.a.iii, 3.b.ii, 4.c	general chain recursion

Table 1: Correspondence between V-graphs and recursions.

linear recursive rule is a **n-chain recursion** if after finite expansions its expansions can be expressed in n disjoint chains along with some base predicates where each chain consists of a sequence of base predicates connected in a periodic way. Two distinguished variables are **bound** to each other if they are connected by a sequence of base predicates after certain number of expansions.

Theorem 4.1. *Each class of linear recursive rules from the above classification belong to either one of the two categories: bounded recursion or chain recursions.*

In particular, the popular transitive closure recursions are properly included in chain recursion with $n = 1$. Depending on the complexity of the connection patterns of the chains, chain recursions can be further divided into two subclasses: **simple** chain recursion, which has simple chain connections and variable binding, and **general** chain recursions. The difference results in different implementations, as will be seen in section 4.4. Table 1 lists the correspondence between graph properties and classes of recursions.

Example 4.2. The recursive rule r2 is classified in class 2.b. It is a simple multiple chain recursion as to be shown in Example 4.3.

Each category of recursions can be processed using a special efficient strategy. Bounded recursion can be processed utilizing traditional nonrecursive programs. 1-chain recursions, in particular, can be processed using transitive closure algorithms and their variants. In general, chain recursions can be processed using synchronous counting methods and the likes.

Regarding the implementation of this rule classification, a divide-and-conquer approach can be adopted in which each connected component of the corresponding V-graph is partitioned to trees and 2-connected components, and the latter is further decomposed to a composition of cycles. Variations of graph traversal algorithms and articulation point algorithms on the V-graphs will suffice for such a task.

4.3 Parameter determination

Variable connections in rule expansions represents the information passing among query instantiations and inquisitions. For each class of rules, a set of quantitative parameters are needed for characterizing the connections in the rule expansions. For a bounded rule, it is the number of the expansions needed to find all the nonrecursive rules which together are equivalent to the recursive rule. For a chain recursion, it is the number of chains, the period of the chains, and the expansions starting from which the chains start to emerge. These parameters are used to determine the size of the data structures for storing the information about the connections in the rule expansions in the next step and, more importantly, to generate the EDB program in the compilation stage.

The following theorem determines the parameters for the connections in the rule expansions in terms of the properties of the graph representations.

Theorem 4.2. *The number of nonredundant expansions of a bounded recursion is the length of the corresponding V-graph. The number of nonredundant expansions of a chain recursion is the sum of the length and the weight of its V-graph.*

Example 4.3. Rule r2 has two chains starting from expansion 2, with period 2. Thus, three expansions are necessary for collecting information about all rule expansions.

For rules in class 1 and 2, these parameters can be easily determined by performing traversals on their V-graphs and are guaranteed to be minimal. Parameter determination becomes more complex for some rules of class 3 or 4, as many cycles may exist in one connected component of the V-graph. In these cases, exhaustive traversals for determining and minimizing the parameters could result in exponential time performance with respect to the size of the rule (e.g., the number of vertices and the edges in the V-graph). The requirement of minimality can be relaxed in order to make sure parameter determination can be done in polynomial times. Such a compromise might increase the cost of compilation but will not affect query processing performance. Thus, it can be considered a worthwhile tradeoff. For instance, because the number of expansions needed for a bounded rule is upper-bounded by len, which is in turn bounded by the arity of the rule, the arity of the rule can serve as the upper bound for the number of necessary expansions.

Similar approach can be adopted to determine the bindings of simple chain recursions. Since the variables bound to one another will connect to the same chain and since they are bound if and only if they are pairwise associated to a D-pair on some path of length no greater than len, the number of chains can be determined by tracing the expansions len times.

To find the period for a complex unbounded rule which is a general chain recursion, the connected component can be decomposed into nondegenerate cycles of nonzero weight that cover the connected component. Then the expansions of the rule can be derived by tracing the expansions of any of these cycle decompositions [10]. The least common multiples of the cycles in such a decomposition (no greater than the weight of the V-graph by definition) can be taken as the period of the periodic connections in the rule expansions. Note that finding such a cycle decomposition and thus the least common multiple of those cycles in the decomposition takes polynomial time [10].

4.4 Establishing connections of rule expansions

The connections of recursive expansions are established based on the classification and parameter determination. The connections record the detailed base predicate connections among distinguished variables in all expansions. For a bounded rule, only len expansions are needed; for chain recursion, at most $len + w$ expansions are needed. Thus, the connection information can be stored in a fixed-size data structure upper-bounded by the parameters and the size of the rule.

The establishment of the connections can be realized by traversing the V-graph starting at the distinguished variables along the paths and cycles that cover the V-graph. Depending on the complexity, the variable connections in the rule expansions should be represented by different types of data structures. Simple chain recursions have simple chain patterns in their expansions, so a simple array structure is a suitable choice. On the other hand, general chain recursions need more complex structures such as graph structures to represent the expansions.

4.5 Implementation

As a summary of the above discussion on the functions of the analysis stage, the following algorithm implements the analysis component by collecting the complete information about the connections of the rule expansions. In order to express the idea in a concise way, we choose to use an array $Conn$ for information storage.

Algorithm: (Finding the connections (formulations) of rule expansions)

Input: a linear recursive rule in the V-graph representation with weight w and length len.

Output: the complete information about the connections of rule expansions.

Data Structures:

(1) An array $Conn(1 : -, 1 : n)$ for storing the information, where n is the number of distinguished variables of the recursion and $-$ means a dynamic bound. $Conn(i, j)$ can hold several sequences of base predicates generated in expansion i. Each sequence is generated from some path p_i or cycle c_i of the V-graph decomposition and is associated to the base predicate connections for the distinguished variable x_j. The ID p_i (or c_i) is attached to each sequence of $Conn(i, j)$ indicating the path or cycle from which the sequence is generated. Hence, the sequences with the same ID in $Conn(i, j)$ for $(i = 1$ to $n)$ together are the base predicate sequence connected to x_j along the path or cycle indicated by the ID in expansion n. Row i contains all the base predicates generated in expansion i.

(2) A variable, $Center$, for storing the exit predicate along with the base predicates connected only to the exit predicate.

Begin

1. Simplify the base predicate connections of the rule;

2. Record all the degenerate cycles and their connections with the remaining part of the V-graph;

3. Decompose the remaining V-graph into cycles and trees, each associated to a distinguished ID;

4. Determine the class of the linear recursive rule;

5. Find all the parameters and record all the bindings;

5. For $k = 1$ to len do

6.1. for each distinguished variable x_i, find the sequence of base predicates grown in expansion k along the cycle or path and store it into $Conn(k, i)$ with an ID for that cycle or path;

6.2. for variables that become bound in expansion k via a sequence of base predicates, stop recording this sequence in further expansions.

7. (Only for chain recursion) For $k = len+1$ to $len+w$ do

for each distinguished variable x_i, find the sequence of base predicates grown in expansion k along the cycle or

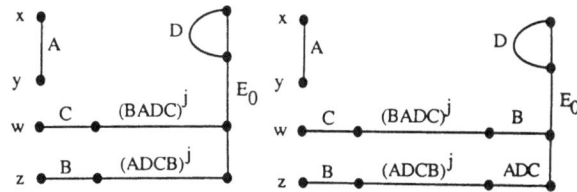

Figure 4: The expansions of rule r2.

0	x	y	z	w
1	A	A	B	C
2	-	-	ADC	B
3	-	-	B	ADC

Table 2: The $Conn$ of rule r2.

path and store it into $Conn(k, i)$ with an ID for that cycle or path;

End.

Example 4.4. We inspect r2 again. The connections of the expansions of r2 are shown in Fig. 4, in which the edges represent base predicate sequences and the end vertices represent distinguished variables. One can see clearly that the periodic change of the connections with rule expansions starts at expansion 2. They are expressed in the array $Conn$ as shown in Table 2. $Conn$ has 3 rows because the chains start at expansion 2 with period 2. It has 4 columns each corresponding to a distinguished variable of the rule. $Center$ is $E_0 D$.

5 Compilation

In this stage, an input query is compiled into an EDB program using the information about the rule expansions obtained from the analysis component. In the process, the query constants are inserted into the $Conn$ to determine the directions along which processing should be conducted. Based on the query instantiations, the information about the classes of the recursive rules and $Conn$, an EDB program is generated for that query. Here we describe the compilation in the context of a sample query to a simple 2-chain recursion. We use $\pi_B(A \bowtie B)$ to represent the

454

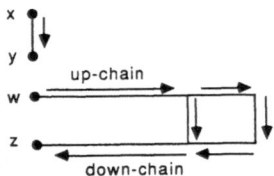

Figure 5: The processing direction of the sample query to rule r2.

join of A and B on their common attributes followed by a projection on the attributes of $B - A$.

Example 5.1.

Input:

(1) $Conn$ for rule r2 and $Center$: $E_0 D$.

(2) A query $?R(a, ?y, c, ?w)$. (According to the instantiations, the processing directions are determined, as indicated by the arrows in Fig. 5.)

Output: The set of answers $Answer$ to the query.

Data Structures:

(1) a dynamic array of sets $ST(1 \ldots, z)$, in which $ST(j, z)$ stores the facts generated along the base predicate connections associated to z, the instantiated variable in expansion j;

(2) two sets $Result(y)$ and $Result(w)$ for storing all the relevant facts during down-chain processing (see 10 to 13 of the algorithm) and finally the values of y and w. $Result(y)|_{level}$ is the subset of $Result(y)$, in which all the facts are associated to expansion $level$. $Result(z)|_{level}$ has the similar meaning. (3) We use P to represent ADC or B interleaved in the expansions.

Begin

1. $Answer \leftarrow Empty$.

[* Processing exit rule *]

2. $Answer \leftarrow Answer \cup \pi_{2,4}\sigma_{x=a,z=c}E_0$.

[* Processing first expansion *]

3. $Result(y) \leftarrow \pi_2\sigma_{x=a}A$.

4. $Result(w) \leftarrow \pi_C(B \bowtie E_0 D \bowtie C)$.

5. $Answer \leftarrow Answer \cup (Result(y) \times Result(w))$.

[* Up-chain processing *]

6. For $k := 2$ to forever do begin

7. $ST(k, z) \leftarrow \pi_P(ST(k-1, z) \bowtie P)$.

8. If $ST(k, z) = Empty$ then goto 10.

9. end.

[* Down-chain processing *]

10. For $l := k - 1$ down to 1 do begin

11. $Result(w) \leftarrow Result(w) \cup \pi_{E_0 - D}(ST(l, z) \bowtie E_0 D)$;

12. $Result(w) \leftarrow \pi_P(Result(w) \bowtie P)$;

13. end;

[* Generate the answer *]

14. For $level := 2$ to $k - 1$ do

15. $Answer \leftarrow Answer \cup Result(y) \times Result(w)|_{level}$.

16. Return $Answer$.

end.

Notice that the array ST may contain the whole relation for some queries, e.g., total closures. Thus, it may not be appropriate to store it in main memory. Cache techniques and parallelism can be implemented at lower levels to at least alleviate the storage problems.

6 Performance Consideration

One of the important criteria for the feasibility of the processor is that the overheads in the analysis and compilation phases can not be too high, compared with the saving in query processing. We study the complexity of the algorithms needed for implementing the processor as follows.

1. Converting a linear recursive rule to its corresponding V-graph representation is performed by graph traversal which takes $O(ne)$ time where n is the arity of the rule (also the number of the vertices) and e is the number of edges in the V-graph.

2. The time for establishing the connections for a rule depends on the complexity of the rule. Because the algorithm mainly uses the idea of graph traversal, for simple chain recursions, the complexity of the algorithm is bounded by the size of the V-graph, which is $O(ne)$. For more complex rules, polynomial-time heuristics can be adopted by relaxing the minimal conditions as discussed in Section 4.3.

3. The complexity of generating the EDB program is in the same order of the size of $Conn$ which is upper-bounded by $O((len + w)ne)$.

In summary, the algorithms for implementing the processor have polynomial time complexity with respect to the size of the rules, thus demonstrating the feasibility of the approach. Furthermore, the saving in expensive secondary storage accesses resulting from a more efficient EDB program more than offsets the preprocessing costs.

As far as the performance is concerned, related studies can be found in [1,13]. A common measure for efficiency is the number of times a base relation is accessed and searched in answering a query. In [11], we proved that the performance of this processor is optimal with respect to this measure. In particular, it outperforms the magic set methods. Such superiority comes as no surprise, since a rather sophisticated analysis on the rules is performed in the preprocessing stages.

7 Conclusion

We have proposed a design of a logic query processor for linear recursive rules. Besides efficiency, the design has another advantage, that is, it is extensible and portable since the processing algorithms for each class can be easily migrated to other systems. Algorithms for new classes of recursions can be easily integrated into the processor. We focus on the single linear recursive rules in this paper. A natural question is whether this design can be further extended to more general types of recursions such as multiple linear recursions, nonlinear recursions, recursions with function symbols, and mutual recursions. Studies have shown that special forms of these types of recursions can also be identified for efficient processing [5,9]. Since the basic idea behind these studies is to reduce complex types of recursions to the processing of single linear recursive rules, the results from these studies might be adopted in our design to include more general recursions.

References

[1] H. Aly & Z. M. Ozsoyoglu, "Synchronized Counting Method," *Proceedings of the Fifth International Conference on Data Engineering*, Los Angeles, Feb. 1989.

[2] F. Bancilhon & R. Ramakrishnan, "An amateur's introduction to recursive query processing strategies," *Proceedings of the 1986 SIGMOD Conference*, Washington, D.C., May 1986, 16–52.

[3] C. Beeri & R. Ramakrishnan, "On the power of magic," *Proceedings of the Sixth ACM SIGACT-SIGMOD-SIGART Symposium on Principles of Database Systems*, San Diego, CA, Mar. 1987.

[4] J. Han, "Compiling General Linear Recursions by Variable Connection Graph Analysis," *Computational Intelligence*, Vol. 5, No. 1, 1989.

[5] J. Han & L. Liu, "North America Logic Programming Conference," Cleveland, Ohio, Oct. 1989.

[6] J. Han & W. Lu, "Asynchronous Chain Recursions," *IEEE Transactions on Knowledge and Data Engineering*, Vol. 1, No. 2, June 1989.

[7] L. Henschen & S. Naqvi, "On compiling queries in recursive first-order data bases," *J. ACM*, Vol. 31, No. 1, Jan. 1984, 47–85.

[8] Y.E. Ioannidis, "A Time Bound on the Materialization of Some Recursively Defined Views," *Proceedings of the Eleventh International Conference on Very Large Data Bases*, Stockholm, Sweden, Aug. 1985.

[9] Y.E. Ioannidis, "Commutativity and Its Role in the Processing of Linear Recursion," *Proceedings of the Fifteenth International Conference on Very Large Data Bases*, Amsterdam, The Netherlands, August, 1989.

[10] D. L. Lee & W. Y. Lu, "Graph Modeling and Analysis of Linear Recursive Queries," *PARBASE-90: International Conference on Database, Parallel Architectures, and Their Applications*, Miami, FL, Mar. 1990, 44–53.

[11] W. Y. Lu & D. L. Lee, "Characterization and Processing of Simple Prefixed-Chain Recursions," *submitted for publication*.

[12] W. Y. Lu & D. L. Lee, "Query Processing Based on Program Structure," *Methodologies for Intelligent Systems*, Vol. 5, 1990.

[13] A. Marchetti-Spaccamela, A. Pelaggi & D. Sacca, "Worst-case Complexity Analysis of Methods for Logic Query Implementation," *Proceedings of the Sixth ACM SIGACT-SIGMOD-SIGART Symposium on Principles of Database Systems*, San Diego, CA, Mar. 1987.

[14] J. Naughton, "One-Sided Recursions," *Proceedings of the Sixth ACM SIGACT-SIGMOD-SIGART Symposium on Principles of Database Systems*, San Diego, CA, Mar. 1987, 340–348.

[15] D. Sacca & C. Zaniolo, "The Generalized Counting Method for Recursive Logic Queries," *Proc. 1st International Conference on Database Theory*, 1986.

[16] C. Youn, L. Henschen & J. Han, "Classification of Recursive Formulas in Deductive Databases," *Proceedings of the 1988 SIGMOD Conference*, Chicago, IL, June 1988.

PERSISTENT DATA STORAGE FOR PROLOG

Monika Danielsson and Jonas Barklund
Uppsala University

UPMAIL, Computing Science Dept., Box 520, S-751 20 Uppsala, Sweden
MONIKA@EMIL.CSD.UU.SE or JONAS@EMIL.CSD.UU.SE

Abstract

To provide persistent data storage for Prolog programs we propose a simple interface between Prolog and relational data bases with SQL. The intention has been to make relations stored in data base tables behave as much as possible like relations defined by Prolog clauses, except for ordering of solutions. We introduce a syntactical device for simplifying translation of data base relations to efficient SQL queries and we describe the translation. A non-trivial problem has been to implement backtracking over data base relations, simulating the behaviour of Prolog. We suggest three different implementations and provide some benchmark figures for two of them. The data base system and our Prolog system are two components of a distributed and modular tool for writing applications such as expert systems.

1. INTRODUCTION

The logic programming language Prolog (Colmerauer, Kanoui, Pasero, & Roussel, 1973) has been found appropriate for expert systems applications but the language lacks persistent data storage. We have studied how relations can be stored as data base tables while still behaving almost like relations defined by Prolog clauses.

Our ambition has been to propose a simple but practical interface between Prolog and standard SQL (Date, 1987) for storing and retrieving "reasonably" large amounts of data. We attempt to take advantage of the data base system's facilities for joining and uniting tables when retrieving information, but otherwise the computation is expected to be done in Prolog. In particular all recursive computations are done in Prolog.

Although it has not been our main concern so far, Prolog extended with a data base interface such as ours may function as a more powerful query language for the data base than SQL or other data base languages. This is particularly true when the Prolog system, like Upmail Prolog (Barklund, Danielsson, Gabrielsson, Millroth & Wünsche, 1990) acts as an inference machine embedded in a system (MAKS) which also includes a multimedia system for man-machine interaction (Hamfelt & Barklund, 1990; Barklund, Hamfelt & Wünsche, 1990).

We have used Oracle (1989) as data base system but we have taken care to use only standard SQL which means that our interface, which is implemented in C with embedded SQL, and Prolog, should be fairly easily portable. We believe that restricting ourselves to SQL data base systems does not seriously reduce the usefulness of our approach.

The reader is assumed to have basic knowledge of Prolog and SQL but let us make explicit a few assumptions. A relational data base can be regarded as a collection of tables. Each relation is represented by a named table. A table consists of named columns, one for each attribute in the relation. There is one row in the table for each instance of the relation. Rows are not ordered.

2. PHILOSOPHY

Preferably, we would like the tables to look and behave as ordinary Prolog predicates, i.e., they should be written using Prolog syntax, and unification, backtracking, etc., should work in the same way as for ordinary Prolog predicates.

A table named p, with n columns and m rows would be appear as a Prolog predicate p of arity n with m clauses, one for each row. Column k of the table corresponds to argument position k of the predicate. The only clauses that can be stored in a data base like this are clauses with ground heads and empty bodies. The terms in the clauses may be constants such as integer numbers, floating point numbers and symbols. (The range and precision of numbers is limited.) For example, the table

Teaches:

Name	Course
john	ai2
mary	data_bases
david	theory of programs

corresponds to a Prolog predicate `teaches(Name, Course)`, defined as follows:

```
teaches(john, ai2).
teaches(mary, data_bases).
teaches(david, 'theory of programs').
```

Assuming SQL embedded in some host language, the code

needed to achieve the desired behaviour is approximately

```
EXEC SQL DECLARE C CURSOR FOR
    "SELECT ... FROM ... WHERE ...";
EXEC SQL OPEN C;
more: EXEC SQL FETCH C INTO SQLVars;
if (SQLCODE == NO_MORE_SOLUTIONS) goto lose;
unify(PrologVars, SQLVars);
RETURN;
lose: EXEC SQL CLOSE C;
FAIL;.
```

This code fetches a row, unifies the values with Prolog variables and returns. If control is resumed at label `more`, another row is fetched. Finally, when there are no more solutions, the cursor is closed and the computation fails.

Embedding SQL in Prolog. One way to achieve this is to embed SQL in Prolog, much like the embedded SQL for COBOL or C. All SQL operations would be written explicitly, and a preprocessor would be used to convert the SQL statements into runnable code. The `teaches` predicate could then be defined as

```
teaches(Name, Course) :-
    EXEC SQL declare c cursor for
        "select name, course from teaches",
    EXEC SQL open c,
    teaches_aux(Name, Course).
teaches_aux(Name, Course) :-
    EXEC SQL fetch c into :N, :C,
    !,
    (Name=N, Course=C ; teaches_aux(Name, Course)).
teaches_aux(Name, Course) :-
    EXEC SQL close c,
    fail.
```

Hiding cursor management. In the interface above, all cursor management has to be done explicitly. But of all the code above only the query, the cursor name and the variables are unique for each query; the rest of the code looks the same for all queries. A slightly nicer interface would hide the cursor operations and just send the query, possibly along with some variables, to SQL. In case of a query, the variables would get unified with the selected values, or otherwise the command would be executed. For example,

```
sqlcall('SELECT name, course FROM teaches',
        [Name, Course])
```

unifies the list `[Name, Course]` with a list of two values; a name and a course. The predicate `sqlcall` should essentially do the same things as the more explicit code above: declare a cursor for the query, fetch the values, and close the cursor. The parameters given are the query and the variables; the cursor name could be generated automatically. The predicate `teaches` could then be defined as follows:

```
teaches(Name, Course) :-
    sqlcall('SELECT name, course FROM teaches',
            [Name, Course]).
```

This approach is similar to that taken in PROSQL (Chang & Walker, 1986).

Hiding SQL. The predicates above could either be written manually or generated automatically by the compiler or a preprocessor. If they are written manually, the programmer is required to learn SQL as well as Prolog. Also, SQL implementations do not always follow the standard, and everything is not standardized (e.g., removing tables), so the interface might behave differently depending on the data base system used; a quite undesirable behavior.

If these predicates are generated by the compiler from declarations given by the user, it is sufficient for accessing tables. However, this does not utilize SQL's efficient primitives for constrained searching. We have two solutions to this problem. Either we introduce Prolog relations which play the role of views in SQL and are translated as such, or we introduce a general notation for identifying data base calls and their constraints.

This interface is implemented with an `sqlcall` predicate as above. A Prolog query is translated into a call to `sqlcall(SQLQuery, ListOfVars)`, where `SQLQuery` is the SQL statement corresponding to the Prolog query and `ListOfVars` is the variables to be selected.

3. CONJUNCTIVE QUERIES

Query groups and view predicates. Following the second proposal above we adopt a syntax for data base calls: a *query group* is a conjunctive Prolog goal which is intended to be translatable into an SQL query. We choose to write a query group by surrounding it with vertical bars (|). A query group may contain data base calls and simple tests, mainly comparisons (arithmetic and others) which are easily translated into SQL constraints. For a further description of the translation see section 8.

Our intention is that a formula in a query group should have the same declarative meaning as the corresponding formula in Prolog, but the operational behaviour may be different. In particular we do not define the order in which solutions to a query group are found. This allows the data base system to do optimizations such as indexing.

Other implementations have chosen to introduce *data base predicates* and *view predicates*, e.g., Quintus Prolog[1] (Quintus, 1988) and ZYX Prolog[2] (ZYX, 1990). A data base predicate corresponds to a table and a view predicate corresponds to an SQL view (although it need not be translated to one).

There is a simple relationship between query groups and view predicates: a query group $|G_1, \ldots, G_n|$ is equivalent to an atomic goal H where H :- $G_1, \ldots, G_n$ has been defined as a view predicate. One advantage with the view predicate is that the user could declare information about the relation H, as if it were a normal Prolog predicate. However, it seems unnecessary to force the user to introduce

---

[1] Quintus Prolog is a trademark of Quintus Computer Systems.

[2] ZYX Prolog is a trademark of ZYX Sweden AB.

458

named view predicates whenever accessing the data base, hence query groups are still useful.

A conjunction, which is either a query group or the body of a view predicate, of data base calls and tests is translated into a single SQL query

```
SELECT ⟨columns⟩
FROM ⟨tables⟩
WHERE ⟨constraints⟩
```

where the ⟨tables⟩ are determined by the data base calls, the ⟨columns⟩ are determined by the variables, and the ⟨constraints⟩ are determined by the non-variables and the given constraints. (Similarly, other discussions below about query groups apply to bodies of view predicates as well.)

Local variables. Suppose that the variable Publisher in the goal

```
|books(Author, Title, Publisher)|
```

is not used outside the query but is just a "placeholder". It is a waste of time to SELECT and unify such variables. They could be detected by a static analysis of the whole clause. Alternatively, we could define the syntax Var^Goal in query groups to mean ∃Var(Goal), i.e., that Var is existentially quantified in Goal, much like in Prolog's "all solutions" predicates. The goal above would then be rewritten as

```
|Publisher^books(Author, Title, Publisher)|
```

resulting in SQL code which selects only Author and Title for each row. This also works if the variable occurs more than once, e.g., the query group

```
|Author^Title^(teacher(Author),
               books(Author, Title, Publisher))|
```

retrieves a publisher which has published a book by a teacher. The only column in the resulting SELECT statement is publisher.

4. DISJUNCTIVE QUERIES

It is desirable and meaningful to also allow disjunctions in query groups. This is non-trivial and NU-Prolog does not allow disjunctions at all (Zobel & Ramamohanarao, 1986), while Quintus Prolog allows disjunctions only between tests. For example, not all disjunctive goals can be translated into a single SELECT query. Some disjunctive goals must be translated into compound SELECT queries or more than one query.

1. The disjunctive goals that can be translated into efficient code are primarily those which can be rewritten into a database call and a disjunction between the conditions. E.g., the goal

```
|teaches(Name, data_bases) ;
 teaches(Name, ai2)|
```

can be rewritten into the goal

```
|teaches(Name, Course),
 (Course = ai2 ; Course = data_bases)|
```

and is thus easily translated into SQL as a single SELECT statement with a disjunctive condition

```
teaches.course = 'ai2' OR
teaches.course = 'data_bases'.
```

2. A disjunction between two different predicates can be translated into one SQL statement if both disjuncts instantiates the same variables, and the corresponding columns are of the same type. This is translated into an SQL UNION. For an example, see p. 12.

3. A disjunction between two predicates of different arity is more difficult. In general it is necessary to translate it into two queries. Consider the goal

```
|teacher(Author) ;
 books(Author, Title, Publisher)|
```

where none of the variables are instantiated. This is translated in the same way as

```
|teacher(Author)| ;
|books(Author, Title, Publisher)|
```

because SELECT cannot return rows of different size. On the other hand, if the values of Title and Publisher are not used later, the goal would be equivalent to

```
|teacher(Author) ;
 Title^Publisher^
   books(Author, Title, Publisher)|
```

which can be translated into a UNION.

Order of solutions. The previous example

```
|teaches(Name, data_bases) ;
 teaches(Name, ai2)|
```

retrieves the rows where course is either data_bases or ai2 in an order determined by the database system. This results in a different operational behaviour than that of Prolog, where disjunction is computed left to right and depth first; solutions for teaches(Name, ai2) are not sought until all solutions for teaches(Name, data_bases) have been found.

First, we believe that this is only a small inconvenience in practice. Second, the behaviour is consistent with our design decision that the order of solutions of a query group is not defined.

If the order of solutions does matter, one makes two query groups, as in

```
|teaches(Name, data_bases)| ;
|teaches(Name, ai2)|,
```

which translates into two SQL queries.

5. BACKTRACKING

In Prolog "backtracking" over multiple answers to nondeterministic relations is realized by keeping a stack of *choice
points* (Warren, 1983) which contain enough information to
restart the computation at earlier points. Choice points are
generated whenever Prolog enters a predicate whose definition has more than one clause which can match the goal.
Apart from a description of the machine state, each choice
point contains a pointer which identifies the next clause to
be tried. (That pointer is updated each time another clause
is tried; when the last clause is tried the choice point is
discarded.)

These pointers corresponds to SQL *cursors*, which are
used to iterate through the answers to a query. To preserve
Prolog's behaviour it would, conceptually, be necessary to
associate a cursor with each SQL query in the translation.
This could be accomplished by storing a cursor in a Prolog
choice point when the predicate to be backtracked upon is a
data base predicate. Regrettably, a cursor is not necessarily
something we can move, rename or save, but rather a lexical
entity that must be explicitly declared to the preprocessor.

The problem is that it is not possible to determine in
advance how many cursors are needed to run a Prolog program as is shown by the following Prolog predicate:

```
ancestor(X,Z):- |parent(X,Z)|.
ancestor(X,Z):- |parent(X,Y)|, ancestor(Y,Z).
```

which might have any number of calls to `parent` "open" at
the same time. And since we have a fixed number of cursors,
it is in general not possible to assign a new cursor to each
query. We try to solve this in three different ways. The first
two solutions require only one cursor to be defined for the
whole program.

1. Retrieve the set of answers for a query immediately and
   represent the collection of answers as a Prolog term
   (as if they had been collected with Prolog's `bagof` construct). Then use Prolog's `member` predicate (or a similar predicate) to generate answers one at a time. This
   is the simplest way, but a drawback is that it is very
   slow if many values are selected and only one or a few
   are really used. If many values are selected, there might
   also be memory capacity problems.

2. Let the cursor always be associated with the most recent query and store for each query how many of its
   answers have already been retrieved, say n. Generating another answer to the most recent query (so-called
   shallow backtracking) is inexpensive. When there are no
   more solutions to the most recent query and backtracking to an older query occurs (so-called *deep backtracking*) it is necessary to reparse the previous SQL query
   (though not redoing the translation from Prolog), then
   fetch and throw away the first n answers. This is easily
   programmed but has quadratic worst case complexity.
   It may be worthwhile if shallow backtracking is much

more common than deep backtracking. It also assumes
that the same n first answers are found each time, a
reasonable although not quite safe assumption.

3. Define a multitude of cursors, say k, ($k = 10$ in our
   actual implementation) and a collection of subroutines
   for each cursor. Each cursor and collection of subroutines is associated with a name and unused names are
   assigned dynamically to new queries. The name is used
   when fetching consecutive answers to a query. When
   all answers to a query have been found the name associated with the query can be reused. If there are more
   open queries than defined cursors it is necessary to re-
   sort to the previous solution (or signal an error). By
   employing a stack (identifying up to k choice points)
   it is easy to ensure that the k most recent queries are
   associated with cursors until deep backtracking occurs,
   therefore this solution can be seen as a generalization of
   the previous approach. The *cut* operator can be used
   in Prolog to prune all solutions, except the first, to a
   query. Basically, its operational semantics is to remove
   some of the most recent choice points. If a removed
   choice point corresponds to a data base query the cursor associated with the query (if any) could be released
   immediately, rather than when backtracking actually
   occurs.

As expected, the two latter methods are equally fast
for queries which do only shallow backtracking of data base
queries. The multiple cursor solution is—also as expected—
faster for deeper backtracking. See the appendix for more
precise run times.

ZYX Prolog allows the use of explicit cursors to iterate
over tables without backtracking. This may be efficient but
is not elegant, nor does it correspond to any form of Prolog
control structure. Also it requires the use of multiple cursors
which must be handled through dynamic definition of cursors or along the lines of the third solution above (but note
that this may break the stack-like behaviour assumed previously). Although we are aware that some data base systems
provide facilities for dynamic definition of "cursors," it is
not represented at all in the *de facto* standard for embedded SQL (Date, 1987) we prefer to use.

6. ALL SOLUTIONS

To collect all answers to a Prolog query, one can use "all
solutions" predicates, e.g., `bagof`, `setof` or `findall`. It is
possible to call data base predicates inside an "all solutions"
predicate, e.g., the goal

```
bagof(Name, |Course^teaches(Name,Course)|, L)
```

would unify L with a list of the names of all teachers.
"All solutions" predicates are usually implemented in Prolog through repeated backtracking and copying of solutions.
In the previous section we discussed backtracking over the
solutions to a query group. Although it is clear that any

460

of the strategies proposed for implementing backtracking would work also in this context, it is also obvious that the first strategy is superior since it generates all solutions immediately. To recognize this case without complicating Prolog's ordinary "all solutions" predicates we propose to allow "all solutions" predicates to appear also inside query groups. The previous goal would be equivalent to

|bagof(Name, Course^teaches(Name,Course), L)|,

but the latter could be translated into a version of `sql-call` which collects all solutions to the query immediately, without actually going through Prolog's backtracking mechanism.

7. UPDATING THE DATA BASE

We also want to allow other operations than queries to the data base, e.g., updating the data base. One could either define an entirely new syntax for that, or extend query groups to contain non-queries. We choose the latter solution, and let occurrences of Prolog's data base updating predicates inside query groups be translated into data base updates. The mapping between SQL's updating predicates and their Prolog counterparts is unfortunately not one-to-one, so some restrictions are needed.

Inserting a row. A row can only be asserted into an existing table; if the table does not exist, an error is signalled. The asserted data must be of the correct type. Under these restrictions `assert` can be translated into SQL INSERT.

Deleting a row. In Prolog, `retract(Clause)` normally removes the first clause matching `Clause`. Since SQL rows are not considered ordered, a concept such as "the first row" is not meaningful. Instead, one row is removed, but we cannot control which one. This is, however, consistent with our earlier decision: within query groups, the order of solutions is unknown. There is no SQL command exactly corresponding to `retract`; it would have to be translated into a SELECT where the "first" matching row is found, and a DELETE which removes that, and only that, row (*positioned* DELETE). Retracting many rows with a repeat-fail loop, as is sometimes done in Prolog, would thus not be particularly efficient.

Deleting many rows. The `retractall(Clause)` predicate, which removes all rows matching `Clause`, is probably more useful in a data base context, except for when one wants to do something with the retracted `Clause`, e.g., change it and assert it. It can be translated to a *searched* DELETE statement.

Updating one or more rows. A common operation in a database is to modify one or more rows of a table. In SQL that is done using the UPDATE primitive. Updating a single row is accomplished in Prolog by a goal on the form

retract(X_1), R(X_1, X_2), assert(X_2)

(where R(X_1,X_2) means any formula which expresses a new row X_2 in terms of an old row X_1), since there is no updating

primitive in Prolog. A query group of this form, with certain restrictions on the formula R(X_1, X_2), could be translated to an SQL *positioned* UPDATE. For example, the formula

|retract(salary(tom, Salary)),
NewSalary is Salary + 100,
assert(salary(tom, NewSalary))|.

is translatable. Recognizing such query groups is clearly possible, but it would be more difficult to handle certain simple generalizations of that scheme with, e.g., nested `retract-assert` pairs. The obvious translation of a formula such as the one above would otherwise be a *positioned* DELETE and an INSERT but between the DELETE and the INSERT the data base would be inconsistent. That might lead to problems if a crash occurred or if another user queried or modified the table in the meantime. Therefore a *positioned* UPDATE is more secure, apart from being more efficient.

The problem with multiple users querying and modifying the data base at the same time could have been solved by implicitly enclosing all query groups with LOCK and UNLOCK statements, had such primitives been available in standard SQL. On the other hand, this is a situation which has no correspondence in Prolog's data base operations, so it would not have been unreasonable to explicit locking primitives to query groups.

Another solution than recognizing certain `retract-assert` pairs would be to extend Prolog with an updating primitive (also outside query groups). This is a situation where extending Prolog with a functional notation would simplify matters, because update(X_1, F(X_1)) could then mean to (atomically) replace the row X_1 with a row F(X_1), expressed in terms of X_1. The previous example could then be written

|update(salary(tom, Salary),
        salary(tom, Salary ++ 100))|,

where the addition function is written as ++. Lacking such a syntax, we could instead define

update(X_1, X_2) where R(X_1, X_2)

to mean the same thing. Thus

|update(salary(tom, Salary),
      salary(tom, NewSalary))
        where NewSalary is Salary + 100|.

updateall would then relate to update as retractall to retract and could be translated into a *searched* UPDATE statement.

Transactions. Naish, Thom & Ramamohanarao have proposed a transaction primitive (1986)

all Local_vars transaction Goal

which means that the statements in `Goal` are performed for all instances of `Local_vars` satisfying `Goal`. Moreover, data base modifications are saved and not done until the transaction succeeds.

We consider allowing a statement like this inside query groups, for similar purposes. We expect that many updates inside transactions can be translated to *searched* `UPDATE` statements. (The construction would also be meaningful for deleting many rows, as a more general device than `retract-all`, or even for inserting many rows.) The transaction is completed by one of the SQL primitives `COMMIT` and `ROLL-BACK`, corresponding to a successful or failing computation, respectively.

8. TRANSLATION OF QUERIES

The translation into SQL is straightforward—we do not attempt to optimize the queries although that subject has an interesting potential for the future. We assume that the reader is familiar with the general form of SQL queries.

Conjunctions. Let us begin with an example:

```
bar(42,Name), |teaches(Name, Course),
              credits(Course, Credits),
              Credits < 6|.
```

The calls to `teaches`, `credits` and `<` are all assembled into one SQL query, instead of making two separate queries for `teaches` and `credits`, and let Prolog check the constraint on `Credits`. If we assume that `Name` is instantiated to `john` by `bar(42, Name)`, the SQL query corresponding to the query group is

```
SELECT teaches.course, credits.credits
FROM teaches, credits
WHERE teaches.name = 'john' AND
      teaches.course = credits.course AND
      credits.credits < 6.
```

One of the columns `teaches.course` and `credits.course` needs not be retrieved since they refer to the same variable. Only if `bar` does not instantiate `Name`, the column `teaches.name` (which corresponds to `Name`) will appear among the columns to be selected, instead of among the constraints.

Usually it is not possible to completely translate a query group into SQL at compile time since we might not know, e.g., which variables will be instantiated at runtime. To save time, the query group is translated as far as possible at compile time, and the instantiation information is used at runtime to assemble the SQL query.

In general we consider conjunctive goals on the form

$$|P_1(t_{1,1},\ldots,t_{1,k_1}),\ \ldots,\ P_l(t_{l,1},\ldots,t_{l,k_l}),$$
$$C_1,\ \ldots,\ C_m|$$

where the symbols P_1 to P_l are data base predicates and C_1 to C_m are test predicates. The order of the conjuncts is irrelevant The formula is translated into a single SQL query, referring to a set of columns, a set of tables, and a conjunction of constraints. The predicate symbols P_1 to P_l determine the set of tables; multiple occurrences of a predicate symbol are translated into aliased tables. The test predicates C_1 to C_m are immediately translated into constraints. A non-variable term t_{i_j} is translated into a constraint `column` = t_{i_j} where the column is identified by its position in the predicate. A variable term which occurs n times, $n > 1$ is translated into $n - 1$ constraints $\text{column}_a = \text{column}_b$, where the columns are identified by the occurrences of the variable. The set of columns is defined by the set of all variables in $t_{1,1}$ to t_{l,k_l}. (If none of those terms is a variable, one of them is chosen to be selected anyway since at least one column must be specified in the SQL query, but its value is discarded.)

Disjunctions. Consider a disjunctive goal $|G_1\ ;\ \ldots\ ;\ G_k|$ where each G_i is a conjunctive goal. It can be translated in one of three ways.

1. If the disjunctive goal can be rewritten as $|G,\ (C_1\ ;\ \ldots\ ;\ C_k)|$, it becomes a conjunctive goal and is translated as above. This should be used whenever possible since it results in the most efficient SQL code. See p. 6 for an example.

2. If all G_i instantiate the same variables, the goal can be translated into G_1' `UNION ... UNION` G_k', where each G_i is translated as a conjunctive query. E.g., the goal

   ```
   |teacher(Name) ; student(Name)|
   ```

   is translated into

   ```
   SELECT teacher.name
   FROM teacher
   UNION
   SELECT student.name
   FROM student.
   ```

3. Otherwise, the goal cannot be translated into a single SQL query but is translated as if it were the Prolog disjunction $|G_1|\ ;\ \ldots\ ;\ |G_k|$.

Comparisons. There is no one-to-one mapping between the Prolog comparison predicates and the SQL comparisons. In SQL the relations =, <, >, <=, >= and <> are used to compare either numbers or strings. It is an error to compare items of different types. In Prolog there is a distinction between arithmetic comparison (=:=, <, >, =<, >= and =\=), and term comparison (==, @<, @>, @=<, @>= and \==). It is an error to compare non-numbers arithmetically. Term comparison is meaningful for all types and a standard order is defined where, e.g., all numbers precede all strings. There is also unification (=) which can act as a comparison but also instantiate variables.

Prolog's arithmetical comparisons can be translated directly to the corresponding SQL comparisons, with a few minor exceptions; the arguments to SQL comparisons must be numbers, additions, subtractions, multiplications or divisions, although Prolog allows a richer set of expressions. For example,

```
|credits(Course, Credits), Credits*2 > 42|
```

is translated into

```
SELECT ... FROM ...
WHERE credits.credits * 2 > 42.
```

When Prolog's term comparisons are applied to arguments of the same type they can be immediately translated into the corresponding SQL comparisons. When the arguments are of different types SQL comparisons cannot be used but instead it is possible to deduce at translation time the outcome of the comparison. For example,

```
foo(X), |books(Author, 'Logic and Data Bases',
              'Plenum Press'), Author @> 'X|
```

is translated into

```
SELECT ... FROM ...
WHERE books.author > 'Hemingway'
```

if `foo` instantiates `X` to `Hemingway`, while the `WHERE` part can be omitted completely if `X` is instantiated to a number.

SQL also has other tests, e.g., LIKE, BETWEEN and IN, which lack Prolog equivalents. In standard Prolog these relations could be programmed by the user, but of course it would be advantageous to use the SQL tests when possible. If the corresponding relations were incorporated as primitives in Prolog, their occurrences within query groups would translate immediately into SQL.

Other functions. Prolog's `findall` which computes a list of solutions to an (implicitly) existentially quantified goal could be generalized to a class of predicates which compute other functions of the solutions. Many of these predicates, when occurring inside query groups, could be translated immediately into searched SQL statements. For example,

```
|max(Credits, credits(Course, Credits), M)|
```

would unify `M` with the maximum number of credits for a course and could be translated into

```
SELECT MAX(credits.credits) FROM credits.
```

Other new predicates would be `count` (COUNT), `sum` (SUM), `average` (AVG), and `min` (MIN). They would compute the number of solutions to a goal, the sum of solutions, the average of the solutions, and the minimum of the solutions, respectively. (It would be an error for `max`, `min` and `average` if there were no solutions at all.)

9. CONCLUSIONS AND FUTURE WORK

We believe that our ambition, to propose a simple but practical interface between Prolog and standard SQL, has been accomplished.

A fairly obvious observation was that it is important to combine conjunctive queries when possible, to avoid unnecessary and inefficient backtracking. To simplify this we have proposed a syntactical construction, query groups, which delimits data base calls. An important design decision was that the goals in a query group should have the same declarative behaviour as in ordinary Prolog but without a defined order between solutions.

The main obstacles have been translating disjunctions and implementing backtracking over data base queries to simulate the behaviour of Prolog. We have discussed several methods for this and presented some measures of their efficiency.

The translation into SQL has suggested some extensions to Prolog which are meaningful also when data bases are not considered.

Some interesting future problems are Prolog-like negation (probably quite easy), transaction processing, and more sophisticated optimizations inside query groups (probably quite hard). In a single-user application it would be possible to "cache" recently used table rows in Prolog, if care is taken to keep it consistent with the actual table. This is worth investigating to reduce the number of accesses to the data base system.

The first application for our data base interface is as a part of a real-time expert system for process control.

ACKNOWLEDGEMENTS

This research was supported by the National Board for Technical Development (STU) through UPMAIL, directed by Sten-Åke Tärnlund. Credits to the anonymous referees for suggestions and to our colleagues at UPMAIL and the Computing Science Department for creative discussions. Special thanks to Per-Eric and to Anna and Ellin.

REFERENCES

Barklund, J., Danielsson, M., Gabrielsson, J., Millroth, H., and Wünsche, J., 1990, *The Basic UPMAIL Prolog Manual*, Comp. Sci. Dept., Uppsala Univ.

Barklund, J., Hamfeldt, A., and Wünsche, J., 1990, A Modular Architecture for Knowledge Systems. *Proc. Computational Intelligence '90* (ed. F. Gardini). To be published by North-Holland, New York.

Chang, C. L., and Walker, A., 1986, PROSQL: A PROLOG Programming Interface with SQL/DS. *Expert Database Systems* (ed. L. Kerschberg), pp. 233–246. Benjamin/Cummins, Menlo Park, Calif.

Colmerauer, A., Kanoui, H., Pasero, R., and Roussel, P., 1972, *Un Système de Communication Homme-Machine en Français*. Groupe de Recherche en Intelligence Artificielle, Univ. d'Aix-Marseille, Luminy.

Date, C. J., 1987, *A Guide to The SQL Standard*. Addison-Wesley, Reading, Mass.

Hamfelt, A., and Barklund, J., 1990, An Intelligent Interface to Legal Data Bases—Combining Logic Programming and Hypertext. *Proc. DEXA '90* (ed. A. M. Tjoa). Springer-Verlag, Berlin.

Naish, L., Thom, J. A., and Ramamohanarao, K., 1986, Concurrent Database Updates in Prolog. *Technical Report* 86/12. Dept. of Comp. Sci., Univ. of Melbourne.

Oracle, 1989, *ORACLE for Macintosh: References, Version 1.1*. Oracle Corp.

Quintus, 1989, *Quintus Prolog Data Base Interface Manual*. Quintus Computer Systems, Mountain View, Calif.

Warren, D. H. D., 1983, An Abstract Prolog Instruction Set. *Technical Note* 309. SRI International, Menlo Park, Calif.

Zobel, J., and Ramamohanarao, K., 1986, Accessing existing databases from Prolog. *Technical Report* 86/17. Dept. of Comp. Sci., Univ. of Melbourne.

ZYX, 1989, *ZYX Prolog Reference Manual*. ZYX Sweden AB, Stockholm.

APPENDIX. RUN TIMES

These queries were run for the last two backtracking methods, and the time was measured. As expected, the two methods were equally fast when the query only involved backtracking to the most recent goal, and the multiple-cursor method was faster on deeper backtracking. (Queries 1, 2 and 3.) We have not measured the first version (the "setof"-like solution), but it is probably much slower than these two, at least for queries involving many answers, and not much faster for deterministic queries.

Grouped queries were *much* faster than Prolog conjunctions. (Queries 4, 5, 6 and 7.) Query 5 has not been tested with the "recompute".method, but because of its complexity, we expect the query to take significantly longer time than 17 minutes.

1. ```
   :- |books(A, T, P)|, fail.
   ```
   Fetch all rows (494 rows returned).

2. ```
   :- |teaches(N1, C1), teaches(N2, C2)|, fail.
   ```
   Cartesian product (400 rows returned).

3. ```
   :- |teaches(N1, C1)|, |teaches(N2, C2)|,
      fail.
   ```
   As 2 but not grouped.

4. ```
   :- |books(A, T1, P1), books(A, T2, P2),
      T1 \== T2|, fail.
   ```
   Get two titles for the same author (104 rows returned).

5. ```
   :- |books(A, T1, P1)|, |books(A, T2, P2),
      T1 \== T2|, fail.
   ```
   As 4 but not grouped.

6. ```
   :- |books(A, T1, P1), books(A, T2, P2),
      T1 \== T2|.
   ```
   As 4 but get only the first answer.

7. ```
   :- |books(A, T1, P1)|, |books(A, T2, P2),
      T1 \== T2|.
   ```
   As 5 but get only the first answer.

The following figures are approximate and includes the time spent on translating Prolog goals into SQL statements (a quite insignificant part of the total times). All figures were measured without any indexing in the data base. For example, with an index on the first column (author) of the table **books** the time for query 6 goes down to approximately 2 seconds.

Timings:

Query	Recompute	Multiple Cursors
1	19 s	19 s
2	18 s	16 s
3	24 s	20 s
4	16 s	16 s
5	--	17.40 min
6	9 s	9 s
7	1.20 min	41 s

The queries were run with Oracle on a Macintosh II. This implementation of SQL is comparatively slow so the actual figures are quite bad overall.
   ```

A Knowledge-Based Design for Hypertext-Based Document Retrieval Systems

Hsinchun Chen

MIS Department, University of Arizona
Tucson, Arizona 85721, USA

Abstract

This paper presents some aspects of an ongoing research that aims at incorporating knowledge-based search mechanisms into hypertext-based document retrieval systems. We propose an information structure that is grounded on a semantic network-based thesaurus. It serves to represent the documents and concepts (terms) involved in information retrieval. The second important component of our design is heuristics-based search mechanisms that were derived from our prior cognitive modeling study (which investigated the search strategies of expert searchers). By incorporating these components into a navigation-based hypertext, we attempt to create a system that facilitates effective and efficient information retrieval in a complex retrieval environment.

1 Introduction

During the past decade the advancement of hypertext-based researches has brought about significant changes in the design and use of information systems. Graphic display and online navigation that are available in hypertext systems have been proven to be useful to organize ideas, store information, and facilitate information retrieval. This positive impact is most evident upon document retrieval systems. This type of system typically consists of a database of documents, a classification scheme to index the documents, and an online system to access the documents. Unlike traditional document retrieval systems in which users access information using keyword searches, users of hypertext systems navigate through the database by following the "links" from one datum to another. Such an architecture encourages users to find information by "browsing", i.e., following a likely path from one node (concept, object, data, etc.) to another until they obtain their goal. This problem-solving process is similar to a search in the problem space [1]. However, in the absence of effective search assistance, this method of search may require a lot of browsing and backtracking, and can cause users to become lost in the search space.

Information science researchers are also concerned about the process of information retrieval and their findings in search strategies are most relevant to the hypertext systems. These strategies indicate the general approaches or plans searchers have adopted to perform a search. The strategies employed by expert searchers (such as reference librarians) are generally more effective and are considered "strong" methods of problem solving [15]. In a series of studies conducted by Chen and Dhar [6] [7], we developed a semantic network-based representation for information retrieval and identified various search strategies that had been used by expert searchers in a real-life setting. We propose to use this information network as the basis for a hypertext system. The search strategies were simulated as algorithms that can help users search in a complex information network.

As Croft [9] commented:

> The important issue from an IR (Information Retrieval) perspective is the choice of a retrieval model, and consequently a retrieval strategy, for hypertext. This choice will have an impact on the effectiveness of retrieval and the system implementation.

In Section 2, we present previous researches in document retrieval which are relevant to our work. A complex information network that is based on an existing thesaurus is proposed and discussed in Section 3. In Section 4, we describe the search strategies used in our system. We conclude this report in the final section.

2 Process of Document Retrieval

One of the most widely used types of document-based retrieval systems is the online catalog, which is commonly found in university and public libraries. An understanding of the functionality and working of such retrieval systems is essential in order to perform a successful search. The classification scheme used for organizing the information provides index terms for documents, thereby defining access points to information. These terms constitute a very restricted vocabulary (of which users in general have little knowledge) for classifying documents (such as books or articles), based on their semantic content. The process of searching for documents within a subject area is referred to as *subject-based search*. It is the most difficult and least supported type of search. The following paragraphs describe why the subject-based search is difficult:

1. *Terms Matching:* There is a high degree of variance in search terms that different users tend to apply in seeking some piece of information. Studies have revealed that on average, the probability of any two people using the same term to describe an object is less than 20 percent [12] [11]. Thus an exact match between users' search terms and the index terms is unlikely. This is referred to as the problem of terms matching and is a fundamental property of language that limits the success of various design methodologies for controlled vocabulary-driven interaction [11].

2. *Query Refinement:* Users tend to approach a search by specifying broad terms first. There might be several reasons for this. One hypothesis is that users often do not have "queries," but what Belkin calls an *anomalous state of knowledge* [2] [3]. Users often expect to refine this anomalous state into a query through an interactive process. Taylor suggests that a user's queries start from an actual but unexpressed need (visceral need). The visceral need is refined to a conscious description of the need (conscious need), which is finally formalized as a statement (formalized need). The actual query presented to the information system, however, may be compromised due to the user's expectation of the system (compromised need) [18]. Reference librarians appear to be particularly adept at performing this function. However, the organization of a catalog or a system does not always facilitate this type of query refinement.

3. *Search Strategies:* A *search strategy* is referred to as the plan or approach to conducting a search. Two search strategies were identified by Bourne. In the *building-block* strategy, a user enters various terms as separate search statements. After the search results are derived, the user combines all search statements into a single final statement using the Boolean operator, AND. This strategy contrasts with the *pearl-growing* strategy, in which a user first searches on a few specific terms to retrieve initial citations, which are then examined carefully for new candidate search terms that will be added for subsequent searching [14]. In summarizing the results of several online search studies, Fenichel [10] concluded that, for both experienced and inexperienced users, the problems of information retrieval were with search strategy, not the capabilities of the system. Users did not know how to apply appropriate search strategies under various conditions. He found that a substantial number of users performed simple searches making little use of the capabilities of online systems.

In a recent study by Chen and Dhar [5], we identified five search strategies used by searchers of online cataloging systems. Two strategies were considered "weak" methods of searching. They required little knowledge and were often ineffective. The first strategy is referred to as the *trial-and-error strategy*. Searchers generated terms without applying knowledge about the system or the classification scheme. The second strategy was the *screen-browsing strategy*, in which the searchers browsed the screens extensively in an attempt to find new clues for their searches. Three "strong" search strategies were observed. These strategies required good knowledge about the subject area, the classification scheme, or the functionality of the system. In the *known-item-instantiation strategy*, the searcher's knowledge about citations that were relevant to the query were applied. Information within the known citations was used to generate new clues for search (the author, title, subject headings, etc.). This is a strategy that can be used iteratively. Searchers who were familiar with the system search options employed the *search-options-heuristics strategy*, where different search options (author search, title search, subject search, keyword search, etc.) were used to find matches. This strategy is useful because different search options were appropriate for certain type of queries. Finally, in what is referred to as the *thesaurus-activation strategy*, searchers consulted the terms and the cross-reference structure of the thesaurus extensively to determine the appropriate search terms. Both subject area knowledge and classification scheme knowledge are essential for successful use of this strategy.

3 A Hypertext-Based Network

In a previous article [7] we proposed a semantic network-based online thesaurus to represent the subject area knowledge and classification scheme knowledge essential for information retrieval. The existing thesaurus (hardcopy) contains not only index terms (subject headings), but also non-index terms which point to the index terms. The thesaurus can be viewed as a large semantic network of terms (concepts) where links are of two types: relations between non-index and index terms, and set-superset relationships (like ISA links). The top part of Figure 1 shows a portion of the semantic network corresponding to the Library of Congress Subject Headings (LCSH) classification scheme. Terms and the cross referencing structure of the LCSH are incorporated. This structure serves as the knowledge base for information retrieval.

In order to expand the semantic structure of this information network, we incorporated actual documents and names of the authors of those documents into this network. Books are indexed by the various index terms in the thesaurus (the "Heading" links in Figure 1). Information is embedded in the book entry, such as title, publisher, year of publication, notes, and call number. Each book can be perceived as a notecard (the box in Figure 1). Authors of books are also important entities in this information network and are represented as nodes in this network (the round-cornered boxes in Figure 1).

We define the nodes and links in our network more precisely as follows:

1. **Nodes:**

   Nodes represent information about terms, books, or authors that are stored in the online thesaurus and databases.

- *Terms:* Terms represent concepts. These terms may be used to index documents (index terms, shown as un-darkened ovals in Figure 1). Other synonymous terms are considered non-index terms (the darkened ovals in Figure 1). Both types of terms serve to represent subject area knowledge. They constitute the knowledge base of the system.

- *Books:* Books indicate the information to be sought by the searchers. They are the final search outputs. They may also be used by searchers to identify other similar books. Typically, a book contains information about its authors, subject headings, publisher, year of publication, call numbers, etc. They are shown as the boxes in Figure 1.

- *Authors:* The third type of node that is important for information retrieval is the author node. Often authors are known for their research in specific areas. Searching for a particular author's publications frequently has been used as a way to identify relevant works in the areas. Authors are shown as round-cornered boxes in Figure 1.

2. **Links:** Three types of links are used in our network. They are links for terms, subject heading links, and author links.

- *Links for terms:* Three types of links collects the index terms and the non-index terms. The ST (synonymous term) link leads a no-index term to its synonymous index term. The NT (narrower term) link leads a broader index term to a narrower index term. The reverse direction of the NT link indicates the BT (broader term) link (not shown in Figure 1). The RT (related term) link connects two related index terms. These links enhance the semantic structure of our information network (the links appear at the top part of Figure 1). Searchers can traverse these links to identify terms of interest to them. For example, a searcher who is interested in the medical applications in AI may start from the node: "Artificial Intelligence", follow the NT link, and identify a more relevant term: "Medicine in AI" (see Figure 1). Browsing this knowledge base helps articulate queries.

- *Heading link:* Heading links connect index terms with book records. The relationship is many to many and bidirectional. A book can be classified by more than one heading and a heading typically classifies more than one book. Searchers can navigate from headings to the relevant books or vice versa. For example, by following the heading links of the node: "Expert Systems" in Figure 1, a searcher can obtain books like: "Rule-Based Expert Systems," "Introduction to ES," etc.

- *Author link:* Author links connect authors with book records. The relationship also is many to many and bidirectional. Again, searchers can browse

the links associated with some authors to identify relevant citations. For example, a searcher can search for all the books authored by "Shortliffe" by tracing the author links associated with the nodes. As shown in Figure 1, at least two books can be retrieved.

We derived our semantic network-based online thesaurus by extracting a portion of the computer readable form of the LCSH Handbook (with the assistance of OCLC[1]). Our online thesaurus consists of nearly 3,500 terms (both index terms and non-index terms) in the areas of computer science. Each term has between a couple of and a few hundred relevant terms associated via the cross referencing structure of the thesaurus. In our prototype system, we have included a few hundred books and authors. The terms in our thesaurus, the books, and the authors constitute our information network. We are in the process of generating a hypertext interface for our information network.

Our information network represents the essential knowledge elements for information retrieval. With proper search mechanisms, this network can be extremely useful in assisting users in information retrieval.

Figure 1: A portion of an information network

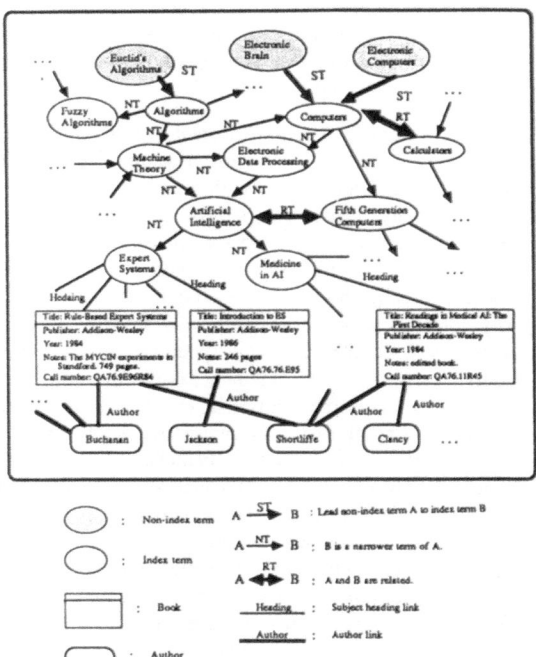

4 Search in the Information Network

As Halasz indicated in [13], search and query in a hypertext network is one of the top issues for the next generation of hypertext systems. Specifically, he commented that:

---

[1]Online Computer Library Center, Inc., Dublin, Ohio

The NoteCards experience suggests, however, that navigational access by itself is not sufficient. Effective access to information stored in a hypermedia network requires query-based access to complement navigation.

Salton [16] presented a glimpse of a future hypertext system. He argued that vocabulary matching methods and link traversal algorithms (spreading activation) can be used to retrieve related parts of a documents (corresponding to related nodes in a hypertext network). We believe the same argument can be applied to a hypertext that represents concepts and documents for information retrieval. A powerful search mechanism is necessary for alleviating the disorientation problem in a large information network.

We earlier had developed a few heuristics-based search strategies from a previous empirical study [5]. This study used a cognitive modeling technique in investigating expert searchers' strategies for information retrieval. Two of these strategies appear to be useful for automatic searching in a large information network. They are the *known-item-instantiation* strategy and the *thesaurus-activation* strategy.

4.1 Known-Item-Instantiation Strategy

The *known-item-instantiation* strategy was derived from the observation that some users used the known item search options first (author, title, and call number) to locate some initial relevant documents. After those relevant documents were retrieved, users could obtain the index terms that describe the contents of these documents. This process of instantiating the information in known citations is iterative in nature. We can think of this strategy as an online variant of the *pearl-growing* strategy identified by Bourne [14]. This strategy is appropriate for performing search of the following nature:

Find documents which are similar to this one.

We developed an algorithm that simulates this strategy. Users are first asked to identify some relevant citations through the use of the conventional known item search options. These include: author search, title search, and call number search. Our program then uses the index terms assigned to these retrieved citations to perform a subject search. This strategy is applied continuously in a "chain reaction" manner. When a new citation is derived, the system can obtain a few new index terms. These new index terms may lead to other new citations, which in turn may suggest other new index terms. By following this process continuously, we can identify a set of relevant index terms and citations.

In Figure 2 we illustrate graphically this chain reaction of known item instantiation in our proposed information network. For example, by identifying the author of BOOK1 ("Salton," as shown in Figure 2), a user can find an initial relevant citation (BOOK1). Book1 is classified under SUB1 (follow the *Heading* link in Figure 2). Following the links associated with SUB1, the system identifies BOOK2 and BOOK3. These two books lead to two new index terms, SUB2 and SUB4. These

two index terms link to BOOK4, BOOK5, and BOOK6, which in turn generate SUB3 and BOOK7. This instantiation process is continued until no links can be instantiated further. Our algorithm displays the "activated" index terms and citations in some ranked order. For example, our program will display the matched books in the order of: BOOK1, BOOK2, BOOK3, BOOK4, etc. (follows the sequence of activation). By using this strategy, a search process in a large network can become productive and efficient.

Figure 2: A graphic representation of known item instantiation

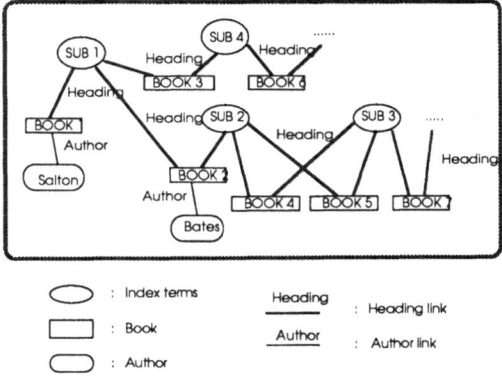

4.2 Thesaurus-Activation Strategy

Many reference librarians in our prior study adopted the *thesaurus-activation* strategy in assisting users. In order to retrieve documents that would address the specific needs of the user, the librarian solicited search terms from the user. These user-supplied terms then had to be sharpened and translated into *index terms*. The chance of terms in the user's query matching index terms is generally low. The librarian therefore initiated a *terms translation* process which included consulting the thesaurus (possibly involving a tracing of the cross referencing structure of the thesaurus) and a brainstorming process. The goal of this process was to identify the most specific terms to represent the query. In this stage of the consultation, both the user's and the librarian's familiarity with the subject area played an important role in determining the appropriate terms.

The consultation terminated when a reasonable number of relevant documents had been found. This strategy is similar to the *building-block* strategy proposed by Bourne [14]. Using it, a human information specialist should be able to generate index terms systematically. A detailed discussion of the role of the information specialists in reducing search indeterminism appears in [4].

This strategy is appropriate for a query of the following nature:

Find all documents that are related to the following concepts: expert systems, fifth generation language, etc.

We developed a program to simulate the thesaurus-activation strategy. During a search, our system first used terms supplied

468

by the searchers that matched with some nodes in our online thesaurus. These nodes were taken as *source nodes*, with which there were associated links. Our system applies a heuristic spreading activation process (a similar process has been described in [17] and [8]) on the semantic network-based thesaurus to generate relevant terms. We developed a few heuristics to guide this activation process. They are presented as follows:

1. **The Specific Terms First Heuristic:** Based on the analysis of the LCSH structure, we observed that nodes (terms) which have fewer neighbors in the semantic network are generally more specific (in content) than nodes (terms) which have more neighbors. Since users have a tendency to state their information needs more broadly than they should, our system applies a heuristic which expands the nodes with fewer neighbors first (the more specific terms).

2. **The Specific Links First Heuristic:** Links associated with the index terms are of three types: NT, RT, and BT (the reverse of NT). Our system adopts a heuristic for expanding the links in the order of: NT, RT, and BT. That is, our system will search the NT links before it searches the RT links and before it searches the BT links. This heuristic guides our system in activating the more specific links first (which will eventually lead to more specific terms).

3. **The Shorter Distance First Heuristic:** This heuristic is related to the distance of a node from the source nodes. During the activation process, our system will expand the nodes which are closer to the source nodes (shorter distance) before expanding nodes which are farther away from the source nodes (longer distance). The rationale is that terms which are more remote (from the source nodes) are less relevant to the source terms than terms which are closer to the source nodes and therefore, should be expanded only after the more relevant terms (closer nodes) are expanded.

4. **The Two-Level Expansion Heuristic:** The number of links between two nodes (terms) in a semantic network indicates the semantic proximity of the terms. In order to find only terms which are closely relevant to the source nodes, our system expands the source nodes by two levels. That is, we activate only nodes that are two links away from the source nodes. (Because each node in the network may have between a few dozen and a few hundred links, two-level expansion still requires a lot of computation.) This two-level expansion heuristic was derived from observation of the query articulation characteristic of users (they rarely broadened or narrowed the specificity of their search terms for more than two levels) and an analysis of the cross referencing structure of LCSH. This heuristic ensures that the system only finds terms that are semantically close to the source nodes (terms).

The four heuristics described, which consider the specificity of the nodes, the specificity of the links, the distance between

nodes, and the expansion level, are used to direct our system's spreading activation effort. We represent the problem as a search task. We assign costs to each expanded path based on the nodes visited, the types of links traversed, and the number of links in the path. We develop a branch-and-bound algorithm to guide the search. This algorithm computes costs for each partial path and expands the least-cost path. After the expansion, new costs are assigned to the newly expanded paths and the expansion process is repeated. This algorithm is able to alleviate the computational explosion problem that frequently occurred in the semantic network spreading activation process.

After expanding each source node by two levels, our system classifies the expanded paths into different concept groups. Paths that are connected are considered to be in the same concept group. Nodes (terms) on the paths within the same concept group address a similar underlying concept. For queries which involve one concept (topic), our system will generate one concept group. For queries which involve multiple concepts (topics), our system is able to recognize all the concepts involved in the queries and to generate multiple concept groups. This concept grouping process frequently has been used by human information specialists (reference librarians often attempt to identify the various topics patrons try to address during a consultation session). New terms (terms which are different from the source terms) found in each concept group will become good candidate terms for the user's queries. Our algorithm ranks the concept groups in order (based on the number of source terms involved in each concept group) and suggests new terms to the users. A session of user relevance feedback then follows. This thesaurus activation process is useful in helping users articulate their queries.

Figure 3: A graphic representation of thesaurus activation

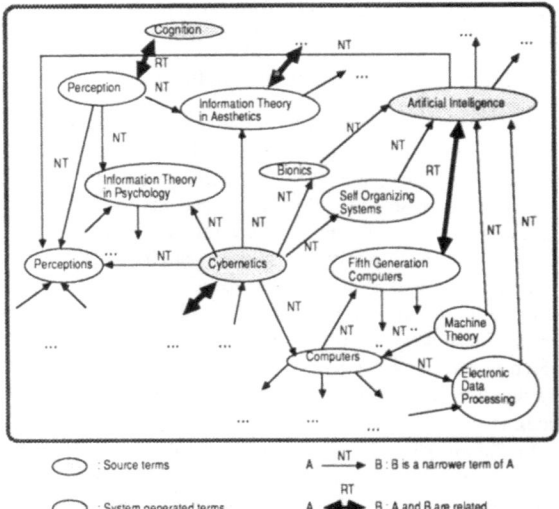

In summary, the thesaurus activation process generates relevant terms by activating the links in the semantic network-based online thesaurus. This process has been made possible by means of a heuristic-based branch-and-bound algorithm. In Figure 3 we present a sample session of thesaurus activation.

We list the source terms (nodes in shaded ovals) and the relevant paths and terms generated from the browsing process (nodes in un-shaded ovals). The initial terms consist of: "Cognition," "Artificial Intelligence," and "Cybernetics." The thesaurus activation algorithm suggested other relevant terms in ranked order to the user (e.g., "Perception," "Bionics," "Information Theory in Psychology," etc. in Figure 3). This example involved only one concept group (all terms are linked together). There were a few hundred nodes and links in our information network that were related to the initial query. Our branch-and-bound algorithm helped obtain a reasonable search time. In a complex information network like this, manual navigation for a query of this nature would be a major undertaking (there would be too many nodes and links to be explored). Using our algorithm, the activation process explored 345 paths in about 15 seconds.

Our current prototype was developed in Franz Lisp, Opus 42, and run on the SUN. It was implemented as a menu-driven system. We are in the process of migrating our system to a hypertext environment. With the visual display and browsing mechanisms associated with the hypertext system and the powerful search mechanisms our system exhibits, we can realistically create a useful hypertext-based document retrieval system.

5   Conclusion

We believe merging the idea of hypertext with information retrieval mechanisms is essential for creating a flexible and "intelligent" retrieval environment. In this paper, we have demonstrated the feasibility of creating a hypertext-based information network. Most importantly, we have proposed two heuristics-based search strategies that make search in a large information network possible. Both strategies perform a spreading activation process in our information network. Our empirically-derived heuristics helped alleviate the computational explosion problem that frequently occurs in a semantic network structure.

We are in the process of investigating various hypertext environments that may be appropriate to serve as a platform for our system. A series of experiments that study the effects of our design on online searchers will follow after successful system migration.

References

[1] J. R. Anderson. *Cognitive Psychology and Its Implications, 2nd Ed.* W. H. Freeman and Company, New York, NY, 1985.

[2] N. J. Belkin, R. N. Oddy, and H. M. Brooks. Ask for information retrieval: Part I. background and theory. *Journal of Documentation*, 38(2):61–71, June 1982.

[3] N. J. Belkin, R. N. Oddy, and H. M. Brooks. Ask for information retrieval: Part II. results of a design study. *Journal of Documentation*, 38(3):145–164, September 1982.

[4] Hsinchun Chen and Vasant Dhar. Reducing indeterminism in consultation: a cognitive model of user/librarian interaction. In *Proceedings of the 6th National Conference on Artificial Intelligence (AAAI-87)*, 1987.

[5] Hsinchun Chen and Vasant Dhar. Cognitive process as a basis for document-based retrieval systems design. *submitted for publication*, 1990.

[6] Hsinchun Chen and Vasant Dhar. A knowledge-based approach to the design of document-based retrieval systems. In *Proceedings of the 5th Conference on Office Information Systems*, Cambridge, MA, 1990.

[7] Hsinchun Chen and Vasant Dhar. User misconceptions of online information retrieval systems. *International Journal of Man-Machine Studies*, forthcoming, 1990.

[8] Paul R. Cohen and Rick Kjeldsen. Information retrieval by constrained spreading activation in semantic networks. *Information Processing and Management*, 23(4):255–268, 1987.

[9] W. B. Croft and H. Turtle. A retrieval model for incorporating hypertext links. In *Proceedings of HYPERTEXT'89*, pages 213–224, Pittsburgh, PA, November 1989.

[10] Carol Hansen Fenichel. The process of searching online bibliographic database: a review of research. *Library Research*, 2(2):107–127, Summer 1980.

[11] G. W. Furnas, T. K. Landauer, L. M. Gomez, and S. T. Dumais. The vocabulary problem in human-system communication. *Communications of the ACM*, 30(11):964–971, November 1987.

[12] M. D. Good, J. A. Whiteside, D. R. Wixon, and S. J. Jones. Building a user-derived interface. *Communications of the ACM*, 27(10):1032–1043, October 1984.

[13] F. Halasz. Reflections on notecards: Seven issues for the next generation of hypermedia systems. *Communications of the ACM*, 31(7):836–852, July 1988.

[14] Karen Markey and Pauline Atherton. *Online Training and Practice Manual for ERIC Data Base Searchers.* Syracuse, NY: ERIC Clearinghouse on Information Resources, ERIC: ED 160109, 1978.

[15] A. Newell and H. A. Simon. *Human Problem Solving.* Prentice-Hall, Englewood Cliffs, NJ, 1972.

[16] G. Salton. Automatic text indexing using complex identifiers. In *Proceedings of ACM Conference on Document Processing Systems*, Santa Fe, NM, December 1988.

[17] Peretz Shoval. Principles, procedures and rules in an expert system for information retrieval. *Information Processing and Management*, 21(6):475–487, 1985.

[18] Rober S. Taylor. Question-negotiation and information seeking in libraries. *College and Research Libraries*, 29:178–194, May 1968.

The Process of Knowledge Structuring Supported by a Hypertext System

M.Hofmann   U.Schreiweis   H.Langendörfer

TU Braunschweig
Inst. für Betriebssysteme und Rechnerverbund

Abstract

We[1] introduce the features of a hypertext system called CON-CORDE, its basic objects and its software-architecture. It is shown how this system will support the knowledge engineering process.

1 Goals of Research; Structure of the Paper

The process of structuring the knowledge of experts is often seen as the most critical issue of the development of *expert systems*. We are convinced that the new type of information system called hypertext system can fill an existing gap of today's knowledge engineering. This gap exists between the very early work of a knowledge engineer and the experts and the final structuring of the expertise. Hypertext systems prepared for user-support necessary in intelligent applications have been described by [8], and [12].

Hypertext resp. *hypermedia systems* are able to relate information of different data types in a flexible manner [4]. Information is divided into isolated portions; these portions are called *nodes*. Individual relationships between node instances are expressed by *links* [5]. A hypertext system is not only a system storing and managing this kind of information; a real important part of any system is the *presentation* of nodes and links [7].

In a current project concerning the development of an expert system managing and diagnosing a sewage filter plant (This project is sponsored by the German minister of research and technology (BMFT) under grant 02WA8828/7), knowledge acquisition support is urgently needed. So we decided to use a hypertext system implemented at our institute to supply the help needed in this case.

---
[1]Authors' address: TU Braunschweig, Inst. für Betriebssysteme, Bültenweg 74/75, D-3300 Braunschweig, Fed. Rep. Germany; E-Mail: unido!infbs!hofmann.uucp or hofmann@dbsinf6.BITNET

2 Knowledge Acquisition

Knowledge acquisition is a crucial stage in the development of an expert system. As a process, it involves eliciting, analyzing and interpreting the knowledge that a human expert uses when solving a particular problem and transforming this knowledge into a suitable machine representation. Knowledge acquisition is crucial since the power and utility of the resulting expert system depend on the quality of the underlying representation of expert knowledge.

The basic idea is to view the process of knowledge-based system development as a *modelling* activity [11]. Given this distinction, knowledge engineering can be seen as going through a number of phases (see fig. 1).

Raw data in the figure refers to the input data from the real world: text books, interviews, thinking aloud protocols, etc. The *conceptual model* is real-world oriented in the sense that it only describes the competence in expert problem solving. The *design model* is a model at the same level of abstraction. It is a high-level logic system design. The major difference between the conceptual model and the design model thus is that the design model takes into account external requirements.

Therefore knowledge acqustion is divided into three major phases:

1. knowledge elicitation

2. analysis and interpretation,
   where the structure of the problem solving process and the relevant types of knowledge are identified from the elicited data, in order to build an epistemological model of expertise.

3. operationalization of the interpreted and analysed data.

In essence the developing of an expert system involves *modelling* of expertise, i.e., the structuring of the required knowledge, inference competence and *flexible* use of knowledge.

3 The Hypertext System

This section describes the hypertext system CONCORDE (**Connected Card-oriented Entities**), a research prototype

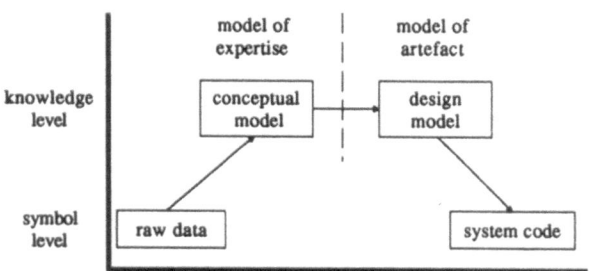

Fig. 1: Models in knowledge-based system development

suited for active hypertext applications, e.g. decision support, authoring, or knowledge structuring. A first prototype of **CONCORDE** is implemented in Smalltalk-80 on a SUN-3/60. The navigation tool of it is described in [9]. In the following, we briefly discuss its object management.

Two parts of the system have to be differentiated: a global hypertext and local contexts. The *global hypertext* contains the information that is common to all users. Any information item of the global hypertext is accessible to any user (read access). The information items are stored in a global database and managed by a global object manager.

A *local context* supports individual user views of the global hypertext. Any local context contains a subset of information items copied from the global hypertext, a set of tools for manipulating these items, a local object manager to handle the information, and a local storage. Manipulation of the information items can only take place in local contexts not in the global hypertext. The distinction between global hypertext and local context is also supported by the *client-server-configuration* of **CONCORDE**. While the global hypertext is stored at the server, any user environment is placed at a client (see fig. 2).

Basic object of the hypertext **CONCORDE**'s is the *card*. We are dedicated to the current fashion to call the basic information nodes cards. A card is a good symbol for a unit whose content is presented as a whole. In addition, the use of cards in hypertext systems is analogous to the usage of notecards in office environments. A card is made of a unique surrogate, a content of datatype text, graphics, or bitmap, a list of system attributes, a list of application attributes, and a set of links.

System attributes are properties independent of an application. Examples for such attributes are the access rights of a card (reading access is always guaranteed), the mode (cards can be archived or editable), the class of the card etc. Other attributes are application-dependent. Usually, their presentation differs from the presentation of the system attributes. Application attributes are presented by default while system attributes are only shown by demand. A *link*, instantiating a relation between two cards, is the second basic object of **CONCORDE**. We differentiate two categories of links: individual links and constrained links.

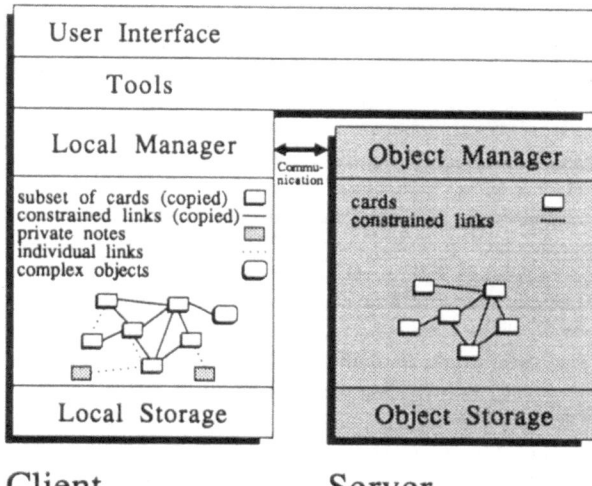

Fig. 2: Software-architecture of **CONCORDE**

Constrained links are typed links defined in the global hypertext (see fig. 2). For any link type, two sets of card classes are defined. One set contains the classes whose instances are valid link sources, the other set contains the classes whose instances are valid to be link destinations. In addition, constraints of the link types are defined as a set of predicates concerning operations such as adding a link, deleting a link, and renaming a link.

Therefore, constrained link types are well suited for an adaption to a special application. The given types of links serve as a restricting structure for the knowledge engineering process. The placement of links can be controlled. An example of a constraint of a link type looks as follows:

$$causes \ insert\_link \ \exists \ N_m, \ \exists \ N_t, \ \exists \ N_s :$$
$$N_m \in [Measure], N_t \in [Threshold], N_s \in [Symptom]$$
$$insert\_link(causes(N_m, N_s)) \rightarrow \exists \ L_c \in [causes] : (L_c(N_t, N_s))$$

with N_m, N_t, N_s card instances, L_c link instance, and *[Name]* symbolizing a card class respective a link type called *Name*. The first keyword (*causes*) names the concerned link type, the second one the operation (*insert_link*) where the constraint is triggered. This is followed by a predicate that expresses the constraint.

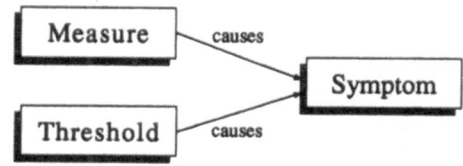

Fig. 3: Relationships between Cards defined by Constraints

This constraint describes a relationship in a knowledge base containing symptoms, measures causing symptoms, thresholds of these measures, etc. The relationship expresses that a measure causes a symptom since a threshold is exceeded. So, a relationship between the measure and the symptom exists as well as the relation between a threshold and the symptom (here, we neglect the relationship between a measure and its threshold). If the entities of the knowledge base are expressed by card instances of CONCORDE, the insertion of a *causes*-link from a *measure*-card N_m to a *symptom*-card N_s only is allowed if a *causes*-link L_c exists from a *threshold*-card N_t to the same *symptom*-instance N_s. If a user wants to insert such a link, the link only becomes valid if the second link already exists. Then the predicate will evaluate true.

Individual links are untyped. They can be named but cannot be controlled. Links of this category are unconstrained. In opposite to constrained links of the global hypertext, they exist only in local contexts. They are kept in a local storage (see fig. 2), even if the cards they relate to are written back to the global hypertext ("check_in"). We see the following advantages in this approach.

Firstly, we are able to protect private links against the access of other users. We can guarantee the privacy of information. CONCORDE offers the special card class *PrivateNote* in every local context; instances of this class are never inserted into the global hypertext but kept locally. So, not only private link structures can be created, also private remarks are possible. Secondly, a lot of links not relevant to any other user are kept locally. This makes our global hypertext "more readable". Especially, the danger of the effects of disorientation will be reduced. These advantages overcome the disadvantage of the management overhead.

Beside individual links and private cards, local contexts show a third additional structure of information. Cards can be aggregated to *complex objects*; their structure is manipulated with the help of structure cards. All links of the separate cards are still visible in complex objects made of these cards.

3 Knowledge Engineering Support by CONCORDE

At various places, attempts are being made to integrate the idea of hypertext and expert systems. Hypertext is used to relate the network of objects, rules, and properties. The result is just a graphical presentation of relationships. Other applications (beyond them knowledge-based systems) use a hypertext network as an online-help system.

In this section, we describe an approach using hypertext for more than simple presentation and help tasks. We think that this tool bridges the gap between existing expert systems shells and current knowledge acquisition research prototypes. It will at least enable the knowledge engineer to develop *maintainable* expert systems.

Taking advantage of CONCORDE's concepts the three main phases of the knowledge acquisition process are supported by the following functionalities:

1. Any source used in knowledge engineering and accessible in machine-readable form can be made into a hypertext node. E.g. references of the expert to a source in form of an image become a link to this source. So, for the first time the knowledge engineer is able to manage all existing different knowledge sources in an *integrated environment*.

   A scanner enables CONCORDE to include drawings, scribbled notes etc. In all knowledge-based applications, this informal kind of information is of great importance. E.g. the blueprint of the sewage filter had shown a basin where it had not been built. This was *manually* corrected by the expert.

2. Some knowledge elicitation methods are easily integrated. The structure formation techniques like *Networking*, *Heidelberger Structure Formation Technique* or *Card-Sort* methods are based on the fact of being able to present knowledge-structures graphically or visually. These techniques make available an exactly specified visual system for representing the structure of a particular knowledge-domain [3]. In all approaches, the most important concepts of the knowledge domain are written onto cards and arranged on the screen. The relations between them are presented together with the concerning typed links.

   Complex objects can be aggregated of cards belonging together very closely (for instance, cards related by *analogous*-links should be grouped to one complex object).

3. In a more common fashion, the knowledge engineer is able to create his set of relation types (links) specially adapted to the domain. This naturally involves some background understanding of the particular expertise.

   In a case where none of the methods presented above seem adequate to the expert, he or she is capable of using the underlying hypertext system. He or she selects information or sources of his or her area of expertise, defines fitting link types, and relates the information written on cards by links of these types. A knowledge engineer can get an idea of the relationships of the application by looking at the created hypertext. Also, the expert is able to select subsets of the global hypertext and to *criticize* the relations placed by the knowledge engineer by a predefined constrained link type.

   A related kind of method is the following: Using constrained links, the knowledge engineer presents "exercises". These "exercises" are made of relations the knowledge engineer inferenced from the elicited knowledge. If the relation is valid, the expert creates a complex object containing the cards and links of the "exercise". A *valid*-link is placed with the complex object as its destination. If something is wrong, a better solution can be proposed by use of (new) cards and (new) links. These procedures result in a *temporal independent cooperation* of expert and knowledge engineer.

4. Up to now one of the most important methods for knowledge elicitation has been *interviewing*. While modelling the "universe of discourse" of an application the knowledge engineer is able to mark ambiguous points with *question-cards*.

   The knowledge engineer is able to write down immediately his or her intended question in the right context. The question-card is then related to the card containing the questionable content by a *query*-link. Later on a *collector-modul* accumulates these cards: It presents all cards a *query*-link points to. The browser shows the surrounding of these cards, and knowledge engineer and expert can reorganize content and structure.

5. Expert systems require extensive maintenance. Maintenance problems are not so much due to the fact that in many domains of expertise knowledge may change, but rather that systems are so opaque and unstructured that it is hard to tell where updates and modifications should be applied [2]. Simply adding a new rule may affect the way other rules interact.
   The knowledge engineer builds a hypertext-model of the entire domain. So the hypertext contains formal expert knowledge as well as knowledge components only important for the knowledge engineer him- or herself. The hypertext includes also the knowledge sources the rules are based on. So, if a rule is modified the knowledge engineer is aware of all pieces of knowledge relating to this appropriated rule.

4 Conclusion

In this paper, we introduced a prototypical hypertext system that is able to manage relationships between individual nodes containing information. We showed some possibilities to take advantage of the properties of our hypertext systems to support knowledge structuring.

It hasn't been our goal to introduce a new knowledge engineering methodology nor to present a knowledge-acquisition workbench for expert systems either. But we are convinced that our *integrated approach* of collecting knowledge, managing sources of this knowledge, supporting its structuring, and the facility to maintain the knowledge by hypertext links is an important step to the integration of databases, expert systems, and hypermedia systems.

In the next future, we want to extend our prototype. At the moment, the manager of the global hypertext checks only the static constraints of the typed links. We plan to "activate" this module of CONCORDE. It must be able to interpret the structures of the hypertext. For instance, it should look for forbidden cycles of an argumentation. But we will not make an inferencing module of it. Another task for this module would be the automatic leading of a user to open questions marked by the concerning link.

[1] **J.Boose, B.Gaines, M.Linster**, Proceedings of the European Knowledge Acquisition Workshop (EKAW'88), GMD-Studien Nr. 143, June 1988

[2] **J.Breuker, B.Wielinga**, Use of Models in the Interpretation of Verbal Data, in: [10]

[3] **M.Bonato**, Knowledge elicitation with structure formation techniques, in: [6]

[4] **R.Cordes, M.Hofmann, H.Langendörfer**, Layered Object-oriented Techniques Supporting Hypermedia and Multimedia Applications; in: Proc. WOODMAN'89, Rennes, May 1989, pp.286–296

[5] **J.Conklin**, Hypertext: An Introduction and Survey; in: IEEE Computer, Vol.20, No.9, September 1987, pp.17–41

[6] **J.Diederich, T.Uthmann**, Knowledge Acquisition for Expert Systems, Arbeitspapiere der GMD 281, December 1987

[7] **M.Hofmann, R.Cordes, H.Langendörfer**, Hypertext/Hypermedia; in: Informatik–Spektrum, Vol.12, No.4, August 1989, pp.218–220

[8] **F.G.Halasz, T.P.Moran, R.N.Randall**, NoteCards in a Nutshell; in: Proc. ACM Conference CHI/GI'87, Toronto, 1987, pp.45–52

[9] **M.Hofmann, H.Langendörfer**, Browsing as Incremental Access of Information in the Hypertext System CONCORDE; in: Proc. Interactive Communication, Paris, May 1990

[10] **A.L.Kidd**, Knowledge acquisition for expert systems, Plenum Press, 1987

[11] **G.Schreiber, J.Breuker, B.Bredeweg, B.Wielinga**, Modelling in KBS Development, in: [1]

[12] **N.A.Streitz, J.Hannemann, M.Thüring**, From Ideas and Arguments to Hyperdocuments: Travelling through Activity Spaces; in: Proc. Hypertext'89, Pittsburgh, November 1989, pp.343–364

CONCEPTS OF INTEGRATING EXPERT SYSTEMS AND VISUAL DATABASES

Matthias Rhiner

Multimedia Laboratory
Computer Science Department
University of Zurich

Advanced Software Systems
IBM Switzerland

ABSTRACT

Modern application development tendencies put more and more importance on the integration of expert systems with other system components. Besides embedding in operational environments the connection with *databases* and *sophisticated user-interfaces* are emerging points of interest.
Basic concepts for the integration of *Expert Systems and Visual Databases* are discussed in this paper. Visual Databases extend beyond the conventional range of alphanumerical data in that they incorporate also *graphics and images*. The main purpose of this paper is to show how *visual objects* can be organized in an expert system and database environment and so that they can be used for more *sophisticated problem visualization, knowledge representation* and *user interaction* in the domain of expert system applications.

KEYWORDS

Expert systems, knowledge based systems, knowledge representation; visual databases, visual objects, object representation; visualization, visual user interface;

1. INTRODUCTION

Data Processing is going through major changes in various aspects. Typical components of interactive applications (main processing, data access and user interaction) show new conceptual and implementational functionality compared to former traditional ones.

The main *processing and controlling part* of applications is subject to new influences. Besides the still very useful and in many cases inevitable *procedural* processing tendencies of *declarative* programming (e.g. rule-based systems) came up. 'Expert systems' - with all the positive and negative implications of this term - became an exponent of this programming techniques. To prevent further misuse of the already overloaded term 'Expert Systems' we will use 'Knowledge Based Systems' (KBS) for the rest of this paper.

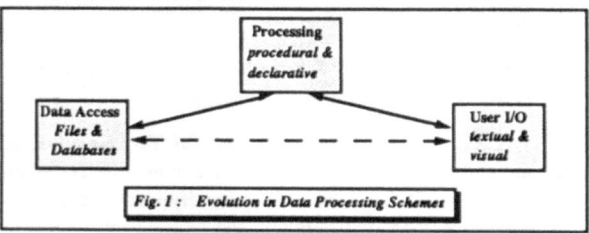

Fig. 1 : Evolution in Data Processing Schemes

Data manipulation changed from simple file handling to a higher level of database mechanisms. Previously procedural-oriented hierarchical and network-type databases get replaced by the more *declarative* concepts of relational and lately by object-oriented databases.

The *user interface*, as the third major component, has been profiting very much by progresses made in the development of peripheral devices. Mainly high resolution displays with color features are an important basis for advanced information exchange between application and user.
In classical on-line applications the main parts of an application were processing and data manipulation. Recent tendencies put more and more emphasis on the user interaction that should go beyond simple text-I/O based communication. New media as windowing techniques, supporting graphics and images, are essential methods for the target of *visualization*.

Visual representation of facts can replace (or support) long textual questions and explanations that might be difficult to understand or take a long time to be processed mentally if expressed only in an alphanumerical way [1]. This kind of visual knowledge representation can be of major interest in various application domains of KBS, as for knowledge based diagnosis and configuration, on-line documentation, tutoring-systems etc.
In order to build a KBS that makes extensive use of visual data, all representative objects must be organized and prepared for further consistent manipulation as any other data in a complex application environment. Therefore the principle of storing also visual objects and related metadata in a database can be considered as a consequence of typical requirements like *maintenance, consistency, durability, indexing and query facilities.*

Various aspects and implications of integrating *KBS-Techniques* with *Visual Databases* will be developed and discussed in the following paragraphs:

In paragraph 2) some considerations to the *areas involved* in the integration of KBS and Visual databases are made. 3) describes a more specific *scenario* of integration. In 4) different, conceptual techniques and levels of *coupling* KBS and Visual DB are discussed. Combining KBS and Visual DB allows various models of *knowledge representation*, related aspects can be found in paragraph 5). 6) presents an early prototype and testbed *implementation model*, based on existing software-components. 7) contains criticism related to various aspects of this work and an outlook to future improvements.

2. RELATED AREAS OF INTEREST

There is a kind of advanced representatives for the main parts of a complex application environment when looking at the the domains of *KBS* (main processing part), *database techniques* (data manipulation) and *multimedia techniques*, mainly graphics and images (user interface).

In a general, not yet application dependent context, there are various relations between these domains (cf. Fig. 2) that build a basis for specific types of interaction and (mutual) support:

- Expert systems using databases as an information-base
- Expert systems using advanced user-I/O for visualization of complex facts
- Databases using KBS as 'intelligent' frontends
- Databases using advanced user-I/O for representation of structure and data
- Advanced visual interfaces using databases as object servers (text, graphics, images)
- Advanced visual interfaces using KBS for special, complex tasks

Some of the major relations in this scheme are target of intensive, on-going research. Principles of interaction between *KBS and databases* can be found in [2], two specific examples in [3], [4].

The idea of using *Visual Databases* (also called *Pictorial Databases*) is not only related to the here involved field of KBS but has been promoted in various other application domains for more than a decade [5], [6]. Other tendencies in this domain concentrate on *Multimedia Databases* that go even further in handling unconventional dataobjects (animation, video, audio) than visual databases. Related articles can be found in [7] and [6].

The possibilities of combining *KBS with Multimedia* are the latest techniques to come up. For that reason there still seems to be a lack of experience. Recent trends start using multimedia as high-level interfaces to KBS (*visualization*) or take profit from KBS for certain hypermedia applications (*'intelligent' navigation, object recognition and management* etc.). Principles of these concepts are shown in [8], [9]; an interesting application example is given in [10].

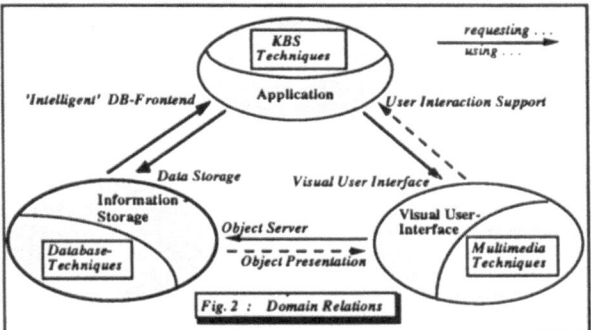

Fig. 2 : Domain Relations

In complex applications various combinations of relations and interactions between the domains presented can occur, depending on different constellations and requirements. In the following paragraphs such a specific scenario will be presented.

3. INTEGRATION SCENARIO

The integration scenario to be described consists of an application scheme using KBS techniques for the main knowledge representation and processing part. Besides the 'internal knowledge' of the KBS additional information (and/or knowledge) can be retrieved dynamically from a database. User interaction is done on an interactive visual level. In addition to the application driven representation of facts and data, *direct, mainly implicit* DB-accesses can be done by the user interface. In this way it is possible to get further information (e.g. help, explanations in a hypertext-style) concerning the problem domain without steady regressing to the main processing KBS-part.

The main idea of this concept is to use advanced visualization and interaction techniques for appropriate KBS applications. The dynamic functionality and flexibility required for the interface part can be realized by combining suitable *visual dataobjects* with related and dedicated *operations*. These components will be integrated in the symbiosis of KBS and database in order to take profit of the DB-specific advantages and facilities. Therefore the database will act as a kind of object-server for the active KBS and user interaction parts.

Analyzing this scenario there are two main points of interest to consider:

- Visual objects with related operations as active application components
- Visual objects as a method of knowledge representation

The first point expresses a requirement to consider visual data as an integral part of the whole system. This will be realized by adding operations (*methods*) to the normally passive visual components (*objects*). Both, *objects and methods*, will be stored in an application related database and can therefore be handled by existing DB-mechanisms.

For the second point considerations must be made if it is possible to combine data in the database used as information for the main KBS application and data mainly used for visualization. Pursuing this concept further on leads to a point where active visual objects can be considered as an alternative or additional way of *knowledge representation*.

We resume these principles by saying that visual objects and their respective methods can have a *structural* and *operational* meaning in the scenario specified. The following paragraph will discuss several different possibilities of integration with regard to the whole system environment..

4. METHODS OF COUPLING SYSTEM COMPONENTS

There are various methods and levels how to connect the components in a complex application environment as mentioned above and how to define their way of interaction:

In a first scenario the KBS is the main and only controlling part. It retrieves all additional, not KBS-local data necessary for processing and visual user interaction from the database (except the binary visual objects and corresponding methods themselves).

The visual user interface acts as a mere *display server* that retrieves visual objects and related display-methods from the database and presents them to the user according to requests from the KBS. There is only textual input from the user to the processing part. According to this separation of main processing and representation part, also data in the database is dedicated to corresponding different purposes.

In a second scenario the visual user interface is still kind of a dumb server. Besides simple displaying of objects, other operations for more advanced user interaction can be executed. These operations are specified and activated, one by one, by the controlling KBS-part. But there are not only display-methods anymore, but also additional, more complex ones: Showing details of an object, highlighting areas of interest etc. Besides the *passive display part* such complex methods also have an *active operation part* that mainly supports the selection of previously marked object features.

The results of such an operation (e.g. an implicitly defined text string, the code of an area of interest) are returned to the KBS and influence further inferencing. In this case visual interaction is a more sophisticated way of conversation with the processing part than just user-depending textual I/O. To enable implicit relations between the main KBS and the visual interaction part the data and knowledge structuring of the two components cannot be done in a complete independent way anymore. There must be common data in the database.

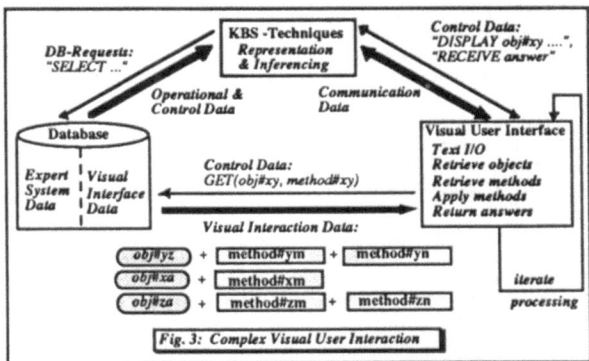

Fig. 3: Complex Visual User Interaction

In a third and last scenario (Fig. 3) much more of *direct control* is given to the visual user interface. Instead of defining each object and each method to apply explicitly in the main KBS part, tasks on a higher level are set up to be fulfilled during a user interaction cycle. Therefore the interface component (under user control) is more independent in how to reach the target set: Direct textual user I/O, one complex single step-operation, iterating simple steps of visual interaction etc. In the end a specific answer-type (textstring, code etc.) or a predefined default value ('unknown', 'no answer possible' etc.) must be returned to the KBS according to the pending request.

To fulfil these requirements there must be additional functionality in the objects and methods used. Specially there must be a way of directly retrieving further information from the database without awaiting other commands or requests from the controlling KBS part. Considering these prerequisites for advanced operations it is obvious that the separation between processing and visualization data in the database is weaker again and that there is a need for linking metadata. More and more it is also *structural application knowledge* that must be accessible or that is integrated in the complex operations of the user interface.

Some of the concepts introduced in the scenarios above can be enlightened by applying the following example. We assume a KBS application for the analysis and diagnosis of pollution data. Input for the specialists to work with this system are satellite pictures and numerical data. Beside this input data there are numerous visual and alphanumerical tools to give *visual support* to the analysis process:

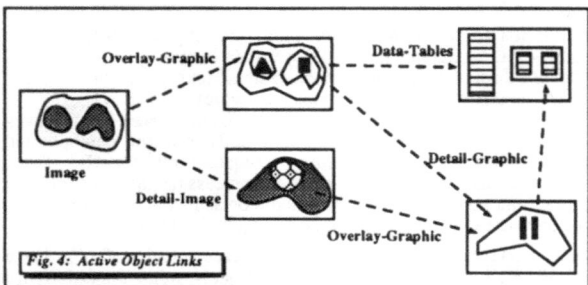

Fig. 4: Active Object Links

Existing maps containing geographical or dedicated thematical information (e.g. industry, population density) can be used as overlays or explanatory images to the incoming ones. Exact graphical contours, grids and symbols can be accessed to provide links between *implicit visual image* data and *explicit alphanumerical* data.

In the interaction with the KBS application the specialist can use and process all this information in a very dynamical, hypermedia-like style. Methods operating on the visual objects show him active components triggering the appearance of additional supporting data, allow the implicit access to related information and return keywords, codes etc. as input to the KBS application part.

5. DISTRIBUTION OF KNOWLDEGE REPRESENTATION

The scenarios in the former paragraph brought up the topic of *knowledge representation*. With regard to the different system parts it is possible (by using appropriate techniques) to structure and represent knowledge of importance to more than one application component, conceptually and physically, by using various methods (cf. Fig. 5):

1.) In the most common way all direct application relevant knowledge is represented within the proper KBS part itself using the specific structures provided by the KBS. Databases are accessed only to provide operational data and the user interface acts as a simple question-and-answer tool.

2.) By extending function and meaning of the *database usage* there are new ways to represent application specific knowledge in database structures that can be mapped into corresponding KBS structures during an intialization phase or dynamically while processing. In this way a database provides *operational data* and *structural knowledge* (in many cases it may even be difficult to distinguish between the two of them).

3.) Using *active visual objects* is another means of representing not only display but also application relevant knowledge. This knowledge is represented on one side by the structure and the visual content of these objects. On the other side there are *methods* related to them. These methods can contain additional (operational or structural) knowledge in the way they operate on the respective objects, interact with users, return data to the controlling KBS and how they retrieve other objects and methods from the datal...e.

Defining an integrated application based on these components therefore needs careful modelling of the knowledge representation and considerations where to put which aspects of functionality.

	KBS	Database	Visual objects & methods	
'Plain' KBS	*Knowl. Rep. Inferencing Control*	*operational data only*	*textual I/O*	
& Database		*Data in DB Knowl. Rep.*	*textual I/O*	
& Visual Objects			*Visual Objects Knowl. Rep.*	
& Methods				*Active objects Knowl. Rep.*

Fig. 5 : Knowledge Representation Scheme

Various factors like *clarity, transparency, updating possibilities, performance* etc. are deciding factors for keeping all relevant knowledge in the main KBS part (homogeneous model) or to distribute it to the appropriate components. There are different reasons for separating: Dynamic and often changed knowledge might better be handled by the flexible and error excluding database mechanisms than by rather static KBS data. Knowledge difficult to transform into textual representation structures should be stored in its original form (graphics, images) and only have symbolic alphanumerical references to the KBS.
One of the major challenges in designing a correct and suitable model is the discrimination between *implicit* and *explicit* knowledge: On one side the two forms of knowledge should complement each other intuitively in a self-explaining way or rather by the definition of appropriate, linking *metadata*. On the other side unwanted *redundancy* must be avoided whenever possible for reasons of consistency and efficiency.

6. IMPLEMENTATION MODELS

An implementation of the model developed in the previous paragraphs, schematically shown in Fig. 6, can be realized in various ways. The current environment used for prototyping and testing the concepts suggested is based on the integration of three *existing* software-components running on the same PS/2 workstation (Model 80-111). All of the three parts offer an application program interfaces (API) and are therefore open to interact with each other making use of the various facilities for interprocess communication in the OS/2 multitasking operating system environment [11].

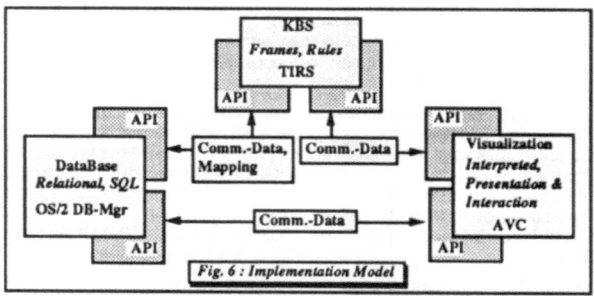

Fig. 6 : Implementation Model

The *KBS part* consists of a rule-based KBS-shell called TIRS (The Integrated Reasoning Shell [12]) providing a development and execution environment. Unstructured parameters, structured frames and rules are the means provided for knowledge representation. Communication and interaction with external programs during execution time is done by calling (synchronously or asynchronously operating) procedural C-programs from the KBS.

The *database* used is a conventional relational database with SQL as query language (OS/2 Database Manager [13]). For dynamic and program driven data requests SQL statements can be imbedded in C-programs.

The *visualization* and *user interaction* part is based on the interpreted multimedia tool AVC (AVC, Audio-Visual Connection [14]). The main concept of this program consists in *objects* (text, graphics, images, simple animations) that are presented according to a controlling program (method, *story* - the correct AVC term) which is dynamically interpreted. User communication can be done by keyboard (textual input, function keys) and mouse interactions (triggers, active elements).

The two concepts of objects and related methods/stories and the flexibility of interpreting can be used to emulate a kind of restricted, object-oriented database environment using conventional programming and database techniques. All dataobjects and related stories are stored as unstructured, binary files in a LONG field of a relational table. Retrieving a dataobject from the database means also retrieving a corresponding presentation method (story). The method gets interpreted and processes the dataobject according to the defined instructions. By calling or retrieving other stories the same dataobjects can be processed dynamically in a different way (different method).

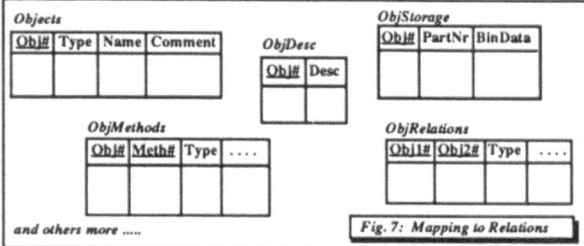

Fig. 7: Mapping to Relations

The simple presenting of objects in AVC is augmented by the functionality of the *controlling stories* that are written in a subset of the structured programming language REXX (Restructured Extended Executor Command Language [15]). The fact that REXX is interpreted has two major advantages:

1.) Turn-around time while developing an adequate user-interface is very reasonable. New objects and processing steps can be integrated and tested interactively without need for recompilation. This is a very important fact when considering that most of the work done for visually oriented applications is put in the development of the user interface.

2.) As stories get interpreted it is possible to call dynamically other stories and execute them according to parameters passed. There is no need for previous linking and related static definitions.

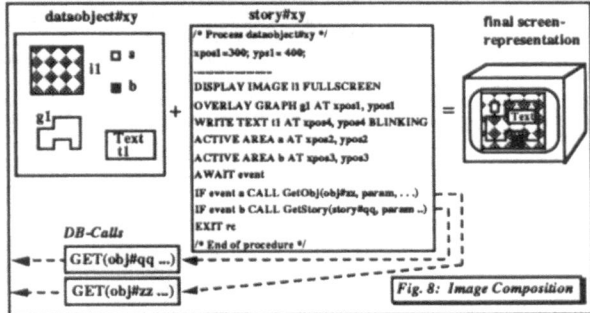

Fig. 8: Image Composition

In order to decrease system overhead different, also non-related objectparts can be stored physically in the same dataobject. In this case the controlling story is responsible for correct logical interpretation, for the extraction of specific parts, for their positioning and timing during representation. As REXX knows the concepts of subroutine calls, stories can be structured in a similar way. Stories likely to be called by a dominating one can be stored (and therefore also be retrieved) physically together with the calling as just one database object. If additional dataobjects and/or stories are used during a complex operation tests can be done if the corresponding objects are already

in memory, on an intermediate file or if they have to be retrieved from the database. In this way a *hierarchy of storage levels* can built that may influence processing time considerably.

The constellation shown in Fig. 6 does not specify any specific interprocess scheme apriori. The components making part of the whole integrated system may be distributed to different physical machines, running even different operating systems. These principles are the starting point for a second implementation scenario to be tested in the same application environment of integrating KBS and Visual Databases. Again existing software-components will be the basis for the development of this scenario.

The mainframe KB system KnowledgeTool [16] already offers an integrated, direct interface to AVC. Via certain communication mechanisms common variables can be exchanged and maintained between a controlling KBS application running on a /370-host and the AVC counterpart [17] running on a PS/2 workstation, acting as a multimedia user interface. In this loosely-coupled environment the possibilities for the overall system configurations are even broader than in a dedicated local one. Mainly there is the option to use a distributed databases as well: Operational data used by the KBS originating from the respective DB-systems on the host, visual and interaction dataobjects from the local DB on the workstation. It is also a seducing idea to use large host data repositories as storage media for a heavily space consuming distributed Visual Database. But the drawbacks of such a solution currently are found in the transfer time of large visual objects between host and the local enduser-workstation.

As a conclusion it can be said that such a scenario of distributed resources offers quite a lot of interesting features. But the overall system design and related performance considerations have to be done even more careful than in a dedicated local environment.

7. CRITICISM AND OUTLOOK

The principles of the integrated KBS and Visual Database System presented in the previous paragraphs are based mainly on conceptual considerations. A testbed environment has been created using system components that allow efficient and illustrative prototyping to a certain extent. But there are quite a few factors that do not match yet a thorough overall system design and that need new conceptualization for future improvement:

1.) *Allow real structure and dynamics in the visualization part:*

In the current model the visualization part is mainly based on static, predefined flat images. Structured objects like graphics and text are mapped into images (bytemaps) during the development process. Element structure and dynamics for the runtime process are simulated by means of parameter controlled stories explicitly retrieving and reconstructing the features wanted (quite in contrast to the concepts of object-oriented models).

2.) *Allow large, structured objects in the database:*

There are structured objects like graphics, hierarchical images structures etc. that must be 'flattened' for storage in a relational database. Other objects larger than 32 KByte must be split in subparts because of the 32 KByte restriction of the LONG field datatype. For the reconstruction of these objects again additional information must be stored in the methods handling them and/or in additional, merely administrative database elements. Thereby immanent information must be mapped to heterogeneous forms using utility-data and utility-methods.

3.) *Define a common knowledge representation form:*

Knowledge is represented in quite different ways in the three system components. In the KBS it is mainly *frames*, in the DB *tuples in tables* and in the visualization part *"semi-structured"* objects (bytemaps consisting of distinct components) that are used for static knowledge representation. On the side of dynamic processing it is *rules* (declarative) in the KBS, *relational queries* (declarative) in the DB and *procedural code* in the operations for visualization.
A more common way of knowledge representation could be of great importance to define a homogeneous datamodel and perform the respective mapping to actual datastructures thereby reinforcing the synergy of the various components and reducing redundancy.

478

4.) *Find methods for tighter coupling of the various system components:*

By now the three system components are coupled in a very loose way (Fig. 9-a). A more common data representation and processing model as required above would be a first requirement for bringing them closer together. Data transfer and conversion overhead could be remarkably reduced in a more tightly coupled or even closed model (Fig. 9-b).

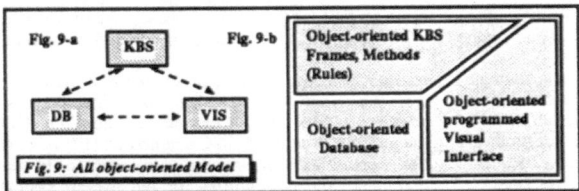

Regarding modern tendencies of software modeling and development, the requirements above are very similar to the main arguments for object oriented-application design and development. Even with respect to the specific particularities of the components involved, a thorough object-oriented approach conceptually seems to be the most adequate and homogeneous one.

In the domain of KBS object-oriented techniques have a long tradition using *frames* and *methods* for knowledge representation [18]. On the conceptual side of description techniques for visual objects frames have been a representation model that has been adopted for quite a time. It has mainly been used to represent passive image structures in *vision recognition systems* [19]. But many of these concepts can be transferred also to *active image-objects* where structure is related to processing functionality.

Also object-oriented databases show many concepts originating from the frame model [8]. They are still in a process of evolution and being approved for realistic applications, but research and commercial development [20] are consequently going on.

For the active part of visualization and user-interaction, object-oriented techniques can be applied as well. Corresponding programming environments (e.g. Smalltalk/V PM for OS/2) provide interfaces to standard user-environments like OS/2 Presentation Manager. The Presentation Manager itself is principally based on conventional programming techniques (function oriented API) but has adapted additionally many of the main object-oriented concepts (classes of windows, implicitly related procedures, message-concept [21]).

Resuming all these facts there is an obvious tendency that the main techniques to adopt for future consistent development in the complex domain of integrating KBS and Visual Databases may be given by *frame and object-oriented representation models* for the knowledge structuring and *respective methods* for the active processing part.

8. CONCLUSION

Integrating Knowledge Based Systems with Visual Databases and supporting a highly interactive user interface is a promising and challenging domain for specific application types. Well known conventional and approved software methods currently allow the realization of a testbed-environment to evaluate some of the concepts proposed in this paper but do not completely correspond to the particular properties of this field.

Shortcomings concerning a homogeneous knowledge representation model and adequate related processing methods are the main disadvantages of the current implementation. But on-going tendencies in the development of widely adaptable object-oriented models seem to provide elegant solutions for future development in this problem domain.

ACKNOWLEDGMENTS

Thanks are due to Prof. Dr. P. Stucki, University of Zurich, for his motivation and help to write this article and to Dr. G. Mahler, IBM Switzerland, for providing the support of IBM.

REFERENCES

[1] G. Rahmstorf : "Graphische Funktionen in der Künstlichen Intelligenz"; in W. Brauer, W. Wahlster ed.: Proceedings 2. Internationaler GI-Kongress, München, October 1987; Informatik Fachberichte Bd. 155, Springer Verlag, Berlin Heidelberg New York, 1987; pp. 207-216.

[2] M.L. Brodie and J. Mylopoulos ed. : "On Knowledge Base Management Systems, Integrating Artificial Intelligence and Database Technologies"; Springer Verlag, New York Berlin Heidelberg, 1986.

[3] S. Tsur : "LDL - A Technology for the Realization of Tightly Coupled Expert Database Systems"; IEEE EXPERT, Vol. 4, No. 2, Fall 1988; pp. 41-51.

[4] B. Cohen: "Merging Expert Systems and Databases", AI EXPERT, Vol. 4, No. 2, February 1989; pp. 22-31.

[5] S.-K.Chang: "Principles of Pictorial Information Systems Design", Prentice Hall International Editions, Englewood Cliffs, 1989.

[6] Kunii T.L. ed.: "Visual Database Systems", Proceedings of the IFIP TC 2/WG 2.6 Working Conference on Visual Database Systems, Tokyo, Japan, 3-7 April 1989; NORTH-HOLLAND, 1989.

[7] IEEE COMPUTER SOCIETY: "Multimedia Systems", Proceedings of the IEEE Computer Society Office Automation Symposium, National Bureau of Standards, Gaitersburgh, MD, 27-29 April 1987; Computer Society Press of the IEEE, Washington, 1987; pp. 36-66, 180-204.

[8] K. Parsaye et al. : "Intelligent Databases, Object-Oriented, Deductive Hypermedia Technologies", John Wiley & Sons, Inc., New York, 1989.

[9] P. Carando : "SHADOW - Fusing Hypertext with AI"; IEEE EXPERT, Vol. 4, No. 4, Winter 1989; pp. 65-78.

[10] J.-P. A Barthès : "A Command and Control System Based on a Multi-Media Object-Oriented Data Base and a Logic Programming Language"; in Proceedings of The Annual AI Systems in Government Conference, Washington, D.C., March 27-31, 1989; IEEE Computer Society Press, Washington, 1989

[11] E. Iacobucci : "OS/2 Programmer's Guide". Osborne McGraw-Hill, Berkely California, 1988

[12] IBM : "IBM TIRS Development/2, Knowledge Base Developer's Guide", IBM Form-Nr. SH21-1006, IBM Corporation, 1990.

[13] IBM : "IBM OS/2 DB Manager, Programming Guide and Reference", IBM Form-Nr. 90X7772, IBM Corporation, 1988.

[14] IBM : "IBM Audio Visual Connection, Audio Visual Authoring Language Reference", IBM Form-Nr. S15F-7134-00, IBM Corporation, 1989.

[15] IBM : "IBM Common Programming Interface Procedure Language Reference", IBM Form-Nr. SC26-4358-1, IBM Corporation, 1988.

[16] IBM : "IBM KnowledgeTool Application Development Guide", IBM Form-Nr. SH20-9262, IBM Corporation, 1989.

[17] IBM : "IBM Programmable Workstation Services Guide", IBM Form-Nr. SH20-9448, IBM Corporation, 1989.

[18] M. Minsky : "A Framework for Representing Knowledge"; in P. Winston ed. : The Psychology of Computer Vision; McGraw-Hill, New York, 1975.

[19] A. R. Rao : "Knowledge Representation and Control in Computer Vision Systems"; IEEE EXPERT, Vol.4, No. 1, Spring 1988; pp. 64-79.

[20] M. J. Tucker : "Object-Oriented Databases Arrive"; UNIXWORLD, August 1989; pp. 62-66.

[21] C. Petzold : "Programming the OS/2 Presentation Manager"; Microsoft Press, Redmond Washington, 1989.

Database Models for Textual Documents: User Needs and System Capabilities

B.N. Rossiter
Computing Laboratory
University of Newcastle upon Tyne
Newcastle upon Tyne
England NE1 7RU

M.A. Heather
Sutherland Building
Newcastle Polytechnic
Newcastle upon Tyne
England NE1 8ST

Users' needs in large and complex textbases are itemised and discussed in the light of current models. Examples applying relational and semantic models, such as the E-R and Taxis, suggest criteria for a more fundamental approach involving the merger of object-oriented programming techniques with database methods in future complex object textbases. Current object-oriented database systems have a number of significant weaknesses which need to be remedied before they can be adopted for textual document applications.

1: Introduction

Little attention has been paid to text as structured data. Much of administrative data is in the form of textual strings but these tend to be treated as atomic entities independent of any relationship between words. Text retrieval and hypertext systems are based on physical divisions in documents and physical positions of words and rely on features like inversion, position operators and physical connections. By exploiting fully current technology such as multi-windowing and the emerging object-oriented programming, there have been significant advances in document manipulation in the provision of natural user interfaces [1] and browsing systems [2,3]. There has been little regard for the very fine logical structure that lies beneath the physical form, even in recent data models for hypertext [4]. Recognizing the need for more advanced advanced file handling techniques to handle large amounts of complex office data, Croft and Temple [5] developed a model with constrained types ADABTPL to represent ODA. Unfortunately ODA has considerable limitations as a document description language through the inability to specify methods [6]. It would be interesting to see the representation of more complete document semantics in ADABTPL. The current work is concerned with the complete spectrum of textual applications: full text information systems, electronic publishing, email, office automation, hypertext, bulletin boards and conferencing [7].

2: Textual Applications and Filing Systems

As a first step to formulating a model, the demands made by textual applications on the technology of filing systems have been analyzed by drawing on applications at both Newcastle and elsewhere. The first two columns of Figure 1 summarize the results which have been reported more fully elsewhere [8].

This paper considers the implications of the requirements for database systems. Besides the obvious structural properties listed in section 1 of Figure 1, many of the other needs also place demands on textual filing systems: context and proximity matching require fine index structures; thesauri introduce further types of data; referential transparency, to provide navigational facilities as in hypertext, requires links from one text to another ideally using symbolic identifiers; trails made while navigating text structures need to be recorded as fully-fledged data [9,10]; and updating involves the major problems of version management and the modelling of dynamic behaviour such as the life cycle of a document.

2.1 Data Structures and Models

Examination of applications at Newcastle shows that text plays an important part in many research databases [11]. Natural history collections and biographies of politicians employ text at a vital elementary level: a text field is used to supplement highly formatted data to record comments and observations which do not fit the highly-structured classification scheme designed at the outset. Medical research databases, in addition to storing many items of numerical and coded information on subjects such as biochemistry, can hold large bodies of text to record complete details of operations, surgical procedures and unexpected complications. Genealogical databases involve complex relationships between people with identifiable objects such as branch, family, marriages and individuals. Uncertainty over exact relationships means that textual evidence such as wills and litigation should be recorded verbatim.

In a further broad class of applications, text comprises the most important part of each record. Thus in Hansard, the main data is the verbatim record of business in the UK Parliament although ancillary classifiable data such as dates and names of bills and speakers also need to be held in formatted form. Identifiable objects in Hansard include days of business, debates, speakers and speeches. In the Bible, the text in the verses is the critical part of the data. Identifiable objects are testament, book, chapter and verse, and a symbolic key comprising book, chapter and verse is a natural choice for addressing the data. However, for some biblical applications such as a commentary, where opinion and factors influencing judgement are considered, the structure of book, chapter and verse is too coarse: words and their variants or even individual characters are the basic units [12].

	Free Text	Relational stand.	Relational extend.	Semantic E-R extend.	Taxis	Object-oriented
1. Design of STRUCTURE for holding text						
. unlimited size of fields and records	yes	not yet	not yet	-	-	-
. symbolic identification of records	limited	yes	yes	yes	yes	yes
. data models						
. hierarchical	yes	yes	yes	yes	yes	yes
. non-hierarchical (shared sub-obj.)	no	no	diff.	yes	yes	yes
. ability to retain un-normalized data	yes	no	no	-	yes	yes
. dynamic control of unit size (aggreg)	no	diff.	diff.	no	yes	diff.
. generalization and specialization (inher.)	no	no	no	yes	yes	yes
2. VIEWS						
. derived structures	no	yes	yes	no	yes	yes
. parallel texts	no	no	poss.	-	poss.	poss.
3. RETRIEVAL						
. fast	yes	no	yes	-	-	-
. non-procedural interactive languages	yes	yes	yes	-	no	no
. closure	no	yes	yes	-	no	no
. words + phrases in text						
. context	yes	yes	yes	-	yes	yes
. proximity matching	yes	no	yes	-	yes	yes
. keywords						
. free vocabulary	yes	yes	yes	-	yes	yes
. controlled vocabulary (thesauri, stop)	yes	yes	yes	-	yes	yes
. 'formatted' data	limited	yes	yes	-	yes	yes
. identifiers of text (symbolic key)	limited	yes	yes	-	yes	yes
4. Various formats for DISPLAY						
. human	yes	yes	yes	-	-	-
. machine-machine (wp, mark-up)	yes	yes	yes	-	-	-
5. TEMPORAL management with consistent updating						
. in-place modification, addition of data,	yes	yes	yes	-	yes	yes
. dynamic behaviour - control of doc. life	no	no	no	no	yes	yes
. version management	no	no	no	no	yes	yes
. concurrent access	yes	yes	yes	-	-	diff.
. value inheritance for natural data loading	no	no	no	yes	yes	yes
6. INTEGRITY						
. protection against hardware failures	yes	yes	yes	-	-	-
. referential	no	yes	yes	no	yes	yes
. value	yes	yes	yes	-	yes	yes
7. SECURITY						
. whole file	yes	yes	yes	-	yes	yes
. designated fields, data driven	yes	yes	yes	-	yes	yes
8. NAVIGATION through texts following conceptual paths						
. referential transparency (hypertext)	no	yes	yes	-	yes	yes
. trail maintenance	no	yes	yes	-	yes	yes
9. Textual ANALYSIS						
. function integrated with data	no	no	no	no	yes	yes
. word frequency lists, distrib. freq.	yes	no	yes	no	yes	yes
. statistical tests e.g. sentence length	yes	no	yes	no	yes	yes
. word co-occurrences	yes	no	yes	no	yes	yes
10. SEMANTIC aids						
. parsing	no	no	poss.	-	poss.	poss.
. predicate logic, machine translation	no	no	poss.	-	poss.	poss.
. cognitive textual types	no	no	poss.	-	poss.	poss.
11. MULTI-MEDIA						
. integration of text and other data	no	no	poss.	poss.	poss.	poss.

Figure 1: User Requirements for Textbases and their Satisfaction
by Database Techniques.

The applications so far discussed in this section basically involve text in hierarchical structures with a choice of unit size for manipulation ranging from word or character up through various intermediate text units to virtually complete texts. This gives rise to the major problem of the choice of unit size.

Choice of Unit: Unlike informal systems which might store text as a continuous stream of characters, formal systems need an object unit [13]. Traditionally a choice has had to be made which is usually governed by the storage capability of the system (e.g. block sizes), by the human capacity for searching, retrieving and comprehending the information and by the character of the document which will often be determined by traditional printing techniques. Thus, for example, the size of a legal statute is controlled by parliamentary business and other political factors. However, one unit alone is insufficient for all purposes. With text objects, it should be possible, in principle, to retain the ability of natural language to keep the choice of unit dynamic and with the option of lazy evaluation to postpone any decision until the full circumstances and context of the use are known.

Non-hierarchical Text Structures: There are texts for which hierarchical structures are inadequate. Shakespeare and legal texts are good examples. Such texts need to be represented in terms of semantic models. Their essential characteristic is that units may need to be linked to multiple units at higher levels of the tree structure rather than the single unit allowed in hierarchical structures. These structures suggest the need to examine models described later where words are considered as atoms of data to be built dynamically into a variety of complex molecular objects.

Generalization and Specialization: Linked particularly with the navigation requirements described earlier is the need to generalise when describing text structures. Thus, for example, in a hierarchical text structure, any one part of the tree may usually cite any other part. The textbase can be viewed at two levels: generalisation for an abstract overview in which any type of text object cites any other type; and specialization for a more detailed representation in which a specific type of text object cites another specific type. The two levels are discussed later.

Multi-Media Systems: Of increasing importance is the storage and manipulation of textual, image and formatted data in an integrated fashion by a single system. Even in pure text systems some of the principles of a multi-media approach may need to be adopted. Multilingual textbases involving languages such as Russian, Greek and Japanese present some of the problems of multi-media systems with the need for ideographic representations of such basic text entities as characters and words.

3: Database Models and Textual Structures

Practical work at Newcastle [8], with the emphasis on legal texts, has demonstrated the potential of database technology for handling text and provided a favourable environment for formulating principles to develop a new generation of textbases. Text volumes can be very large (>100Gb). The texts need to be represented using a semantic or other model such as the basic relational, network and hierarchical methods. There has to be efficient access on both symbolic keys and words. The more expressive semantic models will be considered first.

3.1 Semantic Models

The range of semantic models includes RM/T [14], the E-R Model [15], the Borkin Semantic Model [16], and Taxis [17]. Text because of its complex nature usually requires full semantic models and a range of abstract data types to capture completely its structure and examples of Chen, Borkin and Taxis have been developed at Newcastle.

Models for Expressing Static Aspects: An E-R diagram of a UK statute is shown in Figure 2(a). A relationship flagged '*' is mandatory, otherwise it is optional. All relationships are 1:N bar one. In addition the idea of generalisation is employed with the scope of a generic entity-type being delineated by the enclosure of its associated specializations within a thickly-lined rectangle. The generic structures defined here are *node* to represent all possible text units from an act through parts and schedules to subsections and subparagraphs and *text* to represent the units holding the main part of the text - section, subsection, paragraph and subparagraph.

The idea behind *text* has already been introduced: its creation enables the involuted N:M *XRef* relationship to be simplified into an occurrence of the *text* entity-type may cite another occurrence of the *text* entity-type. In the absence of the generalization, sixteen different cross–reference relationships would be required to handle all the possible combinations: one of the occurrences of the entity-types *section*, *subsection*, *paragraph* and *subparagraph* may cite any other occurrence of the entity-types *section*, *subsection*, *paragraph* and *subparagraph*. The idea behind *node* is that a generic identifier can greatly simplify addressing and aggregation operations by removing the need for end-users to know the specific structures involved.

The base object in the E-R diagram is *word.placement* whose identifier contains two attributes *all.unit.id*, the symbolic identifier for the generalization *node*, and *word#* the physical position of the word in the unit addressed by *all.unit.id*. The entity-type *word*, representing in effect a word list, is in a 1:N relationship with *word.placement*. The nature of the identifier *all.unit.id* is described later.

Class Structures: The structure of the statutes in Figure 2(a) can be viewed as the complex object shown in Figure 3. Two types of hierarchy are embedded within the class structure:

- An aggregation hierarchy represented by solid lines to indicate potential groupings of data through 'isPartOf' relationships. The structure illustrates well the problem of unit size in which a user may seek to aggregate data at any level of the structure or search for data in the context of any simple or aggregated unit. A common aggregation will be of *word.placement* to create dynamically any specialization of the generic object *node*. This hierarchy represents incidental inheritance [18].

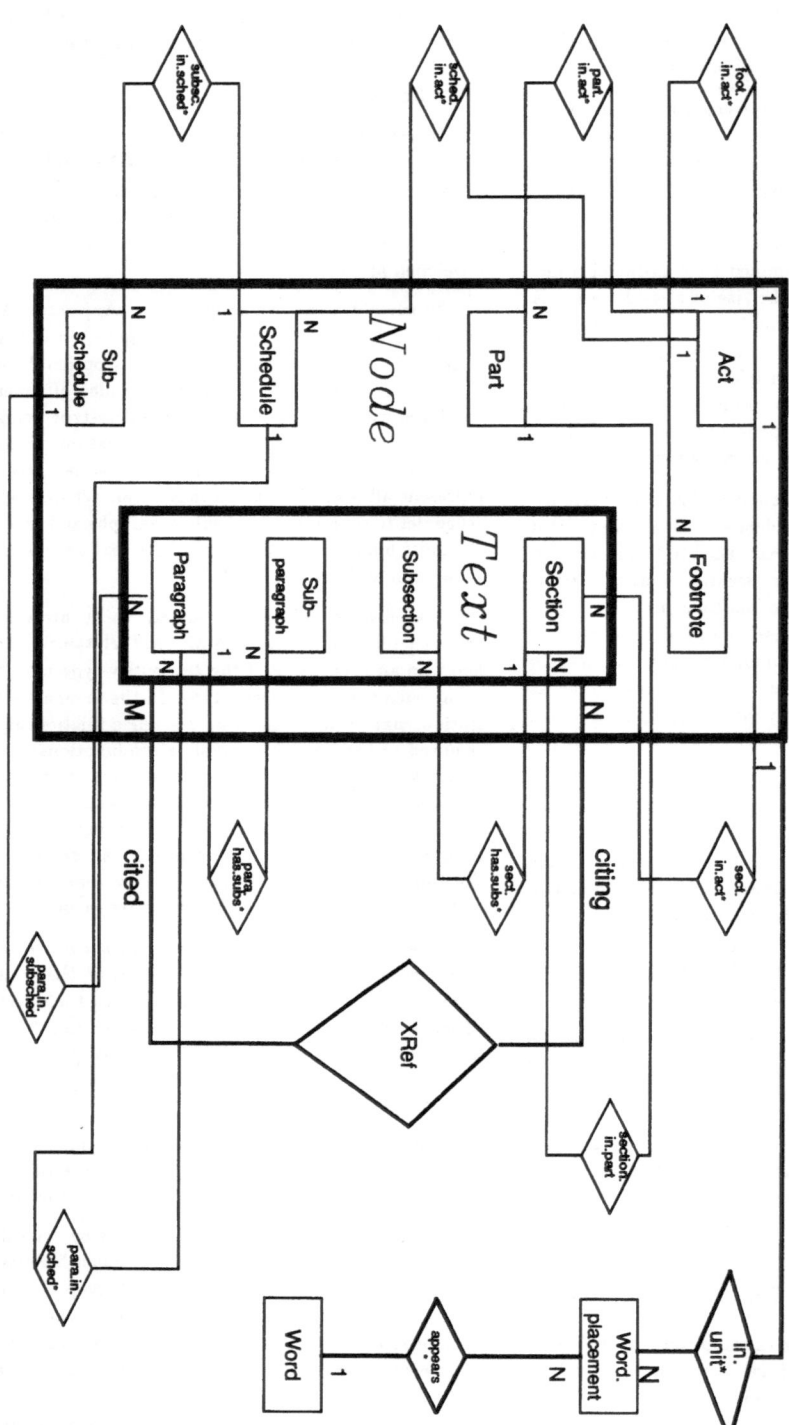

Figure 2: The Chen Entity-Relationship Model of Statutes:

(a) Diagram

Figure 2: The Chen Entity-Relationship Model of Statutes:
(b) Partially-normalized Table-types

```
Act(year, chapter, title, date, preamble, arrangements,
    crossnotes, + 14 formatting attributes)
Part(part#, year, chapter, part.headings,
    part.subheadings, crossnotes, footnotes.old.stats,
    + 5 formatting.attributes)
Section(section#, year, chapter)
Section.in.Part(section#, part#, year, chapter)
Subsection(ss#, section#, year, chapter)
Schedule(schedule#, year, chapter, schedule.headings,
    crossnotes, omissions, footnotes.old.stats,
    + 29 formatting attributes)
Subschedule(subschedule#, schedule#, year, chapter,
    subschedule.headings, crossnotes, omissions,
    footnotes.old.stats, + 29 formatting attributes)
Paragraph(para#, schedule#, year, chapter)
Para.in.Subsched(para#, subschedule#, schedule#, year,
    chapter)
Subparagraph(subp#, para#, schedule#, year, chapter)
Footnote(footnote#, year, chapter, footnote.text)
Word(word, word.description attributes)
Word.placement(all.unit.id, word#, word)
Node(all.unit.id)
Text(text.id, marginal.note.other, crossnotes,
    omissions, footnotes.old.stats,
    + 20 formatting attributes)
XRef(citing.text.id, cited.text.id)
```

Notes: 1) The italicised attributes comprise the
identifier.
2) all.unit.id, text.id, citing.text.id and
cited.text.id are defined in Figure 5.

Figure 3: Class Structure for Objects Occurring in Legal Text

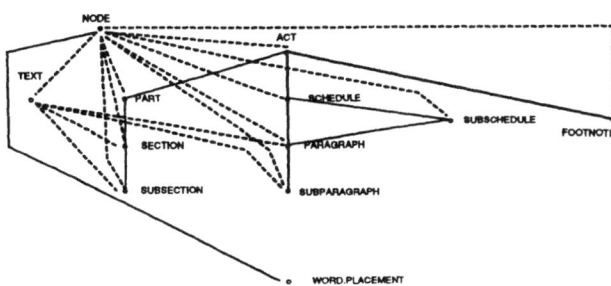

• An inheritance hierarchy represented by dotted lines to indicate the automatic inheritance of properties (attributes) by lower level objects from higher ones through 'isA' relationships. Thus *text* is a generic object from which the subobjects *section, subsection, paragraph* and *subparagraph* inherit properties such as text formatting attributes. Other forms of inheritance are for identifiers: all textual objects can inherit their identifiers from *node* as described later. This hierarchy represents essential inheritance [18].

Figure 4: Class Structure for Objects Occurring in Shakespeare's Plays

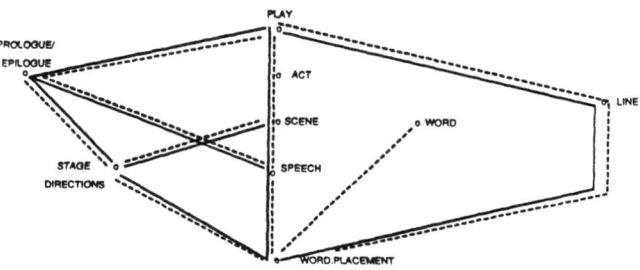

Similar rich structures are encountered in other texts such as Shakespeare's plays where the terminology of overlapping fields is used in the humanities to describe the structures. Fields are neither contiguous to each other nor contained completely within one another: lines, stage directions and speeches overlap each other with no clear structure other than that they each contain one or more words of text. This structure can be represented by the complex object shown in Figure 4 [19]. The complex object comprises one subobject *word.placement* shared by four objects: *speech, stage.directions, line* and *word*, and further subobjects *speech* and *stage.directions* shared by the same two objects *scene* and *prologue/epilogue*. The relatively physical object *line* has a well-defined relationship only with *play* and *word.placement* (a play can have numbered lines and words) and no precise mapping to the logical objects such as *speech* and *stage.directions* which may share lines of text.

Identifiers: To complete the E-R model, Figure 2(b) shows the table-types with their attributes and identifiers. It should be noted that many of the tables are not fully normalised: secondary attributes such as the text formatting ones may have multiple values associated with each identifier value. To remove such dependencies through further normalisation would require the creation of more entity-types which would complicate the model considerably and produce an un-natural structure.

For the generalization *node*, the identifier is *all.unit.id* which can be represented by the Taxis-like class structure shown in Figure 5. Each attribute qualifies one aspect of the content of an object so that the key represented by the attribute *all.unit.id* of the class *node* is a polynomial consisting of the hierarchical sequence of any object in the statute law structure. In this study, all the attributes are of type integer within the permitted ranges shown: for example, *part#* can take values between *partmin* and *partmax*. The identifier of the other generic entity-type *text* is defined also in Figure 5 as *text.id* with a subset of the attributes of *all.unit.id* inherited in the 'isA' relationship between *node* and *text*. The attributes of the entity *XRef* are the keys of the citing and cited text units *citing.text.id* and *cited.text.id* respectively. These attributes draw their values from the domain *text.id* as also shown in Figure 5.

Figure 5. Taxis-like Specification of Symbolic Key for Statutes

```
define AnyDataClass Node with
     ss#: {| ssmin:ssmax |}
     section#: {| sectmin:sectmax |}
     part#: {| partmin:partmax |}
     subp#: {| subpmin:subpmax |}
     para#: {| paramin:paramax |}
     subschedule#: {| subsmin:subsmax |}
     schedule#: {| schmin:schmax |}
     footnote#: {| footmin:footmax |}
     year: {| yearmin:yearmax |}
     chapter: {| chapmin:chapmax |}
  unique
     all.unit.id: (year, chapter, part#,
        section#, ss#, schedule#, subschedule#,
        para#, subp#, footnote#)

define AnyDataClass Text isA Node with
  changeable
     marginal.note.other: string
     crossnotes: string
     omissions: string
     footnotes.old.stats: string
     formatting.attribute1: string
     formatting.attribute2: string ... etc
  unique
     text.id: (year, chapter,
        section#, ss#, schedule#, para#, subp#)

define AnyDataClass XRef with
     citing.text.id: set of Text
     cited.text.id: set of Text
  unique
     ref.id: (citing.text.id, cited.text.id)
```

The mechanism used throughout our work for implementation of the cross-referencing process and for generality in addressing textual units is to employ generic symbolic keys as in Figure 5 to provide a powerful mechanism for flexibly manipulating the complex object structure of Figure 3 [20]. This general mechanism does not preclude direct addressing of a particular specialization such as *section* using one of the specific identifiers shown in Figure 2(b).

Models for Expressing Dynamic Aspects: Major deficiencies of the E-R and Borkin models are that they have no defined operations and thus cannot handle dynamic control of the life-cycle of entities. Semantic models which enable such dynamic structures to be expressed as well as static ones have therefore also been examined such as Taxis, the Event Model and SHM+. The model Taxis illustrates the potential of this approach and its use is being explored at Newcastle for control of the legal drafting process [8] in addition to its earlier usage for exploring structural aspects.

3.2 Basic Models

None of the basic models is rich enough in capability to satisfy all requirements in manipulating complex textual structures. The hierarchical and network models can be quickly discounted but a more detailed discussion is necessary to illustrate weaknesses in a relational approach employing 'flattening' of data.

The Relational Model: Relational systems have been used with success in administrative areas where fixed units are adequate although Codd in 1979 [14] suggested that even here variable units using a supertype-subtype approach would be useful. The E-R model given earlier for law can in principle be implemented directly by mapping the table-types in Figure 2(b) on to conventional relations, each table-type being represented by a relation. However, the semantics of the E-R diagram are now represented implicitly and the basic hierarchical structure is not explicitly conveyed to the user. To a user with detailed knowledge of relational data structures and manipulation, a clear advantage of the relational model is the ease with which keys in the form of formatted data can be manipulated giving flexibility in the choice of units for display purposes and logical addressing on symbolic keys for navigation purposes: the use of standard set operators can provide aggregation of data, dynamic variation of the unit of retrieval as users' needs change, cross-referencing and closure since each operation on a relation produces another relation [21]. To a user with little knowledge of relational structures, the disadvantage of the relational approach is that he is dependent on views predefined as external schemata by the database administrator to achieve abstractions such as aggregation. There is also no ability to retain un-normalized data in the relational model as is strictly required by the table-types of Figure 2(b).

Of equal importance, not only with most current implementations but also in developing flexible systems for the future, is the problem of indexing text in a versatile manner. There is no real concept of a global index in relational databases: a single index cannot readily be constructed for a series of attributes in different relations across the textbase to facilitate searching on a particular generalized abstraction. In Figure 2(b), it is not easy to build a single index on the abstraction *text* of data-type *word*. Lynch and Stonebraker discuss this problem further [22].

Extended Relational Approach: The logical approach to improve the flexibility of relational systems in manipulating text is to flatten the data so that it is completely normalized down to the word level. In principle, the existence of relations holding words, together with their positions in the text, and of the base relations shown in Figure 2(b) provides data structures which can satisfy most user requirements. However, some features of Figure 2(b) are not easy to represent relationally. The key attributes *text.id*, *citing.text.id* and *cited.text.id* which are essential for generalization cannot strictly be defined in the manner of Figure 5 as that conflicts with the entity integrity rule. A further disadvantage in the approach of flattening the data is that no standard set operators exist for constructing the word indexes and it is not realistic to expect users to input such structures manually. Operators to perform the flattening of normal text could be user-written but this would involve additional effort and would be likely to result in inefficient code.

In an earlier paper [23], the manipulation of text in relational databases was considered in detail using the example of the Bible. It was found feasible to normalize textual data to at least the word level and to employ SQL or relational algebra for searching the data against different unit sizes and for aggregating the data as necessary. The biblical data were represented by a complex object with the single path:

testament -> book -> chapter -> verse -> word.placement

Even with the relatively simple biblical example, the approach of 'flattening' the data was found to be cumbersome for data manipulation, to hide the natural structure of the data from the user and to have adverse performance implications when reconstituting aggregations for documents in large textbases. Current work at Newcastle on Shakespeare's "The Tempest" [19] has shown that, for the complex object with multiple paths and shared subobjects shown in Figure 4, it is possible to give a user all facilities with standard set operators. However, only with extensive mediation, between the system and the user, is a natural interface provided with a high level of data abstraction.

4: Object Oriented Systems

In advanced languages such as Ada and Simula, the concept of class structure and variable unit size is well established through the extensible type system with the ability to declare abstract data types. These languages also allow subobjects to inherit properties from higher-level objects and provide communication between objects. Systems based on the object-oriented paradigm readily facilitate iterative searching of complex objects and multiple levels of abstraction and have a natural ability to handle dynamic aspects with function fully integrated with data [24], all important issues for textbases.

The use of object-oriented programs for database management is in its early stages. Advances depend on programming systems being developed to handle persistent data such as in the early work by Atkinson with PS-Algol [25]. One of the first developments was GemStone [26] which is related to SmallTalk. Here, class structures with inheritance abstractions can be defined, object identity is preserved and objects participate in one or more collections to provide a shared subobject facility. Behavioural aspects are handled by messaging. Aggregation of objects can be handled only by external operations on the participating objects: the aggregation abstraction cannot be directly represented.

The strengths of the object-oriented approach lie in the ability to import advanced programming techniques into areas of data modelling in which database technology has been traditionally weak. However, in the management of persistent data, object-oriented systems have a number of significant weaknesses. These include many of the standard functions which are an essential part of any database system. Thus security, concurrency, transaction control, archiving and some aspects of integrity are achieved by primitive methods, if at all. Optimisation of data storage and indexing are at an early stage perhaps analagous to that of the first relational systems but there are perhaps some more fundamental problems [27] relating to the variable depths of the paths needed to realise object values and the need to respect the encapsulation of objects. In the area of office automation, Weiser & Lochovsky have employed a relational database system to provide the persistent data management component of the object-oriented system OZ+ [28]. Whilst this is adequate for short- to medium-sized textual strings, there would be considerable problems in indexing and searching the large volumes of text found in full-text documents which is a major feature of our type of application.

Of greatest significance, perhaps, is that owing to their procedural nature, many object-oriented systems do not provide the non-procedural interactive languages that end-users require for data manipulation. Procedural interfaces requiring some knowledge of high-level programming languages may be acceptable in engineering applications where the clientale usually has a relatively sophisticated programming background. However, in areas such as text and office automation, it is considered that procedural interfaces are not appropriate. Clearly, ad hoc query languages could be designed for applications by writing an interface program in a host language. The more durable non-procedural languages have been based on mathematical methods, such as relational calculus and algebra, applied to a conceptual model of the data. There is thus, owing to a lack of emphasis on conceptual modelling techniques, a layer of control missing from current object-oriented systems to provide the necessary user environment. There are also difficulties with closure: if the result of a query is presented as a table, that is not a viable structure for further work.

Other work has centred on extending the relational model in an object-oriented manner. Stonebraker has considered how relational systems can be extended to be applied to a wider range of applications. In Postgres [29], abstract data types with property inheritance can be defined by the user and attributes can be of type *procedure* calling code written by the user in C or QUEL. This system also provides rules which enable constraints to be readily applied and time-stamps all data as a first step towards version management. One of the problems with the procedures is that, on execution, the return of a multi-valued set as an attribute value produces an un-normalized relation so that the property of closure is lost. Further, the reliance on procedures to achieve abstractions rather than on higher-level modelling constructions offends end-users who require non-procedural access.

5: Discussion

The last six columns of Figure 1 show the extent to which our critical requirements for textbases are met by the techniques of free text retrieval, ISO-standard relational database, extended relational database with facilities to flatten textual data, semantic models oriented towards static and dynamic aspects such as E-R and Taxis respectively, and object-oriented systems. A hyphen in a column indicates incomplete information is available.

Free text retrieval systems suffer from limited data structuring ability, lack of navigational aids and an inability to model dynamic behaviour. Standard relational systems provide better data structuring and navigational facilities but their performance in context searching, other than on base units, is questionable and proximity searching is not available. Extended relational

486

systems with flattened textual data can achieve a better performance and, through some ability to model complex objects, provide the basis of a unified model for multi-media data and of initiatives in advanced text processing such as semantic parsing. However, aggregation is a cumbersome task for a user and dynamic behaviour is not addressed. The E-R model has not been directly implemented so the information in the figure is incomplete but, with the lack of defined operations, it cannot be a complete answer to users' problems. The object-oriented approaches appear to offer the most promise whether in the guise of semantic models like Taxis or databases such as Gem-Stone. Such systems handle quite naturally variable unit size, shared subobjects, dynamic behaviour and integration of function and data, and have considerable promise in multi-media modelling. The semantic models, in particular, also handle aggregation well through subtyping declarations. However, so far, object-oriented systems have presented relatively procedural interfaces to users, do not readily provide closure, are rather limited in standard database functions such as concurrent access and have not proved themselves in terms of performance. The optimum solution for users of textbases would therefore appear to be a merger of advanced database technology as in semantically-enriched relational systems with advanced object-oriented programming to create object-oriented textbases. Such textbases should be thought of as object-bases rather than pure database or object-oriented systems. It should not be pretended that such a merger will be easy. The cultural differences between the two approaches present many difficulties [30] and much research of a fundamental nature is still required to attain a single complete multi-media model.

REFERENCES

[1] Pasquier-Boltuck, J, Grossman, E, & Collaud, G, (1988), Prototyping an Interactive Electronic Book System using an Object Oriented Approach, in: *Lect. Notes Comp. Sci.*, Springer-Verlag **322** 177-190.

[2] Brown, P J, (1988), Hypertext: the way forward, in: *Document Manipulation and Typography*, ed. van Vliet, J C, Cambridge 183-191.

[3] Furuta, R, & Stotts, P D, (1989), Programmable Browsing Semantics in Trellis, in: *Hypertext'89 Proc.*, Special Issue - SIGCHI Bull. 27-42.

[4] Tompa, F W, (1989), A Data Model for Flexible Hypertext Data Base Systems, *ACM Trans Information Systems* 7(1) 85-106.

[5] Croft, W B, & Stemple, D W, (1987), Supporting Office Document Architectures with Constrained Types, *ACM SIGMOD Rec*, **16**(3) 504-509.

[6] Murata, M, (1989), Object-oriented Interpretation of ODA, in: *WOODMAN'89*, edd. André, J, & Bézivin, J, BIGRE **63-64** 91-100.

[7] Heather, M A, & Rossiter, B N, (1989), Theoretical Structures for Object-based Text, in: *WOODMAN'89*, edd. André, J, & Bézivin, J, BIGRE **63-64** 178-192.

[8] Rossiter, B N, & Heather, M A, (1990), *Towards the Object Oriented Text Base*, Computing Lab., University of Newcastle upon Tyne, Tech. Rep. 297.

[9] Zellweger, P T, (1989), Scripted Documents: A Hypermedia Path Mechanism, in: *Hypertext'89 Proc.*, Special Issue - SIGCHI Bull. 1-14.

[10] T J Sillitoe, B N Rossiter and M A Heather (1990), Trail Management in Hypertext: in: *BNCOD-8 Proc.*, ed. A Brown, Pitman.

[11] Rossiter, B N, Davis, P, Goodman, D S G, Ward, M K, & Heather, M A (1988), Generalised DBMS as a tool for research, *University Computing* **10**(2) 71-79.

[12] Heather, M A, & Rossiter, B N, (1989), A Generalized Database Management Approach to Textual Analysis, in: *Proc. 2nd Int. Colloq. Bible and Computer: Methods, Tools, Results*, ed. Poswick, R-F, Champion-Slatkine, Paris-Geneva 519-535.

[13] Heather, M A, (1986), Future Generation Systems in the Service of the Law, in: *Automated Analysis of Legal Texts*, edd. Martino, A A, Socci Natali, F, North-Holland 643-660.

[14] Codd, E F, (1979), Extending the Database Relational Model to capture more meaning, *ACM TODS* **4** 397-434.

[15] Chen, P P-S, (1976), The Entity-Relationship Model - towards a unified view of data, *ACM TODS* **1**(1) 9-36.

[16] Borkin, S A, (1979), *Equivalence properties of semantic data bases for database systems*, Tech. Rep. Lab. Computing Science, MIT, TR-206.

[17] Mylopoulos, J, Bernstein, P A, & Wong, H K T, (1980), A Language Facility for Designing Database-Intensive Facilities, *ACM TODS* **5** 185-207.

[18] Sakkinen, M, (1989), Disciplined Inheritance, *ECOOP'89 Proceedings*, ed. Cook, S, Cambridge 39-56.

[19] Mitchell, J S, (1989), *Implementation of a Relational Textbase*, M.Sc. Dissertation, Computing Laboratory, University of Newcastle upon Tyne D429.

[20] Rossiter, B N, & Heather, M A, (1988), Data Models and Legal Text, *CC-AI* **5**(1) 39-55.

[21] Rossiter, B N, (1986), Full Text Database Management Systems: A Model and Implementation for Law, in: *Automated Analysis of Legal Texts*, edd. Martino, A A, & Socci Natali, F, North-Holland, Amsterdam 899-916.

[22] Lynch, C, & Stonebraker, M, (1988), Extended User-defined Indexing with Application to Textual Databases, in: *Proc. 14th Int. Conf. on VLDB*, Los Angeles 1988.

[23] Heather, M A, & Rossiter, B N, (in press), Syntactical Relations in Parallel Text, in: *Proc. 15th Int. ALLC Conf.*, ed. Choueka, Y, Jerusalem 1988.

[24] Bloom, T, & Zdonik, S B, (1987), Issues in the Design of Object-oriented Database Languages, *OOPSLA'87 Conf. Proc.*, ACM SIGPLAN **22**(12) 441-451.

[25] Atkinson, M P, Chisholm, K J, & Cockshott, W P, (July 1981), PS-Algol: an Algol with a persistent heap, *ACM SIGPLAN* **17**(7).

[26] Bretl, R, Maier, D, Otis, A, Penney, J, Schuchardt, B, Stein, J, Williams, E H, & Williams, M, (1989), The GemStone Data Management System, in: *Object-Oriented Concepts, Databases, & Applications*, edd. Kim, W, & Lochovsky, F H, Addison-Wesley 283-308.

[27] Maier, D, (1986), Indexing in an Object-Oriented DBMS, *Proceedings International Workshop on Object-Oriented Database Systems*, IEEE 171-182.

[28] Weiser, S P, & Lochovsky, F H, (1989), OZ+: An Object-Oriented Database System, in: *Object-Oriented Concepts, Data Bases, & Applications*, edd. Kim, W, & Lochovsky, F H, Addison-Wesley 309-337.

[29] Stonebraker, M, Anton, J, & Hanson, E, (1987), Extending a Database System with Procedures, *ACM TODS* **12**(3) 350-376.

[30] Tsichritzis, D C, & Nierstrasz, O M, (1988), Fitting Round Objects into Square Databases, in: *Lect. Notes Comp. Sci.*, Springer-Verlag **322** 283-299.

Machine Accessible Communications for the Office Environment

Sashidhar P. Reddi

The Wharton School of the University of Pennsylvania

Abstract

A significant number of communications within an organization are routine but essential for conducting business. We propose a means by which such routine activities may be transferred to an intelligent communications system. This paper presents a rich and theoretically founded language, that provides the user with great expressibility in stating his message, and the design of a system to support the language. The precise structure and definition of the language makes the content of the messages accessible to processing by computers and facilitates inferencing. We have also included an overview of a language-based system's implementation and functionality for the domain of office communications.

1 Current means of electronic communication

1.1 Electronic mail and Tagged messages

Electronic mail, in the form that it is currently used, typically consists of a header that indicates the sender and the receiver of the message, the time of transmission and an address or a path to be used in transmitting the message to the receiver. The body of the message is written in natural language text. So currently the use of electronic mail for business communications would entail the active participation of a human being. The person who receives the message, however rudimentary the content, would need to read the message and manually update his/her database to incorporate the new information.

To overcome the hurdles posed by a message with purely a natural language content an appealing step would be to structure the message in a manner that makes at least a part of the message open to computer processing. The message may now consist of a set of fields and possibly an accompanying body of text. The sender and the receiver of the message agree on the meaning of the values placed in each of the fields. If one wanted to send a message indicating that some person A was interested in selling some item X for Y dollars, then the message would have a field to indicate the type of message, "an offer to sell" in this case, the potential seller, A, the type of item, X, and the price, Y. A system that receives a number of these messages could prune out the ones with less attractive offers and inform the user of the better options he/she has for buying the item X.

Tagged messages, as we shall refer to them, allow us to realize some of our goals of finding a good means of business communication. They may be used to eliminate the need for constant human intervention when dealing with messages of the most routine kind. In fact, these semi-structured messages have been the focus of research in developing intelligence-based electronic mail systems ([16], [17], [18], [3], [4], [5], [8], [9]). Tagged messages, however, suffer from their inability to deal with a large segment of business communications. We would be hard pressed to say

(1) Mr. Smith offers to sell X to Ms. Brown for Y dollars if Ms. Brown promises to make the payment by the 10th of June.

(1) is an ordinary enough message and one may be tempted to state that we could build a message which has the necessary fields. That may be true but a message like (2) would demand another message structure.

(2) Mr. Smith offers to sell X to Ms. Brown for Y dollars if Steve also offers to sell X to Ms. Brown for Y dollars.

And there is no end to the number of message types we need to handle the different kinds of messages possible in a typical business transaction. It is possible that an organization would just like to automate the handling of its most frequently used messages in which case tagged messages are indeed an useful tool. However tags make it difficult to quantify over terms in the message or to capture messages like the one below where there is a possibly large set of iterations in the statement.

(3) The President requested the CFO to order his subordinates to send a reply to the company's clients within three working days.

If one sees the difficulty in the construction of tags that permit one to convey non-trivial information, he may discover that the development of a language is a natural next step to overcoming the problems posed by tagged messages. Stating how different tags combine to form a statement is equivalent to defining a language and if that language is extended to allow for quantification and iteration then we are in possession of a more powerful and convenient tool for representing messages. We will present a language based method by which messages like (1), (2) and (3) are represented and dealt with in a relatively easy manner.

0.1 EDI

Electronic Data Interchange (EDI) is an electronic form of communication that is beginning to get noticed by a growing number of organizations interested in capitalizing on the progress made in computer networking (see [6], [7]). The aim of EDI is also to capture the more routine messages in a manner that allows the information to be processed by a computer. If we intended to automate a "sales" message then the potential users of the message need to agree on the various fields that such a message would need to have. This list of fields must be complete. It must also be determined what the size of each of these fields will be and the type of values they can hold. When this is done, the protocol for the new message type is added to the EDI system at some cost. Unlike a tagged message system that lies on top of the network software, an EDI based system is implemented at a lower level, thereby making the modification of an existing protocol expensive and time consuming.

As the information to be conveyed by organizations involved in different businesses would be different, there are a number of EDI protocols in use. If an organization were involved in diverse business activities, it would need to use different protocols. It is not uncommon to find more than one protocol in a given sphere of business activity. Though the benefits of EDI are sufficiently great to lure the business community, EDI's growth is hampered by this proliferation of protocols.Modifying an EDI protocol involves a substantial cost thus forcing EDI users to build/buy software to translate from one protocol to another. There are attempts underway to remedy the situation, however EDI like the tagged messages suffers from its short sighted approach at providing a means of dealing with only the rigidly structured messages. Current EDI protocols would be incapable of dealing with messages of the form (1), (2) or (3).

0.2 Formal languages

There is a growing interest in the use of *formal languages* for communications (see [10], [11], [12], [13], [14]). Statements written in first order logic can be manipulated to make inferences that are provably correct with respect to the assumptions made during the manipulations. Literature in Artificial Intelligence and other related fields provides us with an ample number of such examples. Moreover first order logic is well understood and theoretically founded so that for any inferences drawn from a given set of statements in first order logic and a set of accompanying assumptions one may provide a correctness proof to support the conclusions. Inspired by this one may attempt to see if some use could be made of first order logic to represent the typical statements encountered in our domain. Consider the earlier example of person A offering to sell item X for Y dollars.

(4) A offers to sell item X for Y dollars.

Drawing on work in *Speech Act Theory* (see [19], [1], [2], [15]), one may visualize this statement as consisting of two parts. One is the predication which in this case may be

((predicate sell) (seller A) (buyer ?B) (item X) (price-in-dollars Y) ....)

The predicate may have other arguments like the place of sale and the time of sale. "?B" is a variable that is currently uninstantiated. This predication does not completely capture the meaning of (4). The second part of the statement is A's attitude towards the predication. The complete translation of (4) may be

((attitude offer) (holder-of-attitude A) (towards-whom-the-attitude-is-held ?B) (predication ((predicate sell) (seller A) (buyer ?B) (item X) (price-in-dollars Y) ....))

Say we decide on the arguments of the predicate "sell". Then the statement (4) may be simply written as

(offer A ?B (sell A ?B X Y ....))

This representation of sentences has its roots in work in linguistic philosophy. If we accept the view of certain philosophers like Searle, then we can treat all utterances as consisting of two parts, the attitude and the content. Consider the following examples to appreciate the distinction between the attitude and the content.

(5) Would you like me to sign the contract ?
(6) Would you like me to SIGN THE CONTRACT ?
(7) Sign the contract.
(8) Please sign the contract.

Sentences (4) to (7) use the same predicate "sign" and if the name of the speaker were Mr. Smith and that of the hearer Ms. Brown, then the relevant predication for the four sentences would be

((predicate sign) (who-should-sign ?X) (what-should-be-signed ?Y) ...)

But the different meanings of the sentences is captured by using the correct attitude. We may rewrite sentences (4) to (7) as

(5') (query Mr. Smith Ms. Brown (sign Mr. Smith contract-26 ...))
(6') (protest Mr. Smith Ms. Brown (sign Mr. Smith contract-26 ...))
(7') (order Mr. Smith Ms. Brown (sign Ms. Brown contract-26 ...))
(8') (request Mr. Smith Ms. Brown (sign Ms. Brown contract-26 ...))

Once we accept the need for propositional attitudes we may begin a more detailed study of their role in communication. The sentences (1) and (2), if said by Tom to Dick, may be represented as

(1) Tom writes to Dick that " Mr. Smith offers to sell X to Ms. Brown for Y dollars if Ms. Brown promises to make the payment by the 10th of June."

(assert Tom Dick (if (promise Ms. Brown Mr. Smith (pay Ms. Brown Mr. Smith Y 10th-June ...)) then (offer Mr. Smith Ms. Brown (sell Mr. Smith Ms. Brown X Y ...))))

(2) Tom writes to Dick that " Mr. Smith offers to sell X to Ms. Brown for Y dollars if Steve also offers to sell X to Ms. Brown for Y dollars."

(assert Tom Dick (if (offer Steve Ms. Brown (sell Steve Ms. Brown X Y ...)) then (offer Mr. Smith Ms. Brown (sell Mr. Smith Ms. Brown X Y ...))))

It may be seen that a large subset of business communications can be represented correctly using a combination of predicates and attitudes. The exact syntactic and semantic constraints required to ensure the construction of a precise and unambiguous message is discussed in the next section. Please note that logical operators like "and", "or" and "not" as well as the quantifiers of first order logic may be used in the construction of the message. The current implementation does not support quantification since the message becomes difficult to process, however the rest of the ideas described have been implemented and the types of inferences that can be drawn is the topic of a later section of this paper.

1 Specification of the language

1.1 Language must be complete

Any system attempting to capture the information being communicated in a message must address the issue of being able to correctly represent any valid sentence of the English language. This is a tall order. One may come up with a means of representing each and every English sentence but such a representation would inevitably run the risk of being so complex that its use in automating communications would be questionable. There is a compromise to be reached between having a powerful language capable of conveying every nuance of the written word and having a language that is simple enough to lend itself naturally to computer processing. Where one must draw the line is open to debate and hence our language (or any language) may be termed inadequate in either one or both of these respects.

The language that we have chosen allows the use of an arbitrary number of predicates and arguments combined by one or more logical operators. The exact form of a sentence in the language is governed by the BNF rules that have been specified later in the paper.

Every communication must state
The Sender : The person who originates the message
The Receiver : The person to whom the message is addressed
The Content : The information being conveyed is the content of the message and is represented in the language specified so as to make it accessible to the computer.
The Context : This indicates the context in which this message is being sent.
The Message Id : This is an unique alphanumeric string that may be used to refer to this message.

Though one is tempted to allow the context to contain any and all information relevant to this communication, pragmatic concerns (similar to the compromise reached in the design of the language) prompted us to restrict it to be a list of the message-ids that were sent prior to this communication and have a direct bearing on its contents.

1.2 A BNF specification of the language

message ::= (<sender> <receiver> <content> <context> <message-id>)

sender ::= <address-term>
receiver ::= <address-term>
address-term ::= reddi@cs.nyu.edu / kimbrough@wharton.upenn
/ ......

content ::= <message-statement> / (and <message-statement> <message-statement-list>)
message-statement-list ::= <message-statement> / <message-statement> <message-statement-list>
message-statement ::= (<attitude> <sender> <receiver> <statement> <context> <statement-id>) context ::= (<message-id-list>) / nil
message-id-list ::= <message-id> <message-id-list> / <message-id>
message-id ::= (<sender> <time-point>)

The *content* of the message is always a *message-statement* or a conjunction of *message-statement*. A *message-statement* has the *sender* expressing something to the *receiver*.

attitudinal-statement ::= (<attitude> <holder-of-attitude> <towards-whom-this-attitude-is-held> <statement> <context> <statement-id>)

attitude ::= assert / request / command / offer / ......
(* possibly domain independent *)
holder-of-attitude ::= <name-term>
towards-whom-this-attitude-is-held ::= <name-term>

The *context* allows us to refer to other statements inside the same message or in other messages. The nature of *statement* is very important and determines the expressability of the language. We would like to allow an *attitudinal-statement* to be nested inside another such statement. For example we might want to say "A requests B to offer C SomeThing."

(request A B (offer B C SomeThing ....) ....)

We would also like to be able to say sentences such as "A asserts to B that C is absent from date-1 to date-2."

(assert A B (is (absent C) date-1 date-2))

So we allow *predicate-statements* and also logical combinations of attitudinal-statements and predicate-statements to be nested in the outer attitudinal statement. We would also want to allow quantification over the *statement*. Two other types of structures that we would like to allow for are *conditional-statements* and *temporal-statements*.

statement ::= <attitudinal-statement> / <predicate-statement> / (<logical-operator> <statement> <statement-list>) / (not <statement>) / <quantified-statement> / <conditional-statement> / <temporal-statement>

quantified-statement ::= (<quantifier> <variable> <statement>

quantifier ::= there-exists / forall

conditional-statement ::= (if <condition> then <statement> [else <statement>])
condition ::= <statement> / true / false

logical-operator ::= and / exclusive-or / inclusive-or

The *predicate-statement* may be describing a state or a process in which case we need two time points to demarcate the interval over which the corresponding *predication* holds. If the predicate-statement is an event then we associate the "event time" with the predication.

> *predicate-statement ::= (is/occurs <predication> <time-point> <time-point>) / (occur <predication> <time-point>)*
>
> *predication ::= (<predicate> <argument-list>)*
> *argument-list ::= <argument> <argument-list> / <argument>*
>
> *argument ::= <ground-term> / <function>*
> *function ::= (<functor> <argument-list>)*
> *functor ::= name-of-person / time-of-message-transmission / ..... (* domain dependent *)*
> *predicate ::= sell / buy / deliver / ..... (* domain dependent *)*
> *ground-term ::= "Mr. Smith" / contract-2639 / project-39.9 / ..... (* data dependent *)*

The *temporal-statement* is interesting in that it should allow reasonably complex temporal information to be conveyed without being prone to large amounts of ambiguity. This ambiguity would have to be removed using semantic rules to identify which of the possible interpretations is the intended one.

> *temporal-statement ::= (<temporal-operator> <temporal-argument> <temporal-argument>)*
>
> *temporal-argument ::= <attitudinal-statement> / <predicate-statement> / (<logical-operator> <statement> <statement-list>) / (not <statement>) / <quantified-statement>*
>
> *temporal-operator ::= after / before / until / while......*
> *(* domain independent *)*

The basic intuition behind the syntax of the language is to provide for the recursive use of constructs up to an indefinite depth. The meaning of the predication may be obtained by unfolding the predication methodically using well-understood principles of first order logic.

The above BNF describes the structure of the language as being implemented in our messaging system. The current implementation does not support temporal operators or quantification. Most messages convey some temporal information and this is indeed an important requirement and is currently being addressed. One may get around the absence of explicit temporal operators by having temporal arguments within the predicates.

1.3 Language must be unambiguous

The logical operators, "and", "exclusive-or", "inclusive-or" and "not", do not behave the same way they do in first order logic. The presence of propositional attitudes modify their behavior. Consider the following sentences.

> (9) (offer Mr. Jones Ms. Brown (and (sell Mr. Jones Ms. Brown widgets ....) (sell Mr. Jones Ms. Brown gadgets ....)))
>
> (10) (and (offer Mr. Jones Ms. Brown (sell Mr. Jones Ms. Brown widgets ....) (offer Mr. Jones Ms. Brown (sell Mr. Jones Ms. Brown gadgets ....)))

(9) seems to imply that Ms. Brown may choose to buy both widgets and gadgets but not just one of them. (10) on the other hand gives Ms. Brown the choice of agreeing to buy only widgets or only gadgets or both widgets and gadgets. Consider the same sentences with "or" instead of "and".

> (11) (offer Mr. Jones Ms. Brown (or (sell Mr. Jones Ms. Brown widgets ....) (sell Mr. Jones Ms. Brown gadgets ....)))
>
> (12) (or (offer Mr. Jones Ms. Brown (sell Mr. Jones Ms. Brown widgets ....) (offer Mr. Jones Ms. Brown (sell Mr. Jones Ms. Brown gadgets ....)))

Whether the "or" is exclusive or inclusive, both (11) and (12) seem to imply the same thing. Consider the two sentences below.

> (13) (.... (assert Mr. Jones Ms. Brown (and (is-a-holiday Christmas) (is-a-holiday Easter))) ....)
>
> (14) (.... (and (assert Mr. Jones Ms. Brown (is-a-holiday Christmas)) (assert Mr. Jones Ms. Brown (is-a-holiday Easter))) ....)

Here (13) and (14) have the same meaning. This implies that the interpretation of the logical operators changes with the propositional attitudes present in their scope. Since the number of propositional attitudes and the number of logical operators is small and domain independent, it is possible to write semantic rules that describe the interpretation of the message.

2 The office domain

The first domain for which our language-based messaging system was tested was office communications. Any communication that is typically used within an organization may be considered to fall within this domain.

We have identified seven general message types for the office context (see [11] for a more complete discussion of the seven message types). The names we have selected for these seven message types hopefully reflect the purpose that they usually serve. Note that the system is in no way restricted to these seven messages. As will be explained when discussing the functionality of the system the system administrator may see fit to introduce other message types or predicates. These are the message types we used to test the inferencing capability of our system:

- **read/review/comment** : Read/review/comment (RRC) provides the speaker with the capability to distribute documents and messages to people and to assign one or more people to read, act upon as appropriate, and possibly critique a document. The speaker may request the hearer to send an acknowledgement upon receipt of the message.

- **appointment** : Appointments play an important role in the functioning of an organization. This message may be used to request for an appointment or a meeting. The recipient of the message may reply by either accepting the request or by giving an appropriate reason for denying the request. The elaborateness of the reason given would naturally depend on the relationship between the speaker and the hearer.

- **dissemination of information** : The manager may want to disseminate some interesting information to people in the organization. It is up to the recipients of this message to act, or not act, upon receiving this message.

- **staff action** : This message type is used to issue directives such as assigning a person to attend a meeting, or an entire office to work on a project. Normally, one or more responses by the hearer are required. When the speaker desires additional responses, such as message receipt confirmation, capability of meeting project due date, and acknowledgement of intermediate due dates (milestones), then these must be explicitly requested by the speaker.

- **query for information** : A query for information is closely related to a staff action. The information requested in a query is expected to exist already and the effort to collect the information is thought to be minor. A staff action would be used to produce, or substantially process, the information, while a query is intended to result in a relatively easy retrieval of information.

- **absence** : The absence message type allows speakers to give notification of planned and authorized future absences. When such an announcement is appropriately made, office procedures may be more or less automatically altered in order to maintain office functionality at a high level.

- **statement** : While a dissemination of information carries with it only the implication that the speaker thinks the content might be of interest to the hearer, a statement message is an assertion by the speaker, to the hearer, that the content of the message is in fact true.

Given this general description of the seven message types and their uses in existing (not automated) office contexts, we now proceed to a brief description of the system and its current functionality.

3 The design and functionality of the system

3.1 The design

The system may be functionally divided into three components. One component, referred to as the sender's component, helps the user construct his message and transmit it. The second component, called the receiver's component, helps the user interpret any message he receives and update his database with any new information that he receives. This component, in a sense, provides tools to help manage information. The third component, called the superuser's component, allows the superuser to define/modify message types and the predicates that constitute a particular message and also add/delete users from the system. The design of the first two components are illustrated in figures 1 and 2. The superuser's component may be considered to be a collection of independent modules performing the administrative functions outlined later in this section. Below, we have provided a brief description of the modules that constitute the sender's and the receiver's components.

3.1.1 message construction

It would be unrealistic to expect the user to learn the syntax and the semantics of the language described earlier and input his/her messages in that language to the system. This module is responsible for guiding the user through the construction of the message and concurrently capturing the contents of the message in the language's representation.The construction of the message proceeds with a menu-based prompting for the predicates the user wants to use and the successful filling of those predicates with the correct types of arguments. The defined syntax of the language determines the nature of the menu displayed. If the user selects a predicate to be used then the system prompts for its arguments, some of which may be optional.

3.1.2 constraint checker

For each argument, to the predicate, that the user provides the constraint checker module ensures that the argument satisfies all the specified constraints on the argument's value. This enables the user to construct a meaningful and unambiguous message quickly.

Assuming that the superuser uses meaningful names to denote arguments, we have a way of learning something about the type of value that the argument should be given. The system scans the argument for familiar strings like *when*, *time* and *date* and infers that a temporal argument is expected. It then ensures that a valid date/time is being specified by the user.

3.1.3 the regeneration module

Once the system has represented the message in an acceptable logical form that conforms to the syntax of our language, it regenerates the message so that the user may check the message before approving its transmission. The message regeneration module is also required when a message is received by the system and is to be displayed to the user. The regeneration module may be a simple predicate expander which ensures the correct use of number and gender. The system currently does not have a sophisticated regeneration module. It does have a simple reformatting module that displays the message in a readable manner so that the user can check it before committing himself to sending it or acting upon it in any way.

3.1.4 the message transmission module

When a message needs to be sent the system retrieves the recipient's name or designation (depending on what was provided) and searches its mailing-address database to find the recipient's address and transmits the message through the network. During the construction of the message itself the system checks to ensure that the recipient specified is indeed a valid user known to the system thus preventing the user from wasting time in the construction of a message that cannot be sent.

3.1.5 the message reception module

When a system receives a message it retrieves, from the recipient's **message database**, all those messages mentioned in the context of the new message and passes the set of messages to the inference module. When the inference module has understood the contents and the purpose of the message it forwards the relevant parts of the message (modified to reflect the context in which it was sent)

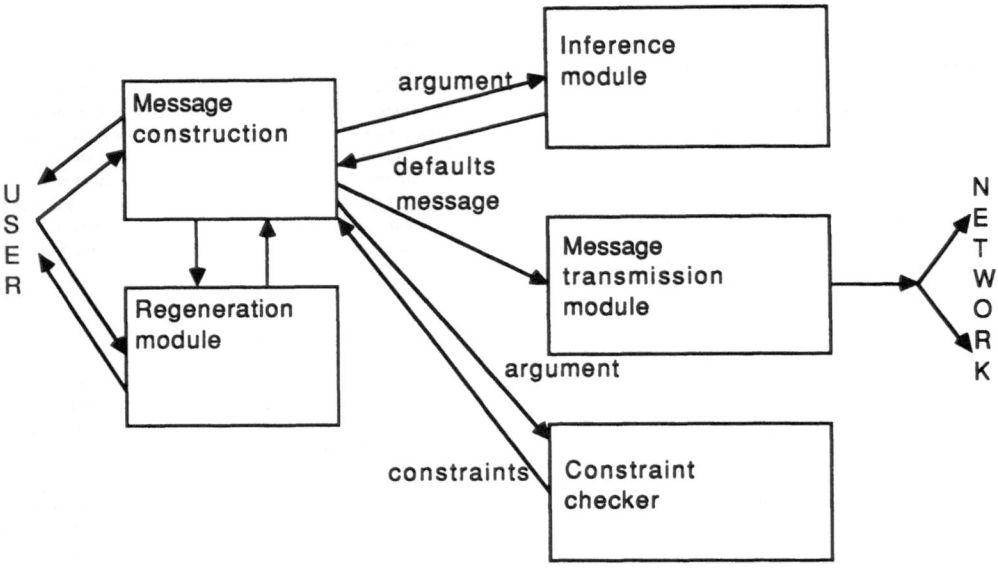

Figure 1: the sender's component

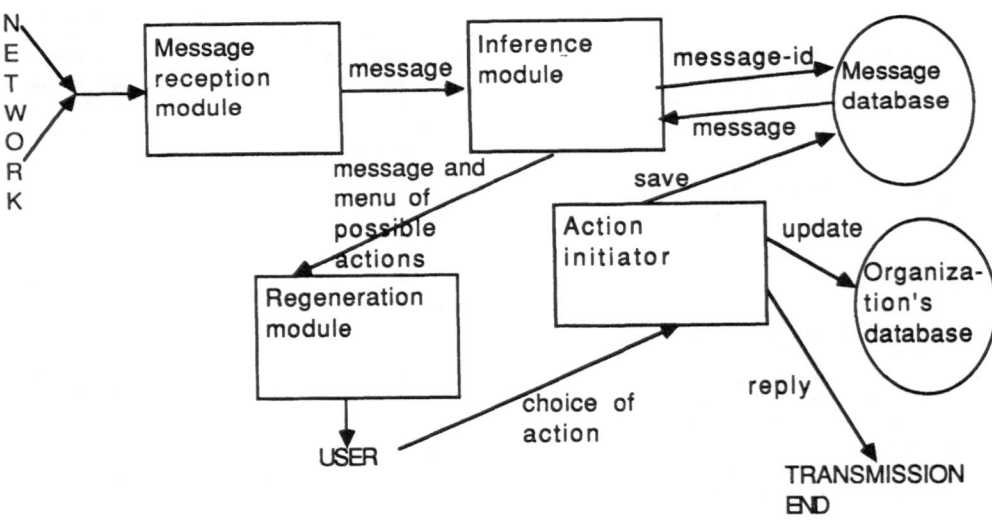

Figure 2: the receiver's component

to the user interface which displays the message in simple natural language using the regeneration module.

3.1.6 action initiator

After the received message is displayed to the user, the action initiator informs the user about the actions available to him. He may decide to *save* the message in his message database, or *reply* to it, or *forward* the message and his reply to someone that he thinks may find it interesting, or *update* his own database (which is a part of the organization's database). He also has the option of asking the system to remind him, with the contents of the message, at a later time.

3.1.7 the inference module

This is naturally the most important component of a messaging system and the work done in the development of the language was aimed at facilitating the design of this module. Though one would like to see an inference engine that would serve well in many diverse domains, AI research literature has repeatedly proved the impracticality of the idea. It is only natural that the system would need detailed and specific knowledge of the domain to draw any non-trivial inference.

Domain information plays a role at every stage of the system's operation. When constructing a message the user must be provided access to only those message types that are relevant to the domain. Within a message he can only use those predicates which convey meaningful information in that domain. The inference module is responsible for providing the message construction module with the acceptable message types and predicates. It also provides the message construction module with default values to save the user time in constructing his message.

When a message is received, the inference module must interpret its content and find out what options are available to the user. These options are forwarded to the action initiator which may then perform whatever action the user requests. It must be said that, at this stage, the system is not capable of general reasoning. It is, however, aware of the message types in the domain and their structure. It has in its possession simple rules regarding what action to take under what circumstances. For example, if it sees that the message is from the recipient's direct supervisor, it informs the user that he has an important message. If the user is absent, the message is forwarded to the user's current location (if that location is known to the system).

3.2 Functionality of the implemented system

In this section we shall present some of the features of our system that provide us with an idea as to the potential of the language based approach. We do not claim that similar features cannot be obtained by other methods but only that there is a marked ease with which a system's functionality may be modified to suit changing needs.

- The user may send a message either by using the available language constructs or by selecting the domain in which he/she wants to send the message. If a domain like "office messaging" is selected, the user is provided a menu containing the message types he/she may choose from. The list of office messages is compiled by the system administrator and may be modified as the needs of the users change.

- The user selects the message type he/she wants and the system guides the user through the construction of the message. The system prompts the user with default values whenever possible and does error checking on the values assigned to each of the arguments of a predicate.

- Before transmitting the message, the system checks to see if the recipient of the message is currently available or not by peeking at his/her schedule. If the recipient is present the message is transmitted. If the recipient were currently absent the sender is informed and is provided with an alternate address/person to whom the message may be sent. This alternate address/person is obtained from the information-base of the recipient.

- When the recipient logs onto the system, he/she is reminded of any appointments or work that needs to be attended to. The list of things to remind is updated automatically to contain any new requests received in the user's mail. The use of propositional attitudes in our language permits the system to select the appropriate parts of an incoming message to add to the recipient's reminder list.

- The system constructs an acknowledgement and transmits it if the user so desires. If the person receives an acknowledgement for some message that he/she had sent, the system searches its database to retrieve the message to which the current message is an acknowledgement.

- If the user receives a request for an appointment the system checks his/her schedule to see whether the user is free at the requested time. Depending on whether the user would be available at the requested time the system generates an appropriate response to the request. If the user accepts the appointment, his/her schedule is updated accordingly.

- If the user had requested someone for an appointment and he receives a message from that person confirming the appointment, the system updates his/her schedule to reflect this commitment.

- The system provides tools with which the system administrator (or the person responsible for the organization's communication needs) may define new message types or modify existing ones to suit the requirements of the users. He/she may also define new predicates or modify existing ones. The system uses certain key words in the predicate's arguments to infer the nature of the values that each argument expects. This information is passed on to the validity checker to be used during message construction.

4 Current work

The next domain that we are exploring is "purchasing", the selling and buying of goods under the provisions of the UCC (Uniform Commercial Code) that regulates all such transactions. This is a far more complex domain where each transaction involves the exchange of a number of pieces of communication, each written in the context of some earlier communication. Communications typically refer to one or more offers, acceptances, refusals and promises made in some earlier communication and hence the correct representation of the context is crucial to successfully dealing with this domain. The approach that we are studying is the use of conversational grammars to model the various types of conversations that take place when negotiating a contract. Most messages are elements of some previously initiated conversation or are initiators of

494

a new conversation. The motivation for adopting this approach is that when we move from one domain to another we only need to rewrite the conversation grammar for that domain. The interpreter of the grammar remains unchanged.

The manner in which a particular organization deals with other organizations differs from one organization to another. Also the same organization would deal differently with its preferred clients in contrast to "bad" clients. Thus the manner in which our system responds to communications from various organizations should be controlled in some way by the users of the system. Towards this end, we have established the distinction between three types of rules that govern a messaging system's behavior in the sales domain : (1) UCC (2) Company policy (3) Semantic rules. The UCC changes very little, if at all, over time and hence may be incorporated in the programming code, beyond the control of the user. Semantic rules are important to constrain the message content to meaningful statements and hence may also be incorporated into the code. Company policy, however, is determined by the user and hence the user must be provided with some means by which he/she may state the action to be taken upon the receipt of a particular type of communication from a particular organization. To leave the complexity of the action to be taken in the hands of the user, the system provides a distinct module "action initiator" which the user may modify to suit his/her requirements.

The messages, or more accurately the syntax of the messages, lacks an explicit representation for tense. One may get around it by defining temporal predicates to convey the appropriate meaning, however it appears more appealing and intuitive to deal with time in a more explicit manner. Towards this end, we hope to arrive at a small set of temporal operators that may be used to express, to a reasonable extent, the sort of temporal information that is important to business communications.

To conclude, we believe that a step has been taken in the right direction towards automating business communications. Formal languages provide the necessary expressibility that is lacking in the rigidly structured EDI approach and the computability that is not possible in paper or electronic mail. The idea of formal languages has been tested and found successful in the office messaging domain. We do, however, acknowledge that much has to be done before it becomes a viable alternative to voice and paper communication.

References

[1] Austin, John L., *How to Do Things with Words*, Oxford at the Clarendon Press, Oxford, England, 1962.

[2] Bach, Kent and Robert M. Harnish, *Linguistic Communication and Speech Acts*, The MIT Press, Cambridge, Massachusetts, 1979.

[3] Chang, S. K. and L. Leung, "A Knowledge–Based Message Management System," *ACM Transactions on Office Information Systems*, **5**, no. 3, (1987), 213-236.

[4] Comer, D. E. and L. L. Peterson, "Conversations—An Alternative to Memos and Conferences," *Byte,* **10**, no. 13, (1985), 263-272.

[5] Comer, D. E. and L. L. Peterson, "Conversation Based Mail," *ACM Transactions on Computer Systems*, **4**, no. 4, (1986), 299-319.

[6] Edwards, Daniel W., "Electronic Data Interchange: A Senior Management Overview," International Center for Information Technologies, 2000 M Street, N.W., Washington, D.C. 20036, 202-659-1314, 1987.

[7] Frost and Sullivan, Inc., *The Electronic Data Interchange (EDI) Market in the U.S.,* Frost and Sullivan, Inc., 106 Fulton Street, New York, NY 10038, 212-233-1080, April 1988.

[8] Hiltz, S.R., K. Johnson, and M. Turoff, "Experiments in Group Decision Making—Communication Process and Outcome in Face–to–Face Versus Computerized Conferences," *Human Communication Research*, **13**, no. 2, (1986), 225-252.

[9] Hiltz, S.R. and M. Turoff, "Structuring Computer–Mediated Communications Systems to Avoid Information Overload," *Communications of the ACM*, **28**, no. 7, (1985), 680-9.

[10] Kimbrough, Steven O., "On Representation Schemes for Electronic Promising," forthcoming in *Decision Support Systems,* (1989).

[11] Kimbrough, Steven O., Sashidhar P. Reddi and Michael Thornburg, "On Messaging with Semantic Access in an Office Environment," University of Pennsylvania, Department of Decision Sciences, working paper, 1989. (forthcoming, Journal of Management Information Systems)

[12] Kimbrough, Steven O. and Ronald M. Lee, "On Illocutionary Logic as a Telecommunications Language," *Proceedings of the Seventh International Conference on Information Systems,* Leslie Maggi et al., eds., San Diego, CA, (December 15-7, 1986), 15-26.

[13] Lee, Ronald M. "CANDID - A Logical Calculus for Describing Financial Contracts, " Ph.D thesis, University of Pennsylvania, Department of Decision Sciences, working paper 80-06-2, 1980.

[14] Lee, Ronald M. and Ranjit Bose, "Deontic Reasoning in Bureaucratic Systems," *Proceedings of the 21st Hawaii International Conference on System Sciences*, (January 1988).

[15] Levinson, Stephen C., *Pragmatics*, Cambridge University Press, Cambridge, England, 1983.

[16] Malone, Thomas W., Kenneth R. Grant, Franklyn A. Turbak, Stephen A. Brobst, and Michael D. Cohen, "Intelligent Information–Sharing Systems," *Communications of the ACM,* **30**, no. 5, (1987), 390-402.

[17] Malone, Thomas W., Kenneth R. Grant, Kum–Yew Lai, Ramana Rao, and David Rosenblitt, "Semistructured Messages Are Surprisingly Useful for Computer–Supported Coordination," *ACM Transactions on Office Information Systems*, **5**, no. 2, (1987).

[18] Malone, T. W., J. Yates, and R. I. Benjamin, "Electronic Markets and Electronic Hierarchies," *Communications of the ACM,* **30**, no. 6, (1987), 484-497.

[19] Searle, John R. and Daniel Vanderveken, *Foundations of Illocutionary Logic*, Cambridge University Press, Cambridge, England, 1985.

A System for Knowledge-Based Information Extraction

Frank von Martial, Frank Victor
German National Research Center for Computer Science (GMD)
Schloss Birlinghoven, P.O.B. 1240
D-5205 St. Augustin 1, West Germany

Hiroshi Ishii
NTT Human Interface Laboratories
1-2356 Take, Yokosuka-Shi, 238-03 Japan

ABSTRACT

In this paper, we deal with the problem of gaining insight into the structure of an office knowledge base. In a dynamic environment, like the office, often changes occur which have to be reflected in the knowledge base. Now, two questions arise: What part of the knowledge base is relevant concerning the changes? How can the relevant information be displayed appropriately? Concerning these two questions, we propose a retrieval technique that supports knowledge-based extraction (filtering) and presentation (visualizing) of relevant information.

1. Introduction

In the last years several information systems have been developed that rely on huge knowledge bases, e.g. [1, 6, 9]. Although a lot of work has been and is being done on embedding methods of artificial intelligence into information retrieval research - e.g. natural language processing, user modelling, knowledge representation or inference mechanisms [2, 3, 4] - we are concerned with a problem that has not yet been solved adequately in this field: Retrieving information in a knowledge-based system to support a knowledge engineer.

Our retrieval problem has arisen during our research activities at GMD for the long-term key project *Assistant Computer* [12] which is to be a system with assistant properties, e.g. for intelligent support of planning, design tasks, communication and cooperation. The *Assistant Computer* will rely on a large knowledge base representing organizational knowledge about our own company. To get a feeling for the representation of organizational knowledge, we have experimented some years with various knowledge representation formalisms [22, 24]. Since the nature of organizations is that they change frequently, we have made the experience that parts of our knowledge base often had to be changed, e.g. by a knowledge engineer or application domain expert. The main problems are:

- How can the user be supported in selecting the knowledge that is currently relevant for him? Which knowledge, i.e. which excerpt of the knowledge base, is selected to be offered to the user?

- How is the knowledge presented to the user? What is the most suitable graphical form to show the selected knowledge on screen?

To solve these problems, we use a retrieval technique that consists of two main components: a **knowledge filter** and a **visualizer**. The filter automatically extracts relevant information from the knowledge base according to the user's role, post, working context, etc. The visualizer generates appropriate graphics for the selected information using knowledge about various graph types and layout strategies.

Based on this retrieving technique, we have implemented a prototype system in Allegro Common Lisp which runs on an Apple Macintosh II. The prototype consists of three knowledge sources, i.e. office knowledge, user profile knowledge, visualization knowledge, and two modules: the *filter* and the *visualizer*, which can be either used standalone or as one integrated system (see figure 1). The modules can be easily used in other configurations and make the system smoothly tailorable for a variety of applications.

We have not seen any other approach which supports both the filtering of knowledge and the visualization of the selected information using an adaptive knowledge-based approach. But there exist several systems which support one of these aspects. The filtering of information is addressed in Malone's Information Lens system [17]. The goal of this system is the filtering and extraction of information in a mail system and not, as in our case, a knowledge base. Another system which also takes a user model for the finding of information is described in [20]. In this case the underlying system is a hypertext system. In [8] an approach is described in which the user himself can define filtering mechanisms with the help of a graphical tool. In [10] a system is proposed which helps preparing already selected information. In this system conventional styles of graph presentation like pie or bar charts are incorporated. Many papers address the problem of layouting a graph on the screen, see [7] for an overview. Some researchers such as Tichy [28] pursue a knowledge-based approach for graph presentation.

There exist several approaches to provide graphic support in an office environment. Lochovsky et al. have developed an icon-based programming language which permits the graphical specification of office procedures [16, 25]. DACRON [18, 19] is an interface for graphically acquiring and manipulating office activities.

496

2. Filtering and visualizing knowledge

The overall configuration of our retrieval system and the flow of knowledge is shown in figure 1. The main knowledge sources and modules are: the domain knowledge base, the user profile knowledge base, the visualization knowledge base, the filter and the visualizer.

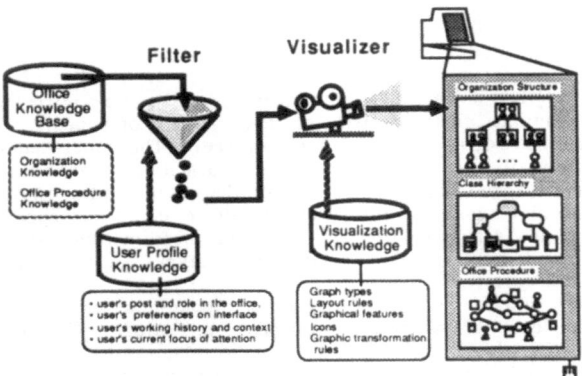

Figure 1: The main components of our retrieval system

2.1. The knowledge bases

Our application domain is the office world and we are building an **organizational knowledge base** that models aspects of this domain, including common sense knowledge [21]. The final system should contain relevant information about our company. In our case the initial source of knowledge is the organizational manual of our company [11]. This extensive manual describes on more than 300 pages the structure and the organizational rules of GMD.

We have represented a portion of that knowledge using the hybrid knowledge engineering tool *BABYLON* [5, 26]. BABYLON comprises representation formalisms and inference strategies for frames, rules, constraints and Horn clauses. Mainly we have represented knowledge concerning the purchasing domain. The object classes we have used are: purchase objects, forms, organizational structure, actions and roles.

The **user profile knowledge base** contains knowledge about the potential users for our office knowledge base. These users can have different requirements and preferences. Moreover, our system allows different forms of interactions for browsing and planning [22, 29]. Thus, it is necessary for the system to adapt its behaviour to individual users. In this situation a user model is beneficial [15].

The user model is kept as a separate knowledge base with frames and rules. The *user frame* has more than 20 slots, each of which can be split up in further dimensions. It captures three kinds of information about users:

• User supplied information: The user contributes various information about himself, e.g. information of her/his post in the organization, her/his interface preferences, the mode s/he wants to use the system such as browsing, knowledge acquisition or planning.

• Bookkeeping information: This part of the user model is updated as the user interacts with the system. It contains mainly statistical information such as the times of system usage, the medium intensity of usage, the record of current interactions. An important constituent is information about the already presented knowledge items. For every selected knowledge base item the times of selection and when it was last presented is stored.

• Rule determined information: The values of this kind of user information are inferred by a rule base after the user has finished a session. This part has, for example, slots for *memory-forget-type* ranging from *extreme-short-term* to *long-term* or the *level-of-knowledge-about-organization*. The condition part of a rule may consider values of slots of kind one or two in order to determine the values of this part. Example for a rule: "IF there are numerous knowledge items in already-presented-knowledge-items with high numbers, THEN set memory-forget-type = short-term".

The **visualization knowledge base** supports three graph types: trees, semantic nets and office procedure nets. Trees and semantic nets have been used in the system BOOK [13, 14]. The net formalism for office procedures has been developed for the system VIPS [23] which relies on a graphical language based on Petri nets [27] and is used for the representation of actions and plans. For each graph type the system has heuristics for its graphical representation. An important factor for displaying information is the arrangement (layout) of objects on screen. Currently, we are experimenting with several strategies.

2.2. The knowledge filter

When the user requests information out of a large mass of knowledge stored in an application domain knowledge base, the system considers the user profile knowledge, such as her/his role, working context and history. The *knowledge filter* extracts parts of knowledge from the big chunk. The user's authority can also be taken into consideration by the filter to restrict the access to knowledge. The knowledge extraction can be done by:

- selecting automatically parts of office procedures
- selecting specified objects, e.g. documents relevant to a special task
- selecting a subnet of objects connected by a specified relation, e.g. *part-of* or *is-a* relation of office objects, set of activities and agents connected by a *responsible-for* relation

We now briefly describe how the filter works: The user selects a cluster of objects, i.e. frames or instances, in which s/he is interested. S/he can specify these objects by menus listing all frames or instances. In addition to that, s/he has to identify a selection strategy. The choice of knowledge extraction strategies is dependent on the type and number of selected objects. In case of *classes*: If the selected object is a single class, the following selections are possible: 'has slots', 'has instance', 'has instance and subclasses', 'object hierarchy', 'is referenced in', 'semantic environment'. For 'semantic environment' the adjacent objects are added in an iterative procedure for which the user can specify the number of loops. If several classes are selected the resulting structure can either be determined by 'semantic net' or 'semantic environment'. 'Semantic net' transforms the current selection into a net denoting the objects as nodes and the slots as edges. In case of *instances*: If the selected object is a single instance, these options are possible: 'is a', 'has slots', 'refers to', 'is referenced in', 'semantic environment'. If there are several instances selected, the alternatives are 'semantic net', 'semantic environment' and 'classes'.

2.3. The visualizer

The extracted knowledge is transformed into an adequate graphic form and displayed on a screen by the *visualizer*. Depending on the information which is to be presented, our system will use different strategies. The visualizer provides the user with an easy-to-understand graph representation. In this process the visualizer uses, for example, the knowledge for automatic graph layout, icons for each object, rules of colour combination and animation techniques for smooth view change. This information is stored in the visualization knowledge base. For each visualized object several values, e.g. its shape or size, can be inferred.

Each office object has its special icon. The visualizer provides these icons to display the corresponding objects on a screen. Office objects are represented as nodes and the relationships among office objects are represented as arcs. All icons are mouse-sensitive. When the user clicks the mouse button on an icon, a pop-up menu for information retrieval and editing comes up.

The visualizer consists of two modules: the **layouter** and the **grapher**. The layouter calculates relative node positions using various strategies, the grapher displays the resulting graph taking into account several parameters like window size, size of nodes or distances between nodes.

The **layouter** positions the nodes of a graph using several heuristics. If the layouter gets its input from the knowledge filter the selected objects are interpreted as a graph structure, consisting of nodes and edges. The frames or instances are the nodes and the slots are the arcs of the graph (semantic net). The layout process is highly parameterized. For example, a strategy is expressed as a list of values. So, it is easy to modify or add heuristics. The layouter creates relative node positions which are, for instance, independent from the size of the display window, the position of the window on a screen, the size of the nodes and the length of text strings. It is the task of the grapher to determine the final layout in dependence of hardware and size restrictions. The system currently comprises the following strategies to generate the layout of a graph, see figure 2:

- *South-east*: The graph is expanded in south east direction.

- *South or tree*: A "hanging" tree is produced (a most adequate strategy for tree structured graphs).
- *Flat*: A symmetrical layout is produced.
- *North*: A "standing" tree is produced.
- *Random1*: Adjacent nodes are positioned in direct neighbourhood to each other in a random direction.
- *Random2*: Distances between adjacent nodes may become longer.
- *My layout*: The user can define her/his own expansion strategy.

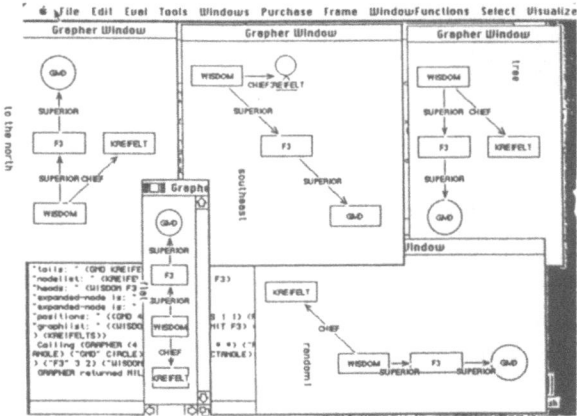

Figure 2: Visualization of the semantic neighbourhood of the object WISDOM

All strategies except Random1 and Random2 contain implicit heuristics to prevent the arcs of the arranged graph from crossing each other. It is not intended to reach an optimal solution concerning arc crossing as this an NP-complete problem and the response time for an optimal layout can not be accepted for an interactive program.

The layouter is flexible and not bound for a dedicated application. However, this means also that a layout of a given graph is created independently of its semantics. For dedicated applications or graph types it is desirable to use semantic information to guide the layout process. In case of a plan layout, it is, for instance, desirable to arrange the objects (activities) according to their time or causal relationship.

The *grapher* can not only display a graph but can also be used to edit and create a graph; see, for example, figure 3. As input, this module gets a graph structure with relative node positions and performs some adjustments: According to the screensize and the number of objects which are to be displayed, the grapher adjusts several attributes of the graph: the window size, the fontsize of text strings, the size of nodes and the distance between the nodes (edge length). The nodes and edges of a graph are mouse-sensitive. The user gets more information about an object by a doubleclick.

498

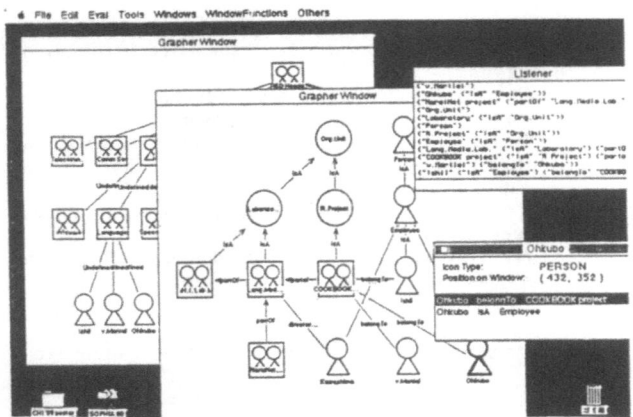

Figure 3: A graph created by the *grapher*

3. Examples

In this section, we will give some examples showing our current prototype at work. It also contains some of our ideas concerning the planned extension of the system illustrated by some scenarios. In fact, what we have not yet fully implemented is a flexible inference mechanism for the user profile knowledge base, nevertheless we find it worthwhile to mention these ideas here.

Our first example is based on a knowledge base which models the organizational structure of the GMD and the activities in the purchasing domain. Let us assume that some changes have occurred in the organization; in our case, the joint project WISDOM has been finished. Now, the knowledge engineer has to update the organizational knowledge base. So, first, s/he is interested in some frames according to the frame WISDOM. S/he wants to know whether and what relationships exist among these objects in the neighbourhood of WISDOM and selects the 'semantic environment' option with the value 1, i.e. s/he is only interested in the objects which have a direct relationship with the instance WISDOM. The system extracts (filters) the corresponding semantic net structure. Then, the user can select according to which strategy the result is to be displayed. Figure 2 shows some possible results.

The next example concerns the extraction and presentation of office procedure knowledge. Now, our knowledge engineer has to modify the office procedure for purchasing, which also is represented in the knowledge base, because two departments involved in this procedure have been joined (for details concerning the representation of office procedures, see [21, 29]). The user profile knowledge base contains some information about our knowledge engineer; for instance, the parameter 'specialization for extracting procedural knowledge' which specifies the depth that the user prefers when knowledge about activities is extracted, e.g. the value 'low' means that the user should not be bothered with every detail of an office procedure. This information is then used, for instance, in the following rule:

IF   'retrieved object' = 'office activity' AND
        'specialization for extracting procedural knowledge' = 'low'
THEN   'extract activities to depth two'

Now, the extracted part of the procedure is sent to the visualizer. For the layout of office procedures the following rule will be applied:

IF   'retrieved object' = 'office activity'
THEN   'place activities along the center horizontal line according to their chronological order, and arrange other icons such as documents or agents around that line'

The visualizer generates the graph on the screen using layout and icon knowledge of the visualization knowledge base, see figure 4.

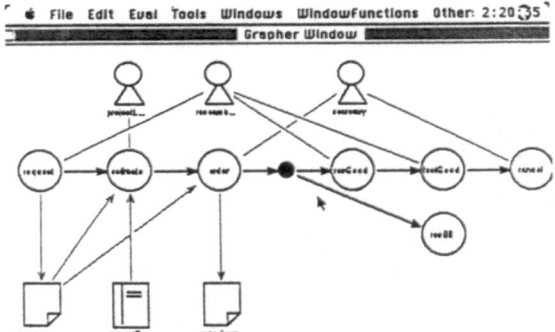

Figure 4: Rule-based office procedure layout

The main advantage of using a knowledge base as described, is that the displayed graph contains only information which is relevant and of interest for the user in her/his situation. Thus, hopefully s/he can easily understand the output and does not have to read a lot of redundant information.

4. Conclusion and future work

We have represented a knowledge based adaptive retrieval system which gives insight into the structure of a knowledge base depending on a user model. Our prototype is composed of a knowledge filter for extracting knowledge and a visualizer for presenting the extracted knowledge on screen. Three knowledge sources are used: an application domain knowledge base, an user profile knowledge base, and a visualization knowledge base. As an example, we have applied the concepts for intelligent filtering and visualization to an office knowledge base. We hope that we have clearly demonstrated how a user model can be successfully utilized to adapt the system behaviour depending on user and situation.

There are many aspects of the system which have to be evaluated more carefully, refined and improved. Concerning the extraction we will: experiment with more features for the user model, enlarge the underlying knowledge base, look for more rules to adapt the user model and investigate cognitive aspects of human computer interaction. Concerning the graphic interface we will: integrate more strategies for generating more sophisticated presentations, use icons for more objects, introduce more types of edges, e.g. bidirectional, dotted or multirelational and develop techniques for focussing, zooming and shrinking.

Acknowledgements: Most of the work described in this paper was performed during Frank von Martial´s one-year stay in the Language Media Group at NTT Human Interface Laboratories in Japan. Especially, we would like to express our gratitude to Masaaki Ohkubo who implemented the *grapher*.

REFERENCES

[1] G. Barber, *"Supporting Organizational Problem Solving with a Work Station,"* ACM Transactions on Office Information Systems, Jan. 1983, pp. 45-67

[2] N. J. Belkin, *"Tutorial on Information Retrieval and Artificial Intelligence,"* Workshop on Artificial Intelligence in Economics and Management, Singapore, 1989

[3] N. J. Belkin, W. B. Croft, *"Retrieval Techniques"*, in: Annual Review of Information Science and Technology, 22 (1987), pp. 109-145

[4] N. J. Belkin, A. Vickery, "Interaction in Informations Systems: ·A Review of Research from Document Retrieval to Knowledge-based Systems", The British Library, London, 1985

[5] Th. Christaller, F. di Primio, A. Voss (eds.), "Die KI-Werkbank BABYLON," (an English translation will be published this year), Addison-Wesley, Amsterdam, 1989

[6] W.B. Croft, "Representing Office Work with Goals and Constraints," Proceedings of the IFIP WG8.4 Workshop on Office Knowledge, Toronto, Canada, August 1987

[7] P. Eades, R. Tamassia, "Algorithms for Drawing Graphs: An Annotated Bibliography," Technical Report No. 82, University of Queensland, Australia, July 1987

[8] R. K. Ege, D. Maier, A. Borning, "The Filter Browser - Defining Interfaces Graphically", ECOOP'87, European Conference on Object-oriented Programming, June, 1987

[9] R. Fikes, "ODYSSEY: A Knowledge-based Assistant," Artificial Intelligence, 16, 1981, pp. 331-361

[10] R. A. Gargan Jr., J. W. Sullivan, S. W. Tyler, "Multimodal Response Planning: An Adaptive Rule Based Approach," CHI'88-Conf. on Human Factors in Computing Systems, Washington, DC, pp.229-234, 1988

[11] "Geschäfts- und Betriebsordnung (GBO) der Gesellschaft für Mathematik und Datenverarbeitung mbH", GMD, St. Augustin, 1985

[12] "Forschungs- und Entwicklungsprogramm 1989/90," Gesellschaft für Mathematik und Datenverarbeitung mbH (GMD), 1988, pp. 61-68

[13] H. Ishii, "Office Modeling and Analysis by OM-1," (in Japanese), Paper of the Technical Group on Office Systems (OS86-24), IEICI Japan, Sep. 1986, pp. 39-46

[14] H. Ishii and K. Kubota, "Office Procedure Knowledge Base for Organizational Office Work Support," IFIP WG8.4 Working Conference on OIS, Aug. 1988

[15] R. Kass, T. Finin, "A General User Modelling Facility," CHI'88-Conf. on Human Factors in Computing Systems, Washington, DC, 1988

[16] F. H. Lochovsky, J. S. Hogg, S. P. Weiser, A. O. Mendelzon, "OTM: Specifying Office Tasks", Conf. on Office Information Systems, Palo Alto, California, March 1988

[17] Th. W. Malone, K. R. Grant, F. A. Turbak, St. A. Brobst, M. D. Cohen, "Intelligent Information-Sharing Systems," Communications of the ACM, Vol.30, No.5, May 1987, pp.390-402

[18] D. E. Mahling, W. B. Croft, "An Interface for the Specification of Office Activities," IFIP WG 8.4, "IFIP Working· Conference on Office Information Systems," Linz, Austria, August 1988

[19] D. E. Mahling, W. B. Croft, "Knowledge Acquisition for Planners", Third AAAI-Sponsored Acquisition for Knowledge-Based Systems Workshop, Banff, Canada, November 1988

[20] G. Marchionini and B. Shneiderman, "Finding Facts vs. Browsing Knowledge in Hypertext Systems," IEEE COMPUTER, Jan. 1988, pp. 70-80

[21] F. von Martial, F. Victor, "The Electronic Organizational Handbook: Requirements and Specification" (in German), WISDOM Research Report FB-GMD-87-16, Gesellschaft für Mathematik und Datenverarbeitung, St. Augustin, July 1987

[22] F. von Martial, F. Victor, "Collaborative Construction of an Office Knowledge Base: Experiences and Suggestions," Proc. of the 2nd European Knowledge Acquisition for Knowledge-Based Systems Workshop, Bonn, West Germany, June 1988

[23] F. von Martial, F. Victor, "An Interactive Planner for Open Systems," Proc. of the Fourth IEEE Conference on Artificial Intelligence Applications in San Diego, IEEE Computer Society Press, Washington, D.C. 1988

[24] F. von Martial, F. Victor, "Knowledge Acquisition for an Electronic Organizational Handbook," Proc. of the Fifth Australian Conf. on Applications of Expert Systems, Sydney, May 1989

[25] T. Mosser, P. Di Felice, F. Lochovsky, "Specifying Office Tasks by Example," IFIP WG 8.4, "IFIP Working Conference on Office Information Systems", Linz, Austria, August 1988

[26] F. di Primio, G. Brewka, "BABYLON: Kernel System of an Integrated Environment for Expert System Development and Operation", in: Proc. of Fifth International Workshop on Expert Systems and their Applications", Avignon, 1985

[27] L. Peterson, "Petri Nets," ACM Computing Surveys, Vol. 9, No. 3, Sept. 1983

[28] W. F. Tichy et al., "A Knowledge-Based Graphical Editor," Technical Report, University of Karlsruhe, Jan. 1986

[29] F. Victor, E. Sommer, F. von Martial, "The Planning Support System VIPS: Creating and Analyzing Office Procedures Using an Electronic Organizational Handbook" (in German), in: Conf. Proc. of the GI-89 in: M. Paul (ed.), Reihe Informatik-Fachberichte, Springer, Heidelberg

Design and Development of a Document Management System for Banking Applications: an Example of Office Automation

E.Bertino, D.Montesi

Istituto di Elaborazione dell'Informazione - C.N.R.

Via S.Maria, 46 - 56100 Pisa (Italy)

Abstract

In this paper we describe the design and development of a document management system. The documents contain regulations that are imparted by the bank management. These documents are consulted by a large number of users for carrying out their tasks. An important aspect in the design of the system is the definition of an appropriate authorization model and of a query language for document selection. In this paper, we discuss the requirements that have a major impact on the design and we present the document authorization model.

1 Introduction

The automation of an office involves several technical and non-technical aspects. Among the non-technical aspects, the choice of the methodology is a crucial one. An important component in the methodology is the type of conceptual model of the office used during the analysis of the office. As in the design of conventional information systems, we can classify the various approaches in the case of Office Information Systems into technical, organizational, and socio-technical [BRAC84].

- The technical approach takes office activities into account in great detail by considering the operations and tasks to be executed and the expected execution times. However, the model mainly considers the physical characteristics of office activities without paying attention to the intellectual aspects. From the analysis of these data, an evaluation of the office productivity is obtained.

- The organizational approach considers the organizational structure of the office and the enterprise goals. Therefore, this model reflects the entire (hierarchical) structure of the considered organization.

- The socio-technical approach sees the office in terms of the tasks that must be executed by each of the units into which the office is broken down. Each unit is assigned some resources for the execution of unit tasks. In this model, the office activities are not analyzed to the same level of detail as in the technical model.

In this paper we describe the design and development of a document management system based on the third approach. However, the organizational approach has also influenced the design of the overall office model. The documents contain regulations for banking applications. Even if this office model is specific to these applications, its design has highlighted, some of the capabilities that an office automation system must provide.

The organization we consider is a financial institution in central Italy. Within this organization, we can identify a number of Organizational Micro Units (OMUs). Some OMUs are illustrated as a box in Figure 1 [BPA88]. An OMU:

- is a *working subsystem* in a system for service production;

- has the task of providing a specific set of services to other OMUs, within the same organization, or to external organizations;

- implements its tasks via information processing.

The Organization & Method Unit and the Information Processing Unit have the task of designing and developing the document management system. In general, the tasks of each OMU can be looked at as processes requiring two types of information flow:

- information to be processed, called service information

- control information.

The information to be processed is the usual information circulating within the offices of each OMU. The control information consists of triples, where each triple has the following structure: *(rule, procedure, form)*.

The control information is organized in this way to better manage the consistency and completeness of the managed information, that is, the service information. The *rule* determines what can be done; the *procedure* specifies how, and the *form* specifies which objects are needed to process a specific set of service information. By using these triples it is possible to specify how to process the service information within a specific OMU to obtain other information which are the input to other OMUs.

A triple constitutes what is called protocol bulletin. These protocol bulletins are distributed and consulted by the people working in the various OMUs. A protocol bulletin, henceforth called document, is a structured object containing text and attributive data. The overall goal of the research described in this paper was to design and develop a system for managing these documents: said system will be referred to as SAD.

The set of documents managed by the SAD can be in either the *active* or *archived* state. A document is active if it can be accessed by all users, except where restricted for security reasons. The set of active documents constitutes the Active Document Archive. A document is in a non-active state if it has been inactivated. The set of inactivated documents constitutes the Non-Active Document Archive. The archived (inactive) documents are not used by the majority of users, since they contain some control information that is no longer valid. They are only accessible to users with tasks of management and control over the entire SAD. Therefore, the SAD consists of two archival subsystems.

The goals that we intend to achieve by automating the management of these documents are as follows:

- To modify the current filing system, which is based on 160 paper files located at the Main Office and at each of the various branch offices.

- To modify the current retrieval and updating procedures. In the current paper files these operations are performed manually, by using some indexes, and by physically substituting the modified documents with the new versions.

- To modify the current access control mechanism, which is very simple and based on two levels of access to documents.

An important aspect in the SAD design is the development of a sophisticated access control mechanism, which could not be achieved with the paper archives. In order to better understand the types of access control required, we must take into account the document content and usage. The documents are used by the management as a tool to impart rules to the other OMUs. Therefore, a few users have the task of ensuring the completeness, consistency, and security of the information contained in these documents, while a large number of users read these documents to perform their specific tasks. Thus it is clear that the SAD concentrates information concerning all levels and sectors within the organization. Therefore, there is a need for both a vertical and horizontal partitioning of the information. The goals of the access control mechanisms are partially opposed:

- On one hand there is the need for the **completeness** of the information that each user must receive.

- On the other hand there is the need for **discretion** in distributing the information.

The information needed by each user is a pair:

1. Basic information

   This information is common (and accessible) to all users at all levels.

2. Information specific to the user's sector

   This information must be distributed in a controlled way to the various users.

A major difficulty in the design of this system is that there are a number of structural, organizational, and economical constraints. The structural constraints basically concern the hardware and software architectures. These architectures were preexisting and used by other applications, and for cost reasons they had to be used for document management, as well.

The chief results obtained by the design phase are as follows:

- The definition of an access control model specific to this system, and the development of a mechanism for access control based on this model. Two requirements were to support restrictive viewing of the active document set and a simple user interface for authorization management.

- The determination of the software components that can be implemented by acquiring available software products and of those that must be implemented "ad hoc". For example, the document storage subsystem has been implemented with the IRIDIS system. IRIDIS is an Information Retrieval System that provides document management functions available from a fourth-generation language [LOGO86]. The authorization subsystem has, instead, been implemented directly since there were no available products.

- The definition of a simple but powerful query language to be used as a filter in accessing the documents [AGOS85].

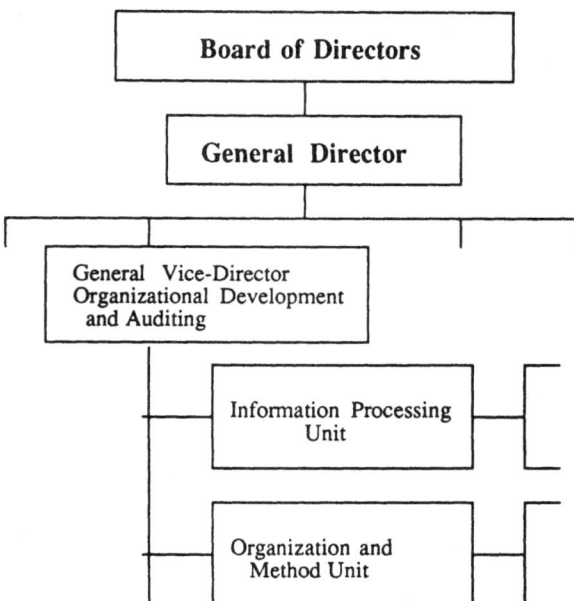

Figure 1. Section from the hierarchical tree of the Institute's Management

The query language allows the user to formulate queries by successive approximations.

The design activity has followed a methodology organized into four steps:

1. requirement analysis

2. conceptual design

3. design of the functional architecture

4. mapping of the functional architecture onto the existing hw/sw architecture.

The requirement analysis has been carried out by interacting with the various users in order to understand all the issues involved in automating this application environment. We note that in this case all the needed information was distributed among a small number of people [HIGG84] that have/had the task of managing the archival system. Particular care has been dedicated to the definition of the access control mechanism. This mechanism must fulfill several organizational constraints (both present and future) and be in accordance with the organizational policy. The conceptual design has been performed by using the Galileo [ALBA85] language, extended with primitives for the management of text data types.

The functional architecture has been defined according to the architecture model defined for the MULTOS system [BERT88]. The factors that have a major impact are related to the various types of users that will have to interact with the system. The mapping has been performed starting from the components defined in the previous phase and analyzing the existing architecture.

The remainder of the paper is organized as follows. Section 2 describes the requirement analysis and the conceptual model. Section 3 presents the formal definition of the authorization model. Section 4 briefly describes the functional architecture and discusses the mapping. Finally, Section 5 presents some conclusions.

2 Requirement Analysis and Conceptual Model

The operations that users execute on the documents are categorized as follows:

- query formulation on the Active Document Archive
- query formulation on the Non-Active Document Archive
- document management
- authorization and access rights management.

Queries are formulated by using a query language, defined as part of the conceptual model. The major requirement for the query language is to allow the users to formulate queries containing conditions on both the attributive and the textual components of the documents. Conditions on textual components are those typical of text retrieval, such as that two words are contiguous. Attributive data include information such as the document creation date, or the version. The document structure is the same for both documents in the Active Document Archive and the Non-Active Document Archive. The only difference is that the inactive documents (stored in the Non-Active Document Archive) contain an inactivation date indicating when the documents migrated from the Active Document Archive to the Non-Active Document Archive.

The document management operations involve the Active Document Archive, the Non-Active Document Archive, and the access control subsystem. The required functions involve inserting a new document in the Active Document Archive, transferring a document from the Active Document Archive to the Non-Active Document Archive, and modifying a document in the Active Document Archive. The last operation creates a copy of the old document, which is transfered to the Non-Active Document Archive, and inserts the new version in the Active Document Archive.

As concerns authorization, different user profiles must be supported. A user profile determines the activities that the user can perform on the SAD. An activity is defined by specifying a SAD component (among the Active Document Archive, the Non-Active Document Archive, and the Authorization Subsystem) and a set of operations that can be invoked from the component. The required profiles are the following:

- Inquiring users (I)

    These users may only formulate queries on documents stored in the Active Document Archive. They represent the majority of the user population and use the information stored in the SAD to perform their clerical tasks. These tasks are related to typical bank activities, such as customer loans.

- System Managers (SM)

    These users have complete control over document management. A manager can execute queries on both the Active Document Archive and the Non-Active Document Archive, modify, create, or transfer documents, and manage the assignment of classes and levels to documents. In general, these users have specific a technical competence. Their tasks are mainly related to the management of the computer system and, therefore, they may not have a precise knowledge of banking procedures. Thus, these users do not decide which documents can be accessed by which users or offices.

- Authorization Managers (AM)

    These users can execute queries only on the Active Document Archive and manage the authorization rights. In general, these users have a precise knowledge of the document contents and of the various user tasks. Therefore, they decide which documents can be accessed by which users and offices.

- Supervisors (S)

    These users can formulate queries on the Active Document Archive, and on the Authorization Subsystem. These users are not technical, unlike the managers. Their major task is to verify that all the organizational procedures are followed in the proper way. Therefore, they need to inspect the current documents and to verify that the authorizations are correctly granted.

This organization of the users into various profiles, or roles, is the basis for the definition of the authorization model, described in the following section.

The conceptual model of SAD has been defined by using the Galileo language [ALBA85], which has been extended in [MONT88] to support information retrieval applications for document management. A new data type, "txt" has been introduced. This type has, as values, alphabetic strings of arbitrary length. It differs with respect to the string data type in that some special predicates are defined for this new type. Furthermore, it is possible to associate to each text component a thesaurus. The definition of the conceptual model in Galileo is presented in [MONT88].

3 Authorization Model

Before describing the authorization model, we need to briefly analyze the structure of the application environment. An important factor in the environment is that there is a small number of users (4-8) producing documents, while there is a large number of users (more than 1000) accessing, in read mode, the documents. The number of active documents is about 40,000. Both the users and the documents are organized hierarchically. Furthermore, the users are orthogonally partitioned into offices and the documents into classes. Each office can access only certain classes of documents. A user can access all the documents that can be accessed from the office to which the user belongs.

Therefore each user is characterized by a profile, an access level, and an office. The profile determines the operations the user can execute. The access level determines the "height" of the accesses the user can execute. Finally the office determines the activity performed by the user in the organization and therefore determines the information need of the user.

Each document is characterized by an access level and a class. The access level determines the discretion level of the document. A class groups documents concerning the same organization sector or area. All documents in a class are visible to the same offices.

Similar models are defined in the literature [LAND81]. However, these models were not suited to our situation because of the requirement that the user access level be a higher priority than the document class. In our authorization model, a user can read all documents at a lower level, independently of user office and document class. However, a user can read a document, D, at his/her same level only if the user office is authorized to access the document class to which D belongs. Figure 2 presents the authorization model schema.

The model is based on three structures. The first, T_1, contains authorization information about each user; in particular it specifies the user office and level. The second, T_2, contains authorization information about each document; in particular, it specifies the

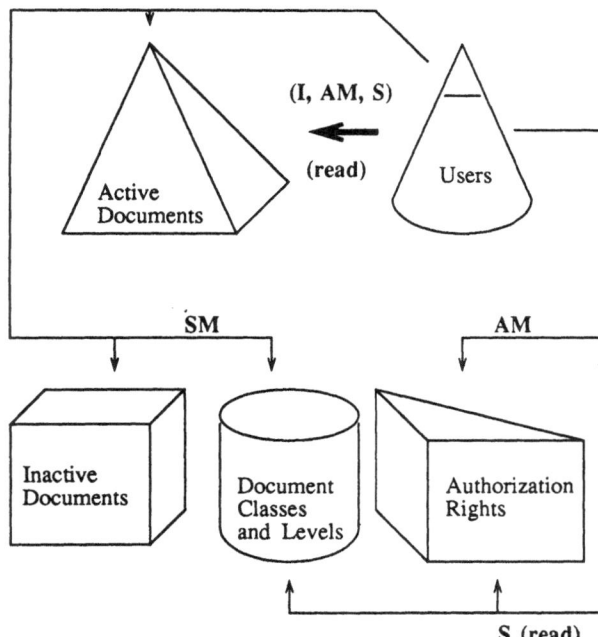

Figure 2. Schema of the authorization model

document class and level. The third, T_3, is an object-subject matrix that specifies which offices can access which document classes. This matrix is used in query operations to determine the user authorization to access a specified document. The authorization of the user to execute other operations are directly determined from the user profile.

The model is composed of seven elements:

the Users (U), the Levels (L), the Profiles (P), the Classes (C), the Offices (O), the Documents (D), and the Authorization (A).

The operations that each user can execute are specified by the user profile (P). Each user with profile I, AM, or S can only access documents that belong to the user window. A **user window** consists of all documents that are at a lower level with respect to the user and of all documents, of the same level as the user, that can be accessed by the user office.

In the following, $P_i(t)$ $(i > 0)$ denotes the projection on the i-th component of a given tuple t.

User Tuple

A user tuple defines the user authorization information. Each tuple has the following structure:

$(u_i, k_j, lm_w, o_x) \in T_1$ with
$u_i \in U, k_j \in Q, lm_w \in L$, and $O_x \in O$ where

- U is the set of all users. Each user is identified by a *user code*.

- Q is the set of passwords

- P is the set of profiles

- L is the set of levels. Five levels are defined in our model: $L = \{L_0, L_1, L_2, L_3, L_4\}$, where $L_0 < L_1 < L_2 < L_3 < L_4$.

- O is the set of all offices.

The set of users belonging to an office o_x is denoted as U_{o_x}. The following constraint holds:

$$\forall i, j, i \neq j, o_i \in O, \text{ and } o_j \in O, U_{o_i} \cap U_{o_j} = \emptyset.$$

This constraint states that a user cannot belong to more than one office.

We define a function f that determines the user profile, after a user has requested to be acknowledged. The user requires to be identified by providing the pair (user code, password).

$\mathbf{f}: U \times Q \times T_1 \to P \cup \{\text{Unknown}\}$
$\mathbf{f}(u_i, k_j, T_1) = $ if $pred_1$ then $P_3(fp(u_i))$ else $\{\text{Unknown}\}$
where

- $pred_1$ is a predicate that returns TRUE if and only if u_i is the user code of some user u and k_j is the password of u

- fp is a function that returns the tuple of a user whose user code is specified, that is:

$$fp(u_i) = \{t \in T_1/P_1(t) = u_i\}.$$

Document Tuple

Each document tuple defines the document level and class. Each tuple has the structure
$(d_i, ld_w, c_y) \in T_2$ with
$d_i \in D, ld_w \in L, c_y \in C$ where

- D is the set of all documents. Each document is identified by a *document code*

- L is the set of levels (defined in the previous subsection)

- C is the set of all classes.

A document cannot belong to more than one class.

Subject-Object Matrix

This matrix is defined as a set of tuples. A tuple specifies that a given office has authorization to access a certain class of documents. Each tuple has the structure
$(o_x, c_y, a_i) \in T_3$ with
$o_x \in O, c_y \in C, a_i \in A$ where

- O is the set of all offices (subjects)

- C is the set of all document classes (objects)

- A is the set of authorization types. In our case, only the Read authorization type occurs, that is, $A = \{\text{read}\}$.

The following function is defined
$\mathbf{h}: O \times C \times A \to \{\text{TRUE, FALSE}\}$.

Given a tuple (o_x, c_y, a_i), the function $\mathbf{h}$ determines whether the subject o_x has the authorization type a_i on the object c_y.

To define the user window with respect to an authorization type A_i, for a user u with level l_w and belonging to an office o_x, we use the following function
$\sqrt{}: L \times O \times A \to L \times C$
$\sqrt{}(l_w, o_x, a_i) = [P_1(l_w, o_x, a_i) \times C_u] \cup [LD \times C]$
where

- $C_u = \{c_j / \mathbf{h}(o_x, c_j, a_i) = TRUE\}$

C_u contains all classes, at the same level of the user u, that are visible to u.

- $LD = \{ld_j / ld_j < l_w\}$

LD contains all levels that are lower than the level of user u.

In our case, the type a_i is always equal to Read. However, the model has been defined in a general way and it permits the introduction of other authorization types.

Definition. Given a user with level $l_w \in L$, and office $o_x \in O$, and given an authorization type $a_i \in A$, the **user window** is the set of pairs (l_i, c_y) with $l_i \in L$ and $c_y \in C$, defined by $\sqrt{}(l_w, o_x, a_i)$.

Figure 3 presents an example of a user window. In the example, we consider a user belonging to an office Off_2 and with level L_2. The document classes that can be accessed from the office Off_2 are C_1 and C_3. From the figure, we can see the portion of active

504

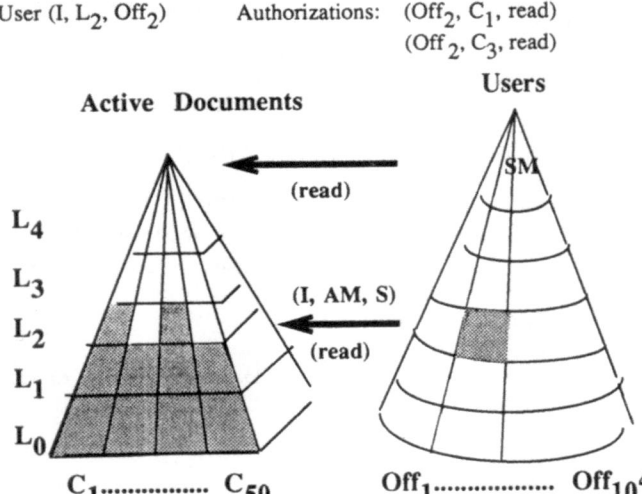

User (I, L_2, Off$_2$)　　　Authorizations:　(Off$_2$, C_1, read)
　　　　　　　　　　　　　　　　　　　　(Off$_2$, C_3, read)

Figure 3. Example of a user window

documents that the user can access (the portion is shown by the shaded area). This portion consists of the classes C_1 and C_3 at level L_2 and of all the classes at lower levels L_0 and L_1.

4　Functional Architecture and Mapping

The SAD architecture is based on the client-server paradigm [SVOB84]. This architecture has been chosen since it leads to an open system consisting of loosely coupled components - the servers and their clients- and so is appropriate for such office systems and other applications where flexibility and extensibility are required.

An office system network may contain storage devices with greatly differing capacities and access times. Because of the range of retrieval requirements and hardware capabilities it is useful to divide document filing systems into three categories:

- **Dynamic document filing systems** are used essentially as buffers allowing local storage of documents being manipulated (edited) and of documents received in response to queries issued to other document filing systems. Generally a dynamic document filing system is accessed by a single user. Since the number of documents held in a dynamic filing system is very small, retrieval can be simply by file name or some mnemonic.

- **Current document filing systems** are used for documents that are frequently accessed and so of current interest to the office. Current documents may be shared and updated (subject to authorization and concurrency constraints). Retrieval is by content, collection and document identifier.

- **Archive document filing systems** are used for less frequently accessed documents which have reached a stable state where modification is infrequent. If modification is necessary a new version of the document is created and the previous version retained. Document retrieval is again by content, collection and document identifier.

These three categories of systems are also correlated to the document life cycle. Our system uses all these different types or archive systems. The document management clients, used for document editing and manipulation, have a small dynamic archive

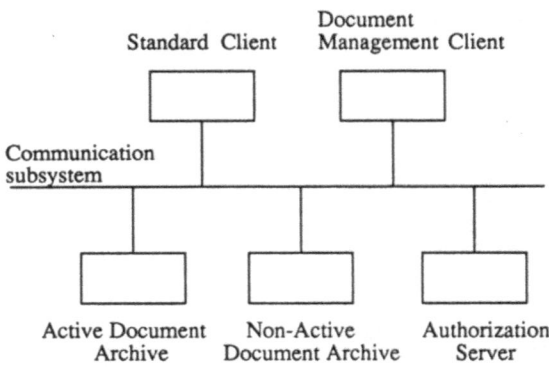

Figura 4. SAD functional architecture

used to store documents while being prepared. Upon completion, a document is transferred to the Active Document Archive, so that all authorized users can consult it. Therefore the Active Document Archive provides the function of current archive. The Non-Active Document Archive supports the archival function for documents that are not used and that must be stored for historical and audit purposes.

Figure 4 illustrates the SAD functional architecture. In general, the servers are located on specialized nodes and the clients on single-user workstations. The functions of current and archival document filing are supported by the Active Document Archive and Non-Active Document Archive respectively. The dynamic filing is supported by the client subsystem. Finally, the access control functions are supported by a special purpose *Access Control Server*.

In SAD there are two types of clients

- Standard client - This client can execute queries and manage the authorization rights; however does not have functions for document editing.

- Document management client - This client can execute all the operations of a standard client, and all operations concerning document input and manipulation. It contains a dynamic filing system to hold the documents being prepared.

The Active Document Archive and the Non-Active Document Archive have a similar internal architecture, which is illustrated in Figure 5. The only difference is that the Active Document Archive

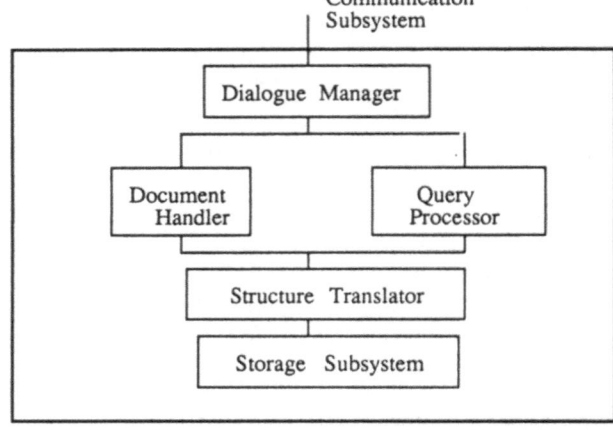

Figure 5. Internal architecture of document archives

provides support for the user-window. The Non-Active Document Archive being accessed only by the managers does not have the user-window mechanism, since the managers can access all documents. The internal component of an Active Document Archive or an Non-Active Document Archive server are the following

- **Dialogue Manager.** This component mediates all the communications between client and server. The client requests are received by the dialogue manager that performs a syntactical analysis and passes them to other server components. The dialogue manager has also the task of preparing the replies for the transmission and to manage the dialogue context for the duration of the client-server interaction.

- **Document Handler.** This component acts as mediator between the dialogue manager and the storage subsystem. The main task of this component is to return to the client only the documents belonging to the window of the user that has formulated the query. To execute this filtering operation, the documents result of a query are passed to the document handler that returns only the document in the user window. This component is only present in the Active Document Archive. No filtering operations are required for the documents stored in the Non-Active Document Archive, since the only users accessing the Non-Active Document Archive are the managers and they can access all documents.

- **Query Processor.** This component has the task of executing queries. It checks the syntactic correctness of the query and performs query decomposition and query optimization. The result of the query execution is the set of identifiers of all documents satisfying the query.

- **Structure Translator.** The structure handles the conversion between the document representation used for exchange with the client and the storage format in the storage subsystem. It also maps the commands issued by the server controller for the storage of documents onto corresponding operations for the storage subsystem.

- **Storage Subsystem.** The storage subsystem provides functions for the storage and retrieval of documents, maintains access methods for document retrieval and allows the storage of large data values. Different access methods are supported for formatted data and for text components.

The storage subsystem has been implemented by acquiring the information retrieval system IRIDIS. The other components have been developed "ad hoc". The reason why the IRIDIS system cannot be used directly but other components (such as the query processor) had to developed is that the functionalities it provides are not exactly those required by the applications. For example, the data model and query language provided by the IRIDIS system are slightly different from those designed as part of the conceptual model under the user requirements. The choice of this information retrieval system has been rather based on economic - its cost - and logistic reasons - its availability through an italian vendor. Therefore an important part of the functional design has been to identify the discrepancies between the functionalities required and those provided by the IRIDIS system. The required functionalities, not provided by IRIDIS, are supported by the other server components, designed on purpose.

In addition to the Active Document Archive and Non-Active Document Archive servers, the SAD architecture contains an Authorization Server. This server has the task of supporting the access controls. The authorization mechanism implemented by the server is based on the model described in the previous section.

This server has also been designed and implemented "ad hoc" since the IRIDIS system does not provide the required authorization functionalities. The internal server architecture is described in [MONT88].

A standard client contains several components, such as a dialogue manager, a user interface management system, a multiserver coordinator. The last component is used to support operations that involve several servers, such as the transfer of a document from the Active Document Archive to the Non-Active Document Archive. A document management client contains the same components and in addition a document editor and a local dynamic archive. The first type of client is used by the majority of users, while the second is used by users with document management responsibilities.

4.1 Hardware and software architecture

The organization had a preexisting hw/ws architecture, illustrated in Figure 6 that for economic reasons has also to support the document management system previously described. This architecture is based on two types of processing unit. The first is a computer of the IBM 30xx series. There are two computers of this type to ensure service continuity, operating in a configuration masterslave. The commutation between master and slave is executed manually. These two systems, called central units, are located at the organization management.

The second type has the function of departmental unit and is a computer of the family 470x. There is a computer of this type at each of the organization agencies and branches. These units have the task of managing all local information and they are seen as remote nodes from the central units. A department unit manages a number of terminals and personal computers, that are used for local applications. The organization is also connected to an Interbanking Network for operations with other organizations.

4.2 Mapping

The mapping of the functional architecture illustrated in Figure 4 on the architecture in Figure 6 has been quite simple. Since the documents are generated and controlled by users residing at the organization management, all servers (Active Document Archive, Non-Active Document Archive, Authorization Server) have been allocated at the central units. They are therefore mapped as processes on these units. All the communications among them are supported by interprocess communication mechanisms.

The standard clients have been mapped as terminals. These terminals can be local or remote with respect to the central units. In the latter case, the department units with the associated communication units make the remote access transparent. In this way, from a branch it is possible to consult the documents stored in the servers. The document management clients have been mapped on personal computers and located only the organization management.

From the point of view of the document management system, the entire hw/sw architecture can be seen as the system illustrated in Figure 7.

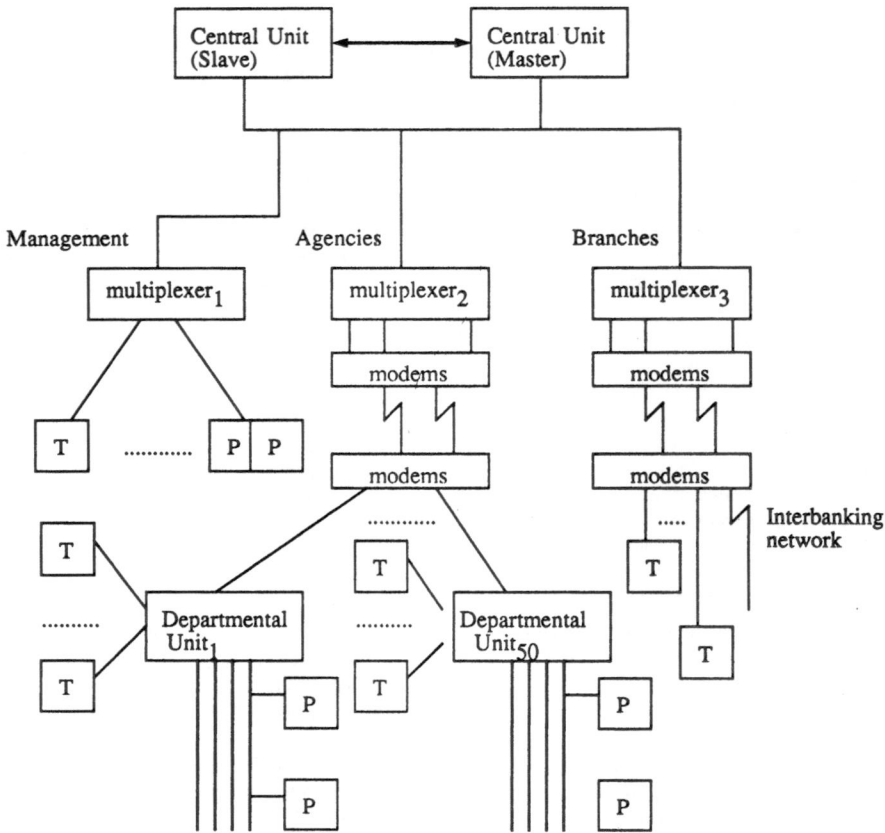

Figure 6. Hw/Sw Architecture

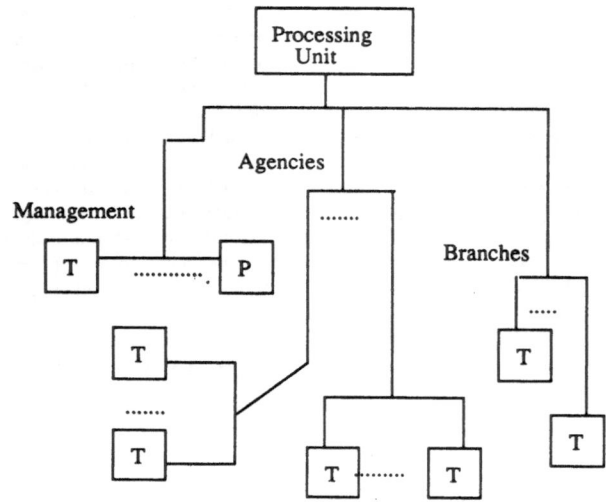

Figure 7. Hw/Sw Architecture from a functional viewpoint

5   Conclusions

The introduction of a document management system has a considerable impact within the organization. Very often, the introduction of new systems is the opportunity for executing additional modifications concerning other aspects such as the work organization. In our case for example, the preexisting authorization mechanism has been modified by introducing a greater number of discretionality levels and refining the authorization granularities. Supporting such extended authorization model would not have been possible without computer support. This new authorization model is supported by a specific architecture component - the Authorization Server - which has been fully implemented. Other architecture components, such as the Active Document Archive and Non-Active Document Archive, are under implementation.

Even if the implementation has not been completed, it is possible to make some points. Very often the office automation systems are developed without particular restrictions. Therefore it is possible to choose the most appropriate hw/sw environments. In our case, instead, two constraints concerning the preexisting hw/sw architecture have heavily influenced the design and the future usage of the system:

- the document management applications must share the hardware architecture with other 100 different applications that execute around 100,000 daily transactions;
- the communication subsystem has not enough capacity to support the amount of information that will have to transmitted.

Finally we note that in most situations the office automation is an evolutionary (often slow) process. Usually an organization starts automating some applications - checking and saving accounts in our example. Other applications are automated later on - the document management in our example. To support this evolutionary process it is necessary to develop adequate design tools, that take into account constraints deriving from existing applications and hw/sw environments, and integration tools [BERT89] for the interconnection of these preexisting applications.

References

[AGOS85]   Agosti M.S., "Un Sistema per la Gestione di Documenti Multimediali", *Congresso AICA*, Padova 1985.

[ALBA85]   Albano A., Cardelli L., Orsini R., "A Strongly Typed, Interactive Conceptual Language", *ACM Transactions on Database Systems*, Vol.10, N.2, March 1985.

[BERT88]   Bertino E., Rabitti F., Gibbs S., "Query Processing in a Multimedia Document Systems", *ACM Transactions on Office Information Systems*, Vol.6, N.1, 1-43 January 1988.

[BERT89]   Bertino E., Negri M., Pelagatti G., Sbattella L., "Integration of Heterogeneous Database Integration through an Object-Oriented Interface", *Information Systems*, Vol.14, No. 5, 1989.

[BPA88]   Servizio Organizzazione e Metodi (ed.), "Elenco Posizioni Circolari", *Documenti Interni della Banca Popolare di Ancona*, January 1988.

[BRAC84]   Bracchi G., and Pernici B., "The Design Requirements of Office Systems", *ACM Transactions on Office Information Systems*, Vol.2, N.2, 151-170 April 1984.

[HIGG84]   Higgins C.A., and Safayeni F.R., "A Critical Appraisal of Task Taxonomies as a Tool for Studying Office Activities", *ACM Transactions on Office Information Systems*, Vol.2, N.4, 131-139 October 1984.

[LAND81]   Landwehr C.E., "Formal Model for Computer Security", *ACM Computing Surveys*, Vol.13, No. 3, 247-278 September 1981.

[LOGO86]   Logos Progetti (ed.), "IRIDIS Descrizione Generale", *Documentazione IRIDIS*, Vol.1, 1986.

[MONT88]   Montesi D., "Progettazione e Sviluppo di un Sistema di Gestione di Documenti in Ambito Bancario: un Esempio di Automazione di Ufficio", Doctorate Thesis, Computer Science Department, Pisa University, Dec. 1988.

[SVOB84]   Svobodova L., "File Servers for Network-Based Distributed Systems", *ACM Comp. Surveys*, Vol.16, No.4, 353-398 December 1984.

ALADIN: A knowledge based data analysis in an industrial field

Abdelkébir ABDALI
I.N.S.A de LYON
Laboratoire d'Informatique Appliquée
Bâtiment 502 IF
69621 VILLEURBANNE CEDEX   FRANCE

ABSTRACT

The main problem with data analysis packages, although quite powerful and interactive, is the lack of statistical knowledge.

To overcome this deficiency, one of the possibilities lies in applying expert system techniques to improve the existing programs.

This paper is intented to describe our experience in the special field of industrial processes where data analysis methods are widely used and where ALADIN a prototype of a knowledge-based system is being developed to give advice to a statistically naive user.

Keywords: Knowledge based systems, Statistics, Multidimensional data analysis, Industrial processes

1. INTRODUCTION

In order to study the behavior of an industrial process, the use of statistical and data analysis methods is appropriate and efficient ([11]).

Unfortunately, once the data acquired on plant and organized into a database, the difficulties attached to the application of data analysis techniques are just one end of the problem for the naive user. The other end is the difficulties associated to the domain and mainly due to the diversity and the disparity of data and entities to study, and to the considerable pile of knowledge about processes which may be taken into account and considered for interpreting correctly the results.

These observations led us to the design and implementation of ALADIN, a prototype of a knwoledge-based system that can assist such user. Its validation is performed on continuous manufacturing processes: cement and cast iron processes.

2. AI AND DATA ANALYSIS

It is now widely recognized that the proliferation of personal computers and the development of cheap statistical software has led to an easy use of data analysis. But the main problem with current statistical packages, although quite powerful and interactive, is the lack of statistical knowledge.

Moreover, data analysis practice (figure 1) is an iterative process and several cycles are usually required before a satisfactory description of the data is found. Through its maze, the data analyst must in progressing think about different aspects simultaneously and has to make decisions according to the nature of the problem and the kind of the data.

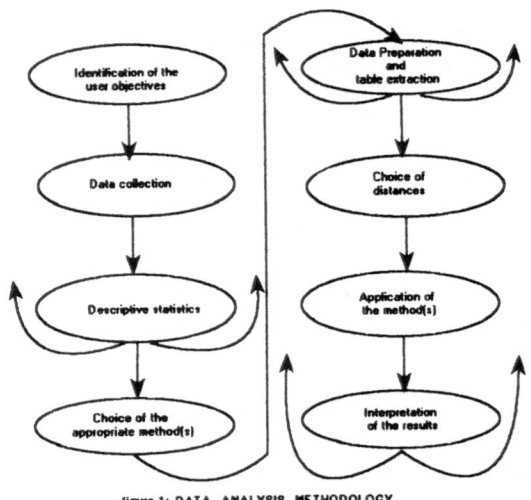

figure 1: DATA ANALYSIS METHODOLOGY.

Therefore, it appears that combining expert system (ES) techniques with the existing statistical software can provide assistance to novice users in the course of a data analysis. Thus, recently a number of studies have been published on the subject of statistical expert systems (SES) (e.g [4], [5], [6], [7] and [10]).

An ideal SES should do, guide, explain, and even teach the statistical techniques; that is, it would among other things:
   * interact with the user to define the research aims,
   * check the validity of the assumptions underlying the methods,
   * guide in selecting the appropriate statistical technique,
   * help in applying the chosen methods in a proper way,
   * suggest possible data transformations if the assumptions are violated,
   * explain the meaning of technical terms,
   * assist in the results interpretation, ...

3. ALADIN STRUCTURE

Our own work, ALADIN, advises the inexperienced user in each stage of the industrial data analysis process and its novelty compared with other SES largely results from the preparation phase of data which is costly and time consuming ([2]).

Obviously, the purpose is not to automate completely the analysis process because of the size of knowledge that a statistician is expected to do but to provide intelligent suggestions, to interactively guide the user and to help him to understand the results throught interpretation.

ALADIN is basically a production system written in Turbo-Prolog and developed to run on an IBM-PC or compatible computer. It is linked to the MODULAD package ([9]) (written in Fortran) that offers the main useful tools in multivariate analysis and to some graphical tools for the required plots.

At present time, ALADIN is limited at the Principal Component Analysis (PCA) problems. Nevertheless, its architecture (i.e the separation of the statistical expertise from the knowledge about the subject matter from which the data are) will permit to add new techniques and to introduce new knowledge about other industrial processes. It could also be extented to other softwares with small modifications.

ALADIN consists of four modules:
* preparation of data module,
* choice of techniques module (limited at PCA),
* application of chosen techniques module,
* and interpretation of results module.

ALADIN knowledge (figure 2) has three parts:

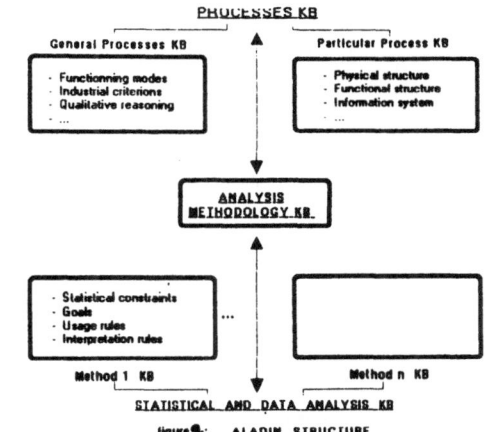

figure 2: ALADIN STRUCTURE

3.1 Knowledge about industrial processes

This Knowledge was described in ([1]) and embodies:

3.1.1 Knowledge about general processes and processes type to study:

It comprises knowledge about:
   * indexed functionning modes,
   * industrial criterions to be satisfied (energy, pollution, security, ...),

* qualitative reasoning ([3]), ...

3.1.2 Knowledge about the particular process under study:

It concerns:
* its physical structure: the process is represented in terms of a hierarchy: each component is viewed as consisting of a number of component parts and each component, in turn, may consist of other component parts (figure 3),
* its functional structure: each component has a characteristic behavior,
* its information system: the sensory system, the variables, the time lags, ...
* its behavior, ...

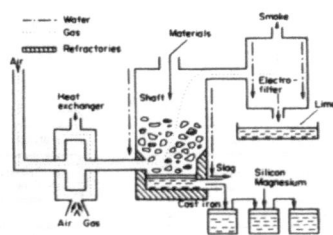

Hot blast cupola: scheme

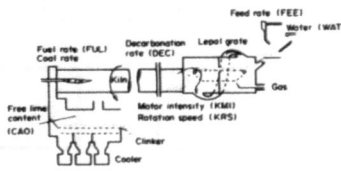

Rotary cement kiln: scheme

figure 3

3.2 Knowledge about statistical methods

There are three groups of methods: descriptive methods (mainly factor analysis), explaining methods (segmentation, discriminant analysis, ...) and classification procedures (cluster analysis, metric and nonmetric classification, ...).

To each method, are associated:
* statistical constraints and required assumptions in the data table,
* goals,
* usage rules (specification of control parameters, ...) which depend on the MODULAD manual,
* "elementary" rules of interpretation and typical situations (classical formes of the cluster, ...) that offer precious suggestions for a quick interpretation of the results.

3.3 Meta-knowledge

It contains the analysis methodology: when, why, and how to conduct the analysis.

This knowledge is still under development.

4. ALADIN AND DATA PREPARATION

ALADIN starts by breaking the industrial objectives of the user expressed in natural language and translates them in elementary statistical goals already known and associated to the available methods.

Example of industrial objectives:
* Determination of the delays and time constants
* Synchronization of numerical information
* Representation of the interactions between the variables
* Detection of cycles, trends, ...
* Detection of process functionning modes, ...

Next ALADIN performs some checks and transformations. Amongst these are:

1. The static analysis of a process means that the phenomena in the process must appear as synchronous: we must therefore neutralize the dynamics of the phenomena by taking into account the delays and time constants which link the variables describing these phenomena.
ALADIN performs this especially by using the cross-correlation functions

between the variables considered in pairs in order to detect the shift for which the information expressed by the first variable is best explained by the second.

Example:
* **IF** dependency sense between two variables is known
THEN look for (the maximum or the minimum) of the function.
* **IF** causality sense between two variables is known
THEN look for the (right-hand or left-hand) side where the extremum is

2. ALADIN identifies the statistical type of the table (of measurements, of categories or heterogeneous) and participates to the variables classification: numerical or categorical.

3. To check the data likelihood and to detect the anomalous values (due to sensor degradation, spurious readings, etc.), ALADIN uses rules concerning the interval allowed, the variation speed, the relationships between variables, ...
According to their number, ALADIN suggests their elimination or estimation.

4. When necessary, ALADIN transforms the qualitative variables into homogeneous variables using some coding techniques.

5. ALADIN AND PRINCIPAL COMPONENT ANALYSIS

The central purpose of PCA is to reduce the dimensionality of a data set in which there are a large number (p) of interrelated variables to a much small number of Principal Components (PCs) whilst retaining as much as possible of the variation present in the original data set ([8]).

The main objective of ALADIN in this stage is to guide the user to identify the relevant results throught interpretation using graphics, etc.

For a PCA using a correlation matrix, the following process is adopted:

5.1 Examination of the egeinvalues of the correlation matrix

The examination of the eigenvalues sequence $(l_i)_i$ offers precious suggestions.

ALADIN uses rules such as:
* **IF** l_i is "close to p"
THEN there is a linear relationship between all the variables
* **IF** l_i is "large"
THEN the ith PC should be interesting

To decide how many PCs should be retained in order to account for most of the variation in the original variables, ALADIN uses rules of thumb like the criterion:
* Plot l_k against k and find at which value of k the slopes of lines joining the plotted points are steep to the left of k and not steep to the right. This value of k is the number of components to be retained.

5.2 Interpretation of PCs

The advantage of a two -or three-dimensional representation is that all the dependences can be displayed.

First, for each PC, the variables on which it has large coefficients are detected and interpreted. For instance:
* **IF** all there variables are in the same side of the axis
THEN this PC is a 'size' component
* The "closer geographically" two variables are, and the further are from the origin, the more similar their evolution
* The closer an experiment point is to a variable, the more it corresponds to a large value of that variable

Next it translates the output in a report in trying to find a satisfactory physical interpretation like:
* The clear opposition on axis 1 between "pig iron" and "returns" comes from the fact that total

512

quantity of iron charged is kept constant.
* The opposition on axis 2 between "wear and tear" and "iron temperature" is due to an increase in thermal loss caused by the continual wear and tear on the refractory lining

Then ALADIN looks at the observations cluster, tries to point out patterns and peculiarities (groups, outliers, etc) and draws the user attention to those.

6. CONCLUSION

Statistics is a big subject. The complete expertise of an expert data analyst incorporates a vaste range of different kinds of knowledge. That it is still hard today to build an automated statistical consultant.

Focussing on industrial processes subdomain and containing knowledge about the domain where the data come from, ALADIN is able to help efficiently the naive user.

Further research is needed before a sophisticated system is available. Some points like the following must be studied:
    * extension to other data analysis techniques (such as segmentation): it poses the problem of the choice of the most appropriate technique for a given problem,
    * improvement of the user interface (windowing techniques, bit mapped terminal, ...),
    * justification of reasoning and recommendations, explanation capabilities (e.g visual lexicon approach to explain unkown technical terms)
    * qualitative reasoning.

ACKNOWLEDGMENTS

The author gratefully acknowledges the contribution of Professor P. Prévôt (INSA-Lyon), director of this research project, for the helpful discussions on industrial processes.

REFERENCES

[1] Abdali A. and Prévôt P. 89
ALADIN: Prototype d'un Système Expert pour l'Analyse de Données Industrielles, Proc. of the 9th International Workshop on Expert Systems and their Applications, p.613-625, EC2 (ed.)

[2] Abdali A. and Prévôt P. 89
L'Analyse de Données Industrielles par ALADIN, Proc. of EXPERSYS-89, p.139-144, Liebowitz J. and IITT International (eds.)

[3] Cohn A.G. 89
Approches to Qualitative Reasoning, Artificial Intelligence Review, n°3

[4] Diday E. (ed.) 89
Proc. of the Conference on Data Analysis, Learning Symbolic and Numeric Knowledge, New York: Nova Science Publishers

[5] Edwards D. and Raun N.E. (eds.) 88
Proc. of COMPSTAT 1988, Heidelberg: Physica-Verlag

[6] Gale W.A. (ed.) 86
Artificial Intelligence and Statistics, Addison Wesley: Reading Massachussetts

[7] Haux R. (ed.) 86
Expert Systems in Statistics, Stuttgart: Gustav Fischer

[8] Jolliffe I.T. 86
Principal Component Analysis, New York: Springer-Verlag

[9] MODULAD 87
Bibliothèque FORTRAN 77 pour l'Analyse des Données, INRIA Rocquencourt

[10] Phelps B. (ed.) 87
Interactions in Artificial Intelligence and Statistical Methods, Aldershot: Gower Technical Press Ltd.

[11] Prévôt P. 86
Data Analysis and Interaction Evaluation, Encyclopedia of Systems and Control, Pergamon Press

A FUNCTIONAL MODEL FOR STATISTICAL ENTITIES

M. Rafanelli *, F.L. Ricci +

(*) Istituto di Analisi dei Sistemi ed Informatica, CNR, viale Manzoni 30, 00185 Roma
(+) Istituto di Studi per la Ricerca e la Documentazione Scientifica, CNR, via De Lollis 12, 00185 Roma
Italy

ABSTRACT

In this paper the Authors discuss a functional model, in which a new data structure, called Statistical Entity, and a set of new operators are proposed. The aim is to have an algebra able to manipulate summary data starting from the descriptive attribuites of these data, with the automatic management of the summary type (rate, average, etc.).

1. INTRODUCTION

The representation of summary data by tables is widely used in statistical applications, such as census data analysis, economic planning, health care organization, etc. Hereafter we will call "statistical entity" (SE) any representation of data structures for summary data (relation, vector, table, etc.) in statistical databases. These SEs need both proper logical modeling tools [1], [11], [7], [10] and data definition and data manipulation language [5], [2]. In this paper we propose a functional model, in which a new data structure and new operations, able to operate on such a data structure, working only on the descriptive part of it, are defined; the computation of the summary values is automatic, as well as the management of the summary type (average, rate, etc.).

2. STATISTICAL MACRO DATA APPLICATIONS

In recent years, there has been a growing interest in studying macro data representation and manipulation; these data are often called statistical data and by the term *statistical databases* (SDB) we refer to databases that represent statistical or summary infor-mation and are used for statistical analysis. SDBs are different from conventional Data Bases (DBs) in the following ways:

a) *the data structure* - SDBs support *complex data structures* which contain quantitative informations (such as "population counts") and a combination of descriptive informations (such as "state", "sex", "race", etc.);

b) *the data manipulation* - boolean operations or logical asso-ciations between data are not of prime importance to statisticians; in addition, updating and deleting data is forbidden, because data are generally *static* (i.e., events consolidated in time);

c) *the data processing* - the statistician uses the techniques of *missing data estimation* or *outlyers estimation* for modifying the data and not *updating;* moreover, the use of statistical packages, which supply a support for the *data analysis*, is necessary.

2.1. MICRO AND MACRO SDBs

Generally there are two broad classes of SDBs, micro and macro SDBs. The former refers to SDBs containing disag-gregate data (i.e., records of individual entities or events). The latter refers to SDBs containing aggregate data, often shown as statistical tables, that result from the application of statistical-mathematical operations (i.e., count or average) on micro data. These two classes are different from various points of view: for example, from a descriptive point of view, there is, for the macro data, an intentional and an extensional level of the meta-data; from the querying point of view, the relational algebra operators are suitably modified so as to correctly carry out que-ries on the relations which represent the above structures.

Let us look at the dynamic aspect (i.e., the querying point of view). In a relational database, the table in Fig.1 is stored by the relation shown in Fig.2. If the user wishes to know "how is average age distributed in countries", the result of the query is the relation in Fig.3. As we can see, in order to obtain a correct result, the numeric value of the attribute "life expectancy" has to be recomputed.

Life expectancy in the 1981	Sex Male	Female
Country Japan	75	81
.....	....	....
Canada	73	81
....	....	....
Gambia	38	43

Figure 1 - Life expectancy table in the world in the 1981

(from a statistical research of Jo Ann Tooley and Lynn Anderson Carle,

U.S. News & World Report, March 1989)

Life expectancy in the 1981

Country	Life expectancy	Sex
Japan	75	Male
Japan	81	Female
.....	.....	.....
Canada	73	Male
Canada	80	Female
.....	......	......
Gambia	38	Male
Gambia	43	Female

Figure 2 - Life expectancy in the world in the 1981 represented by a relation (same information source of Fig.1)

In order to carry out the data analysis, a statistical user, that has only summary data, has often to manipulate the descriptive part of these data, before making such a data analysis. This phase is characterized by the homogenization of the macro data which are

Life expectancy in the 1981

Country	Life expectancy
Japan	78
.....	.....
Canada	77
.....	.....
Gambia	41

Figure 3 - Relation with "Life expectancy in the world in the 1981" without "sex" (same information source of Fig.1)

often distributed among different data owners, and by verifying the semantic consistency and comparability among different levels of aggregation of the available data. Two different paths have been followed for the manipulation of macro data: to extend the relational model (for example, [6]), or to propose a new model, i.e., a new data structure and new operations with their semantics to manipulate it. We have chosen the second solution, proposing the Mefisto functional model, in which a new data structure, the *statistical entity (SE),* and new operators are defined.

The models based on the relational model are an appropriate tool for the logical representation and the manipulation of micro-SDBs. Instead they present various disadvantages when are used as logical model for macro data; the more relevant of them is when the user has to express the usual queries using extremally complex statements [9].

In fact, at the level of micro data, the only things that need to be represented are the concepts and the associations among such concepts: on the other hand, at the level of macro data the operation of aggregation, carried out on micro data, renders such associations implicit to the summary datum; we must express, for each summary attribute, the category attributes which define it and viceversa [1].

2.2 THE DATA STRUCTURE

A Statistical Entity is represented by an ordered pair $< r, g >$,

where: r is a relation whose attributes are category attributes which describe an SE to which the pair refers;

g is a function which maps from the category attributes which describe the macro data to the macro data itself.

The aggregation function, applied to micro data to obtain the SE, generates the summary type (average, count, etc.) of the SE. As we will see, the operators defined in the following do not change the summary type of the SE to which they are applied.

3. DEFINITIONS AND TERMINOLOGIES

The elements that characterize a SE are:

a) a single *summary attribute* (quantitative data) representing a property of the statistical phenomenon described in the SE; its instances (summary values) are the numeric values inside the table. Its *summary type* depends on the particular aggregation function that generated it.

b) a set of *category attributes* (qualitative data), that is, the variables which describe the quantitative data.

c) *statistical entity category attribute domain (secad)*, that is, a set of values corresponding to every category attribute.

The Cartesian product of all the statistical entity variable domains of the SE represents the *statistical entity space*.

3.1 THE DATA MODEL

Let $\mathfrak{V} = \{C_1, \ldots, C_m\}$ be a *universe of category attributes*.
Let *dom* be a function that associates to each category attribute C_i an underlying domain, $dom(C_i)$.

A *statistical entity scheme S* is a pair $< \underline{C}, t >$, where " $\underline{C}$ " ($\mathfrak{V} \supseteq \underline{C}$) is a set of the category attributes of S and " t " is the summary type (for instance, "rate") of the summary attribute.

Let $S = < \underline{C}, t >$ be an SE scheme, with $\underline{C} = \{C_1, \ldots, C_n\}$ with $n \leq m$: a *statistical entity instance s* on S is a pair $< \underline{D}, g >$, where $\underline{D} = \{D_i\}$, with $1 \leq i \leq n$, $dom(C_i) \supseteq D_i$ and D_i finite

set, and g is a function (according to t) which maps from the *statistical entity space*

$$r^+(s) = D_1 \times D_2 \times \ldots \times D_n \quad \text{to} \quad \mathfrak{R} \cup \{NV\},$$

where $\mathfrak{R}$ is the set of real numbers and NV means "null value".
We denoted by $r(s)$ a relation which is a subset of the statistical entity space $r^+(s)$, that is, $r^+(s) \supset r(s)$. The relations $r(s)$ and $r^+(s)$ are defined on the relation scheme $\underline{C}$ (that is, the set of category attributes previously defined).

Let $p = (d_1, \ldots, d_n)$ be a *tuple* which represents an element of $r^+(s)$, with $d_i \in D_i$ ($1 \leq i \leq n$), and let Z be a non empty subset of $\underline{C}$, that is, $\underline{C} \supset Z$; we denote by $p(C_j)$ the instance of the attribute C_j ($C_j \in \underline{C}$) into the tuple p, and by $p[Z]$ the tuple, whose values are the corresponding instances, in p, of the attributes of Z. Let r be a relation defined on $\underline{C}$ and let Z be a non empty subset of $\underline{C}$; the *projection* of r on Z, that is $\pi_Z(r)$, is the set $\{p[Z] \mid p \in r\}$. Finally, let $\underline{R}$ be a relation scheme, and let Z be a non empty subset of $\underline{R}$. Z is *key* for $\underline{R}$ if:
$\forall$ r (defined on $\underline{R}$) and $\forall$ $p_1, p_2 \in r \quad \dashrightarrow \quad p_1[Z] = p_2[Z]$
implies $p_1[\underline{R}\text{-}Z] = p_2[\underline{R}\text{-}Z]$.

4. THE ALGEBRA OPERATORS

In order to schematically represent the operations of the Mefisto model we use the graph in Fig.4, where the orientated edge goes from the input data structure to the output data structure, with regard to the operations associated with the edge itself. The algebra operations can have one or two statistical entities in input, or the couple < relation, statistical entity >; output is one statistical entity.

4.1. OPERATOR WITH ONE OPERAND AND RECOMPUTATION OF THE SUMMARY VALUE

Summarization

One of the operations performed in the statistical entity manipulation is the elimination of one category attribute. This operation is carried out by the summarization operation, which provides in output a statistical entity in which the category attributes are the same (except the deleted category attribute) of the statistical entity in input and the summary values are recomputed according to the new statistical entity space of the output statistical entity.   Let $s_1 = <\underline{D}_1, g_1>$ be a statistical entity defined on $S_1 = <\underline{C}_1, t>$ and let $C_i \in \underline{C}_1$; the **summarization** of s_1, with respect to C_i, is the statistical entity s defined on $<\underline{C}_1 - \{C_i\}, t>$;   then we have:

$s = \Sigma_{C_i}(s_1) = <\underline{D}_1-\{D_i\}, g>$ with each summary value:

$g(p) = f_t (\{ g_1(p_1) \mid p_1 \in r^+(s_1) \wedge p = p_1[\underline{C}_1 - \{C_i\}] \})$

with $p \in r^+(s)$.

By f_t we represent a function which depends on the summary type of the statistical entity and which permits the recomputation of the summary attribute values. This means that this operator is, in reality, a *family* of operators, each of them doing the same operation (the summarization) but by different f_t.

tributes. The resulting statistical entity is a reorganization of the starting data, with (in general) an aggregation of data (recomputation of the summary values). In this case the concepts which are reclassified by the operator change. Let us consider, for example, the statistical entity "Number_of_ cars_produced" of Fig. 5-a, characterized by the category attributes "model" and "years"; if we wish to have the same statistical entity described by the category attributes "displacement" and "years" (the link between the "model and "displacement" is the relation "r" of Fig.5-b), we perform the classification of "Number_of_cars_ produced" by the relation "r" along the category attributes "displacement" and "years", obtaining the SE of Fig. 6.

Let $s_1 = <\underline{D}_1, g_1>$ be a statistical entity on $S_1 = <\underline{C}_1, t>$; let $\underline{R}$ be a relation scheme; let $\underline{C}_1 \cap \underline{R}$ be a key of $\underline{R}$; let $\underline{C}$ be a set of attributes such that $\underline{C}_1 U \underline{R} \supset \underline{C}$; let r be a relation defined on $\underline{R}$. The **classification** of s_1 by r along $\underline{C}$ is a statistical entity s

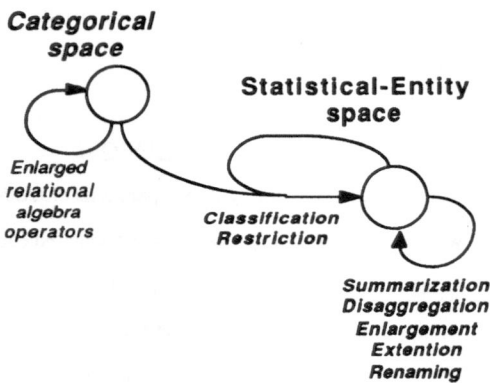

Fig. 4

4.2. OPERATOR WITH TWO OPERANDS AND RECOM-
PUTATION OF THE SUMMARY TYPE

Classification

This operation classifies one category attribute of an SE according to a given relation in which the new classification criteria are specified. The scheme of this relation contains both the category attributes which must be substituted, and the category attributes which must substitute the above mentioned

#_OF_CARS_PRODUCED_ IN_JAPAN (by Model and Years) (absol. values, by thousands)	MODEL		
	Corolla	Civic	Corona
1983	536	438	317
YEARS 1984	601	496	369
1985	710	580	421
. . . .	. . .	. . .	. . .

(a)

r

MODEL	DISPLACEMENT
Corolla	1,200
Civic	1,200
Corona	1,800

(b)

Fig. 5

#_OF_CARS_PRODUCED (absol. values, by thousands)	DISPLACEMENT	
	1,200	1,800
YEARS 1980	768	220
1981	831	249
1982	900	285
1983	974	317
1984	1,097	369
1985	1,290	421
. . . .	. . .	. . .

Fig. 6

r e l

MODEL	YEARS
Corolla	1981
Civic	1981
Corolla	1982
Civic	1982

Fig. 7

#_OF_CARS_PRODUCED (absol. values, by thousands)	MODEL	
	Corolla	Civic
YEARS 1981	458	373
1982	499	401

Fig. 8

defined on $S = <\underline{C}, t>$:

$s = \zeta_{\underline{C}}(T_1, r) = <\{D_i \mid D_i \in \underline{D}_1 \wedge C_i \in \underline{C}_1 \cap \underline{C}\} \cup \{D_i \mid D_i = \pi_{C_i}(r) \wedge C_i \in \underline{R} - \underline{C}_1\}, g>$

with summary value: $g(p) = f_t (\{ g_1(p_1) \mid p_1 \in r^+(s_1) \wedge p_r \in r \wedge p_1 [\underline{C}_1 \cap \underline{C}] = p [\underline{C}_1 \cap \underline{C}] \wedge p_r [\underline{R} \cap \underline{C}] = p [\underline{R} \cap \underline{C}] \wedge p_1 [\underline{R} - \underline{C}] = p_r [\underline{R} - \underline{C}] \})$,   where $p \in r^+(s)$.

Besides, if $\{g_1(p_1)\} = \varnothing$ then $g(p) = f_t(\varnothing) = $ null value.

Restriction

This operation gives in output an SE whose statistical entity space is restricted to the elements of a set described by a given relation.

The result of its application is a new statistical entity, defined on the same statistical entity scheme as the input SE.

For instance, let us consider the SE "Number_of_cars_produced" (Fig. 5-a); if we only want to have the production of "Civic, Corolla" and in "1981, 1982", we perform the restriction of "Number_of_cars_produced" by the relation "rel" of Fig. 7, obtaining the SE of Fig. 8 (sometimes this operation involves a recomputation of the summary values).

Let $s_1 = <\underline{D}_1, g_1>$ be an SE on $S_1 = <\underline{C}_1, t>$; further, let r_1 be a relation defined on the relation scheme $\underline{R}_1$ (this relation represents a set of element of the statistical entity space of s_1) and let $\underline{C}_1 \supseteq \underline{R}_1$ and $\pi_{\underline{R}_1}(r^+(s_1)) \supseteq r_1$.

The **restriction** of s_1 by r_1 is a statistical entity s defined on the same statistical entity scheme S_1:

$s = \sigma_M(r_1, s_1) = < \{ D_i \mid D_i = D_{i1} \wedge C_{i1} \notin \underline{R}_1 \} \cup \{ D_i \mid D_i = \pi_{C_i}(r_1) \wedge C_i \in \underline{R}_1 \}, g >$

with summary value: $g(p) = f_t (g_1(p_1) \mid p_1 \in r^+(s_1) \wedge p_1 = p)$ where $p \in r^+(s)$.

Enlargement

Let us consider, as an example, the two SEs of Figures 9 and 10; if we are interesting to have the SE "Employees in 1980 by "States and Industry" (where the category attribute domain of "States" is {Alabama, California, Oregon, Texas}), that is, we are interesting to "union" of the previous two SEs, we perform the enlargement of these SEs and we obtain the SE of Fig. 11. To perform this operation we have to know or the population, with regard to which the percentages have been computed, or the partial percentages of the single state with regard to the total of the population.

Let $s_1 = < \{D_1', D_2, \ldots, D_n\}, g_1 >$ and $s_2 = < \{D_1'', D_2, \ldots, D_n\}, g_2 >$ be two statistical entities defined $S_1 = < \underline{C}_1, t >$, so

EMPLOYEES (by Industry and State = Ca, Tx) (1980) (rate per industry and state)		INDUSTRY			
		Agricolture	Metal	Other	Total
STATE	California	2.72	19.51	18.08	40.31
	Texas	10.08	19.12	30.49	59.69
	Total	12.80	38.63	48.57	100.00

Fig. 9

EMPLOYEES (by Industry and State = Al, Or)) (1980) (rate per industry and state)		INDUSTRY			
		Agricolture	Metal	Other	Total
STATE	Alabama	2.93	15.41	24.45	42.79
	Oregon	3.67	24.94	28.68	57.21
	Total	6.60	40.35	53.05	100.00

Fig. 10

EMPLOYEES_in_1980 (rate per industry and states)		INDUSTRY			
		Agricolture	Metal	Other	Total
STATES	Alabama	1.01	5.33	8.45	14.79
	California	1.78	12.76	11.83	26.37
	Oregon	1.27	8.63	9.89	19.79
	Texas	6.59	12.51	19.95	39.05
	Total	10.65	39.23	50.12	100.00

Fig. 11

that $D_1' \cap D_1'' = \emptyset$, the **enlargement** of s_1 and s_2 is a statistical entity s defined on the same table scheme S_1:

$$s = s_1 \, \Omega \, s_2 = < \{ D_1' \cup D_1'', D_2, \ldots, D_n \}, g >$$

with the summary value characterized, for $p \in r^+(s)$, by the following function:

$$g(p) = \begin{cases} f_t(g_1(p_1)) & \text{if } p_1 \in r^+(s_1) \wedge p_1 = p \\ f_t(g_2(p_2)) & \text{if } p_2 \in r^+(s_2) \wedge p_2 = p. \end{cases}$$

Disaggregation

This operation is related to the problem of the estimation. It is a binary operation which, starting from two SEs **s** and s_d, provides a new SE which is the estimation of s by s_d; the statistical entity of disaggregation s_d contains, in its summary values, the way to disaggregate the summary values of the starting SE.

Let $s_1 = < \underline{D}_1, g_1 >$ be a statistical entity on $S_1 = <\underline{C}_1, t >$; in addition let $s_d = < \underline{D}_d, g_d >$ (that expresses the disaggregation law regarding s_1) be a statistical entity on $S_d = < \underline{C}_d, t_d >$, with $\underline{C}_1 \neq \underline{C}_d$ and $\forall \, C_i \in \underline{C}_1 \cap \underline{C}_d : D_{i1} = D_{i\,d}$.

The **disaggregation** of s_1 by s_d is a statistical entity s defined on $<\underline{C}_1 \cup \{C_i\}, t >$: $\quad \Sigma^{-1}_{s_d}(s_1) = < \underline{D}_1 \cup \underline{D}_d, g >$

with summary value: $\quad g(p) = (\, g_1(p_1) \cdot g_d(p_d) \, |$

$$p_1 \in r^+(s_1) \wedge p_d \in r^+(s_d) \wedge p_1 = p[\underline{C}_1] \wedge p_d = p[\underline{C}_d] \,)$$

where $p \in r^+(s)$ and the symbol $\cdot$ represents the multiplication between real numbers.

4.3   OPERATOR WITH ONE OPERAND, WITHOUT RE-COMPUTATION OF THE SUMMARY TYPE

Extension

This operation works on one SE and provides as output an SE in which a new category attribute is added with a unique value in the corresponding underlying domain.

The values of the summary attribute are equal to those of the input SE, but the dimension of the SE (that is, the number of the category attributes) is increased by one.

Let $s_1 = < \underline{D}_1, g_1 >$ be a statistical entity on $S_1 = < \underline{C}_1, t >$ and let $C_{n+1} \notin \underline{C}_1$ and $v_{n+1} \in dom(C_{n+1})$. The **extension** of s_1 by C_{n+1} with value v_{n+1} is a statistical entity s defined on $< \underline{C}_1 \cup \{C_{n+1}\}, t >$:

$$s = \varepsilon_{< C_{n+1}, v_{n+1} >}(s_1) = < \underline{D}_1 \cup \{ \{v_{n+1}\} \}, g >$$

with the summary value characterized by the following function:

$$g(p) = (\, g_1(p_1) \, | \, p_1 \in r^+(s_1) \wedge p_1 = p[\underline{C}_1] \,)$$

518

and with $p \in r^+(s)$.

The extension operation ensures that the statistical entity space $r^+(s)$ of the resulting SE coincides with the Cartesian product between the statistical entity space $r^+(s_1)$ of the input SE and the relation composed by the tuple $(C_{n+1} = v_{n+1})$, whose schema consists only of the attribute C_{n+1}.

Renaming

This operation works on one SE and provides as output an SE in which the name of the category attribute is changed.

Let $s_1 = < \underline{D}_1, g_1 >$ be a statistical entity on $S_1 = < \underline{C}_1, t >$ and let $C_i \in \underline{C}_1$ and $Y_i \notin \underline{C}_1$. The **renaming** of C_i (of s_1) with Y_i is a statistical entity s defined on $<(\underline{C}_1 - \{C_i\}) \cup \{Y_i\}, t >$:

$$s = \delta_{C_i \rightarrow Y_i}(s_1) = < \underline{D}_1, g >$$

with the summary value characterized by the following function:

$$g(p) = (g_1(p_1) \mid p_1 \in r^+(s_1) \wedge p[\underline{C} - \{Y_i\}] = p_1[\underline{C}_1 - \{C_i\}]$$
$$\wedge p[Y_i] = p_1[C_i]) \qquad \text{and with } p \in r^+(s) .$$

5. STATISTICAL EXPERTISE ELICITATION

In this section the authors discuss the problem regarding the automatic management of the summary type in the operations previously described, without having to define a special procedure for each SE considered. It must be realized that it is impossible a priori to know which summary types should be considered in a macro-SDB, in that there is always the possibility of defining new ones; it follows that the world of the summary type is an open world. In order to do this, a set of summary type has to be defined and the database administrator (DBA) must supply to the system, for each summary type, the information (condition of applicability, formulae for the computation of the different f_t) which enables the system to construct the recomputation procedures of the summary attribute values. In the following the instances of these informations with regard to the types "absolute value", "min", "max", "average" and "percentage" are given [3].

For the sake of simplicity, a notation like "matrix algebra" are used, where a summary value is represented by $t_{i,j}$.

Absolute value

condition of applicability : none

formulae : summarization and classification

$$t_i = \sum_j t^1_{i,j}$$

restriction

$$t_i = t^1_i$$

enlargement

$$t_i = t^1_i$$

Minimum

condition of applicability : none

formulae : summarization and classification

$$t_i = MIN_j (t^1_{i,j})$$

restriction

$$t_i = t^1_i$$

enlargement

$$t_i = t^1_i$$

Maximum

condition of applicability : none

formulae : summarization and classification

$$t_i = MAX_j (t^1_{i,j})$$

restriction

$$t_i = t^1_i$$

enlargement

$$t_i = t^1_i$$

Average

condition of applicability : the availability of a statistical entity with the same table space obtained by means of an aggregate function of the type count (T_c) or sum (T_s)

formulae : summarization and classification

a) in the presence of the count statistical entity (T_c):

$$t_i = \frac{\sum_j t^c_{i,j} t^1_{i,j}}{\sum_j t^c_{i,j}}$$

520

b) in the presence of the sum statistical entity (T_S):

$$t_i = \left.\sum_j t^s_{i,j}\middle/\sum_j t^s_{i,j} \middle/ t^1_{i,j}\right.$$

restriction

$$t_i = t^1_i$$

enlargement

$$t_i = t^1_i$$

Percentage

condition of applicability . It is needed to know the value of t_S

formulae : <u>summarization</u> and <u>classification</u>

$$t_i = \sum_k t^1_{i,k}$$

restriction

$$t_{i,j} = 100 * \left. t^1_{i,j} \middle/ \sum_k t^1_{k,j}\right.$$

<u>enlargement</u> (in presence of the values t_{S1} and t_{S2})

$$t_{i,j} = \left. t^1_{i,j} * t_{s_1} \middle/ t_{s_1} + t_{s_2}\right.$$

6. <u>CONCLUSIONS</u>

In this paper the authors have proposed and discussed a functional model, in which a new data structure and a set of new operations are presented, in order to manipulate aggregate data. A discussion about a comparison between this model and other previous proposals and some limitations of the relational algebra operators (with regard to the macro data) is made in [10]. A Data Definition Language, defining the SE data structure in a SDB [Meo Evoli 90], and a Visual Query Language, based on the above discussed set of operations [10], has been implemented on Macintosh II, using the MPW environment and the Pascal-object language.

REFERENCES

[1] Chan P., Shoshani A. "SUBJECT: a directory driven system for organizing and accessing large statistical databases" Proceed. 7th Very Large Data Bases, Cannes, France, September 1981

[2] Ghosh S.P. "Categorical numerical relational operations for statistical database management" Tech. Rep. IBM, RJ 5780, Nov. 1987

[3] Falcitelli G., Meo Evoli L., Nardelli E., Ricci F.L. "The Mefisto model: an object oriented representation for statistical data management" in "Data analysis, Learning Symbolic and Numeric Knowledge", Nova Science Pub., 1989

[4] Meo Evoli L. "Interaction model for Man-Table Base System" Proceed. 7th Intern. Symp. on Applied Informatics, Innsbruck, Austria, Febr. 1990

[5] Ozsoyoglu G., Ozsoyoglu Z.M. "Statistical database query language" IEEE Transactions on Software Engineering, Vol.SE-11, No.10, October 1985

[6] Ozsoyoglu G., Ozsoyoglu Z.M. , Matos V. "Extending Relational Algebra and Relational Calculus with Set-Valued Attributes and Aggregate Functions" ACM ToDS, Vol.12, No.4, Dec. 1987

[7] M.Rafanelli, F.L.Ricci "Proposal of a logical model for statistical database" Proceed. 2th Int. Workshop on Statistical Database Management, Los Altos, CA, Sept. 1983

[8] Rafanelli M., Shoshani A. "Storm: a statistical object representation model" Lecture Notes in Computer Science, N. 420, Springer Verlag Publ., 1990

[9] Rafanelli M., Ricci F.L. "Mefisto: a functional model for statistical entities" Tech. Rep. IASI (in press)

[10] Rafanelli M., Ricci F.L. "A visual interface for brawsing and manipulating statistical entities" Lecture Notes in Computer Science, N. 420, Springer Verlag Publ., 1990

[11] Su S.Y.W. "SAM*: a semantic association model for corporate and scientific/statistical databases" Information Sciences, Vol.29, No.2-3, May - June 1983

Exploratory data analysis using data semantics

Friedrich Gebhardt

Gesellschaft für Mathematik und Datenverarbeitung mbH (GMD)
Institut für Angewandte Informationstechnik (F3)
Schloß Birlinghoven, Postfach 1240, D-5205 Sankt Augustin 1
e-mail: gebhardt@kmx.gmd.dbp.de

Abstract. In our project EXPLORA, we try to utilize the semantics of the data for their exploratory statistical interpretation. The kernel of the system supplies a set of tools built around a search algorithm that exploits the semantic structures among variables, variable values and other objects. When a data set (or a type of data sets) is set up, these objects and relations have to be initialized; this includes defining the evaluation methods applicable to this particular data set. The system finds the most interesting statements about the data and thereby suppresses statements that are redundant or uninteresting relative to other ones that have been displayed. We propose an algorithm working on the data objects covered by a statement rather than on its syntactical form for suppressing results that apply to nearly the same data objects as another one even though the syntactical forms may – or may not – be quite different.

1   Essential components

1.1   Structure of the EXPLORA system

In our project EXPLORA, we are looking for conspicuous, non-redundant results extracted from data sets. For this objective, we try to utilize the semantics of data as far as they can be formalized when the data set or the type of data sets is being prepared for analysis [6; 11 – 13]. This will now be elaborated in more detail.

We want to explore a data set which is too big or too complex as to find the interesting or surprising properties just by looking at the original or aggregated data or at the customary describing statistics. The system essentially searches for statements about the data that are

- correct,
- conspicuous,
- non-redundant and
- not uninteresting in view of other statements.

In this context, "conspicuous" means that the fact underlying the statement exhibits some outstanding property or irregularity in the data such as values above or below certain limits or outside a statistical confidence interval. "Non-redundant" excludes statements that follow from some other, usually broader statement that is reported. "Uninteresting in view of other statements" are those that do not exactly follow but nevertheless loose their importance once that the other statement is known. Typical examples: If a rare property is true for all members of a set, it would be redundant to state this also for subsets; if a rare property holds for most members of a set, this need not hold for all subsets but is uninteresting if it does.

Conceptually the system consists of three main parts, the kernel system, the data manipulator and the user interface.

The kernel system is built in an object-oriented manner; it provides all the structures and procedures that are independent of the particular data set. This includes objects for data structures such as ordinal (linear) and hierarchical order, sets of sets and means for composing new structures from existing ones (e.g. Cartesian products). In addition, the kernel system contains a search algorithm for searching in those structures under control of several alternative redundancy properties such as "If a statement is true, then its predecessor (or successor) with respect to the given (partial) order is redundant (or uninteresting)". Utilizing this property amounts to pruning parts of the search space.

As an example let us examine the ordinal structure for a variable. To each interval of values of the variable there corresponds an object in the system; these objects are connected by a successor relation: The highest-level object comprises all possible data values. Each object at any level (except the lowest one) has two successors: one where the highest and one where the lowest potential value is cut off. On the lowest level, each object corresponds to exactly one data value; to this object, all data objects (representations of the external entities for which data had been acquired) having just this value are attached. Once the data values are declared to have an ordinal structure, all these objects are created automatically. The structure on the values of a variable induces a class structure on the set of data objects.

The data manipulator provides the means for setting up a particular data set (or a collection of similar data sets). This includes defining objects by specializing the objects included in the kernel system, setting up relations between these objects, attaching to them the actual data, establishing the validation methods that incorporate the meaning of the statements to be produced. More details will be given later.

The user interface permits the user to select variables, validation methods, subsets of the data, to set certain parameters and otherwise to control the search process. He may choose those parts of the entire search space that he momentarily is interested in. In addition it is possible to navigate in the search spaces in order to get statements on objects selected directly or through various relations with other objects previously found thereby using or neglecting the redundancy relations. The user interface will not be described here.

1.2   Main goal of the project

Our system differs in its underlying philosophy fundamentally from most statistical expert systems. Its goal is not to select more or less automatically statistical routines that are suitable for a given data set, perhaps also helping in the statistical interpretation of the results. There are already many systems of this type; some surveys are compiled by Gale [3] and Hand [9; 10] and more extensively by Chowdhury [1]. Some systems exploit semantical properties of the data to guide the selection of applicable statistical routines, exemplarily that by Wittkowski [16].

In contrast, our system is first of all a frame that permits the person who sets up a new application to define all those structures that convey the semantics of the data; during this process he chooses among other things the statistical routines (if any) to be used as verification methods and possibly in other contexts (e.g. for defining relations of uninterestingness).

Since this is still a major task, the system is meant to support multiple analyses, in particular evaluations of a repeating nature or of complex data sets that are inspected by many people.

We try to capture as many and as diverse means as possible for expressing the semantics of data. In this way we produce semantic analyses of the data instead of analyses based entirely or mainly on syntactic structures and verifiable properties of the data (such as normal distribution) only.

2   The search procedure

2.1   Overview
The theoretical foundation for the kernel system is a formal language based on categorical grammars. Primary syntactical categories are objects and statements; predicates and operations belong to the derived syntactical categories. All categories are subcategories of object. A detailed description is given in [14; 15].

Examples of objects in a given application include the variables, their potential values including sets of values if an order (most important types: hierarchic, ordinal) is given, the statements corresponding to potential facts in the data as determined by verification methods.

A search space is given by a predicate and a set of arguments on which the predicate operates. The arguments may be variables or derived objects. The order defined for the variables induces an order on the search space. Together with the predicate the proper redundancy relation for each argument is fixed from a set of predefined redundancy relations; these are of the type "If a statement is true for a certain set of arguments, then it is true (false, uninteresting) for its successors (predecessors) with respect to the given partial order on this argument". The search algorithm exploits this property for pruning the search space. Usually there exist many search spaces for a data set; they correspond to different predicates and to different sets of arguments for a given predicate.

The evaluation methods yield either a truth value or a numeric value from which the truth value is derived (e.g. "true" if outside a certain boundary). In the latter case, the user can alter the boundary according to his present needs. In addition, the system can compare two statements for different values of the arguments; as an example, a subset of a conspicuous set can be displayed if its value of the evaluation function exceeds that for the superset by a given amount.

It is possible to attach properties to objects. This permits the system to generalize results, that is to combine statements if they are valid for all (or most) objects with a common property. The properties are not used to define an order (hierarchical or otherwise) on the set of objects since different properties may belong to overlapping sets of objects and some objects may have no property at all. They are not exploited during the search phase but rather afterwards for reducing the number of facts to be stated.

As a next step, relations between properties or objects can be defined such as "contrasting". Then the user may ask to get together with any statement the contrasting ones (if there are any), that is the corresponding statements for contrasting objects or for objects with a contrasting property.

The searching procedure as outlined above has to be modified in order to avoid certain unwanted effects. Some important cases will be discussed in the following Sections.

The class structure is also utilized to arrange the results with headings, subheadings and, finally, statements that do not repeat those parts that are already present in the headings. The objects associated with predicates, variables and classes have slots for the necessary text constituents.

2.2   Ordinal structure
Very often, one is interested in the broadest groups that exhibit some conspicuous behaviour; this means that the search process should find statements on the highest level possible in the structure of a variable. However, some caution is necessary.

Consider a variable with ordinal structure and an ordinary verification method for finding conspicuous sets of data objects such as the percentage of conspicuous objects exceeding a limit or the mean of a variable deviating from the overall mean (or some other value) by more than a certain multiple of the standard deviation.

The search procedure might find an interval in the values of the describing variable, say (m, n) (meaning the ordered values $v_m, v_{m+1}, ..., v_n$). This does not imply that all these groups deviate at all or in that particular direction. It is e.g. possible that group n deviates into the negative direction even though the interval (m, n) deviates strongly into the positive direction in terms of the chosen verification method.

Then certainly only the interval $(m, n-1)$ should be found. Thus the search procedure cannot be cut off at this point; either it must continue on the next lower level (thus loosing some of its efficiency gained by pruning the search space) or special checks have to be added.

Even more complicated situations are possible. Let us indicate by single or double signs a moderate or strong deviation of a group into positive or negative direction and consider this situation:

$$++ \; ++ \; - \; + \; -- \; --$$

Then the procedure would tell the user "Groups 1 to 4 deviate in positive direction" and "Groups 3 to 6 deviate in negative direction". This will certainly surprise and possibly annoy him.

The following solution is possible: If an interval is found, the system has to check if there are sub-intervals starting at the lower or upper end of the entire interval that produce a deviation in the opposite direction; if so, they are cut off.

In our simple example, groups 3 and 4 are attached to the positively deviating interval only if their combined effect is positive.

Let us mention that there may be exceptions to this rule. In a situation like this

$$- \; ++ \; ++ \; + \; - \; -- \; --$$

it may be more meaningful to state positive deviations for groups 1 to 4, in particular if the first group is small, assuming the result for the first group is negative purely by chance.

Furthermore, there exist verification methods where a positive deviation of a group does not imply a positive contribution to the interval. Example: an essentially monotone dependency; the last group may by itself show a decreasing effect while nevertheless strengthening the increasing effect within the interval.

2.3 Hierarchic structure

If a variable has a hierarchic structure, similar problems arise but the solution is not as simple. Assume a class C in a hierarchy shows conspicuous results, perhaps a significant positive deviation. If all its subclasses show essentially the same behaviour, it should be displayed. It should also be displayed if only a minority of its subclasses (possibly weighted by the number of elements) deviates in the other direction. But what if C has just two or three subclasses and one of them is indifferent or even negative?

It seems that this question cannot be solved by just counting the number of positively or negatively deviating subclasses. Generally, one has to take into account the size or weight of the subclasses, the amount of deviation and also the importance of the particular hierarchical subdivision.

A hierarchy level may have been defined just as a means for a simpler description of results if they happen to come out that way, e.g. a division of the Federal Republic of Germany into North, Middle and South; other levels may have strong implications such as the Länder (States). If a statement holds for three of the four Länder in Northern Germany, the three Länder would be displayed separately; if it holds for three of the four Regierungsbezirke (administrational districts) of Baden-Württemberg, they would not be listed.

2.4 Complementary classes

If a subset of the data objects is conspicuous in one direction, then its complement very often is conspicuous in the other direction. If the election result for a party in the northern half of Germany is clearly above average, then it must be below average in the southern part.

Should both results be displayed? If not so, which one?

A simple strategy would be to show the smaller group and to suppress its complement. As an example, the portion of people having a banking account is significantly below average in the income group below 500 DM per month and consequently above average above 500 DM. Stating the latter result is uninteresting. But the search algorithm has to be careful; otherwise the subgroups (500 to 750 DM, 750 to 1000 DM etc.) would now be found and displayed since they are no longer suppressed by the high-level interval "above 500 DM". The same holds for combinations with other variables like "above 500 DM and male".

2.5 Overlapping classes

There exists another type of problems which the searching procedure alone cannot solve. It may find two or more interesting statements that have no syntactical relationship but nevertheless describe approximately the same situation.

For instance, the algorithm could find remarkable results for the classes "age below 20" and "occupation: high school student". These two groups of course overlap strongly.

Both classes belong to different structures and no relation has been defined explicitly; therefore the search procedure does not notice any relationship. To take account of such situations, statistical procedures have to be applied. We shall come back to this in Section 4.

A danger of omitting one of the two results shall be mentioned, however. If only one statement is displayed, the user might wonder why the other one does not hold or even consider it false without thinking about it. This is the more true the less obvious to the user the overlapping is.

3 Statistical criteria

3.1 Exploratory analysis

When a new type of data is being prepared for analysis, a main task is to define (and, possibly, program) the evaluation methods that are applicable in this context. Only the evaluation criteria included at that time can later be used.

The criteria may be descriptive or statistical in nature.

Examples of descriptive criteria that have been used are the length of runs in time series, statements like "second best result since n years", percentage of data objects with a desired property like "more than p% of the election districts in class C belong to the best n districts of party P", coverage of a set of data objects with a desired property like "contains p% of the best n election districts of party P" and others. We will not expand on this sort of statements.

By statistical criteria we mean those that apply statistical tests. Three caveats have to be made beforehand.

In the context of exploratory data analysis, it is neither possible nor even desirable to look for exact tests. The data are screened in many directions. Setting up in advance exact tests allowing for all kinds of unexpected irregularities would be an enormous task not worth the effort if at all manageable.

Secondly, the result of one test is not taken into account when looking for the next one unless explicitly so specified in the evaluation method. For instance, an outlier detected in a test is not omitted before performing the next one; if people under 20 years of age deviate significantly from the general mean, the next group (people over 60; unemployed) is still compared to the general mean and not to the mean of persons over 20. This course of action is necessary here since otherwise the results would depend on the sequence in which the tests are made but it does not agree with the usual principles of testing theory. Exploratory analysis does not verify or falsify previously fixed hypotheses but produces hypotheses that have to be verified in a second step (ideally with a new data set).

Thirdly, there is no overall error probability. Since a huge number of tests is performed (either actually or only in principle but omitted due to redundancy relations or other knowledge incorporated into the search algorithm), one has to use sufficiently small formal error probabilities for each single test; otherwise one is flooded with chance results. But there is no way to accumulate all these diverse error probabilities into a gross value. Nevertheless, one should strive not to perform excessive testing and to restrict oneself to some general, perhaps even crude procedures rather than to check for all abnormalities one can think of.

Because exact tests are not possible anyways, as we have demonstrated, it is not necessary to attach too much importance to this issue. More important are fast approximate tests that can be performed even if the usual regularity assumptions such as normal distribution or independence do not hold. However, distribution-free tests are often too crude and robust tests too time-consuming.

3.2 Searching for conspicuous classes

While many ways for an exploratory analysis of a data set are possible, three important patterns are:

- Given a dependent variable; are there any patterns such as linear dependency or monotony with respect to some explanatory variables considering the entire data set? Such a situation of exploratory analysis is discussed in [4; 5].
- Given a dependent variable; for which classes of data objects describable by the values of one or more explanatory

variables has the dependent variable a mean significantly above (below) average (or above or below a predefined value)?

- Given several explanatory variables; for which classes of data objects describable by the values of two or more of them is the size of that class significantly larger or smaller than expected under assumptions of independence of the variables involved?

We shall concentrate here on the third situation and for simplicity discuss it for two variables only. In this Section, we want to convey an idea of how the analysis works.

To have a concrete example, consider those persons within a sufficiently big sample that own shares; one would like to find population subgroups in terms of various demographic variables where the portion of share holders is significantly above or below average.

We can estimate the overall portion of share holders from the whole sample unless we know that figure from some other source; next, we test population subgroups on deviations taking the size of the subgroup as fixed and the number of share holders within that group as a binomial variable. Thus we may find that the goal set is overproportional within higher income groups.

One could object that the test is not correct if the null hypothesis (overall portion of share holders) is taken from our sample. But this is unimportant because in exploratory analysis we are content with approximate tests anyways.

Similarly one finds that the portion of persons owning a banking account is overproportional in the age group "above 20". All right. Really?

In this case we would expect at least that we get the result "underproportional in the age group below 20" and that the first statement is suppressed; even better would be "persons *not* owning a banking account overproportional in the age group below 20" since almost everyone owns an account and the not-owners are the exceptional and therefore interesting case. Two problems arise: If the search algorithm just ignores the result "above 20", it would find on the next levels subgroups such as "above 30" or "20 to 59". These must also be suppressed unless they are so much more significant that they should again be stated. Secondly, in such completely unbalanced cases it is easy to ignore the large group; but what about sex or other classes that comprise about half the population? Here supposedly both groups are to be stated, but where to set the limit?

Essentially, the situation can alternatively be described by a 2×2 contingency table. In one direction one has the goal set (here: share holders) and the rest of the population, in the other direction the test group (here: class of persons described by one or two demographic variables) and its complement. The usual χ^2-test is completely symmetric in all four table values and somewhat stronger than our proposed test; it could be used as well. We prefer our approach for two reasons: It does not tacitly assume that the complementary classes are homogeneous and it devalues classes containing a large portion of the total population (the group "above 20 years of age" automatically receives a considerably lower significance than the group "below 20 years of age").

Let us come back to the question: Which one of the four fields of a 2×2 table is the most important one, the one that should be shown to the user as anomalous? Certainly it has no general solution, but there are some guidelines to be used by a system utilizing domain knowledge: The class selected by the user or by the person setting up the system as goal class is more important than its complement; a class described by simple terms is more important than its complement (e.g. with variables A and B "A = a" vs. "A ≠ a" or "A ≤ a and B < b" vs. "A > a or B ≥ b"); a small

class is more important than a big one. Of course, these criteria may in a given situation prefer different solutions.

We see that not nearly all statistically significant classes are interesting and that there exist intricate dependencies.

3.3 Competing classes

Exploratory analysis aims not only at finding conspicuous results but also at suppressing uninteresting ones even if statistically significant lest the "data cemetery" becomes a "fact cemetery". One step in this direction was the concentration on one of the four fields of a 2×2 table. Another way is to combine results. This is largely done by our search algorithm; some problems in finding sensible aggregations have been discussed in Section 2.2.

In a statistical context, finding and selecting interesting results is not just a question of distinguishing positive and negative deviations. We shall assume now that the evaluation function measures the deviation of a class from normal (however "normal" may be defined) by a statistical variable that is additive; by this we mean that the evaluation function yields for the union of two disjoint classes (approximately) the sum of the values for the two classes and that also the variances are (approximately) additive. We judge the significance of a class by its evaluation function in terms of multiples of its (estimated) standard deviation.

It may happen that several disjoint classes are all insignificant but that its union is significant. This is not a problem if – as is the case – the search algorithm starts at the top (with the largest classes). But the first significant class found may be too large. If the evaluation function yields for a class and for the set difference of this class and one of its subclasses on the next-lower level values with opposite sign (deviation into the opposite direction), then clearly the subclass rather than the class has to be reported; it is the essential source for the deviation. If the significance of the class is larger than that of the subclass, then clearly the class has to be reported. For the cases in between, we have left some freedom in choosing the class or the subclass or both.

In the interval situation of Section 2.2, this freedom permits to drop border classes that have the correct sign but deviate too little from zero.

In its simpler version, the search algorithm just looks for a conspicuous class and then stops that branch. Exploiting the value of the evaluation function makes the results more meaningful but also complicates the search: Having found a class one has to check if there is a considerably more significant class one or more levels further down.

If the order on the variables and, therefore, on the search space has been defined in proper accordance with the semantics of the variable, it will usually suffice to stop the search if the next lower level in a hierarchy does not produce more significant results. In an ordinal structure, the situation is somewhat more complicated since a few bordering values of the interval just under consideration may taken together have an opposite contribution (or a negligible contribution in the correct direction); the remaining interval is then formally several levels lower, but not all sub-intervals need to be checked. Of course, in a more-dimensional setting new problems arise that cannot be explicated here.

The search algorithm stops as soon as the expected class size becomes too small. Not only does the approximation by normal distributions become too crude but there is also the danger of a few outliers producing too many spurious statements, and in large data sets there just have to be some objects exhibiting unusual combinations of variable values.

4 Selecting good representatives

4.1 Suppression of redundant results

The search algorithm suppresses many redundant results, in particular subclasses of a class that is already reported unless the result for the subclass is considerably stronger. There remain cases where a guidance is needed whether a class or a subclass or both should be reported, and there are more complicated cases (partially overlapping classes) when more than one variable is involved. Moreover and more importantly, the search algorithm cannot find relationships between classes when these relationships have not been defined together with the data; in particular it recognizes no similarities between classes described by different variables but covering largely the same data objects.

We shall sketch now an algorithm that has been designed to suppress results that on the level of data objects are similar to other, stronger results and thus are redundant. It selects from a collection of statements those that in a way are good representatives also for those that are dropped. For a complete description, see [7]. In the terminology of artificial intelligence, the situation can be described as a generalization or machine learning problem in the presence of noise [2]. This heuristic algorithm has some desirable properties and shows good results in practice.

We assume that with each class (more exactly: with each statement on a class) is associated a numerical measure for its conspicuousness, its degree of unexpectedness, its importance to the user; we call it *evidence* and denote it by V.

We further assume that there exists a numerical measure for the similarity of any two classes primarily on the basis of their data objects; we call it *affinity*. The affinity S need not be symmetric. We assume $S \leq 1$ with $S = 1$ signaling close agreement.

Selection procedure: The class C_j will be suppressed by the class C_k, if

$$V(C_j) < S(C_j, C_k) V(C_k).$$

This procedure assures that the better statement cannot be suppressed by a worse one. The smaller the affinity, the smaller can the evidence of C_j become without C_k suppressing C_j.

Practice has shown that this basic procedure should be modified slightly to suppress one of two classes with virtually the same evidence but with an affinity slightly below 1.

As evidence, one may take the evaluation function described earlier or a measure derived from it.

As affinity one is tempted to use $|C_j \cap C_k| / |C_j \cup C_k|$ or a power of it where $|C|$ is a suitably chosen weight of C, perhaps the number of data objects. However, this measure has some undesirable properties; in particular, subsets of a conspicuous set would also be displayed if they are much smaller even if they are considerably less conspicuous.

The affinity $S = S_0^\kappa$ has led to useful results where

$$S_0(C_j, C_k) = |C_j \cap C_k| / |C_j|,$$
$$\kappa \leq 0.5.$$

If $C_j \subset C_k$, then $S_0(C_j, C_k) = 1$ but $S_0(C_k, C_j) < 1$. Thus, a subclass will always be suppressed unless it has a larger evidence; in that case, the class may or may not be suppressed depending on the evidences, on S_0 and on κ.

The smaller κ, the fewer statements are in general retained; the user can in this way control the amount of output. So far, values for κ between 0.25 and 0.4 have produced reasonable results.

4.2 Statistical evidences

The selection procedure can be used with descriptive as well as with statistical evidences. An example of the first type is the portion of objects of a goal set G within a class C, e.g. the portion of constituencies where a party has gained votes within a geographical region or a set described by demographic variables. However, rather than $|G \cap C| / |C|$ one should use $|G \cap C| / (c+|C|)$ with a small addend c lest one gets together with a class too many subclasses that happen to have a portion of goal objects just a little bit larger.

We consider now an additive statistical evidence. A typical situation is this:

Each data object ω has attached to it a random variable $\xi(\omega)$ which is standardized to $E(\xi) = 0$ under a suitable null hypothesis of "everything is normal"; the variables for different data objects are independent; the conspicuousness of a class C is a function of the sum $\xi(C) = \Sigma_{\omega \in C} \xi(\omega)$. The variance $\sigma^2(\xi(C))$ plays the role of a weight of the class C. An obvious choice for our procedure is

$$|C| = \sigma^2(\xi(C)),$$
$$V(C) = \xi(C) / \sigma(\xi(C)).$$

Under these assumptions, one can show: If $\kappa = 1/2$ and $C_1 \cap C_2 = \emptyset$, $C_1 \cup C_2 = C$ and $\xi(C_1)$ and $\xi(C)$ have the same sign (say, positive), then C_1 suppresses C if and only if $\xi(C_2) < 0$.

This means: Assuming $V(C_1) > V(C) > 0$, then C_1 as well as C are displayed if and only if C_2 adds a positive contribution to C_1.

Therefore, $\kappa = 1/2$ is a boundary case for meaningful choices; usually one will prefer some $\kappa < 1/2$ permitting C_1 and C to be displayed only if C_2 adds some appropriate amount of evidence. Of course, $V(C_1) > V(C)$ implies that the average value of ξ, $\xi(C) / |C|$, which usually indicates the amount by which the null hypothesis is false, is considerably larger for C_1.

In practice, the independence assumption will rarely be exactly true; e.g. the sum of ξ over all data objects may be given. However, this does not change the situation drastically except perhaps for very large C.

4.3 Some variants to the selection procedure

In the way as it has been stated, the selection procedure is based entirely on the extension of classes. A class may suppress another one that has an entirely different description (using other variables) if only it is better and both are similar on the basis of the affinity S. Thus the user will not be bored by finding several results that essentially describe the same fact as "below 20 years of age", "high-school student", "little or no personal income", "single and living in a household of 3 or more persons".

The procedure also gives a solution to the problem of overlapping classes within a class structure (Section 2.5), in particular where classes are defined by the combination of two or more variables each having a hierarchic or ordinal order.

It does not find situations where a class is largely contained in the union of two or more classes unless the union is itself a candidate for the search algorithm.

The algorithm can be modified in order to reflect special goals of the user. As an example, the evidence may be devalued for classes with a complicated description thus preferring simple classes. If in an ordinal structure closed intervals are devalued against open ones, the algorithm may prefer "$v \leq v_m$" over "$v_2 \leq v \leq v_m$" even if the class $v = v_1$ tends into the opposite direction.

Of course, if the selection procedure is modified, the properties such as the special behaviour of $\kappa = 1/2$ for certain statistical evidences no longer hold exactly; but these properties anyways served only to show the rough behaviour.

A more serious objection against the use of modifications to the selection procedure is that they introduce new parameters that must be adjusted by the user and whose effect is not obvious.

526

This is a general problem with procedures that permit diverse adaptations to user needs. Such modifications should therefore be used with care.

The user must also be warned, and be aware of, that results that do not show up may nevertheless be valid; they may be suppressed by another statement whose relatedness is not apparent to the user. From "statement not shown" he should not, perhaps unconciously, conclude "statement not valid".

Our system permits the user to check such situations either by selecting only certain variables for the search procedure (reducing the search to a subspace of the entire search space) or by looking for selected results by means of navigation; various relations for linking statements have been defined and implemented.

Together with the textual result the user may of course see the original or derived data that produced the statement.

5   Some experiences

The EXPLORA system is running on Macintosh II computers using Allegro Common Lisp and CLOS; it is not yet documented. Space limitations unfortunately prevent the exhibition of an example; a short one can be found in [8], mor elaborate ones in [5; 7]. The system has been set up for several quite diverse data sets:

- Federal elections, election results and a dozen demographic variables for all 248 constituencies of the Federal Republic of Germany. The evaluation methods are of a descriptive nature such as "very high proportion of the best 50 constituencies for party P within the constiuencies with low population density and moderate or high proportion of Roman Catholics" [4; 5; 8].
- Federal elections, results for all elections on the basis of the Länder (States). The evaluation methods are simple time series results such as "highest losses for both major parties since <year> in <Land>".
- Use of computers in industry based on a sample of several thousand firms. Important data are the size, branch of industry and geographical region of firms and number and price class of the computers. The evaluation methods look for unusually high or low computer use. The evaluation is hampered by extremely diverse weights attached to the firms.
- Financial business connections of people. Data on 20000 persons including business connections with banks, insurances and building societies, kinds of business and 20 demographic variables. The evaluation methods look for unusual proportions of demographic groups within customers of an institution or of a kind of service.

It takes some effort to set up such an application. Each one so far showed a number of peculiarities that implied extensions to our system but in that way made it more flexible.

The system is not yet connected to a database system; there was no need to do so. For commercial applications, this would be necessary but we foresee no severe problems.

The goal is to find explanations of the data and their peculiarities in the light of subject knowledge. Where is this subject knowledge in our system? It is spread over various components; primarily it governs the definition of the objects and their relations (including class structures, redundancy relations) and the choice of evaluation methods.

We are not aware of other work where the semantics of the data governs the exploration in a comparable way and we are convinced that this concept can be extended. It will be necessary to find and to exploit other structures that on the one hand permit to deal with semantic peculiarities of data sets and on the other hand are general enough for wide application.

Acknowledgement
The results reported in this paper include work of the whole project. At present, project members are (besides the author) Fred Kellermann, Willi Klösgen, Peter Latocha and Claes Valentin.

References

[1] Chowdhury, Shamsul I.: Statistical expert systems – a special application area for knowledge–based computer methodology. Linköping : University, 1987. – 109 pp.

[2] Ellman, Thomas: Explanation-based learning: a survey of programs and perspectives. In: Computing Surveys 21 (1989), pp. 163 – 221.

[3] Gale, William A.: Statistical applications of artificial intelligence and knowledge engineering. In: Knowledge Engineering Review 2 (1988), pp. 227 – 247.

[4] Gebhardt, Friedrich: Prospects for expert systems to analyze election data. In: Classification and related methods of data analysis : proceedings of the First Conference of the International Federation of Classification Societies (IFCS) (Aachen, Juni 1987) / Hans H. Bock (ed.). Amsterdam : North-Holland, 1988, pp. 691 – 696.

[5] Gebhardt, Friedrich : Statistische Fragestellungen bei einem Expertensystem zur explorativen Datenanalyse. Sankt Augustin : GMD, 1988 (GMD-Studien 137). – 123 pp.

[6] Gebhardt, Friedrich : An expert system strategy for selecting interesting results. In: COMPSTAT 90 : proceedings (Dubrovnik, Sept. 1990). Heidelberg : Physica, 1990. To be printed.

[7] Gebhardt, Friedrich: Choosing among competing generalizations. Sankt Augustin : GMD, 1989 (Arbeitspapiere der GMD, 421). – 16 pp. – Preprint, to be published elsewhere.

[8] Gebhardt, Friedrich: Choice among overlapping classifications. Submitted to the proceedings of 14. Jahrestagung der Gesellschaft für Klassifikation (Marburg, March 1990) / P. Ihm (ed.) ; H.-H. Bock (ed.). Berlin : Springer, 1990.

[9] Hand, David J.: Expert systems in statistics. In: Knowledge Engineering Review 1, Nr. 3 (1986), pp. 2 – 10.

[10] and, David J.: The application of expert systems in statistics. In: Interactions in artificial intelligence and statistical methods / Bob Phelps (ed.). Aldershot : Gower Technical Press, 1987, pp. 3 – 17.

[11] Hoschka, Peter ; Klösgen, Willi : A support system for interpreting statistical data. In: Knowledge discovery in databases / G. Piatetsky-Shapiro (ed.); W. Frawley (ed.). Cambridge, Mass. : MIT-Press. – In preparation, 1990.

[12] Klösgen, Willi: The generalization step in a statistics interpreter. In: Data Analysis, Learning Symbolic and Numeric Knowledge / E. Diday (ed.). New York : Nova Science, 1989, pp. 473 - 480.

[13] Klösgen, Willi: EXPLORA: content interpretation of statistical data. In: Fortschritte der Statistik-Software / F. Faulbaum (ed.) ; H.M. Kehlinger (ed.). Stuttgart : G. Fischer, 1990. In print.

[14] Latocha, Peter: Searching for the most interesting facts. In: Proceedings of the IASTED International Symposium on Expert Systems : theory and applications. Zürich : Acta Press, 1989, pp. 90 – 93.

[15] Latocha, Peter: Exploration von Aussagenräumen : ein semantischer Ansatz. Sankt Augustin : GMD, 1989 (GMD-Studien 164). – 144 pp.

[16] Wittkowski, Knut M.: Knowledge based support for the management of statistical databases. In: Statistical and scientific database management: 4th International Working Conference SSDBM (Rom, Juni 1988) / M. Rafanelli (ed.) ; J.C. Klensin (ed.) ; P. Svensson (ed.). Berlin : Springer, 1989, pp. 62 – 71.

An Expert System Interface for Consultation of Decision Table Systems

F. Hazevoets   B. Vanhoutte   J. Vanthienen

Katholieke Universiteit Leuven
Department of Applied Economics
Dekenstraat 2
B-3000 Leuven (Belgium)

ABSTRACT

In this paper, a decision table consultation environment is proposed, based on a decision table engineering workbench, which combines the advantages of decision tables (table based verification and modelling) with those of common expert system shells, incorporating rule based knowledge representation, extensive consultation facilities (explanation, specific help, selective restart, case archivation) and interfaces to existing procedures and databases.

Introduction

As a lot of expert systems which are being built nowadays use the rule based paradigm to develop systems which are essentially deterministic decision trees, it seems that mainly two aspects of current commercial expert system shells are used : a *question driven user interface*, and second, a *rule based knowledge representation and acquisition*. Other facilities (uncertainty, complex inference strategies, explanation facilities, heuristics, inductive learning) are often not considered. This raises the question whether decision trees are expert systems (HAYWARD [85]) or need expert system shells (see also LEITH [90]).

Irrespective of the answer to these questions, it therefore seems useful to consider other alternatives in order to obtain both desired aspects (the user interface and the rule based design/representation/specification) for handling deterministic decision situations. The use of decision tables (using a decision table engineering workbench) is a promising alternative, as it easily enables the designer to check for contradictions, inconsistencies, incompleteness, redundancy, etc. in the rule base (VANTHIENEN [86], MAES & VAN DIJK [88]), which is one of the major problems in building and maintaining expert systems (see e.g. LOVELAND & VALTORTA [83], SUWA, SCOTT & SHORTLIFFE [84]).

For this purpose, a decision table consultation environment has been developed, similar to an expert system shell, which incorporates rule based knowledge representation, table based verification, extensive consultation facilities (explanation, specific help, selective restart, case archivation) and interfaces to existing procedures and databases.

The system is built in two research versions : DECADE, implemented in VM/PROLOG on IBM 9370 (VANHOUTTE [90]), and DETACONSULT, implemented in Turbo Pascal on PS/2 (HAZEVOETS [90]).

The proposed system

The **DECADE/DETACONSULT** system operates on information supplied in the form of decision table rules and supporting material. These decision tables are imported form the decision table engineering workbench **PROLOGA** where they have been constructed by the knowledge engineer.

The **PROLOGA** (PROcedural LOGic Analyzer) system is an interactive rule-based design tool for computer-supported construction and manipulation of decision tables (MAES, VANTHIENEN & VERHELST [82], VANTHIENEN [86]). The system not only applies the manual design techniques, but also offers additional features such that it is easier to construct and manipulate decision tables.

The connection between the design and consultation environment is shown in figure 1.

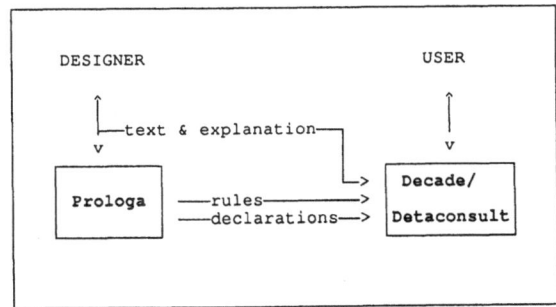

Fig. 1 : The Design - Consultation Environment

Decision tables and knowledge engineering

Although the decision table still looks almost the same as in the early days of its first developments, some profound changes can be noted concerning the contents and the application field of the decision table technique (see e.g. VERHELST [80], CODASYL [82], REILLY, SALAH & YANG [87], VANTHIENEN [88]).

A decision table is a tabular representation of a *procedural decision situation*, where the state of a number of conditions determines the execution of a set of actions. Not just any representation, however, but one in which all distinct situations are shown as columns in a table, such that every possible case is included in one and only one column (completeness and exclusivity).

The tabular representation of the decision situation is characterised by the separation between conditions and actions, on one hand, and between subjects and conditional expressions, on the other. Every table column (decision column) indicates which actions should (or should not) be executed for a specific combination of condition states. The condition oriented approach of the decision table makes it very useful to *display* procedural knowledge, with such advantages as : overview, readability, consistency and completeness. For most of the common validation problems in rule based systems (see e.g. NGUYEN et al. [87], AYEL [88], LIU & DILLON [88]) can easily be solved using decision tables, e.g. redundant rules, conflicting rules, subsumed rules, unnecessary conditions, circular rules, missing rules or combinations, unreferenced attribute values, illegal attribute values, dead end clauses.

An simple example of a (partial) decision table for animal classification is shown in figure 2.

ANIMAL CLASSIFICATION

1. Skin ?	feathers	hair		other		
2. Flies ?	-	Y	N	Y		N
3. Lays eggs ?	-	Y	N	-	Y	N	-
4. Gives milk ?	-	-	-	-	-	Y	N	Y	N
1. Table BIRDS	x	x	.	.	x	.	.	.	.
2. Table MAMMALS	.	.	x	x	.	x	.	x	.

Fig. 2 : Example of a decision table

This enumeration of decision columns, however, is not the way in which procedural knowledge is acquired or specified. To this end, the decision situation is gradually formalised in action oriented or partial decision rules, which constitute a modular description of knowledge (analogous to the use of "rules" in expert systems).

A set of rules for the above example might e.g. be specified as follows (the decision table in figure 2 has been constructed automatically from these rules) :

[1]	IF	animal has feathers
	THEN	animal is a bird
[2]	IF	animal flies
	AND	animal lays eggs
	THEN	animal is a bird
[3]	IF	NOT animal is a bird
	AND	animal has hair
	THEN	animal is a mammal
[4]	IF	NOT animal is a bird
	AND	animal gives milk
	THEN	animal is a mammal

The rule based *specification* method, however, does not offer the representational advantages of the decision columns (easy checking for completeness, consistency and correctness).

Hence the need for an automated decision table tool like PROLOGA, which is able to build and manipulate (a) condition oriented decision table(s) from a given set of partial specifications.

In this way a two step approach is really taken, in order to deal with three important problem views :

Rule based specification —PROLOGA→ Table based representation —DECADE→ Dialog based consultation

Knowledge representation and inference in DECADE/DETACONSULT

The knowledge base consists of rules, being the rules of the decision table(s), provided with the necessary descriptive information.

As the decision table is already condition oriented, decision making is straightforward, eliminating complex search and scheduling at consultation time.

A table in DECADE/DETACONSULT is seen as a sheer description of a decision table. It consists of two files, which are automatically derived from the PROLOGA system, and one optional file drawn up by the knowledge engineer.

The first two contain the contracted table(s), with the actual rule base of the system, and a brief description of the conditions, condition states and actions of the table(s) involved. Furthermore, as a result of the table decomposition of a DECADE/DETACONSULT application in several tables, the table hierarchy is implicitly included.

Although the information stated in these two files enables one to work with DECADE/DETACONSULT (on a prototyping basis), the real strength and flexibility of the proposed system lies in the use of a third file, offering the possibility of adding powerful functionalities to a DECADE/DETACONSULT application.

First of all, **help texts** can be supplied as to inform the user about the specific problem domain. These help texts are possible at three different levels : a global text at the *application level*; a more specific *subject level* help text for each condition and action; and a two-line description of each table element (conditions, states and actions) at the *detail level*, in order to express questions, possible answers and results.

Secondly, it is possible to link conditions and actions with **executable code**. This code is activated each time the corresponding condition or action is met during a consultation. The file does not contain the code itself, but refers to programs, written in Prolog. In the future, other programming languages will be supported.

DECADE and data bases

Current expert system shells often operate in isolation, with no connection to company data bases for retrieving or storing information.

DECADE provides a triple link with data bases :
- *data base consultation through condition programs*
- *data base update via action programs*
- *case archivation*

As stated earlier, the knowledge engineer can link programs to the conditions of a table. Instead of asking the user to select one of several alternative states, a program may be provided to determine the appropriate state.

Such a program could be a data base query, which tries to fetch the necessary information from a certain data base. For example, it is possible to link DECADE with an **SQL data base**. E.g. in a sales discount problem, one of the conditions which determines the discount offered could be the total sales to the customer under consideration. This information can easily be extracted from the corporate customer data base.

The advantage of linking DECADE with other Prolog queries, is that these queries can use the Prolog rules of DECADE itself. This still enables a program to ask the state from the user if a query should fail to find the required information.

The second way of linking DECADE with data bases through the use of data base access programs, is to link actions with such programs. When in a consultation for a specific problem an action is found to be applicable, the program is triggered and the required **data base updates** or queries are performed on the basis of the conditon states

that were previously entered or other information provided by previously encountered actions.

E.g. the final action in the sales discount problem could be to print the actual bill and to update the customer information or other data bases

Finally, there exist an option to **save a consultation** for later use. This also permits the use of standard cases, where only a few modifications are needed to complete a consultation.

E.g. a consultation could be stored for each customer, or for a certain type of customer, with customer dependent information that does not change regularly. For instance, the distance from a client to the nearest warehouse.

Features of a DECADE/DETACONSULT consultation

During a consultation, the user is asked to select the appropriate condition states in order to find a unique column in the decision table (or all relevant decision tables). Only conditions relevant to the specific situation are presented, in the order in which they are included in the decision tables. As soon as such a unique column is discovered, the relevant actions are shown to the user or in case a program is linked to it, these actions are performed.

It is also possible for a condition or action to call subtables. The process of switching from one table to another in a hierarchy of decision tables is performed entirely by the system and is transparent to the user. He does not (have to) know the exact structure of the application.

DECADE/DETACONSULT also offers some features which help the user to navigate through the application and find the right action(s).

For instance, there exists an option to change an answer that was previously entered (all other selections remaining equal) or to restart decision making from a certain condition onward. Together with the case archivation option this enables one to perform 'what-if' analyses or to use the standard cases discussed earlier.

Another important function is the **review** option, which can be called at the end of the consultation. It redisplays all the relevant actions, including those reached in the subtables. This provides the user with a quick resume of the conclusion.

Finally but not less important is the **help function**, which enables the user to consult the help texts at various levels, provided by the knowledge engineer. This can be extremely important for applications which are to be used by non-experts.

530

An example of a DETACONSULT screen for the above animal classification problem is shown in figure 3.

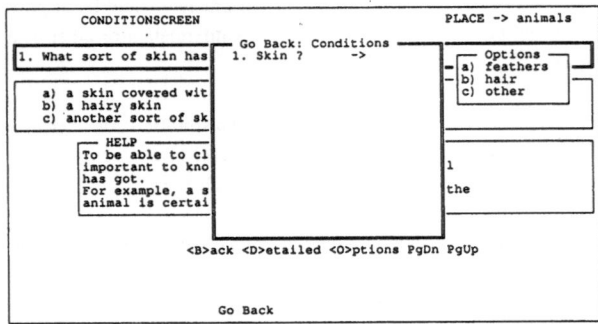

Fig. 3 : Example of a DETACONSULT screen

Conclusions

As indicated, decision tables and expert systems show some striking similarities, although both approaches put strongly different emphases. While decision tables traditionally stress the representation facilities (with the resulting additional checking capabilities), expert systems are mainly dealing with knowledge formulation and inference.

By using rule based design of decision tables, combined with a user friendly consultation mechanism, the strong points of both approaches can largely be incorporated in the proposed decision table systems :

- advantages of rule based knowledge specification (modularity, flexibility and simplicity)
- easy checking for completeness, consistency and correctness by designing decision tables;
- high performance of the search process;
- user friendly question driven interface.

REFERENCES

[1] AYEL, M. [88], *A Conceptual Model for Consistency of Knowledge Bases*, in : O'SHEA, T & SGUREV, V. (Ed.), *Artificial Intelligence III : Methodology, Systems, Applications*, North-Holland, 1988, pp. 75-82.

[2] CODASYL [82], *A modern appraisal of decision tables*, Report of the Decision Table Task Group, ACM, New York, 1982.

[3] HAYWARD, S. [85], *Is a Decision Tree an Expert System*, in : BRAMER, M. (Ed.), *Research & Development in Expert Systems*, Proc. Fourth Technical Conf. on Expert Systems, Cambridge University Press, 1985, 228 pp., pp. 185-192.

[4] HAZEVOETS, F. [90], *Ontwikkeling en Implementatie van een Omgeving voor het Konsulteren van Beslissingstabellen (Turbo Pascal Implementatie)*, dissertation, K.U.Leuven, Dept. Applied Econ., 1990, 65+45 pp.

[5] LEITH, P. [90], *Formalism in AI and Computer Science*, Ellis Horwood Limited, Chichester, 1990, 225 pp.

[6] LIU, N., DILLON, T. [88], *Detecting of Consistency and Completeness in Expert Systems using Numerical Petri Nets*, in : GERO, J. & STANTON, R. (Ed.), *Artificial Intelligence Developments and Applications*, North-Holland, 1988, pp. 119-134.

[7] LOVELAND, D., VALTORTA, M. [83], *Detecting Ambiguity : An Example in Knowledge Evaluation*, Proc. Eighth Int. Joint Conf. on Artificial Intelligence, Karlsruhe, Aug. 1983, Vol. 1, pp. 182-184.

[8] MAES, R., VAN DIJK, J. [88], *On the Role of Ambiguity and Incompleteness in the Design of Decision Tables and Rule Base Systems*, ISRA Report 88/01, Universiteit van Amsterdam, 1988, 21 pp.

[9] MAES, R., VANTHIENEN, J., VERHELST, M. [82], *Practical experiences with the procedural decision modeling system*, Proc. Joint IFIP WG 8.3/IIASA Working Conference on Processes and Tools for Decision Support, Laxenburg (Austria), July 19-21, 1982, pp. 139-154.

[10] NGUYEN, T., PERKINS, W., LAFFEY, T., PECORA, D. [87], *Knowledge Base Verification*, AI Magazine, 8(2), 1987, pp. 69-75.

[11] REILLY, K., SALAH, A., YANG, C. [87], *A Logic Programming Perspective on Decision Table Theory and Practice*, Data & Knowledge Engineering, 87(2), pp. 191-212.

[12] SUWA, M., SCOTT, A., SHORTLIFFE, E. [84], *Completeness and Consistency in a Rule-Based System*, in : BUCHANAN B., SHORTLIFFE E., *Rule Based Expert Systems*, Addison Wesley Publishing Co., Reading (Mass.), 1984, pp. 159-170.

[13] VANHOUTTE, B. [90], *Ontwikkeling en Implementatie in VM-Prolog van een Pakket voor de Konsultatie van Beslissingstabellen*, Dissertation, K.U.Leuven, Dept. Applied Econ., 1990, 72 pp.

[14] VANTHIENEN, J. [86], *Automatiseringsaspecten van de specificatie, constructie en manipulatie van beslissingstabellen*, Doctoral Dissertation, K.U.Leuven, Dept. Applied Econ., 1986, 378 pp.

[15] VANTHIENEN, J. [88], *Een moderne kijk op beslissingstabellen*, Informatie, December 1988, pp. 912-937.

[16] VERHELST, M. [80], *De praktijk van beslissingstabellen*, Kluwer, Deventer/Antwerpen, 1980, 175 pp.

Coupling Knowledge Base and Database in a Productive Environment

Hans-Peter Hoidn
IFA, Institut für Automation AG, Zürich

Riccardo von Vintschger
SBG, Schweizerische Bankgesellschaft, Zürich

Abstract

Integration of database and expert system methods, in particular of object oriented evironments is crucial for future information systems. This paper presents an example of an object oriented system coupled with a relational database, which combines the strengths of both environments. We present a modelling approach which can be applied to both the database and the object oriented environment. Crucial for the implementation is the one–to–one transformation of values in the database (stored in rows) into facts of the object system as well as the transaction design. In this paper, along with general questions, we present some details of the implementation of this coupling issue in a productive expert system.

1 Introduction

One of the major issues for productive expert systems is the integration of their problem solving features with data-handling capabilities. Object oriented databases would be suited best, but they can not be used yet in a productive environment. Thus, the only practicable approach is the coupling of a classical database with an object oriented environment. This solution offers the possibility of developing an integrated system supporting object oriented functionalities as well as traditional data management features (e.g. consistency, persistency, multiuser environments) but it requires a sophisticated mapping between the two environments. As a first step of a coupling approach we had to find a model which allows an adequate description of the database and of the object structure. In addition, transfer mechanisms for the translation of fields in the database into complex objects must be provided, and a clean design supporting the strengths of both systems has to be found.

The paper is organized as follows. A brief overview describes the main functionalities of *MetaPSS* , a productive expert system dealing with large amounts of data (Section 2). In Section 3 a modelling approach for the design of the data structure of the coupled system is described. Section 4 focusses on the translation module and the last section deals with the problem of defining a transaction for such hybrid systems. Throughout this paper, along with theoretical discussions, examples and solutions drawn from *MetaPSS* are provided.

2 METAPSS: An expert system for production planning of batch processing

This section gives a brief description of the project *MetaPSS* , which will be the example for our coupling approach throughout this paper. More about *MetaPSS* can be found in [6].

2.1 The application background

Production planning for batch processing at *UBS* (*Union Bank of Switzerland*) is done with the dedicated language *PSS*, developed by *UBS* and *UNISYS* . Cobol programs (or *tasks*) belonging to the same application are grouped in *runs*, and *PSS* provides a means of defining static resource allocation and rollback points as well as precedence relations between tasks (*flow*). A *run* is a program written in *PSS* containing the description of the tasks and the relations between them: for each task *PSS* describes the referenced files or areas, the reference mode (read, write), its successors and the *rollback cycles*; this information in turn is input for the actual job control, which executes Cobol programs at run time. *MetaPSS* is an expert system supporting an intelligent and highly graphical editing of *runs*.

2.2 Knowledge base design and system architecture

MetaPSS is a *LISP*-based system and it is implemented with *KEE*, an object oriented environment which provides canonical object features like classes, inheritance, methods and message passing.

Following the terminology of *KEE* [4] an object is called *unit* and the instance variable names are called *slots*. *KEE* provides *classes* and *instances* of classes. Inheritance may occur between a class and a subclass as well as between classes and units.

The abstract knowledge about runs (applicatorial rules and the syntax of *PSS* itself) is stored in permanently loaded *knowledge bases*. *Frame knowledge bases* contain the methods and the abstract structure, like classes RUN, TASKS, FILES, PSS-EXPRESSIONS. A representation of a specific *run* (an *instance*) consists of units (*instances*) which inherit the behavior and the structure from the corresponding *frame knowledge base* classes and which only own the *values* of the instance variables.

Since runs are crucial for the whole EDP environment, there is a need of permanently storing them, and the rest of this paper deals with problems related to the issue of coupling expert systems with traditional data bases. The clean separation of abstract knowledge from the actual data mentioned above, only requires to store the values of the instance variables, and this is crucial for the whole coupling design.

3 Modelling

Modelling in an object-oriented programming environment is based on objects. But *modelling* to design a relational database system mainly uses an entity-relationship-model. For the integration of an object-oriented environment with a database system *modelling* must support both. The need of an "unifying design" is widely accepted (see i.e. [5]). We intend to use proven design methods, not to develop new ones and to respect the conceptual, logical and physical levels of design (see [1] where DB and AI design levels are compared).

3.1 Object oriented design

In the terminology of Smalltalk [2], the state of an *object* (in *KEE* called *unit*) is represented as a set of instance variables. Our modelling considers only the state of an object (in *KEE* represented by *value slots*), not the operations and their implementation (in *KEE* represented by *method slots*). Classification assigns *units* to *classes*. *Classes* can be grouped

in order to use the code–sharing capability of an *inheritance mechanism*. Thus, we obtain a *class structure* which structures the real world in a static model. (For example: The *classes* LOCAL–FILES and GLOBAL–FILES can be composed to the *superclass* FILES. LOCAL–FILES can be divided in two *subclasses* SPECIAL–FILES and DEFAULT–FILES.)

The *class structure* is transformed to an *entity–relationship–model* which uses the concepts of entities, relationships and attributes to represent data.

- Each *class* corresponds to an *entity set*, each *slot* (of a class) corresponds to an *attribute*. A *value slot* may have multiple values (in the terminology of Smalltalk a *collection class*).

- A *relationship* between two units (n:m-relationships are allowed) is represented by slot values. For example: The relationship A–B is represented by the value B in object A. Allowing redundancy, A–B may be represented by the value A in object B too (see Table 1).

3.2 The design of the relational database

For the design of the database the main task is the normalisation of the class structure into relations. *Relations* are built for all *classes* which have instances (each instance belongs to one and only one class). The *class structure* is not transformed to the database.

- One unit (i.e. one entity) corresponds to one tuple in the so–called *primary table* (the *primary tables* in the example are GLOBAL_FILES, SPECIAL_FILES and DEFAULT_FILES). A column of the *primary table* corresponds to a slot (i.e. an attribute) with cardinality 1.

- Due to the normalisation, a slot (i.e. an attribute) with multiple values corresponds to a so called *secondary table*. Such a slot of one unit may contain a set of values which must be mapped one-to-one to a set of tuples in the corresponding *secondary table*.

- A relationship of two units is represented by one tuple in a so called *relationship table*.

One unit is usually mapped onto a bunch of tuples in different database tables. Thus the advantages of encapsulation which preserves some integrity is lost.

Table 1 shows the representation (e.g. the *slot values*) of the attribute REFERENCED-RESOURCES for the *entity set* TASK (describing the resource allocation for an application program). The same information is stored in the redundant slot REFERENCED-BY for the class RESOURCES. Since it may be multi-valued (the application program may reference several files) it has to be split into several lines of the corresponding *secondary table*. We consider a task (#[Unit: 'EBLINF+8912] in the *KEE* notation for those *LISP* -objects) referencing the areas (application databases) KONTO and DEPOT (both being *units* in their own rights, too).

3.3 The integrity of data and supported functionalities

Due to the fact that object oriented environments are primarily not designed to deal with large amounts of data, they often support *local reasoning* only. The facts in the object world are only partial views of the application domain. In a multi user environment, an union of these partial views stored as a whole along with integrity requirements imposed by the database itself may significantly enhance the quality of reasoning.

In *MetaPSS* the database contains the data of all runs. Therefore we have to deal with the problem of data integrity covering all data. In order to identify the tupels corresponding to some unit we need to build a unique key for each table composed of some attribute combinations of the entities, which is supposed to be unique over all instances. Furthermore, runs are the largest logical entities and there are only a few entities (mainly some files which are explicitly marked as strategic files and which are used by different applications) which are shared by more than one run and for which a local approach has to be widened.

Uniqueness of the keys may be implemented with unique indexes and this simple integrity requirement may significantly enhance the discipline of editing a run (e.g. it is not allowed to use the same name for different tasks).

It should be mentioned that a database storing all the information about batch control is an excellent starting point for an information system, which, in a read only mode, may be much more widely used than *MetaPSS* itself, providing an online information and help system about batch control. Such an information system is planned for the near future.

#[Unit:EBINF+8912]
IDENTIFICATION
EBINF+8912
.....
.....
REFERENCED RESOURCES
#[Unit: KONTO] #[Unit: DEPOT]

TASKS		
IDENTIFICATION	..	..
..	..	..
EBLINF+8912	..	..

#[Unit:KONTO]
IDENTIFICATION
KONTO
.....
.....
REFERENCED-BY
(#[Unit: EBLINF+8912])

TASK-RES-REF		
TASK-ID	**RES-ID**	..
..	..	..
EBLINF+8912	KONTO	..
EBLINF+8912	DEPOT	..

#[Unit:DEPOT]
IDENTIFICATION
DEPOT
.....
.....
REFERENCED-BY
(#[Unit: EBLINF+8912])

RESOURCES	
IDENTIFICATION	:
..	..
KONTO	..
DEPOT	..

Table 1: database design

4 Mapping and translation

4.1 The mapping and translation module

As its main task this module supports the translation between equivalent representations of the same entity. For each entity has to be specified:

1. the way columns (from the primary table or from the secondary tables) map onto the slots of the corresponding frame knowledge base class (*logical mapping design*)

2. the function providing the translation between a set of database fields (a row in the database) and *KEE* objects as well as its inverse (*implementation*)

Since frame knowledge base *classes* and *relations* in the database are equivalent representations of the same *entity sets*, both representations share a lot of structure. Nevertheless there is still some work to do in order to uniquely transform flat database strings into highly aggregated and potentially unlimited *LISP* structures, as can be seen from Table 2. Joins require the definition of a one–to–one mapping between sets of strings and sets of *LISP* structures.

4.2 Implementation details

The *MetaPSS* database is *ORACLE* and it resides on a dedicated database server (at the moment *SUN* 3). The software basis for the translation and the mapping is *KEEconnection*: it provides a server module (basically a *Pro*C* application accessing the database), the connection between the server and the client (using remote procedure calls) and the translation module integrated in *KEE* . In later versions the communication will be supplied by *SQL*NET* . This facility will be extensively exploited with the *MetaPSS* -Information system; *SQL*FORMS* applications will be installed on several PC's, providing fast access to data about runs.

The logical design of the mapping is entirely specified using the development interface provided by *KEEconnection* .

This powerful graphical tool (the *Mapping editor*) provides an adequate way to define the structure of the mapping as well as of the joins between primary and secondary tables. The structure is then stored in a *mapping knowledge base*, which contains all the information needed to map the *tables* onto the corresponding *classes* and which is loaded together with the *MetaPSS* knowledge bases. *KEEconnection* provides some elementary translation functions, but there is also the possibility of defining such individual functions to cover further needs.

5 Transaction design

The transaction module provides the user with the required data, stores the results of a user session back in the database and supplies some features of a multi-user environment. It has the following basic functionality, which will be described in this section:

1. Consistency of data in a multi-user environment

2. Transactions in *MetaPSS*

   - Providing the user with the needed data (*download*)
   - Modifying a run
   - Updating the database (*upload*)

We will close this chapter with a brief description of some shortcomings of our approach and point out some issues in the current discussion of integrating knowledge based systems and databases.

#[Unit: EB+8912.03]
identification
EB+8912.03
....
#[Unit: IN]
....
HTO
....
((#[Unit: OPTIONS].T) (#[Unit: NOUGHT]))

TASK-E-EXPRESSIONS

IDENT	ENV-SEL	KEY-TOKEN	PARAMETER
...	...	...	...
EB+8912.03	HTO	IN	/OPTIONS./T;NOUGTH
...	...	...	...

Table 2: KB-DB translations

5.1 Consistency of data in a multiuser environment

Due to long transactions and to database locking the trade-off between data consistency and an efficient multiuser environment had to be seriously considered in the integration of databases and knowledge bases (see also [3] and its approach of *disjunct objects* for locking strategies in object oriented databases). From an application point of view, a run is the main logical entity. Thus, the parallel editing of the same run by several users is not allowed. As a second restriction, the parallel editing of a run and of a strategic resource referenced by this run is not allowed either. *MetaPSS* overcomes these consistency problems with the concept of *disjunct database partitions*: since there is no sharing of database rows between runs (except for global resources) the database is partitioned into disjunct subsets, each belonging to a different run, thus minimizing locking. On modifications of a run consistency is ensured with only one exclusive row lock (on the row in the primary table corresponding to the run being modified). Modifications of resources need exclusive row locking for all rows corresponding to the runs which reference them.

At the beginning of a session, users try to lock some rows in the database in an exclusive mode; if they succeed, there is no consistency problem with other concurrent edit sessions, if not, a message tells the user that for consistency reasons the editing of this particular run (or resource) is not allowed.

5.2 Transactions in MetaPSS

In a system like *MetaPSS* , supporting a variety of editing facilities which can be exploited in almost any order, the definition of a transaction, i.e. of the portion of work which might be rolled back, is crucial. Unfortunately, the lack of integration seems not to allow a general strategy, and very much will depend on the implementation.

In *MetaPSS* the user must be able to stop a session at any moment, leaving the database in an unchanged state. Consequently we define a transaction as *the whole set of SQL statements resulting from the user session.*

5.2.1 Providing the user with data (DOWNLOAD)

Due to the considerable amount of data, an efficient download strategy is crucial: at the beginning of a session the data most likely to be used (e.g. for the initial display) is downloaded. For the download *KEEconnection* provides an *SQL* -like and fully integrated query language; it allows an efficient and packed download of all data needed (which then passes through the translation module) and it is integrated in *KEE* 's rule-system, thus allowing reasoning about data in the database. Here are two examples drawn from the productive code:

- (DOWNLOAD '(AND (?TG IS IN (TASK-GROUPS))
  ((THE IDENTIFICATION OF ?TG)
  IS LIKE "WH1%"))))
  (downloads all the taskgroups of the run WH1)

- (DOWNLOAD '(AND (?T IS IN (TASKS)
  ((THE IDENTIFICATION OF ?T)
  IS CONTAINED IN
  '("WH1START" "WH1POST")))))
  (downloads all tasks whose identification is
  "WH1START" or "WH1POST")

In addition to this query language *KEE* provides a selective download: data are fetched as they are needed (in a transparent way for the programmer). Despite the conceptual elegance, performance problems do not allow a very extensive use of this feature.

5.2.2 Modifying a run

The *MetaPSS* interface provides local save features during the session: a user can rollback all changes when quitting a window, and only after closing it, the changes become part of the (temporary) units representing a run. For rare changes the selective download fetches all needed data and translates it into *KEE* structures at run time. The system itself keeps track of downloaded or updated slot values.

5.2.3 Updating the database (UPLOAD)

As a final result of the user session, insert, delete and update statements have to be applied to the database . *KEEconnection* provides some functions which take care of updates and deletes in a selective and efficient way; those functions provide a selective update of the concerned fields. Moreover there are means of specifying a correct handling of joins: e.g. a new relationship between units results in an insertion of a whole row in the corresponding secondary table.

In our implementation all updates are collected at the end of a session: to prevent deadlocks, the actual SAVE is performed in a single user mode: all tables are exclusively locked at the beginning of it and concurrent SAVES have to wait until the locks are released, removing all conflicts due to the lack of integration at the expense of a reasonably small amount of multiuser comfort.

KEEconnection is primarily download–oriented and mainly supports an intelligent reasoning about data in a database and selective updates of an existing database . In *MetaPSS* , however, the database is gradually built by the system itself, the insertion of new rows in the database is a serious performance problem. It required an in-house extension of *KEEconnection* so that new rows are inserted efficiently.

5.3 Problems in a non–integrated approach

There are serious conflicts between an object oriented environment and a conventional database:

- An object oriented system supports data abstractions which are far beyond the scope of available DBMS

- Databases provide some classical facilities (persistency, queries, integrity, concurrency, etc.) which are not yet implemented by object oriented systems

- The classical database approach implies the independence of data and programs. This is contrary to basic concepts of object oriented programming.

- Impedance mismatch.

Presently, a divide and conquer approach to combine the strengths of both systems is most promising to develop software with productive standards. However it is obvious that a highly aggregated entity must be split into many tables (also due to the normalisation process on the database).

Thus, minor changes in the underlying structure of the object oriented environment may result in very complicated and tedious changes of the database structure. This may be a severe restriction of the fast prototyping features of many object oriented systems. In addition, a slight change in some objects may often be a (very) long transaction for the database. This in turn may cause serious problems (performance, deadlocks).

In the design of the user session, the statements representing a database transaction are either collected at the end of the session or applied gradually on the database with a final database *commit*. The first case, as implemented in *MetaPSS* , amounts to enormous transactions with hundreds (sometimes even thousands) of *SQL* statements. Incremental updates of the database, with a final *commit* or with user defined and/or automatic *commits* could be applied if the definition of transaction is somewhat relaxed. But this approach largely depends on the specific DBMS: in the case of exclusive table locking before a *commit* this approach is not practicable. Due to the fact that even slight changes in the objects might produce a lot of *SQL* statements, the risk of deadlocks and of sometimes irrational reactions of the DBMS in the case of detection would be too high in a real multi–user environment. As an alternative to the incremental update a global transaction could be split into many local transactions with local save features, but they should never affect data integrity. In *MetaPSS* , as explained before, the problem of data integrity is solved from the very beginning of a session (with a disjunct partition of the database) and the collection of all updates at the end is a practicable strategy.

References

[1] **Brodie, M.L.** *Future Intelligent Information Systems: AI and Database Technologies Working Together* in **Mylopoulos, J. & Brodie, M.L.** (eds.), *Artificial Intelligence & Databases* Morgan Kaufmann Publishers Inc. (1989).

[2] **Goldberg, A. & Robson, D.**, *Smalltalk 80: The Language and its Implementation* Addison-Wesley, 1983.

[3] **Herrmann, U. & Dadam, P. & Küspert, K. & Schlageter G.** *Sperren disjunkter, nicht–rekursiver komplexer Objekte mittels objekt– und anfragespezifischer Sperrgraphen* in **Härder, T. (Hrsg.)** *Tagungsband der GI/SI-Fachtagung "Datenbanksysteme in Büro, Technik und Wissenschaft" Zürich, März 1989*, Informatik–Fachberichte 204, Springer–Verlag, 1989, 98-113

[4] **IntelliCorp** *KEE Version 3.1* Software Development System User's Manual, 1986.

[5] **Risch, R. & Reboh, R. & Hart, P. & Duda, R.**, *A Functional Approach to Integrating Database and Expert System.* Communications of the ACM, *31* 12(1988), 1424-1437

[6] **Schlegel, D.** *MetaPSS - A Knowledge System for the Design and Maintenance of an Automated Batch Processing*, Tagungsband der SGAICO–Tagung, Lugano, Mai 1989.

Artificial Intelligence Techniques for Bibliographies

Johannes Gordesch, Hartmut Salzwedel, Ingeborg Siggelkow

Freie Universität Berlin

ABSTRACT

Conventional bibliographies are, from the view point of EDP, mere data bases. Despite their extensive use of key words they often do not provide the appropriate information. Hence expert system techniques are introduced to guarantee an improved representation of knowledge as well as the deduction of new interrelations, and thus to furnish broader and more profound information. Besides the exposition of the technical and logical aspects two instances of application are dealt with:

- a bibliography on Soviet research on China: economics, technology, and ethnic groups;
- sociological categories in theory and practice: time, space, symbols, rules, and norms as an expression of cultural identity.

1 Introduction

Even extensive bibliographies do not always furnish the desired information. Key words are often too vague, and their mutual relationship is not made explicit. In the sequel, we introduce a knowledge based system consisting of a bibliographic knowledge base, i. e. the conventional bibliography, and in addition, of an inferential system for the derivation of bibliographic references. We follow the path of formal conceptual analysis, for the annotations comprise a set of interrelated concepts describing the characteristic features of each literary document. The selection of concepts (and accordingly of key words) is guided by social theory rather than left to mere intuition.

2 Databases and expert systems

Expert (Knowledge-based) systems [1] are used for an intelligent "inductional leap" from past to present to future, and should at least diminish uncertainty by e. g. switching from an n-dimensional distribution to an (n-m)-dimensional (less unknown factors) or by an increase of the a priori probability of events or hypotheses. They are no oracle for the nonprofessional but assist the expert; when no elaborate theory or algorithms are available, they may be of great advantage.

An expert system provides a dialogue between a computer and a human being. With regard to efficiency, its advantages are:

- availability and easiness of use
- independence of the actual condition
- lack of personality with all its preferences, emotions etc.
- generation of a new expert by copying the program from one machine to another

It consists of a *knowledge base* characterizing the related objects, and of an *inferential system* ("inference engine"). More refined techniques of *knowledge representation* are indispensable. Predicate calculus, semantic nets, frames, conceptual dependency and scripts are well-known instances. In most practical cases an object can be characterized by a list of attributes this object possesses or does not possess. Lattice theory [2] has proven a valuable tool, for most logical systems can be represented by particular types of lattices or semilattices (e. g. propositional calculus by distributive lattices which correspond to set theory, quantum logic by modular lattices, etc.). Concept lattices have been the hub of formal conceptual analysis [3]. If the attributes form a distributive lattice, the calculus of boolean algebra or equivalent systems apply, and any expression may be transformed to its additive or multiplicative normal form, etc. Especially, propositional calculus, theory of probability, systems for the formulation and evaluation of rules and so forth can be achieved by mappings of special types of lattices [4], thus yielding a rather general tool.

The inferential system may operate in one of the following ways:

Forward chaining starts with some pertinent information and looks for the appropriate object (building up a tree as in plant identification). Redundant information is discarded.

Backward chaining commences with a plausible hypothesis (an object the attributes apply to). The system asks for information in order to verify or falsify the hypothesis (trimming a tree). It is best if only one object is wanted. As it is goal-oriented, only relevant information is taken into account.

Rule-based (Evaluation, Heuristic) methods try to maximize the reduction of uncertainty at each step of the algorithm. Because of the complexity of thought this objective is hardly ever attained.

It is professional standard that knowledge base and inferential system are separate, and objects and their attributes are not tied to the program (not "hard-coded"). This ensures easily augmenting, correcting etc. the knowledge base, and no access to the source code of the program is necessary.

Knowledge engineering: A rather crude approach is to select one object after another and to check whether it matches the goal (simple backward chaining). This can be done by uncomplicated SQL commands, making allowance for the distribution of the information over several files (relational database). A more refined technique is to confine the set of all feasible objects to classes with known probability of containing the desired objects, and to search these classes in the order of the decreasing probability of success. This reduction of the number of cases to be searched could be done by the user who ought to be an expert. The pertaining subclasses of the total knowledge base, then, are searched by straightforward SQL commands. It is, however, more appealing to perform this reduction automatically, i. e. by some heuristic algorithm.

Testing large knowledge bases in total is hardly possible; therefore sampling techniques have to be used. For that purpose, special algorithms constructing an appropriate sample must be designed. Then some coefficient of reliability may be computed.

Experts may differ in essential points; a test of compatibility will be necessary (ranging from simply computing Kendall's coefficient of concordance to rather refined models). The inability of some experts to explicate what they know ("experts do not know what they know") is conspicuous. Unfortunately, no computer program and no algorithm will do away with it.

3 Areas of Application

We use the same expert system techniques to represent knowledge in two different fields. Both cases involve bibliographical data that is selected, documented, and prepared in a form suitable for research work in sociology and economics. The areas of application are very different, which shows that the system can be applied in other areas without difficulty, in accordance with the special interests of the respective users.

The development of the system is based on actual research work on the following subjects:

- "Sociological categories in theory and practice: time, space, symbols, rules, and norms as an expression of cultural identity";
- "Soviet research on China: economics, technology, and ethnic groups".

3.1 The first topic resulted from attempts to answer a number of theoretical and practical questions, namely

- questions on sociocultural theory aimed at giving it a new direction in Germany;
- in order to create links between the practical experiences of social workers and community workers and an expanded base of knowledge that benefit their daily work, in particular to promote

intercultural understanding and action based on interdisciplinary insights.

For this purpose, bibliographical references from the fields of philosophy, sociology, psychology, ethnology, and education to be found in collections scattered throughout a number of libraries, above all in Berlin, are being prepared in a manner suitable for data processing.

Lecturers at university institutes and specialized institutions of higher learning as well as experienced community workers and social workers can use this knowledge-based information system, now in its initial phase of development, for the purpose of information and further training. Since very little staff is available for data entry, one of the main problems is the current quantitative limitation on inputting data into the information system; selection of material is based on qualitative criteria. The goal of the information system, to have it include approximately 30,000 titles along with key words, requires careful selection and limitation of material - for example, just for the category of "time" the number of articles in periodical literature is estimated by Fraser at 40,000 during the 1965 - 1980 period [5].

The organizational principle underlying both information systems is identical; each system consists of two data sets:

The first includes: consecutive number, identifying character and number ("D" for dissertation, etc.), author/editor, title/subtitle, translation of title, periodical, place of publication, publisher, year, number of pages, bibliographical information, series, language, and location.

The second data set includes: consecutive number, identifying character and number (dissertation, bibliography, article in a periodical / location / whether already used in cultural sociology), group of words / single key word with the respective number, and page references if applicable.

The following example is intended to illustrate the structure and functioning of the second data set in the first information system:

"Sociological categories in theory and practice: time, space, symbols, rules, and norms as an expression of cultural identity".

Excerpt from the second data set:

1
D 2 I
1. time in philosophy
2. the relationship between space and time
3. how time is experienced"

The numbers and characters stand for:

1 = consecutive number
D = identifying character (dissertation)
2 = location (Free University Berlin)
I = already used in cultural sociology

This hypothetical statement can serve as an example:

"Concepts of time in developing countries and in industrialised countries are not connected" ("either ha or hb").

The following lists of key words and rules were conceived:

Categories (Key words)
aa time as a category
ab space as a category
ba social time / time and social class / time and social structure
bb time and empirical methods
ca how time is experienced
cb how space is experienced
da time orientation
ea past
eb present
ec future
fa cyclical time
fb linear time
ga time and identity
gb time and action
ha time in developing countries
hb time in industrialised countries
ia time perspective
ib synchronization
ic lack of time
id autonomy
ie heteronomy
if morality
ig control of emotion
ih trust
ii deferred gratification
ik anxiety / disturbed attitude toward the future

Rules

aa or ab	either ha or ic
aa and ab	ha and ie
ba and bb	either ha or ih
ca or cb	either ha or ii
ca and cb	*ha and ik*
da and ea	hb and ia
da and eb	hb and ib
da and ec	hb and ic
ea or eb	hb and id
ea or ec	hb and if
eb or ec	hb and ig
either fa or fb	hb and ih
ga and gb	hb and ii
either ha or hb	*hb and ik*
either ha or ia	

We easily derive

(ha and ik) and (hb and ik) ⇒ ha and hb.

Thus the system disproved the initial hypothesis ("either ha or hb") by connecting "ha" with "hb" via "ik" and thereby creating an indirect link between concepts of time in industrial countries (time, identity, and jobless) and developing countries.

3.2 With regard to the second topic, the development of a knowledge-based system on Soviet research on China is intended to provide basic information for the German media and German policy-makers. The system focuses on analyses of the economy and technology as well as the problems of ethnic groups in areas close to the Soviet border.

In addition, the system includes an index of geographical and ethnic designations plus names that lists the transliterated transcription used by libraries opposite the transcribed (i.e. phonetic) transcription, because in the system concerning Soviet research on China the second data set will employ the latter form of transcription until various technical questions are resolved. Thus far approximately 6000 book titles have been entered in the expert system about Soviet research on China, whereas the ultimate goal is to encompass 30,000 book titles.

Selecting Russian, German, and English bibliographies, monographs, papers on specialized subjects, and conference reports was only the first step, one that immediately revealed a number of deficiencies in the way this information was prepared for data processing by a number of otherwise highly respected research institutes. The team's approach was developed on the basis of its observations and experience. To ensure that the results are useful, particularly for work in the public and private sectors (the media, policy-making, economic affairs), the index provides a special form of access to economically and technologically significant material. It seeks the middle ground between the general practice of recording only titles on the one hand and providing a detailed description of content on the other hand. The further development of the software is tied closely to this approach, which goes far beyond simple documentation. Such an index represents an intentional break with the approach generally used by librarians to formulate key words. This means avoiding the use of key words that, in our opinion, are not very meaningful (e.g. "foreign policy") in favour of key words chosen for their significance in the fields of Slavic studies and sociology.

3.3 At first glance it might seem possible to develop an expert system for Soviet research on China strictly on the basis of bibliographical considerations. However, in reality Russian and Soviet policy on China have always been closely linked to the leading researchers of the respective historical period. This applies both to the present and to the past. Only looking back at the beginnings of Soviet research on China and how it changed over the course of time makes it possible to understand continuities and discern radical changes in Soviet policy. It is therefore of crucial importance to work with bio-bibliographical materials from earlier periods when the first efforts were made in this field. The innovative potential of such authors should not be underestimated, even though technical resources were inadequate at the time. Some particularly important examples are:

Miliband's [6] bio-bibliography supplements the work of Skačkov [7,8,9] and Nikiforov [10]. It deals exclusively with work by Soviet Orientalists published after 1917. Of the more than 260 authors whose publications contained references to China, the work of approximately 220 researchers dealt with China as the main subject. The 1977 edition, which includes more material than the first edition that appeared in 1975, provides information about Soviet research work published up to April of 1976.

The need to put bibliographic and historiographic information about Russian and Soviet research on China into usable form was already recognized by P.E. Skačkov (1892-1964) - and, incidentally, also by M.F. Dostoevskij (1884-1944), a great-nephew of the famous author [11]. Skačkov's first bibliography appeared in 1932. It contained all work including references to China that had been published in Russia since 1730. The fact that a new American edition of this bibliography about research on China was published in Ann Arbor, Michigan in 1948 shows that Skačkov's work meets high international standards.

In continuation of his work, a second edition by Skačkov appeared in 1960 that took research until 1957 into account and included almost 20,000 titles of publications. During his lifetime, Skačkov could not realize his plan to compile a bibliography about research on China by foreign Sinologists, nor was it possible for him to prepare a bio-bibliographical reference book about Russian Sinologists.

In addition to his bibliographic research, Skačkov laid the foundations for work in the field of historiography. He wanted to write a book describing the development and history of Russian Sinology, but unfortunately he was unable to complete it - his daughter finally published "Očerki istorii russkogo kitaevedenija" in 1977.

V.N. Nikiforov also takes historical aspects into account in his book entitled "Sovetskie istoriki o problemach Kitaja", which was published in 1970. Its first chapter deals with the pre-revolutionary period. The book is primarily concerned with Soviet research on China from 1917 to 1949. It offers the possibility of understanding the connections between historical conditions, leading researchers, and policy formulation, which is also a major concern of the team of experts.

Thus both projects ("Soviet research..." and "Sociological categories...") are currently making a transition from typical bibliographical data bases to information data bases [12].

3.4 The following example shows how information about a publication is entered and how key words are used to describe it:

Kitaj posle "kul'turnoj revoljucii". <Političeskaja sistema, vnutripolitičeskoe položenie.>
Institut Dal'nego Vostoka AN SSSR. Avt. koll.: L.M. Gudošnikov
Moskva: Mysl' 1979. 359 S.
Key words: Domestic policy / Contemporary political issues: China

We propose providing the following information in place of the key words "domestic policy" and "contemporary political issues: China".

"cultural revolution"
10th party congress of the Chinese Communist Party
Mao Tse-tung
campaign on "criticism of Lin Piao and Confucius"
mass campaigns 1975-1977
11th party congress of the Chinese Communist Party
constitution of 1975
constitution of 1978
China after Mao Tse-tung

Initially all data are assigned equal status. This eliminates the traditional hierarchy set up by libraries when they distinguish between the alphabetical and the systematic catalogue, and the same applies to key words as a group.

There are many explanations for the frequent occurrence of meaningless, superfluous key words: these include the formalistic rules followed by librarians, as well as political constraints (that also apply to the formulation of book titles) which have placed, or still place, limitations on (Soviet) research. The latter have sometimes led to ritualistic word combinations devoid of meaning, such as "socialist democracy". However, similar or frequently repeated, and therefore apparently boring titles can conceal highly interesting details that are only revealed to the scrutiny of an alert researcher. His assessment of such details naturally makes it necessary to adopt a point of view much broader than that prevailing among librarians; feedback from the researcher's expanded possibilities for systematic classification is part of the concept being discussed here.

In connection with setting up and using the information system, one aspect applicable to different periods of time is the planned reconstruction of how Soviet research on China was organized in past years. It is significant, because the formal hierarchy of Soviet political advisors (and the views of individual researchers or groups within this hierarchy) has influenced, and continues to influence, the policies implemented. An organizational chart on Soviet studies about China like that provided by Rozman [13] can be brought up to date or used for earlier periods, and some aspects can be expanded on the basis of extensive bibliographical and biographical material.

Both systems of bibliographical documentation and information are intended to assist the expert who provides information, not to replace him.

4 Practical aspects of EDP

As a large amount of bibliographic data and annotations have to be processed, the selection of an efficient professional system for data handling (inputting, correcting, retrieving etc.) is imperative. We use the relational database system Oracle, albeit experiments with a system based on semantic nets (Kleio, κλειω, developed at the Max-Planck-Institut für Geschichte at Göttingen) [14] are made.

Bibliographical data are not restricted to ASCII characters (diacritical symbols, also non-Latin alphabets). For data entry, WordPerfect 5.1 is used because of its inherent multilingual abilities. PostScript printers (or Post-Script emulations like UltraScript from QMS) provide most of the necessary diacritical symbols and guarantee an easy extension to non-Latin alphabets.

The main problems arise with database systems, for most software is written in the United States, and the English speaking programmers cannot imagine what other languages involve. DataPerfect, the database related to WordPerfect, does not show most of the multilingual capabilities of WordPerfect, and is a rather restricted MS-DOS program. Hence the bibliographical data have either to be kept separate, or to be transformed to ASCII for processing, and afterwards to be transformed back. Even problems with the sorting algorithms arise (the authors do not know any US software which could perform German sorting correctly). Oracle (and other systems) allow for switching to C programs, where the necessary operations can be effectuated.

Fortunately, most key words (except proper names) can be spelled using standard Latin alphabetic characters, and the more sophisticated operations in analyzing data are not hindered by spelling or typographic problems. For the rest, cumbersome transliterations are unavoidable, at least for the time being.

Ordinary SQL is used for standard retrieval problems. The artificial intelligence techniques are prototyped by a Prolog front end [15], though predicate calculus is restricted to Horn clauses. The authors do not know any total integration of Prolog into a DBMS; perhaps PROSQL [16] comes close to that goal. Because of memory requirements and speed, the Prolog front end will be replaced by more efficient C programs in the final version. Prolog dialects show a great variety (Edinburgh or Marseille standard, typed versions like PDC Prolog): another reason for discarding it eventually.

A user-friendly front end and the reduction of search time for large data sets are the most pressing problems. In a first step, we pursue both goals by the use of standardized logic forms. The set of key words with the connectives "and", "or", "not" is isomorphic to propositional calculus. Various normal forms are known; the Gentzen normal form seems to be the most natural for our purpose: a conjunction of "premisses" and a disjunction of "conclusions" match ordinary thinking better than the disjunctive or conjunctive normal forms do.

A Gentzen formula is of type

$$P_1 \wedge P_2 \wedge \ldots \wedge P_n \quad \rightarrow \quad Q_1 \vee Q_2 \vee \ldots \vee Q_m$$

where P_i $(1 \leq i \leq n)$ and Q_j $(1 \leq j \leq m)$ denote atomic formulae. For $m = 0$ or $n = 0$ or both the conjunctions resp. disjunctions reduce to the logic constants T or F (true or false). Horn clauses as employed in Prolog are derived if we substitute a single Q for the disjunction of several Q_j $(m = 1)$. For more intricate semantic problems, Herbrand structures and Herbrand models are chosen [17].

A somewhat different interpretation leads to phrase-structure grammars (PSGs) where the use of key words is formalized as a system of generative rules. The key words correspond to the linguistic elements, and the logical operators to the metalinguistic symbols. A substitution rule exists such that the PSG takes the form of "rewrite rules". Even the distinction between context free and context sensitive grammars is applicable. Generalized phrase-structure grammars (GPSGs, [18]) would reflect the interrelation of key words even better; e. g. categories are sets of feature specifications, while in traditional PSGs category labels have no internal structure. In practice, however, the required effort would be tremendous.

Throughout, portability is achieved by the use of software systems and programming languages which are available at various computer systems and are identical in the majority of relevant features. This is the case with the language C and databases as Oracle or Kleio, while Prolog interpreters or compilers may differ widely.

UNIX resp. UNIX substitutes like MKS serve as programming environment, and extensive use is made of piping of small independent modules. As far as linguistic manipulations are necessary, standard UNIX utilities as well as AWK [19,20] are used.

REFERENCES

[1] R.-D. HENNINGS. "Informations- und Wissensverarbeitung." Berlin: Freie Universität, 1989.

[2] G. BIRKHOFF. "Lattice Theory." 2nd ed. New York: AMS, 1948.

[3] B. GANTER, R. WILLE and K. E. WOLFF. "Beiträge zur Begriffsanalyse." Mannheim : BI Wissenschaftsverlag, 1987.

[4] J. GORDESCH. "A generalized concept of probability." COMPSTAT 1976. Proceedings in Computational Statistics. Wien-Würzburg: Physica, pp. 18-29, 1976.

[5] J. T. FRASER, N. LAWRENCE and D. PARK. " The Study of Time IV." Berlin: Springer, p. 267, 1981.

[6] S. D. MILIBAND. "Bio-bibliografičeskij slovar' sovetskich vostokovedov." Moskva: Nauka, 1977.

[7] P. E. SKAČKOV. "Bibliografija Kitaja. Sist. ukaz. knig i žurn. statej o Kitae na rus. jazyke, 1730-1930." Moskva-Leningrad: Socėkgiz, 1932.

[8] P. E. SKAČKOV. "Bibliografija Kitaja." Moskva: Izd. vost. lit., 1960.

[9] P. E. SKAČKOV. "Očerki istorii russkogo kitaevedenija." Moskva: Nauka, 1977.

[10] V. N. NIKIFOROV. "Sovetskie istoriki o problemach Kitaja." Moskva: Nauka, 1970.

[11] P. E. SKAČKOV. "Očerki istorii russkogo kitaevedenija." Moskva: Nauka, pp. 353-357, 1977.

[12] F.-J. LAND. "Computergestützte Literatur- und Dokumentationsarbeit in den Sozialwissenschaften." Zeitschrift für Soziologie, vol. 16, no. 6, p.474, 1987.

[13] G. ROZMAN. "Soviet Studies of Premodern China. Assessments of Recent Scholarship." Ann Arbor, Mich.: Univ. of Michigan, pp. 197-198, 1984.

[14] M. THALLER. "Κλειω. Ein fachspezifisches Datenbanksystem für die Historischen Wissenschaften." Göttingen: Max-Planck-Institut für Geschichte, 1988.

[15] C. ZANIOLO. "Prolog. A Database Query Language for all Seasons." Expert Database Systems. Reading, Mass.: Cummings Publication, 1986.

[16] C. L. CHANG and A. WALKER. "PROSQL: A Prolog Programming Interface with SQL/DS." Expert Database Systems. Reading/Mass.: Cummings Publishing, 1986.

[17] D. HOFBAUER and R.-D. KUTSCHE. "Grundlagen des maschinellen Beweisens." Braunschweig: Vieweg, 1989.

[18] G. GAZDAR, E. KLEIN, G. K. PULLUM and I. A. SAG. "Generalized Phrase Structure Grammar." Oxford, 1985.

[19] A. V. AHO, B. W. KERNIGHAN and P. J. WEINBERGER. "The AWK Programmming Language." Reading, Mass.: Addison-Wesley, 1988.

[20] G. STAUBACH. "UNIX Werkzeuge zur Textmusterverarbeitung: Awk, Lex und Yacc." Berlin: Springer, 1989.

INTENSIONAL QUERY PROCESSING: A THREE-STEP APPROACH

Il-Yeol Song

Drexel University
College of Information Studies
Philadelphia, PA 19104

Hyoung-Joo Kim, Petra Geutner

Georgia Institute of Technology
College of Computing
Atlanta, GA 30093

Abstract

When processing a query in a conventional database a set of facts are usually returned for an answer. This can be different in a deductive or expert database system. Users may, as before, be interested in a set of facts to answer their query, but in certain queries users are also able to get the answer of a query as a set of formulas (e.g., facts, intensional answers).

These "intensional answers" can greatly reduce the costs of processing a query, can be represented in a more compact way than a large set of facts, and are moreover independent of the current state of the database. In this paper, we introduce an intensional query processing technique composed of 3 steps. Our approach is more efficient than previous works on intentional query processing and provides guidelines of implementation details of intentional query processor.

1   Introduction and Motivation

When querying a deductive or expert database for intensional answers, we are not interested in the set of objects which satisfy a given query in a particular database state. We rather want to know the conditions that objects must satisfy, in any state, to belong to an answer.

But why are we dealing with intensional query processing at all? As we get intensional answers as a set of rules, they are independent of the particular circumstances in the database. Displaying the output of a query in terms of a formula gives us the answer in a more compact form than a set of rules could ever do. Intensional query processing has also an advantage in computation compared with extensional answers. Most of the time intensional answers can be computed without accessing the database which saves a lot of time. Also, intensional answers tell us exactly what conditions must be fulfilled to get a certain extensional answer. That means intensional answers can help us to interpret extensional answers.

This paper looks closely at some work dealing with the topic of intensional answers and suggests a technique composed of 3 steps. Our approach is more efficient than previous works on intentional query processing and provides guidelines of implementation details of intentional query processor. It is organized as follows.

Section 2 provides the terminology that is necessary to understand intensional query processing. Section 3 is a short introduction into the previous works that have been done in intensional query processing. The following section, section 4, gives a definition of both extensional and intensional answers. Section 5 formalizes intensional answers and gives our strategy consisting of 3 steps to obtain them. Next, section 6 describes some properties of intensional answers. Section 7 summarizes the improvements of our work over previous works concerning processing intensional queries. Finally section 8 gives an outlook to further problems in intensional query processing and summarizes the paper.

2   Terminology

We assume that the reader is familiar with the terminologies of first-order logic which are normally defined in standard logic references [1], such as formulas, atomic formulas, free variables, bound variables, ground formulas, and etc.

2.1   Deductive Databases

A *Deductive Database* (*DDB*) is a database in which new facts may be derived from the facts that were explicitly stored by using an inference system. The database of a DDB can be divided in an *extensional database* (*EDB*), which consists of a set of facts explicitly stored in a physical database, and an *intensional database* (*IDB*) consisting of a set of deductive rules. These rules can be used to derive new facts out of the facts in the EDB. Deductive databases deal with two different types of queries which can be distinguished by the kind of answer they are providing. These two are known as:

- extensional answers
- intensional answers

Whereas an *extensional answer* just consists of a set of facts, an *intensional answer* is a set of non-ground first-order logic formulas. So an *extensional query* is a query which has only extensional answers and an *intensional query* has only intensional answers.

2.2   Rules and Horn clauses

Previous works in intensional query processing used resolution to generate answer formulas for a given query. In order to deal with resolution, we first must introduce the terms of rules and clauses.

A *rule* has the form $a \longleftarrow b_1, b_2, ..., b_m$, $m \geq 0$ where a is an atomic formula and the b_i's are literals. All the variables occuring in the rule are assumed to be universally quantified. The literal a is called the *head* of the formula, the b_i's are referred to as the *body*.

A *clause* is a finite disjunction of zero or more literals. Every rule can be represented as a clause, so our rule from above would look like:

$$a \vee \neg b_1 \vee \neg b_2 \vee ... \vee \neg b_m$$

Here in this paper we are only dealing with *Horn clauses* which are a subset of clauses that have at most one positive literal.

2.3 Example

The following example illustrates the notion of intensional answers. Suppose we have a database for students, consisting of 3 relations representing the extensional database and 4 rules constituting the intensional database.

EDB:

- (relation 1:)   student(S_name,Year)

- (relation 2:)   course(C_number,C_name,C_hrs)

- (relation 3:)   has_taken(S_name,C_number)

The relation *student* contains information about student names (S_name) and the years, they have been studying (Year). The relation *course* contains a course number (C_number), the course name (C_name) and the number of credit hours (C_hrs). The relation *has_taken* describes who (S_name) has already taken what courses (C_number).

IDB:

- (rule 1:)   pre_req(S_name,4402)

    ← has_taken(S_name,3102)

- (rule 2:)   cannot_take(S_name,C_number)

    ← student(S_name, 1), C_number = 3102

- (rule 3:)   cannot_take(S_name,C_number)

    ← ¬ pre_req(S_name,C_number)

- (rule 4:)   cannot_take(S_name,C_number)

    ← student(S_name,1) , C_number > 4000

Rule 1 states that course number 3102 is a prerequisite for course 4402. Rule 2 says that a freshman cannot take course 3102. The third rule tells us that if the student does not satisfy the prerequisite of a course, then he cannot take that course. Finally, rule 4 states that freshmen cannot take courses above the 4000 level.

Suppose we have a query *cannot_take(X,4402)?*, asking "Who cannot take course 4402?". In a conventional database system which computes only extensional answers, the answer might be a long list of student names who either did not take course 3102 or who are freshmen. However , if a database system can process intensional queries, the answers can be represented as a set of simple formulas such as

$$ans_1 = student(X,1)$$

and

$$ans_2 = \neg \ has\_taken(X,3102)$$

The first answer implies that if any student is a freshman, then he cannot take 4402. The second one implies that if any student has not taken 3102, then he cannot take 4402.

This example shows that whereas intensional answers distinguish between two cases in which a student cannot take 4402, extensional answers would only provide a set of facts. The user would not be able to conclude for which reason a student could not take that particular course. Thus, by telling us what conditions or formulas constitute the answers, intensional answers are more informative than extensional ones in some cases.

2.4 Resolution

Resolution is an automatic theorem proving method that uses a refutation proof procedure. So, in order to prove that a theorem F follows from a set of axioms T, we prove that the formula $T \wedge \neg \ F$ is unsatisfiable.

For query processing, when resolution is used in the context of databases, a query formula is negated, converted into clause form and unioned with a set of database axioms. All the possible resolvents are computed afterwards. The query is proved if we derive the empty clause in the end. The unification process extracts answers to the query throughout the whole resolution process.

Consider C_1 and C_2 being two clauses of the form

$$C_1 = p_1 \vee C_1'$$

and

$$C_2 = \neg p_1 \vee C_2'$$

with no variables in common. Let p_1 and $\neg p_1$ have a unifier θ with as few substitutions as possible. Using resolution will lead to the new clause

$$C_3 = \theta(C_1') \vee \theta(C_2').$$

C_3 is called a *resolvent*. Thus if a literal p from a clause C_1 can be unified with the literal $\neg p$ from a clause C_2, then applying the unifier to the remaining literals in C_1 and C_2 and combining them, will result in the resolvent of a resolution step.

3 Previous Works

There has been done a lot of research in the area of deductive or expert databases for last several years. The interesting works for this paper are two different approaches. They both have in common that all or part of their answers to a given query consist of a set of first-order logic formulas rather than a set of facts.

Cholvy and Demolombe [2] study the idea of having a set of formulas as an answer set and Pascual and Cholvy [4] improves an algorithm based on this research, while Imielinski [3] tries to incorporate intensional predicates as a part of the answers.

Whereas Cholvy and Demolombe use resolution to generate answer formulas for a query in a logical formula, the latter uses relational algebra to transform the rules and process a query in relational algebra expressions.

In the context of deductive databases usually general rules are used to compute complete answers to a certain query. The rules are used to derive new facts from a set of elementary facts. Cholvy and Demolombe want to provide answers which are independent of these facts, that means answers which are valid in all the states associated to the set of facts. Their answers are a set of formulas defining the conditions that a given tuple would satisfy to be an answer for a given query.

In their work [2], a method for generating answers is developed. The basic assumptions are:

- the rule base is a non-recursive set of rules

- the answer to a query is a formula (instead of a set of tuples)

- the formalism of the first-order predicate is used.

Only non-recursive rules are allowed to make sure that the algorithm for generating answers terminates.

Based on the research by Cholvy and Demolombe, Pascual and Cholvy [4] developed an improved algorithm to retrieve an answer set of a given query. The former approach accepts any form of clauses and therefore is inefficient in the case of Horn clauses. Horn clauses permit avoiding numerous tests while generating the answer set. Thus they help to accelerate the resolution process.

Also [2] proves that tautologies and subsumed clauses have to be eliminated when generated. Tautologies are never generated when the clauses, that can be used, are restricted to Horn clauses. So this test doesn't have to be done in Pascual and Cholvy's algorithm. Moreover Horn clauses do only have one positive literal. So only this particular literal has to be examined if it matches either one of the negative literals of another clause or the negation of a query. Before, all positive literals had to be tested if they were unifiable with a negative literal of a clause or a query.

Imielinsky [3] introduces a new concept of an answer for a query. His answer can be composed of atomic facts and general rules built from projection, join and selection, so that they can be incorporated into the answer of a query.

Pirottr and Roelants use integrity constraints to filter out inadequate answers [5].

4 Definition of Intensional and Extensional Answers

4.1 Definition

First of all, a formal definition of query answers given [2]. We define T as the database theory consisting of a set of facts and rules. $Q(X)$ represents a query where X is a tuple of free variables.

So, the intensional answer to a certain query $Q(X)$, ANS(Q) is defined as:

$$ANS(Q) = \{\ ans_i(X) : T \vdash \forall\ X(ans_i(X) \rightarrow Q(X))\}$$

The literal $ans_i(X)$ is defined that under the theory T, any element X, where $X \in ans_i(X)$, must satisfy $Q(X)$. $Ans_i(X)$ now can be any formula in a logical sense, that means we don't care about its semantics and its truth value.

As we are only interested in meaningful answers, which means answers within a defined domain of interest, we try to put some restrictions on the intensional answer set. Above all, this means that our intensional answers consist of only predicates out of T. Also we don't allow contradictory formulas or redundant answers.

So let $DP = P_1,...,P_n$ be a set of predicate symbols either of the IDB or the EDB. Let L(DP) be the first-order language whose predicate symbols are $P_1,...,P_n$. Thus an intensional answer set ANS(Q,DP) to a query $Q(X)$ is defined by:

$$ANS(Q,DP) = \{\ ans_i(x): ans_i(X) \in L(DP)\ and$$

$$T \vdash \forall\ X\ (ans_i(X) \rightarrow Q(X))\ and$$

$$(ans_i(X)\ is\ not\ the\ negation\ of\ a\ tautology)$$

and

$$(each\ ans_i(X)\ is\ not\ redundant)\}$$

If a query is formulated as a formula with free variables it is also possible to try to find bindings for these variables as the answering process. An extensional answer set then would be defined as:

$$ANS_E\ (Q) = \{X \mid T \wedge [\ \forall\ X\ (Q(X) \rightarrow ans_e(X))]\}$$

An extensional answer is defined as a tuple X which makes $Q(X)$ true in the database theory T. To use resolution a special literal called answer literal was added. It contains the same variables as the query and its purpose is to collect all substitutions made by the resolution process.

4.2 Resolution

While evaluating a query the basic idea is to use the database theory T and the negation of the theorem defining either intensional or extensional answers.

In the first case, resolution will be applied to the theorem

$$\forall\ X\ (ans_i(X) \rightarrow Q(X))$$

and the database theory T. The negation of the theorem above is

$$\neg\ \forall\ X\ (ans_i(X) \rightarrow Q(X))$$

which is equal to

$$\exists X \, (ans_i \, (X) \wedge \neg \, Q(X))$$

That leads to the clause form

$$\{ans_i(x0), \neg \, Q(X)\}$$

where x0 is a tuple of skolem constants introduced to remove the existential quantifier.

Using the database theory T for resolution, all facts have to be converted into rules. The set of clauses transformed from the theory T is called S. So the basis from which the resolution is starting is:

$$S \cup \{ans_i(x0), \neg \, Q(x0)\}$$

As it is not known what $ans_i(x0)$ actually is, it will be removed at the beginning and the resolution process will be started off with:

$$S \cup \neg \, Q(x0).$$

Resolving this will result in a resolvent R(x0). To finally get the empty clause, R(x0) has to be resolved with $ans_i(x0)$. That means that $ans_i(x0)$ must be equal to $\neg$ R(x0) in the most simple case.

In the second case, by using the added answer literal together with the query and then apply resolution to it, the theorem to start with would be

$$\forall X \, (Q(X) \rightarrow ans_e(X))$$

which is equal to

$$\neg \, Q(X) \vee ans_e(X).$$

So the following is to be resolved:

$$S \cup \{\neg \, Q(X) \vee ans_e(X)\}.$$

In this case not the empty clause can be derived but a clause that consists only of one answer literal $ans_e(X)$. The instantiated values of the variables in $ans_e(X)$ are now the answers for the variables of the query.

4.3 Example

The following example shows, how we get an intensional answer by using resolution. Suppose our database consists of two rules and a fact as follows:

- at(mary,X) ← at(john,X)

- at(john,X) ← at(bob,X)

- at(bob,school)

The first rule says that Mary goes wherever John does, and the second rule says that John goes wherever Bob does. The fact says that Bob is at school. The clause form of the rules and the fact are:

- $\neg$ at(john,X) $\vee$ at(mary,X)

- $\neg$ at(bob,Z) $\vee$ at(john,Z)

- at(bob,school)

Note that the variable X in the second rule has to be renamed to Z to make variable names unique in the clause set. In this example, a possible form of a query is $at(mary, Y)$, which asks "Where is Mary?". An initial set of clauses for resolution to derive an intensional answer for the query above is:

- (clause 1:) $\neg$ at(john,X) $\vee$ at(mary,X)

- (clause 2:) $\neg$ at(bob,Z) $\vee$ at(john,Z)

- (clause 3:)   at(bob,school)

- (query:) $\neg$ at(mary,y0)

The resolution proof for the goal $\neg$ at(mary,y0) will look as follows:

```
                              ¬ at(mary,y0)    ¬ at(john,X)
∨ at(mary,X)
                                    |
                                    |              {y0|X}
                                    |
                              ¬ at(john,y0)    ¬ at(bob,Z)
∨ at(john,Z)
                                    |
                                    |              {y0|Z}
                                    |
                                at(bob,y0)
```

Since we have two resolvents, we have two intensional answers as follows:

$$ans_i^1(Y) = at(john,Y)$$

$$ans_i^2(Y) = at(bob,Y)$$

The answers can be read, according to the definition of an intensional answer, as "if John is at Y then Mary is at Y" and "if Bob is at Y then Mary is at Y".

The two intensional answers we get are ans_i^1 and ans_i^2. The extensional answer $< Y = school>$ would satisfy both of them. It satisfies $at(bob, Y)$ because $at(bob, school)$ exists in the database. It also satisfies the second intensional answer because $at(john, school)$ is implied by the rule $at(john,X) \leftarrow at(bob, Y)$ and the fact $at(bob, school)$.

5 Formalization of Intensional Answers

As already stated, here it has only been dealt with a non-recursive set of rules – in order to get the algorithm, that generates the answers, terminating – and with Horn clauses. Early works on this topic allowed any form of clauses and presented algorithms inefficient for Horn clauses [2]. The exploitation of Horn clauses avoids numerous tests and thus accelerates the resolution method.

The former algorithms also had to eliminate tautologies after generating intensional answers. By using Horn clauses we never produce tautologies and can save time by not testing if an intensional answer is a tautology or not [4]. Also, the algorithm, generating intensional answers is more efficient when using Horn clauses. We only have to test the one positive literal of each clause to find out if it is unifiable with one of the negative literals of the clauses of the negation of the query.

Nevertheless there are still a lot of problems left:

[2] didnot suggest any particular resolution method, while [4] used Prolog-like resolution. However, the detailed resolution steps to remove redundant resolution steps or meaningless answers were not discussed.

Also, no solution was given to deal with a large number of facts in the extensional database. Converting all facts to rules as in [2] is neither efficient nor practical and should therefore be avoided.

Moreover the relationships between intensional answers and extensional answers was never examined. This is an important point to connect intensional query processing with conventional databases.

Another disadvantage was the fact that all intermediate resolvents of the resolution process were converted to rules whereas the last resolvent maybe could have been enough.

Trying to solve all of these problems, we [6] divide the resolution process into three steps : pre-resolution, resolution and post-resolution.

5.1 Pre-Resolution

In the first step some rule transformations will be done in order to get unique intensional literals and extended term-restricted rules. Moreover the relevant literals of a query will be identified.

Unique intensional literals means that a literal should either be extensionally or intensionally defined but not both. Users can always get rid of this equality of names by renaming the existential literal to p* and introducing the rule p ← p*. The reason to force unique literals is to get a unique resolution tree.

Extended term-restricted rules have the following characteristics:

1. All the variables in the head of the rule appear also in the body.

2. The rule does not have any constant in the head.

Converting our rules to extended term-restricted rules provides that all the information in the head of a rule also appears in the body. That keeps us from losing this information while doing resolution because the subsequent resolvent will also contain it.

Identifying relevant literals and clauses avoids getting meaningless answers. *Relevant literals* are any literals contained in the query or that can be unifieds with relevant literals. Relevant clauses are those that contaon relevant literals.

5.2 Resolution

We use SLD-like resolution with the notions of relevant literals and clauses. Using the notion of relevant literals and caluses have two advantages over [2] and [4]. First, it can eliminate unnecessary rules which are used for the derivation of intensional answers. Second, certain meaningless intensional anmswers, as in [2], can be avoided.

The resolution stage serves to either simplify or discard resolvents. We do it by factoring, subsuming clauses or evaluating comparison literals.

Once a resolvent is derived from two parent clauses, it may have unifiable literals within a resolvent. In this case, we say that a clause has a *factor* and a factoring rule can be applied to simplify the resolvent. The simplified clause then will be obtained by removing all but one of the unified literals.

The subsumption strategy allows the deletion of a clause based on other clauses. A clause S_1 *subsumes* a clause S_2 if there exists a substitution σ such that the literals of $S_1\sigma$ are a subset of the literals of S_2. Then we are able to delete the subsumed clause S_2. However, [6] shows that, in SLD resolutions, since we are always performing resolution between either a query clause or a resolvent and a rule in IDB, we do not need subsumption test against rules in IDB. We need to test only subsumption of each resolvent against the last resolvent of the any previous branches in a SLD tree.

Evaluating comparison literals as far as possible helps to simplify the resolvent. After evaluating literals, users might be able to reduce the number of literals used, or users might be even able to discard the resolvent itself totally.

5.3 Post-Resolution

The last step is post-resolution. Here the last resolvent of resolution will be negated and taken as a candidate for intensional answers. Considering only the last resolvent instead of all the resolvents ever generated in the whole resolution process is much more efficient and can easily be justified. As the last resolvent is the logical consequence of the union of the negated query clause and the intensional database, as well as all the intermediate resolvents and the intensional database, it is the candidate for an intensional answer.

5.4 Algorithm

All these steps can be done in the order the following algorithm presents.

1. Pre-Resolution

   - transform rules which have constants in their heads into extended term-restricted rules

   - negate the query and convert it into the clause form

   - compute non-relevant clauses and remove them

2. Resolution

   - repeat for all branches of the resolution tree

     – perform resolution

     – for each evaluable comparison literal in the resolvent

       * if it is contradictory, then discard the current branch

       * perform subsumption test against the last resolvent of any previous branches

       * perform factoring, if necessary and if the result of factoring is consistent with database semantics

   - until a resolvent consists only of non-intensional literals or it cannot be further resolved

3. Post-Resolution

   - generate the candidates of intensional answers by negating all the last resolvents of the success branches of the resolution tree

   - for all candidates, evaluate evaluable formulas against the EDB

     – remove any contradictory formula

     – remove any subformula which is a tautology against EDB

   - now the answers are meaningful intensional answers

4. Minimal Intensional Answers

   - remove redundant answers from the answer set

Note that the steps of accessing the EDB in the post-resolution step can be skipped for the efficient processing of intensional answers. However, the step is necessary if a user is interested in pure intensional answers under the current EDB status. The soundness and completeness of this algorithm is proven in [6].

5.5 Example

This example shows the application of the algorithm introduced in the section above. Suppose we have the following EDB and IDB schema about car-dealership.

EDB:

- (relation 1:)   emp(name,salary,job_type)

- (relation 2:)   car(cno,model,year,price)

- (relation 3:)   sold(name,cno)

The relation *emp* stores employees' name, salary and job type. The relation *car* stores car number, model, year and the price of the car. The relation *sold* stores which salesmen sold out which cars.

IDB:

- (rule 1:) $expensive\_car(c1) \leftarrow car(c1,m1,y1,p1), gt(p1,20)$

- (rule 2:) $economic\_car(c2) \leftarrow car(c2,m2,y2,p2), \neg gt(p2,5)$

- (rule 3:) $gt(s3,20) \leftarrow emp(n3,s3,manager)$

- (rule 4:) $gt(p3,20) \leftarrow car(c3,benz,y3,p3)$

The IDB consists of four rules. The first rule says "Car c1 is an expensive car if its price is over 20000". The second one says "Car c2 is an economic car if its price is not greater than 5000". The third rule says "A manager's salary is greater than 20000". Finally, rule 4 says "The price of a Benz is over 20000".

Note that rules 4 and 5 are not extended term-restricted rules. So we transform them into extended term-restricted rules as follows:

- (rule 3':) $gt(s3,w3) \leftarrow emp(n3,s3,manager), (w3 = 20)$

- (rule 4':) $gt(p3,w4) \leftarrow car(c3,benz,y3,p3), (w4 = 20)$

Now let us consider the query *"Find all expensive cars that are sold out"*. The query can be written as $Q(N,C) = sold(N,C), expensive\_car(C)?$ Then the goal clause is

$$\leftarrow sold(n0,c0), expensive\_car(c0)$$

where n0 and c0 are Skolem constants. The directly relevant literals are {*sold, expensive_car*}. The directly relevant literal *expensive_car* makes *car* and *gt* relevant literals and the clause (rule 1) a relevant clause. The new literal *car* is an extensional literal, thus it does not introduce any new relevant literal. The literal *gt* in clause (rule1) can unify with *gt* in the rules 3' and 4'. However, by the definition of relevant literal, the rule 3' does not introduce any new relevant literals since it does not have any relevant literals in its body. Thus rule 3' is not a relevant clause either. The rule 4' is a relevant clause because its body contains a relevant literal by the definition of a relevant clause. Thus the set L_r of relevant literals is {*sold, expensive_car, car, gt*} . The rule 2 is not a relevant clause because its head cannot be unified with any other relevant literals. The set C_r of relevant clauses is {*Q, relation 2, relation 3, rule 1, rule 3'*}. Since rule 3' is not a relevant clause it will not be used to build a resolution tree, thus avoiding meaningless resolution. The tree is shown below.

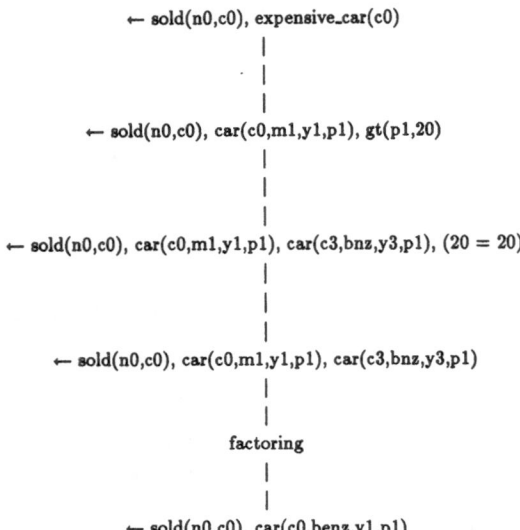

$\leftarrow$ sold(n0,c0), expensive_car(c0)

$\leftarrow$ sold(n0,c0), car(c0,m1,y1,p1), gt(p1,20)

$\leftarrow$ sold(n0,c0), car(c0,m1,y1,p1), car(c3,bnz,y3,p1), (20 = 20)

$\leftarrow$ sold(n0,c0), car(c0,m1,y1,p1), car(c3,bnz,y3,p1)

factoring

$\leftarrow$ sold(n0,c0), car(c0,benz,y1,p1)

Since the leaf in this resolution tree consists only of extensional literals, it becomes the last resolvent. The candidate for an intensional answer is:

$$ans_i(X) = \exists y1 \ \exists \ p1 \ sold(N,C), car(C,benz,y1,p1)$$

No subformula is evaluable aginst the EDB, so the above formula becomes an intensional answer. By the definition of intensional answers, we can interpret that as follows: "If a salesman N sold out the car C whose model is Benz, then it is an expensive car that is sold out".

5.6 Meaningful answers

The term meaningful answers was already used before to describe all the interesting answers for a certain query. The definition of an intensional meaningful answer is the following.

A *meaningful answer* is

- relevant to a given query

- a negated formula of the last resolvent

- a non-contradictory formula

- not containing a tautology

The intensional answer being developed throughout the resolution process should not only be meaningful but also non-redundant, as stated before. An intensional answer that is not only meaningful but also non-redundant is called *minimal*.

6 Properties of Intensional Answers

Talking about intensional answers, the theorem $\forall \ X \ (ans_i(X) \rightarrow Q(X)$ has always been the basis for it. So every formula $ans_i(X)$ derived is a sufficient condition for $Q(X)$ under the database theory T. Having a logically equivalent relationship, raher than efficient conditions, would be more preferable but cannot be derived by the means of resolution. This kind of relationship is called *syntactic* whereas a logically equivalence would be called *semantic*.

Concerning the relationship between intensional and extensional answers there can exist a syntactic or semantic relationship. A *syntactic relationship* would mean that any X that satisfies an intensional answer, is an extensional answer. In a *semantic relationship*, any X that satisfies an intensional answer, is an extensional answer, and all extensional answers can be derived by evaluating all intensional answers against the extensional database.

If a database is correctly modeled the semantic relationship should always hold true.

A database is *globally complete* if the semantic relationship of intensional and extensional answers holds true for any given query. It is *locally complete* if it depends on the query whether this relationship holds or doesn't. This is true for most databases.

7 Innovations

Our work [6] was based on research made by Cholvy and Demolombe. We did not only try to extend this previous work but also provided new relationships between intensional and extensional answers.

All previous works concerning intensional query processing used resolution to derive their intensional answers. Nevertheless it was never stated which resolution strategy should be used. Without a specific strategy for resolution a lot of redundant resolvents can be derived. We solved this problem by introducing a SLD resolution strategy which is based on the notions of relevant literals and relevant clauses.

Moreover no specific methodologies and procedures had been given so far, to remove the redundant resolution steps or meaningless answers in an answer set. In order to reduce the initial set of clauses, we introduced a formalization process of intensional answers. It consists of the three steps: pre-resolution, resolution and post-resolution. This process also shows what operations have to be performed to each resolvent.

Cholvy and Demolombe didn't solve the problem of a large number of facts in an extensional database. They just converted all the facts into rules and didn't care about the rules which were converted in vain, because they were never needed for the resolution process. We deferred the access to an extensional database until the resolution process is completed and no further resolution can be done, thereby being much more efficient than the former approach.

Also, the blind application of resolution can lead to meaningless intensional answers. To avoid meaningless intensional answers, the idea of relevant literals and clauses was introduced and used for our particular resolution strategy.

The relationships between extensional and intensional answers had never been studied before. This issue is necessary to connect intensional query processing with conventional database systems.

Finally, Cholvy and Demolombe converted all intermediate resolvents to intensional answers, which takes a lot of time and is not necessary at all. We showed that the last resolvent is logically implied by both an intermediate resolvent and an intensional database and thus justifies the omission of converting all intermediate resolvents.

Finally we can say the follwing about this work: all the improvements described above lead to a much more efficient algorithm to derive intensional answers than all previous works could provide.

Also our work gives a guideline for implementing the three steps of the resolution. [6] even provides a more detailed algorithm than this work could do.

Further, we implemented an intensional query processor in Prolog and reported in elsewhere [7].

8 Outlook

All the time only non-recursive clauses were dealt with. Query processing algorithms applying recursive rules usually have difficulties in termination because recursion cannot tell when a complete answer is found. Therefore the extensional database would have to be accessed, which has been avoided in this work.

Also only Horn clauses have been used whereas this restriction might be desirable to be changed. Dealing with non-recursive Horn clauses is not well-developed yet and therefore is a matter of interest.

It may be interesting to use different computational methodologies to get intensional answers. Another method besides resolution might help to use the logical definition of intensional answers and extensional answers described in the previous section.

Further the idea of incorporating intensional predicates in conventional query answers [3] might be significant. Hybrid answers consisting of both formulas and facts in addition to these two types would be a more general approach than strictly separating them.

References

[1] C. Chang and R. Lee. Symolic Logic and Mechanical Theorem Proving. Academic Press, 1973.

[2] L. Cholvy and R. Demolombe. *Querying a Rule Base*. In *Proceedings of the First International Conference on Expert Database Systems*, pages 365–371, Charleston, South Carolina, April 1-4 1986. Kerschberg, L.

[3] L. Imielinski. *Intelligent Query Answering in Rule Based Systems*. *Journal of Logic Programming*, 4(3):229–258, September 1987.

[4] E. Pascual and L. Cholvy. *Answering Queries Addressed to the Rule Base of a Deductive Database*. In *Proceedings of Second International Conference on Information Processing and Management of Uncertainty in Knowledgebased Systems*, pages 138–145, Urbino, Italy, July 1988. Springer-Verlag. Lecture Notes in Computer Sciences 313.

[5] A. Pirotte and D. Roelants. *Constraints for Improving the Generation of Intensional Answers in a Deductive Answer*. In *Proceedings of the International Conference on Data Engineering*, Los Angeles, California, Feb 6-10 1989.

[6] Il-Yeol Song. Intensional Query Processing in Deductive Database Systems. PhD thesis, Louisiana State University, August 1988.

[7] Il-Yeol Song and David Dubin. *An Intensional Query Processor in Prolog*. In *submitted for publication*, 1990.

AN ALGORITHM FOR SELECTION OPERATOR PROPAGATION IN RESOLUTION GRAPH

A. Hameurlain, F. Morvan

Université Paul Sabatier, Lab. IRIT
118, Route de Narbonne 31062 Toulouse Cédex

ABSTRACT

Data structures used to describe queries and rules systems strongly influence the optimization of the performances of deductive DBMS and more precisely evaluation methods for recursive queries.The scope of the optimization problem led to us study data structures derived from several research areas in the domain of deductive databases. From our results we propose a data structure called Resolution Graph, with a double objective : to maintain homogeneity with relational systems, and to help for the realization of the resolution and evaluation process. We also describe an algorithm which uses the Resolution Graph during the propagation of the selection operator. Comparing our Resolution Graph to other data structures and our algorithm to other methods of recursive queries optimization shows the strength of our method.

INTRODUCTION

A deductive database consits of a set of base relations called extensional database , and a set of deduced relations defined using rules, called intentional database. Recently, several researchers studied and proposed evaluation methods for recursive queries in the domain of deductive databases [1][2][8][[16][18][28][30][31]. The study of these evaluation methods for recursive queries enables us to establish that the main problem of deductive DBMS (database management system) is the optimization of the performances of deductive DBMS and not the problem of feasibility. The main factors which influence the optimization of the performances of recursive queries evaluation strategies are :

i) duplication of the computation of intermediate steps
ii) the generation of useless facts
iii) data structures based on graphic models, often called semantic networks [22], to describe queries and rules. These graphic models are similar to the tree structure of algebraic operators.

In a context of deductive databases [9], the modelized objects are the deduction rules and the relational predicates. The nodes represent the rules and the predicates, while arcs represent links between the rules and the predicates . Among the main data structures born from research areas in the domain of deductive databases , we can enumerate : Actifs Graphs Connection (ACG), Rules/Goals Graphs (RGG), Systems Graphs (SG), and Predicates Transitions Nets (PrTN).

i) The Active Connection Graphs (ACG) were introduced by Mac Kay [26] and implemented in the SNIP system. The elaboration of ACG is based on Predicate Connection Graphs (PCG). Nevertheless, a PCG is mainly used , for a DATALOG program (Horn clauses without symbol function and without negation)[24], to find all the formulae that unify with a given formula [6][7][27].

ii) The Rules/Goals Graphs (RGG), introduced by Ullman [29] corresponds to a generalization of PCG in the way it specifies how variable values move through predicates during the evaluation of a DATALOG query . The rule to elaborate such a graph is based on the concept of signature of predicates and rules [8][29] .

iii) The Systems Graphs (SG) have been introduced by Lozinskii and Kifer [18][20] and have been implemented in the system PROD [18], and have properties for propagating filters (selection criteria) in some favorable cases [19].

iv) The Predicates Transition Nets (PrTN) [23][24], have been introduced by Genrich [10], derived from Petri Nets which have been adjusted for the context of relational databases. The network tokens are structured objects with multiple values and they correspond to the tuples of relations and passing the transitions corresponds to joining conditions. The main feature of the PrTN is their ability to modelize RDL1 type programs (extension of DATALOG to integrate a production rule) [23].

In our work, the relevant systems rules and the queries are represented by a data structure called Resolution Graph. The essential specifications of Resolution Graph, represented below, are the use views mechanisms to define deduced relations from a query or a union of queries formulated in SQL relational language. This paper is organized as follows : we recall briefly the language used to define the rules . Then specifications of Resolution Graph are described. We then compare Resolution Graph to other cited graphic models such as the System Graph proposed by Lozinskii and Kifer. Our selection propagation algorithm is evaluated with respect to other recursive queries optimization methods.

RESOLUTION GRAPH

Before describing the specification of the Resolution Graph, it is necessary to briefly recall the formalism we proposed and used in order to define deduction rules and to handle deductive databases [4][5][11][12].

RULES LANGUAGE

A deductive DBMS has to propose a language of rules which allows to specify rules. These rules (recursive or not) define, deduced relations starting from base relations or deduced relations . With an aim to ease the resolution process and optimize the performance of the evaluation process, the language of rules we choose for our prototype is based on the views concept, which defines the deduced relations from relational queries . Indeed, in the prototype realized, the premise of the rules are expressed by a query or queries union written with the relational language SQL without use of arithmetic operations, aggregation functions or grouping. The deduced tuples are assigned in a deduced relation whose name corresponds to the conclusion query of the rule. Let us consider the system of recursive rules defining hierarchy between company employees :

(r1)   S_O(X,Y) <-- COM(X,Y).
(r2)   S_O(X, Y) <-- S_O(X,Z), COM(Z,Y).
where COM(X, Y) is a base predicate and means that X is ordered by Y and S_O(X, Y) is a deduced predicate and means that X is under order of Y.

This rules system specifies a recursive deduced relation which may be expressed by a SQL queries union :

S_O(NAME, NAME-S) =
    SELECT C.NAME   C.NAME-C ⎤
    FROM   COM C   ⎟ QR (COM)
    UNION   ⎦
    SELECT S.NAME   C.NAME-C ⎤
    FROM   COM C , S_O S   ⎬ QR (S_O,COM)
    WHERE S.NAME-S= C.NAME   ⎦

This tool corresponds to an extension of relational systems. Even though rules systems expressed in terms of Horn clauses are more concise, they are less homogeneous with relational systems.

SPECIFICATION OF THE RESOLUTION GRAPH

A Resolution Graph is a quadruplet (X, Y, Z, A) where :

- X : is a set of "oval" nodes which represent a deduced relation. These nodes correspond either to whole tuples in a base relation, or to whole or part of tuples which may be deduced.
- Y : is a set of "square" nodes, where each node represents a SQL query specifying a deduced relation.
- Z : is a set of "round" nodes which represent the union operator for the results of several queries in order to entirely evaluate the deduced relation .
- A : is a set of arcs connecting :

a) either a relation-node(X) to a query-node (Y)
b) either a query-node (Y) to a deduced relation-node
c) either a query-node (Y) to a relation-node through a union node (Z).

a) If a query Q refers to a relation R then one creates an arc which connects R to Q (If R appears several times in Q, there are as many arcs connecting R to Q).This type of arc corresponds to a flow of tuples which are issued from the relation R.

b) If R is a deduced relation defined by only one SQL query Q then one creates an arc connecting Q to R.
c) If R is a deduced relation defined by an union of SQL queries UQ$_i$ then, for each query Q$_i$ i [1..N] one creates an arc which connects the union node to the R node. This type of arc corresponds to a flow of computed tuples during the evaluation of queries defining deduced relations. This flow may be reduced by a selection enclosed in the formulation of the user query.

Example : the Resolution Graph bound to the query " who are the hierarchical superiors of Mike " (and bound to the system of linear recursive rules defining the hierarchies between employees of the same factory) <-- S_O (Mike, Y) would be :

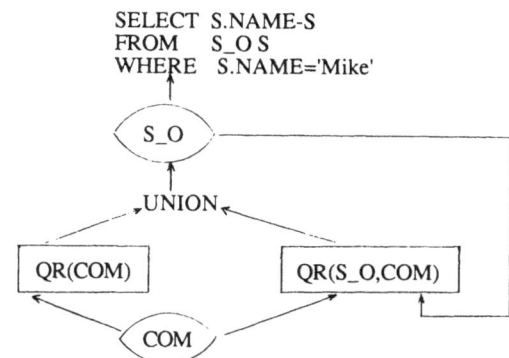

Figure1: Resolution Graph bound to the query <- S_O(Mike, Y)

SELECTION OPERATOR PROPAGATION ALGORITHM

For simplicity and conciseness, we will represent the definitions of recursive relations according to Horn clauses. We have studied the problem of propagation of the selections by taking into account a set of rules systems and queries [3].

System 1: Linear recursive system
A(X,Y) <-- P(X,Y).   where P is a base predicate and 'a' is
A(X,Y) <-- P(X,Z), A(Z,Y).   a constant.
REQ(X) <-- A(a,Y).

Systeme 2: Linear recursive system
A(X,Y) <-- P(X,Y).   where P is a base predicate and 'b' is
A(X,Y) <-- P(X,Z), A(Z,Y).   a constant.
REQ(X) <-- A(X,b).

Système 3: Strongly linear recursive system
C(X,Y) <-- H(X,Y).   where H, B, D are base predicates
C(X,Y) <-- B(X,Z), C(Z,T), D(Y,T).   and 'a' is a constant.
REQ(X) <-- C(a,Y).

Système 4: Quadratic recursive system
A(X,Y) <-- P(X,Y).   where P is a base predicate and 'a' is
A(X,Y) <-- A(X,Z), A(Z,Y).   a constant
REQ(X) <-- A(a,Y).

The principle of the method consists in propagating the selection in the Resolution Graph as far a possible, instead of pushing-down the selection as in algebraic operator tree structures [17]. The selection operator propagation process, in the Resolution Graph, uses a data structure representing the correspondance between target attributes (t_attr) and the source attributes (s_attr) of the relations referenced in the definition queries. An index allows to determine the relation to which belongs the source attribute. The selection operator propagation algorithm works starting on the relation-node (X) representing the result . This algorithm is as follws :

```
procedure selection_propagation (filter, attr_c, rel_node)
    /* filter : selection criterium */
if(rel_node) is a deduced relation and (not Marked( rel_node ))
then
begin    /*  For a given deduced relation DR=U query_i /SQL  */
        Marked( rel_node );
        /* Use substructure t_corresp to rel_node structure to
        determine source attribute corresponding to target
        attribute */
        Obtain_source_attr (attr_c, attr_s);
        Search_recursive_query ;
        if ∃ i / type(query_i) is recursive  then
                begin  get_name_rel_recursive;
                    if attr_s ∈ recursive relation then
                /*insert selection criterium in the request node */
                        query_node_i <-- query_node_i + filter;
                end
        else /* for any i∈[1..N] type(query_i) is no recursive*/
                begin
                for each query_i  (i∈[1..N]) do
                        begin
                        query_node_i <-- query_node_i + filter ;
                        selection_propagation(filter,attr_s,rel_node.son[i]);
                        end;
                end;
end;
```

For example, to the question " is Mike under the orders of John", by applying the above algorithm, one obtains the following optimized Resolution Graph :

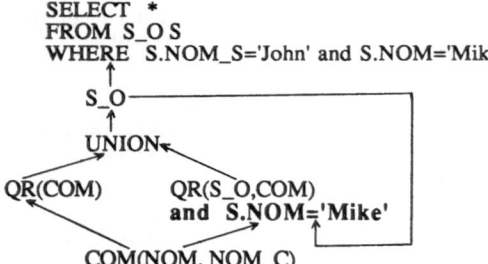

Figure 2 : Optimized Resolution Graph.

Consequently we noted that the selections which could be propagated are those concerning the attributes of the deduced relation defined in a recursive fashion. On the other hand, the selection S.NAME_S='John', cannot be propagated because it concerns an attribute of a base relation which figures in the premise of a recursive deduced relation. This propagation rule for selections ensure the completeness of the answers.

COMPARISON WITH OTHER METHODS

Resolution Graphs closely resemble System Graphs introduced by Lozinskii and Kifer. The difference in our approach is that the rules language is based on the views concept (defining deduced relations from SQL relational queries), whereas in System Graphs the language of deduction rules is based on the use of Horn clauses, occasionally incorporating function symbols [21]. The main advantage of our choice is that, during the evaluation process, the Resolution Graph leads directly to the SQL sequence of queries to send to the DBMS. This avoids the time consuming process of translating the Horn clauses into a pre-compiled relational program and considerably improves the performances of the deductive system.

The Henschen-Naqvi method [14] applies to strongly linear rules. The magic sets method [2] which consists in incorparating 'magic' predicates in the rules, applies to linear rules, strongly linear rules, and acyclic data [15]. The method of selection operator propagation in the Resolution Graph behaves as a static filter method in the case of linear rules.Nevertheless, it applise to quadratic rules.

The System Graphs and the Resolution Graphs differ from Active Connection Graphs in that the later can create more than on target-node by relation. As to Predicates Transition Nets the transitions and positive arcs (to model a DATALOG program) play the same role as query-nodes in the Resolution Graph. The positions correspond exactly to the relation-nodes of the Resolution Graph. Furthermore, we can establish that all these data structures represent a monotonous increasing evaluation (execution model based on the forward chaining up to the base saturation) except for the PrTN because there are negative arcs modelizing the deletion of tuples.

The optimization method called static filter [19] applies to linear rules when the filter concerns the attribute of a recursive relation. This filtering method boils down to a semi-naive method in case of strongly linear rules and quadratic rules. In addition, the method has been expanded to include functional terms in order to represent DATALOG^{func} [21].

IMPLEMENTATION

Thus, we have conceived and realized an experimental prototype for a deductive DBMS on a SUN (UNIX) station by using the relational DBMS ORACLE. Programs are written in PRO*C language. From the architectural point of view, the prototype we have realized stongly approximates an extension of a relational DBMS to recursive definitions (integration approach). The join loop is perfomed by a semi-naîve iterative algorithm.

One of the main goals of the deductive database is to integrate a maximum of deduction rules in the intentional database part. In addition, to ensure correct performances during the elaboration process of the Resolution Graph (selection of the pertinent rules bound to the query) it is important, before the elaboration of a rules base, to specify data structures which enable :
- an effective research of pertinent rules from of the rules base during the course of the resolution process
- a flexible update of rules base keeping its coherence.

We choose to represent the rules base by a relational structure which will be managed by the relational DBMS ORACLE.

553

The main advantage of our choice lies in the fact that the searching of pertinent rules, from the rules base and the update of the base, is done with the help of the relational language SQL. In this manner the optimization techniques implanted in the relational system can be advantageously exlpoited.

CONCLUSION

In this paper we have proposed a formalism which is homogeneous and compatible with that of relational systems in that the definition of rules, the handling of deductive databases and the search for deduction rules are caried out with the same SQL language. An overview of our work shows that the principal characteristics of data structures which strongly influence performance optimization of recursive queries evaluation methods are :

- the construction cost of a data structures which depends on the query (number of rules and predicates) and not on the size of the data base
- the possibility to include optimization techniques and in particular the propagation of the selections and projections in order to decrease data size.

Taking into consideration the importance of the optimization problem we are working on parallel execution strategies in order to implement the transitive closure operator more efficiently and on performance evaluation in order to demonstrate the contribution of parallel execution. We propose, on one hand, a multiprocessor architecture approach suited for parallel transitive closure, and on the other hand, a parallel algorithm based on the hashing technique to evaluate the transitive closure of a binary relation. The results of this work are presented in another publication [13].

REFERENCES

[1] R. Agrawall and H.V. Jagadish, "Efficient search in very large database," Proc. of the 14th VLDB Conference, Los Angeles, California, p. 40, 1988.
[2] F. Bancilhon and R. Ramakrishan, "An amateur's introduction to recursive query processing strategies," Proc. of ACM-SIGMOD Washington D.C., p. 16, 1986.
[3] F. Bancilhon and R. Ramakrishan,"Performance Evaluation of Data Intensive Logic Programs," Foundations of Deductive Databases and Logic Programming. Morgan Kaufman Publi., Los Altas, California, Minker Edit. p. 439, 1988.
[4] P. Bazex and A. Hameurlain."Evaluation optimisée de relations virtuelles par parcours de structures arborescentes," Journées des Bases de Données aux bases de Connaissances", Sophia-Antipolis, France, p. 265, 1987.
[5] P. Bazex et al., "L'inférence dans les bases de données relationnlles : approche PROLOG / approche relationnelle". 1ère Conf. Européenne sur les techniques et les application de l'intelligence artificielle en milieu industriel et de service, Paris, vol. 1, p. 11, 1989.
[6] A. Colmerauer et al., "PROLOG, bases théoriques et développement actuels," TSI, vol. 2, no. 4, p. 271, 1983.
[7] H. Farreny and M. Ghallab, "Eléments d'Intelligence Artificielle,". Ed. Hermes, 1988.
[8] G. Gardarin and E. Simon, "Les systèmes de gestion de bases de données déductives," TSI, vol. 6, no. 5, p. 347, 1987.
[9] H. Gallaire et al., "Logic and Databases: a deductive approach," ACM Computing Surveys, vol.16, no. 2, p. 15, 1984.

[10] H.J. Genrich, "Predicate / Transition Nets ," in Advances in Petri Nets' 86. Springer-Verlag, 1987.
[11] A. Hameurlain, "Optimization for recursive queries in relational Databases," 12 th Intl. Information Technologies Conference. Sarajevo YU , vol. 2, p. 601, 1988.
[12] A. Hameurlain et al., "Conception et réalisation d'un évaluateur de règles de déduction dans un environnement relationnel," Convention Informatique Latine , Barcelona, p. 445, 1989.
[13] A. Hameurlain and F. Morvan, "Deductive databases: Parallel Transitive Closure," Intl. Conf. On Operations Research,Vienna, 1990, to appear in the DGOR Proceedings, Springer-Verlag.
[14] L.J. Henschen and S.A. Naqvi, "On compiling queries in recursive first-order data bases", Journal of the ACM., Vol. 31,, p. 47, 1984.
[15] L.J. Henschen and C.S. Wu, "Answering Linear Recursive Queries in Cyclic Databases," Proc. of Intl on Fifth Generation Computer System, ICOT,·JAPAN, p. 727, 1988.
[16] Y.E. Ioannidis and R. Ramakrishan "Efficient Transitive Closure Algorithms," Proc. of the 14th VLDB Conference, Los Angeles, California, p. 382, 1988.
[17] M. Jarke and J.Koch, "Query Optimization in Database System," ACM Computing Surveys, vol. 16, no. 2, p.111, 1984.
[18] E.L. Lozinskii, "Evaluating Queries in Deductive Databases by Generating," Proc. 9th Intl. Joint Conf. on Artificial Intelligence, Los Angeles, p. 173, 1985.
[19] E.L. Lozinskii, "A Problem-Oriented Inferential Database System," ACM trans. on Database Systems, vol. 11, no. 3, p. 323, 1986.
[20] M. Kifer and E.L. Lozinskii, "Filtering Data Flow in Deductive Databases,"Proc. of the Intl. Conf. on Database Theory, Lecture Notes in Computer Science, no. 243, Springer-Verlag, p. 186, 1986.
[21] M. Kifer and E.L. Lozinskii, "Implementation Logic Programs as a Database System," Proc. of 3th Intl. Conf. on Data Engineering, Los Angeles, 1987
[22] R. Kowalski, "A Proof Procedure using connection graphs," Journal of the ACM, vol. 22, no. 4, 1975.
[23] C. DE Maindreville and E. Simon , "A Predicat Transition Net for Evaluation Queries Against Rules in a DBMS," Abstract in Proc of 3th JBDA, Port-Camargue, France, p. 347, 1987.
[24] C. DE Maindreville and E. Simon, "A Production Rule Based Approach to deductive Databases," Proc. of 4th International Conference on Data Engineering, Los Angeles, p. 234, 1988.
[25] C. DE Maindreville and E. Simon, "Modeling Non Deterministic Queries and Update In Deductive Databases," Proc. of the 14th VLDB Conference, Los Angeles, California, p. 39, 1988.
[26] D.P. Mckay and S.C. Shapiro, "Using Active Connection Graphs for Reasoning with Recursive Rules", Intl. Joint Conf. on Artificial Intelligence, p. 368, 1981.
[27] N.J. Nillson, "Principles of Artificial Intelligence"; Tioga Publishing company, 1980.
[28] J. Rohmer et al.,"The alexandre method, A technique for the processing of recursive Axioms in Deductive Databases," New Generation Computing ,vol. 4, no. 3, p. 273, 1986.
[29] J.D. Ullman, "Implementation of logical query languages for data bases," ACM Trans. Data Base Systems, vol. 10, no. 3, p. 289, 1985.
[30] L. Vieille, "Recursive Axioms in Deductive Databases : The Query - Subquery Approch," Proc. First Intl. Confrence on Expert Database Systems, Charleston, p. 179, 1986.
[31] L. Vieille, "BD déductive : DEDGIN, un évaluateur de requêtes récursives," Journées des Bases de Données aux bases de Connaissances, Sophia-Antipolis, France, p. 247, 1987.

Database – Knowledge Base Consistency Monitor

W. Cellary[1], A. Jaeschke[2], T. Morzy[1]
H. Orth[2], G. Zilly[2]

[1] Technical University of Poznań
60-965 Poznań, Poland

[2] Kernforschungszentrum Karlsruhe GmbH
7500 Karlsruhe, West Germany

Abstract

Expert systems composed of a database and a knowledge base, which cooperate, are considered. In such systems mutual consistency of the database and the knowledge base must be enforced. A consistency monitor is proposed for this purpose, whose task is double: to enforce internal consistency of the database and mutual consistency of the database and the knowledge base. The first task comprise enforcement of referential constraints imposed on the database. An efficient technique is proposed. Referential constraints are enforced by the use of DBMS journals instead of looking up the entire database. The consistency monitor described in this paper is applied in the laboratory information and management system *ELAN* installed in the analytical laboratories of the nuclear fuel reprocessing pilot plan at the Nuclear Center of Karlsruhe.

1 Introduction

Many expert systems are composed of a database and a knowledge base, which cooperate. In such systems an important problem is mutual consistency of the database and the knowledge base. To solve this problem, in this paper, a *consistency monitor* is proposed, whose task is automatic enforcement of consistency. It was developed for expert system *ELAN* installed in the analytical laboratories of the nuclear fuel reprocessing pilot plant at the Nuclear Center of Karlsruhe [10,11,14].

To control the process of nuclear fuel reprocessing, efficient analytical laboratories are needed for physical and chemical assay of various process constituents and products. The main aim of the *ELAN* system is to support the plant operator in the preparation of process measurement plans including: selection of the appropriate analytical methods, determination of analytical steps (sample preparation, measurement procedure, evaluation procedure, choice of measurement devices, etc.) and dispatching measurement tasks among laboratories.

System *ELAN* is two computer. Its both components are specialized. The first one, *VAX* equipped with the *INGRES* database, is dedicated for data acquisition and storing. It is a multiuser system, whose terminals are dispersed over work -

posts in laboratories. The second one, actually equipped with *TI-Explorer*, is dedicated for knowledge base storing and reasoning. It is a single user system. Its aim is to support the plant operator in decision making concerning measurement plans. Both components of the system are weakly coupled to preserve their autonomy (Figure 1.)

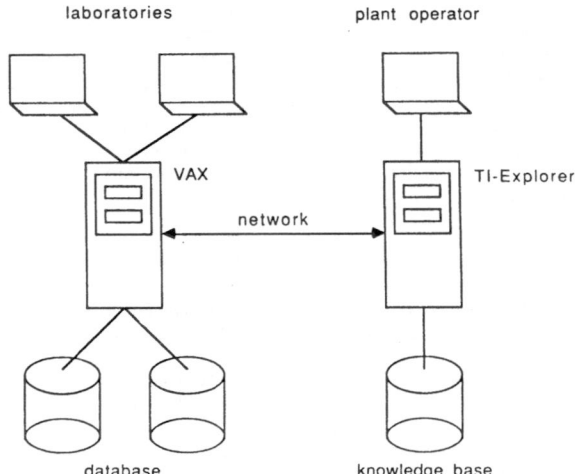

Figure 1. Structure of the *ELAN* system

Some information stored in the system are replicated in both computers. Replication follows from the necessity of different representations of information in both computers and from relatively slow communication between them. By data replication, the system was optimized to minimize the volume of data transferred and transformed. For this reason, maintenance of data replication in the system is indispensable.

Cooperation between the database and the knowledge base is not continuous. It is required only when a new measurement plan is prepared by the plant operator. Thus, the *ELAN* system operates as follows: data are continuously collected and processed at the *VAX*, and from time to time a new measurement plan is generated by the use of the knowledge base at *TI-Explorer*. Precisely at these moments, mutual database – knowledge base consistency is required. It is enforced by in-

---

[1]This work was supported in part by the Polish Academy of Sciences under the contract CPBP 2.17.

serting some new facts to the knowledge base or deleting some existing ones following database modifications, which were made since the last generation of a measurement plan.

To solve the problem of mutual database – knowledge base consistency, the database itself must be consistent. Otherwise, some false facts may be inserted to the knowledge base or some true facts may be deleted from it, making reasoning false. Internal database consistency is preserved if two kinds of database integrity constraints are observed: value constraints and referential constraints [5]. The first ones are automatically enforced by the $INGRES$ DBMS, not the second ones. Up to date, enforcement of referential constraints was particularly inefficient, because it required looking up the entire database. In this paper, a technique is proposed of the use of the DBMS journaling system to enforce referential constraints without looking up the entire database.

The paper is organized as follows. In Section 2 the solution to the problem of enforcing internal database consistency by the use of journals is presented. Section 3 is devoted to the problem of mutual database – knowledge base consistency. Section 4 contains conclusions.

2 Enforcing Internal Consistency of the Database

Integrity constraints represent time-invariant semantics of data stored in the database [5]. They must be obeyed to guarantee that a database correctly reflects the real world it models. A database state is consistent if it satisfies all the integrity constraints imposed on the database. The database management system (DBMS) should ensure consistency of each database state by enforcing integrity constraints whenever the database is modified.

Two types of integrity constraints are distinguished: *value constraints* and *referential constraints*. The former ones encode information about allowable values of objects stored in the database, e. g. values of an attribute representing the age of a person can be neither less than 0 nor greater than 110. Integrity constraints of this type are automatically enforced by the $INGRES$ DBMS, if they were expressed by the mean of the $DEFINE\ INTEGRITY$ statement. The later constraints encode the structural relationships among relations describing real world objects. They arise whenever one relation includes references to another relation. For example, values of an attribute $Employee\_name$ in a relation $University\_teachers$ must appear as the value of the $Employee\_name$ attribute in some tuple of the $University\_employee$ relation. More formally, a referential constraint states that if a relation R_2 includes a foreign key FK matching the primary key PK of some other relation R_1, then every value of FK in R_2 must either be equal to the value of PK in some tuple of R_1, or be entirely null. A relation such as R_2 is called *referencing*; a relation such as R_1 is called *referenced*. Attributes FK and PK are called *referential attributes*. For one referenced relation there may exist several referencing relations. Also, one referential constraint may involve several referential attributes. We denote a referential constraint as follows:

$$RX : R_2.Y \rightarrow\rightarrow R_1.X,$$

where RX is the label of the referential constraint, Y is the foreign key of R_2, and X is the primary key of R_1. This constraint may be informally read as "Given an R_2 tuple with value y for a foreign key Y, there exists an R_1 tuple having that value y for the primary key X".

Referential constraint enforcement has been proved to be very difficult to implement efficiently [1,2,6,8,9,12,15,16,17]. The major reason is that referential constraints, unlike the value constraints, involve comparison of attribute values of two relations to verify whether the value of a foreign key of the referencing relation is a key value in the referenced one. Therefore, large amount of data must be accessed to determine consistency of a database state. This is time-consuming, and this is why existing commercial DBMSs, including $INGRES$, do not enforce automatically referential constraints. Therefore, in the expert systems like $ELAN$ they must be enforced by some extra software like the consistency monitor described here.

Two different approaches may be applied to enforce referential constraints by the consistency monitor. In the first one, the consistency monitor acts as a front-end to the DBMS. It controls the stream of database operations and enforce database state consistency by the use of triggers and demons [4,18]. While this ensures database consistency all the time, involved overhead is very high [7,13]. In the second approach, referential constraint enforcement is deferred [3]. In this approach, update anomalies, which violate referential constraints, are not blocked or prevented. Consistency monitor performs a complete "sweep" of the whole database at some intervals notifying the users of inconsistencies or enforcing referential constraints. Unfortunately, sweeping the whole database is also very time consuming [7,13].

In the consistency monitor developed for the $ELAN$ system the second approach is adopted, however, sweeping the whole database is avoided. This approach might be adopted, because in the $ELAN$ system database consistency is not required all the time. It is required only when mutual database – knowledge base consistency is enforced. To avoid sweeping the whole database, $INGRES$ journaling system is used. Originally, a journal serves for two purposes. First, it maintains a backup copy of the database for recovery. Second, it maintains transactions logs. This means that all the update operations—insertion, deletion and updating—on relations created under $WITH\ JOURNALING$ option are automatically logged in the journal file. Two system commands: $CKPDB$ and $AUDITDB$, permit users to manipulate with the journal. The $CKPDB$ command makes a new checkpoint for the database and destroy all the journal entries up to this checkpoint. The $AUDITDB$ command permits the user to read the database journal since the last checkpoint and to create a readable audit trail of the changes made to a particular relation. The trail is made in a file, in a form suitable for coping through the $COPY$ command into an $INGRES$ relation, called *audit relation*. The audit relation contains all the information concerning modifications made on a given relation since the last checkpoint. Thus, the audit relations contain all the information necessary for the consistency monitor to enforce consistency. Processing audit relations is much more efficient than sweeping the whole database.

The consistency monitor works as follows.

Tuple Insertion

Tuple insertion to a referenced relation is ignored by the consistency monitor, because the propagation of insertions to the referencing relation may lead to indeterminacies. Indeed, in the case of a constraint $RX : R_2.Y \rightarrow\rightarrow R_1.X$, an insertion into R_1 determines only the value of attribute Y. Hence, if some attribute Z of R_2 does not admit the null value, the propagation of the insertion would have to arbitrate some non-null value for Z, which is not reasonable. The $INGRES$ DBMS does not support null values in attributes that are relation keys or parts of them.

Tuple Deletion

Tuple deletion from a referencing relation is ignored by the consistency monitor. On the contrary, if a tuple is deleted from a referenced relation, the consistency monitor propagates the deletion to the referencing relation.

Tuple Updating

The consistency monitor ignores updating a non-referential attribute of a referenced or referencing relation. It ignores also updating a referential attribute of a referencing relation. On the contrary, if a referential attribute of a referenced relation is updated, the consistency monitor propagates the update to the referencing relation.

To specify referential constraints, the tables similar to the ones described in [5] are used. They contain information on referencing and referenced relations, as well as referential attributes and their types.

3 Enforcing Mutual Database – Knowledge Base Consistency

Information is stored in the database in the from of relations, and in the knowledge base in the form of sets of facts. Replicated information corresponds, on the one hand, to some sets of facts, and on the other hand, to derived relations following from the evaluation of some relational expressions over a database instance. Expressions are combinations of *project*, *select*, *join* and *group by* operations. An expression can be written in the following form:

$$E = \pi_A \sigma_C(R_{i_1} \bowtie R_{i_2} \bowtie \ldots R_{i_K}),$$

where $R_{i_1}, R_{i_2}, \ldots, R_{i_K}$ are relations, π denotes the *project* operator, σ denotes the *select* or *group by* operator, $\bowtie$ denotes the *join* operator, C is a selection condition, and $A = \{A_1, \ldots, A_L\}$ is a set of attributes of the projection. Set of attributes A corresponds to the set of fields of a fact in the knowledge base.

As an illustration consider the following example. Assume that the knowledge base contains a set of facts KB_fact, each fact of the following form:

$$KB\_fact \ (cleaning\_period, box\_type, device\_type),$$

where $cleaning\_period$, box_type and $device\_type$ are fact fields. Assume that the set of facts KB_fact corresponds to the derived relation defined upon the set R_1, R_2, R_3 of relations of the following schemes:

$$R_1(box\#, device\#, cleaning\_period),$$
$$R_2(box\#, box\_type),$$
$$R_3(device\#, device\_type).$$

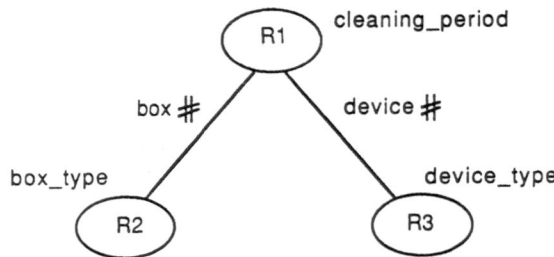

Figure 2. Relationships between R_1, R_2 and R_3

The part of the database containing relations R_1, R_2 and R_3 has the structure presented in Figure 2. Relational algebra expression E has the following form:

$$E = \pi_{\{cleaning\_period, box\_type, device\_type\}}(R_1 \bowtie R_2 \bowtie R_3).$$

This expression corresponds to the following QUEL command:

Retrieve ($R_1.cleaning\_period, R_2.box\_type, R_3.device\_type$),
where $R_1.box\# = R_2.box\#$
and $R_1.device\# = R_3.device\#$

The execution of this command for the database instance presented in Figure 3 gives as a result the derived relations, whose tuples correspond to the following set of facts:

$$KB\_fact(50, entry\_box, spectrometer)$$
$$KB\_fact(60, entry\_box, thermometer)$$
$$KB\_fact(04, gamma\_box, thermometer)$$
$$KB\_fact(16, cleaning\_box, thermometer)$$
$$KB\_fact(18, cleaning\_box, ph\_meter)$$

Modification of the database relations, whose attributes correspond to fields of facts in the knowledge base, may, but must not, be followed by the generation or deletion of facts. For example, adding a new tuple (B_4, new_box) to relation R_2 (Figure 3) is not followed by the generation of a new fact, because information is incomplete: $KB\_fact(?, new\_box, ?)$. A new fact will be generated if also R_1 is updated by adding, for example, a tuple ($B_4, D_3, 45$). Then, the new fact is:

$$KB\_fact(45, new\_box, ph\_meter).$$

To enforce mutual consistency between replicated parts of the database and the knowledge base, consistency monitor propagates to the knowledge base all the database modifications that lead to the generation or deletion of facts. These modifications are determined by the use of the following state differencing technique.

R₁

box#	device#	cleaning_period
B_1	D_1	50
B_1	D_2	60
B_2	D_2	04
B_3	D_2	16
B_3	D_3	18

R₂

box#	box_type
B_1	entry_box
B_2	gamma_box
B_3	cleaning_box

R₃

device#	device_type
D_1	spectrometer
D_2	thermometer
D_3	ph-meter

Figure 3. Database instance

We denote *Fact_1, Fact_2,..., Fact_i,..., Fact_m* the sets of facts containing replicated information. We introduce three kinds of relations related with these sets of facts. Relations *Fact_1_new, Fact_2_new,..., Fact_i_new,..., Fact_m_new* represent the current state of the database. Relations *Fact_1_dif, Fact_2_dif,..., Fact_i_dif,..., Fact_m_dif* contain the difference between the new and the old knowledge base state, i. e. they contain tuples, which have to be send to the knowledge base to update it by the generation or deletion of some facts. To distinguish between the generation and deletion, an extra attribute is used, called *operation*. Two values of this attribute are allowed: "+" and "−". All the relations mentioned above are stored only for the purpose of the consistency monitor and they are not accessible for the users.

The following algorithm is applied to verify whether database modifications lead to some knowledge base modifications and, then, to enforce the mutual database – knowledge base consistency.

For each set of facts *Fact_i*, i=1,...,m, do:

1. Derive relation *Fact_i_new*.

2. Create in two steps the content of relation *Fact_i_dif* (\ denotes the difference operator):

   - Append to *Fact_i_dif* all the tuples from the set *Fact_i_new\ Fact_i_old*. Attribute *operation* set to "+". (Facts corresponding to these tuples have to be inserted to the knowledge base.)

   - Append to *Fact_i_dif* all the tuples from the set *Fact_i_old\ Fact_i_new*. Attribute *operation* set to "−". (Facts corresponding to these tuples have to be removed from the knowledge base.)

3. Send *Fact_i_dif* to the knowledge base to update it.

4. Memorize the new state of the knowledge base: *Fact_i_old ← Fact_i_new*.

5. Clear relations *Fact_i_dif* and *Fact_i_new*.

4   Conclusions

The key problem of functional correctness of the *ELAN* expert system was mutual consistency of the database and the knowledge base that compose it. Traditional techniques that require looking up the entire database could not be applied, because the time required to enforce database – knowledge base consistency was longer than the interval of measurement plan generation by the plant operator. The use of DBMS journals, which permits to avoid looking up the entire database, improved efficiency of the consistency monitor radically. Thus, the problem has been solved.

Efficiency of the consistency monitor can be further improved at the level of its implementation. The original *AUDITDB* command used in it creates the readable audit trail of the changes made to only one relation. Therefore, in the consistency monitor, it has to be executed as many times as many relations are monitored. To execute an *AUDITDB* command, it is necessary to exit the *INGRES* database, while to execute a *COPY* command (to create the audit relation) it is necessary to re-enter to the *INGRES* database. The sequence of: exit database – enter database is time consuming. It may be avoided by rewriting the *AUDITDB* command in such a way that it makes a readable audit trail of changes of all the monitored relations at one execution.

References

[1] Badal, D., Popek, G., *Cost Performance Analysis of Semantic Integrity Validation Methods*, Proc. SIGMOD Conf. on Management of Data, Austin, 1979, pp. 109–115

[2] Bernstein, P.A., Blaustein, B.T., *Fast Method for Testing Quantified Relational Calculus Assertions*, Proc. SIGMOD Conf. on Management of Data, Orlando, 1982, pp. 39–50

[3] Cammarata, S., Ramachandra, P., Shane, D., *Extending a Relational Database with Deferred Referential Integrity Checking and Intelligent Joins*, Proc. SIGMOD Conf. on Management of Data, Austin, 1989, pp. 88–97

[4] Casanova, M.A., Tucherman, L., Furtado, A.L., *Enforcing Inclusion Dependencies and Referential Integrity*, Proc. 14th VLDB Conf. Los Angeles, 1988, pp. 38–49

[5] Date, C.J., *Referential Integrity*, Proc. 7th VLDB Conf. Cannes (France), 1981, pp. 2–12

[6] Furtado, A., dos Santos, D., de Castilho, J., *Dynamic Modeling of a Simple Existence Constraints*, Information Systems 6, 1981, pp. 73–80

[7] Hatonn, T., *Deferred vs Immediate Checking for Consistency of Databases*, Management Information System Week (June 1988)

[8] Hsu, A., Imielinski, T., *Integrity Checking for Multiple Updates*, Proc. SIGMOD Conf. on Management of Data, Austin, 1985, pp. 152–168

558

[9] Hammer, M., Sarin, S., *Efficient Monitoring of Database Assertions*, Proc. SIGMOD Conf. on Management of Data, Austin, 1978, pp. 38–49

[10] Jaeschke, A., Orth, H., Zilly, G., *Expertensystemgesteuertes Informationssystem fuer ein chemisch- analytisches Betriebslabor*, Fachtagung Prozessrechensysteme '88, Stuttgart, Maerz 1988, Berlin (u.a.): Springer, 1988, pp. 376–382 (Informatik Fachberichte; 167)

[11] Jaeschke, A., Orth, H., Zilly, G., *Expertensystemgestuetztes Informations – und Managementsystem fuer die Laboranalytik*, G. Schmidt (Hrsg.) *Mit vernetzten, intelligenten Komponenten zu leistungsfaehigeren Mess – und Automatisierungssystemen*, Fachbeitraege INTERKAMA Kongress 89, Muenchen (u.a.): Oldenbourg, Oktober 1989, pp. 633–641

[12] Kobayashi, I., *Validating Database Updates*, Information Systems 9, 1, 1986, pp. 1–17

[13] Lafue, G.M.F., *Semantic Integrity Dependencies and Delayed Integrity Checking*, Proc. 8th VLDB Conf. Mexico, 1982, pp. 292–299

[14] Orth, H., Zilly, G., *Expertensystem hilft Experten im Labor*, Ingres News, Ausgabe II, 1988, U. Parthier, *Ingres: Datenbankmanagement der Zukunft*, Wuerzburg, Vogel, 1989, pp. 94–98

[15] Qian, X., Smith, D.R., *Integrity Constraint Reformulation for Efficient Validation*, Proc. 13th VLDB Conf. Brighton, 1987, pp. 417–425

[16] Qian, X., *Effective Method for Integrity Constraint Simplification*, Proc. 4th Conf. on Data Engineering, Los Angeles, 1988

[17] Stonebraker, M., *Implementation of Integrity Constraints and Views by Query Modification*, Proc. SIGMOD Conf. on Management of Data, San Jose, 1985, pp. 65–78

[18] Stonebraker, M., Rowe, L., *The Design of POSTGRES*, Proc. SIGMOD Conf. on Management of Data, Washington, 1986, pp. 340–354